Legal Executions
in Tennessee

Legal Executions in Tennessee

A Comprehensive Registry, 1782–2009

Lewis L. Laska

McFarland & Company, Inc., Publishers
Jefferson, North Carolina, and London

Library of Congress Cataloguing-in-Publication Data

Laska, Lewis L.
Legal executions in Tennessee : a comprehensive registry, 1782–2009 / Lewis L. Laska.
p. cm.
Includes bibliographical references and index.

ISBN 978-0-7864-5975-9
softcover : 50# alkaline paper ∞

1. Executions and executioners — Tennessee — History — Chronology.
2. Capital punishment — Tennessee — History. 3. Criminal justice, Administration of — Tennessee — History. I. Title.
HV8699.U6T285 2011 364.6609768 — dc22 2011000789

British Library cataloguing data are available

Manufactured in the United States of America

McFarland & Company, Inc., Publishers
Box 611, Jefferson, North Carolina 28640
www.mcfarlandpub.com

Contents

Preface 1

PERSONS EXECUTED AND THEIR CRIMES
(*Listed Chronologically*) 7

Notes 421

Index 469

Preface

No one likes the death penalty. Even proponents blanch at the prospect of executing the very young and recoil at learning that Tennessee hanged a 13-year-old slave girl in 1833 — and that one of the most notorious hangings came in 1872 when about 10,000 people came to watch 17-year-old John Presswood, Jr., die in tiny Smithville. His corpse, shown in a white shroud, is one of the few photographs of a Tennessee execution.[1] But what of modern times? What *should* Tennessee have done with Lawrence West, who coolly killed a farm couple in 1941? When executed he was 16 years old. Why, then, write a book about every known legal execution in what is now called Tennessee?

The answer is this: respect for the truth. What do we know about capital punishment aside from so-called statistical analysis — when the underlying data are known to be faulty? To understand the issue, every execution in the United States must be researched and described. Toward that end, a new form of research, called fact-based death penalty research, was pioneered by Daniel Allen Hearn, a public scholar, whose question was simple: What are the *facts* that the jury heard and saw?[2] That is, the Hearn model emphasizes facts and eschews overemphasis on due process, which changes from time to time. Instead, the fundamental question is this: What did this man *do* that caused *that jury* to impose *this punishment*?

Ideally, a reader would see a flat narrative account of what happened, free from the writer's bias. This scientific reporting of these crimes and their aftermath would be value-free. This author has an opinion about capital punishment. But fact-based death penalty researchers are forbidden to speak publicly about their opinions. Personal views have no place in good research and writing. Neither does slanted language. A killing is simply a murder, not a slaughter, although five people may have died. The defendant is not a "brute" or a pervert. He may have been of low intelligence, but the term mentally retarded (with its due process consequences today) was not even used until the late 1950s. Prior to that time, persons were labeled idiots, morons or imbeciles, but the science of measuring intelligence was not accredited by the courts.

Meanwhile, capital crimes do not "occur," as many researchers assert. They are *committed*. This author uses the "committed" language because it is more accurate. The difference is important. In Tennessee, lightning "occurs" and kills about two people per year. The death penalty is much rarer and happens only when someone does wrong, a very serious wrong.

Fact-based death penalty research questions whether the death penalty, as imposed, is *still* random (and racist), and hence amounts to cruel and unusual punishment.[3] That thesis got its origin in Justice Potter Stewart's statement in *Furman v. Georgia*, 408 U.S. 238 (1972): "These death sentences are cruel and unusual in the same way that being struck by lightening [*sic*] is cruel and unusual."

The lightning analogy fails by looking at the facts. First, *most* people (victims) who are struck by lightning have *done* something that was a factor in their deaths, such as standing under tall trees in a thunderstorm. But most victims in capital cases were true victims, such as the four children of Daryl Keith Holton (q.v.), whom he killed execution-style in 1997. Lightning is a true act of God. Legal executions are the work of imperfect man. But even here, the analogy fails. Consider July 12, 1887. During a funeral that afternoon in Maury County, nine black mourners took refuge under a tree atop the cemetery. It was struck by lightning and all were killed.[4] At no time in Tennessee has the state executed nine people on the same day, much less nine black people. Moreover, most people who die from lightning do so in Southern states — just like most executions occur in Southern states. There were 82 lightning deaths per year nationally from 1980 through 1995, four times the number legally executed during that period, and twice the number executed annually nationwide from 1981 through 2008.[5]

In recent years, the death penalty debate has been dominated by concern that factually innocent people have suffered a wrongful death. Indeed, when this author began research for this book in 1999 his chief motive was to describe those cases of "wrong man" execution. Readers will have to decide for themselves who among the 524 people listed here were truly innocent ("wrong man") as opposed to those who were "wrongly convicted," like Ephriam Shelby Dodd, hanged as a spy in Knoxville by vengeful Yankees. Again, the latter is a due process issue, not truly the scope of this book.

This author fully expects this book to germinate a host of term papers and scholarly presentations "proving" the Tennessee death penalty is "wrong" when viewed through the lens of contemporary standards of decency. Meanwhile, this book shatters some conventional wisdom about the death penalty in Tennessee. For example, in civilian cases, facts show that all the men had at least one lawyer, sometimes as many as four, appointed by the court, regardless of race or rank. Some had *several* appeals to the Tennessee Supreme Court. These men were by no means rushed to their deaths. Still, until recent times, most men were executed within a year of their crime, including a trip to the Supreme Court. (The men's ages are their age at the time of the crime.)

What endures is not so-called analysis, but facts. This is a collection of facts, drawn from every known source: court records and opinions, newspaper accounts, published "confessions" of a few killers, and even the lowly detective magazine. This book challenges the assumption that our ancestors were benighted racists eager to send black men (and poor whites) to hasty deaths. Rather, they were just like people today, trying to reach a difficult decision based on the information in front of them. Unfortunately, some of the language used in past trials sounds racist to the modern ear. For example, the fact that "the odor of the Negro was still present in the room," was relevant in a 1918 rape — in the days before air conditioning — and the rapist had walked several miles on a summer day.

This author is confident that he has captured 99 percent of all legal executions in Tennessee. Missing cases might still be found for the antebellum period. They were either not documented (no newspaper coverage) or the records are gone. For example, a Nashville newspaper account from 1810 briefly mentions a slave who had been sentenced to die the next day for killing another slave. But there was no follow-up story and extant records make no mention of his hanging. In 1821 a white man named Adkins (Adkinson) killed his wife with a shoe last and was supposedly hanged in Franklin County, but surviving records only begin in 1824. Likewise, a young slave killed his owner and another man in Cocke County in 1842, news that reached newspapers beyond the state, but local records were destroyed when the courthouse burned in 1879.

Virtually predicting that law would some day hold that the punishment of death must only be visited on "the worst of the worst," Tennessee passed a unique statute in 1838, which allowed the jury to find the defendant guilty of first-degree murder, but "with mitigating circumstances," which allowed the judge to impose a life sentence. An untold number of killers benefited from the law. This likely accounts for the fact that no white woman has been executed in Tennessee since 1829. Likewise, a similar law allowed the Tennessee Supreme Court to send the governor a certificate suggesting he commute (pardon was the word used for decades) the death sentence to life imprisonment. The statute remains today. Criminal law experts observe, "Tennessee does not share the mind set of its Southern counterparts."[6]

Capital punishment law in this state may be summarized as follows: Tennessee has *never* had a mandatory death penalty law for white or black people. The condemned had the right to beg for mercy (called benefit of clergy) and receive an alternate punishment — placement in a pillory, ears nailed to the pillory and usually cut off, whipping and/or branding on the thumb. Technically, benefit of clergy was abolished in 1829 with the adoption of a law reform (the penitentiary), but the practice of a court remitting punishment continued. For example, black child rapist Dan Cherry got a new trial, but instead of a retrial his lawyers negotiated what was an "appropriate" punishment in 1851: fifty lashes. Likewise, the condemned, bondsman or free, has always had a right to ask the Tennessee Supreme Court to hear all the issues he deemed worthy of appeal. That is, the court could not pick and choose which cases it wanted to hear, as is the case in Missouri.

Death penalty opponents have seized on the issue of a condemned man asserting his innocence to the last as proof of "wrong man" convictions or wrongful convictions. This book shows that scores of men have "met their Maker with a lie on their lips." It is time to put to rest the notion of factual innocence based on a final protest of innocence. Men proclaim their innocence to the end for two reasons. First, they hope for a commutation to the last. Why not? In several instances the governor commuted the sentence of a man the day before his execution — and let another die the next day. (Indeed, according to one source, a man was on the gallows with a rope around his neck in 1819 when a rider appeared with a gubernatorial commutation.) Second, most of the men who proclaim innocence do so because they leave a wife, children and extended family behind. They simply do not want to dishonor their families.

A careful reading of Maurice Mays's case (1922), thought by many to be innocent (wrong man), shows he was not innocent and could have avoided death by agreeing to say he was insane at the time of the killing. Mays's death was a failure of commutation. Four white men (the most executed in Tennessee on the same day in the 20th century) protested their innocence despite overwhelming evidence of their guilt. Because they did so at the same time that Mays's case was under consideration for mercy, the governor was placed in a dilemma from which he could not escape. If he had granted mercy to the so-called Christmas Killers, he would have to do the same for Mays. All died in the electric chair within two weeks of each other. This is another value of a descriptive compilation of all legal executions in Tennessee. The deaths are placed in context.

Today, juries and appellate courts accredit scientific evidence (not eyewitness testimony) as the most reliable, both to convict and to exonerate. But both death penalty opponents and proponents do not know that the first death penalty in Tennessee traceable to crime lab work came in 1949. No ballistic evidence was used by either side in the Mays case, which turned on whether his pistol had been recently fired. Mays had two trials and a "dream team" of lawyers. In the past, witnesses at executions were eager to hear the condemned man admit his crime because technology-based evidence was lacking. Moreover, legal executions were public until 1883, made quasi-private that year (the public could see the man on the gallows but not the actual drop), and finally removed to the Main Prison in Nashville in 1909. For 100 years, executions were quasi-religious ceremonies. It was common in a Bible Belt state like Tennessee for several ministers to speak, pray and lead hymn-singing while standing on the gallows with the condemned man.

The Hearn model mandates a discussion of the victims, ignored by opponents, who usually focus attention on the condemned in order to show him as a victim of a racist culture, especially in the South. Opponents tend to overlook Anthony Blair, a black lawyer, who was legally executed in 1879. In today's language he was a "volunteer" because he chose not to appeal to the Tennessee Supreme Court. Recently, Daryl Keith Holton was another "volunteer" who chose not to pursue federal appeals, and literally chose to die in the Tennessee electric chair. This book hopes to give some life back to the victims, who are at least as important as the killers and rapists. They are described with the same demographics as the condemned.

Authors of similar books in this series, e.g., California, usually ignore military executions. (There were at least four in California. One was botched, killing a bystander.) However, military executions must necessarily be included in a Tennessee book, because they shed light on a poorly understood aspect of the Civil War. Moreover, they help explain why the years after that conflict were so bloody. For example, the 15,000 or so Confederate Army of Tennessee soldiers, camped across the state line in Georgia, saw 12 former comrades tied to posts and shot at the same time.[7] An illustrative anecdote: Two years after the Civil War was over, a Tennessee Confederate tracked down a man in Kentucky who had wrongfully put his eye out during the conflict. The Kentuckian tried to hail the Tennessean in a friendly manner. It didn't work. The Tennessean promptly shot and killed him, but suffered no punishment. The shooter was the father of Cordell Hull, who later won the Nobel Peace Prize.

This book contains the largest description of persons executed under Confederate and Union authority in any state. But Tennessee did not have the largest number of Civil War executions because Tennessee did not have retribution executions, like Missouri. Nor did it have mass executions as in Texas and North Carolina. Most non–mass executions under Confederate authority occurred in Virginia, but no book has captured them. The problem is record-keeping. To fully understand a Confederate execution (procedures were very similar to USA courts-martial) a researcher must consider three different records.[8] First are the General Orders (G.O.), which were printed documents that briefly described the charges and the verdict. Second are the actual court-martial files (again similar to USA courts-martial). Third is the Compiled Service Record (CSR) of the individual soldier. But here are the problems. First, the General Orders for the Army of Tennessee are incomplete. Next, the actual court-martial files were intentionally destroyed with the fall of Richmond in 1865. The CSRs for Confederate soldiers are incomplete. For these reasons, the CSA executions shown here include only men whose executions can be documented by *two* sources such as G.O.s and a diary, CSR, or newspaper account. The scope of the problem is this: there are at least eight men who were ordered shot in Tennessee for whom there are no Compiled Service Records. Conversely, there are five whose CSR says they were shot in Tennessee but no G.O. can be found for them. Furthermore, there is rudimentary documentation that at least two more civilians were executed for spying by the Confederate military in Tennessee, but information is lacking. Finally, there is rudimentary information that the Confederacy hanged four slaves in Tennessee, but the reasons are unknown. Similar, but lesser, problems exist for Union executions. After this book was submitted for publication, a detailed letter from a soldier posted at Memphis (June 11, 1863) came to light. It described the shooting of three federal soldiers for rape/murder. No court-martial records exist for these unnamed New Jersey miscreants.

This author suffered a major disappointment in researching this book. Despite an 1829 statute requiring written opinions by the Tennessee Supreme Court, at least 60 opinions cannot be located. That alone feels like a gross violation of due process. To make it clear, these are *unpublished* opinions, that is, they were never offered for publication in a law book by the Supreme Court. Compounding the problem is that the author uncovered many unpublished opinions. Some are literally reprinted in this book. Many have never been seen by anyone except the lawyers involved in the case until this author "discovered" them in court files. Regarding opinions, a fact-based death penalty researcher has a duty to look for and use handwritten opinions. Typewritten opinions began in Tennessee in 1903.

The Tennessee Supreme Court reverses or affirms convictions based on the *facts* as shown in the appellate record. It can do no more and must not do less. This discussion of Tennessee's "dead men walking" (a phrase never used in the state) differs from the Hearn model in this important feature: it includes a discussion of what the Supreme Court said were the facts. For example, in one case the newspaper account said the defendant (on the gallows) claimed the killing was in self-defense and maintained his innocence to the end. However, the Tennessee Supreme Court's opinion makes clear the killer drew the unarmed victim into a physical fight, shot him, and "finished him with a club." Furthermore, the reason for today's post-conviction relief is to bring before a court facts that were not brought out in the man's original trial (DNA evidence, details of ineffective assistance of counsel). In other words, today's post-conviction procedures and habeas corpus are chances for the defendant to "tell the whole story," and this author is well aware that "the facts" and "the story" depend on who is doing the telling.

This book is the first comprehensive accounting of legal executions in a Southern state. Certainly, the penalty of death was visited more on persons of African descent than whites. But generalizations should be avoided. By definition, a person who kills his owner is black. Likewise, it is clear that the Tennessee criminal justice system simply stopped killing black men who killed their black wives in 1910—does that make capital punishment more or less racist? The last white wife-killer was executed in 1943.

One of the goals of fact-based death penalty research is to find common patterns surrounding *why* this person was actually executed. The concept is simple but heroic. Once books are published cataloging all executions in every state, a careful observer might divine common threads that run through all executions nationwide. For example, a disproportionate percentage of men shown here were convicted of killing someone on Christmas Eve or Christmas Day. Can that be a factor? Likewise, killing a pregnant wife seems to raise the likelihood of state-imposed death. Although the last execution for killing a pregnant wife came in 1899, these executions may return. In 2010, the legislature decided that killing a pregnant woman, when the defendant knows she is pregnant, becomes an aggravating factor for purposes of imposing the death penalty in first degree murder cases (T.C.A. 39-13-204[i]). Two men cut their wives' throats on a Memphis street 42 days apart. They were hanged on the same day—although the white man was hanged separately from the black man a few minutes later.

Folklore is the natural enemy of truth, but every culture uses folklore to ease the tension caused by conflicting values. This book attempts to expiate folklore by telling the truth. Yes, there were newspaper accounts of men said to be walking about who were seen hanged a few days before. But does that make it so? A vile form of folklore arises from newspaper accounts of someone allegedly confessing to a crime for which a man was hanged years earlier. This is journalistic negligence, although on one occasion the offending paper ran down the story and found it false.

Death penalty opponents focus on botched executions to show the cruel and inhumane nature of the death penalty. This book will serve their argument. The number of botched hangings in Tennessee is alarming. While there were no botched electrocutions in Tennessee, it is true that the lights dimmed and an odor of burnt flesh could be smelled for an hour or two. But the reason is known: Tennessee administered 2300 volts. In the most recent electrocution, only 1750 volts were used. To this author's knowledge, there are no written firsthand accounts of the actual electrocutions of the men executed in the Tennessee electric chair between 1916 and 1960.

All fact-based death penalty researchers owe a debt to the late Major Watt Espy, Jr., who began a life's work capturing information about every known legal execution in 1970. The famous Espy List was first published in 1987. Espy was a death penalty opponent who soon disavowed his own list because he was not allowed to correct it before it was published. This author spoke with Espy several times regarding his list. His research strategy was to write every county clerk and county librarian in the nation asking for information. In Tennessee, many librarians responded by sending him short entries about hangings that had been published in a venerable multi-county history called Goodspeed's published in 1886.[9] Espy acknowledged that he confirmed no facts regarding the 335 names on his Tennessee list. For example, it contains three men who were not executed and a woman (Eve Martin) who was a victim. The Espy list was by no means complete; this book attempts to remedy that.

Espy included only two Civil War–era legal executions, namely Confederate martyr Sam Davis and Unionist mass murderer Champ Ferguson (1865). But that is the posture of most opponents. They ignore Civil War *legal* executions because of two inconvenient truths. Most of the men executed were white, and most of the court-martial files bear the notation, "Sentence approved A. Lincoln." Civil War executions have been a blind spot for most fact-based researchers too. Like Daniel Hearn, they have not had to contend with Confederate executions. The death by musketry of a Confederate deserter (Asa Lewis) may have been a factor in the Confederate defeat at the Battle of Murfreesboro five days later.[10] Maybe we are all — North and South — in this together, as most death penalty authors insist.

Persons Executed and Their Crimes

(Listed Chronologically)

1782

Isaac Choate, white, age unknown. *Horse stealing.*
John Vann, white, age unknown. *Horse stealing.*
William White, white, age unknown. *Horse stealing.*

Executed under authority of North Carolina.

The dates and locations of the crimes are unknown except that they were committed in Washington County near the time the first court was established in what is now Tennessee, but was then North Carolina. This was the court of Oyer and Terminer, presided over by Judge Spruce Macay,[11] in whose office the teenage Andrew Jackson would briefly study law two years later.

Macay had lost a hand. In its place he wore a brass ball. When necessary to make his point or keep order, the irascible Macay slammed the ball down on a table or the bench and it rang like a bell. Macay was considered a heartless and tyrannical judge.[12]

William White, who had earlier been convicted of improperly indenturing a woman, had been convicted of horse stealing at an earlier "tryal." John McCain and Thomas Mitchell testified against Vann, who challenged five jurors.[13] He was convicted on "Fryday, the 16th" [of August 1782]. Choate was tried on "Satturday the 17th" and pled guilty and "put himself on God and his country" (i.e., asked for mercy). By law, it was still necessary for a jury to convict him, which it did, after he challenged three jurors.

Although the jury had recommended mercy for Vann, Judge Macay sentenced all three to be hanged on September 10, 1782, and by tradition they were executed that day in Jonesboro, Washington County.[14] Horse stealing was a capital crime because a horse not only provided the muscle power needed to pull a plow and drag fallen logs, it was the primary means of escaping an attack by Native Americans.

North Carolina abolished capital punishment for horse stealing in 1786 and substituted in its place the following punishment: one hour in the pillory, 39 lashes on the back well laid on, ears cut off ("cropped") and nailed to the pillory, and branding on the cheek the letters "H" and "T." However, for the second offense, the punishment was death without benefit of clergy.[15]

When North Carolina ceded its Tennessee counties to the United States to become the Southwest Territory in 1786 (and again in 1789) the cession act provided that North Carolina laws were to stay in effect. Therefore, capital punishment was effectively abolished for horse stealing, except for second offenders. For the next decade numerous men were whipped and "cropped" in what is now Tennessee. John Vann had been easy to recognize. His ears had been cropped sometime before in North Carolina. In 1799 the State of Tennessee reenacted capital punishment for horse stealing and did not repeal the law until 1809.

1784

Unnamed female slave, black, age unknown. *Murder.*

Executed under authority of North Carolina.

The crime was committed at an unknown date in 1784 in the French Broad River in what is now Cocke County, but was then Greene County, still a part of North Carolina. The woman was present at the "Slave Block" while her grandson, age eight, was being sold at auction. She had been weeping. He was her only grandchild.[16]

As the bidding began, she was heard to say, "That man will never get him!" As the auction ended, she quickly grabbed the boy and put him on her back. She ran to the ford of the French Broad River about fifty yards west of the Old Town bridge. As she attempted to swim the river, the boy became frightened. Apparently, he lost his grip and drowned.

She was convicted by a special jury consisting of slave-owners. It concluded that her statement, coupled with his disappearance into the river, suggested she purposely drowned him. She was immediately tried and hanged. No contemporaneous documentation supports these facts.

1786

Tom, black, age unknown. *Murder.*

Executed under authority of North Carolina.

The facts of the case are unknown except that Tom, a slave, poisoned John Fuller Sain (possibly Lain), white, age unknown, somewhere in Sullivan County in 1786. He was tried on August 8, 1786, and was hanged the next day. His owner, William Evans, claimed he had hired counsel for Tom, but the court refused to allow him to argue the case.[17]

Evans filed suit against James Allison, the sheriff, for wrongful destruction of his property, but the suit was dismissed by the court.[18] Finally, in 1799 Evans filed a petition asking the General Assembly to compensate him for what Tom was worth in 1786, namely "one hundred Virginia pounds," because Tom was a "faithful, industrious, healthy slave and in the prime of life."[19] The petition was signed by a hundred citizens but was ignored by the Tennessee General Assembly.

1787

George Middleton Clarkston (aka George Middleton Clarkson), white, age unknown. *Murder.*

Executed under authority of the State of Franklin.

The crime was committed in the Sequatchie Valley sometime in 1787 at a cabin the killer and the victim, brother-in-law George Middleton, were building. Tradition has it that the two began arguing, variously about slavery or the purported new State of Franklin. Persons who supported the new state were called Franklinites; those opposed were called Tiptonites. Clarkston was a Tiptonite and antislavery. Middleton was a Franklinite and proslavery. The two got into an argument and the victim was killed with an axe. Clarkston was tried before Franklinite judge David Campbell of the Superior Court of the State of Franklin, and condemned before the Tiptonite family and friends could seek revenge. That is, the judge was seeking to prevent more of the bloodshed which had wracked the area. Clarkston was convicted at Jonesborough on April 2, 1787, and was hanged there on April 13, 1787.[20]

1792

Absalom Morris, white, age 30. *Burglary.*
Welcome Hodge, white, age unknown. *Burglary.*

The details of these men's crimes are unknown except they were found guilty by the Superior Court of Washington County on April 15, 1792. Operating under Territorial (federal) law, this court consisted of three judges, David Campbell, John McNairy and Joseph Anderson, but it is not clear whether all presided, or just the judge from that area, Joseph Anderson, with the aid of a jury. The two were publicly hanged in Jonesborough on April 22, 1792.[21] Absalom and brothers Gideon and Daniel were among the first families of the region, for whom Morristown is named. Brother Gideon was hanged in 1806.

John A. Herrin (aka John Aherrin and John O'Herrin), white, age unknown. *Murder.*

The facts of the crime are unknown other than Herrin shot Christian Distow in the back opposite the heart, killing him instantly on September 27, 1790. He was sentenced to hang at Nashville on June 3, 1792.[22] According to tradition he was hanged that day, the first legal execution in Nashville. Much confusion surrounds the defendant's name.

1794

Obongpohego (aka Abongpohigo), Native American, age unknown. *Murder.*

Technically, because Tennessee was a territory, not a state, at the time Obongpohego was executed, it was conducted under federal authority.

On July 24, 1794, a Creek war party headed by

Obongpohego killed John Ish, white, age unknown, who headed a station (reinforced blockhouse) eighteen miles from Knoxville. Ish was plowing a field about two hundred yards from his house. He was killed without warning and scalped.[23] He was survived by his wife Elizabeth and eight children, the eldest about twelve years old.

Obongpohego would not have been captured without active help from Hanging Maw, head chief of the Cherokees. Hanging Maw was attempting to curry favor with the white settlers, who had begun a policy of punitive reprisals against Cherokee towns for raids emanating from both Cherokee and Creek towns. Hanging Maw's son, Willioe, was one of the four warriors who captured the killer, bound him, and delivered him to the white men.[24] This was during a period of constant attacks from Indians.[25]

On July 29, 1794, Territorial Governor William Blount signed a special warrant authorizing David Campbell, John McNairy and Joseph Anderson to serve as judges of a Court of Oyer and Terminer to try Obongpohego for murder. The warrant allowed them three days to conduct the trial.[26]

At trial, Obongpohego actually pled guilty, saying, "The white men are determined to weigh [hang] me anyhow."[27] He was asked to withdraw the plea, which he did. According to one account, he was convicted by a jury, but more likely the three judges tried the case themselves, with Anderson presiding. When asked if he had anything to say before sentence was pronounced, Obongponhego said, "I have nothing to say. I came out to take hair and horses, or to be killed. I killed John Ish, and have fallen into the hands of the whites. I would have escaped if it had not been for the Cherokees. If I am now to be killed, there are enough of my Nation to avenge my death."[28]

Obongpohego's execution on August 4, 1794, did not go smoothly. He was mounted on his horse with his hands tied at his sides. The noose was placed around his neck. The sheriff threw the rope over a tree limb, but concluded that the doomed man was too tall for the length of rope the sheriff held. He told Obongpohego to stand up in order to decide how much rope was needed. As he did this, the brave's horse shifted and Obongpohego fell off. With the sheriff holding the rope, Obongpohego was strangled. His death widened the split in relations between the Cherokees and the always menacing Creeks. The latter sent warriors into Cherokee towns and extracted bloody revenge.[29]

1797

Robert Parker, white, age unknown. *Burglary.*

The crime was committed on the night of March 31, 1797, at the home of Thomas Humes in Grainger County. Parker, a laborer, stole five hundred Spanish milled dollars. He was convicted before the Superior Court of Law and Equity on April 11, 1797, and was ordered hanged in Grainger County. He was executed on April 28, 1797, in Rutledge by the Knox County sheriff in charge.[30]

1800

Shawney George (aka Tellico George and Nasuate), Native American, age unknown. *Murder.*

The crime was committed at an unknown location in Kentucky on May 15, 1800, on unspecified Indian land. The indictment charged George with shooting James Johnston, white, age unknown, in the side with a rifle and then striking him with "a knife and tomahock on the body and head."[31] Shawney George was captured in Knox County on June 28, 1800. He was tried and convicted on July 10, 1800, and was hanged in Knoxville the next day.[32]

1801

Jack Pate (aka Jack), black, age unknown. *Murder.*

The crime was committed on the night of July 28, 1801. Jack raped and killed Mrs. Sarah Crawford, white, age unknown, whose husband was away. Jack had entered the house to rape her, but she fought and he strangled and beat her with a claw hammer. The bed and an infant were found covered with blood. Jack dragged her into the yard, where her body was found with fourteen wounds to the head and breasts and an arm broken.[33] She was survived by three children. Jack was a slave owned by Stephen Pate.[34] Discovered the next day covered with blood, he quickly confessed. Jack was tried before a slave court and convicted on August 3, 1801. He was executed the next day in Knoxville.

Gov. John Sevier, in Knoxville, attended the trial. The execution method, set by the court, was the worst punishment known in law. Jack was burned alive.

Gov. Sevier wrote in his diary, "August Sunday 2 Very warm and dry. Mon. 3 Ditto a called court on negro Jack the property of Stephen Pate for the murder of Sarah Crawford was held & the negro found guilty & sentenced to be burnt on the morrow between the hours of 12 & 4 o'clock. Tue. 4 Negro Jack was agreeably to the sentence of yesterday executed in the presence of a great number of spectators."[35]

It is not clear whether Governor Sevier attended the execution.[36] The Knox County sheriff reported that it cost twenty-one dollars to execute Jack.[37]

Within months, the legislature received a petition signed by eighty-three leading citizens of Knox County. It said, "Said Stephen Pate is a good honest citizen and a man of but low Circumstances of property by a Misfortune which of late befell him — he is Incapable of providing for himself and family by labour. That a Negro man Jack which was his principle dependence for Support has lately been Executed at Knoxville agreeable to the Law of the State. We therefore pray that your honorable body would take under your Consideration the said Citizen and allow him such Compensation for the Loss of his Slave as you in your wisdom may think just and Right, and your petitioners shall ever pray...." The legislature denied the request as "unreasonable."[38]

Aaron Gist (aka Aaron Guiss), white, age unknown. *Horse stealing.*

The details of the crime are unknown except that Gist was convicted by a jury in front of the Superior Court of Law and Equity on October 6, 1801, and three days later was ordered hanged at the public gallows in Knox County on October 14, 1801.[39] He was hanged that day.[40]

Samuel Carman (aka Samuel Carmon), white, age unknown. *Burglary.*

The crime was committed on March 18, 1801, at 11:00 P.M. at the house of William Stewart in Davidson County. Carman broke into the house and stole "one hundred silver Spanish milled dollars of the value of one hundred cents each" that were owned by Samuel Walker. No other details of the crime are known. Carman was tried on May 18, 1801, before a jury and a Superior Court of Law and Equity consisting of Archibald Roane, David Campbell, and Andrew Jackson.

The jury convicted Carman. His lawyer, George Washington Campbell, immediately moved to quash the verdict. He argued that not all the grand jurors were from the Mero District, nor were there twelve or more such jurors. He argued the grand jury indictment recited the state of Tennessee, but not Mero District. Further, it did not say it was "by the oaths" of the grand jurors, nor did it mention the name of the judge or judges who presided, or the day of court. Finally, it did not state that Carman entered the house with the intent to commit a felony. The court took the matter under advisement.[41]

No opinion was filed. The court minutes state: "On argument of the reasons in arrest of Judgment, heretofore filed in this case, it is the opinion of the Court, that the reasons aforesaid are not sufficient in law to arrest the judgment and that the same be overruled. And the said Samuel Carmon, who stands convicted of Burglary was again led to the Bar in custody of the sheriff of Davidson county and thereupon it being demanded of him, if anything for himself he had or knew to say why the Court here to judgment and execution of and upon the premises should not proceed, he said, he had nothing, but what he had before said — Therefore, it is considered by this Court that he be hanged by the neck until he be dead, and that execution of this judgment be made and done upon him the said Samuel Carmon by the sheriff of Davidson County, on Tuesday the twenty ninth day of December next, between the hours of twelve in the forenoon and five in the afternoon of the same day at the public gallows in the county of Davidson — and that the said Samuel Carmon be remanded to jail."[42]

Setting the execution date this far into the future ensured that the person elected governor to succeed Gov. John Sevier would have the power to pardon Carman. That person was Archibald Roane, and Samuel Carman was hanged on the appointed day.

1802

Charles Powel (aka Charles Powell and Charles Foster), white, age unknown. *Horse stealing.*
Michael West, white, age unknown. *Horse stealing.*

Charles Powel committed the crime on August 7, 1801. Powel, alias Charles Foster, a laborer, stole a ten-year-old gelding branded with an "S" from

Thomas Draper at Dixon Springs, Smith County. The horse was worth sixty dollars. The Superior Court of Law and Equity, with a jury, convicted Powel on May 18, 1802, and he was sentenced to hang on June 25, 1802.[43]

Similarly, Michael West, a laborer, stole a bay mare worth $100 from William Marshall of Sumner County on February 18, 1802. He was also tried before the Superior Court of Law and Equity and convicted in May 20, 1802.[44] He was sentenced to hang on June 25, 1802.[45]

Samuel Black was convicted of stealing a young bay mare, worth $100, from William Marshall on January 18, 1802, and was tried on May 20, 1802, along with West and was sentenced to die with him on June 25, 1802.[46]

The Superior Court of Law and Equity was composed of David Campbell, Andrew Jackson and Hugh L. White. They recommended clemency for Black because of his youth and he was pardoned by the governor. Powel and West were executed at Nashville on the appointed day.[47]

1804

Samuel Inman, white, age unknown. *Horse stealing.*

On May 10, 1803, Inman stole a black mare "the value of one hundred dollars" owned by Nancy Cortney. He was tried by the Superior Court of Law and Equity on May 21, 1804, and found guilty. He was hanged in Nashville, Davidson County, on June 22, 1804.[48]

1805

Samuel Forrester, white, age unknown. *Murder.*

The details of the crime are unknown except that Forrester and Joseph Duncan were the subject of a governor's reward of $200 after they were accused of shooting a negro woman named Millie on March 26, 1803, in Jackson County.[49] According to the indictment, Millie was shot with a "riffle gun" in and upon "the left side of the belly near the short ribs" and died April 4, 1803. This is the first known case where a reward posted by a Tennessee slave owner for the death of a slave bore fruit. The reward notice said that Forrester had a scar under his right nipple due to a penknife wound.[50]

Joseph Duncan was arrested in Knoxville on June 8, 1803, and was convicted in some manner but was pardoned by the governor in 1803.[51]

Forrester was tried in Nashville on May 20, 1805.[52] He was convicted by a jury before the Superior Court of Law and Equity [53] of murdering "a certain female negro slave named Mille, the property of a certain Garrett Fitzgerald," and was sentenced to die on June 15, 1805.[54] The governor respited him until August 20, 1805, when he was hanged in Davidson County.[55]

1806

Gideon Morris, white, age unknown. *Horse stealing.*
William Evans, white, age unknown. *Horse stealing.*

The facts of the cases are unknown.[56] The defendants were tried together and convicted before the Superior Court on October 7, 1806, and ordered hanged in Knoxville on October 23, 1806.[57] The exact location of the crime cannot be determined because they were tried under the jurisdiction of the Hamilton District, which comprised the counties of Anderson, Bledsoe, Blount, Cocke, Jefferson, Knox, Rhea, Roane, and Sevier. Hamilton District trials were held in Knoxville and unless the judgment spelled otherwise, executions were conducted there. Gideon was the brother of Absalom Morris, who was hanged in 1792.

James Clements, white, age unknown. *Murder.*

The details of the crime are unknown except that it was committed somewhere in Davidson County on June 6, 1806, when Clements killed Edward Steel (Steele), white, age unknown, by shooting him in the left side near the short ribs with a "riffle gun." Steel died the next day. "He left a wife and several small children in very indigent circumstances to lament his death."[58] Clements was tried on November 15, 1806, and was hanged as ordered on December 15, 1806.[59]

1807

Unnamed male slave, black, age unknown. *Rape and murder.*

The crime was committed on February 9, 1807, within a mile of the three forks of the Duck River in Bedford County at the home of Mr. and Mrs. Philip Burrow. The husband was away and the slave, owned by Captain W. Wilborne, came to the house in secret. When Mrs. Burrow, white, age unknown, went outside, he knocked her to the ground and tied her with his belt and raped her. She asked to see her children before he killed her. He took her into the house, raped her again, beat her and three of the children (two remained hidden). He stole from the house and set fire to it. The older children helped her from the house but at least one child, an infant, burned to death. The slave was captured the next day. He was tried by a slave court. He admitted the crime and said his intent was to murder the whole family. He was hanged February 10, 1807.[60]

Molly (aka Molly Holevine and Molly Holcomb), a slave, black, age unknown. *Murder.*

Molly was convicted by a special slave court in Williamson County of murdering her child, age and gender unknown. She was convicted on February 28, 1807, and hanged on March 20, 1807, in Franklin.[61]

Moses Penrice (aka Moses), black, age unknown. *Murder.*

The crime was committed near the home of a man named Penrice at a place called Southside, in Montgomery County. The exact date of the crime is unknown, but it was March or April 1807. Moses, a slave, was being sold by Joseph Penrice because he was obstinate. He was being bought by Samuel Minott, white, age unknown. He was a severe master. When Minott and two guards came to get Moses, he took a hidden gun from behind a log and shot Minott dead.

The guards nearly beat Moses to death. Fearing he would die, the authorities quickly brought him to town for a trial. A slave-holder jury consisting of six justices of the peace and four slaveholders found him guilty. He was ordered "hung by the neck until he is dead, dead, dead, and that his head be severed from his body and placed upon a pole as a warning to all evil doers."[62]

Moses was hanged before a large crowd on March 30, 1807, at a vacant lot between Franklin and Main Streets. The severed head was placed on a pole at the corner of Main and Fourth. It remained on the pole until all the flesh disappeared and the sun bleached the skull white.

In 1809 his owner petitioned the General Assembly for compensation for his value. His petition was ignored.[63]

Henry McNight (aka Thomas Pate), white, age unknown. *Horse stealing.*

The details of the crime are unknown except that McNight was tried before the Superior Court of Hamilton District on October 7, 1807, and ordered hanged on November 6, 1807. He was executed that day in Knoxville.[64]

1808

Frank, black, age unknown. *Rape and murder.*

Frank, a slave belonging to John Howard Sr., raped and murdered Betsy Osborn, white, age unknown, on February 14, 1808. He killed her by "tying a skain of thread around her neck by which she instantly died."[65] Arrested the next day, he was tried and convicted on February 22, 1808, by a special court consisting of seven slaveholders, two justices of the peace, and four freeholders. He was hanged in Dandridge, Jefferson County, on February 28, 1808.[66]

1809

Jesse Ward, black, a slave, age 12. *House burning (arson).*

Details of the crime are unknown except that Ward burned the dwelling house and several barns belonging to the man who owned him and told the court he did so because he had been whipped. Convicted by the Superior Court, not a slave court, on October 3, 1809, he was ordered hanged on October 31, 1809, and died that day in Knoxville.[67]

1810

Unnamed male slave, age unknown, black. *Rape.*

According to Goodspeed's, "about 1810 a black man was hanged for rape in Sumner County."[68]

The execution cannot be confirmed by diligent search of Sumner County records for the period.

Goodspeed may have confused this case with Israel (1819), which he did not report.

1811

Jacob Pickering, white, age unknown. *Murder.*
Stewart W. Thornton, white, age unknown. *Murder.*

The crime was committed on a road from Clarksville to Springfield, somewhere in either Robertson County or Montgomery County in early 1810. Jacob Pickering was a tavern keeper and jailer of the town of Springfield. Stewart W. Thornton was the town's only tailor and was custodian of the courthouse. It was his duty to see that the doors were kept closed to "prevent any gambling in the house or damage."

Elijah Gardner, white, age unknown, had been taken from the jail by Pickering and made to work, but eloped. He was captured in Montgomery County. Pickering and Thornton were sent to bring him back. In Clarksville, the pair began drinking and became increasingly intoxicated as they returned with Gardner. His hands were tied and he was riding on the same horse as one of his captors. He angered the two and shortly before reaching Port Royal they gave him a savage beating. He was told to walk behind the pair, his neck tied to a rope fastened to one of their saddles. In time, he fell and was dragged and stabbed to death. The pair said he ran away and pretended to help look for him when the body was found two hundred yards from the road. The pair was indicted in Robertson County and sought a change of venue to Davidson County.

The pair received separate trials beginning September 14, 1810, and were convicted on consecutive days. Their new trial motions were denied sometime after March 22, 1811.[69] Both appealed, but the records cannot be located. They were executed in Nashville on July 13, 1811, before a "concourse of spectators greater than ever before known in this country."[70] The newspaper reported that both confessed their crime on the gallows and their confessions would be published. No record of such documents can be located.[71]

John Cunningham, white, age unknown. *Murder.*

The details of the crime are unknown, but Cunningham killed his wife, white, name and age unknown, at their home in Bledsoe County in 1810 or 1811. He was hanged at Pikeville, Bledsoe County, on October 4, 1811. "The particulars are shocking," said a Nashville newspaper, without describing them.[72]

1813

Jessee (aka Jess), a slave, black, age unknown. *Burglary.*

The facts of the case are unknown except that Jessee broke into the Rutherford County home of Edward Ward and stole unspecified property belonging to Samuel Smith. The crime was committed in August 1813 and Jessee was executed by hanging in Murfreesboro on September 3, 1813.[73] Goodspeed says Jessee was found guilty of "house breaking" and "according to superstition of the time, bits of the hangman's rope were in great demand as a talisman against many ills that human flesh was heir to."[74]

Jessee was the property of Col. George M. Sanders of White County. In November 1813, Sanders petitioned the General Assembly for compensation for Jessee's life. He explained he did not know Jessee had been charged with a crime until after he was dead. He argued that unless he was compensated "the negro property of no person in this county would be secure from malicious prosecution."[75] Sanders argued he was a poor man who was a "tiller of the property he is in possession of by the labor of his hands."

Smith's petition said that the prosecutor, Samuel Smith, really did think that Jessee was guilty, but was mistaken. He offered the affidavit of John Edwards (not identified), which said that Smith told him shortly before he died that Jessee had "suffered death for which one or two other Negros was guilty of" and that he said Jessee was innocent.

Smith offered a second petition. This was signed by about a hundred people (county not identified) which said they were informed that the charges were "incorrect" and "the trial was conducted with that sort of prejudice and heat which too often is manifested in this country in trials in which white and free persons are concerned, and which seldom or never fails to show itself in a tenfold degree when slaves are tried for offences either real or imaginary."[76] The petition repeated the assertion that

Smith had said he thought Jessee was guilty at the trial but before his execution changed his mind and Jessee "died entirely innocent of the crime charged upon him."[77]

Neither petition asked for a specific amount. The Tennessee General Assembly rejected the petitions by "laying them on the table." There is no record of Tennessee's ever paying compensation to any slave owner regardless of whether the slave was executed by law or wrongly executed.

1814

James Brice, white, age unknown. *Slave stealing.*

The details of the Blount County crime are unknown except that on February 5, 1813, Brice absconded with a "negro slave man, called and known by the name of Charles, the property of and owned and employed by a certain Parmer Shields."[78] Brice was a member of a gang that stole slaves. The ringleader was never caught.[79]

Popular accounts of the case describe it as unusual because he was "convicted under a statute that was never enacted in Tennessee."[80] This was partially true. The North Carolina legislature passed a statute making slave stealing a capital offense in 1779. Blount County was still a part of North Carolina at the time. In 1789 the present Tennessee was ceded to the United States and became a territory, with the cession act stating that all North Carolina laws remained in effect. This provision was carried over when Tennessee became a state in 1796.[81]

However, in 1807 the Tennessee capital punishment law was revised. The new statute did not expressly repeal the North Carolina law nor mention slave stealing. It plainly repealed capital punishment for *horse* stealing.[82]

Brice's appeal to the Tennessee Supreme Court insisted that the practical affect of the 1807 statute was the implicit repeal of the North Carolina statute. The court said no. The act of slave stealing was a worse crime than larceny (horse theft) because it usually involved "seducing" the slave to leave his owner.[83] James Brice was hanged in Blount County on July 20, 1814. Shortly before the rope was placed he collapsed with fright and had to be lifted to his feet.[84]

The next year, the court said the horse-theft provision was retroactive, overturning the death sentence of a man whose theft of a horse had occurred in 1801 but was not caught and convicted until 1813.[85]

John Jones, white, age 33. *Desertion.*
William Myers, white, age 19. *Desertion.*
Jacob King, white, age 20. *Desertion.*
Benjamin Harris, white, age 38. *Desertion.*
John Young, white, age unknown. *Desertion.*
Nathaniel Chester, white, age unknown. *Desertion.*
Drury Puckett, white, age 36. *Desertion.*
James McBride, white, age 21. *Desertion.*

The crimes were committed at various times but the men were court-martialed in Nashville during October and November 1814. The declaration of war against England (June 18, 1812) had little practical effect in Tennessee until August 30, 1813, when the Creeks massacred civilians at Fort Mims, Alabama. A shiver of fear struck Tennesseans because a charismatic chief, Tecumseh, seemed able to bind the northern tribes and southern ones, commonly called Creeks, into a full frontier war on the whites. Major General Andrew Jackson led men south to punish the Creeks, who were supplied with British weapons and supplies. However, the Tennessee militiamen had enlisted for short terms (three to six months). What constituted desertion was confusing because the militiamen took the position they could return home when their enlistments expired. Many did. Soldiers in regular Army units such as the hard-fighting 39th Regiment and the lackluster 24th Regiment could not use this excuse. The number charged with desertion is unknown but could have reached two hundred, including militiamen. Unknown is when the court-martial findings were received by Gen. Andrew Jackson in West Florida or after he arrived in New Orleans (December 1, 1814). But he affirmed the sentences in an order dated January 28, 1815, twenty days after the Battle of New Orleans.

Private Jones had enlisted for five years on July 25, 1814, at Farquier, Virginia.[86] He was a member of the 2nd Rifle Regiment. Private William Myers was born in Georgia. He enlisted on March 27, 1814, for the war's duration. Artilleryman Myers deserted at New Orleans on July 30, 1814. Private Jacob King was a member of the 1st U.S. Artillery. Born in Adams, Pennsylvania, he enlisted at Fort Fayette on March 28, 1814, for five years. He deserted on July 12, 1814. Private Benjamin Harris was born in Orange, Virginia, and was a member of the 44th Regiment, which had been raised in New Orleans. He had enlisted on March 26, 1814, for the duration but deserted on July 1, 1814. Private John Young had enlisted on October 3, 1813, at

Winchester, Virginia, for one year. A member of the 39th Regiment, he deserted October 8, 1813, (this may have been October 3, 1814). Private Nathaniel Chester was a member of the Corp of Artillery; no other information has been discovered about him. Private Drury Puckett was born in Russell, Virginia, and had enlisted there on September 24, 1814, for five years. He was a member of the 2nd Infantry. The date of his desertion is confusing, shown in the records as December 31, 1814, which was after he had been sentenced to die by the court-martial. Private James McBride, born in Patrick County, Virginia, had enlisted at McMinnville, Tennessee, on July 22, 1814. Other records show him having enlisted for the duration on April 20, 1813, but later deserting that company.

One version of the famous "Coffin Handbill" (below) says Private Joseph Muckelroy was executed with these men. He had enlisted on August 28, 1814, location unknown, for five years. Muckelroy's service record includes the execution order, but it also shows him on several attached duty details; he was "sent to" Newport, Kentucky, and was at Portage de Sioux in August 1815. It says he drowned on November 1, 1816.

The men were kept confined in a house waiting news of whether Major General Andrew Jackson had affirmed their sentences. The death order was received in Nashville on February 15 and the men were executed two days later. They were taken from the house separately, in part, because there was concern that there were not enough soldiers available to make up a large firing squad that could kill all of the condemned at the same time. What was done with their bodies is unknown.

The executions were criticized in both Nashville newspapers even as they praised Jackson's victories, notably New Orleans.[87] These executions, plus others on March 14, 1814 (John Woods in Alabama), two British subjects in Florida on April 29, 1818, and six Tennessee militiamen shot on February 21, 1815, at Mobile, followed Jackson the rest of his life. They became a volatile issue when he ran for president in 1828. It took the form of a handbill called the "Coffin Handbill."[88] Less known is the fact that Jackson pardoned five others at the same time as he condemned these eight. One was Thomas Puckett, apparently an eighteen-year-old kinsman of Drury Puckett. (He deserted again for good in 1816.) On October 17, 1814, Jackson had pardoned four of six deserters court-martialed in Knoxville in trials lasting from September 19 to 29, 1814.[89] The fate of two not pardoned, John Haygood and Henry McCurdy, is unknown.

The actual court-martial files for those executed in Tennessee cannot be found in the National Archives. Records can be found for only four others sentenced to die at a Nashville court-martial on April 28, 1814, but their fate cannot be determined from known documents. They were Pvt. Robert Williams, Capt. Reynold's Company, 39th Infantry, who deserted the Nashville garrison on January 13, 1814. Privates John Hutchinson and William Dunning (Denny), members of Capt. Sturges' Company, 24th Infantry, deserted the regiment at Newport, Kentucky, on February 5, 1814.[90] Private Leonard Belau (Belew) had deserted with Hutchinson and Dunning and was sentenced to be shot, but with a recommendation for mercy because of his youth.

During the War of 1812 about thirteen percent of all soldiers deserted.[91] The execution of these eight soldiers at Nashville remains the largest execution in Tennessee history.

1819

Unnamed female slave, black, age unknown. *Murder.*

The details of the crime are unknown except that the slave murdered her mistress owner somewhere in Sumner County in late 1818 or early 1819. The owner is thought to be either Abagail Gardner Clark or Mary Brigance, who both died at this time survived by their husbands. The execution took place prior to February 25, 1819, the day the sheriff was paid for hanging her.[92] The account that her head was put on public display at the forks of the Nashville Turnpike near Gallatin cannot be confirmed."

Benjamin Bridges, white, age unknown. *Murder.*

The details of the crime are unknown except that Bridges killed Evan Anders (sometimes Andries or Adres) by shooting him in the back of the neck somewhere in Franklin County on June 18, 1818. The victim was white, age unknown, a peddler.[93] Bridges was tried in Bledsoe County.[94] He and Charles L. Bennett (see below) had several venue changes, a matter noted in Bennett Dula's case, which referred to them as "culprits."[95] Bridges was ordered hanged in Pulaski, Giles County, on November 12, 1819, and was hanged that day.[96]

Charles L. Bennett, white, age unknown. *Murder.*

The crime was committed after dark on September 27, 1816, at the defendant's home at an unknown location in Wilson County.[97] According to Bennett's published confession, he and the victim, William T. Hay, white, age unknown, planned to travel from his home to that of Mr. Clack Stone, where Bennett was to arrange the purchase of some land. But they were distracted by Hay's shooting of squirrels and a trip to the blacksmith's. They returned to the Bennett home, having decided to go the next day.

At home, they began to play cards and Bennett became convinced Hay was dealing from the bottom of the deck. The amount at stake was ten dollars. The two began arguing. Bennett said that Hay picked up a stick and swung it at him. Bennett got the stick away and threw it in the garden, but Hay picked up an ax and swung it at him. Bennett could not find anything by which to defend himself except a pair of smoothing irons tied together with a string. He flung them at Hay, striking his head, killing him.

Said Bennett, "I left him in his gore as he fell and started to go to Mr. Robb's, to make known my misfortune, in a state of distress which almost took away my senses. I stopped at the creek and sat down on a log and was deliberating what would be best for me to do."[98]

Here is what happened next:

> I saw a young man passing by with whom I was acquainted; I harked him; I went to him with a flood of tears flowing from my eyes, and related to him the dreadful accident that had just taken place. I told him I was awfully afraid my life would be taken on account of it, as I was not able to prove the cause I had or doing what was done. Another thing I told him, that I had been informed by Mr. Hay, that he had left home with about $2,300 and that he had gambled away the principal part of it, and his friends would readily conclude that I had taken the part that was deficient. He gave it as his opinion, that the thing had best be concealed, and his money at some time conveyed into the hands of his friends in such a manner so as for no person to be suspected. I then asked him to assist me in concealing my misfortune, which he at first denied, and said he was afraid of being brought into a preminary [sic; mispronunciation of preliminary]. I told him it was impossible for me to accomplish it without help, and if he would assist me, I never would disclose to him, not even to save my own life. I hope that will never be urged, for I never will give insinuations that will accuse him.[99]

The young man helped bury the body, took Hay's mare "to a considerable distance to destroy her in order to remove every vestige that might lead to detection."[100]

The newspaper that reported his "confession" spoke on his behalf. "There can be no doubt but Bennett, if he was this day discharged, would be a *pious, industrious, orderly* man, and he might so continue to the day of his death. To hang him can do society no good: The example has no effect, for where most men are hung we have positive history for it that crimes are common."[101]

Bennett's case was appealed to the Tennessee Supreme Court, but only a portion of the bill of exceptions can be located, notably the indictment. He was indicted in Wilson County on October 26, 1818, but the trial was moved to Bedford County. The indictment recites that he struck William T. Hay on the back part of the right ear with an axe, then took a bandana and "choked and strangled" him to death.[102]

The execution of Charles L. Bennett became a part of Tennessee folklore. Bennett had been defended by the most famous criminal lawyer of his day, Felix Grundy, later United States Senator and Attorney General. According to much-repeated lore, Grundy had defended 165 men and only Bennett was found guilty and executed.[103] "The Bennett case was the only capital criminal case he ever lost."[104] For the rest of his life, when Grundy appeared to give a political speech or debate, someone in the audience taunted him, "This will be a Bennett case!" Charles L. Bennett was hanged in Franklin, Williamson County, on November 20, 1819.

Bennett was likely the first man in Tennessee who underwent attempts to bring him back to life. After hanging thirty-two minutes, his body was taken down. Doctors and friends used unspecified means to animate him. Some claimed they saw his legs move; he was buried at dark. By the next day, so many rumors of a successful resuscitation were repeated that the sheriff ordered the body exhumed and displayed for several hours on the courthouse square.[105]

Israel, black, a slave, age unknown. *Murder.*

The details of the crime are unknown except that it was committed in October 1819, at Soldier's Rest, the plantation of Gen. Thomas Overton in Davidson County, near Andrew Jackson's home, the Hermitage.[106] The victim was William O'Bryant (Obrien, O'Bryan), white, age unknown. He was the overseer on the plantation. O'Bryant was found beaten to death by a fellow employee, Nelson Jones, who promptly took Israel into custody. On November 4, 1819, Israel was tried before a slave court. The witnesses called by the state were Thomas

Overton, Nelson Jones, William Bell, Edward D. Hobbs, William Chappell, George Wartlow, and two of Overton's slaves, Lydia and Billy.[107] The slave court found Israel guilty and he was ordered hanged on November 28, 1819. Testimony implicated Mrs. Mary Ann O'Bryant, the victim's wife, and she was tried on November 10, 1819, as an accessory.

A report of the slave trial was offered the jury over the defendant's objection. Nelson Jones attempted to testify but was barred from repeating anything Israel had said to him that incriminated Mrs. O'Bryant, the defense asserting the rule that a black person could not testify against a white person.[108] Mrs. O'Bryant was acquitted and Israel was hanged on the appointed day.[109]

1820

John Lusk, white, age unknown. *Rape.*

The crime was committed in Rutherford County on August 3, 1819, and the victim was Catherine Daniel, white, age twenty-five. She was the wife of James Daniel. The details of the crime are unknown. Persons placed under bond for appearance were Mr. Daniel, Charles Read, Peter Moon, Pious Brawley, George M. Lee, Alexander Lorance (for his wife Margaret), Richard Burge (for his wife Nancy), William Stephens, Moses Pasley and Richard Stephens.[110]

Due to the excitement generated by the charge, and to the inadequacy of the Rutherford County Jail, the case was transferred to Nashville. Lusk was tried on November 23 and 24, 1819. His defense was impotency. According to the bill of exceptions, Lusk was unable to find a physician to testify because he had sent a messenger twice (while sitting in jail) to summon "lawyer Hayes" to represent him. The lawyer never appeared. Unknown to both Lusk and the messenger, there were two lawyers named Hayes. One was Alexander Hayes, the district attorney. The other was O.B. Hayes, who was not timely contacted. Apparently, O.B. Hayes actually represented Lusk at his trial. The state allowed the defense to read a letter to the jury regarding Lusk's impotency from "Brawley," but it is not clear whether this was Pious Brawley or a physician by that name.[111]

Lusk's case was appealed to the Tennessee Supreme Court, but no opinion can be located. There was an opinion because it was mentioned in passing in Burrell Cornwell's case in 1827, dealing with an asserted flaw in the bill of exceptions, namely whether the affidavit supporting a new trial could be heard by the court, despite the fact that it was not in the bill of exceptions. According to Peck's dissent, the court in Lusk's case held the omission from the bill of exceptions preventing the court from considering the affidavit.[112] The district attorney in this case was named Sam Houston.

Lusk was hanged on June 26, 1820, on a gallows on the "bank of the Cumberland River opposite Nashville on the land of Doctor Shelby above the road leading from the middle ferry."[113] Details of the execution are unknown.[114]

1821

Robert Delap, white, age unknown. *Murder.*
Mitchell Marcum (aka Mitchell Markum), white, age unknown. *Murder.*

The crime was committed at the victim's home somewhere in Campbell (now Scott) County in 1819. The victim was Mrs. Eve Martin, white, age unknown. According to local belief, she was the widow of former North Carolina governor and United States Senator Alexander Martin (1740–1807).[115] According to local tradition, she was murdered because she was a witness to a prior killing by Delap. The pair were tried in either Campbell or Hawkins County and found guilty on April 8, 1820. Marcum was found guilty of killing Martin, with Delap guilty of aiding and abetting. The convictions were reversed by the Supreme Court of Errors and Appeals, but neither the transcript nor an opinion can be located.

They received separate trials the second time. Farmhand Marcum was again found guilty and was hanged at Rutledge, Grainger County, on May 24, 1821.[116] Marcum admitted his guilt. From the gallows he said, "I was working at the house of Robert Delap on the day Mrs. Martin was murdered. Later on in the evening Delap asked me to accompany him to the hog pen. He told me that he wanted me to kill the governor's wife, Mrs. Martin. He offered me $150 and I told him no. After my reply, Delap said, 'Life is uncertain. Death is certain and money is damn good.'"[117] He explained that Delap had aimed Marcum's rifle through a hole in the wall near the chimney, hitting the victim as she sat on a bed.

Said Marcum, "Her brains had been blown out. I ran out and Delap followed, him asking that I not report her death till morning. I agreed. Later Delap and I were taken into custody. Delap told me to confess to the murder and as it was my first offense I would not be punished."[118] Delap promised that no expense would be spared for Marcum's legal defense and Marcum finally offered a written confession.

Marcum continued, "About four years ago last September, I met a peddler in the woods. I asked him if he had passed by Delap's. He said that his name was Sturgeon and that he was going to the Elk River in White County. He went on to Delap's. Later about two miles below Delap's, I was butchering a deer. I followed him. I saw him shoot and murder Sturgeon. About three years ago, Delap had murdered another peddler. I do not know his name."[119]

Robert Delap was tried and convicted, but the trial court granted a new trial on April 7, 1821, because of juror misconduct. Delap was tried again in Hawkins County on April 4, 1822, and was convicted as an accessory. His conviction was affirmed in July 1822, by the Supreme Court of Errors and Appeals, then sitting in Hawkins County, but neither the record nor an opinion can be located. Delap was hanged at Rogersville on May 17, 1823.[120]

Kinchen (aka Kinchen Sullivan), a slave, black, age unknown. *Murder.*

The details of Kinchen's crime are unknown except that he was found guilty of poisoning Mrs. Elizabeth Crockett. Kinchen and his father, Travis, were slaves owned by William Sullivan and they were tried before a special slave court. Travis was tried first on May 24, 1821, and the trial lasted until eleven o'clock at night, when he was acquitted. Kinchen's trial began the next day and he was found guilty and ordered executed on June 8, 1821.[121] He was executed that day. The details of Kinchen's hanging are unknown except that a large crowd gathered and stood in heavy rain from the time he was taken from the jail until the hanging was completed.[122]

1823

Allen (aka Allen Russell), black, age unknown. *Rape of a white woman.*

Allen raped Phoebe Powell, white, age twenty-three, in Williamson County on February 2, 1822. She had left her house to visit a neighbor when Allen met her on a path and struck her five times on the head with a large stick. Dr. McGee, who attended her, did not think she would live. Allen was convicted within a month by a special slave court consisting of three justices of the peace and twelve slaveholders. On May 19, 1822, the circuit court granted a new trial from the slave court. He was tried a second time and convicted on February 22, 1823.[123]

Allen was hanged in Franklin on March 1, 1823. "He appeared perfectly resigned to his fate, and died with great fortitude. His behavior was characterized by none of that audacity and impudence which was displayed on his trial. On the contrary, he exhorted the negroes, of whom a great number were present, to take warning by his fate, and forsake their vicious ways. He denied the commission of the rape to the last, though he confessed that was his intention when he first attacked the young woman."[124]

Jim (aka Jim Ragsdale), black, age unknown. *Burglary.*

Jim, a slave of John Ragsdale, was convicted of burglary by entering the Williamson County house of Robert Beard and his wife and striking both with an ax. Beard's slave, Harry, was also convicted and sentenced to die, but reprieved. Harry was "pardoned" (sentence commuted) in part because of the gallows confession of Jim. Jim was hanged in Franklin on May 31, 1823.

"Jim was swung off after making a full confession of his crime in which a white man of this county was strongly implicated. Jim died with a great firmness. He had been baptized a day or two previous and expressed full confidence in the mercy of a savior. He exhorted the negroes to quit their evil practices. Three instances of theft occurred that evening. One fellow was detected who had stolen some money from a store, was imprisoned and whipped on Monday."[125]

1826

Unnamed female slave, black, age unknown. *Murder.*

The details of the crime are unknown except the crime was committed somewhere in Henderson

County when the female slave drowned the small daughter of Dr. John A. Wilson, who was the first physician in the county (1821). The killing and the execution took place in 1826.[126]

1827

James R. Bennett (aka Charles R. Bennett), white, age unknown. *Murder.*

The crime was committed on February 17, 1826, at the farm and distillery owned by the defendant in Maury County. The victim, Thomas Callahan, white, was an elderly Revolutionary War veteran, largely a vagabond. He had visited the farm/distillery previously and both had imbibed. After he left, some of Bennett's chickens began to die of chicken cholera. Bennett blamed Callahan.

When Callahan returned he was told to leave but he sneaked back. The day of the killing, the two were seen drinking together outside. When it got dark, they went into Bennett's house. Both continued drinking and the veteran boasted of his war exploits, saying the bullet had not been made that could kill him. Bennett took down his rifle, loaded it and shot Callahan in the side. The bullet went through the body and several witnesses who came into the house heard Callahan say, "I am dead. Bennett, you are a murderer, you killed me for nothing," as he writhed on the floor.[127] The old man died the next day.

Bennett told everyone who came by that night what he had done.[128] To one person he said Callahan was a "pilfering old villain," and he had aimed for his heart but missed.[129] Several witnesses who arrived after the shooting saw Callahan on the floor. They heard him say, "Bennett, you are a murderer. You have murdered me. I am a dead man."[130] Most witnesses said Bennett was not drunk, but that drinking made him talk and act crazy. Two years earlier, his property had been auctioned at a judicial sale. At the sale he was clearly drunk, but was not as drunk at the time of the shooting.

Bennett's chief defense was intoxication, or in the alternative, that he was insane by intoxication and lacked the requisite intent to commit murder. The Tennessee Supreme Court said that a "temporary frenzy" was no excuse for the act and affirmed the verdict.[131]

Bennett was hanged on April 2, 1827, in front of a large crowd gathered at Columbia. Sheriff Nimrod Porter (famous today for his Civil War diary) supposedly began crying during the execution.

Bennett was the first white man executed in Maury County. The body was left hanging to serve as a warning to others. His execution is one of the few described by a woman. "A number of us girls went around to Mrs. Vorhees' to get a good look at him. We saw him come out of the jail and get into a cart to be driven to the gallows which stood in the bottom north of the old cemetery. It was long left there as a warning to evil doers. I don't believe a gallows would frighten folks so much now. Dearly did I pay for my idle curiosity; for months afterward I was haunted by the uncanny face of the doomed man."[132]

Bennett's grandson (his daughter's son), Israel Thomason, was convicted of murdering R.C. Jackson in 1875 and ordered executed. The conviction was upheld on appeal but his sentence was commuted by the governor at the recommendation of the Tennessee Supreme Court. Outraged townsfolk burned the court and the governor in effigy.[133] Barely two months later, both of Thomason's parents died suddenly, possibly a double suicide, and were buried on the same day.

Over a hundred years later, a journalist had this to say about the Thomason commutation: "The wisdom of his action was confirmed 15 years later when another man confessed on his deathbed to the murder. The grandson was then pardoned."[134] There is no truth to the report. Thomason's commutation record says nothing about innocence. Rather, he served the amount of time most killers suffer in a penitentiary that was riven with tuberculosis.

Burrell Cornwell, white, age 20. *Murder.*

The crime was committed on the evening of February 21, 1826, in Nashville, Davidson County, in the saloon of Mr. Mackey. The victim was Owen Hughes, white, age unknown, a patron who was known to the killer because of an earlier altercation with him. Cornwell's family was from southern Kentucky and his nickname was "Kentuck."

Burrell Cornwell, Moses McCallahan, and Owen Hughes had a fight about three months prior to the killing in a house of ill fame called McRaymonds. Hughes was sitting on a bed when McCallahan "knocked him off the bed and Cornwell stamped upon him and blacked his eyes."[135] There was conflicting testimony about whether the pair knew they were beating Hughes because he was actually wearing the clothes and hat usually worn by a man named Connor.

The court allowed lawyer David Craighead, who represented McCallahan in a murder indictment for the Hughes killing, to testify about the mistaken identity and how the trio "met, explained the matter, made friends and drank together."[136] The purpose of this testimony was to show that Cornwell had no ill will toward Hughes before the killing. The district attorney told the jury that McCallahan had been acquitted of "aiding, helping, abling and comforting" in the killing. He did not testify at Cornwell's trial.

On the night of the slaying, Cornwell and McCallahan went to Lewis Carter's saloon about two hours before the homicide. Carter testified that McCallahan asked if he had seen a man named Hughes and ordered a gill of liquor which he shared with Cornwell. "The two men touched glasses and drank. McCallahan said there was but one man that he had any animosity against, and struck his knife several times into the baluster and said if he caught him that night he would give him first hell, then said to Cornwell, 'Let us go.'"[137]

Arriving at Mackey's saloon, the pair found Hughes. He had been drinking. The men stood in a small room between the counter and the fireplace and exchanged "fierce words" with Hughes. Mackey told them there would be no quarreling in his place. Mackey slipped out and was not present when Hughes was stabbed.

Lewis Sutton testified that Hughes said to Cornwell, "If you want to quarrel choose your friend and I'll fight you tomorrow morning."[138] Cornwell and McCallahan moved away from Hughes to talk, and exchanged hats.[139] Suddenly Cornwell stepped toward Hughes and asked, "Did you say you could whip me, or any of my friends? Did you?" Without waiting for a reply, Cornwell struck Hughes with his hand and stabbed him in his left breast. Sutton had been offered as a defense witness, but the district attorney threatened to remove him because he appeared intoxicated in court.

Another witness affirmed that Cornwell said he could "whip Hughes or any of his friends," after which Cornwell and McCallahan stepped back and appeared to talk. Then Cornwell struck Hughes and knifed him. The pair left the place, but Cornwell returned some time later.

Cornwell was still at the saloon when Hughes's father Murdock Hughes arrived. He had been summoned by a witness. The father shoved Cornwell, who then yelled, "Don't push me!" (It is likely this was an attempt by the father to provoke Cornwell to attack so he could kill him.)

The town marshall, Captain Drew, was nearby. When he heard what had happened he came to Mackey's immediately. He touched Cornwell and said, "I hope you are not the man who did the murder."[140] Cornwell replied in a bold daring manner, "I am the man that done it," and brandished the knife. Drew asked Cornwell to step outside to show him how he had done it. The clearly intoxicated Cornwell drew his knife in a "very abrupt manner" and said he would show the captain how he did it.

Captain Drew caught hold of Cornwell's arm with his club. This caused the knife to drop. The officer told him to pick up his knife. By now, McCallahan had returned, the pair left together, Cornwell swearing about what he would do to anyone who threatened him.

Cornwell later told the court he did not intend to kill anyone but had made those remarks in jest. He said that if he had killed a man, he would not "be fool enough to tell of it."[141]

Cornwell and McCallahan went to Louther's saloon. Here, Cornwell appeared intoxicated and said he had just killed a man and brandished a knife. Cornwell stated he had "slipped it into a man up to the handle," and wanted to kill two more. Louther thought Cornwell was joking because he was clearly intoxicated.

It was noted that the small knife used to kill Hughes was not the much bigger one McCallahan had used earlier at Lewis Carter's saloon. The knife used in the killing "was a common pocket knife without a spring back — the blade about three inches long." (The purpose of this testimony was apparently to absolve McCallahan of any complicity in the killing.)

Cornwell's chief defense was intoxication, that he was so intoxicated he did not have the intent to murder. His mother testified that when he was intoxicated he became insane and was not responsible for his actions. The Tennessee Supreme Court ruled that "temporary insanity" brought about by drunkenness or intoxication is not a defense to a murder charge.[142] Cornwell had asked for a change of venue because all the Irishmen in town were prejudiced against him for the killing and he could not get a fair trial; it was denied. The court did not discuss this issue. Burrell Cornwell's case is the cornerstone law on insanity by intoxication and is the longest published criminal case up to that time. It contains an unusually long dissent by Judge Peck, who said that McCallahan's words and actions at Carter's saloon were not part of the res gestae and should not have been allowed. He raised several other issues relating to matters missing from the papers, such as a showing of why a different judge tried the case from the one who normally heard cases in Nashville. The normal circuit judge had been replaced by William E. Kennedy of a different circuit.[143]

The details of Burrell Cornwell's hanging in Nashville on April 2, 1827, are unknown.[144] At this time, Tennessee did not have a statute setting out various degrees of murder. It is likely that Cornwell's case was used as a reason why such a statute was necessary. This occurred when the state's criminal laws were revised and codified in 1829.

Thomas Jameson (aka Thomas Jamerson; Thomas Jamison), white, age 23. *Murder.*
Randal, black, age unknown. *Accessory to murder.*

The crime was committed on the afternoon of February 15, 1826, on the Madison County plantation of the victim, Francis Sanders, white, age fifty. Sanders was a prosperous, pious and well-connected planter. Jameson was a tenant on Sanders' land and sought to court his landlord's daughter. The victim refused the request.

Eleven days before the murder, Sanders was fired on by an unknown person in hiding. "Who it could be, or what extraordinary motive the assassin could be actuated by, it was impossible to conjecture."[145] The evening of the murder, "while returning to his house from a piece of new ground, where he had been superintending his negroes, he suddenly received a blow, without knowing at the time from whence it came, on his head, which instantly brought him senseless to the ground." Sanders was struck several times while on the ground. He was discovered within a few hours and was taken to his house where he languished for two days, "having previously recovered his senses."[146] One of Sanders's slaves, Randal, had agreed to assist Jameson in the killing.[147]

The pair was implicated immediately but Jameson was not indicted until July 27, 1826.[148] Jameson received several continuances due to inability to locate witnesses and was brought to trial in October 1826, but a jury could not be seated. His trial began on January 27, 1827, and he was convicted three days later.[149]

Randal was tried on March 20, 1827, before a three-member slaveholder court. He was charged with being an accessory to the murder. "After a full and impartial examination of the testimony, which the guilt of the defendant was clearly established, the Jury retired, and after a short absence brought in a verdict of Guilty."[150] Randal was ordered hanged the same day as Jameson, May 4, 1827.

The largest crowd in Jackson history to that time, estimated at from three to five thousand, witnessed the dual hanging on the appointed day. The multitude heard "an appropriate prayer and sermon from the Rev. John P. Harton (from 23 Luke 42–43), during which time the most profound silence was observed; at the close the Rev. Benjamin P. Seawell rose, and closed the service by a most solemn address."[151]

"Jameson rose and addressed the multitude, acknowledged his guilt, and the justice of the punishment, and closed by a most fervent prayer, which had a visible effect on the crowd. Next followed Randal, who also addressed the people, and closed in like manner. They both seemed very penitent, and expressed a firm hope that their sins were forgiven. At 20 minutes past one o'clock they were launched into eternity."[152] This was the only time in Tennessee history that a white and black man were hanged at the same time for the same crime.

Duncan Bonds, white, age unknown. *Murder.*

The details of the crime are unknown except that on August 2, 1826, Bonds, "without any known provocation, and without the least previous intimation, deliberately stabbed Mr. Felix Crunk," a citizen of Lincoln County, "so as to cause his death on the Sunday following."[153] (It was erroneously reported that the victim was Felix Grundy. Crunk was white, age thirty-one.) Bonds was convicted in Lincoln County in October 1826.[154] His case was decided by the Tennessee Supreme Court in 1827. The question before it was whether Bonds was properly sentenced to death because in a motion for a new trial, his lawyer pled Bonds's insanity.

The Supreme Court said that no evidence was shown in the record to support this contention, and the conviction was affirmed.[155] The practice at the time was this: If at sentencing the defendant was found to be insane, he was simply kept in jail until such time as the court determined that he was sane, and then could be executed. Here, while the case was under review, the judge was given affidavits supporting Bonds's lunacy. "The Court, with the assistance of several eminent physicians, investigated the matter, and with great patience and assiduity, and became fully satisfied that the prisoner was in a deranged state of mind; his execution was, therefore, respited until the further order of the Court."[156] Bonds was kept in the Davidson County Jail pending his execution.[157] Bonds apparently regained his sanity. He was executed on May 7, 1827, at Fayetteville.

1828

John Mitchum, white, age unknown. *Murder.*

The details of the crime are unknown except that Milley Mitchum, white, age unknown, the killer's wife, was killed by him in Hardeman County on December 1, 1827.[158] He was tried on June 5, 1828, and was hanged at Bolivar, Hardeman County, on August 22, 1828. The travel fees of nine witnesses were paid by the state, a total of $45.34, while all other costs totaled $205.12. His estate paid none of these fees assessed to it.

Henry Lunsford, white, age unknown. *Murder.*

The crime was committed on March 25, 1828, at a log-rolling at an unknown location in Blount County. At least a dozen people were present. Most saw Lunsford strike the victim, Berry Thompson, white, age unknown, on the side of the head near the crown with a large stick of wood. Thompson was rendered unconscious and died on April 2, 1828.[159]

The case was appealed to the Tennessee Supreme Court but its opinion cannot be located.[160] An issue on appeal was whether Miss Keziah Thompson, apparently related to the victim, was a woman of good character whose testimony could be believed. Another issue was whether she violated the rule of sequestration of witnesses by talking to the other witnesses after her testimony. Lunsford was hanged on September 26, 1828, in Maryville. A large crowd came and was not disappointed. From the gallows Lunsford sang along with the hymn, "Why Should We Start and Fear to Die?" The spectators were greatly impressed by the strange appearance of a white dove over the gallows.[161]

In 1868, Henry Lunsford's son was murdered by a man named John Murphy. He was described as a popular "handsome part–Cherokee," and the son was known as a bad man. He had earlier gotten into a fight at a country dance and gouged out the eye of Bill Yarber, his sweetheart's brother. The details of the son's killing are unknown, but Murphy's conviction was appealed to the Tennessee Supreme Court, which ordered a new trial.

Before he could be retried, Murphy escaped and hid in Kentucky. He was discovered and brought back for trial. In the meantime (1870), Loudon County had been created out of Blount County. Appearing before the circuit judge in Maryville (Blount County), Murphy was ordered tried in Loudon County because it was the actual location of the killing. Taken to Loudon County, the same judge ruled that Blount County had jurisdiction and promptly dismissed the charges, which were not brought again.[162] "Murphy later met his match in Campbell County and was killed in a brawl."[163]

1829

Samuel McClure, white, age unknown. *Murder.*

The crime was committed in September 1828 in the town of Fayetteville, in Lincoln County, about four hundred yards east of the public square. McClure was the town's cobbler. Across the street was the blacksmith shop owned by the victim, Edward McBride, white, age unknown. The pair had quarreled for some time, but the mediation of a mutual friend was thought to have settled their differences.

McClure took a shoe knife, which by frequent sharpening had been ground down to a fine point, and hid it up his sleeve. He went across to the blacksmith shop and began cursing McBride, whom he knew to have a fiery, impetuous temperament. McBride took a pair of tongs from an anvil and began chasing McClure, who appeared to flee across the street, but all the time cursing the blacksmith. "As soon as they crossed the street, McClure drew his knife and before the blacksmith could realize the danger, made a rush at him and cut his throat. McBride fell dead."[164] McClure thought that because he killed McBride after being chased back to his side of the street, the jury would think it was self-defense.

The Tennessee Supreme Court said, "The evidence proves this to have been a case of clear and aggravated murder: the defendant can truly be said to have been regardless of all social order and fatally bent upon mischief."[165]

But an important issue was raised. The defendant did not find out until after the trial that one of the jurors, William Neeld, was an atheist. The majority said this did not matter because a statute describing juror qualifications did not require otherwise, and the defendant's counsel should have addressed this issue in voir dire.[166]

Judge Peck dissented, saying the Tennessee Constitution barred atheists from holding office, since such people could not take an oath and were considered untrustworthy.[167] He said, "The Constitution has pointed her artillery against such as avow themselves to be atheists. No law can place an atheist upon a footing with a Christian, because the

Constitution has placed a barrier between them."[168] Judge Peck was so convinced an injustice had been done he wrote Gov. Sam Houston asking clemency for McClure.[169]

McClure was hanged on April 12, 1829. He was taken by horseback to the gallows. He wore a white burial shroud, which he held up around himself like a woman holds her skirts, to keep it clean because the road was dry and dusty. He mounted the gallows with a firm tread. Apparently, there was no speaking or preaching, and he was promptly hanged from a tree onto which a cross-bar and upright post had been attached. For years afterward, small boys dreaded and shunned the tree, and when they had to go to the nearby mill they were particular to "get by it on the return home before nightfall."[170]

James White, white, age 24. *Murder.*

The crime was committed on December 13, 1828, in the farmhouse of Mr. and Mrs. George W. Brown in rural Marion County. The defendant and the victim, Mr. Brown, knew each other because the defendant had worked as a farmhand for the couple. James White struck Brown, who was asleep, with two ax blows to the head. According to White's florid account of the murder, the prime cause of Brown's death was his wife, her first name not known.[171]

In February 1828, White had been courting "the daughter of Boaz Still"; the couple were engaged and the bride's wedding dress was prepared. White asked Mrs. Brown to sew him a pair of trousers suitable for the wedding. In short order Mrs. Brown began to warn White about the woman, saying she had been too familiar with a married man. White stopped seeing Miss Still.

In the evenings, White held the candle while Mrs. White sewed. "She soon asked me to let her feel my pulse, to which I agreed."[172] White explained, "By her beauty and enticing arts, I was seduced to accept her evil offers."[173] White moved in with the couple in March, staying until May. The Browns separated from time to time, but got back together. During the time White lived there and for several months after he left, Mrs. Brown pleaded with him to kill her husband. She threatened to get rat poison and used every device she could to win the young man to her bidding.

Said he, "My ill-fated and unconquerable attachment to her, aided by the instigation of the devil, absorbed my reason and finally seduced me into the assent to her fatal proposition. I ought, however, to have mentioned another powerful influence over me. Her tears! These were her last resort. She besought me with tears in her eyes! I was conquered!"[174]

They planned to place a rolled-up sheet for Mr. Brown to use as a pillow, which could be used to catch the blood, and kill him as he slept. The pair carried the body to the river, weighted it down with two large rocks, and threw it into the water from a canoe. They burned his bloody clothes and concocted a story that he had gone to another county.

Although Mrs. Brown professed glee that her husband was dead, White's reaction was different: "During the next day, I was overwhelmed with horror and despair, and shed tears copiously and constantly. I seemed totally abandoned to despair. It appeared to me that every person I saw, looked at me suspiciously; and that the very clouds were frowning the wrath and impending vengeance of my Maker."[175]

White was stunned to learn that ten days later Brown's body was found floating in the river. How blame was fixed on White is not known, nor whether Mrs. Brown was charged as well. He was convicted in June 1828, but the conviction was reversed on appeal. He was convicted a second time and ordered executed on August 17, 1829.[176] White's published "confession" document is a testament to the danger "from the embraces of a lewd woman" and one's own "high-handed rebellion against His righteous law."[177]

James White was hanged on August 17, 1829, in Knoxville in front of a large crowd. The details of the execution are unknown except he was executed alongside Joshua Young, who had killed his wife because he had grown fond of another woman.

Joshua Young, white, age 67. *Murder.*

The crime was committed the morning of February 21, 1828, on the Knox County farm near Campbell's Station, owned by the killer and his wife, Margaret Young.[178] Two years earlier, Young began an affair with a younger woman, Elizabeth Pennington, who "she suggested that my old wife was much in the way of our intercourse."[179]

Young's wife, age sixty-four, had borne him seven children. Five had reached adulthood by the time of her death. Young asked his wife to help him prepare a plant bed. As she was stooping down, he attempted to shoot her in the back with a homemade wooden gun. The gun merely exploded, knocking her down. Young picked up a hickory stick the size of a common chair leg and struck her twice in the head, killing her instantly.

The issue on appeal was whether the jury had to accept all or none of his various statements to law enforcement officers, referred to as confessions. The Tennessee Supreme Court said the jury could believe whatever it wanted, based on all the testimony.[180]

Young was executed on a gallows at Knoxville on

August 17, 1829, alongside James White, age twenty-four, who had killed a husband at the wife's urging.

Mrs. Polly Hughes, white, age unknown. *Murder.*

The crime was committed sometime in 1829 in the rural cabin owned by Polly Hughes and her husband in Hardin County. Polly Hughes killed her husband as he lay sleeping in a drunken stupor. According to Polly's testimony, her husband had repeatedly threatened to kill her when he was drinking and she feared for her life. While he was asleep in their cabin, she took an ax and struck him on the head. He drew up his shoulders and groaned. She gave another blow, which killed him. She then went to bed herself and attempted to escape the next day but was quickly arrested. Because she had laid out his burial clothes prior to the killing, her act was deemed premeditated and the death penalty was warranted.[181] No record of an appeal can be located.

On November 13, 1829, Polly Hughes was taken in a cart to the river bank in Savannah, Hardin County. The rope had been placed around her neck for the last ride. She fainted when the cart approached the hanging tree and was placed on her feet with great difficulty. She had been sobbing on the way to the gallows and was hanged in the traditional manner. She said nothing prior to the cart's being pulled away.

According to one account, the execution was seen by an immense crowd.[182] According to another, the crowd, estimated from five hundred to eight hundred, was not as large as anticipated.[183] The account said, "The scene was awful, indeed — and the sympathies of the crowd greatly excited, not only for the wretched woman, but for her hapless offspring, who are of tender years, and very poor."[184] Polly Hughes is the only white woman legally executed in Tennessee.

1830

Henry Nunnelly, black, age unknown. *Murder.*

The crime was committed in the Gray's Bend area of Hickman County near the victim's home. She was Tampay Carlisle, white, age fifteen, who was raped and murdered by Nunnelly. She was alone at the time and he attempted to force entrance to her home. She escaped through a window and ran toward a neighbor's house but was overtaken and dragged into bushes. Nunnelly tried to conceal her body by covering it with stones. Tracking dogs found Nunnelly hiding under a barn. He was hanged in Centerville in 1830. Details of the execution are unknown. It is also unclear whether the defendant was a slave or free. His brother Carter Nunnelly was hanged for murder in 1861.[185]

Joe Bearden, white, age unknown. *Murder.*

The crime was committed in Perry County sometime in 1829 or early 1830. Bearden and the victim, name unknown, had been working on a government project at Muscle Shoals, Alabama. They traveled together back to Tennessee. When the companion was overdue, his relatives inquired about him and began a search which revealed his body half-buried in southern Perry County. Joe Bearden was said to be the last person seen with him alive. After the body was found, a man named Thomas Green, who lived in that part of Perry County, recognized the coat Bearden was wearing as the property of the dead man. Green made a citizen's arrest and authorities communicated by mail with the dead man's family. A sister responded by letter describing a unique patch she had sown on the coat.[186]

The case was tried in Humphreys County at Reynoldsville, then the county seat. Bearden was described as a degenerate and no appeal was taken from his conviction.

While in jail, Bearden told everyone that if he was hanged, the meeting between him and the devil would be a "stormy affair." Bearden was hanged in Reynoldsville on May 31, 1830. That night, a tornado wrecked Hickman, Perry and Humphreys counties and almost destroyed the town of Shelbyville in Bedford County.[187] For decades, the people in the area referred to this as the "Bearden Storm."[188]

Bearden had sold his body to Dr. Marable of Reynoldsville for ten dollars. The doctor extracted and preserved Bearden's heart in a glass jar and kept it on display in his office, where it was a frequent topic of conversation.[189]

1831

Charles (aka Charles Turner), black, age 16. *Murder.*

The details of the crime are unknown except that Charles, a slave, killed his owner, John Turner, in

Williamson County on October 6, 1830, and was hanged in 1831.[190]

1833

Joe, black, age unknown. *Murder.*

The details of the crime are unknown, except that Joe, a young slave owned by George Gillespie, was hanged for murder in Winchester, Franklin County, in June 1833.[191] Gillespie's petition to the General Assembly for compensation was rejected.[192]

William Ford (aka William Fad), white, age 18. *Murder.*

The crime was committed on May 28, 1832, about four hundred yards from the farm home the victim shared with her grandfather and extended family in Roane County. The victim was Patsy Wiggins, white, age twelve. Ford took the girl into the woods, raped and killed her. Ford was a farm hand on a nearby farm. His employer testified he was "not qualified to make a living, or to attend to the ordinary transactions of life for the want of intellect." He was "a silly boy with little sense."[193]

Ford smashed the side of Patsy's head with a rock. He was tricked into confessing. Ford denied the killing to a friend Samuel Bowman. At this time, Bowman thought the girl was dead but did not know the location of the body. Bowman told Ford to confess if he was guilty or run away if he was not. Ford responded that Bowman would find him if he ran away.

The body was found the next day and constables Jeremiah Monday and John Hickey arrived and arrested Ford. Bowman said he would take Ford to where the body was found and make him look at it unless Ford pointed out where it was. Ford took the three men to within a short distance of the body but Ford stopped, turned, and kept looking back over his shoulder in the direction of the body.

Several witnesses put Ford near the girl when she was last seen alive, playing in her doorway with a pet rabbit. After the killing, Ford went to a neighbor, inquiring about the girl, and attempted to fix blame on three negroes he claimed had recently passed by. But he gave conflicting statements about the girl's whereabouts when he last saw her.

Patsy had stayed at the farm where Ford lived the night before the killing. Ford's sister, Rhoda Ford, testified that when she told him that Patsy had been murdered, the killer said, "Lord, have mercy on me. I am ruined in soul and body!" Rhoda was in such bad health that she seemed ready to faint on the witness stand. Bowman also asked Ford if he killed the girl. Ford responded that if he did, he did not know it. Bowman also said there was blood on the private parts of the girl. Ford was convicted at Knoxville in August 1832.[194] The Tennessee Supreme Court affirmed the conviction but the opinion cannot be located. The court ordered Ford hanged August 15, 1833, in Knoxville with the Roane County sheriff in charge.[195]

Harriet, black, age 13. *Murder.*

The date the crime was committed is unknown. Harriet, the slave of James H. Shepperd, Jr., drowned the five-year-old son of Alexander McKenzie, in a common flour barrel at his home. The barrel was fixed to a spring near the Hardeman County residence. "The circumstances as detailed by the witnesses on the trial, show the transaction to have been one of the most wanton and aggravated murders, perhaps ever committed by a female so young, and created considerable excitement in the minds of a virtuous community."[196] She was convicted on July 23, 1833, and was hanged on August 23, 1833, in Bolivar. So far as known, Harriet is the youngest female executed in Tennessee.

In 1806, another slave girl also named Harriet, age twelve, had strangled Polly, white, age eight, in a creek in Williamson County. The victim was the daughter of the Rev. John Record. She was sentenced to hang, and her case was not appealed. Harriet's lawyer, a young Thomas Hart Benton, provided the governor a petition of numerous citizens, including the victim's father, which argued Harriet's immaturity and mental capacity, and the fact her confession was extracted by physical abuse. The governor spared the girl's life and her fate is unknown.[197] In 1850, a slave girl named Ann, age fifteen, was taken from the slave quarters to attend a five-week-old child. She was told by a male slave to give the baby laudanum to keep it quiet so they could get together. Without knowledge of the consequences, she gave it too much, killing it. Her conviction was reversed because her confession had been coerced.[198]

Wiley (aka Wiley Bird), black, age unknown. *Murder.*

The crime was committed on November 23, 1833, at an unknown location in Dickson County. Wiley, described as "a recalcitrant negro," clubbed to death his owner William G. Bird, white, age unknown, a slaveholder and member of the patrol. Wiley was quickly captured and his three-day trial began on December 19, 1833. There was no appeal.

Wiley was hanged in a creek bottom about one-half mile from Charlotte on December 28, 1833, before a crowd of several thousand. Many blacks were present, including those brought by their owners to teach them the consequence of disobedience. He was swung off in the traditional manner.[199]

1835

Bennett Dula, white, age 29. *Murder.*

The crime was committed on June 10, 1833, on a remote hilltop in Marion County "on the Cumberland Mountain near Higgenbather's trace," about three miles from Jasper. The victim was William Patton, white, age sixty-five, who was traveling from South Carolina to West Tennessee in order to purchase land. "William Patton was a man who might be called wealthy," testified his son.[200] Dula bludgeoned him with a weighted horsewhip, which bent under the blows and was left near the scene covered in blood and hair. Several witnesses said the horsewhip was like the one Dula carried.[201]

Patton was known to be carrying a large amount of money, variously eight hundred dollars or ten thousand dollars.[202] Dula, who was reputed to have some connection with the Murrell gang, was seen by several people traveling with the victim. Patton's body was covered with bushes and rocks and was found within a week because of the smell.[203] The face was obliterated, but his clothing was identified by witnesses and his son, who came from South Carolina. Numerous personal items such as his hat, saddle blanket, saddlebags and personal papers were found nearby.

The pair had spent the night before the killing with a witness, who explained that Dula seemed to intentionally mislead Patton about the proper way to travel to the next town, and repeated several times that he liked Patton's horse. The horse had a distinctive tail, but when Dula was seen later with the horse, he had cropped the tail. When captured in Cherokee Nation (Georgia), Dula was carrying a distinctive watch worth $250. It belonged to Patton.[204]

Dula gave conflicting accounts of how he came by the horse and watch, asserting that two benefactors had given him money which he had used to purchase these from Patton. The benefactors, he suggested, were supporting him because he had allegedly made a strike in a popular gold field in Georgia, and he had flashed some gold nuggets to various witnesses to prove his gold-field ventures.

After several delays and a change of venue, Bennett Dula was convicted in Warren County circuit court and hanged in Sparta, White County, on September 14, 1835.[205]

Sampson, black, age unknown. *Assault with intent to rape.*

The crime was committed somewhere in Davidson County on September 8, 1835, apparently near the home of the victim, white, described as a "respectable girl, not more than twelve years old."[206] Sampson was a slave owned by John Boyd, who provided two lawyers. They offered no proof, but argued for mercy. The case was heard by a special slave court composed of three Justices of the Peace and twelve jurors. "The proof was clear, and of the most unquestionable character." The jury rendered a guilty verdict without retiring from the box. "This offense, when committed by a colored person, being capital by the laws of the State, the prisoner was sentenced to hang on Friday, the 25th inst." Sampson was hanged on that day "on the road running out by the grave-yard."[207]

Jesse Mitchell, white, age unknown. *Murder.*

The crime was committed on March 5, 1832, on a farm very close to the Kentucky border in Jackson County. The killing arose out of a dispute over the setting of a boundary line. The victim was Samuel Wilson, white, age unknown. Mitchell and Wilson and several others, including some boys who were the sons of both, were attempting to locate a corner[208] in order to mark off the land separating Wilson's tenant, Woodson Cummins, and the land occupied by Mitchell's mother.

Mitchell had been summoned to assist. His mother insisted he take part in the surveying, taking him away from splitting rails with another neighbor. For this reason, Mitchell was carrying his axe. Mitchell was described as peaceful and hard-working, but hard of hearing and "weak-minded and could not take learning."[209]

As Mitchell, Wilson and Woodson Cummins were walking the line single-file, aided by a compass, it appeared that Mitchell had encroached on the tenant's land. Wilson said, "Jesse, my son, you have plowed a little too far over." The defendant responded, "Well, if I have, I will tend it." Wilson replied, "I suppose not, Jesse; but you and Cummins go for that." At this point, Mitchell said in a loud voice, "I will show you whether I will tend it or not," and instantly struck Wilson on the back of the neck with his axe. The blow was deep and Wilson died quickly.

Mitchell's first conviction was reversed on appeal.[210] The issue on the second appeal concerned whether the indictment, prepared in common-law form, was appropriate under the new murder statute of 1829, which separated murder into degrees. The court found no error in the use of the old form.[211]

Judge Peck strongly dissented. He said the indictment did not inform the defendant that his life was in peril and was therefore defective. Furthermore, he was moved by an issue raised for the first time on appeal. The land where Wilson was killed was shown to be north of thirty-six degrees, thirty minutes, and was therefore in Kentucky. The old state line was still the North Carolina line. Although Tennessee and Kentucky had agreed on the line, this had never been approved by Congress, as the Constitution required.[212]

Jesse Mitchell was executed at Gainesboro, Jackson County, on October 1, 1835.[213]

1836

Clayton, black, age unknown. *Murder.*

The details of the crimes are unknown except that Clayton committed the crimes in Wilson County by killing Thomas Hunt, white, age unknown, and an unnamed daughter, white, age unknown, on September 17, 1836. Clayton and another slave named Charles were charged with murder, assault with intent to commit murder, and arson. Charles was owned by a man named Samuel B. Smith. Charles was tried first on November 10, 1836.[214] Clayton was owned by a man named Henry F. Smith. One of the jurors was a man named John Y. Smith. (The relationship of these men, if any, is unknown.) During the trial, juror Smith "absconded and absented himself from the rest of the jury without permission of the court."[215] This prompted a mistrial and a fifty-dollar fine imposed on juror Smith.

Clayton's trial began on November 14, 1836. Apparently, Charles testified against Clayton, who was convicted two days later. He was sentenced to hang on November 26, 1836, and died that day.[216] At this time, Hunt's surviving children, minor daughters Sophia and Martha Hunt, were described as orphans.[217]

Charles went to trial again on March 9, 1837. Former juror John Y. Smith (and a negro boy he owned) were summoned to testify for Charles. Whether they did is unknown, but Charles was acquitted of murder.[218] The other charges were nulled.

1837

Charles (aka Charles Maney), black, age unknown. *Rape.*

The details of the crime are unknown except that Charles was executed for rape of a white woman. Goodspeed reports the crime in 1838, but 1837 is more likely.[219] No circuit or criminal court records for Rutherford County survived the Civil War and no known newspaper reported the execution.

The county court record for December 4, 1837, indirectly supports the fact of his execution. On that day the court approved payment of court costs: James Maney, clerk, $5.25; C.W. Head, $42.50 (probably his lawyer); Sheriff Watkins, $12.50 (the statutory fee for hanging); and Attorney General Whiteside, $20.00.[220]

According to Goodspeed, "The evidence was wholly circumstantial but seemed pretty clear, and on the strength he was tried, convicted and executed. There was a strong suspicion at the time that he was not the guilty party. Later a negro was executed in Mississippi for a similar crime, and while under sentence of death owned to have committed the crime in Rutherford for which Charles was hanged."[221] No evidence in Tennessee supports this statement.

Julius, black, age 20. *Assault with intent to murder a white person.*

The crime was committed about 8:00 P.M. on January 4, 1837, in the farm home of John and his wife Rebecca Matthews in Maury County. Julius had been owned by John Matthews since he was ten years old. He was described by her as much attached to the family, a great coward, and "has but half sense." Her husband said Julius was docile and obedient, but quite dull and "had just sense enough to make a good negro."[222] The victim was Rebecca Matthews, white, age thirty-two.

Present in the house were the couple's three children, the youngest of whom was three years old. The husband was away on business. At trial, John Matthews[223] refused to hire counsel. The court appointed two lawyers. One was Alfred O.P. Nicholson, who became a member of the Tennessee Supreme Court in 1870.

Early on the day of the crime, Littlebury Fallen, white, had come to Mrs. Matthews's house to seek help shucking corn. Julius left with him and returned about 6:00 P.M. smelling of liquor. After doing some chores, he made an extra large fire in the fireplace, explaining he was going to sleep by the fire, as was his custom. About 7:00 P.M. Mrs. Matthews heard several keen whistles at the back of the house. She asked Julius what they meant, and he replied that he did not know. He went outside and returned with an ax, saying he would defend her with it. She fastened the windows and bolted the door. She began spinning and he turned the wheel crank.

"She stooped down to pick up something when he seized her by the throat, and told her he was going to kill her, to take the money in the house, and run off to a free state."[224] She grabbed the ax and they struggled over it. He threw her to the hearth, saying he had made the fire large to throw her into it. She recovered her feet and they continued struggling over the ax. She did not know how the door was unlocked but he opened it and threw her outside on the rocks. She held the ax but threw it away. He came upon her, put his knees to her breast and tried to hit her with a three-pound rock. She grabbed his arm and he dropped the rock. He dragged her to the gatepost some fifteen steps. Here she got to her feet, put her arms around Julius and held onto the post, screaming. He pulled his pocket knife and managed to open it. She grabbed his wrist and held it as he attempted to stab her several times. She gave his hand a sudden jerk, which caused the blade to cut his throat three inches. Holding his throat with one hand, Julius attempted to choke her with the other. As they struggled up a hill ten steps she began to choke him with both hands. "She felt his strength giving way and called to her little daughter. Julius then let loose and ran."

Rebecca picked up the little girl and ran to neighbor David Breckenridge's house. She noticed William and Littlebury Fallen behind her. Julius was arrested and jailed the next day.

At trial, Julius explained that Littlebury Fallen and his uncle William Fallen, white, had started a drinking contest at the corn shucking and urged him to kill Rebecca and take her money, and William Fallen, who lived in Kentucky, would help him get to a free state. The bottle was placed in front of the shuckers and whoever got to it first could take a large drink. The bottle was nicknamed Swigley, and Julius usually won. Julius explained the whistles were the sign that the Fallens were present and he was to kill her and they were to search the house.

Littlebury Fallen testified he knew nothing about a plot to kill Rebecca. He came only when he heard screaming; the bottle had no nickname. Another witness who was present at the shucking and took part in the contest confirmed the bottle's nickname. The deputy who arrested Julius told him he would be hanged, and it would make matters no better or worse to tell about it. The deputy said he told Julius to get religion. He said Julius confessed to the crime, said he was intoxicated, sorrowful and wished she had killed him in the struggle. To the deputy, Julius implicated the Fallens and the plot to kill Mrs. Matthews and take him to a free state. William Fallen did not testify.

The jury deliberated overnight and the next day returned a guilty verdict with a recommendation for executive clemency because of his prior good character, his youth, and the strong suspicion resting upon others. The judge sentenced Julius to die on March 1, 1837.

On February 2, 1837, Nicholson wrote Governor Newton Cannon asking for a pardon so that Julius could be sold instead of hanged. He explained that the sale would keep the family from poverty. He said the family wanted mercy for Julius so he could be sold. He cited six other reasons: "1. The negro is shown to have had a most excellent character. 2. He was quite young. 3. He was proved to have but a very limited portion of intellect. 4. He was shown to be in liquor and the circumstances raised a strong presumption that he was induced by white men to drink for the very purpose of being instigated to commit the murder. 5. The circumstances rendered it certain that he was instigated by white men, and with his limited sense, and in liquor, that he was almost a passive instrument in their hands. 6. He was the only slave of his master."[225]

Nicholson finished his letter by explaining that "it struck many as an unusual and severe punishment to take away a life when no murder had been committed." He explained that the Matthews couple now thought that Julius "was not himself when he did the act — that they knew in his common senses he could not conceive such a design.... They would therefore prefer that he was pardoned and sent out of the state."[226]

The governor had already received a petition from Maury County arguing against a pardon for Julius. It contained the familiar statement that slaves boasted: "White men love money too well to have a negro hung, that the only punishment will be a change of masters and that perhaps for the better." The petition explained that Julius had a fair trial with able counsel. Sparing Julius would jeopardize the lives of free citizens of the county. "For what is to restrain the slave from imbuing his hands on his masters' blood, with whom he is incensed, if he had good reason to believe that his punishment, if caught, is to be only a change of masters, and a chance that the may be for the better?"[227]

Julius was hanged at Columbia, Maury County, on March 1, 1837, at 2:30 P.M. before an immense crowd. "The negro first appeared entirely composed — in the course of divine ceremony, administered on the occasion, however, he was much affected, and wept." The newspaper reported, "He confessed his guilt, and deplored his error; spoke of his mistress with much tenderness and warned the colored persons present to remember his fate." The newspaper concluded, "He said he had been instigated to the horrid attempt by a white man, (whose name he repeated, aloud, but) whom we forbear to mention."[228]

1839

George Long, white, age unknown. *Murder.*

The crime was committed on December 15, 1835, in Sevier County. The victim was the killer's wife, Elizabeth Manning Long, white, age unknown. She was killed when he shot her with a rifle "a little above the left nipple."[229] Other details of the crime are unknown, except Long had left the county with Jane Manning ("spinster"), who was her sister, and was living elsewhere until brought back for trial in 1837. After 250 veniremen were called, it was decided that Long could not get a fair trial in Sevier County and the trial was moved to Knox County. Jane was originally charged with "inciting, procuring and counseling" the murder, but was tried separately and acquitted. George Long was convicted on June 19, 1837, and ordered hanged on August 12, 1837.

Long's appeal to the Tennessee Supreme Court argued error because the bill of exceptions did not show the grand jury had been "sworn and charged."[230] The court held the case over for a second argument, but concluded the error did not affect the conviction, relying on Samuel McClure's case.[231] It ordered Long executed on August 12, 1839.

Governor Newton Cannon was asked to pardon Long. The petitioners asserted he should invoke the spirit of a new law allowing him to commute death sentences to life, although the statute was passed after Long's conviction. The petition also contained the names of several members of the Manning family, who said "we do not believe the accused to be guilty of this murder."[232] Also accompanying the petition was an affidavit from Jane Manning, who said that while she was waiting trial in the Knoxville jail, Barnabas Thurman came to the window of the jail and said, "I made a damned mistake. Instead of killing Long, I killed your sister; but I don't care, I have got you both safe anyhow."[233] Two other family members, William Manning and Nancy Manning, provided an affidavit saying that Barnabas Thurman "was at great enmity with the said Long, for a great while previous to, and up to the time of the murder." (Thurman was dead by the time the July 19, 1839, petition reached the governor.) The governor was unmoved.

Long was hanged in Knoxville on August 12, 1839. Following remarks and prayers by three ministers, one of them said he had been requested by Long to say that he was not guilty of the crime charged against him, and should die innocent. "Many people were under the impression that Long would confess his guilt under the gallows, but he persisted in declaring his innocence to the last."[234]

The newspaper said about the crowd, "The number of persons who witnessed the execution has been variously estimated by good judges present. We should think the number could not have been less than 3,000, *many of whom were women!* We have always questioned the propriety of *public executions*, and the scenes exhibited here yesterday have only served to strengthen our belief of their impolicy."[235]

Charles Cox, a slave, black, age unknown. *Murder.*

The date and place of the Blount County killing are unknown but was possibly January 25, 1839. Cox was a slave. His wife was owned by David Humes, white, age unknown. Humes had whipped the woman. In revenge, Cox shot him through a window as he sat playing checkers with William J.

Hackney. The murder weapon had been borrowed from a free negro, Andy Tedford, who was charged as an accessory but was acquitted.[236] Cox was convicted on September 26, 1839.

Charles Cox was hanged on October 25, 1839, before a large crowd. Despite having asserted his innocence to that time, on the gallows Cox said he had "killed old Humes and was proud of it." He died with a curse on his lips against Humes and all slaveholders.[237] The details of the execution are unknown except he and Lunsford (1828) were hanged by the same sheriff, William Wallace. All three antebellum Blount County executions, Brice, Lunsford and Cox , took place "on top of the hill at the head of McGhee Street" in Maryville.[238]

1840

Bob, black, age 22. *Murder.*
Jacob, black, age unknown. *Murder.*

The crime was committed about 11:00 P.M. on September 11, 1838, in the rural Fentress County farmhouse of Samuel Blair, white, age sixty-two, and wife, Nancy Blair, white, age fifty-nine. Bob, a slave owned by the couple, had told several people that he would kill them the first chance he got. Jacob had told others he would beat "old Mr. Blair's soul case out" if Blair attempted to cane him.[239] He was angry at Mrs. Blair because she had damaged a fiddle he owned.[240]

Bob led the plot. His friend Jacob, a slave on a nearby farm, went along because he wanted to share in the couple's money. Bob had planned the crime carefully. After the couple had been killed, Bob was to pretend he had seen two strangers near the Blair house and pretend to shoot at them. Jacob was to come running to the house to support the ruse.[241]

The pair played cards until about 11:00 P.M. and went to the Blair house but found it locked. They prized open a window using Jacob's comb. With Bob leading Jacob by the hand through the dark house, they came upon the couple in bed. Jacob began choking the man, Bob the woman. The latter struggled and both victims ended up on the floor. Both had handprints and severe scratches on their faces and necks.

Bob and Jacob looked throughout the house but found only one silver dollar and a fifty-cent piece. The latter was given to Jacob, who hid it near a fence post on his owner's farm and covered it with a shingle. It was later found there. After finding the money, the pair put the bodies back in bed and partially covered them.

The ruse began to fall apart when one of the neighbors awoke at the sound of the gunshot and saw Bob, who was wearing distinctive yellow pantaloons. As both Bob and Jacob attempted to put forth their story, they drew suspicion to themselves. First, Bob volunteered the fact that the Blairs had only one and a half dollars in their possession because they had loaned the rest of the money to Moses Pool two days earlier. The investigation which followed showed that Bob had given a distinctive silver dollar to a boy the day after the murder. It was recovered and identified by Pool and another witness, Irvin Frogg. Bob's pantaloons were bloody. He said this was from a nosebleed a few days earlier, but one of Bob's eyes was bloody and swollen as if someone had struck him. The blood on his clothes did not look like it came from drops of blood. Under questioning, the killers' story fell apart. Bob said that after he shot at the mystery pair he turned and saw the Blair house front door was open. However, the door could not be seen from that point.

Held in jail, the pair were told it would be better for their souls if they confessed. Jacob did so and told the details of the crime. Several witnesses of both races said that Bob had threatened to kill the old man. One reason was that he had the opportunity to go to Missouri and operate a store for a man who wanted to buy him. Another reason was that Blair had accused him of stealing chickens and threatened to beat him in the house.[242] The state's last witness was Moses Pool, who owned Jacob. He said the two slaves were close friends and he feared Bob would ruin Jacob and forbade him from going to Bob's or associating with him.[243]

Bob and Jacob were convicted by a Fentress County jury, but the judge granted a new trial because the court had run out of qualified veniremen and was forced to seat five jurors who were seated by consent. The case was then moved to Overton County and tried in the June 1839 term.

The only issue on appeal was whether one of the jurors had separated himself from the rest. The facts showed that one of the jurors had walked about twenty yards away to a blacksmith shop, but he had not spoken to anyone nor was he out of sight of the deputy in charge, and when called, immediately returned. This was not grounds for a new trial, ruled the Tennessee Supreme Court.[244]

Bob and Jacob were executed in Nashville on January 20, 1840, before a large and festive crowd, but the details of the hanging are unknown. One witness said the spectacle did nothing to lessen crime and wrote a letter to a newspaper insisting the legislature bar public executions.[245]

Peter, black, age unknown. *Murder.*

The crime was committed on November 15, 1841, at the victims' home in McMinn County, about four miles north of Athens. Initial accounts said that four members of the McMahan family were ax-murdered by their slave, but in fact only two were killed.[246] The victims were Mrs. Esther McMahan, white, age thirty-five, and her daughter, Mary McMahan, white, age thirteen. They were the wife and daughter of John McMahan, who owned Peter.[247]

The crime was planned by Peter and Jim, another slave owned by John McMahan. He had taken Jim to Decatur, in Meigs County. While they were gone, Peter came to the house and entered the back door. He struck Mary's head with two blows from an ax and she fell in the kitchen. The mother heard the noise and was felled with two blows, a third nearly severing her head as she lay on the floor. As Jim and McMahan neared the house, Jim suddenly blurted a warning not to enter the house or McMahan would be killed.[248] Jim soon told him about the plot and testified against Peter. Following a slave-court trial, Peter was hanged in McMinn County on December 28, 1841.

1842

Dick (aka Dick Dyer), black, age unknown. *Attempted rape of white woman.*

Dick, the slave of Isaiah Dyer, attempted to rape Elizabeth Hodges, white, age fifteen, on July 11, 1842. Elizabeth was returning from school "when Dick came up behind her and overtook her and told her he wanted to do his bidding." She testified, "He caught hold of me and threw me on my back and pulled off my clothes and said that if I didn't let him do what he wanted to do that he would kill me and got upon me with his britches loose and with the thought to ravish me, but failed.... I said I saw a man coming."[249] A white man testified he saw Dick near the schoolhouse, appearing to be looking for something. Dick said his horse had gotten away near the schoolhouse. Rosannah, a slave of George A. House, said she saw Dick come running away from the direction of the schoolhouse.

Dick remained mute through all legal proceedings. He was tried on July 21, 1842. There was no appeal and he was hanged in Franklin on August 15, 1842. The details of the hanging are unknown.

1843

Jacob (aka Jake and Jake Bradford), black, age 30. *Murder.*

The crime was committed on August 17, 1840, on the Davidson County farm owned by the victim, Robert Bradford, white, age forty-two. Bradford rebuked Jacob on August 11 for not doing his work and threatened to whip him and sell him. Bradford then got a switch and attempted to whip Jacob, who snatched the switch out of his hands, broke it up, and ran off.[250]

In a day or two, Jacob returned. Bradford ordered him to go off until he was willing to be tied and whipped. Jacob returned on the 16th and was asked again if he was willing to be tied and whipped. Again, Jacob said no. Bradford told him to take food and leave again and not come back until he would accept his punishment. Jacob returned the next day.

This time, Bradford and his brother, Frederick Bradford, grabbed Jacob. A struggle ensued and Frederick "struck [Jacob] two blows on the head with a stick," but "did not knock him down or draw blood." The brothers then threw Jacob to the ground on his back. He arose and grabbed the stick. This time the brothers threw him to the ground on his face. Just as Frederick took the stick away, "Jacob drew a knife from his bosom, the lower part of the hand next to the blade, and raising it up at arm's length, struck Robert Bradford on the left side, exclaiming, 'Damn it, clear the way!'"[251] Robert Bradford died in about five minutes. Jacob escaped and was found some months later in Arkansas.

The issue before the Tennessee Supreme Court was whether there was such provocation to vitiate the case to manslaughter. The court said that the slave's personal injury, "if it exceeds not the bonds of moderation, is lawful correction," which was "necessary for the proper organization and due discipline of society." Simply stated, "the law did not recognize the violence of the master as a legitimate cause of provocation."[252] The case did not show any mitigating facts; it was "most clearly one of murder."[253]

Jacob was hanged in Nashville on January 29, 1843, before "an immense crowd that contained women." From the gallows Jacob sang a hymn that could be heard "two squares away," and "his fortitude was manifest, even unto death."[254] Jacob confessed that he had killed his master, but it was not done willfully. A newspaper said public executions were improper and that hangings should be conducted inside a prison.[255] The body was taken into the woods for burial. By 1887, the site was no longer woods. It became a site at the corner of Belmont Boulevard and Hawkins Street, where the grave was uncovered on May 19, 1887.[256]

Hannibal (aka Ham), black, age unknown. *Murder.*

The crime was committed on January 5, 1843, on the victim's farm near Greeneville, Greene County. The victim was John Rhea, white, age fifty-three. He was Hannibal's owner. Rhea and two slaves were engaged in covering a coal-pit when some altercation took place between the master and servant about his manner of working, which caused Hannibal to strike Rhea with a coal shovel. "The first blow entered the edge of the hair, passing down to the ear, severing all the flesh from the bone. The second blow was just above the eyes, across the forehead, penetrating half through the skull. The third blow, after Rhea had fallen, was across the throat, severing both arteries of the neck, and cutting the throat from ear to ear. The demon in human form finally took a mattock and stuck it through the neck bone leaving the corpse fastened to the earth."[257] Hannibal was tried in circuit court on February 15, 1843. One of his lawyers was Robert J. McKinney, who served on the Tennessee Supreme Court, 1847–1861. Hannibal was hanged at Greeneville on March 3, 1843. Placed in a coffin and buried, Hannibal was dug up that night and his body was publicly displayed to terrorize other slaves.[258]

Archibald Kirby, white, age 47. *Murder.*

The crime was committed on the night of May 11, 1842, in White County, at the rural home of Mrs. Polly Hunter. But Kirby's walk to the gallows began on February 22, 1831, with his killing of Peter Elrod on Pine Mountain in White County.

Elrod was a gunpowder miller and needed saltpeter. Kirby knew this and lured him to a remote spot, where he had supposedly found a saltpeter cave, and killed him. Kirby was tried for murder and convicted, but was granted a new trial by the Tennessee Supreme Court. This was because some of the men who testified spoke of a conversation they had with Elrod, who said that he and Kirby were planning to explore Pine Mountain to look for the saltpeter cave, but some of the conversations were too far removed from the time of the killing to be part of the res gestae.[259] One testified that Kirby had told him that the saltpeter samples he had shown Elrod had come from a known source, not the cave.

Kirby was tried a second time and convicted. Again, the case was reversed on appeal, in part, because one of the witnesses' testimony was different in the second trial from what it had been in the first. The difference was whether the witness (Baker) was testifying about what Elrod had said about the upcoming trip to Pine Mountain, or whether Baker himself was traveling in that direction.[260]

When the case came for trial a third time, witnesses failed to appear and Judge Abraham (Abram) Caruthers angrily dismissed it. The sheriff said, "I will have to set you at liberty, a murderer as you are, and turn you out upon the community though you are not fit to be a member of society."[261] Kirby's lawyer, Sam Turney, said, "You're as guilty as hell and if you ever murder again I'll volunteer to hang you."[262] By now, Kirby had spent nearly six years in jail. During that time he had learned to read and became an accomplished shoemaker. He returned to his wife and family in February 1837.

"About a hour into the night" of May 11, 1842, Mrs. Polly Hunter, white, age unknown, a widow, was sitting in her cabin on Blue Springs Cove with two other women.[263] One was Mary Ann Todd. As they sat talking, a rifle shot was fired which broke the glass and struck Polly in the neck a little below the ear. Shoe prints on the ground outside showed where the killer had been standing. The mashed bullet was found inside the house.[264] All the evidence against Kirby was circumstantial.[265] No motive was assigned for the killing, although none is needed when a killing is done while lying in wait.[266] Kirby was an immediate suspect and was charged with the crime within two weeks.[267]

The June 6, 1842, trial in Sparta, White County, was presided over by Judge Abram Caruthers. Kirby did not take the stand. His lawyer insinuated that Mrs. Hunter's slaves were responsible for her death, on the belief they would be emancipated on her death. A witness, Matthew Wallis, who apparently stood to gain by her death, testified that her husband's will contained no emancipation provision.[268]

In an elaborate opinion recounting the testimony of many witnesses, the Tennessee Supreme Court outlined facts which pointed to Kirby. The mashed bullet (ball) was identical to those made by a man for Gideon Anderson's gun. Anderson had given the gun, bullets and powder to Kirby the day before the killing. (Kirby was told he could keep the gun if he found Anderson's lost cow, which he did.) Kirby was seen with the gun, but not on the evening of the shooting — the court said he likely hid the gun near her house the night before. His heel shoe prints fit those at the scene exactly, although the shoe length was a little shorter. The unique footprints left by his horse were found near the shooting site, the horse having been tied there.[269]

Kirby's own actions made little sense. He told a friend that he was going to a certain store to buy shirts for his small sons the night of the murder, but seemed to have changed his mind and rode off in the wrong direction. Likewise, he claimed to have walked back to another person's house, taking a route he said was clear. But it was not, having grown up since the time he had apparently taken it several years before.

Regarding the most compelling evidence, the shoe prints, Kirby actually served to draw attention to himself. When arrested, he pointedly asked if the heel prints showed the presence of heel irons. When told they did not, he quickly pointed to his shoes, which contained irons, asserting they had been put on the Saturday after the shooting. (The irons were clearly old, but the nails were new.) But this was contradicted by a witness for Kirby, who said the irons were on his shoes in April. The court said that Kirby must have taken them off for the killing and put them back on afterward.[270]

Regarding the misfitting shoe prints, the court said, "The tracks were made in ploughed ground, across the ridges. The prisoner had on shoes, when apprehended, that he had worn a considerable time. The toe of a coarse shoe, after it has been worn some time, turns up somewhat, so that in walking across the ploughing it would not press firmly on the ground so as to press the earth together and make the track distinct as it would be at the heel and ball of the foot."[271]

The court said that some of the evidence pointed to Anderson, who fled the county on hearing the news of Polly's killing, and "their concert of action and probable presence of both at Mrs. Hunter's on the night of the murder, is established beyond a reasonable doubt."[272]

The February 13, 1843, execution of Kirby (and the two men who were hanged with him for separate crimes, Willis Carroll and Zeb Payne) was filled with drama and became a part of Tennessee folklore for decades. First, it was thought that Governor James "Lean Jimmy" Jones was likely to pardon Kirby because the evidence was poor. On the gallows, Kirby stooped down to bid good-bye to a friend. This was mistaken as evidence of clemency: "He is descending — the governor has pardoned him!" said the crowd, unhappy at the prospect. But it was not so.

The three men had been dressed in "winding sheets," white shrouds, and taken by wagon to the gallows on a hill in south Nashville. After Carroll asserted his innocence, Kirby did the same. "I am to be murdered this day for the murder of Polly Hunter, a lady I have not seen in 26 or 27 years."[273] Over a thousand people watched the executions.

After the two ministers said a prayer, the ropes were placed, then caps, and the trap was sprung. Folklore suggests that Carroll's sister was in the crowd and emitted a piercing scream which sent another woman into a swoon and brought about her death two days later. Contemporary accounts mention nothing about a scream, but suggest that as the death procession crowd passed the home of Mrs. Nancy Taylor, age 46, it caused a "violent nervous excitement and congestion of the brain, of which she died on Sunday morning."[274]

While in jail awaiting execution for killing Mrs. Hunter, Kirby explained what happened with Elrod. About five years before the killing, Kirby met and began to live with a young woman who had an illegitimate daughter. The girl had been fathered by Elrod. In time, Kirby's anger grew toward him, especially after the girl was taken to live with Elrod and his wife; and the girl clearly preferred him over Kirby. First, Kirby tried to shoot Elrod but the gun misfired. Then he tried to put an explosive under the couple's bed, but the fuse went out. Finally, he lured Elrod to the remote Pine Mountain location and split his head with a tomahawk.[275]

The coroner at first balked at recommending Kirby be charged. He resorted to an old superstition. He told Kirby to pick up the body — if it did not bleed this meant that Kirby was innocent. Kirby agreed. He lifted the body and it did not bleed.[276] The public first thought the "lessen" of the body was the truth. But testimony at the two trials showed otherwise, and the public was outraged over the reversals based on technicalities. Public sentiment at his release from the Elrod killing was so intense that it carried over to the prosecution of Mrs. Hunter's case—for which some doubted Kirby was responsible. These included his lawyer, who wrote the pamphlet telling what happened to Elrod, and describing the crimes of Carroll and Payne.

One person who shared no doubt about Kirby's guilt was Judge Nathan Green, who denounced him in giving the court's order for his execution:

> Your victim was an unoffensive female. Stimulated most probably by a reward bestowed from some person who was interested in the death, you were induced to act the part of a cold blooded assassin. Soon after dark, on Wednesday night the 11th of May, you approached her dwelling, armed with a deadly rifle. A light was in the room and you saw her, in the midst of her female friends, sitting around the candle, engaged in cheerful conversation. You approached, silently and stealthily, the window near which she sat, and fired your gun upon her through the glass. Your aim was but too sure. The fatal ball had done it's work of death, and in a few minutes she was a lifeless corpse.[277]

The jurist continued:

> You have shown in this transaction that you have a heart utterly void of social duty, and fatally bent on mischief. As a terror to others, and a means of safety to the community, the law pronounces that you must die. If you were permitted to go abroad in the community, no man's life would be safe, who you might be tempted to destroy, or whose destruction would benefit any person willing to pray the price of blood. Is it not, therefore, fit that you should go at large, in terror to mankind, and the *law deems* that it is fit that you suffer an ignominious death, as a terror to evil doers who might be tempted to follow in your steps. And the judgment of the law is that you be hanged by the neck until you are dead.[278]

Zebadiah Payne, white, age 19. *Murder.*

The crime was committed about 1:00 P.M. on June 12, 1840, outside of Shelbyville, near the community of Roseville, in Bedford County. The victim, William Coltart (Colthart), white, age unknown, was riding his horse down a lonely road and Payne came upon him on his horse. Coltart said he had done well opening a store in Franklin, Williamson County, and was going to Winchester to start another. This gave Payne the idea that Coltart was carrying a lot of money.

After traveling together, they came to a road leading to a house where they planned to stop. Dismounting, and leaving their horses tied at the road, the pair walked toward the house, the victim leading. Payne hit Coltart on the head with his pistol and slashed at Coltart's throat fifteen or twenty times with a pocket knife. He then robbed the body, also taking Coltart's horse, which he soon abandoned.

Payne fled to Galveston, Texas, but was apprehended because Governor James K. Polk had placed reward notices in Texas newspapers.[279] He was helped to hide by friends and family in Texas, and on one occasion was released from the custody of bounty hunters by former Tennessee Governor Sam Houston. He and another man killed a peddler in Texas. Bounty hunters brought him back to Tennessee via New Orleans and he was tried in Franklin County on July 22, 1842.

Numerous witnesses testified they had seen Payne with the victim and remembered Payne because of a distinctive white hat he wore.[280] Payne insisted that his meeting with Coltart was purely accidental and they had parted shortly after riding together and Coltart saw another man on horseback and decided to ride with him.[281]

The issue before the Tennessee Supreme Court was whether two jurors had heard so much about the case, namely that a man had been killed, the defendant was charged with the killing and had tried to escape, that they should not have been seated. The court said this was a matter for the judge's discretion, that the test was whether the potential jurors had been asked and answered whether their minds were made up, not whether they had an opinion.[282]

Payne was one of three men hanged on February 13, 1843, on a hill in south Nashville. They were Archibald Kirby, Willis Green Carroll, and Payne. This was the first triple execution in Nashville and about a thousand people came to witness it, in part because there was a rumor that one of the men, Archibald Kirby, would receive a gallows pardon (commutation).

The reason the three men were hanged in Nashville is unknown because none of the crimes occurred in Davidson County. The three were taken to the gallows in a wagon and were dressed in "winding sheets," namely white shrouds. All had been attended by ministers who proclaimed them ready for death. After the Rev. A.L.P. Green made some remarks and a prayer, Payne spoke first: "I am this day to die for the murder of William Coltart, of which I am innocent. I pray God that He may so shake the earth, as to convince the world of my innocence. Since the laws of my country have doomed me to die, I yield up my life cheerfully." Kirby made similar remarks. Carroll could not be heard, for his voice was too low.

According to folklore, moments before the men were dropped, Payne's sister gave out a piercing scream. This caused another woman present to fall into a swoon and die three days later.[283] No contemporary accounts mention anyone screaming. Rather, the death procession crowd passed the home of Mrs. Nancy Taylor, age 46. "The sight of the prisoners and the crowd passing her residence brought on violent nervous excitement and congestion of the brain, of which she died on Sunday morning."[284]

Shortly after the executions, lawyer Milton Haynes, who had represented Kirby, published a pamphlet describing the men's lives and crimes. He reported that Payne had told another prisoner that he had killed Coltart. He said, "I made another cut at this throat, and broke off the blade. Picking up the blade, I thrust it into his neck, on the left side, and cut the neck vein. I only got about $60 in Alabama money."[285]

Willis Green Carroll (aka Willis Green), white, age unknown. *Murder.*

The crime was committed on the bank of the Cumberland River near Saunder's Ferry in Sumner County on the late afternoon of December 14, 1840. The victim was the Rev. Isaac Lindsey, white, age fifty-six. He was from a pioneer middle Tennessee family for whom Lindsey Ridge was named. He had been a circuit-riding minister whose religious ardor had cooled and had been replaced by a desire for money and wealth.[286]

Carroll, a mysterious loner, was reputed to have been at one time a member of the infamous Murrel gang, but at the time of the killing was acting alone. Carroll had earlier befriended Lindsey. He convinced Lindsey that he had discovered a silver mine on a bank of the Cumberland River. The pair went searching for the mine. Lindsey was riding, Carroll walking behind carrying a rifle.[287] As they approached Saunder's Ferry they turned to walk along the river bank. They were seen by a ferryman's daughter, who recognized Carroll because he had stayed with the family a few days earlier.

About an hour after they passed, the young woman heard a gunshot and exclaimed, "Carroll has killed that man!"[288] A few days later, Lindsey's body was found in a swampy area beside the river. Carroll was gone. William R. Saunders, a Lindsey neighbor, pursued the killer and finally found him in Indian Territory (Oklahoma) and personally brought him back for trial.

The most compelling evidence was the gun that Carroll always carried. Saunders was able to purchase it from a man Carroll had sold it to for much below its real value. The size of the ball it shot was exactly the same as that recovered from Lindsey's body.[289]

Carroll maintained his innocence to the end, including a letter he wrote to Lindsey's widow. He denied any involvement with an alleged silver mine, directly controverting several witnesses who heard him talk about it. Lindsey had told his family the morning of his death that he was going "speculating" with Carroll.[290]

The chief issue on appeal was whether the testimony of several witnesses who heard Carroll talk about the silver mine, and the testimony of the Lindsey family about the venture, were admissible. The Tennessee Supreme Court said they were part of the res gestae.[291]

Judge Nathan Green had read the Tennessee Supreme Court's sentence of Carroll, Kirby and Payne. He concluded, "You are soon to appear before a tribunal, where falsehood cannot avail, and where justice cannot be eluded. Let penitence and faith prepare you for that last awful trial, for enormous as your guilt, it does not exceed the mercies of God, in Jesus Christ. Employ all the means to bring your hearts in deep humility, and hearty confession to this mercy seat. Engage the service, advice, and prayers of the Rev. Clergy of the city, and let your remaining days be days of penitence and your nights of devotion and prayer."[292]

Carroll, along with Archibald Kirby and Zebediah Payne, were kept in the Nashville penitentiary while their cases were on appeal. They were executed on February 13, 1843. They were placed in a cart and taken to a hill in south Nashville wearing "winding sheets" (shrouds). Kirby and Payne were attended by Methodist ministers, Carroll a Catholic priest.

On the gallows, both Kirby and Payne asserted their innocence, but Carroll spoke in such a low voice he could not be heard. In the written "confessions" of the three men, Carroll never admitted his crime. He only promised to haunt the jail and his enemies.[293] Just before the men dropped, Payne's sister is said to have uttered a piercing scream. At the drop, another woman, a stranger to the three men, fell into a swoon and died the next day, a Sunday. The incident was repeated in Tennessee folklore for decades.[294] This was the first triple execution in Tennessee.

The Rev. John B. McFerrin, a notable in the Tennessee Methodist church, had attended the trio in prison. He said about Carroll, "He died without any seeming emotion, and had the sympathy of no one. His crime was so shocking, and betrayed such a heartless and bloody disposition, that every one felt he was justly executed upon the gallows."[295]

Henry (aka Henry Kelly), black, age unknown. *Murder.*

The killer was an escaped slave belonging to Mrs. Ann Kelly of Shelby County. He and another escaped slave, John, broke into the Gibson County home of a widow, Mrs. Franklin, white, and raped and attacked her with an ax on May 13, 1842. William C. Franklin, white, age thirteen, came to his mother's aid and was killed with "a certain chopping axe of the value of fifty cents."[296] One blow went to the left side of the neck, another to the left side of the head, "the breadth of five inches and of the depth of six inches, said mortal wounds the said William C. Franklin then and there instantly died."[297] Henry was not captured until November 1842. John was shot while being captured and died in the Gibson County jail.

Henry's appointed lawyers got the case continued until March 10, 1843. Seven people were called as witnesses. Henry was convicted and sentenced to hang on April 4, 1843. There was no appeal and Henry was hanged on the courthouse lawn at Trenton on the appointed day by sheriff L.P. Seay.[298]

Louis (aka Lewis), black, age unknown. *Murder.*

The crime was committed on March 20, 1843, in Tipton County. Louis was a slave owned by Rachael S. Cannon, administrator of the Estate of Newton Cannon.[299] Details of the crime are unknown except he struck John Ethridge, white, age unknown, on the left side of the head with an ax. He was tried by a circuit court jury.[300] There was no appeal and Louis was hanged at Covington on August 23, 1843. Details of the execution are unknown.

Buckner, black, a slave, age unknown. *Murder.*
Three unnamed slaves, black, slaves, ages unknown. *Murder.*

The crime was committed on the night of May 24, 1843, somewhere in Haywood County. In December 1842 and January 1843 there were a series of runaways in Haywood and neighboring counties which triggered fears of a slave insurrection. The slaves were caught and dealt with harshly. But the tactics failed to prevent four slaves belonging to Benjamin B. Branch from eloping. The victim, Thomas Branch, white, a young adult, was looking for them when he was stopped, robbed of two hundred dollars and shot.[301] Initial accounts of the crime reported the victim was in bed asleep when killed by the four slaves owned by his father.[302]

The shooters were arrested with a white man (he was charged with forging a note) and jailed on May 30, 1843. The shooters were formally charged on June 15, 1843. Fifteen days later, the father of Thomas Branch had one of the defendants whipped in the jail to get a confession and to reveal where the stolen two hundred dollars was hidden. The latter was discovered but there was no confession.

The supposed ringleader, named Buckner, was tried and found guilty on October 14, 1843. The other three were tried and found guilty on November 16, 1843.

Buckner and the other three were hanged at the same time in Brownsville on December 22, 1843. Within two days the county doctors were busy dissecting one of the dead.

1844

Lucy, black, age unknown. *Murder.*

The crime was committed on May 4, 1844, on the farm of James W. Hayley and his wife Eliza in Madison County. The victim was the couple's son, white, age sixteen, name unknown. He had attempted to whip Lucy for not working properly when she grabbed a hoe and mangled his face and head, then cut his throat from ear to ear. The boy's parents testified at Lucy's trial. She was convicted on April 27, 1844, and was hanged on June 21, 1844, in Jackson, Madison County.[303] Because Lucy was the Hayleys' property, they were required to pay the costs of her trial.

1845

Jim Payne (aka Jim), black, age unknown. *Murder.*

The crime was committed at midnight in a cabin located in DeKalb County owned by a white man, William Williams, on January 14, 1843. The victim, Isaac, was a slave who was killed by a single shot while he was asleep on the floor of the kitchen. He was shot by one of two bullets fired from outside through a hole near the door.[304]

Jim, the shooter, was accompanied by a slave named George. Judgments had been gotten against their owners and the creditors were attempting to execute (levy) on the negroes in order to sell them. The pair was hiding from the sheriff and anyone else they suspected of attempting to apprehend them. Both Jim and George had heard that Isaac had been hired to capture them, especially George. In the presence of other slaves, George said, "If Isaac was one of the sort that would betray black people, he would be none too good to hurt him."[305] The witness who heard this (Sam) said that George had "agged" Jim to kill Isaac.[306] Jim's conviction at his first trial was overturned on appeal because the jury had engaged in two experiments testing whether a voice could be heard through a door and whether a footprint of a person running was shorter than the person walking.[307]

Most of the key witnesses were slaves and the issue before the court was whether the jury was correct in believing one slave, Cindy, over two others, Nancy and Becky. Jim's lawyers said Cindy should not be accredited because she was George's wife and had a reason to fix blame on Jim in order to spare her husband. The court said that her testimony at both trials inculpated both men but fixed the shooter as Jim.

Moreover, Jim's testimony was shown to be false. He insisted he had sold his pistol to Peter Creps two or three weeks prior to the killing, but various witnesses saw him with the pistol a few days prior to the killing. Said the court, "To one witness he said he had seen Isaac coming from the mill, and could have shot him then, but there was a white boy along."[308] His assertion that he did not know Isaac was shown to be false, since he had been seen with him at the Williamses' still-house. The most damning evidence was a shoe print showing a hole in the sole which fit a shoe Jim was wearing. Finally, several whites said that Cindy was more credible than Nancy and Becky, who were "in the habit of telling stories, and are not entitled to full credit."[309]

Jim Payne was executed in Smithville, DeKalb County, in early 1845 on a gallows erected about a half mile from the town. Several thousand attended the execution, one of them was "about ten years old" and later wrote that the execution "made a very deep impression on me."[310] The viewer was John A. Fite, who became a lawyer and judge. His is one of the few eyewitness accounts of an antebellum execution, written when Fite was seventy-eight years old:

> There was a negro named Jim Payne, he had been sold down South. He came back up Dry Creek, near where my grandfather lived. My grandfather had a negro named Isaac. Isaac married a negro girl that lived with the old man Williams. This runaway negro Jim Payne had been informed that Isaac had betrayed him and was going to have him caught. One night when Isaac was at his wife's house at old man Williams and was lying in front of the fire on a pallet with the little girl by his side, this negro Jim Payne slipped up back of the cabin and shot him through the crack in the cabin.[311]
>
> Sometime after that Payne was caught and indicted and tried for murder at Smithville, and sentenced to be hung. It was sometime after the killing before he was caught and tried, for at that time I was living in Alexandria, I, with my grandfather had moved there.[312]
>
> With a lot of other boys I went to see him hung. He was hung about one half mile from Smithville, in a hollow. He was sitting on his coffin in a wagon, and before he was hung the sheriff asked if he had anything he wanted to say to the people. He said, "Yes," and got up on his feet and asked for Henry Hart, and nobody answered. He then asked for Peter Crepes, and nobody answered. Then he asked for Terry Williams. Terry Williams was sitting on the ground a few feet from me. Somebody told him to get up and see what the negro wanted. He said, "If it hadn't been for you and Henry Hart and Peter Crepes, I would never have killed Isaac. Henry Hart furnished me the pistol, you promised to give me money, and Peter Crepes was to put me in his wagon and conceal me and take me to Nashville, you came to me that night that I killed Isaac and showed me where Isaac was lying. Sometime before that I had hid in the hollow of a sycamore tree on Dry Creek, and I had seen Isaac and a little white boy going by, going up to the mill, when he came back I didn't want to scare the little boy so I did not shoot, and he never knew I was there at that time.[313]

Fite concluded, "I remember distinctly going with Isaac up from the mill to grandfather's and when he told that I was satisfied that if he had shot at that time I should have been scared to death."[314] Fite did not describe the details of the execution.

While it seems clear that Peter Creps, race unknown, was known to be a half mile from the Williamses' house at ten or eleven o'clock the night Isaac was killed, no information is available whether he was charged in the matter.[315] No information is available regarding Terry Williams or Henry Hart.

The Tennessee Supreme Court explained the murder motive. "The truth seems to be that Isaac had not only excited the enmity of George and Jim, but he seems to have lost *caste* with the other negroes in the neighborhood. He had combined with the white folks to betray George to the sheriff, and it was thought he was also engaged to apprehend Jim. This was no slight offence in their eyes; that one of their own color, subject to like servitude, should abandon the interests of his *caste*, and, for hire, betray black folks to the white people, rendered him an object of general aversion. Hence it was that George and Jim felt so little hesitation in the utterance of their threats; and hence it was that Cindy did not wish to destroy Jim for such a fellow."[316]

Lize, black, age unknown. *Murder.*

The crime was committed on the night of May 14, 1845, at the farm of Wilson Turnar Meador and his wife in Macon County. Lize had been purchased some months earlier for $1,250. It was suspected she had killed several persons before Meador bought her, but was never charged with murder. Within a few months she had taken a knife to the smokehouse to kill Mrs. Meador, but changed her mind because she realized she could not find a place to hide the body.[317]

One night she took one of the Meador children, Jim, age four, from where he was sleeping and tied a handkerchief around his throat, thinking it would choke him. She put the child outside on the doorstep, but the couple heard the noise and rescued the child. Lize attempted to fix blame on Jack, another slave. Lize was apparently whipped for her misbehavior.

On the night of May 14, 1845, she took Thomas J. Meador, Jr., age two and one-half, to the milking shed and beat him to death with a calf stick, the device used to separate a calf from its mother.

She was soon convicted and sentenced to hang. She was hanged at Lafayette, Macon County, sometime in late 1845. Before the execution, she sold her head to a Dr. Flippin, of Lafayette, in exchange for all the cider and ginger cakes she could eat. Immediately after the hanging, Dr. Flippin cut off her head, tied it with a handkerchief and later placed it in a bottle. Upon his death it was inherited by his son-in-law, Dr. Bratton, who then willed it to his son, also named Dr. R.E. Bratton.

During the Civil War, a troop of Union soldiers stayed at the Meador home, bringing with them smallpox. Thomas J. Meador and his wife died on the same day, January 16, 1863.

Bill (aka Bill Moore), black, age unknown. *Assault with intent to rape.*

The crime was committed about 9:00 P.M. on September 28, 1843, on a road leading out of Fayetteville, in Lincoln County. Mrs. Mary Smith, white, age unknown, was riding a slow horse, carrying a bundle of clothes and a baby. She was riding out of town and was accompanied by a boy slave. Bill, on horseback, met them. Mrs. Smith thought he was a slave owned by her mother who had been sent to assist her. Unable to recognize him because of the darkness, she asked who he was and he replied, "One." He proceeded toward town.

The proof showed that he hitched his horse to a rail and ran on foot to her. This was possible because the road took a right angle and he ran the hypotenuse of the triangle. He pulled Mrs. Smith from her horse and attempted to rape her (saying this was his intent) but was attacked by the slave boy. She dropped the clothes bundle. She took the baby and ran to a neighboring house.[318] The defendant was found with the clothing and the testimony of other slaves placed him in the area at the time of the crime. He was hanged on March 14, 1845, in Fayetteville.[319]

Skelt, black, age unknown. *Murder.*

The details of the crime are unknown except it was committed in 1845. Skelt, a slave of Bird Greer, killed a traveling tailor, whose last name was Dupree. He was white, age unknown. The hatchet murder was committed on the Huntingdon road about four miles south of Paris, in Henry County. Skelt was charged on September 17, 1845. His owner provided two lawyers and he was tried beginning on March 19, 1846. The jury had difficulty making up its mind but Skelt was convicted on March 23, 1846. He made a full confession before his hanging in Paris on April 10, 1846.[320]

Ned (aka Ned Walton), black, age unknown. *Murder.*

The crime was committed on August 17, 1845, on the farm of David J. Walton, white, age unknown, in northern Robertson County. Ned and another slave, Peter, were chopping wood on new ground when the victim, their owner, arrived and an argument ensued. He was struck in the back of the head by an ax swung by Ned. The pair was tried on October 10, 1845, and Peter was found not guilty but Ned was convicted. He was ordered hanged on October 31, 1845. There was no appeal. Ned was hanged on the appointed day from a tree in a field on the south side of Fifth Avenue West, in Springfield, Robertson County.[321]

1846

Claricy (aka Clarissa), black, age unknown. *Murder.*

The crime was committed on February 23, 1846, on the farm of William Dawson in Franklin County. Claricy was "a slave for life" of Dawson. That day, "being big with child" she gave birth to the victim, a female infant child "without a Christian name." She strangled the infant, beat it with her fist, threw it to the ground and kicked it. She took a stone and smashed the right side of its head and face, killing it instantly. Claricy was convicted in circuit court and ordered hanged on June 12, 1846.[322] On June 10, 1846, Gov. Aaron V. Brown, who opposed the death penalty, granted a respite until July 3, 1846, so that her case could be "more fully inquired of and examined by me."[323] Claricy was hanged in Winchester, Franklin County, on August 3, 1846.

1847

Thomas, black, age 16. *Murder.*

The details of the crime are unknown except that Thomas, a slave, killed a free white woman, Miss Pollock, age unknown, about five miles from Shelbyville in Bedford County on June 23, 1846. He smashed her head with a rock and she was "dreadfully mangled."[324] He was owned by James P. Couch. Thomas was hanged sometime in 1847 in Shelbyville. Because Thomas was the only property of value owned by Couch and he was "left without any help by which to make a living except his own labors," Couch petitioned the General Assembly to compensate him for the loss.[325] It rejected the petition on January 14, 1848.

Frank Oliver, a slave, age unknown. *Murder.*

The facts of the crime are unknown except that Frank was a slave and the victim was Mrs. Elizabeth Rumley, white, a widow, age unknown. She was murdered with an ax on September 5, 1846, at her home somewhere in Carroll County. Oliver was hanged on a gallows in Huntington in May 1847 in front of a crowd of ten thousand.[326]

1848

Gilbert, black, age unknown. *Murder.*

The crime was committed sometime in 1847 at an unknown location in a tobacco barn owned by the victim, in Henry County. The victim was Armstead Forrest, white, elderly and nearly blind. He was Gilbert's owner. The motive was Gilbert's desire to leave his wife, also owned by Forrest, and take a different wife at a neighboring plantation.

Gilbert frequently carried a hickory stick which he called "the peace-maker." On the murder day, Forrest went to the tobacco barn and was seated stripping tobacco. Gilbert crept up behind him. Holding the stick with both hands he struck the old man's head. He fell forward without crying out. Gilbert sent Jackson, black, age seventeen, who was Gilbert's half-brother, to "get fire" and set the barn on fire. When neighbors appeared, Gilbert told them the barn had caught fire and the old man's clothes had caught fire and the pair could not get him out.[327]

The neighbors did not believe the story. They tied Jackson to a log on the ground and threatened to kill him unless he told the truth. He told them what happened and was the chief witness against Gilbert at trial. Forrest had refused Gilbert's request to take a new wife at a neighboring plantation. Gilbert had threatened to kill Forrest, according to the testimony of another slave, Coleman.[328]

Gilbert's story of the barn catching fire did not make sense because the barn had been a dwelling house with a proper hearth. The jury and the Tennessee Supreme Court did not believe the fire escaped from it to the building. "It is not to be believed that, if the flame had got to the house and had risen beyond the control of the parties, two young, athletic men could not have rescued the old man from the burning house."[329] Also, Gilbert could not explain why he had Forrest's wallet.

Gilbert was executed in Paris on May 21, 1848. Details of the execution are unknown.

Sarah, black, age unknown. *Murder.*

The crime was committed on March 16, 1848, in Rutherford County, at the home of the victim, Mrs. Catherine Smith, white, described as aged. Sarah entered the victim's bedchamber during the night and crushed her skull with a hammer. She took the woman's body from the bed and laid her on the fireplace hearth with her head in the fire. When the body was discovered, the head was almost completely consumed.[330] Sarah was captured with the victim's goods, hiding in the woods in a remote area called Fall Creek. She was tried soon after March 21, 1848, and was hanged in Murfreesboro, Rutherford County, on June 15, 1848. The cost of her execution was $12.50 to the sheriff to hang her, $5.00 for erection of the gallows, $5.00 for a coffin, $3.00 for her grave (including digging), and seventy-five cents for a shroud.[331]

David Deakins, black, age seventeen. *Murder.*

The crime was committed sometime in 1848, seven miles northeast of Jonesboro, in Washington County. The victim was William Deakins, white, age unknown, the slave's owner. The slave had not done some work to his owner's satisfaction. The owner, a young man, attempted to whip him with a hickory switch, called "hoop poles." David picked up an ax to ward off the blows, but in doing so, struck the owner behind the right ear, fracturing his skill and causing his death on September 6, 1848.[332] The slave insisted the blow was accidental. David had two appointed lawyers. He was convicted on October 25, 1848, and sentenced to die the next day.

David Deakins was hanged in Jonesboro on November 24, 1848. He was buried in a rude coffin fifty yards from where he was hanged. That evening the coffin was removed from the ground. The body was placed on a horse in front of a young doctor's office and later used for dissection.[333]

1849

John Milton Riley (aka Milton Riley and Milton Reilley), white, age unknown. *Murder.*

The crime was committed on the night of February 5, 1848, at a grocery in the town of Independence, in Henderson County.[334] A number of people had gathered at the grocery that day, including the defendant, his cousin William H. Spain, and the victim, William "Buck" Willis, white, age unknown. Spain and Willis had been quarreling off and on all day.

On one occasion a witness saw Riley go into the store and put a steelyard pea (a heavy sliding weight) in his pocket. Riley told another witness that he had armed himself with the steelyard pea so that if the two began fighting he could use it on Willis. Later, Riley told the same witness that he had put the steelyard pea back and showed him a rock he carried for that purpose. Another witness said he was playing cards with Riley in the early afternoon, and when laughter was heard outside which was attributed to Willis, Riley said, "If he does not mind, I will lay him in his tomb before night."[335]

Throughout the day and evening Riley kept urging Spain to provoke Willis into a fight. Spain challenged Willis, but the latter said he would cut him if he attacked, and friends interceded. Spain (testifying as a hostile witness) said that Riley had shown him some fist-sized rocks he would use if a fight later ensued. Riley also passed a rock to the hand of another witness, Pope. Shortly thereafter, another witness saw Riley with a brickbat and stick and heard him say, regarding Willis, "God damn him, I will fix him before he leaves here." Another witness heard Riley try to get another person to quarrel with Riley so that he could "give him Hell." This witness saw the same brickbat and stick.[336]

Shortly after sunset, while another witness was talking with Riley, the defendant approached and challenged him to a fight, at which time Willis told him to go away or he would cut his guts out because Riley had been following him all day. Another witness heard Riley say, in company with Spain and another man, "Let him alone; I will fix him directly."[337]

About an hour later, when it was dark, the men began drinking before they started to ride their horses home. The only light came from the open door of the grocery. The defendant was offered a ride home, but declined, saying he was going to stay with a man named Joseph White. Within minutes, a sharp crack was heard which sounded like a gunshot. It became evident that Willis had been struck over the head, breaking the skull badly, leaving a wound in the shape of a letter V. No one saw who struck the blow. Willis died four days later.

Shortly after the blow was struck and Willis was taken inside, Riley appeared and Spain told him that someone had killed Willis. Riley said he "reckoned not," but that he had "knocked him down," and showed him the piece of timber he had used, saying he had struck him over the head. Riley told several other people the same story, despite Spain's telling him to hush. Within the hour, Riley gave conflicting versions as to where he was going, an apparent attempt to prevent his capture.

Apparently, Riley did not take the stand. His chief defense was that the element necessary to show murder, namely "lying in wait," was not proven.[338] The court said these facts clearly showed both malice and lying in wait. Judge Nathan Green's sentence was filled with Biblical allusions and included, "The blood of Willis cries from the ground for vengeance upon his murderer! and the stern voice of the law declares that you must die."[339]

Although Riley was convicted in Henderson County, he was taken to nearby Madison County for execution on June 8, 1849.[340] Confusion surrounds the case. It can be traced to a presentation made to the Madison County Historical Society in 1946. A history professor at Union University told the group that a man named Reilly (Riley) had killed a man named Willis with a brickbat sometime in 1838 (ten years earlier than it actually happened). Although Reilly admitted the killing at the time, when he sobered up the next day he denied the crime.[341]

According to the professor's account, thousands came to the hanging, with many perched in trees to get a better view. Riley made a great show of protesting his innocence, including a loud prayer asking the Lord to give a sign from heaven showing him guiltless. Just as the rope was placed around his neck, a black cloud appeared in the otherwise clear day and issued forth thunder, lightning and heavy rain. This caused the crowd to disperse, leaving Riley and the sheriff standing on the gallows.

According to the professor's account, when the crowd returned, a large cracking sound was heard as a large tree limb came crashing down on a man's head, pushing his hat over his eyes. This delighted the crowd, which then became silent. Riley was promptly hanged.

The case has become a popular item of Tennessee folklore. According to the college professor, "Years later a preacher holding a revival meeting in a nearby state took a deathbed confession from an old man who said it was he who killed Willis at Cotton Grove in Madison County, Tennessee."[342] By the time the case was mentioned in a history book it was recorded as follows: "Years later a man on his death bed in Obion County confessed that he had committed the murder for which Reilly had been hanged."[343] No evidence can be located to support these contentions, which were of a sort common in the 19th century.

A contemporary account of the execution mentions the massive crowd and the storm: "A single blaze of lightning in its gyrations, struck a tree near where the gallows was erected, and lighted it up in one sulfurous flame."[344] The account continued, "The rain descended in torrents — the vivid lightning flashed around — the muttering thunder rumbled along the thick fold of clouds, and horror seized the hearts of the people. The women fell in swoons, and the people trampled upon them as they hurried to and fro, frightened out of their wits. All was confusion and uproar! Trees falling on every side — the thunder roaring overhead and the lightning flashing in their faces, caused in the crowd a panic never before witnessed."[345]

The contemporary account gives no mention of Riley's saying anything. "His eyes wandered to and fro, restless and untamed. With his heart centered on earth, and with not one link of affection blinding him to heaven, he died as he had lived, with no more just conceptions of religion than a hog."[346] Like the history professor's account, the contemporary account fails to mention a booklet, *Life and Confessions of John M. Riley*, sold at the time, in which Riley admitted the crime. It has not been located.

John Inman (aka John Hill), black, age unknown. *Assault with intent to rape a free white woman.*

The crime was committed at 10:00 A.M. on September 22, 1848, at the farm of Mr. and Mrs. William Bettis, at an unspecified location in Jefferson County. The defendant was known to the defendants as John Hill, and was prosecuted in that name. He was described as a free mulatto. The victim was Mrs. Mariah Bettis, white, age fifty-four. Hill's lawyers got the trial continued until August 1849.

Hill and another man named Laferty came to the Bettis house and asked for a dram. A Bettis daughter and daughter-in-law were making ready to go to Dandridge. Hill buckled the saddles and assisted the women on their way. Mrs. Bettis gave Hill a "half a tea cup of spiritous liquors and no more."[347] Bettis and Laferty left for Massengill's for a workbench, leaving Hill and Mrs. Bettis behind alone. Bettis yelled for Hill to come but heard no answer.

The two proceeded to Massingill's and Bettis returned an hour later. He heard screaming and ran in the direction of the cornfield and heard another scream. He found his wife screaming and crying. Her neck was very red and scratched, and bore fingerprints where she had been choked. By now Laferty had returned. The area in the cornfield showed signs of a scuffle and twenty stalks of corn were down. Two pairs of footprints led to the cornfield. The larger pair were shown to match Hill's shoes, including his footprints to a fence where he had escaped. The shoes had distinctive tacks on the ball of the foot.[348]

Mrs. Bettis said she had gone to the cornfield to

gather beans growing along it and Hill had followed her. He threw her down and "done to her as a man does his wife." He had sexual intercourse with her violently and against her will, and repeated the act. According to her, Hill said she was a white woman and he was going to be hanged for raping her and "he might as well be hanged for her as another woman." She was able to scream when he loosened his grip on her neck. Hill's lawyers argued there was no proof, except opinion, that Mrs. Bettis was a white woman and that Acts of 1833, chapter 75, and Acts of 1842, chapter 193, were unconstitutional.[349]

The case was appealed to the Tennessee Supreme Court, which affirmed the conviction, but an opinion cannot be located. John Hill (Inman) was hanged on November 16, 1849, in Dandridge.

1850

David (aka Dave), black, age unknown. *Assault with intent to kill a white person.*

The details of the Hardin County crime are unknown except that on July 6, 1850, David intentionally shot a rifle at Elizabeth McCarn, the bullet striking her, but the nature of her injury is unknown. Because she was a free white woman, this was a capital offense. The facts showed that Daniel G. McCarn, David's owner, age twenty-five, apparently the woman's husband, instigated the crime. The reasons are unknown. Although the general rule was that an accessory before the fact could be punished the same as the principal, the Tennessee Supreme Court held that only David could suffer death, because the punishment for a white person assaulting another white person was limited to a prison term not to exceed twenty-one years.[350] David was hanged in Savannah, Hardin County, sometime before October 7, 1850.[351] Daniel McCarn was ultimately convicted as an accessory before the fact in Wayne County and was sent to prison for twelve years in 1853. Military governor Andrew Johnson pardoned him on July 24, 1862.

Hiram "Hyde" Godsey (aka Hyde Godfrey), white, age unknown. *Murder.*

The crime was committed in late 1849 or early 1850 somewhere in Bledsoe County at the home of the victim, John D. Morris, white, age thirty-two. Godsey's younger brother John had borrowed his "hog" rifle and gone hunting with Morris, who asked questions about the gun. When told it was his brother's, Morris took the weapon and shattered it against a tree. John took the pieces home. Godsey said, "I'll kill the son of a bitch before sundown tomorrow."[352]

Taking a jug of apple brandy, Godsey made his way to Morris's house and was welcomed inside by Mrs. Polly Morris. The murder weapon was left hidden outside. Godsey was cordial but remarked that both Polly and his wife would soon be widows. Polly took this to mean the men would be gone for a length of time, logging and taking the logs to market by river.

Morris shortly arrived and found Godsey holding Patsy, his two-year-old daughter, on his lap. When Godsey attempted to give the baby a drink of brandy, Polly said, "Don't do that, Hyde!" This caused him to get up and leave. He left and made a large noise soon after he got outside. This made the couple think he had fallen against the house. As John Morris peered outside the windowless cabin through a crack near the chimney, he was shot near the eye.

Polly ran from the cabin, leaving her two small children behind, a fact that gave rise to the belief that she had played some part in the killing.[353] Godsey found her and held her captive in the woods for a time, reluctantly allowing her to return to the cabin to nurse an infant. Godsey was finally captured in the woods by a deputy sheriff. Several kinsmen were arrested too. They all broke jail and it was a considerable time before Godsey was arrested again.

This time he was kept in the Athens jail. Details of the trial are unknown and no record of an appeal can be located. Godsey lived at the head of Sequatchie Valley, in Cumberland County today, but in Bledsoe County at the time. The execution took place near Pikeville, on the east side of the Sequatchie River, known as Hangman's Basin, or Gallows Bottom. Godsey was hanged on April 26, 1850.[354]

According to a witness, a large crowd assembled, overcoming unusually wet weather. The witness saw Godsey drop but the rope broke and he landed on the ground and was briefly rendered unconscious. "Oh! Don't put me up there again!" he said. The incident caused Sheriff A.M. Anderson to faint. The chief deputy took over and completed the task. Some witnesses fainted.[355]

The story of the rope breaking has been disputed. But the folklore continues. After Godsey's body was cut down and placed in a coffin it was taken to his home. His wife sat with the body until the burial the next day. During the night the body groaned and even sat up in the coffin.[356]

Ransom (aka Rans Overall), black, age unknown. *Rape of a white woman by a slave.*

The details of the crime are unknown except that it was committed in May 1850 in Rutherford County and the victim was a Miss Eliza Ivie, white, age forty-nine. The details of the trial and execution are unknown except that Ransom was hanged on October 25, 1850, in Murfreesboro.[357] Conventional wisdom that allowing or bringing slaves to witness an execution imbued them with respect for authority did not always hold true. A slave of Robert Jones had gone to Ransom's execution and came home under the influence of liquor. He attacked his master with a knife and succeeded in getting him down, when Mr. Jones drew a knife and cut the slave's throat in self-defense.[358]

Moses, black, age unknown. *Murder.*

The details of the crime are unknown except that it was committed somewhere in Lauderdale County on July 3, 1847, when Moses, a slave belonging to Mr. Cogshaw, struck Benjamin Huckaby, white, an aged Revolutionary War veteran, on the back of the head with a stick, killing him instantly.[359] Moses had come to the man's house to rob him, and some of the victim's property was found on him. Moses was convicted in Lauderdale County, but the Tennessee Supreme Court ordered a new trial based on doubt about an impartial juror.[360] Moses was retried in Haywood County on November 7, 1850, and was hanged in Brownsville, Haywood County, on December 27, 1850.[361]

1851

Moses, black, age 17. *Murder.*

The crime was committed on September 12, 1849, near the Sumner County rock quarry owned by John W. Lauderdale, white, age forty, the victim. He owned Moses and had raised him. About a year before, Moses had run off and was gone several weeks. When he returned home he was greatly emaciated.[362] "After he had been at home some time, and had recovered his health, the deceased whipped him, somewhat severely, but not cruelly."[363]

Shortly before the time of the murder, Moses had run away again and was gone several weeks.[364] On Sunday night a week before the killing, while Moses was a runaway, he went to a neighboring farm and told another slave that he was going home, and if his master "got close to him" and he could not get out, "he would knock him down and kill him before he would be beaten as he had been."

Moses went home and was not chastised. Several days passed. On the morning of the killing, the slaves were building a rock fence. Moses was hauling rock. He had broken an ox-bow that morning, and was sent to borrow another.[365] As he was driving down a hill one of the keys came out of the ox-bow and the ox got away. While Moses and another slave were trying to yoke the ox, Lauderdale came up, took hold of Moses and ordered two slaves to hold him. He sent for a padlock and when it was brought, he tied a log chain on Moses's leg and sent him to the quarry to work, striking him several blows with the ox switch as he went off.

Lauderdale went to his house and got some rope. He tied a piece of leather, seven inches long and three inches wide, to a handle, and left them in the stable. He then went to the quarry and told Moses to follow him to the stable. Moses did so, carrying a mattock and a knife. As they approached the stable, Moses struck Lauderdale five blows to the head with the mattock. He stabbed Lauderdale five times with the knife. Blood, brains and hair were found on the mattock.

"After the killing, Moses went back to where the other slaves were at work, and told them he had killed his master. When asked why he had done it, he replied, he was obliged to do it."[366]

The jury rejected a manslaughter defense and convicted Moses of murder.[367] The Tennessee Supreme Court said the facts showed all the elements of murder, especially malice, which was evidenced by the earlier statement to the other slaves that "if he got in a close place he would kill his master," and his deliberate arming of himself with a mattock and knife.

Moses was hanged alongside Henry in Nashville on February 21, 1851. On the gallows, Moses said, "I have but one word to say. I never murdered any man; if I did, I don't know it."[368] The pair was attended by the Rev. Brown, a Roman Catholic priest, who gave them extreme unction. He said from the gallows he thought both men were innocent. Said the newspaper, "That's all humbug. No sane man who heard the evidence in the case of Henry believes for one moment that he was innocent and the mere declaration of his innocence ought not to have led a man occupying the position of Minister of the Gospel into any such expression of opinion, especially as he had been fairly tried by two respectable courts and fully convicted. We apprehend that 'father Brown' is rather a credulous sort of a fellow, who is not hard to impose upon. Would he have believed them innocent had they not professed the faith of his church? We guess not."[369]

Henry (aka Henry Bennett), black, age unknown. *Murder.*

The crime was committed at 11:00 P.M. on Sunday, February 24, 1850, on Margin Street in the town of Franklin, in Williamson County.[370] Henry, a slave, had stolen several hams from a home on Main Street and was walking swiftly out of town with the hams on his shoulder. Several slaves saw him both before and after the killing, but none saw the killing. The other slaves were returning from a church meeting. As he walked quickly down the street, he carried a three-foot-long stick of apple or plum, which contained thirteen trimmed knots.[371]

Henry was confronted by two white men, John G. Eelbeck, age twenty-six, and William P. Barham, age twenty. One of them said, "We must see about this."[372] The three were seen to scuffle. Following the scuffle, one of the men (Eelbeck) was seen running after Henry until he fell to the ground. Within minutes, a doctor was called. He found both Eelbeck and Barham dead with knife wounds to the heart. The hams were found nearby. Barham had the stick in his hand; there was a split on the large end of it. It was thought that Barham wrested the stick from Henry and struck him or the ground with it, and was the first one stabbed. Henry, formerly a butcher, was seen carrying a large butcher knife "in his bosom" the night of the killing.

Henry proceeded to his home about fifty yards away and the next morning claimed not have any knowledge of the killing. He was seen the next day washing something; the water from the basin was red when he threw it out. Henry gave no account of his movements on the night of the murder; he was not with the other negroes of the town at the church service. Henry was charged with the murder of Eelbeck.

Henry was convicted on the testimony of the other slaves, notably Oney, who identified him as present near the killing. Others identified his clothing, the stick, the butcher knife, and his long goatee. The reason none saw the actual killing was that they thought the pair were going to whip Henry and they did not want the same to happen to them. They "pushed on home."[373]

From the gallows, Henry said, "Gentlemen, I am innocent. I never did any murder, and when you take my blood, you take innocent blood."[374] The statement outraged the four to five thousand people watching. The newspapers agreed that giving voice to such lying meant the gallows no longer held a terror and if that was so, the executions should be done in private. One paper said it doubted the value of capital punishment anyway, but public executions were degrading and demoralizing to the thousands of men, women and children who watched. Henry was hanged in Nashville on February 21, 1851. He was hanged alongside Moses.

1852

Ellick (aka Alec), black, age unknown. *Assault with intent to rape a free white woman.*
Jerry, black, age unknown. *Murder.*
Arbert, black, age unknown. *Assault with intent to rape a free white woman. Murder.*

Ellick (Alec), a slave, was convicted of assault with intent to commit rape on a free white woman, Sarah E. Tidwell. Ellick had been charged and convicted in Giles County, where the crime was committed, but the conviction was overturned. After a venue change and considerable delay, he was convicted a second time in Maury County and the conviction was affirmed. The Tennessee Supreme Court did not discuss any facts.[375] He was hanged in Nashville under the name Alec.

Jerry was a slave owned by William W. Ross. He killed a slave named Nancy, black, age unknown, also owned by Ross. He struck her head with an ax somewhere in Rutherford County on May 9, 1851, and was convicted on May 17, 1851.[376]

Arbert (a version of Robert), was also known as Albert, but was hanged under his shortened name, Bob. On May 13, 1850, he attempted to rape Miss Delilah McGaughan, white, age unknown, somewhere in Montgomery County and was sentenced to hang on July 10, 1851.[377]

On the gallows at Nashville on April 16, 1852, Alec and Jerry said they were innocent. Bob said little and spoke so low he could not be heard. "They conducted themselves with that calmness and composure, characteristic of persons to whom all chance of life is denied, and with whom resignation has taken the place of hope or struggle."[378]

1853

Alfred, black, age unknown. *Murder.*
Anthony, black, age unknown. *Murder.*

The details of the crime are unknown except that Alfred and Anthony were slaves owned by John Peck, white, age sixty-one. He was a prosperous planter in Weakley County.[379] The slaves robbed and killed him at his plantation in Weakley County on December 17, 1851. They avoided capture for a year and were tried with another slave, Isham, who was acquitted.[380] The Supreme Court found no error in the trial. The men's confessions had been freely given to the committing magistrate. These were admissible because they had been reduced to writing.[381] The Supreme Court set the day of execution as June 8, 1853, and they were hanged at Dresden, Weakley County, on that day.

Isom (aka Isham and Isaac), black, age unknown. *Assault on white woman with intent to rape.*

The facts are unknown except that Isom, a slave, committed an assault with intent to commit rape on sixty-nine-year-old Mary W. Riggs, a free white woman in Jefferson County, on June 27, 1852.[382] His trial was continued several times and he was convicted on August 16, 1853.[383]

The Tennessee Supreme Court's opinion contains no facts. It said, "The objections in this case are all purely technical, and have no reference to the merits."[384] Said the court, "The proof is not even given on which the conviction was founded. From which fact it must be inferred that it was entirely conclusive of guilt."[385]

Although there was no bill of exceptions as to the facts, there were two issues relating to procedural matters. One involved error in the court's hearing the case out of order. The other found fault in the court's refusing to delay the testimony of someone who heard Isom's confession until others could testify about the circumstances of his giving it.[386] An issue raised after the appeal was filed was whether the case should have been continued because Isom's lawyer was taken ill and another lawyer represented him.

Said the court, "The technical errors in the indictment had been rendered harmless error by a recent statute.[387] Said the court, "The day has now passed for rescuing the guilty upon mere technicalities. The Legislature has wisely willed it, and it is not for the courts to resist the great reform. We would favor rather than obstruct it."[388] Isom was executed on November 30, 1853, in Dandridge.

However, both Nashville newspapers questioned whether the executions accomplished their purpose. One newspaper said that public executions, when the condemned asserted their innocence and met death without quivering, defied the purpose of such executions, namely to strike fear in the hearts of other potential lawbreakers. "The assertion of their innocence, under circumstances which the sense of mankind and the law itself, regards as the highest test of truth, excited a feeling of defiance for its justice, and almost conviction of its injustice. The act of death developed no physical pain. How then could it terrify? It did not."[389] For this reason, executions should not be public, argued the editorial. A rival newspaper echoed those sentiments and asserted the legislature should have abolished public executions in a bill posed in the last session.[390]

1855

Elias, black, age unknown. *Rape of a free white woman.*

The crime was committed on November 4, 1852, on the farm of the victim, Mrs. Sarah Bristow, white, age seventeen, in Montgomery County. Elias may have escaped because he was not indicted until May 11, 1853. The details of the crime are unknown although there were eighteen state's witnesses, including William Bristow, the victim's husband, age nineteen, and four slaves owned by another state's witness, Ben Hatcher. The defense offered nine witnesses including two slaves.

Elias was a slave of William C. Adams, who declined to provide counsel, as a result of which the court appointed two lawyers for Elias. They sought numerous continuances and Elias was finally tried on February 14, 1854. The case was appealed but the Tennessee Supreme Court opinion cannot be located.[391] Elias was hanged on April 7, 1855, in Montgomery County, but details of the execution are unknown. The sheriff was paid $12.50 to perform the duty.

Martin, black, age unknown. *Murder.*

The facts of the case are unknown other than

that Martin killed his owner, David T. Lawrence, white, age forty-two, in Marshall County on August 17, 1854. Martin was tried in Giles County in March 1855. Martin was returned to Marshall County and executed there on April 12, 1855.[392]

Gardner R. Earles, white, age unknown. *Murder.*

The crime was committed on November 19, 1849, at the rural farm home the killer shared with his wife at an unknown location in Campbell County. The victim was Rhoda Earles, white, age unknown, the killer's wife. He struck her on the side of the head with a board. She died three days later. The reason for her killing is unknown.

Earles was not immediately arrested. He was brought to trial in Campbell County, but a jury could not be seated. The case was transferred to Scott County with the same result. After another delay, including a jail break, he was finally tried in Knox County and convicted on June 20, 1854.[393] The case was appealed to the Tennessee Supreme Court and affirmed on October 23, 1855, but an opinion cannot be located.[394] The reason for the delay on appeal is unknown.

Gardner R. Earles was hanged a Jacksboro on December 7, 1855. The six-year period between the date of the crime and the execution was the longest in the history of Tennessee in peacetime, until the late 20th and early 21st centuries.

1856

Ben Harbert, black, age unknown. *Murder.*

The crime was committed on April 29, 1853, at the victim's small home on the Charlotte Road a mile from Clarksville, in Montgomery County. Ben Harbert, a free black man, was a long-time thief and known as a "rascal." The victim, Hannah Frazier, a black woman in her sixties, had charged Harbert with stealing from her and he had been kept in jail waiting trial.[395] She asked that he be released pending trial.

Harbert was seen at her home the day of the murder. Several asked the whereabouts of Hannah. He answered, "It's none of your business!" To another he said, "Hannah has gone to the spring and I'm waiting for her to come back." Later in the day a passing teamster noticed blood and discovered the body. Hannah had been struck on the temple with an ax. Harbert was soon arrested and confessed in the jail.[396] He told a fellow inmate that he had knocked her down, "using vulgar language implying that he had carnal knowledge of her," and that "she looked so mean he thought he would finish her."[397]

Harbert was convicted and kept in the Nashville jail awaiting an appeal. During the appeal, which ordered a new trial because of improperly admitted testimony, Harbert escaped. He was finally caught and convicted the second time. He then escaped from the Montgomery County jail. The Tennessee Supreme Court opinion in his second appeal cannot be located.

Ben Harbert was hanged at Gallows Hollow in Clarksville on March 7, 1856. The Rev. J.B. Jackson addressed the large crowd. Ben confessed and blamed his fate on liquor.[398] He was swung off in the traditional manner.

Jack, black, age 16. *Murder.*

The crime was committed on the night of February 25, 1856, in the small store of the victim William Rowland, white, age forty, in the Double Spring community of McMinn County. Two friends had left Rowland at 9:00 P.M. that night. He was dressed in pantaloons and a nightshirt. Jack, a slave owned by O.P. Hall, came to the store that night and sought to purchase sugar on credit. Rowland said no. Jack left and came back later, announcing that he had borrowed the money. As Rowland was stooping to go under the counter, Jack struck him on the back of the neck with the pole of an ax. After he fell, Jack used the ax to cut his throat from ear to ear. Jack took $125 from a strongbox, along with other items. Suspicion fell on Jack immediately because he was found with some store items.[399] Jack explained in court that a white man, William Williams, visiting the area from North Carolina, had told him and another slave that if they got together enough money he would take them to a free state. Williams was arrested but later released.[400] Jack was hanged on a gallows in Athens on June 25, 1856, in front of a crowd of four to seven thousand. He explained that Williams had not actually told him to kill Rowland and played no part in the killing.[401]

Old Hal, black, age unknown. *Slave insurrection.*
Amos, black, age unknown. *Slave insurrection.*
Anderson, black, age unknown. *Slave insurrection.*
Grey, black, age unknown. *Slave insurrection.*
Ishmael, black, age unknown. *Slave insurrection.*
Charlie Napier, black, age unknown. *Slave insurrection.*

The crimes were committed by male slaves between November 28, 1856, and December 10, 1856, at several iron works, usually called furnaces, in Stewart County. The details of the crimes and the executions are unknown. Whether these were legal executions remains a matter of debate, but they are included here because they were conducted under purported legal authority.

The so-called slave insurrection of 1856 has been the subject of considerable research.[402] Today, most historians insist there was no clear evidence of a slave revolt in Tennessee. Rather, whites in Tennessee and throughout the South became victims of their own anti-black propaganda in the weeks prior to and after the presidential election of November 1856. This was the first national election with a so-called "Black Republican" nominee (John C. Frémont), and Democrats had canvassed the populace decrying the danger of his potential election.

Stewart County, with a slave population that exceeded whites by a substantial margin, was unique in Tennessee because the slaves were employed in working at several iron works. They worked in close contact with each other, including slaves at other furnaces. Fear of a slave revolt had worried whites in Stewart County for decades, but by November 26, 1856, the "excitement" in Montgomery County seemed over.[403] But the shooting of an unruly slave pushed fear into panic. Hence, it is more accurate to say there was a slave insurrection panic in late 1856.

On the morning of November 28, 1856, a slave named Brittain, owned by Solomon D. Rainey, was heard just before daybreak approaching Louisa Furnace making a great noise and exclaiming at intervals, "Wake up, boys! Wake up!" He also said many other things that could not be understood by the whites who heard him.[404] He went to the house of William Nicks, white, about three hundred yards from the furnace. Nicks was away because he was on a patrolling expedition.[405] J.N. Puckett, a lawyer, who was the father-in-law of Nicks, went outside and stood on the porch.

"As the negro came up to the yard gate, which is about twenty steps from the house, the dogs ran out and commenced barking at him, whereupon he exclaimed, 'I am not afraid of dogs!'"[406] As he entered the gate toward the house, he dropped aside two coats, or roundabouts, and advanced to the steps of the porch. As he started up the steps Puckett shot and killed him. The alarm was given by Puckett and within minutes a dozen white men were on the scene and "found the negro dead, with his head resting upon the steps, just as he had fallen."[407]

A Committee of Safety was formed by December 3, 1856, and within days at least sixty slaves were taken into custody. Many were severely whipped and some began describing a purported revolt scheduled for Christmas Day.[408] Various details emerged. The insurrection was to begin on Christmas Eve night. Ishmael was to kill a white furnace manager and take his wife. By December 5, 1856, the Committee had concluded four ringleaders should die. They were given some sort of "trial" and hanged near the courthouse at Dover that day. Three of the four were deemed preachers, which sealed their doom. The last one executed was Ishmael. Charles Napier was hanged privately.[409] His body was allowed to hang overnight. Two whites reportedly singled out for death by the insurrectionists, George Lewis and Henry Erwin, publicly whipped Bob Murrell until he died.[410]

The matter was reported in the Nashville press. "Seven negroes have been executed in the county — four at Dover and three at the Forge; and all by a verdict of a committee of responsible citizens, rendered after a calm and careful investigation of the circumstances."[411] The report continued, "Five white men, whose complicity with the insurrectionary movements of the slaves were established beyond the possibility of question, were severely whipped and driven out of the country."[412] With this, the excitement had almost entirely ceased.

Virtually all reports of the episode assert that four of the slaves who died were "the property of U.S. Senator John Bell."[413] Some reports suggest the dead men's heads were placed on poles and paraded through the streets of Dover, possibly viewed by slaves who were summoned to look at them.[414] Neither assertion can be verified.

No circuit court or county court records (or minutes) exist regarding the trials. But county court minutes ratified the hangings. On January 6, 1857, the court approved the payment of $40 for boarding negro prisoners "from November 25, 1856, to December 10, 1856." Another $40 was paid O.P. Thomson for guarding negroes "during the excitement from 28th November to 5 December 1856." Likewise, the court approved payment to "E.P. Lemaster of $7.50 for making three coffins for three negroes hung by the Committee of Safety at Dover on December 5, 1856."[415]

The number of slaves executed in Montgomery and Stewart Counties during the "excitement" has been estimated as high as nineteen, but no records exist of any trials. Cryptic news reports said, "The report of the execution of the four negroes at Dover, mentioned in our last, was premature, though since that time six have been hanged at Dover, one at Dover Furnace."[416] In Sumner County, four slaves allegedly implicated in the revolt were taken from the jail on December 23, 1856, and hanged by "a large and respectable body of our first citizens," said a newspaper.[417]

During the insurrection panic of 1856, a slave named Hard was tied up by three men in Gibson County. When he attempted to escape, one of the men killed him. The owner sued. The defendants asserted the purported slave insurrection was a complete defense. They offered newspaper accounts to support the claim. The jury returned a verdict for the trio.

The Tennessee Supreme Court reversed, holding that an honest belief in a slave insurrection was not a defense, especially when the slave was already tied and could do no harm to anyone. The court said, "We find no justifiable cause, in the proof, for the capture and confinement of the slave, in the first instance, even under the acts of Assembly to which we are referred. He had not misbehaved himself in any way, had done no wrong, threatened none, and was entirely submissive and docile. After being thus unlawfully tied with a rope, he became alarmed at what he saw and heard around him, and in endeavoring to make his escape from this unlawful confinement, was slain by one of his pursuers."[418]

On retrial, the jury returned an $800 verdict for the slave's life. On appeal, two of the men insisted liability should attach only to the actual killer. The Tennessee Supreme Court ruled that each joint tortfeasor was liable for the actions of the others. "They are all answerable for any injury done by either, in the common enterprise."[419] Said the court, "The wild panic, and vague, undefined apprehensions about a 'rising or insurrection of the slaves' at that time, cannot be allowed to save parties from liability for the destruction of their neighbor's property."[420]

In 1858, the legislature ordained a new procedure available in times of slave insurrection panics. Upon a petition of five persons, the circuit court was to impanel a grand jury immediately and the slaves should be questioned by it. If cause were found, the court was to begin prosecution immediately.

1859

John, black, age unknown. *Murder.*

The crime was committed on December 25, 1857, at the farm of Octavius Yoe, John's owner, somewhere in Grainger County. Betsey, black, age unknown, the killer's wife, was owned by a different family. For unknown reasons, John struck her in the back with an ax, making a wound four inches wide and five inches deep. She died five days later. A slave Harriet and three whites testified against John and he was convicted on June 25, 1858.[421] Because the trial court refused to grant a continuance, the Tennessee Supreme Court reversed.[422] John was retried in Hawkins County and convicted on April 15, 1859. His second appeal cannot be located and he was hanged in Rutledge, Grainger County, on October 12, 1859.[423]

William "Tom" Holt, white, age unknown. *Murder.*

The crime was committed on August 7, 1858, at a house in Marion County near "the slope of the mountain and the rail road" occupied by Mrs. Mary Jenkins and a couple named Rainwater and their young adult daughters. The immediate cause of the killing was a dispute over peaches between Holt and William Cox, white, age unknown, the victim.

Cox was in the yard gathering peaches when he was told by Mrs. Jenkins not to get all the good ones, that he was only to get them from a certain tree. Holt suddenly appeared (from where is not clear) and swore at Cox, "God damn you, I'm going to kill you!" Cox was holding a knife in one hand and peaches in both hands, having cut a peach he was eating. Holt picked up a stick two inches thick and four feet long and hit Cox over the head. Cox fell to the ground. He was hit again in the neck. The second blow dislocated his neck, killing him.[424]

A witness said he heard Holt swear he was going to kill Cox after he saw Cox paying too much attention to the Rainwater girls. At the time of trial the entire household had moved to northern Alabama, but Mrs. Jenkins came back for the trial, which began on August 16, 1859.[425]

A witness said Mrs. Jenkins should not be accredited because she was a woman of low character and allowed unwed couples to live in her house. Furthermore, men came at all hours of the day and night, including Cox and Holt, and the Rainwater girls were of low character.[426]

The Tennessee Supreme Court affirmed the conviction but did not issue an opinion. It simply affirmed the judgment in an undated per curiam order signed by Judge Carruthers shown on the cover of the bill of exceptions.[427] William Holt was hanged at Jasper on December 15, 1859.[428] Details of the execution are unknown.

John Lewis, white, age 21. *Murder.*
Jesse Lewis, white, age 23. *Murder.*

The crime was committed on the afternoon of August 3, 1858, on a road outside Jacksboro, in Campbell County. The victims were Travis Gibson, white, age forty-one, and Sampson D. Queener, white, age thirty-seven, who were attempting to arrest the killers for counterfeiting.

The Lewis brothers had spent the night at a roadhouse owned by Sharp. The next morning, Jesse Lewis gave John Sharp a twenty-dollar bill, purporting to be on the Bank of Hamburg, South Carolina, to pay their bill, $1.25. Sharp thought the bill was counterfeit and refused to take it, but said he would accompany the pair to Jacksboro to get it changed. He left with them on horseback. The pair acted suspiciously, and finally told Sharp they had the proper money he needed and gave it to him as they reached the town. The two asked where they could get some liquor and their horses shod, and were directed to a nearby grocery and blacksmith shop.

Sharp immediately went to a justice of the peace to swear out a counterfeiting warrant. It was denied because Sharp did not know the men's first names. It soon became apparent that the pair had not stopped at all, but had turned north, out of town, at a rapid gait. Sheriff S.D. Queener asked a citizen, Travis Gibson, to help apprehend the pair. After a hard twenty-minute ride the two were overtaken.

Queener put his hand on Jesse's shoulder and said, "I take you as a State's prisoner." Jesse pulled a pistol and snapped it at Queener. As Queener was getting off his horse, he was shot in the chest by Jesse. Meanwhile, Queener saw that Gibson was tussling with John. As Queener went to help, Jesse came up, stabbed Gibson and cut his throat. He died instantly. Queener, left for dead, was discovered by Sharp and others, who recounted the facts of Queener's dying declaration.[429] The circumstances of the killers' arrest are unknown.

A month after the killings, a passerby found a bundle of counterfeit bills ($175) near the murder site. These were identified by Sharp as similar to the one the pair had attempted to pass. Other evidence of the pair's counterfeiting was offered at trial. Numerous objections to this evidence, the seating of several jurors, and the legality of the citizen's arrest were rejected by the Tennessee Supreme Court.[430]

The chief issue on appeal concerned sentencing. Under the recodification of 1858, an 1838 statute had been changed. The statute allowed the jury to convict of first-degree murder but allowed it to report there were mitigating circumstances. The statute originally said that when this happened, "it *shall* be the duty of the court" to commute the punishment. Now, the code section said "it *may* be the duty of the court" to commute. The Tennessee Supreme Court said this change was intentional and pointed to other code sections which changed the discretionary powers of the governor to commute sentences. Furthermore, the language of the new code expressly repealed the old statute.[431]

Said the court, "We are of the opinion, therefore, that the object and intention of this section was to change the rule by which the opinion of the jury was made obligatory on the court, and leave it in the sound discretion of the court, upon an unbiased and discriminating survey of the whole case, to give effect to the opinion of the jury, or to refuse to do so, as the ends of public justice might seem to dictate."

The court continued, "Experience has fully shown, that such a discretion intrusted absolutely to juries, is subject to abuse; and that its exercise is sometimes so indiscriminate and improper as to defeat, in some degree, the objects of criminal punishment. The present case is an illustration of the fact, that such an expression of opinion by the jury is only to be accounted for, in some instances, on the supposition of undue influence or a false sympathy, or as a compromise."[432]

The Lewis case established the rule that the judge could disregard the jury's recommendation of mercy and impose the death penalty. It remained Tennessee law until the death penalty for murder was repealed. When reinstated, the new death penalty law did not contain the provision. Plainly stated, from 1838 until 1917, Tennessee had a discretionary death penalty.[433] Unaffected by the repeal and re-enactment was an 1838 statute that continued to allow the Tennessee Supreme Court to recommend mercy when it upheld death sentences.

At the time, the law provided that when any felony case was appealed the defendant had a right to be present when the case was argued (and decided). This meant the defendants had to be transported to the appropriate location, here, Knoxville. A newspaper described what happened when the Tennessee Supreme Court announced its decision, always referred to as "sentencing" the defendant. "One of the prisoners was considerably affected; asked an interest in the prayers of the people, and announced his purpose by penitence and prayer, to seek and obtain an incorruptable inheritance above. The other was very little moved, and only stated in the Court that he had not had justice done him. The first of the two spoke fondly of his parents, and regretted his fate more on their account than on his own, as their fond hopes had been blighted."[434]

The Lewis brothers were hanged at 1:15 P.M. December 23, 1859, in Jacksboro. They were taken to the gallows in a two-horse wagon, sitting on their coffins. A minister read from Psalm 119:9 and gave a one and one-half hour sermon. Fervent prayers were offered for the killers and the widows and orphans of the victims. The Lewis brothers were "swung off" in the traditional manner, but they "died very hard." They made no statements on the gallows.[435] These were the first brothers in Tennessee executed for a common crime.

1860

Joe, black, age unknown. *Assault with intent to commit rape on a white woman.*

Joe, a slave, committed the crime on the night of February 25, 1860, in the home of John C. Jones and his wife, Sarah K. Jones, white, age twenty-one, in Roane County. Joe broke into the Jones home and sexually assaulted Mrs. Jones, whose husband was not present. Joe escaped and returned on the night of March 1, 1860. This time he carried an ax and knife and seriously wounded Paulina (sometimes called Patience), a black woman, probably a slave, who was sleeping in the same bedroom as Mrs. Jones.

Joe was captured on March 2, 1860, and after hearing seven witnesses, including the Jones couple and Paulina, the jury convicted him on March 9, 1860. There was no appeal. Joe was ordered executed on May 4, 1860, and was hanged that day in Kingston, Roane County.[436]

Henry (aka Henry Erwin), black, age unknown. *Murder.*

The crime was committed in McNairy County on April 22, 1860, several miles south of Purdy near the community of Stantonville, at the log home of John Pinkney Erwin and his wife Diana, white, age forty-two. The killer entered the home at night to kill the couple and steal purportedly hidden gold. The couple were asleep in the same bed. Henry was carrying a hatchet. Diana was sleeping on a different side of the bed from which she usually slept. She recognized Henry, who immediately struck her. She died within minutes; Mr. Erwin was badly injured.[437]

A niece of the Erwins was sleeping in an adjoining room of the log house. She witnessed the attack but hid outside in a thicket with a small child belonging to the Erwins. Henry looked but could not find them, returning to his nearby cabin. The niece went back inside and, discovering the bodies, tricked Henry by telling him the couple had both been killed. She told him to saddle a fast horse to ride for help. As soon as neighbors gathered and Henry returned she named him as the killer.

Henry was convicted on July 12, 1860, and sentenced to hang on September 7. He was hanged that day in Purdy, then the county seat, in front of four thousand, which included Mr. Erwin. On the gallows Henry said he was sorry he had killed Mrs. Erwin, but her husband was abusive and had mistreated him and he was not sorry for attacking him. Henry was swung off in the traditional manner.

Jo Harrison (aka Negro Sam), black, age 22. *Murder.*

The crime was committed on the afternoon of December 8, 1860, on the plantation of John Harrison Trice, white, age thirty-eight, the victim. Called Jo Harrison by his mother, the killer was born on the plantation and was formerly owned by the victim's father. Jo had been engaged in splitting fence rails. Trice was unhappy with his work and tied him with his own suspenders and began to walk Jo to a barn on the property in order to whip him. As they walked, Jo freed himself from the suspenders and they began to fight. Jo soon got the better of Trice.

Jo's confession said he saw Trice's pocket knife on the ground. It apparently fell from the victim's pocket as they struggled. "I put my left hand on his chin and cut his throat from ear to ear at two licks. When he attempted to rise and while on his hands and knees, I thought him not yet dead, I picked up a chunk of wood and struck him on the head which I concluded would do the work. During the time we scuffled he told me not to kill him and said if I did my old master would hang me. He begged me twice to quit and called a little boy, Frank, to come there."[438] Harrison carried the body several miles over five fences to place it where it would look as if Trice was murdered on a different side of the farm from where Jo worked.

Jo was captured the same day. His trial was irregular and may be characterized as a formal lynching — technically not the subject of this book. A group of seventeen men acted as a jury and tried

Jo at the location where he killed Trice. They issued a written opinion:

> We, the undersigned citizens of the state and county aforesaid, having been called upon and selected to investigate the case of the murder of John H. Trice, said to have been committed on Saturday, the 8th instant, by a negro named Jo Harrison, the property of John H. Trice, deceased, after having heard all the evidence adduced in the case, have come to the conclusion, to wit: That the said Jo Harrison is guilty of the murder of his master, John H. Trice, by his own admission, and from other evidence; and that the murder was committed by cutting the throat of the deceased with his own pocket knife and that our verdict is that for the offense aforesaid the boy Jo Harrison be hung by the neck until he is dead, on Tuesday, the 11th instant, at 2:00 o'clock P.M. And we hereby take the responsibility of our acts. Given under our hands, on this 10th day of December 1860.[439]

The location of the hanging remains unclear, but apparently took place in Lexington, Henderson County, before a crowd of one thousand.[440] At the gallows, Jo Harrison said, "My master was always good and kind to me. I always had plenty to eat and good clothes to wear and now I do not know what reasons I had for killing him. I know that I have to die. I want my life, conduct and death to be a warning to all who may hear me. I freely forgive all my enemies and ask both friends and foes to remember one who is no longer worthy to live but soon must go and meet the great and powerful God in the skies."[441]

1861

Carter Nunnelly, black, age unknown. *Murder.*

The details of the crime are unknown, except that the September 15, 1861, killing was committed in the Gray's Bend area, the same location as the rape-murder of Tampay Carlisle, a white girl who was killed by Carter's brother Henry Nunnelly who was hanged in 1829. The victim was Andrew Jackson Baldwin Nunnelly, white, age forty-three, possibly Carter's owner. He was murdered by the ax-wielding Carter. The killer's status as a slave or free man is unknown. Carter Nunnelly was also charged with the murder of an unnamed white woman.[442] The details of Carter Nunnelly's 1861 hanging in Centerville are unknown, like the hanging of his brother.

Alfred (aka Alfred Stephens), black, age unknown. *Murder.*

The details of the crime are unknown except that Alfred murdered his owner, William Stephens, by striking him on the head with a stick on November 3, 1859. He hid the body in a cave.[443] He was convicted in July 1860 and the Tennessee Supreme Court affirmed the conviction, but the opinion cannot be located.

Alfred was hanged in Fayetteville, Lincoln County, on March 1, 1861. On the gallows he made a rambling, disjointed speech of about twenty minutes in which he tried to shift responsibility for the murder to his mother and another slave named Jake. Following an "earnest and impressive prayer" by the Rev. M.B. DeWitt, he was dropped at 12:52 P.M. The newspaper praised the citizens of Lincoln County for "adherence to the forms of law in this case. The murder was of an aggravated kind, yet the people submitted to the 'law's delay,' and allowed justice to take its tardy but certain course through the proper tribunals."[444]

Moses, black, age unknown. *Murder.*
Isaac, black, age unknown. *Murder.*

These were the first legal executions in Shelby County.[445] Moses was the slave of Mr. Worsham. On November 14, 1860, he beat an Italian organ grinder, Giacomo Passagno, on the head with an iron gate hinge and left him for dead. He took a small amount of money from him along with the hurdy-gurdy, which he tried to sell in Memphis. This prompted his arrest. Passagno lingered in the hospital until his death on November 17. Its not clear whether he named Moses as his assailant. Moses's conviction was upheld by the Tennessee Supreme Court but the opinion cannot be located.

Isaac, described as a mulatto, was a slave of Major Berry. He ran away and was concealed near Nonconnah Creek. On the morning of August 31, 1858, a Mr. Mack, who was out hunting, came upon him and two other runaways. He attempted to take them, but they took his gun from him. Gideon Bauden, white, age unknown, overseer of Col. F.R. Sledge of Arkansas, then tried to take them. Isaac shot and killed him with Mr. Mack's gun. Isaac was captured on September 8, 1858, and confessed to the killing.

Isaac's first trial resulted in a reversal because one of the jurors, W.W. Ritchie, refused to take the juror's oath because of "conscientious scruples in regard to capital punishment."[446] Ritchie was then placed in jail by the trial judge. Fifteen hours later, Ritchie sent word that he would serve. The judge then allowed him to serve. When the state challenged him for cause, the judge overruled the challenge. All this was error, ruled the Tennessee Supreme Court, because a juror once discharged may not later be allowed a seat on the jury. Isaac was convicted in a second trial. Whether he appealed is unknown.

In jail, Moses and Isaac were visited by many people concerned about their souls. Isaac, described as very intelligent, became a dedicated and overt Christian, professing his faith and urging others to accept religion as well, including Moses.

On May 31, 1861, the pair were taken on a furniture wagon, which carried their coffins, to an execution site near the fairgrounds. The ropes were strung from a beam held by two trees, but the platform had a trap door in the center. The pair were guarded by two companies of militia, the Bluff City Guards and the Italian company called Garibaldi Guards, carrying muskets with bayonets attached. A large but orderly crowd was present, including females in carriages, in wagons and on horseback.

The men were dressed in long white shrouds (called surplices) over their clothing and wore white gloves. On the platform with them was their minister, Mr. Merriman, two religious friends, and Sheriff Felts and the jailor. Merriman announced that the men had been given the opportunity to speak.

Isaac spoke in a calm and self-possessed manner. His lengthy and well-crafted speech was a call for spectators to receive Christ and admit sin: "I have committed murder, but God is merciful. Many of you, I am afraid, have done or will do the same; then repent in time. You soldiers that are fixing for battle, you are only fixing for your ruin, unless you prepare for the great change that is to come."[447]

Isaac continued, "If all would pray, there would be no need of fighting; God would stop all the mad careers that men are running in the United States. Mr. Abraham Lincoln is nothing to God, and if you will seek God's aid, He will bring back peace. I wish you would forget what is gone by and all be Union again. God told me while I was lying in my bed that I was forgiven; he told me this, and I tell you now. Your eyes are perhaps as blind as mine were. If I had repented when I was a young boy, I might perhaps have been a preacher and have been able to lead souls to Christ."[448]

Isaac concluded his remarks by asking those who feel like it to come forward and shake his hand. Many of his race came forward. Their tear-streamed faces caused Moses to break down crying. Finally, when Moses was allowed to speak, he said simply, "I hope God will forgive me. I know I have done wrong. I hope you will all meet me in Heaven. I have no more to say to you. Farewell, farewell forever!"[449]

At this point, Mr. Merriman sang the hymn "Mansions in the Sky," and gave an earnest prayer. The men were pinioned and white caps placed over their heads. The sheriff drew the bolt from the trap at 1:10 P.M. and the men dropped three feet. They struggled briefly and were allowed to hang for thirty minutes. They were cut down and placed in coffins. The place of burial is unknown.

Earlier that month, Confederate authorities had hanged a Mr. Morton, described as a "sporting man" who used to drive his two horses through the streets, for being a northerner. They also hanged Sampson Kennedy, a local man, for expressing his Unionist sentiments. Neither had been given a trial.[450]

John, black, age unknown. *Murder.*
Ned, black, age unknown. *Murder.*

The firing upon Ft. Sumter in April 1861 prompted this crime because the killers thought the coming of war was the best time to instigate a slave revolt. The killings were done on May 1, 1861, while the county was swept with war fever and many white males in Tennessee were taking steps to join the Confederate Army. The crimes were committed at the farm home of Mrs. Mary Hale Haynes, white, age sixty, in Hawkins County. The widow Haynes operated a sizeable farm with slave labor and help from her son-in-law, George Rufus Kite, who operated his own farm a few miles away on Dobson Creek.

On the evening of the killings, George Rufus Kite, white, age thirty-four, took his young son Benjamin, age eight, and daughter Rachel, age eleven, to spend the night with the widow Haynes and her crippled daughter, Louisa Haynes, age thirty-nine. The killers took Mrs. Haynes out of the house and shot her. Next they shot Louisa Haynes, followed by George Rufus Kite. Finally, they killed his daughter Rachel Kite. Following this, they set fire to the Haynes home. Benjamin was overlooked in the killing and escaped from the burning house and ran to a neighboring house.

The murders prompted fear of a slave insurrection and runners were sent in all directions warning of the danger. No insurrection occurred and the killers were easily captured. John and Ned were tried in Rogersville, Hawkins County, on May 9, 1861, and were executed by hanging on June 12, 1861.[451]

Levy Stover (aka Levi Stover), white, age 45. *Murder.*

The crime was committed on November 26, 1856, on President's Island in the Mississippi River off Memphis, in Shelby County. The victim was Aaron B. Stearns (Starnes), white, age unknown. The victim and his adult son had come to Stover's home to collect money he owed them for tearing down a cabin and selling the lumber. According to Stover, as he turned to get the money, he was knocked to the floor by Stearns. The son knocked Mrs. Stover to the floor. Regaining his feet, Stover stabbed Stearns with a Bowie knife.

Stover crossed the river and summoned a physician. While he was gone, Stearns was moved to a different house, where he lingered four weeks before death. At the time of his execution, Stover had been in the Shelby County jail since his arrest. Stover had several trials. This accounted for the delay from the arrest to his ultimate conviction on June 26, 1860.[452] During this time his hair turned gray. The conviction was affirmed by the Tennessee Supreme Court, but the opinion cannot be located.

The day before his execution, Stover was taken from the jail and allowed to have his photograph taken with his wife at a studio. Stover was a Mexican War veteran and received a pension. A "numerously signed" petition (238 names) had been sent to the governor seeking a commutation.

Stover told the newspapers that many other Memphis men (he gave their names) had killed but had received light sentences and he said the conviction was wrong, that he should only have received a four- or five-year sentence. "But I was a sort of stranger, and besides, when a man has money, he can do as he pleases. If he be poor, he stands no chance."[453]

A deputy sheriff had been left at the telegraph office to await last-minute action by the governor. Stover felt he would receive a commutation until the deputy arrived with bad news. Levy Stover's wife rode with him in a wagon to the gallows, followed by about two thousand people. Stover was dressed in a white burial shroud. His eight-year-old son was taken to the execution in a carriage by others.[454]

Levy Stover was hanged on June 28, 1861. The death ceremony began in earnest when the deputy sheriff arrived. A minister made a brief statement and said Stover would speak. Stover walked to the edge of the gallows. He said:

> You have all come here to see me hung. I am poor, but endeavor to die like a man. I served two terms in Mexico with Frank Cheatham, and he will tell you I never flinched. I want you all to be good boys. The little ones, I hope, will all behave themselves, and mind their fathers and mothers. You soldiers, I hope, will serve your country bravely and faithfully. I wish I could go along with you. I die an innocent man; and I call upon God to witness that I speak the truth. A great many lies were sworn about me on my trial. I see a good many here that I know. I hope you will look after my wife and little boy. He is a smart boy, and will make a smart man if he is brought up right. I bid you good-bye.[455]

Mrs. Stover turned to embrace him and he took her hands and told her not to "take on," that he had to die but once, and he might as well do it now. She left the gallows sobbing and went to the ground in front of it where she fell to her knees in prayer. She stayed that way, with her back to the gallows, until the execution was complete.

Several men came forward to shake Stover's hand good-bye. "At last his little son climbed the steps of the gallows, sobbing, as if his heart would break. 'Kiss me, my boy!' cried the condemned parent; and as this act of filial affection was performed, tears gushed from the eyes of every beholder."

The newspaper reported, "Cheeks bronzed and hardened by age felt the warm tears coursing their way upon them for the first time in years. Women sobbed and children were convulsed with pity. Not an eye was dry while this heartrending spectacle was being enacted. The prisoner alone remained seemingly unmoved. Not a muscle of his countenance betrayed the tumultuous emotions that agitated his breast. The affecting scene ended by the removal of the little boy."[456]

The minister led the throng in singing the hymn "Alas! And Did My Savior Bleed." Stover was dropped without warning or signal. "A more audible sob [from Mrs. Stover] betokened that she had heard the fall, when her son, bursting through the line of soldiers that surrounded the place, threw himself, screaming into her arms." Said the newspaper, "The sight was too much. We hastened from the accursed spot, in company with the horror-stricken crowd, and trust that it may never be our fate to witness such another scene."[457]

Levy Stover was the first white man hanged in Shelby County. Stover told the newspaper that it had been suggested to him that his son should change his name. "He expressed his disapprobation of this in strong terms, and declared that his son should retain his name. The little fellow is an interesting child, and we understand will be properly cared for by some benevolent citizens."[458]

Henry Fry, white, age 38. *Sabotage in wartime.*
Jacob Madison Hinshaw (aka Jacob Hensie and Matt Hensie; pronounced "Hinchey"), white, age 20. *Sabotage in wartime.*

Executed under authority of the Confederate States of America.

When Tennessee seceded from the Union in April 1861, many of the inhabitants of East Tennessee did not support the decision. In August 1861, an insurgency plan was devised by the Rev. William B. Carter, an East Tennessee Unionist. It called for the destruction of nine wooden railroad bridges on the line from Virginia to Georgia. Carter met personally with President Lincoln, who approved the plan, which was set to coincide with an invasion of Tennessee from Kentucky, under the command of General George Thomas.

Fry and Hinshaw were among the group of insurgents who met at the house of Jacob Harmon, Jr., on the night of November 8, 1861, and took an oath of secrecy and Union loyalty by placing their left hands on a United States flag with their right hands uplifted. Technically, they were also mustered into Company F, 2nd Tennessee Volunteer Infantry, under the command of Capt. David Fry (no relation to Henry Fry).[459]

At two o'clock on the morning of November 9, 1861, two bands of Unionist insurgents made separate attacks on the bridges, burning five. The burnings sent a spasm of panic among the Confederates and slowed enlistments.[460] The Confederate authorities considered these acts war crimes because they were not committed by organized military units operating by command and commission.[461] The insurgents did not kill the Confederates who were guarding the bridges. Instead, they allowed the guards to live if they swore allegiance to the Union. The guards promptly informed authorities of the insurgents' identities.

The burned bridges were soon restored and the roundup of insurgents began. These included Fry and Hinshaw (and a dimwitted sixteen-year-old). All three admitted burning the Lick Creek bridge, some fifteen miles west of Greeneville, near the present-day town of Mohawk. These were the last insurgents arrested, but the first to die.

The general in charge asked the Confederate War Department what to do. He received a telegram from Confederate Secretary of War Judah P. Benjamin: "That all those implicated in burning the bridges should be tried by drumhead court-martial, and, if found guilty, publicly hanged in the vicinity of the burned bridges; and that their bodies should be left hanging for several days as a warning to the Union men of East Tennessee."[462] Colonel Danville Leadbetter and a company of troops were sent to protect the bridges and punish the insurgents.

Col. Leadbetter quickly ordered a general court-martial.[463] It convened on November 30, 1861, and all three were convicted, with Fry and Hinshaw to be hanged that day in Greeneville, Greene County. Leadbetter had ordered the bodies to hang four days, but they were cut down the next afternoon. Col. Leadbetter telegraphed the war department, "Two insurgents have today been tried for bridge-burning, found guilty and hanged."[464] On December 11, 1861, martial law was declared in Knoxville. This was the day Christopher A. Haun was executed. Other insurgents, the Harmons (father and son) were executed on December 17, 1861. The teen-ager was later released.

On the gallows, Fry was told his life would be spared if he swore loyalty to the Confederacy. He responded, "When there ceases to be fleas in a hog pen and rebels in Hell is when I will pledge allegiance to the Confederacy."[465]

According to William G. "Parson" Brownlow, later governor of Tennessee, Col. Leadbetter had hanged the pair on a tree next to the railroad. This allowed passengers in the cars to strike the bodies with outstretched canes, which they did.[466] In fact, the men were hanged several hundred yards from the track.

Later, Fry and Hinshaw were considered Union army soldiers and their widows given federal pensions. Hinshaw's wife gave birth to a son two months after his execution. He was given his father's name. The execution prompted Solomon Fry, age seventeen, to join the Union Army. Likewise, the execution caused William Hinshaw, Jacob's father, to enlist in the Union Army at the age of fifty-three. He was badly wounded in the Battle of Blue Springs in Tennessee. The Union invasion of East Tennessee finally came in 1863.

Charles Alexander Haun, white, age 40. *Sabotage in wartime.*

Executed under authority of the Confederate States of America.

The crime was committed on November 9, 1861, and was a pro–Union insurgent attack on railroad bridges, planned by the Rev. William B. Carter, an East Tennessee Unionist, who personally presented it to President Lincoln, who approved it. The purpose was to prevent escape (or reinforcements) of Confederate soldiers and sympathizers in East Tennessee in the wake of a planned invasion by Union forces under Gen. George Thomas. His army was gathered in Kentucky in late 1861.

Christopher Alexander Haun was one of the foremost potters in Tennessee and was an outspoken Unionist.[467] He took part in a secrecy and loyalty oath performed at Jacob Harmon's house the night of the bridge-burning. The insurgents placed their left hands on the United States flag and upheld their right hands during the ceremony, each promising to "do what was ordered of him that night and never to disclose what he had done."[468]

The bridge-burning by pro–Union insurgents on the night of November 9, 1861, had been predicted by Confederate Sen. Landon C. Haynes, an East Tennessean. The attacks on nine railroad bridges along the lines from Virginia to Georgia were deemed war crimes, and resulted in the prompt hangings of Jacob M. Hinshaw and Henry Fry on November 30, 1861. The pair were part of a group led by Jacob Harmon, Jr., and his two sons, Thomas and Henry, which included Haun. The insurgents who burned the Lick Creek bridge in Greene County, near the present town of Mohawk, included Haun.

The bridge-burners allowed the Confederate soldiers who guarded the bridge to live if they took an oath supporting the Union. This they did, but promptly reported the insurgents' names to authorities. Haun, arrested a few days after the burning, was represented by counsel, whose primary task was to ask for mercy.

Haun's trial presented a legal problem. The Confederate District Court was open and Knoxville was not under martial law. In fact, the regular state courts also had jurisdiction to try Haun for treason, a matter clearly stated under Confederate law.

As soon as the court-martial, consisting of thirteen officers, had been convened, it was presented with a writ of habeas corpus from the District Court. The officer in charge, Col. Robert F. Looney, took the position that the case was a matter of war crimes, not treason, and the District Court had no jurisdiction.[469] But martial law had not been declared until December 11, 1861, which was after the bridge-burning. Moreover, the state courts were still functioning.[470]

On December 10, 1861, Haun was convicted, but the Confederate general in charge asked the war department for instructions. The next day he received a telegram reaffirming that all bridge-burners like Haun should be executed immediately and that this was a standing order from Confederate President Jefferson Davis, not requiring his personal approval.

Haun was hanged in Knoxville on December 11, 1861. According to William G. "Parson" Brownlow, later governor of Tennessee, Haun was denied a minister at the gallows and executed on one hour's notice. The newspaper reported, "Men are required to pay dearly in this country for the sport of bridge burning. The price, however, is by no means too extravagant."[471]

Haun was survived by a wife and four children.[472] He wrote the following letter to his wife: "Dear Elizabeth: I have the promise this morning that my body shall be sent home to you. Oh, live for heaven. Oh, my bosom friend and Children, live for Heaven. I pray my time is almost out Dear Friends. Farewell to this World. Farewell Earth and Earthly Troubles."[473] Mrs. Haun gave birth to a baby girl two months after the execution.

Later, federal officials approved a pension for Haun's widow by acknowledging he and the other executed bridge-burners were properly enlisted soldiers in Company F, 2nd Tennessee Volunteer Infantry, having been placed on the official rolls the night of the bridge-burning.

The Union invasion of East Tennessee did not come until 1863. In 1865, four members of the Haun court-martial were placed on trial in Knoxville, charged with the murder of Haun in a closely-watched trial. As officers of the Confederacy, they did not come within the terms of President Andrew Johnson's amnesty proclamation. To the chagrin of Union loyalists such as Governor Brownlow, the jury acquitted them.[474]

Henry Harmon, white, age 43. *Sabotage during wartime.*

Jacob Harmon, Jr., white, age 22. *Sabotage during wartime.*

Executed under authority of the Confederate States of America.

The crimes were committed on November 9, 1861, when all of Tennessee was under Confederate authority, no Union forces having entered the state. The crimes were pro–Union insurgent attacks planned on nine railroad bridges on the Virginia to Georgia rail lines. The attacks had been urged by Union officials, who promised that East Tennessee would be invaded promptly by Gen. George Thomas, whose army was in Kentucky. Earlier, Confederate officials had warned the public in East Tennessee, which had been largely pro–Union, that "no aid shall be given within Tennessee borders to the arms of the tyrant Lincoln."[475]

The plan had been conceived by an East Tennessee loyalist, the Rev. William B. Carter, who approached General Thomas at the federal recruitment site, Camp Dick Robinson, in Kentucky.

Gen. Thomas liked the plan and sent the Rev. Carter to Washington, where he met with President Lincoln and Gen. McClellan, who quickly approved the plan. Upon his return to Camp Dick Robinson, final preparations were made, which included the Rev. Carter's return to Greene County to help burn the bridges, along with Captain David Fry, also from Greene County.

Dressed in civilian clothes and posing as a Confederate Army hog buyer, Captain Fry finally met the other insurgents at Jacob Harmon's house the night of November 8, 1861. Technically, each was sworn into Company F, Second Tennessee Volunteer Regiment, which was Capt. Fry's unit.

The leader of one insurgent group was Jacob Harmon, Jr., a potter and a staunch Unionist. His group, consisting of himself, his son Thomas, Henry Fry (not related to Capt. Fry), Jacob Hinshaw, Charles A. Haun, and others, met at the elder Harmon's house on the night of November 8, 1861, to plan their attacks. At Harmon's house they took an oath of secrecy and loyalty by placing their left hands on a United States flag with their right hands uplifted.

At two o'clock on the morning of November 9, 1861, Harmon's group went to the Lick Creek bridge in Greene County, near the present-day town of Mohawk, captured the guard detail, and burned the wooden bridge of the East Tennessee and Virginia Railroad. They gave the Confederate guards the choice of being shot on the spot or taking an oath to the Union, which the guards promptly did.

Leniency toward the guards meant the insurgents were easily identified, and they were arrested within days. Jacob Harmon, Jr., and his two sons, Thomas Harmon and Henry Harmon, were arrested the next day and taken to the Knoxville jail. C.A. Haun was arrested next, and taken to Knoxville. Later, Henry Fry and Jacob M. "Matt" Hinshaw were arrested in Cocke County and jailed in Greeneville.

All of the insurgents were tried before courts-martial by direct orders of Confederate Secretary of War Judah Benjamin, who said that President Jefferson Davis had issued a standing order that all such traitors be hanged promptly. The Confederate officer in charge, Col. Danville Leadbetter, born in Maine, had been a regular Army officer for fifteen years, but opted for the South in the war.

The courts-martial of the Harmons were held in Knoxville. The elder Harmon transferred all his land to the four lawyers who represented him and his surviving sons.[476] One of the lawyers was retained by Haun to seek clemency. Jacob Harmon, Jr., was required to testify at the court-martial of Harrison Self on December 17, 1861. All the Harmons were convicted, with Thomas Harmon receiving a prison sentence. Jacob and Henry Harmon were ordered hanged on December 17, 1861, in Knoxville and died that day.

The authorities made Jacob's punishment worse because he was a ringleader. He was forced to watch as his son Henry was hanged first. It is possible that the rope was intentionally weakened so that it broke and Henry was hanged twice. A few minutes later Jacob Harmon, Jr., was hanged.[477]

The widow Malinda Self Harmon was forced to pay $45 for the transport of the bodies to the train depot nearest their home, called Pottertown. Col. Leadbetter interfered with the burial by insisting the pair be buried outside the family cemetery as befitted felons and traitors. Son Thomas was released from prison several months later when it became obvious he was gravely ill. He died within days of reaching home. The heartbroken Malinda Harmon died a few years later.

In 1862 the federal government acknowledged the five hanged bridge-burners as official Union soldiers and awarded pensions to their survivors. The hangings had left twenty children without fathers. His execution prompted Haun's oldest child, fifteen-year-old Jacob Daniel Haun, to join the Union Army.

The Union invasion of East Tennessee did not come until 1863.

1862

Michael Connel, white, age 24. *Crime unknown.*

Private Connel's crime remains unknown. Born in Ireland, he enlisted for three months' service on April 28, 1861, but records indicate he enlisted for three years' service at Camp Jackson, Columbus, Ohio, on that day. He was a member of Company E, 24th Ohio Volunteers. He saw fighting in the Cheat Mountain campaign and his regiment was on its way to Shiloh when he committed an offense for which he was executed by musketry on March 5, 1862, at Camp Andrew Jackson (Nashville).[478] He was executed under a general court-martial, the legal term for a drumhead court-martial. This accounts for the lack of paperwork. He was probably not given a formal trial.[479] He was the first Union Army soldier executed in Tennessee during the Civil War.

Alexander M. Beadle (aka Alexander Beadles), white, age 37. *Treason in wartime.*

The crime was the classic Civil War guerrilla operation. A small band of Confederate partisans lay waiting in ambush to attack a squad of Union soldiers. Gunfire erupted. A soldier or two fell. A chase ensued and the partisans scattered. Reinforcements arrived and a few of the partisans were captured. Some were simply shot without trial. Others were brought in for questioning, received a general court-martial and were hanged or shot. A general court-martial is better known as a drumhead court-martial. Sometimes a sign or note was pinned to the body as a warning to other traitors (partisans).

Beadle's case is shown here to illustrate the *scores* of Tennesseans who were killed by Union forces (and Union partisans) without a formal trial during 1862–1865. The drumhead court-martial was undertaken to provide a gloss of legitimacy to the summary execution, and to serve as a warning to spectators and lurking partisans. Few records exist of the general court-martial. None were appealed. Neither the War Department nor President Lincoln were informed of them.

In fact, many *hundreds* more were simply shot or hanged without the pretense of a drumhead court-martial. In Middle Tennessee, the term Milroyism has been used to describe the acts of Union troops who captured and summarily executed their enemies. These killings were ordered by Union Gen. Robert H. Milroy, who had the responsibility to protect the railways in Middle Tennessee.

Gen. Milroy was angry because of his loss at the Battle of Winchester, Virginia (June 13–15, 1863), and extremely bitter at West Point–trained officers who refused to give him another regular command. Milroy took out his anger in a manner little known outside Civil War justice scholars. He sent death squads to kill partisans.

Milroy's biographer admits the killings and quotes a letter to his wife describing his soldiers killing captives without trial: "This suits me exactly and they know it so I never see any guerilla prisoners and frequently hear of them being killed and see their horses and arms."[480] Milroy got the idea from Union General Eleazer Paine, a West Point graduate, who was originally posted in Gallatin, Sumner County, Tennessee. "He has had about 200 gerillas shot since he has been stationed here. He orders Confederate prisoners quietly walked outside of the pickets and shot. I would not have known anything of it had I not happened on their dead bodies."[481]

Death lists were drawn up by Gen. Milroy and men were summarily executed. For example, orders issued to Capt. William H. Lewis, Company A, 42nd Missouri Infantry, listed four names. Three of those named were found. They were Leroy Moore, age seventy; Thomas Saunders, age fifty-five; and William Saunders, age fourteen. Their hands were tied behind their backs. They were forced to wade into a millpond at Huffers Mill. They were shot in the back and their bodies were guarded for three days before the families were allowed to remove them for burial. The killings were retribution for a similar killing of three Union soldiers in a millpond at Mullberry in 1863.[482] The dead had played no role in the Mullberry shootings, however.

Civil War narratives abound with accounts of superior officers urging drumhead courts-martial. For example, in October 1862, General William Rosecrans cabled Gen. George Thomas, in charge of the area immediately west of Nashville, that Morgan's raiders seemed to be loafing around in civilian dress unmolested by Union forces. The army was to make the acquaintance of these "settlers" in the areas and arrest intruders. Above all, "who ever cannot give a good account of themselves shoot or hang to the nearest tree."[483] Later, after he lost at Chickamauga, Rosecrans was sent to Missouri. He ordered the retaliation execution of six Confederates at St. Louis.

One of the most notable examples of federal retribution was the shooting near Clarksville of brothers John and George Henson (Hinson). In turn, their father waged a one-man sniper war, killing Yankee pickets, stragglers and boatmen with a heavy custom-made rifle. Each "kill" was marked on the long barrel. By war's end it bore thirty-six marks.[484]

Alexander M. Beadle's road to death began with the arrival near Humbolt, Gibson County, of two hundred Confederate cavalry soldiers under the command of Capt. John C. Jackson. They came to Beadle's house because he had agreed to lead them by a hidden path to a bridge inside Union lines, which they sought to destroy. On the way, they came upon six federal scouts riding towards them. Beadle directed the Confederate cavalry to hide in order to ambush the scouts.

The plan was foiled when a young slave belonging to Beadle risked his life by running through a corn field to warn the scouts. Shooting began and three of the scouts were captured. Two escaped, but one was shot in the chest. After riding six miles back to the town of Humbolt, the wounded soldier fell from his horse and died. The Confederates attacked the bridge, but it was only partially burned because the federals had been alerted and arrived in time to put out the blaze before it spread. However, Capt. Jackson's men burned another bridge closer to Memphis.[485]

The Union Army sent reinforced scouting parties to look for Beadle. He and four other rebel leaders were captured. Beadle was recognized by the surviving scouts. He was found carrying a written oath of Union allegiance, which he obviously had not followed. He was given a drumhead court-martial and hanged the next day, July 29, 1862, in Trenton. The Union Army then burned down Beadle's house and the houses of the four other men captured with him.[486]

The following are some examples of persons known to have been captured (or arrested) by the Union Army in Tennessee, or by militia known as the Home Guard, or by gangs loosely organized around a leader, more properly known as guerrillas or bushwhackers, who, following some sort of "trial," executed other Tennesseans. In later years, these killings might have been called lynchings. But this is not a book about lynching. It is a book of legal executions. These persons were deemed *legally* executed, much like Beadle. This much is certain: the persons who performed the killings thought their actions were within the law. None were ever punished or apologized for the killings.

Lewis M. Kirk, white, age forty, deserves special mention among the Confederate lawless. A blacksmith, he had killed a man named William Kelly in a brawl before the war and in 1859 was convicted of killing a man named Westmoreland and given a fifteen-year sentence.[487] Upon the recommendation of two influential men of Maury County, Andrew Jackson Polk and W.V. Thompson, Gov. Isham Harris commuted his sentence on condition that Kirk join the Confederate Army.[488] This he did on July 5, 1861, joining the Maury Braves, namely Company F, 1st Tennessee Cavalry. The nature of his service in that unit is unknown.

By August 31, 1862, Kirk was something of a free agent on behalf of the Confederacy. On that day he gathered enough men to form his own company, of which he was chosen captain, called Company D, 19th (Biffle's) Tennessee Cavalry Regiment. Composed of partisans from Lawrence County, the unit under Kirk harassed Union forces and pro–Union civilians in small vicious attacks. Part of his duties included enforcing the Confederate draft law, which he did with special joy, rounding up elderly Union civilians and holding them hostage.[489] Wrote a federal spy on October 14, 1863, "Kirk has killed several Union men in cold blood and is a terror to all Union sentiment."[490]

In late July 1865, when the war was over, a squad of federal soldiers stationed at Pulaski arrested Kirk and subjected him to a drumhead court-martial. They shot him in early August 1865 at Pulaski.[491] Locals took a different view of Kirk's death. One writer said the federals "murdered him in one of the most cold blooded murders ever perpetuated in the county."[492] Fifteen years after his death he was still remembered as a vicious killer.[493]

Colonel William W. Lowe, 8th Iowa Cavalry, was placed in command of the "twin forts" (Donelson and Henry) after their capture and ordered counterinsurgency actions from that base. In time, the depredations conducted under his command in sacking Clarksville (September 1862) resulted in the Confederacy's placing a price on his head as a common felon. In early 1863, his troops marched to a church two miles northeast of Erin. They arrested James Rushing and Hub Edmunson, both white, ages unknown, and marched them a half mile to a clump of trees. A death warrant was read to them and they were given time to say a prayer. While kneeling in prayer they were shot. Later that day, the soldiers did the same to Frank Warden.

On January 7, 1865, a group of Union soldiers under Lt. Clarke, Company A, 83rd Illinois, crossed the Cumberland River at Clarksville and captured James Jacob Sly, James S. Finley and William H. Moore. Sly had earlier offered a reward for Clarke's head. The trio was captured that day and shot the next day on Clarke's orders.[494] Guerrilla Samuel Ellis was also shot that day.

Colonel Fielding Hurst, a West Tennessee resident, was an ardent Unionist in an overwhelmingly rebel area. His land, together with that of his four brothers, was so extensive in the McNairy County area that it was called "Hurst Nation." After Shiloh, Hurst raised six companies and was placed at its head, called the 1st West Tennessee (6th Tennessee U.S.) Cavalry.

Col. Hurst began a terrorist campaign against his neighbors in McNairy, Chester and Hardeman counties and struck north to Madison County, primarily destroying property. He burned most of the town of Purdy, the seat of McNairy County, in 1863.

Under Col. Hurst, persons known to be members of Newsome's 18th Cavalry, CSA, were simply shot following capture. These included Lt. Joseph Stewart, Pvt. John Wilson, and Pvt. Samuel Osborn, who were shot in Haywood County. Pvt. Alex Vale of the 18th was shot in Madison County.

Sgt. Leanders McAuliff of the 18th was shot at LaGrange, Fayette County. On March 9, 1864, Lt. J. Willis Dodds, also from the 18th Cavalry, was captured at home on furlough. His face was skinned, nose and genitals were cut off and the body lacerated.

By late 1864, the Union Army had lost confidence in Hurst. He resigned on December 10, 1864. He served briefly in the infamous Brownlow legislature until the governor appointed him a circuit judge.[495]

Like Sam Davis a member of Coleman's Scouts, Dewitt Smith Jobe was captured by Union Army patrols on August 29, 1864. Carrying dispatches, he attempted to chew and swallow them. The scout troop of the 115th Ohio Cavalry beat him, tied his hands and neck with a leather strap and choked him. Still refusing to talk, he was beaten over the head, his front teeth were knocked out, and he was dragged by the leather straps around his neck until he strangled to death. Jobe's cousin, Dewitt Smith, had been in the Confederate Army, but became a guerrilla to avenge Jobe's death. He bragged of killing about fifty wounded soldiers, often by slitting their throats. He was badly wounded when captured near Nolensville in 1864 and was taken to Murfreesboro for a summary hanging but died the next day just hours before his execution.[496]

Lincoln County, which bordered Alabama, was a microcosm of vigilante justice and unlawful killing. Before the Civil War, three men had been legally executed there. But the war changed everybody's life. In faraway Lynchburg, Virginia, Lt. Joseph G. Davidson, a local man, was shot and killed while attempting to break up a fight among his troops, which included Private Joseph C. Taylor, also from Lincoln County. The shooting was done on April 29, 1861. Somehow Taylor made his way back to Fayetteville in early October 1861. Breathing defiance and threatening other citizens, he was taken by a mob and lynched on October 20, 1861. Later, a member of Davidson's regiment, Private Marion Rice Cobb, and his brother Asbury, killed two federal soldiers in cold blood in a neighboring county.

On June 15, 1864, a large body of federal troops under General Paine entered Fayetteville (Lincoln County) and demanded three men said to be guerrillas. They were Thomas Massey, William Picket,[497] and Finis Burroughs.[498] The three were handed over. John R. Massey,[499] who had been discharged from the Confederate Army two years earlier, stepped forward and said his brother, Thomas, was not a bushwhacker and had never been in the Confederate forces. He said that Thomas had small children and that if Massey blood had to be shed, it should be his because he had been a Confederate soldier. The men were exchanged. Five minutes later, the three men were riddled with bullets and General Paine ordered the bodies to lie undisturbed on the ground all day as a warning against bushwhacking.

These retribution killings were prompted by the work of Young C. "Tobe" Edmondson, a former member of G Company, Turley's 1st Tennessee, and bushwhackers like William Lemmonds (q.v.). Edmondson was a Lincoln County native. Wounded at Gettysburg, Tobe had been furloughed in Georgia, where he deserted on October 13, 1863. He returned to Lincoln County and became a bushwhacker. He was tried for murder and robbery by a military commission and sentenced to hang.[500] But his mother and another woman, both reputed as the most beautiful women in the county, went to Governor Andrew Johnson, who fell to their pleading. He referred them to President Lincoln. When the mother finally got to see the president, she could not speak, saying only, "My son; my son!" The president said he would look into the matter. When she returned a few days later, Lincoln asked, "Your boy has been to my men, and if I do anything for your boy, what will you do for me?" She replied, "I will pray for you always." Following a second delay, she was again before the president. He said, "Cheer up; cheer up. There is brightness in the world, and there may be a share for you." Edmondson was pardoned but spent the rest of the war in a federal prison. After the war he settled in Texas.

Finally, not included in this book are the several summary executions ordered (or personally performed) by Confederate General Nathan Bedford Forrest. The reason is that no documents were generated or have survived regarding these deaths. Forrest got into a fight with one of his officers, who shot him, and the officer died from a knife wielded by the commander. On another occasion, Forrest literally thrashed a runaway soldier to death. He fired a shotgun at some retreating soldiers and shot and killed a cowardly color bearer.[501] He ordered shot a Union soldier who had set fire to the Murfreesboro jail, which was filled with Confederate soldiers.[502] They were freed in a raid on the town. He ordered two black Union soldiers (or civilians dressed in federal uniforms) taken into the woods and shot near Trenton in December 1862.[503]

Francis M. Samples, white, age unknown. *Desertion.*

Executed under authority of the Confederate States of America.

Private Samples was a member of Company C, 28th Alabama. He deserted from Tines Station, Tennessee, on August 18, 1862, but was seen and arrested in Blount County, Alabama, by Lt. H.H. Green on November 10, 1862. He was subjected to a general court-martial at Murfreesboro on December 15, 1862, and executed there by musketry on December 19, 1862.[504] Inexplicably, the execution was botched. "Owing to some blunder, the squad fired three volleys into him before he was killed. It made a deep impression. I think any man who witnessed it would resolve never to die such a death," wrote a soldier.[505]

Asa Lewis, white, age 26. *Desertion.*
William Litterall, white, age unknown. *Desertion.*
Edward P. Norman, white, age unknown. *Desertion.*
Zachariah Phillips, white, age unknown. *Desertion.*
Samuel Gray, white, age unknown. *Spying.*

Executed under authority of the Confederate States of America.

Private Asa Lewis was a member of Company E, 6th Kentucky Infantry. He had enlisted for twelve months, which had expired, and he went home in 1862, but the facts are not clear. He contended he was not bound by the new reorganization law which extended enlistments. Now his father had recently died and his mother needed him to help harvest the crops and care for three younger siblings. He had asked for a furlough but it was denied.[506] He left anyway, intending to return. At trial, it was shown that he had been granted an audience with the commanding general, Braxton Bragg, who denied the furlough. He began cursing Bragg and was arrested. He escaped and was captured by a bounty hunter in December 1862, apparently before he got home.

The Kentuckians, known as the "Orphan Brigade," pled for a commutation of the sentence by Bragg.[507] This included a personal appeal by Kentuckian Gen. Breckinridge to Bragg, who was unmoved, possibly because this was Lewis's second desertion. Confederate President Jefferson Davis had traveled to the Confederate encampment to calm the near-mutiny that was occurring in the ranks, a three-way split between the Kentuckians, the Alabamians and the Tennesseans.[508] But President Davis had left the camp on December 15, 1862, to return to Richmond.

Confederate writer Bromfield Ridley (who was likely present) described the Lewis execution as "most affecting," and explained:

> A Kentuckian had disappeared from his regiment and gone home. A scout captured him in the Federal lines. He claimed to be returning; that he had gone hence on a plea from his wife and children of being in want; that on supplying them he was in route to join his command. A court-martial was demanded. Gen. Breckenridge, it is said, urged the prisoner to wait until after the battle, then in contemplation, before being tried. The soldier declined, saying that he was no deserter, that the trial must come. The court-martial sat, the prisoner was condemned, and shot. It created a profound sensation in the Army of Tennessee, and incensed Hanson's Kentucky Brigade beyond measure.[509]

The execution of Private Lewis caused a permanent rift between Bragg and the Kentuckians.[510] Generals Breckinridge and Hanson watched Lewis's execution on horseback. On his way to the shooting ground, Lewis was allowed to speak to the officers, who saluted him. Lewis had fought well at Shiloh. Lewis was allowed to speak to the squad that was about to shoot him. "Comrades, I know you are all grieved to do this work but don't be distressed; none of you will know who kills me for you know one of your guns has no ball in it. Each man may think his was the harmless gun. But I beg of you to aim to kill when the command "fire" is given; it will be merciful to me. Good-bye."[511]

William Litterall had enlisted on May 16, 1862, for the duration and was from Buncombe County, North Carolina. He was a member of F Company, 60th North Carolina Infantry.[512] He deserted on October 1, 1862. Accounts differ on whether he was returning from desertion when apprehended. He was court-martialed on December 3, 1862.

The details of the other men's desertion are unknown other than some had been absent without leave for as much as six months. All were members of the Army of Tennessee, Polk's Corps.[513]

They were executed on December 26, 1862, at the Confederate encampment at Murfreesboro under the command of Gen. Bragg. Private Norman, age unknown, was a member of Company C, 28th Alabama Infantry. Private Phillips, age unknown, was a member of Company B, 28th Alabama Infantry. They were executed in a heavy rainstorm in front of the entire brigade formed up to make three sides of a square.

Their executions were done separately, each man brought to the killing ground on a wagon, followed by a hearse. Each man was allowed to shake hands with his friends and bid them good-bye. Each was blindfolded; some chose to die while kneeling in prayer. The firing squad consisted of fifteen members with three rifles shooting blanks. The best marksmen in the man's company served as shooters, and most men were hit by eleven bullets (balls). Asa Lewis was shot first at precisely 12:00 noon. At that moment, "General Breckenridge was seized with a deathly sickness, doubled forward on the neck of his horse, and had to be caught by some of his staff."[514]

Dr. V.W. Cooper, surgeon of the 60th North Carolina, who watched the execution, remained bitter about the experience for the rest of his long life. He was especially touched by the death of William Litterall, "a good soldier, a true Christian and a praying member of the Baptist Church."[515]

A newspaper reporter writing for a pro–Union newspaper said sarcastically, "I would advise all deserters who may be skulking around the cities of the Confederacy, to return while Gen. Bragg offers them pardon."[516] Reuben Searcy, of Lumsden's Artillery Battery, Alabama, had been elected a third lieutenant only two weeks earlier. The nineteen-year-old officer wrote, "I wrote to cousin Sue a week ago — in which I spoke of a deserter from the 28th Ala. Reg't. being shot. Today we had to witness two more from the same regiment. Our brigade was marched out fully accoutered — in the midst of a heavy rain to witness their execution. It was hard to witness it."[517]

The executions were not without drama. A soldier of the 24th Tennessee was taken to the shooting ground, but just as he was about to be executed a courier arrived, bringing a reprieve from General Bragg.

The military executions were designed to strengthen discipline in the Army of Tennessee. At the same time, a signal was being sent to the civilian population. Samuel Gray, a civilian described as a "spy and traitor and a thief" was tried on December 20, 1862, and ordered hanged the same day as the four were shot.[518] This was done near the Murfreesboro train depot before an immense crowd of soldiers and civilians.[519] The details of Gray's activities are unknown. To show his disdain for his executioners, Gray literally jumped off the gallows the instant the rope was placed, not waiting to hear the death warrant read.[520]

On December 31, 1862, the Union Army under Gen. Rosecrans threw itself against Bragg's army at the Battle of Stones River (Murfreesboro) forcing it to withdraw to Tullahoma. Bragg ordered the Kentuckians to attack at a place Breckenridge and others protested because it was vulnerable to Union artillery. Following orders, some 1,197 Kentuckians surged forward. Within twenty minutes, 431 were dead or wounded. It was the highest loss of any brigade in the battle. A weeping Breckenridge exclaimed, "My poor Orphans! My poor Orphans!"[521] In time, a bitter jest followed the overall Confederate commander: "Bragg had no army: he had shot half of it and the other half he lost at Murfreesboro."[522] Also killed was Reuben Searcy.

1863

William Ackerman, white, age 22. *Desertion.*

Executed under authority of the Confederate States of America.

Private Ackerman was a member of Company E, 1st (Strawbridge's) Louisiana. He had enlisted at New Orleans on April 15, 1861. He was released as a prisoner of war on October 16, 1862, but was arrested at Lancaster, Kentucky, on October 18, 1862, wearing a federal uniform. He was court-martialed at Tullahoma on January 23, 1863, and shot there seven days later.[523]

Ambrose Clark, white, age 22. *Desertion.*

Executed under authority of the Confederate States of America.

Private Clark was a member of Company F, 51st Alabama. He had deserted shortly before the Battle of Murfreesboro. He was court-martialed and shot at the Confederate camp at Tullahoma on February 12, 1863.[524]

William M. Meadows, white, age 32. *Desertion and willful failure to follow orders.*

Executed under authority of the Confederate States of America.

Private Meadows was a member of Company D, Col. Stearns Cavalry Regiment (Tennessee), and had enlisted on November 16, 1861, at Camp Cheatham. After refusing to obey an order at the camp at Murfreesboro, he got into an altercation with an officer and deserted on December 1, 1862. He was discovered in a house in Cornersville, Tennessee, and fired at the squad sent to arrest him. He killed a member of the squad and was captured when it burned down the house.

Court-martialed on December 12, 1862, he was ordered shot on December 26, 1862, but this was not done because he was sick. He was shot by the provost guard at Tullahoma on February 13, 1863.[525]

Samuel W. Kenny, white, age unknown. *Spying.*

Executed under authority of the Confederate States of America.

Kenny was a civilian who was captured within the lines of the Army of Tennessee in early January 1863 and was immediately identified as a spy. The details of his spying and trial are unknown but he was executed by hanging on February 13, 1863, at the Confederate encampment at Tullahoma.[526]

Cornelius Kennedy, white, age 20. *Conduct prejudicial to military discipline.*
W. S. Brakefield, white, age 20. *Cowardice in face of the enemy.*

Executed under authority of the Confederate States of America.

Private Kennedy was a member of Company C, 5th Confederate (Tennessee) Regiment. On December 2, 1862, he attempted to rescue a fellow soldier, William Rouch, from the guardhouse at Shelbyville. He struck the sergeant of the guard a severe blow in the face and when taken by guard officer Lt. William P. Wilson, Kennedy struck him and escaped. Captured, he struck his captain, W.A. Brown, on February 4, 1863, at Tullahoma. He also called Capt. Brown a "damned son of a bitch."[527]

Private Brakefield was a member of Company D, 17th Tennessee. At the Battle of Murfreesboro, on December 31, 1862, "while his comrades were moving on, and driving the enemy successfully before them, he did refuse to follow them."[528] He and Kennedy were executed by musketry at the camp at Tullahoma on March 13, 1863.

Michael LaVoi Keener (aka Michael LaVoi), white, age 23. *Desertion.*

Executed under authority of the Confederate States of America.

Private Michael LaVoi, who enlisted under the name Keener, was a native of Alsace, France. He enlisted in the DeKalb Riflemen on January 11, 1862. On January 22, 1863, he attempted to desert with a comrade. The comrade committed suicide. LaVoi shot at an officer attempting to arrest him. Private LaVoi was executed by musketry on April 10, 1863, near Savannah, in Hardin County.[529]

James Welch, white, age unknown. *Desertion in wartime.*

Private Welch was a member of the 40th Indiana Infantry. On December 31, 1862, on the battlefield of Stones River, he abandoned his company and did not return "until the enemy were drawn from the field, Sunday, January 4, 1863." He was court-martialed on March 11, 1863, and shot on April 14, 1863, at Murfreesboro.[530] Francis D. Cain, C Company, 18th United States Infantry, and Ezekiel Ennis, 6th Kentucky Infantry, were to be executed on April 10 and 14, but their sentences were remitted. Cain had led a mutiny at the Louisville barracks when he threatened a sergeant with a musket and bayonet. Ennis was a deserter.[531]

Joseph Smith, white, age unknown. *Spying and theft.*

Joseph Smith was a civilian. During March and April 1863 he spied on the camp of Crook's Division near Carthage and obtained information about the strength, position and appearance of the forces. He spied from an overlook on a mountain across the river from the camp. Smith was convicted solely on his own words. He was tried before a general court-martial, not a military commission, on April 20 and 21, 1863, at the federal camp in Carthage, and ordered "hanged by the neck until he is dead at such time and place as the commanding general may direct."[532]

Five Union soldiers from Crook's Division, dressed as rebels and claiming to have been cut off from Confederate forces in Kentucky, approached Smith's house across the river about three miles from Carthage at dawn on April 19, 1863. They explained they were trying to link up with Morgan's forces. Smith served them breakfast, gave corn to their horses, and explained that he was a Confederate soldier on leave after he had been wounded at Shiloh.

In conversation with the five soldiers he explained that he was doing better service as a spy than as a soldier because he watched the Yankee troops and sent messages to Bragg's army. He said that from six to seven thousand troops were camped on the Carthage side of the river, but were making their way across to his side. He explained he had watched the camp from a bluff. When asked why he didn't tell the Confederate Army to attack the camp, he explained, "It would be a damned dirty hole to get them out of."[533]

Smith also boasted that he had "snapped three good horses from the Yankees," which had strayed from the camp. One was purchased for two hundred dollars by one of Morgan's men, the others were given to Confederates. He explained that he hid in a canebrake near his house and boasted that no one could find him there.[534] When asked if he would take the oath of allegiance to the United States, he said that no oath would hinder him from what he thought to be his duty.[535]

Smith volunteered to ride with the five men to show them a crossroads that would take them to Rome, where he said they would find Confederate forces. As they rode, the sergeant in charge of the squad drew his pistol on Smith and arrested him. "After that he was not very communicative."[536]

On the issue of whether Smith was actually a soldier, the Army offered the testimony of George McGee, a private in Company C, 4th Tennessee (Confederate) Cavalry. Smith asked him, "Do you know by what authority I am now away from the Southern Army?" McGee replied, "I do not know what authority. He has not been with the Southern Army that I know of since about the first of January."[537] Joseph Smith was hanged at 4:00 P.M. at the Union encampment near Carthage on May 12, 1863.[538]

Julius Milika (aka Julius Mileka and Julien Milaka), white, age 30. *Desertion.*

Private Milika was a member of Company E, 10th Michigan Infantry. He deserted the unit on September 14, 1862, near Nashville. On November 6, 1862, he enlisted in Company K, 1st Tennessee (Federal) Infantry. He deserted again and was captured on February 8, 1863.[539] He was court-martialed on May 5 and sentenced to be shot ten days later. He was executed on May 15, 1863.[540] This is among the few executions for desertion that were not sent to the president for review. The reason is unknown.

Milika, a native of Prussia, sent a letter to the Commanding General asking for mercy. The letter was most likely written with the aid of someone more literate than Milika. It reads:

> Nashville Jail, May 12, To Genl Morgan, Comdg Post, Sir, I am sentenced to be shot on the 15th Instant and before that time arrives, I would say a few words to you hoping that they may be of aid. In my trial, the witness for me did not appear in court by forgetting his name therefore I was left in the lurch. His name is August Wald belonging to the first Tenn Infantry Company K. I saw him today. He was present when his Lieut. persuaded me to join his Company, his (the Lieut.) told me that the pay coming to me from my Reg he would get for me and that I would not be harmed. All this, this man Wald was present and heard. How sir can you not assist me in this hour of great need. I do not wish to have it said that I was shot for deserting the flag of my adopted country. Then I have no one left to support the declining years of my poor old mother. Please sir exert your energy on behalf of a soldier who erred but who is repentant and you shall command the lasting gratitude of a fellow mortal. And can you say that I may have a prospect in that my case may be petitioned as life is very sweet — especially when one is not prepared. And in conclusion can you let me know today what you can do for me. I have been a soldier now for some 10 years and never thought for once that I would come to this for I have always tried to do my duty ever since this war I have been in the army. Yours most Respfly, Julius Milika 10th Reg. Mich. Vol. I should like to have the Art of War read to me here as I do not fully comprehend it. Yours, J.M.[541]

An eyewitness to Milika's execution was Cpl. Henry Carlton of Company A, 18th Michigan Infantry, who wrote in his diary:

> May 15th, 1863. 15th Fridy, Warm & pleasant. Were relieved at the usual time and have had a very pleasant time. Were ordered out the rest of the troops in the vicinity of the city to witness the execution of Julius Milika, who deserted from the 10th Mich. & afterward joined the 1st Tenn receiving $80 bounty shortly after deserted from them & went to Louisville, & was taken & brought to Nashville & confined in the city jail. He had his trial & was sentenced to be shot at 12 M. Milika was a native of Prussia but for the last 10 yrs. prior to his enlisting was a citizen of Mich. He was a sober and hard working man supporting himself & aged mother (a cripple) by his industry. He had a good religious education in his youthful days & had always led an exemplary life prior to his enlistment. But after he got into the Army (like many others) he forgot his religious duties took to drinking kept bad company & gave loose rein to his sinful desires until it led him far.

The diary continues:

> At noon he was brought into the hollow sq. (into which the troops were formed) in an ambulance accompanied by a squad of Cavalry. The coffin was set down on a knoll in full view of the whole troops. The doomed man was led to the fatal spot by the Clergyman in attendance accompanied by 2 other gentlemen he was seated on his coffin & then a gentleman read something from a paper probably his sentence after which a prayer was offered by Mr. Egyerz the clergyman the prisoner bowing his head after this was done he sat up very straight shaking hands with the several gentlemen & some Officers bidding they "good-bye." Then the bandage was placed over his eyes & the executioners of the Kansas 8th who were formed in front 10 paces (14 in number) recd the orders to "ready, aim Fire," the poor devil fell over only waving one hand a little. 5 of the balls hit his breast in the space the size of a mans hand. Thus the man was hurled into eternity with scarcely a moments notice. He said that he tho't that the authorities would not punish him to the full extent of the law yet he said he deserved the full extent of the punishment. His last words were "Take good aim men, all is over now!" He sat

> very firm & put on a bold front. He was buried on a beautiful hill side beneath a tree 1½ miles south of the city near the "Granny White" pike.

Corporal Carlton concluded:

> There has been a great many deserters from the Union army of late & it is high time that there is some stringent measuring taken to prevent it. I believe this is the first execution of the Kind that has taken place in the Union army. God grant that I may never forget my early training & fall into evil habits & finally end in destruction. What must be the feelings of that aged mother as she sits in her helplessness & contemplates the sad fate of her only son. One she had fondly hoped, perchance would be a comfort to her in her declining years, but alas for human hopes they very often fall to the ground without a moments warning. How essential then it is, then that we have an interest in Others that can comfort us in our afflictions.[542]

The grave was temporary. He was later buried in grave 4553 of the Nashville City Cemetery. He was the second Union soldier executed in Nashville.[543]

Joseph Manning, white, age 25. *Desertion.*
Executed under authority of the Confederate States of America.

Private Manning joined B Company, 5th Regiment Provisional Army, Mountain Rifle Regiment, renamed the 35th Regiment, on September 6, 1861. Initially thought dead in the retreat from Corinth, he rejoined his company but deserted on August 16, 1862. He was captured by bounty hunters, court-martialed on May 28, 1863, and shot at Tullahoma in front of Hardee's division on June 1, 1863.[544]

William A. Selkirk, white, age unknown. *Murder.*
George W. Williams (aka Thomas Brown), white, age unknown. *Murder.*
George Lyles (aka Mansfield Rhodes), white, age unknown. *Murder.*

The crime was committed about 8:00 P.M. on March 9, 1863, at the rural farm home of Adam Weaver in Wilson County. The victim was Weaver, white, age fifty-four, and the killing was part of a home robbery. Weaver shared the house with his daughter, Sarah Ann Weaver, white, age twenty, and a negro named John. The robbery was largely the work of Williams and Lyles, who knew that Weaver was a Union man and was thought to keep about a thousand dollars in his house. Weaver was killed because he had far less money in the house than supposed. The defendants were tried by a military commission, Selkirk first on May 5, 1863, then Williams and Lyles on June 13, 1863.[545]

Williams and Lyles, known to be a members of Bond's Guerrillas, began drinking about noon on the murder day and by nightfall had been joined by Selkirk. They went to Weaver's house and knocked on the door. Weaver asked, "Who's there?" Lyles answered, "Favor Cason," the name of a neighbor who was in the Union Army.[546] When Weaver opened the door, Selkirk and Lyles pushed their way inside. After candles were lit, they called Weaver a damned Union man and demanded his money.[547]

When only eighty-five dollars was produced, he was taken outside. A rope was placed around his neck then thrown over a log that extended from the house. Lyles pulled the rope, lifting Weaver off the ground. He was then dropped. Money was demanded. He was hanged again, this time a little longer. Dropped again, he was unable to speak for awhile, but finally told where to find about three hundred dollars. Still unhappy, one of the trio took Weaver about a hundred yards from the house, shot him once in the neck, and returned to the house. Weaver "kept struggling" on the ground.[548] Someone went to him, shot him twice and cut out his tongue. Sarah A. Weaver asked neighbors to find her father. C.R. Puckett testified, "I found the body of Mr. Weaver near a half a mile from his house with a shot through the head, one through the neck, and one near the heart. The head was on the back part, badly broken up and beaten to a jelly and the tongue was cut out."[549]

The killers pointed to each other. Selkirk said he had tried to persuade Williams not to shoot Weaver and when he (Selkirk) was ordered to silence the man by Lyles he simply shot in the air over him.[550] Williams blamed Lyles and Selkirk.[551] Lyles and Williams, represented by lawyers, made a defense that the testimony of the other two was inadmissible, especially Selkirk's written statement naming Lyles as the first shooter. Lyles's chief defense was that he was an unwilling participant, threatened by Selkirk.[552] Williams likewise said he was a threat victim of Selkirk.

Sarah A. Weaver did not know who actually killed her father, but disputed the testimony of Selkirk, who maintained he had tried to talk the others out of killing her father. He insisted that but for his intervention both she and John would have been killed.

Selkirk had been arrested on March 11, 1863, but broke free. The other two were captured a week later at a house of ill fame. The trio was transferred to various jails as far away as Chattanooga. They escaped from the Harrison (Hamilton County) jail but were recaptured in Wilson County. Each implicated the other when finally recaptured. Williams was the first to name Selkirk, who replied in kind.[553] Williams gave a written statement after arrest in which he said that after Selkirk came back after shooting Weaver, Selkirk said, "He was the damnedst hardest man to kill he ever tried."[554]

Selkirk addressed the commission: "I wanted to say to the court that I don't think the evidence proves that I committed the murder. God in Heaven knows that I am innocent of it. It would not be just for me to suffer for another man's crime. If it had not been for me, Williams would have killed the girl."[555]

William A. Selkirk was hanged near the Union military encampment near Murfreesboro on June 4, 1863, a day earlier than his sentence ordered. The newspaper said, "The wagon containing the convict and coffin was driven from prison through the town, and was followed by an immense concourse of citizens and soldiers. The gallows was erected in an open field about half a mile from town, and was surrounded by at least ten thousand spectators. The daughter and son of the murdered man stood immediately in front of the scaffold. The former asked the privilege of adjusting the rope."[556]

The Selkirk execution was the subject of hundreds, perhaps thousands, of soldiers' letters to home folk. All mentioned the cutting out of Weaver's tongue, which was probably done by Lyles, whom both Selkirk and Williams called "Captain." Some say he cut off Weaver's ears too. Others say the daughter actually placed the rope around his neck.

Williams and Lyles were hanged together on June 18, 1863, on the same gallows used to hang Selkirk. Five thousand soldiers watched.[557]

Solomon Wright, white, age 18. *Desertion.*

Executed under authority of the Confederate States of America.

Private Wright was a member of H Company, 8th Tennessee Infantry.[558] The facts of his desertion are unknown, but his June 8, 1863, execution was recorded in the remarkable Civil War memoirs of Samuel Watkins. His regiment, the First Tennessee, was encamped near Shelbyville, in Bedford County.

Watkins wrote, "I saw a young boy about seventeen or eighteen years old, by the name of Wright, and belonging to Gen. Marcus J. Wright's brigade, shot to death with musketry at this place. The whole of Cheatham's division had to march out and witness the horrid scene. Now, I have no doubt that many, if not all, would have gone without being forced to do so, but then you know that was Bragg's style. He wanted always to display his tyranny, and to intimidate his privates as much as possible."[559]

Watkins explained:

> The young man was hauled in a wagon, sitting on his coffin, to the place where the grave was to be dug, and a post was planted in the ground. He had to sit there for more than two hours, looking at the preparations for his death. I went up to the wagon, like many others, to have a look at the doomed man. He had his hat pulled down over his eyes, and was busily picking at the ends of his fingers. The guard who then had him in charge told me that one of the culprit's own brothers was one of the detail to shoot him. I went up to the wagon and called to him, "Wright!" He made no reply, and did not even look up. Then I said, "Wright, why don't you jump out of that wagon and run?" He was callous to everything. I was sorry for him.

Watkins continued:

> When the division was all assembled, and the grave dug, and the post set, he was taken out of the wagon, and tied to the post. He was first tied facing the post, and consequently would have been shot in the back, but was afterwards tied with his back to the post. The chaplain of the regiment read a chapter in the Bible, sang a hymn, and then all knelt down and prayed. General Wright went up to the pinioned man, shook hands with him, and told him good-bye, as did many others, and then the shooting detail came up, and the officer in charge gave the command, "Ready, aim, fire!"

Concluded Watkins, "The crash of musketry broke upon the morning air. I was looking at Wright. I heard him almost shriek, 'Oh, Oh, God!' His head dropped forward, the rope with which he was pinioned keeping him from falling. I turned away and thought how long, how long will I have to witness these things?"[560]

William Orton Williams (aka Lawrence Williams Orton, sometimes Auton or Austin, and Lawrence Orton Williams), white, age unknown. *Spying.*
Walter G. Peter (aka Major Dunlop), white, age unknown. *Spying.*

The crime was committed on June 8, 1863, at the Union Army encampment at Franklin, Williamson County, called Fort Granger. The defendants were Confederate officers. Lt. Walter Peter and Col. William Orton Williams rode their horses boldly into the federal camp and introduced themselves as having been sent by the Inspector General of the Union army. Peter introduced himself as Major George Dunlop, and Williams called himself

Col. Lawrence W. Auton (Orton). They were wearing partial federal uniforms consisting of military pants and caps, the latter covered with white flannel havelocks. They wore civilian jackets. Each was carrying a sidearm and sword.[561]

The pair explained to the colonel in charge that they had been held up by Confederate soldiers who stole both their jackets and wallets. The pair displayed papers from both Gen. Rosecrans and headquarters in Washington attesting to their mission.[562] They said they came from Murfreesboro (Rosecrans's headquarters) and were on their way to Nashville.

The officer in charge, Col. John P. Baird, examined their papers, which appeared to be in order. The men made little effort to examine the camp. An officer, Col. Van Vleck, told Baird the men's story didn't make sense. The army was already served by several kinds of inspectors and the men would have traveled with an escort. How had the men lost their one servant, coats and money, but got away safely? Telling Col. Baird they needed to leave, although it was now dark, the pair asked him to loan them fifty dollars each to purchase goods that had been stolen. The colonel gave Williams fifty dollars and took a promissory note from him. Col. Williams gave them a written pass and told them the countersign.

Within minutes of their departure, Col. Baird concluded the two were spies. He ordered Col. Lewis D. Watkins to arrest them. Overtaken by Watkins and a carbine-armed soldier, the two agreed to return to the camp. They were placed in a tent surrounded by several armed guards. They did not think they were under arrest until one of the guards prevented one from leaving.

They were brought to Col. Baird, who said he thought they were spies, which they vigorously denied. Baird replied that if they were loyal, they would not object to the caution he was showing, and he formally placed them under arrest. Baird telegraphed Gen. Rosecrans asking about the pair. He received this reply: "There are no such men as Insp. Gen. Lawrence Orton, Colonel, U.S. Army, and Assistant Major Dunlop, in this army, nor in any army, so far as we know. Why do you ask?"[563] After further messaging, the following came from Rosecrans's Chief of Staff, Brig. Gen. James A. Garfield, later president of the United States: "The two men are no doubt spies. Call a drum head court martial tonight and if they are found to be spies, hang them before morning, without fail. No such men have been accredited from these headquarters."[564]

The men were searched and Major Dunlop's sword bore the marking, "Lt. W.G. Peter, C.S.A." Col. Baird said to his captives, "Gentlemen, you have played this damned well." "Yes," remarked Lt. Peter, "and it came near being a perfect success."[565] Other incriminating documents were found on the men, and Lt. Peter's Confederate cap was found inside a rolled-up white flannel havelock.

The pair were tried before a military commission in the middle of the night. They vigorously denied being spies. They insisted their plan was simply to pass through federal lines because they wanted to visit friends in the North and in Europe. They were ordered hanged the next day, June 9, 1863. Colonel Baird did not want to oversee the actual hanging and telegraphed Rosecrans asking what to do. Gen. Garfield telegraphed orders to hang the men promptly.

Col. Williams was allowed to send a telegram to Rosecrans. "Will you not have any clemency for the son of Captain Williams, who fell at Monterey, Mexico? As my dying speech, I protest our innocence as spies. Save also my friend." It was signed Lawrence W. Orton (formerly W. Orton Williams). Rosecrans never replied.[566]

The men were allowed to write letters. Col. Williams penned these words to his betrothed: "When this reaches you I will be no more. Had I succeeded I would have been able to marry you in Europe in a month. The fate of war has decided against us. I have been condemned as a spy — you know I am not."[567]

At daylight the men were attended by a minister to whom they gave personal items such as jewelry and silver cups. The men had protested death by hanging, asking to be shot. The guards who marched them to their deaths did them the honor to march with arms reversed.

The two were taken to a wild cherry tree near the train depot and two coffins were placed near their feet. Without fear the men stepped upon the platform of the cart and took their places. White linen handkerchiefs were placed around their eyes. At this moment the men asked to be given a chance to say good-bye to each other. This was allowed and the men embraced. Lt. Peter sobbed and said, "Oh, Colonel, have we come to this!" Williams replied, "Let us die like men."[568] No one noticed the men's hands were not tied. This was Col. Baird's first execution. The cart was driven away at nine-thirty in the morning.

Shortly before the hanging, Col. Williams (Orton) explained that he had recognized Col. Watkins, who captured him, because they had served together in the Army before the war. Williams explained that he had his hand on his pistol when Watkins drew near and would have killed him if it had been anyone else. Watkins did not recognize Williams until this was explained. Col. Williams gave his two pistols and sword to Col. Watkins, along with his horse, which he said was worth five thousand dollars, and asked him to treat it kindly.

Col. Williams had been aide-de-camp and private secretary to Gen. Winfield Scott when the war broke out and was privy to all the details of Scott's plans to end the rebellion. When Williams announced his sympathies were for the Confederacy, he was jailed on Governor's Island for three months. Following the first Battle of Bull Run, he was released and was known to have joined the Confederate army. He had served as chief of Bragg's artillery and was a cousin of Robert E. Lee's wife. His last letters were to his sister and his fiancée. One source says he had a brother serving in the Union Army.[569] This was the reason he dropped the use of his last name.

Col. Williams was hanged with a gold locket around his neck. It contained the portrait and a braid of hair of his intended wife. Her photograph was in his pocket. These were buried with him at his request.

Lt. Peters's neck was broken and he died quickly. Col. Williams grasped the rope for about three minutes and ceased to struggle in about five. Two doctors found the men's hearts still beating at seventeen minutes, but they were pronounced dead three minutes later. The pair were buried on top of each other in a common grave.

One of the doctors wrote, "We are all sad over this event. There is a gloom upon every face. Although we are fully satisfied that the mission of these men was to plan our destruction and that even they recognized their punishment just according to the accepted rules of war among all nations, still to see such men suffer such a penalty has filled our garrison with sadness."[570]

The mission of Williams and Peter remains a mystery.[571] One theory holds they were bound for Ireland to inform the public that so-called emigration experts were actually Army agents whose job was to provide soldiers for the Union Army. An image, purportedly drawn from life, shows the men hanging. It was published in *Harper's Weekly* and remains one of the notable images of Civil War justice.[572] The execution has been a favorite topic of writers on the Civil War.[573] The illustration of the midnight court-martial, drawn by noted artist Howard Pyle, has become a fixture of Civil War iconography.[574]

Col. Williams's death was not mourned by the Confederate Army. "The general belief about the man was that he was out of balance, erratic, full of conceit, personal vanity and distorted views of his military importance and dignity. To sum up — he was not entirely sane." Early in the war, a soldier refused to salute him the second time he passed him in his morning visit to the stable. Williams thrust his sword into the hapless man. Williams's written report was remembered by all who knew him: "For his ignorance, I pitied him; for his insolence, I forgave him; for his insubordination, I slew him." When he was assigned to a Tennessee regiment in 1863, the other officers refused to allow him to take command. General Van Dorn acquiesced, as did Gen. Bragg. This left Williams and Peter in "unassigned" status at the time they were executed.[575] According to a fellow officer, Williams was court-martialed at Columbus, Kentucky, and the "eccentric officer" was regarded as "mentally unbalanced."[576]

Col. John Pierson Baird (1830–1881), the officer in charge of Ft. Granger and the hanging, was severely affected by the episode and had a mental breakdown in 1875. He died in the Indiana Hospital for the Insane on March 7, 1881.

William Minix, white, age 25. *Desertion.*

The crime was committed on September 20, 1862, near Bowling Green, Kentucky. Private Minix, of the 9th Kentucky Infantry, was a cook who also personally served the company commander.[577] The company was ordered to march from Nashville to Bowling Green. Minix was given strict orders to stay with the company baggage and wagons. Apparently becoming fearful because the baggage actually preceded the marching troops and provided an easy target for bushwhackers, Minix deserted along the way.

He was arrested on April 14, 1863, and court-martialed at the Union Army camp at Murfreesboro. He offered no testimony or statement and was ordered shot on June 16, 1863. He wrote the company commander: "Sir as you are doubtless aware I am sentenced to be shot on Tuesday next, others have also been sentenced the same as my self who have done much worse than my self and yet have been reprieved and feel shure if you would interest your self in my behalf my life mite be saved. And I will promise to swear if I escape that, awful degrading death I will hence forth be a true and loyal and law abiding soldier. May God help me for I cannot help my self."[578]

Minix was shot by a firing squad in Murfreesboro

on June 14, 1863, (two days early), in full view of General Horatio P. Van Cleve's division. The division was marched to the site and the men waited for the ambulance bearing Minix to arrive. He declined, saying, "Oh, no. I think a walk will make me feel better." He was preceded by a wagon carrying his coffin and the chaplain walked with him. The band played the "Dead March" and his head was slightly bowed. He walked around the whole square "without the least faltering in his step."

Wrote a fellow soldier:

> A short prayer was uttered by the Chaplain and thus the prisoner was secured to his coffin and in a sitting position and the twelve were marched up a short distance in front of him and brought to a front. I involuntarily turned my eyes away from the scene and waited several seconds which seemed like hours, of the most tormenting suspense when the almost death-like silence was broke by one of the most irregular volleys I ever heard, and a glance toward the prisoner told me he was no more. As I stood a moment as if in breathless suspense and then a long breath apparently from each one broke the spell of suspense and immediately we were deployed and formed into columns of companies and marched in this order over by the spot where the victim lay and then filed off toward the camp.[579]

Concluded the soldier, "A great many executions of this kind occurred during our stay in Murfreesboro."

Unnamed Union soldier, white, age 17.

This unknown Union soldier was a member of the 4th Indiana Battery and a few weeks before he was executed he deserted and was captured by a scouting patrol wearing a Confederate uniform, claiming to be from John Hunt Morgan's command. He was executed by musketry on June 20, 1863, at the Union encampment near Murfreesboro. A contemporary account reads:

> The entire division was formed into two lines, each facing the other about ten paces apart. The prisoner, under a strong guard, was made to walk the length of these lines. Four men marched behind him carrying his coffin. Upon arriving at the prepared grave the coffin was set down. He was made to kneel beside it, his sentence was read to him, a cap was drawn over his face, the order was given to "Fire" and the full penalty for desertion had been paid in his case. I knew this boy — only about seventeen years of age — he was physically weak, and regarded as rather weak-minded, and this was evident by the fact that he enlisted with the enemy so near to our lines. He appeared to be incapable of realizing that he had done anything wrong. I think it was too bad to shoot the poor fellow. The mistake was made in enlisting him in the first place.[580]

David Blazer, white, age 22. *Desertion.*
John Shockman (aka John Schockman), white, age 20. *Desertion; offering violence to a superior officer.*

Private David Blazer had been mustered into the 4th Indiana Light Artillery on February 18, 1863, at Nashville and deserted in the face of the enemy near Liberty, DeKalb County, Tennessee, on April 24, 1863. He was arrested by Union cavalry near Alexandria, Tennessee, three days later. Out of uniform, he was wearing gray pants and a checked coat and an altered black brimmed hat. He told his captors he was a member of Floyd's Command, CSA, and was from "northern Tennessee."

He was court-martialed on May 6, 1863, and said the following: "When I went from the Battery, it was not my intention to desert the Army at all. When I went out with the train [horse drawn supply wagons], I went to get some eggs. I went a little too far from the camp, between three and four miles, I got captured out there. They thought I had so much better clothes on than they had, they would take mine off and give me a different suit."[581] He was ordered shot on June 23, 1863, and this was done at the Battery's camp near Cripple Creek, Rutherford County.

John Shockman had enlisted in I Company, 1st Kentucky Infantry on June 1, 1861, and deserted the company on December 4, 1861, while on the march from Camp Gauley to Charleston, Virginia (West Virginia). He later joined Company M, 4th Ohio Infantry. At Cincinnati, Ohio, on August 25, 1862, his former company commander, Capt. A.J. Hogan, recognized him and attempted an arrest. Shockman resisted with great violence and escaped. He disappeared and was not arrested until May 11, 1863. He was court-martialed and ordered shot on June 23, 1863.[582] He and Blazer where shot at the same time.

George M. Holmes (aka George M. Homes), white, age 25. *Disobedience of officer in execution of his duties.*

Executed under authority of the Confederate States of America.

The crime was committed on December 27, 1861, on a road five miles outside Tazewell, Tennessee, about fifteen miles from the Confederate camp at Cumberland Gap. The victim was Lt. Alexander H. Vaughan, Company H, 11th Tennessee, white, age twenty-eight. Vaughan was the duty officer. Members of a Confederate cavalry regiment were carousing and harassing the neighborhood and Vaughan was under orders to arrest drunk and disorderly Confederate soldiers. Vaughan set out alone toward Tazewell and encountered a drunk and unruly Private Howell Ambrose, a member of Company F, 1st (Carter's) Tennessee Cavalry. He put Ambrose under arrest. Suddenly two horsemen rode by at a quick pace. A few minutes later, the two and another man appeared with pistols drawn, and began threatening Lt. Vaughan. He told them not to shoot him, that he was under orders from Col. James Rains, his commander, to arrest drunks. Ambrose also begged the men not to shoot. According to Vaughan's dying declaration, "One [a fourth man] came from behind the others and shot me."[583] Vaughan could not name his shooter, but said he recognized one of the men, George M. Holmes, by his horse. The four men were soon captured. The killers were Privates Thomas Crupper, William Ivy, George M. Holmes, and Joel T. Taylor, all members of Company F, 1st (Carter's) Tennessee Cavalry. Holmes was a member of Company K of this regiment.

This is one of the few Confederate death sentences for which the trial records have survived. The soldiers were charged with violating Articles of War No. 9, disobedience of officer in the execution of his duties. The gravamen of this offense is disobedience. Merely killing a superior officer was not punishable under military law unless the victim was killed "in the execution of his office."[584] The court-martial began on January 11, 1862. Private Ambrose said Taylor had fired the shot, but was not asked any questions about Crupper and Ivy. There was conflicting testimony about how many shots were fired, but Lt. Vaughan had not fired his pistol. None of the defendants testified. Crupper and Ivy were convicted as accessories. Holmes was ordered hanged; the other three were to be shot. The court-martial findings were sent to the chief commanding officer, Gen. P.G.T. Beauregard, camped in Mississippi. He affirmed the death sentences on June 14, 1862.[585] The thirty-nine-year-old Ivy, a forage master, somehow escaped punishment, as did Thomas Crupper. The latter joined Gen. Forrest's command, was captured twice by the Federal army, and ended the war in a Northern prison. Joel T. Taylor died in jail waiting execution.[586] At the time the order affirming the death sentences was received, Vaughan's regiment was camped at Bean Station, Grainger County, Tennessee. It was there on July 3, 1863, that Holmes was shot by members of Vaughan's regiment.

John Caio (aka John K. Ould), white, age 23. *Spying.*
Joseph Ford, white, age 20. *Spying.*
Executed under authority of the Confederate States of America.

The pair was accused of posing as Confederate soldiers when passing through Centerville, Hickman County, on or about February 26, 1863, heading south. Then about March 12, 1863, they were seen returning on their way north. They were arrested in Maury County. In addition to the charge of spying, each was convicted of the crime of "depredation upon the property of private individuals."[587] Caio and Ford claimed to be members of the 10th Ohio Infantry, but records do not support their enlistment in any Ohio regiment. Details of their spying are unknown. They were executed by hanging at Gen. Van Dorn's headquarters in Maury County on July 3, 1863.

William Whitehead, white, age 20. *Desertion.*
Executed under authority of the Confederate States of America.

Private Whitehead was a member of Company K, 2nd Tennessee Cavalry. He had joined the Confederate army in August 1861 and was a member of McClellan's battalion. He became separated from his unit at the Battle of Fishing Creek. Word was sent out that all absentees were to report to Knoxville by February 28, 1862. The night before, he stole his brother's horse and went to Kentucky and joined the Union army under Morgan.[588]

Whitehead came to Cumberland Gap with the Union army and while foraging was captured by rebel troops and brought to Tazewell. Here, Captain Holland recognized him, as did many members of his old company. He was placed in the Confederate military prison in Knoxville to await charges, but he became ill and was sent to the hospital. When his health improved, he eloped from the hospital and went to his home in Blount County.

Following his Confederate unit's fighting at Bell's Bridge, he was induced by some members of his company to think that his former actions would be forgiven if he returned to his regiment. Instead, he was promptly arrested and given a court-martial. The purpose was to make an example of him: "The sad end of this unfortunate youth shall be a warning to all soldiers who are prone to be derelict in their duties; and especially those who are absent without leave. Steps are being taken by Col. Scott to enforce discipline, the only odium by which our cavalry can be made effective, and the severest penalty of military law will be visited on those who lay themselves liable to punishment, irrespective of position."[589]

Prior to his execution, Whitehead was taken to a rural church where an army chaplain sang and prayed for him, but with the same result as similar visits in prison, "perfect indifference to his eternal welfare."[590] Fellow prisoners and numerous visitors had implored Whitehead to consider his "hopes beyond the tomb." His only reply was that he did not care what they did with him, that he knew he was not prepared for death, but had no fears as to its horrors.

Whitehead was executed at 3:00 P.M. on July 18, 1863, in a meadow above the church. A grave had been dug in the center, where Whitehead was to be shot. He was brought from Knoxville by ambulance along with his coffin. After the coffin was placed on the ground, Whitehead knelt near the grave as the charges were read to him. "During all this time he manifested a stoic indifference seldom ever witnessed. Not a feature was changed or a muscle moved. He seemed perfectly calm and composed."[591]

Virtually the entire command was present on three sides of an open square. A white handkerchief was placed over his face and he began to utter a few words, apparently a prayer. Without delay, the squad was given the order, "Make ready, fire!" He was hit by two balls, one in the heart and another in the side, and he fell over without a groan or struggle. His body was placed in the coffin, deposited in the grave and covered without ceremony. The command marched slowly back to its encampment, all of its members "deeply impressed with the importance of the occasion."[592] Whitehead was survived by his widowed mother and several sisters.

John C. Kerr, white, age unknown. *Desertion.*

Private Kerr was a member of B Company, 1st Battalion, 16th United States Infantry. He deserted his company near Tyree Springs in Sumner County on September 12, 1862, after he was sent with three canteens to fetch water. According to him, there were so many people at the spring that he had to wait an hour. When he finally got underway, he had to wait for two divisions to march by.

He walked four miles after his regiment and sat down with sore feet. That evening it began to rain and he stayed in a friendly house. The next morning he was sick but hitched a ride on a wagon, which took him to a hotel where he remained sick for five days. Next, he got aboard a train at Franklin, Kentucky, but did not find his regiment at Bowling Green. Still sick, he went out into the country and stayed with a farm family for three weeks. By now he was out of money and had no idea where the regiment had gone, nor any way to find out. He got a job as a clerk in the Quartermaster Department for two months. Then he decided he could make money "buying different kinds of goods in Kentucky and shipping them to Nashville."[593] He was arrested there on April 14, 1863.

"When I was with the Regiment I think I was as good a soldier as their was in the Regiment. I allways don my duty as a Soldier. I was ingaged in the Battles of Shilo and Corinth and don my duty as a soldier."[594] John C. Kerr was ordered shot on June 24, 1863, but the day before, the Union Army mounted an offensive known as the Tullahoma Campaign. When it was over, Kerr was shot at the regiment encampment at Tullahoma, Franklin County, on July 20, 1863.[595]

Wyley Brown, white, age 20. *Desertion.*

Executed under authority of the Confederate States of America.

Private Brown enlisted in Company B, Kain's Light Artillery (Tennessee) on January 4, 1862. Colonel Leadbetter placed him on detached service on January 12, 1862. Brown was ordered to return to his company on February 12, 1862, to go toward Mill Springs, Kentucky. He never returned. According to his compiled service record, he was shot at Strawberry Plains, Tennessee, on July 31, 1863.

Hiram Reynolds, white, age 51. *Murder.*

The crime was committed about 12:30 P.M. on May 19, 1863, at the camp of the 82nd Indiana Infantry at Triune, in Williamson County. The victim was another soldier, Private Washington Moser (sometimes Mozier), a camp cook.

Reynolds claimed to have fought in the Mexican War and said he joined the 27th Indiana Infantry at the outbreak of the Civil War. He said he transferred to the Navy but received a disability discharge. Recovering, he joined the 82nd Indiana. Reynolds had been born in Tennessee. He was a widower with several children and made his living as a professional gambler.[596]

Reynolds's luck ran out when he was accused of murdering Pvt. Washington Moser at the regimental camp following a quarrel that was witnessed by numerous soldiers, many of whom also saw the shooting. Prior to the shooting, Reynolds's captain had confiscated his rifle and a pistol after he threatened members of his company with the rifle.

The pair began to argue in the serving area after Moser accused Reynolds of taking a large serving pan. "If Jesus Christ came down from Heaven and swore [Reynolds had taken it] it would be a lie," he said. Other soldiers entered the quarrel and Reynolds said they were all afraid of him and afraid he would steal something. Moser said he was not afraid of him and told him to leave. Reynolds got up, started to walk away, halted, turned around and said, "Mr. Moser, are you in earnest?" Moser replied, "You fool around and I will show you." Reynolds said, "I know what I have got to fight." Witnesses said Reynolds was enraged.

Moser, from the cook shanty, fired his rifle toward Reynolds's tent. At once, Reynolds emerged with his rifle and said, "Boys, get out of the way!" and fired one shot from his rifle that struck Moser in the head. The captain grabbed the rifle away as Reynolds was reloading.

The court-martial rejected Reynolds's claim of self-defense, focusing on the fact that he had improperly taken back, that is, stolen the rifle from the captain's tent and was bent on shooting others.

Reynolds sought mercy from the court and commanding General Rosecrans, citing his prior military service, his claim of self-defense and his two children. His August 13, 1863, letter also asked for "a few days to prepare for death."[597]

When nothing was heard from Rosecrans, Reynolds was taken to the gallows in the yard of the Nashville prison on August 14, 1863. With about five minutes remaining before Reynolds was dropped, a courier appeared who dashed into the midst of the guard and shouted news of a respite.[598] The general had given him three days.

Reynolds was hanged on August 17, 1863.[599] On the gallows, Reynolds said the sentence was fair and the cause of the murder was "the monster intemperance," and he warned his fellow soldiers to "beware of its meshes."[600]

Henry McLean, white, age 19. *Desertion and theft.*

Private McLean joined Battery C, 2nd Illinois Light Artillery at Paducah, Kentucky, on July 10, 1862. On December 22, 1862, he entered the home of a citizen near Bucksnort, Tennessee, and stole a gold locket, six hundred dollars and other personal articles.[601]

McLean bragged to his captain about his catch. The captain took the locket from him and said he would try to locate the owner. An investigation showed McLean had also stolen bedding, clothing and meat. He was arrested on December 24 and charged with robbery. He was hung by his thumbs until he told where the money was hidden. After hanging an hour and one-half, he told where the money could be found, in a rolled-up shirt hidden in a caisson. It was not there and was never found.

During the court-martial he admitted he had served two years in the Iowa penitentiary. He said he had once killed a man in a knifing, but blamed his conduct on the loss of his parents at an early age. McLean escaped from custody on December 27, 1862. The date of his recapture is unknown. He was court-martialed on January 22, 1863, at Fort Heiman, Kentucky, and ordered shot. The sentence was approved by the president and he was shot on August 25, 1863, at Fort Donelson in Stewart County.[602]

William Jasper Whitehead, white, age 20. *Desertion.*

Executed under authority of the Confederate States of America.

Private Whitehead joined Company H, 2nd Kentucky Regiment. He had enlisted on May 13, 1862. He deserted during the Battle of Murfreesboro on December 30, 1862. After deserting, he joined Company D, 28th (Gray's) Louisiana. He was court-martialed for desertion on May 1, 1863, but no execution date was set. Somehow he escaped from Camp Taylor on August 21, 1863. Captured, he was shot on September 1, 1863, near Chattanooga.[603]

Jabez R. Rhodes, white, age 38. *Advising soldiers to desert; making false muster.*

William H. White, white, age unknown. *Quitting guard; advising desertion; corresponding with the enemy.*

J.P. Pledger, white, age unknown. *Unknown crime.*

Executed under authority of the Confederate States of America.

Captain Rhodes, of the 1st Infantry, Georgia Volunteers, was charged with knowingly making a false muster, conduct unbecoming an officer, advising a soldier to desert, positive and willful disobedience of orders, and drunkenness on duty. His crimes were committed during January–March 1863 in Bridgeport, Alabama.[604]

On at least two occasions, he allowed a soldier to be discharged upon finding a substitute. When the substitute was provided, he kept the man's bounty (variously $1,800 or $2,000) and told the man it had not been paid, giving the man about twenty dollars to pay his expenses home. Others may have played some role in the scheme. For example, a lieutenant who resigned was reenlisted as a private in another company. Captain Rhodes likewise encouraged at least two of his men to desert by telling them the bounty had not been paid. His willful disobedience was violation of General Orders No. 29, which allowed only one substitute per month in each company.[605]

A contemporary account said, "His offence consisted of having encouraged men of his own command to desert and receiving men as substitutes, knowing them to belong to the service, and then discharging them for a bonus."[606] The court-martial convicted him on all charges except embezzlement.[607] The court-martial returned its verdict on August 30, 1863, while Bragg's army was near Chattanooga, and he was shot there at noon on September 4, 1863.[608]

While the accounts of Rhodes's wrongdoing differ, there is no conflict about the details of his death. He walked to the execution spot with a firm step, agreed to the justice of his sentence, "manifested but little concern, and died without a struggle."[609] Until recent times, Capt. Rhodes was generally thought to be the only Confederate officer executed for wrongdoing.

No details are available about the crime for which Pledger was executed on the same day as Rhodes. He was probably a civilian.

Also executed was Lt. William H. White, Company C, 4th Georgia Cavalry (Col. Isaac W. Avery's), General John A. Wharton's Division. He was charged with advising Private William White, Private James White (both probably related to him) and Private W.H. Nabors to desert at various times between May 1, 1863, and June 11, 1863. He was charged with quitting his guard at Cross Keys, Tennessee, on June 14, 1863. He was also charged with failing to follow an order to take a squad of men and post them as pickets at that time and place. He was charged with having correspondence with the enemy on July 14, 1863, and other times prior to July 21, 1863. He corresponded with Col. George W. Bridges and Brig. Gen. R.S. Granger at those times.

Lt. White was tried by a court-martial on August 13, 1863, and found guilty on August 22. General Bragg ordered White executed but he was not executed until September 4, 1863.[610] At least twenty Union Army officers were sentenced to death during the Civil War. All were commuted or escaped and none was executed.[611]

Henry Roberts, white, age 23. *Desertion.*

Executed under authority of the Confederate States of America.

Private Roberts was a member of Company K, 26th Tennessee Infantry (D.H. Hill's Corps), Army of Tennessee. He had enlisted on February 19, 1863, at Bristol. He deserted from Tullahoma on July 1, 1863. On September 26, 1863, he was captured in a skirmish after the Battle of Chickamauga wearing a blue uniform. His court-martial was irregularly formed, more akin to a drumhead court-martial. Kneeling beside his coffin, he was executed by musketry on September 28, 1863, three miles outside Chattanooga.[612] Roberts fell "limp as a rag," and a sergeant came forward and fired a pistol coup de grace.[613]

William R. Silvey, white, age 22. *Desertion.*

William Franklin Dabney, white, age 20. *Desertion.*

Abraham Hamilton, white, age 20. *Desertion.*

Executed under authority of the Confederate States of America.

William R. Silvey and another man were on their way from Roane County to Kentucky to join the Federal army when they were arrested by Confederate soldiers. Both men agreed to join the Confederate army as a way of escaping the draft. They enlisted in an unspecified Confederate unit known only as Company K, at Winter's Gap, Tennessee, on February 27, 1863. They deserted at Winter's Gap on April 9, 1863, and enlisted in Company B, 2nd Tennessee (Union), at Stanford, Kentucky, on April 15, 1863. Silvey was a wagoner. Many of his regiment were captured by Confederate forces on November 6, 1863, near Rogersville. Silvey and the two others were "court-martialed and shot at the stake" at Blountville, Sullivan County, on November 13, 1863.[614]

Private William Franklin Dabney came out of a Knoxville saloon on January 16, 1862, somewhat intoxicated and was immediately surrounded by Confederate soldiers. To escape arrest and imprisonment in Alabama, he agreed to join the Confederate army. A few days later he deserted and joined the 2nd Tennessee (Union) at Somerset, Kentucky, on February 2, 1862. He was the regimental bugler and was captured by the Confederates along with Silvey and Hamilton.[615]

Private Abraham Hamilton, a Sullivan County native, was arrested at his home on October 25, 1862, and threatened into joining the Confederate forces. He was never assigned to a regiment, but was assigned to a military hospital in Knoxville. He deserted on Christmas Day, 1862, and joined Company F, 2nd Tennessee (Union) in Kentucky on January 16, 1863. He was among those captured by Confederate forces in November 1863. Accounts differ on the details of his shooting, most saying that he was executed alongside Silvey and Dabney. His fellow soldiers called him Lincoln because he looked like the president.

These executions were designed as a lesson to others, including Silvey's family members. Two other men named Silvey (James M. and Peter) had enlisted in the Confederate army at Winter's Gap in September and November 1862. James was reported as present for duty only until June 30, 1863. James was reported absent without leave from November 1863 to February 1864, and by April 1864 he was reported as "sick in enemy's lines."

Erastus C. Daley (aka Erastus C. Daily), white, age 30. *Desertion.*
Valentine Benjamin (aka Benjamin Valentine; also Balentine, Volentine, Volatine), white, age 45. *Desertion.*

Private Erastus Daley had enlisted on August 5, 1862, and was mustered into service at Chicago on September 4, 1862, joining what would become Company D, 88th Illinois Infantry. His regiment was sent south and was pursuing Baxton Bragg's army when he deserted near Harrodsburg, Kentucky, on October 13, 1862. Two weeks later, a friend at Polo, Ogle County, Illinois, wrote to his commanding officer that Daley was very ill and was recovering at the friend's home. The letter explained that he had been picked up by the rear guard and sent to a hospital. According to the letter, the hospital surgeon told him to find a private house in which to recover because the hospital was full. That prompted Daley to go home to get well and he ended up at the friend's house. The letter asked for a furlough and explained that Daley's gun, knapsack and personal items had been left with a member of his company. The letter promised that Daley "would soon be around."

Daley did not join his company. He was arrested by the provost marshal at the friend's house on August 6, 1863. Daley went before a court-martial on August 25, 1863, at Bridgeport, Alabama. He raised the defense that he had not actually completed the enlistment process and was never sworn into service and had never received his bounty.[616]

Private Valentine Benjamin had enlisted on July 1, 1861, and was mustered into service on September 13, 1861, at Chicago in what was later known as Company C, 44th Infantry Regiment. He was the regimental carpenter. On May 27, 1862, Private Benjamin deserted at Hamburg Landing, Tennessee, as the regiment was advancing toward battle at Corinth, Mississippi.

On June 11, 1862, his company commander wrote the Provost Marshal in Chicago that Benjamin was working his trade (carpentry) there and to go to a hospital where another man would help identify Benjamin. It is not clear when he was returned. Private Benjamin went before a court-martial at Camp Harrington, Alabama, on August 17, 1863. Private Benjamin offered the court a statement, prepared by a lawyer, emphasizing his good character and asking for mercy.[617]

By the time Daley's and Benjamin's sentences were approved, the army had moved to Chattanooga. Both men were executed by musketry at the federal encampment there on November 13, 1863. Daley "seated himself upon his coffin, opened his shirt-bosom, and tapped his fingers on his heart, to show the marksmen where to direct their aim."[618] "There were five holes in Daley's breast very near the spot he had directed the marksmen to aim at; one bullet, however, passed through his neck, cutting the jugular vein, from which the blood flowed profusely."[619]

Lawson Camp (aka Lawson Kemp), black, age 19. *Rape.*

Private Camp (Kemp) was a member of Company A, 1st Alabama Infantry, A.D. (African Descent).[620] He enlisted on May 1, 1863, and was mustered into service twenty days later. He was promoted to sergeant, but reduced to private for drunkenness and neglect of duty on June 3, 1863. A commanding officer wrote, "This man was a desperate villain. I sent him from Fort Flood, Tennessee to the stockade at Corinth, Mississippi for swindling, with a request that he be kept until I could prefer charges."[621] The company captain personally removed him from the jail.

On November 18, 1863, Camp (Kemp) was engaged in a scouting party five miles from the town of Pocahontas, in Hardeman County, when he came to the home of a Mr. Keith. He asked Ann Keith, age seventeen, and her sister-in-law if there were any men kinfolk around. The girls ran into the house. He followed and they ran out. He laid down his gun and began choking and attempting to rape Ann. Her sister-in-law grabbed his gun. He took it from her and raped Ann in full view of the sister-in-law. The women complained to the federal officers in the vicinity and Camp was quickly tried by court-martial and sentenced to be hanged.[622]

A contemporary account tells what happened next: "Colonel Fielding Hurst, 6th Tennessee cavalry,[623] commanding the post, approved the sentence, and ordered the execution to take place at 8 o'clock [November 19, 1863] but afterward commuted the sentence to shooting. At the appointed time the 1st Alabama was drawn up, and after some very pointed talk from Col. Alexander, 1st Alabama, showing his intention to enforce the strictest discipline, they marched out, and he was shot."[624]

The account concludes: "Twelve muskets were on detail, one loaded with blank cartridge; ten balls were lodged in his body. He expired without a struggle, and bore his fate with a great deal of fortitude, not seeming to be affected at all. He has always been a bad, unruly man, and richly merited his punishment. The effect, it is hoped, will be most salutary. The young lady upon whom he committed the deed bore an excellent character."[625]

Samuel C. Davis, white, age 21. *Spying.*

The most famous execution in Tennessee history was the hanging of Sam Davis on a hill in Pulaski, Giles County, on November 27, 1863. At one time, every schoolchild in Tennessee was taught the story of Sam Davis.[626] A statue of Davis, sometimes known as the "Boy Hero of the Confederacy," stands on the capitol grounds in Nashville, facing south.[627] His ancestral home (Sam Davis Home), in Rutherford County, Tennessee, was purchased by the state in 1927. The place was once known as the Shrine of the Confederacy, after a small shrine built there by the United Daughters of the Confederacy.

Davis was an eighteen-year-old student at a military school in Nashville when the war broke out. He enlisted in Company D, 1st (Field's) Tennessee regiment, Army of Tennessee, saw service in the Cheat Mountain campaign, was ordered back to Tennessee to help relieve Ft. Donelson (arriving too late), apparently fought at Shiloh and was wounded at Perryville on October 8, 1862.[628]

Sam Davis's unit was camped at Shelbyville with Gen. Braxton Bragg's army, when in April 1863 he was placed on detached duty. He became a member of a Confederate cavalry group of about forty which spied on Union troop movements in middle Tennessee. It was called Coleman's Scouts.[629]

There remains a dispute about what Davis was wearing when he was captured. Most insist Davis was wearing what many people would call a Confederate "uniform," gray pants and short gray jacket, over which he wore a blue Union coat that had been died with butternut, rendering it black. His uniform bore no military insignia and he wore a black brimmed hat (not a cap) of civilian nature, but favored by most soldiers in the Army of Tennessee. R.S. King, one of the scouts who captured Davis, was asked by the judge advocate, "Did he wear the uniform of the Confederate Army?" He answered, "Yes, sir, he did."[630] The officer in command, Gen. Dodge, said that Davis was wearing a "faded Federal coat, an army soft hat, and top-boots." Others say he was wearing a "mixed uniform," part blue and part gray.[631] All agree that the federal buttons had not been removed from the coat.

General Grenville M. Dodge, commanding the "west wing of the 16th Army," was headquartered at Pulaski and forces were being marshaled to push east. Both sides needed intelligence on troop size and movement. Gen. Dodge's own scouts were dressed as Confederates or civilians. They were under the command of a Mississippi native, a civilian. He was L.H. Naron, known as "Captain Chickasaw." On November 20, 1863, two scouts, posing as Confederate conscription agents, encountered Davis on Lamb's Ferry Road, near Minor Hill, in Giles County. Davis carried a message intended for Gen. Bragg. Most accounts suggest that Captain Coleman himself had given Davis the critical information at a rendezvous the night before. Davis was behind federal lines and carried a pass from Captain Coleman. Davis rode with the pair willingly, having been tricked into thinking they were allies.

The message Davis carried contained precise information about troop strength and positions in the Pulaski area. The message was carried in a hollowed-out boot heel. In a saddlebag he carried personal mail, along with personal items such as toothbrushes and recent newspapers. When it became clear to Davis that he was being carried toward the federal camp, not away from it, he attempted to escape, but one of the federal scouts grabbed his horse's bridle. A gun was leveled at Davis and he was soon placed in the jail at Pulaski.

The boot-heel message was soon discovered and Davis was immediately brought before Gen. Dodge. The general offered Davis his freedom if he would tell how to locate Coleman so he could "ascertain, if possible, who was furnishing information so accurate and valuable to General Bragg."[632] Davis demurred. General Dodge said he pleaded "with all the power I possessed to give me some chance to save his life." Finally, Davis said, "I know, General, that I will have to die; but I will not tell where I got the information, and there is no power on earth that can make me tell. You are doing your duty as a soldier, and if I have to die I shall be doing my duty to God and my country."[633]

General Grenville M. Dodge brought charges against Davis under a general orders court-martial, which meant Davis was tried before a military commission.[634] It was convened on November 25, 1863. Davis pled guilty to carrying the mail, but not guilty to spying. The military commission found him guilty on both charges. He was ordered hanged on November 27, 1863, and died that day.

General Dodge was proud of the speedy manner in which the case was handled. He wrote his commanding general, "I have the honor to enclose General Orders No. 74. I tried, convicted and hung the man in three days. I considered it our safest policy to act promptly; and did not send up the record from the fact, this I supposed the General would prefer that I should act in such cases, and not wait the delay necessarily occasioned by sending the record for his approval, with the present uncertainty of its speedily reaching his Head Quarters."[635]

General Dodge was angry because so many locals still supported the Confederacy, so he ordered Davis hanged on a hill overlooking the town.[636] When townsfolk complained, he replied, "I want him hung where you all can see him. There are more of you guilty of his crime — I know it — and if I ever get my hands upon you, damned you, I'll hang you upon the same gallows."[637]

Visited by townsfolk the night before his execution, Davis insisted he was not a spy, rather a scout, and was wearing the same clothes, all gray, that he was wearing for the visitors. He cried a little, as well.

Taken to the gallows in a wagon sitting on his coffin, Davis was wearing his hat, and his hands were tied to prevent any chance of escape. It was ten o'clock. Five minutes later he stepped from the wagon and sat on a bench beneath the gallows. He turned to Captain Armstrong, in charge of the hanging, and asked how long he had to live. The captain said fifteen minutes. At this point he asked what had happened recently in Bragg's command, which had faced a loss.[638] Davis said he was sorry to hear it, and said, "We would have to fight the rest of the battles alone."[639] Here is what was said.

> *Capt. Armstrong:* "I am sorry to be compelled to perform this painful duty."
>
> *Prisoner* (with a smile): "It does not hurt me, Captain: I am innocent, though I am prepared to die, and do not think hard of it."

At this time, Captain Chickasaw arrived on horseback and spoke to Davis, reminding him again that his life would be spared if he revealed the source of his information.

Said the newspaper report, "Captain Chickasaw then asked the prisoner if it would not have been better for him to have accepted his offer of life, upon the disclosure of facts in his possession when the prisoner answered with much indignation: 'Do you suppose I would betray a friend? No, sir, I would die a thousand times first!'[640] He was questioned upon other matters, but refused to give any information, which could be of service."[641]

Naron's own account, written in 1865, was this: "When he was taken to the scaffold I was permitted to talk to him. I addressed him thus: 'Davis, you are not the man that should be hung, and if you would yet tell me who General Bragg's chief of scouts was, so I might capture him, your life would yet be spared.' He looked me steadily in the eye and said, 'Do you suppose, were I your friend, that I would betray you?' I told him I did not know, but life was sweet to all men. His reply to this was: 'Sir, if you think I am that kind of man you have missed your mark. You may hang me a thousand times and I would not betray my friends.'"[642]

Most accounts of the execution suggest that Captain Coleman was actually in the Pulaski jail, having been brought in the same day as Davis, but under disguise as a civilian named H.B. Shaw, who traveled about selling herbs. Accounts suggest that Coleman/Shaw and another scout, Joshua Brown, were ordered transferred to a Northern prison. On the way, Captain Coleman jumped to freedom from the moving train outside Louisville.

The newspaper account of the Davis execution continued: "The prisoner then mounted the scaffold, accompanied by the chaplain, James Young, whom he requested to pray with him at his execution. The prisoner then stepped upon the trap; the rope was adjusted about his neck, and the cap drawn over his head. In a moment, the trap was sprung, and the prisoner fell suspended in the air."[643]

The reporter concluded, "So fell one who the fate of war cut down in early youth, and who exhibited traits of character which, under other circumstances, might have made him a valuable friend and member of society."[644]

The newspaper reporter said, "For a few moments he struggled with his hands and feet; this was succeeded by a slight quivering of the body, which ceased at three and a half minutes from the time he fell. After being suspended seventeen and a half minutes, the officiating surgeon (D.W. Voyles, 68th Indiana) pronounced the prisoner dead and he was cut down and placed in his coffin. It was supposed, from the protracted animation which the prisoner exhibited, the fall had not broken his neck, and that he died by strangulation, but upon subsequent examination, his neck was found to be completely broken."[645]

Lt. George Bargus, 64th Illinois, described the execution in his diary:

> It is a Lovely Morning the Sun shines Bright and the air is just Cool Enough to make it both Healthy and comfortable yet by the Laws of Nations a fellow human being must be hurried to Eternity by hanging, his name is Samuel Davis a member of Colemans Scouts he has been convicted of being a spy found Guilty and hung Col. [Madison] Miller of the 18th Mo was President of the Court that sentenced him he behaved very well and showed a great deal of Courage he stepped out of the Wagon and Marched up to the Scaffold Mounted it and would have put his own head in the noose without any help but was prevented by Capt. [William F.] Armstrong who took of [off] his hat and then a Chaplain Made a long Prayer which sounded to me a great Deal more like abusing the Man than Praying for him after the Prayer was ended the Provost Marshal put a white bag over the head of the Prisoner arraingned the Rope Dismounted the scaffold when the drop was [illegible word] the Prisoner launched into Eternity there are two more in the Guard house that are guilty of the same offence and I presume will be hung we are going to have a Skirmish Drill this afternoon.[646]

The next day Bargus wrote, "It Rained all night and this morning it is very Disagreeable. Capt. Armstrong eat Dinner with us to-day and he informed us that the Prisoner Davis that was hung yesterday was offered his life on the scaffold if he would answer certain questions but said questions involved the Betrayal of a Friend and he Absolutely Refused to Purchase his life by sacrificing that of his friend. Such Courage was worthy a Better Cause."[647]

On April 2, 1864, at a meeting of the "Rutherford Rifles," composed of members of the 1st Tennessee Regiment, a "Tribute of Respect" was prepared and sent to the press. Under the direction of Lt. Hardy Murfree, chairman, and T.M. King, secretary, the memorial condemned the death of their former comrade at the "hands of the hated vandal foe of his country" for the "alleged crime of being a spy." The group "treasure with solace and admiration that sublime attitude assumed by him in that sad hour to his ignorant executioners, in refusing and disdainfully declining to purchase dear life itself at the price of betraying a friend."[648] The document called for an investigation (none was ever done), expressed condolence to his parents and siblings, and called Davis "a brave and heroic martyr of the cause."[649]

The story of Sam Davis became a focal point in the collective history of the Confederacy because the editor of the magazine *Confederate Veteran* saw Davis as the model of Southern youth lost during the Civil War. In the 1890s editor Sumner A. Cunningham, himself a lackluster Confederate soldier, worked tirelessly to promote the image of Sam Davis, who in time became known as the "Boy Hero of the Confederacy." Cunningham was largely responsible for raising money for the statue of Davis that stands on the grounds of the Tennessee capitol.

Another account of the Davis execution confirms his statement about boys having to fight without him, and says he was asked three times if he would name the source of his information. The implication was that he might be given his horse, his side arm and a pass if he did. Davis replied, "I would rather die a thousand deaths."[650] In time, with Cunningham's editing, the statement became, "I would rather die a thousand deaths than to betray a friend." In time, the coat Davis wore, which he gave to Chaplain Young, was returned to Tennessee. The soldier who pulled the trap came forward to say Davis died manfully.[651]

Likewise, in time it was argued that Sam's execution was wrongful because the charges were defective.[652] The specifications failed to state that he was dressed in disguise, a prerequisite for the charge of spying. Davis vigorously denied he was a spy, saying rather he was a scout whose duties include carrying messages, and was therefore a prisoner of war because he was wearing a uniform. However, a General Orders from the Department of the Ohio said that carriers of secret mail and anyone who protects rebels would be treated as a spy.[653] Finally, it was asserted that because the records in his trial were not forwarded to Gen. Dodge's commanding general until after Sam's death, or to the War Department in Washington, that the proceeding was entirely without the law.

The execution was witnessed by several hundred people, including six companies of Union troops, along with numerous frowning civilians. Davis was quickly buried in a shallow grave. Later, his body was moved to his ancestral home, near which was built the Shrine of the Confederacy. The Sam Davis Home has taken on the role of an interpreter of Southern history and the Shrine has taken a secondary role today. The historiography of Sam Davis continues to the present day.[654]

Captain Coleman's (Henry B. Shaw) seemingly

charmed life came to a tragic end. He returned to the river after the war and was half-owner of the steamer *David White*. Its boiler exploded near Vicksburg on February 16, 1867, killing him and several others, including John Davis, brother of Sam Davis.

James Roll, white, age 32. *Desertion.*

Private James Roll was a member of Company H, 23rd Kentucky Infantry. On August 8, 1862, his regiment was ordered to march from Murfreesboro to McMinnville. Roll told his captain that he had been on picket duty the night before and was physically unable to make the march. He was told to continue. "The march was hard, warm, and dusty and a great many men fell out."[655] One of these was Private Roll.

A witness said Roll told him he had been captured by Forrest's men and paroled. He came to the witness, an officer, unobserved, at Cincinnati and asked whether he should report to Camp Chase and was told to do so. This was October 15, 1862. Roll said he had soldiered long enough and said he would report by letter.[656] Roll was also seen at his home in Covington, Kentucky, in October 1862. He was arrested by bounty hunters on October 28, 1863. They received ten dollars for the arrest and another eight and one-half dollars for transporting him to Chattanooga. At the court-martial Roll made no statement. He was ordered shot on December 4, 1863.

Private James Roll was shot in front of his regiment on December 4, 1863, near Chattanooga. His record was received at the Judge Advocate General's office on February 1, 1864.

L.L. Elkines (aka L.L. Elkins and B.F. Elkins), white, age 23. *Desertion.*

Executed under authority of the Confederate States of America.

Private Elkines was a member of Company C, 18th Tennessee. He had joined the army on May 23, 1861, at Murfreesboro. He was captured in enemy ranks near Lookout Mountain on October 27, 1863. He was hanged there on December 10, 1863.[657]

1864

Ephraim Shelby Dodd (aka E.S. Dodd), white, age 24. *Spying.*

The crime was committed between December 1 and 18, 1863, on the road from Maryville to Sevierville, in Sevier County. The charge against Dodd was: "Being found and apprehended within our lines as a spy." The specifications against Dodd were two. First, he disguised himself as belonging to the United States military and sought to procure information concerning the strength and position of United States forces, and did procure such information. Second, that he was secreted within federal lines, and in the vicinity of federal pickets, disguised in a United States uniform.[658]

Dodd was a private in Company D, 8th Texas Cavalry (Terry's Texas Rangers). His own words suggest he was a private, but he never expressly stated his rank.[659] Dodd's case is among the few Tennessee executions mentioned in the Official Records of the Civil War, but without any factual details.[660]

Dodd was arrested on December 18, 1863, and tried before a general court-martial beginning on December 23. The court met continuously (including Christmas Day), reaching its decision on December 28.

Dodd explained to his captors and the court that he was the wagon master of his company and had gotten separated from it. He was seeking to rejoin Wheeler's cavalry forces, with two other Confederate soldiers, and except for the blue overcoat which was clearly a Union uniform, was always dressed as a Confederate soldier. He and his companions had been given the names of "Southern men" and he had stopped at their houses to seek food and directions. After getting directions at the last house, he became lost and was found in "Timothy Chandler's Cow-house."[661]

Crucial to the government's case was a diary Dodd kept. He would not have been executed but for it. The diary was offered at the trial but its contents were not discussed. It was included in the record but did not resurface until 1914.[662]

Dodd questioned the officer who had arrested him, "Was there any pickets on the road anywhere near where I was captured?" The response: "There was a good many soldiers around and from that fact it was thought unnecessary to have pickets."[663] Dodd's argument was that he was not within Union lines because the rules of war recognize only lines protected by pickets.

He argued, "I am arraigned before you, as being found and apprehended within your lines as a spy. Inside the lines, I understand to be inside the pickets. The lines of an Army do not extend beyond the pickets, if outside the pickets you may be in the vicinity of the lines and yet not in them. I have proved by Lieut. Criswell that there were no pickets on the road. There were none probably near than 12 or 15 miles of where I was captured, as the Troops from above had all come down the day before."[664]

The witnesses against Dodd were members of the Home Guard who arrested him and a few citizens where he stopped. At each house he asked if there were any federal troops ahead. All the witnesses said he was dressed in the Union army overcoat, usually buttoned to the top. The few witnesses who saw his companions described one as dressed as a Confederate soldier and the other as a civilian.

Dodd vigorously denied spying. Admitting he wore the overcoat, he insisted the rest of his clothing was official Confederate issue, including the blue pants. He explained that they had been issued to him and most other Confederate soldiers from captured Union stores because the Confederacy lacked clothing.

He argued to the court, "What does it take to constitute a Rebel Spy? A Texas Ranger dressed in a gray jacket, blue pants (which is the prescribed uniform of the Confederate States) with a Mexican hat and Texas Star, armed with a gun and a six shooter, and a Yankee overcoat on, cut off from his command and making his way through to it." He concluded, "Gentlemen, I leave the case with you only asking you to *act upon the square with me.*"[665]

The court-martial "acted upon the square" and found Dodd not guilty of both counts. Dodd wrote to his father on December 31, 1863, "I was tried by the court-martial as a spy, but the charge and specifications could not be sustained."[666] The decision did not rest well with Commanding General Foster. His adjutant wrote to the court-martial, "The General Commanding returns to the Court Martial the proceedings in the case of E.S. Dodd accused of being a spy on the ground that the verdict is contrary to the evidence. The record is defective in not showing the contents of the Diary in the possession of the prisoner to which reference is made by witness for the prosecution and by the prisoner in his defense."[667]

The memorandum explained that Home Guards "were part of our forces and paid by the Government as officers and soldiers." "The General Commanding desires to impress upon the Court that our lines include any portions of the Country occupied and protected by U.S. Troops and that the Home Guards organized by Gen. Burnside is an important element of the force of the United States."[668]

The memorandum concluded, "Unless officers and soldiers of the enemy found within our lines seeking information in the U.S. uniform are punished, it gives the enemy an advantage which is not recognized by the rules of war."

The court-martial reconvened on January 1, 1864, for reconsideration and the next day, without taking any more evidence or explaining its thinking, found Dodd guilty on both counts and ordered him hanged "at such time and place as the Commanding General may direct." On January 5 the Commanding General approved the sentence and ordered Dodd hanged on January 8, 1864. Dodd wrote his parents, "Do not grieve for me, dear parents, for I am leaving a world of sin and misery for one of perfect bliss. I can say no more. Your loving son, E.S. Dodd."[669]

Numerous townsfolk, including some known Unionists, petitioned for Dodd's life. But Gen. Foster was determined. Two incidents had hardened him. After Longstreet aborted his siege of Knoxville, he left in his abandoned lines two Yankee spies dangling at the ends of hanging ropes.[670] "It never ought to have been done," wrote a young female diarist, who befriended Dodd. She continued, "I think they are expecting him [Longstreet] in here and that is one reason Mr. Dodd's sentence is to be carried into execution so soon. They are afraid of his being rescued."[671]

An historian explained that the day Dodd was executed Gen. Foster complained about a large number of Union pickets and outposts recently "overpowered and captured by the enemy's troops, disguised as Federal soldiers." He ordered commanders "to cause to be shot dead all the rebel officers and soldiers (wearing the uniform of the U.S. Army) captured within our lines." General Foster also forwarded a copy of the proceedings and findings of Dodd's case to Gen. Longstreet, a clear warning to the rebel chieftain.[672]

Dodd was executed on January 8, 1864. Snow covered the ground as Dodd's wagon was drawn through the streets of Knoxville. He was seated on his coffin wearing his Texas Ranger hat and a serape. On the gallows, a federal officer looked him in the eye and asked again if he was a spy. Dodd replied, "I die innocent of the charge against me."[673]

Dodd was hanged at the same location as Henry Harmon and his son, Jacob Harmon, Jr., the bridge burners. The transaction was cruelly similar. The trap was released at 11:00 A.M. and Dodd plunged downward, the rope breaking. Writhing in agony, he whispered, "Release me quick, if you please."[674] The soldiers crowded around, rubbed and rolled his body for fifteen minutes to make sure his blood was circulating so he could walk. In excruciating pain from torn muscles and weakened by the fall, he was assisted in standing on the gallows while the rope was placed a second time.[675] He died at 11:30.

A reporter for the *Boston Evening Transcript* reported the common belief that the diary contained lists of Union forces and officers, and that Dodd admitted he had been a spy for two years. The reporter said the information was wrong. "There was little or nothing in his diary to incriminate him; and I saw a touching and yet manly letter written by him to his relatives, in which he affirms, as a dying man, his innocence of everything except reckless imprudence."[676]

The reporter concluded, "The impression at Knoxville was, that he was not guilty enough to deserve death, and that his execution was not so much a punishment as a necessary act of retaliation; since the rebels had recently murdered, in the most brutal manner a Federal soldier belonging to an Indiana regiment, who should have been held a prisoner of war. These are not important matters; but they serve to show how difficult it is to be accurate."[677]

E.S. Dodd's death was reported across the Confederacy in the form of a letter written by the Presbyterian minister, the Rev. Joseph H. Martin, who baptized him the day before his execution and stood with him near the gallows. Martin wrote that Dodd was born in Lancaster County, Kentucky, and had gone to Texas four years earlier.[678] Dodd was teaching school when the war broke out and was apparently in another regiment when he joined Terry's Texas Rangers on the march on December 4, 1862.

Before his death, he wrote six letters: one to his father in Kentucky, one to his grandfather in Mississippi, one to a Mr. Maxwell, near Austin, Texas, and the others to persons in Texas and Mississippi. The Chaplain of the Rangers, Robert F. Bunting, told Dodd's story as well. He explained that Dodd was a "bright Mason" who called upon the members of that order to assist him after he was arrested. According to Bunting, they did all they could. Three federal chaplains and the Rev. Martin (later sent through lines) thought he was innocent of spying. "The guards who were with him were of the same opinion."[679]

What can be made of Dodd's assertion he was only guilty of "reckless imprudence"? Amid his attacking Union wagons, grabbing food wherever he found it, dodging Union attacks, and moving though Middle Tennessee in December rains, he had time for other matters. On December 4, 1863, he wrote, "I took supper there but did not know where I was until the young ladies came down. Miss Mollie came in glad to see me, was then introduced to Miss Mollie Turner and Miss Alice Hord, staid till 11 o'clock, time passed very pleasantly. Came on to Camp."[680]

George Smith, white, age unknown. *Desertion. Executed under authority of the Confederate States of America.*

The details of his desertion are unknown. Private George Smith, Company A, 43rd Alabama, was shot by musketry on February 6, 1864, near Morristown in Hamblen County.[681]

Joseph Cornell, white, age unknown. *Desertion.*

Private Cornell was a member of Company I of the 105th New York Infantry. He deserted the company near Frederick, Maryland, on June 30, 1863, and was returned to the company on July 5, 1863, having avoided the Battle of Gettysburg. He was found traveling as fast as he could away from his regiment. He deserted the second time on July 14, 1863, near Fairplay (or Falling Waters), Missouri, and was returned to his company on December 17, 1863.

By the time of his court-martial on January 13, 1864, his regiment was camped near Tullahoma, Franklin County. He stood mute before the court-martial, which ordered him shot. This was carried out in front of his division on February 26, 1864.[682]

Richard H. Carney (aka Dick Carney), white, age 27. *Murder.*

The crime was committed about 9:30 P.M. on June 25, 1863, on the bank of the Red River in Montgomery County near a fish trap. The land was leased by the shooter. It was owned by the estate of his recently deceased uncle, Harry Carney. The fish trap had been built six years earlier by Harry Carney, a man named Pride, and the victim, Lawson P. Murphy, white, age thirty. Murphy kept it in repair.[683]

Prior to the shooting, Dick Carney had complained that Murphy, a wealthy man, who served as administrator of Harry Carney's estate, had been slow in closing the estate despite knowing that Dick's wife would be a beneficiary.[684] He also complained that the fish trap was his, since he leased the land, but Murphy had continued to take fish from the trap and had allowed his slaves to get fish from it. He had told another cousin, James Carney, that he had both a squirrel gun and a pistol and he intended to keep "varmints" away from the trap.

The night of the shooting Murphy walked down the river bank toward the trap. Carney, sitting under a tree with the rifle on his lap, yelled, "Halt!" Murphy replied, "Halt, the devil, Dick! I am going down to get some fish!"[685] Carney, with the rifle aimed at Murphy, replied, "Lawson Murphy, I don't know what to make of you anyhow!" as Murphy approached.

When Murphy was ten steps away, Carney fired the rifle, which was loaded with buckshot. Murphy received seven or eight wounds, including at least two that penetrated his lungs. He staggered and Carney ran away. Then Carney turned and shot a pistol in his direction. The bullet missed. Carney ran to his father's house and explained what happened.

There were two other people at the fish trap at the time. One was a Negro boy and the other was assumed to be Wright B. Carney (Richard's father), who was tried as an aider and abettor but was acquitted. The acquittal came mid-trial and the father testified for his son.

The facts of the shooting were heard by two doctors who attended Murphy and were treated as a dying declaration. Murphy did not recognize anyone else at the trap. Murphy died forty-five hours after he was shot. When asked on his deathbed if Carney had any grounds for the shooting, if they had any previous difficulty, Murphy replied, "None in the world; they had no previous difficulty."[686]

Cousin James Carney, age nineteen, lived with Lawson Murphy, his legal guardian.[687] James testified, "Two days before Lawson Murphy was shot I heard Richard Carney, the prisoner, say that his father Wright Carney had told him whenever Lawson Murphy came to the trap and attempted to go on it to halt him and if he did not stop to shoot him, and that he intended to do it, in the same conversation. He showed me a gun and pistol, which he said were both loaded, and had water proof caps on them and did not think either would flicker. About two or three days previous to this he also stated to me that he or Lawson Murphy would be hurt at that trap."[688]

The cousin said, "From my numerous conversations with the prisoner Richard Carney I know that his feeling toward Murphy had been of an angry and hostile character for six or eight months, previous to the shooting."[689]

The night before the shooting, cousin James told Dick Carney, "Uncle Lawson had said that if he found Dick near the fish trap he would take the gun and 'wear it out on him' or throw it in the river." The reason given was that "uncle Lawson had heard he had threatened to shoot his negroes at the trap."[690]

Another witness heard Carney say that two-legged varmints were taking fish and he intended to stop it. One was a "big dog among big dogs."[691] Another witness said he had told Carney he had a claim against the Harry Carney estate, to which Carney said the estate owed him twenty-five dollars but Lawson Murphy would not pay it.[692]

Proof showed that Dick Carney was a "delicate and weak man" because he has been "afflicted a good deal" and suffered a very serious hand injury several months earlier which had caused his hand to wither.[693]

The case was tried before a military commission at the military camp near Clarksville beginning August 4, 1863, because martial law had been declared in the area and the civil courts were closed. The commission allowed a private lawyer to serve as a special prosecutor and he offered a lengthy written closing argument summarizing the case. Both sides agreed Tennessee law applied and the special prosecutor explained the facts showed motive, malice and the criminal act. Carney's prior anger at the victim, the several threats, and the act of shooting him with a pistol were the important issues. Another issue raised in testimony but not argued by either side was the fact that Murphy's estate would benefit Richard Carney's wife — if Murphy died without a will, which he did.

Richard Carney and his father were defended by A.O.P. Nicholson, one of the best lawyers in the state. He became the leader of the Tennessee Constitutional Convention in 1869 and the chief justice of the Tennessee Supreme Court in 1870. Nicholson's argument said Murphy was a trespasser because the land (and fish trap) were rightfully in the possession of the defendant.

Furthermore, Dick Carney had warned Murphy not to come closer and that Murphy had actually threatened Carney, who was "weak and afflicted," so that he shot in self-defense.

The military commission found Carney guilty and ordered him hanged. The evidence was summarized by Advocate General Holt as clearly supporting the commission's finding. The file bears the notation, "Sentence approved. A. Lincoln." It is dated February 9, 1864.

An affidavit signed by several Carney relatives asked the president to reconsider the case because the defendant was a poor loyal subject and Murphy had been a wealthy supporter of the rebellion. Holt wrote the affidavit added nothing to change his opinion about the case and he apparently declined to pass it along to the president.

Richard Carney was hanged at the main prison in Nashville on April 17, 1864.

John W. Johnson, white, age unknown. *Bushwhacking and murder.*

The crime was committed about 8:00 P.M. on September 4, 1863, on a rural road three miles north of the village of Hillsboro, in Coffee County. Before the war, Johnson had been a circuit-riding minister and had served as a chaplain in the Confederate Army. At this time, he was out of service and was home helping with the harvest. He was one of five men who captured two Union soldiers, apparently stragglers, and shot one of them, Private Abner Tull, a member of Company C, 13th Michigan Infantry. The body was found the next day where the other soldier said Tull fell. It was "literally riddled with bullets and his face all shot away."[694]

The other soldier, named Wiley, said that Johnson was among the five heavily armed men who captured him and Private Tull. The pair was made to take off their clothes, abandon their possessions and weapons, then told to leave. After the pair got about three rods away, the bushwhackers began shooting. Tull fell with a groan. Wiley made an abrupt turn and escaped. He returned the next day with scouts. They examined footprints and determined one was unusually long, and Johnson was immediately implicated.

Within a week Home Guards had surrounded a house where Johnson and a man named Anderson were barricaded. They refused to surrender, saying they had done nothing wrong, but attempted to negotiate. Johnson promised he would name the actual shooter. They gave up when persuaded they would get a fair trial.

Johnson was tried before a military commission on September 12, 1863, at the federal camp at Murfreesboro.[695] Johnson admitted he was a secessionist and had served in the Confederate Army. He offered a dual defense. First, he was not a member of the five-man bushwhacking group and shot no one. Second, he was not a bushwhacker. He had this to say about bushwhackers: "No proof of a positive character has been made that I ever reduced the theory of Bushwacking to practice. On the other hand it has always been entertained by me that bushwhacking would bring vice upon citizens without accomplishing any good for our government."[696] He continued, "Bushwackers are generally desperados. My moral character is good. This lessens the probability of my Bushwhacking. If men Bushwack at all they are not likely to wish themselves or friends to suffer for it. Some of my best friends, my Father included, live in the vicinity of the avowed Bushwacking. Can it be supposed that I would be senseless or ungrateful enough to lay a snare for their ruin? And try to get them arrested and their property burned?"[697] However, he felt that actions taken against Union soldiers were properly called guerrilla warfare, if done under authority and command.[698]

Johnson said that it was so dark that Wiley could not see his face, there was no evidence he was armed on the night of the killing, and the shoe print was clearly not his. Wiley did not know how tall Johnson was because he was sitting on a box in the military courtroom when identified. Wrote Johnson, "Men are identified (if identified at all) by features, voices, complexions, eyes, height & make as formations." He asserted, "I was not identified by either or all of these combined. I was not identified at all."[699]

Johnson challenged everything Wiley said such as he "knows my coat and hat." He wrote, "Furthermore, there is nothing remarkable about my hat or coat. One is an old gray jeans and the other is a dilapidated old coon colored hat. Just such as are fashionable in this Confederacy. Viewed through the inky blackness of the night they would not be known by my most intimate friends."[700]

Johnson's defense displayed a prickly nature. "It was testified that Mr. Anderson said that he would not surrender to Rosecran's [*sic*] Army but I have nothing to do with that. I only said that I would fight Moses or anybody before I would surrender to a set of men that were talking about padlocking me. Further those men did not demand a surrender in that genteel manner which they ought. The insulting summons ought to have been hurled back upon them."[701]

Johnson's attempt to portray himself as a gentleman of moral character concluded: "With my thanks as compliments for the gentlemanly manner in which I have been treated by the court since my trial commenced I respectfully submit my defense. So wrote it he. Very Respectfully, John W. Johnson."[702]

Placing his character in evidence may have been Johnson's undoing. In a March 29, 1864, memorandum to President Lincoln, Judge Advocate General Holt wrote, "A neighbor of the prisoner, being asked as to his character for morality and good conduct, answered—'I really can't say what you have been for the last four years. I have understood you were preaching. When I knew you as a boy, you were a good hand at cards; and after you had rode the circuit three years, I understood you were a chaplain in the rebel army twelve months.'"[703]

Holt continued, "A witness called by the prisoner on his defense, testified that the people had not recently had confidence in him, and that he believed he would fire on a prisoner who had surrendered."[704]

Holt continued, "It may not be that the prisoner fired the fatal shots; it is not necessary that this should be proved to make him out guilty of the charge, nor would it be to convict him of murder. But that he was present, aiding and abetting in the cowardly and fiendish crime, by which an unarmed and defenseless soldier of our army was deliberately shot in the back and killed like a dog, is a conclusion from which it is believed that the Court could not escape."

Holt concluded, "The penalty is hanging. The crime is one only to be expiated by the most ignominious death; and the enforcement of this sharp sentence is proper, not only as inflicting a fit punishment for a violation of the rules of civilized warfare and the commission of an inhuman murder, but as terror to those who, like the prisoner, believe that they may rightfully and with impunity turn guerillas and 'bushwackers,' assassins and highwaymen."[705]

John W. Johnson was hanged at the prison in Nashville on April 28, 1864.

John Meyers, white, age 39. *Murder.*

The crime was committed on the evening of December 3, 1863, at the Union Army encampment near Corinth, Mississippi, but had its origins the day before. An elderly black man had come to camp to see his wife, a cook. He was knocked down by a soldier and when an officer asked who had done it, the soldier admitted he had. The officer placed him in the guardhouse. Sergeant Meyers said he should be released, and began cursing the officer who ordered it.

On the day of the murder, Meyers continued his loud protest that the soldier should be released from the guardhouse. The company commander ordered Meyers arrested. Captain Henry W. Allen, white, age unknown, was Meyers's company commander. He said, "Meyers, I will have you arrested and put in the guardhouse if you don't keep still."[706] (Meyers had earlier sought a transfer to another company.)

Meyers continued to rage all day and Capt. Allen came to get him. As the captain came walking down a tent street toward Meyers, the killer said, "Captain Allen, you are the son of a bitch, I mean, I will kill you." He held his rifle aimed at the captain as the officer came forward.

The captain shouted in desperation, "Why don't someone get hold of him and get the gun away from him?" As three soldiers started for Meyers, he fired his rifle, striking the captain. "I have done what I wanted to do," said the killer as he was seized. He continued to rage at the captain, saying he was the only man that had the heart to do it. The captain died that evening.

At his court-martial Meyers explained he was a Mexican War veteran, had never been in trouble before, but "Captain Allen, on the last day of his life, gave me unlimited permission to get whiskey from his quarters, as I was at work for him."[707] Meyers explained he had no malice toward the captain: "I committed the act in a moment of intense excitement, caused by whiskey and the circumstances which surrounded that evening."[708] He begged the court for mercy.

Meyers's sentence was approved up the chain of command and bears the notation, "Sentence approved. A. Lincoln."[709] By the time the record was returned to the Army Headquarters, Meyers's regiment was encamped at Pulaski, Giles County. Meyers was hanged there on April 28, 1864, from the same gallows that took the life of Sam Davis five months earlier.[710]

Thomas Martin Smith, white, age 29. *Smuggling and trading with the enemy.*

The crime was committed about 5:00 P.M. on the afternoon of June 7, 1864, on Pigeon Roost Road a mile and one-half outside the federal lines at Memphis "beyond Mrs. Logan's boarding house," on the way to Nonconnah.[711] A ten-member squad of Union cavalry, under the command of Lt. J.W. Fackenthal, had been sent to scout the road to "see what was going on towards Nonconnah." As the squad progressed, it happened to meet Smith, who was walking, coming from the opposite direction. Lt. Fackenthal stopped Smith, demanded his pass and asked his business. Smith said he was a cotton dealer, had no pass, but was a boarder at Mrs. Logan's.

As the two were speaking, a wagon suddenly came out of the woods a half mile away. Fackenthal told four soldiers to inspect the wagon, which abruptly took off away from the soldiers. As soon as the soldiers left his view, a gunshot was heard coming from the wagon's direction. Soon one of his soldiers came riding back and said the wagon was loaded with gunpowder and percussion caps. The soldier pointed to Smith, saying he was the owner of the wagon.

The wagon was driven by Bill McKinney, black. On the wagon with him was his owner, Jim Shangles. As the soldiers approached, Shangles jumped from the wagon and ran into the woods. He was never captured. With Smith in custody, the soldiers searched the woods and found two small barrels of gunpowder (in flour barrels) and one million eight hundred thousand percussion caps in sacks cached in hollowed-out trees, or still on the wagon.

Investigation showed that Smith lived at a hotel in Memphis as well as the boarding house. A year earlier he had signed a written oath to the United States. He had told everyone he was a cotton speculator. He had been a railroad conductor, as was Shangles. How the investigation focused on the hotel was not shown in the record, but a trunk found in the hotel bore papers with Smith's name, as well as his clothing, which he admitted were his.

The Army's theory of the case was seemingly supported by the testimony of McKinney, who said that Negroes had been hired to transport small quantities of the contraband materials to the pair at or near the boarding house, who then hid it in the woods. He seemed to say that the trio was doing this at the time of capture.

Smith was tried before a military commission on April 14, 1864, convicted a week later and sentenced to be hanged. The three charges were smuggling, spying, and war treason. He was acquitted of spying.[712]

Smith did not testify. He had asked for a continuance until Shangles could be compelled to testify and asserted it was error for the commission to proceed without him.

His chief defense was a forced confession. Lt. Fackenthal admitted, "When I came up to him, I drew my revolver and told him that he had to tell everything he knew about it and that I had a great mind to shoot him right there as a spy. He begged off and told me he would tell me all he knew and show me where the powder was. He took me two places where he had hid it in the hollow trees."[713]

Lt. Fackenthal continued by quoting Smith as saying that supplies had come from Negroes, but he did not know where they got the materials, although he had offered as much as fifty dollars for the information. "I asked him what he intended to do with this powder and he told me that he intended to speculate on it and that the man who was on the wagon intended to take it off his hands. He was to give him [Smith] $3,500 for the lot."[714] Continued Lt. Fackenthal, "I asked him where this man took it. He said he knew nothing more than that he took it down to Hernando."

Lt. Fackenthal said, "I asked him then how long had he carried this on. He told me that it was his first offense in powder and caps, but he took through cloth and shoes and other things."[715] Fackenthal asked where Smith got the materials. He replied that he did not know and could not tell even if "they killed him for it." Said the officer, "He told me he got the powder from negroes who took it through the lines at night in small quantities, on the Germantown Road. He took it through the woods on the Pigeon Roost Road at night and put it in those trees."[716]

The commission sustained Smith's objection to Fackenthal's testimony, but did not rule it poisoned the hearing itself. Here, Smith had provided "certain facts," such as pointing out the trees where the contraband was hidden. The existence of "certain facts" overcomes the presumption that the confession was untrue. The court quoted a legal treatise, "Such portion of a confession as leads to the discovery of 'certain facts' proved satisfactorily without the confession is competent."[717]

At first, McKinney played dumb in front of the commission — they had difficulty getting him to say he knew what an oath meant — but he said that Smith had helped hide the powder and caps in the woods, but at the time they were caught were removing part of it.

McKinney also drove the captured goods and wagon (with Smith aboard) back to Memphis. He did not hear the conversation between Smith and any of the soldiers, but did hear Smith say, "I would give a thousand dollars to be a thousand yards away from this wagon."[718] This was an apparent attempt to bribe his captors.

Smith offered two witnesses who said he was a loyal citizen, but they did not know anything about his background or livelihood other than he said he was a cotton broker.

Smith's civilian lawyer, John McHenry, filed a lengthy brief attacking the conviction, asserting the lack of Shangles as a witness and the forced confession. The judge advocate general replied that the elements of the crime were proven by McKinney and the totality of the circumstances showed that Smith was violating his oath at the time of his capture.

Thomas Martin Smith was executed by hanging at Ft. Pickering near Memphis on April 29, 1864.[719] The Provost Marshal was in charge of the hanging and virtually all of the spectators were black Union Army soldiers, including the man who put the rope around Martin's neck. Martin admitted smuggling the caps, but not the powder, and expressed the deepest remorse. His accomplice was also named Smith, he said, but refused to name him further. Mrs. Logan had no part in the matter, he said.

Most of Smith's time on the gallows was spent urging the throng to repent their sins. He repeated, "All is well. All is well. Angels are here to welcome my spirt home — I do not fear."[720]

When the Provost Marshal waved a handkerchief to signal release of the trap, nothing happened. Because it had rained the day before, the boards had swelled together and would not move under Smith's weight. The carpenter pulled on the boards and Smith dropped. He was pronounced dead twenty minutes later.

A notation on Smith's file, made by A.A. Hosmer at the Judge Advocate General's office on May 7, 1864, says, "The proceedings in this case are irregular, but the record was not received at this office until after the sentence had been executed."

Hugh Fraley (aka James F. Fraley), white, age 25. *Highway robbery; engaging in guerrilla warfare; murder.*

The chief crime was committed on the night of November 6, 1863, at the home of James Swafford, white, age twenty-five, a civilian whose home was in Bledsoe County. Swafford was killed by someone in a guerrilla band that included Captain Fraley.

Captain Hugh Fraley (James F. Fraley) was a member of the Fourth Tennessee Cavalry, C.S.A.[721] A native of Rhea County, in east Tennessee, he had been detailed by Gen. Wheeler to act as a guide to a guerrilla band under the command of Captain Carter. The band was charged with acquiring horses and "navies"[722] and arresting deserters. But the charges levied against Fraley were quite different.

The military commission which heard charges against Fraley was informed he "straggled from the so-called Confederate states" in the vicinity of Sparta, while on a raid on October 3, 1863. From that day until he was captured on December 20, 1863, he "joined other stragglers and marauders in arms and began prowling around the country robbing, thieving and committing depredations on loyal citizens and the armies of the United States." He was charged with shooting a civilian, James Swafford, and helping to rob his body of about two thousand dollars.

Fraley had been captured in White County in December 1863 by a detail of the 39th Indiana and 15th Pennsylvania Cavalry.

Mrs. James Swafford testified that a group of ten or twelve guerrillas came to the home she shared with her husband at midnight on November 5, 1863. They demanded all the weapons in the house, but her husband refused to let the men inside to search. She went to the second floor and threw down a Navy Colt. As she did this, her husband ran out the back door to get away. She heard two shots. The next day she found his body a hundred yards from the house. His pocketbook containing about $500 was found nearby covered with blood. About two thousand dollars was missing. She testified she recognized Fraley among the group by his voice and image in the moonlit night. She knew Fraley had been in the Confederate Army because she saw him in uniform, but that night he was wearing civilian clothes.

Fraley contended he was a considerable distance from the house attempting to ford a creek when the shooting occurred and he played no role in it. He insisted he was a Confederate soldier under the command of Captain Carter. Several witnesses, former Confederate soldiers, supported parts of Fraley's defense. One said he had seen the orders from Wheeler. Another said Fraley always acted under the command of Capt. Carter. Several said there was no moon that night and it was cloudy. Another heard him tell Capt. Carter not to let the men stop at Swafford's house.

The military commission found him guilty on February 8, 1864, and ordered him hanged. General Thomas approved the sentence. On March 4, 1864, Judge Advocate General Holt briefly summarized the case and wrote the president, "The case seems to be one that calls for the rigid enforcement of the death penalty." The file is marked, "Sentence approved. April 14, 1864. A. Lincoln."

Fraley was executed at the prison in Nashville at 2:25 P.M. on May 20, 1864. Tall and slim, with a slight moustache and "imperial and long black hair," he mounted the gallows "firm and erect," and remained unmoved as the Rev. Dr. Wharton delivered a "brief but impressive address to the assembled multitude."[723] Capt. Fraley spoke: "Gentlemen: I am about to die for a crime of which I am innocent. As to the charge of my being a guerilla, I never was one, and have never shed innocent blood. But if there was ever a true Rebel soldier I am one. That's all I have to say."[724] Fraley was dressed in butternut clothing.

Every available space in the prison yard and walls was occupied by onlookers, including women, a near-mob which pushed and cursed each other to gain a good view. The crowd hushed as Fraley's hands were tied, the rope was placed around his neck and a white cap was placed over his head. The executioner stepped down from the gallows and gave a signal to a guard who used an ax to cut the rope holding the drop. The fall was deemed too short and Fraley's neck was not broken. He struggled for fourteen minutes. His body was placed in a pine coffin. Its place of burial is unknown.

Cpl. Henry Carlton, who had been sent to serve as a guard at the capitol and later sent to escort three hundred captives to the prison, wrote in his diary on May 20, "A reb capt. was hung today in the prison yard. He is said to have been engaged in the Fort Pillow massacre. *Served him right.* I would like to see more of the kind served the same luxury."[725] Captain Hugh Fraley was in the military prison at Chattanooga on April 12, 1864, the day of the Fort Pillow massacre.

Abe (aka Abe Henry), black, age unknown. *Rape.*

The crime was committed about 6:30 P.M. on July 26, 1863, on a road near Baker's Creek, Blount County. Confederate forces still controlled this area at the time. The victim was Mrs. Martha Creger, white, age twenty-four, a widow. She had gone to a neighbor's house to visit a sick woman and was walking home with her five-year-old son. Abe, a slave owned by four members of the Henry family, had passed the house where Mrs. Creger was visiting about fifteen minutes earlier. He was known to her because he had a wife at a nearby farm and had passed her house on several occasions. She knew one of his owners, Rufus Henry.

Abe sprang from the woods naked with his face covered with flour. He grabbed her arms from behind and wrestled her to the ground. She fought back but after a fifteen-minute struggle in which he began to choke her, her strength gave out while he was on top of her and "he done what he pleased to me."[726] During the struggle her son pummeled Abe's head with his fists. When Martha realized she was unable to escape, she told her son to run home and tell his grandmother that "a nigger was trying to kill his Ma."[727] After the rape she said, "Abe, I'll have Rufus Henry to kill you for this if it is the last thing I ever do." He replied that he was not Abe; he was a volunteer.[728] She went home with torn and muddy clothes, told what had happened and collapsed.

Rufus Henry was called and came to Mrs. Creger's house. His brother William R. Henry, a co-owner of Abe, and Jim Logan (owner of Abe's wife) arrested Abe that night. He was charged on a warrant the next day. When asked by the military commission why the case had lingered, she said, "Because it was at the time the Rebels were in here, and there were no Union men at home in the neighborhood but three or four old men, and the Rebels didn't care I reckon."[729] Abe escaped the day after his arrest and went to Kentucky.

He "fell in with Wolford's men, came to Knoxville after Burnside occupied it, and was at work there for a citizen when a man calling himself the Provost Marshall, induced me to enlist and I was sworn into the service of the United States."[730] He offered a torn piece of paper purporting to be a document affirming his enlistment, which was made a part of the trial record. It showed his name as Abe Henry.

Abe testified that he had not actually raped Mrs. Creger, "I endeavored to raise her clothes but did not succeed; she was too strong for me, and I let go."[731] He acknowledged her threat to have him killed and admitted saying, "I ain't Abe." He said that on the way to Logan's he fell in with a Rebel volunteer who had two canteens of whiskey, from which he took two drinks, and was "drunk and crazy" at the time of the assault: "I have always been a well behaved man, respected by both white and black. I know I did wrong, but I was not myself when I did it."[732] No witnesses, including Mrs. Creger, said he was under the influence of alcohol. "I was not naked nor did I have flour on my face at the time of the assault."[733]

Abe was tried before a military commission on February 14, 1864, at Loudon and found guilty four days later. It recommended death by hanging. Abe's case was sent through military channels, each commanding officer (Schofield and Sherman) approving the verdict, along with Judge Advocate General Holt. The last notation on Abe's file bore unmistakable handwriting—"Sentence approved A. Lincoln April 26, 1864." Abe was hanged in Knoxville on or about June 1, 1864, but details of his execution are unknown.[734]

John Callahan, white, age 18. *Theft and rape.*
Thomas Johnson (aka Thomas Johnston), white, age 18. *Theft and rape.*
John Snover (aka Jacob Snover), white, age 40. *Theft and rape.*

The crime was committed about 6:00 P.M. on March 12, 1864, at Nonconnah Creek, in Shelby County. The trio, all members of the same cavalry regiment (2nd New Jersey), had been sent to investigate a robbery. At the creek they came upon a wagon stuck in the mud. In a buggy nearby was Mrs. Margaret Brooks, white, age unknown, the victim.

Mrs. Brooks, a servant named Moore, and George W. Bradshaw, an employee of Mrs. Brooks, had been taking a loaded wagon and buggy to the Brooks residence outside Memphis, when the wagon got stuck. Bradshaw unhitched one of the mules and rode it to seek help. Mrs. Brooks and Moore stayed in the buggy. When the three soldiers appeared, Moore vanished and was not seen again, including at the military commission trial.

Callahan demanded the woman's money. She said she had none. He demanded sex and she replied, "I will die right here before I will submit to any such thing!"[735] He placed a gun to her head and repeated his demand. When she refused, he began choking her into semiconsciousness. He raped her while the others held her. She was then raped by Snover and Johnson. Callahan said she had not permitted him to penetrate her and raped her again. The trio searched her body and found $250 in her bosom and $100 in her purse.

When Bradshaw returned he found Mrs. Brooks, a mother of two, in serious condition. He took her to a doctor who confirmed the rape.

Callahan and Snover were tried before a military commission on March 21, 1864. Neither testified. Mrs. Brooks was certain about their identity, especially Callahan, a recent Irish immigrant. She was less certain about Johnson, who was tried separately on March 31, 1864. A civilian testified the trio had stopped at his house the evening of the rape and demanded supper. Another soldier testified that Callahan told him that he and two other soldiers had got some "screwing" and it occurred while they were drunk.[736]

At his trial, Johnson denied any involvement and insisted he received no money. A reason Mrs. Brooks had difficulty recognizing him was that he had been held in the guardhouse from the time of the arrest until the day of his trial several weeks later. He had lost considerable weight and bore a sallow color. The guard in charge testified, "I can't tell what his disease was."[737] The trio was executed by firing squad at Ft. Pickering on June 10, 1864.[738] They were buried at the National Cemetery at Memphis. Their headstones contain only their names and state of origin.[739]

William Lemmons (aka William P. Lemond), white, age unknown. *Murder; assault with intent to kill.*
Cyrus Lee Cathie (aka Lee Cathey, Cyrus Lee Cathey), white, age unknown. *Murder; assault with intent to kill.*
Jessee B. Neven (aka Jesse Nearing, Jesse B. Nerron), white, age unknown. *Murder; assault with intent to kill.*
Thomas R. West, white, age 18. *Murder; assault with intent to kill.*
Benjamin F. West, white, age unknown. *Murder; assault with intent to kill.*

The crimes were committed in December 1863 and January 1864 in Lincoln and Bedford counties.[740] The five were former Confederate soldiers who joined a guerrilla band headed by Major Blackwell and Captain Mosely. Its purpose was to punish deserters and to capture horses and weapons for Forrest's command. The group met in the woods many times "to raise a company for Gen. Forrest and sometimes to go on raids."[741] None of the members had been mustered into service under these officers. They had simply left their units, returned home and fallen in with the Blackwell-Mosely gang.[742] The charges against all five were identical.

All of the men were from the Lincoln County area when the war broke out. Benjamin F. West had been a member of Company A, 32nd Tennessee. He had joined October 19, 1861, and left in June 1863.[743] Lemmons had been a member of the 17th Mississippi; Cathie a member of the 44th Tennessee and had been wounded at Chickamauga; Neven had been a member of the 32nd Tennessee. Thomas R. West, Benjamin's cousin, had been a member of the 32nd Tennessee.

According to a former gang member, Blackwell held a commission from President Jefferson Davis to raise as many men as he could for service under Forrest. The commission did not give him authority to do anything else besides raise recruits.[744] A gang member who testified against the five said he saw himself as "belonging to the Confederate government, but not as a soldier."[745] The problem was the gang, about forty in number, was never large enough to constitute a company.

The five were charged with killing a citizen, Irvin E. McLean, of Marshall County, on December 14, 1863, and killing citizen Samuel "Jack" Wakefield, of Lincoln County, the same day. The next day, they killed William White, a Shelbyville citizen, and Grey Hyde, a federal soldier, at his Shelbyville home.[746] They were charged with assault with intent to kill by firing on a "waggon train" in Bedford County on January 15, 1864, and shooting at soldiers trying to capture them at Boon's Hill, Lincoln County, on February 5, 1864.

The officer in charge described the capture of Lemmons:

> On this Friday morning, I was going up Fishing Ford road — we were hunting guerillas — and I noticed a house where the women were running

> backward and forward, a sure sign that something was up. I sent on two men and followed up and when I arrived there found that two men had just left there. We saw the men ride into the woods and followed them. I lost their trail but found it again, and finally getting near ordered him to halt and which he disregarded, and I then ordered my men to fire, rule being to fire after a second halt; he kept up, and we followed, he fired at us I thought five times but he said he had fired seven times. No one was hit, he fired too high and we fired too low. We both did the best we could. He then got away from us and after hunting awhile for him we finally found him hid behind a log. We took him and delivered him over to Col. McDougal.[747]

The military commission, headed by Col. E.A. Cannon, 13th New Jersey, heard the cases at the federal camp in Tullahoma between March 2 and 25, 1864. A dozen witnesses, each with specific but limited firsthand knowledge, placed all of the defendants among the group (numbering has high as thirty-three) that killed the four men, although none was charged with the actual shooting.[748]

Several of the witnesses had been members of the gang itself. They confirmed that the group met in the woods, shared in the proceeds of robberies (including the men that were killed), and in thefts of mules, saddles and guns. The liberated property was auctioned among the gang members. For example, of the ten mules taken from a man named Thompson, Lemmons got one.[749] The actual shooters were named by a few witnesses.[750] Most of the gang member witnesses admitted they and the defendants had left Confederate service without leave.[751]

Grey Hyde, dressed in a Union uniform, was shot through a window of his home, with his family present.[752] His sister, who was there, said, "They just came up and shot him through the window with a pistol." Q: How many shots were fired? A: Three. Do you know who fired the shots? A: No, sir, the pistol put the light out but I saw Bob Blackwell."[753]

Hyde's sister told what happened next: "Yes, sir, they robbed him; they took his horse, saddle, pistol, overcoat, knife, boots and things out of his pockets, his money and other things. They took off with them, and they told my mother they would burn up the whole house and everything there. I asked Blackwell why did he do it, and he said because my brother joined the Northern Army."[754]

McLean was taken from his home in the early morning hours, robbed, and released. He was promised that if he "would bring up the right kind of man to show that he was a Southern man they would return him his money."[755] He was re-arrested that afternoon, taken away to the woods and shot in the head.[756] A gang member said that Blackwell told him to shoot McLean but he refused. Blackwell said McLean and Wakefield deserved shooting because they had been "stealing mules from the citizens and selling them to the Yankees."[757]

Wakefield was placed on the same horse with Tobe Edmondson. He was shot and his body was thrown in Elk River.[758] White, in full uniform, was called out of his house and shot by Eastland.[759] The defendants were found guilty of most, but not all of the charges. For example, Lemmons, Cathie and Neven were found not guilty in the McLean and Wakefield killings.

The five were represented by the same lawyer, William A. Wisener, who cross-examined witnesses and offered detailed written arguments on their behalf.[760] The common defense was they were acting under orders from Blackwell and Mosely and their actions were within the rules of war. Argued Neven, "I was under Blackwell's command, and am, I believe protected by his orders, under the circumstances, as proved in the case, under consideration."[761]

A defense witness was asked, "Did you consider yourselves as in the service of the so-called Confederate States at this time? Answer: "I suppose they did but don't know what they did." Question: "Who mustered you into that service?" Answer: "I don't know that anybody did. I was not mustered at all."[762] McLean and Wakefield asserted they were Confederate deserters who had taken the oath.[763] They argued the deaths of Hyde and White were protected by the law of war (military necessity). However, a former gang member testified that Blackwell had told White to surrender and he would be treated as a prisoner of war.[764] When White stepped out the door and into the yard, he was simply shot. Benjamin F. West was present at both killings.[765]

The military commission refused to disallow the testimony of a black man who testified against them, saying Tennessee law did not apply and there was no federal bar against black witnesses.[766] Citing authority, their lawyer argued the proceedings were illegal because there was no showing the civil courts were not operating at the time of the trials.[767] The testimony of Daniel Woods, black, was clear. He saw Thomas R. West riding alongside McClean with a pistol in his right hand. On cross-examination, he was asked, "Don't you know that the prisoner [Thomas West] left at the creek when Mosely said, "shoot him if he does?" Woods answered,

"The crowd that [Thomas West] was with never halted. They went straight up the hill with McLean."[768] Wisener's detailed written arguments on behalf of each were also fact-specific. For example, Neven said he never received any share of the robbery money or goods.[769]

The military commission ordered the men hanged. General Slokum strongly endorsed the finding. He wrote, "The outrages committed in this region of the state of Tennessee during the past four months, by organized bands of outlaws known as guerillas, and the fact that the crimes of murder and robbery are still weekly occurrences, demand the execution of those who are convicted of these crimes a matter of necessity, as it is the only course that can, in my opinion, be adopted, which will restore peace and order in this locality."[770] Advocate General Holt echoed Slokum's language in his recommendation to the president. The file bears the notation, "Sentences approved. A. Lincoln." It was dated April 21, 1864.

The week before the execution the men were attended by two ministers attached to the Union Army. Cathie and Neven were deemed sincere in their search for religion and Lemmons and Benjamin West were baptized. Cathie's wife and small child were allowed to remain at the prison all night with him the night before his execution. The men were executed in the yard of the Nashville prison on June 17, 1864. Only about fifty spectators witnessed their deaths.

All five mounted the scaffold with firm steps and listened attentively to the ministers' comments ("fervent appeals to the Throne of Grace") and prayers. Each was allowed some last words. All proclaimed their innocence, Cathie and Neven the most earnestly, but said they were willing to die and felt assured of immortal happiness. Lemmons's speech was broken and could not be understood. The two Wests, speaking last, spoke at length, seemed less penitent. After asserting their freedom from guilt, stated they were honest Rebel soldiers and "affirmed their belief in the justness of the Rebel cause, and said they would die true Rebel soldiers."[771]

After their arms were bound and white caps placed over their heads, the ropes were placed. At this point Cathie fainted, falling the length of the rope.[772] He was lifted to his feet and held erect by soldiers. The drop was made at 11:00 A.M. The men dropped cleanly. Their bodies were borne away by relatives and taken to Lincoln County for burial.

Writing from Richmond on March 22, 1865, Robert Ould, the Confederate official in charge of prisoner exchange, said that eight or nine Federal officers sent to him concur in the statement that a number of Confederate soldiers had been hanged at Nashville. He listed the names:

"Lieut. Mosely, on the 30th of September 1864; Capt. J.F. Fraley, Fourth Tennessee Cavalry, in May 1864; Private Lee Cathey, Forty-first Tennessee, in June 1864; Private William Lemmon [*sic*], Seventeenth Mississippi, in June 1864; Private Jesse Nearing, Thirty-second Tennessee, in June 1864; Private Robert T. Gossett, Forty-second Tennessee, on the 8th of July 1864; two brothers by the name of West, belonging to the Thirty-second Tennessee, in June 1864."[773]

Agent Ould said that these men belonged to regular commands and were in the discharge of their duty when captured. "I will thank you to inform me why these executions took place, and why Confederate soldiers, whom the fortune of war has thrown in the hands of your military authorities, are thus treated. It is very easy for you to find out the truth or falsity of this representation, and I therefore request an early response to this communication."[774] No record of a reply has been located.

Captain Mosely was, in fact, executed for the same crimes as his men, and died a "true Rebel" on September 30, 1864.

Robert T. Gossett, white, age unknown. *Murder.*
Preston Pollock, white, age unknown. *Murder.*

The crime was committed on the late afternoon of Christmas Day, 1863, on an unspecified road in Cheatham County. The shooter, Robert T. Gossett, and co-shooter, Pres Pollock, were former Confederates who had joined a guerrilla band headed by Thomas Perkins. The band, nineteen in number, had plagued Dixon, Cheatham and Rutherford counties throughout the year.[775] The victim was John T. Allbright, white, age unknown, a civilian. The fate of Perkins is confusing: he was reported captured on Christmas Day, but testimony in Pollock's case (March 1864) asserted he was dead.[776] Gossett and Pollack were arrested a few days after they signed formal allegiance papers on February 1, 1864.[777]

The military commission tried Gossett and Pollock separately for stealing horses from George A. Washington and attempting to shoot him, robbing E.P. Follis, and killing B.F. Binkley and Allbright.

The commission focused on the killing of John T. Allbright. Several witnesses said he was taken from a house, put on his mule, taken away and shot. He was found by the roadside and he lived seven days. Several witnesses heard him say, "Leave me alone!" as Gossett seized the mule's bridle. Others had heard Gossett, in the presence of Pollock, brag about the killing. They said Pollock described shooting him after his hands were up, begging for mercy.[778] They said Pollock had shot him in the chin, but the bullet went straight down into his chest. The pair discussed whether the shot was fatal. To be sure, Gossett turned his horse and shot Allbright in the head. According to the witnesses, who heard the account from Pollock, he said the next time he killed a man he would stick a knife in the bottom of his foot to make sure he was dead.[779] He told witnesses that Allbright was "too dead to skin."[780]

At trial, Gossett denied shooting Allbright and offered alibi witnesses who said that he was home all day.[781] Pres Pollock testified about the shooting, both to free Gossett and himself.

Pollock explained he had lost a pistol crossing the river and he and Gossett were looking for it. They came upon Allbright riding a mule. They asked him if he had seen it and he said no. They continued, but several people they encountered revealed that Allbright had told them he found a pistol and showed it. The pair turned around and caught up with Allbright, riding with him to a house. After leaving the house, the trio rode alone and Pollock asked Allbright if he knew a man named Pollock. Allbright responded, "God damn him. I would like to come across him. I have been watching the road for him several days with a double barrel shot gun, a mighty good one, as good one as ever fired." According to Pollock, Allbright said, "If I ever get sight of him, I intend to kill him." Pollock replied, "What would you think if I tell you my name is Pollock?" He looked surprised and says he would not know what to think. "I says, my name is Pollock. You have found the boy you have been looking for!"

According to Pollock, here is what happened next: "He had his breeches in his boots, long legged, sort of cavalry boots, and reached down to his boots and got hold of the butt end of a pistol and attempted to draw it when the cock on the hammer caught or hung in his breeches, and I jerked out mine then. I shot him."[782] That was Pollock's testimony at Gossett's trial.

At Pollock's trial a few days after his, Gossett explained the problem with the missing pistol, the fact that Pollock identified himself to a surprised Allbright, and the shooting. "And he [Allbright] just whirled his mule around and I looked back and threw himself down as though he attempted to draw a pistol from his boot, and I looked forward then. I expected they was going to shoot and my mare was afraid of a gun. I check up and by the time I looked they was together and Mr. Pollock he shot and their pistols might have went off at the same time. My mare sprung off and by the time I turned around, he was attempting to get up again and was cussing and Mr. Pollock shot him a second time."[783]

The military commission in Nashville found Gossett guilty of murder in the Allbright killing and ordered him hanged. A few days later, a similar verdict was reached in Pollock's case. Adjutant General Holt wrote the president regarding Gossett, "Prisoner's conduct for many months has been the cause of terror to his neighbors, and he has stained his hands with the blood of many an unoffending victim."[784] The file contains the notation, "Sentence approved. A. Lincoln."[785] Pollock's case reached the president, who affirmed his death sentence on August 16, 1864.

On June 22, 1864, seventy citizens of Robertson County signed a petition to the president asking for mercy for Gossett, suggesting he was intoxicated at the time of the killing. Military Governor Andrew Johnson, only months away from election as vice-president, wrote the president saying the persons were reliable. But he made no recommendation. The president asked Holt to examine the record in light of the petition. On July 5, 1864, Holt wrote the president that the record "gives no support to the suggestion made in his favor in within letter.... The sentence should certainly be enforced."[786]

Robert T. Gossett was hanged at the main prison in Nashville on July 8, 1864. Hanged at his side was Obed C. Crossland, bushwacker.[787] Pres Pollock was hanged at the main prison in Nashville on September 15, 1864.

On July 30, 1864, a guerrilla band under the command of a Captain Porter surrounded Union Lt. Gamble and four others and took them six miles into the woods. All were ordered to disrobe. Captain Porter said, "We have but one way of parolling Federal prisoners, and that is with our revolvers." Gamble ran and was not hit. He hid in the woods. A Union scouting party found him on August 2.

Gamble led the party back to the woods and found the bodies of Ira Butcher, an Illinois soldier; Christopher McCarty, a sixteen-year-old teamster; and an unnamed government laborer. The fourth person was not found. Pinned to the breast of each was a strip of paper, dated July 30, with the following words written in pencil: "These boys were executed in retaliation for our friends hung in

Nashville." According to the newspaper, the friends referred to in the notes "are presumed to be guerillas recently hung in Nashville, one of them was named Gossett, a notorious robber and murderer of Cheatham County."[788]

Obed C. Crossland, white, age 40. *Being a guerrilla and murder.*

The crimes were committed in Marion County, Tennessee, on May 1, 1863, and Jackson County, Alabama, on June 7, 1863. Crossland was a civilian. He was a member of William Gunter's guerrilla band. Among its members was a Confederate conscript agent named Hornbeck. There were six or seven others in the band operating in the area. The victims were Napoleon Hedrick, white, age twenty-five; William Ridge, white, age sixty; and his son, James Ridge, white, age unknown.[789]

Hedrick, a Unionist, was at his Marion County home ten miles from Bridgeport, Alabama. He was standing near an outdoor fire with five or six other men. The Gunter band arrived and began shooting. Hedrick pulled out a pistol and got off one shot. Accounts differ on what happened next. One witness said Hedrick was then hit by five or six bullets. Another said he was taken between the smokehouse and another house and shot in the back, "right across his galluses," and shot about four more times. "I heard Gunter say when Hedrick was lying with his head sorter against the steps that it was a damned pity and shame for a man to fetch themselves to such as that rather than go out and fight for the country like a man."[790]

Crossland's name was mentioned because he robbed one of the men, John Doss, of his pocket knife. The men still present after the shooting were ordered to their knees and told to beg for their lives, with threats of being shot in the head. Three were tied with their hands behind their backs and taken to a Confederate-controlled jail in Bridgeport, Alabama, and were charged with being bushwackers. All of the jailed men were Unionists. Some had brothers or close relatives in the federal army. All, like Hedrick, were hiding out from Confederate conscription.

Crossland was also charged with being a guerrilla from July 1, 1862, until January 1, 1864, when he was captured.

Frank Ridge, a Unionist, had been wounded in some manner. He was recovering at his father's house in Jackson County, Alabama. Crossland came in and told him he was sorry it was not a center shot.[791] The band then tied up both father and son and took them away. Several weeks later, after Bragg's army had passed through and the area came under federal control, Crossland was heard to say that the pair had "gone up." George Ridge, another brother, was later taken prisoner by the Gunter gang and Crossland, and said "he would build breastworks of me, as he had built with the others, my father and brother."[792] Crossland said the bodies would be found somewhere between Stevenson and Bridgeport. Frank found the decayed body of his brother James at that location in September. The father's body was never found.

Crossland said he happened to be with Gunter on the two occasions mentioned, but was not a member of the band. "I was as afraid of Gunter as anybody.... As to this Hedrick scrape I happened to be with them."[793] He insisted that an official at the provost marshal's office at Bridgeport be summoned to swear he was not a member of Gunter's band. "Some of them witnesses swore mighty hard. I felt just that way [shaking his hand in tremulous manner] all the time. I never told them where to find Ridge." He concluded, "I hardly ever went armed."[794]

The military commission which met in Nashville on March 22, 1864, found Crossland guilty of all three counts and ordered him hanged. Judge Advocate Holt recounted the evidence in a memorandum to the president and recommended the sentence be "rigidly enforced."[795] The file bears the notation, "Sentence approved. A. Lincoln."

Obed C. Crossland was hanged at the prison in Nashville on July 8, 1864. Hanged beside him was Robert T. Gossett, bushwacker.[796]

On July 30, 1864, bushwackers under the command of Captain Porter surrounded five men under the command of a Union lieutenant named Gamble. They were taken six miles into the woods and ordered to disrobe. The bushwackers began shooting the men with pistols. Gamble ran and escaped. When he led troops back to the killing spot, three bodies were found with written notes pinned to their bodies, "These boys were executed in retaliation for our friends hung in Nashville." A newspaper reported the friends referred to "are presumed to be guerillas recently hung in Nashville, one of them was named Gossett, a notorious robber and murderer of Cheatham County."[797]

Aaron, black, age 16. *Murder.*

The crime was committed about 9:00 A.M., April 29, 1864, in the stables of the Union cavalry headquarters in Chattanooga, Hamilton County. Aaron and the victim, William Henry Maston, black, age twenty, were civilian groomers. Maston had been picking on Aaron for several months. On the morning of the killing, the two had quarreled when Aaron would not give Maston a curry comb which belonged to an officer. Earlier that morning, Aaron told William Holland, black, a servant for another officer, "I will kill him [Maston] before night."[798] Aaron drew a hidden pistol and shot Maston in the shoulder. No one saw this shot being fired, but Holland saw the second shot strike Maston in the back as he staggered away. An officer arrived in moments and saw Maston die. He asked Aaron why he did it and Aaron said he was willing to die now as he had accomplished his purpose. The court asked whether Aaron had fired in self-defense, but Holland answered only that they had been quarreling over the curry comb. Aaron was not represented by counsel and offered no proof. He told the court, "He [Aaron] was imposed on frequently by this William Henry Maston, and he [Maston] was always quarreling with him." The court ordered Aaron hanged.

Judge Advocate Holt said the facts made out murder under Tennessee law. Holt wrote the president:

> The finding of the Court is sustained by the evidence, and the case falls entirely within the terms of the statute. That the killing was premeditated is shown by his declaration to the witness Holland of his intent to take the life of Maston before night, that it was "willful" and "malicious," his avowal to Captain Jacobs of a willingness to die for what he had done, and his firing a second shot at the deceased, amply prove. That Maston was attempting to take away a curry comb at the time is no excuse for putting him to death, while prisoner's own statement that Maston was constantly quarreling with him, only confirms the belief that the crime of which he was guilty was conceived not in the heat of passion, but was prompted by malice and a desire for revenge.[799]

The file is marked, "Sentence approved. A. Lincoln." Aaron was hanged on August 12, 1864, at the federal camp outside Chattanooga.

George Nelson, black, age unknown. *Rape.*

The crime was committed on the afternoon of November 13, 1863, on the Nashville Pike a mile outside Dickson, in Dickson County. Private Nelson was a member of Company F of the 13th U.S.C.T. and one of three men who met the victim on the road, riding in the opposite direction. She was alone. Her name was Indiana Jones, white, age unknown. She was unmarried.

The soldiers asked where she had been and she replied at Mr. Jones's house just over a mile away. Asked where she lived, she said about a mile away. Nelson said he had been in a fight with some rebels near her house and insisted she go with him and the other two soldiers. She said she did not want to go. Nelson threatened to shoot her. "I went with him about two hundred and fifty yards."[800]

One of the soldiers also held his rifle on her. "I begged and prayed of him to let me go. He then put his bayonet against my side and said that if I did not follow him into the woods that he would run it through me. I started with him and commenced crying."[801] Nelson told her that if she did not stop he would hang her with a rope in his pocket. They walked further. The three of them whispered together. Two stayed behind and held the horse.

Nelson took her farther away. "I again begged of him to let me go, when he cocked his gun and said if I did not be still that he would blow my brains out. He then took hold of me, threw me down, and committed a rape on my person." After this, he forced her to empty her pockets, taking a dollar and a half. The other two soldiers made him give the money back. During the trial of the other two, Miss Jones was asked, "Did you use your utmost endeavors to prevent him from executing his desires, or did you simply cry out, thus yielding a tacit consent?"[802] The other two were sentenced to twelve and ten years in prison.

President Lincoln approved the sentence in August 1864 and George Nelson was hanged at the Nashville prison on September 12, 1864.

Jourdan C. Mosely, white, age 27. *Murder.*

The crimes were committed in December 1863 and January 1864 in Lincoln and Bedford counties. Mosely was sometimes referred to as Lieutenant (or Captain) Mosely because he helped lead a guerrilla band headed by Major Blackwell, who was a recruiting agent for Gen. Nathan Bedford Forrest. Witnesses at Mosely's military commission trial said Blackwell offered to show them his commission, if they wanted to see it, and because Mosely acted like second in command, they assumed he had been elected lieutenant.

Mosely was actually a private, and never offered any documents showing he was commissioned. He maintained he was simply a private who followed Blackwell's orders.[803] Mosely was charged as a citizen, not a soldier, although there was some proof that he had been elected a lieutenant under Captain Elliott, who served under Major Blackwell. All witnesses agreed that Blackwell had never sworn the men into service. The reason was there were too few to make up a company to send to Gen. Forrest.

The Union newspapers described Mosely and his band as bushwackers who "lay in wait by roadsides and kill the drivers of stray Government teams, burn the wagons, sell the horses or mules, and pocket the proceeds."[804] He was charged with killing citizen Irvin E. McLean and citizen Samuel "Jack" Wakefield on December 14, 1863. The next day, he was charged with killing William White, a Shelbyville citizen, and Grey Hyde, a federal soldier, at his Shelbyville home. He was also charged with killing Thomas Y. Brown on November 22, 1863, near the village of Richmond, in Bedford County.[805] He was also charged with assault to kill by firing on a "waggon train" in Bedford County on January 15, 1864, and shooting at soldiers trying to capture him. Some who testified against Mosely were former gang members waiting trial on the same charges.[806]

Precisely, he was found guilty in only the last three murders and firing on the wagon train. He pled guilty to the last charge. The press reported he was guilty of three murders and "for being a guerilla."[807] These killings were done with his guerrilla band. Mosely was present but was not accused of actually shooting the men. The details of the band's actions are discussed under the cases of Lemmons, Cathie, Neven, and two men named West (q.v.).

Following his capture, Mosely was held under guard at Shelbyville, but was not placed in the local guardhouse. On the evening of January 19, 1864, he escaped because he had been taken to the house of "Mrs. Blackwell, the wife of Capt. Blackwell, the guerilla chief, accompanied by a single guard, to stay all night." Said a report, "The guard went to bed, and of course, to sleep, when Capt. Mosely took a revolver from under his head, and the horse of a lady friend of Mrs. Blackwell, conveniently near, and made off."[808] While a captive, Mosely had been given great freedom, receiving many friends and sympathizers "who chose to call on him; was never sent to the guard-house or turned over to the commander of this post, but, on the contrary, rather treated as a guest, who was entitled to a guard of honor."[809]

Following his escape, "Several messages have been reported as coming from Capt. Mosely since his escape, of an unpleasant nature."[810] The reason he was allowed to stay at Mrs. Blackwell's was probably to entice the gang to rescue him, but facts are unclear. What is clear is that Grey Hyde was the husband of Mrs. Blackwell's sister. Mrs. Blackwell testified against Mosely and five other members of his gang. Hyde had been shot through a window in his home. Present were Mrs. Blackwell, her sister (Mrs. Hyde) and their mother. His body was stripped to his underwear, and Major Blackwell personally removed Hyde's boots and took them.

In the early morning hours of March 27, 1864, a squad of Union soldiers sent to find him noticed a horse hitched to some bushes near a roadside at Boon's Hill, in Lincoln County. As they approached, three figures sleeping on the ground jumped up and ran away in their bare feet. The soldiers shot at them, and Mosely was hit in the fleshy part of his thigh and captured, as was another. The third hid in a hollow log but was captured because his feet stuck out.[811]

Mosely was convicted before a military commission at Tullahoma on April 16, 1864. His death sentence was endorsed by Gen. Thomas and made its way to Advocate General Holt, who eagerly endorsed it. An entry reads, "Sentence Approved. A. Lincoln. July 8, 1864." Meanwhile, Mosely's mother had made an appeal for her son's life, which was sent to the president by Military Governor Andrew Johnson. It was also accompanied by a petition signed by three loyal citizens asking Lincoln not to grant clemency. Lincoln gave the file back to Holt, who wrote a lengthy memorandum urging the sentence be upheld. Secretary Nicolay wrote on the file: "The President declines to interfere with the due execution of the sentence in this case." This was September 7, 1864.

Jourdan Mosely was hanged at the Nashville prison on September 30, 1864. By orders of Gen. Thomas, only a few spectators were allowed to watch Mosely mount the gallows "with a firm free step and there was no tremor or emotion as he looked to be almost indifferent to his fate." Following a reading of the charges, Mosely was asked if he had anything to say.

Mosely responded in a clear firm voice:

> Gentlemen, I am a Confederate soldier. I have always been a Confederate soldier and I shall die one. I am innocent of murdering those men. If I had been allowed to get my witnesses I could have proved myself innocent. I was when captured, with my superior officer, and acting under orders from the Commanding General. I do not fear to die. I have been a true soldier to my country and her cause. I have never disgraced. I have done nothing but my duty. I enlisted in the Confederate service in Okalona, Miss., in January or February 1862, I disremember which. I have never been anything but a true

> soldier. I was tried as a citizen of Tennessee. I am not a citizen of Tennessee, but a native of Okalona, Mississippi, where I lived up to the time that I entered the Confederate service.[812]

He stopped speaking at this point and was asked if he had anything more to say. He replied, "I believe that is all that I have to say." A white cap was placed over his head, the chaplain offered a prayer and he was dropped. But the knot shifted to behind his head and he struggled for five minutes. Left hanging for twenty minutes, he was cut down and his body was placed in a plain coffin and turned over to his "afflicted mother."[813]

Alexander Vest (aka Vass, Ness, Vest, Voss), black, age 21. *Murder.*
Henry Irving, black, age unknown. *Murder.*

Private Vest was a member of Company E, 3rd Regiment, 1st West Tennessee Heavy Artillery (USCT). On January 15, 1864, he and four other soldiers, all black, plundered the Griffiths (Griffis) Plantation on Horn Lake Road in Shelby County. The group included Henry Irving, George W. Pope, John Wilks, and Manuel Clark. Irving was also a member of Company E.

The soldiers came to the house about 7:00 P.M. and Irving ordered the owner, Wiley P. Griffiths (Griffis), white, age 34, taken outside. "Sergeant, shoot this man down," said Irving. No witnesses identified the shooter, but Griffiths was heard to say, "I am shot!"[814] He was shot in the bowels and died the next day. The killing outraged Memphis citizens because all the soldiers were from the Memphis area. The group was identified when it was discovered that parts of a shattered musket near the shooting scene were traced to the weapon owned by one of the group. Griffiths had been hit over the head with the musket and bled profusely.[815]

The soldiers were brought before a court-martial on February 27, 1864.[816] Most of the witnesses were black, but included two white women, Miss Mary Bell and the victim's wife. Vest and Irving were clearly identified by most of the witnesses. This was because they led plundering the house by gathering goods in quilts. Pope had not been arrested at the time of the Vest and Irving court-martial.

All the defendants were convicted and sentenced to be hanged. Most of the court-martial members signed a petition asking mercy for Wilks and Clark. The commanding general said the original sentence should be carried out, writing, "Rigid example is necessary." This notation was placed on the file on August 9, 1864: "Sentence approved as to Irving and Vest, and not approved as to others. A. Lincoln."[817] Alexander Vest and Henry Irving were hanged at Ft. Pickering, in Shelby County, on December 16, 1864.[818]

Dick Davis (aka John W. Smith), white, age 25. *Murder.*

The crime was committed on the afternoon of June 13, 1864, in the woods near Germantown, one and one half miles west of Collierville, in Shelby County. Dick Davis was a Confederate guerrilla, the leader of a band that terrorized Shelby County and Marshall and DeSoto counties in Mississippi. He and his gang (about fifteen men) were hiding in the woods, waiting to pick off Union soldiers by robbing and killing them as they came down State Line Road.

Two days earlier, a Union force had been sent east to Mississippi to crush a brigade commanded by Gen. Nathan B. Forrest. In a skirmish known as the Battle of Brice's Crossroads, the Union forces were routed. Scared, tired and hungry soldiers were streaming back to the safety of Ft. Pickering in Shelby County. It was known as the Guntown retreat, named for a Mississippi town by that name.

The victims were Capt. Henry C. Somers, of the 108th Illinois, Pvt. Frank Panky, 120th Illinois, and Sgt. James Mitchell, also from the same regiment.[819] Only Capt. Somers was armed at the time of his capture, the others having thrown down their weapons. They were approached by Captain Davis, as he was called, and ordered into the woods, with Capt. Somers brought in about an hour later. At least seven were captured.

The men were ordered to sit on a log. They were robbed of their money, shirts and rings. (One of the ways captives knew the identity of the guerrilla band leader was that all the booty was placed at his feet for distribution.) Davis was told by one of his band, "We have enough to retaliate now."[820]

According to the testimony of two surviving soldiers, who were wounded as they ran away when the shooting started, Captain Davis came up to them and said, "Boys, you have got to go overboard, every one of you."[821] Although one of Davis's men protested the order to shoot, Davis said, "Tut, tut, shoot."[822] Said the witness, James E. Guernes, "They fired, being at a distance from three or four feet to three or four yards." He said, "I jumped up and turned around and immediately they fired. I was shot in the arm which in consequence has since been amputated." When asked how many shots were fired, he answered, "They all fired in a volley, all at once. I could not tell how many there were."[823]

Another soldier, Pvt. John H. Parks, 120th Illinois, who escaped the shooting, confirmed that the man in charge of the shooting was called Dick Davis by his men.[824] Prior to the shooting, Parks said he heard one of his captors say they belonged to Forrest's command and heard Davis say he belonged to a command of his own.[825] Another soldier who was captured by Davis in September 1864 identified him. He had escaped when the Davis gang was attacked by a squad of Union soldiers.[826] A civilian who had been the subject of a death threat unless he turned over $8,000 in federal money, some gray cloth and some cavalry boots, also testified that Davis seemed to be the man in charge of a gang that came to his house.[827]

The unburied bodies were found June 24, 1864.[828] Dick Davis was captured in a skirmish in Cold Water, Mississippi, on October 2, 1864. He was tried before a military commission from October 10 intermittently until he was convicted on December 15, 1864.[829]

The chief defense was mistaken identity. The man on trial insisted he was John W. Smith, of the 6th Missouri Cavalry, and he was not Dick Davis. He offered the testimony of a fellow inmate of the military prison in Memphis to assert the same. But his chief witness was Miss Annie Talley, who said she had known him for six months, that he went by the name of J.W. Smith, and that she knew Dick Davis, and they did not look alike.

Miss Talley had visited the defendant in jail and he had concocted a scheme to cut through the bars and drug a guard with laudanum-laced whiskey, in addition to paying a guard one thousand dollars for help. The scheme was detected and Miss Talley had signed an affidavit on November 13, 1864, in which she described the plot. "Mr. Newton Davis furnished me with one hundred dollars to be applied in procuring the release of Mr. Smith from prison," it said.[830] It was shown that Newton Davis, a Memphis resident, was a cousin of Dick Davis. A near contemporary account of the Dick Davis case was written by General Thomas M. Browne, who as a lieutenant colonel was president of the military commission which tried him.

According to Browne, Davis was raised in Kentucky, where he joined a Confederate cavalry unit, fought under Morgan, and served as a spy in Ohio. While there, he stole a horse, was arrested and charged with spying, but was released on condition that he join the Union army. He did so, but soon deserted. Captured and jailed as a spy in Memphis, he escaped through the complicity of a guard.[831] Dick Davis became the most notorious guerrilla in the Memphis area. "His men were principally deserters, some from the rebel and some from the Union army. In his exploits as a highwayman, he made no distinction between loyal and disloyal, white and black, nor did he respect age, sex or condition."[832]

Browne described Davis's last days: "He received the information of his sentence with apparent unconcern, immediately assumed his true name, and commenced preparations for death. He wrote to his friends, instructing them what disposition to make of his property, and in what manner to pay his debts. He made but one bequest, and that was of his favorite race horse, which had been his companion in his expeditions of blood, and that he directed to be given to his friend, Miss Anna Talley. To the members of his band he wrote a touching farewell, requesting them not to avenge his death by retaliating upon innocent men."[833]

Dick Davis was hanged at Fort Pickering on December 23, 1864. He was attended by a Catholic priest and ascended the steps of the scaffold to the platform in a bold, firm step. "While the rope was being adjusted about his neck, he stood erect, exhibiting no signs of emotion or fear. For a few moments after his fall there was no motion except a slight pendulum-like vibration of the body, that was soon succeeded by a spasmodic shrugging of the shoulders, then there was a quivering of the limbs, and then — Dick Davis, the Guerilla Chief, was no more. His spirit had passed from earth and stood before its God."[834]

1865

Champ Ferguson, white, age 44. *Murder.*

The most widely-known execution in Tennessee occurred on October 20, 1865, and was the result of the Civil War.[835] Champ Ferguson was a Confederate guerrilla. Capt. Ferguson, as he was called, had raised a band of killers that preyed on both Union military and Union partisans in the upper Cumberland area. By war's end, Ferguson had boasted of killing over a hundred men.

Union authorities refused to recognize his purported military status and arrested him for murder on May 26, 1865.[836] Most of the killings occurred in southern Kentucky and the prosecution was not based on an investigation. When news circulated that Ferguson was to be charged, his victims' families besieged the federal authorities with stories of atrocities and eagerly came to Nashville for the trial.

Ferguson was brought before a six-member military commission in July and his trial ended in September.[837] Twenty-three specific charges were brought against Ferguson, accusing him of murdering fifty-three persons. He simply shot people dead, sometimes in their own homes in the presence of wives and children.[838]

Some of the victims were like Reuben Wood, white, age unknown, who had known Ferguson as a child. Ferguson and two other men rode up to Wood's house near Albany, Kentucky, on December 2, 1861. After inquiring whether Wood had been to a Union mustering ground (Camp Dick Robinson) and being told yes, Ferguson began cursing him, calling him a damned Lincolnite, and shot him in the chest with a pistol in front of his grown daughter.[839]

Ferguson insisted that Wood was a member of a Union partisan gang with shoot-to-kill orders on Ferguson. "If I had not shot Reuben Wood, I would not likely have been here, for he would have shot me. I never expressed a regret for committing the act, and never will. He was in open war against me."[840] Contemporary Southern writers refused to condemn Ferguson's actions, insisting his actions matched those of equally bloodthirsty Union guerrillas such as the infamous Tinker Dave Beatty, who operated in the same area.[841] They accredit the story, never mentioned at trial, that early in the war, Ferguson was standing on his porch when a troop of federal soldiers marched by. His three-year-old child came to his side waving a Confederate flag. One or more of the soldiers fired at Ferguson but killed the child.[842]

Other charges included killing Alex Huff in Fentress County in 1862, and the killing of David Delk, by chopping and cutting him to pieces, at the home of Mrs. Alex Huff, in Fentress County in 1863.

He was also charged with killing nineteen soldiers of the 5th Cavalry, names unknown, on February 22, 1862.[843] This has come to be called the Saltville Massacre. The Confederates won a battle at this obscure southwest Virginia town the day before and the Union troops left the field that night, although they kept large campfires burning to trick the Confederates into thinking they were still present. When the morning came, the field was littered with wounded federal soldiers, most of them black.

The Confederates simply shot the wounded. Notable among the killers was Ferguson. Explained a wounded federal soldier, "I saw him pointing down at prisoners lying on the ground, and heard the reports of the pistol and the screams of the men."[844] Ferguson walked up to Crawford Hazelwood, white, a wounded soldier, and asked, "Why did you come up here to fight with damn niggers?" Then he asked Hazelwood, "Where will you have it, in the back or the face?" Hazelwood pleaded for his life as Ferguson shot him in the face. A short while later, Ferguson killed four wounded black soldiers in a house nearby.[845]

Elijah Kogier was shot at his home in Clinton County, Kentucky, in 1862 while his little daughter clung to him, pleading for his life. Ferguson killed William Fogg, who was sick in bed, in 1861, and did the same to Peter Zachery at Rufus Dowdy's house in Russell County, Kentucky, in January 1863.

Ferguson's most notorious murder occurred in Emory, Virginia, on November 7, 1864.[846] This killing followed the Saltville Massacre. Ferguson entered a Confederate hospital and went to the bed of a Union officer, Lt. Ezra C. Smith, 13th Kentucky Cavalry. Ferguson said, "Smith, do you see this?" Pointing the pistol directly at his head, he fired three times. The first two were misfires. The third killed Smith in his bed.[847] This particular killing caused Ferguson to be arrested and held for court-martial by the Confederate army, but he was released because the Confederate forces were falling apart. At trial, Ferguson was mute regarding Lt. Smith, but his defense to the other murders was simply that he killed people who were trying to kill him, if they had the chance. According to Confederate lore, Lt. Smith had "mistreated Ferguson's family; that he had made Ferguson's wife undress and marched her before him along the public road in a nude state."[848]

Regarding Lt. Smith, Ferguson spoke freely after his trial ended. "I acknowledge that I killed Lt. Smith in Emory and Henry Hospital. I had a motive in committing the act. He captured a number of my men at different times, and always killed the last one of them. I was instigated to kill him, but I will not say by whom, as I do not wish to criminate my friends. [Smith] is the only man I killed at or near Saltville [the battle that sent Smith to the hospital], and I am not sorry for killing him."[849] Ferguson's notoriety prompted his guards to have their picture taken with him and several images survive. The trial received daily verbatim newspaper coverage in Nashville and was reported in the northern press.

Ferguson's chief defense was that he fell within the terms of the surrender which barred punishment for actions committed during the war. His lawyers convinced former Confederate General "Fighting Joe" Wheeler to attend. His testimony was generally favorable to Ferguson, but failed to establish clear evidence that Ferguson held a commission or received and obeyed orders in killing any of the persons named in the indictment.[850]

The military commission convicted Ferguson in September and he was hanged on October 20, 1865, at the Nashville prison on Church Street in front of three hundred people who had received passes to witness his death. The prison itself was protected by soldiers from the 15th United States Colored Infantry, which irritated the townsfolk.

Ferguson walked the six steps up the gallows with a firm step and erect bearing. "Ferguson was dressed with scrupulous neatness in a black frock coat with vest and pants of the same material and black gloves and new gainters. The neatness of the prisoner has always been one of his peculiarites and was a noticeable feature of his character during the trial."[851] It took twenty-three minutes for the officer in charge, Colonel Shafter, to read the sentence. As it was being read, Ferguson stood on the gallows alternately nodding or shaking his head at various charges. When Colonel Shafter said, "to all which the accused pleads not guilty," Ferguson said, "But I don't now!" Shafter replied, "In accordance with this sentence, I am now going to have you executed." Ferguson replied, "Very well." The Rev. Bunting offered a prayer, and the killer bowed low, thanking him in an inaudible voice.

Colonel Shafter asked if he had any last words, to which Ferguson responded, "Nothing to say particularly at all. No, I don't think I have." When the noose was placed around his neck, Ferguson's face flushed a deep scarlet, perspiration broke forth profusely and his lips closed in a convulsive quiver. Colonel Shafter wiped the sweat from his face, and Ferguson seemed to regain his composure. The colonel called for a handkerchief to be placed around Ferguson's eyes, which he rejected.

Ferguson began speaking, "I don't know some things in those specifications, but I don't deny anything I ever done." He seemed unable to continue, but said, "I want to be sent to my family. I don't want to be buried in this soil." He paused again, "Don't give me to the doctors. I don't want to be cut up here." The colonel replied, "You shan't, Mr. Ferguson." More silence. "I want to be put in that thing," gesturing to the coffin, "and taken to White County, where I can have my family around me. If I had only had my way I wouldn't have been here. Whenever you are ready, I am done. My last request is to be sent away with my wife." The cap was placed over his head. Champ Ferguson's last words were, "Oh, Lord, have mercy on me!"[852]

Without warning, the trip rope was severed by a hatchet blow from a federal detective at 11:43 A.M. and the body dropped two feet with a heavy thud. Twice he slightly shrugged his shoulders. At thirteen and eighteen minutes his heart was still beating; after another four and one-half it stopped. The rope had embedded itself in the front of his neck and the knot in the back. Blood gushed from his nose onto the cap. The body hung until 12:24 P.M. and was placed in the coffin with the lid screwed down.

Champ Ferguson's execution started a folklore tradition that endured for decades, namely that he was not actually hanged, but his body was spirited away in a coffin and given to his wife and teen-age daughter, who were present at his execution, but went unnoticed. The folklore arose out of the fact that supposedly no one actually saw Ferguson's body hanging. The area below the gallows was obscured by wooden planking. Hence, he was alleged to have been placed in his coffin alive. The *Harper's Weekly* illustration of the hanging shows Ferguson dropping but also shows the planking.[853] Another version holds that Ferguson's pillaging during the war made him wealthy and his wife bribed the hangmen, who placed the body of a recently deceased black man in the coffin.[854] The folklore was further enhanced because his wife and daughter left Tennessee for the west and were never heard from again — and the fact that Ferguson's name was misspelled on his gravestone. The story was retold every time a man was hanged in late 19th-century Tennessee. For this reason, the man's body was often placed in a coffin near the jail or place of execution for all to see.

1866

George Craft (aka George Kraft; George Crabb; George Reid; George Red), white, age 17. *Murder.*
James Lysaught (aka James Lycought), white, age 16. *Murder.*
Thomas Perry (aka Thomas Ferry), white, age 20. *Murder.*
James Knight (aka William McClusky; William Dran; William Dean), white, age 17. *Murder.*

Craft was prosecuted and executed under the name George Craft but insisted his name was

Crabb.[855] He had used the alias Reid or George Red. Perry was sometimes known as Ferry. Knight had used the alias William McClusky, and was arrested under that name, but also used the alias William Dran or Dean. He was prosecuted and executed under the name William Dean. Lysaught's name has been reported as Lycought.

The crime was committed on the night of November 22, 1865, while Nashville was still under federal control. The killers were civilians employed as hands in the Army corrals. Knight had served in an Arkansas regiment in Confederate service. Perry had served in the 11th Tennessee and claimed to have been among those captured at Ft. Donelson. Kraft had been a teamster in the Eleventh Army Corps under Gen. Hooker. The killers lived in the back of a low saloon (referred to as a "doggery") on Jefferson Street, then occupied by federal soldiers of both races.

William Hefferman (sometimes spelled Heffran, Heffernan, Hufferman), white, age sixty, was a wealthy and respected street and railway contractor. Hefferman, his wife, adult daughter, and her husband Mr. Tracy were returning to their home from a musical program at St. Cecilia Convent. As their carriage came near the doggery, four to six young men came out and suddenly turned toward them. Perry stopped the horse. Mr. Tracy asked, "What do you want?" Hefferman said, "Surely you don't mean to hurt anyone here." Perry, closest to Hefferman, said, "Yes, goddamned quick, if you don't give up your money." Hefferman replied, "I am a private citizen, near my own home, just from an evening party and have no money."[856] Craft seized Hefferman, pulled him to the ground and beat him with a billy club. Mrs. Hefferman got out to help her injured husband.

Mr. Tracy shot a pistol at Craft. The bullet struck a glancing blow at the nipple and came out the chest. Craft returned fire. His bullet grazed Mrs. Hefferman's face and entered her husband's nose, passing into his skull. The buggy bolted, still carrying the Tracys, and by the time Mr. Tracy was able to control it, the killers had escaped. Taken to his home, Hefferman was able to describe both the incident and the killers, although he was bleeding badly and brains were coming out his nose. Hefferman died on November 26.

News of the incident stunned the city, and the next day two prostitutes led the town marshal to the injured Craft, who quickly confessed and implicated the others. Perry had escaped to Murfreesboro, where he was arrested after breaking into a shed.[857]

Taken to jail, Craft and his accomplices were visited by East Tennessee Unionists, Gen. Thomas Brownlow and Col. Horace Maynard. They identified Craft as the person who had robbed them a few days earlier on the Franklin turnpike.

A three-member military commission heard evidence against all but Perry in November. Perry's trial began on December 3, 1865. Co-defendant Joseph A. Jones (alias Tom Carter) denied involvement. Perry insisted he had not actually stopped the horse, only stood in front of it. He said Craft was the shooter. Witnesses included persons the killers had confided in, such as Perry's supervisor at the corral, who said that Perry had told him the details of the crime, which he relayed to the tribunal.[858] Another person, George Leonard, was originally charged with the five but did not face trial.

All but Jones were found guilty of a multiple-count indictment.[859] They appealed to Gen. Thomas, who affirmed the sentence January 16, 1866. He sent the case to General Grant. Grant refused clemency, as did President Andrew Johnson.

Throughout the trial and the appeal, the defendants maintained a confident and defiant manner, convinced they would be granted clemency. They broke only briefly, but generally maintained bravado, including joking, up to the moment they were pinioned and taken to the scaffold.[860] Then they began to tremble and sob.

The killers were seated on coffins and taken to the gallows on two wagons, each pulled by four white horses. The execution was at the state prison on Church Street on January 26, 1866. It was witnessed by a solemn and orderly crowd of ten thousand. Knight exhorted the onlookers, "I wish to say to all, don't swear, don't visit low houses, don't gamble, don't do anything wrong. If you take warning by me, you will never meet my fate, but I am going to a better world."[861]

Lysaught, the youngest, who had earlier joked that he weighed so little he might not actually die by the hanging, said, "I am no scholar; I have no education, but I wish, gentlemen, to say, that I hope I am going to a better world. I forgive everybody, and I hope no man in this crowd has anything against me. If he has, I hope he will forgive me." After thanking the military jailers for treating him kindly, and stating that if he had stayed in the city jail he would have starved to death, Lysaught concluded, "That is all, gentlemen, I am going to a better world and I hope to meet you all there."[862] Each bid the other farewell as the caps were being drawn over their heads.

Lysaught's neck was broken; the other three were

strangled, notably Perry. The knot had slipped around to the back of his neck. The killers were buried in unmarked graves at the National Cemetery in Nashville. Later in 1866, the United States Supreme Court ruled that criminal trials by military commissions were unconstitutional where the state courts were open, as they were in Nashville at this time.[863] But the result would not likely have been different.

At the time of the Hefferman murder in November 1865, the military was still trying to keep the peace in middle Tennessee. The newspapers carried frequent accounts of gangs robbing civilians.[864] Most of the gangs were garbed in at least partial blue uniforms. The execution of the Hefferman killers was a signal that the Army would punish federal lawbreakers as well as local criminals. Coming on the heels of the Ferguson execution, it showed fairness to all, regardless of prior allegiance.

Columbus C. German (aka Lum German), black (Melungeon), age 25. *Murder.*

The crime was committed sometime in the spring of 1864 on the victim's farm near Mill Creek, located three miles from Hilham, in rural Overton County.[865] The victim was Solomon "Lee" Hays, white, age thirty-three, a Union sympathizer.[866] The killing was a typical Civil War–era military-related, but civilian death, whereby Confederate partisans, sent as a foraging party, encounter a man determined to prevent what he deems theft of his property. He strikes or threatens them with a gun and is shot.

Here, Lum German and Evander Turner Deck, former Confederate soldiers who had deserted, joined a partisan group loosely under the command of Col. John M. Hughs, after they were cut off behind Union lines. The two-man foraging party, under the influence of whiskey, got into an argument with Hays. He was shot in the chest with a pistol held by German. Hays's wife had tried to intervene and witnessed the shooting.

Accounts of the trial differ; one said German was tried by military authority and released, but German appears to be the only Tennessee man convicted and executed by a civil jury for a wartime killing that was arguably military-related.

After the killing German rejoined his unit and was captured near Petersburg, Virginia. He was imprisoned in Elmira until March 1865, but upon release was sent to a military hospital in Richmond. He was indicted in September 1865 for the rape of Miss Jane Osborn, white, age unknown, during the war, and the killing of Hays. Evander Turner Deck was also indicted for the rape.[867]

The date of German's arrest is unknown but he was kept in the military prison in Nashville because the Overton County jail had been destroyed by fire. On the way to Nashville, he attempted suicide by cutting his throat. A newspaper reported, "He is represented as a notorious and desperate character, and will be held to answer the charges of rape and murder."[868] Lum German begged military authorities to release him.[869] They refused and he was returned to Overton County for trial in January 1866.

German's defense was that Deck had been ordered to get a horse and German had accompanied him. Asking that the trial be postponed, he explained that he was "very much intoxicated" at the time. Hays knocked him down with a large stick. He got up and was knocked down again. "Deck seeing the difficulty ran up and shot deceased."[870] The motion for continuance said that Deck was a necessary witness. Also necessary were Thomas Davis, Marion Gore, Carter A. Allison and William German (his brother). These witnesses were needed to show that when Columbus German was intoxicated Deck commonly disarmed him "because of his condition."

The trial went forward under Judge Hauk, a Brownlow appointee, who was a "better judge of whiskey than he is of law," who interrupted the trial to drink and made "nightly raids into the country after certain lewd women, and would return of a morning wet, muddy, and red-eyed; and his red eyes, and the unmistakable drunken leer, proclaimed his intoxication on the bench to the most casual observer."[871] No ex–Confederates or sympathizers were allowed on the jury.

The details of the trial are unknown, but Deck did not testify. About the same time German had returned to the Confederate Army, Deck became a turncoat and joined the Union Army. He was never tried for the rape charge. He did return to Overton County in 1868 after German's hanging and died twenty years later. The newspaper reported German's case: "There seems to be no palliating circumstances in this case. It appeared that the accused went to the home of the deceased for the purpose of taking the latter's horse, when the deceased resisted, whereupon the accused drew his revolver and shot him dead."[872] German was convicted on May 29, 1866, and sentenced to hang on June 4, 1866. No effort to appeal has been discovered. The Overton County sheriff returned German to Livingston from the Fentress County jail accompanied by six guards.[873] This number was likely deemed necessary to prevent his rescue.

Columbus German was hanged before a large

crowd in Livingston on July 28, 1866.[874] Handcuffed and taken in a cart sitting on his coffin, German was placed under an oak tree and the rope placed around his neck. He showed little emotion. Following the reading of scripture and a prayer, the sheriff asked German if he had anything to say. He replied, "I am not guilty."[875] He was swung off in the traditional manner.

Lum German's case would likely have been lost to history but for an incident three years later. His brother, William German, who had also served in the Confederate Army, was jealous of a former slave named Bill Cullum. William German was told to vacate the farm he and his family were renting from the white landowner, Alvin Cullum, so the former slave could live there. Dressed in Klan garb, German and another man met Bill Cullum on the road, shot him several times, and left him for dead. He was able to crawl to a house and name German before he died.

The "official" Klan was outraged. In a widely distributed news report, it took William German from his home on the night of January 13, 1869. He was hanged in a nearby barn with the following sign placed on the body, "Hung for shooting [n — er] Bill Cullum and violating the laws of the KKK."[876] Lum German's death was mentioned along with his brother's.[877]

W.W. "Tobe" Thornton, white, age 40. *Murder.*

The details of the crime are unknown except that Thornton and several others were brought to trial on November 14, 1866, for the killing of Sam W. Broyles, white, twenty-one, a respected citizen of Hardin County. The trial lasted five days and only Thornton was convicted. There was no appeal. Thornton was hanged in Savannah on December 21, 1866.[878] The judge in this case was the notorious Fielding Hurst.[879] This was the last execution in Hardin County.

1867

Joseph Huff (aka Jacob Huff and Joseph Hough), black, age 32. *Murder.*

The crime was committed on the afternoon of August 25, 1866, in a rural area outside of Chattanooga, between Ooltaway and Tyner's Station, in Hamilton County. The victim was John Jones Killpatrick, white, age thirty-six, a farmer. Killpatrick had a contract to sell timber (lumber) to the railroad. He had been sick with a fever and was well enough to go outside for the first time. He and his wife Margaret were taking a short walk and were returning to their house, when they were met by Huff, carrying a shotgun.

The victim had earlier told his partner in the timber contract that some of the lumber was missing and he suspected Huff had taken it. He had reported this to the railroad officials. Although Killpatrick was carrying a pistol in his waistband, he was not fearful of Huff. When told about Huff's anger and a threat to beat him up, Killpatrick said, "I don't think I will let him get hold of me."[880]

As they met, Huff angrily said to Killpatrick, "You have been talking about me and I'm going to kill you." By this time, the couple had passed Huff. The wife turned and saw the shotgun pointed at her husband and knocked it up. Killpatrick began to scuffle with Huff for the gun. During the scuffle, Killpatrick fell to the ground on his face. Huff placed the muzzle of the gun directly toward the victim's back, shooting him in the spine.[881]

Several witnesses said they heard Huff say ten days before the killing he was going to beat up the victim, or be killed doing so. Huff told one witness he would give Killpatrick a "damn good beating." The witness told Huff he had better not because one of them might get killed. Huff replied he was as good a killer as the victim. The witness said he might get hung for it. Huff replied, "Catching comes before hanging and if I get to the bushes, not ten white men could take me."[882] Huff was arrested two weeks after the killing.

Huff's conviction was affirmed by the Tennessee Supreme Court but the opinion cannot be located, only a per curiam order entered on the bill of exceptions.[883]

Huff was executed on December 27, 1867, in Harrison, then the county seat of Hamilton County. The sheriff in charge was Asbury Conner. John Nance was hanged the same day in Rutledge.

John Nance, white, age 26. *Murder.*

The crime was committed on the afternoon of October 8, 1864, near Blain's Cross Roads in Grainger County. At the time of the killing, Nance claimed he was home on military leave. He said he had enlisted in the 17th Tennessee Cavalry (Federal) early in the war and had been captured and his enlistment had expired. Following his leave, he planned to reenlist in another Federal regiment. The victim was William P. McBee, white, age twenty-four. The men knew each other prior to the killing and were on good terms. The day before the killing they had gone to the Blain's Cross Roads mustering center, where Nance claimed he had reenlisted as a soldier and McBee as a militiaman.[884]

There is much confusion regarding McBee's status. The contemporary view was that McBee was a Confederate, or at least had Confederate sympathies, due in part to Nance's statement when passing the Strawberry Plains graveyard where McBee was buried, "There lies one damned rebel I have killed, and if they don't mind, I will kill several more of them."[885] In his published "confession," Nance has McBee saying that a certain man would not sell him whiskey (and he therefore asked Nance to buy it) because "he was a rebel."[886] Nance's own words can be interpreted three ways — the victim (McBee) was a rebel or the person who sold the whiskey was a rebel, or the seller thought McBee was a rebel.

The victim, William P. McBee, had enlisted in the Union Army's 1st Tennessee Infantry (1st East Tennessee Infantry Regiment) as a private.[887] This regiment served throughout Tennessee and Kentucky. When the three-year enlistments were up, the entire regiment was mustered out of service on September 17, 1864.[888] It is likely that private McBee would still have possession of his mustering-out pay on October 8, 1864.

The confusion was likely enhanced by a defense that Nance was a member of the regular army at the time of the killing, and therefore civil authorities had no jurisdiction, especially since he had been tried (apparently) under military authority for the McBee murder on March 30, 1865, and was convicted.[889] He escaped from jail and the federal authorities made little attempt to capture him, but a reward was offered for his arrest. This produced his body for a second trial. Nance was tried again by civil authority in January 1, 1867, in Grainger County, and was convicted by a jury.[890]

As Nance and McBee were coming back from the muster, they rode together. "McBee became very sick and made attempts to vomit, and finally fell from his horse. We were both very drunk."[891] A short while later, Nance bought two and a half pints of whiskey and "I let McBee have one pint of it." Said Nance, "I then went out, and John Rice was standing in the yard. I told Rice to keep McBee there — that I didn't want him to go with me any further — that I was going to Laurence's."[892]

Despite the detail in Nance's "confession," he provides no information about the killing. Rather, he continued to his destination, which included crossing the Holston River on a puncheon, and staying with friends and going to a party — but he was so intoxicated that he remembered little of what he had done — and had no knowledge of McBee's death until he was told about it.[893] Said Nance, "I believe the public think I killed William McBee; but now, in the face of death, with only a few days to live, if I murdered him, I do not know it. I was drunk at the time."[894]

No one actually saw the killing. Several persons saw the two quarreling as McBee rode his horse and Nance walked.[895]

Twenty-three witnesses appeared at the trial. The state's witnesses asserted that Nance was not actually in the federal army at the time of the killing, that he had told several of them that he had killed McBee and would do the same to others. The most compelling witness was Prissilla Maples, who said Nance came to her house the night of the killing, explained he had killed McBee, was so nervous he refused to eat supper or breakfast the next morning, and said he had taken $500 from McBee. The defense responded that she had a bad reputation and if her testimony had been true he would have shown her the money. Several witnesses testified that Nance had actually been in the Rebel army.[896] His brother-in-law testified he had never been in the federal army.[897]

Nance's own witnesses were fellow jail inmates who spent most of their time on the witness stand denying they had been paid to tell a story that another soldier probably killed McBee or that Nance was actually in federal service at the time. On one issue, all witnesses seemed to agree: "Liquor makes Nance talk pretty wildly."[898]

The rest of Nance's "confession" was a litany of jailings, the opportunity to escape which he declined, a successful escape, re-arrest, a release, another re-arrest. It is also clear that the men who finally brought Nance back to Grainger County were motivated by a reward and were not lawmen.

Nance's argument to the Tennessee Supreme Court raised only one issue, whether the facts of first-degree murder were shown, rather than second-degree, because every witness agreed that Nance was highly intoxicated at the time of the killing. Precisely, there was no evidence of premeditation. Further, McBee's pocketbook was found near his body and it still contained money. Nance's brief seemed to say that McBee was killed while Nance was in a drunken haze. No issue of his federal status or the prior court-martial was raised in the appeal.

The Tennessee Supreme Court, sitting in Knoxville, affirmed the death sentence, in an opinion by Justice Nicholson, and ordered him hanged on December 27, 1867. The opinion cannot be located.[899] By the time of his execution, Nance spent most of his time in Bible-reading and prayer, and promised that if his sentence were commuted, he would never touch alcohol.[900] The details of Nance's execution are unknown except that he was hanged on December 27, 1867, in Rutledge, Grainger County, and his death was witnessed by three thousand people.

The issue of whether a prior court-martial or military commission conviction served to bar a later civil court conviction had been (seemingly) answered by the Tennessee Supreme Court sometime in 1867.[901] A federal officer, Lt. Rankin, a member of the 9th Tennessee Cavalry, had killed John Thornhill in Jefferson County on June 1, 1865. Details of the case are unknown. He was acquitted by a court-martial on October 5, 1865. Meanwhile, in August 1865, he was indicted in the Jefferson County circuit court, but the indictment was dismissed for double jeopardy. Reversing, the Supreme Court held the prior adjudication did not result in double jeopardy because these were different governments. It allowed the second case to go forward.[902]

The issue remained before the Tennessee courts at least until 1876. Sometime during the war, Pryor Coleman, a Union Army soldier, had killed Mourning Ann Bell in Knox County. Coleman was convicted by a court-martial in 1865 and sentenced to die. But he was released. In 1873, he was arrested upon an indictment for the murder. He sought a writ of habeas corpus and the district court freed him.[903] However, the state went forward with its case upon Coleman's demurrer and the Tennessee Supreme Court said that Coleman could be tried for the crime. Again, this was because two separate governments were involved, Coleman had not been punished, and the facts "make a clear case of murder in the first degree."[904] The United States Supreme Court reversed the conviction, but said Coleman could still be punished under the court-martial. He was ultimately imprisoned for life in a New York prison and served ten years.

Mitch Pearson, purportedly acting under federal authority from General Milroy[905] to recover all federal horses found in Bedford County, killed William Cheek, whom he accused of stealing Pearson's own horse during the war. Cheek's dying declaration said he knew nothing about Pearson's horse. The case came to trial in 1873. The Tennessee Supreme Court's opinion ignored Pearson's military status and seemed to agree that the facts likely supported a murder conviction, but reversed because Pearson had not been given enough opportunity to locate a crucial witness. He had been kept in jail for a long period prior to trial and the witness had moved to a different county years earlier.[906]

1869

James Galvin, white, age 25. *Murder.*

The crime was committed about 12:30 P.M. Christmas Day, 1867, near a saloon on Main Street between Winchester and Commerce Streets, in Memphis, Shelby County. The killer and two friends, Connell and McGrain, had been drinking in the Delta saloon. Two Negroes were passing the entrance just as the trio left. Someone in the Galvin party (said to be Connell) knocked down one of the Negroes and a brawl erupted. The Negroes hailed the victim, John Fenton, white, age thirty-one, a policeman in uniform who was walking home.

Fenton attempted to arrest Connell, who knocked him into a gutter. Connell wrested the policeman's billy club and began beating Fenton with it. A witness testified that while Fenton was down, Connell was over him and Galvin held him. Fenton rose and struggled with Connell in the street. Galvin drew a pistol and said nobody would arrest him, or Connell said this; the witness did not know.

Another policeman, Chamberlain, arrived and Fenton said, "Arrest that man," indicating Galvin. Chamberlain moved toward Galvin, who drew his pistol. Chamberlain stopped because Galvin said to him, "If you go for your pistol you are a dead man."[907] Chamberlain, who had been walking with his wife, was not carrying a pistol.

Getting free from Connell, who with McGrain apparently ran away, Fenton came across the street toward Galvin, who had turned to go away, saying to him, "I want you!" Galvin stopped, turned, and with a pistol in hand said to the advancing officer, "Don't you come any nearer, or I'll shoot you."[908] Fenton drew his pistol and as he was cocking it, Galvin fired one shot, grazing his arm. The bullet killed a German boy, Joseph Schellen, age ten, who was standing behind Fenton. Galvin fired two more shots as Fenton fired at him. Fenton was hit by the third and died within hours. The trio were arrested within hours. Galvin escaped from jail and was finally arrested six months later, having stayed in the Memphis area.

Two defense witnesses (unnamed but probably

Connell and McGrain) said that Fenton fired first. The Tennessee Supreme Court said, "This testimony is contradicted by such amount of testimony as to be incredible."[909]

The chief defense was that the shooting was in "defense of his person against an assault or unlawful arrest" and was justifiable homicide, or manslaughter.[910] The court said the notion that homicide committed in response to an illegal arrest equaled manslaughter was not the law.[911] Here, Fenton technically did not have authority to arrest Galvin or Connell because the assault on the Negro did not occur in his presence. The amount of force Galvin could use to resist arrest must be "proportioned to the emergency," but here, the shooting was done because the officer was attempting to arrest Connell.

Galvin had no right to assault the officer or use a dangerous weapon. Said the court, "He had not the right to interfere for the assistance or rescue of Connell who stood in no relation to him justifying such interference, by assaulting the officer or displaying deadly weapons."[912] Actually, ruled the court, Fenton had the right to arrest Galvin the moment he drew his pistol on the public street."[913] Premeditation was shown here because "design or intention may be conceived, and deliberately formed in an instant."[914]

The judge who sentenced Galvin signed a petition asking the governor to commute his sentence. A lengthy commutation petition was sent to Gov. Sentor, who also received a long counter-petition.

In jail, Galvin became a changed man, forsaking his "reckless and violent speech," in part due to the efforts of Father O'Brien, to whom he confessed. Interviewed in his cell, he showed a "calm and peaceful state of mind."[915] The priest and Galvin walked to the gallows together, repeating a liturgy. Galvin wore a new shirt and suit provided by his brother. A Negro barber had come to his cell that morning to shave him and oil his hair. Before stepping out of his cell, Galvin buffed his shoes with a towel.[916]

James Galvin was executed at 1:43 P.M. on August 20, 1869, on a gallows erected inside the yard of the Shelby County jail in front of three hundred witnesses in the yard and at least a thousand (mostly black) seated or standing on roofs, railroad cars, and balconies. Several thousand waited in the streets, unable to see anything except the coffin as it was taken from the jail. As Galvin was being taken to the gallows a shed outside the jail collapsed under the weight of spectators. This caused the crowd to stampede, seriously injuring one man. Among the spectators inside the yard were Mrs. Fenton and Mrs. Perry, wives of the policemen killed by Galvin and Samuel Moody (q.v.).

Following reading of the death warrant, Father O'Brien gave the service for the dead, responses given by Galvin. He stepped forward and said, "I appear before you today for the last time on earth. I have a few remarks to make, however, before leaving this world forever. It is true I killed officer Fenton, but I did it in self-defense. If I had not thought I should be killed by him, I would not have shot him. I forgive all who had a hand in bringing me to this ignominious death, as I have been forgiven by God. Good-bye and God bless all."[917]

Galvin was pinioned with leather straps with buckles, said to be much better than traditional ropes. The cap and rope were placed and without verbal warning the trap was sprung. He gave a few convulsive shudders and a partial drawing up of the legs. He was cut down fifteen minutes later and his body turned over to his brother and friends.

The newspaper said this was the first execution in Memphis since John [*sic*] Stover in June 1860 [*sic*], overlooking the fact that others had been executed as spies and deserters during the war. It reported that since 1860 hundreds of men had been murdered in Memphis but less than five percent had "condign punishment meted out to them." It was thought the execution of Galvin, an Irish brawler, and Moody, a black, would send the message that law and order had returned to Memphis.[918]

Samuel Moody, black, age 20. *Murder.*

The crime was committed about 9:00 P.M. on June 4, 1868, at Price & Yeatman's store in downtown Memphis, in Shelby County. The killer was burglarizing the store when the victim, Capt. James Perry, white, age forty, suspected a burglary was in progress. He lit a match and was shot one time by K.G. "Cagey" Bedford, black, age unknown.

According to Moody's last statement, he happened upon Bedford while walking down Main Street between Union and Monroe. Bedford, a much older, experienced criminal, induced Moody to go with him to burglarize the store, in part by showing him a pistol. There is some inference from Moody's statement that Bedford shamed him into taking part. They removed the grate from the sidewalk and Moody entered the service door. They looked around the building holding candles and Bedford took a few things.

As they were leaving, two police officers appeared. The leader, Capt. Perry, struck a match and asked, "Who's in there?" At that moment, Bedford fired one shot which killed the policeman instantly. Bedford jumped over the body and ran away. Moody followed, but was seen and identified by the other officer. He was arrested two days later.

Moody insisted to the end that he had not shot Perry (which was generally believed by most people), but was convicted and sentenced to death. At the time of Moody's execution, Bedford was in prison but it is not known whether this was related to the Perry killing. The file in Moody's appeal to the Tennessee Supreme Court cannot be located.

In jail, Moody found religion under the care of the Rev. W.R. Revels and the Rev. B.M. Williamson, both black, Methodists. He had another black inmate read the Bible to him. The gallows were built inside the courtyard of the Shelby County jail, and had to be mounted by a ladder. The black ministers and two white ones accompanied Moody to the top. Once there, the Rev. Revels read II Corinthians, chapter four, and offered a short homily. Moody was asked to make a last statement and he said he was ready to meet his God who had forgiven him and urged young men to stay away from bad company. He insisted he was innocent because he had not actually fired the fatal bullet.[919] The hymn was sung, "There is a Fountain Filled With Blood," followed by a prayer from Rev. Revels. Throughout the death ceremony Moody's whole body trembled in fear like an "aspen in the wind."[920]

Samuel Moody was hanged at 2:26 P.M. on August 20, 1869, by Sheriff Cupp, following the execution of James Galvin at 1:43 P.M. The same crowd saw both executions and in the jail yard were both Mrs. Fenton and Mrs. Perry. After being pinioned, Moody kept repeating, "Jesus, receive me! Lord, have mercy! Oh, Lamb of God, take me!" while the noose and cap were placed. The sheriff triggered the trap without warning and Moody fell cleanly. He was declared dead eleven minutes later, put in a walnut coffin, and taken by friends to his mother's house.

Five days later, the following appeared in a Memphis newspaper:

> Moody — he that was thought to have been hanged by the neck until he was dead, dead, dead! on Friday last — was seen taking a drink in the "Fixed Bayonets" saloon, on Gayoso street, yesterday afternoon. His neck having been broken, he experiences a little inconvenience from the liability of his head to suddenly drop over on one side; but beyond this, he is all right. Woods and Givens slept the better last night for the announcement of a morning cotemporary yesterday that Moody stood the hanging so well.[921]

The executions of Galvin and Moody were the first legal executions in Memphis since 1860, according to the newspapers, which ignored Civil War spying and desertion executions. At least a thousand people perched on rooftops, balconies and railroad cars outside the jail to watch them drop. Many had paid twenty-five cents to watch from the windows and rooftop of a nearby mill. Earlier, some had filed through the jail to glimpse Galvin and Moody, who said nothing. They also looked at the newly-made (in Memphis) rope which was heavily waxed and bore the hangman's noose. With each drop, the crowd let out a thunderous cheer. Likewise, each time, the crowd began to panic and several policemen received injuries, as did some in the crowd who were slightly bayoneted by the policemen.

A carriage filled with prostitutes was turned over, dropping the "whole dirty crowd into the street," along with a horse that fell on a child, who was seriously injured.[922] Another woman, Mrs. Marie Golay, age sixty, was thrown down and run over by a wagon. She died four days later.[923]

1870

Henry Williams (aka Andy Williams), black, age 20. *Murder.*

The crime was committed about 1:30 P.M. on November 5, 1867, on a road five miles outside of Chattanooga, in the direction of Lovingood. The killer was a career thief who had stolen some watches from the victim's jewelry store. Most had been recovered, but Williams was serving a twenty-day sentence for theft. A jail guard told the victim, Adolph Duetch, white, age thirty-three, that Williams would take him or his brother Henry to where two of the watches were hidden near Bird's Mill, if they came and got him from the jail and took him there.

With only eight more days to serve, Williams was released from the jail in the victim's custody and they began walking toward the location on the morning of November 5, 1867. Adolph Duetch spoke to his brother that morning and told him where the two were going. The victim wore gloves and comfort, and his brother's coat to wear as an overcoat. The black coat had a distinctive velvet collar. He also wore pants, boots, his coat, and a hat. He carried a hidden Navy revolver and said he would return about 3:00 P.M. Adolph Duetch did not return on time, and his brother began a search the next day.

The victim was found about five miles from Chattanooga, near a road where he had been dragged some ten feet into the bushes on his face. The body was found wearing only a "shirt, vest, slips and socks."[924] The skull had been crushed from several blows from behind, and a bloody stick (wagon standard) was found near the body. A witness identified the wagon standard as one he had made that was missing from his wagon about a mile from where Duetch's body was found.

Another witness who lived in the area testified that Duetch and the defendant had stopped by his house and asked directions to Lovingood. The defendant was carrying a stick that looked like the one found near the body. Another witness said she saw the defendant wearing a dark-colored coat with a velvet collar, similar to the one exhibited at trial, and carrying a pair of black pants on his arm, and carrying a pair of boots in his hand. He had on a dirty shirt and a pair of old shoes.

The sheriff testified that two days after Duetch's death he began a hunt for Williams, who had obviously not returned to the jail, and saw him come out of a rural cabin. He said Williams ran into a thicket wearing the hat, coat and pants of the victim, as identified by the brother. Williams was still wearing the same clothes when he was captured two days later.[925] The sheriff testified that following the arrest, Williams said he had killed the man to get his clothes and get away.

The chief issue on appeal was whether a confession made by Williams to Henry Duetch, in jail after he was first tried and convicted of killing the brother, was properly admitted. The Tennessee Supreme Court said it was, but recounted the facts to show that the crime was proven by the evidence without the confession.[926] (This confession was made after the brother approached Williams wanting to know if his brother had suffered.) The court found the proof clearly supported the finding of guilt.

This was Williams's second trial. In a decision that cannot be located, the Tennessee Supreme Court held the original indictment was defective. Williams's counsel in the first appeal was Thomas A.R. Nelson. As a senator, he had defended President Johnson at his impeachment trial. He had been elected to the Tennessee Supreme Court under the new Constitution of 1870, which was designed to sweep incumbents from office. Nelson was very unhappy as a judge and resigned after about a year's service, in December 1871.[927] Nelson did not hear the case as a member of the Supreme Court. Henry Williams (known to most as Andy) was executed on cold December 16, 1870, amid blowing snow.

A hundred passengers paid $1.50 for a round trip steamboat ride from Chattanooga to Harrison, then the county seat of Hamilton County. Williams smoked cigars and laughed with the passengers. He was shown a pamphlet that supposedly contained his written "confession" and said it was inaccurate. From the steamboat he was taken to the jail in Harrison and covered with a shroud.

About 500 people were gathered around the gallows when Williams was finally brought there in a wagon. The crowd was boisterous. "Well, I want to see him dance on nothing," said one. "Well, I thought I'd come to see the hanging, my wife is sick," said another. "One less Radical vote," chimed another. The spectators built small bonfires to warm themselves. Williams sat on a chair on the gallows.

The minister Williams had asked to attend did not arrive and the sheriff asked for a volunteer. The Rev. Hubbard Clark came forth and led the hymn, "And Am I Only Born to Die?" After this, Williams said the death sentence was just and asked Duetch's brother for forgiveness. He replied, "Andy, I have done my duty towards my brother." Next, Williams asked a notorious courtesan to come forward and he asked her to take care of his child in Knoxville. Williams asked to be baptized and the Rev. Clark performed this duty by sprinkling him. Another hymn was sung, "Back From the Tomb a Soulful Sound."

Williams spotted the doctor in the crowd and asked that his body remain untouched. The doctor said it wasn't wanted. As the cap was placed over his head and the rope adjusted, the crowd continued loud talking and joking, described as "drunken wit." Without warning the trap was loosened and the body fell. It trembled and quivered and the feet jerked. Williams was cut down after eighteen minutes. The rope and knot were placed in the coffin, "to let the Old Man know what death he died." Williams was buried beside Huff.

The story that the rope was too long, which caused a deputy sheriff to hastily begin digging under Williams's feet, was false. The grave had already been dug, but no shovels were present. The deputies and others were forced to kick the dirt over the coffin with their feet, as if planting a tree. Adolph Duetch had been buried in the first Jewish cemetery in Chattanooga. His tombstone reads, "Died by the hand of an assassin."

1872

Edmund Lea (aka Edmond Lee), black, age 22. *Murder.*

The crime was committed about 8:00 P.M. on October 3, 1871, on the victim's farm in a rural area of Haywood County. The killer was a farmhand employed by the victim, Elias King, Jr., white, age twenty-three. The King family had large land holdings in Haywood County. The King patriarch had landed at Jamestown, Virginia, in 1620.

Edmund Lea was known as a wild and reckless young man who enjoyed getting intoxicated and taking the finest of Elias King's horses and riding around the country at full gallop, shooting weapons in all directions. About two months before the killing, Lea rode a horse into the town of Brownsville, firing shots and scaring people. Arrested, King posted his bond, securing his release.[928]

On September 30, 1871, the killer was hauling a load of cotton to a gin house when the mules stopped and could not be budged. Lea savagely beat the animals with a club. Still they would not move. Lea took a knife and opened a mule's mouth and slashed the inside of its mouth. Then he "carved their heads to ribbons." King was nearby, but did not see the actual cutting. He reprimanded Lea, who then sassed him. This caused King to hit Lea on the head and back with a small board lying on the ground. The next day, Lea came to work complaining of head and back pain. King told him to go inside the house, where Mrs. King dressed his wounds and applied salve.

Lea continued to brood. He crept up to the house and fired a rifle through an open window. King was inside reading a newspaper, his wife nearby. The rifle's muzzle was inside the open window and Lea had prepared what was called a rude scaffold to reach the window.

He was soon arrested and promptly confessed, insisting he was urged to kill King by the man who had raised him, his "Pappy," Robert Carter. According to Lea, when he told Carter about being hit by King, Carter told him he "must kill that gentleman." He said Carter furnished him an Enfield rifle, told him to make lead bullets for it, loaded the bullets and the powder, and put the percussion cap in place for him. Carter told him to take good aim. After killing King, he was to take the victim's best horse and come back to Carter's, where he would be given money to leave for Texas.

It cannot be determined whether Carter was ever charged in the matter, but Lea did not follow the plan. He went straight to Memphis, spent money foolishly, and end up at his sister's house in Shelby County, where he was arrested without a struggle.

Lea was quickly convicted by the Haywood County jury but it cannot be determined whether he appealed to the Tennessee Supreme Court. Because the date of the conviction, December 7, 1871, and the date of execution, February 2, 1872, were close, an appeal seems unlikely. A reporter from a Memphis newspaper visited Lea the day before the execution. Asked how he spent the night, Lea answered, "All right." Asked about the crime, Lea said he didn't want to talk about it. Lea spent his time in jail playing his Jew's harp or cursing everyone he saw. The newspaper called him a "quarrelsome, turbulent full-blooded negro."

After he was taken from the jail to the gallows by a dozen armed guards, Lea's execution followed the typical order of ministers exhorting the mostly black crowd of one thousand to live a proper life. Several hymns were sung, including the gallows standard, "There is a Fountain Filled with Blood." The ceremony included reading of the 92nd Psalm and Lea was asked for last words. Lea said little, but asked to sing several hymns, which he was allowed to do. He said he was convinced he was going to heaven.

In the absence of an appropriate cap, a black gauze was placed around his eyes. When the drop fell, a gust of wind took the gauze from his head. Floating upward it seemed to signal to spectators that Lea's soul was likewise wending its way to heaven.

Robert Beatty, black, age 29. *Murder.*

The crime was committed on May 25, 1871, in a rural area on a farm owned by a white couple, Mr. and Mrs. Whittaker, in Maury County. The victim, Mary Jane Beatty, black, age twenty-four, was the cook for the Whittaker household. The kitchen was separate from the house and Mrs. Whittaker heard the Beattys arguing. The victim's body was found in Fountain Creek, a mile and one-half downstream from the murder scene. Mary Jane had been hacked in the back of the head and neck.

Beatty's conviction was affirmed by the Tennessee Supreme Court. It said the proof showed that Beatty had quarreled violently with his wife, told an acquaintance that he was going to kill someone and brandished a knife. He told several people that he had two wives, that the other one "hugged him and kissed him" but Mary Jane did not. Likewise, Mrs. Whittaker testified that the quilt and blanket found around Mary Jane's body, which was bound with a grass rope, had been given to her by the Whittaker family.[929] The jury found Beatty guilty but with mitigating circumstances. The trial judge disregarded the recommendation and sentenced Beatty to death. The Supreme Court said this was a matter for the trial court's discretion.[930]

Beatty maintained his innocence to the end. In jail, he was attended by the Rev. Blackman Williams, black, who rode with him on the wagon taking him to the gallows.

Beatty was hanged at 1:30 P.M. April 5, 1872, on a gallows on the bank of the Duck River, about a mile from Columbia. At least ten thousand people watched his death. Two-thirds were black.

After reaching the gallows, the Rev. Williams read the 22nd Psalm and made a "very feeling talk to Beatty." The minister led the masses in singing the hymn "Show Pity, Lord; Oh, Lord, Forgive." The Rev. Smith, black, offered a fervent prayer for Beatty.

Beatty then spoke to the crowd saying he had stolen watermelons and chickens, but never wheat, corn or bacon, and insisted he was innocent. He spoke for over half an hour on disconnected topics, apparently trying to delay the hanging as long as possible. Sheriff Latta kept looking at his watch but did not stop him. A number of his friends made their way close to the gallows to tell him good-bye, but he ignored them.

When Beatty stopped talking, the sheriff adjusted the rope and cap and said farewell. Without verbal warning, the sheriff cut the rope with one hatchet chop. Beatty plunged to his death "amidst the most deafening and unearthly religious yells it is possible to imagine, from the throats of at least a thousand horror-stricken negroes." Said the newspaper, "The women, especially, showed great excitement, some of them shouting, 'Glory! Glory!' and even rolling upon the ground in their frantic demonstrations."[931] Said the newspaper, "This is explained by the fact that Beatty told them all he had repented and wanted to meet them in heaven. His colored sisters really thought they were helping him on the road to immortal bliss."[932]

After hanging twenty minutes, the body was cut down and buried by some of Beatty's friends on the river bank a few steps from the gallows. "Then they had another big singing and praying, after which all quietly dispersed." Said the newspaper, "There were no disturbances throughout the day, though there were more negroes in Columbia than had ever been seen at any one time before."[933]

In 1875, the following appeared in the local newspaper: "Several years ago Bob Beatty, col., was hanged at the old wharf below town. It will be remembered by those present that Bob stated a few minutes before he was hung that he did not kill his wife, for which he was about to be hanged, and pointed his finger at Warren Childrey and Dock Harris, in the crowd, and said they did it. Nobody believed Bob. Well, last Sunday a report was freely circulated in town that Childrey had died the day before, and just before he died had called his family to his bedside and told them that he and Capt. Dock Hart had killed Bob Beatty's wife."[934]

The paper continued: "The report was freely circulated and stated confidently. Monday morning the rumor was found to have no foundation whatever. Childrey had not been sick even. We cannot find out who started the lying report. Surely he ought to be punished, whoever he be. The evidence against Beatty was strong as it could be almost — his own children testifying against him; besides he ran off, and when caught, confessed to the deed."[935]

James Calvin Logston (aka Calvin Logston and Calvin Logsdon), white, age 24. *Murder.*

The crime was committed late in the night of November 19, 1868, at the rural home of Mrs. Catherine Galloway, a widow, at a place called Three Forks of Wolf River, in Fentress County. Her husband had been a Union soldier during the Civil War but had not received a bounty for enlistment, nor back pay due at the time of his death.[936] His widow had recently gotten the money, \$300.[937] Logston had come from his home in Kentucky to visit his grandfather, William Brown, who lived near the Galloway family. He was a known criminal; by the time of his execution he boasted of killing eight people. Two women who were the killer's aunts, Eliza (Lizzie) and Jane Brown, played a role in the crime.

The victims were killed by blows from an ax and possibly a shovel. The victims were all members of the same family. They were Mrs. Catherine Galloway, white, age twenty-six; one of her children, William B. Galloway, white, age four; and Lucinda Galloway, white, age fifty-three.[938] Lucinda was Catherine's mother-in-law. The chief witness against Logston was James Hill Galloway, age six at the time of the killings. He was Catherine's son. He had been seriously injured from a shovel blow to the head after the killings and was unconscious for two days.

Logston was first convicted in Scott County. Logston's appeal to the Tennessee Supreme Court found that the change of venue was without the defendant's request or approval, and a new trial was granted.[939]

The second conviction in Fentress County was reversed on appeal because the indictment was defectively drawn. Because it charged Logston with the death of three people in a single count, the indictment was not clear. The Supreme Court said the indictment should inform the defendant whether these were separate and distinct killings, or three all at once.[940] The court declined to pass on the question of whether (now) eight-year-old James Galloway was too young to testify, the court ruled that this must be decided on a case-by-case basis.

Logston's third trial was for Lucinda Galloway's death alone. The details remain unclear except the two Brown women came to the house supposedly to warn the family that Logston was on his way to kill them. When Logston arrived he brandished a pistol and demanded money. When this was refused, Logston took an ax and struck Catherine first. Then he hit granny Lucinda, and finally little brother William. The cabin was awash with brains and blood, as Logston left with the women's money. James also testified Jane Brown hit him with the shovel.[941]

The coroner's jury the next day determined that the killing was done by a left-handed person and Logston, left-handed, was immediately suspected. He was also missing. Within three days he was found at his father's house in Kentucky. His clothing was blood-spattered.

Logston's third trial was held in Overton County and the conviction was upheld by the Tennessee Supreme Court. The court said the testimony of Dr. J.H. Storie, who examined the bodies, was proper since it was needed to show a full description of the position of Mrs. Galloway in relation to things and persons present.[942] The court said the fact there were dead people with her tended to "destroy the hypothesis of their guilt, as inconsistent with the guilt of the accused."[943]

The court held that young James Galloway's testimony was proper because he had been properly qualified by being asked what would become of him if he lied. He answered, "Yes; the bad man will get me." He was asked who told him so. He said his mother. The court characterized his testimony as remarkably intelligent and said his testimony, "given on former trials, discovers an honesty the absence of which in many older and more mature persons, is to be regretted."[944]

Following his arrest, Logston had confessed the killing to various constables and deputies. The court ruled that Logston's confessions were made freely and voluntarily, "without the least inducement of hope or fear."[945]

When the Tennessee Supreme Court announced its decision and asked Logston if he had anything to say, he did not respond, but within days he sent the court a short note proclaiming his innocence and blaming his conviction on a conspiracy and the fact that he was a stranger in the community.[946]

Calvin Logston claimed to have served in the Civil War. "He remembered with remarkable accuracy everything he had seen or heard through life, and read a great deal while in prison."[947] Said the newspaper, "His mother was an industrious woman and gave him good counsel, but without effect. She and her four children now live in Campbell County, East Tennessee."[948] His parents had divorced, and his father lived in southern Kentucky.

Prior to his return to Jamestown, Logston had been visited in the Nashville jail by Governor John C. Brown. The visit lasted an hour. The governor said three juries were convincing enough for him and that Logston should prepare to meet his fate. The governor also met with John Presswood at this time and gave the same advice.[949] Formal photographs of the killers were taken at their request.

It was generally thought that an attempt to rescue Logston would occur when he was brought from Nashville to the jail in Jamestown. There the Supreme Court had heard his case. The trip was made largely by steamboat, and Logston's father was seen on the boat with several friends. But the attempt, if any, was averted when the sheriff asked more deputies to board the ship at Carthage, and by the sheriff's taking the last part of the trip overland.

Logston became friendly with the sheriff. In the Jamestown jail, he entrusted the sheriff with his photographs and with letters to be sent to his mother and brother. At the jail, Logston dropped his claim of innocence, but insisted the two women, Eliza Brown, white, age twenty-one, and Jane Brown, white, age twenty-six, who had been indicted with him, were guilty as well. They had turned state's evidence.[950]

The evidence that sent Logston to the gallows also implicated the Brown women. Jane had hit James Galloway with a shovel, and prior to the killings there was a "passel" of women in the house. Folklore insists the reason the women wanted Catherine Galloway out of the way was that their widower father had decided to marry her. They objected because she was a woman of low virtue and her children were illegitimate.[951]

Calvin Logston was hanged in Jamestown on

April 5, 1872, the same day that Bob Beatty was executed in Columbia. Four thousand people watched him die. The Rev. Absalom B. Wright saw Logston the day before his execution and counseled him. He baptized Logston by pouring, as he had done with Calvin's mother years earlier. He had preached the funerals of the women and child Logston had killed. The Rev. Wright accompanied Logston on the wagon to the gallows, singing hymns along the way, notably, "I Ask Not to Live Always, I Ask Not to Stay." The shrouded Logston heard the Rev. Wright give a sermon from Genesis 9:6: "Whoso sheddeth man's blood." The crowd heard Logston say that he had come to this end by keeping bad company.

The trap was sprung at exactly 1:30 P.M. "As soon as he was dropped, the rope broke, and he fell suddenly to the ground. Another rope was placed around his neck, and he was drawn up, but had scarcely hung one-half minute when the rope broke a second time, and again he fell to the ground. He then uttered a word or two before they raised him the second time."[952]

The scene was more graphically described by a newspaper:

> The weight of the prisoner snapped the rope and he fell to the ground with a dull, heavy thud. He was immediately seized by the Sheriff and his guard, who put a new rope on him, throwing it over the gallows, and three or four men taking the end, they hoisted him up again very much after the fashion of hanging a dog. This time he hung some two minutes, swinging around five or six times, when, his feet getting near the ground, in an attempt to raise him a little higher, he again broke the rope, coming to the ground a second time. Once more he was seized and hoisted, the blood running from his mouth and nose, and his shroud nearly off of him. This time the rope proved sufficient and the poor fellow was launched into eternity. Such was the fate of Cal Logston, the murderer of the Galloway family.[953]

The body hung twenty-five minutes before being cut down. Because the Rev. Wright had promised to do so, he stayed with Logston the entire time and oversaw his burial. Calvin Logston is one of the few persons executed in Tennessee buried in a marked grave. According to one source, the execution had such a profound affect on the spectators there was not another homicide in Fentress County for the next twenty-five years.[954]

John Presswood (aka John Presswood, Jr.), white, age 17. *Murder.*

The crime was committed on the night of January 29, 1871, at the cabin of James Billings and his wife in rural DeKalb County. The killer was a neighbor whose "manner of looking at deceased attracted the attention of a female witness" the day before.[955] He was at the house earlier on the night of the killing, having been told by the victim to tell one of his sisters to come and stay with her that night. The victim was Mrs. Rachael Fowler Billings, white, age thirty-six. Presswood knew that her husband was out of town because he was floating logs down the river on a raft.

Presswood came to the house on the cold night barefoot and dressed only in his underwear. His presence was announced by the dog's barking, which was silenced by a rock. He put his hand through a crack in the door and unlatched it. He came in and saw Rachael Billings sitting on the bed. She took a rifle from its rack and pointed it at him. He came forward quickly and pulled it from her hands. As this was happening, Inez Certain, Rachael's daughter by a previous marriage, age eleven, grabbed an ax. Presswood pulled it from her hand and struck her in the head, knocking her to her knees. She then laid down behind a chair and looked through it, feigning death.[956]

"The man then struck her mother down; he was then down on the floor with her mother, who was groaning; he remained a short time and left. He came in at the upper door, and went out the lower door, washed his hands in the water bucket and left."[957] Inez went back to bed and stayed there because she was afraid to leave and tried to calm two other siblings, ages two and three, who began crying. The next morning she gave the alarm to a neighbor, Mrs. Rigsby, who called other neighbors and the sheriff.

Inez had seen John Presswood before. She said he was barefoot, wore no hat, coat or pants. Barefoot prints that were found leading to and from Presswood's house matched his feet. Also, at the jail his underwear was found to have been recently bloody and washed. His feet and ankles were scratched and bloody.

The defense was an alibi offered by his father and two sisters, that he had stayed with them the entire night, after going with them to Mrs. Rigsby's house, staying up until nine or ten o'clock, and then going to bed. The sisters were impeached by their inconsistent statements made before the justice court in a preliminary examination. Their own statements showed that it was possible for Presswood to have left the house without their knowledge.

In affirming the conviction, the Tennessee

Supreme Court said, "Upon these facts is there any room to doubt? The evidence did not cast the slightest suspicion upon anyone else." It concluded, "It was in the winter season. The fact that the guilty man was barefooted, without a hat or coat, would clearly indicate that he had come but a short distance."[958] The court said he had committed the murder "most probably in the perpetuation of, or attempt to perpetuate, another most brutal crime."[959]

John Presswood maintained his innocence until a week before his execution, when the governor came to visit him at the Nashville jail and refused to commute his sentence. Presswood confessed, in part, to contemplate his afterlife (and be baptized) and to ask the governor again for a commutation.[960] Presswood said his confession was due to the work of the Rev. Mason, who visited him at the Nashville jail, and the Rev. Brien, who baptized him by sprinkling.

He said, "I could not hold it any longer. I am guilty. I have repented of what I have done, and cannot die without a full and true confession. I had hoped that by keeping it to myself, Governor Brown would commute my sentence. I am very sorry I did not confess the whole thing to Governor Brown, when he visited me yesterday, because I believe it would have been better for me. I hadn't the heart to do it."[961]

In his first confession, he said Mrs. Billings said, "Go back! Go back!" when he entered and pulled the rifle out of her hands. He said he thought the girl hit her mother with the ax in trying to hit him. "I seized the ax and gave Mrs. Billings what I thought would be a light tap on the head, and then struck the girl." He continued, "The girl said, in her evidence, that after I struck her mother, I attempted to accomplish a certain purpose, but in this she was wrong, for I did nothing more than put my hand upon her person, and then left, going home in a different direction to that by which I had come through the wood and a hollow where I was for a time lost."[962] Presswood concluded by saying that he did not know he had killed her until the next day and he had not intended to kill her.

Presswood gave a final written confession which was taken by jailor G.W. Cameron and witnessed by J.M. Allen and Thomas N. Christian. Presswood signed with an "X." The confession was given on May 19, 1872. In it he admitted to having propositioned another woman a year or so before and had struck her with a hoe on the forehead when she refused his advances. For this, his father had administered thirty-nine lashes, he said. Presswood said he was influenced to approach Mrs. Billings by the statements of two friends, Steve Johnson and Dan Kerby, who talked about her, and the fact he had a dream about her, in which her husband was gone. On the fatal night he had gone to bed but did not fall asleep: "I was studying about the women, and wished I had a wife." After falling asleep, he had the dream, and acted upon it, going to the house in his underwear.

After hitting Mrs. Billings and her daughter, he explained:

> I then turned around and went to where the woman was laying on the floor, and got down by her side and put my right hand flat upon the floor in a puddle of blood, and my shirt sleeve was down over my hand and I got it all bloody, and about the same time I put my left hand on her bowels. I then became scared, from finding so much blood upon the floor; all my feelings left me. I did not do what I went there to do, nor did I know she was killed until informed the next morning. The report of my having intercourse with Mrs. Billings is false. I will state here that I never had sexual intercourse with any woman.[963]

Presswood repeated his motive: "I was led to make this attempt from what the boys had told me, and the dream I had that night; for I had never heard anything against Mrs. Billings' character, but I thought at the time that I could go and persuade her into it, without any intention of harming her in any way."[964]

On the gallows, he admitted deceiving his parents and sisters about his guilt, and turned his attention to religious matters. He said, "I want everybody to read the Bible that can read, and those that cannot read to get some person to read for them, for that is the way that I have done, and it has been a great comfort to me to hear the Bible read."[965] John Presswood had a specific request about his execution: "I want Sheriff Blackburn to get a good strong rope, so it will not break, for I want the thing all over as soon as possible, and I don't want to suffer like Logston did. When the time comes, I want the thing all over."[966]

John Presswood was baptized a second time the day before his execution. This was a full immersion in Town Creek, by the Rev. Green Magness, a Primitive Baptist minister. Jail guards held a long rope that was tied to Presswood's leg.

John Presswood was hanged at 1:30 P.M. on a gallows erected on the public square, about one hundred and fifty yards from the jail, on the south side of the courthouse. He was taken to the gallows in a one-horse wagon, seated on his coffin. He sat on a box on the gallows while the death ceremony was conducted. The circuit court clerk, Thomas Christian, read Presswood's lengthy confession and when finished asked if it was correct, and he answered it was "all just right." This immediately halted demand for the published confession, which was being sold for ten cents a copy.

The Rev. Brien read the sixth chapter of Romans, and then led in a hymn, "Am I Born to Die, to Lay This Body Down?" which many in the crowd sang as well. The Rev. Brien offered a prayer and addressed the group briefly. The clerk announced that Presswood wanted it said that he had been treated well by the sheriff and the jailer. The Rev. Jerry W. Cullom, a Methodist minister, spoke a few words, followed by the Rev. Brien who said that Presswood told him he was glad he had not been given a life sentence because he would not have been so well prepared to die as he was at present. More hymns were sung.

John Presswood made his final statement:

> Gentlemen and Ladies — I bid you all farewell. I hope you will meet me in Heaven for there I am going. I feel the Savior is with me this day. I feel in my soul he is with me. I have no fear but that I will go above there, where I hope to see all my friends, my grandfather and grandmother. I have also a little brother dead. I know that he has gone there. That is a good place. There are no pardons there. That is a heap better world than this. You have not got a better friend on earth than the good Savior. You can be saved by nobody else except through his blood. Farewell, all of you. I want all to meet me in heaven, for there I am going.

Presswood continued:

> Tell the little girl to tell Mr. Billings that I am sorry that I killed his wife, also am very sorry that I murdered her mother. I feel sorry, but the sense unto my heart tells me that I am forgiven for my sins — not only for one, but for all. I feel fully satisfied. I am willing to die and want to go. I will meet the Lord when the breath leaves me. I invite you all to take warning by me. Don't get scared. Don't drop your heads to keep from looking at me. All take warning. Don't any of you get in the trouble that I have. I say to you, be prepared to meet me in Heaven. I know that I am bound to go now in a few minutes; cannot tell exactly how long, but I know it is not long. I am well prepared to go and I am willing to go.

Presswood concluded:

> There is no other chance for me except this gallows right here. I do not care for the gallows. All that is on my mind is the Savior. Mr. Christian and Jim Allen and others have been good to me; they have done everything I wanted them to do. I want them to stay by me when I am dead and see me put in the coffin and buried like other men. I have nothing against anybody, even those who swore against me. They were right and I was wrong. I wanted you all to know that before I leave this world I have nothing against any of you.[967]

A hymn was sung, "Alas, and Did my Savior Bleed?" after which Presswood became very agitated because moments before he had been told by the sheriff that he had ten minutes more. After the last hymn, Sheriff Blackburn unfastened the handcuffs and Presswood was pinioned. Just before the sheriff placed the white cap over his face, Presswood cried out, "Fare you well, gentlemen and ladies, farewell this world, for I am going...."

The sheriff announced at one-minute intervals how much time Presswood had left as Presswood sobbed under the cap. Finally, he said, "Presswood, you die." At that moment the sheriff cut the trap rope and Presswood fell cleanly. He struggled slightly for six minutes and was cut down in twenty minutes and placed in his coffin. Just as the rope was cut several people fainted and mournful groans could be heard throughout the crowd.[968] His body was taken to within a mile or two of Alexandria, where his father and two sisters were waiting for him.

The execution of John Presswood in Smithville on May 24, 1872, drew such a large crowd, estimated at eight to ten thousand, that well into the 1960s all large gatherings were compared to it: "This is the largest crowd since the Presswood hanging."[969] The Presswood execution, showing him dressed in a white robe and cap, is one of the few Tennessee executions for which a photograph exists.[970]

1874

Professor Bryant (aka Prof London, Progue London, Progue Bryant), black, age 43. *Murder.*

The crime was committed in the early afternoon of April 11, 1872, on the farm of Alexander Steele near Chicken Creek, Giles County. The victim was Alexander Steele, white, age sixty-five. Bryant had been hired to plow for Steele. Bryant's wife, Mattie Ray, also worked for Steele that day. On the day of the murder, she had a heated argument with Steele, which prompted the killing.

Steele asked her how many rows of cotton she had hoed and she flew into a rage, saying, "When I work, I work, and I don't count the rows for any man, white or black!"[971] She kept haranguing Steele as he walked from a side gate of his yard back to his house. Near his house he picked up a small rock and threatened to hit her with it. She responded, "I wish to God you would hit me. I would go straight to town and report you and have you arrested, dirty and ragged as I am."[972] Seeing this from horseback at the front gate of the yard, Bryant said, "If you hit my wife, we'll all have a fuss!" Steele dropped the rock and went into the house and took a pistol out of a drawer. Mattie was near the south gate of the yard when Steele returned.

By the time Steele had returned, Bryant (on horseback) had come near the south gate. He held five large stones under his left arm. He said to Steele, "What did you say to my wife?" Witnesses could not hear what Steele said in reply. Bryant got off his horse and began throwing the stones at Steele. As he did so, Steele reached for his pistol but it fired as soon as he clutched it and he never raised it toward Bryant. By now, Mrs. Oliver, Steele's daughter, tried to protect her father by putting herself between the rock-throwing Bryant and her father. As she did so, the last rock flew past and struck him on the left side of his head. He fell to the ground senseless and died without speaking two days later.

Bryant claimed self-defense. But the state urged the facts showed murder because the size and type of stones (flint) were not present on the ground where the killing took place. Bryant had ridden his horse to Chicken Creek, some 175 yards away, and gathered the stones even before Steele reappeared and before he got his pistol. All the witnesses said there were no similar stones closer, in particular, near the south gate. A witness said he heard Bryant say to his wife, "I've killed him! Damn his old soul, I've killed him!"[973]

Bryant appealed his conviction to the Tennessee Supreme Court. It reversed, saying the jury instruction was defective because it did not require the jury to find malice, although as a matter of law malice could be shown by the use of a deadly weapon, and the offense could be shown by all the facts and circumstances.[974]

At the second trial, several witnesses attested that rocks similar to those thrown were not on the ground in the location of the killing, except for the ones thrown by Bryant. The killing rock weighed six pounds and seven ounces. Also at the second trial it was shown that Mattie Ray and the defendant were never married. According to a witness, about a week before the killing the couple had argued and Mattie came to the Steele house complaining about her husband's mistreatment. When Bryant arrived to get her he said, "She is not my wife and that's not the worst of it. She never will be!"[975] Convicted after a second trial, Bryant appealed in 1874 but the handwritten opinion affirming his conviction is wholly illegible.

Bryant had been kept in the Nashville jail until shortly before the execution when he was taken to the Pulaski jail. There he was attended by friends and the Rev. A.H. Newton, black. He spent most of his time in prayer and hymn singing. A newspaper said that he had a half pint of ginger brandy the morning of his execution and a half a glass of wine. It described as false a report in another newspaper that he had consumed a quart of whiskey a day for two weeks leading up to his execution.[976]

According to the newspaper, "Bryant said that he did not bring any rocks with him to the place where the assault was made, and that he never had but two rocks and they were procured at the place. He said that Mr. Steele had fired his pistol at him once and was trying to fire again when he (Bryant) threw the rock that killed him. He stated that he had no object now in telling a lie, and asserted emphatically that he killed Mr. Steele in self-defense."[977]

Bryant was taken by wagon to the gallows. In the wagon with him were black ministers, the Rev. Nelson Merry and the Rev. A.H. Newton, plus the sheriff and the jailer. He jumped nimbly from the wagon. He was dressed in a black suit, with white vest and gloves. He mounted the gallows with a firm step and sat on a chair. He was hanged at 2:20 P.M. on April 10, 1874, on a gallows two hundred yards from the Pulaski jail "on the banks of Pleasant Run, immediately in the rear of Mr. Jno. B. Ezzelle's residence."[978]

The death ceremony began with remarks from the Rev. Nelson Merry, the foremost black Baptist minister in Tennessee. He said, "I came not here to plead the innocence of crime but to rebuke sin. I taught the criminal standing here before you the way of Christ while in Nashville last winter and he believed and was baptized." At this point, the Rev. Merry was overcome with emotion and stopped speaking. Gathering himself, he led in singing a hymn. Bryant's voice could be heard as well. The Rev. Merry then offered a prayer. The Rev. Newton read the 25th Psalm at Bryant's request. Then Bryant gave an "enthusiastic and incoherent" statement, in which he claimed innocence but forgave those who testified against him and asserted he was going to heaven.[979] The crowd of five thousand, mostly black, responded with "Amens" and the women cried out laments. Bryant dropped to his knees and gave a long earnest prayer which brought forth even more "Amens" and "Hallelujahs" from the crowd.

Bryant began a kind of religious wailing as he stood on the trap. The sheriff placed the black cap and noose, then pinioned Bryant with his hands behind him. Without verbal warning, the sheriff cut the trap rope with a hatchet, and the drop was clean. The body was motionless, then at one minute began twitching. "At the end of five minutes a desperate effort was made by the dying man to loosen his hands, his legs and shoulders drawn up in a mighty effort to get his breath."[980]

"When the drop fell great cries and prayers arose from the congregation, and the crowd, as if sickening at the scene, commenced to scatter."[981] He was declared dead in fourteen minutes and cut down in thirty. The body was put in a coffin and taken to Elk Ridge near Lynnville, where a service was conducted by the Rev. Nelson Merry. Despite the large crowd, there was no disorder in Pulaski because the sheriff had ordered all the saloons closed by eleven o'clock that morning.

Bill Kelly, black, age 38. *Rape.*

Few details of the crime are known except that it was committed on July 30, 1873, at the victim's home ten miles west of Nashville and the victim was Mrs. Sarah E. Moore, white, age unknown. The victim said that after Kelly raped her he put a straight razor to her neck, then put it in his pocket and dragged her outside. As they struggled, she pulled the razor from his pocket and threw it into the woods. She continued fighting and he ran away.

Kelly was a cook in a Nashville house of ill fame and was familiar to police because of his record of small crimes, mostly gambling. Two years earlier he had been indicted for the attempted rape of a ten-year-old white girl, but was released from jail prior to that trial. He was hiding out in the country at the time of the rape of Mrs. Moore. Kelly contended that the sex was consensual. He said it was instigated by Moore, who demanded two dollars, and that intercourse occurred after he gave her the money.

Kelly was charged with both rape and assault with intent to commit rape. When the jury came back with a general verdict imposing the death sentence, Kelly contended on appeal that this was a defective verdict requiring a new trial. The Tennessee Supreme Court ruled that when the indictment charges the same species of offense, a general verdict meant the jury has found the defendant guilty of the higher offense, especially when the verdict clearly imposes the punishment allowed in the higher offense.[982]

The Supreme Court also said that it was proper to admit the victim's testimony. The court said there was no doubt as to the defendant's guilt: "The proof is full and conclusive, showing a case of unquestionable guilt."[983] Kelly begged Governor Brown to visit him in jail. The governor appeared a week before the execution. Kelly's pleas were rejected. The governor said it was a heinous crime and that Kelly should "fix his thoughts upon the life beyond."[984]

Bill Kelly had been kept in the Nashville jail for eight months prior to his execution. When asked on the morning of his execution how he had slept, he remarked he had not slept better in eight months. Kelly was very eager that the newspapers tell his version of the case and not quote him using such words as "dis" and "dat." He said he was not tired from the people coming to see him, a total of 1069 the day before, and said he would have gladly talked to more if they had kept coming. When one man offered his condolence, Kelly snapped, "Don't talk to me that way! I don't want any consolation, I've made up my mind to die, I'm ready to die, and what do I want of your consolation?[985]

The sheriff had difficulty finding a suitable place for the execution. Several sites had to be rejected because neighbors strongly objected. A circuit judge suggested the courthouse yard, but another judge strongly objected, saying the courthouse was county property and this was a state hanging.[986] Bill Kelly was hanged on a gallows built "just south of the Rock City paper mills, and to the west of Murfreesboro Pike," in a natural amphitheater that easily held two thousand people. This was the same spot where Carroll, Kirby and Payne were executed for murder in 1843.

By the time Kelly was executed about ten thousand people were present. The crowd itself was quiet, but considerable noise was caused by the steam engine of the paper mill and the neighing of horses and braying of mules. Two-thirds of the crowd was black. Every prostitute in town was present, dressed in their finest clothes, seated in elaborate carriages.[987] "A general air joyousness and reckless insouciance pervaded the throng."[988]

Kelly rode to the execution in a wagon drawn by two white horses. In the wagon were the sheriff and several deputies, two black men, Jesse Hightower and Ike Smith, and the Rev. W.R. Cobb, black. Kelly was dressed in a fine black coat and pants, white Marseilles vest, silk hat, and black velvet slippers. He wore white gloves and held in his hand a small Bible, held partly open with his index finger.[989]

The foremost black Nashville minister of this time, the Rev. Nelson Merry, who had ridden to the execution in his own buggy, addressed the crowd and offered a prayer. Next, the Rev. Cobb, who had attended Kelly in the jail and had been asked by him to speak, gave the following prayer: "Oh, Son of God, Thou who knowest the terribleness of death, help this, thy servant, to bear it. He clings to Thee alone, in this, his hour of direst need. Forsake him not—forsake him not, nor do Thou suffer the curse of human law to reach beyond the grave. Lord, unto Thee we commend his spirit. God of pity, save his soul."[990]

Kelly then gave his last statement. "Friends, both white and colored: I am here today to suffer death, but as Paul said when the crowd gathered to see his head chopped off: They may murder my flesh but my soul they cannot kill. Jesus is with me. I am here today to be offered up, I am ready to die—hear me, I am prepared to die, I have religion and I don't fear death, I'm going home. Some of you here today are not prepared for death, and I have to say to such, 'Prepare yourselves for death and the judgment.' Don't put it off until tomorrow. Why? Tomorrow belongs to eternity."[991] Kelly said he had been treated well by the sheriff, who treated him like a gentleman. Kelly next said that he had traveled all over the world and had two children in Indiana.

Kelly continued:

> I am willing to be offered up between heaven and earth because of the small sum of two dollars. This person who charged me swore false against me. She made an offer to me. I went to the spring at her request. I brought her a couple of buckets of water. After I brought the water, her request to me was to go for wood. I went as she asked me, as a servant would. You know, friends, that sometimes, if you should be waiting on anybody and they told you to do something, you go and do it. Well, just so it was with me. When I went to the house that morning, she invited me in, I stayed awhile and talked to her and then went for the water. Then I came back and went around on the hill and cut her some wood. After I came with the wood she said to me that one of her neighbor's chickens came into the house and her request was for me to kill it, and I did so. In the mean time she dressed the chicken, she asked me for the pitiful sum of $2. I told her I hadn't the money to spare, had some debts to pay, but she said to me, "You can pay your debts, let me have the two dollars." I told her I couldn't do it; yet she kept insistin' on me for the money. I gave it to her, then I walked back to the bedside. She sat down on the bed after she had made the offer.[992]

Kelly concluded: "But friends I say to you. I am here today innocent of the charge, but thanks be to God, I am willing to go by the laws of Tennessee. Friends, I hope that you will all remember me, I will bid you a long farewell. Farewell! Farewell!"[993] During the Rev. Merry's speech and Kelly's the black audience frequently responded with "Amens" and the like, and called "Farewell" to Kelly. Bill Kelly then offered his own prayer that brought cries and groans from the black listeners.

Kelly was pinioned by the deputy and asked if the noose was too tight; he said no. At this point, the crowd began to surge: "The excitement among the colored people became fearful." Sheriff Whitworth turned to the crowd and said in a loud voice, "I am willing at all times to do my duty, but this is a painful one to me."[994] He then rapidly descended the steps and cut the trap rope with a small hatchet. Bill Kelly fell cleanly at 2:01 P.M. on May 8, 1874. His body moved sluggishly to and fro and gave a few convulsive tremors. The body was cut down thirty minutes later.

About two or three minutes after the drop the crowd seemed to surge forward, as if to rescue him, and the fifty guards pointed their bayoneted rifles toward the crowd. But the cause was actually the crowd's attempt to move away from a frightened horse. The crowd was stopped when police Sergeant McAllister dashed into the crowd on horseback with revolver in hand. It soon became clear that the crowd also had moved forward to avoid people who were falling inside an overcrowded ravine. There were no serious injuries except for "Squire William Butler, colored, who had a leg broken by falling into the ditch."[995]

Kelly's body was placed in a coffin and taken to Mt. Ararat Cemetery, followed by a large crowd. Before it was placed in a vault, the coffin was opened so all could look at him, and a funeral service was conducted. "Kelly was exceedingly anxious that his body should not fall into the clutches of 'body snatchers' and on this account it will remain in the vault some days before final interment."[996]

The placement of Kelly's body in the vault was a factor in what happened next. When the vault was opened for burial, Kelly was supposedly found sitting on his coffin shouting. He was then taken to the Capitol, where hundreds supposedly saw him. When a white newspaper reporter inquired about the matter at a black church, he found no one who could claim to have seen him, but many who said they knew someone who had. The black minister told the congregation the story was a fabrication and told them to ignore it. The reporter wrote, "Thousands of negroes in Nashville believe, however, that Kelly is still alive and kicking."[997]

Robert Baskin (aka Robert Bascom), black, age 20. *Murder.*

The crime was committed on August 7, 1873, on a road near the community of Pocahontas in Hardeman County. The victim, John Marlow, white, age unknown, had been to the town of Bolivar, where he had purchased some books. He had ridden out of town. Along the way he realized he had dropped a spelling book. Turning his horse around, he came upon Baskin. Marlow asked if Baskin had seen the book and he said no.

Marlow became angry. According to Baskin, "He called me a liar and got off his horse to search me, saying that I was the only one that had passed along the road since he had lost the book. We got into a scuffle, when I broke loose from him, and pulling my revolver, shot him twice, both bullets entering just over the right eye and killing him."[998]

Baskin took Marlow's horse, escaped to Mississippi and was arrested a week later. He was tried in July 1874. Because Baskin was hanged at Bolivar on September 26, 1874, it seems unlikely his case was appealed. As execution day approached, "Baskin made a full confession of his crime to the clergymen and officers and stated that he felt he had made the necessary preparations for death."[999]

Robert Baskin's execution took place amid heavy rain in front of two thousand spectators of both races. "Rev. Mr. Gray alighted from the wagon and ascended the slippery steps of the gallows, the service as laid down for public executions in the Book of Common Prayer was read by the clergyman to which the culprit seemed to pay strict attention."[1000] The heavy rain saturated the white shroud that covered Baskin.

With the rope around his neck, Baskin spoke his last words, "Don't let the devil work with you. If I had worked with God as I have worked for the devil I would not be here in this fix today. That is all I have to say."[1001] After this, the cap was placed and the sheriff told Baskin he had three minutes to live. Baskin neither moved nor spoke and the crowd waited in breathless anticipation for three minutes, when the trap was released without warning.[1002]

Two hours before the hanging, Baskin was interviewed in jail. Q: Did you kill John Marlow? A: Yes. Q: What did you kill him for? A: I don't know; I was mad. Q: Was you mad with him? A: No, I didn't know him. I was mad because I couldn't get work. I had been to Ubet, and was going to Corinth, but I got to foolin' with a white man and the cars left me. Q: Did you kill him to get his horse? A: No, I don't know what I killed him for. Q: Did you take anything but Marlow's horse? A: I took his knife. Q: Did you quarrel with him or say anything to him before that? A: No. Q: Do you think justice has been done you? That all the witnesses against you told the truth? A: Yes. Q: How many times did you shoot Marlow? A: Twice; first in the side and then in the face. He never spoke to me afterwards nor me to him. I pulled him from the road into the bushes; then got on his horse and left.[1003]

The townsfolk said they were glad the execution was over. "Very many negroes have this evening expressed themselves satisfied as to the justice of the execution, and bow submissively to the stern decree of the law."[1004]

Shade Woods Westmoreland, white, age 36. *Murder.*

The crime was committed in rural Hamilton County on May 24, 1873. Westmoreland's parents had died when he was young and he was raised by a brother and sister, growing up "with very little education, under no control, with vigorous health, he filled up the measure of his days in hard work on farms, fishing, hunting and occasionally drinking."[1005] Another account said that his real name was Shade Woods, but he took the name Westmoreland after the man that raised him, his maternal uncle.[1006] He served in a Tennessee regiment of federal cavalry during the Civil War, under the command of Col. Thornburgh. In 1868 Westmoreland leased some farmland from the victim, William Emberlin, white, age forty-five, and lived with the family, which consisted of the Emberlin couple and five children.

William Emberlin was lame and carried a walking stick. But he was a "hard character, and was often heard to boast that he had killed four men."[1007]

According to Westmoreland's written "confession" released the day of his execution, trouble began when Emberlin was involved in stealing some hogs and fled. Westmoreland stayed in the house. Two months later Emberlin returned and a dispute arose because Westmoreland would not keep quiet about Emberlin's plan to steal salt from a neighbor. Westmoreland confronted Emberlin on a neighbor's porch, but claimed that he shot in self-defense. The chief purpose of the "confession" appears to have been to preserve Mrs. Emberlin's reputation: "I hereby make this, my last assertion, in behalf of Mrs. Emberlin. She is not guilty, directly or indirectly, of the charges preferred by an excited and prejudiced community."[1008]

The Tennessee Supreme Court summarized the case: "The proof makes out a case in which one friend, about to leave home, procures another friend to take charge of his wife and children and property, during his absence. Before his return the affections of his wife have been alienated and the purpose formed by his trusted friend to destroy his life and take possession of his wife and children. The purpose is carried out soon after the return of the deceased, by seeking to provoke an altercation, and failing in this, by executing his purpose, long before formed, by shooting the deceased, and afterwards, finishing the work with a club."[1009]

Said the Supreme Court:

> It appears that the deceased William Emberlin, was a married man with a wife and five small children. He had occasion to leave home to be absent several months and left the defendant at his home with his family in charge of his affairs. During his absence, an intimacy seems to have been formed between defendant and the wife of the deceased. After the deceased had been absent about six months, the defendant learned that he would soon return and about ten days before the killing, defendant passed the home of Mrs. Jane Bowers who states that defendant said he was going to meet Emberlin, who was coming home that day. About an hour afterwards, Emberlin and another man stopped at the gate. Emberlin looked badly, like he had been sick and would not live long. While Bowers and Emberlin were talking, the defendant came up [and] Emberlin went to the home. The defendant told Bowers, "You never saw me any madder; I have a good pistol and it's well loaded and damn me if I don't kill Bill Emberlin before he gets home. I'm going to run that shebang myself. I can dress Mrs. Emberlin like a lady and take care of the children.[1010]

Mrs. Emberlin had left the home the Friday night before the Sunday killing, and the husband had taken the children to her father's (Alan Varner). That morning another witness said that Westmoreland came by searching for the children, and that Mrs. Emberlin had sent him after them, and "told him to bring the children to her or to kill Bill Emberlin, that [he] was going to scalp him with his own [walking] stick." According to the witness, Westmoreland had "made Emberlin knuckle to him three times and he was going to make him knuckle the fourth and last that day, and that he was able to take care of Mrs. Emberlin and the children."[1011]

The killing occurred outside in the yard of a house near Varner's, where one of the witnesses had taken Emberlin to avoid a conflict with Westmoreland. The latter accused Emberlin of throwing his clothes on the ground back at the house and was cursing him. By now, Mrs. Emberlin arrived and she said, "Shade, did you throw me up to Will?" (This question was designed to provoke Westmoreland by making him confront Emberlin in front of his wife.) When Westmoreland said no, the two began to quarrel, with the killer saying, "Bill Emberlin, don't you deny it, God damn you!" He warned, "Don't rush on me," several times, but the purported warning was false, because Emberlin was doing and saying nothing to provoke a fight. For example, he never picked up his walking stick, which remained on the floor. Westmoreland drew a pistol and fired into the ground, but this caused Emberlin to run into the house, where he literally hid behind one of the witnesses, Miss Serepia Crawford.

The two men ended up in the yard struggling on the ground when Westmoreland pulled the pistol and fired three times, hitting Emberlin in the foot and arm, and a bullet piercing the body from the back. Emberlin staggered off, moaning loudly. One of the witnesses saw Westmoreland standing over him with a club, but did not see the blows. The body was found with a deep head wound. One of the witnesses attempted to ameliorate the effect of her testimony by repeating several times that Emberlin was very sick and was "going to die anyway."[1012] The killing was witnessed by the children, all under the age of eight. Mrs. Emberlin was charged with complicity in the murder, but the jury acquitted her.

A legal issue at Westmoreland's trial was whether a juror was properly seated who was not a "citizen" of the judicial district because he had not lived there a year, only eight months. The Tennessee Supreme Court said this was not error. Another issue was whether the judge erred in allowing the trial to continue while Westmoreland was taken from the courtroom to answer a call of nature.[1013]

Shade Westmoreland was the first civilian executed in Chattanooga under civil authority. Prior executions of Joe Huff and Andy Williams occurred in Harrison, when it was the Hamilton County seat. Five thousand people witnessed his death. After hearing the words of two ministers, the crowd sang "Amazing Grace," as tears streamed down hundreds of faces. Several women came forward to kiss him good-bye, as did a boyhood friend; acts that brought tears to more eyes.

Westmoreland was executed at 1:25 P.M. on November 20, 1874. The scaffold was built on a hill where the University of Tennessee at Chattanooga now stands.[1014] His last words thanked those who had helped him such as the ministers and his lawyer, forgave those who testified wrongly against him, and asserted that he was redeemed in the eyes of God, having been baptized recently. As the cap was drawn over his head he said, "Meet me in Heaven, everybody!"[1015]

1875

William Nicholas Berry, white, age 47. *Murder.*

The crime was committed on October 11, 1872, on the killer's farm in rural Hawkins County. Berry, a farmer, claimed he had been drafted into the Confederate Army, Col. Rucker's regiment, General Pegram's brigade. He claimed to have deserted in July 1863 to return to his wife, who he said was sick.

The victim was Berry's wife, Alzira "Allie" Berry, white, age forty-eight. At the time of the murder, the couple had four daughters, Sarah, age twenty-five; Mary, twenty-one; Matilda, seventeen; and Amanda, eight. The couple had many violent quarrels, and the morning of the murder her screams could be heard a mile away.[1016] Berry told family and neighbors that she had simply left him when they inquired about her whereabouts.

After three weeks, Berry's father and brother came looking for her. They discovered her naked body ninety feet from the house, at the foot of a tree that had been blown over. The body had been covered with a large stone and some clay. Care had been taken to leave no traces behind where the ground had been disturbed.[1017] She had been killed by blows to the head, and a mattock with a gap in its blade was found. It had been used to dig her shallow grave. Her body was covered with a coat Berry often wore. Investigators found a place near the house where a struggle had ensued and blood was on the ground.[1018] A posse went searching for Berry. He was brought back to view the body and claimed not to recognize it. He was taken to jail but escaped. Months later he was located in Texas and brought back for trial in Morristown, Hamblen County.

During the trial, the elder daughters described a household of constant violence and incest when they lived at home. After trial, one of the daughters said she saw the killing.[1019] The Tennessee Supreme Court opinion cannot be located.

In an interview the day before his execution, he named the real culprits: "My father, Patsy Dotson, James McFerin, Hanna Berry, my cousin, and Henderson Berry, my half brother, as my father and others of the party named had threatened to kill her on various occasions."[1020]

When confronted by a newspaper reporter that his daughter had recently declared she had seen her father kill the mother, Berry replied, "She was scared into such a statement by my father and other enemies of myself and family. They also promised if she would turn against me they would get up a petition for the pardon of her husband who was sent to the state prison some time ago for stealing a hog."[1021]

Earnestly asked to confess his crime by two ministers, Berry steadfastly maintained his innocence. According to a reporter who interviewed him the night before the execution, "Many believed that the reason why Berry did not confess was through pure malice towards his father, brother and the others who he implicated, while others thought that he had told so many falsehoods about the affair that he really believed he was then telling the truth."[1022]

The reporter continued, "It is claimed, sometime before murdering his wife, whom he had sworn to protect, that he killed his own son, and then declared he was kicked to death by a mule."[1023]

Berry was the first man executed in Hawkins County in postwar Tennessee. Berry was executed in the traditional manner. Two posts with a bar across were erected and the rope strung from the bar. Berry and the sheriff stood on a wagon. Before the cap was pulled over his face, Berry asked the sheriff, "How do you feel about this?" The sheriff replied, "Very badly, Nick."

Berry refused to make a last statement, but allowed a Presbyterian minister to offer the typical "wages of sin" homily and a fervent prayer. Berry's last words were, "I bid this world farewell and hope to meet you in the better world where parting is not known."[1024] Moments later the sheriff cracked a whip and the horses moved forward. Because this manner of hanging causes the body to swing, it gave rise to the term "swung off." The August 13, 1875, execution was witnessed by 7,000 people who came from all neighboring counties including those in Virginia. This was "the largest crowd that had ever assembled in Rogersville on any occasion."[1025]

Berry was one of three men who were executed in different parts of East Tennessee that day; the others were John C. Webb in Knoxville and Ananias Honeycutt in Tazewell.

Ananias Honeycutt, white, age 24. *Murder.*

The crime was committed on the morning of January 30, 1874, in a rural part of Claiborne County at a place called Wagon Hollow near the farm and leather shop of a neighbor, the victim. He was Thomas Ausmus, white, age forty. Newspaper accounts of the crime sometimes asserted Honeycutt was part Cherokee.

Honeycutt went to Ausmus's house the day before the murder and they had a conversation in which they seemed to make an appointment for the next day. Honeycutt returned the next day and both men walked into the woods together, Ausmus telling his family that he would be gone an hour. Honeycutt told them it might be an hour and a half. Several hours later, about noon, Honeycutt returned to the house and inquired about Ausmus's whereabouts, suggesting that the two had conducted some business, but that Honeycutt needed to talk to him more. Honeycutt would later explain that the two had agreed on the boundaries of land he would farm, but the second meeting was necessary to formalize the matter in writing.[1026]

Later that day, Ausmus's body was found in the woods of Wagon Hollow. His skull had been struck by a rock from behind, several rocks with brains on them were found nearby. Ausmus was found on his back. His face had been smashed with a club and hatchet. There was no sign of a struggle. His pocketbook, known to contain money, was missing.

Honeycutt was the prime suspect from the first. A small boy claimed to have seen him with Ausmus. His flight was considered the best evidence of guilt. He procured a canoe and was nearly a hundred miles away by nightfall. One witness said he overheard a conversation between Honeycutt (in the canoe) and his father-in-law on the river bank. He heard the words "Wagon Hollow" mentioned. Honeycutt would later explain that he fled because he was fearful the killing would be blamed on him and that his father-in-law told him to claim self-defense.

Honeycutt's final explanation of the killing was this. After he left Ausmus he encountered his brother-in-law Wesley Mayers, who admitted he had killed the man. He told Honeycutt where the man's pocketbook would be found. Honeycutt said he swore to Mayers he would not tell anyone and invoked his heritage. "I will also say that the red race of men, from whom I descended, have given up their lives rather than divulge the secrets of their fellow men. But I knew I must tell it or leave the country, and for this reason I left the country and went away."[1027] Honeycutt's loyalties to the Mayers family were mixed. He was married to a daughter of Henry W. Mayers, but the man frequently abused him.[1028]

All of Honeycutt's later statements were influenced by this decision to follow his father-in-law's advice, and later by threats to his life after capture. When Honeycutt was arrested he immediately claimed self-defense. From that point on, Honeycutt kept changing his story, sometimes in the face of real or imagined threats.

When told that the murder scene showed no sign of struggle, Honeycutt said that Ausmus was alive when he left him and was in the company of a man named Greenlee. This story failed when it was shown that Greenlee was elsewhere all day. But in order to embellish his claim against Greenlee, Honeycutt offered to take the sheriff to where he claimed to have seen Greenlee hide the victim's wallet. This Honeycutt did and the wallet was found, but the act served only to implicate him further.

Honeycutt was incriminated by his own foot. He had deformed toes which stuck straight up and he wore an unusual shoe. Footprints near the body matched Honeycutt's unusual print — but Honeycutt maintained to the end that he wore a plain shoe on the day of Ausmus's death. According to one writer, "From one confession or statement Honeycutt would take refuge in another, and managed to hopelessly entangle himself in their mazes."[1029]

Honeycutt's return in handcuffs to the murder scene involved several stops, one at the victim's leather workshop, where he was confronted by the victim's adult son. Noticing that Honeycutt was wearing a new store-bought shirt, the son attempted to take it off, but was held at bay by a sheriff's deputy pulling a pistol.

Fearing a lynching ("a burning" he called it), Honeycutt variously admitted and denied the killing. His father-in-law had told him to claim self-defense, apparently at the riverside meeting.

Honeycutt did not understand the implication of this defense, namely, it put him at the crime scene, but since he had not visited the actual body, he did not know there had been no struggle and Ausmus was clearly struck from behind.

But when asked directly by Ausmus's son at the leather shop whether Wesley Mayers was involved in the killing, he said no. Then he claimed that the son threatened to "fill me with pine splinters and set me on fire" unless he implicated Mayers, who by then had been jailed on suspicion of the crime — a fact unknown to Honeycutt when he spoke.

Honeycutt's appeal to the Tennessee Supreme Court dealt largely with whether the various confessions he gave were admissible, but the opinion did not recount the facts of the crime in detail other than to describe the murder scene. The court ruled that Honeycutt lost his credibility by asserting that he had struck Ausmus in self-defense and implicated Greenlee (who was shown to be innocent) and the various statements he gave were not caused by his being placed in fear nor "offered a promise or benefit."[1030] His demand for a change of venue was not supported because the "excitement" manifested in the community was limited to the time of his arrest and was largely limited to Ausmus's family and friends. There was no evidence that it existed at the time of the trial.[1031]

Ananias Honeycutt was executed on August 13, 1875, one of three men executed that day in East Tennessee. The others were John Webb in Knoxville and William N. Berry in Rogersville. Honeycutt's gallows consisted of an upright post with a crosspiece sticking out, upon which hung the rope. Two ministers gave homilies, and Honeycutt spoke in a halting voice, "Had I taken my mother's advice, would not have been here today; kept bad company, went astray; 'tis hard to die such a death; am willing to go to God who made me, in peace, will die soon; home to meet all my friends in Heaven; hold no enmity against no man; want all to meet me there; want my friends not to grieve after me; lament your case, and meet me in Heaven."[1032]

Honeycutt's published "Confession" states, "I am innocent of the murder. But my ignorance of the law and the false swearing of witnesses together with the money and influence of the Ausmus family, have heaped upon me the highest crime known in the law."[1033] On the gallows, he was pointedly asked by one of the ministers whether he was guilty or innocent, Honeycutt replied, "I've told it time and again, and will not tell another tale than the one told heretofore."[1034]

Moments later the sheriff ordered the two-horse wagon forward and Honeycutt was "swung off" in the manner of William N. Berry, who was executed at almost the same moment in Rogersville. Between five and six thousand people came to Tazewell to witness the execution. The report of his execution described Honeycutt as "medium height, and would weigh about 150 pounds, left foot turned up, making a shorter track than the right."[1035]

The execution of Ananias Honeycutt has entered Tennessee folklore. According to a popular account, the minister who asked the killer if he was guilty or innocent gave him a white handkerchief and told him to move it from one hand to the other if he was innocent. When the drop came, Honeycutt was seen to move the handkerchief from one hand to the other — and back.[1036] Supposedly this caused spectators to scream, sob and faint.[1037]

The notion of a man on the gallows proclaiming his innocence and shifting something to another hand can be traced back to at least 1825. Stephen Videts, convicted of murdering Mrs. Fanny Mosely, wrote a statement that was read by a man from the gallows in which he asserted innocence and said he would die with the document in his right hand. The document was placed in his left hand. As the drop fell "he changed it from his left hand into his right, and, for a minute or two, seemed as if waving it by design."[1038]

Another version has Honeycutt standing on his tiptoes to get the noose around his neck, but when the wagon pulled away the rope was too long and his toes touched the ground. This caused some deputies to grab shovels to dig the ground at his feet. As late as 1979 the Honeycutt story was being retold in the local newspaper. By now, the outlaw Frank James (brother of Jesse James) was said to be present at the execution and supposedly helped Honeycutt to escape. He was finally executed for another murder in Kansas — after admitting that he had already been once hanged for murdering a man named Ausmus in Tennessee.[1039] No contemporary account mentions the handkerchief, the shovels or Frank James.

John C. Webb, white, age 34. *Murder.*

The crime was committed at 8:30 P.M. on the night of March 5, 1874, in rural Beaver Creek in Knox County. Webb had served in the 2nd Tennessee (Federal) Infantry under Col. Carter, at the age of fifteen. "But like many others, he could not return to the quiet ways of peace, and first became reckless and finally developed into a desperado."[1040] The victim was a farmer, Richard F. Reynolds, white, age fifty-four, who was thought to have several hundred dollars hidden in his house.

The robbery-killing was planned by Jasper Ayers, a career criminal who was in jail at the time of Webb's execution, and apparently testified against Webb in return for leniency. Webb and another gunman, Dave Duncan, white, entered the home of Reynolds and his wife, Barbara Reynolds, white, age fifty-six. Also present was an unnamed black boy and a nephew, Richard F. Reynolds, white, age unknown.

The robbers tied up the hostages individually and searched the house for money after Mr. Reynolds refused to give them anything except a pocketbook containing only a quarter. The gunmen became enraged and treated the captives roughly. At one point, Webb took Mrs. Reynolds outside and raped her on the ground, then brought her back into the house when she promised to give him four hundred dollars if he would leave. Webb ordered Duncan around as though he were one of the captives, but when the couple were placed side-by-side, he shot the older Mr. Reynolds four times. In the melee the black boy was shot, but not killed. Mrs. Reynolds apparently told the gunmen where the money was hidden after her husband was shot, and they took a gun, a shawl, jewelry, and the money.

The outlaws made a getaway but Duncan was "shot down like a wild animal [by Ayers and Webb] in the weird and lonely mountain when they thought he might inform upon them."[1041]

At trial, Webb cursed the court, the jury, the witnesses and everyone in the courtroom. He maintained his innocence. The case was appealed to the Tennessee Supreme Court but its opinion cannot be located. John C. Webb was executed a mile from the Knox County courthouse on August 13, 1875.

Leaving the jail to be executed, Webb said to Ayers, "Old fellow, you'll have to pray mighty hard for forgiveness for murders you've caused, if you get to heaven." He claimed to have received religion by that time and was offered a cross to kiss by a Catholic priest present at the execution.

Still maintaining his innocence, Webb was asked by Mayor Staub of Knoxville if he knew who the killer was if he was not. Webb refused to answer, saying that a newspaperman, Capt. Washington, had a true statement and it would be given to the public.[1042]

Instead of confessing, Webb asked the sheriff to summon certain people near the gallows: "The defiant manner in which he directed the Sheriff to call before him respectable men and women — who had testified against him — in order that he might insultingly denounce them as liars and perjurers, irresistibly impressed us with the idea that he was entitled only to a short shrift and a strong cord, and the sooner the shocking performances were concluded, the better for the dignity of the occasion, at least."[1043]

In order to induce a gallows confession, Webb was allowed to talk to his wife while both stood on the wagon.[1044] She implored him to tell all he knew, saying, "Pray for pardon!" At that moment a rider appeared with news that his sister had died and she was to be buried that same day. It was another attempt to manipulate him into confessing. He said, "My dear wife, I would rather be in my place than that of many I see here."

As he was bound around the feet and legs, he said to the sheriff, "You have hold of the best soldier you ever had." He told the spectators, "I thank you all for coming out to see me hung. I forgive all and hope God will forgive me. Good-bye. God bless you!" Turning to his wife he said, "I'll try and meet you in heaven." Then turning to the sheriff, he said, "I'm the best piece of furniture you have seen in many a day."[1045]

The gallows consisted of two upright posts with a crossbar, from which hung the rope. Like Berry and Honeycutt, Webb was "swung off" when the sheriff ordered the horses forward, moving the wagon on which he was standing. The body swung back and forth three times and twisted slowly. The sheriff gently stopped the motion.

Two days later a newspaper published two letters from Ayers, dated before the murder, showing that it was he who had offered Webb a large reward for killing Reynolds, and Webb's own statement implicating himself along with Richard Dowell, who had committed suicide some months before, as the first person who brought the proposition of robbing Reynolds to him.[1046]

In the letters Ayers wrote, "We are going to kill an old rebel tonight and burn his house, for he killed my father." He continued, "If you haint got a rig it don't matter for I have got plenty of black muslin." The killers were pretending to be KKK members. Webb's payment was to be one hundred dollars up front and a horse after the killing was done, according to Webb's written but incomplete statement, in which he claimed to have refused to carry out the murder, but said that Duncan and a man he did not know had committed the crime.[1047]

According to the newspaper, Webb was the first white man to be legally executed in Knox County.[1048] The clergy of Knoxville requested on the grounds of public morals that Webb be hanged privately but the sheriff said no. Webb's execution occurred the same day as the executions of William Berry in Rogersville and Ananias Honeycutt in Tazewell. One newspaper reported fifteen thousand people saw Webb's execution and compared it to only five thousand who attended the funeral of former President Andrew Johnson about ten days before.[1049]

1876

Milton McLean, white, age 54. *Murder.*

The crime was committed on April 25, 1874, on the killer's farm in rural Madison County. The victim was Thaddeus Pope, white, age forty-seven. A black man, George Redd, was a farmhand on McLean's farm, but they had a falling out and Redd had found work with Thaddeus Pope. Redd left and a few days later returned with Pope to gather his belongings, which included some farm implements. The decision by Redd to leave likely meant other farm hands would follow.

McLean met them carrying a double-barreled shotgun, but said nothing in anger. While talking to George Redd, McLean suddenly turned his double-barreled shotgun toward Pope (who was loading a wagon with Redd's belongings) and shot him in the back. This spun Pope around and McLean shot him in the chest with the other barrel. Pope lived long enough to tell witnesses that he knew of no reason why McLean shot him. After the shooting, McLean made no effort to escape and went home. He surrendered peacefully to the sheriff and deputies. The defense was insanity.[1050]

McLean was convicted in a September 1874 trial, but a new trial was ordered by the judge and the second trial began in August 1875. Issues in the case involved insanity, in particular, whether the suicide of a member of the defendant's family was evidence of McLean's insanity.

The Tennessee Supreme Court said, "Suicide per se in not evidence of insanity."[1051] McLean was vigorously defended in a sixteen-day trial. His lawyer made an array of objections. One involved the calling of juror "J.E. Askew" but when "J.C. Askew" stepped forward and said there was no "J.E." he was allowed to be seated. Another involved whether a juror who had heard a discussion of the facts of the first trial accredited it. The Tennessee Supreme Court said the seating of both jurors was proper, saying the record showed the second juror had "given no ear" to the discussion of the first trial.

The decision of the Tennessee Supreme Court did not discuss any facts. The chief legal issue was whether the judge who tried the case was properly selected. A new statute, passed on March 19, 1875, had established a new "law and chancery court" for Madison County, and the governor appointed a judge to the new post. The defendant said this was error, that the judge should have been elected. The Supreme Court said this was proper because there was no intervening election scheduled.[1052]

This obscure capital case would have been entirely forgotten to history but for another fact. The appointed judge recused himself from the case and a statute provided that when this happened the local lawyers were to elect a temporary judge from among their number. There were twenty-six lawyers in the circuit, but only eleven were at the courthouse when the temporary judge was selected by them. He was Howell E. Jackson. Twenty years later he was appointed to the United States Supreme Court.[1053]

The Tennessee Supreme Court also approved, apparently for the first time, trial judge Jackson's charge that the jury was the sole judge of the facts. But if the jury was certain the judge had made an error of law in his charge, "you may disregard its instructions and adopt your own view of the law, but before you do so you should feel convinced of the court's error."[1054] This instruction, which seems to endorse the concept of jury nullification, was proper because it simply meant that the jury had "the right and duty of finding a general verdict under the law and facts, under the direction of the court."[1055] When the Tennessee Supreme Court announced its decision in front of McLean, he said nothing. He pulled an apple from his pocket and took a large bite from it.[1056]

McLean was executed on January 7, 1876, in Jackson.[1057] Two other Tennessee executions occurred that day. Frank Scott was hanged in Memphis and William Williams was executed in Bartlett.

Milton McLean had fought in a North Carolina Confederate regiment for the entire Civil War. He had siblings in North Carolina and his mother was kept uninformed about the case. About seven hundred people signed a commutation request, which was rejected by Governor Porter.

McLean was taciturn during his trial and appeal and while awaiting execution. His wife visited him often and he comforted her flow of tears. He steadfastly denied any recollection of the killing. He met his children with good cheer and throngs came to see him, largely to urge him to confess and seek redemption. These visitors included several ministers whom he greeted respectfully, but explained he had read the Bible many times but it remained a mystery to him. He never joined a church because of the uncharitable conflicts among the sects, he explained.[1058]

McLean was taken to the gallows in a one-horse wagon, seated on his coffin. The gallows was located a half-mile from the courthouse near the bank of the Forked Deer River. On each side sat a minister. During the ride he was asked how he felt and responded, "I am prepared to die, and feel at peace with earth and heaven." He also revealed that he remembered full well the killing of Pope and said that he did it under a strange and mysterious impulse.[1059]

An immense crowd attended the execution, which followed the tradition of two ministers speaking and praying, while McLean sat calmly on a chair. The traditional execution hymn, "There Is a Fountain Filled with Blood," was sung. When asked if he had anything to say, McLean replied, "Nothing." The crowd fell silent. The ministers left the gallows and the sheriff let McLean sit alone for ten minutes, hoping he would say something. Finally, the sheriff motioned him to come forward to stand on the trap.

The nervous sheriff had some difficulty placing the noose around McLean's neck because his beard, which hung nearly to his waist, got in the way. The sheriff then placed a black veil over his head. This was the signal for the drop.

McLean weighed about two hundred pounds but the rope slipped to the back of the neck and he strangled to death. His only movement was a fierce clenching of his hands. His heart beat for nearly thirty minutes before he was cut down and his body was turned over to his wife and friends. He was buried in Hardeman County.

William Williams (aka Billy Williams), black, age 40. *Murder.*

The crime was committed at 7:00 P.M. on September 7, 1874, in the Shelby Depot area about eighteen miles from Memphis, in Shelby County. The killer, Billy Williams, was a widower. He was a landowner-farmer and the victim was his tenant. The victim, Joe Fields, black, age forty-four, was indebted to the killer. Williams was having sexual relations with the victim's wife. According to the chief prosecution witness, the victim had threatened to bring rape charges against Williams, if pressed too hard for the money. The chief prosecution witness was Sampson Pryor, black.

The killer came to Pryor's house the afternoon of the killing. He was carrying a large hickory stick. When Pryor asked what he needed the stick for, Williams said that when he "wanted to mash a negro's head, he took the stick."[1060] That day, Williams and the victim met at the house of Branch Grinnell, black, where they drank. Pryor was also present. Williams and the victim left together, walking to their homes about a mile apart.

Williams struck Fields in the head with the stick. A black woman heard a man's cries from her house but did not investigate. A couple of hours later, Williams came to Pryor, who was getting corn from a crib for his cattle, and told Pryor what he had done, saying, "I have killed Fields because he threatened to have me indicted for raping his wife, and I thought my life was as dear to me as his was to him, and threw him over the fence, so that Billy Mitchell would not see him when he came along with the wagon."[1061]

Williams demanded that Pryor assist in moving the body. Williams took a fence rail and they tied the victim's hands and feet together in order to carry him on the rail as if they were carrying a dead deer. Pryor stumbled and the body slid toward him, "The body fell back toward me, and I was afraid to let it touch me, and I ain't touched it till yet."[1062] Pryor continued, "I dropped my end and ran back a little. I then went up and took the other end of the rail and Billy came and took my end, and we dragged him up the bank. Then we went on about 150 yards, and I told him I wouldn't go any farther, and we put him between two logs, and Billy took the rail on his shoulder and carried it about a hundred yards and threw it down. We then came up on the mouth of the lane and we then parted and I went home."[1063]

The large pool of blood in the road where Fields had been killed aroused suspicion, but the body was not found for two more days. Williams pretended to help search. When it was found, Williams was promptly jailed. By this time Pryor had disappeared. He was located in Mississippi, arrested and described the facts. Pryor was charged with being an accessory, but his trial was severed.

Pryor was the chief witness against Williams. The first trial resulted in a conviction, but the verdict was overturned by the Tennessee Supreme Court. The opinion cannot be located.[1064] Williams was given the death penalty in the second trial.

The issue before the Tennessee Supreme Court was whether it was error for the court to allow the testimony of Pryor, who had been charged with the same crime, but the state had asked for a nolle prosequi on him. The defendant insisted that the testimony of a co-defendant should not have been allowed. The court ruled that the testimony was proper. Pryor was not an accomplice, but at most an accessory after the fact, and there was corroboration of Pryor's testimony on several material points.[1065]

The court said there was no error in the jury's having seen a file folder, reused from the first trial, on which someone had written guilty of first-degree murder. It was obvious, said the court, that the reason Williams was being tried the second time was that he had been given a new trial, and this point could have been a matter of testimony, had either side wanted to ask about it.[1066]

The Tennessee Supreme Court ordered Williams executed on December 24, 1875, within a mile of the courthouse in Bartlett, then the county seat of Shelby County.[1067] That day presented a problem. A petition was circulated asking Governor Porter to move the date and William Williams was hanged on January 7, 1876. As it happened, Frank Scott had been ordered executed on December 24 as well. His execution was also moved to January 7.

William Williams was visited in the Shelby County jail by numerous ministers. He became disenchanted with them. He said, "They bother me a great deal, each one insisting that I must join his church, as his is the only right way to heaven; but I do not listen to that. You can look in the Bible there and see what religion is, but you feel it in your heart here when you get it."[1068] He continued, "I don't want to see the clergy any more. My sins are forgiven, and I know God will take care of me. I am a Baptist and will die in that faith."[1069]

Williams's principal concern awaiting death was the fact that one of his chief creditors had taken over his farm and stock and sold them while he was in jail, cheating him and his children in the process. One of the creditors had told him (and showed him a document) that made it appear that the property was to be held in trust until Williams's oldest son came of age and could manage the property. The creditor responded with a long explanation and denial that was published the day of Williams's execution, which showed that everything was in order. Williams was illiterate and the documents he signed were clearly different from what he understood them to reflect.

Williams was kept in a cell next to Frank Scott, who shot a man over a ninety-cent debt on Christmas Eve in front of several witnesses. Scott had recently embraced Catholicism and the two discussed religion. Williams was firm in his belief that Scott would not participate in the resurrection if he died a Catholic.[1070]

Williams and Scott had been supplied with new suits of clothes, paid for by the county. Williams's death party took the train to Bartlett. Then a wagon took Williams, his coffin, several deputies, and the Rev. Nightingale, black, who sat beside the driver, to the Bartlett courthouse. They waited there where several prayers and hymns were sung. Williams told everyone that he did not want any man to be his confessor, nor to act as a witness to God for him. He confessed his sins to God, and having been baptized, was ready to die and be buried in the graveyard at Hatchie Church.

The death party walked to the gallows in the courthouse yard. Williams mounted the gallows with a firm step and sat down in a chair. The execution was overseen by a deputy sheriff because the high sheriff was attending the hanging of Scott at the county jail in Memphis. William Williams was hanged at 1:25 P.M. in front of a mostly black crowd of about three thousand. As he sat on the gallows the crowd became silent, except for persons on the outer edges who talked among themselves.

Williams said the following:

> Good-bye to all brothers and sisters. I am going right home. I have been from home a long while, and feel as if I just now have a chance to return there. I have not got any book religion, but I have a religion of the heart, and feel it. I have got no hard feelings against the world, nor against anyone in it, not even my enemies, and I don't want any of you to think otherwise. I am going right home, and expect to see my wife right soon, and have got nothing to come back for. If you get a religion of the heart you'll love your enemies and the man who hates you even better than your friends, but will get lost if you have only got book religion. I have nothing against the world or anybody in it. Good-bye to all.[1071]

Someone in the crowd asked, "I'd like to ask you one question. Are you guilty of this crime?" Williams made no answer and stood under the gallows unmoved. The Rev. Nightingale, standing near him, said, "He need not answer that question, for it has been asked him five hundred times. It is now between him and his God."[1072]

Williams was pinioned and capped, and the noose placed. The drop was made without warning and he fell with a thud. A great sigh came from the crowd. Williams's neck was not broken. His hands clasped, his body quivered, his feet jerked up and down. Gurgling sounds, like strangulation, were heard for two and a half minutes, and "the shoulders shrugged as if it were the last convulsive throes of a horrible death."[1073] The action caused the body to swing to and fro. He was pronounced dead in twelve minutes and cut down in twenty. His body was placed in the coffin.

But for the fact that the Supreme Court's order specifically mentioned Bartlett as the place of execution, Williams would have been hanged alongside Frank Scott in the Shelby County jail yard.

Frank Scott, black, age 40. *Murder.*

The crime was committed on the afternoon of December 24, 1874, on the Wolf River bridge, near Memphis, in Shelby County. Scott knew the victim because he had sold him a load of timber cut from a field Scott was clearing. The victim was Ransom Phipps, black, age unknown. Scott had a contract to clear 27 acres and his compensation included anything he received in payment for timber. Scott was described as a mulatto "with a cross of Indian blood, straight black hair, dark eyes, copper color, and weighed one hundred seventy-five pounds."[1074]

On December 20, Phipps had taken a load of timber and promised to pay for it (ninety cents) in three days. When that day passed, Scott saw Phipps on the bridge, in a logging wagon with his son beside him. Scott pulled up beside and demanded the money. Phipps said he did not have the money. Scott drew a pistol.

What happened next was in dispute. Scott said Phipps came down from the wagon and struck him with a whip handle. Scott's pistol was knocked from his hand and picked up by Phipps's son. The three struggled and Scott knocked it from the boy's hand, picking it up while defending himself with his left hand. He said he shot Phipps in self-defense.[1075] He said that when Phipps's body was picked up a pistol fell from it and was snatched up by his daughter. Scott insisted that the witnesses (all black) were friends of Phipps and shaded their testimony because Scott was a stranger.

The witnesses, all black, told a different story. The Tennessee Supreme Court said, "There is no serious conflict in the proof."[1076] After explaining that Scott met the victim on the bridge, it said, "The deceased was driving a wagon and was sitting on the wagon with his little boy. The prisoner asked him for the money. The deceased replied, 'I have not got it now, but will give it to you this evening.' The prisoner replied that would not do him, that he was going to have it then. The deceased replied, 'You can't get it now, for I have not got it.' The prisoner replied that 'I will kill you or shoot you if you do not pay me now,' the deceased 'said you will have it to do then, for I cannot pay you now.'"[1077]

The Supreme Court opinion continued, "The prisoner then drew a pistol and snapped it at the deceased. The deceased jumped up and said, 'Do you snap a pistol at me?' and jumped down on the ground. The prisoner said 'don't you come on' and fired — deceased immediately sprang at him, and struck him with his whip, they fought for a little while, but Phipps soon fell down, and immediately died from the effects of the pistol shot." Continued the court, "The prisoner started away but bystanders arrested him and brought him back. When asked why he killed Phipps, he said he had to do it, to get his rights."[1078]

Scott's lawyer had argued these facts showed second-degree murder. The court said this was premeditated murder: "There was no provocation, nothing to incite passion. The purpose was deliberately commenced, and deliberately executed."[1079] Scott's execution was set for December 24, 1875, but city officials and townsfolk objected and the governor moved the date to January 7, 1876.[1080]

In jail, Scott had become a member of the Catholic Church under the care of Father Aloysius ("Father Lucius') of St. Mary's Church, who took a special interest in condemned men. One of the reasons Scott converted to Catholicism was the assurance of a Christian burial and an undisturbed grave. He was concerned because he was a young, stout, healthy man that the doctors might want his body. The Catholic Church said it would protect his body as well as his soul.[1081] He told the newspaper that he wanted to be hanged at 1:40 because, "My church has some reason for it."[1082] Scott spent most of his time reading Life of Christ and said, "I have been to a good many hangings and know just how the people feel. It is nothing to be hung; it is what comes afterward that most concerns me."[1083]

Scott's Catholicism was rejected by William Williams, who was executed the same day. They shared adjoining cells and Williams clung to his Baptist beliefs. He rejected the idea of confessing to a person, rather than directly to God. Williams told Scott that his Catholic faith would bar him from the resurrection. Both men were given as much whiskey as they wanted. Scott helped himself.

Both Scott and Williams were provided new suits of clothes costing ten dollars, courtesy of the County Court. Scott went to his death dressed in a white linen shirt, black cassimere vest and pants, black alpaca coat, and goat-skin slippers. His long black hair was combed straight back and hung in ringlets almost to his shoulders. Throughout the last days, he teased and joked with Williams. "Put on your fine clothes, Billy, and when you mount the scaffold, instead of looking like a stinking nigger, you must look like a South Carolina Senator!"[1084]

Hundreds of Negroes claiming to know Scott had attempted to see him in the jail and secure a good view of the hanging. Only those arriving early were allowed inside and the yard was quickly filled. Spectators sat on roofs and railroad cars, several thousand in all, mostly black. Latecomers wishing entrance had to present a card (ticket) issued by the sheriff. At the door to the inner courtyard was posted a sign, "Notice — Only those holding cards admitted. Ladies excluded. Gate closed until 12:30 P.M. Signed, Ch. Anderson, Sheriff."[1085] Because of the sign, no women watched the execution in the jail yard.[1086]

About 10 o'clock William Williams was taken from his cell for transport to his death in Bartlett. He shook hands with Scott, saying, "We will soon meet in heaven." Scott replied laconically, "We will start on one journey about the same hour, but I am rather inclined to the opinion that we will travel in contrary directions; however, keep a stiff upper lip, Billy: we'll die game."[1087] At noon, Father Aloysius came to Scott's cell and conducted a service and put a blue ribbon around his neck which held a crucifix.

Frank Scott was taken from his cell at exactly 1:00 P.M. on January 7, 1876, and walked to the gallows with a firm and steady step. He sat on a bench beside the sheriff, his two lawyers, two doctors and Father Aloysius. Gazing around at the crowd, he turned to the group and remarked that he never thought he would be such an important character. Sheriff Anderson told him that he could make a last statement, to be followed by Father Aloysius.

Scott addressed the crowd, telling them he was perfectly ready to die, that he was innocent because the killing was in self-defense, that he was lucky that he knew when his death would come and could be prepared for it. "I die a Catholic. It is a safe church and it is my religion. I am doomed to die, but I am perfectly willing, understand me all. I prefer this to dying in bed."[1088]

He then turned to the priest. Scott and the priest knelt on the platform and the priest conducted a short service, with Scott moving his lips as if praying. When this was done, Scott said, "Come on now, Captain, I am in a hurry to go; my arms and hands are hurting me, and I had rather go now than endure the pain."[1089] He shook his hat from his head and told the sheriff to give it to one of the jail inmates. At this moment, a cart filled with spectators collapsed on the outside of the walls, causing a commotion, and Scott looked in the direction and chuckled.

Scott then stepped on the trap. He was pinioned; he tilted his head so the rope could be placed. The sheriff stood back ready to give the signal. "Ain't you going to put on the cap?" asked Scott. The sheriff then placed the cap. Without a verbal signal the sheriff counted one, two, three to himself and sprung the trap. Scott dropped cleanly with a thud. A minute after the fall his bosom heaved slightly, breathing exertions continued for two minutes. The body quivered, then began violent convulsions at about four minutes, then stopped. As the body was dropped, the crowd gave out a "kind of half-groan and half-grunt."[1090] Scott's body was taken down in fifteen minutes, placed in a coffin and given to the county undertaker, who was told to take it to the Catholic Calvary cemetery for burial.

Frank Scott had been dropped at exactly the time he had requested, namely, 1:40 P.M. Also hanged that day in Bartlett (Shelby County) was William Williams, and Milton McClean in Madison County. Scott, single, was born a slave in Athens, Georgia, and was brought by his owner, George Reese, to Chambers County, Alabama. He had lived in Memphis several years.

Burr Beggarly (aka Burrell Sphynx, Burr Spinks), black, age 24. *Murder.*

The crime was committed on the night of March 16, 1875, at the victim's home in rural Wilson County. The victim was a Robert Hamilton, white, age forty, who was shot from ambush as he stepped outside his house. Beggarly, Porter Williamson and George Kelly had gone to the man's house to steal chickens, but the noise attracted Hamilton's attention. Because Beggarly's hat was found at the scene, he was arrested but gave conflicting statements (called confessions). Beggarly and Williamson were convicted, but granted new trials.[1091] Williamson was lynched. Beggarly was convicted a second time.

The Tennessee Supreme Court found that his conflicting statements were properly admitted because they were not given under force or promise. Furthermore, the evidence showed that Hamilton was killed with a "short Army musket," the kind which was found at Beggarly's house, instead of a shotgun, which was found at Williamson's house.[1092]

Beggarly maintained his innocence to the end. In the Nashville jail he was attended by the Rev. Nelson Merry, foremost Tennessee African American Baptist minister of his day. The Rev. Merry had baptized Beggarly at the jail.

Burr Beggarly was hanged at 1:11 P.M. on May 31, 1876, on a gallows three-quarters of a mile from the jail in Lebanon. The newspaper said this was the first legal execution in Wilson County in forty years. Five thousand people witnessed the execution, standing in the boiling sun.[1093]

Taken from the jail and placed in a wagon, he went to the gallows accompanied by the Rev. Bond, black, and the Rev. Merry, who rode in the wagon with him, along with the sheriff and deputies. The wagon was surrounded by sixty-two armed guards. Beggarly mounted the trap-door gallows with a firm step. Sheriff Grandstaff spoke to the crowd, saying this was the "most awful" duty required of him, but he would accomplish it with uplifted hands and a fearless heart. He did not decide Beggarly's fate. The law had decided it and he was there to do his duty.

As soon as he finished, a gun carried by one of the guards accidentally discharged and the vast crowd surged in all directions. Those on the outside ran away, others were pushed in all directions while horses plunged and reared. Witnesses on the scaffold waved handkerchiefs and shouted until order was restored. No one was hurt.[1094]

The Rev. Merry explained that he did not know Beggarly until a few weeks earlier and did not know anything about his crime except that he was convicted of murder. The minister said that life was a vapor, vanishing like a shadow. He said he believed that Beggarly had repented, and his purpose in coming was to see that he passed out of life with some degree of comfort. Then the Rev. Bond led singing the hymn, "Death Cannot Make Our Soul Afraid." The Rev. Bond offered a prayer and another hymn was sung, "Must I Be to Judgment Brought."

At this point, Beggarly gave his last statement in a loud clear voice. He said:

> I want to speak a few words to these people, now that my last time on earth has come. We will talk again together if we meet in Heaven. I shall be hung to pay the debt of another man. I am going where there are some of my friends, and where some of my relatives are too. I am not going to suffer pain. I am ready and willing to die. As God is my witness, I am innocent, and witnesses will be found yet to prove it. I have been overpowered by men — overpowered by false witnesses. As God is my judge, today, I did not do the killing, and all my hope is in Him. My life has been sworn away by false-testimony — not by truth at all. I hope God will forgive all who swore falsely against me. I have forgiven them, and hope they may never have an hour of pain for the way they have treated me. All you white and black people, both Christians and not Christians, I have a sister, talk to her and help her take away some of the damnation she heaped on her head when she swore falsely against me. When she came home and said, "Brother Barnes has baptized me and I am saved," what did she do the very next day? She went up to the courthouse and swore that I came home that night covered with blood, and with a gun in my hand, said that I killed Mr. Hamilton. If Mr. Hamilton was here today, he would stand up before you and say: "No, Burr, you did not murder me." And some of you tell Elzy Hewgly to repent of the wrong she did me, and try to meet me in Heaven. Remember me in a particular manner. Have mercy on this crowd, and make them repent. Remember me today, who is under prosecution on false pretense. May all these people obtain full satisfaction in their minds. Oh, Lord, I come to die in the place of another man. All of you take warning from me and listen to my last prayer.[1095]

After saying this, he fell to his knees and said a prayer that was virtually the same as his last statement. Rising to his feet, he said to the sheriff, "You can go on now." One of the ministers began singing a hymn and when it was finished, Beggarly called for a black man in the crowd to come forward. He told the man to bury him beside his wife and tell his parents not to grieve.

The sheriff put the noose around his neck and said, "Beggarly, you told me this morning that you knew who did the killing. Who was it?" Beggarly replied, "I can't tell, Mr. Grandstaff. I don't want to say anything more."[1096] Beggarly was pinioned and before the cap was placed he said, "Good-bye to all, both black and white." Everyone left the platform and the sheriff walked to the bottom and used a mallet to remove the peg holding the trap. Beggarly fell cleanly, his body making a few convulsive shudders. He was taken down seventeen minutes later and his neck was found not broken. According to the newspaper, "Although Beggarly used some very strong language in protesting his innocence, still it was almost the unanimous verdict of the crowd that he died with a falsehood on his lips."[1097]

Hawson Clark (aka Hanson Clark and Howson Clark), black, age 55. *Murder.*

The details of the crime are unknown except that Clark killed his uncle in Fayette County on September 10, 1875, with a carbine. The victim's name was William Gaines, black, age forty-four. Clark was indicted on October 19, 1875. He was convicted after a two-day trial on March 4, 1876.[1098]

The opinion of the Tennessee Supreme Court did not recite any of the facts, saying, "We forbear to criticize the facts of the case. It is sufficient to say that the case lacks not one of the elements of that high crime and that the prisoner's conduct in the transactions which so tragically was characterized by a wanton barbarity seldom to be seen in the annals of crime."[1099]

The jury had found guilt but with mitigating

circumstances; the judge disregarded this recommendation. The defendant asserted this was error. The Supreme Court said that it had several times ruled this was a matter for the trial court's discretion and affirmed the death sentence.[1100]

The only legal issue raised was whether it was necessary for the record to show that the officer in charge of the jury had been sworn. Here the record showed that the jury was attended by a deputy sheriff whose name was given, but there was no showing he had been sworn. The court said that because it was not necessary for the record to show that a sheriff doing this task was sworn, it was not necessary for the record to show such for a deputy. It suggested there might be a situation where a person who performed this duty on an irregular basis would have to be sworn separately, but the record would have to show this affirmatively.[1101]

Hawson Clark was hanged at Somerville on December 15, 1876. The details of his execution are unknown.[1102]

1877

Frank Wilson (aka Jack Seefly), black, age unknown. *Murder.*

The crime was committed on August 7, 1876, in a rural area near Aaron Springs Road five miles from Dover, in Stewart County. The killers, Frank Wilson and Bill Mockbee, black, age unknown, knew the victim, Wiley McClish, white, age twenty-six, a local farmer. McClish had told the men that he was going to Dover to get a large amount of money. He had stopped at Walter's Store and purchased a pound of copperas and a sieve. He was walking on a footpath toward his home when he was struck from behind with an ax.[1103]

Wilson said that as McClish approached, he let him pass, and Mockbee struck him with his brother's ax from the rear. Wilson then cut off McClish's head. They found ten cents on his body. They took his shoes, his hat and the sieve. The body was found five days later. Found at the scene was an old felt hat that did not belong to McClish, and the copperas.

The sheriff began canvassing the neighborhood and came to Mockbee's cabin. His wife was washing clothes, and seemed to be in hurry to scrub a shirt. The sheriff asked why the shirt was bloody and she explained that her husband had shot a rabbit and carried it close to his chest. The sheriff noticed a sieve and asked who owned it. She said it belonged to Frank Seefly. On the way out, he noticed a spool of green silk thread. He asked what she had last sewn with the thread and she replied Frank Seefly's hat. The sheriff confiscated the thread and it matched the thread on the old felt hat.

The pair was arrested and Wilson began confessing and implicated Mockbee, who was found wearing McClish's shoes. Wilson explained that when McClish was struck he said, "Oh, Lord!"

Wilson said that a few hours after the killing he went back to examine the body to make sure he was dead. He explained he had no grudge against McClish and when asked why he had killed him, Wilson said the devil made him do it. When asked how he felt the night of the killing, Wilson replied, "Oh, bully; I never slept better in my life."[1104]

Wilson and Mockbee's conviction was appealed to the Tennessee Supreme Court, which granted a new trial. The opinion cannot be located. Mockbee was held for trial following the second trial (and appeal) of Wilson. The conviction was upheld, but the opinion cannot be located. By this time, Mockbee had been granted a change of venue.

Three weeks before Wilson's execution, Mockbee was taken from the jail in Dover by about thirty armed men. They took him to a tree and lynched him, riddling his body with bullets.[1105]

Frank Wilson was executed at 1:00 P.M. on May 25, 1877, not far from where Mockbee was shot, near Dover. The execution was witnessed by two thousand five hundred people. Wilson made a rambling last speech in which he admitted his guilt and said that Mockbee was as guilty as he. He said he deserved to die.

A year later, Robert Mockbee, Bill's brother, was convicted of infanticide and sentenced to be hanged. A new trial was granted after an appeal and he received a seventeen-year sentence.[1106]

Millard Filmore Wilson (aka Min Wilson), black, age 21. *Murder.*

The crime was committed at 11:30 P.M. on July 13, 1876, at the intersection of Liberty and LaFayette Streets in downtown Jackson, in Madison County. The killer, a servant/houseboy for a prominent white family, knew the victim because he had been arrested by the victim several times. Capt. Newton C. Perkins, white, age thirty-eight, was the victim. He was a policeman for the city of Jackson. Wilson had frequently boasted that he would kill Perkins if provoked. One of Perkins's children had died the previous day and Wilson was heard to say the father would be next. Perkins was known to flaunt his authority.

Min Wilson, sometimes called "Ninrod," was raised in the home of a prominent white family. "He was possessed of a rare degree of intelligence for one of his race."[1107] He was born a slave and was owned by Mrs. Weakly Wilson. His mother died shortly after his birth. He was raised with affection and care. He was considered one of the best waiters in the city, talented and charming. He gathered flowers and arranged them in baskets which he sold to white men as gifts for their girlfriends. He did not associate with black people until he was seventeen years old. From that time he was in constant trouble with the law for minor infractions.[1108]

The death of Capt. Perkins was caused by a combination of personal insult, invasion of one's "space," youthful boastfulness, and wine. In simple terms, as policeman Perkins confronted Wilson on the street and attempted to search him for a weapon, Wilson pulled a pistol and shot Perkins point-blank in the chest. Perkins said, "Send for a physician!" but died within minutes on the street.[1109] The shooting had a complicated origin.

Following an evening church service, the well-dressed Min Wilson, together with three other young black friends, bootblack Matt Bradford, Phoebe Oliver and Anna Wilson, decided to take an extended walk about the town. It was a full-moon night. After walking some time, they went to a barber shop where Bradford worked and to which he had the key. When Wilson entered the shop he put a concealed pistol on a table. The party lit lamps and proceeded to drink and frolic, but noticed they were being watched by two policeman across the street. Seeing this, Wilson and the girls left by the back door, Bradford the front, locking it behind him. Wilson realized he had left the pistol and went back inside and got it.

Although the foursome had done nothing wrong, they were engaged in loud talking and laughing. This made policeman Perkins suspicious. He came up behind the girls and took them by the sleeve and asked them where they were going. Wilson said, "Mr. Perkins, what do you intend to do with these girls?" Perkins replied, "Wait until Bob comes and I will show you." The reference was to the other policeman, Robert Rawles.

Wilson said, "Let them girls loose," and said to them, "Come on, girls," and the three started to go. Perkins pulled them back. Wilson turned his back to the group. He pulled out his pistol. He then turned around toward Officer Perkins, who asked, "Wilson, are you going to shoot me?"

"No," said Wilson, "I have nothing to shoot you with."[1110]

Wilson was holding the pistol close to his side. Perkins approached Wilson and put one arm around him and felt around him with the other. Wilson shifted the pistol from hand to hand while this was being done. Wilson then said, "Oh, God damn it, Mr. Perkins, let me loose!" Without further warning, he put the pistol to the policeman's chest and fired.

The three ran. Wilson caught up with them and asked them not to tell who did it. Apparently, one of them, at least, did. Wilson was found at an old black man's house the next day. To gain permission to spend the night, he told the man that he'd had a "little scrimmage" with policeman Perkins. He was allowed to sleep on a pallet on the floor. When officers arrived they found Wilson hiding between two mattresses. He blamed the shooting on Matt Bradford.

At trial, he offered the defense that officer Perkins had no right to stop the women and the shooting was in self-defense against an illegal arrest. The facts did not support a conviction of first-degree murder, but at most, a conviction of second-degree murder, namely, a killing in the heat of passion.

The Tennessee Supreme Court affirmed the conviction in a three-to-two decision, emphasizing the fact that he had turned away before drawing his gun and had asked his friends to cover up for him. The dissenters, Freeman and McFarland, said the facts warranted only a second-degree murder conviction.[1111]

The trial and execution of Min Wilson presented a special problem for the sheriff because Capt. Perkins was his brother. For example, the duty of summoning a jury, normally part of the sheriff's job, had to be done by a person specially appointed for the task, as well as guarding and tending to the jurors. Sheriff George Perkins supervised the hanging and put the rope around Wilson's neck, however.[1112]

Millard Filmore Wilson was hanged at 11:46 A.M. on July 13, 1877, on a gallows on the south of the city of Jackson, on a river bank of the Forked Deer River. Following the prayers offered by three ministers, and several hymns including "There Is a Fountain Filled with Blood," he was pinioned and the rope placed. He looked straight at a cross that was held before him. He made no last statement.[1113] The cap was placed and he was dropped without verbal warning from the sheriff. His neck was not broken, and he was cut down fifteen minutes later.

Andrew J. Hunt (aka Jackon Hunt and Jack Hunt), white, age 23. *Murder.*

The crime was committed on the afternoon of July 27, 1875, in a rural farmhouse owned by Mr. and Mrs. John Farmer in the White Cliff Springs area of Monroe County. Mrs. Farmer was the killer's sister. The victim was the killer's wife, Margaret Ann Davis Hunt, white, age nineteen. The couple had married on November 18, 1874. Margaret was visibly pregnant at the time of her death.

Hunt, the eighth of ten children,[1114] was described as "an unsteady fellow, dissipated at times and frequently abused his wife."[1115] He whipped her, locked her in the house, left for awhile and would only return when he felt like it. Sometimes when he abused her, she would seek refuge at a neighbor's house, which in turn further enraged Hunt.

On the evening before and again on the morning on which the killing took place, Hunt gave his wife a terrible beating, and while he was temporarily away from the house, she fled to the Farmer home. In a rage, Hunt confronted her and demanded that she leave with him. When she refused, he struck her. She still refused, saying that she was going to her father's house in North Carolina. He took a Navy pistol (.40 caliber) and shot her through the wrist.[1116] He turned and walked out the door. Here is what happened next:

> The wife, still true to her womanly instincts, with a broken arm and staggering toward the door called out to him, "Oh, Jack, don't kill me. I love you, come back and I will forgive you all." But this appeal, which was enough to have melted the heart of a savage had no effect on his pitiless nature, for he turned back and with a steady aim at her breast fired the fatal shot, the bullet passing entirely through her body and burying itself in the door shutter. Crying out, "Oh! I am killed," the beautiful young wife fell bleeding on the floor, and in gasping tones, begged Mrs. Farmer to pray for her, and immediately expired.[1117]

Hunt put the pistol in his pocket and without looking at his wife, walked out of the house into the woods. He was discovered two days later and jailed. He escaped from the jail ten days later, but made no effort to flee, although one of his brothers offered him money to aid in his doing so. Jack Hunt insisted on borrowing a horse, but the brother refused, saying the missing horse would implicate him.

Brother-in-law John Farmer was instrumental in leading the effort to recapture Hunt, finally finding him deep in the forest, sheltered by a blown-down tree. Jack Hunt gave up without a struggle, begging Farmer not to shoot him. Hunt had many times threatened to kill Farmer for shielding Margaret.

According to the newspaper:

> On his way to prison, Hunt betrayed a variety of conflicting emotions. He descanted on the beauties of nature so smilingly spread out before his view, though taking no pleasure in them. He expressed the deepest remorse for his crime, saying if wealth and liberty were offered him he would accept neither unless his murdered wife could be re-endowed with life. He said his grief would be somewhat alleviated if he could feel assured that his wife had been prepared for heaven, and alleged at one moment that he had killed her to save his own life, as he had treated her so badly that he feared her relations would murder him for so doing. Another time he said that he could scarcely realize having committed so heinous a crime avowing that he had always loved his wife, and he certainly had been instigated by the devil.[1118]

The trial was moved to McMinn County and Hunt was convicted in April 1877. The Tennessee Supreme Court said it was not error for the state to challenge a juror who had a case pending in the same court, as mandated by a statute. Furthermore, Hunt had not exhausted his challenges.[1119]

It was likewise all right for the court to give the written jury instructions offered by defense counsel, with the notation to the jury that they were offered by the defense. The statute requiring written instructions was designed to prevent judges from making verbal comments on evidence and was not violated by this procedure.[1120]

The court's insanity charge was somewhat truncated but still satisfactory. Here the court said, "The theories of those who make the subject of insanity a study, tend strongly to the conclusion that all criminals are insane. No matter how plausible such theories are in a metaphysical sense, they cannot be allowed to prevail in the trial and punishment of criminals. The man who possesses in a healthy condition the ordinary qualities of a mind must be punished as a sane man."[1121]

The proof of insanity was deficient. Family members spoke of "strange looks, conduct, and conversations by the prisoner on a few occasions shortly before the killing, all of which was supposed by them to have resulted from an attack of fever he had some twelve months before, but these symptoms are not satisfactorily described, nor does it appear to us that there is anything in this testimony showing insanity."[1122]

Kept in the Knoxville jail until thirty days before his execution, Hunt was visited by his mother and one of his brothers in the Monroe County jail the night before his execution. Around midnight, he took a large dose of morphine but was discovered. Two doctors administered emetics and saved his life for the hanging. Hunt refused to say who gave him the drug.

After this, he was allowed no private visitors. The next morning he was attended by his weeping mother, who kept saying, "My boy, my boy!" Hunt repeatedly told her to quit crying. Just before leaving, his mother asked him why he had committed the crime. He replied that "he had a cause and I would do more if I could."[1123] The last utterance was understood to mean that he wished he had killed Farmer too.

Hunt rode a wagon, sitting on his coffin, and in the wagon were sheriff's deputies and one of Jack's brothers-in-law. Fifty-six armed guards accompanied the wagon. The rope was attached to an iron ring on the crossbeam. The sheriff addressed the crowd by saying this was the saddest duty of his life and then read the death warrant. He said twenty-six minutes would be allowed for devotional exercises. The Rev. G.H. Colthorpe and the Rev. J.P. Kefauver (Baptists) were present. The former read from the 13th chapter of Romans and said to the crowd that this was the result of carrying concealed weapons. The Rev. Kefauver then read the 10th chapter of Romans. He said that he had talked a great deal with the prisoner concerning his future and while he hoped Hunt's faith was well founded, he feared Hunt was unprepared for the great eternity into which he would soon launch. Hunt seemed largely unconcerned with the proceedings.

The Rev. Kefauver announced he had been asked to read the following letter:

> Mother, Father and Brothers:
> I will try to write you a few lines to bid you all a final farewell. I do not want you, Dear Mother, to be more troubled about me than you are already, I want you to prepare to meet me in a better world, where sin and sorrow is not found. Will and Sam, I want you to be good boys, and try to get to Heaven when you die. There is more pleasure in living the life of a Christian, it looks plain to me now, though I did not think so, nor see it in that light, before I sought and believe I found pardon in a merciful Savior. I do not want any of you all to grieve for me, but take warning by my misfortune and try to do better than it has been my misfortune to do. Farewell to you all and may God bless and save you all. A.J. Hunt[1124]

Hunt's letter also thanked the jailer and his family for their kind treatment. The Rev. Colthorpe said that Hunt had requested him to say that he felt his sins had been forgiven and desired all present to meet him in heaven. The Rev. Colthorpe offered a final prayer.

Andrew Jackson Hunt was hanged at 1:42 P.M. on December 18, 1877, from a gallows one-half mile west of Madisonville in an open field in front of about four thousand five hundred people. As usual, none who were asked said they came to see him hang. All said the same thing: "I just want to hear what Jack has to say."[1125] All were disappointed.

Jack Hunt stepped upon the platform on the wagon, but began to weaken and had to be supported by a deputy. He said good-bye to the sheriff just before the rope and noose were placed around his neck. The sheriff said nothing. He ordered the horses forward and Jack Hunt was "swung off" in the traditional manner. His neck was not broken. He was dead in eight minutes and taken down twenty-seven minutes later, placed in the coffin, and given to his brother-in-law. He was buried in the family cemetery in Tellico Plains.

Jack Hunt was hanged with the same rope used to hang John Webb two years earlier in Knoxville. Plans were to use it in hanging Jacob Harris in Clinton the next month. The crowd was orderly, due in part to the "public spirit of Mr. W.W. Wooten, proprietor of the saloon, who closed his place of business for the day."[1126] Said the newspaper, "We saw no cases of drunkenness."[1127]

Jacob Harness, white, age 36 (at the time of the crime), 49 (when executed). *Murder.*

The crime was committed on July 15, 1863, on the killer's farm in rural Anderson County. Harness, age thirty-six, had a reputation for violence and had quarreled with the victim about the sale of some whiskey. The victim, Isaac White, white, age fifty-two, was a distiller. The killing was indirectly related to Civil War allegiances. In addition to the dispute over the whiskey, Harness was angry that White, a Confederate sympathizer, had turned him in to Southern officials, and he had been held for a time in Castle Fox, a military prison in Knoxville. While there, he told cell mates that when he got out he would kill Isaac White and another man, Dick Webb.

Harness said he had served twenty months in the Mexican War and said he had been a member of Company H, 1st Tennessee Infantry Regiment (Federal).[1128] In London, Kentucky, in 1864, Harness boasted about killing White to a member of the regiment, Pvt. Daniel Vann.[1129] The relationship, if any, between Daniel Vann and Ebb (sometimes Ed)

Vann is unknown. The latter testified he saw the body the day after the murder.

Harness planned the killing by stealing some of White's "doublings" (a part of the process of whiskey making) and carrying the keg in such a way that White would follow the trail. The path ultimately led to Harness's property. As White followed the trail he came to a field in which Harness, his wife and a black girl were working.

Harness raised his rifle to kill White, but his wife stopped him. "Shaking her off with brutal threats, he took deliberate aim and fired, the ball crashing through the breast of his victim."[1130] As White lay on the ground begging for his life, Harness taunted him, made him drink his own (stolen) whiskey, and fired a shot into his head.

After killing White, Harness cut off his head with the large knife he always carried, and "rolled it down the ridge like a damned old pumpkin."[1131] With the help of the black girl, the headless body was carried from the field and placed between two logs. Sometime later, remnants of the body and clothing were found, remnants left by circling buzzards, but no charges were brought against Harness or anyone, in part, due to wartime conditions.

Shortly after the killing, the Harness family moved to Wayne County, Kentucky, and the matter was largely forgotten. Not forgotten by those who remained behind were his threats on the lives of people he did not like. He had attacked and wounded several men, including stabbing Thomas Russell with what was later shown to be the knife used to cut off White's head. Later, the family moved to Scott County, Tennessee. At the time of his arrest, Harness had a wife and seven living children.

The Tennessee Supreme Court's opinion explained: "Daniel Vann says himself and Harness were military prisoners in the Knoxville Jail, three or four months before White was killed, defendant then said he aimed to kill White and Dick Webb before he went back to his regiment. After the killing, a good while after, I was in London, Kentucky, and came to Camp Nelson where defendant was, about two or three months after I heard of the killing, defendant asked if I had got the news he sent me. He said he had killed White and aimed to kill Dick Webb but could not get a chance."[1132]

The testimony of Daniel Vann included all the details of the killing, including the wife's attempting to stop him, the rolling of the head down the ridge like an old pumpkin, and the hiding of the body. The opinion explained the disarrayed nature of the body, scattered "as if by dogs."[1133]

The court's opinion continued: "Thomas Russell, State; that in November 1863 at Jim Philip's on New River when a good deal of whiskey was around and fighting going on defendant drew out a large pocket knife and cut right and left, I remonstrated with him, he said that knife made peace, it had cut Isaac White's head off and he would cut off some more heads if he was fooled with."[1134]

Ebb Vann said he saw White's body in the field about a quarter of a mile from Harness's house. He and Warren Jones were traveling through the country from Kentucky as recruiters. When they came into the house they heard two sounds like a gun being cocked. When they identified themselves as federal recruiters, Harness came out from under the bed and told them he was glad they said who they were because he had killed one man that day and would just soon kill another. Harness showed them White's body and said it grew out of the time Ebb Vann, the victim and Harness had been in the Knoxville jail together. This is apparently the incident in which White had revealed Harness's Unionist sentiment.[1135]

Mary Doughtery Jones, daughter of Isaac White, testified about the money he was carrying, including a two-dollar bill with amber spots in one corner. She saw it later in the possession of Liz Phillips, who testified that she had received it from Harness's wife to purchase some tobacco. This was after White was killed, but before his body was found. Both women were sure about the amber spots because they were "about as large as a fly's head, or a pin head."[1136]

Jacob Harness's adult daughters, carefully coached to name Ebb Vann and Warren Jones as the killers, fell apart under cross-examination, unable to tell any consistent facts. For example, at the beginning of her testimony, one of the daughters was asked her age. She replied she was twenty-five. When asked on cross-examination, she said she was "twenty, last May."[1137]

The Supreme Court said, "We are satisfied the testimony of the daughters of the accused is the work of the prisoner impressed on their minds by constant drilling on his part. It is clear from the record that no pains were spared on the part of the defendant, by himself and through his wife to impress upon his children the importance of understanding the story they were to tell and of "telling it all alike."[1138]

The court said, "The disposition to protect the father was a natural one and easily excited to the use of such means as would most likely accomplish that protection. Yet the story bears the unmistakable evidence of fabrication."[1139]

Harness asserted error in the trial court's refusal to allow a question to Daniel Vann, asking if he had not been indicted several times. The court said this ruling was proper because it did not ask about any specific indictments.[1140] Harness asserted error in the trial court's not writing on the jury instructions the volume and page of the Tennessee Reports from which he took the language. The court said this was proper; the law only required a full citation and recitation of any statute charged.[1141]

Harness was convicted in July 1876. This was thirteen years after the crime. He was ordered hanged on September 10, 1876. The Supreme Court's order set December 29, 1877, as the day. Despite a mixture of rain and snow, Jacob Harness, age forty-nine, was hanged at 1:20 P.M. on December 29, 1877, on a gallows a half-mile from the town of Clinton in front of two thousand people, half of them women.[1142] Harness steadfastly maintained his innocence, still naming Ebb Vann as the real killer. At the time of his execution, Harness had seven living children.

The month before his execution, he gave a written statement which included:

> I am not a member of the church but I am a firm believer in the Missionary Baptists. I have been in my young days, a bad man. About nine years ago my eyes were opened and I firmly resolved to abandon my wicked ways, which resolution by help of a living and just God, I have most sacredly kept. It has long been my intention to unite with the church and be baptized, and if I have to expiate on the scaffold for a crime I never committed I sincerely pray God that I may have an opportunity of being baptized by immersion. I have no fears of death and find great consolation in the words of my dear Savior, who died upon the cross, that we might live eternally.[1143]

He told the sheriff he wanted to be buried in the clothes he was wearing, that no money should be spent on new clothes. Taken from his cell to the execution site, Harness "remained unmoved in the presence of his wife and children leaving them without an affectionate embrace."[1144]

Harness was placed in a wagon and sat on his coffin while being taken to the gallows. His wife was allowed to stay with him in his cell the night before his execution provided she changed her clothing and was thoroughly searched. Harness thought he would be rescued because someone had told him "all of Scott County will be here."[1145]

Seated in a chair on the gallows wagon, Harness remained unmoved as a prayer was offered, then got to his knees as a hymn was sung, "Teach Me the Measure of My Days," and another he requested, "Oh, Where Shall Rest Be Found?" Another minister offered a prayer, and Sheriff Gibbs asked Harness if he had anything to say. Harness replied, "Nothing."

Harness rose deliberately and threw off his coat and stepped up on the gallows wagon platform. The noose was placed over his head and the black cap was placed. He asked Thomas Duncan to take care of his body and see to it that he was buried on the premises of his brother, Thomas Harness. (A James Harness was in the group in front, but his relationship to the defendant, if any, is unknown.)

At that moment, Sheriff Gibbs discovered he had forgotten the death warrant. He told the guards to remove the noose and cap while he rode his horse back to the jail.

While the sheriff was gone, Harness finally addressed the crowd, "Friends, I want to say to you all just one more thing, and that is, that Dan and Ed Vann have caused my death by swearing lies. They are responsible for my death. I am not guilty of this as charged. That's all I have to say to you. I look to God knowing I am prepared for a better life."[1146]

When the sheriff returned, Harness listened unconcernedly to the reading of the death warrant.

Again, he stepped on the wagon platform and the noose and cap were placed. He asked, "How long is the rope?" He asked to be notified when all was ready. Nobody answered. The sheriff ordered the horses forward and Harness was "swung off" in the traditional manner.[1147]

The newspaper noted, "He was a bad, bad man and his sentence was looked upon by the community as just." It said, "That this fearful crime should be left unatoned for twelve long years, while the perpetrator quietly pursued his avocation in an adjoining State, probably not a hundred miles from the scene of its commission, will not particularly surprise the older citizens of this section of the State by whom it will be remembered that lawlessness and crime were rife in those perilous times."[1148] The head of Isaac White was never found.

1878

Rev. Brown Coble, black, age 31. *Murder.*

The crime was committed on June 23, 1876, on a farm outside Winchester, Franklin County. Coble and the victim, Felix Gardner, black, age unknown, were tenant farmers living in the same house with their wives on the land of W.J. Woods, white. The two had quarreled publicly on several occasions and Coble pulled a pistol and threatened to kill Gardner, but violence was prevented because the men's wives intervened. The chief disagreement between the men was the accusation that Coble and Gardner's wife were too intimate.

Shortly before the killing Coble asked Woods, "If two men were together and no other person present, and one was to kill the other, what would be done with the one doing the killing?" Woods replied that it depended on what he said afterward.[1149] For a year prior to the killing, Coble told people that he could kill a man and make it look like suicide. A week before the killing, Coble told a state's witness (Wilson) that he regretted not killing Gardner at the time the wives intervened.

The day of the murder Wilson brought home a mare that needed to be broken and asked Coble to get a set of gears. Coble replied the gears were at his house and the two walked in that direction together. Suddenly, Coble ran ahead. By the time Wilson arrived, Coble ran from the house exclaiming that Gardner had killed himself. Wilson found Gardner across a chair with his hands and feet on the floor, his throat cut from ear to ear. Bread was found in the victim's mouth and some was protruding from the wound. A half-closed razor was found in his hand. There was considerable blood on the floor, but none on the victim below the shirt collar. The scene did not look like a suicide.

Wilson testified that he saw fresh blood between Coble's eyes and blood on his pants as if someone had smeared dust on them. Coble had not worn shoes that day, which Wilson said was unusual for him. The implication of this testimony was that Coble's shoes had gotten blood on them during the killing.

Gardner was buried on Saturday but the investigation required exhumation. The skull was severely fractured above and behind the right ear, the fracture extending in different directions as if he had been struck from behind. Wilson found in a shed room a "dog-block" weighing twelve pounds, some twelve inches long, and three and one-half inches wide. A chain attached to it was bloody.

Coble's first trial resulted in a death sentence but the verdict was overturned by the Supreme Court because the indictment was not properly signed by the district attorney and did not contain the word "willful" in describing the crime.[1150]

Following the second trial, the Supreme Court rejected a double jeopardy objection, and said the facts were overwhelming, setting the execution for March 14, 1878.[1151] The Rev. Brown Coble was hanged that day. Seven thousand people poured into Winchester to witness the execution, with "saloons allowed to remain open; whiskey was consumed freely and began to show its demoralizing effects long before noon."[1152] Said the paper, "One of them, Mr. Seth Green, had not visited the town for forty-one years."[1153]

Dressed in a white robe, Coble told the crowd he was innocent, that his words had been misconstrued. His statement to the crowd was rambling, "The dog-block that he produced before the Court as the instrument that fractured Felix Garnder's skull — it may be true, but it is him or some other man that used it for I will not tell you a lie about it. I am as clear as the angels in Heaven, and I guess you will admit that they are."[1154]

Notwithstanding Coble's status as a part-time minister, no one seemed to show any sympathy for him, including his wife, who was kept in the jail for eight months because she had become insane after the killing. The newspaper observed, "Coble appeared to have no friends, and everyone, both white and black, seemed to think he deserved his fate."[1155]

The facts of the execution are conflicting because the same newspaper account that said he died instantly, also said the rope was too long and his feet touched the ground. "But he was lifted up and placed higher by four strong men." It said because he showed signs of life after the doctor pronounced him dead, Coble was allowed to hang for twenty-six minutes.[1156]

Joseph Lewis Brassell, white, age 19/22. *Murder.*
George Andrew "Teek" Brassell, white, age 18/21. *Murder.*

The crime was committed on the late evening of November 29, 1875, nine miles west of Cookeville, Putnam County, where the Nashville Road intersects the Sparta Road, some two hundred yards distant, at a large home used by travelers, called Allison's Stand Inn. The victim was Russell Allison, white, age eighteen.

The inn was built and operated by Joseph Allison and his wife Angeline. When he died, she married James Isbell and was then known as Mrs. Isbell. Living at the inn were her two adult sons, Russell Allison and Joseph Allison, Jr. Present in the inn at the time of the shooting, in addition to Mrs. Isbell and Russell Allison, were Miss Amanda Pippin (sleeping in the same bed as Mrs. Isbell), Arch

Bryant (who was sleeping upstairs in the same bed as Russell), and the youngest Allison brother, a teen-ager, Joseph Allison, who was sleeping in the dining room.

The Brassell brothers had criminal records and were part of an extended family of moonshiners. The plan to rob Allison's Stand Inn was devised by their brother, James Brassell. Because the county tax collector, W.J. Isbell, was the son of inn owner James Isbell, it was thought he would be at the inn on the murder night. He was thought to be carrying four thousand dollars in cash, and that four hundred dollars was hidden in the inn clock. The plan called for a robbery of the inn. The robbers were Joseph, then age nineteen, and Teek Brassell, then age eighteen, Dobson Johnson, and Dol Bates.

The Brassell brothers, on horseback, called out to the house demanding supper and lodging for four men from the railroad. (Johnson and Bates stayed some distance away and never went inside.) When Mrs. Isbell heard the calling, she asked who it was. The voice came back, "It's Mansfield Howell, by God!" She replied that it was not because Howell did not swear. At this time, Russell Allison came downstairs, lit a candle, and opened the door. In rushed the Brassells, with faces blackened and their red coats turned inside out, with white linings showing. Russell had gone to school with the Brassells and recognized them at once. He said, "Don't be frightened, it's Teek and Joe Braswell," or "It's the Braswell boys."[1157] (People used the name Braswell and Brassell interchangeably in describing the family.)

Seeing a drawn pistol in Teek's hand, Russell Allison grabbed it and a scuffle ensued in which Teek soon held Russell in a bear hug from the back. Russell said, "Teek, don't do that." Teek said, "Turn my pistol loose." Joe came to his brother's aid and said, "Damn him, I can make him turn it loose." He fired one shot in Russell's direction but missed. Russell escaped Teek's grip and ran to the dining room, probably to get a weapon or to draw the men away from the bed in which the women were sleeping. Joe followed a few steps and fired at Russell Allison at close range. The bullet entered his abdomen. The women screamed and Joe fired into the bed, missing them. Russell was met by his brother Joseph who had come downstairs. Realizing they had been recognized, the Brassell brothers fled without taking anything. On the way out, they shot the barking family dog, and fired several shots in the yard outside.[1158]

Russell Allison, holding his abdomen, went to his mother's bedside and said, "Angie, I'm shot and Teek and Joe Brassell are the ones that shot me." Russell lived another thirty-six hours and told several people (physicians and clergymen) as well as friends, who had shot him.[1159]

The four would-be robbers were seen on the road by various people. They split up but the next day they were present at the Brassell still-house and seen by several other people. Bates and Johnson left for DeKalb County.

That evening, a posse came to the still-house and immediately arrested an intoxicated Joe Brassell. Asked his whereabouts, Joe said Teek had gone to a nearby mill but would return shortly. In the posse was John Allison, age forty-one, the oldest of the Allison brothers. When Teek appeared, John approached him angrily and they began fighting. As before, Teek held John Allison in a bear-hug from behind. As they struggled, Teek pulled out his pistol and fired it into John's side. Not realizing the nature of his wound, John exclaimed, "I'm shot in the leg." He died in the early morning hours the next day. From this was born the legend of two brothers who were hanged for killing two brothers two days apart, a fact which captured national media attention. (Actually, Teek was given a twenty-year sentence for killing John Allison, in a separate trial.)

The brothers were taken to the inn for identification. By now, the posse included a surprise, namely Buck Brassell, another brother.[1160] Seeing him, Teek jumped up, popped his hands together and said, "I'm a horse's ass yet."[1161]

With able lawyers, the Brassell's case was continued from term to term while they stayed in the Nashville jail. Trial finally began on June 23, 1877, and numerous witnesses appeared for both sides. This trial was only for the death of Russell Allison. (Joe was not charged with John Allison's death.) The key witness was Dobson Johnson, a conspirator whose case had been severed from theirs. He testified at length about both the plan to rob the inn and what the four had discussed following the shooting, namely to "go into the spurs of the mountains and engage in the business of highway robbery."[1162]

Joe Brassell offered the testimony of his mother and sister that he had spent the night at their house. The sister said she remembered it well because she was up and down during the night with a toothache.[1163] Teek's sister-in-law, Harriet Z. Brassell,[1164] insisted that Teek had spent the evening and all night in a chair by the fireplace because he had gotten his feet wet and had become chilled. She said that when her husband arrived later in the evening he placed a blanket over his brother. Unconvinced, the jury convicted Joe and Teek of first-degree murder. When the judge asked if they had anything to say, only Teek spoke up: "Yes, I'm not guilty."[1165]

The Tennessee Supreme Court said the statement of gravely wounded Russell Allison to his mother was part of the res gestae and was properly admitted because it was made so close to the shooting and the defendants could hear them.[1166] It was also proper to ask a defense witness if he had been indicted for counterfeiting. This did not require the witness to incriminate himself.[1167] Finally, it was proper for the state to argue that the failure of James Brassell, a brother and Harriett's husband, to testify about Teek's presence could be used to show a weakness in the alibi.[1168]

At the time, it was the custom to bring defendants to the location where the Supreme Court announced its decision. In this case, it was Nashville. When the Brassells were read the opinion, Justice Sneed asked if either had anything to say. The two had been convinced their convictions would be reversed. Joe said, "I am an innocent man. I have to suffer for what someone else has done!" Then Teek, in a very excited manner, blubbered, "The witnesses against me have sworn positive lies, for the purpose of taking my life. I am able to show it, but I am too excited now; I will have it written out by someone who understands how to fix up such things, and send it to the Court." Sneed cut him off, saying, "If you can make these matters plain to the Governor, there might be some hope for you yet." Teek spoke again, "The evidence of Mrs. Isbell and Johnson varied; Johnson was there, and he turned state's evidence against us; in his evidence he said four railroad men came to the house and asked for supper; Allison himself swore falsely against me; it was all done through malice, for the purpose of taking my life, and they have accomplished what they aimed to do; that is all I have to say at present."[1169]

The brothers were visited by over a thousand people in the Nashville jail, many bearing food, but most wanting to help save their souls or just gawk. The Rev. J.P. McFerrin was the most constant and effective minister. He and his brother the Rev. Sumner McFerrin (Methodists) finally baptized them the day before they were executed.

The legend of the Brassell brothers was heightened by their escapades in the Nashville jail. Their father had sent them liquor (bitters) but it was given to them in half-pint portions. They managed to accumulate a large quantity to use in getting up their courage for a jailbreak. Just before Christmas 1877, they managed to saw through the chain holding their door, and were about to escape, when a guard heard the chain drop to the floor. Instead of coming inside the cell block, the jailer summoned help and the brothers were captured — but not until after they offered to shake hands with their captor.

Teek was placed in shackles, but soon found he was able to remove them. A few days later, Teek tried to crawl under the bars of the door to the cell in which he and Joe were confined. He got stuck and was removed with difficulty. The pair somehow got arsenic into their cells. They planned to poison apples which they were to give to the guards taking them back to Cookeville for their execution. Another inmate tipped off the guards to the plan. The brothers were thought to have some other plan to escape during the trip back to Cookeville, but were thwarted when the sheriff decided to return them by steamboat.[1170]

On the way back, Teek said he had shot nine men while under the influence of whiskey, but did not provide any details about deaths. Joe said the only thing he had ever done to deserve the death penalty was to beat a woman and shoot her over a dispute involving a watermelon. She had died.[1171] Their escapades were published by the county clerk, Henry Polk Davis, but the pamphlet did not sell as expected because the men refused to discuss the Allison killing.[1172]

Joseph, now age twenty-two, and Teek Brassell, now age twenty-one, were hanged at 1:30 P.M. on a cold March 27, 1878, on a gallows one mile from the courthouse on Billy Goat Hill. It had two trap doors. The deaths were witnessed by a crowd estimated between ten and twenty thousand. The men were taken by wagon to the scaffold; they were seated on their coffins. Their sister Amanda Brassell rode behind on horseback. Just before they stepped up on the scaffold, she hugged each good-bye in a flood of tears. They asked her not to watch the actual hanging. Accounts differ on whether she watched.

The men were placed on chairs. The McFerrin ministers and the Rev. John H. Nichols were on the gallows with them. The death ceremony began with the Rev. Sumner McFerrin reading the Bible, with his brother offering a prayer and a short homily addressed to young men, warning of the evils of liquor and bad company. At 12:08 the minister asked exactly when the men were to be executed; the sheriff said they had asked to be executed at 1:00. The minister said he did not want to take up more of their time, and turning to the brothers said he hoped they had made their peace with God. The Rev. Nichols made remarks about the responsibility of parents to raise their children properly, then commended the men to the mercy of God. The three ministers sang a hymn, and a prayer was offered by the Rev. Sumner McFerrin. The ministers huddled with the brothers, asking if they felt secure in their souls. They responded they did and the ministers left the gallows.

Joe spoke to the crowd:

> Gentlemen and ladies, I will speak a few words to you if you will give me your attention. I am here today, and what is it for? Murder. What were the causes of it? They were whisky, hard seeking after money, and association with drunken reckless boys — and there are hundreds here today. I will give you some advice. Boys, let whisky alone. Above all things have nothing to do with whisky. Take warning by this. It brought me here in this fix, and your are liable to be put in this condition by following the same course. Young men, take warning and be good to one another. Go to meeting and keep the Sabbath holy. Farewell to you all. Meet me in heaven.[1173]

Now Teek had his turn: "This is a solemn hour. It is told me that I must die. I am ready, waiting, prepared and willing to die." There was a long pause. "I hope to meet you all in heaven." When it became clear that he was not going to say any more — he had maintained he was innocent all along — Mr. J.W. Isbell, who came up on the scaffold, asked Joe, "Were you at my house the night the murder was committed?" Joe answered, "I was there and I am guilty." Teek still insisted his innocent life had been sworn away.[1174]

The brothers were pinioned, nooses placed and white caps were put over their heads. The brothers asked for a few more minutes. It was granted. The hoods were removed and Joe said, "Boys, let this be a warning to you." Mr. Isbell saw another chance to ask Teek, "Wasn't you at my house that night?" Teek did not answer the question. Instead, he turned to the crowd and said, "All of you in hearing, listen! I have this to say. I am an innocent man, and have got to die for what someone else has done. I am paying another man's just debt." Mr. Isbell then asked Joe if Teek was present. Joe whispered, "Don't press me on that."

Mr. Isbell tried to get Joe to say more, apparently trying to get him to implicate his brother. But someone in the crowd said, "Don't press him too far," and Isbell left the scaffold area.

With the caps placed over their heads, the sheriff announced they had five more minutes because Teek had asked to be told when the trap was to be released. The sheriff announced each minute. With thirty seconds left, Joe said, "Good-bye, Mr. Bohannon." The sheriff said, "Good-bye, Joe." Joe's last words were, "Lord Jesus be with me." Teek spoke last, saying, "Lord, have mercy on those who swore my life away!"[1175] At this point, the sheriff used a hatchet to cut the trap rope and the pair fell cleanly. Their necks were broken and contractions were minimal. The bodies twisted under the rope and stopped facing each other. They were cut down in fifteen minutes and placed in coffins which were claimed by their sister Amanda and another brother. They were buried in the same grave in the family cemetery in Baxter.

The night before his execution, Joe Brassell wrote a letter to his family acknowledging that his family had worked on his behalf because he had told them he was innocent. This was not so. "I cannot go hence with a falsehood on my lips. Forgive, that you may be forgiven. I have no malice or ill will towards anyone on earth. Meet me in Heaven, for I am doing all I can to go there."[1176]

Teek Brassell's steadfast assertion of innocence gave rise to all manner of folklore about the case. One version says Amanda Brassell was the shooter, with her hair tucked inside her hat. The other belief was that the shooter was James Brassell, the brother who did not come forward to support Teek's alibi. This was supported in some measure by his obituary in the January 25, 1894, issue of the *Cookeville Free Press*. It said, "James Brassell, brother to the notorious Teek and Joe, who were hanged at this place several years ago for the murder of Russell Allison, died last week at his home about 8 miles west of Cookeville. It is said he made a confession to the effect that he did the murder instead of his brothers."[1177]

Another supposed complicating factor is this: At the time of the execution, tax collector W.J. Isbell (now County Trustee) was married to "the sister of the boys."[1178] It is not clear who this sister was, or if it was true. Another legend is this. Seen in the crowd were two men living in the Nashville area under false names. In fact, they were hiding out from the law following a bungled bank robbery in Northfield, Minnesota. Their real names were Jesse and Frank James.[1179]

And a final bit of folklore. As soon as Teek's body was cut down, the rope was removed from around his neck, but not Joe's. Taken to their father's house, Teek's body was said to have been rolled on the floor, air was breathed into his mouth, hartshorn and camphor were sprinkled into his nostrils, and within a few hours he was fully conscious and alive. Thereafter, he roamed the "desert wild," living in the mountains and never coming near areas where he might be known.[1180]

Accounts conflict about what happened to Dobson Johnson and Dol Bates. One account says they were still in the Putnam County jail at the time of the execution. Another account holds that Johnson escaped, or was allowed to escape from jail and disappeared.

George Howell, black, age 17. *Murder.*

The crime was committed on the evening of December 28, 1877, on the farm of Joseph Martin in rural Greene County. The killer knew the victim because he was employed by him as a farm worker for eight dollars a month. He had been employed for six months. The victim was Joseph Martin, white, age forty-four.

Howell shot a rifle through the farmhouse window where Martin and his wife and children were eating their evening meal. The bullet wounded Martin, who was able to come out of the house with his son Bob, age sixteen. In the yard he met Howell, who had first gone behind a barn to reload.

Howell said he had shot the rifle at some tramps who were passing through, shooting in the direction of the house. Martin and his son started across a field in search of the tramps, but Martin fell to the ground and died a few minutes later. Martin did not suspect that Howell had intentionally shot him. While on the ground, Martin asked Howell to return to the house and protect his wife and daughters. A few days later, Howell fled but was soon captured.

The testimony against Howell came from several people he confessed to immediately after his capture. Howell did not take the stand. There was no appeal. After the conviction, Howell sought executive clemency by asserting that Martin's family urged the killing.

His elaborate "confession" recounted in detail domestic turmoil and violence in the Martin household, due in part to Mrs. Martin's refusal to sleep with her husband after she accused him of visiting a local house of ill fame.[1181] Howell said Mrs. Martin told him she would bake him cakes for Christmas if he killed her husband and told him that he would be killed soon unless he killed the husband first. Bob had promised to give him two calves and a pig if he killed the father, and the two girls, Margaret and Teenie, urged him as well. He said the son gave him the weapon, a muzzle-loading Enfield rifle. Howell said he tried to kill Martin a day or so before but was prevented by runaway horses. He said the family urged him to flee earlier than he did by telling him he was a suspect. The story was not generally believed. Rather, Howell's motive was his anger over being rebuked for not cutting enough wood on the murder day.[1182]

Howell's execution was set for August 5, 1878, and several thousand people arrived in Greeneville for the event. They were disappointed when the governor, at the urging of William B. Yardley, a black lawyer, granted a reprieve to consider Howell's clemency petition.

George Howell was executed at 1:49 P.M. September 5, 1878, on a gallows near the fairgrounds, with about three thousand people watching. Howell had expressly asked for a trap-door gallows, not the traditional "swung off" method because he did not want to strangle to death.

No minister assisted in the death ceremony because many had visited him in the jail "apparently without producing any impression."[1183] A devotional exercise was led by a county official. Most of his last words were unintelligible except he warned young men from keeping bad company and continued to assert the victim's family had urged him to do the killing. Just before the trap was sprung, he said, "I ought not to have done it." His gave his body to the doctor who pronounced him dead with the understanding it would be subject to a "slight surgical examination" and not an out-and-out dissection.[1184]

Stephen Griffee (aka Stephen Griffey), white, age 21. *Rape of child under age of ten.*

The crime was committed on February 18, 1877, on a rural road in Cocke County. Griffee was a local man who had been accused of several crimes but had never been convicted. He was illiterate and drank heavily. He did not know the victim personally, but had seen her before because she lived in the area. The victim was Evaline Clark, white, age nine. She had gone to a country store with her brother, white, age seven.

Griffee and two or three friends were at the store when the children arrived. He had been drinking. In front of the friends he forced the children to drink some whiskey, although they protested. When they left, he followed them, again offering them whiskey. When they refused, he grabbed the boy and ordered him to drink to a certain point on the bottle or he would kill him. Then he did the same with Evaline.

The three continued walking toward the children's home. Griffee pretended he had found a rabbit by the side of the road. When the brother went to look, Griffee ordered him away with a threat to his life. A little farther along, he said he spotted another rabbit (some distance from the road) and both children went to the spot. Griffee again ordered the boy away. He left, but did not go as far as Griffee wanted. Griffee came after him, frightening him away. Griffee came back to the girl. Here is what happened:

> Seizing her, he forced her to the ground, and meeting difficulty on account of the girl's tender years, took out a sharp knife and cutting a horrible gash, finally accomplished his purpose, the girl being almost too drunk to comprehend the situation. Afterwards he and the girl went to where the boy was waiting and the three walked half a mile or so along the road. Griffee left them, telling Eva that if anybody asked what was the matter with her to say she had snagged herself; if she revealed what had happened he would kill her. He then left, but soon returned. The girl, seeing him coming back, tried to escape, but fell over the fence. Griffee then repeated his threats. A woman passing on the road, after some time, heard the child's cries of distress and carried her to a house. Her wounds were examined and attended to and to those present she told the story of the crime.[1185]

Griffee went to the house of a friend. When asked about the blood on his hand and pants, Griffee said he had a nosebleed and that he had had difficulty with a man named Hall and would have to leave the country. He was arrested a short time later.

Griffee went to trial in October 1877. One evening two jurors who were being sequestered left the control of the sheriff (who was asleep) and went to a grocery a few hundred yards away.[1186] When this was discovered, the two were fined and put in jail for five days. The offenders had spent the night with four other jurors. The four were offered to the defendant as a part of voir dire, but counsel declined to accept or reject them. This caused the court to strike the entire panel, and ordered the sheriff to bring in a new panel, but these four were directed by the court to be on this panel. The state challenged one, and the other three were offered to the defendant, but counsel again declined to accept or reject them. Counsel said in open court that the judge had punished the first two, and he did not know what effect it would have on the other three. The court then discharged the other three. As a full jury was picked, the defendant had not exhausted his challenges, having stricken only eight persons. Griffee's defense was a general denial of any involvement, emphasizing his prior quarrels with the girl's father.

In affirming Griffee's conviction, the Tennessee Supreme Court said there was no reversible error in the jury selection, because "it is settled in our State that the court may discharge a juror, even in a capital case, before he is sworn, for sufficient cause."[1187] The court said that Griffee was not prejudiced by this event because the jury was seated without Griffee's having exhausted his challenges.[1188] The court said, "The punishment may seem severe, but the offense is one of the most shocking that can be conceived, and well deserves the most emphatic reproof which the law has given a jury the right to inflict for such brutality."[1189] Griffee was ordered hanged on November 22, 1878, and was executed that day.

Stephen Griffee was executed at 2:00 P.M. on a public gallows a short distance from Newport. He had asked for a private execution, but the sheriff, citing the law, denied the request. He also asked for the traditional "swung off" hanging instead of a trap door. This was done as Griffee stood on a wagon pulled by two horses. On the scaffold, his last statement was an admission he had raped the child, but he denied cutting her vagina.[1190] He expressed full confidence that he was in the process of being converted into an angel.[1191]

Newport had a population of three hundred, but over two thousand people attended Griffee's execution. Petitions to commute his sentence to life imprisonment were based on his age. "It was also said that he was of a weak mind; had been subject to fits, and that in one of these moments of dementia he committed the deed. The petitions for mercy were unaccompanied by any papers of record, but rested solely on the opinion of the signers."[1192] Among the signers were the parents of Evaline Clark.

While being kept in the Knox County jail, Griffee made a statement that was written for him by a fellow prisoner. A great portion of the document recounted his quarrels with Evaline's father, whom he asserted was the force behind the prosecution. He denied burning down a church he had attended, as well as a man's home. The statement, written a week before his execution, at a time when he was still hoping for a commutation, said:

> Hasty and inconsiderate people frequently come to grief, and much of every man's good or evil fortune depends on the choice of his friends. It is true that I have led a dissipated life, but I am innocent of the charge alleged, and as I feel my own innocence, cannot help wanting other people to know I was falsely convicted. This seems to me a cruel world and cruel people that want

> to punish an innocent man, but it may be all for the better. I hope my parents may never be upbraided for my crime. My counsel, as well as the witnesses, is to blame for my conviction. I hope no one will ever meet a similar sad fate is my prayer. To young men, my advice is, by all means avoid strong drink and bad company. You see what it has brought on me. While I am still young, I have felt the bitter punishment of a prison life, and unless some unseen hand interferes, I expect soon to taste the bitter cup of death — the effect of bad company, bad habits, etc. I would advise all young men who are trodding down the broad road to everlasting punishment, to turn back, lest like in my case, it is too late, and you are placed in the condition of your sorrowful friend.[1193]

According to the newspaper, Griffee was the first person executed in Cocke County, and the first white man executed for rape in Tennessee. Joshua Franks, one of the posse that pursued and captured Griffee, was awaiting trial in the Cocke County jail charged with a similar crime on Debby Roland, a ten-year-old girl.[1194] A Knoxville newspaper used his execution to call for an end to public executions, suggesting they be conducted in the jail yard. Of Griffee, "He is said to be an imbecile almost to idiocy."[1195]

1879

Knox Martin, black, age 21. *Murder.*

The crime was committed on the night of January 13, 1879, in the Bell's Bend area in Nashville, in Davidson County, a rural farming area across the Cumberland River from the city, reachable only by two ferryboats. The killer had worked some months as a farm worker for the victims. They were John Wittemeier, white, age forty-six, and his wife, Lucinda Foster Wittemeier, white, age forty-one. They were murdered in their beds.

Knox Martin had come from Alabama to seek work on railroad construction and had a brother, Peter Martin, living in Nashville. The killer had signed a two-year contract to work for the victims, but decided to quit several weeks before the end of the first year and return to Alabama. He went south, changed his mind, and returned to the victims' farm and sought money he was owed, namely, four dollars and fifty cents. John Wittemeier was angry that Martin had breached his contract and left at a time he was needed. He refused to give Martin any money.[1196]

Martin came to Nashville and met up with George Berry, whom he knew growing up in Alabama. According to Martin, the two decided to return on the night of the 13th to kill the couple and burglarize their house. They went across on different ferries and hid in the woods.

According to Martin, Berry entered the house and struck the man with a rock, killing him. Martin was right behind him. He struck the woman with a wagon wheel spoke, killing her. The spoke was thrown into the fireplace. Berry took the rock with him. Berry found a quantity of cash, but Martin only got fifty cents, and Berry did not share any of his money with Martin. When Berry saw that Martin had not found any money or valuables, he told Martin to take clothing. He took an overcoat, pants and a hat. The pair hid in the woods for two hours and returned to the city, going separate ways. Martin went to his brother's house.[1197]

Martin's statement implicating Berry, given after conviction, was not believed by police. Berry had been kept in jail as a material witness and was paid thirty dollars for his trouble. At no time prior to conviction did Martin accuse Berry of complicity. Berry left town as soon as he was released, fearing a possible lynching if Martin's story was believed.

The bodies were found the next morning by one of the couple's adult children who lived nearby. The room was covered in blood. The couple's two infant children had crawled upon their mother's dead body and were blood covered. From the condition of Mrs. Wittemeier's bed clothing, it appeared she had been raped. Martin denied she had been raped by either himself or Berry. The bodies had been disemboweled. For years, the crime was known as "The Bell's Bend Murders." It was the subject of national news.[1198]

Within a week after the killings, suspicion had focused on Berry and Martin. Berry implicated Martin, who was arrested that day. Martin promptly confessed, was tried on February 20, and was sentenced to die on March 28, 1879. Efforts were made to convince Martin to appeal but he rejected them, saying he did not want to sit in jail for a year and still be hanged.

Martin was attended in the jail by the Rev. Nelson Merry, a nationally known black Baptist minister, and by Roman Catholic priest Father Veale, as well as two nuns. Martin became a Catholic and was baptized into that faith the day before his death. On the night before his execution, he asked for a glass of wine and was given it. His brother visited him that same night and he cried. The next day, his picture was taken by a photographer. Martin had been given all manner of small gifts, mostly food, by visitors. He asked that it be given to the female jail inmates.[1199]

Martin had been given new clothing for his death. He wore a silk hat (which he never took off), a black cloth coat and vest, navy blue trousers, a clean white shirt, a white linen necktie, and a pair of size-ten shoes. The wardrobe had been provided by the doctors to whom he had willed his body. He granted the press a lengthy interview in which he confessed the crimes.

Knox Martin was hanged at 1:33 P.M. on March 28, 1879, on a gallows located in the Brown's Creek area of south Nashville "in a hollow between two hills, about midway between the Tennessee & Pacific Railroad and the Catholic orphan asylum." This was deemed the best location in Nashville because it formed a natural amphitheater. The execution was seen by about twelve to fifteen thousand people of all classes, mostly black. Parents had allowed their children to miss school for the event. One of these children was injured. As Martin was being cut down, the pistol a man held in his back pocket accidentally discharged when he sat on it. A little girl, Lilly Meyers, was shot in the leg. The entire Wittemeier family watched the execution hoping Martin would confess the crime. He said nothing.[1200]

Martin was taken by large furniture wagon to the site. Seated on a chair, he smoked a cigar and wore his new hat. (He wore the detached shirt collar upside down.) The wagon carried several deputies and had difficulty making its way through the three thousand people surrounding the jail. Following the wagon was the famous Father Ryan riding in a buggy. As the wagon was nearing the execution site, a floor plank under Martin gave way and he fell through the wagon with only his head and shoulders appearing. He was pulled up and smiled at his rescuers.

Martin began trembling as he stepped upon the gallows, assisted by the two priests. Martin and the two priests knelt on the gallows, a Latin prayer was offered and Martin was granted absolution. The priests said good-bye, with Father Veale saying, "I will pray for you, Knox. I am with you. Put your trust in God." Sheriff Price put the rope and cap over Martin's head after Martin was pinioned. The sheriff gave a hand signal to a deputy and the trap rope was released.[1201]

Martin fell cleanly and was allowed to hang for fifteen minutes. Cut down, his body was immediately taken to a cow shed for experiments by doctors to bring him back to life. Most people thought this was laughable, but "to the little knot of professional men about the scaffold, the matter was a serious one."[1202] The doctors told the sheriff that Martin was dead ten minutes after the drop, but before they were allowed to take his body, the sheriff required the doctors to look him in the eye and repeat their pronouncement.

The doctors cut the rope and quickly put the body in a coffin and carried it fifty yards to the shed. The new clothes were cut off and artificial respiration by hand was vigorously done. Then electrical batteries were connected to the head and neck:

> Immediately upon turning on the current the contortions of the muscles were visible. Every expression of emotion was manifested — pain, fear, anxiety, hope, delight, anger and disgust. Once the experiments seemed to offer hope for success. Artificial respiration having been kept up from the beginning, the body showed signs of life in about five minutes. The pulse came back, the hands were clenched and a deep breath indicated returning vitality. The eyes opened and stared vacantly while the muscles of the face played actively under the electric influence. A very strong current was used — the equivalent of fifty cells of Grove's battery.[1203]

The account concluded, "The most interesting result of the experiment was the spontaneous erection of the head and neck of the body in the coffin. There seemed a perfect expression of life and it seemed Knox Martin was once more a living man. Great excitement prevailed and threats of mob violence were made if the experiments proved successful."[1204] After the initial experiments were conducted, the body was taken to the Nashville Medical College, where more were attempted. The body was then dissected.

The location where Martin was executed had been used since 1843 for hangings. Three white men were executed nearby in 1843, three black men in 1852, and Bill Kelly had died there in 1871. Knox Martin was born a slave in 1858 in Jackson County, Alabama, and was owned by a man named John Martin, who owned several slaves and "ran twelve or fourteen plows."

Anthony Blair, black, age 50. *Murder.*

The crime was committed about 9:00 P.M. on July 30, 1879, on a road in the community of Russellville, in Hamblen County. The killer was a practicing lawyer in Jonesboro, in Washington County. The victim was his stepdaughter, Maggie Walker, but generally known as Maggie Blair, black, age nineteen. She was described as a "very smart, industrious girl."[1205]

Blair had married the girl's mother when Maggie was an infant and she grew up in his household. The mother died two years before the shooting, entrusting Maggie's care to Blair, who was a respected member of the community. In May 1879, Maggie left the home and did not tell Blair where she was going. He finally found her working as a servant in the home of Squire William Donaldson, in Hamblen County. Blair came to the house as Maggie and Mrs. Donaldson were preparing dinner. He asked her to come outside and talk with him. She refused, saying he should say what he wanted in front of Mrs. Donaldson. About this time, Squire Donaldson rode up and Blair left without saying more.

Three days later, July 30, 1879, Maggie and some friends had attended a Wednesday night prayer meeting at a black church. They were walking home. She was talking with a young black man, Henry Taylor. Blair came up, pushed Taylor away and caught Maggie's hand. The friends heard him say, "You must go home with me on the train tonight to your Grandpap's."[1206]

Here is what happened next: "The crowd was so stunned by his vehemence that it stood paralyzed as Blair literally dragged the struggling Maggie down the road about a hundred yards. She was screaming that she would rather die than go with him. Whereupon he drew a pistol and shot her twice, from the effects of which she died the following Saturday."[1207]

Although Blair ran away, he was soon captured and put on trial on August 7, 1879. His appointed counsel were Capt. J.C. Hodges and Maj. Joseph Grigsby. The state's witnesses said that the reason she left Blair's house and would not return was that he forced her to perform the duties of a wife, including sexual relations.

Forceful arguments were offered in Blair's behalf. He admitted shooting Maggie, but steadfastly denied any improper relationship. The jury heard the case overnight and convicted him of first-degree murder without mitigating circumstances. Blair's lawyers told the court no appeal would be made and sought mercy. The court asked Blair if he had anything to say before sentencing. He replied no. The judge sentenced Blair to be executed on September 26, 1879.

As he was being taken back to the jail following his trial, Blair said the sentence was just and he was sorry his execution did not come off "today or tomorrow."[1208]

Anthony Blair had arranged with a printer to publish his version of the case, which was sold on execution day for a nickel. The eight-page pamphlet contained advertisements (called "cards") on the back.[1209] One was from A.T. Newman, who sold pure medicinal liquors in two-, three-, and four-gallon packages, at wholesale prices. He offered good whiskies, cold beer, fine wines, the best cigars, oysters, crackers, etc. His advertisement proclaimed, "On Hanging Occasions I Hang Prices Very Low. Come and Let Me Hang You on to a Drink or Pint of Pure Medicinal Whiskey."

Hanged on the day set, Blair was taken to the gallows in a wagon, riding on his coffin with the rope around his neck. The streets were choked with dust because a crowd of eight to ten thousand had been coming from neighboring counties since the day before. The gallows was erected "at the hollow at the foot of Lula Street, just west of and parallel to Henry Street" in Morristown. One version says he was hanged from a persimmon tree which from that day never bore fruit. Another explains that he was "swung off" in the traditional method while standing on the wagon. It says he held on to the wagon with his feet as long as he could.[1210]

Blair was composed and clear-spoken on the gallows. He spoke for nearly an hour, giving the discourse that was printed in his "Confessions." He said:

> I am not satisfied with the testimony of some of the witnesses. They do not do me justice. They are unfit to appear on the witness stand, and they perjured themselves before leaving it. For the enlightenment of my friends, I will state here that Bertha Taylor and Lee Scott were both prejudiced against me, I am satisfied, and swore falsehoods. This is the truth, as God in heaven knows it. Bertha said that I said to Maggie, "God damn you, I've got something in my pocket to make you go." It was a lie. I never uttered a word of it and she knows it. Also, after I shot Maggie, "Now you'll go, God damn you!" That is also false. I never used such language.

Blair continued:

> Scott swore that I said that I would have Maggie or drink her heart's blood. It is false. I never made such remarks. I simply said I would rather see Maggie lay down and die and that I would follow her to the grave, than see her go astray. For on her mother's deathbed she said to Maggie, "Stay with pappy and take care of him. He has been good and kind to me all my life and as I am going to leave you both, I want you to be good and kind to him." With regards to the statement about my "sneaking off" when I saw Squire Donaldson coming up to the house I have only to say that it is false. In the first place, I did not enter the kitchen as stated by Mrs. Donaldson on trial, but was sitting on the porch

when Mr. Donaldson came up. I had been coaxing Maggie to go home with me — she being in the kitchen. Finally, I went to the door and said, "Sis, come and shake hands with me." She did. I then took a silver-mounted tucking comb from my satchel and gave it to her." Said Blair, "I saw Squire Donaldson take a sack of something from the wagon, Charlie Carmichael was sitting in the wagon. I then got up and went down where they were and spoke to them. I talked several minutes and did not scare off nor sneak off as stated on the witness stand.

He continued:

I will say this much for the benefit of Lee Scott and Bertha Taylor: (1) If the old Devil has any claims upon liars in this world, he has a dead mortgage on their black souls, (2) that their hearts are as foul and corrupt as hell, the Devil and all his angels, (3) that no one who has acted as they have toward me should ever expect to prosper in this world or reach heaven when they die, (4) that if my spirit should return to this world and haunt and terrify them, they need not be surprised: I will do so if I can, (5) that when they die, they will die perjurers, double-damned and will go into the Devil's clutches and remain with him forever, unless they heartily repent of their damnable sins and receive forgiveness from my gracious Lord.

Blair said:

With regard to my ravishing Maggie, either before or after shooting her, I deny the charge and pronounce it false to the last. I entertained for her that feeling and respect that is characteristic of a natural parent. Indeed I should have been a brute had I done otherwise. I can prove that from the time she came into my hands in her infancy up to the time she left my house, that I treated her as kind and fatherly as a parent could. I can also prove that I am not as mean a man as was sworn on trial. I appear from the statements that I was a most infernal human being.

He said:

I find a deal of truth in the old saying when a man takes a start downhill everybody will help him along by giving him a push. I find it so in my case — those who once professed to be my friends are now my enemies and are anxious to see me hung. I have this consolation, however, my God and myself alone know just how mean a man I am. There are people who will never give the devil his due; there are some such in my case, and they say I am so monstrously mean that I will get all my just dues and the devil with it. Let such cruel remarks pass into nothingness. They don't know whether I will or not. They might be deceived. Possibly I might take the other track and beat them to heaven in the end. At least I hope so. The Lord saith: "He that believeth on Me, I will in no wise cast out." Is there not some consolation in these words for a poor sinner? I think there is. Does He mean saint, devil or what? Perhaps one of the pious fellows who are troubled about my welfare can tell. I don't mean those kind, fatherly and Christian advisers who visited me during my confinement, and to whom I owe a lasting debt of gratitude and return my sincere thanks, but those who manifest a deep interest in my conviction, earthly and future punishment and who unjustly and unchristianly remarked that I would go hell-ward at the first drop of the rope.

Blair continued:

I will admit that I am a bad man — a very bad man — or I would never have committed the crime I did. Well, before I leave this world, I will give myself credit for some good points in my life. I was never in jail before, for any crime, until I was placed in the Hamblen County jail upon this charge, I have always borne a good character, I was never charged with theft in my life, nor prosecuted for any violation of civil law until this time. I was never arrested by any public officer before. I always tended to my own business. I was always kind to my family.

Said Blair:

I have never intentionally insulted a white man or woman, but was always ever ready to obey and respect their command. I have always showed a kind and respectful disposition toward my own color, when they were so inclined to do likewise to me. I have always had contempt for gossipers and have never spread evil reports. I never carried a pistol before, never indulged in whiskey drinking, no card playing nor any vice whatsoever since my connection with the church. Last but not least — I never made a direct or indirect statement to anyone that I would be satisfied to die and leave this world if I could kill three persons before doing so.

Blair concluded:

This is an honest statement of facts whether taken as true or false. I desire the prayers of all Christians in my behalf and trust they will all meet me in heaven. A jury of my countrymen have found me guilty of a crime for which I stood indicted. For this I entertain not the slightest feeling of resentment. I now bid farewell to the country of my birth, my friends and my relations. I trust I shall be prepared to meet its execution. I hope to be able, with a pure heart and perfect composure, to appear before a higher tribunal — a tribunal where a Judge of infinite goodness as well as of justice will preside and where — Judge, jury, dear friends and relatives — many, many judgments of this earth will be reversed. Hoping to meet you all in heaven, I submit myself.

His words were not well received by newspaper reporters. A reporter said Blair "lumbered away in jargonesque hymn and made a speech an hour in length."[1211] The reporter closed his story with a poem:

But Blair, Blair, Anthony Blair,
You have passed away to — the Lord knows where.
Yet it to Heaven, you did repair,
Excuse me, Anthony, Anthony Blair,
I'd rather not, rather not travel up there.[1212]

The newspapers ignored the fact that Blair was a lawyer. He was described thus by a newspaper: "The most hideous, repulsive, semi-gorilla looking mortal in appearance we ever saw."[1213] Another described him, "Body and limbs shaped and hung like a turtle's; the head presenting the contour of a ram's, and surmounted with a black cap fashioned with angles at the top like that worn by Jesuits."[1214] The hat was a scholar's cap. The reporter had apparently not seen one before.

1880

John Hall, black, age 50. *Murder.*
Burrell Smith, black, age 52. *Murder.*

The crime was committed about 11:30 P.M., May 16, 1879, at the farm home of Major Henry S. Pugh in Rutherford County. The killers were part of a gang that had burglarized homes and businesses for several months. Their trademark was arson. They frequently burned the businesses they had entered. The victim was Major Pugh, white, age forty-nine, who lived in the house with his wife. Nearby was his small store, the pair's target.

In April 1879, the pair had tried to burglarize the Pugh home but had been scared away by Mrs. Pugh, who fired a pistol shot through an open window. The night Mr. Pugh was killed the pair waited in Pugh's stable for his dog to stop barking. Major Pugh was aroused by the noise, and carrying a kerosene lantern in one hand and a pistol in the other, walked toward the stable.[1215] Hall and Smith had separated by the time he got close enough to shoot, and when he started walking in Smith's direction, Hall fired at him. Pugh returned the fire and Hall shot again, the second bullet striking his left side, causing his death the next day.

Hall and Smith, and as many as fifteen other criminals of both races, had formed a secret "society" of criminals who took an oath that if any member got in trouble the others would assist him with "money or fire." The gang had held the town of Murfreesboro in terror during 1878–1879 as some fifty thousand dollars in fire losses had been incurred. No one had lost his life until the Pugh killing. Both men were career criminals. Hall had served a five-year sentence for stealing cotton, beginning in 1868. Smith had been sentenced to a five-year term for stealing meat but was released a year early in 1878. The two rented a farm in 1878 and began a crime spree that culminated with the Pugh shooting.

One of the gang members, Bill Smith (not related to Burrell Smith), turned state's evidence against the gang, including the murder of Major Pugh. When the gang was rounded up, a large mob formed to lynch them. When word reached Governor Albert Marks, he promptly took a train from Nashville to Murfreesboro and addressed the mob, finally convincing them that the law should take its course. The arsonists were convicted, but these convictions were overturned on appeal, except for one of the white defendants.[1216] The arsonists were tried again and received long sentences, including Hall and Smith. Meanwhile, they were charged with the Pugh murder.

The case went to trial and they were convicted on June 30, 1879, and given death sentences. The Tennessee Supreme Court opinion affirming the conviction cannot be located, but it was paraphrased in a Nashville newspaper. After reciting the facts, the court said that the separate confessions of the pair, each naming the other as the shooter, together with their tracks and the pistol which was found under trash in the barn, were sufficient to convict. Their common purpose established guilt regardless of who fired the fatal bullet. Furthermore, it did not matter whether they had actually entered Pugh's store (they ran off with nothing), since their admitted common purpose was complete when they entered his property with the resolve to kill if they had to.

When Judge Freeman finished reading the Supreme Court's "sentence" (final order), he asked the men if they wanted to speak. Hall attempted to speak on Smith's behalf. The judge cut him off, "You will be allowed to speak for yourself only." Hall seemed affected by the sentence, but Smith remained unmoved.

The execution of Hall and Smith presented a serious problem for the Rutherford County sheriff because he could not find a suitable place within a mile of the courthouse, as required by law. Finally, he made an agreement with a man named Mr.

Kerr, who owned land on an island in the Stones River. The execution was several times delayed and by the time it took place on February 20, 1880, Kerr had built a temporary grandstand and charged twenty-five cents admission to watch the execution. He also sold peanuts and lemonade and made a large amount of money.

Adding to the excitement of the day, both men had given permission for local doctors to attempt to revive them with electricity. In short, the crowd came to see not only an execution, but a resurrection. Because the execution was announced in many newspapers, which by this time enjoyed wide readership, about fifteen thousand people came to watch, enjoying barbecue, lemonade and liquor.

The death ceremony began at the jail with a service conducted by black ministers the Rev. G.D. Olden and the Rev. Dempsey Childress. The pair had received a full immersion baptism by the Rev. G.D. Olden in the jail a month before in front of a large group. Witness Bill Smith came by the jail on the day of execution to talk with the pair. They told him to go to hell.

Hall and Smith were taken to the gallows wearing black gowns (shrouds), smiling but trembling. The wagon was drawn by two horses and the men sat on their coffins. Smith asked for a piece of pound cake which was being sold, and said he would die in peace if it was granted. It was. His lusty eating and exclaiming how much he enjoyed the cake greatly amused the crowd.

On the scaffold the Rev. Childress led the hymn, "And Must I Go to Judgment Brought." The Rev. Olden offered prayer; the Rev. Robert Bond led a hymn, "My Lord, the Appointed Way." The Rev. Olden read from Jeremiah and gave a short homily. He read the men's confession. They specified nine robberies (actually burglaries) they had committed. But they said that six other men had no role in those crimes and they denied responsibility for four other similar crimes. In the confession, John Hall admitted firing the shot that killed Pugh, but he insisted that Bill Smith had lied at the trial.

At 1:30 P.M. February 20, 1880, the trap was sprung. This caused witness Bill Smith to fall into a swoon. The crowd surged forward (caused by some attempting to get a better look) and the wood bleachers, described as circus seats, began collapsing. No one was seriously hurt.

The spectacle of the Hall and Smith execution was described with scorn by the state's reputable newspapers.[1217] "The land on which the scaffold was erected was owned by Mr. Kerr, who was the only person in the vicinity who was willing to allow the use of his property for the execution. Sheriff Arnold is censured for allowing persons to erect reserved seats near the scaffold and for preparing barbecue on the grounds but he could not help it, as he had no authority to dislodge Kerr from his own land."[1218]

The hangings came on the heels of the Bill Kelly execution in Nashville, complete with electrical experiments and rumors that Kelly was actually revived by them. The legislature changed the law forbidding truly public executions. After March 22, 1883, the public would no longer be allowed to see the actual drop.[1219] Although the execution could still be held outdoors, allowing the public to hear the man's last words and the words of his ministers, the actual hanging had to be obscured from public view. From 1883 until 1909 (when executions were moved to the Main Prison in Nashville), all Tennessee executions were "semi-private."

Sheriffs used several means to follow the law. In some places the gallows was obscured by a canvas drape. Sometimes a rude wooden wall, called a stockade, surrounded the gallows. In others, the hanging was undertaken inside the jail yard. Finally, the hangings were performed inside the jail itself, either in a hallway or a special gallows built in the upper floors or in the basement.

Burrell Smith had been a slave owned by Gen. W.H. Smith and he grew up in Rutherford County. Unmarried, "he lavished his affection upon a mistress, who recently bore him a child."

Daniel C. Potter, white, age 37. *Murder.*

The crime was committed on the evening of April 8, 1879, on a road outside Newport in Cocke County. The killer and victim knew each other. Potter had a reputation for criminal activities and drinking. Potter had a feud with Dave McMahan (known as Dave Mac). His brother, Willis McMahan, had tried for years to heal the breach between the two. On the night of the killing, Potter, his fourteen-year-old son, and Willis McMahan were walking toward the McMahan home where the killer had been invited for dinner and brandy. As they approached the Black River Bridge, Potter told his son Tom to run ahead. The boy only partially complied. He stayed far enough ahead to see his father stab Willis McMahan, white, age forty-four.

Potter hit McMahan a terrific blow in the face and then stabbed him. McMahan fell to the ground and Potter stabbed him again. Potter left and went home, but returned several hours later, fearful that McMahan might not be dead. He stabbed him again. He dragged McMahan's body to a ravine under the bridge. His intestines were protruding.

McMahan lay under the bridge all night and was found the next morning. He was taken to a neighboring house where he named Potter as his attacker. When Potter found out that McMahan was still alive, he rushed to his bedside, thinking he was too badly injured to talk.

McMahan appeared unconscious and bore seventeen stab wounds. After looking at him, Potter turned to others in the room and said, "The man who did that ought to be hung." McMahan rose up from the bloody bed. He pointed his finger at Potter and said, "Yes, he ought to be hung, and you are the man and you will be hung!"[1220] Potter's son testified against him at a preliminary hearing. Potter was kept in the Knox County jail but escaped with a notorious bad man named Hutchinson Amarine. They dug into a sewer line and crawled to the Tennessee River. Several months later Potter was recaptured hiding in a mountain cabin not far from his own neighborhood. In jail, he bragged he had killed seven men.[1221]

At trial, Daniel Potter's son again testified against his father, as did the people who heard McMahan's dying declarations. The conviction was affirmed by the Tennessee Supreme Court but the opinion cannot be located.

Daniel C. Potter was hanged at 12:30 P.M. on November 12, 1880, on a gallows built on the muster grounds one mile from Newport, a location that afforded ample viewing from all sides. The gallows had been used to execute Stephen Griffee a year earlier. Griffee's death was witnessed by a crowd estimated from four to six thousand. Potter's crowd was estimated at ten thousand. Potter had served as a guard at Griffee's execution and had told people he wanted to die before a large crowd.[1222]

Potter had been attended by Father Welch of the Roman Catholic Church in Knoxville, but observers said the priest seemed to have little effect on Potter's demeanor. "He talked very recklessly and profanely regarding his death and the future."[1223] Said one account, "The efforts of the priest, however, have not been crowned with the most signal success as it has been a habit with him to call down severest imprecations upon all connected with his trial, the witnesses, judge, jury and counsel."[1224] Potter had been raised in the Catholic faith.

Potter was taken to the scaffold in a wagon. Riding with him were his wife and two children, a son age twelve and a daughter age nineteen. The priest read from a Catholic book on the way. The crowd was kept thirty feet away from the gallows by a rope. "There was very little sympathy for the criminal."[1225]

Potter regaled the crowd: "If I could only kill three more men the powers that be could cut me up and saw me in two, skin me, burn me, do anything to me that they might choose to do." It was understood the intended victims were the sheriff, the mayor and his son, Tom Potter.[1226] By the time of the execution, his arch-enemy David McMahan had also died. Potter said, "I hope I will be hung in time to get to hell to eat dinner with Dave Mac."[1227]

Potter spoke his last words: "I wish to say to you ladies and gentlemen, and everybody, that you have come here to see an innocent man die a cruel death. But if men are willing to perjure themselves to destroy my life, I am willing to give it; let it go." Then turning around with a wave of his hand, said, "I bid everybody farewell."

Potter had asked that the noose be placed so that it broke his neck. But when the noose was placed around his neck Potter jumped, kicked and plunged terribly, which served to move the knot under his chin. The sheriff was forced to turn the wagon around and rearrange the knot under Potter's ear. But it slipped again when Potter was swung off. The rope caught under the chin and the body swung several minutes with violent convulsions and hard breathing sounds, audible for some distance. Potter was declared dead in nineteen minutes and cut down within thirty minutes. His body was taken to Bridgeport and buried near relatives.

Edward Long, black, age 22. *Murder.*

The crime was committed on the afternoon of June 30, 1880, on a farm in Madison County. Ed Long lived in the home of Titus (Tito) Rogers, the black victim, age thirty-four. Long and Rogers's wife, Mollie, had worked together and had been sexually intimate prior to and during the marriage. Rogers worked land about a mile away and was seldom home. Mollie told Long that if he could get her husband out of the way she would live with him.

On the day of the murder, Long picked up an iron bolt as he and Rogers walked toward another house where Mollie was working. Several times Long lost his nerve, but eventually he stepped behind Rogers as they were crossing a bridge and struck him on the back of the head. Rogers fell and Long continued across the bridge. He looked back and was surprised to see Rogers staggering to his feet. Long battered the victim again and threw his body into the creek, where it was found the next day.

When Mollie was questioned, she quickly implicated Long. He confessed to authorities but maintained his innocence during the trial. The jury heard testimony from thirteen people regarding his confessions. The jury was instructed to use caution accrediting verbal confessions. Long's counsel persuaded the court to give the instruction that merely because evidence of a confession had been allowed did not mean that the jury has to believe the testimony; rather, it was the duty of the jury to decide this factual matter.[1228] The court also instructed the jury to decide the degree of murder and that it could mitigate the punishment to life imprisonment. Mollie was subpoenaed to testify and did so under the name Mollie Brunner. It is unclear whether Mollie was still a widow at the time of the trial, had remarried, or had never been married to Rogers.

Long was heartbroken that Mollie had turned against him and had neither hope nor care to appeal his case.[1229] Long was baptized the day before his execution by the same black minister who delivered a homily from the gallows. Long had admitted full guilt and said he had no fear, desired death and was ready to go. Long said that his mother always told him that if he made his bed, he must lie in it. He was executed in Jackson on December 18, 1880, before a crowd of four thousand.

1881

John Williams (aka Thomas Prewitt), black, age 40. *Murder.*

The crime was committed in the afternoon on April 27, 1877, on a farm in rural Humphreys County. The killer was the estranged husband of the victim, Sallie Williams, black, age twenty-six.

The Williams marriage was stormy because of John's drinking. He became especially abusive when intoxicated and Sallie had left him several times. The last time, she was staying with a friend. This woman agreed to let the killer see his wife because he promised he carried no weapon. Sallie steadfastly refused to go home with him. He remarked he was going to let her do as she pleased, turned and walked out. She was at the door. He walked ten steps, quickly turned and emptied a double-barreled shotgun into her chest. She lived two days. Williams was captured immediately, but escaped from the jail. Williams fled to Paducah, Kentucky, where he remarried and lived under the name Thomas Prewitt. The circumstances of his capture and trial are unknown except that the jury returned a guilty verdict in fifteen minutes. The case was appealed to the Tennessee Supreme Court, but the opinion cannot be located.[1230]

Williams had been kept in the Nashville jail until a few days before the execution. In jail, he became religious and spent most of his time in Bible study with various spiritual advisors. These included Roman Catholics. Back at the Waverly jail, he said he appreciated the Catholic Church's attention, but had been raised a Baptist, so he sought a Baptist clergyman, Elder Caleb T. Thomas. The morning of his execution, Williams was baptized in Trace Creek two hundred yards from the jail in front of five hundred black people. They sang several hymns, including "On Jordan's Stormy Banks I Stand." The full-immersion ceremony was assisted by the sheriff, who helped lift Williams from the water. He came out of the water in a religious frenzy, shouting, "Thank God, I am willing to die!" "O, Lord, have mercy on my soul!" "Holy, holy, Lord!" "Thanks to the name of Jesus!"[1231]

He was so frantic that it took six stout men to hold him until he quieted down. As he was taken back to the jail, the black women shrieked and cried, "Praise be the name of the Lord!" and "He has been saved in Jesus and will ascend to the heavenly heights." Back at the jail he was given "enough whisky to nerve him for his doom," and he called for Priscilla Banks, a bright mulatto girl whom he had helped raise. He asked her to ride on the wagon with him to the gallows. She said that if she attended she would walk. John Williams was executed at 2:09 P.M. on April 8, 1881, at Waverly.

Williams was taken from the jail and put on the wagon. He was told to sit on his coffin, but his weight immediately broke the thin poplar wood. He was accompanied on the wagon by the sheriffs of four counties, all anticipating upcoming executions. The gallows was built in a ravine which provided a good view for the three thousand people who came to town to see Williams's death. A misty rain began to fall, and the area was a sea of umbrellas. Williams "fairly danced up the steps of the scaffold with a light and airy step, bounding to the platform in three jumps and bowing his head to the crowd."[1232]

He told the crowd he had prayed to God for forgiveness and had been forgiven and was bound for heaven. The sentence of the court was just, he said, but he would not have been brought to this bad end but for the unfaithfulness of his wife. Williams explained that he would never have been recaptured but for his taking one extra drink of whiskey, but that he didn't mind death because it was little more than a drink of water. He said he almost had enough money to send his body to Johnsonville for burial next to his children. When he stopped speaking, "Oh, That I Might Find a Secret Place," was sung, followed by a prayer from a black Presbyterian minister, the Rev. Randall Whylie. Three more hymns were sung.

Williams began to address the crowd again. He told about his wife in Kentucky and asked that someone tell her she could no longer look for support from him. He repeated the theme of his prior statement that everyone needed to meet him "on the right side of Jesus." He remarked with a laugh that he was heavy enough the rope would break his neck. A voice from the crowd told him to get up and run. He responded that if he were not hanged for killing his wife somebody would shoot him.

The sheriff announced to the crowd that he had a painful duty to perform. The noose was placed around Williams's neck, and he exclaimed, "I did not expect to see the noose put over my neck, but I have." When the cap was brought out, he said, "Why, it is a little blacker than I am!"[1233] Then he complained the noose was too tight: "You are about to smother me before I swing." The noose was loosened. He responded, "That will do, thank God. Here's the last of John Williams in this world. Here I go!" Without warning the sheriff loosened the trap and Williams fell cleanly, breaking his neck. The body was cut down twenty-one minutes later. It was placed in the coffin and taken to Johnsonville.

Williams had been born a slave in Maryland, was sold at Baltimore, taken to Richmond, and sold to Dick Prewitt, who had a plantation near Courtland, Alabama. Since the war, he had lived mostly in Johnsonville, working as a barber. He did not know his exact age but said he weighed two hundred pounds.

Andrew Saunders (aka Andrew Sanders), black, age 19. *Murder.*

The crime was committed about 3:30 P.M. on August 3, 1880, at the large three-room home of Mr. and Mrs. Michael Miller in rural Tipton County. The killer was a farm worker whose purported wife Lina had worked as a cook for the Miller family for several months. The victim was Michael Miller, white, age seventy-seven. He was described as a respected planter. The killer's purported wife, Lina Fritz, black, age twenty, had been living in the Miller home. Saunders was angry she would not return to him. He felt the Miller family was preventing a reconciliation. On Saturday before the shooting, Saunders talked with Lina outside near the front gate. They began quarreling and Michael Miller told him to leave. She had been impregnated by Jesse H. Miller, white, age thirty-two, one of Michael Miller's sons, and her condition was obvious. She enjoyed some status as Jesse's mistress.

Saunders returned on Tuesday, August 3, and asked to speak to his wife. She refused, in part because she was busy, but she told Miller she was afraid. Saunders left and returned. Another family had come to the Miller house and they were playing croquet on the east side of the house. Again Miller went back to the gate, located on the south side of the house, and told Saunders to leave. Saunders became enraged and pulled a single-barreled shotgun from the brush near the gate.[1234]

Saunders ran around the west side of the house (avoiding the croquet players, which included Sydney Miller, a sixteen-year-old son) and ran to the north end of the house. He entered the door with Miller chasing him. The three-room house (from the north) consisted of a parlor, then a door to the chamber (or family room) where there were beds, and then a door to the kitchen. Saunders, carrying the shotgun at his waist, searched all three rooms but did not find Lina. By this time, the croquet party heard Saunders bellowing, and one of the adults slipped inside the house and took a shotgun outside, placing it on a shelf. Saunders did not see this.

As Michael Miller stood in the door between the chamber and the kitchen, he said to Saunders, who was holding the shotgun at his waist, "You wouldn't shoot an old man as me would you, Andrew?"[1235] Without answering, Saunders fired. The blast hit Miller's left side near the lower ribs. Immediately, Sydney Miller, who had taken the shotgun from the shelf, opened a side door and fired one shotgun blast at Saunders.

The shot was high, but grazed Saunders's head. He dropped his shotgun and fell to his knees. Sydney Miller, thinking Saunders was surrendering, threw down his shotgun. Suddenly, Saunders jumped to his feet, pulled a dagger from under his shirt, and slashed Sidney, who picked up Saunders's shotgun, breaking it over his head. Saunders ran outside to the croquet field and Sydney followed. They tangled again, Sydney receiving a knife wound in the back as he twisted away, but also hitting Saunders with a croquet mallet.[1236] Saunders ran away but was found a few days later.

Michael Miller lingered until his death on

August 6. He told his sons, three doctors at three different times, and several other people what had happened. They repeated his dying declarations in court and Saunders's claim of self-defense was rejected by the jury. The case was appealed to the Tennessee Supreme Court but the opinion cannot be located.

Saunders was kept in the Shelby County jail for his safety and brought to Covington the day before his execution. In jail while his case was on appeal, he got religion, read his Bible constantly, sang and exhorted. Saunders claimed to know more about the Bible than the ministers who came to him.

Saunders contended that the men intended to kill him when he came for his wife and he was within his rights to fight back. "Now, what was I to do? To go with de law? I s'pose I ought to stood still an' let 'em shoot me. If dey had come to arrest me or keep me from hurting my wife I wouldn't have pestered any of 'em; but I had to fight or be killed."[1237] Sympathetic white men gave him new clothes to wear on the gallows, everything from underwear to a new suit. On the train to Covington, Saunders drew out a harmonica and played mournful sounds on it. "The air was weird and mysterious. It struck the ears of those present like the wail of a lost spirit."[1238]

The trap door gallows was built on the courthouse yard about a hundred yards from the jail. He was taken from the jail and put on a wagon; twenty-five armed guards protected him. On the way, Saunders became angry and shouted, "Do the very same I have done if any man comes in your way interfering with your wife. I just wish I had one of those guns in here a little while."[1239]

On the gallows, he asked for "Uncle" Jupiter Williams, the elderly minister who had married him and had counseled him in the jail the morning of his execution. For some time, Saunders had told everyone that he was going home and dwelling with his Savior, and that he preferred death to a lifetime in the penitentiary, although he was confident to the end that the governor would commute his sentence.

Jupiter Williams had to be summoned several times by the sheriff before he made his way to the platform. "Jupiter came forward with an ancient pair of saddle-bags, a solemn countenance, a long beard, and a still longer stick."[1240] Saunders told the crowd not to worry, he would speak to them.

Jupiter Williams told him to keep quiet. "Jupiter then delivered a mighty oration and also a prayer, which was a perfect menagerie of big words assembled together without the least distinction on account of use or meaning, declaring, however, that Sanders [*sic*] had not followed his advice."[1241] When he was finished, he said, "Farewell, Andrew; farewell from now until the morning of the resurrection when I trust I will meet you at the right hand of your Savior."[1242] "Well, I trust I will meet you," responded Saunders. The divine then gathered his things (which now included Saunders's new hat and coat which he had placed before the old man) and left the area.

Andrew Saunders was hanged at 1:24 P.M. on August 26, 1881, before a crowd of three thousand. His last words angered many in the crowd. Sheriff Reeves had asked if he had anything to say. He answered, "I have nothing to say, Mr. Reeves, that would be of any profit to your people at all. If I was to speak anything, I would speak altogether against your people. I feel justifiable in what I done, I feel that I done right. If a white man interferes with a colored man's wife he passes on. If a colored man interferes with a white man's wife he dies. Don't let your hearts be troubled by this scene. If you colored people do not do something to protect your wives, what will you come to? You will come back to bondage."[1243] These words caused a commotion in the mixed-race audience.

As the rope was put over his head and he was being pinioned, Saunders said, "Understand me, Sheriff Reeves, if you are going to hang me, hang me; don't fix a way to have no fooling about me; break my neck, if you want to, and let me go along. Tie my hands behind me; I have done give up. If I had a gun today and anyone was to face me, why then I'd try him. But you have got me. Tie my hands and fix me just like you want to. Now, I will say to all you, both white and black, I wish you all well, and I am in hopes that you will meet me in heaven."[1244]

When the cap was put over his head, Saunders said, "Captain Leslie, farewell." "Good-bye, Andrew," came the reply from the jailer. At that moment the trap was sprung and Saunders's neck was broken. He struggled little and his body was cut down thirty minutes later. "He was a big bull-headed negro," said Captain Leslie, "afraid of nothing, but he would do anything if spoken to kindly."[1245]

Andrew Saunders's purported wife, the woman he claimed to be protecting, never visited him while he was in jail, despite numerous requests that she come. "I got them to go for her in a horse and buggy, but she wouldn't come. I wanted to see her to tell her something. I don't think my wife wanted to face me. She is sorry and don't want to face me.

She knows that she is the cause of all this. I wanted to talk to her, though, for her own good. I had something in view that I could tell her. I only wanted to say a few words."[1246]

Henry Lawson, black, age 32. *Rape.*

The crime was committed at 2:00 P.M. on July 4, 1881, on the farm of James Donaldson, three miles south of Chattanooga, in Hamilton County. The rapist was a farm worker in the neighborhood and had worked on the Donaldson farm in the past. He had irregular work habits. The victim was Miss Nancy Donaldson, white, age nineteen, the oldest daughter of James Donaldson.

The Donaldson family forbore participation in the holiday festivities in favor of working, and Nancy was plowing a small field some distance from the house. It was assumed that Lawson had approached the farm with the intention of burglarizing the house, thinking the family was gone, when he saw Nancy and decided to rape her. He hid in a clump of bushes and sprang upon her, pulling her clothes over her head. She struggled but he managed to tie her hands with hickory thongs, dragged her away and raped her several times. Because she continued struggling, he pulled out a straight razor and cut her face, body and legs, and raped her again, threatening her life.[1247]

Nancy gnawed through the thongs and her screaming attracted her father. A small posse went looking for Lawson and found him home in his bed the next night. When an officer appeared, Lawson ran, but a bullet fired by the officer grazed him slightly. In his coat pocket was found the razor with blood on it. He was taken to the Donaldson home and positively identified. He was later jailed without bond. After news of the rape was carried in the newspapers, mobs twice appeared at the jail, but without a leader, they were dispersed by the sheriff and deputies.

Lawson went to trial on July 26. One hundred and forty veniremen were called before a jury was seated. Lawson did not take the stand and his defense was an alibi that was quickly discredited. Lawson's conviction was not appealed to the Tennessee Supreme Court.[1248] The reason is unknown.

The black ministers of Chattanooga asked the governor to grant Lawson a reprieve "because he has not made any preparations to meet his Master, and that if he were given a few more days he might repent of his sins and be prepared for eternity."[1249] The governor said no. The ministers visited him daily and Lawson could not make up his mind whether he was saved or not. He listened to the ministers and for a while "imagined" that he was converted, but "a change came over him and he refused to listen to them and grew more boisterous than before."[1250] He had told the Rev. J.S. Shaw of the A.M.E. Church that he had sex with the woman but that it was with her consent. Fifteen minutes before he was taken from his cell to the gallows, Lawson was baptized by one of the ministers.

Wearing new clothes, he was taken by wagon to the execution site, located in a deep basin near "Swartz's beer garden, in the eastern portion of the city, about one-half mile from the courthouse and due east of it."[1251] The location provided hills on every side where thousands watched the execution. Over his clothes, Lawson wore a white shroud which covered his whole body. He sat on his coffin and the wagon carried deputies. It was escorted by one hundred armed special deputies. The wagon had some difficulty making its way to the gallows. The surrounding crowd was estimated at between five and ten thousand. On the scaffold were three black ministers, the Rev. H.N. Hutchinson, the Rev. William Marsh, and the Rev. J.S. Shaw.

Lawson had told the newspapers that he would make a statement from the gallows. On the gallows he was asked if he was going to say anything, and he said no. Henry Lawson was executed at 11:42 A.M. on September 2, 1881. "As he fell an involuntary shriek arose from several women in the crowd, and men turned their heads so as not to witness the death throes."[1252]

Lawson said that all he wanted was the ministers to sing and pray. He said he had not attempted to ravish a girl in Georgia, as reported in the newspaper. He was pleased when it was announced that a collection of $50.59 had been raised for his wife and five children (the oldest was eleven) so they could get back to Georgia, his home, where he had been born a slave.

Following the prayers, he was asked again if he had forced himself on Miss Donaldson. He replied that he "would not answer any man, as he had already made up with God."[1253] Finally, as he was standing on the trap with the rope around his neck he was asked again by the reporters if he was innocent or guilty. "He gave an evasive, non-committal reply, and neither denied or affirmed."[1254]

The deputy who placed the cap on Lawson's head said, "Ready," and Sheriff Springfield immediately sprung the trap. The fall was clean, but his neck was not broken and he struggled violently for four minutes, drawing up his shoulders. He was declared dead in thirteen minutes and cut down three minutes later. The body was placed in a coffin and taken by a deputy to the county cemetery, where it was buried without mourners.

Henry Lawson was described as "far from the ignorant man he was supposed to be," and the crowd was greatly disappointed that he did not make a final statement.[1255] The crowd was orderly, and although there was some drunkenness, not a single fight occurred, "not even a disturbance around the gallows."[1256]

Lawson's wife was interviewed by the newspaper. She described him as an "unpleasant companion," who made her life an almost continual burden with his cursing and abusive behavior, and his running after other women. She did not think he had raped the woman, but repeated what she had said in similar interviews: "I have told Henry many times that women will yet be the death of him."[1257]

Henry Lawson told the newspaper he had seen a man hanged in Georgia: "You could hear his neck pop for 100 yards, but then he didn't suffer long." He continued, "I once saw a young woman going to be hung; she went singing; I was so sorry for her, and didn't think that I would ever be hung." He concluded, "Yes, I will go singing too. I want 'em to break my neck the first pop, but I'm mighty 'fraid I will hang a long time and be chocked [*sic*] to death."[1258]

Joseph Harris, white, age 25. *Murder.*

The crime was committed at night on November 22, 1880, at a large house converted to an inn called Marble Hall four miles from Rogersville in Hawkins County. The killer knew the victims because he was a vagabond laborer who performed work for them such as taking cattle to market and cutting wood. The victims were Charlie Brown, age twenty-five, and Andy Heck, age eighteen, both white. Harris was charged only with the murder of Brown. He was to face a second trial if acquitted in the Brown case.

Joseph Harris was the eldest (but illegitimate) son of a woman who wandered from place to place in East Tennessee, carrying her illegitimate children with her. He was known throughout the area as a vagrant and thief. His mother finally married a respectable man who tried to influence Harris but to no avail. "He continued to grow worse and became more and more of a pest and a dread to all the neighborhoods which he frequented. His conduct was so bad that it was impossible for him to stay in one neighborhood long at a time, and this floating, drifting life which he led, he was made acquainted with more neighborhoods."[1259]

Harris had been a wood chopper for Charlie Brown and had been hired by his father, John Brown, to drive some hogs to Whitesburg, where they were sold. Harris and the Browns took the hogs there and Charlie was paid $260 in cash. The father left for Bristol, where he planned to open a manufacturing plant. Charlie returned to Marble Hall to finish up some business before leaving for Bristol. Harris came back with him and bought some ammunition in Rogersville and attempted to borrow a gun. He knew that Brown was leaving for Bristol on the morning of November 23.

On the night of the 22nd, a Mr. Price and his son, Charlie Brown and Andy Heck obtained three quarts of whiskey and were drinking and playing cards. The Prices left, but the father came back and found Harris with them. At three o'clock in the morning Mr. Price smelled smoke and determined that it came from Brown's room. He opened the door and found the room filled with smoke. He fumbled towards the bed and discovered two bodies in it. He pulled the bed into the hall. It contained the bodies of Charlie Brown and Andy Heck. A search showed that Brown's coat was missing along with the $260.

The sheriff and a deputy found Harris at another man's house the next morning, highly intoxicated and wearing Brown's coat containing the money. The coat had a distinctive patch and the money was in recognizable denominations. Harris was brought back to Marble Hall to view the bodies. He remained impassive.

Harris was tried in January 1881 and was defended by three lawyers. He did not take the stand. During his confinement he refused to discuss the crime.

The Tennessee Supreme Court's decision in his case is unique. What seems to be an opinion is actually a lengthy dissent by Justice Freeman, who said an error in the judge's charge warranted a new trial, but "a majority of the court thinking otherwise, the judgment will be affirmed."[1260]

The trial court had given all the proper instructions, but said, "The jury are also judges of the law. Should you conclude that the court has not given you the law correctly, and should you conclude you know the law is otherwise than as given by the court, then you may pass upon the law in this case as you may know it."[1261]

Judge Freeman emphasized this was clear error because it allowed the jury to decide for itself what the law was. He traced the development of the common law of jury trials as mandating the separation of functions — judges to determine the law, juries to decide the facts — said that allowing a jury to decide the law was wrong because it might do what it wanted. He said, "We are always likely to have the law given by the court disregarded, and the crude or corrupt conclusions of ignorance or corruption made the standard for decision."[1262] He said the majority of the court found no prejudicial error because the instruction, in effect, operated in this case to Harris's benefit.[1263]

The day before his execution, Joe Harris was given a shave and haircut and a photograph was taken which was sold the next day. Joseph Harris rode to the gallows in a wagon sitting on his coffin. "Harris was almost staggering drunk, having been stealthily furnished with whisky by someone."[1264] The wagon was filled with men and boys. He was taken to the gallows located a mile from Rogersville with a noose around his neck. On the gallows he spoke in an incoherent and indistinct manner, claiming that he had made peace with his Maker and was prepared to die.

Joseph Harris was hanged at 1:30 P.M. on November 25, 1881. This was the same spot where Berry was executed a few years earlier. He was "swung off" in the traditional manner with the wagon being pulled from under him. When the wagon was driven out Sheriff Blevins gave Harris a push, remarking, "If this isn't a gilt-edged affair, you may have my hat!"[1265] The body was cut down in thirty-five minutes, placed in a coffin and taken for burial by a cousin. Harris had refused the request of local doctors to experiment on his body in an effort to restore life.

Harris made a written confession two days before his execution. Here are his words:

> We played [cards] till we got very tight, and the young man (Heck) would look in my hand and tell Charlie what I had. At last Charlie got so mad because I was beating him that he struck at me, but I did not care for it, and I played on with him. There was on the fire board a butcher knife, and he got it and ran at me with it. I tried to get out of the house but he was on me so close with the knife that I grabbed a piece of split ash wood with a sharp edge and big end which was in the corner and struck him with the big end of it on the head and knocked him in the fire. The other one was coming on me so fast, that I turned around and struck him and knocked him back on the bed. Then I pulled Charlie out of the fire and threw him on the bed. As it was a cold night I expected to lay out, I grabbed the overcoat and ran out of doors. I did not know that I had killed them, for I did not aim to. When I left they were trying to get up. I do not know how the fire got on the bed, unless Charlie was afire when I jerked him out. I burnt the stick up. I did not kill them for their money; I did not know that they had it. The money was in the overcoat pocket and I did not know that I had it until I had gone away from there. When I felt the pocketbook I pulled it out and opened it and found the money in it, but I did now know how much, and I did not know what to do with it. It made me feel bad, because I did not intend to kill the men or take anything they had. If I had not taken the coat I would not have had the money, but it was cold, and the coat was on the chair, and I took it, intending to wear it home, but not to keep it. I did not know how hard I struck. I was very drunk and the rest were too. If we had been in our right minds we would not have gotten into a row. I went there to stay all night with him, and I didn't think that I would kill or hurt anyone till the knife was drawn on me. God will forgive me for all my sins, and I do thank God for the name of Jesus. I know that Jesus died for us all, and I am going to that happy land where Jesus is, and were troubles never come.[1266]

No one believed his story of self-defense and innocent flight with the coat. A newspaper reporter had spent the night before the execution in a cell next to Harris and asked numerous questions, Harris taking a long time to answer, but often refusing a full answer. The reporter concluded after the hanging, "The miserable carcass will mingle with the earth, and Joe Harris will only be remembered because of the notoriety his heinous crimes gave him."[1267]

The inclement weather kept the crowd to two thousand five hundred, but they were warmed by liquor. "The crowd was very boisterous and unruly; several fights occurred. Harris feared lynching, but no attempt was made."[1268] This was the last public execution in Rogersville. Harris's obvious intoxication and that of many spectators was frequently cited as a reason for making executions semi-public in 1883.

1882

William W. Rea, white, age 30. *Murder.*

The crime was committed at 9:00 P.M. on July 23, 1881, in the back room of a store located in the community of Diana, about twelve miles east of Pulaski, in rural Giles County. The killer lived about two hundred yards from the store. The victim, James R. Goodrum, white, age twenty-nine, was a clerk in the store. The killer and victim knew each other.

On November 30, 1880, Rea had been the prosecution witness in a criminal case against a man named Clark. On the witness stand, the victim and another man said that Rea did not have a good reputation and they would not believe anything he said under oath. The jury could not agree and a mistrial was granted. The state decided not to prosecute the case again. Said the Tennessee Supreme Court, "The defendant was greatly enraged at Goodrum for discrediting him, and used threatening language on the subject."[1269]

The court continued, "There was a wedding at Rea's house on the 2nd of December after the trial, to which Goodrum had been invited. Rea wrote Goodrum a letter forbidding him to come to his house. And on that evening, he repeatedly said to several persons, and while at the table with his guests, that he would kill Goodrum, as one witness testified, but most of them say he would kill him if he came upon his premises. There is testimony of hostile language on other occasions. And one witness testified that on May 1, defendant said to him that these fellows in the store were mad at him, and he would oust them yet."[1270]

Rea had borrowed a shotgun which was loaded with squirrel shot and told the lender that he needed it to kill a squirrel for his wife. A few days before the killing, Rea fired some shots at a tree in his back yard. Paper from that shooting and some large shot were found about the area later. This paper had been used to pack the barrels of the muzzle-loading shotgun.

Goodrum was seated by a kerosene lamp studying Latin with a schoolteacher, Professor M. Dwyer. The window was open. Rea stood about twelve yards from the window and shot through it, hitting Goodrum with shot entering his head and heart. He cried, "O, God, I'm shot!" Pieces of paper similar to those found at Rea's home were found at both the place the gun was fired and inside the room where Goodrum fell. The blast caused Goodrum's death in a matter of minutes. He was attended by the professor, the store owner, J.K. Trigg, and the store owner's brother, W.H. Trigg, who were summoned moments after the shooting.

Five minutes after the shooting, Rea was heard to ask, "What's the matter down there?" calling to J.K. Trigg. The area where the shooter stood was cordoned off until the next morning. Careful examination of the shoe prints showed tracks from a size seven shoe (Rea's size) in a circuitous route from his house to the shooting point. When Rea was asked if he saw anyone come by his house the night before, he said no. Later, he said he saw three men because the dogs had barked. Rea offered to help look for the killer(s) and led the searchers in what seemed to them the wrong direction. Following his arrest, he agreed to walk in the area where the tracks were seen. But he walked on his toes.[1271] He said he had gravel in his shoes, and stopped two or three times to take the gravel out, but continued to walk on his toes, without making full tracks.

Rea offered the alibi that he was in his kitchen (located a few steps from his house) at the time of the shooting. He said he was making a poultice for his wife, who was sick in bed. At trial, his wife, mother and brother supported his alibi.

A reconstruction of the shooting showed that it was clearly possible for a man walking "beyond the ordinary pace," to make it to Rea's house by the circular route shown by the tracks within the time he called out to Trigg inquiring what happened.[1272]

The circumstantial evidence that persuaded the jury to find guilt were the pieces of paper found in three places. When the shards were gathered it was possible to make out full sentences from them. They came from the weekly edition of the *Nashville Banner*, March 24, 1881, and the *Pulaski Citizen*, June 5, 1879. The Nashville paper contained an advertisement for medicine to kill tapeworms, and showed a picture of a tapeworm. The shards had been carefully collected and lodged with the court for safekeeping. The owner of the gun did not take the *Banner*, but said he was certain that he loaded the gun with wadding from one of the Pulaski papers. Professor Dwyer, the schoolteacher, had received twelve copies of the March 24, 1881, *Banner*, sent to him as specimen copies for distribution, and he had given one of the copies to Rea.

The chief prosecuting witness was the Rev. W.J. Brown, Goodrum's brother-in-law. After Rea's conviction was upheld by the Tennessee Supreme Court, a Nashville newspaper carried an interview with Rea in which he said he was the victim of a plot. This prompted the Rev. Brown to write an extensive account of the case demonstrating that it was literally impossible for there to have been a plot.

Wrote the Rev. Brown:

> Could W.W. Rea, an innocent party, knowing nothing of these circumstances, take his gun, take duplicate copies of the same date, the same sized balls, tear these same papers so as to divide the same letters, the same words, the same sentences, the same tape worm, etc., exactly in the same direction and in the same place, so as to geometrically and literally dove tail into each

other, paper, letters, words and sentences? He says he is innocent and that some other party did the killing. If he is innocent he has done exactly what the unknown and guilty third party has done with the Banner of the 24th of March 1881, and the Citizen of the 5th of June 1879, for he confessed to loading his gun, and these papers were found in his lot, in his pouch, in his gun and at the window through which Goodrum was killed, torn and fitting exactly as described. That he can be innocent in the light of these facts is not only improbable, but impossible — a perfect paradox.[1273]

The Rev. Brown went on to describe in detail how the words and sentences fit together, for example, "Buttram (M.K.), a member of the present legislature, part of the name found in the left hand barrel of Rea's gun, and the other part at the window through which Goodrum was killed."[1274] The Rev. Brown concluded, "This case is one of the simplest and strongest, and the most extraordinary and exceptional in its nature that it will form a test case for future reference — so say the lawyers. The crime, the victim, and the assassin from one of the bloodiest pictures in the book of time."[1275]

The case did capture some national attention. It was discussed in the *National Police Gazette*, a newspaper supposedly designed to assist law officers in solving crime, but in reality a series of accounts of lurid crimes.[1276]

On May 1, 1882, a letter was received in the office of Governor Hawkins from a man signing his name as Samuel Fisher, in which he declared Rea was innocent because he had committed the crime.[1277] A diligent search was made to locate Samuel Fisher. He was not found until the day before the execution, too late to stop it. A post-execution letter from Fisher (coupled with his affidavit) made it clear that he had not sent the first letter.[1278]

William W. Rea was hanged in the yard of the Pulaski jail on May 19, 1882. Rea had managed to take a teaspoon of morphine at daybreak on that day and called for a toddy. But he vomited before it could be delivered.

Rea was dropped seven feet at 3:00 P.M. Here is what happened:

> The noose having been left too loose, and the knot not having been properly adjusted, when the body fell with a jerk, the knot slipped around in front, and slipping up off his neck, cut through the superficial facia, breaking some small blood vessels in the neck and scraping the great part of the whiskers off his chin. There he hung groaning for a minute — it seemed an age. Then his left arm released itself from the rope which bound it and raised the quivering hand with its twitching fingers to the throat, clutching at the throat and rubbing off the blood which was running several places. The black cap had been thrown nearly off, so that every twitching of the facial muscles could be seen. Sheriff and jailer Arrowsmith, with an assistant, raised the body in their arms and adjusted the rope again, while the poor wretch again repeated, "Oh, Lord, my God, is there no help for the widow's son?" and said, appealing, "Oh! Henry, Oh! Henry," to the sheriff.[1279]

The account of Rea's death continued: "He was let fall and the sickening sight was again beheld, which horrified the entire assembly as the first effort, as the rope again slipped up. A bystander now rushed down and suggested that the noose be drawn tightly and the knot be placed behind the ear. This was done, and for a third time the body was let fall. The neck was not broken and the poor fellow slowly choked to death."[1280]

By now the jailer had fainted. Someone remarked the death was itself a murder. This threw the sheriff into a rage and he threatened death to the critic. "Quite a stampede was caused by the affair, several falling in the adjoining creek in their haste to get out of the way of a row."[1281]

Sandy Matthews, black, age 46. *Murder.*

The crime was committed on the afternoon of October 6, 1881, in the rural community of Lucy, about sixteen miles northwest of Memphis, in Shelby County. The killer had come home after having left it for some time to work in the city. He said the victim had convinced his wife, Delia Matthews, black, age forty-one, to leave the farm home to work in Memphis. She was living with the victim. Matthews was carrying on an incestuous relationship with his adult stepdaughter (his wife's daughter), Bettie Hicks. The victim, Essiah Polk, black, age forty, had come to talk to Bettie Hicks about her moving to Memphis as well.

When Matthews arrived at the house, Polk and Bettie were sitting on the porch talking. Matthews said nothing to Polk but asked Bettie where his ax was located. She told him it was at the woodpile. He walked through the house, got the ax, came back through the house and without warning struck Polk on the head with it. Polk fell to the ground, exclaiming, "Lord, have mercy on me! Don't kill me!" Matthews struck another blow.[1282] He dragged the body to the back of the house near the chimney and cut off the head. The body was then dragged to a shed and covered with cotton seed. What happened to the head is unknown.

A few hours later, Matthews ordered Bettie

Hicks to help him bury the body about two hundred yards from the house near a dike. The hole Matthews dug was too small for the body. It was then pulled out of the hole. Matthews cut off the arms and legs with the ax. These and the body now fit the hole. It was covered. Matthews told Bettie that if she told anyone about the killing it would be her fate too.[1283]

Polk's disappearance caused suspicion to fall on Matthews, in part because it was well-known that Matthews was sexually involved with Hicks (against her will). Matthews had a poor reputation already. He was the "champion hog thief in the neighborhood."[1284] After several months, Hicks told what happened to a white landowner, Coleman, who did not believe her. Later, he undertook a search when she was gone and after he had dug for the body for two days, he found it through the use of a sounding stick.[1285] Matthews was arrested and denied any involvement. He was then questioned by the police chief, who told him the details of the murder. The chief said, "Come on, confession is good for the soul."[1286] Matthews then confessed to the crime.

At trial, the issue was whether it was proper for the court to allow the testimony of the police chief regarding the confession. The court said there was no evidence that any "promise or intimation of temporal benefit was held out as an inducement to confess," and the confession was admissible.[1287] Two other issues were also turned aside. The defendant had been chained in the courtroom while the jury was out, and when it came back he remained shackled for a few minutes. This was not error. Nor was the fact that on one occasion the jury came back in two groups. That is, there was no improper separation of the jury.[1288] Bettie Hicks testified against Matthews and the attempt to impeach her by questioning her relationship with Matthews failed. The Supreme Court ordered Matthews hanged on June 2, 1882, and he was executed that day.

Sandy Matthews was attended in the jail by Roman Catholic priest Father Aloyisus (whom everyone called Father Lucius) and converted to that faith. Said Matthews, "I was a Baptist about ten years ago, but I stumbled and wallowed, and fell away from grace." He continued, "But God has brought me back. Once I didn't want to know when I was to die; but it is better as it is. A few weeks ago a prisoner fell and broke his head; he suffered and groaned all night and then died. I would rather die as I shall than like him."[1289] Matthews's wife and small son visited him inside his jail cell. He asked for donations for his wife, saying she was a good woman. But he continued to denounce her daughter.

Matthews was executed at 2:03 P.M. June 2, 1882, on a gallows built inside the jail yard of the Shelby County jail. About five hundred people were inside the yard, and about three thousand were watching from afar, including rooftops and parked railroad cars.

Matthews mounted the steps wearing a black jacket, jeans pants, slippers, a white shirt and a black tie. He walked with a "quick, springy step," and as soon as he was on the scaffold began a wild and incoherent speech. He frequently offered questions such as, "Will you come to the fold of mercy?"

He exclaimed, "I was a Baptist long ago, but was tempted by the devil. But I have come back to God. If it hadn't been for the good sisters and Father Lucius, I might have been lost. We know the Son of Man appeared after death. I tell you today, come to the fold of mercy. I hope I may be the last man to die this way. I am done. The papers will stop telling all over the world about Sandy Matthews. They may kill the body, but they cannot kill the soul. I am going to Jesus — to the great city. I don't know fear. Go to Jesus with all your soul. He is your only friend. I ask all, in the name of God, come and join the true church."[1290]

After Matthews was finished, he knelt in front of the priest and they said the Lord's Prayer, followed by the Apostles' Creed. The priest gave the prayer for the dying. While this was going on, Matthews's small son began to cry and this brought tears to several women.

The noose and black cap were placed and Matthews said, "Farewell, O Lord! In Jesus trust!" At that moment the trap was sprung and the drop was clean. His neck was broken and except for a flutter of the hands, there was no movement. The body was taken down twenty-two minutes later. It was placed in a coffin and taken to St. Mary's Church for a service and burial in Calvary Cemetery. The coffin had a silver cross on the lid.

The newspaper described Matthews: "Sandy Matthews is a negro, black, of large frame of body, and in endurance betrays all of the impulses of his inhuman nature; an absence of intellectual capabilities, and full development of the usual, brutal conditions from which, according to the Darwinian theory, he has progressed but a step or two."[1291]

Samuel Hodge, black, age 23. *Murder.*
Milton Hodge, black, age 22. *Murder.*

The crime was committed at 4:00 P.M. on September 5, 1881, in a rural area called Black Oak

Ridge, in Knox County, where railroad construction was underway. The killers were brothers. Their sister was married to the victim. Her son had come to them saying that the victim had beaten her and threatened to kill her. The victim was James McFarland, black, age thirty. He was working at the construction site.

Shortly after the beating, the Hodge brothers had gone to their sister's house and confirmed the beating and the threat. They swore out a warrant for McFarland and brought him before Constable Pinkney Northern. He told them to watch McFarland while he left to gather witnesses. McFarland escaped from their custody. When Constable Northern returned he told the brothers to re-arrest him and to "take him wherever found."[1292] He did not tell them to take McFarland "dead or alive" and gave them no written warrant to arrest him.

The brothers, armed with shotguns, looked for McFarland and told several people they would shoot him on sight. They went to Knoxville, where they asked an uncle, Henry McBee, to assist them. They went to the railroad work area (called a cut) and McBee went inside a tent and found McFarland. He returned and told the brothers where he could be found.

The brothers rode their horses up to the tent. Brandishing weapons, they demanded McFarland come out because they had a warrant for his arrest. (They did not show a warrant.) They threatened to take him dead or alive. When he came out, a fistfight erupted and the four men ended up on the ground, struggling. The fight was broken up by the crew boss. He ordered the brothers and McFarland off the property.

As they walked away, another scuffle began and the brothers managed to tie McFarland's hands in front. However, he broke free and struck Sam in the face with a rock. Sam said, "Let him have it." Milton shot McFarland in the temple. McBee was arrested on the spot. The brothers fled and surrendered to the sheriff of Jefferson County, saying they feared for their lives. The newspaper said much indignation was felt in the colored community regarding the murder. It said there is a "universal desire to have the matter speedily investigated, and the majesty of the law maintained."[1293]

The trial went forward against the brothers as principals and McBee as an accomplice. On February 9, 1882, the Knoxville jury convicted the brothers but could not make up its mind about McBee. He had testified against them and was tried three times. At the time of their execution he had been indicted for assault and was waiting trial.

The brothers were represented by William F. Yardley, the premier black Tennessee lawyer of his day.[1294] The brothers claimed error in the failure of the grand jury to have included any blacks, that is, none had been called to serve on the grand jury. The court said this issue had not been raised in the trial court, only by affidavit after the conviction, and this was too late. Likewise, there was no error in charging the jury that when the facts of the killing were proven by the state, malice was shown, and the "onus of exculpation is on the prisoners."[1295]

The Hodge brothers were visited by earnest members of the Young Men's Christian Association, and found religion in jail under the care of several black ministers, notably the Rev. C.C. Russell of First Baptist Church, the Rev. B.H. Johnson, and the Rev. Masterson of Second Baptist Church. They spent most of their time "singing, praying and shouting."[1296]

The night before the execution, the men ate five beefsteaks, biscuits, sweet cakes and coffee. The next morning they insisted that "ol' Satan" had tried to come to their cell that night but they had driven him away with their prayers. The pair were "dressed in new cheap cassimere suits," and were seated on a wagon and taken to the execution spot. Samuel's wife rode in the wagon with them, along with the three black ministers.[1297]

The gallows was erected "three hundred yards from the south end of the bridge," and the wagon had some difficulty moving through the assembled crowd. The estimate ranged from five to fifteen thousand, but the best guess was eight thousand. The crowd was half black, but contained women and children of both races. Samuel Hodge's wife got off the wagon when it arrived at the gallows and she left the scene. Samuel and Milton Hodge were hanged at 1:30 P.M. on November 10, 1882. It was the last truly public execution in Knox County and Sheriff Homer Gilmore was in charge.

The execution method was the traditional "swung off" method whereby the men stood on the wagon with ropes and caps over their necks and the wagon pulled away. For that reason, the wagon became a platform for the last religious service. The Rev. Russell exhorted the crowd regarding the men's crime and offered a prayer in which he called for the men to confess. The Rev. Johnson led singing a Presbyterian hymn, "Stoop Down My Thoughts That Need to Rise." The Rev. Russell offered another prayer. Then the Rev. Johnson said the men would speak to the throng.

Before anything was said, lawyer Yardley spoke something in Sam's ear. Sam began a rambling statement that included, "It seemed there was a large congregation assembled to see the death of two poor prisoners, who had been confined in the prison house for fifteen long months." He continued, "None but Jesus knows whether this death is just or not." Sam's speech was so long Sheriff Gilmore told him to sit down.[1298]

Milton stood on the wagon seat to address the crowd and said: "God knows what is just. Let this be a warning to all, not for my sake, but for God's sake." It was evil passions, he said, that brought him to this, but Jesus had pardoned his sins and he knew he had a home to go to. He said he was tempted after he got into the right path. Even this morning Satan was at his cell door jumping and hopping in, but thanks to God, he didn't stay long because Milton "loaded and shot him with the gospel gun." He said he had not a bit of malice towards anyone. He hoped to meet all in heaven. McFarland, poor fellow, was gone, and he was sorry. Speaking about the same length as his brother, but in a more cogent manner, he too was finally told to sit down by the sheriff.

Next, the Rev. Johnson asked that a collection be taken up for the benefit of Samuel's wife and two children, but the sheriff said there was not enough time. This could be done after the execution. Finally, the Rev. Masterson gave a benediction.

The men's hands were cuffed behind their backs and they were pinioned. As this was being done, they "kept talking, looking up, laughing and danced around, expressing thanks to God, saying, "Do what you please with our bodies, thank God, Jesus will take care of our souls."[1299]

After the caps were placed, Milton began singing, "I'm Going to Ride on the Evening Train," and Sam said, "I see Jesus." Milton's legs seemed to give way, but at that moment the sheriff ordered the wagon away. At the drop, several women in the crowd began sobbing. The men's hearts stopped beating in ten minutes.

After the men were cut down, their shoes were taken off and given to the family. The bodies were placed in simple coffins with the caps still on their heads. At this time, the Rev. Johnson announced that people could purchase a part of the noose upon giving a contribution to Sam's wife and children. It is not known how many took the offer.

Concluded the newspaper, "They were born in Jefferson County at Hodges Tank, slaves of Joseph C. Hodges, and their father is yet living, an invalid. They were entirely illiterate, and ignorant, and in their life time had been considered rather bad fellows."[1300]

1883

Robert Wilson, black, age 23. *Murder.*

The crime was committed about 9:00 P.M. on September 29, 1882, at Stafford's Drug Store near the corner of Vance and Hernando Streets in downtown Memphis, in Shelby County. The killer was a trotting horse jockey and horse trainer who traveled the country on the horse racing circuit. He had been in Memphis a month before the shooting. His foster sister Anna Dunn, black, lived there. The victim was Frank P. Ruppell, white, age forty-four, a grocery store owner. He went by the name Russell. The shooting occurred as a result of Russell's attempt to make a citizen's arrest following Wilson's theft of a bucket of lard from Russell's Grocery.

Wilson and another man had burglarized Russell's store the night before the shooting and had hidden the goods near the store under a building. Russell saw Wilson walk by with the bucket of lard. Armed with a pistol, he followed and said, "Halt!" three times. When Wilson ignored him, Russell shot him "in the rear part of the leg just below the hip joint."[1301]

Wilson fell to the sidewalk and begged not to be shot again. Russell said, "Damn you, I've got you, have I? Get up from there, I want to see if I know you." Wilson was helped to his feet and taken inside a nearby drug store and placed on a stool. He wailed and talked excitedly.

Russell asked the clerk to telephone the police. Russell said the bucket of lard was his. Wilson did not respond. While the clerk was making the call, Wilson suddenly sprang for the door, but was grabbed by Russell and another man. Wilson bit the man's wrist and he let go. Russell and Wilson struggled over the pistol Russell was still holding. As they struggled, Wilson reached into his back pocket and pulled a small pistol and fired three shots at Russell. He died seventy-two hours later.

Wilson ran away but was quickly caught. Both pistols were found in his possession. At the jail, Wilson told of the burglary and where some of the goods could still be found hidden.[1302] He later complained about the "harsh words and threats" the police made toward him during the interrogation. He was taken to the Nashville jail for safekeeping.

The issue before the Tennessee Supreme Court was whether these facts supported first-degree murder. Ruling that they did, the court said the statute[1303] allowing for citizens' arrests made lawful an arrest where a crime has been committed and the citizen-arrester is in pursuit. The court said, "The arrest in the present case was on pursuit and the fact already cited shows that the prisoner was fully advised of the cause of which he was arrested, and by his silence confessed to the larceny of the bucket of lard. There is ample proof in the record to convict him, at least of the larceny."[1304]

Wilson had the duty to submit to the arrest until "he might be within a reasonable time turned over to the officers of the law."[1305] Russell had reasonable grounds to arrest Wilson, regardless of whether the facts showed there could be a conviction of the underlying felony. Said the court, "The conduct of the prisoner after he was arrested, his feigned suffering to throw parties having him in custody off their guard, showed conclusively that he fully understood the situation. He had, we have no doubt, armed himself to kill if it became necessary to complete the felony he had undertaken. His plans were well formed."[1306] Robert Wilson was ordered executed on July 20, 1883, and was hanged on that day.

Wilson maintained to the last the he should not have been convicted of first-degree murder because he did not intend to kill Russell, whose death was "unpremeditated and happened when both were excited, and when he had a reasonable right to suppose he was in danger."[1307]

For Wilson's execution the gallows in the jail yard was taken down and moved inside the Shelby County jail. It had been used to hang Sandy Matthews, but a new law required semi-private executions with only designated people allowed to witness the actual drop. Robert Wilson was the first person in Shelby County to be executed inside the jail. On the gallows were benches where the witnesses sat. These included ministers, the press, and some deputies.

In jail, Wilson was given as much ice cream and cake as he wanted. He was visited by several ministers, in particular a Roman Catholic priest Father Aloysius, under whom he converted to that faith a week before his execution. Father Aloysius had attended Sandy Matthews the year before and Frank Scott in 1875. Wilson was hanged with the same rope used to execute Sandy Matthews. It had been greased with tallow to slip properly.

Wilson was also seen by his foster sister. Both had been adopted as infants. She told him to stop complaining about the poor treatment he had received from the police following his arrest, saying, "Never mind, Robert, that is all over now." Her words made him angry and he blew cigar smoke in her face.[1308] Visitors brought him food and on his last full day he ate chicken, sardines and crackers.

Wilson was described as a very intelligent Negro. The day of the execution he asked the sheriff when the execution would take place, having learned that it could be as late as four o'clock. He asked that his execution take place at that time but the sheriff said he had waited too long to ask. The execution was set for noon and would be carried out at that time.[1309]

Father Aloysius administered Wilson's last rites in his cell and walked with him to the gallows. Wilson wore black pants, a black alpaca coat and a white tie given to him by Sheriff Cannon.[1310] Wilson mounted the gallows with a firm step and was "the coolest man on the scaffold and was almost lively."[1311]

At the priest's motion, Wilson fell to his knees for a benediction and recitation of the Lord's Prayer. Wilson had earlier proclaimed, "I feel that Jesus is with me," and went to his death with a crucifix around his neck. He recited the Apostles' Creed and without any hesitation spoke the Act of Contrition, following which the priest announced absolution. Wilson declined to make any last statement on the gallows, but shook hands with everyone seated on the benches. This included the Rev. T.H. McAuley, a black Baptist minister, who had also attended him.

Wilson's hands were cuffed and he was pinioned. After the cap was placed on his head, he was heard to pray, "Jesus, Mary and Joseph, assist me in the hour of my death. Amen."[1312]

The word "Amen" was the agreed signal for his death. At 12:22 the trap was sprung and the drop was clean. At intervals his shoulders drew up as if he were attempting to lift a heavy weight. His heart stopped beating fourteen minutes later and when he was cut down flies immediately beset the body.[1313] The neck was broken. "The ugly protrusion of the tongue and the ghastly swollen countenance usually worn by those who have gone before in like manner, was not there."[1314] The body was placed in a casket and taken to St. Mary's Church, where Father Aloysius conducted a service and Wilson was buried in the Catholic cemetery.

Andrew Taylor (aka John Purnell), white, age 23. *Murder.*

The crime was committed on the afternoon of September 14, 1882, near the community of Philadelphia, eight miles east of Sweetwater, in Loudon County, on a moving train underway from Chattanooga to Knoxville. The victims were William T. Cate, white, age fifty-two, and John J. Conway, white, age thirty.[1315]

The facts were described by the Tennessee Supreme Court as follows: "On September 14, 1882, Sheriff William T. Cate of Hamilton County and John J. Conway, his deputy, were in the smoking car of the railroad train in charge of three prisoners, bringing them from Chattanooga to Knoxville for a hearing of their causes by this court upon appeal. One of the prisoners was John Taylor, a brother of the defendant, Andrew Taylor, who had been convicted of the crime of voluntary manslaughter, and sentenced to ten years of confinement in the penitentiary."[1316]

The court continued:

> Andrew Taylor, and another brother, Robert Taylor, had been waiting a week or two at different points on the railroad, and watching the trains in expectation that their brother John would be conveyed by rail to this place. They manifestly conspired together to attempt to release their brother. On the day mentioned, they got on the train at a way station, entered the car in which the sheriff and his deputy were sitting with the prisoners, and took a distant seat. When the train stopped at the next station, Robert Taylor strode up the aisle of the car, and with, according to the principal witness, a "steely appearance in his eyes," was followed by the defendant Andrew Taylor.

The court said:

> Conway was sitting next to, and looking out of the window of the car. One of the prisoners was occupying the same seat, while the other two prisoners were on the seat in front of them handcuffed together, John Taylor being nearest to the aisle. When within one step of Conway's seat, Robert Taylor drew a revolver from his pocket, and presented it at his hand, saying with an oath, "cross your hands." Before the startled officer could do anything except turn his face toward him, dropping at the same time his left hand from the back seat on which it rested, Robert Taylor fired his pistol and killed him, the ball passing through the head of Conway.

Said the court, "The sheriff, who was sitting on the other side of aisle two or three seats further on, rose to his feet and presented his pistol at Robert Taylor, saying, "Hold on there!" At that moment the defendant, Andrew Taylor, fired his pistol at the sheriff, the ball striking him."

The court continued, "The sheriff also fired at Robert, but the pistol was struck up by John Taylor, and Robert Taylor then shot the sheriff over John's shoulder. As the sheriff retreated towards the door of the car, Robert and Andrew both again fired at him. Andrew Taylor also continued to snap his pistol two or three times at the sheriff, and when the latter had fallen to the ground, and, as the witnesses say, was pointing his pistol aimlessly "like a dying man," the defendant gave him a final shot from the steps of the car, which "straightened him out."[1317]

Taking the keys from Conway's pocket, the shooters released their brother. They ordered the conductor not to stop the train at the next station, but made their escape at the one following. Robert Taylor escaped to Cincinnati and then to Missouri. John and Andrew went south, mostly by foot, pretending to be hoboes, with John acting brain-injured, supposedly from a mining accident, according to what they told anyone who met them. John had been slightly wounded in the shoulder, and Andrew in the arm, from the shots fired by the sheriff.

The getaway prompted national newspaper attention, with the press likening them to "the Harps, Murrell and the James boys." Ultimately, the reward for their capture reached a staggering fifteen thousand dollars. The governor's already large five-thousand-dollar reward was double-matched by the railroad to show it tolerated no violence on its trains.[1318] Images of the Taylors appeared in the *National Police Gazette*, ostensibly a newspaper covering new methods of crime detection, but in reality, the scandal sheet of its day.[1319] At one point, the pair actually met a sheriff's posse looking for them but their disguise worked.

News of the reward reached the sheriff of LaClede County, Missouri, who was watching for the brothers and happened to be at the train station in Lebanon, Missouri, on October 12, 1882, when he overheard a stranger he suspected might be one of the brothers ask about a train the next day. The sheriff boarded the train at an earlier stop the next day. As the sheriff hoped, Robert Taylor boarded the train.

According to a news account, "Robert Taylor had an oil coat thrown over his lap, under which he held a pistol in his hand — being aware doubtless that he was shadowed. When the train neared Marshall, Missouri, the sheriff notified Taylor that he was his prisoner." Said the account, "Bob Taylor immediately drew his pistol, but the sheriff was too quick for the outlaw and pulled down on him, sending a bullet through his brain. The prisoner dropped dead in his tracks and the body was brought to Chattanooga and fully identified."[1320] It was thought that one of the brothers may have been aboard the train because the pistol that fell from Robert's hand was picked up by someone during the excitement attending the shooting. The snatcher passed into another car and was seen no more.

Andrew and John continued hiding out in Missouri and Kansas. The newspaper said, "In an isolated portion of the country, a swampy, malarial section, and twenty miles from a physician, John died of flux, after much physical and mental suffering, aggravated by remorse of conscience, which made life a burden from the day the crime was perpetuated. Away from friends, self-ostracized, it remained for Andy to make a rude plank coffin and bury his brother in the swamps of Kansas."[1321]

In April 1883, Andrew was working for a Missouri farmer named T.N. Dixon under the assumed name of John Purnell. On a visit to town, he became highly intoxicated and told Dixon his real name and details of the crime. At first, Dixon paid little heed, but when Andrew became even more intoxicated and began shooting his pistol, Dixon became alarmed.

One of the bullets grazed Taylor's own head. In his drunken stupor he concluded he was going to die. He made a confession that was heard by Mrs. Dixon. Over the next few days, Dixon telegraphed the governor of Tennessee to confirm the story. By then, Andrew had sobered up and attempted to escape, but a posse captured him near Newton, Kansas, and brought him back to Loudon County.

Virtually the entire male population of Loudon County was summoned for jury duty and scores were challenged because they said they had made up their minds regarding Andrew Taylor's guilt. He was only charged with the killing of deputy Conway. The conductor who witnessed the killing was the chief witness. Taylor was convicted after a week-long trial in May 1883.

Robert Taylor was represented by two lawyers and their appeal to the Tennessee Supreme Court raised two issues. First, it was claimed that one of the potential jurors had expressed his opinion of guilt in such a manner as to have tainted the entire jury. The venireman said, "He ought to be hung without law, or gospel, or judge, or jury."[1322] The court did not find this reversible error because there was nothing to indicate the entire panel was somehow influenced by these remarks. However, Judge Freeman dissented. This was sufficient as a matter of law to have tainted the entire panel. The second error involved an unsupported affidavit offered by Taylor that a witness was not available for trial, who would supposedly endorse the notion that Andrew, who was much younger than his brothers, was a somewhat reluctant participant in the scheme and lacked the intent to kill. The court said because the affidavit was unsupported by any other evidence it should be ignored.

Taylor had been kept in the Knoxville jail for his safety during his appeal. At the jail he had been given liquor by other inmates and visitors, a common practice at the time. As Taylor was being transported back to Loudon County for execution, he managed to pull a pistol from the holster of a guard and aim it at Sheriff Foute, pulling the trigger. However, the pistol was a single-action model and did not fire. As he was trying to cock the pistol, it was wrested from his hand.[1323]

Andrew Taylor was executed at 3:15 P.M. November 23, 1883, on a gallows in Lenoir City. He was the first man executed under a new statute that forbade the public from seeing the actual drop. Although the hanging was outdoors, Taylor died inside a canvas-enclosed gallows. Thousands viewed the body in its coffin afterward.

Taylor was described as both cool and nervous in the hours before his death. He refused to talk to a minister and turned away a sister who brought her small daughter to ask him to consider his mortal soul. He snapped, "There is no damnation hereafter!" He ate his noonday dinner with great relish as the sheriff stalled the execution hoping Taylor would confess and seek redemption. Instead, in the hours before his death he attempted to sell his confessions for $150 to various newspapers, but none met his price.

After the noose was placed around his neck, he was asked by the sheriff if he had anything to say, to which he responded that he didn't want to say a "goddamned word." He said to the sheriff, "God damn you, I could drink your heart's blood!"[1324] At that moment the trap was sprung and Andrew Taylor strangled to death although his heart continued beating for eight minutes.

The practice of bringing a defendant from the local jail (or the penitentiary) to the sitting of the Tennessee Supreme Court when his appeal was heard, was finally stopped in 1901. A statute that year said that all convicted felons should be taken immediately to the penitentiary upon conviction.[1325] In 1915, a defendant in a non-capital felony case said he had a right under the Tennessee Constitution to appear at the Supreme Court argument, with the state responsible for getting him there. The Tennessee Supreme Court said no.[1326] Said the court, "It is quite inconvenient and very expensive, to say nothing of the danger of escape, to have the prisoner, under the care of guards, transported some hundreds of miles from the penitentiary to the place of the court's sitting."[1327] Andrew Taylor's name was not mentioned.

1884

Shim Forrest, white, age 24. *Murder.*

The crime was committed shortly after midnight on December 1, 1882, in the home of David Cruse (Cruise) in the rural community of Mansfield, in Henry County. The killer lived with the victims. They were Shim Forrest's mother, Jane Forrest, white, age forty-seven, and his grandfather, David Cruise, white, age seventy-four. Jane Cruse was not married when Shim was born. She later married a man named Forrest and Shim took that name. It is not known whether Forrest was even alive, but he did not live at the Cruse home at the time of the killings. The murders were prompted by a dispute over a five-dollar gold piece.

Forrest arose in the night while the family was sleeping. He entered his mother's bedroom and struck her head with an ax. She made a sound which awakened her father, David Cruise, who was sleeping in a different room. The old man was partially paralyzed and begged for his life. Shim struck him in the head, scattering his brains about the room.[1328]

Shim's defense was insanity. The Tennessee Supreme Court stated, "There was not a particle of proof tending to show the existence of any form of insanity. The witnesses who depose upon the subject speak of the prisoner as having a good ordinary natural sense but extremely ignorant. The ignoble motive to this hideous tragedy seems to have been to get rid of a bed-ridden grandfather and a petulant mother."[1329]

Shim was illiterate, and "kept at home with his father, who was a man of bad character generally."[1330] The newspaper said, "His mother and his sisters were all women of bad repute, one having given birth to a negro child. All were addicted to drink and swearing."[1331] The grandfather had drunk and gambled away his money until finding religion late in life. The newspaper said, "Shim Forrest's excuse for committing the crime was that they treated him badly at home and he thought he would dispose of them and get what they had and marry a girl to whom he was engaged, she objecting to marry him while his mother lived."[1332]

Forrest said, "My mother never took me to church or Sunday School in her life. She used profane language and drank whisky, and has often brought me to Paris, carried me in a saloon, and called for two drinks, one for herself, the other for me."[1333]

Forrest was attended by the Rev. G.K. Brooks while in jail awaiting death. On July 1, 1884, he professed religion and was baptized. He fully confessed his crimes and said that he was satisfied that God had pardoned him. He said a great burden had been lifted from his heart and for the first time he could pray. For lunch on execution day he was given his choice of food. He selected oysters. He also asked for musk to perfume himself, which was given.

About three thousand people came to Paris for the execution and were in a festive mood on July 11, 1884. At least fifteen hundred crowded around the execution stand and cheered as Shim began to mount the scaffold. He lost his nerve. He began crying and he fell on the stairs. He began to call out for his mother. His crying brought a hush to the crowd. Sheriff M.H. Freeman put his arm around Shim and helped him up the stairs.

On the scaffold, he gave a four-and-a-half-minute speech admitting his crime. He also said he was sorry to die this way but was prepared to go. He said he was sorry more of his relatives had not come to see him die. "He said goodbye to his friends, both black and white."[1334] Two-thirds of the crowd was black.

As soon as he finished talking, with tears streaming down his cheeks, he turned to the sheriff and asked to be disposed of at once. He was pinioned. The noose and cap were placed and without warning the trap was sprung at 2:22 P.M. Shim Forrest's neck was broken and he died without a struggle.

The sheriff had not fully complied with the statute mandating private hangings and the crowd had maneuvered to get a glimpse of the drop. The sheriff said he was opposed to public hangings because they were not fit for women and children to see and they brought out the worst in men. The newspaper criticized Sheriff Freeman for not making the execution a truly private matter as mandated.[1335]

Charles Phillips (aka Charley Phillips), black, age 53. *Murder.*

The crime was committed at 8:00 P.M. November 10, 1883, on the platform (porch-sidewalk) of Spellings' Store in a rural area called Hollow Rock in Carroll County. The killer and victim knew each other. The victim was Frank Prince, black, age unknown. Prince was stabbed and died on the porch.

Gambling among a group of black men that began at the small train depot moved to the store at nightfall. Before this, Phillips, somewhat intoxicated, had brandished a long-bladed pocketknife, slashed the air, and said several times that someone would die before daybreak.[1336]

About 8:00 P.M. Phillips came into the store and complained loudly about "negroes who stick their noses in white men's sterns."[1337] Phillips went outside and others followed, Frank Prince among them. Prince asked if Phillips meant him. Phillips replied, "Any damn man that takes it up!"[1338] As Phillips came closer, Prince put his hand on Phillips's shoulder and pushed him away "very lightly."[1339]

Phillips stepped off the platform (he later said he was pushed) and came around, again facing Prince. Phillips said, "If any damned nigger wants to fight me, let him come."[1340] A few mumbled words were passed. Suddenly Phillips raised his hand high and with an overhand blow, thrust his knife into Prince's neck near the collarbone. The blade broke off. Prince said, "Charley, what are you striking me for?"[1341] Phillips backed away cursing and said to Prince, "Don't come on me!" He had his hand on his back pocket, saying, "I'll shoot your damn heart out!" Then he ran away.

The witnesses, mostly black, said Prince offered no threat to Phillips and was not armed, and that Phillips's threat to shoot came after the stabbing, with the knife handle breaking off and falling at the victim's feet. The blade had lacerated the upper subclavian artery and Prince died within minutes of a doctor's arrival.

Phillips's defenses of self-defense and intoxication were rejected by the jury. His defense raised the victim's character. Most witnesses said Prince was a "bad, fussy sort of man, especially when drinking." But he was not dangerous.[1342] A state's witness said Prince had knocked Phillips down with a wagon standard a year earlier and Phillips said he "had not gotten it out of him" and "would kill him yet."[1343] The conviction was affirmed by the Tennessee Supreme Court but the opinion cannot be located.

Charles Phillips was executed on July 31, 1884, on a gallows at Huntington in Carroll County. Dressed in a new suit given to him by the sheriff, he said, "I am glad to see you all. I am going away. I am not grieving about going. Whiskey was the cause of all of this trouble. I advise all young men to let whiskey alone. I never wanted to destroy any of my fellow beings. I charge all my trouble to whiskey. If I have an enemy in the crowd let him come forward and shake hands with me in peace."[1344]

The district attorney came forward and shook his hand. Phillips said he had made peace with God and hoped to meet everyone in heaven. He was then taken inside the enclosed gallows. At 2:29 P.M. the drop was made and his neck broken.

Initially, the newspaper reported that a large crowd had witnessed the execution and criticized Sheriff Pate for allowing the public to engage in this illegal spectacle and called for his indictment. The next day, the newspaper said its report was erroneous and blamed its correspondent, who "failed to state facts sufficiently exact and left the inference that the execution had been in the presence of a large crowd."[1345]

Isaac "Ike" Fain, black, age 21. *Murder.*

The crime was committed in the afternoon of March 29, 1884, in a rural part of Roane County called Emory Gap where railroad construction was underway. Fain was a laborer and the victim was his supervisor, called a section boss. He was Frank Curran, white, age thirty-one, who oversaw seven workers at the site called a "cut."

Fain was tamping, but Curran told him he was not doing the job right. Fain replied angrily, "What do you take me for!" Curran said, "A man." Fain replied, "Then treat me like a man or I can quit." Curran replied, "All right."[1346] After Fain left, Curran said to the other men, "I suppose Ike has quit us."[1347]

Fain grabbed his hat and coat and went to where he boarded. There he grabbed his double-barreled shotgun and went to the store of the depot agent, W.B. Love, at Emory Gap and bought some buckshot. Love said that it seemed a strange time to be hunting when he was working on the railroad. "Oh," replied Fain, "I am just going out to shoot some fresh meat."

Fain returned to the work area. Hiding behind the cut, he raised the gun and motioned the other men away. Curran was looking down with his hands behind his back. Fain shouted, "Damned son of a bitch!" just as Curran lifted his head to face him. Fain said, "Shot about is fair play!" and shot Curran's face and neck. He died on the spot. Fain was under the impression that Curran carried a pistol and did not want the victim to get the drop on him. A pistol was found in a pocket of Curran's underwear.

Fain was captured four days later and tried at Kingston, where he received the death penalty. His conviction was upheld by the Tennessee Supreme Court but the opinion cannot be located. When the Supreme Court announced its decision on September 16, 1884, Fain said to the court he was glad, "Dey 'firmed da sentence for I get to glory long 'fore any of 'em, and hab' a much better time."[1348]

Ike Fain was hanged at 1:15 P.M. on October 31, 1884, on a public gallows in Kingston. He spoke to four thousand people.

Fain said he had left home four years earlier because his stepmother was cruel to him. She never visited him in jail, although his father came often. Fain admitted that his greatest fault was his fiery temper. He admitted he had done wrong in killing Curran, but said he did not regret it.

The newspaper reported, "Much of his time was taken up reading his Bible; and although he never made a public confession he got very good, like other criminals of his kind, and said that he was going straight to glory."[1349]

When time came for the drop, a canvas curtain was placed around the gallows. The crowd heard Fain's last words: "May the Lord have mercy on me!" The newspaper said, "From the above a number of morals can be drawn. Among them: Children, obey your parents. Parents: Show more respect for your children than [as] if they were brutes, and treat them kindly. A bad temper always needs watching, and often gets one into trouble."[1350]

1885

Joseph Clark, black, age 28. *Murder.*

The crime was committed on March 15, 1884, in a rural farmhouse in Saulsbury, Hardeman County. The killer was known to the victim, Peter Wooten, black, age thirty-seven. Joe Clark was intimately involved with the victim's wife.

The purpose of the killing was to get Wooten out of the way so that Clark could have his wife.[1351]

Clark went to the victim's house at night armed with an old musket. He found Wooten at his corncrib, and as Wooten made his way to the house, Clark fired. The shot only wounded Wooten, who ran to his door. Clark pursued and began to beat Wooten with the musket. Just as he reached the steps, Wooten fell to the ground. Clark used the gun to hit Wooten on the head, splattering his brains on the cabin walls. Wooten's wife arrived in time to see Clark deliver the two fatal blows. Clark ran away, leaving part of the gun at the scene, along with his hat.

Clark was apprehended almost immediately and soon confessed. He told authorities where the rest of the musket could be found. The victim's wife also testified at the trial. The conviction was affirmed by the Tennessee Supreme Court, but the opinion cannot be located.

Joe Clark was executed on a gallows erected in a shed across from the jail in Bolivar at 1:55 P.M. on June 5, 1885. He had been attended by a black minister, the Rev. Williams, and seemed resigned to his fate. He had already admitted the killing after his conviction was affirmed. Clark addressed a crowd of three hundred people in front of the jail. His speech was rambling and was not recorded except insofar as he said that "his fate was an example to all."

Clark mounted the gallows with a firm step and made another rambling statement, but never addressed the issue of whether he had been aided in the killing by anyone else, a matter of considerable interest in the community. The gallows was designed so that the trap would be sprung by knocking out an upright support that held the trapdoor. As the cap was placed over his head, Clark's body shivered. The Reverend Williams then offered a prayer. When the minister finished, Sheriff Yoppe sprung the trap without warning. Clark's neck was broken and he was cut down sixteen minutes later. The newspaper described Clark as a tall man with sharp features, saying, "His bump of intelligence was not very great."[1352]

William Morrow, white, age 36. *Murder.*

The crime was committed shortly after 8:00 P.M. on August 9, 1883, on a rural farm owned by the killer in Montgomery County. The farm was about a half-mile from the massive Bellamy Cave. The killer knew the victim, who worked for the killer's father, Ransom Morrow, white, age sixty-six. The victim, Dick Overton, black, age forty-eight, a farm worker, had been employed by the father for six years and lived about a mile away from the elder Morrow's farm.

Dick Overton had been lured to the killer's house, but the reason for the murder was never fully explained. One theory held that Ransom Morrow put his weak-minded son up to the killing in order to avoid a debt of sixty dollars he owed Overton. Another theory, based on a claim made by the killer, was that it was a revenge killing for an attempted rape on the killer's three-year-old daughter.

Morrow's wife had gone to a church service, leaving him in charge of their four small children. About 8:00 P.M. Overton arrived. According to Morrow, Overton went inside the house (Morrow was in the yard) and would not open the door when Morrow called to him. When Overton finally came out, Morrow went inside and determined that his three-year-old daughter had been raped by Overton. Morrow went out and knocked Overton to the ground, tied his hands and brought him to his feet.

At trial, three witnesses testified that Morrow told them later that he had marched Overton to the cave and shot him there. The next day the killer and his brother, Charles Morrow, carried the body farther into the cave and threw it into a deep crevice called Hell's Hole. One witness had gone into the cave at Morrow's request in 1883 and had seen the body. Overton's coat had caught on a sharp rock and so he had not plummeted to the bottom as planned.[1353] The witness said he told Morrow about seeing the body, but was threatened with death if he told anyone.[1354]

The Morrow family told Overton's family and friends that the victim had gone to Alabama. The body was not found until May 1884 and Bill Morrow was soon arrested. Morrow maintained the killing was justified because of the attempted rape. The Tennessee Supreme Court ruled that the manner of the killing showed it was first-degree murder, regardless of motive.[1355] Morrow's chief issue on appeal was the failure to grant a continuance so that the child's grandmother, who was sick, could come to court and testify about the child's condition the night of the killing. The court said that Morrow's father-in-law (the woman's husband) testified that his wife had rheumatism, which made it impossible for her to come to court on horseback, but that she was able to "go about and do her own work." The trial court had offered to issue an attachment and send a buggy for the woman, but the defendant had not demanded this be done. For this reason, there was no error in denying the continuance.[1356]

The jury chose not to recommend mitigating circumstances, which would have allowed the judge to give a life sentence instead of death. The likely reason was this was not the first time William Morrow had shot a black man accused of raping a family member. In 1877, Morrow's sister, Mrs. Bellamy (wife of Dr. P.F. Bellamy) told her husband that she had been assaulted by a black man, Jim Brown, age fifty-seven. This reportedly occurred on a Sunday night. On Monday, Dr. Bellamy told William Morrow that he wanted him to kill Brown. This Morrow did on Wednesday, going to the man's house and shooting him six times with a pistol as Brown was whittling on his porch. He then partially cremated the body. Then Morrow went to church. The case was not prosecuted until 1884.

Dr. Bellamy had been charged with the Brown murder, but was acquitted. The facts presented at that trial caused William Morrow to be charged with the Overton killing, with Dr. Bellamy and Ransom Morrow as accessories. All were convicted, but the latter with mitigating circumstances, and each given a life sentence. All were kept in the Montgomery County jail pending their appeals. Three weeks after William Morrow's execution, the Tennessee Supreme Court granted new trials because overlapping (but sometimes inconsistent) confessions warranted separate trials.[1357]

William Morrow was hanged at 2:16 P.M. on June 20, 1885, inside the Montgomery County jail. The gallows was actually outdoors in an alley between parts of the old and new jail and the gallows would have been seen from across the river but for the erection of a stockade. Fewer than a dozen spectators, including two friends of the doomed man, were allowed to watch the actual execution.

The day before his death, Morrow was visited by his wife and her mother, Mrs. Hambric (who could not come to testify on his behalf) and all three wept bitterly. Morrow had earlier said that his father had put him up to the shooting, much as Dr. Bellamy had done with the shooting of Brown. When William's last letter to his father was read aloud to him inside the jail, the father became angry and shouted, "It's a lie!"[1358] The newspapers believed the son, explaining he was "hardly up to the average in intelligence, and it is the general opinion that in the commission of the murders he confessed he was a tool of other parties who did the planning."[1359]

Morrow had been attended by a well-known Baptist minister, the Rev. A.D. Sears, and was confident that he was going to heaven, having left a letter to his wife in which he paraphrased a popular poem: "'Tis sweet to rest in lively hope that when my change has come, angels will hover round my bed, and waft my spirit home."[1360]

Bill Morrow walked to the gallows with a firm step and was asked if he had anything to say. He replied no. His long stenographic last statement contained a confession and explanation of both killings. It was given before the Rev. Sears and two others. In it, he took full responsibility for the Overton killing, saying his father had nothing to do with it.

When asked by Sheriff Collier if he was ready, he responded, "I am ready at any minute."[1361] Following a prayer by the Rev. Spears and the Lord's Prayer, which Morrow joined, he was pinioned. After the cap and rope were placed, he was dropped without warning at 2:16 P.M. His neck was broken and he was cut down twenty minutes later. His body was placed in an imitation rosewood casket with silver handles and taken for burial at the cemetery of Blooming Grove Church. William Morrow was the first white man executed in Tennessee for murdering a black man.

John McKeever, black, age 23. *Murder.*

The crime was committed on December 17, 1884, in a rural area near the railroad tracks in the direction of Vicksburg, in Shelby County. This was a hunting area and McKeever and a small black boy named Lindsey Long had gone hunting that morning. McKeever carried a musket he had borrowed from John Long. The victim was William I. Trainor, white, age twenty-nine, who was hunting in the same area. He carried a double-barreled shotgun which he had borrowed. It had been repaired with a distinctive wire holding the trigger and trigger guard in place.

According to the boy, when they encountered Trainor, McKeever asked him for chewing tobacco, which was shared. McKeever told the boy to go home and have breakfast. The boy balked until McKeever promised he would remain in the area until he returned. When he returned (several times) neither man was in sight.

The afternoon of the killing, McKeever entered a small rural grocery store carrying a bundle of clothes, which he placed on the floor upon entering. With him was a "small negro man" and both carried weapons.[1362] McKeever, wearing a dark-colored coat, attempted to sell the shotgun to the store owner.[1363]

Three days later, Trainor's body, stripped of all outer clothing except boots, was discovered hidden in a thicket. He had been shot at very close range in the back of his head with a large-bore weapon. A button from the dark-colored coat he had been wearing was found near the body.

The same day, McKeever was arrested. In his pocket were two pawnbroker tickets. At one shop he had pawned Trainor's initialed pocket watch. At the other he pawned the dark coat. A search of his home produced Trainor's other clothing and the musket belonging to Long. Distinctive sewing and mending patterns made by Trainor's wife showed they were his. Blood was found on McKeever's own coat, offered to police by Mrs. Trainor.

At trial, McKeever said the blood on his coat came from assisting a man he could not identify in slaughtering a steer. His brother offered an alibi, but on cross-examination he admitted he could not be sure regarding the day they had spent together, whether it was a week or two weeks and a few days before Christmas. In closing arguments, McKeever's lawyer argued the death was a suicide or an accident. McKeever was sullen, surly and threatening toward the jury, which he looked at with a fixed gaze.

The Tennessee Supreme Court said the proof clearly showed that McKeever was guilty, the only legal issue being whether it was proper to allow Mrs. McKeever to testify over his objection. The proof showed, however, that she was married to a man named Brown who was in prison, never having gotten a divorce, and the license for her marriage to McKeever had never been signed and returned by the minister who married them. Therefore, her testimony was proper.[1364] McKeever cursed the woman to the newspapers. On the day he was executed they published a copy of a letter she had sent him explaining she had not been paid to testify and had done so out of civil and religious duty.

McKeever was suspected in six other killings and apparently had narrowly avoided conviction of an earlier murder. He was profane and acted strangely in his last days, prancing naked and howling. He gave an elaborate description of how Trainor met his death at the hands of John Long, admitting he was present. The newspaper described this version as a "romance."[1365] McKeever's father came to his cell on the day before his hanging and asked if he had raised him right. McKeever said yes and assured him they would both meet in heaven. A few days earlier, a Catholic priest had attended him for several hours. The night before his execution McKeever slashed himself in several places with a snuffbox remnant. He claimed bad luck had interfered because his candle went out prematurely.[1366]

The condemned man was given all the brandy and whiskey he wanted the night before and the day of his execution. He hiccupped like a drunkard when the death warrant was read to him in his cell. He ate as much food as he could get and said he wanted to make it "lively for the worms when he was planted."[1367] John McKeever was hanged on a gallows built in a corridor of the Shelby County jail on June 26, 1885, the same gallows used to hang Sandy Matthews and Robert Wilson.

McKeever walked with a steady step to the gallows, dressed in a white shirt and dark pants. He was accompanied on the gallows by the priest. "I'm not afraid of that rope," he said, mounting the gallows. "I intend to die game." Asked if he had anything to say, he failed to respond. After the rope was placed around his neck he was asked again. He replied, "All I have to say is I am no murderer."[1368]

Here is what happened next: "Absolution was then given him, and though he repeated the prayer after the priest, he declined to kiss the crucifix which was held before his lips."[1369] Without prompting, he said, "You bet I'm ready. Go ahead, you can't scare me, I'm ready." His arms and legs were pinioned and he said, "Good-bye, Mr. Moss."[1370] The cap was put over his head and without warning the sheriff loosened the trap and McKeever fell. The sound of the trap door hitting the gallows prompted "a large group of negroes outside the jail to give out a half groan, half howl." The body was taken away by his father.

At the time McKeever arrived on the gallows, he found Mrs. Trainor and a female friend already seated there. Both watched the death ceremony in silence. Asked by the newspaper how she felt, Mrs. Trainor replied, "My nerves were as much composed as they are at this moment. I felt proud to see him hung, and I don't think I would have been satisfied if I had not. I have never seen him or talked to him since he was first arrested. I believe he would have confessed on the scaffold if he had not been so much excited."[1371]

Jim Baxter, black, age 24. *Murder.*

The crime was committed about 8:30 P.M. September 12, 1885, at the residence of Mrs. Martha Lane, located on the corner of Market Street and College Street in Lebanon, in Wilson County. The killers were small-time criminals who decided to rob the victim, Mrs. Lane, white, age sixty-seven, a widow who lived alone in her house.

The killers were Jim Baxter and Andrew Church, black. While Church served as a lookout, Baxter entered the house. Using a three-pound rock, he struck several blows to her head. Just as he did so, Church sounded the alarm and Baxter left the house without taking anything. Mrs. Lane crawled through her back yard to a servant's house and within fifteen minutes her physician, Dr. Kidder, was at her side.[1372]

Said the Tennessee Supreme Court, "Her physician stated that he regarded her wounds as fatal, but at first did not regard the case as utterly hopeless. She was unable to articulate for several days. The blows were inflicted on Saturday night, and the next Thursday thereafter she expressed her conviction that she would die. She lived about sixteen days after the wounds were inflicted of which she died."[1373]

By means of signs and pointing, Mrs. Lane was able to tell Dr. Kidder that the person who assaulted her was a Negro. Names were repeated to her and she said no, until she was told Jim Baxter's name and she said yes. "Defendant was arrested and brought into her presence, and she recognized him, and said he was the one. Defendant denied it and Mrs. Lane replied, "Yes, you did, you know it." The defendant was removed and Mrs. Lane said, "Jim knew he did it. He looked like it."[1374]

The issue before the Supreme Court was whether Mrs. Lane's statements could be admitted as a dying declaration. Besides the statement in front of the doctor and a law enforcement officer, another witness, Dinah Robertson, heard Mrs. Lane say that Baxter struck her. On cross-examination, she was asked if someone in Mrs. Lane's presence had asked if Jim Baxter had any folks in the area and she said, "No; he is nothing but a loafer." The third witness, Mrs. Yeargin, stated that Mrs. Lane told her Jim Baxter struck her, and said, "I wish you had been here Sunday to see Jim Baxter, the one that hit me. He would not look at me."[1375]

Because Mrs. Lane made the statements after she said she did not think she would live, the statements were properly admitted as dying declarations.[1376]

Also important in the conviction was the testimony of a Negro detective who had been placed in the same jail cell as the killers. Church told the detective the crime facts. He repeated them in court.

Baxter received a death sentence. Church was convicted of first-degree murder with mitigating circumstances and was given a life sentence by Judge Robert Cantrell. Church was in prison at the time of Baxter's execution. The Supreme Court set April 8, 1886, as the execution date but the governor granted a reprieve to review the case.

Baxter was kept in the Davidson County jail until the day before his execution. He had been baptized in the jail by the Rev. Luke Mason, black, who became the favorite minister for black condemned men following the death of the Rev. Nelson Merry, black, who had attended several men. Telling his Nashville jail friends good-bye, Baxter said he was not afraid to die.

Jim Baxter also asserted his innocence. "I don't know why Andrew Church made the statement that he did about me and mixing me up in the killing, for I don't know nothing about it and never did. I wasn't there and never saw it." But when asked pointed questions about the crime, he never gave a straight answer, reported the newspaper.[1377]

Jim Baxter was hanged at 11:32 A.M. June 4, 1886. The exact location of the gallows is unknown. Baxter died of strangulation and was cut down in fifteen minutes. His body was given to friends for burial.

1887

Ben Brown, black, age 43. *Murder.*

The crime was committed about 9:00 P.M. November 9, 1885, six miles outside of Nashville off Harding Pike on a four-acre farm one mile from the famous Belle Meade Plantation, in Davidson County. The killer and the victim knew each other. The victim, Frank Arnold, a bright mulatto, age fifty-five, and known as Uncle Ben, lived in a one-room house. Also living there was a sixteen-year-old black boy Arnold had adopted, Noshey Lane. On the night of the killing, Ben Brown came to the house and told the boy to tell Arnold to meet him later that night to go possum hunting. When Arnold returned, he received this information and left, taking his dog with him. Arnold never returned, although his dog did about 11:00 P.M. with a gash on its head.

The details of the killing came from the testimony of Bill Brown, who turned state's evidence and was in prison at the time of Ben Brown's execution. (Bill Brown's real name was William Taylor; he had married Ben Brown's sister and simply took the name Brown.)[1378] The murder party consisted of Bill and Ben Brown, Nelson and his son Foster Joslin, Simon Fox and Robert Maclin, all black. They lived on a nearby farm. Simon Fox was a nephew. Fox lived with the Joslins. All were angry at Arnold for varying reasons, chiefly Arnold's lawsuit (which failed) to dispossess them of land upon which they lived which had belonged to Arnold's sister-in-law.

According to Bill's testimony, he served as a lookout while Ben lured the victim out of the house. As they walked into a thicket, Simon Fox shot Arnold, Ben hit him on the head with an iron bar, and someone stabbed him. The body was carried to a shallow grave, but as it was being placed in the ground, it groaned. Ben struck Arnold's head with an iron bar.[1379] The next evening, the body was dug up and taken to a stable. It was decapitated and dismembered, and the parts were brought to Nashville in a wagon and buried throughout a tanbark (tannery) on Belleville Street in a black part of town. On January 18, 1886, a worker saw an arm protruding from the bark — seven body parts were found. The head was placed in a creek for two weeks, then put in a bee gum which was placed in the henhouse.[1380]

According to the Tennessee Supreme Court, at 5:00 A.M. the day after the killing Ben Brown appeared at the house and told the boy (Noshey Lane) that Arnold had gone to Nashville to attend business and then was going to Kentucky to see his kinfolk. Because there was enough food in the house, the boy was to stay home. Brown also told the boy to say that Arnold had left the morning of the previous day to go to Nashville and "to say this when he got into court; that the lawyers would halloo him, and put him off in a little room."[1381]

According to the Supreme Court's opinion, "In explanation of the cut on the dog's head, he explained to the boy that the dog was trying to get on the railroad car with Arnold and the driving wheel struck its head, and he thought killed it."[1382] According to the boy, when Arnold left the evening before, he had locked the horse in the barn. This meant that the next morning, the boy could not enter the barn to feed or use the horse. Ben Brown returned the evening of the next day and gave him the key. Before the body was found, Ben Brown moved into Arnold's house, saying he had bought it and began to expand it.

According to the Supreme Court, "Brown came to Nashville, got someone to impersonate Arnold and procured a forgery of a note on Arnold, dated the 10th day of November 1885, payable to himself for $100, and also a conveyance of Arnold's horse and wagon and feed, at the recited consideration of $150 paid, and moved into Arnold's house, taking possession of all his property. He procured witnesses to agree to swear that Arnold had come to Nashville on the 10th of November 1885 and spent three days here, and then left for Kentucky."[1383]

In January of 1886, Arnold's body and "dissevered"[1384] limbs were found in Nashville and after a lengthy search, the head was discovered on Arnold's property. Upon this discovery, Brown began telling contradictory stories, chiefly that the actual killer was Bill Brown, who was charged as an accessory. According to Ben Brown, he saw Arnold's body on the night of the killing, and "Bill hired him to bring the body to town."[1385]

Ben Brown was tried with the Joslins and Fox; all were convicted on March 6, 1886, with Brown given death, the others life sentences. His appeal raised two issues. First, he was denied a continuance in order to procure witnesses. Second, an article regarding the case had appeared in a leading newspaper, the *Daily American*, prior to the trial.

The Tennessee Supreme Court stated that the defendant's affidavit failed to show how he was prejudiced by a lack of a continuance or the article. Likewise, while the court said that anyone who came near the defendant during the trial would be arrested, this did not show a level of "hostility and excitement inconsistent with a fair trial."[1386]

The undated newspaper article, included in the appellate record, contained firsthand accounts by several of Ben Brown's comrades-in-arms (black) who served with him in the United States Colored Troops during the Civil War. They explained how he shot and killed two fellow soldiers in cold blood, nearly beat an Irish lady to death, drowned another soldier, and robbed several others. The article quoted one former soldier: "If he is not hung by the law for what he is in jail for now, if they will just give the colored people a chance at him they'll fix him."[1387]

Without reciting the facts, the Supreme Court explained that Bill Brown testified that Ben Brown and others (including Simon Fox) were involved in a plot to quickly bury Arnold, and then later to remove, mutilate and dispose of the body. The Supreme Court said, "That the defendant participated in the murder for which he was convicted no member of this Court entertains any doubt whatsoever from this record."[1388]

A few days before Brown's execution, a report circulated that Simon Fox had died in prison and had given a deathbed statement that Bill Brown had stuck the first blow. The statement was disputed. The governor refused to accredit it, remarking that it did not mean that Ben Brown was not guilty or should not hang.

Ben Brown allowed all who wanted to see him in jail before his execution to say good-bye and throngs of blacks did so. He maintained his innocence and said that his conscience was clear and the scaffold was "free transportation to heaven." Likewise, "He urged upon each of his acquaintances to trust in God and lead a better life."[1389] The Rev. Luke Mason, black, who attended Brown on his last days, said that Brown did not want the local doctors to perform any experiments on his body to attempt to bring him back to life.

Under the statute passed in 1883, the Supreme Court's death warrant now ordered that capital defendants be executed inside the jail or in an "inclosure erected for that purpose ... adjacent to the prison, higher than the gallows, or so constructed to exclude the view of persons outside thereof, and in the presence of no more or other persons than are allowed by law to be present."[1390] For this reason, Ben Brown was the first person in Davidson County executed inside the Nashville jail, meeting his death on the morning of April 15, 1887. An editorial remarking on his protestation of innocence while guilty, yet asserting that he was heaven-bound, presented "a metaphysical study" that was "not without some solemnly ludicrous features."[1391]

1888

Napoleon B. Lester, white, age 50. *Murder.*

The crime was committed at 7:00 P.M. on July 26, 1887, on East Main Street in the town of Lebanon, in Wilson County. The killer was a harness maker who was disgruntled by actions of the victim, John T. Lane, white, age forty-seven. Lane was a lawyer and claim agent.

Lane was sitting in a chair outside his office when Lester suddenly appeared carrying a double-barreled shotgun. Just before he was shot, Lane said, "Lord God, Lester!" Lester then shot Lane at close range. As he lay on the sidewalk, Lane begged Lester not to shoot him again. Lester fired the second shot into Lane's side, killing him. Several witnesses saw the shooting. "Lester seemed to be laboring under great mental strain and soon became so weak he was seated in the chair that a moment or two before had been occupied by the man whose life he had taken."[1392] The dissembling Lester was taken to jail and he offered several reasons for killing the lawyer.

Lester had divorced his first wife in order to marry Mrs. Al Gibson, a wealthy widow. She was expecting a sizable insurance payment from the Knights of Pythias for her husband's death. Lane was retained for this purpose, but he arranged for the payments to be made in installments directly to the widow. Mrs. Gibson was unable to handle Lester's badgering her about money and sued for divorce. She retained Lane for this purpose. Lester vowed revenge but was not deemed a threat, in part because he had made threats against the local members of the Knights as well.[1393]

Lester's defense at trial was insanity. No expert testimony was offered and the only lay testimony came from a witness who stated that Lester had said, after the shooting, he had seen God in the vicinity of Lebanon who had told him to do it. On the stand, Lester said, "I killed him because he disgraced my wife and children and God told me to go and kill Lane. I was going to kill the negro woman also, but God told me just to kill Lane. God had also told me to kill the negro woman. I saw God at the cow pen and also on Academy Hill.

God looked like a large man and at that time had no wings."[1394] Lester asserted that Lane and his wife had been sexually intimate and this caused the breakup of their marriage. With no witnesses prepared to support this contention, the judge refused to allow Lester to assert this defense. The conviction was affirmed by the Tennessee Supreme Court, but the opinion cannot be located.

Lester was kept in the Davidson County jail until the day before his execution. While there, he was ministered to by women from the Salvation Army. He became religious and published a long letter complimenting the women on their great work in saving his soul and others. His letter said, "I will approach the throne of grace and mercy truthfully declaring that it was a desire to cherish and protect such chaste womanhood as yours that impelled the commission of the act for which I die."[1395] A lethal quantity of morphine had been found in his cell earlier.

Lester was taken to the Wilson County jail the day before his execution. As he was being driven from the train station to the jail, crowds gathered to look at him. He waved and bowed to them. He examined the gallows, which was inside the jail, and suggested a few changes. He was taken that afternoon to a photographer for some pictures with the handcuffs removed. When he returned to the jail, his speech was "nonsensical and disconnected, suggesting great nervousness."[1396] He sent word that he wanted to speak with his now ex-wife. She refused to come but sent a message that she would raise his children (her stepchildren) as her own.

Lester made a will in which he gave the murder weapon and his pocketknife to his son in Nashville, the money on his person to a fellow inmate and his real estate to be divided among his children. He also said that his sister had eight thousand dollars in a Nashville bank which he also wanted divided among his children.

Napoleon B. Lester went to the gallows in front of thirty witnesses, six of whom were invited by Lester. After he mounted the gallows, Lester was asked if he had anything to say. Lester gave a "lengthy and disconnected" speech in which he blasted the newspapers for saying that Mrs. Gibson was "as pure a woman as ever lived in Lebanon." He insisted that George Gibson, her son, had told Lester that his mother and Lane had spent two nights together in a Nashville hotel the previous April. He said that Maggie Gibson, her daughter, had said she saw the two in a room together.

Lester took special aim at Circuit Judge Cantrell, who was in attendance, and criticized him for not allowing him to speak against his wife and her relationship with Lane. "You, sir, spoke of me in the crowded courtroom with a forward mouth and a false tongue, and God will be the judge between you and I." Lester finished his speech by saying he was going to heaven and forgave everyone.[1397]

The Reverend B.F. Haynes of Nashville's McKendree Methodist Church offered a prayer. Afterwards, Lester said good-bye to all the officials and exacted a promise from Sheriff W.P. Brandy that he would meet him in heaven.

As Lester's arms were pinioned, he said with a laugh, "Don't tie them too tight." Then the trap was sprung without warning. Lester dropped cleanly at 11:55 A.M. on April 20, 1888, and his pulse stopped at 12:06. He was cut down four minutes later. Lester was placed in a coffin and taken to Nashville for burial.

None of Lester's brothers or relatives were present at the execution. A white artificial rose that had been pinned to his lapel came off during the hanging. This was placed on his body in the coffin. Lester was the first white man legally executed in Wilson County since the Civil War.

Hicks Carmichael, black, age 24. *Murder.*

The crime was committed at 10:00 A.M. on May 20, 1888, at a railroad work camp fifteen miles north of Knoxville. The killer was a laborer at the camp. Because it was Sunday, Carmichael was relaxing in his tent. The victim was deputy sheriff Doctor A. Shipe, white, age thirty-nine, known as John Shipe.

Deputy Shipe and a constable had come to the camp to arrest Carmichael on an outstanding robbery warrant from Morgan County. Carmichael was sitting half-dressed on a cot when the men came in and asked if Carmichael was present, whereupon he identified himself.

The deputy said, "You are our prisoner." Carmichael replied, "Please read your warrant and let me know what charge you have." The deputy replied, "You are wanted for robbery," and began reading the warrant aloud. Without warning, Carmichael sprang forward with a pistol in each hand and began shooting. One of the bullets hit the deputy in the heart and he died instantly. The constable was not hit by the fusillade of bullets, which pierced his clothing.[1398]

Carmichael made a dash for the woods. The constable aimed at him but the revolver misfired. A coroner's jury was promptly convened and with three witnesses to the shooting it was quickly decided Hicks Carmichael was the shooter. In short order, over a hundred men began looking for Carmichael, encouraged by a $350 reward offered by the county and another $300 offered by the governor.

Carmichael had been reared in Cocke County and made his way there. He hired a friend to take him through rural North Carolina to escape. He was spotted and shots were fired. A citizen later saw him in the woods near the French Broad River. When he refused to surrender, the citizen shot him with a buckshot-filled shotgun. The wound looked serious, but it did not prevent Carmichael from jumping into the river. He swam across it and hid under hay in a barn. The citizen followed by holding onto a saw log. He and others came upon the barn and Carmichael was captured without more violence.[1399]

After the prisoner was taken to the jail, the sheriff had great difficulty in keeping Carmichael safe from a lynch mob. The "bright yellow" Carmichael was said to have some Indian blood. His mother had brought him from North Carolina at the age of nine, and he had learned to read and write on his own. At the time of his arrest he was wanted on an Alabama murder charge. He had a brother who was reportedly hanged for murder, location unknown.[1400]

Carmichael's trial, with appointed counsel Gen. R.N. Hood, lasted only two hours because the defense put on no proof. The jury found him guilty in fifteen minutes. It cannot be determined whether there was an appeal to the Tennessee Supreme Court, but because of the proximity of the crime to the date of execution, July 20, 1888, an appeal was unlikely.

During his time in the Knoxville jail, Carmichael was visited by over five thousand people. Two black ministers attended him and after some effort convinced him to profess religion. Three days before his death, he sent a letter to his mother. The letter contained two gold dollars, one for his mother and the other for his infant son, whom he had conceived with a woman known as Dicey Smith. The letter concluded, "I am prepared to meet my doom. Meet me in heaven. Tell Charley Carmichael to be sure and come after my body. Farewell, Your Son, Hicks Carmichael."[1401]

The morning of the execution was spent in a prolonged session of prayer, singing and Bible reading with cell mates and ministers. The jailers had given them bananas and melons, and they sang, "Going to Join the Angels," "Beautiful Home," "Sowing the Seed," "The Old Ark Is Moving," and "Trouble in the Mind."

The gallows was built outside his cell inside the Knox County jail. Carmichael was provided new clothes for his death: a new shirt, a collar, a black tie, a handsome cutaway suit and glossy shoes. When he was dressed, he was visited by his mother, two family friends, and Dicey Smith, who was holding his six-month-old baby. Carmichael wept bitterly during the visit and began to break down but was cheered up by one of the guards. The cell mates sang, "When I Am Dead and in My Grave, Don't Weep for Me," and a photographer took pictures of Carmichael for the baby and Carmichael's mother.

The ministers returned, read the 14th chapter of Job, sang "Jesus, Lover of My Soul," and prayed fervently for him. Carmichael, bent over a chair, wept bitterly, but steadied himself when he heard the hymn, "There Is a Fountain Filled with Blood."

At 12:45 P.M. on July 20, 1888, Carmichael was taken from his cell. He was executed fifteen minutes later. When asked if he had anything to say to the handful of spectators, he said, "I am going fast to heaven. I don't fear it. I am trusting in Him, and thank Him for it. I want to state I am dying this evening for Jesus. I feel that I am as bold as a lion and not afraid to die. I feel that I am bound for heaven and a soldier for Jesus. Though I have been sadly scorned by this world, I forgive everyone. I give my thanks to Sheriff Lones, his assistants and others who have shown me so much kindness while here. I expect to meet you all in heaven; meet me there. Farewell."[1402]

At Carmichael's request, two ministers sang "I Am Going Home to Die No More," and the noose and cap were placed over his head. Sheriff Lones asked if he was ready and Carmichael gave a faint, "Yes." The trap was sprung at exactly one o'clock. The drop was clean and the heart was still beating two minutes later.

The body was cut down eighteen minutes later. He was placed in a casket donated by undertaker H.B. Rule. The body was taken to the jail yard and over one thousand people passed by to look at it. Later, his cousin Charley Carmichael came and got the body. Charley sent it by train to Cocke County for burial.

Deputy Sheriff Shipe was survived by his mother, an invalid sister, his wife and four small children who depended on him for support. One of the Knoxville newspapers started a campaign to raise money for the needy and sorrow-stricken family and over one thousand dollars was raised.[1403]

1889

Mack Francis, black, age 62. *Murder.*
Jim "Blue Jim" Turney, black, age 63. *Murder.*

The crime was committed on the evening of August 31, 1888, on a road about a mile from the community of Round Top near the old Woodbury and Murfreesboro Pike, in rural Wilson County. The killers were longtime criminals. Turney had been released from prison a few weeks prior to the killing. The killers knew the victim, who had attended a service at a black church called Prosperity Church. A special collection had been taken in order to hold a revival, and the killers noticed the victim seemed to have a lot of money. They decided to kill him as he walked home. The victim, Leonard Martin, was white, age forty-three.

Len Martin was described as a "half-wit, semi-imbecile, yet harmless and well-meaning." The newspaper said, "His practice of associating with negroes was his chief fault. He was a good worker but a very poor manager."[1404] Martin lived with his mother, white, age sixty-two. In order to earn money which he spent at black gatherings, he went from place to place to perform odd jobs with black folk.

As Martin walked down the road, the killers came up behind him. Jim Turney fired the first two shots with his pistol. Martin cried, "Jim! Jim!" and then Jim Turney said to Francis, "Shoot! Why don't you shoot?" Francis then shot Martin twice. Turney then shot him twice again. The killers took seven dollars from the body. They were disappointed because they thought Martin had more. Turney took four dollars and Francis three.[1405] The pair then dragged the body into the woods, where it was found the next day.

Turney said to his stepson the following day, "If anyone asks you where I was last night, tell them that I came home with you and your mother from church, and that I stayed home."[1406] When authorities announced that they were looking for Turney and Francis, the two men left town and were captured in different parts of middle Tennessee within a few days.

The details of the trial are unknown. The case was appealed to the Tennessee Supreme Court, but the opinion cannot be located.

The men were kept in the Davidson County jail for their safety; the circuit judge made a specific finding that the Wilson County jail was not suitable. In jail, the men were visited by scores of people, including ministers and reporters. Turney angrily turned away the reporters and denounced the judge. He explained that he had voted for Judge Cantrell, but he had not "treated him right in sending his papers to the Supreme Court."[1407]

As the execution day approached, both men professed religion and were convinced their souls were saved. Francis left a letter that advised his friends to mend their ways and announced, "I have joined the Primitive Baptist Church, that is, the Hardside Baptist Church."[1408] Francis also confessed the details of the crime and told the newspapers that the Reverend Luke Mason, the Nashville minister who had baptized them, would read their last statement from the gallows. Francis and Turney also confessed to the murder of a peddler they had killed before Martin.

The Wilson County sheriff went to Nashville and prevailed upon the General Assembly to set the limit of the place of execution to two miles because there was no suitable location within the mandatory one mile of the courthouse.[1409] The new statute also required that if the condemned was taken outside of the jail for the execution then he must be taken in a closed vehicle. Mack Francis and Jim Turney were executed at 12:19 P.M. March 26, 1889. The exact outdoor location is unknown.

On the gallows, the Rev. Mason read a statement which described the murder, and sheriff W.P. Bandy asked if they agreed with what he read. The men replied, "We do." Then Francis was asked if it were true that Turney had threatened him unless he shot Martin. Francis said he was afraid Turney would shoot him if he failed to act, but Turney had not actually threatened him.[1410]

After the prayers and songs by the Reverend Mason and another minister, the men said to the small group that they hoped to meet them in heaven. By this time Turney had weakened and could hardly stand. The caps and ropes were placed on the men. Deputy Mount began to count and when he said "Four," Deputy Baird, who was standing below, took a hammer and struck the pin that held the trap.

The pin did not budge at first but deputy Baird's second attempt was successful. The bodies dropped cleanly. Turney's neck was broken by the three-and-a-half-foot drop. Mack Francis "struggled for life for some time, and the noise made by him in strangling to death was simply awful and it was about twenty minutes before his pulse was gone." Turney and Francis were cut down at 12:38 and 12:44 P.M. respectively. An undertaker took charge of the bodies. Francis was to buried in Auburn,

Cannon County, and Turney was to be buried in Liberty, Wilson County.

It was soon believed that Mack Francis was not actually killed by the rope. This was because few people saw the drop, because he struggled so long, and because the bodies were quickly put into coffins and carried away.

By April 6, 1889, the newspapers had given wide support to the notion that the wagon's jostling had brought Mack Francis back to life and that he began to move about in his coffin. The newspaper reported, "News reached here tonight that a strange negro passed through Dekalb County. He stayed with a negro man all night and told him that he was Mack Francis, in proof of which he showed the marks on his neck made by the rope." The newspaper continued, "The news came from a reliable source and it is stated that the people are greatly excited over the presence of a live dead man in their midst.[1411]

Charles Wirt, black, age 30. *Murder.*

The crime was committed on Christmas Eve, 1888, on a road near the black community of Warren in rural Fayette County. The killer was the victim's paramour. The victim was Evaline Hester, black, age twenty-two. Wirt had repeatedly warned and threatened Evaline that if he saw her with another man he would kill her. On the day of the killing Wirt saw her walking with another man. Intoxicated, he flew into a rage. He chased her and shot her in the heart. The next day he turned himself in to the sheriff. Wirt's defense was that the shooting was accidental. It cannot be determined whether the case was appealed to the Tennessee Supreme Court.

Charles Wirt was hanged at 1:00 P.M. on July 13, 1889, on a specially built gallows in sight of the Fayette County jail in Somerville. It was eighteen feet square and built around two trees which had been cut off to serve as uprights for the crossbeam. Thomas Jefferson was executed the same day in Memphis.

Two thousand people stood around the gallows and those on the heights could see something of the execution. Mounting the gallows with a firm step, Wirt stood on the platform as the Rev. William McMichael, a black Baptist minister, exhorted him to confess. When he was done, the Rev. B.M. Cowan of the Presbyterian Church tried to induce the same. Both failed. Wirt still insisted the killing was an accident, and his sin was getting involved with a woman not his wife who was the cause of his ruin. He said he had unshaken confidence in the Lord and would be saved. He said, "I am safe. I want to meet you all in heaven. I can look you all in the face and say that I am innocent."[1412]

Wirt continued talking about his family and said, "I am done. I have nothing more to say." The Rev. McMichael then offered a prayer asking mercy on the soul of the condemned man. The sheriff toyed with the rope in an attempt to give Wirt more time to confess. Wirt became nervous, started patting the floor with his feet, and sang a Negro spiritual.

As the noose was slipped over his head, he said, "Gentlemen, I am now standing on the gallows, but God says his children don't fear to die." Turning to the victim's brother, in the small group inside the stockade, he said, "Brother Jim, I am not afraid." When the town clock struck one, the sheriff said, "Good-bye, Charlie," and pulled the trap. Wirt's neck was broken and he was taken down thirty minutes later. Wirt's body was placed in a plain pine coffin and given to his brother, who took it to the community of Warren, where Wirt's wife lived.

The local militia company, called the Phelan Light Guards, was credited with keeping order throughout the day. It brandished rifles with bayonets. The weather may have been a factor as well. It rained heavily throughout the day and most of the spectators stood in two inches of water attempting to see the execution.

Thomas Jefferson, black, age 32. *Murder.*

The crime was committed about midnight on October 20, 1888, in the apartment of William Ragland at 363 Union Street in Memphis, in Shelby County. The killer was angry that his former girlfriend, with whom he had lived for a time, was seeing another man. She was Alice Rogers, black, age unknown, a woman of bad reputation. A few months before, Jefferson had married a young black woman to avoid a bastardy charge, but they had not lived together. The victim was William Ragland, black, age thirty-eight. He and Jefferson had quarreled openly over Alice Rogers's attention. Jefferson had brandished a knife and told several people he was ready to use it on Ragland. He told some that if he found her with Ragland again, "Jack Walsh would haul his dead body off."[1413]

On the night of the murder, Jefferson went to Alice's house. Finding her not home, he went to the Ragland apartment. It consisted of two rooms over the stable of a white man's house. It was entered by an outside stairway. He called Ragland, who opened the door. Alice, who was a co-defendant,[1414] testified she saw Ragland strike Jefferson, but did not see the killing. She said she ran down the steps when it began. The proof showed the room was showered with blood. There was no blood underneath a piece of scantling beside the bed, but blood on it. There was blood on a pair of woman's shoes and bloody female footprints leading outside.

Jefferson insisted the killing was self-defense. According to the newspaper, by the time of his execution, he had rehearsed the story so many times that he believed it himself.[1415] "It was just this very way," he said. "When I went to Ragland's house, I was looking for my woman so that I could get my clothes. It was raining and I was wet. Ragland insisted on my coming in, and when I finally entered he assaulted me with a piece of scantling. He hit me several times and I thought of the razor which I had borrowed to shave with next morning. The room was dark because Ragland put out the light and I couldn't see him. I tried to escape but fell over a trunk, and in rising I made a slash at him with my razor and cut him. I couldn't tell where or how. I then got to the door and escaped."[1416]

Jefferson said, "I feel satisfied that what I have done was done in self-defense. If I had not killed him, he would have killed me. I feel certain that he would have done so."[1417] The conviction was affirmed by the Tennessee Supreme Court, but the opinion cannot be located. Jefferson was convinced his lawyer, a former judge, would get his sentence commuted to life imprisonment. He was encouraged because the sheriff delayed the noon execution until one o'clock. The newspaper described Jefferson as a mulatto. "He is not ill favored and does not resemble the orthodox murderer. There is a sinister sneer about the corners of his mouth when he laughs."[1418]

Jefferson was eager to talk to everyone who came to the jail whether they offered cigars, liquor or salvation. When told the governor would not intervene, he said he was not afraid:

> No sir. I never weakened from the time I was arrested and I'm not going to weaken. You see, when a poor man can't help himself he must make the worst the best and trust in God. Of course, I am a poor man and have no money. If I had money I could save my life; but I haven't, and I must die. But what does it matter? They can hurt my body but they cannot hurt my soul. This trouble is my first and greatest, and it will be my last. It will soon be over, and when it is over there can be no more trouble in the grave. A man's trouble ends there, if he makes his peace with God and trusts in Him, and I trust in Him. A man who has no money must make the worst his best and be satisfied. Death comes only once, and after death there is no trouble.[1419]

When the sheriff asked him how tall he was in order to give him a new suit, Jefferson said he was six foot, three inches. Measured, he was six feet tall. Jefferson had been visited by four black ministers, notably the Rev. T.H. McCauley of Beale Street Baptist Church. The ministers insisted Jefferson was saved. He had a large quantity of beer with his breakfast and continued to drink "whiskey and cocktails" until taken to the scaffold.

A 10:40 A.M. a woman named Nancy Perkins came to the jail and brought her infant son, who had been fathered by Jefferson. He carried the boy around the jail proudly. Later, he was taken to see his coffin and seemed concerned that it was not big enough. He lay on top to satisfy himself. He was given a "bottle of cocktail," and asked if it had been poisoned. "You people must hang me, but not poison me," and insisted the sheriff take a drink. Afterward, he wanted to drink the rest of the bottle, but it was taken away. Back at his cell, he did not want to wear his coat, but finally relented, and put on white gloves.

Thomas Jefferson was hanged on July 13, 1889, at 1:37 P.M. inside the Shelby County jail using the rope and gallows material previously used to hang John McKeever outside in the jail courtyard. He was executed the same day as Charles Wirt in Somerville.

Jefferson stumbled at the gallows steps, but then "ran nimbly" up them. At this point, he began complaining bitterly about being handcuffed. The small crowd waited for Jefferson to make his final statement. He had promised to give an account of the crime from the scaffold. "I have a little speech to make on the place [motioning toward the scaffold] and I will make my speech there. I don't think it is any use to put anything in the papers now until it is over. I will make my speech on the place."[1420]

Just as he was about to speak, a "peal of thunder broke over the building and sounded through the jail," and Jefferson could not talk. "Be a man, Tom," urged the sheriff, "and now say what you are going to say." Jefferson replied that he would, but could not talk properly with his hands in handcuffs. "Come, Tom, say what you're going to say like a man. Begin and go ahead," repeated the sheriff.

Jefferson raised his voice, "Gentlemen, loose my hands and let me talk. Let me do as I want to this once; it's the last time. I'm in your power and can't get away and there is no danger. There's Mr. Mason. He's a good man. He knows me since I was a boy, long before this trouble. He knows me, and he is a good man. I want to step out on the trap door and make a speech. You gentlemen ought to allow me to be free for a few minutes, it will soon be over."[1421]

"Go on, Tom, say what you're going to say," replied the sheriff, ignoring his request. According to the newspaper:

> But Tom wouldn't. He was struggling for time. Minutes became ages to him. Finally the clergymen arose and began reading. Tom would turn from the right to the left and now and then burst out in a great laugh. When the services were over the parson gave out a hymn, "Am I Born to Die?" while Jefferson was asking, "Let me pray." When the clergymen began singing, Jefferson sang too — sometimes behind them and sometimes before them and sometimes between them, but always loud, sonorous and strong, balancing from one foot to the other and clapping his manacled hands. Sometimes when the preachers were filling the building with their swelling notes, Tom would stop suddenly, say something to one of the attendants and then break out in a great loud laugh, but presently realizing that now was the time to be devout, he would join in and try to make up for lost time by good and generous measure.[1422]

After the preacher bent down and gave an earnest prayer, Jefferson asked to speak. But when be did, all he could say was that his hands were tied and he could not speak. The newspaper described what happened next: "He raised his white gloved hands and blew his nose, then spit on the floor and watched it fall. He had to be lifted on the scaffold, and when the black cap was being placed on his head he asked again to be heard. He was apparently earnest this time and the Sheriff paused, leaving the black cap on his head, his face exposed, giving him a ludicrous appearance."[1423]

Jefferson stood awhile and said he wanted to speak, but when urged to do so, said, "Friends, meet me in glory!" The noose was now placed and the cap returned over his head. Suddenly, he complained that the rope was too tight, that it was pulling him upward. When the rope was loosened, it came down too far and he grabbed it with his gloved hands. Again, he asked to say a few words. "Go on, Tom," said the sheriff. He began dissembling and when he said, "Friends and relations, meet me in glory. Good-bye!" the sheriff tripped the lever.[1424]

The drop was clean. His pulse stopped in six minutes and he was cut down in twenty. The body was placed in a coffin and removed by the undertaker, whose vehicle had difficulty making its way through hundreds waiting outside. The sheriff told the jailer to take the rope outside and show it to the crowd.[1425] Commenting on the delay caused by Jefferson's stalling, the sheriff remarked, "Twenty-three minutes more and I would have been a murderer."[1426] At the time of Jefferson's execution, Alice Rogers was at the county work farm serving a one-year sentence for larceny.

Tom Yates Condor, white, age 43. *Murder.*

The crime was committed on September 12, 1888, on the rural farm some two miles west of Troy (then the county seat of Obion County) in the cabin occupied by Mr. and Mrs. Jack Riley. The killing occurred during daylight hours and was staged to look like a suicide. The killer was the victim's son-in-law. The victim was Jackson Riley, white, age fifty-four. Condor had been carrying on a sexual liaison with Mrs. Riley.[1427]

Condor had been trying for months to get Mrs. Riley to agree with his plan. She finally assented. While the husband was sleeping, Condor crept close and shot him with a shotgun, putting the gun down so as to look as if Riley had shot himself. The couple told neighbors that Riley had been complaining about headaches and had long threatened to kill himself. A coroner's jury was summoned and it ruled "that Mr. Riley had come to his death in some unknown manner, Thomas Condor and Mrs. Riley being present in or near the house at the time of the death of Mr. Riley."[1428]

Mr. Riley was buried that afternoon. But the couple departed too quickly. They were seen heading out of town with all their belongings the next day, bound for Missouri. Someone alerted district attorney James G. Smith and he prepared an indictment. The couple was arrested shortly before crossing the state line. They were placed in different parts of the jail, and Mrs. Riley began confessing immediately. Condor, barely literate, sent her notes telling her to be quiet. In one he said he would put the "fire-fenes of hell" on her if she didn't stop talking. (He meant fiends).

The pair was convicted, largely on Mrs. Riley's testimony. Condor was found guilty with mitigating circumstances, but the judge ordered the death penalty. Mrs. Riley was tried separately and given life imprisonment. The cases were appealed to the Tennessee Supreme Court, but the opinion cannot be located. Condor insisted to the last that he was innocent. He had two adult children living in Perry County at the time.

Thomas Condor was executed on July 16, 1889

(the date sometimes given as July 13 or May 10), in an enclosed gallows surrounded by a plank wall, inside which only a few spectators were allowed. Condor was taken to the gallows in a wagon and over one hundred special deputies were present carrying weapons. The exact time of the execution is unknown, but when the cap was placed over his head he was asked if he was ready. He replied, "Yes. Good-bye, gentlemen."[1429] About a thousand people had come to town the day of the execution, but they saw little except Condor's trip to the gallows.

This was the first and only legal execution in Obion County. The trap was pulled by Sheriff F.B. "Dick" Taylor, a stern and fearless former Confederate soldier. He was one of the survivors of his regiment that surrendered at Greensboro, North Carolina. Only fourteen of the original regiment of one thousand were present. There was some question in the community whether Condor was actually going to heaven as he said he was. Seven years earlier Condor had become a Mormon. He was buried in an unmarked grave in Ebenezer Cemetery. Mrs. Riley was in the penitentiary in Nashville at the time of his execution. The extensive coverage of the Condor trial and execution captured the attention of the community and ensured the success of a fledgling newspaper, the *Troy News-Banner*.[1430]

John Hanner, black, age 28. *Murder.*

The crime was committed at 10:00 P.M. on July 14, 1887, at the victim's home in a rural area of Henry County. The killer, whose farm was next to the victim's, was carrying on an illicit affair with the victim's wife, Hannah Ellis, black, age thirty-seven. The victim, Joe Ellis, black, age forty-two, was shot at a close distance, less than twelve feet. He was shot while standing on his porch smoking his pipe.

Hanner was the prime suspect in the case, but an unusual piece of evidence convicted him. Ellis had been shot by a muzzle-loading shotgun. A piece of paper from the gun wadding was compared to a paper found at Hanner's house which had been torn to form the wadding. The paper and the wadding found near Ellis's body tallied precisely, being an advertisement for "Three C's, Certain Chill Cure." The paper was distinctive because it was printed in German on one side and English on the other.[1431] The same type evidence had sent William R. Rea to the Giles County gallows on May 19, 1882.[1432]

Hanner was tried with Hannah Ellis. She received life imprisonment, but her conviction was overturned on appeal to the Tennessee Supreme Court. The opinion in the joint cases cannot be located.

The details of the execution are unknown except that Hanner was hanged on August 13, 1889, in Paris on a scaffold which adjoined the jail. He told his employer that he was innocent, but confessed his sins to two ministers and said he was prepared to die.[1433] Fifteen minutes before the execution he asked for a knife to peel a peach. It was denied. He sent everyone away and promptly took a whiskey bottle, broke it, and slashed his leg and neck, coming close to the jugular vein. He bled profusely and refused to wipe the blood away, forcing the jailer to do it. After the wound was bandaged, Hanner then dressed for the execution. He was given a large quantity of whiskey.

On the way to the gallows he gave way and had to be assisted down the jail stairs and up the gallows steps. He shook hands with the sheriff and chief deputy and bade everyone good-bye. Sheriff Blakemore loosened the trap at 1:10 P.M. and Hanner fell cleanly, breaking his neck, and he was declared dead in ten minutes. He was cut down in eighteen minutes. About two thousand people had come to town on the day of the execution, but few saw it. Hannah Ellis was awaiting a second trial at the time of Hanner's execution. The outcome of her case is unknown.

1890

Edward Carr, black, age 28. *Murder*

The crime was committed on the evening of November 9, 1889, on Court Street in Memphis, in Shelby County. The victim was the killer's wife, Sallie Carr, black, age twenty-four. The couple had moved from Somerville, where they had married in August. Carr was a laborer helping build a railroad caisson, but was unhappy with the cost of living in Memphis. He wanted to move to Mississippi, but Sallie refused and moved in with another woman. On the day of the killing, the two were walking down the street.

Meeting the women on the street carrying washed clothing, Carr said, "Well, Sallie, I am going to kill you."[1434] He shot her and she ran into a nearby icehouse. He followed and shot her three more times, once in the mouth. Comforted by her friend, she said, "I will never see my Mamma anymore."[1435] Carr walked briskly away. Three days later he surrendered at a police station. He explained he had bought the pistol the morning of the killing at a "Jew store" on Beale Street. He said he needed it for self-defense because his co-workers were "very disagreeable and quarrelsome."

A witness said he had talked with Carr about the Parker Harris (q.v.) trial and Carr said that he could kill a woman. Carr denied having had the conversation.[1436] Carr attempted to plead guilty, but his court-appointed lawyer, Col. Nate Taylor, convinced him to plead not guilty after explaining the charge carried the death penalty.

At trial, Carr said, "I do not know why I killed her. It was not because she offended me. We had lived happily together. I loved her. I loved her well enough to die for her. It grieved me to think that I loved her so well, and she would not go with me. I thought she was persuaded to leave me, or she would not have done so. I was troubled to death. I could not sleep. I worked on the Midland railroad for two years." He was convicted December 17, 1889. The conviction was appealed to the Tennessee Supreme Court, but the opinion cannot be located.

Carr was one of three men executed at 11:20 A.M. inside the Shelby County jail on June 24, 1890. He stood in the middle and was hanged with Hardy Ballard and Parker Harris. The triple gallows was used on them first. Frank Brenish, white, had insisted he not be executed with the others because they were black. The sheriff accommodated his request by enlarging the gallows trap from two to three, and allowing Brenish to die alone after them. The blacks loudly proclaimed their indignation.[1437]

The same gallows had been used to execute Sandy Matthews, John McKeever, and Thomas Jefferson. The rope had been borrowed from Fayette County, where it had been used to hang Charles Wirt on July 13, 1889. It had been soaped to slip smoothly.[1438] Carr and Ballard had spent the day before their execution singing and praying. Carr had been given several glasses of beer the night before his execution to help him go to sleep. But he consumed no alcohol the day of the execution.

He had been ministered to by the Rev. Taylor Nightengale of Beale Street Baptist Church. Carr was very nervous on the gallows and could hardly stand. He shook "like an aspen leaf," his chest heaved and tears streamed from his eyes. His last words were largely unintelligible but he asked that his picture be sent to relatives in the town of Echo, in Middle Tennessee. He warned young men to beware of evil and stopped abruptly.

Following prayers and remarks by the three black ministers, who concurred that the three were saved and going to heaven, the ropes and caps were placed. The sheriff's pull on the trigger lever sent the bodies downward but the rope on Carr had shifted to under his chin and his body convulsed for several minutes. He was cut down twenty-four minutes later. The bodies were placed in bunks in empty cells in the jail where they were viewed by a multitude who wished to see them.

Parker Harris, black, age 30. *Murder.*

The crime was committed at 7:30 P.M. August 18, 1889, at 258 Hernando Street, in downtown Memphis, in Shelby County. The victim was Letha "Lettie" Harris, black, age twenty-five, the killer's wife. She was described as a beautiful octoroon, he a magnificently proportioned mulatto.

Lettie had been out for a buggy ride with two other black women. The buggy was stopped in front of her home and she had just gotten out. Parker Harris suddenly approached and asked to talk to her. "She turned from him haughtily, remarking that she never intended to have anything to do with him again while she lived."[1439] "Then you shall not live!" he shouted, slashing a large knife across her throat, severing the jugular vein. He then slashed his own throat, falling on top of her. He got up and ran away but was found collapsed several blocks away from loss of blood.

The case was identical to Frank Brenish's killing of his wife a few weeks before on July 5, 1889. Each had also slashed his own windpipe, but was saved by medical treatment that was not expected to save him. The similarity was such that the newspaper speculated they might have a joint trial.[1440] They did not. Brenish was convicted first.[1441] It cannot be determined whether Parker Harris appealed his conviction, but it seems likely.

As his execution date drew near, Harris wrote a letter that was published in the newspaper, saying that a black Memphis lawyer, Madison Vonner, had taken advantage of him to get his hands on Lettie and had turned her affection away from him.[1442]

Harris was given as much liquor as he wanted in the jail the days before his execution, and spent most of his time "keeping his system inoculated with alcohol." He was angry and surly and rarely talked to visitors. He said he would walk firmly to the gallows and die like a man. He said he was not afraid to die and "has had all the religion he wants."[1443]

Harris was executed at 11:20 A.M., June 24, 1890, on the gallows inside the Shelby County jail along side Ed Carr and Hardy Ballard. The three had complained loudly about the sheriff's decision to execute them separately from Frank Brenish. Because Brenish had complained he didn't want to be hanged with the three black men, the sheriff allowed him to die alone, after them. The gallows was designed to hold two. The sheriff modified it to hold three but it was too small for four.

Harris was attended by the Rev. Robert Talley, black, a Methodist minister. After the execution he told the newspaper, "Brother Harris made one of the brightest professions I ever heard."[1444] He had also baptized Harris, he said.

Harris had been given a new suit, compliments of the sheriff. "We're going to get a present now," he said with a hearty laugh as the sheriff came with the clothes. All three wore gloves to their deaths. Harris and the other two condemned men walked to the gallows with four black ministers. Each said something on behalf of the men, and several hymns were sung.

Each man was asked if he wanted to make a statement. Harris spoke last. He said he had been forgiven for all his sins. He had committed a great crime, but he had repented and would be welcomed by the angels. "This is no death at all. It's only heaven," he said in a loud voice.[1445]

After the prayers and hymns, the ropes and caps were placed and Sheriff McLendon sprung the trap without warning. The drop was clean.

Harris swung half around once and his legs drew up convulsively one time. The knot had slipped to the back of his head, but he died in three minutes. The five-eighths-inch robe which had been used to hang Thomas Jefferson and John McKeever had cut into his neck and had to be removed with a knife. He was cut down with the others twenty-four minutes later. All the bodies, including that of Brenish, were placed in bunks in empty cells in the jail. At least a thousand visitors walked by to gaze at them.

Hardy Ballard, black, age 45. *Murder.*

The crime was committed about 8:00 P.M. on Christmas night, 1889, on South Main Street in Memphis in Shelby County. The victim was streetcar driver G. Emmett Pinkston, white, age twenty-one. Pinkston had told Ballard to get off the car because he had not paid his fare. Ballard got off. He continued walking in the same direction as the horse-drawn streetcar. A few blocks away, the car entered the turntable, turned around and stopped. Ballard approached the car and demanded to know why Pinkston had ordered him off the car. Pinkston replied, "Because, you black son of a bitch, I did." Ballard insisted he had paid the nickel fare. "You are a damned liar!" replied Pinkston. The pair traded insults, Ballard saying, "I'll knock the hell out of you," and Pinkston replying, "I can give as much hell as you can."[1446]

Ballard struck Pinkston over the eye with his fist. Pinkston retrieved an iron hook from beside his seat and hit Ballard on the top of the head. Using his left arm to ward off further blows, Ballard lunged forward and stabbed Pinkston three times. The victim exclaimed, "Oh, God, I am stabbed!" He died in a passenger's arms in the car. Witnesses heard the fleeing Ballard say, "I got the son of a bitch." Other witnesses heard him say that evening, "The fellow got my money, but he got my knife with it." A fifteen-year-old boy, Jesse Cates, watched where Ballard ran, took two policemen to the area, and identified Ballard, who was arrested the next day.[1447] Ballard vigorously denied any wrongdoing, but admitted he had returned to the car to get "satisfaction" but not to get his money back nor to cause injury. Ballard claimed self-defense, but no witnesses offered proof on this issue and he was convicted January 2, 1890. The conviction was affirmed by the Tennessee Supreme Court, but the opinion cannot be located.

Ballard was given as much beer as he wanted to help him go to sleep the night before his execution. He was ministered to by the Rev. Robert Talley, black, a Methodist minister, who baptized him two days earlier and who gave him the last sacrament, as well as the Rev. W.F.H. Morgan, black, who accompanied him to the gallows. Ballard and fellow jail inmate Ed Carr were given new suits in which to die, compliments of the sheriff.

Hardy Ballard was executed at 11:20 A.M. on June 24, 1890, on the gallows with Ed Carr and Parker Harris, both wife-killers. He was the first to address the small crowd allowed to see the executions. "I've been in this world a long time and now I'm going to meet my God. I haven't got much sense, but I know what I done. I done it and I done wrong. God has forgiven though, and I am not afraid. Please give my body to Brother Frank Morgan, and let him have everything I leave behind."[1448]

After Carr and Harris spoke, the three ministers gave remarks and prayers. The ropes and caps were placed. Without warning Sheriff McLendon pulled the lever and Ballard fell with the others. His neck was broken and there was no movement. He hung twenty-four minutes before being cut down and his body was placed in a bunk in an empty jail cell for viewing. Over a thousand filed by gawking at the bodies.

Ballard and the others came near to death a few

minutes before the actual drop. A young man was seen approaching the trip lever and had his hand on it when a spectator said, "Let go of that lever, you chump!" A black minister grabbed the man's arm and pulled him away. But the young man returned when the sheriff turned his back and went upon the gallows to help adjust Carr's rope. This time the minister put his full body between the lever and the young man. He was W.M. Pinkston, white, half-brother of the murdered streetcar driver, G. Emmett Pinkston.[1449]

In many cities in the United States at this time it was the custom of streetcar drivers to allow riders whom they knew to ride free on Christmas Day. Apparently, Ballard assumed he enjoyed the privilege.

Frank Brenish, white, age 36. *Murder.*

The crime was committed at 9:30 P.M. July 5, 1889, at Third Street between Union and Monroe in downtown Memphis, in Shelby County. The victim, Mary Brenish, white, age thirty-eight, was the killer's wife. They had been married two years. Mary had two children from her first marriage; the elder was Florence, age fourteen. At the time she was killed, the couple were separated and she was working as a chambermaid at the Clarendon Hotel. Frank had threatened to kill her if she did not return and live with him, but his drinking and failure to support the family by not working had destroyed the marriage. She had spoken to the chief of police about the threats made by Frank. When questioned, he promised to leave her alone.

On the night of the murder, Mary and Florence were walking together, followed by Mary's sister Mrs. Ellen Hickey and Mr. James Sanoni. They were walking as a group to protect her from possible attack by Frank. As they passed a dark alley, he burst forth and exclaimed, "Did you tell Chief Davis you wouldn't live with me?" She ignored him and he asked the question again. She said, "Go on, Frank, and leave me alone." He grabbed her and made a slashing thrust to her neck with a large butcher knife, nearly cutting off her head. Brenish walked a few steps, leaned against a wall and slashed his own throat. He threw himself forward so that his blood would run into the gutter.[1450]

Both Mary and Frank were carried into a nearby livery stable. A doctor came and hurriedly sewed up Frank's trachea and esophagus, saving his life, "much to the surprise of the surgical fraternity."[1451] Brenish was tried in October 1889 and the jury ignored his claim of insanity.[1452] His conviction was affirmed by the Tennessee Supreme Court, but the opinion cannot be located.

Brenish died much as he lived, in an alcoholic daze. Jail officials allowed him to have liquor and he consumed as much as he could. He also had taken morphine, but it was unknown how he got it. Brenish still had the large gash on his throat and it bled from time to time. The night before his execution he attempted suicide by slashing his wrist with a homemade saw made from the handle of a tin cup.

Brenish was attended by both an Episcopalian priest and a Roman Catholic priest. When the latter insisted that his confession be heard alone, Brenish could not decide what to do. When the jailer was summoned, Brenish was asked whether he wanted the Episcopalian priest to stay. Brenish replied he did. The Catholic priest left. Earlier, Brenish had been befriended by the Rev. H.A. Jones of the Cumberland Presbyterian Church. After the Episcopalian minister left, Brenish said he didn't know a thing about religion. Although he had been raised Catholic, he liked the Rev. Jones the best, in part because his wife had attended his church.

Brenish was one of four men executed inside the Shelby County jail on June 24, 1890. The others, Ed Carr, Parker Harris, and Hardy Ballard, were black. Brenish had complained that he did not want to be executed with them because of their race. The sheriff obliged and executed him fifteen minutes after them. The blacks complained loudly about this special treatment, especially since it meant that the gallows trap had to be enlarged to accommodate three, rather than two, meaning one would die earlier than planned.[1453] When Brenish heard the trap fall on the three, he said, "Gimmie a drink of whiskey!"[1454]

Brenish said he was ready to die but his nervous condition suggested otherwise. He had to be assisted to his feet for the reading of the death warrant. "He was so nearly stupefied that he could not walk without assistance. The pupils of his eyes were dilated, his face was livid and he did not look as though he could live three hours longer."[1455] Brenish died wearing his own clothes, except for new and ill-fitting pants. He took several drinks of whiskey before putting on each garment.

On the gallows, Father Sargent read a portion of the Episcopalian service. Brenish's eyes closed several times while the priest was reading the service and he seemed to reopen them with difficulty. Father Sargent asked him if he desired to say anything and he replied, "They oughtn't to hang a man when he ain't in his right mind."[1456]

Frank Brenish was hanged by Sheriff McLendon at 12:20 P.M. on June 24, 1890, on the gallows inside the Shelby County jail. His heart stopped beating within one minute and his body was taken down twenty minutes later.

The officers had difficulty in placing the handcuffs because of his bandaged wrist. Blood trickled down his white gloves. With the noose and cap placed, he swayed to and fro and had to be held up. When the lever was pulled and he dropped there was a pop (his neck was broken) and a hissing sound. The drop had opened the hole in his throat from the attempted suicide on the night of the killing. The hole was large enough to hold a cigar. As he hung, his wrist wound bled profusely.[1457] Brenish's body was placed on a jail cell cot and over a thousand people walked by to look at it and the other three men executed that day.

Witnessing the execution were Mrs. Ellen Hickey and his wife's friend, Mrs. Hattie McKee, both white. "Both watched every detail of the execution and seemed to enjoy it." When Mrs. Hickey was asked if she thought Brenish went to heaven, she replied emphatically, "No, sireee." A bystander said, "He repented his sins." "I can't help it," replied Mrs. McKee, "I ain't afraid of meeting him when I go to heaven." Mrs. Hickey said he deserved his fate and worse. Mrs. Brenish's daughters, age fourteen and ten, had asked to see their stepfather hanged, but the sheriff had refused. Brenish's body was taken to an undertaker's parlor. His mother had requested that no one be allowed to see the body. She, a sister and a niece attended his funeral.

Jackson Staples (aka Jack Staples), black, age 18. *Rape.*

The crime was committed in the afternoon on February 18, 1890, near Heiskell's Station, in northern Knox County on a road near the home of William Connor. The victim was Mrs. Rufus (Luda) Lewis, Connor's niece, who was visiting from her home in Missouri. Luda, white, age thirty, had walked to the post office at Heiskell's and was returning on foot. Staples accosted her with an "indecent proposal," and she cursed him in return. He threatened to kill her with a club he was carrying and when he approached, she began fighting him. During the fight she grabbed his shirt collar and a collar button came off.

He knocked her down with the club, which he dropped. They continued fighting on the ground and he ripped off virtually all of her clothes.[1458] He held her arms with one hand and choked her nearly senseless with the other. He repeatedly raped her.

As he finished, she regained her senses and hit him over the eye with his club. The wound bled profusely. Staples ran off. Mrs. Lewis staggered to her uncle's house several hundred yards away, holding her shredded clothing to her body. She told William Connor about the rape and he immediately set out on horseback and was joined by a man named Swan. They followed Staples's tracks in a circuitous route and finally found him twelve miles away.

With weapons pointed at him, he surrendered. While Connor stood guard, Swan went for a rope. Staples sensed an opportunity to escape and bolted. Connor fired a warning shot and then shot him in the thigh as he climbed over a fence. Sheriff's deputies arrived and they returned to the disturbed muddy ground where the rape had been committed. Staples was held at Heiskell's station. Mrs. Lewis positively identified him as her rapist. A lynching was murmured as he was jailed in Knoxville.

Staples was tried on September 4, 1890. One of his three lawyers was J.M. Hargo, described as a prominent colored lawyer. Mrs. Lewis and her cousin, Miss Connor, said that Staples had passed their house two or three weeks before the rape and leered at the women, making them uncomfortable. Staples then turned and stopped at the gate and asked for food, explaining he had no money. He wore a distinctive watch chain. They fed him and he left without incident.

Miss Connor gave similar testimony. She said that Staples had come to the house the morning of the rape and again asked for food. Luda Lewis had recently left for Heiskell's Station. Miss Connor again gave Staples food and saw him walk down the railroad track and across a trestle. Luda Lewis said she saw him coming down the hill from the trestle. A railroad section boss said he thought Staples was the man he saw walking on the trestle and down an embankment, although he was not sure.

Staples took the stand and vigorously denied raping Luda Lewis. He said he was at a brick oven at the time of the rape, 12:30 P.M., and offered the names of two men there to fix the time. He said he had lost the collar button on the road as he walked from Knoxville to Anderson County. The injury over his eye was caused by his bumping his head as he climbed up on top of one of the boilers to sleep the night before the alleged rape. None of the several people Staples said could confirm his story appeared on his behalf. In fact, no witnesses appeared for him. The jury was out three hours and returned with a death verdict.

Staples told the newspapers he was sorry to die because it would break his widowed mother's heart. He said he had a brother. The newspapers described his "sickly smile" and said ministers could not understand why he refused to confess the crime. "I have no confession to make," said Jack. "I am an innocent man, have accepted Christ, and feel positive I shall meet Him in heaven above." Reported the newspaper, "It was alarming to the gentlemen. If he was innocent of the crime what a terrible mistake to hang him. If guilty why would he refuse to confess?"

Jack Staples case was appealed to the Tennessee Supreme Court but the opinion cannot be located. He was ordered hanged on November 21, 1890, and died that day. The newspaper reported that a few days before the execution a delegation of colored citizens met with the governor, who was visiting Knoxville. But he refused to intervene.[1459] The newspaper said that some of Staples's statements seemed insane. "I don't hate to die," he said, "but I do hate to think I have to be dead so long."[1460] The day before his execution Staples professed his religion and was baptized. A friend, Nick Wilkinson, black, was allowed to spend the night with him and read the Bible to him. They prayed and sang. The next morning, Wilkinson was given a razor and shaved him.

Jack Staples was hanged on a gallows inside the Knox County jail. A dozen people, including four black ministers, were allowed to witness the execution. The sheriff had provided Staples with new clothes, including shined shoes. Two uncles had come to the jail and cried openly from the time he was brought to the gallows until he was declared dead. Each of the four ministers spoke on the gallows, read from the Bible or led in singing. The hymn "Just As I Am" was sung and Staples seemed to be singing as well. Staples was asked if he had anything to say.[1461]

Staples said, "I want to tell you gentlemen you are hanging an innocent man. I never violated a law in my life as I know of but this thing; will all remember how I wasn't afraid to die." Pointing to Mr. Connor, he said: "There is the man responsible for this execution today. He swore my life away. I had an unfair trial and had no witnesses." At this moment, one of the clergymen asked, "Where will we meet you, Jack?" He shot back, "In heaven."[1462]

"Are you ready, Jack?" asked the sheriff. "Yes," came the reply. The trap was released at 2:42 P.M. and the neck was not broken. The body made four slight convulsions and the heart stopped beating twenty-five minutes later. The body was placed in a coffin and the lid screwed down. The uncles accompanied the body to Anderson County for burial. The fifteen hundred people, mostly black, who had surrounded the jail hoping to see the body were disappointed, including those who had climbed upon the windows to find their view was obstructed by blankets.[1463]

1891

Houston D. Kelley, black, age 24. *Murder.*

The crime was committed on the evening of December 25, 1890, at a black community called Guntown, two miles outside Rogersville, in Hawkins County. Kelley and five companions, Will Christian, Henry Smith, Bud Orange, Frank Johnson, and Lewis Applewhite, had come to a house where a "negro festival and dance party"[1464] was underway. The victim, Daniel Carmichael, was described as an "industrious, and well-behaved and respected mulatto bricklayer and plasterer."[1465] He was twenty-eight.

Kelley, described as a mulatto (his mother was "a white woman of low origin"[1466]) was infatuated with a mulatto woman named Alida Mitchell. Kelley, married with a child, had pursued the woman for some time and was known to quarrel with the victim about her. Several months before the killing Carmichael had pulled a pistol on Kelley at the Rogersville train depot and a shooting was prevented by a third person's pushing the weapon down.[1467]

Everyone at the party was under the influence of whiskey, and a fight broke out between Kelley and Carmichael. Kelley was assisted by his friends and Carmichael was knifed several times in the back. He was taken to a small frame kitchen adjoining the house. Kelley, "not being satisfied with having temporarily overcome his enemy, suddenly pulled aside a little window, or maybe that act was done by one of his accomplices,"[1468] and shot Carmichael at close range with a double-barreled shotgun which he had brought to the festival, having vowed to kill Carmichael if he didn't agree to leave Alida alone for Kelley's attention. Another version of the killing is that Carmichael had fired three pistol shots at

Kelley, one slightly wounding him, prior to the knifing and subsequent shooting.[1469]

Kelley and the others ran away but were quickly captured. Kelley, Henry Smith and William Christian were convicted of first-degree murder, but the judge found mitigating circumstances and remitted the latter two men's sentences to life imprisonment. Applewhite was convicted but the trial court granted him a new trial, which never occurred.

According to one account, "Houston Kelly is the illegitimate son of one Polly Kelley, a white woman living on and owning a prosperous farm about three miles from Rogersville. His father is old Lilbourne Johnson, a coal black negro man bent with age."[1470] The account continued, "His mother's wealth is estimated at from eight to ten thousand and of this amount she spent freely to secure a longer lease of life for her son."[1471] Several attempts were made to seek a rehearing from the Tennessee Supreme Court after it affirmed his conviction. The opinion cannot be located.[1472] Aided by his lawyers, Houston made a vigorous attempt to seek a commutation from the governor.

Three days before his execution Kelley was given permission to have a formal photograph taken. Kelley remained defiant until the day before his execution, when it became clear that the governor would not intervene.

As the execution neared, Kelley became a fervent convert to Christianity and was baptized in his prison cell by a black Presbyterian minister. He proclaimed that he was going to heaven, but asserted, "When I stepped up in the door you all know what he [the victim] said to me. I didn't know he was there. I didn't get justice. I did everything I could to prevent trouble. He borrowed a Winchester and on December 15 drew it down on me. We had always been good friends. I tried to reason with him, but couldn't. That was the evening before the trouble."[1473] Kelley also insisted that Will Christian was innocent of any wrongdoing.

Houston Kelley was executed at 1:50 P.M. on November 10, 1891, on an outside gallows located behind the Rogersville jail. The actual execution was not seen by the public because the gallows was enclosed, including the roof. Although several hundred people had gathered nearby, they left because of a heavy rainstorm. The execution unnerved jailor Fernandez, who wept bitterly for several minutes. "That's the first man I ever hung and it's the last, too," he said.[1474]

1892

Jesse Frierson (aka "Black Diamond" and Jesse McPherson), black, age 26. *Murder.*

The crime was committed about 9:00 P.M. on December 19, 1890, in Irvine's Saloon on Market Street in the Fort Payne area of Chattanooga. The killer was a longtime criminal. The victim, David Crockett Musgrove, white, age fifty, was an eight-year veteran of the Chattanooga police department.

A black man, John "Alabama " Reeves, had gone to a justice of the peace complaining that Frierson had stolen his clothing while Reeves was in jail. Armed with the warrant, Reeves and police officer Musgrove went to the card room of the saloon. Reeves came up behind Frierson, placed his hand on his shoulder and said, "This is the man you want." Frierson jumped to his feet and fired a pistol shot at Musgrove but missed. Frierson, trying to flee, fired a second shot, which hit Musgrove in the side. He fell. At this moment, saloon owner Irvine attempted to grab the gun and another wild shot was fired. Musgrove arose and tried to grab the pistol, resulting in yet another wild shot. Musgrove then pulled his own pistol and fired two shots at the fleeing Frierson. He turned to Irvine, handed him his pistol and said, "Catch him! Catch him!"[1475] Within an hour a wagonload of police had arrived at the saloon. By then, a doctor had arrived to attend Musgrove, but he died there at 10:07 P.M. The next day a railroad detective arrested Frierson, who had been wounded in the leg by Musgrove's shot.

Frierson had a long record of violence and crime. He left his home in Columbia, Tennessee, at seventeen because of his "misdoings," and moved to Birmingham, Alabama, where he lived a criminal life under the name "Black Diamond." He left there after shooting another black man at a dance hall. He moved to Macon, Georgia, and married a schoolteacher in a fashionable wedding. They had a son, but eighteen months after the wedding he left for Chattanooga, taking with him a "yaller gal," and was arrested at least three times for larceny and gaming. Next, he beat his brother-in-law John Reed almost to death with a fence picket.[1476] Then he killed officer Musgrove. Frierson appealed his case to the Tennessee Supreme Court but the opinion cannot be located.

Waiting death in the Hamilton County jail, Frierson said he had found religion without the benefit of a minister. He explained, "One day while standing in his cell all of a sudden he felt so light that he wanted to fly right away to Heaven and he knew that his sins were forgiven and that his soul was saved."[1477] Thereafter, he sang, chanted and exhorted from his cell to groups of people who were allowed to gather in front of it. One of them apparently slipped him a file. Later, both the Catholics and the Baptists vied for his soul. The Baptists won the contest and he was baptized in a jail bathtub.

Frierson was executed in the basement of the Hamilton County jail at 1:52 P.M. on January 2, 1892. About two hundred people watched, including the entire city police department. Hundreds crowded around the jail but saw nothing. The drop was clean and his neck was broken. As usual, the heart continued to beat for six minutes and he was cut down twenty minutes later. About three thousand people surrounded the jail or occupied the courtyard to gaze at his body.

Frierson was cool and "took charge" of the execution. He smoked a cigar until he mounted the gallows and spoke in an even and earnest manner. He still insisted he was innocent, although he had confessed to the crime when held in jail in Knoxville for his own safety. As time for his execution drew near, he blamed the killing on Oscar Barrows, and later on George Montgomery. On the gallows he named Barrows again. When asked by a newspaper reporter why he kept changing the real killer's name, he said it was to protect a friend. Police never located anyone with either name.

The execution followed the usual progress of a quasi-religious service, as two black ministers alternately sang songs and prayed. One prayed, "Help him to clear his soul of all that is false in statement concerning the awful crime that has led up to this hour."[1478] The hymns included "Steal Away," and "Come Thou Fount of Every Blessing." Four black ministers stood with him on the gallows.

Frierson's last statement included:

> I stand on the scaffold, convicted of killing Policeman Musgrove, a crime I never committed. I am not guilty, yet I have to die. But I have made my peace with God and hope to meet all of you in Heaven. Every one of you. I am not mad at anyone. I am not frightened at all, and I thank God for it. I feel at peace with all and am happy. I die for a crime I never committed, by the laws of the State. I did not have a fair trial. It was because I was a poor man, and did not have the money to employ lawyers on my behalf. I have many good friends, who have done all they could for me for the last few days, but they came too late to be of much service. I say I am not guilty as I stand on this scaffold. I am not guilty. I am not guilty. But, thank God, none of you are responsible for my being hung, I am well satisfied. God now had an engine waiting to fly away to Heaven with my soul. He will do it. I know He will. My Gracious Father will remember me and have mercy on my soul and He has done it. I have said all I want to. Good-bye to everyone; good-bye, good-bye.[1479]

This was not all he had to say. He asked the sheriff if he could speak more, and he continued by thanking a "good colored boy" who came to his cell to wish him well, and to remind the crowd to remember his wife and child and his "good old mother," and thanked his brother. "He used to talk to me and tell me to be good, but I got to going to bad places and in bad company and that is what got Jesse into all that trouble."[1480] When the drop came, his relatives gave out "terrible screams."[1481]

Frierson further explained that he had not told a newspaper reporter that he was going to send fire from Heaven and burn up the city. "I said I was going to be hung wrongfully and God would punish the town."[1482]

The Rev. G.D. Olden, who had baptized him in a bathtub a few days earlier, offered a fervent prayer which included, "He says he is innocent and he knows. It is entirely between he and God. A man judges a fellow man by his outward actions. God judges man from his breast. Everyone's heart is revealed to Jesus. Jesus can and is always willing to save."[1483]

Realizing that Frierson was not going to admit his crime, the Rev. Olden addressed another issue. "Nearly all crime is the result of the gilded saloon and gambling hall. The law punishes a man for committing a crime, yet it licenses these vile fountainheads of crime. How can we save our young men from temptation when they are hourly thrust under its very nose? As long as these temptations are allowed to remain in our land just so long may we expect crime. A man whose brain is fired with liquor is not strictly accountable for what he does, and would not think of committing a crime when sober. God will always bless a righteous man and keep him from committing crime."[1484] He said to Frierson, "Now, Jesse, God bless you, and may He receive your soul to heaven, and may there be a crown of glory awaiting you at the splendid throne of God in heaven. Good-bye, Jesse."[1485] Frierson responded, "Good-bye, Dr. Olden. Good-bye, everyone." But these were not Frierson's last words.

The noose was placed over his head by jailer Holt. It was found to be kinked and was removed. Frierson said, "That's right; make it all right; I don't want any trouble; make it good." Then he exclaimed, "I've got nothing against no one. Tell all the people good-bye. I am going home to die no more." At this point, the Rev. Olden decided to sing the hymn "I'm Going Home to Die No More." As the jailer put the black cap over his head, Frierson said, "Let me know just when you are ready, so I can say good-bye." "Say it now," said jailer Holt. "Good-bye," said Frierson, and jailer Holt snapped his fingers. This was the signal and the sheriff pressed his foot on the trigger and the drop fell. The drop was clean and an audible snap indicated his neck was broken. The attending doctor performed a test that was the latest proof of death by "dropping an atom of phreuniscine upon the pupil, they turned a livid green, a sure sign of death."[1486]

Despite Frierson's assertion that he had plenty of friends, when asked for donations to bury him, no money was raised, although his sister wept and begged for money. Even her husband, John "Alabama" Reeves, refused to contribute. The body was finally sent to Columbia for burial at the price of a first-class ticket.

Frierson's reflections on God's word and redemption were likely met with skepticism by some present. The night before the execution, when jailer Holt went to his cell to look for a pistol and a file Frierson had told another inmate he had hidden in the cell, Frierson attacked the jailer. He nearly choked Holt to death, bringing him to his knees and turning his face purple, before several other guards managed to free him by hitting Frierson.[1487]

The cell fight lasted fifteen minutes and the guards were badly bruised. During the fight, "the desperate negro fought as if possessed by a demon. He bit, kicked, tried to brain the officers, and kept up a continual cursing that was frightful to listen to." In his ravings he said he was going to hell and was glad of it; that he was tired of "this religious damn foolishness," and his cursing could be heard outside the jail.[1488]

Later, when the sheriff was still unable to locate the pistol, he ordered six guards back into the cell to shackle Frierson and bind him to his bed. Another fight broke out, "more desperate than the first." This time, the officers were impeded because there were too many of them in the small cell. Another fifteen-minute struggle saw several officers kicked badly in the head and abdomen. The officers had left their pistols outside, "for if they had been armed, Frierson would not have lived to be hanged today." The file was found, however. Concluded the newspaper, "One thing is certain, the religion Frierson professed to have was all poppy cock."[1489]

Finally, Frierson had told the Rev. Olden where the pistol was hidden on the promise not to reveal its location until after the execution. When the minister and deputies looked in cell number two on the fourth floor after Frierson's death, they found nothing. "The entire fourth floor was thoroughly searched and still no weapon was found. After a thorough search it was decided that the murderer never had a pistol and had been simply lying."[1490]

J. Larkin Lancaster, black, age 46/50. *Murder.*

The crime was committed on November 25, 1888, in a rural area called Pisgah Hill outside Pulaski, in Giles County. The killer, age forty-six at the time, was a farmer who lived near the victim and was jealous of the attention the victim was paying to the killer's sister-in-law, Mandy Crittenden, black, age twenty-five. Said the Tennessee Supreme Court, "Zack Dixon, who is alleged to have been murdered, was a black, negro boy, seventeen years of age, and residing on a farm, near Pulaski, in Giles County."[1491]

Dixon was last seen on November 25, 1888, because he bade his mother good-bye that afternoon and said he was going to Lancaster's house. He was seen near the house, but was never seen alive thereafter. Three weeks later, a headless body was found near Hicks's Bluff two and one half miles below Pulaski in Richland Creek, several miles from where he was last seen by the witnesses. The Supreme Court explained what was found: "The trunk with arms attached being confined by a piece of rope in one sack, and the severed legs tied up in another sack." It continued, "In each sack was also a heavy rock, used as a 'sinker' and in the one containing the legs, was a butcher knife. One of these sacks was a tow sack and the other cotton."[1492] The head was never found. Suspicion quickly focused on Lancaster, and a coroner's jury ruled he should be charged. The facts at trial showed a chain of circumstantial evidence that convicted Lancaster. But it took three trials and three appeals to the Tennessee Supreme Court.

Lancaster was very protective of his sister-in-law, who lived with him, his wife and children.[1493] In recent months, Dixon had been showing her attention and Lancaster was angry. "She is mine," he said, and on several occasions threatened Dixon.[1494] One time he shot a gun in Dixon's direction, in front of his father-in-law, Alex Crittenden. On the night in question, Mandy and several others went to a church service where Dixon was expected to appear. Others on their way to the church service came up to the house and yelled for Lancaster to come with them but there was no answer. Several gunshots were heard in the area of Lancaster's house the night of the murder.

Lancaster, riding a horse the day after the disappearance, was met on the road by another rider. Lancaster asked if the other rider had seen Dixon; he had not. The rider noticed that Lancaster was carrying a large tow sack, which he said contained clothes. Lancaster's twelve-year-old son was riding a horse behind him. He was carrying a large cotton sack. Blood was oozing from it.[1495]

Lancaster told several people that he wanted them to say he was with them the night of the murder, but all said they declined to do so. Because Lancaster never took the stand, he never offered evidence of his whereabouts on the night of the murder. His son was not offered as a witness either. The long delay from murder to execution was caused by delays amid rumors that Zack Dixon was seen alive in various locations.

The chief issue before the Tennessee Supreme Court was whether the corpus delicti was proven.[1496] The court's discussion began, "[Dixon] expressed no purpose of leaving the county, made no preparations to leave, and no reason is shown why he should have done so. He was an industrious, well behaved boy, and left behind a matured cotton crop, some clothing and other property, which he made no effort to dispose of in any way, and has never called for himself."[1497]

Regarding the body, the court said that Dixon's mother and others identified two unique scars on the legs. She identified the shirt as one she had made, in part because of the way she hemmed the sleeves, which were too long. She identified a leather wristband he was wearing, which he had made from a piece of bridle. The man Dixon worked for also recognized the scars. His sister, Mattie Dixon, recognized the shirt and saw him put it on the day he left.

Witnesses who saw the body disagreed on one point—whether the body was that of a black person or a mulatto. The problem was that the skin was both colors. This was explained because the water had washed off much of the cuticle. Explained the Supreme Court, "Where cuticle had come off, [it] was 'mulatto or yellow,' but that it was 'black' where no such change had taken place."[1498] There was sharp disagreement on that issue, doctors took both sides on whether water would "lighten" a body.[1499] The court concluded that the scars, the shirt and the wristband were sufficient evidence to show the corpus delicti.[1500]

Turning to the question of whether the evidence showed that Lancaster was the killer, the Supreme Court said that he had a motive, namely, his jealousy about Dixon's attention to Mandy. He had previously acted on that motive, telling another witness that Dixon must leave Mandy alone or "he would kill him and put him away where he won't be found."[1501] No one testified as to Lancaster's whereabouts the night of the killing.

Here is what the court said: "Where he and his son were going that Monday morning, the character of the burdens they bore, and what they did with them, no witness is brought to state. Not even the son, himself, comes to declare that the trunk and limbs of Zack Davis's dead body were not in the two sacks or to explain or deny the dropping of blood from the sack in his charge. He at least knew the facts, and could have unquestionably enlightened the Court and the jury. Though living in the defendant's facility and under his control, he is not introduced and no excuse is given for his non-appearance as a witness."[1502]

Finally, two statements showed an attempt to cover up the crime. First was the testimony of his brother-in-law, Hutch Crittenden, that Lancaster wanted him to say that "Dixon had stolen a horse and gone to Texas." Second was another witness who was told, "Dixon had gotten in a pistol case and ran away."[1503]

The jury returned a verdict of guilty with mitigating circumstances, and the appeal asserted that the jury did not think Lancaster was guilty. Rather, the trial court erred in not questioning the jury about what it meant. The Supreme Court rejected this argument, saying it was within the court's legal discretion to accept or reject the recommendation.[1504]

Larkin Lancaster was interviewed by the newspaper the morning of his execution. When asked how he felt, he replied, "Badly." He insisted he was innocent: "I have told you two or three times that I am not guilty." When asked on what he based his hopes for salvation, he replied, "Because I believe I have been changed from nature to grace."[1505] Larkin Lancaster, now age fifty, was hanged at 1:30 P.M. on April 19, 1892, in Pulaski, but the location of the gallows and the details of the execution are unknown.

Joe Wallace, white, age 30. *Murder.*

The crime was committed on September 30, 1891, off the road about a mile from the community of Shellmound, in Marion County. Wallace and John Smith, white, age thirty, were walking down the road when they met the victim. He was a peddler, John T. Parder, white, age unknown. When Parder asked for directions it became clear to the pair that he was lost. They seized the opportunity to waylay him. The peddler's body was found stripped naked, his throat cut from ear to ear, his skull crushed, and buckshot wounds to the body, which was covered with blood.[1506]

Smith turned state's evidence; he claimed Wallace forced him to participate in stripping the body. At the time of Wallace's execution, he was awaiting trial. Wallace's conviction was affirmed by the Tennessee Supreme Court, but the opinion cannot be located.

Wallace had been kept in the Hamilton County jail for his safety. The accounts of his last days differ. One source said he refused to eat for three days before the hanging; another said he ate heartily in the company of his wife.[1507] According to one account, the sheriff had promised Wallace as much time as possible on his last day, which was deemed to be 3:00 P.M.[1508]

From the Chattanooga jail, Wallace released a written statement insisting the killing was done by Smith alone after he had left him alone on the road. He said Smith's family would try to show he was insane. "John Smith is known as a liar and a rogue in his own county. He is a boy I have known for six years and he has stood with me when they would be after him for his meanness and I have treated him like a brother, and this is the thanks I get for it." He said, "I hope you will respect my wife and children. They are left alone in this world to do the best they can. The men that pretended to be friends to me when out have showed what sort of friends they were. When a laboring man gets so he cannot work they are no more friends to him. So I only have this today — I don't think that I ought to be hung for what they are hanging me for. If my brothers had come to the front and helped me in time, I never would have been hung."[1509]

Taken by train to Jasper, he spent the morning of his execution with his wife and a minister at the jail. The couple were brought a large meal which they ate. Wallace spoke only of his children and their future care. When summoned for the trip to the gallows, he kissed his wife and turned away. She asked, "Are you prepared for death, Joe?" He did not answer.

The sheriff had difficulty getting permission for the execution from landowners within a mile of the courthouse. By execution time, the crowd of at least two thousand had come from every direction, most carrying guns, but fully knowing they would be prevented from seeing the actual drop. The location of the gallows, however, did allow many to see over the thirteen-foot-high stockade. Shortly before the execution someone said the five-foot drop was not enough. Deputies dug a two-foot hole under the drop.

Joe Wallace was executed in Jasper on June 17, 1892. A hundred armed guards escorted his wagon to the gallows located "at the base of one of the mountains surrounding that beautiful town."[1510] Just as Wallace mounted the gallows, a dark rain cloud descended over the town. On the gallows, rain began to fall and "sharp lightning danced from the hill tops." Within minutes everyone was drenched. The minister read from the Bible, gave a prayer and led in singing "There Is a Fountain Filled With Blood." Asked if he had anything to say, Wallace remarked that he had been converted and was prepared to die. "I was led astray, but God has taken me back."

When the rope was placed around his neck, it became apparent that the water had swollen it and the sheriff and a deputy had difficulty tightening it around his neck. Wallace said in a joking manner, "If you had a pair of steers to pull with perhaps you could do it better." These were his last words. The drop came at 2:32 P.M. and his neck was broken. Mrs. Wallace had sat down on the jail steps as Wallace was taken away to the execution. She was still there when his coffined body was brought to her.

George Stone, black, age 24. *Murder.*

The crime was committed on the evening of August 31, 1889, on a road outside Fayetteville, in Lincoln County. The victim was Thornton Burkley, black, age fifty-four. He had taken his wagon to Fayetteville to sell railroad ties and had stopped at a store and a blacksmith shop. At the store, his money, about twelve to fifteen dollars in silver, was seen by several people, including the killer, George Stone. Stone left the store and walked down the road in the direction of Burkley's home and sat on a bridge railing. Within two hours, Burkley came by and Stone asked for a ride. Several people saw Stone on the bridge. Others saw him riding on the back of the wagon holding a stick of the type sometimes used as a wagon wheel brake (i.e., a wagon standard).

The state's proof was circumstantial, but was based in part on Stone's confession given in the Nashville jail sometime after the killing. Burkley had been struck violently on the head by a wagon standard that was left with the body. The face was unrecognizable and the head collapsed into mush when the doctor called to the scene touched it.

At the time of the killing, Stone was seen wearing overalls over his red pants. The day after the murder he had gotten a black woman to wash the overalls and he attended a Baptist church supper that night. He offered to pay the admission of several people and flashed the silver dollars. He spent freely on females at the supper. When several people told of seeing him on Burkley's wagon, he was arrested.

Stone was taken to Nashville for his safety. He told a friend, Mansfield Caughran, who visited him in jail, that the murder was committed by Clem Massey, who had arranged for Stone to be the decoy, and was waiting farther up the road. According to Caughran, Stone said he had not hit Burkley. Rather, Massey had struck the blows, Massey dragged the body into the dry swamp were it was found, and Massey took the money and did not share it with Stone. Several people, including fishermen on the nearby Elk River, testified they saw Stone running through the woods shortly after the time of the killing.

At trial, Stone told the story implicating Massey. He insisted the four dollars he spent at the church supper had come from his mother. His testimony was impeached by other witnesses who testified that his mother and sister had sent word earlier that they would put him in jail if he did not pay over to them money he had collected from others for work they had done.

Stone's lawyer vigorously cross-examined all the witnesses, including whether they really saw George Stone, or his twin brother Tyrone. Stone's mother testified she had given him the four dollars, but was not examined further by either side.[1511]

Following Stone's conviction in early 1890, he was kept in the jail until Massey could be found and tried. Massey was acquitted in 1891. The delay caused Stone to be respited several times.

George Stone's appeal reveals an important fact regarding early Supreme Court opinions and possibly explains why many can't be found, even in unpublished form. The Supreme Court's opinion in Stone's case was given *orally* by Judge Lea. It happened to be captured by a newspaper reporter and it was reported verbatim in an unknown newspaper.

Here is the entire opinion:

> The prisoner was indicted and convicted in the Circuit Court of Lincoln County for the murder of one Burkley, and sentenced to death. The crime was committed August 31, 1889. Burkley, an old colored man, had sold some wood and cross-ties in Fayetteville, and had collected the money for them on that day. On his way to his home some miles in the country, while making change for some money, he exhibited $12 or $15, which the prisoner saw. Thereupon the prisoner got into his wagon and rode with him some miles. When about a half a mile from his home, in a lonely spot in the woods, the prisoner aided by a confederate, killed the old man by crushing his head. They dragged him some distance from the road, and the body still showing some signs of life, the finishing blow was struck by the prisoner with a heavy piece of wood. The prisoner, having rifled the body, returned that night to Fayetteville, where he spent it lavishly at a negro festival.

The court concluded:

> On arrest, he confessed to the crime, but said that the first and fatal blow had been struck by his confederate. It was urged by his counsel that this was an extenuating circumstance. But the court was unable to see an extenuation of the crime, even under the confession of the prisoner. There was error in the charge of the Judge relating to the effect of portions of a confession proved to be untrue, on the other part of the confession, but the error had been in favor of the prisoner. It followed that the judgment of the Circuit Court was affirmed. The execution was fixed for Wednesday, March 18.[1512]

George Stone was hanged on July 6, 1892, inside the Lincoln County jail in front of several official spectators and the press. His last words were taken as a confession. He said that Massey was as guilty as he was and it was not fair that Massey should go free.[1513] The newspaper said, "George Stone was of such a low order of intelligence that he was thought by many to be of unsound mind. He was by no means a vicious Negro but was well thought of by the whites."[1514]

1893

Floyd Woodly (aka Floyd Woodle), black, age 23. *Murder.*
John Turner (aka John Stewart [real name]), black, age 24. *Murder.*

The crime was committed on the night of November 23, 1892, on a road near the town of South Pittsburgh, in Marion County. The killers had extensive criminal records. The victim, George Dawson, white, age unknown, was attacked by the two and another black man named Cal Collins. Dawson was a smelter for the Tennessee Coal & Iron Company. He was one of fifteen men killed within a mile of the spot in a little over a year.

The three men had been attending a Negro dance and were highly intoxicated. Dawson, walking alone, had stopped by the dance and continued down the road. Woodly and Turner had been told by Collins that Dawson was carrying ten or twelve dollars in silver. They decided to rob him.

The killers followed him. He turned around and asked them if they were following him, and Turner said no. Woodly then hit him on the back of the head with a rock. Dawson fell down, saying, "Oh, Lord!" and Turner held his hands while Woodly and Collins beat his head with rocks and Woodly finally cut his throat. His head was beaten to a jelly.[1515]

Woodly went through his pockets but didn't find anything. He got into an argument with the other two over money. Turner and Collins went home and Woodly went back to the dance. Woodly later said, "When I went up and saw the dead man lying there it sobered me up right away." Woodly then noticed a stick he had been seen carrying at the dance and reached down to pick it up. At that moment, the people who had discovered the body saw him reach down and saw some silver money on the ground. The next day, blood was seen on Collins's clothes, and he was arrested. His confession implicated Woodly and Turner. They were given the death penalty and he received a life sentence.

Because of the proximity between the crime, November 23, 1892, and the execution, February 16, 1893, it is unlikely there was an appeal to the Tennessee Supreme Court.

On the morning of the execution, both men gave confessions which were taken down and signed by each. Woodly said his father was a white man. He fully confessed to the crime, and described at least two other murders he had committed in Alabama.

Woodly said that Collins was as guilty as they were but he didn't want him hanged too. His confession concluded, "I have nearly always been caught when I would try to steal anything."[1516]

Turner said his real name was John Stewart, and his story matched Woodly's. He said, "I was mad at Cal for going back on me, but I ain't mad at him now, and I don't want him hung. I feel like the Lord is going to save me."

Floyd Woodly and John Turner were executed at 1:20 P.M. on February 16, 1893, the day the trial court had set for their deaths. The pair were executed on a gallows about a mile east of Jasper, near the foot of a small mountain. An enclosure of rough boards was designed to hold a hundred men, but the number who saw the execution is unknown. About one thousand men, women and children surrounded the gallows, standing in the cold February rain.

On the gallows, Woodly said, "Well, people, I will tell you why I am here. It is whisky that has brought me here, but I feel like the Lord had said mercy on me." Turner said, "Well, whisky did not bring me here. I just did it myself. I have been a bad boy and ran away from home and got into bad company." He said to a black man in the crowd, "Henry, keep out of bad company. I feel like I'm ready to go, but I'm not feeling a bit good about it. I'll not saying anything about the murder."[1517]

Turner began crying on the scaffold. Someone passed a baby for Woodly to kiss. Then the ropes and caps were placed. Without warning, Sheriff D.D. Rogers released the trap. Woodly's neck was broken. Turner died of strangulation. They were cut down twenty-four minutes later.

John Armstrong, black, age 38. *Murder.*

The crime was committed on the evening of April 20, 1893, in a rural area called Red Hill, a black community near Athens, in McMinn County. The killer was the secret paramour of Ellen Sharp, black, age unknown, the victim's wife. The victim, French Sharp, black, age forty-one, was a friend of the killer. Both had a reputation as corn thieves.

French Sharp had been missing for two weeks when his body was found badly mutilated, about three-quarters of a mile from his home. It had been eaten by hogs. The hands were missing, as was the skin on the head. Earlier, his wife had said that if he were found he would be dead with a sack of corn at his side. The statement was taken as a vague confession — it was well known in the black community that Ellen and John Armstrong had been carrying on an illicit relationship.

A coroner's jury quickly decided that the killing was done by John Armstrong with some aid by Ellen Sharp. They were both arrested and indicted together. She soon confessed that Armstrong told her he had killed her husband (his phrase was "left the old man behind") and had shot him three times.[1518] On the night of the murder, Armstrong had come to the Sharp home and lured the victim away with the promise they would steal corn. They apparently had. Two sacks of corn were found near the body. After the killing, Armstrong came back to the house and gave Ellen two of the three spent cartridges as love tokens.[1519] Other testimony showed that Armstrong had bought the cartridges in Athens about three weeks before the killing with money given to him by Ellen. Her case was severed from his after she testified. The conviction was affirmed on appeal to the Tennessee Supreme Court, but the opinion cannot be located.

John Armstrong was executed about 1:30 P.M. on December 13, 1893, on a gallows in the McMinn County jail yard. "Before this, McMinn County has had three public executions, two legal and one lynching, all of which occurred many years ago."[1520]

Armstrong confessed the crime to the sheriff the night before his execution. He suffered from an abscess on his leg, and was unable to stand on the gallows without assistance. He had to be held up for the noose to be placed around his neck. He said he was ready to die and would go to heaven. The details of the execution are unknown. Armstrong was survived by his wife and three small children.

At the time of execution, Ellen Sharp was still in the McMinn County jail awaiting trial. She loudly protested her innocence, saying she did not know of the killing until it was completed. She was twenty-eight years old and had borne ten children. The youngest, age seven weeks, was being cared for by someone else while Ellen was in jail. It was left on a pallet while the caregiver worked in the fields. Hogs came upon it. They ate portions of both ears and a finger. According to the newspaper, this was regarded "by the colored people as a rather singular coincidence," as an "ever-present reminder to the mother, if she lives, of the mutilation by like brutes of the dead body of the father of her babe."[1521]

Allen Cousan, black, age 30. *Murder.*

The crime was committed in the evening of May 21, 1893, at 831 Frounch Street in Knoxville, in Knox County. The killer was the victim's husband. The victim, Mattie Cousan, black, age twenty-eight, was killed in a jealous rage.

Mattie was present in the house of her stepfather, Phillip Cooper, black, age unknown, and was making his bed and assisting him to bed, when Cousan entered the room. Cooper was standing with his back to Mattie. As she turned to face her husband, he shot her twice with a pistol. Cooper then turned and was shot in the arm. Another bullet grazed his head. Cooper tried to get out of the room but found the door locked. He and Cousan struggled and he overpowered the killer. The shots were heard by a constable. He was summoned by cries for help from others who heard the shooting. He arrested Cousan.

Allen Cousan's defense was that he had seen his wife and stepfather in an embrace and flew into a rage. Cooper's testimony and the physical location of Mattie's body and the path of the bullets showed otherwise. Mattie was visibly pregnant at the time of her death. Cousan's conviction was affirmed by the Tennessee Supreme Court, but the opinion cannot be located.[1522]

Cousan was known to police. He bragged he had killed a black man in Mexico, along with four Mexicans, in a row over the Mexican wife of the black man. His brother Mike was in jail at the same time as Allen, serving a term for assault.

Sheriff Fox had provided Cousan with a new black suit and kid slippers, but Cousan complained the bow tie made him look like a "countryman."[1523] The sheriff got him a new scarf-like necktie. The night before his execution, Cousan took what he thought were morphine tablets in an effort at suicide. However, the note he had given his sister seeking the morphine had been intercepted, and he took quinine tablets instead. He denied taking the tablets, however, which he had hidden in another necktie he was wearing at the time.[1524]

Cousan was executed on a gallows located at the top floor at the end of a corridor inside the Knox County jail. Located over a stairway, it had been built for Jack Staples. The day before his execution, his two children, age six and four, were brought to him for a good-bye. He asked the many visitors to give him nickels and dimes so that his sister's ring, which had been pawned, could be reclaimed. The money had been used to hire a lawyer to seek commutation of his sentence. The sheriff had paid for metal handles on Cousan's coffin.

Cousan had found religion in jail and had been baptized by sprinkling the day before the execution. He was visited by several black ministers on his last full day of life. The Rev. Armstrong, black, prayed for him at his cell and the minister "worked himself into a religious frenzy." Cousan remained unmoved, although he said he forgave all and wanted God to remove all doubts from his soul.

Allen Cousan was executed at 10:37 A.M. on December 21, 1893, in front of twenty witnesses. Hundreds clogged the streets outside. Cousan mounted the gallows with nerve, smoking a cigarette. He said, "Well, good people, I've got to die. The instant this trap falls and death takes place I'll be around God's throne. I committed the crime but did not intend to kill the woman. She was my wife and I loved her. I am innocent of what was sworn against me. I love everybody and I am prepared to go. I will die as much a man as any colored man who ever died this death. Now, good people, speak a good word for my little children. They are without a mother and are soon to be without a father. My God speed their mother that she went to heaven. Now brothers, let us sing a hymn and have a prayer."[1525]

Cousan's bright demeanor seemed to place him in charge of the proceeding. He was smoking a cigarette as the hymn was begun by the Rev. Armstrong. He took a last puff and threw it away and joined in the singing. When the song was over, he said, "I'm going to heaven. In a short while I'll be one of God's angels. All of you meet me there. I'll be just as good an angel as there is on the top side of the earth." Turning to the sheriff, he said, "Now, just one prayer, Mr. Fox, and you can let 'er go." As the Rev. Armstrong prayed, Cousan leaned against a gallows post. When they prayer was over, he said, "Now, gentlemen, as many of you as are in sympathy with me raise your right hand." All the hands went up. "Thank God," he said, "I've got some friends yet." Then Cousan started singing a hymn which contained the line, "Say Father, move this bitter cup away."[1526] Following the song, he said good-bye to several people by name. "I'm a poor old darkey, but a better one never lived," he said. Then he called upon the crowd to remember his children and give them a nickel, "not for my sake, but for God's sake. I'm going where I cannot want."[1527]

Finally, he turned to the sheriff and said, "Well, when you're ready, Mr. Fox, I'm ready." As he was being bound, he kept talking, "Well, gentlemen, I'm prepared to go. The instant the trap falls God has received me around his throne. I have faced death many a time. I won't flinch."[1528] He asked that his brothers John and Mike be told that he went like a man, that he died like a soldier. "Good-bye, good-bye to everyone," he said as the cap was pulled over his head. He was heard to sing, "Hark, from my tomb a doleful sound." At that moment without warning the sheriff motioned a deputy to untie the rope holding the trap. Cousan's neck was broken, but the heart beat for seven minutes, and he was cut down fifteen minutes later. Cousan's body was put in the coffin and was put in a corridor where hundreds of people, mostly black, filed by to see it. It was later turned over to his sister.

Lafayette Richie (aka Fate Richie), black, age unknown. *Murder.*

The crime was committed about 10:00 P.M. on December 2, 1892, near Sheely's Knob, about two miles from Gainesboro, in Jackson County. The victim was William Stephens, white, age unknown, a farmer who had just sold his farm for $800 cash, which he was known to be carrying.

Richie had arranged for Stephens to meet with two women, apparently prostitutes, the night of the killing, as a pretense for meeting him and walking with him through a cornfield to a roadside destination. Richie shot Stephens in the head from behind with a Winchester rifle (and possibly a pistol) and robbed the body. This involved cutting the suspenders and removing a carefully crafted money belt in which Stephens carried his money.

The chief evidence against Richie were the distinctive footprints made by his boots. They had been repaired by horseshoe nails on the outside of each heel, three in one and four in the other. The nail in the corner of one of the heels was turned crossways. There was a round-headed tack in one of the boot heels and there was an impression in the back of the footprint that fit the tack in the boot.[1529]

Numerous witnesses testified about Richie's lack of money prior to the killing and his boast that he would have some soon. At trial he explained the money was expected to come from an uncle in Kansas. He offered to purchase land and hogs from virtually everyone who talked to him the day after the killing. His accounts of where he got various sums of money he spent after the killing were inconsistent. Dirt was found on the Winchester he owned and blood was found on Richie's pistol.[1530] He made no attempt to explain these facts. Earlier, at the coroner's inquest, Richie offered to allow the investigators to compare his boots to the tracks found near the body. They did so the next day after he was placed in the jail for safekeeping.

One of the state's witnesses said that Stephens was an eccentric who wore strings around his body and that he (Stephens) had offered to pay him one hundred dollars to kill him because he had gotten himself "in such a fix that he would rather die as to live," which occurred about the time Stephens's wife had suffered an apparent attempted poisoning. This was an unspecified time before the killing, however. The witness said he had seen Richie working for Stephens the week of the murder.

The Tennessee Supreme Court opinion in Richie's case cannot be located.

Richie was executed on May 9, 1894, in Gainesboro, Jackson County.[1531] Details of the execution are unknown except that it drew a large crowd (which could not see the actual drop), but according to local lore the townsfolk eagerly accepted portions of the rope as talismans against bad luck or bad health, and the actual noose still reposes in the Jackson County archives.

1894

Henry Bennett, black, age 28. *Murder.*

The crime was committed at 6:40 P.M. on May 22, 1893, near the Madison Street bridge over the Memphis & Charleston Railroad tracks, in Memphis, Shelby County. The victim was the killer's wife. She was Fannie Bennett, black, age twenty-five. Their five-year marriage had produced five children. Only one, age three, was still alive.

The couple had quarreled for months and were separated at the time of the killing. She had moved into a disreputable building called "Old Charleston Hill House." Fannie admitted she was living a life Henry did not approve of and had been intimate with other men. On the day of the killing, he left his home about six o'clock, telling his wife's grandmother, who lived with the couple, that he was leaving to "have some fun," brandishing a large knife.

Finding Fannie at the house, he intimidated her into leaving with him. Witnesses saw the couple walking and arguing. Henry pulled the large knife and began stabbing Fannie, who fell to the ground screaming. The witnesses came to her after Henry ran away. They helped her to walk to the couple's home on Monroe Street. She had received numerous defensive cuts to her arms and hands, and had two large penetrating wounds to the right and left abdomen, the latter after she had fallen to the ground. Fannie lived three days conscious of her impending death. She said Henry had stabbed her without provocation. Henry Bennett was arrested while she was still alive and said that if she died, he was ready to die for killing her.[1532]

At trial, he contended that she had struck the first blow with a small knife she carried and he had responded in kind, in a fit of anger.[1533] His counsel argued this was second, not first-degree murder. But no witnesses saw her attack him and he was found with her small knife when arrested. It was not bloody. The conviction was affirmed by the Tennessee Supreme Court, but the opinion cannot be located.

Bennett was executed on a gallows built inside the Memphis jail yard. It had served to execute five others, three for the same crime as Bennett, wife murder.[1534] Bennett was converted by the Rev. McCauley, black, a longtime jail minister, and had been baptized some eleven months earlier by the Rev. A.D. Cotton. Bennett said he was convinced he was going to heaven. One hour before the execution, a photographer was summoned. He took several pictures of Bennett, which the condemned wanted given to the sheriff and jailer, among others.

He walked to the gallows with a firm step. He was dressed in a white shirt, a black alpaca coat and vest, a turndown collar, new jeans trousers, a white necktie and a pair of white gloves. His shoes were blackened. Bennett said he was satisfied with his appearance.

Bennett was executed at 12:24 P.M. on July 25, 1894, in front of a dozen witnesses, but hundreds sat on railroad boxcars as others perched on the jail walls (helped up by a man with a ladder), getting a view they were legally barred from seeing.

On the scaffold he said, "My friends, I'm goin' away. I believe that I've been saved, an' that I soon will sit on the right hand of our Lord. I want you all to take warnin' by my fate. I ain't afraid to die. I know that I am goin' to a better world." As soon as he finished, a black female inmate quartet, under the direction of the Rev. Cotton, sang "How Sweet Are the Tidings." Both ministers spoke and offered prayers and another hymn was sung.

At this point Bennett was pinioned, the rope and cap were put over his head. Without warning, Sheriff McLendon pulled the trap lever. The body swung "aimlessly to and fro, and every now and then it would draw up on a convulsive movement, as with great, shuddering gasps the lungs fought for air which was shut out from them forever."[1535] It was determined that Bennet's neck was broken, but his heart beat for eleven minutes, and he was cut down a few minutes later. The body was given to the county undertaker for burial in a pauper's grave.

While incarcerated, Bennett had become infatuated with a woman named Katie Hudson, whom he met in the jail. He gave minister McCaully twenty-five cents to give to the woman, along with his hat. The morning of the execution, he was visited by Annie Edwards, his wife's niece, who was caring for his small daughter. She agreed to continue to care for the girl but received nothing from him for the task.

John S. Kennedy, white, age 25. *Murder.*
General Kennedy, white, age 26. *Murder.*

The crime was committed on the night of October 23, 1893, at the train depot of the Nashville, Chattanooga & St. Louis Railway Company in the community of Shellmound in rural Marion County. The killers were cousins. They had criminal records for larceny. General was largely in the thrall of John, including in the commission of their crimes. The pair had made various unsuccessful "raids" on train depots and trains in the mode of Jesse James, whose exploits they had followed with great interest and sought to emulate.[1536] The victim was John Lowrie, white, age twenty-four, the telegraph operator at the train depot. He worked the night shift and slept on a cot in the office. He was shot while asleep. Because of paper wadding found in the wound, it was determined that he had been shot with a muzzle-loading shotgun.

The killers had come to the depot area three consecutive nights prior to the killing to plot the crime, which involved giving chloroform to Lowrie, but John finally decided to shoot him. John crept up to an open window and shot Lowrie in the face. He climbed through the window and took all the money available, which included a new twenty-dollar bill. General told John not to take the man's watch in case they were found with it, but John did so, along with a pistol. These were hidden on their grandfather's farm in north Georgia where they lived. The pair had taken along Josephus Kennedy, a teen-ager, who was apparently unaware of the plot. He ran away after the shooting.

When Lowrie did not respond to signals, someone was sent to the check on him. At 3:00 A.M. his body was found and detectives from Chattanooga and at least two railway detectives began working on the crime. They quickly made the deduction about the type of shotgun, and within two days at least two groups of witnesses said they saw two men in the depot area the night of the murder. The two met the description of the Kennedys. A large reward was offered for them by name and General was captured "after a hard fight" by a constable in Dade County, Georgia, during which General was shot in the foot.[1537]

General, the weaker of the two, gave a confession implicating John and Josephus. All of the Kennedy clan lived in a place called Egypt Hollow. The detectives went to General's mother's home and lied, telling her that he had escaped from jail. She responded, "It is just what I expected. I knew General would get away from you, for he is sleek as an eel."[1538] The ruse was designed to make the Kennedy clan think the police were looking for General, when in fact, they were looking for the other two. A several-day stakeout showed that John was hiding in his grandfather's house. With the exits covered by lawmen, he was arrested in the house "after a sharp struggle" and the murder weapon was recovered. Josephus was arrested later.

In the jail, General was asked to repeat his confession with John present, but under John's intimidating eyes, he began stammering and stopped. "From that time until the day of the execution, John established the fact that he had a control over General which was almost superhuman. One look from those piercing gray eyes, and the tall mountaineer was absolutely unable to utter a sound."[1539]

General had given the twenty-dollar bill in trade at a saloon, and this had caused suspicion. The barkeeper wrote on the bill the date he received it and hid the bill in a trunk. (The barkeeper was later to share in the reward money.) General said that he had gotten the money in change when he paid a fine at a town near the Lowrie killing, prompting even more suspicion.

General took the witness stand and fell apart when confronted with the twenty-dollar bill. He admitted giving it at the saloon, but said he had gotten it in a store robbery a few nights before the killing. When the robbery victim was put on the stand he said that only silver money had been taken in the robbery. General changed his story, saying that he had exchanged the silver money for the twenty-dollar bill.

During the closing hours of the trial, a tip was received regarding the location of Lowrie's watch. The railroad sent a special train to Georgia with the detectives aboard. They went to the location given by the tipster and found the watch. The special train then returned with the watch. When it was presented to the jury, John Kennedy exclaimed to his lawyer, "By God, that ain't the watch! It don't look like it!" His lawyer turned to him and said, "You keep your damned mouth shut, will you!" but the jury heard both statements. After the trial, it was determined that the watch belonged to Lowrie by tracing its serial number to a Nashville jeweler. John and General Kennedy were convicted. Josephus Kennedy was acquitted. It was later shown that he had been a virtual hostage to the other two. The convictions were upheld on appeal by the Tennessee Supreme Court, but the opinion cannot be located.

The Kennedys escaped from the Marion County jail in March 1894 but were captured a few days later. When they were captured, the sheriff chained them together, which brought an oath from the men that they would kill him. Both men were baptized by the Rev. Cartwright in the jail a few days before the execution. General Kennedy gave his confession to all who would listen. John said nothing. The night before the execution, John's girlfriend, a prostitute named Martha Taylor, "spent the night with him."[1540] The next day, both men gave her their hats. In order to prevent a crowd from coming to the execution (which it could not see), the sheriff allowed the pair to sit in a second-storey window and answer questions from a crowd of five hundred the day before the execution.

The pair was taken in a wagon to a gallows built about a mile from the courthouse in Jasper. It was in an oak enclosure on the Pryor farm, and was built to accommodate one hundred spectators. By execution time, about two thousand five hundred people had crowded around the gallows, making it difficult for the wagon to pass through. This was the fifth legal execution in Jasper since the Civil War, a small-town record. About two hundred boys, perched in trees around the gallows, had the best view. "Will Fischer, a Nashville saloonist, was stricken by violent hysterics during the preparations, but recovered."[1541]

The Kennedys were executed at 1:56 P.M. on December 17, 1894. They had difficulty walking and were seated in chairs. They were accompanied to the gallows by the Rev. Cartwright. Both were shaking badly. General asked for a morphine tablet, which he was given. John asked for and received several large drinks of whiskey.

The Rev. Cartwright, on the gallows, asked General Kennedy if he was satisfied as to his salvation. He answered, "I am trusting to God." Asking John the same question brought no response. However, two minutes before the trap fell, a voice from the crowd asked John if he was guilty and he nodded his head.

After the Rev. Cartwright gave a moving prayer, the pair were pinioned, ropes placed and caps pulled over their heads. The Rev. Cartwright left the gallows at that moment. He later explained, "John said nothing; but General thinks he is forgiven and is going to heaven."[1542] As soon as the caps were pulled, the sheriff left the stand to pull the trap trigger, saying, "Gentlemen, everybody take fair warning." General responded, "Oh, my God!" and the trap was sprung. "As the bodies shot downward, the crowd instinctively drew back and then there was a reaction and a rush for the bodies."[1543] At that same moment, Martha Taylor, in the crowd with her mother and sister, gave out a piercing scream.

An audible crack indicated that General's neck was broken. John struggled with his hands, trying to free himself; his back and abdomen convulsed for six minutes as he tried to breathe. Both were cut down twenty-seven minutes later. Their bodies were placed in coffins and given to their kin for burial in Egypt Hollow. Martha Taylor wore both men's hats proudly.

According to the newspaper, "By 10 o'clock in the morning, three hours before the hanging, a book written by John Kennedy will be on sale here giving, it is said, a full confession and implicating no one but the two who hang. The book gives the life of the boys and is published in small pamphlet form."[1544] The pamphlet was published by Byrne Tatum, the lawyer for the pair.[1545]

John Stanley, white, age 35. *Murder.*
Clarence Cox, white, age 22. *Murder.*

The crime was committed at 6:45 P.M. February 7, 1894, at the house of the victims near their flour mill on Hinds Creek in Union County. The killers were from Knox County. The victims were Henry Snodderly, white, age eighty-nine, and his wife Serene, white, age eighty-two. Mystery surrounds why the couple were killed. The common belief was they were victims of an armed robbery gone bad. The old man reputedly kept a "half bushel of hard money" in the house.[1546]

The Snodderly family had finished supper. Seated in the living room were the elderly couple, a daughter Lucinda Snodderly, age thirty-five, a grandson Sam Guinn, age twenty, and a younger granddaughter, Serene Pyle. Guinn opened the door, responding to a request from outside asking if his uncle, John Snodderly, was still operating the mill at that hour. As he did so, Stanley pushed his way in the house, followed by Cox. Stanley was under the influence of whiskey.[1547] Both were wearing masks.

Seeing the gunmen, Lucinda Snodderly and Serene Pyle bolted from the room, ran to the kitchen and out of the house. They hid underneath the mill. Later, one hid in a field while the other hid in a closet in John Snodderly's house nearby.

Stanley told the old man to keep still. But when he lifted his hand and said, "Oh, Lord, what shall we do?" Stanley shot him once. Serene Snodderly, across the room, stepped toward her husband and Stanley shot her once. She staggered toward the kitchen and fell. The gunmen ordered Sam Guinn to empty all the bureau drawers into the middle of the room, and they continued ransacking on their own. The only money in the house was $117.75, which they overlooked. As the killers lowered their pistols, Guinn slipped out a side door, going to the nearby home of John Snodderly, the couple's son. When they returned, the killers were gone. Because it was raining, it was not thought possible to track the men that night. It was discovered they had taken two horses from the stable.[1548]

Several days later, the sheriff arrested Sam Guinn

but did not hold him. Guinn said he thought the men were Stanley and Cox because they had attended a Sunday School at his house.[1549] Stanley was short and stout and Cox was tall and thin. In time, rewards amounting to $700 were offered. The two were named as suspects in the reward offers. After several weeks, the father of Clarence Cox came forward and offered the sheriff a deal. In return for $300 of the reward money, which was to be used to pay a lawyer, the two would surrender because they had alibis. This was agreed and the men surrendered to the sheriff of Knox County. They feared lynching if they surrendered in Union County.

The trial began on June 28, 1894, in Union County. The pair did not take the stand and their alibi witnesses were largely discredited. The pair had ridden horses from Knoxville to the Snodderly house, taking at least a day to get there. The state presented numerous witnesses who placed them at proper traveling times on the way to the murder house, and saw them entering the woods so as not to be seen, shortly before the shooting.

One witness, whom they had asked for food, had been told by the men that they were from Maynardville. When he asked them about a religious revival being conduced by a man named McCloud, they did not respond. The witness thought this was peculiar.[1550] Another witness directed them to Snodderly's mill when they asked directions.

Stanley was quickly convicted but the jury said it was having difficulty reaching a verdict on Cox. The judge sent them back and Cox was ordered hanged too. The Tennessee Supreme Court affirmed the convictions, but the opinion cannot be located.

The men were kept in the Knoxville jail to prevent a mob from lynching them. The day of their execution they told a newspaper reporter they had secreted morphine in their cells by which to kill themselves if taken by a mob. When the reporter pressed jail officials to search the cells, a box of morphine pills was found containing enough to "kill a couple of horses."[1551]

The gallows on "hangman's hill" in Maynardville had been built for the double execution and was never used again. The enclosure was 21 by 36 feet with a 10-foot fence. The pair was brought to Maynardville from the Knoxville jail the day before the execution. A crowd of five thousand gathered around the enclosure. They were unable to see anything. A group of ruffians led by Dave Turner pressed against the enclosure and knocked it down. The well-armed deputies restored order and rebuilt the enclosure, delaying the execution by about an hour.

Both men professed faith and demanded separate cells so they could each study the Bible and contemplate their condition alone. Both men confessed to the crime while in jail. However, at the gallows Stanley told the crowd he was innocent and had prepared a book-length manuscript about his life which he left with his widow.[1552]

The pair was executed at 2:45 P.M. on December 22, 1894. Stanley asked if he could pray aloud and was given permission. He prayed endlessly in mocking fashion and was stopped by the sheriff. When the sheriff started to put the hood on Stanley, he shouted, "Put it on Cox first!" and the sheriff complied. Because the Union County sheriff had difficulty cutting the trip rope, he was assisted by the Knox County sheriff.

Stanley left his wife a long letter which aroused much speculation. The general feeling was the pair had been put up to the crime, intended as just an armed robbery, but the intoxicated Stanley began shooting when confronted with so many people in the room. Stanley had a reputation as a vicious man and Cox was thought to be under his influence.[1553] Cox was unmarried and his body was delivered to his father.

1895

Buddy Wooden, black, age 18. *Murder.*
George Mapp (aka George Knapp and Mitchell Morgan), black, age 20. *Murder.*

The crime was committed about midnight on December 17, 1892, on Rossville Avenue in downtown Chattanooga, in Hamilton County. The killing occurred in the Last Chance Saloon owned by the victim, Marion Ross, white, age sixty.

The killers were longtime criminals with prior convictions for larceny and burglary. Mapp had been held on a larceny charge in Birmingham, Alabama, but was mistakenly released by the jailer. He went to the rail yards, where he met Wooden for the first time. They took a train to Decatur, Alabama, where Mapp shot a black man named Tom Hopkins. The pair escaped by catching a train to Chattanooga, where they planned to meet at the home of Wooden's aunt. Wooden arrived the next day. As the two slept in the same bed, they planned on getting money by robbing a store. The pair decided not to hold up the store because there were too many people present, and chose the saloon because it appeared empty.[1554] The victim, Marion Ross, was seated alone in his saloon.

The killers waited outside until three men seated together left. They burst into the saloon and pointed pistols at Ross, demanding that he not move. When he seemed to move, he was shot by Mapp, then by Wooden, then by Mapp again, and finally by Wooden. It is not clear how much money they garnered. Police were without any clues until a man living in the neighborhood described the pair he had seen hanging around the saloon earlier on the night of the shooting. Police went to Wooden's mother's house, where they found the two in bed. Wooden was arrested on an outstanding burglary charge. Mapp was not arrested for lack of evidence. He promptly left town.

In jail, Wooden became friends with another inmate, Ed Dillard, black, and told him the crime details. He told the police, and soon Wooden confessed. He was tried and convicted largely on his own confession, and was waiting execution at the time Mapp was arrested many months later. Mapp had an unusual birthmark.

Mapp was caught only because of the perseverance of detective Charles Brock, who traveled some three thousand miles tracking Mapp, finally locating him in the Sioux City, Iowa, jail on June 20, 1893. The cost of his travel was borne by a friend of the Ross family. Wooden testified against Mapp, who protested his innocence to the end. Mapp literally cursed Wooden with his last breaths.

It cannot be determined whether the cases were appealed to the Tennessee Supreme Court.

Wooden had escaped from the Chattanooga jail on December 10, 1893, at a time when Mapp was still at large, but was arrested in a Birmingham saloon on January 3, 1894. He later admitted that he placed himself in the wrong cell two nights before his execution, hoping for another chance to escape.

Mapp had two girlfriends. Lillie Coleman visited him in jail and urged him to consider his soul. The other, Ella Kemp, had been a jail inmate who captured his attention. Mapp spent his last days cursing everyone around him and singing a popular song, "Milwaukee Fire."

The gallows inside the jail were built to handle both executions and engineered so that the deputy who actually pulled the lever would remain unknown. Five deputies were arranged around a table, each pulling a rope under the table that may have actually tripped the trap. This was an innovation suggested by Sheriff F. Scott Hyde, who had never presided over an execution.

The pair were executed at 8:21 A.M. on January 11, 1895, in front of about fifteen witnesses. The sheriff chose this time in order to frustrate the crowds expected to assemble around the jail, having told the media that the executions were to take place at 11:00 A.M.

While in jail awaiting his death, Wooden embraced the Catholic faith and was wearing a crucifix around his neck when executed. Two priests walked with him to the gallows and prayed while he stood waiting to die. Mapp had been visited by the priests and a black Congregationalist minister, but turned them away, saying he did "not want any preachers, nor any of their damn monkey business around him." When asked what he wanted done with his body, Mapp replied, "I don't care a damn. You can give it to the student doctors to cut up or you can throw it into the Tennessee River and let it float to hell!" He said he didn't want to ever see Wooden again, even in hell.[1555]

As the two were being taken to the gallows, with Wooden crying and Mapp "brutally defiant," Wooden was comforted by the priests, and standing on the gallows, responded to a phrase intoned by the priests, "Deliver, O Lord, the soul of Thy servant," by saying, "The soul of Thy servant." He was repeating this at the time of the drop. The pair had been seated on chairs on the gallows, and because of Mapp's cursing, the pair were not asked for any last statements.

Mapp cursed everyone in sight, especially Sheriff Hyde. He had anticipated receiving a commutation, and felt the sheriff was responsible for his not getting it. Mapp "cursed and swore like a trooper." He was now certain what he wanted done with his body: "I want my body to be thrown into the Tennessee River and let it float to hell." He continued, "By Jesus, this is what an innocent boy gets. I am going straight to hell, and I'll meet him [Wooden] there, too." He continued, "I will see you on earth again some day to haunt you, Mr. Hyde." Mapp rambled, "Mr. Easley [his lawyer], give my hat to Ella Kemp and tell her to wear it. She lives at 119 D Street. I hope this will be a warning to all you boys. I hope all those people that have got it in for me will meet me in hell."[1556]

When the sheriff tired of listening to Mapp, he ordered the ropes and caps placed. Without warning he pushed a button that rang a buzzer to the men down below at the lever-table. They pulled their cords and the men dropped cleanly. Wooden's neck was broken, but Mapp strangled to death. They were cut down eighteen minutes later and placed in plain coffins, the lids nailed shut.

The coffins were taken by a black undertaker to

his parlor, but were opened for public viewing. Several men stood at the door demanding a nickel to see the bodies, with the money used to bury the men. The mayor learned of this and came immediately to the parlor and ordered the viewing to stop, but not before $30 had been raised from the mostly black spectators. The undertaker was charged with the crime of operating a museum without a license.[1557]

Wooden was buried in the Catholic cemetery. What happened to Mapp's body is unknown. It was said in the years that followed that Wooden's ghost haunted the gallows. Because he lived a few minutes longer than Mapp, he was the last person to die on the gallows. This gave his ghost the privilege of visiting it from hell, according to local lore.[1558]

Matthew Calloway, black, age 24. *Murder.*

The crime was committed about 6:00 A.M. on July 16, 1894, on a road in a rural area near the town of Santa Fe, in Maury County. The killer was a farm worker who was intimately involved with Mary Walters, black, wife of the victim, James Walters, black, age twenty-six. The couple had been quarreling for six months and had separated. Jim Walters was attempting a reconciliation with his wife at the time he was killed. He was carrying a recently ornamented dress to her, walking to their home.

Calloway met Jim Walters for the purpose of killing him. Said Calloway, "I was sitting on the fence. Jim Walters came up. I stepped out in the road and grabbed him. I told him I was g'wine to whip him and axed him to come out to the road, an' he wouldn't do it. Then I walked to the fence and set the gun down. Then I ketched him by the throat by my left hand and commenced to choke him. He soon said, Lord, Lord, Lord, then I carried him over in the thicket. He wasn't dead when I left him. He had a dress of his wife's and a pair of shoes which he drapped in the road. I carried them and put them by his side."[1559] The body was hidden about 400 yards from Jim and Mary's house.

Calloway continued, "I went to Mary Walters's house and told her I choked Jim down and put him in the thicket and he mought get up, that he wasn't dead when I left. I stayed with Mary the night before I choked Jim." Jim Walters, described as a "timid negro," had been scared away from seeing his wife by Calloway, who was described as a "bad and dangerous negro," who visited her at times when he thought Calloway was not around.

When Walters was not seen for two weeks, his friends began looking for him. They located the body on August 4, 1894, because it had drawn the attention of buzzards and dogs. It was recognizable because of his peculiarly shaped head and the remaining clothing, including the dress for Mary.[1560]

The state's theory was that Mary had gone to where her husband lay and fired three shots into him while he was still alive. She was linked to the crime by the couple's six-year-old son. He had gone to the thicket, where he saw his father, and had told his mother he appeared to be sleeping. Mary scolded him to keep quiet or she would kill him. It was possible that Mary intended to cast blame on Calloway because one of his shirts, with blood on it, was in a hollow log nearby. Calloway denied there was any bleeding involved in killing Walters, and denied the shirt was his.[1561]

The pair was tried together and both were convicted of first-degree murder, but the jury said there were mitigating circumstances regarding Mary Walters. For that reason the judge sentenced her to life imprisonment. Their cases were appealed together to the Tennessee Supreme Court, but the opinion cannot be located.

The exact location of the gallows is unknown, but appears to have been in the yard in front of the Maury County jail. One newspaper said there were rumors that a crowd threatened to tear down the stockade built around the gallows. Another newspaper said that was false.[1562] In order to frustrate the anticipated crowd, Sheriff P.H. Ragsdale refused to announce the time of the execution. Instead, he brought Calloway to the gallows as soon as possible, at 8:00 A.M. on April 20, 1895. Fewer than a dozen people saw Calloway mount the platform with a steady step and speak his last words.

Calloway insisted that he had not meant to kill Walters and had killed him at a different time than the state alleged. He insisted he had not shot him. When finished, the sheriff asked him if he wanted to pray and the doomed man said yes. Calloway had spent virtually all of his time in jail reading his Bible. Calloway fell to his knees and said, "O God! O God, as this is my last hour, oh, take me home. O God! forgive me all my sins. I acknowledge my sins; I open up my eyes to Thee. Oh, carry me to a better place; please carry me safely home. Oh, take me home! Oh, God, who knows the secret of my heart, forgive me for everything; carry me home; send angels to guide me. Oh, my God, take me to a world where I will be free from tribulation anymore."[1563]

As soon as he finished, the rope and cap were placed. The sheriff said, "Matthew, your time has come. Good-bye," and dropped the trap at 8:06 A.M. His neck was broken with an audible snap and he was cut down fifteen minutes later.[1564] Calloway died with his Bible in his pocket. Sheriff Ragsdale gave the $30 he was paid to execute Calloway toward the funeral expenses. The body was taken by the undertaker and placed on view in the undertaker's parlor, where about five hundred people, mostly black, viewed it.

Robert Ford, black, age 19. *Murder.*

The crime was committed at noon on October 21, 1894, at the house of Will Frazier, black, in Mud Bottom, near Ransom's Mill, located behind Jubilee Hall, in Nashville, in Davidson County. The killer was a small-time criminal who had been engaged in a craps game at this location. The victim, Jerry Brown, black, age thirty-five, was a fellow gambler. The shooting arose out of a gambling dispute.

Two weeks before the shooting, Frazier, the killer and the victim had engaged in a craps game and Ford lost $2.25. He laid a $2 bill on the table, and Frazier and Brown began disputing to see how they should divide the money between them. Finally, Ford picked up the money with the remark, "You niggers can settle this thing some other time!" and walked out of the house with the money. Brown and his brother-in-law followed Ford, insisting they should get the money back, but Ford dodged them. After searching Hell's Half Acre, they gave up.

On the day of the shooting, Ford went to Frazier's house to attend a craps game already underway. Ford said on the witness stand that if he had known that Brown was there, "We would not have gone inside." Ford went in, put a quarter on the table and threw the dice. Brown picked up the dice and quarter and told Ford he could not play in the game. At that point, the bouncer, named Crawford, threw Ford out the door.

Now outside, Ford bumped into a friend, Sam Hatchey, alias Hatchett, and they began talking about what happened. Earlier, Ford had borrowed fifty cents from Hatchey. Ford told Hatchey he would go back into the house and get back his quarter in order to pay Hatchey back. Hatchey tried to convince Ford not to go back in the house, fearing trouble from Brown. Ford replied, "I am going in there and make Frazier get my quarter."[1565] He then went to the back door. Some witnesses said he took his pistol from his hip pocket and put it in his coat pocket.

As Ford entered the back door, Brown came at him with one hand in his pocket and grabbed at him. In defense (as he claimed), Ford fired a shot that grazed Brown's abdomen. Brown stepped back and Crawford attempted to close the door to keep Ford out. Ford pushed his way into the room and with Crawford between them, fired a second shot at Brown, underneath Crawford's arm. As Crawford moved to one side, Ford grabbed Brown by the collar and shot him through the heart. Ford then tried to get Hatchey to go back inside with him to get his money. Hatchey refused, realizing the nature of the situation, and took off. He was arrested the next day. Ford was found two days later at a friend's house hiding under a bed.

When arrested, Ford exuded bravado, saying, "Yes, I killed the damn nigger, and I would do it again if necessary. I picked my spots on him before I would fire." The night before his execution, he was asked if he was sorry he had killed Brown. He replied:

> Yes, I am and you bet I would have never done it if I had been in my right mind. I know little of laws and when first arrested I did not comprehend the enormity of my crime. The officers would talk to me in a laughing, careless manner, as though I would come out of the affair all right. I was only 18 years old and their manner made me believe I had done something smart. I afterward learned they used this ruse to pump me up and make me criminate myself. I know that I did wrong in killing Brown but if I knew as much when arrested as I do now, I firmly believe that I would never have been sentenced to death. My advice to folks is never to get in trouble, but if they unfortunately do, the wisest course for them to pursue is not to talk. These policemen don't care for a poor negro, and they think it is a feather in their cap to send one to the gallows.[1566]

Ford and Hatchey went to trial on November 21, 1894, (Hatchey as an accomplice). Ford was convicted of first-degree murder and Hatchey was acquitted. The day before his execution, Ford told this version of what happened: "Brown and I had a dispute about a quarter in a crap game. He was not entitled to the money but took it anyhow. Me and Hatchey left the house, but shortly after we had gotten out Hatchey suggested that I go back and get the money or get him [meaning Brown]. I had been drinking and acted on Hatchey's suggestion. We went back together and met Brown at the door with a deck of cards in his hand. I asked him to refund the money, but he refused, and when he made a step toward me I drew my pistol and fired. He was a much more powerful man than me, and I would have been no match for him without a pistol."[1567] The conviction was upheld by the Tennessee Supreme Court on February 28, 1895, but the opinion cannot be located.

The scaffold built for Ford's death was new; no one had been executed in Nashville since Ben Brown in 1887. It was located inside the Davidson County jail, built in a manner to utilize the space between two walls separating the jailer's living quarters and the kitchen. Except those who stood on the gallows with Ford, no one could see the drop because it was covered by a curtain of white canvas. For several days, the gallows were opened for viewing and about six thousand people came by to look at it.

In the weeks before his execution, Ford had been attended by the Rev. Luke Mason, black, and another black minister, and by the time of his death he was convinced he was saved and was going to heaven. His written statement to the media said, "The Lord has promised good to me and he will go with me through the dark valley and shadow of death. I fear no evil in my soul. My home is heaven."[1568] On the night before his execution, Ford had complained of a headache and was given whiskey and Antikamnia, which put him to sleep, enabling him to pass a restful night.

The Rev. Mason conducted a service at Ford's cell which included the last sacrament. Earlier Ford had requested oyster soup for breakfast, and it was brought to him. Ford had asked for whiskey to fortify him on the way to the gallows, and this was given to him. His other request, that inmate George R. Alexander, awaiting execution for a Fayetteville murder, be allowed to witness his execution, was denied. (Alexander was never executed.)

Ford walked firmly to the gallows wearing new underwear, a light-colored sack coat closely buttoned with the collar turned up, light blue pants, and a new pair of patent leather shoes, all purchased by the sheriff. Ford was executed at 9:49 A.M. on April 25, 1895, in front of a dozen people, but with at least a thousand waiting on the crowded streets outside.

The sheriff asked Ford if he had anything to say. With a voice choked with emotion he said, "I want to say that I have made peace with my God and expect to go to heaven. I acknowledge that I have done wrong, and that I have no hard feelings toward anyone. God has promised to save my soul and I know He will do it. I hope my fate will be a warning to all young men of my race to beware of gambling and drinking. It was not the fault of my mother and father, for they tried to raise me right. I am not afraid to face death, for I know I am going to heaven and hope to meet you all there."[1569] Ford spoke in short, broken sentences in a voice that could only be heard by those standing near by. At the conclusion of his remarks, he turned to Sheriff Sharp and said, "That's all."

The Rev. Mason read a portion of the Fifty-Seventh Psalm. He and the Rev. Nixon sang a hymn. Ford wept bitterly, but regained his composure when the Rev. Mason began a prayer. Ford's hands were then handcuffed, he was pinioned and the rope and cap were put over his head. Said the newspaper, "Although the work was accomplished rapidly the suspense was something terrible. Seconds seemed minutes and minutes seemed hours, but the condemned man never flinched."[1570] As soon as this was done, Sheriff Sharp stepped to the back of the scaffold and pulled the lever. The drop was clean, but Ford strangled to death, making a slight sigh and a gurgling sound. He was cut down thirty-two minutes later.

Thousands waited outside the jail but saw nothing but the hearse leave with Ford's coffin, which was taken to his home for his parents to see, then to Mt. Ararat Cemetery for burial the next day without a funeral service. "Except for a slight discoloration of the face, Ford's body looked quite natural."[1571] Ford had asked Sheriff Sharp to see that he had a decent burial, but since the family had used all its money on his lawyer, Ford doubted it would be likely. The sheriff donated his $30 execution fee for that purpose.

Mike L. King, white, age 23. *Murder.*

The crime was committed in the middle of the night on December 23, 1894, in the killer's house near the community of Isham, in Scott County. The killer had been befriended by the victim, Aaron Beck, white, age forty-seven. He had been lured to King's home for robbery and murder. Beck, a schoolteacher, was thought to carry all his money on his person, as much as three hundred dollars.

Beck had come to Tennessee from Kentucky a couple of years before he was killed. He was a writing and music teacher in Oneida and "bore a good reputation."[1572] He had befriended King and "taught him well enough to teach in a county school, secured him a position, loaned him various amounts of money, and in other ways showed favors that only reaped the basest ingratitude."[1573]

The story of the crime came from King's mouth: "I made up my mind to kill Beck about December 20, 1894. I went to the tunnel on the Oneida & Paint Rock Railroad armed with a Winchester rifle and watched for Beck all day, intending to kill him for his money. He did not come. I then went back to Isham and came to Oneida on Sunday, December 23; met Beck and persuaded him to accompany me home at Isham, where we arrived about 1:00 o'clock and went to bed without supper." King continued, "About 11:00 o'clock I got up and shot Beck through the head with a .38 caliber pistol. He floundered a little and I hit him in the head with a hatchet. He died at once. I rifled his pockets, getting $54 in cash and his watch. I then carried and dragged his body to the woods and covered it up."[1574]

Beck's grave had been dug by nature. The wind had uprooted a large chestnut tree and Beck's body was placed in the hole. It was found on January 20, 1895, by a boy and two women who were looking in the woods for sourwood that could be used as oxen yoke.[1575] Suspicion immediately fell on King and he was taken to the Morgan County jail for safekeeping.

King went on trial in March 1895. His not-guilty plea was based on the defense that the killing occurred in Kentucky, not Tennessee, because his house was close to the line. It cannot be determined whether the case was appealed to the Tennessee Supreme Court, but the proximity of time from trial to execution suggests it was not.

Mike L. King was executed at noon on May 17, 1895, in Huntsville, county seat of Scott County. Details of the execution are unknown except that King's wife and baby said good-bye to him on the scaffold. He trembled in every muscle and told the huge crowd not to sin like he had. "The country preachers exhorted the crowd and then the doomed man stood up for the black cap. At 12:37 the trap was sprung and he strangled to death."[1576] This may have been due to imbalance; King had only one arm.

People came from great distances to see the hanging and the crowd was immense. The effect of the hanging was this: "Scott County is the roughest county in Tennessee. Last night toughs terrorized the town. Horses were driven at break neck speed through the town to the accompaniment of yells and pistol shots. This morning things were quieter, but with moonshine whisky flowing like water. It was still very lively. The people made it a gala occasion. Venders of red lemonade and bologna made a small fortune. Peanuts were everywhere. The women were as numerous as the men and entered as heartily into the fun. It was a regular picnic."[1577]

1896

Bart Green, black, age 46. *Murder.*

The crime was committed about 5:00 A.M. on December 16, 1895, in the barn on the farm of Miles P. Mitchell in the community of Whiteville, in Hardeman County. The killer was a farmer who lived about a mile away. The victim, Miles P. Mitchell, white, age fifty-six, was described as a wealthy and peaceable farmer. He was reputed to carry large sums of money on his person.

Moses Pirtle, black, lived close to the Mitchell farm and worked there. He conspired with Green to rob and kill Mitchell, who was supposed to have as much as eight hundred dollars on his person. The night before the killing, Pirtle loaded Green's shotgun and left it outside his door. Green carried the gun to the barn, where Mitchell was feeding his stock. Green shot him in the head and took money from his body. By prior arrangement, Green put half of the money he got ($70) into a snuff bottle and buried it at a location some distance from Pirtle's house.

As soon as Mrs. Mitchell found her dead husband, she notified the sheriff. He contacted the Madison County sheriff, who brought bloodhounds by a special train. The hounds tracked both Pirtle and Green. In particular, they tracked Green's scent to a smokehouse where Green had originally hidden the gun. Pirtle began confessing and explained that Green had taken the gun from the smokehouse and thrown it into a thicket. It was found at four o'clock in the afternoon and showed evidence of having recently been fired.

The tracks left by Pirtle and Green were distinguishable. Green's footprint and shoes were "a little careened and run down to the outside on both feet."[1578] Likewise, the buckskin gloves which Green was seen to wear every day were discovered and showed evidence they had been rubbed in order to clean something from them. An expert testified that when a portion of the gloves were "saturated with a solution of chloride of sodium and subjected to microscopic examination by an expert in such matters" it was blood.[1579] The expert could not say it was human blood, only mammal blood, as "for instance, the blood of a goat, dog, horse, or cow."[1580]

Pirtle said on several occasions in front of different people, "I didn't do it. I loaded the gun and set it outdoors, and Uncle Bart killed him," or stated it this way, "It's just like I said before: I set the gun out of the house and Uncle Bart killed him and put my money beside the stump."[1581]

The issue before the Supreme Court was whether Pirtle's statements could be repeated to the jury by those who heard them. Moses Pirtle had died in the Nashville jail shortly after he and Green were brought there for safekeeping. He died, "it is supposed, of pure fright."[1582] In ruling the statements were admissible, the court held that where one has heard an accusation and understands it, and has the opportunity to challenge it immediately, but says nothing, the act of not speaking may be taken as a circumstance of guilt.[1583] Also, it was proper for the court to admit the testimony of two women who had said in the presence of Green that he had come to the Pirtle house and hidden the gun, and came back later to hide it again.[1584]

Green had been tried in Madison County instead of Hardeman County. The courts said, "There is little doubt from this record — although a sad commentary upon our institutions — that, had the prisoner been returned to Hardeman County, he would have expiated his crime at the hands of a mob."[1585]

The night before his execution Green was asked if he wanted anything said to his friends. He replied that he had only three friends in the world. They were the sheriffs of Hardeman and Madison Counties (who had taken many steps to save him from lynching), and the Rev. Jesse Normant of Whiteville. While he was in the jail, he had been visited by every minister in town and told them he had no doubt as to his eternal salvation.

Bart Green was executed at 10:56 A.M. July 29, 1896, in the hall of the Madison County jail in Jackson. He walked to the gallows unaided and gave the Rev. Normant two letters, one for the pastor of his wife's church and another for the newspaper, in which he continued to assert his innocence. On the gallows he made a short, disconnected speech asserting his innocence. When the cap and noose were placed on his head he fainted and had to be held on his feet for the drop. When it came, his neck was broken and he was cut down fourteen minutes later. Green was very disappointed that his wife did not stay for his execution, having left on a train after seeing him at the jail that morning. He was survived by five children.

William H. Whitlock, black, age 40. *Murder.*

The crime was committed on the morning of August 9, 1895, at a home in the community of LaGrange in rural Fayette County. Whitlock had been in the area "looking for hidden treasures" (a newspaper euphemism for dealing in stolen property) when another black man complained to the sheriff that Whitlock was carrying a pistol which he had brandished at will.

The warrant for this crime was being served by the victim, sheriff's constable William D. Holliday, white, age forty-three. The victim was "taken unawares" and was shot with the pistol several times.[1586] Holliday left a wife and nine children. The Memphis newspaper predicted Whitlock would be lynched.[1587] Whitlock escaped to Birmingham, Alabama, but was captured a month later. He was brought back for trial, which began on January 25, 1896; all the witnesses against him were black. Prior to trial he admitted doing some shooting, but denied the killing. He was sentenced to death on January 30, 1896, and at a later trial convicted of carrying a pistol.[1588]

Whitlock appealed to the Tennessee Supreme Court but a written opinion cannot be located. It ordered him executed on August 6, 1896.[1589] However, because that was election day for local offices, the governor granted a one-week reprieve and Whitlock was hanged inside an enclosure about a half-mile from Somerville on August 13, 1896. The details of his execution are unknown.

On the gallows Whitlock continued to maintain his innocence, but spoke earnestly of his Christian faith and his confidence in going to heaven. He was attended by white and black ministers who offered prayers inside the enclosed gallows. Whitlock had brought to the gallows a large sign which he asked be hung outside the enclosure. It read, "Jesus hath redeemed; I have a building with God not made with hands, eternal in the heavens."[1590]

Frank Johnson, black, age 18. *Murder.*

The crime was committed about 7:00 P.M. August 1, 1896, on West Seventh Street in Columbia, in Maury County. The killer was an unschooled town rowdy. The victim was Austin Rye, black, age forty-four.

Johnson, somewhat intoxicated, happened upon the victim, described as an "honest old negro," while walking down the street. Johnson was carrying an unseen ax. He struck the victim in the side of the head and robbed him after he fell, taking a small amount of money and personal effects. Coincidentally, the victim was found lying in front of a doctor's house with brains oozing from his head. He lingered a day or so before dying. The bloody ax was found the next day.

Johnson had left town and the circumstances of his arrest and conviction are unknown other than that he confessed. But he also implicated, at various times, three adult white men. Each was found to have credible alibis and were never charged. It cannot be determined whether his case was appealed to the Tennessee Supreme Court. Johnson had been baptized in the Baptist church by a black minister, the Rev. Joe Elder, who was with him on the gallows.

The day before his execution, he was interviewed by the newspaper. He explained that he was "not quite eighteen" years old, that his parents had not visited him in jail, nor had his brothers and sisters, because he did not want them to visit him. Asked why he killed Austin Rye he answered, "I killed him just because I could, I reckon."[1591] He explained that he alone killed Rye and that he had drunk a great deal of whiskey that day.

When asked if he had any word of warning to other people, he said, "No, nothing." Then he was asked, "Now, the most important question of all. How is your soul?" He responded, "Oh, that's all right." Asked again, "And you are sure, then, that all is well, and you are prepared to die?" He answered, "Yes, I am sure; all is well."[1592]

Johnson left a long handwritten last statement which thanked many people, by name, who had tended his needs while in jail, including providing him a large Thanksgiving meal. It said, "Boys, do not commit such a crime as I have committed. George Frierson, try to be a better man and meet me in heaven. I want you all to do right and meet me in heaven. Obey your parents, for my mother taught me to do right. It is not her fault for what I have done. If I had listened and obeyed her, I would have been at home today instead of being a criminal for the gallows."[1593]

He concluded, "Let all who read my statements please take them as a warning, especially the younger boys. Praise the Lord, O, my soul! I am ready to meet my Savior in glory. Amen."[1594]

Frank Johnson was executed at 10:15 A.M. November 27, 1896, on an enclosed gallows in the yard of the Maury County jail. About eighteen people witnessed the hanging, including his minister on the gallows with him. There was little said at the gallows because of a heavy, driving rain, and Johnson spent most of the time on his knees in prayer. He told the gathering that he was the only person involved in the killing and he was very sorry for it.

With the cap and noose around Johnson's neck, the sheriff told him that he had one minute to live. Johnson replied he was glad and he was ready and willing to go. Sheriff Webb pulled the trap trigger without verbal warning and the fall was clean, breaking Johnson's neck. His body was given to a black undertaker who buried him in a black cemetery, reported the newspaper, which had described Johnson as a mulatto.[1595]

Maired Hatfield, white, age 20. *Murder.*

The crime was committed on the evening of March 25, 1896, in a rural area located between the home of C.D. Allen and the victim's "blind tiger," an unlicensed liquor parlor, one mile from Ball Point, near the Grainger County line, in Hancock County. The killer was a young farmer who had been told that the victim often carried one hundred dollars on his person. The victim was Jonas Trail, white, age thirty-nine, owner of the blind tiger.

Hatfield was convicted on the testimony of a friend, Bud Richardson, who said that Hatfield came to his house the morning after the killing wearing soiled and bloody clothes which matched the knee prints found beside Trail's body. When Richardson said the community was upset about the killing and the culprit might be lynched, Hatfield "became uneasy."[1596] Shortly after his arrest, Hatfield confessed, but kept changing his story regarding involvement of others. Another man, Charlie Collins, was tried with him but exonerated when Hatfield named a woman, Hanie Jordan, and his own wife as co-killers. Hatfield's conviction was upheld by the Tennessee Supreme Court, but the opinion cannot be located.[1597]

Shortly before the execution, Hatfield gave a lengthy statement to the newspaper. He said:

> I want to tell you that Hanie Jordan is as much to blame for my fate as I am. She helped me murder Jonas Trail. I would be perfectly satisfied to die if I thought she would hang too, but it seems that she is going to escape punishment for her part of the crime. Hanie Jordan, my wife and myself had talked over the affair for two months before the killing. Hanie had told us that Trail had $100 in cash, and it was our plan to get it at any cost. On the night of March 25th, between seven and eight o'clock, we three got a man named Allen to call Trail out to get some whiskey from a blind tiger he was running. As he returned to his house we assaulted him, having been in hiding behind a fence. Hanie was the first to get behind him. She struck him with a big dogwood stick and the lick knocked him down. I then struck him several times on the head with a big rock, and Hanie finished the job by stabbing him with a case knife that had been sharpened at one point. He fell on his face and turned partially over. We searched him and got his pocketbook, some money and a knife. I kept the knife and Hanie gave me $8 in money. I can't count money, but she said it was half of what he had. The truth is, Hanie Jordan and my wife got me into this scrape to get rid of me. They had never seen Trail with $100, as reported. I got some dirt and blood on my pants and Hanie also some on her clothes. My mother washed my pants after the killing, and said she would swear that I stayed at home on the night of the murder. I told her I did not want anyone to swear a lie for me. After I was arrested I got the money and knife for the officers. I killed Trail because the women told me to, and I don't

> think they ought to hang me and let Hanie Jordan go. Sheriff Buttry has been very kind and good to me, and had done all he could for me. That is all I want to say, and now I am ready to die like a man.[1598]

An earlier confession said the following: "My father has been married eight times, and he is now in Kentucky. He left mother thirteen or fourteen years ago, and I have not seen him since. I have been raised up in ignorance and debauchery all my life. I would advise all parents to train their children better than I have been trained. My mother has always kept a bad house, and never gave me any good counsel."[1599] A few days before the execution, Hatfield made a profession of faith and was baptized. He was under the impression that his sentence would be commuted to life imprisonment until a day or so before the execution, at which time he became "enshrouded with a spirit of melancholy."[1600]

Maried Hatfield was executed at 1:00 P.M. December 16, 1896, inside an enclosure on a recently built gallows about a half-mile from Sneedville. About sixty people were present, but because of the geography, about five thousand people got a good look because they watched from surrounding hills. A rumor had spread that he was kin to the Hatfields of Hatfield-McCoy fame and that they were going to rescue him, but Sheriff M.R. Buttry told the newspaper this was not true.[1601]

It took two hours from the time Hatfield was taken from the jail to the time he died. Among the issues concerning him was that the drop not be so far that it would pull his head off. His footsteps faltered badly and he was nearly carried to the gallows. During the service, which included prayers by two ministers, he became weak and fell to his knees crying.

During the service the Rev. R.M. Burton said that if he had been governor, he would have commuted Hatfield's sentence to life. Later, the sheriff said the same thing. The sobbing, nearly prostrate Hatfield said nothing intelligible on the gallows and the trap was triggered while he was in a kneeling position. His neck was broken. This was the first legal hanging in Hancock County.[1602]

1897

Harvey DeBerry, black, age 23. *Attempted rape of child.*

The crime was committed on the morning of October 8, 1896, in the farm home of Mr. and Mrs. Eigiman, in the Frayser Station community in Shelby County. The rapist was a farmhand on the farm. His wife was the cook and helped with the Eigimans' three children, ages seven, five and two. They lived in the house with the Eigiman family. The victim was Elenora Eigiman, white, age seven.

On the day of the crime, Mrs. Eigiman had gone to Memphis to visit her husband, who was in the hospital with a skull fracture and broken leg. The children were left under the care of DeBerry and his wife. The victim had complained of not feeling well, and the mother left her in bed wearing her bedclothes.

According to Elenora, Harvey entered her room, got on top of her and hurt her. He said he would kill her if she told. That afternoon Mrs. Eigiman found her daughter in bed, nervous and crying as if in pain. Asked what was the matter, the girl refused to answer. Elenora cried and moaned all night.

The next morning, the mother examined the bedclothes and found them bloody. Elenora told what happened and Mrs. Eigiman demanded DeBerry come to the child. He vigorously denied harming her. The girl said, "Yes, you did, Harvey. You know you did."[1603] The mother attempted to restrain DeBerry. He pushed her away and ran off. He was found later working on an Arkansas farm under the name Frank Berry.

The girl was examined by a doctor the day after the assault. Said the Tennessee Supreme Court: "The physician testified that he found the child highly excited, nervous, and trembling; that the person of the child was swollen, and very tender to the touch; that the parts showed acute inflammation and swelling; that he found a purulent discharge, and a slight rupture of the hymen; that penetration had been partial, but not complete; that the acute inflammation, purulent discharge, and swelling indicated that the injury was recent. During the course of the examination the physician asked the child who hurt her, and she replied that 'Harvey hurt her.' The mother was not present when the child made this statement."[1604]

It is unknown whether DeBerry took the stand, but he offered two witnesses. One related to his help harvesting corn on the day of the crime. The other was a washerwoman who testified there was no blood on the girl's clothing. On cross-examination, the corn harvesting was shown to be on a different day, and the clothes washing was a month prior to the assault.

According to the newspaper, this was Shelby

County's first conviction under the statute which made it a crime to commit "assault and battery upon a female under ten years of age, with intent to unlawfully and carnally know her."[1605] It was a new capital crime, different from rape or attempted rape. DeBerry was acquitted of those charges. After the conviction was upheld, a different Memphis physician sent the governor an affidavit saying the girl had not been raped and insisted DeBerry was innocent. This prompted the governor to grant a respite to examine the facts and conclude that DeBerry was properly convicted of the charge of assault on a child under the age of ten with intent to commit rape.[1606]

Harvey DeBerry was executed at 10:31 A.M. on August 19, 1897, inside a newly constructed gallows inside the Shelby County jail in front of about six witnesses, including the noted black minister, the Rev. George Washington.[1607] Deberry's lawyer was in the small crowd to hear what DeBerry had to say, but did not stay to witness the actual execution.

In the weeks before his execution, DeBerry had become very religious under the direction of the Rev. Washington, who baptized him in a bathtub in the jail. Since that time, DeBerry had maintained an unceasing rant about religion and the afterlife. He had been visited by Booker and Julia Hooks, who conducted a Sunday school at the jail. A service conducted by Mrs. Hooks in front of his cell on the day of his execution found him shouting, shrieking with joy, singing loudly with tears running down his cheeks. Bathed, shaven and taken to the gallows in clean clothes, he talked without stopping, but was shaking badly and had to be assisted up the steps.

On the gallows the Rev. Washington conducted a prayer service and one of DeBerry's favorite hymns was sung, "Nearer My God to Thee." Following this, DeBerry let out a shriek.

When asked if he had anything to say, he responded:

> Well, friends and relatives, my mother and father have taught me to pray and serve the Lord. Thank God that I have been saved. I thank God I have committed no crime to be hanged for. The Lord comes to me and says: My little one, don't fear; I'll save your soul. It belongs to me. He has called me His child. If I never see you again, friends, prepare to meet me in heaven. I won't be punished no more in heaven. I won't be lied on in heaven. Tell my mother and my beloved wife to prepare to meet me in heaven. Thank God I have brothers and sisters gone on before me and I will see them. I haven't got a blemish against anybody. I loves everybody. I don't hate the ones that prosecuted me.[1608]

DeBerry continued talking but dissembled. "His talk was nothing more than the ravings of a madman. There was no connection or coherency in what he said. He simply blurted out some sentences expressive of his emotions. What he said probably soothed and pacified him, but it fell harshly on the ears of his listeners. His last words were more of a groaning cry, than anything else. Through the black cloth came a last wailing cry of a man thoroughly terrorized and unnerved."[1609] Finally, out of breath, he said, "Farewell; I'm going home to Jesus. I'm going to die, thank God." At that moment, the sheriff pulled the lever to release the trap but it did not work. A deputy stepped forward and the two pulled it a second time and DeBerry fell cleanly. His neck was broken and he was cut down twelve minutes later.

DeBerry had been represented by two black lawyers, the father-and-son team of Cassells & Cassells. The father explained that he came to the jail that morning to say the following to his client: "Now, Harvey, I have defended you on the presumption that you are innocent. Nothing you can say now will do you any good or harm. I want to know for my own satisfaction whether you are guilty. But the sheriff will not let me see him, so that settles that."[1610]

The media asked the Rev. George Washington, the minister who regularly attended condemned men, whether DeBerry had confessed. The minister demurred, "I won't say anything until after the execution. I have a very difficult duty to perform and don't want to confuse my mind. I won't say anything at all until after it's all over."[1611] DeBerry's wife did not visit him until shortly before the execution when she carried herself in a "haughty manner," and his father refused to visit him when he brought DeBerry's mother to visit him in the jail.[1612] The rope had been used in Shelby County six or seven years earlier, and had been used at Paris and Jackson.

Robert Sims (aka Isham Sims), black, age 25. *Murder.*

The crime was committed in the evening about dark on July 9, 1897, on the farm of Mr. and Mrs. William D. Boring on the Watauga River near Flourville in rural Washington County. The killer was a farmhand employed by the Boring family. The victim, Walter Galloway, white, age twenty-seven, was the fiancé of Miss Effie Viola Boring. He had come to spend time with Miss Boring.

The killing had its origin in a practical joke. Robert Sims had taken to carrying a pistol and drawing it at the slightest provocation. To stop the behavior, Mr. Boring and Walter Galloway had asked a sheriff's deputy to make a mock arrest of Sims, take away the pistol, and briefly jail him. Galloway paid his "fine." In time, Sims discovered the joke and harbored resentment, telling several people he was so angry he could kill Galloway.[1613]

Galloway rode his horse to the Boring farm to eat supper with the family on the porch. He asked Sims to take the horse to the stable and feed it, offering to pay him a nickel. Sims, with "a show of insolence and anger," refused.[1614]

Here is Sims's account of what happened: "I said I would not do it for a nickel or $5.00. He said I had been talking about him and he said if I ever came over about Flourville talking about him anymore he would give me a whipping, and I said if he wanted to fight to fight me in the house, and he said no, but if I would come out in the road he would put a head on me that nobody could get off of me. I told him I would not go in the road, that if he wanted to fight me he would have to fight me in the house."[1615]

Sims continued, "He said he would go and put up his horse, and he started and as he went towards the stile he said, 'I'll get you.'" At this point, Sims went into the house and got Mr. Boring's shotgun, put shells into it, took milk to the basement as asked, and then proceeded to the barn to let out Borings' horses. "The reason I loaded the gun and took it with me was I was afraid he would attack me as I went to turn out the horses." According to Sims, as he was returning to the house, Galloway came up to him and said, "You black rascal, what are you doing with that gun?" Sims said nothing and Galloway repeated the question. Sims did not respond.

According to Sims, "By this time he placed his hand behind him, and reached down to the ground with the other hand, like he was reaching to get something, and I saw something near his hand that I thought was a rock, and I thought I would shoot him in the hand. I fired the gun. I did not intend to kill Mr. Galloway, but fired to keep him from hurting me, and intended to shoot him in the hand."[1616]

Other witnesses said they had heard Sims declare earlier he did not like Galloway because he had gotten him arrested about two years before and wanted to kill him. Mrs. Boring saw Sims carrying the gun toward the barn and heard Sims say the words, "kill you," just before the shot.[1617] According to a newspaper account, Effie went outside and screamed to Galloway to get out of the way, saying that Sims had a gun and was going to shoot him.[1618] Another account says she ran to the barn to warn him and was walking with him to the house when Sims appeared.

The witnesses who came to Galloway after the shooting said his right hand had been largely shot away by the pellets and the blast entered his cheek. They thought the victim had raised his hand to protect himself, or possibly to brush away the barrel, when he was shot. Galloway was unable to speak and died the next day. Sims ran away and was captured in Kentucky three days later. At trial, he vigorously denied telling any of the arresting officers that he disliked Galloway and meant to kill him. Sims was kept in the Knox County jail for his safety. The case was appealed to the Tennessee Supreme Court but the opinion cannot be located.

Robert Sims was executed at 11:00 A.M. on November 17, 1897, on a gallows built on the side of the courthouse in Jonesboro. To mount the gallows, the execution party had to go out a window of the courthouse. The gallows was protected from view below. Sims was attended by six black ministers who prayed and sang hymns. Sims heartily joined the service and read the third chapter of Matthew. Again Sims told the small group of spectators that he had not intended to kill Galloway. He smiled faintly as the cap was put over his head. The drop was clean and his neck was broken. He was taken down eighteen minutes later.[1619]

Miss Effie Viola Boring died on July 30, 1897, only twenty-two days after Galloway was shot. She was thirty-seven years old and Galloway was her last hope for matrimony. She died of "nervous prostration," according to the newspaper, as well as a broken heart.[1620] Effie was the youngest of seven children. She was "the idol of a fond mother's heart," and "a comfort and solace to an aged and paralytic mother."[1621] Her mother passed away on March 14, 1898.

William D. Mays, white, age 23. *Murder.*

The crime was committed on June 15, 1897, at the farm of G.D. Massengill on Hog Ridge, a rural area in Sullivan County. The killer was a farmer with two children. The victim, George D. Massengill, white, age fifty-two, was a neighboring farmer and stock trader with five children. He was shot in the head from the rear while alone, resting from his farm work.

The pair knew each other and Mays had threatened Massengill twice. Once was because the victim had not gotten some money owed to Mays from a county tax collector.[1622] He threatened to burst Massengill's head. The second threat arose out of a dispute regarding tan bark that Mays had hauled from the woods. Massengill threatened to tell the sheriff Mays had taken it from his land without permission. This threat was made in front of a man who pulled logs from the forest. Mays said that if Massengill didn't stop lying he would kill him. The man said he had a good team and could haul the body out, which prompted laughter from Massengill but not Mays.[1623]

Mays and Robert Cole were seen carrying rifles near the time of the killing. They were within a quarter mile of where the body was found. Two shots were heard, one from a large-bore rifle like the one Mays carried, the other from a small bore, like that carried by Cole. Mays was arrested the day the body was found. He was taken to the scene. When asked to look at the body, he looked away toward a clump of trees. Seeing this as a sign of guilt, the coroner's jury went to the spot, where they saw and measured footprints that exactly matched Mays, particularly his boot heels.[1624]

Mays and Cole were taken to the jail in handcuffs. In front of several people, Cole said to Mays that he had said the day before that if any trouble came from Massengill's death that he (Mays) would "make a confession and get him out of trouble."[1625] When this statement was made Mays said nothing. The failure to deny guilt under these circumstances is taken as a sign of guilt. Cole insisted he had met Mays that morning by accident as he was walking in the same direction as Mays. His placing of bee bait was his reason for being there. Cole was given a life sentence.[1626] Mays's case was appealed to the Tennessee Supreme Court, but the opinion cannot be located.

Before Mays stepped on the gallows, he left behind two sworn statements in which he exonerated Cole entirely, but implicated his stepfather Jesse Baker and Godfrey Boling, a constable. (Cole's sentence was commuted later when numerous townsfolk petitioned the governor that enough justice had been done.) Mays was executed at 1:20 P.M. on November 17, 1897, on an enclosed gallows at Blountville. Also executed that day was Robert (Isham) Sims in Jonesboro, Washington County. William Mays said he was not afraid to die and said, "I bid all of you good-bye." One thousand people witnessed the execution, having seen Mays on the scaffold above the partial enclosure. "Mays's wife and two little children were with him to the last. His wife is frantic with grief."[1627]

Mynatt Leach, white, age 37. *Murder.*

The crime was committed on February 17, 1897, near the mine of the Royal Coal & Coke Company near Better Chance, in Anderson County. The killer was a sometime miner who was part of a group of men hostile to the mining company. (The group may have been responsible for the killing of another man, John Craig, who was allied with the mining interests, a year or two earlier. Craig had been shot from ambush as he entered his home.) The victim was John D. Heck, white, age thirty. He was the business manager of the mine.

At noon, Heck was walking up a footpath to his house near the mine, reading a paper. His wife saw him and began running toward him. Only a few steps from his wife, he was hit by a rifle bullet that struck his back and passed through his body. He fell dead at his wife's feet.[1628]

The shot had been fired from a wooded area 247 feet away. Leach threw down the Springfield rifle and ran to the house of Wilburn Leach, his brother, a short distance away. He had borrowed the rifle from his brother that morning. Virtually everything Mynatt Leach did after the killing proved he did the shooting. He told the wife of his brother Calvin Leach that he had been paid $200 to kill Heck. He also said there was a man standing above him at a tree and that if he had not gone through with the killing he would have been killed himself. He said that a number of people had contributed money to kill Heck. Later, he hid in the mountains near Calvin's house and his niece brought him food. She saw him with a large amount of money.

Two people, Amanda Rose, black, and Mrs. Redman ("half Indian and half white"), testified they saw Leach running away after the shooting, although there was some question whether the latter had been threatened with lynching if she did not testify the way she did.[1629] Another woman testified that Leach told her the same thing would happen to Heck as happened to Craig. The Tennessee Supreme Court summarized the evidence: "A circumstantial prediction of a secret murder, followed by the perpetration of exactly such a crime; recent possession and unexplained desertion of the deadly weapon used; suspicious loitering in the vicinity of the victim's well-known pathway to his home; positive incrimination by the consistent statement of an eyewitness; a full and free confession of the deed, and that it was perpetuated for hire; an injunction of secrecy as to money accidentally discovered in his possession; careful hiding before accused — what more could be required or shown in any case?"[1630]

According to newspaper accounts, four men had put up fifty dollars each to be given the man who would kill Heck. These were John Taylor, Sam

Taylor, John Wilson and Henry Goins. Later, four persons drew straws to see who would kill Heck, namely John Taylor, Ahaz Johnson, Rufe Disney and Leach. Leach drew the long straw and thus became the shooter.[1631]

Leach insisted that if he had not gone ahead with the killing, he would have been killed by one of the others, and there is evidence that Ahaz Johnson was nearby when the shooting occurred. He was convicted along with Leach, but the precise charge is unknown. He received a year in the penitentiary. The jury convicted Leach of first-degree murder with mitigating circumstances, but the judge said there were none and ordered Leach hanged.[1632] The Tennessee Supreme Court said this was a matter for the trial court's "legal discretion."[1633]

Because of rumors that fellow miners might attack the Anderson County jail in order to free Leach, he was kept in the Knox County jail until he was brought back to Clinton for his execution. Likewise, extra lawmen were posted at the jail and throughout the town on the execution day to frustrate the rumored plans to tear down the stockade surrounding the gallows. Some of the miners "declaring that if he must be hanged it should be publicly."[1634]

Weeks before the execution Leach confessed to the killing and held to his statement that "it was kill or be killed." He professed religion in jail and said he was ready to die and go to heaven. He also said that he would rather die than go to prison. He had served a term in prison for cattle theft and had only been released a short time before the killing.

When he was taken back to Clinton from Knoxville, he asked to speak to a man named Wallace who lived in a hovel next to the jail and was obviously dying of tuberculosis. Leach brought him a small gift because Wallace had been kind to him during an earlier incarceration. The two talked religion. Leach refused to discuss his crime with anyone, insisting he was only interested in talking religion.

Leach was executed on a gallows erected on the west side of the courthouse surrounded by a stockade. He was hanged on December 8, 1897, in front of a small crowd, none of whom saw the actual drop. On his way to the gallows Leach refused a photographer's request to take his picture, and was visibly weak and walked with faltering steps. The newspaper said his pulse was ninety-seven and his respiration was twenty-eight an hour before the hanging. He had to be helped to walk up the steps to the gallows. Asked if he had anything to say he replied, "Nothing."[1635]

Seated in a chair on the gallows, he was attended by the Rev. J.H. Amis and the Rev. J.R. Lauritzen, who earlier had conducted a religious service for him at the jail. Following their prayers, the noose and cap were placed. The sheriff had told everyone that the execution would take place at noon. As the courthouse clock made its first strike, Sheriff Demarcus tripped the trap and Leach fell cleanly. His neck was broken and he was cut down eleven minutes later. After the body was taken down and placed in a coffin, it was put in a hallway in the courthouse where many of the six thousand people who came to town that day filed by to see it.

Will Johnson (aka George West and George Hunt), black, age 20. *Murder.*

The crime was committed on the morning of August 5, 1897, when Johnson came to a farm where the victim was staying near Idaville, in Tipton County. Johnson came up behind the victim and shot him as he was feeding his chickens. The victim, Walter Boyd, white, age thirty, had recently purchased a Tipton County farm.[1636] He and his wife had gone to Marshall County, Mississippi, to visit his family when the house mysteriously burned on the night of July 31, 1897. Knowing Boyd was away, Johnson had burgled the house, stealing the murder weapon and various items including Mrs. Boyd's ring. He poured coal oil throughout the house and lit it to cover the crime. Then he helped neighbors rescue furniture from the smoking house, which did not burn to the ground. When Boyd returned, he told the sheriff that he suspected Johnson in the house burning. After shooting Boyd, the killer took ten dollars from his body. Earlier he had given the ring to his girlfriend. The sheriff nosed around that Johnson was a suspect in the burning and the girlfriend and her brother were arrested. Johnson was arrested and confessed.[1637]

Johnson explained his crime in a conversation with the Shelby County jail night watchman, Bill Kelly, shortly before he was taken to Tipton County for his execution. "What got into you that made you kill that man?" Kelly asked. "I don't know, Mister Will. I guess it was devilment." "How did you do it?" "Well, ah ain't got any time to be lyin', you know dat, so ahm goin' to tell you de truth. Somebody burned a barn on Boyd's place. He s'picioned me, an' said what he was goin' to do about it. A nigger heard him make his big talk an' come an' tole me. He said Mister Boyd was goin' to shoot me. I made up my min' then to either kill dat' man or get killed nex' mo'nin'. I got up in the mo'nin' an' went to his house. I called him out to the gate an' ak'd him what that he said. He talked 'bout what he was goin' to do in a big way. You ain't goin' to do dat me is you?, ah ak'd him. He sta'ht to run in th' house and I shot him."[1638]

Johnson described how the charge from his gun tore away one side of the victim's skull and how he fell to the ground and died instantly. Johnson was captured a short while later. Because of the danger of lynching, he was kept in the Shelby County jail before and after his trial. At the jail he demanded gin and good food, promising that if they were not granted he would come back and haunt the jail. He received both. Because Johnson's crime was committed on August 5, 1897, and he was tried in October 1897 with his execution set for December 17, it is unlikely that his case was appealed to the Tennessee Supreme Court. Johnson made friends with inmates at the Shelby County jail. On the day he was taken to Covington for his execution, he was given a half-pint of gin which he enjoyed on the way.

Johnson was executed inside an enclosure erected on the south side of the jail, with only those inside the enclosure able to see the hanging. A company of National Guard troops was present to protect Johnson because there had been threats of a lynching. He was executed at 12:09 P.M. on December 17, 1897. His neck was broken and the only twitching was from his hands.

On the gallows, he said, "I am not sorry I am here. I know I did wrong. I have made peace with my Maker. I am glad to go."[1639] He said, "Good-bye, all of you." The small crowd responded in like manner. He was then pinioned and the rope and cap put over his head. Sheriff Lauderdale said, "Good-bye, Will," and took an ax, cutting the rope holding the trap. The body was turned over to his relatives, who had refused to witness the execution.

1898

Dan Harris, black, age 26. *Murder.*

The crime was committed about midnight on June 15, 1896, on an unlit street in a poor black neighborhood called Trimble Bottom in Nashville, in Davidson County. The killer and the victim had lived together "in an unholy alliance" for about a year. "This couple had not lived in that peaceful and quiet manner, which usually marks the lives of the colored people of the South."[1640] The victim, Lizzie Edmonson, black, age twenty-three, was a small, frail woman weighing about 115 pounds who was "patient and submissive," and had suffered beatings from Harris in the past. He was described as "unusually large, tall, well-developed, and robust," weighing 200 pounds.[1641]

The victim had fled from the house she shared with Harris. Fearing that he would injure or kill her mother if she went there, Lizzie escaped to the house of Mary Mayberry, saying, "Oh, Aunt Mary, please don't let Dan hurt me!" When Harris came to the house around midnight he cursed Lizzie and demanded she return both her shoes and the ring she was wearing. Although she complied, he dragged her into the street. He tried to cut her throat, but actually cut the back of her neck. When she was on the ground, he "stamped her in the face, chest, and stomach, first with one foot and then the other, holding on to the fence with first one hand and then the other."[1642]

Lizzie had begged for mercy and for help. "She called him pet names, and pleaded with him to spare her life, until, after repeated blows from his feet, her cries sank into low moans, and she then became unconscious. Defendant, all the time, was cursing the deceased, and saying to her, 'I told you I was going to kill you.'"[1643] Following the beating, he ran away, swam across the Cumberland River, hopped a freight train to Indiana, and settled in Kansas City, Missouri. Lizzie died four days later.

Harris was arrested a year later because he had sent a letter to her mother saying that if Lizzie wanted to get together, he would send money for her travel. He did not know she was dead.

He was arrested in Kansas City and brought back to Nashville for trial. His defense was that he was so intoxicated that he did not have requisite intent to murder, that he did not remember anything of the crime, and because he loved her, he had no reason to kill her.

His brother described seeing Dan "dead drunk" an hour after the assault, but several other witnesses (none of whom had tried to stop him) said Harris was not intoxicated. He was convicted on June 28, 1897.

The Tennessee Supreme Court recounted the facts and concluded, "It appears that on the day before the killing was done, at night, he had been drinking some, but the great weight of the evidence is that he was not drunk, and according to the testimony of his own witnesses, was not so much under the influence of whisky, before and at the time he did the killing, as not to know what he was doing nor so as to affect his walking or actions."[1644] He was not insane. The court noted that Harris was "large, strong, and, the proof shows, was determined, collected, and intelligent."[1645]

The day before Harris was executed, the governor commuted the death sentence of Fred Moore, black, who had raped a white child. Harris said he was happy for Moore, but nothing else.[1646] In the months before his execution, Harris was seen by the Rev. Luke Mason, black, under whose guidance he confessed his sins and became convinced he was going to heaven. Harris spent most of his time reading the Bible.

Dan Harris was executed at 10:00 A.M. March 23, 1898, inside a special gallows built inside the Davidson County jail. The gallows was built into a niche between the jailer's residence and the kitchen, being walled in on three sides by brick buildings.[1647] The gallows could be seen from the windows of a nearby soap factory, but the view was obstructed by a canvas curtain. It was built to execute two men. It had last been used to execute Robert Ford in 1895.

Before going to the gallows, Harris asked the sheriff about the new underwear he had been promised to go along with his new shirt, tie, and coat. It was provided. Harris took a bath and showed special care in dressing. Harris walked steadily to the gallows accompanied by the Rev. Mason and the Rev. Henry Edwards, black. They conducted a service which began by reading from the Bible. Next, the hymn "Show Pity, O Lord, Forgive," was sung, followed by a "rather prolonged and fervent prayer from Rev. Mason."[1648]

The sheriff asked Harris if he had anything to say. He replied, "Take this scene at heart and you will turn and give your heart to God. I feel confident that He has forgiven my sins and I want to meet you all in heaven. Here in my heart I am not ashamed to confess my sins and I am glad to say He has forgiven me."[1649] At this point, the Rev. Mason stepped forward and addressed Harris, saying, "You have stated you are sure God has pardoned your sins. Have you forgiven everybody and cherish no envious feelings toward anybody?" Harris responded, "I have forgiven them all and pardon them freely."[1650]

Two deputies came forward and bound Harris's hands and feet. The black cap was placed over his head, then the rope. As soon as this was done, Sheriff John Sharp pulled the lever to spring the trap. The body fell cleanly and Harris's neck was broken. There was no twitching and the body was cut down fourteen minutes later. The body was placed in a casket and turned over to his mother. Outside the jail over a thousand people, mostly black, milled about hoping to get a look at the body, but saw only the casket.

George Pearson, black, age 42. *Murder.*

The crime was committed about 9:30 P.M. on May 3, 1896, a half-mile from St. John's Colored Baptist Church in a sparsely settled area of Madison County. The killer hid in the darkness waiting for the victim to leave the Sunday night church service and shot him with a pistol and a shotgun. The victim, Sam Walker, black, age twenty-nine, was known to the killer. Pearson was afraid of him because of prior threats. They had argued over the affection of a woman, Ensley Estess, black. The details of the relationship between the two men and Ensley Estess are unknown, but the newspaper said both men had been "criminally intimate" with her.[1651]

Several witnesses had heard Pearson threaten the life of Walker, calling him a "double-headed son of a bitch."[1652] One said he promised to kill Walker if it took seventy-seven years.[1653] Others said Walker told them he was afraid of Pearson. Their troubles went back at least as far as 1894 when they were involved in a lawsuit over the ownership of a gun. Estess, expected to testify for Pearson, stayed home because she was due to deliver a baby.

The facts were complicated because Mat Hudson, black, had shot Sam Walker in 1894 and was the prime suspect in his killing. Pearson was brought before a justice of the peace two times for the 1896 crime but the murder charge was not carried forward for lack of proof. Finally, in order to show he had not killed Walker, Hudson gained Pearson's confidence. He approached Pearson while he was working in a field and told him plenty of people had wanted Walker dead, but he knew Pearson had done it with his shotgun. Flattered, Pearson explained in detail how he had killed his enemy. A few weeks later, Hudson arranged a "chance" meeting with Pearson in a different field, but this time he got Jess Withers to hide in a nearby ditch out of sight while the two discussed the killing a second time. Both Hudson and Withers testified at trial.

As soon as he was arrested, Pearson began confessing to the sheriff, later to a deputy sheriff, and still later to a man who came to advise him spiritually (actually a runner for a lawyer). All testified to what they heard, although reluctantly. Pearson explained he heard Walker's booming voice out the church window and hid in a spot where he knew Walker would pass. He shot him twice in the chest, once with a pistol and then with the shotgun. Pearson had described the killing in great detail. He recounted his thoughts. Seeing Walker talking to a woman, he said to himself, "You are talking to your last woman on earth, you double-headed son of a bitch."[1654] Walker was carrying a concealed pistol. There was a dispute regarding whether it had been fired (only two shots were heard). Pearson's claim of self-defense was rejected. Pearson's case was appealed to the Tennessee Supreme Court, but the opinion cannot be located.

Pearson was executed inside the Madison County jail at 11:02 A.M. on June 18, 1898. Pearson was calm at the gallows, telling everyone that he was saved and going to heaven. After the cap was placed over his head he was told by the sheriff that his time was up. He responded, "All right, sir." His neck was not broken and the body was allowed to hang for fifty minutes before it was cut down.

1899

Hiram Hall, white, age 18. *Murder.*

The crime was committed on the afternoon of August 18, 1897, at the farm home of the killer's parents outside of Crossville in Cumberland County. The killer and his wife lived with his parents. They had been married about two years. The victim, Ida Belle Hassler Hall, white, age nineteen, was the killer's wife. She was visibly pregnant.

The killer confessed the crime both in court and in a later published statement. In the statement, he said that he killed his wife because his mother kept insisting he do so, although no reason was assigned. The couple had separated briefly, shortly after they were married, but had come back to live with Hiram Hall and his parents. After two attempts to push her into the well, which she took as jokes, he finally struck her on the head with a rock and pushed her into the well. Later, according to his statement, when his mother came to him saying it appeared she was trying to get out of the well, he returned and struck her head several times with a plank.[1655]

A coroner's inquest determined that Ida Belle had been struck in the head before she went into the water because there was no water in her lungs. Because this was at odds with the story told by Hall and his mother, both were arrested. She denied any involvement and neither Hall nor his sister, Martha Hall, who was present, could be induced to testify against the mother.

At trial, the mother, Malinda "Lidda" Hall, testified opaquely. "I am the mother of the defendant. I was at home on the morning of Ida's death. There was nobody there but me and Ida and Hiram. Hiram cut some stove wood, got his dinner bucket, and started to school. He had gone some time and I was churning. I told Ida to churn, and I washed out some clothes out of the tub, and I went to the bucket. The water was out, and I told her to go and get some. She picked up the bucket and went to the well. She had been gone so long that I got uneasy about her and went to see about her. When I went to the well I saw nothing but the bucket."[1656] Defense counsel asked if she had pushed Ida into the well. She said no and refused to answer any further questions from defense counsel.[1657] The sister died during the time Hall's case was on appeal to the Tennessee Supreme Court. The opinion cannot be located.

Hall was executed on a gallows in the yard of the Cumberland County jail at 7:05 A.M. on April 13, 1899, in front of barely twenty witnesses, including the sheriff's young son, who had become friendly with Hall and spent the last night with him, sleeping on a cot just outside his cell.

Hall had spent the day before his execution writing letters and was visited by his mother. Deputies and others listened to what the two said, but found nothing incriminating. Hall's written statement, given to the newspaper the morning of his death, followed what he had said since his own conviction, namely that his mother induced the killing. She had tried to get Hiram to kill the father on at least two occasions by shooting him as he worked in the field. The newspaper noted that Hall's implication of his mother came only after his conviction, that Hall had a brother who was serving a second sentence in the penitentiary, and that most people did not accredit the statement blaming the mother.[1658] It was deemed an attempt to gain a commutation of the death sentence.

Hall had professed his faith and was attended by two ministers, one of whom walked with him to the gallows and prayed for him just before the hanging. Until the black cap was placed over his head, Hall smoked a cigar. When asked if he had any last words, he said, "The time is now very short. You all know that I soon must die. I am ready to go. You all should take my advice and never drink any whiskey, carry any pistols or take anyone's life. I am going home to glory, and I hope you all will meet me in heaven. Good-bye."[1659] Sheriff J.L. Garrison said, "May God have mercy on your soul," and pulled the lever. The drop was clean but the rope turned so that the knot went under his chin and he strangled. He was cut down twelve minutes later.

Sheriff Garrison had intentionally held the execution at an early hour to avoid any problems with the crowd that was assembling in Cookeville. In time, it reached two thousand. Many were disappointed they had missed the execution, although none would have been allowed to see it. Virtually all came to see the gallows and filed past Hall's body as it lay in the casket, which was placed outside the front door of the jail.

Hall's written statement concluded, "In view of all the horrible crimes which my mother had caused me to attempt, and knowing she is the cause of me doing all these horrible things, I love her still, and hope to meet her in heaven."[1660] Lidda Hall took custody of his body, although there were objections from other members of the Hall family to his burial next to his kinsmen.

Hiram Hall's parents were divorced by the time of his execution and no charges were ever brought against Lidda Hall. Without shedding any light on the crime, she died on September 22, 1925.[1661] She was eighty-six years old.

Pleasant D. Wynn (aka Pleas Wynn), white, age 30. *Murder.*
James Catlett Tipton (aka Catlett Tipton), white, age 37. *Murder.*

The crime was committed about 7:00 P.M. on the night of December 28, 1896, at the cabin of William Whaley and his wife, Laura Whaley. The cabin was located two miles west of Sevierville, in Sevier County. The killers were members of a vigilante group called White Caps. They had been sent to kill the couple because Mrs. Whaley had violated the strict "code" of confidentiality required of White Cap members, despite the fact she was not a true member of the group. Mr. Whaley was an inactive member. The dispute had its origin in the desire of the leader of the White Caps, Bob Catlett, to control a small piece of land. The victims were William Whaley, white, age twenty-four, and Laura Whaley, white, age twenty-one.

The story of the White Caps has become a matter of East Tennessee folklore. Briefly, in 1892 a group of well-meaning vigilantes, wearing white masks and caps, began whipping prostitutes in the Sevier County region in an attempt to clean up the area. In short order, the group, which had an oath, secret hand signals, and secret membership, became lawless in its own right. It was countered by another group, the Blue Bills, which sought to warn victims, and tension between the groups existed until the White Caps fell following the convictions of Tipton and Wynn. By then (1898) it had become clear that the White Caps had murdered an innocent young couple, the Whaleys. But no White Caps had been brought to justice during the period of its dominance, 1892–1896. This was due, in part, to the influence the group had over the local circuit judge and its influence, usually extralegal, on jurors.[1662]

Catlett Tipton was a leader of the White Caps, and Pleas Wynn a trusted lieutenant. They broke open the cabin door and confronted the couple, who were in bed with their infant daughter. "If you have come to kill us," pleaded William, "we will do anything you say. But spare our lives!" Laura said, "Oh, Lord! Oh, Lord! If you have come to kill us, let me give my little baby to my sister before I die!" She handed the infant, Mollie Lillard Whaley, to her sister, Lizzie Chandler. Tipton was barefaced and unarmed, but Wynn was masked and carried both a shotgun and pistol. He shot William in the mouth. He fell dead at his wife's feet. She was shot in the temple, and the bullet tore away the top of her head.[1663]

The murder was instigated by Bob Catlett, "one of the largest farmers on the French Broad River and one of the largest taxpayers in Sevier County.... For years he had exercised a controlling influence over affairs in the county and had to his credit much that was bad."[1664] Pleas Wynn, who was very short, "was never known to do a day's work, but loafed about town, sometimes fishing and hunting for a pastime." He was "a slave to drink."[1665] His brother, William Wynn, was shot dead by Sheriff M.F. Maples on a Sevierville city street during the trial of Wynn and Tipton.[1666] Pleas Wynn had served as a jailer during the time his father, Captain E.M. Wynn, a Methodist minister, had served as sheriff, 1888–1890.

Catlett Tipton, a carpenter, was a family man who worked at jobs about town and was a good friend of Pleas Wynn. He was a regular member of the United Brethren church, where he was head of the Sunday school. As a carpenter, he had helped build the stockade surrounding the gallows upon which he was later executed.

The problem that led to the couple's death began in December 1895, when Whaley leased from Bob Catlett a tract of land, and with the occupancy of a small house, the rental to be paid in a share of the crop. But the cabin was then occupied by Walter Maples. When the couple came to take possession of the cabin, Maples refused to leave. Catlett let them use another cabin until Maples could be evicted.

This was the White Cap eviction procedure: Bob Catlett and his brother-in-law, Bob Wade, came to the Whaley cabin. Catlett gave Laura a sheet of paper. With a gun pointed at her, Catlett demanded she write a White Cap letter to Maples ordering him to leave the house. She refused, but relented when she saw a gun pointed at her husband. Wade said that Catlett was drunk and she should follow his order or someone would be killed. She wrote the note (her husband was illiterate) as follows:

> Walter Maples:
> If you do not move out of this house in five days, the penalty of the White Caps will be visited on you. The time is half up now.
> White Caps

Catlett then cursed her because she had crossed "t's" and dotted "i's"—apparently genuine White Cap missives omitted this feature.

Catlett then "administered to Laura the fearful oath of the order, which meant certain death if any of the secrets of the clan were revealed. He demanded one of Laura's skirts, which he put over his head in disguise. At gunpoint they were marched to Maples's cabin, where William was forced to nail the notice to the door. The men threw stones at the house and Catlett fired a load of buckshot through the chinks, some of the pellets hitting near the bed where Maples, his wife and children had been sleeping. A few days later, the Maples family left the house and the Whaleys moved in.

As spring came, the Whaleys bought some hogs from Catlett, who recorded the transfer at the courthouse. The record showed the sale was conditioned upon payment in crops and labor. Laura kept strict records of her husband's work for Catlett, and by September, William Whaley had done sufficient work to pay off his debt. He then sold the hogs.

Catlett came to the Whaley house at that time, cursed William Whaley for selling mortgaged property, and threatened to have him arrested. Catlett left in anger and swore a warrant for Whaley's arrest. The couple knew about the warrant but could do nothing at the time. Mrs. Whaley was due to give birth, and the stress was said to have caused her to give premature birth to Mollie Lillard Whaley. Laura was very ill.

At this time, Bob Catlett's daughter, Rou Catlett, a "young and upright schoolteacher," made a call on the Whaleys. She saw their plight, and heard for the first time how her father had acted in the Maples affair, and his stubbornness in the hog transaction.[1667] She confronted her father. He ultimately agreed not to prosecute and to cancel the mortgage. But he exacted a punishment. "For this you shall die!" he said to Laura Whaley, telling them to leave their house immediately.[1668]

Catlett continued to cheat the Whaleys. He never paid them for their share of the corn and failed to release the hog mortgage. Then, in November 1896, Laura's statement had leaked. Deputy Sheriff Davis, a dedicated lawman who opposed the White Caps at every turn, had her brought before the grand jury. When Laura told the truth, her fate was sealed. She had violated the White Cap "oath" and placed her life in danger, a fact well-known to her and everyone else.

Bob Catlett and Bob Wade were arrested for "rocking the house of Walter Maples and for shooting at it." They promptly made bond. On the way out the courthouse door, Catlett threatened Laura's life in the presence of Lizzie Chandler, her sister, who was holding baby Mollie.

The Whaleys made every attempt to leave the area (Lizzie was now living with them), with William taking a money-paying job for awhile to finance the move. He became ill with pneumonia and came home to get well. That was the reason he was home on the murder night.

Bob Catlett had asked the killers several times to kill the Whaleys, but they finally agreed when the price reached two hundred dollars. The pair had arranged multiple alibis, one of which involved meeting with a fellow White Cap at a point three miles from the courthouse at exactly five o'clock in the evening. The agreed time was set based on the bell at the courthouse. The killing went as planned.

Catlett Tipton and Pleas Wynn were the immediate suspects — their shoe prints seemed to match those at the scene — and within days Wynn had told fellow White Caps that he had killed the pair in return for two hundred dollars promised by Bob Catlett, the overall leader of the White Caps.

The pair was arrested and brought to trial because of the courage of Lizzie Chandler, Laura's sister. The pair assumed that Lizzie would be intimidated by the power of the White Caps, or had not actually seen them, but Wynn's mask had partially fallen away from his face and Lizzie had seen it in the light of the fireplace.

The pair was tried for the murder of Laura Whaley in 1897 and would have been easily acquitted but for the act of Deputy Sheriff Davis. He had gone to the legislature in Nashville and it had changed the law, putting Sevier County in the same judicial district as Knoxville. Hence, the trial was held in front of Judge Thomas A.R. Nelson, who was strongly opposed to the White Caps. With the aid of Knoxville prosecutors, the protection of

Deputy Sheriff Davis, and help from the Blue Bills, the trial went forward despite threats.

Lizzie Chandler's testimony at the first trial convicted Pleas Wynn, but Catlett Tipton was acquitted. The second trial, for the murder of William Whaley, finally began in March 1898. By this time the White Cap grip had been broken.

As in the first trial, the evidence against Catlett Tipton was weaker than against Pleas Wynn, but he convicted himself. Holding firm to the White Cap oath of never abandoning a fellow member, Tipton insisted that he was with Wynn the entire evening. Logically, this meant he was in the room and was an accomplice. But he still maintained an alibi, notably a meeting with a fellow White Cap at seven o'clock that evening. To emphasize the point, he was adamant about the time because he heard the court house clock bell. Unfortunately for him, the bell could not be heard at the point he met the fellow White Cap. Both Wynn and Tipton were convicted on April 9, 1898, of killing William Whaley. They spent most of their time in the Knox County jail for their own safety.

The pair was brought to the Sevier County jail and throngs watched from both sides of the road as their jail wagon passed by. Two days before the execution, Pleas Wynn was taken from the Knox County jail to a photographer on the town square, where his picture was taken with his wife. They enjoyed iced refreshments at a parlor before he was returned to the jail.[1669]

The convictions were affirmed by the Tennessee Supreme Court, but the opinion cannot be located.

The two were given several respites in order to testify against Bob Catlett and John Webb, who were charged as accessories. The trial of these two was moved to Morristown, and following a vigorous trial with some of the best lawyers in East Tennessee participating, the jury acquitted John Webb, but could not reach a verdict on Bob Catlett. A new trial was ordered. The state signaled it would not need to use Pleas Wynn and J. Catlett Tipton at Bob Catlett's second trial, opening the door for their execution.

Pleas Wynn and J. Catlett Tipton were executed at 1:02 P.M. (an hour later than scheduled) on July 5, 1899, inside an enclosure (called a stockade) at the Sevier County jail yard. The gallows had never before been used. It was built two and one-half years earlier for the execution of Patton Matthews, but his sentence had been commuted to life imprisonment. Only twenty people were allowed to witness the execution, and even they did not see the actual hanging, while three thousand crowded the town square. Both White Caps and Blue Bills were among the throng.

In the days before their execution, the pair had confessed the crime and professed religion. Under the guidance of several ministers they were convinced they were going to heaven. Catlett Tipton gave a written statement to the newspaper: "My story on the witness stand about the crime, is a true story. Bob Catlett is the cause of my having to die today. He just kept after me, until he overpowered me and now I must say farewell to earth. Let my fate be a lesson to all who are tempted to keep the company of evil doers. It seems hard for me to part from my dear wife and little children, but I feel that I am going home to a happy, peaceful abode, where there are no temptations to sin. Let my evil deeds be forgotten. If I ever did any good, I hope it will be remembered."[1670]

Tipton went on to say that he had actually been convicted by the perjured testimony of two fellow White Caps, one who said he had borrowed a pistol and another who said he had confessed to his part in the killings.[1671] But he continued, "I feel that I should say that we are guilty as charged, but we were convicted on perjured testimony from beginning to end."[1672] Tipton concluded his statement by saying that Bob Catlett would be acquitted because the only evidence against him was the doomed men's testimony. He closed by saying, "I close to permit Sheriff Davis to perform the duty which it seems, to him, will be pleasant."[1673]

The reference to Sheriff Davis (made high sheriff by the recent wounding of the regular sheriff by a White Cap) grew out of a long acquaintance. Davis, as an enemy of the White Caps, had fought them with both gun and law. But he knew the doomed men personally. Years before as youngsters, he was captain of a well-known Enneka baseball team on which they played.

Pleas Wynn's written statement said, "Being guilty, I feel that I should tell all about it, and but for my attorney I would have done it long before I did. I know that my conviction on the evidence, was a mockery of justice, but I know further that the moral turpitude of my crime was such as to merit very severe punishment. Although I did not commit the crime of killing the Whaleys."[1674]

The statement continued:

> Bob Catlett deserves judgment that he may never receive. I hope he will not lead anyone else into trouble. I hope too that the God of mercy will forgive him for his past life. As to my conviction for the Whaley murders I would be glad to have my testimony emphasized by saying that

> I told the truth. I regret that I have brought any trouble on the family to which I belong, and whose name I bear. I would say to every man to keep good company, or none. Be industrious and sober and a life of peace will result. I believe truly that God's eternal word should be the guiding star of our lives, and it is the sheer anchor of my soul today. I do not want my friends to grieve for me. I think that sweet peace is in my future. I bid everyone good-bye, and will close to allow Sheriff Davis to perform the duty which it seems, will be a pleasant one for him.[1675]

The hours before the execution were filled with emotion as numerous relatives, including the men's wives and children, visited them in the jail. The meeting between Tipton and his wife was especially sad because she brought along their five boys, and the oldest, who was fourteen, wept uncontrollably. The pair and others partook of the sacrament of the Last Supper.

The men walked without aid to the top of the gallows and sat in chairs. What followed was largely a funeral service with ministers praying, then singing a hymn, "We Need Thee Every Hour," and another prayer. Catlett Tipton's wife came upon the gallows and knelt in prayer with him.[1676] She cried but both the men remained stoic. The execution was already behind schedule because the wives had asked for more time at the jail. An extra hour was given by Sheriff Davis. Tipton's wife said, "Catlett, I will meet you in heaven." He replied, "I will be there."[1677]

The pair was asked if they had anything to say and they referred to their written statements. The minister in charge, the Rev. Rule, said, "Brethren, I have done all I can for you, my last words and last hope is, that we may meet in heaven and there live forever." The men nodded under their caps. The courthouse clock struck one and the men quivered slightly. Sheriff Davis gave the signal and the trigger was sprung by deputy Keener. The bodies fell cleanly.

Wynn died from strangulation and was pronounced dead in twelve minutes. Tipton's neck was broken, but the rope was so tight it lacerated his throat and blood gushed from under his cap. He was taken down after eighteen minutes. Wynn was placed in a lavish casket, Tipton in a plain one bearing the Odd Fellows insignia. The people inside the stockade filed by and looked at the bodies. Although the outside crowd rushed the stockade, virtually none saw the bodies because the coffins were quickly closed and put in wagons and taken away by the families. Among the many people in the throng were Lizzie Chandler and her niece, Mollie Lillard Whaley, age two. A wrongful death suit was filed against Bob Catlett and the killers, but it was filed too late and was dismissed.[1678]

At the time of the execution, Bob Catlett had jumped bail and was technically a fugitive. He finally surrendered and was brought to trial the second time in Morristown. In all, he was tried four times, spending freely on lawyers. As the fifth trial began the state entered a nolle prosecution against him and he walked free.

1900

John C. Watson (aka Thomas C. Watson), white, age 59. *Murder.*

The crime was committed about 5:30 P.M. on December 21, 1898, at the rural farm home of Jim Hillis outside of McMinnville in Warren County. The killer was a farmer and neighbor of the victim, and the shooting was caused by a dispute over the sharing of recently harvested corn and payment for fence rails. The victim, James Hillis, white, age forty, was the across-the-road neighbor whom the killer thought had cheated him earlier that day.

The dispute was unresolved by the evening of the killing, and Watson, who had been drinking apple brandy all day (which he had produced), was highly intoxicated. He shot Hillis in the front yard of his home. The victim's fourteen-year-old daughter saw her father hit by pellets shot from both barrels of a shotgun held by Watson, who was hiding. Hillis's son-in-law, W.W. Clendenen, who lived nearby, came running and carried Hillis into the house. Hillis named Watson as the shooter and died several hours later.[1679]

John (sometimes Thomas) C. Watson had enlisted in the famous Company "H" of the 16th Tennessee Regiment (Col. Savage's regiment) and had fought throughout the war including Shiloh, Corinth, Jonesboro, Plum Orchard, Atlanta, Decatur, Chickamauga, and Murfreesboro. He had been wounded at the latter two battles. He was known for making and selling untaxed liquor and spent a year in a federal prison. In a drunken row in 1893 he shot and seriously wounded a Negro man but after a hotly contested trial was acquitted.[1680]

On the day of the shooting, Watson and Hillis were at the house of a neighbor, Mrs. A.L. Stepp, where Watson accused Hillis of cheating him on the corn, and of failure to deliver the fence rails. Watson had clearly been drinking and said that Hillis was a rascal and that everybody named Hillis was a dog. Hillis said he would not talk to him under these conditions. Watson then spat on his finger and flipped it in Hillis's face. Hillis slapped Watson, but Mrs. Stepp intervened and ordered Watson out of the house. She saw him standing by the road later with his gun, which he fired twice while waiting.[1681]

Watson was arrested within an hour of the shooting. His defense was temporary insanity, namely that he was so intoxicated that he lacked the mental capacity to kill intentionally. Watson never admitted the wrongfulness of his act because he maintained to the end that he was so intoxicated that he did not remember anything about the day of the killing. He did not take the stand, but his family testified that he was drunk, and that he was a man "whom liquor made almost wild."[1682] He was convicted on September 12, 1899, despite the able defense of two prominent lawyers. The case was appealed to the Tennessee Supreme Court, which affirmed the conviction, but the opinion cannot be located.

Until the end, Watson thought his sentence would be commuted to life imprisonment, and his case was the subject of much rumor. One rumor held that he would be rescued from the jail by the Ku Klux Klan. Watson was questioned about several unsolved crimes going back to 1882, including the shooting death of an internal revenue officer, and a mob that liberated a man from the jail a decade later. He denied any involvement with these crimes.

Watson said, "I feel sick and weak, but as to my hope, it is all right. I realize that I am in a great deal of danger. I don't believe I will ever feel ready to die. But I feel I have forgiven all my enemies and all mankind and I am not uneasy as to the hereafter. I have tried to do my duties in war times and in civil life. They cannot cheat me out of but a few days, and I put my whole trust in the Lord."[1683] After saying this, he broke down crying.

Watson was executed on 11:50 A.M. April 25, 1900, a quarter mile from the Warren County jail on a gallows designed to hold three men. He was executed alongside William Brown, a wife-killer, and Sonnie Crain, who had killed John Brown (William Brown's brother) in the jail. The special gallows had been built on April 17 and was inside a 30-by-30-foot enclosure.[1684] The execution was witnessed by about twenty people, but their view was obscured by a canvas curtain drawn around the top of the gallows. Two thousand waited outside hoping to glimpse the bodies as they were taken down.

Watson had been visited by the Rev. William Weakley of the Methodist Episcopal Church. After making a profession of faith, he was baptized a few days before the execution. Watson had been visited by his five adult children at the jail, but none came to the execution. He had also been visited by a number of former comrades in arms. In the hours before the execution, Watson was emotional to the point of breaking down. He said, "Good-bye, boys," and "I'll meet you in heaven," but unlike the other two, he was trembling and tears flowed down his cheeks. Said the newspaper, "His nerves had failed him entirely."[1685]

On the gallows, the men were attended by four white ministers and two black. The ministers led in singing "Amazing Grace," followed by a prayer, then another hymn, "Lord Jesus, I Long to Be Perfectly Whole." The Rev. Weakley called upon the men to say what they wanted. Watson said, "I don't know that I have anything to say," his voice trembling, "I can forgive all mankind. I am trusting in Him. I fear no danger. Though sometimes I have had doubts, I feel ready."[1686]

The trap was sprung after the sheriff told the men they had thirty seconds to live, and Brown said, "Don't tell us about it." The sheriff said, "Good-bye," and sprung the trap. Watson's fingers twitched a few minutes after the drop. His neck was found to be broken. The bodies were cut down after twenty minutes. Watson's body was placed in a coffin and turned over to his family.[1687]

Sonnie Crain, black, age 40. *Murder.*

The crime was committed in the middle of the night on May 22, 1899, in the punishment cell, called the "dungeon," of the Warren County jail. The killer was being held in the jail while a prior murder conviction was being appealed to the Tennessee Supreme Court. The victim, John "Bud" Brown, white, age thirty-six, was being held in the jail awaiting trial for the murder of his sister-in-law Mrs. Mary Fults Brown. He was kept in the same cell as his brother, William "Bill" Brown, who had been convicted a few days earlier of killing Mary, his wife. The cell was also occupied by John C. Watson, who was waiting an appeal for murdering his neighbor.

Crain was a longtime criminal and gambler who was an expert at craps. In October 1898, he and several other blacks, including Tom Martin and

Will Snellings, had been playing craps on the bank of the river when a dispute arose. Guns were drawn and shots exchanged. Crain was hit in the leg, and Snellings was soon dead. Crain was tried and convicted of second-degree murder and received a ten-year sentence. This case was on appeal and he was in the punishment cell with the three others when he committed the murder.

As the Brown brothers slept, Crain took a bed slat and bludgeoned William "Bill" Brown, cracking his skull. He was not expected to live. Crain then assaulted John "Bud" Brown in the same manner, killing him. Crain's defense was that the brothers had been threatening and ridiculing him for some time and he attacked them in self-defense. There was thought to be another motive. The jailer was away on business and put his wife in charge that day. Witnesses said that the killing was a possible diversion, so that when the jailer's wife came to take Crain away, he and Watson could force an escape.[1688]

Crain was convicted of murder and given the death penalty. This case, and the one involving Snelling's death, were the subject of a single decision from the Tennessee Supreme Court, which affirmed both convictions. The opinion cannot be located. Crain never denied killing Bud Brown and maintained the killing was done because he was afraid of the brothers. He denied the plot to escape the jail.[1689] Crain was visited by two black ministers in the jail and a few days before the execution he professed his faith, saying, "All I want is to be saved in the other world, and I feel that I am saved. I belong to the Lord's church and have been preparing to die."[1690]

Sonnie Crain was executed at 11:50 A.M. on April 25, 1900, a quarter mile from the Warren County jail on a gallows designed to hold three men. He died alongside John C. Watson and William "Bill" Brown. The execution was seen by twenty people who were inside a 30-by-30-foot enclosure which contained the recently built gallows, but their actual view was obstructed by a canvas curtain. Two thousand waited outside the enclosure to glimpse the coffins being taken away.

Crain walked steadily to the gallows and said nothing on the way. The black and white ministers offered prayers and hymns on the scaffold, including "Amazing Grace." When asked if they had anything to say, the men gave short statements. Crain spoke last, saying, "I am willing to die." The sheriff said they had thirty seconds. Brown responded, "Don't tell us about it." The sheriff said, "Good-bye," and both Crain and Brown said, "Good-bye, boys." At that instant the sheriff triggered the trap and Crain fell with the others. His neck was not broken and he strangled. He was cut down in eight minutes. No relatives had visited him in jail or attended the execution. His body was buried at the expense of the county. There are some photos of this triple execution in the photography files of the State Library and Archives.

William "Bill" Brown, white, age 40. *Murder.*

The crime was committed in the middle of the night on May 5, 1898, in the home of Mr. and Mrs. William "Bill" Brown (the killer) in a rural part of Warren County. The killers were Bill Brown, husband of Mary Fults Brown, and his brother, John "Bud" Brown. The victim was Mary Fults Brown (Mrs. Bill Brown), white, age thirty-nine. She was shot by John "Bud" Brown, her brother-in-law, while asleep beside her husband in a bed in their house.

The illiterate Brown couple were tenant farmers. Mary Fults, the mother of an illegitimate child, had married Bill Brown about ten years earlier. A few years later, his brother, Bud Brown, was indicted for having sex with a mare. He evaded arrest, and in some manner Bill and Mary took their savings, forty dollars, and compromised the prosecution. When Bud returned to Warren County a year or so later, he was supposed to repay the money, but made no effort to do so. Mrs. Brown continued to press him for the money. By this time, Bill was tired of the conflict about the money and decided to leave Mary. But the separation was short because it soon became clear that she would follow Bill anywhere.

During the separation, the brothers decided to kill Mary. No motive was ever shown other than their desire to be rid of her. They invited Bill Jeff Calhoun Rogers, an old friend, to stay the night of May 5, 1898. He was to serve as an unwitting witness. The brothers planned that as Bill and Mary slept in the same bed, with Rogers sleeping in the same room, that Bud Brown would come in and shoot Mary. According to plan, Bill left the door unlocked, and Bud came in and shot the sleeping Mary just below the ear, killing her instantly. He ran away. Bill began wailing, "Lordy, lordy, someone's shot Mary!" as a startled Rogers lit a lamp to see the dead woman.

Bill Brown insisted that someone had shot Mary through the open window, but since she was sleeping at his side and he was beside the window, it seemed impossible that the bullet could have come from that direction. A search found a recently fired pistol in a trunk belonging to Bill Brown. He had earlier denied owning a gun. Now he said it had been recently fired because he planned to sell it. When asked what he had shot, he said a piece of planking that had been burned in the stove.

Taken into custody, Bill Brown suffered an anxiety attack. When visited by J.N. Hughes, a neighbor, he suddenly confessed and implicated his brother. The neighbor said the confession should be made to a proper official in order to avoid punishment for his brother's crime. The statement, written by a lawyer summoned for the task, was notarized and given to the sheriff. It served as the basis for Bill Brown's conviction.

The brothers were indicted for Mary's killing, but the trials were severed. Bill Brown, "without sense, money, friends or counsel," was tried first. A young inexperienced lawyer was appointed to represent him. The lawyer prevailed on two more young lawyers to assist. Bill Brown was promptly convicted and given the death penalty.

At a motion for a new trial, defense counsel said that a new trial should be granted because one of the jurors thought he was actually "sitting at the trial of John Brown, not Bill Brown," in part because the two sat next to each other during the trial, in which neither testified. The judge hearing the motion became outraged at the young lawyer, and with a view to punishing him for the statement, commanded another juror to find the confused juror. Brought into court, he confirmed his confusion as to the proper defendant. The astonished judge scolded the juror and ordered a new trial.[1691]

In May 1899, Bill Brown was tried and convicted the second time. The case was appealed to the Tennessee Supreme Court, which affirmed the conviction, but the opinion cannot be located. Bill Brown awaited the Supreme Court's decision in the McMinnville jail. Held along with him, awaiting his trial, was his brother, John "Bud" Brown. A few days after Bill's trial, on May 22, 1899, a fellow inmate at the jail, Sonnie Crain, assaulted Bill Brown with a bed slat, cracking his skull. He then turned to John "Bud" Brown and did the same, killing him. This was the crime for which Crain was hanged alongside Bill Brown on April 25, 1900.

As the execution date neared, Bill Brown professed religion and was baptized. But he repudiated his confession, putting the entire blame on his dead brother. "I ain't guilty. John killed her. I heard him make the threat. The night of the killing the shot woke me. I got up and lit the lamp. I went out and saw John running away. I spoke to him and he hallooed back that he had done what he said he would."[1692]

Brown was executed on 11:50 A.M. April 25, 1900, a quarter mile from the Warren County jail on a gallows designed to hold three men. He died alongside John C. Watson and Sonnie Crain, executed for different crimes. The execution was witnessed by twenty people, but their view was obscured by a canvas curtain drawn around the top of the gallows. The gallows was erected "on the brow of a hill above the power house, across the street from the Falcon Roller Mills." It had been built on April 17 and was "inside of an enclosure 30 by 30 feet in dimensions."[1693] Two thousand waited outside the enclosure hoping to glimpse the bodies as they were taken from the gallows.

Four white and two black ministers tended to the men on the scaffold. Brown knelt on the platform under the rope as the ministers conducted their service. This involved singing "Amazing Grace," followed by a prayer, another hymn and another prayer. As Brown knelt on the gallows he said, "Good-bye, boys, I'll meet you in heaven." Asked if he had anything to say, he responded, "I am going to a better world than this. I put my whole trust in God, though I would like to live as long as I can. I want you all to meet me there."[1694]

After Crain stopped speaking, the sheriff said they had another thirty seconds. Brown said, "Don't tell us about it." The sheriff said, "Good-bye," and sprung the trap. Brown fell cleanly, his neck broken. He died in nine minutes and was cut down at 12:15 P.M.[1695] Spectators saw nothing more than three closed coffins taken from the enclosure. This is one of the few Tennessee executions for which photographs exist showing all three men on the gallows.

Henderson House, black, age 30. *Murder.*

The crime was committed on October 4, 1896, at Isabel Bar on the Mississippi River, one mile north of Plumpoint, in Lauderdale County. A whiskey boat had drawn up at the bank and was selling liquor to a crowd of Negroes and a few white people. About twenty-five yards from the boat a craps game was in progress. Among the players was Duncan Goodrich, white, who lived in Osceola, Arkansas, and four other blacks, including Alf Halliburton and Henderson House. A quarrel arose and Goodrich was shot in the back and died within a few hours.

Halliburton was charged with the shooting and was placed in jail. He escaped and was not captured until 1898. At his trial, Lewis Rice, black, one of the gamblers, testified that Henderson House (still at large) was the shooter and Halliburton was acquitted. An enraged mob lynched Rice on March 23, 1900, for "testifying for one of his own race."

Meanwhile, Henderson House was arrested in Jonesboro, Arkansas, in 1899. He went to trial in April 1900 and was sentenced to hang for the Goodrich killing on May 18, 1900. The Tennessee Supreme Court affirmed the conviction, but the opinion cannot be located. The court set his execution for August 18, 1900, but he was reprieved by Gov. McMillan until September 18, 1900.

House was kept at the Memphis jail and was taken to Ripley for his execution, which was done at 11:00 A.M. on September 18, 1900, on an outside gallows next to a black cemetery. The date was kept secret to prevent any problems with a mob. Only eight people witnessed the execution. A black minister, Romeo Johnson, delivered a short talk and a prayer. House had spent his last days reading a Bible and in fervent prayer.

Asked about the crime, House said he was the shooter, that he was sorry for the crime and was ready to die.[1696] He was taken directly from the gallows to the nearby cemetery.

A. Dillard Warren, white, age 35. *Murder.*

The crime was committed about 9:00 P.M. November 13, 1898, at the rural farmhome of Mr. and Mrs. Elzey Evans in Cannon County. The killers were Warren and Dan Lahue, white, age twenty-five. Warren was a farmer in the neighborhood. Lahue worked on the Dallas Cummings farm nearby. The victim was Elzey Evans, white, age forty-two. He was shot through a window in his house, in the presence of his wife and son. The shot came without warning and he fell into his wife's arms saying, "Oh, Helen, I'm killed."[1697]

Evans's death arose out of a dispute over some lumber. Both Warren and Evans had taken timber to a sawmill. When Evans did not get back two pieces of beech scantling, he went to Warren's house and found the wood hidden under the floor. He told Warren he was going to press charges unless Warren returned the wood himself to the sawmill. Evans met with the grand jury, but it returned a no true bill when Evans did not agree to prosecute. Warren knew only that Evans had met with the grand jury.

Warren tried twice to get Lahue to assist him in killing Evans; in particular, he offered fifty dollars for the actual shooting. Lahue, described as a "man of pliant mind with no power of resistance and partly through fear and partly through a disposition to yield to every request," accompanied Warren to the Evans house.[1698] Under the guise that Warren would pay him to broker an agreement to compromise the lumber-related problem, with the promise that Lahue could farm some of Warren's land in return for his help, Lahue walked slightly behind Warren, who was carrying a double-barreled shotgun.

Accounts differ as to what happened next. Lahue said Warren rebuked him for not going ahead and killing Evans, with Lahue staying behind about twenty yards. Warren then put on a different pair of shoes he had carried hidden in his clothes. He crept up to the house and shot Evans with both barrels through a broken windowpane. At trial, Warren insisted that he had nothing to do with the killing, that it was done by Lahue.

When Mrs. Evans said the only person who was angry with her husband was Dillard Warren, the sheriff went to his house, but was told he had gone rabbit hunting. Riding in the direction Warren had gone, the sheriff encountered some children and asked if they had seen Warren. They said yes, saying he had just passed going toward his house. This time, bloodhounds were used, which tracked Warren to a hiding place in his house.

Both Warren and Lahue were arrested. Because neither implicated the other, both were released. Later, questioning of Warren's wife and a house visitor showed that Warren was gone for a substantial period of time on the murder night. The footprints leading from the murder scene matched Warren's shoes.[1699] Again, both were arrested and put in different parts of the jail.

Taken back to the murder house, Warren refused to go inside, which was taken as a sign of guilt. Back at the jail, Lahue confessed to his part in the matter, naming Warren as the shooter. Warren named Lahue.

The pair were given separate trials. Lahue pled guilty and was given a ten-year sentence. In prison at the time of Warren's execution, he said, "Warren tried to incriminate me in order to save himself. He ought to be hung and I would rather see him hung than anyone I ever met."[1700] Warren's case was appealed to the Tennessee Supreme Court and affirmed, but the opinion cannot be located.

Warren was executed at 1:30 P.M. on September 27, 1900, in the jail yard of the county jail in Woodbury, county seat of Cannon County. It was witnessed by fifteen people, with another one thousand gathered outside the jail. Efforts to gain a full commutation were frustrated because Warren and others had attempted to break out of the jail on August 8, 1900, a few hours before Warren was scheduled to die. He was reprieved until September

27. The reason given was that a number of ministers had asked the governor for more time. They felt Warren was "not satisfied with his future condition," and a respite would allow him to "prepare for death."[1701]

In the days before his death, Warren was attended by two ministers, but refused to make a public statement about his crime. The morning of his execution he said that he had a vision during the night that the Master told him he would die, and he saw his sister in a vision, welcoming him to heaven. Before being led to the gallows, he was brought out in front of the jail and said he was innocent but that others should take warning from him. Wearing his old clothes, but intentionally leaving his jacket in his cell, Warren walked with a steady gait to the gallows, where he was lifted up by several men.

He now complained that the judge was "a little too hard on me in this charge," and said he would gladly have served a life sentence. He said both the judge and jury acted "partially" in giving the guilty man ten years, while hanging an innocent man.[1702] He ended, "That is all I want to say." The cap was put over his head. The noose was adjusted because he said it wasn't right. The trigger was pulled at 1:20 P.M.

The trap failed to release and the spectators watched in stunned silence. Warren calmly said, "I reckon I had better get off." He stepped away from the trap. The scaffold was "rearranged." This time Warren struggled with pinioned hands to grab the rope when the trigger was pulled at 1:30 P.M.[1703] His neck was not broken in the four-foot fall and he strangled. He was cut down after sixteen minutes. The body was placed in a coffin and hundreds passed through the jail to look at it.

None of Warren's relatives came to his execution except his second cousin, Sheriff Shirley, who, at Warren's request, put the noose around his neck because Warren insisted it not be placed by Deputy Sheriff Elkins. As soon as the sheriff sprung the trigger he "turned and buried his face in his hands and wept like a child."[1704] Warren was survived by his wife and five children.

1901

Abe Petway, black, age 33. *Murder.*

The crime was committed on the night of May 31, 1900, in downtown Nashville, Davidson County, at 932 South Cherry Street at a grocery store owned by Michael C. Wrenne.[1705] The killers were Abe Petway, Lewis Bridges, and Eli Webb. The victim was Mr. Wrenne, white, age forty, who had sleeping quarters in the store. He rented the back part of the store as living quarters to the killers. Wrenne lingered in the hospital until his death on June 14, 1900.

Because the men's stories differed, it is not clear how the killing was done, other than Mr. Wrenne was killed with a hatchet and wooden club while asleep in his bed. When Petway was arrested he immediately confessed, but said he had only served as the lookout, and was to receive ten dollars for his part in the crime. Apparently, the other two said he was the actual killer.

The jury convicted all three of first-degree murder, but with mitigating circumstances. The trial judge said the evidence was not strong enough against Webb and granted him a new trial. He disregarded the jury recommendation and ordered Petway and Bridges hanged. Their cases were appealed to the Tennessee Supreme Court, which affirmed Petway's death sentence, but granted Bridges a new trial. The opinion cannot be located.

Petway was respited so he could be used as a witness in the retrial of Webb and Bridges. He was not used, however, because he refused to talk about the crime. The retrial resulted in a hung jury. The pair was waiting a third trial at the time Petway was hanged.[1706]

Petway joined the Catholic Church four months before his execution under the direction of Father Plunkett and Father Morris, who had earlier tended to Duser Thompson. He was executed the same day as Thompson and co-defendant Babe Battise. Both were given last rites in the same cell by the priests.

Petway and the others were executed on a gallows in the Davidson County jail yard at 10:00 A.M. on July 18, 1901. The jail was then located on Front Street. About fifty people were present, with another three thousand, mostly black, waiting outside to get a glimpse of the hearses pulling away. The gallows had remained unused for four years, after it was built for the execution of Dan Harris. Built for the execution of two, the trap had to be enlarged for three.[1707]

Petway, dressed in a new dark suit, white shirt and patent leather shoes provided by the sheriff, mounted the gallows with firm steps. The men were accompanied by the priests and the Rev. Luke Mason, Baptist. On the gallows, Petway said he had nothing to say except that he wanted all to meet him in heaven and that he was going to die without a hard feeling toward anyone. After Babe Battise finished talking, the caps were put over their heads and the nooses placed around their necks. Battise said, "Brother Mason, pray for me." At that moment, a deputy sheriff signaled readiness and Sheriff Hurt sprung the trap. The men fell five feet.[1708]

Petway died without a struggle because his neck was broken, as was Battise's. Petway was holding a rosary in one hand. Battise was placed in a coffin provided by the sheriff, but no one claimed his body and he was buried in the county cemetery.[1709] This was the last triple hanging in Davidson County under county auspices.

Babe H. Battise, black, age 26. *Murder.*
Andrew "Duser" Thompson, black, age 33. *Accessory before murder.*

The crime was committed about 9:00 P.M. on December 8, 1899, near the corner of Cherry Street and Demonbreun Street in downtown Nashville, Davidson County. The shooter was Battise, who was urged to kill the victim, Cain Miller, black, age twenty-nine, by his employer, Andrew "Duser" Thompson. The latter was the owner of the Bucket of Blood saloon and the restaurant next door, located in a slum area of downtown Nashville known as Black Bottom, near the river. Cain Miller was on bad terms with Thompson. According to Battise, the crime was instigated because Miller tried to steer business, especially white patrons, away from the Bucket of Blood, which was known for its back-room gambling. Miller also played the role of a police "spotter," someone who tips off police about illegal activities.

Thompson told Battise where to hide when Miller walked by in the darkness and told him to use the pistol kept in the saloon. Battise shot Miller twice in the back. Miller was found at the shooting site and was brought to the city hospital. Miller lived six hours, unable to name his assailant, but apparently implicated Thompson. Later on the night of the shooting, Battise and Thompson, together with several others described as a gang, were arrested near a Nashville landmark, the Maxwell House Hotel. Under rigid questioning in jail, Thompson named Battise as the triggerman and told where Battise had left the pistol, but denied any involvement. Later he said Battise was angry at Miller over ten cents he had lost in a card game. Confronted with Thompson's statement, Battise bitterly upbraided Thompson for having turned on him. Much of this conversation was overheard by police officers hidden while the pair were placed in nearby jail cells. Battise explained that he had come to work at the Bucket of Blood after Thompson had paid a $19.50 criminal fine which Battise was unable to pay and would have been worked off on the county roads.

At trial, Battise described in elaborate detail how Thompson had shown him the pistol in a drawer in the saloon and told him the street location where Miller was likely to be found after saloon hopping. Thompson was charged with being an accessory before the fact. He vigorously denied involvement: "I had nothing to do with the killing of Cain Miller. I did not beg, buy, ask, incite, threaten or do anything to get Battise to kill him."[1710] The jury returned its verdict on February 9, 1900, finding Thompson guilty and Battise guilty with mitigating circumstances. Judge J.M. Anderson ruled there were no mitigating circumstances and ordered Battise to be hanged as well.

On appeal to the Tennessee Supreme Court, Thompson insisted there was no proof that he had anything to do with the crime except for Battise's testimony.[1711] The Supreme Court's opinion cannot be located, but a newspaper account reported that Governor McMinn had read it along with the entire court record. The governor had been asked by prominent citizens, numerous clergy and eleven members of the jury to commute Battise's sentence to life imprisonment. Petitioners argued that the malleable Battise was under the overwhelming influence of Thompson.[1712]

Battise's lawyer told the Supreme Court: "In view of the infirmities of human nature, and in the light of this influence and control of 'Duser,' from a human standpoint, life imprisonment as a substitute for the death penalty, is overwhelmingly suggested and justified." The argument continued, "Oh!, it is said, just one 'nigger' more to die on the gallows will make no difference! Shall this be the judgment of the Superior race that sits on final appeal? A race that knows the negro race, its faults, its infirmities, its crimes and its temptations and its virtues, if it has any. Shall the Leper be again forbidden to approach Christ?"[1713]

Battise and Thompson were executed by hanging in the Nashville jail courtyard on July 18, 1901. Thompson asserted his innocence to the end. Battise had recently been baptized into the Pentecostal Alliance, affirmed his court testimony against Thompson, and made an earnest plea that all young men "turn away from evil ways, and when tempted, to think of this case." Earlier, after eating his last breakfast, he had told reporters, "A colored man is always doing well when he is eating chicken."

The executions were conducted in front of fifty to seventy-five official observers as four or five thousand people, mostly black, and unable to see anything, gathered outside to see the coffins carried away. Because Abe Petway was executed at the same time, "Sheriff Hurt has the prestige of being the first sheriff in Davidson County to hang three men at one time."[1714] Sheriff Hurt remarked, "This is something I have never done before. It is not very pleasant work, but the mandate of the court must be executed. I hope I won't have to have any more on the scaffold."[1715]

Nathan Caruthers, black, age 18. *Murder.*

The crime was committed on the night of April 7, 1900, at the Anderson-Tully Lumber Company on North Second Street in Memphis, in Shelby County. Caruthers had worked for the company briefly, but was frequently seen on the property. He lived with a relative nearby. Caruthers had been told by Sam Skates, black, that the victim would have about fifty dollars on his person. The victim, Charles Nebe, white, age sixty-eight, was the night watchman at the mill. He was also a moneylender to the workers at the mill, advancing them money in lieu of their weekly pay. The company always paid in cash. It was Saturday (payday) and Nebe was thought to have repaid funds in his pockets, largely in gold.

Nebe worked the night shift and was walking down some stairs when Caruthers struck him with a piece of scantling. Nebe, unarmed, defended himself as best he could, but he was pummeled by Caruthers, rendered semiconscious, and lived four days without identifying his assailant.

The company had two night watchmen. The other man said that Nebe was paid ten dollars a week and likely had two five-dollar gold pieces in his pocket at the time of his death, plus more from his lending. He discovered Nebe on the ground because the two passed each other about every forty-five minutes in making their rounds.[1716] About the same time the other watchman discovered Nebe, a neighbor and his wife appeared. Caruthers had told them that Nebe had been killed. Caruthers accompanied them up to the yard, but did not go near Nebe. Instead, he ran off. He went downtown, looked at some shoes, and caught the train to Covington.

The circumstances of Caruthers's arrest are unknown except insofar as "Sgt. Perry performed a piece of detective work that serves as a model." Taken to the Memphis jail from his uncle's home in Covington, Caruthers was confronted with some of the money (gold coins) he had entrusted to a female relative by marriage. He confessed and implicated Skates.

At trial, Caruthers repudiated his confession, insisting that it was given because the police put a pistol to his stomach and threatened to shoot him. However, by then Skates had turned state's evidence and was dropped as a defendant. Caruthers testified that Skates had nothing to do with the killing.

Caruthers admitted striking Nebe with the scantling, but insisted it was self-defense because Nebe had struck him when he walked across the property. He repeatedly insisted he had not intended to kill Nebe and did not rob him. He insisted the gold money he gave to a relative had been earned the previous summer. However, the relative testified that Caruthers had no money until the night of the killing. "On cross-examination, Caruthers could not give the name of the person who had paid him the gold, nor specify the time in which he had earned the money. He was further asked to exhibit any wound or bruise about his person where Mr. Nebe had struck him and was unable to do so."[1717] Caruthers's case was appealed to the Tennessee Supreme Court but the opinion cannot be located.

After he was brought back from Jackson, where he heard the Supreme Court announce its decision, Caruthers bolted from the Shelby County jail through a door left open, knocking down a guard. Another guard held on to a pants leg and was dragged twenty feet before Caruthers made his escape. He was captured a few days later. The jailbreak was a factor in the governor's denial of mercy, the media saying, "His reputation was altogether too bad to be anything but a detriment to his case."[1718] A few days before his execution, a photographer came to the jail and took an array of pictures of Caruthers. When they were returned, he took great interest in determining which were to be given to family and friends.

In the days before his execution, Caruthers was attended by the Rev. George Washington, who was regarded as the "chaplain-general to the Shelby County hangman." He baptized Caruthers in a bathtub at the jail.[1719] Caruthers had earlier confessed to the killing, and again said that Skates had nothing to do with it, and he had gotten $19.25 from Nebe's body. His sister and a female cousin visited him on execution day. He told the sister, "Good-bye, Channie, be a good girl and meet me on the other side."

Nathan Caruthers was hanged at 2:30 P.M. inside the Shelby County jail on August 6, 1901. About an hour before the execution, he gave the jailer a written statement to be given to the media after his execution. It was an exhortation to live a godly life, and repeated a phrase he used on the gallows, "Never let your mind take control of your body."[1720]

Caruthers had been given liquor throughout the day. Said the newspaper, "Caruthers did not drink copiously during the day, and instead of being drunk, as condemned men sometimes are when they go to the gallows, he was filled with religious fervor, which seemed to stimulate him more than anything."[1721] He walked to the gallows with a steady step. He said, "I could have been a good boy, as good as anybody, but I let my mind control my body. I have bowed down to the Lord and He have forgiven me for what I done."[1722] Caruthers stopped. Somebody in the crowd said, "Good-bye, Nathan." "Good-bye to all," he said, "I'm going on to glory." "I've been praying for you and for myself and when you get over there, jes' tell 'em I'm a coming," said a black woman in the crowd. "All right, I hope you will. I hope I will see you in glory land," said Caruthers. "What will I tell mama, Nathan?" said his cousin who had come by his invitation. "Tell her good-bye and tell her I've gone on to glory," said the doomed man.[1723]

At this point the black cap was put over his head, and his knees quivered. The noose was placed around his neck. Fifty people said good-bye in unison and the sheriff triggered the drop. Caruthers fell cleanly but the knot slipped to the back of his neck and he strangled to death. "Caruthers did not writhe and go through the usual contortions of a man who is hung and whose neck is not broken."[1724] His body quivered slightly and was cut down fourteen minutes later. "A short while before the execution a collection was taken in the crowd to defray the expenses of sending the body to Frayser Station for burial. Over $11 was realized, everyone giving something."[1725]

1902

Armstrong Hensley, white, age 35. *Rape of child; murder.*

The crime was committed on June 27, 1901, in a rural and remote part of Unicoi County, seven miles from Erwin, an area called Flagpond. The rapist-killer had been married to the child's mother for four years. She had two children by her first husband. The victim was one of the children, Minnie, white, age six.

Hensley and Minnie left in the morning to gather huckleberries and blackberries. He returned late in the evening carrying Minnie and placed her in a bed. He said she was badly injured when she walked off by herself and fell while crossing a high foot-log.

Because of her serious injuries, a doctor was called. Minnie explained that she had been raped by Hensley. Her rape injuries were obvious. Minnie said she had not fallen from a foot-log, but that Hensley had beaten her. She died a few hours later. Hensley was immediately arrested. To prevent his lynching, he was kept in the Greeneville jail. He was given what the newspaper called a "hurried trial."[1726] He told his lawyers not to appeal. Apparently, he was convicted of murder and rape of a child under the age of twelve, both capital crimes.

The details of his execution inside the Unicoi County jail on February 6, 1902, are unknown. He was attended by the Rev. A.M. Laughern, who held a religious service in the jail and read the Fifty-first Psalm. By this time, Hensley claimed innocence. He said that his wife, the doctor (Dr. Tilson), and W.N. Quinn, the district attorney, were responsible for his position. The newspaper summed it up: "Armstrong Hensley was a true product of the ignorant mountaineers of East Tennessee."[1727]

Dan Farley, black, age 46. *Murder.*

The crime was committed between one o'clock and three o'clock on the morning on August 6, 1901, beside McLean Avenue, south of Raleigh Road, in a heavily wooded part of Memphis, in Shelby County. The victim was Ada Farley, black, age unknown, the killer's wife. She was a cook for a Memphis family and the night of her death she had gone to a church service. Farley picked her up from that service.

In the buggy on the way back to the city, the two were heard quarreling. Along the way, he pulled her out of the buggy, took her to the side of the road and split her head with a hatchet. He fired a pistol shot into her side.

Farley was described as "an intelligent negro who spent much time among the white people. He knew and believed in them."[1728] He told police what was described as an "improbable story," namely, two men had stopped the buggy, one had pulled Ada from the vehicle and shot her while the other struck her head with a hatchet. They got in the buggy, holding the pistol on him, and took him to a railroad track and let him out.[1729]

The police did not believe the story and arrested Farley. His bloody hatchet was found in mud in a brook near the body. No one saw the killing, but several people testified that Ada was fearful of Dan. He had threatened to kill her previously and was very jealous. He had accused her of being unfaithful to him. The case was appealed to the Tennessee Supreme Court, which affirmed the conviction, but the opinion cannot be located.

Farley was very emotional during the last days of his life, given to rambling accounts of his life and his unfaithful wife. He was attended by the well-respected black minister, the Rev. George Washington. Under his care, Farley embraced religion, and made a plea to be buried in the black church cemetery beside his wife. The congregation objected because they did not believe his story about the killing.

Waiting in jail, Farley smoked cigars and talked about his widowed sister and complained that his young daughter had not been brought to see him. The day before his execution he said, "I am innocent of the murder of Ada and I do not believe that God and the good white folks are going to let me hang because a lot of niggers swore my life away."[1730]

Farley was executed at 12:11 P.M. on July 30, 1902, at the end of a corridor on a gallows built inside the Shelby County jail. About one hundred people witnessed the execution. Walking steadily to the scaffold, he was asked if he wanted to make a statement. He asked how much time he had. Sheriff Blackwell said, "Go ahead, we will give you plenty of time." The Rev. Washington urged him to confess his crime. Farley responded he wanted to talk about God, and then his crime.

After a rambling discourse about religion, he said, "I pay this debt for a crime which Shelby County has worked up on me. It was worked up on me by enemies and the witnesses swore against me. But I promised God I would tell you all when I came to die and would not tell anyone until then. My life is as sweet to me as it is to you and I wanted to live. The weapon at the courthouse was not mine. It was my mother-in-law's hatchet. The other weapon [the pistol] was my property. I could tell you where it is, but you couldn't find it."

Farley continued, "You have the right man. But you just guessed at me, thinking you had the right man. The court was unfair to me, because my crime was transacted in such a way that they could not get at it. I see before me two white faces and two colored faces who know of this trouble and hinted such things to me. They did not testify as they should on the witness stand, but I will not implicate their names. My home was rendered unhappy and this crime happened while I was in a passion. But before the passion was over I had repented. I did the crime, but went to God and asked forgiveness."[1731]

Farley's full statement could not be heard because of the noise of a passing train. His mood had been sustained by an injection of morphine given by a doctor, but he refused whiskey, saying, "I want to leave this world with no unclean things in my body." Farley explained that he was the son of a white man named Daniel Webster and Lucy Farley, black, and was called Webster Farley growing up. When his rambling speech slowed, the black cap was put over his head. He said, "Farewell, world," then said it again.

He began, "I come, oh, Lord," when the trap was sprung. He dropped cleanly. His pulse increased to 90 after the drop, but fell to nothing within four minutes. He was cut down and his body was shipped to his widowed sister in Florence, Alabama. Friends had accumulated $9.80 for his funeral expenses.

The gallows upon which Dan Farley died had been constructed for the execution of Nathan Caruthers, who had been executed on August 6, 1901. Taking a small liberty with the truth, the newspaper reported, "The crime for which the law exacted the life of Farley was committed nearly a year ago. It was on the morning of August 5. On that day Nathan Carruthers [*sic*] was hanged for murder. Farley knew Carruthers [*sic*] and had been at the jail on the day of the execution. He saw the crowd gather and knew that a murder was to be avenged. He left the scene and before the expiration of twenty-four hours had himself committed a murder no less horrible."[1732]

1904

Joe Delp, white, age 28. *Murder.*
John Evans (aka "Slow" John Evans), white, age 26. *Murder.*
Henry Judge (aka James Henry Judge), white, age 37. *Accessory before murder.*

The crime was committed about 6:00 P.M. on August 3, 1903, in the rural cabin of Mr. and Mrs.

Simon Bucher, on the bench of Keith Springs Mountain, in Franklin County. The shooters were Evans and Delp. They had been hired by Henry Judge to kill Mr. Bucher, white, age fifty-five. To cover up the killing they also shot his wife Bettie, white, age forty-three, and set fire to the cabin. Distant neighbors, seeing the smoke, arrived the next morning and discovered Mr. Bucher still alive. His dying declaration was given to several people and was published in two newspapers.[1733]

Henry Judge, a lumber dealer and sawmill operator, was a thief who cut timber on other people's land. He wanted to take lumber from a large plot known as the Sears tract, near where he and Bucher lived, but Bucher would have alerted owners or authorities. Judge wanted him out of the way. Judge also wanted to cut a trail through the property to carry stolen goods, including hogs, to market. "Slow" John Evans was the brother of Judge's wife.

Judge had been urging Evans and Delp to kill Bucher for many weeks. He offered them ten dollars and said that several other people wanted Bucher out of the way and they would actually receive about one hundred and twenty-five dollars. The day before the killing he provided them a shotgun, a rifle and a pistol and plenty of moonshine. They were under the influence when they walked up Keith Springs Mountain and found Bucher sitting on his front porch. Engaging in pleasant conversation, he soon took them to look at his prize sweet potato plants in his garden away from the house. He walked ahead of Delp. Without warning, Delp fired both blasts of the shotgun into Bucher's back between the shoulder blades. Falling face down, Bucher heard his wife scream twice and three pistol shots.

The killers took embers from the stove and threw them on straw mattress ticking to set the house on fire. Paralyzed, Bucher lay on the ground all night praying he would live long enough to name the shooters. Distant neighbors saw the smoking house the next morning and came to Bucher at 7:30 A.M. He was able to describe what happened and died at his son's house that afternoon. The day after the shooting, Delp and Evans told Judge about the killings. He said he would give them the ten dollars the next day. They received nothing. The next day, the dying declaration was published in the newspaper. Delp and Evans turned themselves in to the sheriff. Judge was captured by the sheriff as he attempted to sneak back to his home from a trip to Alabama.

Joe Delp was tried first. Evans insisted he had simply gone along with Delp and did no shooting. Henry Judge denied any involvement. The trials were held in Nashville.

Delp and Evans were woodcutters and log haulers for Judge. They testified the reason Judge gave for wanting Bucher dead was that he "was always stealing from him and had killed two dogs there at his house."[1734] Both said he promised them ten dollars for killing the old man.

The Tennessee Supreme Court's opinion was a recitation of the testimony taken from Delp's trial. It said, "The motive of [Delp] and of Evans for killing these people, as stated by [Delp's] testimony, was that Henry Judge had agreed to give him and said Evans $10.00 to kill these old people, $5.00 a piece. To obtain this trifling sum of money, plaintiff in error was willing to murder, and did murder Simon Bucher. Comment is unnecessary. Nothing could make the statement of the case stronger than the bald facts, thus detailed by Joe Delp himself. There is no error in the record, and the judgment of the Court is affirmed."[1735]

Henry Judge was tried separately and much of the trial concerned what the jurors knew about the case from reading the newspapers and local gossip. Judge appealed his conviction to the Tennessee Supreme Court, but the opinion cannot be located. The defendants were sentenced to hang on May 5, 1904, and died that day in the courtyard of the Franklin County jail in Winchester.

In his final statement on the gallows, Henry Judge explained he was sorry for the record he was leaving his wife and children, but was not guilty. He was going to heaven, he insisted. He and Joe Delp had been baptized Catholics the day before. Delp said, "Well, gentlemen, if I hadn't been ready I never would have been here today. The only thing I have to say is I have got to a better place than this. May God bless you all is my prayer!"[1736] Henry Judge was buried in the woods on his father's farm, not in the family cemetery, as was the custom for people who dishonor their family.

Will Hill, black, age unknown. *Murder.*

The crime was committed on the afternoon of August 17, 1902, in the house of Giles Taylor, near the rural community of Grand Junction, in Hardeman County. The killer was the son-in-law of Giles Taylor. The victim, George Taylor, black, age unknown, was the killer's brother-in-law. George Taylor was the brother of Minnie Hill, black, age unknown, who was also killed that day. Minnie was Will Hill's wife.

Three days prior to the shootings, Will had severely beaten Minnie Hill. She had sworn out a warrant against him and had left him and gone to her father's house. Will waited outside and demanded she return. When she refused, he shot at her, missing. Her father, Giles Taylor, and her brother, George Taylor, went outside to rescue her. The father brought her back inside the house, while her brother confronted Will and there was a slight scuffle. George came back toward the house and got on his horse. Will asked where was he going. He feared George was going to get the sheriff.

Versions differed on what happened next. A witness said George replied that it was none of Hill's business. Hill asserted George replied, "I am going to get my gun and kill you."[1737] Hill shot him, and George fell from the horse, dying instantly. Hill then ran through the yard, entered a side door of the house and shot Minnie Hill twice, killing her. He ran away but was arrested on a Memphis-bound train a few days later.

Hill was tried first for killing his wife. The jury found first-degree murder, but with mitigating circumstances. The judge agreed and sentenced him to life imprisonment. He was then tried for the killing of George Taylor and received the death sentence.

The murder conviction was upheld by the Tennessee Supreme Court, but the opinion cannot be located.

Reported the media, "He stated that if he had been hung for the killing of his wife he would not have thought it wrong as he killed her in cold blood, but when he killed George Taylor, they were in a fight, and he did not think he ought to be hung for that."[1738]

On the front porch of the jail, he was allowed to make a speech. According to the media, "He admitted that he had brought all of this trouble upon himself and censored no one; that if he had listened to the teachings of his mother he would have been a free man today. He advised all colored boys to keep away from railroad work, remain at home and respect the advice of their parents. He stated that he did not intend to kill his wife, but that he did intend to kill Giles Taylor, her father. She received the load intended for him. He said that he had made peace with his God and asked his friends to meet him in heaven."[1739]

Will Hill was taken to a gallows erected "for the purpose in R.N. Mitchell's pasture, near the baseball ground," and executed at 11:30 A.M. on July 28, 1904.[1740] The gallows were inside an enclosure. He walked up the steps without help. Hill was asked if he had anything to say and he said no. Earlier, he had made a last request. He wanted to be executed wearing white socks, white shoes, and white gloves. This was granted.

The Rev. J.T. Strayhorn, black, spoke briefly and asked God's blessing on Hill. The sheriff had already put the rope around Hill's neck, he put the black cap on his head and said good-bye. Hill said farewell. The sheriff snatched the trigger and Hill fell cleanly. His feet twitched a little and he was cut down eighteen minutes later. His body was placed in a coffin and sent to his mother.

Said the media, "The penalty met with general satisfaction with both blacks and whites throughout the county, as Hill was known as a bad and dangerous man."[1741]

Ben Springfield, black, age 18. *Murder.*

The crime was committed in the late afternoon of September 3, 1903, at the home of Annanias Pegues in a rural part of Madison County. He was the father of Willie Pegues Springfield, black, age 18, the killer's purported wife. Springfield weighed over two hundred pounds, his wife less than a hundred.

Willie had left Ben and had gone to her father's house to live. The couple had been keeping house for a year, and had gotten a marriage bond on March 1, 1901, when they were both sixteen, but there is no evidence of a legal marriage. Willie Pegues Springfield was frequently seen with injuries from Ben's beatings. On this occasion, she bore evidence of his mistreatment, and they began quarreling outside the father's house. Earlier, he had gone to his uncle's and gotten a shotgun and shells, saying he wanted to hunt squirrels.

As they were arguing, she put her arms around her father to keep Ben from pulling her away, ultimately hiding behind her father, clinging to him. At the time of the shooting, her head and body were protected by her father's; only her legs were showing.

Springfield insisted the shooting was accidental. He said that as he was climbing through a wire fence the gun was "cocked" by getting caught in the fence. Then it went off accidentally as he was standing close to his father-in-law. He said he intended to shoot the father, not Willie. It was undisputed that the gun was never put to the shoulder. The shot struck Willie in the legs, nearly severing one. She gave a dying declaration explaining what happened and died two hours later.[1742]

Springfield's defense was wholly rejected by the Tennessee Supreme Court in a per curiam opinion.[1743] The court said there was no proof that Springfield meant to shoot the father. "That theory appears only in the argument of counsel."[1744] Rather, the proof showed that after Willie said she was afraid to return with Ben, he told the father to "Look out!" and shot once, with the gun remaining in his hand. These facts supported a first-degree murder conviction.[1745]

Springfield was hanged in the jail yard at the Jackson jail on July 28, 1904, at 12:30 P.M. To the end, he maintained the killing was accidental. Four ministers stood on the scaffold with him. There were few spectators.

Sheriff Mayo said to him, "Now Ben, I have to hang you and I want you to be a man." "Yes, sir, Mr. Mayo, I'll be a man," he replied. When he was told to step upon the trap, he began to falter and the sheriff said strongly, "Remember, Ben." He replied, "Yessir, yessir, Mr. Mayo, sir," and stood erect. The sheriff put the hood over his head and said, "Good-bye, Ben," and instantly released the trap.[1746] Springfield's neck was not broken and he strangled to death. His body was cut down in fourteen minutes. Said one account, "He was regarded as a dangerous negro in the community and his wife bore evidence on her person some time before her death of his cruelty to her."[1747]

Because his family refused to claim the body, it was turned over to a local undertaker. This caused speculation that he had not actually died in the hanging. The mystery was revealed a few days later when the undertaker announced that the body was being used to test a new method of embalming.[1748] It had been given the new treatment and was left in the care of some friends for a week or so to see if it worked. It remained with the undertakers for several years. Later, it was kept in the back room of a local drugstore for a number of years. Its final resting place is unknown.

1905

James Scudder, black, age 58. *Murder.*

The crime was committed about noon on February 24, 1904, beside the road leading from Nashville to Franklin, in Davidson County. The victim was the killer's son, James Alfred Scudder, black, age three. Scudder's wife had died shortly after the boy's birth, and Scudder's mother had cared for him. When she became unable to do so, she sent the boy to his father.[1749] Scudder was a waiter at the Tulane Hotel in Nashville and lived in a boarding house, where no one was available to watch the child, who was crippled.

Scudder was seen walking, carrying the boy south in the direction of Franklin. A few weeks later, the child's body was found in a thicket not far from the Franklin Pike about three miles from Nashville. Jim Scudder's first conviction was overturned because the jurors were allowed to see a copy of the *Nashville American* newspaper with a story about the case cut out, but the headline, which had not been cut out, reported an effort by the parties to settle the case by a plea agreement.[1750]

The body was found in a thicket called a cove. Two front teeth had been knocked out. The head moved easily from side to side. When arrested on March 8, 1903, at the Tulane Hotel, Scudder said the boy had been sent to his uncle's, namely, Uncle John. The latter's wife testified she never heard of Scudder or his son until after the killing and that her husband had been dead for four years. Scudder had told a fellow boarder that he was taking the boy to his uncle's. He left on the morning of February 24 and did not come back until much later.[1751] He told a relative the boy was at his uncle's.

The state's testimony asserted the boy was struck in the face with enough force to break his neck.[1752] A doctor said the movement of a neck from side to side indicated the neck was broken. Several undertakers, offered by the defense, said the necks of all dead people move in this manner. Proof showed that under Scudder's care the boy had sustained a broken leg which did not heal despite hospitalization. He could not walk at the time of his death. The boy's teeth were intact when the boy was delivered to Scudder.[1753]

Scudder testified that as he was taking the boy, wrapped in a blanket, to his rooming house, he encountered his Uncle John driving a wagon. Scudder had not seen him in several years and did not recognize him. The uncle insisted on helping and offered to take the boy. Two weeks later he saw Uncle John, who told him that the boy had died and had been buried. Said Uncle John, "I tried to get you up by telephone, at the Tulane, but couldn't do it."[1754]

Scudder said he later went looking for Uncle John but didn't know where he lived, nor did he have a way to get there. The case was appealed to the Tennessee Supreme Court, which affirmed the conviction, but the opinion cannot be located.

In the days before the execution, over a thousand people came to see the gallows, including a blind man who asked to feel the scaffold and rope. Scudder continued to claim innocence, and constantly asked officials if the governor had sent word of a commutation. He was convinced the governor would spare him, in part because the governor frequently stayed at the downtown Tulane Hotel and apparently knew him. "If the governor don't interfere I reckon my time is about come, but they'll be hanging an innocent man," he said.[1755]

He was given a new suit of black by Sheriff Cartwright. Scudder was hanged at the same time as Andrew Hibbert, who died for an unrelated crime. During their incarceration, both men had embraced the Catholic faith and two priests stood on the gallows with them. Scudder, who had been raised a Baptist, had earlier been attended by the Rev. Luke Mason, of the Baptist church. The Rev. Mason attended the execution. Both men walked steadily to the gallows and stopped by the cell of Tom Cox, scheduled to be executed the next week. "Meet us in heaven," they told him, touching hands through the bars of his cell. (Cox was never executed.)

The execution took place at 7:51 A.M. on April 5, 1905, on a gallows inside a building located inside the south yard of the Davidson County jail. It was built for the execution of Bob Ford, ten years earlier. On the gallows, he and Hibbert were asked if they had anything to say and both replied they did not, but said good-bye to those around them. The sheriff said, "In a moment you will be hurled into eternity." This was the signal to put the caps on their heads. As this was done, Hibbert began singing "That Old-Time Religion," and Scudder joined him in singing. The priests told the men to be silent. Scudder turned his capped head toward the priests and at that moment the sheriff triggered the trap. Both men fell cleanly. Scudder's rope turned and he was strangled to death, struggling for several minutes.

The bodies were turned over to the undertaking firm of Taylor & Company where they were placed in coffins. Nearly a thousand people, mostly black, came to view them. Scudder's nephew finally retrieved the body for burial.

Andrew Hibbert, black, age 21. *Murder.*

The crime was committed on the afternoon of July 14, 1903, at the victim's home at 1268 College Street in Nashville, in Davidson County. The victim was Mary Norvell, black, age forty, the killer's mother-in-law. The victim was seated inside her home with the window open. Hibbert had been seen near the house for several days, complaining about his mother-in-law's interference with his marriage, offering threats and under the influence of alcohol. He was seen sitting in a chair near the window two minutes before the shooting.[1756] The newspapers contained no details of the shooting, but were filled with numerous reports of his sightings in the months that followed.

Hibbert fired a pistol through the open window, the bullet striking Mary in the abdomen. She did not see who shot her, but told friends in the house and medical attendants at the hospital that she thought Hibbert was the shooter. He fled and was not captured for several months. By the time of his capture he had admitted the shooting and eleven black people testified against him at his trial. They explained he told them he loved his wife desperately and could not stand separation from her.

On the stand, Hibbert denied the shooting, denied anything amounting to a confession and insisted he knew nothing of the killing until informed by a little girl months later.[1757] The victim's husband, John Norvell, appeared in court intoxicated the day of the trial. He was promptly held in contempt and jailed; he did not testify.

Hibbert was convicted on January 13, 1904, sentenced to hang on March 25, 1904, and was executed on April 5, 1905. The case was appealed to the Tennessee Supreme Court, but it offered no assistance. Here is why: "There is no bill of exceptions in the case, and we are bound to assume that the evidence introduced warranted the verdict of the jury, and that the trial was conducted without error of law on the part of the judge of the lower court. We are unable to find any error upon the face of the record and it results, therefore, the judgment must be affirmed, and the prisoner be remanded to the custody of the sheriff of Davidson County for execution of the sentence to be pronounced by this court."[1758]

Hibbert's infant child was brought to him in the jail and he kissed it through the bars. He gave it two nickels.[1759] In the days before the execution, over a thousand people came to see the gallows, located in a building inside the south yard of the Davidson County jail. It had been built for the execution of Bob Ford, ten years earlier. Among the visitors was a blind man who asked to feel the rope.

Hibbert was given a new suit of black by Sheriff Cartwright. He was hanged at the same time as James Scudder, who was executed for an unrelated crime. During their incarceration, both men embraced the Catholic faith and two priests stood on the gallows with them. Both men walked steadily to the gallows and stopped by the cell of Tom Cox, scheduled to be executed the next week. "Meet us in heaven," they told him, touching hands through the bars of the cell. (Cox was never executed.)

On the gallows, Hibbert and Scudder were asked if had they anything to say and both replied they did not, merely saying good-bye to those around them. The sheriff said, "In a moment you will be hurled into eternity." This was the signal to put the caps on their heads. As this was done, Hibbert began singing "That Old-Time Religion," and Scudder joined him in singing. The priests told the men to be silent. Scudder turned his capped head toward the priests and at that moment the sheriff triggered the trap. Both men fell cleanly. Hibbert's neck was broken.[1760]

His body and Scudder's were turned over to the black undertaking firm of Taylor & Company, where they were placed in coffins. Nearly a thousand people, mostly black, came by to view them. Hibbert's body was finally claimed by his brother.

Abraham M. Miles, black, age 32. *Murder.*

The crime was committed at 9:00 P.M. on June 7, 1904, in a tenement house on St. Paul Street in Memphis, in Shelby County. The killer was a sawmill worker who had recently lived in Earle, Arkansas. He had returned to Memphis with a pistol he claimed needed repair, and tried to locate his wife. The couple had not lived together for some time. The victim was Mattie Peoples Miles, black, age twenty-five, the killer's wife. Miles had the pistol repaired and went looking for Mattie.

Miles located his wife at the tenement house and in the presence of other unrelated people living there. He urged her to cook him supper. They went to her room. She left the tenement a few minutes later, ostensibly to purchase meat. When she returned, she brought policeman Rice, having told him she feared for her life. Rice went to her room, found a hatchet which he placed in a corner, and talked to Miles, who assured him he had no pistol and denied he planned to harm Mattie. The officer told him to leave, but Miles asked for a brief conversation with his wife. Afterwards, she seemed less afraid, and the policeman left.

Late in the evening the couple came down from her room and went to the porch, where they had a conversation about dishes. Miles wanted Mattie to go upstairs and retrieve some dishes, and they began arguing. She complained that he could have gotten the dishes when both were upstairs. He said, "If you don't [get the dishes], I will pitch you in this bayou."[1761] The couple continued to argue and he said, "You were very smart. You went and got the policeman; and you were going to make me play bad; and I am going to play bad before I leave the State of Tennessee."[1762]

She started up the stairs and he shot her in the back, just above the hip. The bullet passed through her body, coming out the front on the right side. The bullet was imbedded in the tenth step from the bottom. This location forced the conclusion that Miles was much lower than Mattie when he shot her.[1763] Miles then ran from the house.

Miles left town and after spending time in various Arkansas towns was finally arrested in Earle, Arkansas. Under arrest, he was told that he had promised not to harm her. He said, "I did tell you. But I got worked up; and she wouldn't go with me; and I killed her." Asked why he killed Mattie, he said, "Well, she had been doing things she ought not to do, and I killed her."[1764]

Miles took the stand and said that a black man named Bud Taylor was present on the porch, who cursed Miles and told him to leave Mattie alone or he would kill him. Miles responded that Mattie was his wife and Taylor had no business talking to her. Mattie joined the argument and came toward Miles with a hatchet as Taylor's hand was raised to strike him. As he was shooting at Taylor, Mattie ran in front of him and was hit. Miles denied he ran from the house.

Miles's version of the facts directly contradicted that of several other witnesses, who said there was no Negro man with Mattie, and that he simply shot her as she climbed the stairs. The crucial evidence was the "physical fact that the wound upon the wife was in the back, and that it ranged sharply upwards, corroborating the testimony of the other witnesses."[1765]

The jury convicted Miles of first-degree murder with mitigating circumstances, but the trial judge found no such circumstances and imposed the death penalty. On appeal, it was argued that the trial court did not have this power (or should not have exercised it), but the Supreme Court explained the standard: "But it is the opinion of the Court below and of this Court that if such mitigating circumstances cannot be found in the record then it is the duty of this Court to disregard the finding of the jury as to mitigating circumstances, and inflict the extreme penalty of the law."[1766]

Justice Wilkes wrote the following: "So long as the law of capital punishment stands within the statute books it is the duty of this Court to enforce it."[1767] As was the practice at the time, Miles had been taken in person to the courthouse in Jackson, where he heard the Supreme Court announce its decision.[1768]

Under the care of leading black minister the Rev. George Washington, Miles confessed his crime and said he was certain to go to heaven. However, a day before the execution he became unnerved by the gallows testing done with bags of sand.[1769] He was presented with a new suit of clothes by the sheriff.

Miles was executed in a corridor inside the Shelby County jail at 11:30 A.M. on July 18, 1905. He was hanged alongside Toots Taylor, convicted in an unrelated crime, and shortly before the hanging of Major Mills. Accompanied by three black ministers reciting the Lord's Prayer, the two walked with a steady gait.

On the gallows, Miles was asked if he had anything to say and he spoke at length with a trembling voice, saying it was his time to go and he would soon be in the enfolding arms of Jesus. He said that if he had gotten a fair trial he would not be standing where he was, a reference to the issue of mitigating circumstances. He continued and became maudlin, according to the newspaper, and seems to have been cut off by the ministers singing "In the Sweet Bye and Bye." The cap was placed over his head and he shuddered. He gave a deep sigh which caused the spectators to become silent, apparently thinking he was going to faint with the noose around his neck.

Miles said, "Good-bye, Toots." Toots Taylor said, "Good-bye, all," and the sheriff triggered the trap. Miles's body convulsed several times and he made a gurgling sound. His death was caused by strangulation and he was cut down nine minutes later. The body was removed to the morgue in a basket. It was later taken to the county undertaker, who placed it in a casket and put it on view to be seen by "thousands of negroes," along with the bodies of Taylor and Mills.[1770] Miles' brother took the body to Arkansas for burial.

Toots Taylor, black, age 18. *Murder.*

The crime was committed about 4:30 P.M. on August 27, 1904, near the corner of Fourth and Poplar Streets in downtown Memphis, in Shelby County. Both the killer and the victim were paying attention to the same woman, who bore the name "Sam" Eller.[1771] The victim was Samuel Gaines, black, age twenty-seven. Eller had been slapped by a man named Whitlock. She threw a pop bottle at him. It struck Burley Malone, whose bootblack stand was nearby. Soon the three were fighting on the sidewalk, Malone having taken Whitlock's side. Eller summoned help from Bud Wise and the fight continued. Sam Gaines was nearby and entered the fray on Malone's side. Others joined the fray with brickbats and broom handles. Wise drew a knife on Malone. A black woman ran across the street to a dive where Toots Taylor was relaxing and told him that his half-brother Wise was being beaten to death. He grabbed his pistol and ran to the scene. He shot Malone twice, once in the back and another in the hip. Malone hid under a table at his stand. Taylor then went behind Sam Gaines (still fighting) and shot him in the back. He fell face down on the sidewalk. Taylor fired another shot at Malone, then turned to the prostrate Gaines and shot him in the head. Everyone fled when the shooting began; Taylor was captured a few blocks away. He was under the impression that everyone present would either not testify or would support his contention that the shooting was in self-defense. All testified the shooting was unprovoked, including a white city councilman who saw the shooting from a streetcar.

When his trial was set to begin, his two lawyers did not appear and were fined by the judge, who appointed another lawyer to assist Taylor. He was convicted on October 5, 1904, and the jury found no mitigating circumstances. Taylor had sat impassive throughout the trial but when the verdict was read he exclaimed, "My God, I'd a better been born dead."[1772] The case was appealed to the Tennessee Supreme Court, which affirmed the conviction, but the opinion cannot be located.

In the days before the execution, the diminutive Taylor was attended by the respected black minister, the Rev. George Washington, and two other black ministers. Two days before the execution he underwent full-immersion baptism in an overflowing bathtub at the jail, and on his way downstairs for the ceremony asked to see the scaffold. Taken to it he said, smiling, "That scaffold looks strong enough to hold us." Following the baptism, Taylor said he was confident he was going right to the throne of grace and felt much better.[1773] He had earlier confessed to the killing.

Toots Taylor was executed on July 18, 1905, on a gallows designed for three inside a corridor in the Shelby County jail. He was executed beside A.M. Miles. The sheriff had decided that the gallows were not strong enough to accommodate three, in particular, because Major Mills was especially heavy.

Wearing new clothes provided by the sheriff, Taylor walked behind A.M. Miles to the gallows. His steps faltered. Along the way, he asked for a drink of water and it was given. The Rev. Washington, reciting the Lord's Prayer and mounting the gallows with him, reminded him to be strong in the face of death. Taylor steadied but still trembled. He trembled when the rope was placed around his neck. Asked if he wanted to speak, he said he was prepared to go and he was saved, but his tongue was dry and he could not speak further. He was hanged beside Miles, who had given an extended speech, bordering on a sermon. As Miles was apparently winding down, the Rev. Washington led the ministers in singing "In the Sweet Bye and Bye," and when it was done, the caps were placed over the men's heads.

Someone called out, "Good-bye, Toots," and he replied, "Good-bye, all." At that moment, the sheriff triggered the trap and the men fell. Taylor's body convulsed once and he was cut down twelve minutes later. Along with Mills and Miles, Taylor's body was put on display at an undertaker's, where it was viewed by "thousands of negroes."[1774]

Major Mills, black, age 32. *Murder.*

The crime was committed around 6:00 P.M. January 3, 1905, in the home of Alex Gill at 1046 Barton Avenue in Memphis, in Shelby County. The killer was Gill's son-in-law, husband of Gill's stepdaughter, Cora Hayley Gill, black, age twenty-six. The victim was Alex Gill, black, age seventy-two.

Mills and his wife had separated and she went to live with her father. Mills was confident she would return to him, but when she did not, he went to the house. "Baby, get your clothes and let's go home," he said. She replied, "I don't want to go home," and asked her father for help. The father said, "No, I made her go home two or three times, and I ain't going to make her go again. If she wants to go, it is all right with me, and if she wants to stay it is all right."[1775] Gill then got up from his chair and told Mills to leave with him because he did not want Mills alone in the house with his wife.

On the porch, Mills shot Alex Gill twice with a pistol. He staggered off the porch and fell on the ground. Mills shot him again. Police were summoned, and Gill gave a dying declaration to a policeman. He died several hours later at a hospital.[1776] Mills ran away and was later captured in Yazoo City, Mississippi. Mills insisted he had gone to the house only to reclaim belongings taken by his wife. He said that Gill cursed him and brandished a pistol. Mills said he found a pistol on the floor under the bed and had it in his hand to protect himself. But he did not remember any details of the shooting. The prosecution witnesses said Gill was unarmed and Mills pulled his pistol from his pocket and began firing without warning.[1777]

Mills was convicted on February 7, 1905, and sentenced to death. The Tennessee Supreme Court said that Mills gave conflicting testimony in court, namely, that he brought the pistol with him and that he found it on the floor at the foot of the bed.[1778] His story of Gill's pulling a pistol and ordering him to put his hands up was improbable, said the court, including the testimony that "Mills was so excited he remembered little about the shooting."[1779] Mills's lawyer raised another issue. The trial court had ordered him "suspended" by his neck instead of "hanged" by his neck. "The two words are practically synonymous; at any rate one of the primary meanings of the word suspended is hung, or to hang," said the court.[1780]

Major Mills was hanged on July 18, 1905, inside a corridor in the Shelby County jail. This came a few minutes after the execution of Toots Taylor and A.M. Miles. That the three executions were all scheduled for that day was largely happenstance; each had been given one or more reprieves by the governor.

Mills had been attended by a well-regarded black minister, the Rev. George Washington. Under his care Mills confessed his crime, professed religion, and proclaimed he was ready to go. He and A.M. Miles said little to the newspaper, although both complained that "it was awful hot in the cells in which they were confined."[1781] The sheriff provided Mills new clothes for the gallows. Mills was considerably larger than the other two. This, plus the fact that Mills seemed ready to collapse as the 11:00 A.M. execution neared, caused Sheriff Monteverde to hang him separately.

With the other two already dead, black minister the Rev. Searcy offered an earnest prayer for their souls as well as Mills's. At its end, Mills said a fervent, "Amen." When the prayer ended, Mills began his own speech, which was much like a sermon. He said, "I have to go sometime, my white brothers, and I am prepared to go now. I am going to meet my Father beyond the sun, the moon and the stars. I am going to a home where everyone is happy, and I hope that all my white friends and brothers will meet me there." He paused and sighed. He continued in a loud voice, perspiring heavily, "Men, men, men, get ready; for you are all going to go sometime and nobody knows when this call is coming. Be ready so when the call comes you can go to your Father beyond the sun, the moon, and the stars."[1782]

Then Mills paused. He was asked what was to be done with his body. "What do you want done with it, Mills?" asked the sheriff. He wanted it sent to his wife in Jackson, he said, and the sheriff agreed. "Yes, brother, we hear you," said the Rev. Washington. The sheriff asked, "Is that all, Mills?" He replied, "Yes, friends, that is all. Farewell world, farewell all." The cap was put on his head and he stood trembling. At that moment the sheriff triggered the trap and Mills dropped. The scaffold shook slightly because of Mills's size. The drop was clean and his neck was broken. He was cut down twelve minutes later.

Mills's body and those of Taylor and Miles were turned over to the county undertaker, who placed them in coffins which were displayed to "thousands of negroes."[1783]

James Norfleet, black, age 40. *Murder.*

The crime was committed on the evening of July 30, 1904, at a rural home (described as a hut) near the community of Capleville, in Shelby County. The killer shared the home with his wife, the victim, Lucy Norfleet, black, age twenty-nine. They were sharecroppers on the land. Norfleet shot his wife with a shotgun. One blast hit her forehead, the other her breast.

Norfleet had planned the crime and a story to go with it. He appeared at Capleville on the morning of the 31st and told of several men coming to his house the night before. After beating him and his wife, they began to rape her. He said he had escaped and ran to a creek bottom and hid, but when light came he ran to the town. He asked some townsfolk to accompany him back to the house because he was afraid to return alone, concerned that the men might be waiting there and kill him.

Lucy had been shot with squirrel shot and the gun was shown to be his. Only when he gave conflicting accounts of the evening did suspicion focus on him. The blood on his clothing was assumed to be from his wounds. At the jail, he told more conflicting accounts, until it became obvious that he had stayed in the house all night after shooting his wife.

He was tried on October 17, 1904, and the jury took twelve minutes to make up its mind. The conviction was affirmed by the Tennessee Supreme Court, but the opinion cannot be located. Norfleet maintained his innocence until a few days prior to the execution, when he yielded to the influence of leading black minister, the Rev. George Washington. Norfleet asserted he was unafraid of death and was going to heaven.[1784]

Norfleet was executed at 1:00 P.M. on August 18, 1905, an hour behind schedule, because the Rev. Washington asked for more time with General Bone, also executed that day. Norfleet was hanged alongside James Champion. The three were executed the same day, with Boone being last. This was a coincidence. All had been given various reprieves, but they ran out at the same time. Norfleet and Champion had asked that a large number of white people be allowed to witness their executions, and Sheriff Frank L. Monteverde allowed more into the jail than were strictly allowed by law. Special admission cards had been distributed.

On the gallows, Sheriff Monteverde asked, "Have you anything to say, Norfleet?" "No, sir," came the response. Champion, pinioned at Norfleet's side, was asked the same question. He gave a lengthy fervent speech, much like a sermon. Sweat poured off him, and when he seemed to be out of breath, the Rev. Washington began a prayer. When it was done, the sheriff loosened the trap and the pair fell to their deaths. "Norfleet clapped his hands in an irresponsible way, and then hung still without the least contortion."[1785] He was cut down fourteen minutes later. His body was shipped to Eads, in Shelby County, to be buried by his family.

John Champion, black, age 35. *Murder.*

The crime was committed on the evening of December 24, 1904, in the basement of a house of prostitution (called a "resort" at the time). The Mississippi Club at 216 Gayoso Street was located in downtown Memphis, in Shelby County. The killer was a porter at Hammonett's Saloon on Beale Street and DeSoto. He had lived with the victim, his paramour, Orleans (Irene) Jones, black, age twenty-four. Irene had left him and was a maid at the Mississippi Club. She and another woman were ironing in the basement. Champion went to the basement door and as soon as he entered began firing a pistol. Only one of the five bullets hit Jones, who had her back to him. She died at the hospital.

Champion's defense was that he was wholly intoxicated at the time he killed Irene. He maintained to his last that he remembered nothing about the crime until he read about it in the newspaper the next day. Champion's case was appealed to the Tennessee Supreme Court, but the opinion cannot be located. His case was handled and financed entirely by Sandy Carter, a black Memphis lawyer, who witnessed the execution with tears streaming down his cheeks. Carter insisted the death penalty was improper because the jury had found Champion guilty with mitigating circumstances, and Champion never denied the crime.

Champion was executed on August 18, 1905, in a corridor inside the Memphis jail. He was hanged alongside James Norfleet, who was convicted of an unrelated crime. Twenty minutes later, General Bone was hanged. The executions were coincidental, the result of various respites given each man. Sheriff Monteverde was seriously ill at the time, but made his way to the jail with his doctor to do his duty, not wanting to make one of his deputies perform the deed.

Champion was very intelligent and exhorted the crowd to avoid whiskey and lead a proper life. His speech took on the fervor of a impassioned sermon and he was sweating profusely. He explained that he was an orphan who had gone wrong, but the law was just, and his sin had caught up with him. By the time the cap was put over his head he was in a religious frenzy. He kept talking and singing, Sensing the end was near, he exclaimed, "Oh, Lord, oh, God, fortify me with your prayers. I have given God my heart — give God your prayers for me!"[1786]

Here is what happened when he was dropped: "Champion breathed like a child with the croup. It was that wild hopeless struggle for breath denied. His neck was completely broken."[1787]

General Bone (aka General Boone), black, age 29. *Murder.*

The crime was committed on December 31, 1904, at a small cabin occupied by John Maburn, black, and his wife, Mattie Maburn. The cabin was located on the Red Fox Farm in a rural area of Shelby County. The killer was a farm laborer who lived in the area and was known to the Maburns. The victim, Mattie Maburn, black, age thirty-one, and her infant had been left at home by her husband, who went to a New Year's Eve celebration (called a "watch meeting") a mile and a half away.

General Bone (Boone) was present in the house when the husband left. Bone knew he would be gone until well after midnight. When John Maburn returned to the house several hours later he found the bed drenched with blood and the baby in the middle of the bed crying. He summoned help and Mattie's body was found in the daylight hours the next day.

Although Bone initially told several people that he accidentally shot Mattie and then attempted to cover up the crime, he did not testify at trial.[1788] The state's theory was that he propositioned her, was rebuffed, shot her in the face with his pistol, took an ax that was in the house and killed her with it on the bed. Then he took her body and dumped it in some water near the Wolf River.

On the evening of the next day, Bone appeared at a friend's house nearby, barefooted, wearing wet, muddy and torn clothes. He told the friend that somebody had been killed and he feared the neighbors might think he did the killing. While he was at the friend's house, an all-black mob came to the house. Bone wanted to flee but was held at gunpoint away from the mob until a deputy sheriff came and arrested him.

Bone's belt was found near Mattie's nude body. A short distance away, there was evidence that he had built a fire. His pistol was found nearby. Examination showed that all five bullets in the pistol had been "snapped" (attempted firing), but only one had actually fired. Mattie Maburn had a bullet hole above her mouth and her head was a pulpy mass. She had been savagely raped both vaginally and anally.[1789] Bone had told several people who testified against him that if he had not been so hungry, cold, ragged and barefooted, he would never have been caught. He said that he knew in the condition he was in he would attract attention on the road or he would have kept on going.[1790]

Bone's defense was insanity. His father explained that, as a child, he had been in a house fire and was burned (the scars were visible), and was so traumatized that he did not talk until he was nine years old. Later, he began to tell people he had visions, that someone came from either heaven or the devil and told him stories. Said the father, "I would stop him from talking this foolishness whenever I heard it, but the other children would not and then call him a foolish boy. He has never been like other children."[1791]

The uncle with whom Bone had lived the last five years said he was not "peculiar or strange," but seemed backward and afraid of people.[1792] No expert testimony was offered regarding his sanity. Several other people testified there was nothing wrong with him. The Tennessee Supreme Court concluded that Bone had "a dull inferior mind, yet he was not an idiot and was not insane."[1793] It found that his statements made about attempting to escape showed his culpability.

Bone was described in the newspaper as follows: "Bone is a living picture of the 'missing link,' resembling in form and face an ape as much as he does the human family. His arms are greatly elongated and his hands wide spreading and enormous, while his fingers resemble the claw like digits of a monkey really more than they do the fingers of a human being."[1794]

Bone was hanged on August 18, 1905, in a corridor in the Memphis jail, on a gallows that was now described as a permanent fixture, having been used a month before to execute three other men. He was executed the same day as James Norfleet and John Champion, but this was coincidental, each having received various reprieves. The other two were hanged together, in part because it was thought Champion might have to be carried to the gallows, overcome with emotion. Another reason was to give Bone a chance to admit his crime.

Attended by highly regarded Memphis black minister the Rev. George Washington, Bone was indifferent and unmoved. Even after the long sermon-like last statement of John Champion he said nothing. "He looked all that he was, a brute pure and simple. His eyes never once lifted from his feet. He declined to express himself on the scaffold and died, as he had lived, in defiance of the laws of man and God. Standing on the trap, an effort was made to get him to raise his eyes, but he declined to do so."[1795] He was executed about twenty minutes after the others.

John Hill, white, age 44. *Murder.*

The crime was committed at 2:00 A.M. on July 16, 1903, at a tenant house on the property of John Sorras. The scene was fourteen miles from Covington in the Mumford area of Tipton County. The victim was the killer's wife, Sarah Catherine Hill, white, age thirty-five. She was sleeping in a bed with three of her six children. Two were four-month-old twin girls. In the same room were her other three children, the oldest of whom was thirteen. Also sleeping were Mrs. Dyer Ferguson and Miss Grimes, neighbors, who had come to assist her in caring for the twins, who were sickly.

Sarah was fearful that her husband might harm her and this was known to the other women.[1796] She had left the marital home and was living at the tenant house to avoid her husband's wrath over her filing for divorce. She had placed a pair of scissors in the window to jam it shut, along with two boards inside the window to obscure the view inside.

John Hill crept up to the house and pulled at the window, causing the scissors to fall. As he pointed a double-barreled shotgun through the window, his wife sat up in the bed. He emptied the gun. One shot hit her in the chest, the second her leg. She fell face down on the floor. Neither infant on each side of her was hit by the shot. No one saw the shooting. Initially, it was thought Hill would plead insanity because he was a "morphine fiend and addicted to drinking liquor."[1797]

Hill's first trial resulted in a conviction that was overturned on appeal because two jurors said they thought he was guilty based on reading newspaper accounts, but the court refused to discharge them for cause.[1798] At the second trial, the jury found him guilty with mitigating circumstances. The jury was under the impression that this meant Hill would receive life imprisonment, but the judge ignored the recommendation and ordered him hanged.

Sarah had filed for divorce after sixteen years of brutal treatment by John. He appeared in court and asked for a continuance. This was denied and the court ordered him to bring $120 to court on July 16. The night before the court date, Hill killed Sarah. He went to court the next day pretending not to know of his wife's death. His purpose was to tell the court that he still did not have the money. He was arrested and held in jail until his trial.

Proof showed he had repeatedly threatened to kill Sarah unless she dropped the divorce. He was identified as the man who sent her a threatening letter and his handwriting had been identified by his wife shortly before her death. John Hill lived at his sister-in-law's house at the time of the shooting.[1799]

On the night of the shooting, Hill left the house and took a mare from the barn. He also released the mare's colt, a mule, because it brayed constantly when separated from the mare. He was seen leaving the house in the middle of the night. Several people heard the mare ridden past their homes, with the mule following. Hill tied the mare a short distance from his wife's house. The mare and the mule ate the grass where the mare was tied. The mule had a split hoof, making it easy to identify.

Hill's shoe fit the prints found at the window. But he had left the shoes with his lawyer when he came to town. He had put powdered mustard around were he stood. It was shown he had purchased the mustard two weeks earlier.[1800] This was done to throw bloodhounds off his trail. It did not work and the dogs went immediately to where the mare had been tethered. The murder weapon was never found and there was conflicting testimony about whether it came from the house where Hill was staying.

John Hill's defense was an alibi, but this failed, in part because it was shown that he had gotten up in the middle of the night and had the opportunity to ride the horse to his wife's house.[1801] His lawyers insisted that the real killer was someone in the neighborhood who sought to rob the house. The lawyers insisted the shooter was a Negro because they were known to use methods like mustard powder to frustrate search dogs.

The case was appealed to the Tennessee Supreme Court and affirmed, but the opinion cannot be located. It was a 3–2 decision, with Neil and Wilkes dissenting. Both sent letters to the governor urging commutation. A petition for clemency had been sent to the governor but an even larger petition objecting was also sent. Both infants had died before Hill's first trial. Townsfolk held Hill morally responsible because he deprived them of their caring mother.

John Hill was hanged at 11:14 A.M. inside the Tipton County jail on October 10, 1905. Hill asserted his innocence to the end. Standing on the gallows, he spoke in a voice "tremulous with emotion," saying, "I am ready, willing and prepared to go and meet my God in heaven. I am all right." He thanked the sheriff and people of Union City (where he had been kept in jail) for their kindness, and said that he had hoped his children would be present, but that he would see them in heaven.[1802]

He signaled to the sheriff that he had nothing more to say and the black cap was placed over his head and the noose applied. He complained that it was too tight and it was loosened; he was heard saying, "This is awful." A minister offered a fervent prayer and when he was done, the sheriff asked him again if he had anything to say, telling him this was his last chance. When Hill replied in the negative, the sheriff said, "Good-bye, John," and triggered the trap. The fall was clean, but his right leg trembled. He was cut down in thirty minutes. "Dr. L.A. Yarborough, by means of an electric battery, experimented to ascertain whether any life remained, but only a slight muscular contraction rewarded his efforts."[1803]

Finley Preston, black, age 37. *Murder.*

The crime was committed in a wooded area in rural Johnson County on the morning of October 19, 1903. The killer was infatuated with the victim, Lillian Shaw, described as a mulatto, age twenty-two. He came upon her on a path in the woods. The state's theory was that she spurned him, he flew into a rage and shot her with a pistol. Her body was twice hidden and finally burned.

Finley Preston was married and lived with his wife and father on Saw Mill Creek, three miles from Mountain City. "I can neither read nor write, and have never read a chapter in the Bible in my life," he explained to the jury.[1804] The execution of Finley Preston is among the few for which a photograph exists.

Lillian's parentage was unknown to the people in sparsely populated Johnson County, but at age seventeen she had eloped with a white man named Melvin Shaw. To avoid Tennessee's miscegenation statute, they had married in Ohio and lived there until she left him and returned to the Mountain City area. There she was a domestic servant, especially helpful to new mothers by caring for newborns. She was very attractive and at the time of her death was secretly wearing a wedding ring engraved, "From James to Lillian."

The day after she was last seen walking down a road wearing a distinctive red skirt, carrying a small red purse, the people she had been attending became concerned and notified the sheriff. The sheriff followed the forest path she would have taken and found her red purse. Several large search parties were formed but they found nothing. The day after the search was called off, a mountain man came to the sheriff's office and said he had discovered dried blood and hair inside a large hollow log on the enclosed property of Eb Preston, father, and Finley Preston, his son.

The Prestons were arrested but released because no information was forthcoming from them. Two weeks later, another mountain man came to the sheriff's office and described a place in the woods where something had been burned under a pile of wood, which he thought were human remains. As investigators sifted through the ashes, the ring was found, along with enough jaw to allow a dentist to identify a gold tooth he had placed several months earlier. About this time, a landowner came forward to suggest that one of his employees, James Phillips, had been seen with Lillian prior to the murder. Phillips was questioned and he admitted a long-standing relationship with Lillian, including having given her the ring. He said that Finley Preston was very jealous of Lillian's affection for him and that Preston had threatened him and Lillian separately. At least one person for whom she worked had seen Preston lurking near the house in the shadows carrying a shotgun.

Both the Prestons were arrested again. This time the house was searched and Lillian's clothing, including the red skirt, was found in the attic. Confronted with this evidence, the father admitted the son had put the clothing there, saying it was to be given to a young woman he knew in nearby North Carolina. Confronted with this evidence, Finley Preston said, "I guess I was crazy, sheriff. I met her on the trail that morning. She tried to take another man's ring off and hide it, but I saw it. I couldn't stand her turning me down any longer. I made her go with me to that old log and when she wouldn't promise to marry me, I killed her."[1805] His defense was lack of premeditation, and his lawyers asked the jury to convict him of voluntary manslaughter. Later, he explained he had hidden the body in the corncrib but it began to smell badly, so he wrapped it in oilcloth and took it to the mountain spot where it was burned.

At trial, Finley explained that he had allowed James Phillips and Lillian Shaw to stay for several weeks at his house, where they slept together on the floor. Lillian was still married, as was Phillips. He also insisted that he had been offered one hundred dollars by America Phillips, James's wife, to kill Lillian, whom she had named as the correspondent in the divorce petition she had filed against James.

Finley explained that he did not kill Lillian for money, but did not know why he killed her. He explained he had been in the woods looking for his oxen when she came walking down the path, and "after talking to her a few words, I shot her with a .38 pistol."[1806] He said, "My mind was all tore up, and I hardly knew what I was doing. She had stayed at my house the night before, and I do not know why I killed her when I met her, and can give no reason for it, only that I had been urged and hired to do so by America Phillips, and my mind was in such a condition that I did not know what I was doing at the time. I had no ill will whatever against the deceased, and had been furnishing her a home for over two weeks, and had been permitting her and Jim Phillips to sleep there together."[1807]

Preston's disjointed testimony claimed he left the body where it fell for a week, but when he went back it had been moved. A deputy sheriff who had hidden himself in the jail, so that the Prestons did not think anyone was present, testified he heard the two talk about moving the body after they were arrested the second time. "I heard the defendant say to his father, that if they had not been in such a hurry, they would have burned her up, so that no trace could have been found, and the father replied, yes, but we were in too much of a hurry."[1808]

Finley Preston and his father were tried for her murder, but the first conviction was overturned by the Tennessee Supreme Court. Although the opinion cannot be located, the court's minutes reflect that Preston pled guilty. However, the jury was not instructed on the several degrees of murder, and a new trial was ordered.[1809] He was tried alone at his second trial and convicted again on January 3, 1905, and ordered hanged. The crime, trials and execution were among the most sensational in remote Johnson County history, in part because of the dearth of black people in the area.

The second conviction was appealed to the Tennessee Supreme Court, but the opinion did not discuss the facts. The only issue before the court was whether it was fundamental error for the clerk who swore the prospective jurors (talesmen) to fail to ask them to kiss the Bible. The court said this was not error because a variation from the form of the oath does not affect its obligatory character.[1810] It cannot be determined whether Finley's father or America Phillips were ever charged in connection with Lillie's death.

Preston was executed at 11:40 A.M. on November 7, 1905, inside the jail yard of the Mountain City jail. Throngs came to see the execution but few succeeded because the sheriff allowed only about thirty witnesses, including other sheriffs and law enforcement officers.

The gallows was outdoors but the actual execution was obscured from view because a canvas wall was constructed around the gallows. Preston had earlier confessed the crime, professed religion, and declared he was ready to die, but said he did not want to die.[1811] On the scaffold, he read a poem in a faltering voice:

> A great crowd now is gathered,
> Around the jail today,
> To see my execution,
> And hear what I might say.
> I must die on this scaffold,
> For murdering poor Lillie Shaw,
> That others might see me die,
> And learn respect for law.
> Take warning, thoughtless people,
> Remember what I say,
> If you sin against your Maker,
> You're sure to rue the day.
> I've begged Him to forgive me,
> Upon my bended knees,
> And I'm going home to heaven,
> Forgiven and at ease.[1812]

1906

John Mitchell, black, age unknown. *Accessory to murder.*

The crime was committed on the night of December 6, 1905, at the rural farm home of Moses Weddell near the community of Fowlkes, in rural Dyer County. The victim was Moses Weddell, black, age forty-four. There was a serious dispute about the facts. Mitchell said the shooter was Weddell's son, Will Weddell. He also said that Will had told him to say that Will Owens was the shooter. All three were arrested and Mitchell was charged as an accessory to murder.

Mitchell took the stand and said that he had stayed all night with Moses Weddell. The night before the shooting (which he said happened on

December 8) he got up about five o'clock, and the old man was still in bed. As Mitchell was sitting by the fire figuring in a book, the son came into the house, picked up his father's rifle, asked if it was the old man's " bad gun," and shot the old man while he was lying in the bed. Mitchell claimed he started to run, but Will Weddell threatened to kill him unless he helped carry and throw the body into the river. Mitchell said that while the body was in the bed they put a dishpan under it to catch the blood and this was thrown in the river too.[1813]

Mitchell also testified that Will told him to say that Will Owens killed the man and that he could keep half of the old man's money, apparently thirty dollars, and an old gray mare. He also said that Will told him he would give him another twenty dollars to say that Owens was the shooter, after Mitchell was arrested. Will Weddell testified he had nothing to do with his father's death, that he had moved to Crockett County on the day of the murder pursuant to a previous plan, and he had been told on December 6 that his father had gone to another nearby town to visit a sick brother. The state had dropped the charge against Will Owens before trial. Mitchell's confusing testimony and the son's clear alibi determined Mitchell's fate.

The Tennessee Supreme Court said the jury believed the son and not Mitchell, who also gave inconsistent testimony about an alibi, and about whether someone in the jail heard the son promise Mitchell the money.[1814]

Mitchell professed faith a week before his execution and announced he was guilty as an accomplice, maintaining to the end that Will Weddell (who was acquitted) was the actual shooter, and he only shared the money after dumping the body into the river. Two black ministers attended Mitchell in his last hours.

The August 8, 1906, execution was conducted in Dyersburg, but no details are available other than, "It was carried out to perfection in the minutest details."[1815]

Andrew Upton (aka Drew Upton), black, age 50. *Murder.*

Will Upton, black, age 24. *Murder.*

The crime was committed at 8:30 P.M. on January 7, 1906, in the cabin belonging to Richard "Dick" Johnson in rural Monroe County. The killers were Will Upton and his uncle, Andrew "Drew" Upton. The victim was Dick Johnson, black, age sixty-five.

The killing was instigated by William S. Moses, white, age twenty-one, who told the pair that Johnson had a half bushel of money hidden in his cabin and that someone ought to go there and hit him on the head and take it. Although black, Johnson had performed service in a Mississippi regiment throughout the Civil War and was receiving a Tennessee Confederate pension of thirty dollars a month.

The Uptons went to the cabin after dark. Will Upton poured water on the fireplace from a hole in the chimney, so there would be no light by which the robbers could be seen. Drew pushed against the front door as Johnson and his fifteen-year-old daughter struggled to hold it. Drew pushed forward with Will behind him.[1816] Drew fired a musket that hit Johnson's neck. A second blast, from a shotgun, hit Johnson's chest. When Johnson fell to the floor, his eighteen-year-old daughter, who had not seen the shooting, asked him, "Papa, are you ready to die?" He said he was because he had "tried to live right."[1817] He named Drew as the shooter.

Among those who heard his dying declaration were a neighbor and his farm hand, Will Moses. Both Uptons were arrested an hour after the killing and identified by two of the Johnson children. Johnson had about twenty-five dollars in the house. The robbery-murder garnered nothing.

At trial, Drew accused Will of the shooting, and vice versa, each trying to get mercy from the jury. After the verdict was announced a spectator made a loud statement that they should be hanged immediately with different ends of the same rope. The case was appealed to the Tennessee Supreme Court but the opinion cannot be located.[1818]

Will Upton maintained his innocence to the end, claiming he had nothing to do with the killing and sought executive clemency. Drew admitted his role and did not. Poison was found in Drew's cell the day before the execution.

The pair was hanged at 1:21 P.M. side-by-side in a corridor of the jail at Madisonville on December 20, 1906. They had been attended by three ministers, one black. Both professed religion and expected to go to heaven. When Drew's wife was brought to him he broke down crying. He and his wife thought the governor would commute the sentences until an hour or so before the execution. Will busied himself making sure his clothes looked good and his shoes were shined. Under the direction of the ministers, the pair sang hymns, especially "Jesus, Lover of My Soul." They sang "almost frantically and at times they were almost hysterical."[1819] They walked to the gallows with firm steps.

Standing on the gallows, Sheriff P. L. Watson asked for their last words. Will said he had nothing to say other than he was innocent, concluding, "You all prepare to meet me in heaven for God has saved me and I know I am going there." Drew responded, "I know old man Johnson is dead and I hopes he's in heaven and I expects to see him there. White folks, I ain't to tell you no tale. I's goin' to tell you the truth. I and Will was the cause of his death. Will Moses was the planner, but he wasn't there. I and Will went to his house and if the first shot killed him, Will done it. If it was the last shot, I done it."

These words prompted the crowd to respond, "Thank God," because some still doubted the guilt of Will Upton. After they spoke, the sheriff said the only reason he was performing the execution was that it was his duty, but pointed out that he had risked his own life in preventing them from being lynched.

After the caps were put on, the men began singing "I'm Going Home," but Will stopped and asked the sheriff to give his sister his pocketbook and his looking glass. Drew then stopped singing and insisted that the sheriff place a straight stand-up collar around his neck before his coffin was closed. The sheriff assented and the men returned to singing "I'm Going Home." Their singing was silenced when the trap was sprung. Their necks were broken and they were cut down after ten minutes. The bodies were placed in coffins and about half of the one thousand people waiting outside the jail filed through to look at them.[1820]

1907

John Thomas, black, age 20. *Murder.*

The crime was committed on July 21, 1906, close to a railroad construction camp, called Kries Camp, near the community of Strawberry Plains in Knox County. The killer was a laborer on a railroad construction project. The victim, Earnest Perkins, black, age twenty-nine, another laborer, was killed the day after a dispute with Thomas over gambling. Officials said the dispute was over a pint of whiskey; Thomas said it was over a dime. The victim had cheated him and had threatened him. A witness said that when Perkins fell to the ground Thomas continued to fire, picking out buttons on Perkins's jacket as he would shoot at a target. "Thomas then raised his gun in the air and declared that no Tennessee officer could arrest him, that he was a bad negro from Arkansas."[1821] Thomas scurried away, but was recognized by his bowlegged gait; three officers approached and he fired on them until he was surrounded.

The Tennessee Supreme Court said:

> The facts are, briefly, that Thomas and Perkins were working for a railroad contractor in Campbell's Camp, near Strawberry Plains. On the night before the tragedy, they, with some other negroes, were engaged in a game of craps. A controversy arose in regard to a small sum of money, which was put up as a stake in the game. During the controversy, both of them reached for their knives; but the camp cook interfered, and quieted them for the time. Thomas went away, and secured his pistol from a woman in the camp, and returning to where Perkins was, cursed and threatened to shoot him. Perkins did not resent this, but shortly afterwards walked away, when Thomas shot at him, but missed him. Perkins left Campbell's Camp, and went to Kries' Camp, some little distance away, and spent the night.

The court said:

> The next morning some of the other negroes guyed and chafed Thomas about missing Perkins when he shot at him the night before, when he replied, with an oath: "I'll bet I don't miss him a hundred yards this morning." Upon finding that Perkins had passed the night in Kries' Camp, he started out to find him. He concealed himself in a gully, near a path, which Perkins would have to travel upon his return from Kries' Camp to Campbell's Camp, where Thomas was partially screened by some weeds. Here he remained until Perkins appeared walking along near the river bank. Thomas opened fire and Perkins fell at the first shot. Whereupon Thomas ran up to him and continued to shoot him four or five times. This was all in plain view of a number of men connected with the camp, both white and black.

The court continued:

> Thomas's version is that he armed himself with the pistol, because Perkins had stated the night before that he would get a gun and kill him, and that when he left Campbell's Camp in the morning, going up the river towards Kries' Camp, he saw two men standing in the pathway, one of whom was Perkins and the other a man by the name of Manuel. He said that Perkins was armed with a rock and a knife, and attacked him, throwing the rock, and advancing with the knife, and that Manuel shot at him, whereupon he drew his pistol and began to fire, and after having emptied it, ran away into the woods, believing that he was in danger of death or great bodily harm.

The court said:

> There were some seven or eight witnesses to the shooting. All state that at the time he was shot, Perkins was doing nothing whatsoever, and

> upon being searched after he was shot, no weapon of any kind was found upon him. One of the witnesses testified that when the defendant opened fire, Perkins begged him not to shoot. None of these witnesses saw a man by the name of Manuel and none of them refer to him as being present.

The court concluded:

> We are unable to find any error in the charge of the Court; and the able counsel appointed by the Court to defend the defendant has not been able to point out any. The facts present an aggravated case of deliberate and premeditated murder, while lying in wait, and shooting Perkins when he was unarmed, and making no demonstration whatever; and we have not been able to find in the record any mitigating fact or circumstances. We are of the opinion, therefore, that there is no error in the judgment of the Court below; and it must be affirmed.[1822] The court ordered Thomas hanged on January 10, 1907, and he was executed that day.

Described by the newspaper as "an intelligent negro," Thomas had experienced a religious conversion in jail, where he was baptized, and preached constantly to anyone who would listen. He said he wanted his sentence commuted so he could continue preaching and "save others from the path of sin he followed."[1823] At his death cell two ministers, including the black Rev. McCann, conducted a service which included communion and singing the hymn "Saviour, More Than Life to Me," while Thomas talked constantly.

He was taken to the gallows inside the Knox County jail by two deputies, but walked with a firm step. Dressed in a plain black suit, a shirt with black figures, a white collar and a black tie, Thomas mounted the gallows located in a third-floor corridor, and began speaking to the crowd of one hundred. All had been given tickets by the sheriff.

He began, "I am proud to have such a large audience present," and regaled the group with a talk filled with Bible references and explained how he had been responsible for the religious conversion of another inmate, Ed Paris, who was present. He spoke so long the sheriff had to tell him his time was up. The Rev. J.H. Lauritzen gave a prayer. Thomas shook hands with those around him, including Paris. When the cap was put on his head, he was asked if he was ready. He said, "I am ready," and the trap was sprung. "The rope creaked as it tightened on the supporting woodwork. A woman screamed somewhere in the jail. The majesty of the law had been asserted; and a crime expiated."[1824]

After the drop, Thomas's legs and shoulders twitched. His neck was not broken and he strangled to death. He was cut down ten minutes later. His body was carried down to the first floor and placed in a coffin. About a thousand people waited outside. Half came into the jail to view Thomas's body in his coffin, which was then taken to the county cemetery and buried without a service.[1825]

Charles W. Baird (aka William Baird), white, age 39. *Murder.*

The crime was committed on December 1, 1905, about 7:00 P.M. on a road outside Fayetteville in rural Lincoln County. William Baird was a fertilizer (guano) dealer, gin owner, sawmill operator and farm owner. Baird was married to and lived with the victim, Mary Roper Baird, white, age thirty, by whom he had two young daughters. She was his cousin and brought considerable property to the marriage, although it was opposed by her father.

The couple had made a visit to town, where Baird had transacted some banking business. The two had shopped at Cheap Ike's store before heading home in a buggy pulled by a red mule. Their home was twenty miles from town. Baird insisted that two armed men had accosted the buggy shortly after dark and shot Mary in an attempted robbery. He claimed the men were walking in the road. One stopped the slow-walking mule by grabbing its bridle, while the other approached the buggy on Baird's side, brandished a pistol and said, "Hold up!" As Baird leaned backward to retrieve a pistol he carried, Mary leaned forward toward the robber, who shot without warning. Both men fled on foot.

Because Baird did not show proper emotion regarding his wife's death, and the rough manner in which he reluctantly carried her body ("like a dressed hog") to the coroner, his story was deemed not credible. Barely a half-mile from the location of the shooting, Baird had passed the house of a man he knew well, who was standing outside his house. Still carrying his wounded wife, Baird's buggy passed twenty-one houses of people he knew well, a distance of four and one-half miles. He passed the homes of two physicians, as well as the country store where two men he knew well were standing in front holding lanterns. Instead, he went to the house of a cousin.

When asked by the cousin if Mary was dead, Baird said he did not know, but asked the cousin to come and look because Baird did not want to touch her. Mary was clearly dead when taken into the house. Her body was placed on the floor. Baird lay down by the fireplace near the body and fell sound asleep, snoring. When neighbors urged bloodhounds be used, Baird protested this would cost too much money. When the neighbors offered to pay, Baird objected again, saying he feared the wrong man may be caught. A coroner's jury found cause to charge Baird. While jailed, Baird mortgaged his property to pay his lawyers. This aroused the townsfolk because it appeared he was attempting to impoverish his daughters. With a mob on the way, the sheriff took Baird out of the jail and hid him. Baird went on trial February 21, 1906.

The wealthy defendant was served by four lawyers.[1826] The bullet entry wound on the right side of Mary's face was described by a doctor as "cooked to a crisp," as if she had been shot at close range, not by a man standing on the ground beside the buggy. But the doctor was not allowed to testify how close the weapon was to the wound because the doctor had no personal experience with Baird's own pistol, nor had he conducted any tests. A deputy sheriff testified the burn was caused by the flash of the gun and was no more than six inches away. Baird had insisted that the mule began to run away as soon as the first shot was fired, but a large puddle of blood was found on the ground near where Baird said the shooting occurred, indicating that the buggy had been stopped there.

Conflicting evidence suggested that Jean Riley, a single white woman, had become pregnant by Baird. He (not she) had gone across the state line into Alabama and sought the advice of a medical doctor to obtain an abortifacient. Although the doctor refused to assist, Jean Riley's purported son by Baird was either stillborn or died of premature birth. Mrs. Baird had become increasingly angry over her husband's persistent sexual activity with Riley and the sister with whom she lived, Mrs. Faulkenberry. (At trial, Baird described both women as prostitutes.) Numerous witnesses testified as to Baird's sexual infatuation with Riley. One testified about Baird's reading him a letter from Riley in which she implored him to impregnate her and leave his wife. Baird testified matter-of-factly that he had engaged in sex with Riley for four years prior to the killing and that he slept with both women, with Mr. Faulkenberry's approval. Baird also owned property jointly with his wife which he stood to inherit on her death.

The jury found Baird guilty with mitigating circumstances, but the trial judge ruled there were no mitigating circumstances and set Baird's execution for April 13, 1906. The court said, "Any number of instances could be recalled where men of wealth and standing, for instance, the mayor of Charleston, West Virginia, slaughtered his wife not more than eight or ten months ago, for the purpose of getting rid of her, and was afterwards executed for it.[1827] Old Henry the Eighth slaughtered two of his wives, and Emperor after Emperor has killed his wife in order to enjoy the embraces of another woman."[1828]

The trial court refused to accredit anything Baird said or did. Riley was not a prostitute; she was his exclusive mistress. The failure to summon help or seek out the purported robbers was evidence of guilt. The condition of Mary's body, with an arm stuck in the side of the buggy to hold her upright, was evidence he had attempted to show she was alive to anyone who may have met the buggy on the long ride after he shot her.

The case was appealed to the Tennessee Supreme Court.[1829] No record can be found of the court's ruling, although it was reported that the February 28, 1907, opinion was voluminous and the conviction was unanimously affirmed.[1830] Baird, who had been kept in the Nashville jail, expressed shock at the decision.[1831] He released a lengthy written statement denying the crime and blaming the newspapers and public sentiment for his wrongful conviction.[1832]

Baird was executed inside the Lincoln County jail on the morning of May 24, 1907. He maintained his innocence both publicly and in letters to the sheriff and his daughters. Baird had asked the materials not be made public because the newspapers had treated him unfairly. Their full contents were never published. The attending physician and a business associate admonished him not to die with a lie on his lips.[1833] The execution was witnessed by about thirty people, including officers, physicians, ministers and newspaper reporters. A stream of visitors viewed the body as it lay in the undertaker's office. His wife's family refused to allow burial beside the victim.

Moses Walds (aka Mose Walds and Mose Walls), black, age 20. *Murder.*

The crime was committed at 6:45 P.M. on March 30, 1907, in the yard of the home of Mr. and Mrs. Thomas A. Reuland, located at 1297 Thomas Avenue in Memphis, in Shelby County. The killer was a disgruntled employee of the Anderson-Tully Wood Products Company. The victim was his supervisor, Frank A. Deering, white, age thirty-four. He was a widower and the father of a six-year-old girl, Freida. The two boarded with the Reuland family. Deering was engaged to marry Miss Pearl Waller of Paragould, Arkansas. He was on his way to a barbershop prior to seeing her later that evening.

Walds was employed as a laborer in the sawmill,

but for several days he had assumed the duties of a sawyer, which paid more. When his Friday pay envelope contained only his laborer pay, he flew into a rage at the paymaster's window and threw the money down on the counter. Deering was told of the incident. That day at about 5:30 P.M., Walds came to the Reuland house asking for Deering. He said to Mrs. Reuland that he wanted the matter of his wages straightened out. She told him Deering was not there. About that time Deering arrived in a new horse and buggy he had purchased to be used to visit Miss Waller. From the direction he came, and the location he parked the buggy, he could not see Walds waiting at the front of the house. Mrs. Reuland did not tell him about Walds's appearance.[1834] About 6:30 P.M., Deering walked out the front door, after telling his daughter he was going to a barbershop.

As Deering approached bushes at the front gate, Walds came forth. His words were unclear but were angry and surly. Deering was heard to say, "I decline to argue the matter with you."[1835] Walds pulled a pistol from his pocket and shot Deering in the heart. The public was outraged, in part because Freida was now an orphan.

Reuland owned bloodhounds which immediately tracked Walds to his house on Nicholas Avenue, not far from the murder scene. Several women in the house said his whereabouts were unknown, but they became more apprehensive as the days passed without his arrest. The Shelby County sheriff prepared wanted posters, which he sent to neighboring counties. A local deputy in Olive Branch, Mississippi, saw one and arrested Walds on April 2, 1907. A mob threatened the Shelby County jail and Sheriff Monteverde was fearful of a lynching, but the crowd backed down when he said he would use every means at his command to protect Walds and see there was a speedy trial.

At trial, Walds pled self-defense, claiming that Deering moved his hand to his right pocket as if to pull a pistol. However, no weapon of any kind was found on or near Deering's body. The trial court gave the "lying in wait" instruction and Walds was quickly convicted. He appealed to the Tennessee Supreme Court but the opinion cannot be located.

Walds was executed in a corridor inside the Memphis jail on October 31, 1907. He had professed religion and was baptized a few days before his death. He was attended on his last day by leading black minister the Rev. George Washington. He bade a tearful good-bye to his mother, saying, "Don't forget me, mother." He put on new clothes and shoes. When he complained the shoes were too tight, he was given another pair.

Well composed on the gallows, he said:

> I am glad today that I can walk out with a free and good will. I stand on the word of God. I am in no ways scared, ashamed or afraid. Death means no more to me than to stand here and drink a glass of water. God will be with me and lead me to a higher court. I feel no way ashamed or downhearted as I stand here. I don't believe I got justice. We all have to go and I will get justice before God and I know I will have an everlasting home. I am no ways worried, and I stand here humble. The newspapers said I was a desperate negro. I ain't no desperate negro. I only tried to protect my own life. I thought my life was as sweet to me as his was to him. I have been humbugged up to the whole thing. I know I am going to a better world — a world of rest. God is a just God. I hope to meet you all, gentleman and fellow-citizens, in the other world. Good-bye, everybody.[1836]

Sheriff Monteverde waited until the noonday bells and whistles stopped blowing and released the trap at 12:10 P.M. The fall was clean, breaking Walds's neck. He was cut down fifteen minutes later. His body was turned over to his mother.

Bulah McGee (aka Beulah MaGee and Beulah McGee), black, age 24. *Murder.*

The crime was committed on the night of December 16, 1906, in a one-room house owned by Bob Henderson, black, in Athens, in McMinn County. The killer and two other black men, Bob Henderson and Dave Sherman, along with others, were engaged in a craps game. One of the players was the victim, Elisha (Lish) Hicks, white, age thirty-one. Also present was his brother, Jim Hicks, along with John Terry and Henry (Shin) Cleage, both black.[1837] All were drinking. Hicks was carrying $40, enough to carry him through the winter, he boasted.[1838]

The craps game began with Henderson's taking a blanket from a bed and putting it on the floor. John Terry lay across the bed. According to Terry, "When I woke up, Lish Hicks was setting in the chair before the fire. McGee hit Lish and knocked him towards the fire; then he hit him again and knocked him to the floor."[1839] Hicks was struck in the back of his head with a club-like stick with a square edge. Terry was asked in court, "Where was Dave Sherman?" He answered, "He was standing back of Bula." "Did they say anything? He answered, "No, sir." "Did they go up to where he was?" He replied, "They picked him up and put him on the blanket."[1840] "What happened with reference to the other defendants where McGee struck Hicks?" He answered, "They all gathered up right together and Dave Sherman reached and put the light out."[1841] McGee said, "Let's take him out, boys," and, "Let's put him on the railroad, they will think the train hit him."[1842]

According to Terry, Bob Henderson came back and got a shovel, left with it and returned. He said to the others who had returned to the house, "If they ask anything about this, we will say we was drunk and don't know nothing about it." After the train passed, McGee said, "We didn't put him close enough [to the track]."[1843] A witness (Lucy Jackson, described as an aged negress[1844]), who lived in a house next to Henderson, heard "a lick" and "somebody hollering" earlier in the night. She heard Hicks say, "Oh!" and heard him grunting as several men carried him past her house.[1845] Another witness was passing Henderson's house and as he passed the door, he saw three men "jerk" a man "out and carry him down towards the railroad."[1846]

Henderson and Sherman helped McGee carry the body and place it beside the railroad tracks some fifty yards away to make it look like Hicks had been struck by a train. The body was first seen by the town postmaster, who had come to "make up" the mail and saw the body beside the tracks.[1847] He summoned railroad night operator Bishop, who examined the body, thinking it was a railroad employee. Bishop and station agent H.M. Remine took charge of the investigation. The postmaster walked towards the depot and met Bulah McGee and a white man. He sent McGee to look for a doctor.[1848]

Remine could not find any evidence the body had been dragged by the train, nor evidence of its sliding at all. He found clay that had been shoveled from the bank, with blood on it. He also found drops of blood about fifty feet from the cut, nearly halfway to a house near the bank. "I went there to look for the shovel that had been used to shovel this clay. I was looking around Bob Henderson's house and he came out and I asked him if he had heard any fuss or any shooting around his house during the night. He said he had been at home all night but had heard nothing. I took him down and showed him the blood."[1849] The sheriff arrived at this time. A shovel with blood on it was found in the house.[1850]

Remine showed the sheriff what he had found and they entered Henderson's house. They found a three-foot-square puddle of blood on floor matting and blood on the doorstep. The murder weapon was found in the house. A chair was broken and spattered with blood. Remine said, "I asked Henderson what he knew about it. He said that he was there all night, but if anybody else was there he didn't know anything about it. He said to me that he got home and went to bed at 9:00 o'clock."[1851] Henderson denied having seen Lish Hicks the night before.[1852]

According to a newspaper, "They told such conflicting stories in their trial that all three were sentenced to be hanged."[1853] Actually, none of the defendants took the stand. The jury instructions mentioned both aiding and abetting in the killing or "accessories after the fact by assisting in carrying away the body."[1854] The charge also said the jury could not accredit the testimony alone of Terry if it found he was an aider and abettor or an accomplice. His testimony must be corroborated by other independent facts or circumstances."[1855] Sherman and Henderson were convicted as accomplices.

The Tennessee Supreme Court affirmed the convictions. "Bulah McGee seems to have made no statement about the matter, but Bob Henderson and Dave Shearman[1856] denied that they had seen the deceased or knew anything about it. They also denied that there had been any trouble at the house, Henderson claiming at one time that he had gone home at about nine o'clock, and at another saying that he was so drunk he did not know what had happened. These facts, in absence of explanation, to our minds clearly establish the charge against these [defendants]."[1857]

The court recounted verbatim the testimony of John Terry regarding McGee's landing the blows with Sherman standing behind him, and the three men carrying Hicks out of the house on a blanket.[1858] It concluded, "While the credibility of this witness is attacked by the statement he made before the Coroner that he knew nothing of the manner by which Elisha Hicks came to his death, yet it is corroborated in all material particulars by the physical facts and the testimony of other witnesses who were examined in the case. It is probable that he did not see the beginning of the difficulty, being asleep and perhaps to some extent under the influence of liquor when it first began, and that this accounts for the seeming conflict in his account of the homicide and the testimony of Lucy Jackson as to what she heard going on in the house."[1859]

Concluded the Tennessee Supreme Court:

> In any event, all the evidence establishes the guilt of the [defendants]. They did not go upon the witness stand and testify in their own behalf, doubtless under the advice of their counsel because in his opinion, notwithstanding the strong

> case that is made against them, it would avail them nothing. They were represented by able and conscientious counsel who did all that possibly could be done for them, and there can be no doubt that they had a fair and impartial trial, and that all the facts which would in any way establish their innocence or throw any doubt upon the case made by the State were fully developed. We have no doubt of this. No error is assigned upon the rulings of the Court in the admission or exclusion of evidence or upon the charge. We have examined the record, including the charge of the trial Judge, carefully, and we find no error therein. It results, therefore, that the judgment of the trial court must be affirmed, and the sentence of the trial court must be affirmed, and the sentence there pronounced carried into execution.[1860]

The McGee case would have remained in oblivion but for two death penalty opponents, who mentioned it in connection with the subsequent pardon, based on innocence, of Dave Sherman. Here is the opponents' description of the "miscarriage of justice in a potential capital case"[1861]:

> Sherman, David (black). 1907. Tennessee. Sherman was convicted (with two co-defendants) of murder and sentenced to death. No appeal was taken. In 1907, a few days before the scheduled executions, one co-defendant (Beulah McGhee) absolved Sherman of guilt. McGhee was hanged, but Governor Malcolm Patterson granted a reprieve for Sherman and the other co-defendant. In 1908 their sentences were commuted to life. The conviction had been obtained by the "uncorroborated statements of one of the parties who was a witness." Then in 1911 Governor Patterson pardoned Sherman after the Board of Pardons concluded, "This appears to us quite a remarkable case of a miscarriage of justice." The attorney general, who prosecuted the case, wrote that "the prisoner had nothing to do with the murder.[1862]

McGee was hanged inside the Athens jail on November 26, 1907. By local tradition, the sheriff was required to conduct the hanging because a professional hangman hired for that purpose did not show up. Accordingly, Sheriff Bill Shoemaker fortified himself with whiskey and performed the task.

A few days before his execution, McGee stated that Sherman had no role in the killing. On the scaffold he said the same about Henderson. His first statement was put in writing and sent to Governor Patterson, who granted Sherman and Henderson reprieves in order to look into the matter.[1863] On January 23, 1908, the governor commuted their punishment from hanging to life sentences.[1864] In 1910, the men's cases came before the Advisory Board of Pardons. It recommended a pardon for Sherman.

Here is the text of Sherman's pardon:

> This defendant, together with two others, was sentenced to be hanged and on account of developments in the cases after the trial, and the dying statement of one of the parties under trial, who was hanged, the sentences of the other two were commuted to life imprisonment. I now have a report from the Advisory Board of Pardons, on the application for pardon of Sherman. There is filed with this report an affidavit from J.O. Bishop, night operator at Athens, who states among other things that he heard McGee's (the prisoner who was hanged) statements from the scaffold in which he verified the written statement he had given the Sheriff. A letter from the sheriff who hanged McGee stated he heard his statement the morning of the execution and in this statement McGee stated that Sherman knew nothing of the killing until he was told about it the next morning. The sheriff also states that he believes an injustice has been done. A letter from the Attorney-General, in which he states that the prisoner was not put upon the stand as the theory of the defendant's counsel was there was not sufficient corroborative testimony to convict the defendant upon the uncorroborated statements of one of the parties who was a witness in the case, and that he is convinced that the prisoner had nothing to do with the murder, and requests his pardon. The Advisory Board of Pardons in their recommendation, among other things, state: "This appears to us quite a remarkable case of a miscarriage of justice, and that too without any official of Court being to blame. This negro was sentenced by the Circuit Court of McMinn County for life for killing one Hix. There was no appeal. From all the facts connected with the case, as set out above, as referred to, and which are stated in almost concise a manner as we could be able to state them here again, but especially to call your attention to the letter of Attorney-General Fletcher, who prosecuted in this case, the three men charged with the murder of said Hix. The Attorney-General closes his letter by stating that he is convinced that this prisoner had all the facts set out herein above, and the letter of the Attorney-General as a basis, we are clearly of the opinion that the prisoner Sherman should not have been convicted, as he was innocent and not in any way connected with the murder, except that he was asleep in the house at the time the murder occurred, but that he knew nothing of it until the next day. This being true, there is nothing else for us to do but to advise that this prisoner should be pardoned as he ought never to have been sent to prison." In view of all these facts, this prisoner should at once be relieved and I hereby Pardon him.[1865]

The Sherman pardon did not occur in a vacuum. Governor Malcolm Patterson had come to the statehouse in 1907 as a progressive reformer, but did not support statewide Prohibition. His political enemy, Edward Ward Carmack, editor of a new newspaper, the *Nashville Tennessean*, heaped invective on a longtime Patterson supporter, Duncan B. Cooper.[1866] Enraged, Cooper and his son Robin encountered Carmack on a Nashville city street. All were carrying pistols. In the shootout, Carmack was killed. This was November 9, 1908. Seen as a martyr's death, Carmack's killing prompted a tidal wave of sentiment and the legislature passed Prohibition in January 1909.

Patterson began his second term (governors served a two-year term at the time) on January 27, 1909. He was already known as a "pardoning governor," but in April 1910 he pardoned Robin Cooper, whose second-degree murder conviction had been upheld by the Tennessee Supreme Court, which had ordered a new trial for the father. The pardon created a storm of anger and until the end of his term, the pardoning power was virtually the only power Patterson retained, as his party lost control of the legislature. Although Patterson was easily renominated by the regular Democratic party, many had bolted to a so-called Independent Democratic ticket (which included a slate that had removed most of the Tennessee Supreme Court in August 1910). In September 1910, Patterson suddenly withdrew from the race. A Republican, Ben W. Hooper, was elected. On January 13, 1911, Patterson granted the Sherman pardon. It was a gesture showing his charity to both the rich and the poor, and he left office on January 25, 1911. Two accomplishments of his administration were an enhanced pardon and parole procedure (Advisory Board of Pardons, 1909) and a new death penalty procedure. After May 1, 1909, all executions were to take place at the Main Prison in Nashville.[1867]

No clemency waited Henderson. He died of meningitis at the Main Prison on April 20, 1912.

1908

Peter W. Turner, black, age 38. *Murder.*

The crime was committed on the night of March 15, 1907, in the city of Knoxville, outdoors on the back lawn of a house located at Lithgow Street and Church Avenue. It remains one of the most unusual murders in Tennessee history because the defendant asserted that the killing was part of an assisted suicide of the victim, Minnie Scott, black, age twenty-eight.

Turner was described as "an intelligent negro, has some education, and at different times worked as an agent for the *Louisville Courier Journal* and *St. Louis Globe-Democrat.*"[1868] He was married, but had been clandestinely "keeping company" with Minnie Scott, the wife of W.B. Scott, for about four years. According to one source, "She was a good looking negress and she and Turner seemed much infatuated with each other."[1869]

About six months before the killing, according to Turner, Minnie had attempted to shoot herself in the ear with a pistol, but he managed to grab the weapon and she was merely wounded in the head. A mutual friend was nearby when this shooting occurred, but did not witness the event. The matter was brought to the attention of the police, but no charges were brought.[1870]

The day of the killing the couple met and had been drinking beer and whiskey. According to Turner, they lay down on the ground and Minnie urged him to shoot her in the head because she did not want to live any longer as the wife of Mr. Scott. Turner did not have the money to take her away from Knoxville.

Turner testified, "She came back and put her arm around my neck and said, "Now, dear, I am ready to leave this troublesome world with you, and do it before someone comes by that knows me. I don't care after I am dead."[1871] Continued Turner, "So I placed the gun to her head and fired, and she slapped her hand on her stomach and said, "Right here," and I put the gun there and fired, her arm still around my neck and mine around her waist; but when I fired that time she hollowed [*sic*] and said, "Once more, and I'll be dead." So I turned her aloose and put the gun to my own head, and it failed to go off, and I couldn't go on with her. But I am going to her just as willing as she was; for as she is dead, I don't want to live."[1872]

The Supreme Court's opinion explains that when arrested, Turner was carrying a letter from the victim which described her relationship with Turner and their plans to die together. This document was in the hands of a police detective who was out of the city at the time of the trial and was not offered in evidence, although the policeman who took it from Turner described its contents to the jury.[1873]

Turner did not come forward immediately after the shooting. Instead, he hid in a vacant house for two days and was captured attempting to hop a train. He denied his identity and denied any involvement until a sheriff's deputy pointedly recognized him as having worked briefly for a former sheriff. It was at this point that Turner came forth with the 14-page "memoir" which amounted to a confession.[1874] He was tried in April 1907.

These facts supported the jury's verdict of first-degree murder, ruled the Tennessee Supreme Court, because they demonstrated a "willful, deliberate, and premeditated killing."[1875] It said, "The fact that the woman consented and the crime was in execution of a joint agreement would not remove the case from this grade of felonious homicide, since the crime embraced all the elements of malice, deliberation, and premeditation necessary to constitute murder in the first degree."[1876]

The Supreme Court also brushed aside an attempt by counsel to argue that Turner was insane at the time of the crime. The court said that no evidence had been shown at trial to show "hereditary insanity or previous acts tending to show an unbalanced mind," nor was any medical expert testimony shown at trial.[1877]

Awaiting execution while the governor considered commutation (which had been urged by several black ministers), Turner placed paper signs on his cell complaining that he was not a "menagerie" or an "exhibition." However, he brought attention to himself because "he is something of an artist and has drawn a number of pictures and made paintings which he has distributed among his friends."[1878]

In the middle of the night before his execution, Turner secretly attempted suicide by slashing his throat and wrist with a sharpened pewter spoon. This was discovered by the black ministers who came to conduct a worship service. During the service, the victim's husband was allowed to come forward. Turner begged forgiveness for ruining his home: "God has forgiven me and I want you to forgive me," said Turner to Scott. The latter asked Turner if he felt that the law should be executed, and whether he should suffer the death penalty for his crime, and Turner answered in the affirmative. Scott then replied, "I'll have to forgive you, then."[1879]

As Turner stood on the gallows inside the jail, he led the group in singing "Nearer My God to Thee," and kept repeating, "I'm going home." His last full statement to the group was, "I wish to say that I hope that everyone before me will meet me in Heaven." According to an agreement with the sheriff, the minister in charge was allowed to give what was described as a death blessing ritual of the Church of Christ, namely, "Brother Peter Turner, I commend thy spirit and soul unto the tender mercies of God, the Father, God, the Son, and God, the Holy Ghost. Amen." Asked by the sheriff if he was ready, Turner replied in a firm voice, "Yes, I am ready, good-bye to everybody."[1880]

Turner was hanged inside the Knoxville jail on January 11, 1908. Turner's attempted suicide had caused the sheriff to move the execution from two o'clock forward by a hour, lest Turner start bleeding and cheat the gallows. The neck wound itself produced considerable blood as Turner hung from the rope.

Following the time-honored ritual, the physician who pronounced death did so by placing his ear to Turner's heart and saying the words, "dead, dead, dead." The body was placed on a wicker basket and carried to an office in the jail, where over six hundred people walked by in single file to view it.

Arthur Pearson, black, age 25. *Rape.*

The crime was committed about 2:00 P.M. on August 12, 1905, outside the town of Clifton, in Wayne County. The rapist lived about two hundred yards from the victim. The victim was Dora Seiber, white, a twelve-year-old girl. The Seiber family lived in a tent beside the Tennessee River because the girl's father was a commercial fisherman.

Dora Seiber had been sent to a neighbor's house a mile away to purchase potatoes. Her six-year-old sister went with her. They did not procure the potatoes, but on the way back the two were accosted by a black man who asked Dora to go up the hollow and help him turn over a log. She refused and he offered her fifteen cents. When she refused the second time, saying she did not have time, he brandished a knife and grabbed her, saying, "Yes, God damn you, you have got the time!"

He then "put his hand over her mouth and took her up the hollow and laid her down and pulled up her clothes and got upon her and outraged her."[1881] Her sister ran into the woods to hide as this happened. The rapist told Dora he would come and kill her if she told anyone. He then left, walking through the woods. Dora searched the woods for her sister and found her by hearing her crying.

On the way home, crying, shaken and with her dress torn behind and the band of her dress torn loose, she encountered a white man riding a bicycle along the road. She told him what happened and he accompanied her home.[1882] Another man saw Arthur Pearson about five o'clock that evening in the town. His clothing was identical to the rapist's, as described by Dora.[1883] Likewise, another witness testified that, a short while before the girls were sent on the errand, he saw a black man near the place where the rape occurred. This man had his hat pulled down over his eyes, but was wearing the clothing described by Dora.[1884]

When she finally returned to her tent home, she told her mother what happened. Dora's dress was torn and she was bruised and bloody in her vaginal area. The mother washed the girl's wounds and sent word for the sheriff. By then it was nightfall and the search did not begin in earnest until the next day, Saturday.

Dora told the sheriff and others who joined the search that she had been attacked by a "medium sized" Negro with a "short mustache who wore dark pants with a large blue stripe up the leg on the inside and outside, and had on a blue jumper, unbuttoned, and a dark undershirt."[1885] She identified Pearson as the same man at trial. She also identified his clothing at trial.

Bloodhounds were brought from Lawrenceburg and tracked the scent to the river bank. The track was picked up on the other side of the river, along with footprints. The tracks made a long journey around the town of Clifton, finally leading to a river bank. It was now Monday. The steamboat *Clyde* had just been there, loading lumber. The voyage of the steamboat was known and by this time it had landed at another town. While it was docked, the captain was notified that Pearson might be aboard.[1886] He pulled the boat away, but instead of heading downstream, he turned backward toward Clifton. The first mate saw Pearson moving to the side to jump overboard, but pulled a weapon and held him.

Pearson was taken before the girl on Monday and she identified him without hesitation. Her identification was deemed truthful because at least a half dozen other black men had been brought to her and she said none was the attacker. Later, when a mob asked the sheriff whether Pearson had been identified by the girl, the sheriff said no, in order to get Pearson back to the jail. Pearson was harshly interrogated at the jail, but "was never able to give a straight account of his actions during the hours preceding and following the commission of the crime."[1887] The compelling evidence against him was of his own making.

When arrested on Monday, he was cleanshaven. He said that he had gotten a shave and a haircut the previous Tuesday. But the two black barbers he named said otherwise. Barber W.J. Young said Pearson appeared at 8:00 A.M. Saturday morning and asked for a shave. Young said he was busy cleaning some clothes and told Pearson to ask the other barber, Vinyard, to shave him. Vinyard replied he was too nervous to do it and testified that he told Pearson to shave himself. Vinyard saw Pearson lather his face but did not watch the actual shaving, and saw Pearson put a nickel down as payment for use of the shaving tools.[1888] Vinyard also testified that Pearson "appeared a little excited."

Another witness said Pearson seemed a "little rattled" when he appeared at the wharf at 8:00 A.M. on Sunday morning. This witness, John Roberson, said Pearson asked to borrow a skiff to cross the river because he needed to get some money Will Perry owed him. The use of the skiff was refused. Will Perry testified that he did not know Pearson, who never did any work for him and was owed no money.[1889]

At trial, Pearson's major defense was an alibi. He said he had been gambling with other Negroes in Clifton on the day of the rape, and was home from one o'clock until four o'clock that afternoon. He said three adults, including his wife, were home with him during this time. However, two were in the courtroom during his trial and he did not call either to the stand. Likewise, no other person testified on his behalf, except a store clerk who said he had sold Pearson a dress shirt for his wife on the evening of the crime.

Pearson's appeal asserted that there was no evidence that Dora had been raped at all except her testimony and that of her mother. That is, no doctor was asked to examine her. Furthermore, she described the rapist as a "tall and slim black man with thick lips and a short moustache." Pearson was not tall and slim, and initially Dora's father said that Pearson should not even be taken to Dora because he did not meet her description. Likewise, Pearson was not a dark Negro, but was light-skinned.[1890]

Furthermore, Dora was impeached by her own testimony. She said that when Pearson finished raping her and threatening her, he plaited two hickory limbs together. But a witness said that it was he who plaited the limbs together when he visited the rape site with some other men and "did this unthoughtedly" while he was standing there talking, and he left them there.[1891]

There was other startling exculpatory evidence. The year before, Dora had told her mother that a man had tried but failed to rape her at another town called Riverside. Neighbors conducted an investigation but concluded the story was a fabrication. The mother explained that Dora actually said she had been "scared" by a man and there was no rape attempt.[1892] Pearson's appeal also said he had been defended by a young lawyer with very little experience.[1893]

The Tennessee Supreme Court affirmed the conviction, but the opinion cannot be located. The appellate record contains several letters and petitions addressed to the governor, both asking for commutation and objecting to it. Among them is a petition signed by five of the jurors — but the signatures seem to be in the same handwriting. It cannot be determined at this time why these documents appear in the appellate record, nor why the execution was delayed so long (for the time), nearly three years.

Pearson was executed at 10:38 A.M. on February 8, 1908, inside the Waynesboro jail in front of thirty-five witnesses. Asked if he had any last words, Pearson said, "I am not the man. I am ready to go." The sheriff told him to tell the truth. He replied, "I wouldn't tell a lie in the shape I'm in now." He was asked if he was prepared to die. He replied, "Yes. Tell all my folks farewell; same to you gentlemen. You will see this again."

"The Lord be with me," he said as the black cap was placed on his head. The sheriff, hoping another delay would prompt a confession, asked Pearson if the noose was too tight. He replied, "I want it tight enough to break my neck."

The deputy sheriff counted, "one, two, three." As he did so, Pearson said, "Lord have mercy," as he was dropped. His neck was broken and he was cut down thirteen minutes later. The body was given to relatives. This was the first legal hanging in Wayne County.

John Carmack, black, age 31. *Murder.*

The crime was committed about 10:00 P.M. June 20, 1906, at the foot of Seventh Street on the bank of the Tennessee River in downtown Knoxville, in Knox County. The victim's body was found by some boys rowing a boat in the river, who first did not think it was a body. Carmack had served a total of eight years in prison for assault and larceny, and was a Knoxville career criminal. The body was pulled from the water by some railroad workers near a bridge. In the gang was the killer, who proclaimed he was sick and went home.[1894]

The killer and the victim knew each other. Both were born and reared near Rogersville in Hawkins County. The victim was J.H. "Henry" Thomas, black, age twenty-five.[1895] He was five feet, one inch tall and weighed about one hundred and twenty-five pounds. The killer, a railroad construction worker, was familiar with the location of the murder because he worked there. Thomas had come to Knoxville a few weeks earlier and met the killer in a saloon. Thomas was seen carrying a hundred dollars, including two twenty-dollar bills which stuck out of his long black pocketbook.[1896] Carmack struck Thomas in the back of the head and pushed his body into the river. The motive was robbery, netting thirty dollars.

Thomas had a friend, Bob Branner, black, a railroad porter who owned a tailor shop in Knoxville. Branner attempted to keep Thomas away from Carmack by asking him to spend the night of his murder in the Branner household. He had warned that someone might see the money and knock his brains out. Thomas replied, "I am a Christian and God will take care of me."[1897] From his tailor shop window, he saw the pair wandering from saloon to saloon and walk in the direction of Seventh Street.[1898] Thomas's body was pulled from the river the next day. His money was gone, his pockets were turned inside out, and his watch and chain were missing.

Carmack came to Branner's shop the morning after the killing, asking about Thomas's whereabouts. Branner became suspicious after Carmack told him he had left Thomas at the stairs at Seventh Street leading down to the river.[1899] Branner invited himself to go to Carmack's house with him. There he saw Carmack's shoes under the bed, wet with sand on them.[1900] The clothes he had been wearing the day before were muddy. Referring to the muddy clothes, Carmack said to his wife, "That is where you kicked me last night." She replied, "I don't know anything about that." She said she had tried to induce him not to go back to town the night before. "She asked him where he got the watch and chain and he said it was none of her business."[1901]

A witness saw Carmack and a small black man walking to the river.[1902] A saloon owner testified Carmack had used a twenty-dollar bill to purchase a glass of beer on the day he was arrested for the murder.[1903] A few hours before the body was found in the river, Carmack asked fellow railroad workers how long after a body was thrown in the river would it take to surface.[1904]

Branner, convinced Carmack was the killer, followed him to a relative's house in the suburbs. He obtained a warrant and returned with two policemen. They chased Carmack into the woods and captured him. At the police station, Carmack said to the police lieutenant, "I hope God may kill me if I had anything to do with [the killing]."[1905] At that moment, "there was a terrible long thunder clap and just then a quick flash of lightning." The frightened Carmack blurted, "Lieutenant Conners, if you give me a pint of liquor, I will tell you all about it."[1906]

At trial, Carmack said he had been kept in the jail from Thursday until Sunday and had nothing to lie on but the naked floor. He testified:

> They finally took me to a room where there were four or five policemen. They all had on their uniforms and had their billets in their hands. The woman that stays down there had brought me a half a pint of whiskey and told me to drink it, which I did. At the window of the room I saw Bob Branner and James Bradley and a great crowd of negroes. I heard them talking about mobbing me. One of the policemen that told me to tell all about it, that it would be better for me, he says, "You killed Thomas and there is no use your denying it."[1907] He says, "Don't you lie to me. I will break your head with this stick. There was a big storm going on and the room was dark except when it would lighten. They all talked to me in a rough way. I had lost so much sleep and was so scared I don't know what all I did say. I don't know what other statement I made. When I saw those negroes I was afraid. I did not kill Thomas nor did I have anything to do with his killing. I was not down on the river that night or near the place where they say they found the body of Thomas.[1908]

Carmack said he had left Thomas in the company of a "darkey with a gold tooth," name unknown, who without his knowledge took Thomas to the river and killed him. The killer gave Carmack ten dollars and promised to give him ten dollars more.[1909] Branner testified he saw Carmack and Thomas walking toward Seventh Street. There was no gold-tooth person, and there was no mob at the jail, just him and James Bradley. The police said no alcohol was given and there was no mob.[1910] Carmack was convicted with mitigating circumstances. The judge disregarded the recommendation and ordered Carmack executed.

The Tennessee Supreme Court's twenty-one page opinion (lengthy for a criminal case of the era) recounted much of the testimony verbatim (a new practice) and explained the law of confessions, including some new Tennessee cases. It said the confession statements were not coerced and were properly admitted. Carmack's chief defense was alibi (not explained by the court) and there was sufficient independent evidence without the confession statements.

While the close questioning was the reason for his confession, "To these influences, there is at this juncture added a blinding flash of lightning and a deafening clap of thunder."[1911] Said the court, "All these combined have the effect to overcome his resistance, and he at last yields, and makes the confession. And when he makes it, he does so in a way to throw the main blame for the deed on another."[1912]

The court's final orders at the time said that executions were to take place between 10:00 A.M. and 5:00 P.M.[1913] The sheriff sometimes waited until virtually the last minute, in part to give the condemned man the opportunity to make a profession of faith. In Carmack's case, the governor had respited him at least twice at the urging of a group of black ministers who asserted they were working hard to save his soul, not his life.[1914]

On the gallows Carmack gave a rambling speech asserting his innocence. After the cap was placed over his head, he asked that his ten-year-old son be brought forward. With the noose around his neck, Carmack told the boy to shun bad company and asked those in attendance to give the boy pennies. He told the boy never to spend the money.[1915]

Carmack was executed inside the Knoxville jail on February 27, 1908, as hundreds waited outside in a snowstorm to see his body. On this same day, Ed Turner, white wife-killer, was executed in Chattanooga.

Ed Turner, white, age 30. *Murder.*

The crime was committed at 2:00 P.M. on April 2, 1907, on a road on the side of Lookout Mountain, in Chattanooga, in Hamilton County. The victim, Lilly Burcham Turner, white, age seventeen, was the killer's wife. He cut her throat from ear to ear with a pocketknife. The newspaper described her as a "wayward child of the Kentucky mountains."[1916]

The murder outraged the community. Great effort and reward was made for Turner's capture. Dave Edwards, who hailed from the same Breathitt County, Kentucky, area as Turner, was supposedly allowed out of jail to help capture him. Edwards, who was later executed with the same rope as Turner, took credit for Turner's capture. He deserved none. Rather, Turner was found in Estil County, Kentucky, in a barn loft. He told the man who captured him that he had followed his wife to Lookout Mountain, "found her with another man, and in a heat of passion had cut her throat."[1917]

According to Turner's testimony, he and Lilly operated a restaurant in Centerville, Georgia, for a couple of months. The reasons for closing it are conflicting. But it is clear that the police chief ordered Lilly to leave town or be jailed for immoral conduct. Turner stayed behind to close out the restaurant while she went to Atlanta to remain until he could join her.[1918]

According to Turner, at the time he married Lilly a few months earlier he regarded her as a "pure girl," and this was his first knowledge of her sexual misconduct. When he found out, he decided to take Lilly back to her family in Kentucky.

On March 31, 1907, he went to Atlanta to the Germania Hotel, where she was supposed to be staying. (Among his belongings was a letter from her, but he resisted the state's offering the letter as proof because it was illegally obtained.[1919]) He contacted a policeman, and they found her in the Georgia Hotel, in bed with a man named J.E. Jones, white, age twenty-six. The couple had registered as Mitchell and wife. Both were arrested. Turner went to the jail and got Lilly and returned to the same room she and Jones had occupied.

While waiting at the train station the next day, Turner saw his wife talking to the same Jones and another man, later identified as Reeves. Ed and Lilly took the train to Chattanooga, their ultimate destination Kentucky. Because their Kentucky train did not leave until late afternoon, Ed Turner and Lilly took a streetcar to Lookout Mountain for sightseeing. He noticed the two men got on the same car along the way. When he and Lilly alighted, he noticed the men walking toward the incline railroad office. He and Lilly decided to walk up the mountain.

According to Turner: "As we was going along the mountain, I said that she ought to be ashamed of the way she had conducted herself. I said she was a nice girl if she wanted to be. I said it was a shame for her mother to know what she had done. She said, 'I will do as I please, you damned son of a bitch.' I had my knife in my hand and struck her."[1920]

Turner's defense was a form of temporary insanity. That is, the shock of learning of his wife's conduct threw him into such a rage that he lost all reason and impulsively killed her, which the Supreme Court described as a "spasm of momentary insanity."[1921]

Turner's defense angered the community because of the common belief that he killed her, in part, because she refused to prostitute herself for him. She was an especially pretty girl and the newspaper focused on her fair complexion and clothing, "a black silk skirt, a white waist with dark shoulder straps of some sort, and a white hat trimmed with dark red flowers."[1922] Because her body was found by the side of the road in a ditch, a number of people saw it. Many more saw her at the morgue (apparently still dressed) because she was described in the newspaper as an unidentified beauty with her throat bearing five ragged slashes. According to Sheriff Shipp, her head was two-thirds cut off.

To impeach Turner's story, the following facts were elicited. "Some years before, he had contracted a most loathsome private disease, which had greatly impaired his health, the effects of which still remain with him."[1923] He had served nine months in the Kentucky penitentiary for "trying to kill a fellow."[1924] He had no education, religious or otherwise.

Turner had consumed whiskey before they walked up the mountain and on the way. In conversation with Lilly on the streetcar she seemed very angry and her face was red. As the streetcar progressed, Turner kept looking for someone and finally motioned. Shortly thereafter, two men (identified by the conductor as Jones and Reeves) got in the car and sat directly in front of Turner and Lilly. Before they got on the streetcar, according to Jones's testimony, Lilly said in Turner's presence, "She had done something last night that she did not want to do." Said Jones, "I asked her what it was; she said he made her stay with a man last night and I did not want to do it."[1925] Turner said he did not know why the two men followed him and Lilly to Chattanooga.

Turner's insanity defense was supported by two expert witnesses. Dr. McQuillan said that a man under Turner's circumstances "would have a stormy mind, and would not be sane," and had "defective mental responsibility." On cross-examination, he said that only about eighty percent of the human family are sane. The trial judge was called as a witness in rebuttal. He said that Dr. McQuillan had testified in his court in another case in which he said that only about two percent of the human family were sane.[1926]

The other expert, Dr. Kerr, testified that under the circumstances Turner was "simply a moral pervert, a man without power to control his impulses." His standard of right or wrong is lowered and that under the circumstances, the stabbing was " the most natural thing for him, because we must compare this man with a brute."[1927] The court ruled that mere "mental unsoundness" would not excuse one from the consequences of his acts, the test is whether the defendant knew right from wrong, and Dr. Kerr said Turner met this test.[1928]

Lilly Turner had first met E.J. Jones at the Germania Hotel, a sporting house.[1929] The two made arrangements to meet the next morning, along with his friend Reeves, and another "woman of the town," named Effie. When they met, Turner was with Lilly, but he was not introduced as her husband. After the five met, they all became intoxicated and Jones had sex with Lilly along a river bank, while Turner paid particular attention to Effie. The alcohol made Jones and Effie sleepy, and the next thing Jones heard was a ruckus caused by Effie accusing Turner of taking seventeen dollars from her stocking by cutting it. Jones and Effie returned to the Germania Hotel.

Two witnesses said that Turner and a man named Kelly rented a room at the Conner House Hotel in Chattanooga the night before Lilly's death, and that later she went to the room with the pair, and Turner came down and spent the night sleeping in the train station.

The Tennessee Supreme Court said the evidence supported the murder conviction and the jury had the right to decide if Tuner was actually insane.[1930] Turner was convinced the governor would commute his sentence.[1931]

Attended by two ministers the night before his execution, Turner was well composed as he stood on the gallows in the basement of the Hamilton County jail. A theology student led the small group of spectators in singing "Rock of Ages," followed by a prayer from the Rev. J.A. Baylor, minister of Centenary Methodist Church. "Good-bye," was Turner's last word as the cap was placed over his head.

"May God have mercy on your soul," said Sheriff Shipp as he pulled the lever releasing the trap. Turner fell cleanly and was cut down eleven minutes later. His body was sent to his Kentucky relatives.[1932] Among the possessions Turner gave to his cousin before the execution was Lilly's watch.[1933]

This was Shipp's only legal execution. But he became famous in Tennessee history for allowing a black man to be taken from the jail on March 19, 1906, and lynched from a Chattanooga bridge, for which he was held in contempt of court and briefly jailed by order of the United States Supreme Court. This happened over an extended period of time. Shipp and others were tried in a contempt hearing beginning on February 12, 1907, but the Supreme Court did not announce its decision until May 24, 1909, and did not announce its punishment until November 15, 1909. Shipp served ninety days in the federal jail in the District of Columbia before returning to Chattanooga to a hero's welcome. He had been reelected sheriff in 1906, but had been defeated in 1908.[1934]

Sheriff Shipp followed the rare custom of allowing a condemned man as much time as possible on his last day. Because the Supreme Court's order said the execution must occur between ten in the morning and five in the afternoon, Shipp pulled the lever at 4:53 P.M. on February 27, 1908.

John McPherson, white, age 26. *Murder.*

The crime was committed about 11:30 P.M. on July 14, 1906, on the road in front of the house of Thomas Burnett, about six miles outside Knoxville. The road led from Knoxville to Sevier County. The killer was making a hasty escape from an earlier killing and had stopped at the Burnett house to borrow a pistol. Accompanying him was his mistress, a prostitute named Lizzie Winstead, white, and his father, Dr. M.A. "Buck" McPherson. The victim was William F. Walker, white, age thirty-three, a Knox County deputy sheriff who had been summoned to arrest the McPhersons.[1935]

The violent night began about 10:00 P.M. at a house of prostitution in Knoxville when an intoxicated John McPherson got into an argument with Grant Smith (whose wife ran the house) and shot and stabbed him. John was accompanied by his father, Dr. M.A. McPherson, who did not participate in the assault, but quickly learned about it when his son burst from the house, taking along Lizzie Winstead. The three planned to flee to a house in Sevier County owned by Dr. McPherson's brother. They left in a buggy belonging to the father.

Both father and son were familiar with violence. The son was a professional gambler with a long criminal record for minor offenses.[1936] The father, some years before, had killed another man, Dr. Pickens, in a dispute over a woman, and had been sentenced to a ten-year prison term. After shooting Dr. Pickens, Dr. McPherson had helped attend his wounds. He served seven years, having been released four years before the present killing.[1937]

As the buggy hurried out of town, it met a buggy belonging to Dr. Joseph M. Waddell. He had been drinking, but was not intoxicated, and because he was dozing in the moving buggy, it bumped into the McPherson buggy.[1938] The latter sustained some damage, including to the reins of the horse. With the buggies entangled, John McPherson became enraged and struck Dr. Waddell over the head with his pistol. As he arose, Dr. Waddell was struck again, as a female voice said, "Don't kill that man!"

The McPherson buggy continued, first stopping at the house of Constable Peter Doyle. Here Dr. McPherson asked to borrow a pistol, claiming that he needed the weapon to protect himself because he was going to make a call in a dangerous area. Doyle said his pistol was in the possession of Thomas Burnett, further down the road. When they arrived, they explained their need to borrow some rope to fix the harness, and the doctor asked to borrow a pistol.

While the McPhersons were escaping, Dr. Waddell continued towards Knoxville, coming to the house of Deputy Sheriff William Walker. He explained what happened and asked Walker to come with him in his buggy to arrest the son (and perhaps the father) for the assault. Walker got into the buggy. He was armed with a pistol.

The McPhersons heard Dr. Waddell's buggy coming because of its distinctive rattle. Lizzie was in their buggy. The doctor claimed he was just coming out of the house when the shooting occurred. As the buggy went by, Deputy Sheriff Walker stepped out, and walked in a quick pace to the McPherson buggy. He said, "This is William Walker, the deputy sheriff, consider yourselves under arrest."[1939] A shot rang. Waddell said the shooter was on the opposite side of the horse when he shot Walker. Waddell continued to another house to summon more law enforcement officers.

The trio continued to Sevier County, where John McPherson was dropped off. Lizzie and the father returned to Knox County and were arrested. John McPherson was a fugitive for eight months until found in a West Virginia mining town. Meanwhile, the father had been tried for the murder of Grant Smith and acquitted, then tried as an accomplice in Deputy Walker's murder. He was convicted and given a ten-year term. He was in prison at the time of his son's trial and was brought back for it.

McPherson asserted self-defense and no premeditation. John said he thought the person he shot was Dr. Waddell, that Walker did not identify himself as a deputy sheriff, and he thought his life was in danger. Furthermore, when he and his father realized it was Walker, they helped carry him into the house, where the father attempted to dress his wound, taking some thirty minutes.

The state showed that the killing contained the element of premeditation because of the father's attempt to borrow a pistol, and that the shooting was linked to the son by the dying declaration of the victim. Walker gave at least two dying declarations in the period he lived, some four days. He said he had identified himself by name and as a deputy sheriff but the shot came immediately thereafter.[1940] (The bullet entered the shoulder but grazed the spinal cord, paralyzing Walker.) The jury convicted John McPherson on October 23, 1907. The jury said the verdict was first-degree murder with mitigating circumstances. The judge had the power to disregard the finding of mitigating circumstances and he did.

On appeal, the Tennessee Supreme Court turned aside numerous alleged errors: that Walker had not been officially commissioned as a deputy (he had), that Walker did not have the right to arrest without a warrant (he did), and this was manslaughter. It was not.[1941]

Whether John McPherson should actually receive the death penalty split the Knoxville community, and the governor was overwhelmed with extensive petitions on both sides. Mrs. McPherson made an earnest and dramatic plea for her son's life.[1942] A problem was this: no white man had been legally executed in Knox County since 1875.[1943]

A leading Nashville newspaper editorialized: "Thou Shalt Not Kill." It explained, "The size of a petition simply means active solicitation. Most anybody will sign a petition. The one at present in view is that presented to the Governor asking for commutation to life imprisonment for McPherson. McPherson killed two men in one night, and not in one fight, either. The verdict should stand as the twelve men, good and true, handed it in. This man killed more than his share. At this rate nobody will be left alive after tonight."[1944]

While confined at the jail, John McPherson professed religion and was baptized there. To the moment of his execution he hoped the governor would commute his sentence. The newspaper described a "touching scene" when son and father said goodbye at the jail, the latter being taken back to prison.[1945]

John McPherson was described as composed and self-possessed as he walked to and waited at the gallows on March 23, 1908. Asked if he had any last words, a statement he had dictated was read by an unnamed person. It thanked everyone who had tried to seek a commutation. When asked again, he finally spoke. In a low voice he said his father had nothing whatever to do with the Walker killing and the state was holding in custody an innocent man.[1946] About twenty-five hundred asked to see the hanging. All were turned down except those allowed by law. Several thousand waited outside in the rain. The private execution was quite different from John Webb's in 1875, where a crowd estimated as large as twenty thousand saw him die.

Henry Johnson, black, age 19. *Carnal knowledge of a female child under age twelve.*

The crime was committed on October 9, 1907, near the dairy farm home of the Leonard B. Broadway family, on Poplar Avenue six miles outside Memphis, in Shelby County. Johnson had been a farm hand for about two months and lived in a cabin on the farm. The victim was Ida May Broadway, who "was not quite four years of age when the assault was made."[1947] She was assaulted in the rear of a storage room in her parents' house. "On leaving the house, the fiend hurried out of the house and through the back yard to the cow sheds and stable, carefully avoiding other negroes who were working."[1948]

Ida May ran screaming to her grandfather's house nearby, knowing her mother was there.[1949] She was crying and told her mother Johnson had abused her. "When found, Johnson was scrubbing in the milk house and ran before a single question could be asked him."[1950]

After Johnson was named as a rapist he was chased by a posse of neighbors for two miles and would have been lynched but for the intervention of the girl's father and the timely arrival of police officers. "He was taken back to the house where he was identified by the frail little victim, who screamed aloud in her terror at the sight of the black brute."[1951]

A minister of the colored Methodist Church, the Rev. G.A. Griffin, "after a conference with some of the leading negroes decided to employ counsel to represent this man in the Criminal Court in order that he might have a fair and impartial trial on the law and the evidence."[1952] Said the Rev. Griffin, "To that end I went to R.H. Prescott whom I had known for a number of years and knew to be a lawyer who was loyal to his clients, and told him that I could get up a small fee for him to represent this party in the Criminal Court of Shelby County. The defendant in this case had knowledge of this employment, and we considered him to be in desperate straits."[1953]

Robert H. Prescott told the jury that if he had been in the posse that caught Johnson he probably would have helped lynch him, but after studying the case he was convinced his client was innocent and begged the jury not to impose a "legal lynching."[1954] Ida May was placed on the stand but was found incompetent to testify because she could not understand the importance of an oath. The judge then asked her what would happen to her after she died if she told a lie. She said she would be required to stay in the house.

Ida May was not seen by a doctor for her injuries and no doctor testified in court. The father said he found Ida May to have been "slightly abused, evidence of the attack being found upon her clothing, and she being slightly lacerated."[1955] "While the evidence did not show that the negro actually accomplished the crime with which he was charged, the penalty is by statute fixed at death by hanging or such other punishment as the jury may believe to be just, because of the fact that the victim is less than ten years old."[1956]

The jury convicted Henry Johnson on October 20, 1907. The case was appealed to the Tennessee Supreme Court, which expressed its outrage that no bill of exceptions was prepared and provided the court. Justice Neil wrote, "This is the first case since the writer has been on the Bench that a capital case has come to this Court without a bill of exceptions, and no member of the Court remembers such an occurrence as having happened more than once before."

Said the opinion, "The Court was greatly surprised and shocked that any member of the bar who had attended to a capital case in the Court below would consent that his client's cause should come to this Court without a bill of exceptions. That matter has been taken notice of by the Court in a special proceeding addressed to the counsel who represented the prisoner below, and need not be further referred to in the present case."[1957]

The court said: "When records in capital cases are sent to this Court without bills of exceptions, or without anything to show, in express terms, that there was a trial upon the evidence, the judge, attorney general and clerk of the Court below should see to it that a complete, technical record is transmitted."

The court continued:

> It is a great breach of duty upon the part of the attorney representing a prisoner to allow a capital case to come to this Court without a bill of exceptions, and is a matter, as has been held at the present term, for which the counsel can be dealt with by this Court. This, however, does not excuse the Supreme Court from discharging its full duty to the prisoner, by reading the technical record with extreme care to make sure that all the technical requirements of the law have been complied with. It is wholly compatible, however, with the discharge of this duty that the counsel who has imposed it upon the Court by a failure to make out a bill of exceptions should be punished. Such an omission commits a grievous wrong upon the administration of justice, upon the Court, and upon the counsel himself, who is derelict in such a matter.[1958]

The Supreme Court appointed Mr. R.F. Spraggins to represent Johnson on appeal because his trial counsel "did not appear in this Court."[1959] Spraggins was allowed to file a wayside bill of exceptions, a kind of reconstruction of the testimony which was approved by the trial court.[1960]

The document described the facts: "And after a

certain length of time had passed and the little girl was not seen or heard, her mother went to the door where she saw Ida May coming out of the room occupied by Henry Johnson crying. She immediately went to her and carried her into the house, but before going into the house she saw Henry Johnson going hastily out of the room toward the dairy house."

It continued: "After Mrs. Broadway and her child Ida May went into their residence Ida May told her mother that Henry Johnson, the defendant in this case, had abused her, pulling up her dress and showing her mother her private parts. Mrs. Broadway made an examination of her private parts. Mrs. Broadway made an examination of the child immediately upon learning this and found that her private parts were very much irritated and red. Also the inside of her legs adjacent to her private parts were red and inflamed."

The document said, "There was on the child's drawers one or two drops of blood. There was also a greasy substance on the child's drawers which had the appearance of semen and was fresh at that time of examination. These drawers were introduced in evidence on the trial and exhibited to the jury. The spots that were designated as blood had darkened to some extent and the substance designated as semen had dried, yet there were traces of it in considerable quantities."[1961]

Following his capture, Johnson was taken back to the Broadway residence "and confronted with the child who again reiterated in his presence what he had done."[1962] The child's father struck him with his fists, but the Broadway men[1963] persuaded the crowd to let the law take its course. As they were taking Johnson in the wagon to the Poplar Street car line, Johnson confessed that he "sexually used the little girl in the room." The judge told the jury to disregard this testimony because it was not voluntary and made under fear.

As the wagon proceeded about two miles, the defendant seemed to be calm. Asked to make a statement of just exactly how the matter occurred, "he told them that he was very sorry that he did what he had done but he had used the girl in an improper way. They asked him to describe the exact manner in which he had used her, whereupon he said that he had placed his private parts between her legs." That confession was admitted into evidence.[1964]

On the way to the police station, Johnson was accompanied on different occasions by two newspaper reporters from different papers. Both testified that Johnson told them "he misused the girl sexually but said he did not think he had done any wrong."[1965] "The next day Ida May became very sore in her private parts and walked awkwardly, but no physician was called in, she being treated by the common family remedies to allay the inflamation and the swelling of the parts."[1966]

Said the wayside bill of exceptions, "The defendant was introduced as a witness and on the stand made a denial of any intention to rape or sexually know the little girl, and stated that he was playing with her. On cross-examination the defendant admitted that when the child left his room she left crying."[1967]

Spraggins offered a welter of objections, all addressed to the technical record. For example, it did not appear that the court minutes were properly captioned, nor that they described the proceedings day to day, nor that there was even a trial, nor that the jury was properly impaneled, nor that the charge was given to them in writing, nor that they were allowed to take the charge with them, nor that the defendant had counsel at the trial.

To each of these objections the court ruled there was case law or statute saying these errors were not necessarily fatal to a prosecution, or had been waived because there was no evidence to show that proper and timely objections had been made.

The court concluded, "There being no bill of exceptions to enable us to examine the evidence, and no error appearing upon the face of the technical record, there is nothing left to do, and we can do nothing, except to affirm the judgment of the Court below."[1968]

Said the newspaper, "The supreme court spent much time in hearing the case, ordering depositions taken and hearing evidence as to the trial of the negro, no transcript of the evidence having been sent up to the court."[1969]

Robert H. Prescott's defense in the show-cause hearing explains what happened. He argued a motion for a new trial and was given permission to appeal, but did not prepare the bill of exceptions because he was not retained to appeal the case and because a "reversal of the case could not be had in the Supreme Court, and acting at once began a movement toward getting a commutation of the sentence to life imprisonment through the extension of executive clemency by the Governor."[1970] Prescott offered the Rev. Griffith's affidavit to support his own case.

The Rev. Griffith said, "I listened to the evidence and was of the opinion that the only hope of the defendant lay in an appeal to executive clemency for a commutation of the sentence to life imprisonment. There was evidence of a confession on the part of the defendant made at three different times, the last time being made in jail, all of which was admitted by the Court. I advised Mr. Prescott and with the defendant and we came to the conclusion that the best thing to do was not to preserve the evidence in the case by a transcript thereof and a bill of exceptions."[1971]

He continued, "I further make oath that Mr. Prescott was never employed to carry the case further than the Criminal Court of Shelby County. I heard Mr. Prescott tell the court that his connection with the case ceased at that trial but that the prisoner himself desired to appeal the case."[1972] No record can be found regarding what, if anything, the Supreme Court ordered with regard to counsel Prescott.

Counsel Spraggins continued to press Johnson's case after the Tennessee Supreme Court had rendered its decision. In petitions to rehear he argued it was a constitutional violation for the case to go forward without a lawyer at each step.[1973] He also argued that the statute, which made it a crime punishable as rape to "carnally know or abuse" a child under the age of twelve, meant proof of sexual intercourse was necessary.[1974] Spraggins cited no Tennessee cases. The Tennessee Supreme Court issued no opinion or order regarding these petitions.

Henry Johnson was hanged inside the Shelby County jail on August 8, 1908.

Johnson ate well before his execution and was given two cigars with each meal.[1975] He walked to the gallows smoking a cigarette. He was preceded by a notable black minister, the Rev. George Washington, who intoned the 23rd Psalm. The minister then read the 119th Psalm and offered a prayer.

Asked by Sheriff Monteverde if he had anything to say, he denied guilt and insisted he had been wrongly convicted, but he forgave everyone. He asked anyone who was watching to raise their hand if they had "anything against me." The girl's father, uncles and grandfather were present but did not raise their hands, nor did anyone else. Then he asked if there was anyone who "hasn't anything against me." This time the sheriff raised his hand (again no one else did), and the sheriff said that no one had any ill-will against him.[1976]

Johnson concluded, "I am prepared to go and meet my God. Go ahead. May God be with you all." He also declared he believed the Lord had ordained he was to be hanged, and after calling blessings on the head Sheriff Monteverde called to him to go ahead."[1977] Johnson bowed his head toward the deputy sheriff bringing the death cap and said, "Put it on."[1978]

Johnson's mumbled voice was heard under the cap. The drop was clean and his neck was broken. He was cut down ten minutes later. Apparently, no attempt had been made to ask the governor to intervene.[1979]

At the time, the rope that hanged Johnson drew more attention than his culpability. At the time of Johnson's hanging it was owned by Sheriff Shipp of Hamilton County, who loaned it to Sheriff Monteverde. The hemp rope was an inch and one-eighth in diameter.[1980]

A hundred years after Henry Johnson's execution, death penalty researcher Margaret Vandiver refers to Johnson's crime as an "alleged assault."[1981] She offered four reasons for suggesting Johnson was probably innocent. First, he proclaimed his innocence to the end. Second, the jury seemed to have had a difficult time reaching a verdict. It failed to include on its verdict the form language saying guilty "as shown in the indictment." When the judge sent it back to include the language, the jury took three hours to accomplish it. Third, the jury did not actually recommend the death penalty, saying in their verdict, "We leave him to the mercy of the Court."[1982]

But the most compelling reason, according to Vandiver, was Sheriff Frank L. Monteverde's statement, "I do not think that negro is guilty."[1983] Two hours before the execution he read the death warrant to Johnson and made the statement at that time. Much earlier, on June 28, 1908, the sheriff had provided an affidavit in support of lawyer Prescott. The sheriff said he was very much surprised at the conviction. "There was no evidence to the effect that the child had blood upon its clothes or that her undergarments were torn."[1984]

Despite Sheriff Monteverde's belief that Johnson was innocent, he had a motive to say it and to hang him. It was an election year and former members of the grand jury had published notices in the newspaper that the sheriff was not doing his job. "Sheriff Monteverde Refuses to Enforce the Law," said one notice published a week before the execution, complaining about his refusal to take action against "disreputable road houses."[1985]

By hanging Johnson, Sheriff Monteverde demonstrated he was doing his duty to uphold the law regardless of his personal feelings. Apparently, this was the second capital case tried under the new statute which had raised the victim's age from ten to twelve, and some confusion existed about what constituted the crime.[1986] This was because there were two statutes on the same subject. One spoke of "carnally know and abuse" and the other spoke of "an assault and battery with intent to unlawfully and carnally know" a female under the age of ten (or twelve).[1987]

Another Shelby County defendant, Harvey DeBerry, had been executed under the latter statute, but the proof showed a partial penetration and a slight rupture of the hymen.[1988] The first statute encompassed these actions, with the latter statute subsumed in the former. The sheriff was likely confused on the matter. So was Henry Johnson. In his confessions to various people following his arrest, he admitted he *attempted* to have sexual contact with her. However, because he did not succeed he "did not think he had done any wrong."[1989]

1909

Dave D. Edwards, white, age 34. *Murder.*

The crime was committed on March 20, 1908, at 9:30 P.M. in the home of Mr. and Mrs. John W. Davis in the community of Alton Park, near Chattanooga, in Hamilton County. The killer was a notoriously bad man who had been employed by the W.J. Oliver Construction Company, a railroad contractor. He was the conductor of a work train. The victim was John W. Davis, white, age forty-four, the superintendent of the company. The Davis family was from Denmark, South Carolina.

On the day of the shooting, the construction locomotive was being repaired and Edwards and others drank whiskey all day in the roundhouse. The liquor made him violent and he got into a brawl with two fellow workers. His head and face were bloody. Davis appeared. When Edwards tried to talk to him, he refused, citing Edwards's drinking. Edwards boasted he had killed eight men, all Negroes. Davis said he didn't care how many men Edwards had killed; he was fired. When Davis left, Edwards told witnesses he'd killed men for "less than that," and would get even before morning.[1990]

Edwards was staggering drunk by the time he left, about 4:30 P.M. He went to his mother's house, where he lived. Over her protest he left at about 9:00 P.M., taking a streetcar. He did not appear intoxicated to the other riders. Edwards knocked on Davis's door. Davis had been lying in bed fully clothed with his wife and three-year-old daughter. When Davis opened the door, a cursing Edwards pushed his way inside. He fired three fatal shots into Davis, who fell to the floor. Davis's daughter, thinking this was a game, scrambled off the bed and snuggled close to him, trying to awaken him by touching his cheek.

Edwards ran, spending a few days in Georgia and other East Tennessee towns until he was finally captured without a struggle in Trenton, attempting a getaway to Alabama. Brought to Chattanooga, he was tried quickly and given the death sentence. He had three lawyers, all appointed by the court, but insisted upon questioning witnesses and taking the stand. His defense was insanity, in particular, temporary insanity because of intoxication.

On the stand, Edwards's statements failed to support any notion of insanity. First, at the time he killed Davis, he was out on bond for the killing of Sam Brooks, black, age unknown. He claimed the shooting, which occurred in a rail yard, was self-defense. Edwards had been tried three times with hung juries each time. Following the second mistrial, the sheriff had released him because he was too troublesome in the jail, and because Edwards said he knew Breathitt County, Kentucky, and insisted he could help bring wife-killer Ed Turner back to Chattanooga. Edwards's third trial in the Brooks case coincided with Ed Turner's trial, which Edwards watched with great interest.

Edwards's testimony showed him as a boastful killer. He said that he had shot and killed the superintendent of the Black Raven Coal Company in Kentucky eight years earlier — but in self-defense after the man had shot him three times. The Kentucky jury convicted him of malicious shooting, and the jury gave him a seven-year sentence. However, the maximum penalty was five years and the judge imposed that term. The governor commuted this to four years, and he served only two years because of good behavior.

Edwards said he had shot at least fourteen men, but none other than the Kentucky man and Brooks had died. These shootings occurred in various Breathitt County feuds, and during his work as a strikebreaker in Chicago.

The chief issue on appeal was Edwards's sanity at the time of the killing. A doctor testified that Edwards suffered "cyclical insanity" and was insane at the time. However, the doctor said Edwards knew right from wrong, as evidenced by his flight.

The insanity defense was supported by his mother. She explained that she and Edwards's father were first cousins and named several cousins who were insane, some dying in insane asylums. The father was insane at his death and all ten of her children were insane or feeble-minded. She explained that her son suffered a head injury as a child, was epileptic, and frequently had "spells" (which she could see coming) in which he became extremely violent, especially when drinking. He had also been discharged from the Army during the Spanish-American War for shooting at an officer. A medical board found him suffering from "homicidal and suicidal mania."[1991]

The Tennessee Supreme Court found no competent evidence that Edwards was insane at the time of the shooting, citing the rule of voluntary intoxication and the testimony of his threats as well as the circumstances of his flight. His capture, in the Trenton train station, came only when he inadvertently took his hand from the pistol he was carrying in his pocket, while staring directly at law men.[1992]

The practice at the time was to have the defendant in the courtroom when the decision was announced by the Supreme Court. Edwards responded by thanking the judges and said he was sorry his hanging had not been sooner. Because he was such a loud, violent and boisterous prisoner, the Knoxville sheriff and jailors were glad when he was taken back to Chattanooga following the appeal. Every account of Edwards's crime included a discussion of his jail antics. Once he had to be subdued by water from a four-inch hose. Another time he was knocked out with ammonia sprayed into his cell following an aborted hostage taking.

Back in the Chattanooga jail, waiting his execution while family and lawyers appealed for commutation from the governor, Edwards regaled everyone within earshot with profanities mixed with stories of his criminal adventures. He told a long story of walking through the woods for miles following an Ed Turner kinsman, finally going to a cave where he was certain Turner would be hiding, only to discover an old hermit living there. The story included Edwards's assertion that he walked the distance in his stocking feet so he would not be heard. He asserted that his work had led to the capture of Ed Turner. This was false, corrected the newspaper. Turner was simply found in a remote Kentucky jail where he had been held on an old charge.

The appeal for commutation was based on affidavits asserting that Edwards was insane, and asked Governor Ham Patterson to send Edwards to a commission for examination.[1993] The governor respited Edwards seven weeks, but finally decided he did not have the authority to send him to such a commission and concluded from reading the transcript that Edwards deserved no help.

In jail, Edwards spoke lovingly of his mother and sister. The former had given him a hoodoo charm which she had gotten from a fortune teller. He wore the charm around his neck.[1994] He wrote a several-hundred-page memoir which he gave his mother, and on the day of his execution gave the sheriff twelve letters to send to various people. (He broke down sobbing in the night as he wrote one of the letters.) Edwards also told the sheriff that he had two letters in his pocket that the sheriff was to retrieve before burial.

Edwards declared that anyone who wanted to visit him in the jail could do so, provided they paid him twenty-five cents. In this manner, he raised $180 for his mother and sister. One of the visitors who paid a quarter was the Rev. Park W. Taylor. To him, Edwards said, "Go pray for yourself, but don't bother about me." Edwards had earlier professed religion, but by the time of the execution was wholly irreligious, dismissing his earlier statements as occurring during "my crazy days." According to the media, "In his mind there seemed to be no doubt but that perdition was his destiny and he boasted he would hold a high office in that place."[1995] Edwards admitted that he was "in slavery to the liquor habit."[1996]

Sheriff Sam A. Conner delayed the actual hanging until about 4:30 P.M., saying he wanted to give Edwards the full amount of his last day, reckoning that the day ended at sunset. His motive was to give Edwards time to profess religion to the eager throng in the jail, in particular, to the Rev. Mason, pastor of the Methodist Episcopal church. However, Edwards turned him away, saying the congregation needed the prayers, not him.

Edwards continued to shock and amuse until the end. When asked how he liked the jail, he said the food was better than in the Knoxville jail and joked he was being fed well in order to make him heavier so his neck would break. He said, "If I was allowed nothing but the usual fare, I would go up instead of down when the trap was sprung."[1997] When the sheriff came to read the death warrant, he said he had already heard death warrants. He ate a large breakfast, but declined a lunch, saying, "I expect it is easier to die on an empty stomach than a full one." Later, when asked if he wanted a last meal about four o'clock, he demanded oysters. To his delight, they were offered and he ate them with gusto, and looked expectantly for more. When told that the law allowed him to have three friends attend the execution, he replied that anyone who would pay him a dollar could be one of the friends. The sheriff made him take off the hoodoo charm, fearing it might interfere with the noose. Edwards replied he had little faith in its life-giving properties anyway.[1998]

David D. Edwards was hanged inside the Chattanooga jail on January 28, 1909. Edwards mounted the gallows wearing a new shirt, suit and shoes. Someone had given him violets, which he put in his lapel. On the gallows he said he had a clear conscience about killing Davis but did not explain why. He addressed the crowded jail with these words: "I am not a physical coward but if I came here at this time and asked God to save my soul I would be one. My life has been one of shame and crime. When I professed to be religious, I lived the life, but recently I have professed to be a dog. I desire to die like a dog. I could break down here on the gallows and cry, but it would not do any good, so go out and try to save young boys and girls. I am not claiming insanity on this, my last day on earth. I have abused the resources that were given me and I have been guilty of the most wicked deeds. The law is just and I am only about to receive what I deserve."[1999]

When Edwards finished, the Rev. Mason disregarded Edwards's wish that he not intervene, and stepped forward and offered a fervent prayer. Edwards now had the death cap over his head. It was the same one used on Ed Turner the previous year. He said to the minister, "Cut it short." As soon as the minister stopped, Edwards was dropped. His neck was broken and there were no convulsions or contortions. He was allowed to hang twelve minutes before being cut down and his body was placed directly into the coffin. One of the letters in his pocket was for his mother; the other asked the public to assist his mother and sister, whom he feared would starve to death without help. Because neither woman claimed his body, he was buried in a pauper's grave. The newspaper said the cost of prosecuting and executing Edwards was $415, which included $218 for the cost of his trial, and $30 to the sheriff for overseeing the execution.[2000]

In 1932, one of the jailors present explained that Sheriff Conner asked Edwards if he had any last words, apparently hoping for a profession of faith. Edwards, with the cap over his head, said, "I'll see you in hell with a bucket of peas — let her go!"[2001]

Frank Gilbreath, black, age 31. *Murder.*

The crime was committed between 8:00 and 9:00 P.M. on September 24, 1908, on the farm owned by Dr. J.M. Hudson, about ten miles from Fayetteville, in Lincoln County. The killer had been hiding in a peach orchard, waiting to see who came to the back door of a cabin ninety feet away from the main house. The cabin was occupied by Ad Moore, a black woman who served as cook for the Hudson household, and two black field hands, Duke Taylor and Boyd Buchanan. The victim was Ed Pigg, white, age thirty. He was a bachelor farmer who lived a couple of miles from the Hudson house, as did the killer.

The reason for the shooting was explained by the Tennessee Supreme Court: "It is abundantly shown in the proof, that the deceased, Ed Pigg, a bachelor, had been living in an unlawful relation with Ad Moore, and this had continued from the time she cooked at his father's house some years before until the night he was killed."[2002] The killer also had a relationship with Ad Moore, claimed to be engaged to her, but was frustrated that she would not marry him. She had told Gilbreath that on the night in question she would be away from her house. Gilbreath suspected she was welcoming Ed Pigg that night, and he waited for the opportunity to kill him.

Although five people within fifty yards heard the gunshot, no one saw the defendant. Dr. Hudson and his brother were talking on the porch, facing away from the cabin. Even if they had been looking they could not have seen the back door because it was away from them. Their sister was inside the house. The hands had finished eating in another cabin and were walking down the road in the opposite direction. Each person looked around and saw no one, although there was an upset in the chicken yard as if someone had passed through it.

The Hudson men looked around with lanterns, saw nothing and went to bed. At midnight they were awakened by the sound of a bucket being dropped in the well and heard the voices of the hands talking, on their way back to their cabins. When the hands got to Buchanan's cabin, they were surprised to see Gilbreath lying on Buchanan's bed. He got up and left, telling the men not to tell anyone he had been there.

The next day, Ad Moore told a hand she thought she saw a body some distance from the house in a thicket. The body was first seen by Dr. Hudson's brother; he summoned the sheriff, who held a coroner's inquest. The coroner's jury determined that Ed Pigg had been shot once through the neck, which killed him instantly. It also said that Frank Gilbreath was the likely killer and that Ad Moore was an accomplice.

At the jail, Ad Moore explained that Pigg had come to her cabin and said, "Open the door."[2003] It was unlocked and as she opened it partially, Pigg was shot by Gilbreath, although she had not seen or talked to him that evening. When one of the Hudson brothers called out to her inquiring about the gunshot, she had not answered, but a voice (apparently Gilbreath's) said, "She's not here."

Frightened that she might be the shooter's next victim, Ad Moore took a pillow and quilt and hid under her bed. Later that night Gilbreath came to the cabin and told her that he would carry the body away, but he wanted her to clean up the blood on and around the doorway. She agreed to clean up the blood. Gilbreath remarked he had "played the devil." She responded, "Yes, I know you have, and I haven't got narry lie to tell for you."[2004]

With no direct evidence linking Gilbreath to the killing, the state offered the testimony of witnesses, all black, that he had threatened Ad Moore if she continued to see Ed Pigg, that he had aimed a rifle at Pigg on Christmas the year earlier, in company with two witnesses who scolded him not to shoot, in part because they were not sure it was Ed Pigg.[2005] Gilbreath also had gotten into a fight with Green Taylor (father of Duke Taylor) because he had "an improper relation" with Ad Moore.[2006] The defense made an attempt to impeach her by having her admit that she also had such a relation with Boyd Buchanan, some six years before.

Gilbreath insisted that he was at home at the time of the killing and this was supported by the testimony of his parents, although they had not seen him go to bed, but heard him say he was doing so. The court found this circumstantial evidence sufficient to convict, and turned aside the argument that there was no proof of premeditation by ruling that Gilbreath's actions of hiding in the dark constituted "lying in wait."[2007]

A few days before the execution, Gilbreath confessed to the sheriff, admitting he shot Pigg, but he said that Boyd Buchanan was implicated to the extent that he had given Gilbreath an overcoat to wear, as well as the pistol, and that he came back to give him the bullets, which he had forgotten. He said that he had no part in moving the body, which was done by the other farm hands. According to the newspaper, this story was not believed because Gilbreath's bloody overalls and shoes were found hidden in a barn loft.[2008]

Gilbreath was executed on March 2, 1909, inside the Lincoln County jail. He was attended the night before by a black Methodist minister and had asked to be baptized. The sheriff permitted this, but said it had to be inside the jail and by sprinkling.

Gilbreath was pinioned but walked to the trap without faltering. His "voice had a tone of despair and his general appearance bespokened a shrinking from his impending doom."[2009] Once there, he asked to pray and did so kneeling, speaking in a sing-song voice. As the cap was put over his head, he asked to see his father. The sheriff said he would have been glad to have done that but there was not enough time now. Without warning the trap was sprung. Gilbreath dropped four feet and his muscles twitched. He was cut down fourteen minutes later.

Gilbreath was hanged with the same rope used to execute Charles W. Baird in the same jail on May 24, 1907. While Baird had ignored the construction of the gallows outside his cell, Gilbreath studied the apparatus with fixed concentration. The newspaper said, "Frank Gilbreath's parents are good darkies but their boys seem to be a blood-thirsty lot. One of them, John, is in the penitentiary for having killed his wife and a negro man, George Johnson, at Boons Hill. He was sentenced to hang but the Governor commuted it to life imprisonment."[2010]

John Gilbreath's killings were dramatic. He claimed he was taking his shotgun home from his mother's house and left it in the graveyard of a church where his pregnant wife was attending a church supper. Among the crowd was George Johnson, a man Gilbreath and others thought was her paramour. He gave her twenty-five cents "in a tantalizing way" in front of John and the crowd. John went outside and got the double-barreled shotgun. He hid it muzzle down under his long coat. As Johnson stood at a table talking to his wife's sister, Gilbreath shot him, killing him instantly.[2011]

The church members stampeded for the doors. Gilbreath kept the shotgun at his waist, swinging it from side to side, in part to avoid the panic-stricken crowd. As his wife left the relative safety of the crowd and ran along a church wall, Gilbreath shot her in the thigh and she died within an hour. Gilbreath was only tried for murdering his wife. He claimed that after he fired the first shot someone shot him with a pistol. It grazed his nose and cheek. He insisted that his gun's discharge toward his wife was accidental. Witnesses said he was grazed by the pistol shot after he killed his wife, and deliberately watched her running about as he swung the shotgun.

The chief issue on appeal was whether it was prejudicial for the court to order Gilbreath tried for his wife's murder first, when his lawyers were under the impression he was going to be tried that morning for killing Johnson, who was killed first. The Tennessee Supreme Court said there was no error because the facts were similar and close in time.[2012]

Virtually everyone involved in the case, including the judge, district attorney, all the jurors, most of the town lawyers and a host of John Gilbreath's neighbors, signed a petition seeking clemency. They argued that Gilbreath was "insanely jealous of his wife and had some ground therefore." Echoing Judge Wilkes's sentiment, they agreed that Gilbreath "thought no doubt he was upholding the sanctity of his marriage relations." Governor McMinn echoed those words when he commuted the sentence.[2013]

William Mitchell, white, age 42. *Murder.*

The crime was committed at 7:30 P.M. on April 24, 1908, in the store of E.S. Vanderford in the village of Florence, in Rutherford County. The killer was a native of McMinnville, in Warren County, but had spent the last several years moving about various Tennessee cities, and had served as a strikebreaker in Chicago. At the time of the killing, he was the railroad station agent at Florence. He slept upstairs in the station, but took his meals at the Vanderford residence, about one hundred yards from the store, and ninety yards from the depot. The victim was Squire H. William Hindman, white, age forty-four, the store manager. He also took his meals at the Vanderford home.[2014]

Mitchell accompanied Hindman to the store and after Hindman had opened the cash drawer, Mitchell attempted to take it. Hindman put up a struggle. As the two grappled with Mitchell's pistol, a shot was fired, striking the area behind the counter, and another shot hit Mitchell's finger. After shooting Hindman, he took the cash drawer and Hindman's lantern and walked down the track. His bleeding finger left a trail along the ground. He caught several trains and made his way to Smithville, where he saw a doctor. The doctor referred him to a surgeon who amputated the finger.

Hindman's body was found the next day behind the counter. He had been shot four times. There were footprints on his body, caused by Mitchell's getting the cash drawer. Mitchell did not take the stand but a confession he gave was used against him. No one testified on his behalf in any manner.[2015] He tried to argue that first-degree murder was not shown because there was no premeditation. The Tennessee Supreme Court said the felony murder doctrine applied because the killing occurred in the act of larceny.[2016]

Both Mitchell and Cecil Palmer were kept in the Davidson County jail. Many came to see them, often inquiring about their souls. Mitchell had been befriended by the Rev. Oscar Nolen during his trial in Murfreesboro. He continued to counsel Mitchell, who was baptized two days before his execution in a bathtub at the jail. "He seemed to be very strongly affected and shook hands with all present as tears rolled down his face."[2017]

While kept at the Nashville jail waiting transfer to the prison, Mitchell appeared to be in a "state of deep despondency and despair," but by the time of the execution had gathered himself and asserted that he killed Hindman in self-defense. "I have been forgiven of my sins and I am going to Heaven. I feel that I can shake hands with Brother Hindman, and that he will understand. I did not mean to do him any harm."[2018]

The day before the execution, Mitchell and Cecil Palmer (q.v.) were taken in separate open taxicabs to the prison. Mitchell talked freely about places he knew, having worked in Nashville in the past. Townsfolk understood the nature of the last ride and gawked at the condemned men, each accompanied by deputies riding with them. William Mitchell was hanged at the Main Prison in Nashville on October 1, 1909.[2019]

The night before the execution Mitchell was attended by two ministers.[2020] He mounted the gallows with a steady step, but made no last words. He was asked if he had anything to say after the cap was pulled over his head. He said, "All right." This was a double execution. Mitchell was hanged alongside Cecil Palmer, who maintained his innocence. Mitchell was survived by his estranged wife and children, but no arrangements had been made for his body and he was buried in the prison graveyard.

Mitchell and Palmer were the first men to be executed under the new law (1909) that required all executions be held at the Main Prison. The newspaper reported that everyone was pleased with the new system, "doing away, as it does, with the assembling of curious crowds and undue excitement."[2021] Because the statute did not allow any journalists to attend, Warden B.M. Rice, who opposed capital punishment, refused to allow any to watch the actual hangings.

There was one unnamed dissenter. The newspaper explained, "One man said that, as the purpose of an execution is, by the horror of it, to deter others from the commission of crime, no good purpose is served by performing a hanging so privately that those who might be deterred know nothing of it." The man was quoted, "These executions today were a shock to this penal community, which is already expiating its offenses."[2022]

Cecil Palmer (aka Carl Palmer and Carrus Palmer), black, age 23. *Rape.*

The crime was committed at 5:30 P.M. on July 4, 1908, in the victim's home near the railroad water tank in the town of Lebanon, Wilson County. The victim was Mrs. Sophronia J. Yates, white, age thirty-two. Mrs. Yates was home alone with her two small children, a daughter and a deaf-mute son, age nine. Her husband was a railroad superintendent who was at work two hundred yards away.

Palmer, described as a dark mulatto, had gotten off the train at the water tower, somewhat intoxicated. He later claimed to have been drinking with a black woman he knew near the tower. Palmer entered the house and confronted Sophronia. A prolonged struggle took place. She struck him below the eye with an iron stove hook, leaving a gash. She scratched his face with her fingernails. She was beaten severely and was nearly senseless when he pushed her outdoors and raped her. The rape was witnessed by her son.

Palmer ran away and Sophronia's screams attracted her husband, who arrived on a motorcycle. Told what happened, he rode in the direction Palmer had gone, armed with a shotgun. He found Palmer in the woods. "The negro was marched back into the presence of the wife, who positively identified him, and the little mute child showed, in pantomime, signs of both terror and anger."[2023]

A mob formed within minutes and Palmer would have been lynched but for the insistence by the Yateses that he be tried by law. The wounds on his face were still fresh and bleeding, his trousers were still unbuttoned in front and he had dirt on his knees from where Sophronia had been thrown to the ground.

Trial began on September 22, 1908. Palmer denied any involvement in the crime. He insisted the injuries to his face occurred in Nashville when he walked through a thicket. The railroad conductor said he bore no facial injuries when he was allowed off the train at the water tower. Mrs. Yates tearfully testified that she had been raped. Will Davis and Dovey Palmer, whom Palmer said would testify about the time he received the scratches, did not appear at trial.

The Tennessee Supreme Court affirmed the conviction on November 11, 1908, turning aside the contention that jurors had been seated who had read about the case in the newspaper. The court said the proof showed they affirmed they could be fair and had not made up their minds.[2024]

Ordinarily, Palmer would have been executed within thirty to sixty days, but his case was again before the Supreme Court on July 27, 1909. This was because the General Assembly had amended the death penalty statute to provide that all executions must be held at the Main Prison in Nashville, not in the county where the person was convicted.[2025] The new statute said the execution must be held "in privacy and seclusion, and that no witnesses shall be admitted to such executions except a priest or minister of the gospel, the prison physician, the sheriff of the county in which the crime was committed, and such other attendants as are necessary to properly carry out and perform such legal executions."[2026]

The statute also said, "Members of the family of the condemned prisoner may be present and witness the execution."[2027] Palmer's counsel argued this sentence made a substantial change in the statute so that the caption did not sufficiently specify what the amendment actually provided. The Supreme Court said this was not so, and that the caption fully allowed this modest change.

The court also turned aside the argument that when the Supreme Court adjourned its December 1908 term on April 6, 1909, and began hearing cases in Jackson for the April 1909 term, that it had adjourned "finally" and was in error to assemble on July 27, 1909, to continue its December 1908 term.[2028] The court said there was nothing wrong with this because it was not forbidden by statute or the state constitution.[2029] In short, the Supreme Court's decision affirming Palmer's death sentence was reaffirmed.

Each step in the legal wrangling was mentioned in Nashville's new African American newspaper, *The Globe*, and fostered the notion that Palmer was innocent or had been denied a fair trial. He maintained his innocence to the end.

In a taste of what was to come each time the Tennessee General Assembly amended the death penalty law, Palmer's lawyers filed a writ of habeas corpus in state court, which was denied. They went to a federal circuit judge, who denied the writ. Finally, they took the matter to another federal circuit judge, Horace Lurton. (He would be appointed to the United States Supreme Court the next year.) Lurton said the statutory change was de minimus and did not amount to an ex post facto law. The earlier law had allowed three friends, not necessarily family members, to attend the condemned man. He also ruled that there was no sound reason to allow an appeal to the United States Supreme Court.[2030]

Palmer was attended by two black Pentecostal ministers who urged him to admit the rape for the benefit of his soul. Palmer's white lawyer expressed the personal belief that Palmer was innocent and told the newspapers he hoped Palmer had made a private confession to one of the black ministers. He had not.

Cecil Palmer and William Mitchell were kept in the Nashville jail until the day before their executions. Scores of people visited them. They were taken in separate open taxicabs to the prison. Palmer was executed by hanging at the Main Prison on October 1, 1909. He was taken from his cell in the "death house," where he had already been tied with leather cuffs and straps, but was able to make a shuffling walk to the gallows, located on the same level. Both the gallows and the ropes were out of sight, covered by a denim drape, as were the coffins, which were below the trap. The trap itself was initially covered with a rug until the men were told to step on it. The trap was sprung by a lever outside the building, with the executioner unable to see the drop. Palmer was executed alongside William Mitchell, who confessed his crime, but insisted it was self-defense. Each man dropped six feet. Palmer's heart stopped in six minutes, Mitchell's in twelve.

One of the reasons both Palmer and Mitchell asserted some form of innocence was that the day before they were executed Governor Patterson respited the death sentence of Virgil Lee, white, and later commuted his punishment to life imprisonment.[2031] They hoped he would do the same for them.

Witnesses allowed to attend the men were uniformly complimentary of the way Warden B.M. Rice handled the dual execution, which he opposed. Newspaper reporters were barred from seeing the execution because the new statute did not expressly allow them.[2032]

The black minister who attended Palmer, the Rev. George A. Goeing, said, "I have this day received a lesson in the humanitarian method of dealing with condemned men. I want the people of my race to know that the Warden and his assistants did everything possible for the comfort and well being of the two men condemned to death, and that there was no shadow of discrimination or distinction between the treatment accorded the white man and the black one."[2033] Palmer's wife told the warden she would send an undertaker for the body but changed her mind and he was buried beside Mitchell in the prison cemetery.

1910

Bryce McDonald (aka Brice McDonald), black, age 35. *Murder.*

The crime was committed on July 30, 1909, at the rural farm home the victim shared with her husband, who was the killer's brother. The home was near the Perryville community, in Decatur County. The details of the crime are unknown except that Bryce McDonald shot Tishie McDonald, black, age thirty-one, seven times with a pistol. "Jealousy was the cause of the killing."[2034] One account said he shot her, left, but returned and fired another shot into her body.[2035] The killer then turned the gun on himself, firing three times, inflicting superficial wounds. He was arrested and jailed shortly after the killing.

McDonald was highly intoxicated at the time of the killing and said he remembered nothing of the crime. He said he awoke in jail on August 1, 1909, and was told of it. He never denied the killing, but claimed lack of responsibility because of his intoxication. He was brought to trial four months later and ordered executed on February 6, 1910. The governor granted three respites to study the case. McDonald's appeal to the Tennessee Supreme Court cannot be located.

At the time, men waiting execution were kept at the Nashville jail until the day before the execution. No one visited him in the jail and he spent the time from June 20, 1910, until the execution in Bible reading and was never "cast down or boisterous." He graciously offered words of encouragement to everyone who bade him good-bye at the Nashville jail, the day before he was taken to the prison for execution the next day.

At the Nashville jail and prison, McDonald was attended by two black ministers, including the Rev. Preston Taylor, and declared, "I am a very poor man and all I have is my life. The law is perfectly welcome to that. If it will pay the penalty, I am ready to meet death."[2036] But he also said, "I don't worry no more about being hung. The governor has been mighty good to me so far and I know he won't let me swing. I worried a lot before, but I done quit. I know's I's innocent and perhaps you folks might find it out some day."[2037]

Warden B.M. Rice had provided McDonald an entire new suit of clothes for the execution, including underwear. McDonald dressed with care and said, "Clothes make quite a change in a man."[2038]

He was hanged at the Main Prison in Nashville at 6:00 A.M. on October 3, 1910.

McDonald ate a hearty breakfast and went to the gallows without saying a word. Warden Rice, who vocally opposed the death penalty, barred reporters from the execution and refused to give the newspapers any details of the execution. Earlier, it had been reported that McDonald had been joking, playing cards, smoking cigarettes, and saying the governor would commute his sentence. Warden Rice told a reporter this was untrue.

John Casson, black, age 24. *Murder.*

The crime was committed at 2:00 A.M. December 18, 1908, on Florida Street near Gaines Alley, in downtown Memphis, in Shelby County. The killers were John Casson and Mack Collins, alias "River George," black. Both had long police records. They held pistols on the victim, Martin Christenson, white, age twenty-three, and his two white companions, Leo Kirksky and Alfred Houseman. The trio worked for the railroad and had been saloon-hopping.

The other two handed over the little money they had, six dollars. When Christenson was ordered to give up his money he balked. He was carrying a month's salary, twenty-five dollars. He attempted to knock Collins down and was shot in the abdomen by Casson. Christenson, a boilermaker, was taken by ambulance to the city hospital. "Ambulance surgeon Sam Wadley, who examined Christenson's wound as he was placed in the ambulance, stated that there was little hope for his recovery."[2039] Christenson died several days later.

Joe Commel, black, was arrested two days after the Christenson shooting on a charge of killing another black man in a Memphis railroad yard a week earlier. He told the police that he had been robbed of five dollars in the same location a few minutes before the Christenson shooting. He said he saw the robbery-shooting and named Casson and Collins.[2040] Casson was arrested and identified by Kirksky two days later.[2041]

The pair was convicted on November 25, 1909, the jury finding there were mitigating circumstances. "There was much criticism of the verdict by court officials and others who heard the case, it being declared that the evidence showed nothing to warrant the finding of circumstances mitigating the crime."[2042] The judge ordered the men executed. The case was appealed to the Tennessee Supreme Court but the opinion cannot be located. The Supreme Court ordered them executed on August 10, 1910.[2043]

The two escaped from the Shelby County jail about a month before the scheduled execution. Casson was captured shortly thereafter, but Collins was still at large. Collins dictated a letter that was sent to the Memphis Police Chief, in which Collins said that Casson would admit the crime.

When told of the letter, Casson responded, "River George is a bad nigger and the yellow nigger with him was the one. I didn't even know this George and was working at the time of the murder. He says I will confess, does he? Well, you know, boss, I can't confess to anything I didn't do. 'Fo' God, I didn't do it and this nigger George knows I didn't."[2044]

Casson was attended at the prison by three clergymen and asked to be baptized on the morning of his execution in a pool at the prison foundry. He was calm as he mounted the scaffold, saying nothing. His body was sent to his mother in Memphis.

Casson was one of three men executed on November 9, 1910. The others were Moses Cook and Love Bond. Warden B.M. Rice used the opportunity to speak out once more against capital punishment.[2045] "River George" was never executed by the state of Tennessee. What happened to him is unknown.

Moses B. Cook, white, age 30. *Murder.*

The crime was committed at 6:30 P.M. on September 14, 1908, at the corner of Monroe and Third Street, in Memphis, in Shelby County. The victim was Dora Kinger Cook, white, age thirty-one, the killer's wife. No one saw the shooting. Several witnesses saw the couple arguing. Cook claimed he was so intoxicated he did not intend or even understand that he had shot Dora. She was alive when taken to the city hospital. Cook thought he had only shot her in the wrist of her upraised hand, but the bullet had entered her chest. The first witness at the scene said he saw blood on her chest.[2046]

The state's theory was that Cook had waited for his wife to walk by and shot her when she refused to reconcile with him. Dora had left a note the day before saying, "I'm gone." But the note also said where he could find his pistol, which she had hidden. The couple had several loud arguments in the two months before the shooting. On one occasion Cook threatened his wife with a straight razor. After she left home the day of the killing, a friend asked Cook where she was. He replied, "In hell, I hope."

Immediately after the shooting, Cook was knocked to the ground by Reed Ferris, who was walking with his wife, Dora's sister, to meet her. Police were summoned and Cook was arrested and taken to jail. J.E. Currie and his wife, Emma, another of Dora's sisters, identified Dora's body at the hospital.

The case was appealed to the Tennessee Supreme Court but the opinion cannot be located. An issue on appeal was whether certain jurors who had read about the case in the newspaper were properly seated. Cook also asserted that the state failed to prove the corpus delicti because it was not shown that Dora Cook was the same person who had been taken to the hospital from the scene of the shooting. The proof showed that a woman was shot with a revolver at Monroe and Third. "The evidence discloses the fact that she was not killed. The identity of this party shot is not disclosed either by direct proof or by circumstances. There is no evidence that the woman shot was ever removed from this spot. What became of her we do not know, according to his brief."[2047]

Cook maintained his innocence, that is, he did not remember the killing, and was convinced the governor would commute his sentence until an hour before his execution. Cook said, "If I killed my wife, I killed the only woman I ever loved." He continued, "Let whiskey be gone. It has brought me all my troubles and I would give anything if I could recall the past. Not only has it brought trouble and misery to me, but also to my family. I lived happily with my wife — until I began to drink. I want this message given, especially to the young men."[2048]

He said he had made peace with God and was ready to die. He gave a minister a Woodman button to be delivered to J.A. Fowler of Keysburg, Kentucky, an old enemy, saying it would show his forgiveness. The New Testament he had read while in jail he wanted sent to his sister, Mrs. Sarah Fowler, in Armistead, Kentucky.[2049] Moses B. Cook was executed by hanging on November 9, 1910, at the Main Prison in Nashville. This was the same day as Love Bond and John Casson. They died side-by-side. The triple execution prompted Warden Rice to declare once again he was opposed to capital punishment.[2050]

Love Bond, black, age 25. *Murder.*

The crime was committed on the morning of June 13, 1909, at the home of Sallie Cross, near the community of Vildo, in Hardeman County about five miles from the home of Love Bond and his wife. The victim was Bond's wife, Florence Roberson Bond, black, age twenty-eight. The couple had two children from their eight-year marriage. They had many domestic troubles and were frequently separated because he "occasionally whipped her and she usually left him, but after remaining apart a while, she would return to him and live with him again."[2051]

Mrs. Bond's sister was ill and in bed and Florence was sitting next to her. Also present was Tom Norment, black. When Bond asked Florence how she felt, she said to leave her alone and stop following her.[2052] She got up, got her sister a drink of water, and left the room to seek a doctor. The couple had some words and he pushed her arm as she went out. Just outside the house, she said, "Don't follow me, and let me alone!" A shot rang out and Florence came running back into her sister's room. Bond followed and shot her in the back. She fell on the floor beside her sister's bed and he shot her again. Bond ran and was taken by a posse. His empty pistol was found in his pocket.

Proof showed that Bond said the morning of the shooting that his wife would return with him or he would kill her. Norment testified that Bond did the shooting, first in the yard, where the bullet hit her shoulder blade. She then ran back into the house hollering, "Don't shoot! Don't shoot!" He saw Bond shoot her in the back in the house.

Bond's defense was insanity. Two doctors said he had a venous congestion of the brain, a disease of the circulatory system, so that the blood did not return readily from the brain to the heart.[2053] Neither could testify about Bond's mental condition at the time of the shooting, although the next day in the jail he was found in a stupor. He was "depressed, stupid, pupils of the eye dilated, heart beat about 50 beats to the minute, with accelerated breathing."[2054]

This testimony did not rise to the level of insanity. "There is no intimation in the record that defendant's conduct was such as to cause remark or notice before the homicide by his friends or acquaintances." The court said, "Everything indicates that he was in his normal condition on the day of the homicide, and that he killed the deceased because she refused to return and live with him."[2055]

Bond was described as "mentally weak," and kept singing the hymn "Lord Make Me Truly Converted." He became very nervous when it came time to leave his cell, but asked the guards not to help him. He also asked they not touch him as his arms and legs were being strapped, but made no objection when shown that it could not be done without touching him.

Bond insisted he had not received a fair trial and likened his execution to being the victim of a lynch mob.[2056] He insisted to the end that he had not killed his wife, that she was healthy and well when he left her at home the morning of the shooting. He said he had been treated unfairly by both the colored and the white people.[2057]

Bond had been reprieved several times before he was hanged on November 9, 1910, along with John Casson and Moses Cook. The warden used this as an opportunity to voice his opposition to the death penalty.[2058] Bond willed his body to a local medical school for study. This was the last triple hanging in Tennessee.

1911

Thomas F. "Napper" Byrom (aka Napper Byrum, Napper Byram), white, age 46. *Murder.*

The crime was committed at 10:00 P.M. on August 2, 1910, in the community of Silver Springs, in Wilson County. The victim was Ruth Byrom, white, age forty-three, the killer's wife. Byrom quietly approached his house and fired a pistol through an open living room window at a bed where his wife was known to be sleeping. Because Byrom, his wife and one of his daughters had been in a physical fight earlier that day, he was the chief suspect. He was found hiding in a neighbor's house several miles away the next day. Mrs. Byrom had borne her husband twelve children, eleven of whom were living at the time of her death. Most of the children were grown.

Two weeks earlier his brother had killed J.W. Puckett in the same community. At the time of Mrs. Byrom's killing, the cause of Puckett's homicide was still a mystery. Both Byroms had married sisters.[2059] Napper Byrom was wanted as a material witness in his brother's case, but evaded the sheriff by staying on the move and seeing his family only at night. The pistol he carried was for self-defense, he claimed. He was not expected home the night of the killing.

The evidence showed that Byrom fired two shots, one hitting the lung, the other passing through his wife's dress. The state's reconstruction of the crime showed the first shot was the fatal wound. Mrs. Byrom rose up and staggered forward, dying in about fifteen minutes. The chief prosecution witness was an adult daughter who was asleep in an upstairs room at the time of the shooting.[2060]

Byrom did not deny the shooting and offered no reason for his actions. "I don't know what made me shoot her. I couldn't tell you to save my life," he testified.[2061] At trial he made an elaborate and passionate plea that he was a longtime alcoholic. He said he was in a "dream" when he fired the shots, and was not responsible for his actions, having no recollection of the crime.

He said that in 1908 during an altercation with his wife and grown daughter, he had been struck in the head with a fire shovel. "Since that time I have had a great deal of trouble with my head. And at times I do things without knowing what I am doing, especially if I get excited a little, or if I get overheated. I had been hauling hay the day of the killing, and had walked some four or five miles to my home after the day's work. I had been a hard drinker for thirty years and the weakness seems to be growing on me. I often get into a condition when I do not know what I am."[2062]

The Tennessee Supreme Court compared this generalized disorder of mind with his testimony under cross-examination in which he had specific recall of events such as whether his wife had her hands up and where she was standing. The court noted that no medical proof was offered at trial, although the affidavit of a doctor who saw Byrom briefly during the trial said that he might be of unsound mind. But this was offered after the trial during a motion for a new trial.

The court said:

> There is nothing in the conduct of the defendant at the time of the commission of the crime, or upon his examination as a witness in the case to raise the slightest suspicion that he is insane. His own statement of the manner in which the crime was committed shows that it was the act of a deliberate and thoughtful man and that every part of it was planned to a purpose. His examination and cross-examination as a witness show that his mind was alert and entirely coherent and that he saw the effect of damaging statements and worded them with considerable skill and intelligence, and from the whole record, it appears clearly that the claim of his insanity is a mere pretense and device to escape the consequences of his crime."[2063]

A legal issue arose because a juror was overcome with heat stroke during the trial and was treated by the same doctor who saw Byrom. The question arose whether the juror had spoken to a bystander. The court said there was no error if he did. Byrom's lawyers also argued error in limiting closing arguments for each side to two hours. This was not error since the evidence of guilt was convincing, ruled the court.[2064]

Byrom was kept in the Wilson County jail until he was transported to the Nashville jail. The night before his execution he was taken to the penitentiary. He was the seventh person executed in what was now called the "death house" at the prison. Byrom told his brother-in-law Doak Thompson that he wanted good strong boards placed over his coffin, not scrap lumber.[2065] He gave his watch to the minister who consoled him. None of his children were present at the execution although his two youngest daughters said good-bye at the Nashville jail.

Byrom was executed at the Main Prison in Nashville on March 15, 1911, after making no public statement except to say, "God bless you."[2066] At the prison, Byrom made a statement to the warden that his motive for killing his wife was her unfaithfulness, but Byrom declined to release a statement or to talk to reporters. Warden Rice used the Byrom execution to tell the newspaper, "I wish you would state in your story that I am still opposed to capital punishment. I have superintended seven executions since I have been here, and I have never yet seen a man hanged but that I believed the poor fellow was a degenerate, a lunatic or suffering form a diseased mind. I believe that the time will come within the next fifteen years when an intelligent public will shudder at the thought of such punishment."[2067]

Robert Cooke, black, age 22. *Murder.*

The crime was committed at 5:00 o'clock A.M. on June 27, 1910, on a road in a black part of town called Johnsonville in Chattanooga, Hamilton County. The victim was William Houston, black, age fifty.[2068] Cooke was described as a "lazy, thriftless negro, and seldom worked, and had not any regular employment for several months before the homicide."[2069] The victim was described as an "industrious, economical old negro man and, so far as the record shows, without an enemy in the world."[2070]

Cooke had told a friend who wanted him to travel to Cincinnati that he did not have any money to go, but would get some. Later that day, Cooke visited the Houston home. His wife saw the defendant roughhousing Houston; she saw Cooke draw a knife and heard the old man say, "Ole Miss, he is going to cut me." The next morning, Houston left the house at his usual time, 4:30 A.M., to get to his workplace. His body was found on Rogers Road, his usual route of travel, about an hour later. He had been struck with two rocks. The back of his head and face had been smashed. His homemade pocketbook was missing. It was common knowledge that Houston kept all his money in the pocketbook. Houston's employer said the man kept about $300 on his person.

Bloodhounds were brought to the scene. They sniffed the two rocks and took off over a hill past a farmhouse and a grocery store and tracked the scent to the streetcar line a mile away. That same day, Cooke went to a tailor shop and ordered a new suit of clothes, paying $22.50. He also spent that evening with a woman who apparently received remuneration for her companionship. Earlier that morning, he asked a friend to have a beer with him, flashing a ten-dollar bill.

The next day, Houston's son tracked Cooke to his home and waited for him on the streetcar. Cooke got aboard. After ignoring the son, Cooke suddenly came to him and said, "I'm sorry your father got killed." The son replied, "Who told you?" Cooke did not answer.

Convinced that Cooke was the killer, the son and two friends summoned police and told them where to find Cooke, who was apparently headed to his grandmother's house on Ft. Wood. The police arrived by car before Cooke appeared and waited for him. Seeing them in the house, Cooke bolted. A footrace followed in which a policeman wounded Cooke in the leg with a shot from his revolver. Cooke was found hiding under a house. Taken to the police station, he was found with $14.50. Searching under the house, the police found $35.00 in green bills where Cooke had been hiding.

Witnesses at the farmhouse and grocery store placed Cooke walking swiftly past them on the morning of the murder, shortly after it was thought to have occurred. Cooke did not take the stand in his defense. His only witness was the woman he'd spent the evening with, but she offered no exculpatory evidence. The case was appealed to the Tennessee Supreme Court, but the opinion cannot be located.

Because the conviction was based entirely on circumstantial evidence, Governor Hooper took special care to read the record before denying clemency.[2071] Up to that time, the governor had allowed only Napper Byrom to hang, having commuted the sentences of three others. Robert Cooke was hanged at the Main Prison in Nashville on November 18, 1911.

Cook steadfastly maintained his innocence. He prayed and sang with his spiritual advisor, Christian C. Mentzler, the night before the execution, and during the early morning hours. Before walking to the gallows, Cook gave the warden three letters. One was to his mother, another to his sweetheart, and another to the Hamilton County jailor. Their contents were never revealed. While Cooke stood on the death trap, Mentzler asked, "You have only a minute to live, won't you make a confession?" Cook answered, "I am innocent of the crime with which I am to die, but I am ready to meet my God."[2072]

1912

Tom Kinnon, black, age 37. *Rape.*

The crime was committed on October 8, 1911, in the home of Mr. and Mrs. R.M. Watson in the town of Brownsville, in Haywood County. The rapist lived in the area and knew that Mr. Watson was away. The victim, Mrs. Ida Watson, white, age thirty-four, was home caring for her four children. The oldest, a boy, was seven years old.

Kinnon entered the house and grabbed Mrs. Watson, who fought him, as did the boy. Finally, Kinnon found an ax, striking the woman between the eyes. After she passed out, he raped her.[2073] The boy escaped and summoned help. Mrs. Watson was not expected to live. Kinnon was found two hours later hiding in a dense thicket with blood on his clothes.

The trial was moved to Gibson County. According to one account, "The details of the assault as brought out in the evidence was most harrowing. The blood-stained undergarments of the victim were exposed to the court. During the testimony strong men wept like children and many were forced to leave the court room."[2074] It was also reported, "The speech of Attorney-General Tom Rye was one of the best ever heard in a criminal prosecution in Gibson County."[2075] In 1915, the relatively unknown Tom Rye was elected governor. He opposed repeal of the death penalty, saying repeal would "increase crime and encourage mob law."[2076] "This was the first sentence to hang since before the war," reported the newspaper, commenting on life in tranquil Gibson County.[2077]

At the prison, Kinnon was attended by two students from Trevecca College. He prayed and sang with them and seemed indifferent to his impending death until he was about to be taken from his cell. He began shaking. In the cell he had said, "I feel good," but grinned and said, "I ain' satisfied." Kinnon never denied his guilt, but always maintained that if he was guilty, it was because he was under the influence of "whisky and dope."[2078] Because Kinnon's case was not appealed to the Tennessee Supreme Court, he was executed on the day set by the trial court, January 13, 1912. Kinnon maintained an attitude of indifferent acquiescence on the gallows and said nothing. When the trap fell he made one convulsive struggle and then was still. Kinnon was survived by a wife and four children. Because his wife made no arrangements for his body (she had not visited him in jail or the prison), he was buried in the prison graveyard.

John Bailey, white, age 23. *Murder.*
George Shelton, white, age 19. *Murder.*

The crime was committed on December 1, 1911, on a rural road called Blue Hill outside Decaturville, in Decatur County. The killers were farm laborers who had done some work for Ben Pettigrew, black, age thirty-nine, a somewhat prosperous cotton farmer. Pettigrew was driving a mule-drawn wagon containing a load of cotton. Accompanying him were his daughter Pearl, black, age twelve, and son Fred, black, age ten.

The crime was initially called a lynching, but it was actually a robbery-murder. It is the second case in Tennessee where whites were executed for killing blacks, although technically the pair was executed for killing only one person, Pearl, when they actually killed three.

This was one of the most notorious killings in Tennessee history. Initial reports of the deaths described them as a lynching because it appeared so, namely, two blacks found burned to death on a wagonload of cotton. Governor Ben Hooper, a Republican in a solidly Democratic state, had spoken out against lynching and proudly boasted that it was rare in Tennessee because killers of both races received the death penalty for similar crimes.[2079] For this reason, the governor immediately offered a reward for apprehension of the lynchers.

The national African American press noted the difference between what was assumed to have happened and what had actually happened. The initial accounts gave a typical account of a mob of "white land tenants who objected to the occupancy of the land by Negroes."[2080] According to this account, "The three Negroes were traveling to a gin with a load of seed cotton. They were waylaid and tied to the wagonload of cotton. The mob, after building a fire beneath the wagon, stood guard until the Negroes were cremated."[2081] A later account, still wrong, said that Pettigrew was driving his wagon when four white men appeared and shot him dead as he sat in the seat of his wagon. This account continues, "They dragged his two daughters from the top of the load and hanged them to a nearby tree. While their bodies dangled from a limb the slayers drove a load of cotton under them and set fire to it."[2082] In truth, the killings were not a lynching. They were a carefully planned robbery-murder.

Shelton hid in a gully while Bailey drew Ben's attention. He stopped the team by the side of the road. Shelton shot Ben Pettigrew in the back and neck with a shotgun, killing him instantly. A second shot wounded Fred, who jumped down from the wagon near Bailey. A second shot aimed at Fred hit and killed one of the mules. Fred scrambled back up onto the wagon to retrieve a gun his father had hidden. A third shot by Shelton killed Fred. Pearl ran as the shooting began and hid about sixty yards away. The killers followed and when she jumped up and began running, Shelton shot her in the back, while Bailey's shot missed. As she ran again, Shelton shot her in the hip and she fell. Bailey walked up to her and shot the top of her head off. Returning to the wagon, the killers noticed Fred did not appear dead. They each shot him again.

The killers took $24 from Ben Pettigrew's body. They were very disappointed because they thought he was carrying several hundred dollars. They also took Ben's pocket watch and a dollar found on Fred's body. Shelton and Bailey later claimed that the discharge of the weapons caused the cotton to catch fire. The blaze caused Fred's arms to burn off and Ben was burned beyond recognition. The burned bodies gave rise to the notion of a lynching, but more likely the fire was set to make the scene look like a lynching. This was probably staged by Lige Scott, the first white person to discover the bodies.

Because the killers did not take the stand, the chief proof came from seventeen witnesses to whom the killers had confessed the crime. The key evidence was "an oral confession made by each of the defendants, and a written confession made by each of them, and a letter written by one of them to his father in which he admitted their guilt."[2083] Shelton, in jail, had agreed to take the sheriff to where the pair had hidden the money.

Warren Bailey, the forty-five-year-old brother of John, testified about a discussion to kill Pettigrew. When Warren suggested that the murder planned for Blue Hill might not go according to plan because Pettigrew was likely to have his children with him, John replied that he would "kill them too, shoot the damn hell out of them too," and that he would no more mind shooting them than shooting a rabbit.[2084]

An issue on appeal was whether the judge erred in allowing testimony about the killing of Ben and Fred, when the prosecution was only for killing Pearl. The Tennessee Supreme Court said, "The Court in his charge made it quite clear to the jury that the defendants were not on trial for the killing of Ben, nor for the killing of his son Fred Pettigrew, and that the proof of this alleged killing had been permitted to go to the jury to be considered only for the purpose of explaining the situation of the defendants with reference to the deceased Pearl Pettigrew, at the time of the alleged killing of Pearl Pettigrew, and as bearing on the question of the motive, if any, had for the killing of Pearl, if she was killed, and that this proof must not be considered for any other purpose."[2085]

The legality of the confessions was questioned because "the defendants were ignorant and illiterate and the confessions, both written and oral, obtained from them, were the result of efforts of a fellow prisoner in the jail, and of persons not prisoners, who were interested in a reward, which had been offered by the Governor for the arrest and conviction of the persons responsible for the death of the Pettigrew negroes."[2086]

The Tennessee Supreme Court ruled, "We find in this record no evidence that the confessions resulted as above claimed, and upon reading of the entire record, we are much impressed with the idea that the crime of which these defendants are so manifestly guilty should not be palliated or excused by their lack of education, or their unfortunate lot in life. For the purpose of robbery, they deliberately planned and executed the murder of three human beings. Their crime was premeditated, cold blooded and revolting to an unusual degree."[2087]

A strong effort was made to convince Gov. Hooper to commute the sentences to life. Shelton was illiterate, having been reared very poor in the backwoods of Decatur County, and he "was led into the commission of said crime by one Lige Scott, who is a much older man than himself."[2088] Likewise, Bailey was illiterate and very ignorant, "having been reared principally in the poorhouse of Decatur County, led into the commission of the crime by one Lige Scott, who is a much older man than himself."[2089] Apparently, Scott had told the men that they would not be punished for lynching a black man. He had been arrested as an accessory before the fact, but research has failed to discover whether he actually stood trial.

All of the jurors asked in writing for the governor to commute the sentences, as did the local elected officials of Decatur County, who asked that their names not be released by the governor. The trial judge took a middle position, asserting that he could find no mitigating circumstances, but asked the governor to take the commutation requests seriously, opining that he would not be unhappy if the men were not hanged.[2090] Governor Hooper had promised that the "lynchers" would be punished and could not commute the men's sentences, although he commuted the sentence of murderer Stanley Means two days before the executions.

The last days of Bailey and Shelton became even more dramatic because the day before they were to be taken from the Davidson County jail to the prison for execution, the governor granted a twenty-day respite for Emmet Alexander, scheduled to die with them for a separate killing. Alexander's sentence was later commuted.[2091]

Bailey and Shelton went to the gallows confident their souls would enter heaven, having gotten religion in jail. Bailey told a minister to write a letter telling young people not to do what he had done. Dressed in new black clothes with black caps over their heads, the pair was executed beside each other at what was now called the "hanging chamber" at the prison in Nashville on the morning of July 26, 1912.[2092]

The Pettigrew killings had attracted the notice of a fledgling organization, founded only three years before: the National Association for the Advancement of Colored People. Under the editorial pen of the brilliant and scholarly W.E.B. DuBois, the NAACP's magazine *The Crisis* described both the conflicting accounts of the Pettigrew "lynching" and the killers' written confession.[2093] DuBois chose to publish the confession as a powerful testament regarding white ignorance and bigotry:

> To the Publick, and the honor cort of decaturville, Tenn; we was assoated with Mr. J.M. Hill he read the Bible, he read the Bible, to us, and toalked to us, about our soles, and all so Read To Us, in St. Matthews the 10th Chapter, and the 26 Verce, that thire was nothing covered but, what would, be uncovered and nothing hid what would be, be known and, He talked to us about telling, the truth at the blessed Jesus, said that to tell the, truth and, beleave the truth and it would make us, free and we do know that we did a great rong but god has forgive us, as Mr. Hill, has to got to god and, he has forgive us, and now, we with up stretched, ormes, ask the clemences, and mercies, of the, People, and, the cort, to do all they cane, for us, as we, air both maried boyes, and I George Shelton aire only 18 yeares, old, and, never Had, the, chance to go to school and, was raised up by a Good Father. And, Oh, My, Der, ole, Mother, and my Wife, and Little Baby! If, I Had, Onley, of, Knowen at the start what all this would of, cause, me, I would Not, of, done, it, for aney amount of Money. But, Mr. Lige, Scott, tole me, to: That ole Ben ort to be, Killed, and got, out of, the neighborhood. And George Bailey, is a Brothernlaw of, George Shelton, and is, 25 yares, old and His, Parints, Died, when he was a Little Boy, and he, was raised up heare and, yonder, and kid from Piller, to Post and, we Both, have no, Egacation and, never, relised what a Black path, of, sin we had been travling, until Mr. J.M. Hill, Read, the Bible to us, And Praid, for, and with us, and, then, we begin to Relise what we had done."[2094]

George W. Rose, white, age 67. *Murder.*

The crime was committed on August 25, 1911, on the rural farm of James L. Miller in McMinn County. The killers were George W. Rose and his wife, Mary Rose, white, age thirty-eight, along with Thomas Senter, white, age unknown; and Bascomb H. Miller, white, age twenty-five. Bascomb was the adult son of the victim. The victim was James L. Miller, white, age sixty-five. The killers and the victim were neighboring farmers. Miller's body was found in his barn. He had been struck on the head by a sharp object, thought to be an ax or hatchet, and two holes were found in his head.

The trial testimony showed that James L. Miller was held by the arms by Senter and Bascomb Miller while Rose smashed his head with a hatchet. Rose was tried separately. Senter and Bascomb Miller testified that Rose threatened to kill them unless they helped. Mrs. Rose was convicted as an accessory after the fact.[2095] Rose's motive was that Miller had earlier met with the grand jury and had Rose indicted for stealing his corn. Although the matter was settled by Rose's paying for the corn, he was heard by many people to have threatened Miller's life.[2096]

The conviction was upheld by the Tennessee Supreme Court, but the opinion cannot be located. The opinion may have been delivered orally because Rose had been brought to the courthouse where the court was hearing appeals. Rose heard Chief Justice J.K. Shields deliver the opinion from the bench. Rose listened with "his eyes upon the court and he was very nervous."[2097]

After the conviction, a bitter Rose angrily denounced his wife for having testified against him and "fearfully abused" her when she came to see him the afternoon before his execution. She was an inmate at the Main Prison, which still kept women at that time.[2098] He had angrily denounced Governor Hooper, and the sheriff of McMinn County, and had extracted a promise from his son, Hicks Rose, to "attend to" the latter. At the time of Rose's execution, his son Hicks Rose was also in the Main Prison, serving a fifteen-year sentence for murder unrelated to the Miller killing.

George W. Rose was executed at the Main Prison on August 26, 1912. The night before his execution, Rose embraced religion under the guidance of the Rev. Arthur L. Foster, of Rust Memorial Baptist Church. He had scoffed at the idea earlier. On the morning of his execution, Rose said, "I ask God's forgiveness for what I have done. I warn you all to keep away from whiskey, women and bad company." But he added cryptically, "I was not with that crowd that night at all. I can say that before my Maker. I have nothing against anybody. I hold no malice against any persons. My mind is at peace with man and God and I am not afraid to die."[2099]

Minutes before being taken to the gallows, the father told his son, "I am a changed man. Hick, when you get out of here lead a different life from what you have led — and lead a different one from what I have led."[2100] He said not to harm the sheriff or anyone else. Both wept as they parted. Just before he was taken to the gallows, Rose asked to see his wife but was told there was not enough time and he died without seeing her. He weakened with every step to the gallows, and when the black cap was about to be placed over his head, he started to collapse and was held up by Warden Rimmer. He did not struggle after the trap was sprung.[2101]

Rose was buried at the prison cemetery with his wife and son both attending, dressed in prison clothes. The son was shackled and took off his hat to kiss his father's coffin good-bye. Mrs. Rose, standing away, had plucked flowers from the ground to place on the coffin before it was lowered. Hicks Rose sobbed on the way back to the prison, and his mother kept her head bowed.

Rose had left a message to be read by the Rev. Foster after his burial. In it Rose confessed to killing Miller, but said that Miller's son and Senter had not held the man's arms, but had simply said what they had been told to say by the prosecution. He said the murder weapon was an iron bolt, not a hatchet as had been surmised. His motive had nothing to do with the corn theft; rather, it had something to do with his wife. He said, "I love my wife and have not one bitter word to say against her. She has been as good to me as anybody. She alone knows all the facts, and if she refuses to tell the real motive for the crime, I want you to let it remain unknown forever."[2102]

Rose was the oldest man executed by the state of Tennessee.

Sidney Dunlap, black, age 29. *Murder.*

The crime was committed on March 11, 1912, in the home of Miss Mary H. Ewell, white, age sixty, who belonged to one of the most prominent families in Fayette County. The home was near La-Grange. "She was a woman of wealth, owned a large plantation upon which she and her uncle, Robert H. Shepherd, lived. They were the only white people on the plantation, which was worked exclusively by negroes."[2103] Shepherd was seventy-nine.

At noon, Shepherd went to attend some stock, leaving Mary upstairs writing a letter. When he returned, he called for her. Hearing no answer, he went upstairs and found her "unconscious with her head beaten in, her features almost unrecognizable." She died two hours later. Her killer took fifty dollars from the room. He also took an ivory-handled pistol. It was thought that she had taken the pistol from underneath a pillow where it was kept and drew it on ex-convict Dunlap but he quickly overpowered her. After the beating, he took the pistol, but left his own at the scene.

Bloodhounds were called and followed the trail to a place called 45-Mile Siding, where Dunlap was seen boarding the train for Buntyn and was seen in Shelby County the next day. Said the newspaper, "Feeling against Dunlap is very high, and if he be apprehended and carried to the scene of the dastardly crime for preliminary trial, that he will meet summarily the justice his deed merits."[2104]

A fifteen-hundred-dollar reward had been offered for the arrest and conviction of Miss Ewell's killer. A massive posse searched for him, and when he was arrested, a mob formed. He was held in the Shelby County jail, was spirited back to Somerville for his trial, and was convicted on August 2, 1912. He had earlier confessed, but pled not guilty. He did not take the stand. Dunlap maintained he was innocent, but did not appeal to the Tennessee Supreme Court. He was executed at the Main Prison in Nashville on the date set by the trial court, September 4, 1912.

Dunlap had assisted in the execution of others at the main prison during a previous incarceration and had boasted that if he ever came back it would be for something they "would shoot me through the hole for." During his last night he regaled listeners with details about how an execution was carried out.

The night before his execution he asked for the company of inmate Ed Gray, black, a former preacher. The two spent the night in prayer and song. Gray asked, "Is you or is you not guilty of dis crime?" Dunlap answered, "Dey say I is." Gray responded, "Dat ain't what I axed you. Do you say you is?" Dunlap said, "What good would it do if I tell it?" Gray explained that it would help his mother and sisters. Finally, with head bowed, Dunlap said, "Yes, I is de man."[2105]

Dunlap told the guards, "You wants to know how I feel? Well, I feels good. I ain't scared and I don't dread it no more."[2106] When asked if he had the chance, would he try to escape, he replied yes, and admitted that he had helped cut the bars at the Davidson County jail two weeks earlier. Dunlap walked to the gallows with a firm step, shook hands with those around him and announced he was ready. The drop was clean and he did not struggle.

Deputy Sheriff Tom Griffin of Fayette County explained to the newspapers that the townsfolk of LaGrange had taken up a collection to bring Dunlap's body back to "exhibit it as a warning to the lawless element." Griffin explained that many people imagined that men brought to be executed at the prison in Nashville were released after they were brought to Nashville, and "he thought it was best to show them that the law was carried out to the last letter."[2107] Dunlap's body was exhibited in LaGrange and Fayette County.

Leo Temple, black, age 17. *Rape of a child under the age of ten.*

The crime was committed on the afternoon of August 23, 1912, on the Queen farm located near Buntyn, in Shelby County. Temple was a farm worker who raped Clara Queen, white, the seven-year-old daughter of his employer, Thomas F. Queen, white, age thirty-eight. The proof from the girl's parents, as well as her testimony and the "physical facts, left the negro without a defense."[2108] Dr. J.N. Frost confirmed the rape. Temple simply denied everything on the stand.

Clara's father had apprehended Temple after the rape and brought him to the sheriff himself. The trial judge congratulated the father on allowing the law to take its course. It took the jury four minutes to decide the case on September 20, 1912. "The negro received it with a maniacal laugh, seeming to be without realization of the impact."[2109]

The jury instruction said that Temple could be found guilty of rape of a child under the age of ten if, as alleged by the state, he took her or ordered her to go to an outbuilding on the farm and had sex with her without force.[2110] Furthermore, the jury could consider whether both Temple and the victim were diseased.[2111]

Through his regular lawyer, Temple began the process of an appeal, beginning with his signed affidavit and motion for a new trial filed the day after the verdict was rendered. Temple said, "Since the trial of this cause I have in a talk with my lawyer been advised to tell the truth, in fact he advised me to do so before my trial but I was afraid to, I was even afraid to tell the whole truth to my lawyer, P.M.D. Dowdall, I knew I would be tried before a white jury in a white man's court and I thought if I only and truthfully denied the charge brought against me I would be freed, while I feared if I told the rest of the true facts in the case that I would be punished in some way for so doing."

The affidavit continued, "I never did have intercourse with Clara Queen, but she was always hanging around where I worked, and during this time she told me she had intercourse with her brother Carl, 13 years old, and her brother Morris, 9 years old; in fact I and her younger sister Lenie, 5 years old, saw Clara and Morris in the act of intercourse and that evening Lenie tried to tell of what she saw, to the older sister Nora, 14 years old, when Nora and I and some other of the children were in the family kitchen of Mr. Queen, and Nora told Lenie to shut her mouth."

The affidavit said, "Further a short time before I was arrested Carl, 13 years old, told me that he had the 'clap' and that his father Mr. Queen had given him medicine for it and it had stopped hurting him. A short time before this Mr. Queen, during a talk he was having with affiant, told affiant that he had medicine which would cure 'clap' as he called it." It concluded, "The whole of the above is true in substance and in fact, and it was only because affiant is an ignorant, friendless negro that they were not sooner told."[2112]

The trial judge rejected his motion for a new trial and Temple appealed.[2113] He was granted fifteen days to file the bill of exceptions, but on October 12, 1912, he formally withdrew his appeal.[2114] Shortly thereafter, he attempted to reinstate the appeal, but the Supreme Court declined to hear it because no bill of exceptions had been filed. After this, his lawyers filed a writ of common law certiorari.[2115] This procedure startled both the attorney general and the Supreme Court. Could this writ serve as an appeal when no record was before the court? The court entered an order saying no, asserting that Temple's fate was in the hands of the governor.[2116]

Governor Hooper had the case under advisement until December 18, 1912, at which time he refused clemency. Temple's execution would be a lesson to the public: the legal system could be trusted to punish criminals. Said he, "It is my fixed determination to save Tennessee from the disgrace of lynch law in every possible instance. The executive who does not pursue this course violates his oath of office and brings himself and his state into merited public contempt. I have already demonstrated my intention of calling out the militia to prevent lynching, and will continue to offer the largest rewards authorized by statute for the arrest and conviction of any man guilty of this violation of the law."[2117] Hooper had recently attended a governor's conference in Richmond where the overwhelming sentiment of attendees was that lynching could be stopped by proper enforcement of the law against all criminals, including lynchers.

Temple was hanged at the prison in Nashville on December 19, 1912. His last words were, "I do not hate to die, but I sho' do hate to die dis way."[2118] None of his relatives had visited him in the time he spent in the Nashville jail awaiting transfer to the prison for execution.

Temple's novel procedure did produce a written opinion from the Tennessee Supreme Court, but the date of the decision is unclear. The opinion appears to be dated either March 1, 1913, or April 3, 1913, *after* the execution. Most likely, the actual decision was rendered from the bench and enrolled in the court's records later.

Because the writ of certiorari looks exclusively to the law (not facts), no recitation of crime details are included in the opinion. The appeal listed six technical arguments, such as the failure of the technical record to include a caption, the failure of the district attorney general's name to appear on the indictment (only his assistant's name), and that the indictment failed to use the words "true bill." These technical arguments were insufficient, ruled the court, because a statute had specifically said these issues were no basis to overturn a conviction.[2119]

The most important legal argument was that the jury's verdict was general, merely stating that the "defendant was guilty as charged in the indictment," but the jury did not precisely assess punishment. The problem was the language of the child rape statute. Code Section 6458 said that "assault and battery on a female under age of ten with intent to unlawfully and carnally know her shall be punished as in the case of rape." The statute did not assess a punishment. Instead, the rape statute, Code Section 6452, provided the jury could impose hanging, or "commute the punishment for the offense to imprisonment in the penitentiary for life, or for a period of not less than ten years."[2120]

The Supreme Court ruled that the jury's failure to impose a punishment less than hanging was simply its way of refusing to commute the sentence. This was not akin to a case where an indictment contained several lesser included offenses, which would have required the jury to assess a specific punishment. Here, the "grade is in the punishment and not in the offense. There is no uncertainty in the general verdict under this indictment, because there is only the one offense alleged."[2121]

A final technical issue was that the judgment failed to recite that the jury heard evidence and that it was sufficient to sustain a verdict beyond a reasonable doubt. The Court said that it would "conclusively presume in the absence of a bill of exceptions" that the jury heard the evidence and that the trial judge was also satisfied of Temple's guilt beyond a reasonable doubt.[2122]

1913

Pat Malloy (aka Andrew Malloy and John Henry), black, age 25. *Murder.*

The crime was committed about 7:00 P.M. August 6, 1909, in the store of Jewish merchant Herman Henning on Market Street (now Second Avenue) in Nashville, Davidson County. The victim was Herman Henning, white, age fifty-seven.[2123]

The Henning family lived above the store and his wife and young daughter had left the store to run an errand about 6:30 P.M. Henning was last seen alive sitting in a chair in front of his store when the women left. When they returned about thirty minutes later, they found him dead on the floor inside. Some seventy-five to one hundred dollars had been taken from the cash drawer. Henning had been stabbed in the cheek, lip, and neck, and had been killed by a stab in the heart. A bloody ice pick, found at the scene, was identified as the probable murder weapon.[2124] After the body was removed, the building was locked and the family did not return for a week, staying with friends.

When the family returned and ventured upstairs to their living quarters for the first time, a trunk and cedar chest were discovered to have been opened. Missing were striped trousers belonging to Herman's son, Abe Henning. They had been made by tailor B. Friedman. Also missing was a made-to-order blue mohair suit given to Herman Henning by his son-in-law, Henry Zander. A pair of blue trousers, known to have come from the stock of Chas. Levy & Co., where the son-in-law worked, was also missing. They had been a gift of Zander as well. Likewise, a pair of striped trousers of the same origin was missing. The family immediately notified the police of the missing items.

The day after the items were reported missing, several pairs of pants were pawned at Sam Feldman's shop by a person who looked like Pat Malloy. He gave his name as John Henry and his address as 604 5th Ave. South. On August 16, 1909, the mohair suit was pawned at the shop of Sam Silverfield by a black man giving his name as Albert Spraggins, who said he lived at 644 S. 5th Street. Silverfield later positively identified Pat Malloy as the same person who pawned the suit. The suit was of distinctive size because of Henning's build.

In the days following the murder, Pat Malloy was seen by another pawnbroker, who knew him and his family well, in possession of twenty-five to thirty dollars which he flashed. He claimed to have won the money in a craps game, but nevertheless pawned two pairs of brown striped trousers on two separate occasions.

Shortly after the Henning murder he was arrested on an unrelated robbery charge and was placed in jail. The next month (September) he escaped from the jail and went straight to Friedman's pawn shop to redeem one of the pair of pants. He left behind the striped trousers that had been made by tailor Friedman. Finally, in spring 1910, when Malloy (John Henry) had not come back for the pants, the pawnbroker examined them to determine if they could be altered (lengthened) for possible sale. Tailor's markings alerted Friedman that these were Henning's pants. Contemporaneous police records of the bailment (pawning) clearly implicated Malloy, who was positively identified as both the person who pawned the goods and redeemed one pair of pants and left the other.

The only testimony putting Malloy near the crime scene was that of two women who were taking a walk on the night of the killing and were overtaken by a black man who ran by them and kept looking back over his shoulder. He was carrying a bundle of clothing. He matched Malloy's size and color, but was not positively identified.[2125]

Malloy vigorously denied any involvement in crime, although he took the stand and admitted to being a "thief, robber, a gambler and a loafer."[2126] Asked about his numerous prior convictions, Malloy claimed he couldn't remember anything. He denied knowing anyone named Albert Spraggins, who was shown to have been a friend from youth, in whose name he pawned the mohair suit. He claimed to have been living with his mother at 604 Jo Johnston Avenue on the night of the murder, but no one testified about this. Five lawyers defended Malloy, but the newspaper opined, "No Sherlock Holmes could have woven the facts more adroitly and presented them more skillfully than have the state's attorneys and the Nashville detective force that worked up the case."[2127]

The Supreme Court described the circumstantial evidence in detail and concluded, "His examination shows that he was frivolous, impertinent and had a reckless disregard of the truth. So taking into consideration the positive nature of the state's proof establishing the corpus delicti, that the murder was committed in the perpetuation of robbery, that the plaintiff in error was found in possession of the stolen articles almost immediately afterward, that he pawned these articles and appropriated them for his own use, and the evasive and unsatisfactory character of the plaintiff in error's testimony, we think there can be no doubt of his guilt."[2128]

In part because Malloy was so steadfast in denying his guilt, the governor paid special attention to reading "every syllable of proof for both sides, heard every bit of additional evidence presented by the defense, and even examined thoroughly the Henning premises, where the crime was committed."[2129] The governor had granted two stays of execution, one for the purpose of hearing hearsay testimony about a man who claimed to have committed the murder, but who, when brought to the governor, established an alibi. The governor allowed the execution to proceed on May 9, 1913, and Malloy was hanged that day.

When Malloy was taken from the Nashville jail to the prison the day before his execution, a large knife was discovered on his person. He objected to being told to put on the new suit of clothes customarily given to men about to be executed, but relented. A minister was sent to him the night before his execution but Malloy began to cross-examine and ridicule him. Turning to a newspaper reporter, Malloy said, "I suppose that if I tell you I killed that old Jew you will say that I have religion, but I ain't going to say anything of the kind. I am an innocent man."[2130] Malloy was described as having dropped his composure in the hours before his execution, and took on "a frightened look in his eyes, as if he were a hunted animal, starting at the least noise."[2131]

1916

Julius Morgan, black, age 22. *Rape.*

The crime was committed on the afternoon of February 1, 1916, near a farm owned by Morgan's brother-in-law, in a rural area three miles from Bonnicord, in Dyer County. The rapist had lived with his brother-in-law Rob Tate for two years. He had escaped from the Arkansas Prison, a fact unknown at the time of his trial.

The victim, Miss Lura Sutherland, white, age nineteen, was a door-to-door saleswoman. She had made a call on the brother-in-law's house and had left. Morgan saw the direction she was going and ran through the woods to intercept her. He met her face-to-face and "choking her into insensibility," dragged her into a thicket and raped her.[2132] Word of the rape spread quickly and Morgan was soon captured by townsfolk.

Morgan was paraded about the town of Dyersburg as a preview to his lynching. But the sheriff wrested him from the townsfolk. As word of the rape circulated, multiple attempts were made by a mob to convince the Dyer County sheriff to give Morgan over to them, but the sheriff moved him from place to place, promising he would be tried fairly. Morgan was finally kept in the Memphis jail and he was tried in Memphis. The details of the trial are unknown other than that he was convicted on April 3, 1916.

The Tennessee Supreme Court's opinion did not recite the facts, except to say the evidence clearly supported the conviction.[2133] The court turned aside a claim of insanity, saying this had not been raised at the trial (Morgan entered a not guilty plea) and no evidence had been offered on this issue. Likewise, no issue of "idiocy, either at the time of the act, or at the time of trial" had been raised, and the facts showed Morgan knew right from wrong.[2134] Said the court, "That the prisoner had such capacity at the time of the act in this case is clear. The most convincing proof of it is that as soon as the act was done he ran away, fled from pursuit and punishment, from the avenging hand of the law, which he knew he violated."[2135]

Following his conviction Morgan was kept in the Nashville jail, where hundreds of people, mostly black, came to see him and pray for him, many shaking his hand. Governor Rye went to the jail and met privately with Morgan.[2136] But there was no likelihood of a commutation. After the trial it was learned that Morgan was actually an escapee from the Arkansas Prison, serving a sentence for attempted rape on a white woman.

The day before the execution, Morgan was taken by car to the Main Prison directly to the "death house," as it was called, recently built to accommodate the new electric chair. Apparently, Morgan's lawyers made no effort to challenge the constitutionality of the new method of execution. The Tennessee Supreme Court's opinion mentioned the new execution method without comment. It said, "It is therefore the judgment of the court that the warden of the State Penitentiary at Nashville, Tennessee, on Thursday, the 13th day of July 1916, in the death chamber provided by law in said State Penitentiary, shall cause the body of said Julius Morgan, to be subjected by sufficient current of electricity, until he is dead; and may God have mercy on his soul."[2137] Morgan's lawyers did not appeal the constitutionality of the electric chair because it was universally considered more humane than hanging — most men strangled and ropes break.

Julius Morgan met his death on the appointed day, becoming the first person to die in the Tennessee electric chair. The death penalty for murder had been abolished for a few years, but was reinstated in 1917.

The night before his execution Morgan was attended by Prison Chaplain S.F. Sims, and a black minister from the A.M.E. church, W.E. Mitchell. He asked for and was given watermelons throughout the night, and in the morning ate a large breakfast. Morgan had embraced religion and said he was not afraid to die and that he would go to heaven. He blamed alcohol for his crime. "I was good once. Then I went to drinking bootleg whisky and when the showdown come — it got me."[2138] He freely admitted the rape of Miss Sutherland. He also admitted the earlier attempted rape in his home town of Huffman, Arkansas, and his escapee status when he raped Miss Sutherland.

Several times during the night and early morning Morgan began crying and trembling, especially when he first saw the electric chair. He was practically carried to the chair but became calm when seated. Asked for his final words, he asked that his body be sent to his mother in Arkansas. According to the newspaper, the electric chair worked perfectly, with Morgan's body becoming rigid and shooting upward with the first shock. "Morgan received no burns or disfigurements, and he appeared to be dead after the first shock."[2139] Prison guard Tom Hooper pulled the lever that sent the charge through Morgan's body. The newspaper remarked,

"Nothing about the new system has the grim aspect of the gallows. It is rather humanless."[2140]

1918

Eddie James Alsup (aka Eddie Allsup), black, age 17. *Rape.*
John D. Williams (aka J.D. Williams), black, age 15. *Rape.*

The crime was committed about 11:30 A.M. August 30, 1917, at the H.J. Lambert farm near the community of Lynnville, Giles County.[2141] The rapists were farm hands on a nearby farm. Williams, light-skinned, and Alsup, dark-skinned, saw the victim squat down in a sorghum patch, near a melon patch where she had gone to get a melon. She was having a bowel movement, having taken a laxative. The victim was Emma Lambert, white, age sixteen.

Williams ran up behind her and seized her. The pair said they had been watching her for a day or two. She was unable to "hollow" because they were choking her, Williams in front, Alsup behind. They threw her on her back, tore most of her clothes off except her vest and bloomers, then pulled her vest down to her waist.[2142] They pulled off her bloomers. Williams raped her first, then Alsup.[2143] She saw Alsup's privates and he raped her twice.

She struggled against the rapists all the time and kicked Alsup away one time. The pair suddenly said, "Listen!" in hushed tones, thinking someone was near. The sound was made by pigs near the fence and the two began to leave. Alsup abruptly turned around toward her. He kicked her in the side.[2144] There were no menfolk at the Lambert farm. Her father was away at a farmer's institute and her older brother was working on the roads, carrying sand.[2145]

Emma cried out, "Mamma, mamma!" and the mother came to the sorghum patch to find Emma putting on her bloomers. She was muddy, her face blue. She had hand and finger bruises all over her body, including her limbs, hips, neck and groin.[2146] The mother ran to get Charley Lambert, Emma's brother. He went to Lynnville and brought the doctor back to the house. On the way, he saw Williams and Alsup on the road to Lynnville. One was barefoot. The doctor confirmed all the bruising. He said Emma had no hymen, and testified there could have been a penetration.[2147]

After Emma reported the rape, the sheriff and deputies rounded up several young black men of similar age and appearance and brought them to her. She was cautioned to be careful in her identification because "a mistake might send an innocent man to his death."[2148] Without hesitation, she identified Alsup and Williams, who was barefoot.

Both made various statements to several people such as the sheriff, deputy sheriff, and jailor in Pulaski. According to one account, "This confession was corroborated by the young woman in minute detail at the trial. It would have been utterly impossible for the negroes to go into details of the crime as they did, if they had not known about it."[2149]

The trial was conducted quietly. Trial date was not announced, and the case went forward only after the veniremen had been called. The courtroom was nearly empty and the few spectators were told not to talk about the trial. Two respected white lawyers conducted the defense.[2150]

The defendants asserted their statements in the jail were made under fear of lynching (a mob had formed). The pair's lawyers described the two as "small for their ages and are only ignorant little animals," who were frightened into saying they had raped the girl, but were innocent. The defendants said they were working at a nearby farm at the time of the rape. A black man testified Williams was with him earlier that morning, but he let him off his wagon and saw him walk in the direction of the Lambert farm, but he did not know what time. Emma's brother testified he saw tracks where the two had walked from the rape site to the road. One person was barefoot.

In asserting they were not the perpetrators, the pair's lawyers argued that they could only be guilty of assault with intent to commit rape. This was because there was no evidence of penetration since the girl's labia were not bruised or bloody. They insisted, "Mere actual contact of the organs is not sufficient, and there must be actual penetration to some extent to constitute the crime of rape."[2151] No Tennessee case law was cited to support this contention.

The state's brief said there was ample proof of guilt without the confessions. Alsup admitted he had seen Charley Lambert in the road earlier that day. When a deputy sheriff and Charley Lambert came to their house that afternoon, Alsup said, "White folks, we ain't done nothing!" He said this before anyone told him he was charged with committing the offense, but could give no reason why he said it.[2152]

The pair was charged with both rape and assault with intent to commit rape. The jury found the two guilty of rape on October 23, 1917. The Tennessee Supreme Court affirmed the convictions but the opinion cannot be located.[2153]

Another black rapist, Homer Lawson, received a commutation of his sentence from the governor a few days before his execution. He said that he overheard the two laughing about their crime while being held in the Nashville jail about the same time he was there, soon after they were brought to Nashville for their safety.[2154]

Eddie Alsup and J.D. Williams were executed at the main prison on July 8, 1918. Tennessee had briefly abolished the death penalty for murder but had soon reinstated it. "I am prepared to die and I'm not guilty," said Alsup, five minutes before his death. Prison authorities and ministers attending the pair sought last-minute confessions by telling them about Julius Morgan's collapse and confession.

"You can kill me, but I'm innocent," insisted Williams until he heard the buzz of Alsup's execution. He then collapsed and had to be assisted to the electric chair. He gathered his composure and said good-bye to everyone around him.[2155] Williams was executed by prison guard Joe Cope.

1919

Frank Ewing, black, age 21. *Rape.*

The crime was committed at 2:00 P.M. on June 24, 1918, near Stokes Lane, one-half mile west of Hillsboro Pike, about four miles from Nashville. The location was a farmhouse, about two hundred yards from the road. The rapist was a farm hand who wandered from place to place looking for work. He was wanted by police at that time for having stolen a cow. The victim was Mrs. Anna Ferguson, white, age twenty-five. Her husband was three miles away working on a farm he rented.

Anna Ferguson was alone in the garden behind her house when Ewing appeared holding a piece of paper which he asked her to read. As she took the paper, he grabbed her by the back of her neck, drew a knife, and took her into the house, where he raped her at knife point. The rape was committed on a bed in the living room of the house. Mrs. Ferguson and others testified, "There was a very strong sickening odor of the negro in the room a long time after the negro left."[2156]

After the rape, Anna ran to a neighbor's house. The neighbor drove Anna to her husband. Police were notified and brought bloodhounds, but the trail was lost on Hillsboro Road. She was taken to a doctor "with a view of avoiding any infectious disease," and her neck was found to be bruised and scratched.[2157]

When arrested later in Hendersonville, Ewing was brought back and positively identified by Anna Ferguson, who had earlier rejected about six suspects. The piece of paper was also found. A police constable who interrogated Ewing at the jail asked him to describe the location of the furniture. This he did because he initially said the sexual encounter was voluntary. At trial, Ewing denied any involvement with Anna Ferguson at all, but was reminded that he described the location of the furniture. He said nothing.

Squire J.M. Summers of Hendersonville testified to Ewing's alibi, namely that he had seen the defendant at a store in Hendersonville that morning and hired him to work on his farm for the week. Summers explained in detail that he had tried to have Ewing plow corn, but Ewing failed at that because he was so ignorant. He turned Ewing over to his wife, who was also unsuccessful in showing Ewing how to cut weeds. (After the trial Mrs. Summers said she "saw him at work all that afternoon."[2158]) Squire Summers displayed canceled checks made out to another man, which purported to show that Ewing was paid by that man for the full week, and the next week as well.

A death penalty opponent has suggested Ewing was innocent by fully accrediting Squire Summers's testimony and the difficulty Ewing would have had in traveling to the crime site.[2159] Regarding the latter, the bill of exceptions explained:

> He said he and a negro named Sam Johnson started from West Nashville to go together to the power plant to get work. When they got to the Van Barcom station on the Charlotte Pike they decided to follow the Tennessee Central Railroad belt lines that circles the city to the south and did so. This line brought them to the back side of the farm on which Mrs. Ferguson lived and runs within about a quarter of a mile, or a little more, from the house of Mrs. Ferguson. That when they got to this place, Johnson gave him a folded piece of writing paper and Johnson left him there at the railroad, that he then went across a field and up the back way to the Ferguson house, then he went up to the little gate close to the steps of the porch and quieted the dogs, that he spoke to the lady and asked her to read the note to him saying that he could not read, that the lady came to the gate and took the

> paper, that he grabbed her and made her go into the front room, that she laid on the bed and that he had to do with her.[2160]

According to Ewing's version, "He did not force her but that she gave it to him and that he thanked her when he left, and she promised not to tell."[2161]

Against the Summers testimony, the state offered the business records of two other employers to show that it was impossible for Ewing to have worked the whole week(s) involved because he had worked for them. The state argued that Summers simply had his weeks mixed up, and that he met Ewing at the store on July 1, 1918, a week after the rape.

Frank Ewing was tried and convicted in one day, July 31, 1918. His lawyer was Richard S. West, white. The case was appealed to the Tennessee Supreme Court. Lawyer West emphasized both the Summers-supported alibi and Frank Ewing's low mental status. The court's opinion cannot be located.

Gov. Roberts took special care to consider Ewing's case. Besides reading the Supreme Court record, he met with the victim and her husband at the place the rape occurred, and had the defendant examined by a doctor specializing in mental disease.[2162] The doctor opined that Ewing had the mind of an eight-year-old white child, that he was "crafty and cunning," that he knew right from wrong, but said the best thing for him "would be life long employment in custody."[2163]

Roberts also met with Ewing at the prison. Roberts, who had publicly asserted that the cure for lynching was swift due process for accused rapists, concluded he "had no doubt whatsoever as to the guilt of the prisoner," and refused to commute the sentence.[2164] Frank Ewing was electrocuted at the Main Prison in Nashville on May 21, 1919.

Ewing ate two large meals in the twelve hours before his death. He professed religion that night and when asked where he would be the next day, he replied, "In heaven." On his way to the electric chair, he said, "Good-bye to you and I hope to meet you in all heaven." While seated in the electric chair, he was asked if he had any last request or confession. He replied that he wanted his body sent to his mother.[2165]

1920

Winnifred Walker, black, age 18. *Assault with intent to rape a child under the age of twelve.*

The crime was committed in the defendant's home on July 29, 1919, in a rural area outside Jefferson City, in Jefferson County. The victim was a neighbor. She was Frances Rankin, white, age ten. Frances Rankin was walking to her home alone after visiting playmates. She was looking at flowers in the yard of the defendant's house when he asked her to come in and play the organ. "Walker was at home alone at the time. She says that she went into the house accompanied by Walker, and he fastened the door after them. She says she tried to play on the organ a little, after which Walker told her to take off her clothes and lay down on the floor. She says that she obeyed this command, and that Walker laid down on her, and after he got up he told her that if she told anybody what had occurred she would get a whipping."[2166]

The court continued:

> Frances returned to her home immediately after this occurrence, and was upstairs when her mother discovered her. Her mother says that she noticed that Frances was pale and nervous; that she had unusual pallor on her face. She asked her what was the matter, and Frances told her that she could not tell her. Her mother insisted on her telling her what her trouble was, and after some persuasion Frances told her that she would "whisper it to her," and then told her in a whisper what had happened. Mrs. Rankin says that she then immediately examined her person, and found it red and swollen. She immediately sent for Dr. Tittsworth.[2167]

The court said, "Dr. Tittsworth testified that he found the child nervous, and upon an examination of her person found it swollen and presenting a reddened condition, thus indicating that some force had been introduced against it. He says that the inner lip or inner part of the first organ was "bruised, reddened and inflamed." He says the injury that he found indicated the penetration of the labia or vulva, such as would be made by the private organ of a male. He says, however, that the hymen had not been ruptured."[2168]

According to the Supreme Court, the defendant told a deputy sheriff that he knew what he had done with the little girl, but then denied doing it. The defendant did not testify at his trial.

The issue before the Supreme Court was whether it was proper for the jury to have before it a two-count indictment, one for "carnal knowledge of a female under the age of twelve,"[2169] and "assault and battery upon a female under the age of twelve, with the intent to unlawfully carnally know her."[2170] The court ruled that the second count was clearly proven, and explained the law. The second crime is not rape; rather, it is punished as rape.[2171] Thus, while the evidence was not necessarily clear that a penetration occurred (a predicate for rape), the second crime was clear.

The court rejected the defendant's contention that there was "a repugnancy in the verdict," in that "if he were guilty of having carnal knowledge of the female in question, as charged in the first count of the indictment, the offense charged in the second count would necessarily be merged in the offense laid in the first count."[2172] To this, the court said that a conviction on the second count was sufficient, and it did not need to pass on the conviction under the first count.[2173]

The Supreme Court did not set an execution date in its opinion, but Walker was executed on January 8, 1920.

At the time of his execution, Walker had been at the prison five weeks. He confessed the crime to Warden J.T. Lynn when he was taken to the actual "death row," the house-within-the-walls were prisoners were kept within sight of the electric chair. It was always blocked from view by a denim curtain.

His last night he was attended by Prison Chaplain J.C. Miles and two other ministers, one black. Walker ate a hearty last meal of chicken and sausage, apples and oranges. "I am ready to die," he said as he was taken from his cell the last time.[2174]

Lorenzo Young, black, age 39. *Murder.*

The crime was committed on the afternoon of June 13, 1919, at the corner of North Walden Boulevard and Jackson Avenue in Memphis, in Shelby County. The killer was a small-time criminal who that day was accused of selling stolen chickens. The victim was police Sgt. John G. Brinkley, white, age thirty-two, of the Memphis Police Department.

The incident began when a grocer, Frank Micci, owner of Overton Park Market, located at North Walden Boulevard and Poplar Avenue, called police to arrest Young, whom he believed was attempting to sell him stolen chickens. Two police officers arrived, Ed Crume and Patrolman Dan McCarthy. Young asserted his innocence and asked Crume's permission to put the chickens back in his buggy, parked outside. Crume agreed and walked outside with Young. Using the same hand to load the chickens, Young pulled a hidden pistol from the buggy. He shot Crume in the hand, which held a pistol.

Hearing the shooting, McCarthy ran outside and began shooting at Young, who returned fire, wounding McCarthy in the arm. A bullet struck Young in the leg, but he did not yield. Instead, he hobbled around the corner of the store and reloaded his now empty pistol. By this time, Micci came outside. He and Young engaged in a grappling fight, each struggling to get the pistol dropped by wounded officer Crume. Young seized the pistol and shot Micci in the right breast, the bullet traveling down toward his abdomen, but he survived.[2175]

About this time, Sgt. Brinkley, who was at the courthouse, heard a report of the shooting and volunteered to go with others to apprehend the unidentified shooter. The group included Police Chief Burney, detective Hulette Smith and Sgt. John Long. The officers sped to the scene in a car. Young, leaving three wounded behind, hopped into his buggy and lashed the horse, going north on McLean Boulevard. By this time, four more officers joined the others, all giving chase.

The police car driven by Sgt. Brinkley stopped at North Walden Boulevard and Jackson, where Sgt. Brinkley got out and moved to a vacant lot. In a crouching position, he took aim at Young. Seeing him, Young instantly fired at Sgt. Brinkley, hitting him above the heart. He died soon after at a hospital. Young was finally apprehended hiding in weeds near a barn a mile away. When word spread of the shooting, two mobs attempted to stop the train taking him to Nashville for safekeeping. Details of the trial are unknown. The Tennessee Supreme Court affirmed the conviction, but the opinion cannot be located.

Young expressed great remorse for his crime. He was attended by the prison chaplain and a black minister who prayed with him the night before his execution. Lorenzo Young was electrocuted at the Main Prison in Nashville on September 3, 1920. Lorenzo Young's last night was also spent writing letters to his wife in Mississippi and friends in Memphis. He ate a hearty last meal and breakfast and shook hands with all the guards as he walked to the electric chair. Seated, he asked forgiveness of his sins and seemed to be praying along with the ministers who were praying for him. At the time of his execution, no one had received instructions on what to do with his body.[2176]

1921

Taylor Neal, black, age 19. *Murder.*
Cyrenas Jackson, black, age 18. *Murder.*

The crime was committed at 10:00 P.M. on August 21, 1920, on Citico Avenue in the city of Chattanooga. Abraham Baron (also spelled Barron), white, age twenty-four, had been driving a Model T Ford with his date, Miss Jennie Pearlman, white, age unknown, when it started to rain. He got out of the car and was raising a side curtain. Without warning or provocation, he was shot by Neal with a rifle from some thirty feet away. The bullet pierced his arm and entered the chest. Baron died within minutes. Jackson and Neal searched his body and took his money. They came around to the passenger side. Pearlman had a box of candy in her lap. She told the pair, "If that is what you want, you can have these," giving them her wristwatch and ring.[2177]

Neal pulled her from the car and pushed her to the ground, an attempted rape, with the candy falling to the ground. Pearlman scrambled away, but Jackson caught her. Neal put his hand over her mouth, dragged her across the street, and attempted to rape her but was interrupted by an approaching car. The pair ran fifty yards to a cave from which they had come to commit the murder. Pearlman was rescued by another motorist, who also took Baron's lifeless body to the hospital.

Six days later, police arrested the defendants and Woody Smith for a home burglary at the home of a man named Wilson that had occurred a week before the Baron killing. The Wilson home was eight blocks from where the defendants lived. A large quantity of personal items, including clothing and liquor, had been taken. Because Smith was not involved in the Baron killing, he eagerly implicated the defendants in the Wilson burglary. (The defendants were wearing Wilson's clothes and shoes when arrested.) Wilson identified his belongings in the cave and police turned their attention to steel-jacketed bullets found there in connection with the Baron killing.

In short order, both defendants admitted their actions in shooting Baron, but each named the other as the person who attempted to rape Pearlman. Neal insisted he only meant to rob Baron but the cocked rifle accidentally discharged. The defendants' confessions, in writing, were taken by police detectives and were given again several hours later to others, notably the police chief.

At trial, the defendants repudiated their confessions and asserted they were induced by threats of violence and were beaten by police. They were told unless they confessed they would be turned over to a mob. They were taken to Nashville for safekeeping.

The police steadfastly denied any kind of threats or violence and the Supreme Court found no evidence of either. The court said the confessions contained information known only to the actual killers, such as the fallen box of candy and what Pearlman's jewelry looked like. The bullet taken from Baron's body matched those taken from the cave. The Supreme Court concluded, "We do not think there can be a reasonable doubt as to their guilt. We think the jury were warranted in discrediting defendants' claim that the confessions were secured from them by violence, threat of violence or intimidation."[2178]

The defendants' relatives and a girlfriend insisted the pair was at home the entire night of the killing. But Smith said they had left the house shortly before the killing, that he heard a shot and that Neal remarked upon return that Jackson had acted the fool, drunk.[2179]

In the days before their execution, the defendants were attended by several ministers and Jackson was baptized. Neal had professed religion some time before. They talked freely about the crime and joked about who would be the first one executed. "You can say that everything is 'peaches,' and that we are ready to die," said Jackson.[2180] On the day before the execution both men ate hearty meals and smoked cigars and cigarettes.[2181] They continued to assert the confessions were coerced.[2182] They were executed in the early morning of August 3, 1921.

Neal was placed in the electric chair first and was asked if he had anything to say. He shook his head no. Jackson watched Neal's body being taken from the execution chamber. Asked if he had anything to say while seated in the chair, he replied, "Meet me in Heaven."[2183] When asked by prison officials what to do with the bodies, the parents said to bury then in Nashville.

Chesley Graham, black, age 22. *Murder.*
Will Allen, black, age 35. *Murder.*

The crime was committed about 9:00 P.M. April 21, 1920, in the store of Harry H. Allen, on Hooker's Bend, in rural Hardin County. The victim was Harry H. Allen, white, age thirty-four. "He was one of the best citizens of the county and his horrible taking off was an extremely sad shock to everyone."[2184] Six persons were charged in the killing. Charges were dropped against one, another went to prison, and two were acquitted.

Will Allen and Chesley Graham came in the back door of the store and found the victim casing eggs. Will Allen struck him over the head with a sledgehammer and Chesley Graham beat him with an iron bar. George Allen, black, age forty-six, received a life sentence. The three were convicted on the testimony of the other three, who acted as lookouts. These were Will Graham, black, age fifteen; and Ernest Graham, black, age thirteen; and Hurl Yarbro, black, age unknown. The teen-age Graham brothers were acquitted.[2185]

The killers had such a bad reputation they were arrested on suspicion on April 23. They were indicted on April 27 and their trial began on April 30, 1920. The murder weapon had been stolen from the barn of a white neighbor. His boots had been taken from a porch and worn by one of the killers. They poured turpentine on their shoes to confuse bloodhounds. They buried the money in the man's hog lot.[2186] Rumors of an "uprising" of Negro lynchers prompted great concern in the area and National Guard soldiers guarded the men at all times. Courthouse visitors were searched for weapons. The Tennessee Supreme Court affirmed the convictions, but the opinion cannot be located.

Graham and Allen received a large meal of fried chicken, pork, vegetables, white bread and biscuits, watermelon, and soft drinks. They ate heartily. Clean sheets and pillows had been put on their beds. They were sung to by twenty female inmates, listening to hymns and "old darky songs."[2187] This made the men highly nervous, and they did not calm down for another hour after the women left. Prison chaplain J.C. Meyers and four other ministers (two black) stayed with the men all night.

Both men asserted their innocence to the end. Graham said the real killers were his younger brothers who testified against him. He said they had given him the victim's money and the family put the blame on him, in part because he had not seen the family in seven years. He said he signed two confessions because he was afraid of mobs that were forming to lynch him. One of the mobs, it turned out, was actually after a white man who had raped a young girl.

Graham said, "All my people have gone to Arkansas and I haven't heard from them since. I don't care whether I live or not. All my friends have deserted me and even my family refused to write to me much less come to see me."[2188] Graham continued, "I haven't anything to say about my death. I have made it right with God, have joined the church and I am prepared to meet Him on the Day of Judgment. My only hope is that He does not visit punishment on my people for the way they have done me."[2189]

Graham told the newspaper that it was not true that he gave a confession in which he took all the blame for the killing, exonerating Allen.[2190] The Pine Bluff police chief asked authorities to inquire whether Allen would admit any involvement with the killing of a deputy sheriff in 1912. He denied it. Allen declined to talk to the newspapers. Chesley Graham and Will Allen were electrocuted on August 17, 1921, at the Main Prison in Nashville. Also executed that day was Hamp Gohlston.

Graham was the first to die. He said good-bye to everyone he knew, including a captain of the guards, saying good-bye to him through the window. He said a short prayer while in the chair. Hamp Gohlston was second. Allen was last. Governor Taylor had asked the trial judge and the prosecutor if the pair were truly guilty. They said yes. The Hardin County sheriff visited the governor, who afterward said, "There is not a shadow of doubt in my mind about Allen's guilt."[2191] This was the first triple execution in the electric chair.[2192]

Hamp Gohlston (aka Will Brown, Hamp Gholston, Hamp Golston, Ham Gholson), black, age 23. *Murder.*

The crime was committed about 9:30 P.M. on May 31, 1919, at the store of victim Isaac Levy, white, age thirty-seven, at 414 South Main Street, Memphis, in Shelby County. Gohlston had come from Arkansas in 1913 and began a life of crime, he claimed, because he was aided by Beale Street merchants who fenced stolen goods for him. According to Gohlston, at one time he worked as a porter in a jewelry store owned by Abe Narvick along with watchmaker Isaac Levy. He claimed that Levy taught him how to steal watches and bring them to him, including watches belonging to Narvick.[2193] At the time of the killing, Levy had his own store.

Gohlston had lost his money on May 31 in a craps game and had gone to another store to steal a gold watch fob. He was prevented from doing so when the owner's son stood in the door blocking an escape. Later, Gohlston went to Levy's store to steal a gold piece watch fob when he knew Levy would be alone. According to one of three transcribed confessions, he only intended to snatch the fob from Levy, "but Levy jumped at him and that he [Gohlston] had his hand on his pistol and must have lost his nerve and pulled the trigger too hard."[2194] Immediately after the shooting Gohlston used the same gun to rob a black man named Ivory Hines on a street nearby.

Gohlston was convicted and sentenced to die, but the Tennessee Supreme Court reversed. Tennessee death penalty law was confused by passage of the Bowers Law[2195] (1915) which abolished the death penalty except for rape [and] or murder of a prison guard, but this law was itself repealed and the death penalty was reinstated in 1917. However, the reinstatement law was deemed defective because the bill lacked a proper caption.[2196] Confusion prompted the legislature to pass a new death penalty law in 1919.[2197] This law placed the entire burden of finding guilt and setting penalty on the jury. The long-established practice of juries finding guilt "with mitigating circumstances," which allowed the judge to affix punishment at less than death, was gone. Likewise, no more could a judge disregard the recommendation by the jury that the killer be spared.

The jury charge in Gohlston's first trial (June 25, 1919) was defective. The judge had told the jury to first consider whether the crime was murder in the first degree. If so, said the trial court, "If you find beyond a reasonable doubt, the defendant guilty of murder in the first degree, as charged in the indictment, you have nothing to do with the penalty. The law says, 'He shall suffer death by electrocution,' unless you, in your verdict, shall find and say there were mitigating circumstances, in which event the court may commute his punishment for life in the penitentiary of the State."[2198]

Gohlston's second trial included use of his several confessions, one of which was given with a newspaper reporter present. Gohlston's arrest and confessions had caused the police to take him back to the rail yard where the pistol and the clothing he was wearing at the time of the crime were found. The bullet which had completely pierced Levy's skull was found to match the .45 caliber bullets in the pistol.

Gohlston repudiated his confessions, insisting that he had only robbed Hines, but had not killed Levy. But the testimony showed that on his way out of the store after shooting Levy, Gohlston literally ran into a young man named Sellers who recognized him at trial and identified his clothing. Likewise, clerk Fortas, who had barred the door, saw Gohlston both before and after the shooting near Levy's store. Their descriptions had led police to arrest Gohlston that night in the rail yard. He was apparently seeking to hop a train.

A woman who lived near the store testified that she saw Gohlston in the store and saw him running away after the shooting. Her testimony was inconsistent. She first testified she lived a block and one-half away, when she actually lived only four doors away. The Supreme Court found this immaterial since her testimony was merely cumulative.[2199] The clear identification had been made by the clerk and Hines.

Awaiting death, Gohlston joked constantly with guards and inmates and enjoyed talking about his criminal exploits. He asked his spiritual advisers cryptically, "Do you suppose that God will forgive a man who killed six men?"[2200] They said yes. Gohlston died in the electric chair on August 17, 1921. He was heard praying. He asked God to take care of the fatherless children of the men he had slain. His prayer took so long that the electrician thought Gohlston was through and turned on the current just as Gohlston began to say, "Oh, my Father." Gohlston was one of three persons executed on August 17, 1921. It was the first triple electrocution in Tennessee and Gohlston was executed second, after Chesley Graham and before Will Allen.

1922

John Green, white, age 28. *Murder.*

The crime was committed at the home of Robert L. Houston, white, age forty-one, in Watauga in Washington County on July 17, 1921. The facts of the crime are unknown except that Houston was shot with a pistol in the presence of his wife, Ollie Houston, white, age twenty-four, the chief prosecuting witness, and two other men.[2201] A reward prompted a large manhunt.[2202] Green was soon captured and promptly confessed. On June 23, 1910, John Green had stabbed to death a Johnson City policeman, Walter McPeak, white, age twenty-eight. Green had been released from prison after serving nine years.

Green was convicted on December 23, 1921, and the jury found no mitigating circumstances. He was ordered executed on February 17, 1922, but did not appeal his case and was executed at the Main Prison at Nashville on that day.

Green stated repeatedly that he was glad he made the confession that led him to the electric chair because he felt relieved and was ready to meet his Maker. He said, "I'm glad I confessed and I'm so glad that there isn't anyone left behind to care for me for I don't believe I have any relatives in this country." He continued, "Fact is, that I don't even know how old I am, or who my father is, and the only thing that I know is that my mother died when I was born, and I am glad now — for she does not know."[2203]

Green ate a last meal of chicken, country ham, vegetables, fruits and cake. He was attended by Prison Chaplain J.C. Myers, two other ministers, and two young men, L.C. Parsons and S.A. Jones, who "are doing prison work throughout the state."[2204] When asked by the clergymen for a last request, he asked they sing "Nearer My God to Thee." After it was sung, he broke down sobbing. He spent most of the night and morning hours in earnest prayer, on his knees in his cell, perspiring heavily and with tears streaming down his cheeks. He was also attended by a Roman Catholic priest at the end.

Green said, "I have prayed earnestly all day and will do so until I go to my death for those whom I have hurt by my sinful acts. I have, thank God, a clear and undoubted faith in Christ and I have accepted my fate with full resignation to God's will." He continued, "My last request is that by my end all young men will take warning from my fate, which was caused by bad women and drink. That is what it all leads to — the worst end of all."[2205] Green was given new clothes and said nothing on the way or while sitting in the chair. He was the first white man executed in the Tennessee electric chair.[2206]

Asbury Fields, white, age 47. *Murder.*

The crime was committed about 10:00 P.M. July 30, 1921, on a country road eight miles from the victim's home near a road leading from Birchwood to Cleveland, in Bradley County. The victim was James R. Pierce, white, age fifty-eight. The two knew each other because both traded in untaxed whiskey (moonshine). Fields had served two terms in federal prison for selling moonshine, and twenty-seven months at the Nashville prison for forgery. He had been released from prison on December 23, 1920. He had a wife and small son.

Fields arrived in Bradley County two weeks before the killing. He secured room and board at the home of John Thompson. "He was without any means and he and his family were without sufficient clothing."[2207] According to the Tennessee Supreme Court, "He had not worked while at Thompson's. He was out most of the time at nights."[2208]

The killing was committed on Saturday night. Fields was dropped off at the location, a cemetery, where he and Pierce had agreed to meet. Fields walked toward the location. The men who dropped him off had been told by Fields that he was going to sell Pierce two hundred and five gallons of moonshine in barrels. Pierce had told a nephew who dropped him off not to wait. The implication was that Pierce was meeting someone with a truck to carry the liquor and this person would bring him home.

No one witnessed the killing. The state's theory was that Fields lured Pierce into the secluded area to rob and kill him. Pierce carried as much as two thousand dollars on his person. When Pierce did not return, his nephew began searching and he was found near the location where he had been dropped off near the cemetery. His head was battered and he had worn the skin off his fingers attempting to crawl to the road. He died two days later without naming his assailant. The murder weapon, a hammer, was found nearby. The hammer belonged to John Thompson. It had been left at another man's house three days before the killing.

No moonshine was found near Pierce's body, nor any evidence that any had been hidden there. Within days of the killing, Fields had been located in Columbus, Georgia, where he and his wife bought two hundred dollars' worth of clothing. They bought four hundred dollars' worth of furniture and he had just deposited seven hundred dollars in the bank.[2209]

Fields testified that he had sold the whiskey to Pierce on Friday (not Saturday) and was with Pierce at his request because he was meeting three other men, Wyatt Haddock, Bob Williams, and Walter Haddock. Pierce told him there might be a dispute about some money owed to Pierce. Fields described a scene in the dark, lit by lanterns, whereby Wyatt Haddock struck and killed Pierce and Fields could not help because Walter Haddock put a gun to his chest.[2210]

The Tennessee Supreme Court said, "This story is clearly a fabrication pure and simple."[2211] The chief problem was that Fields could not be specific about where he made the moonshine ("down from White Oak Mountain") and did not provide as a witness the man who he said helped deliver this quantity of whiskey and hang it in trees. A former federal prison cell mate testified he saw Fields's still, but he was not specific where it was located and saw no whiskey there.[2212]

Another major inconsistency in Fields's story was that he clearly needed money to pay back Walter Haddock for bringing his wife and child from Cleveland, Tennessee, to the boarding house on the Saturday morning of the killing, but did not have any money. The notion that Pierce was with Fields on Friday night was clearly disproved by several friends and witnesses of the dead man. The nephew was up most of the night because his wife had a baby that night. Pierce slept in the same room as his son, and the nephew had seen him sleeping, and they all had an early breakfast Saturday morning.[2213]

To the last, Fields maintained his innocence. "I absolutely deny the charges made against me, but if I must die I am perfectly reconciled to go. But I want everyone to know that I am dying for a crime committed by someone else. I will go to the chair an innocent man, and I have prayed and settled with my God. If I had not, I would be doing it right now. I have a slight hope that Governor Taylor will act before morning, but I am resigned to the worst."[2214]

Fields's wife visited him the night before the execution. They ate a last meal together. Before his death he was given a bath and new clothes. When he complained the "death house" was too cold, the guards put more coal in the stove. Asbury Fields was electrocuted at 6:15 A.M. February 18, 1922. His last words were not recorded. He was given two thirty-second electric shocks.[2215] John Green had been executed the day before.

Charles Petree, Jr., white, age 23. *Murder.*
Tom Christmas, white, age 26. *Murder.*
Otto Stephens, white, age 29. *Murder.*
John McClure, white, age 26. *Murder.*

The crime was committed about 9:00 P.M. on May 30, 1921, in a secluded area by the side of the road ten miles west of Clinton on Oakdale Pike about a mile from the village of Robertsville, in Anderson County. The killers were Christmas, Stephens, McClure, and Petree.[2216] How they came to know each other is unknown, other than they lived in the same rooming house in Clinton, in Anderson County.[2217]

The motive for the killing was the need for a large fast car because they were planning to rob a bank in tiny Oakdale, in Anderson County. The victim was George A. Lewis, white, age forty-nine, who was a friend of Andrew T. Crumley, white, age twenty-six. It was Crumley's car that attracted the killers' attention. It was a large, fast seven-passenger Chandler touring car.

Crumley was sitting in the car, which served as a private taxi or town car, on Depot Street in Knoxville when he was approached by Petree and McClure, who asked him to drive them to a point a few miles past Clinton. Crumley drove to his boarding house in Knoxville to find a friend to accompany him in the car.[2218] There he met fellow boarder George A. Lewis, who asked Crumley for a free ride to Clinton, where he planned to visit his grown daughter. Crumley drove the car to Clinton, but stopped at a boarding house first. Petree stayed in the car while McClure went inside and brought back Christmas and Stephens. They loaded their luggage in the car and left. It was about 8:00 P.M. Crumley and Lewis sat in the front seat. Three killers sat in the back seat, while the fourth sat in a folding seat in the back. Crumley was told to drive out Oliver Springs Road.

Ten miles out on the Oakdale Pike (as it was now called) and about a mile from the village of Robertsville, Petree told Crumley to stop. Petree got out, looked around, said this was not the place, and stood on the running board as Crumley drove further. Petree was familiar with this area because he had once worked on a farm here. After going another distance, Petree told Crumley to stop the car and asked him if he could see a path leading into the woods.

When Crumley said no, he heard a voice telling him and Lewis to hold up their hands. At first, Crumley thought the voice was a law officer, because he suspected the real purpose of the trip was to purchase whiskey. In fact, it was one of the killers. The two were ordered out of the car and their hands were tied behind them. With Petree leading the way with a flashlight, the captives were marched 350 yards from the road. When they reached the designated spot, Crumley's hands were checked and retied with trotline, tightly cutting into the flesh.

Crumley and Lewis were searched. A few dollars were taken from Crumley, along with a New Testament he had carried since his discharge from the Army. The only thing taken from Lewis was a copy of *Police Gazette*, a popular true-crime magazine. Its discovery prompted jocular remarks from the killers. Crumley began begging for his life, urging the men to take the car and leave him and Lewis. "I pleaded for my life, saying I had a wife and two helpless children," he said, "When I fell I could feel the sharp steel enter my throat."[2219]

As he was begging, he felt his hat come off, and heard a "swishing" sound. He thought he had been struck by lightning and fell down. According to the Tennessee Supreme Court:

> He [Crumley] seems to have regained consciousness in a few moments. He heard one of the men ask, "Have you cut him?" and the reply, "No, I am going to cut him now." Crumley then heard a kind of gurgling noise like blood running and a "squishing sound" and saw one of the men cut Lewis' throat. Lewis had previously been knocked down, as had Crumley. Both of the men had severe scalp wounds apparently made by the butt of a pistol. A piece of the handle of a pistol was found there the next morning. After seeing them cut Lewis' throat, Crumley felt a foot of one of the men on his head and then felt

> his own throat cut. After cutting Crumley's throat the men left. They severed the jugular vein of Lewis. Crumley saw Lewis thrash around awhile and then expire. Crumley's wounds, while severe, were not fatal.[2220]

Getting to his feet, Crumley staggered though the mountains bleeding and running into wire fences. He heard his car return and saw the men looking for him with a flashlight. He and Lewis had been gagged with rags and torn towels tied around their heads to hold the gags in place. The towel holding Crumley's gag slipped down the side of his throat and acted like a bandage to stop the bleeding from his neck. At one farmhouse he was turned away, the male voice inside saying he was attending a sick child. He finally reached a house where he received attention and the alarm was given.

The next day, May 31, 1921, S.N. Oakley, the cashier of the Oakdale Bank & Trust Company, came to open the bank at 8:00 A.M., accompanied by several people who wanted to cash checks as soon as the bank opened. The cashier noticed that a window had been broken or removed and suspected that something was wrong, but he went to his teller's cage to serve the customers. As he did so, two men hiding behind the counter arose with pistols drawn. A pistol was held on the cashier, another on the customers. The men "gathered up their grips," said the Supreme Court, and dashed from the bank. One was recognized as Stephens, who previously lived in Oakdale, and the other was McClure. They ran to the car, which held Petree and Christmas, and sped away.

The police and a posse gave chase but, according to the Supreme Court, "The defendants had the better car and the pursuers were not able to overtake them."[2221] Later, the defendants lost control of the car and wrecked it. They took to the woods as three hundred posse members searched for them, seeking a $900 reward. Oakley and police officers hopped a freight train going in the robbers' direction toward Harriman. The four were spotted sitting beside the track. The train was ordered to stop, and the men were pursued on foot. Petree and McClure were captured immediately; Stephens and Christmas were arrested fifteen days later.

Petree, McClure and Stephens all gave various statements to the police, admitting they were part of the killing, but each vigorously denying actually cutting Lewis's throat. Only Christmas made no statement. It was never determined at trial who cut the victims' throats. None of the defendants took the witness stand, although McClure was adamant that Petree and Christmas were the knife wielders. A sheriff's deputy said Stephens had admitted killing Lewis.[2222] The men had nine lawyers who made a bitter fight.

The only defense raised was on behalf of Petree. His mother testified he was a "weak and backward child; that he had spasms; that his head was hurt by reason of an explosion of a stove when he was a young boy, and she did not think him mentally responsible."[2223] The court said the evidence did not show that he was insane or did not know right from wrong.

The court summarized the case: "These young men planned a bank robbery. They desired a high powered automobile and inveigled Crumley out of Knoxville with his car. Lewis chanced to come along with Crumley. The defendants wanted the car and after getting Crumley and Lewis out of the car, defendants decided to kill them on the theory that dead men tell no tales. Defendants tied these men, knocked them in the head, cut their throats and left them both for dead. All of this was carried through in a perfectly cold blooded and deliberate manner, and there is no controversy about any of the facts."[2224] The men were ordered executed on March 1, 1922.

Three thousand people from Tennessee and neighboring states attended portions of the trial, and seven hundred and fifty veniremen were called before a jury was seated. The courthouse square looked like a county fair with soft-drink sellers and food vendors meeting the crowd's needs. Also present was an evangelist preaching the golden path, ballad singers, a sting quartet, and a Negro minstrel.[2225] The ten-day trial ended July 30, 1921.

With four lives at stake, the governor was besieged with requests from family and friends for commutation. McClure's father had approached the governor of Michigan, who then telegraphed Governor Taylor asking that McClure be given a mental evaluation, which was done. The governor also received counterpetitions from the Clinton area demanding he not grant clemency to the men.

During the trial an attractive young woman, identified as a business college student, had become friendly with McClure and sat close to him throughout the proceeding. He displayed her photograph at the prison in Nashville, and the woman, Grace Brown, captured the newspapers' attention with her frequent visits to McClure in prison and her passionate weeping. Warden J.T. Lynn had initially refused permission for her to visit him, but relented after she agreed to sit in a chair in front of his cell.

When allowed in the death house, she promptly

ran to his arms, and the couple kissed. "Those who were present in the death house respectfully turned their heads, while the couple spoke to each other. They were allowed to remain together for over an hour, when Miss Brown reluctantly, but determinately turned to leave. She kissed McClure for the last time, and then walked down the corridor and shook hands with each of the condemned men, as she reached the exit, she turned her head, gave one departing look at her fiancé and left the death house with bowed head and tears streaming down her cheeks."[2226] McClure had given her a ring. From time to time, she would hold it in her hand and finding a corner, weep softly. McClure's good-bye poem to her was published on the front page of the *Nashville Tennessean*.

Petree and McClure had early said they preferred death to working in the mines for the rest of their lives. But as they waited for clemency, all four maintained they were innocent. McClure's father loudly complained his son was guiltless. The men were attended by Prison Chaplain J.C. Meyers, and all professed they were ready to meet God, upon whom they were depending for salvation. McClure, who asserted he was a Presbyterian, said, "I pray every night. I prayed every night for Asbury Fields and John Green before they were executed. I believe in prayer, and I am going to heaven. Won't you pray for me?"[2227]

Christmas told the media that he was opposed to the death penalty, in part because, "To execute a man is to execute his mother." He quoted the gospel of Matthew as supposedly opposing the punishment. Reading passages from the gospel, he said, "Governor Taylor has a heart, and today he may help us. Bob Taylor and my father knew each other. If the Governor would only read a few verses of St. Matthew, it might help. Here, let me read it to you."[2228] McClure's letter to the governor said, "Governor, I am dying an innocent man. You are sending me to the chair when I am not guilty and God have mercy on your soul."[2229]

Petree assumed an air of bravado, smiling and smoking constantly. He said, "Oh, yes, I have hoped the governor will show leniency, but if he don't, my life's no better than anybody else's."[2230] Stephens agreed with Christmas: "It hurts me because it hurts Mother. Father has been dead many years, and I left school early in life to work and help her." He continued, "Few young men realize the value of a mother. If I'd followed her advice, I wouldn't be here today. She's fifty-four and this will kill her."[2231]

Stephens and McClure complained about the trial. Said Stephens, "Until this day I have never had the opportunity to tell my story to a court. Justice Green of the Supreme Court admitted, in his decision, 'we find error in the court, but the evidence is sufficient.'" He continued, "I am not guilty as charged — of first degree murder. It would do no good to tell it now. Did you know that a member of that jury found a note in his pocket directing him with threats to send us to the chair? Did you know that two of the jurymen decided to convict us before the trial?"[2232]

McClure complained, "It does look like Governor Taylor would give us a little time. He gave Maurice Mays, the negro up the hall, 90 days. Don't you think we deserve that much consideration? They say he is a big-hearted man." McClure continued, "I killed no one. I never intended to kill anyone. The truth of that night is, that we planned to rob a bank and take that man's car to get away. I was two hundred yards away when the cutting was done."[2233] The contention that he was merely an accessory was the basis of his appeal for clemency.

The four were given large meals which they ate, plus plenty of cigarettes, and fresh flowers decorated their cells. They were attended by Allen McNamara, an inmate whose sentence was commuted to life imprisonment eighteen months earlier. The men offered no last words, but left plenty of last writings. McClure read a poem he had written: "To Mother. O Mother of mine, if I had my way, this sorrow would pass you by. But always remember I love you, and as I am innocent, I go without a sigh. Hoping to meet you in Heaven, in the land beyond the sky."[2234]

Stephens's last written words asserted that Petree "is innocent of this. But I feel I will know him as brother in Heaven the same as he has been a brother to me through this."[2235] Petree insisted he was being sent to death for "politic's sake," continuing, "And I can say before my God that I am innocent, and that is more than a lot of the public can say now."[2236] A newspaper reported, "Before it was evident that the defense's case had collapsed, an attempt was made to show that Petree had possessed low mentality since childhood. This effort failed and the defense entered a plea of guilty and begged the court's mercy."[2237]

Tom Christmas's letter said the New Testament did not support capital punishment and quoted long passages of Scripture. He asserted that the people of Anderson County and Knox County just wanted to take his life and "they are guilty of murder in their hearts." He continued, "That is just the same as if they had killed a man, in the sight of God."[2238] His lengthy letter concluded, "So let the people get the murder out of their hearts and come to that God that is all in all."[2239]

Known by now as the "Christmas Killers," the four were electrocuted at the Main Prison in Nashville on March 1, 1922. They were executed in this order: Petree, Christmas, Stephens, and McClure.[2240] The reason Petree was first was that he vomited twice, the latest time an hour before the execution, and a "deadly pallor overspread his face."[2241] The newspaper reported, "It was feared that Petree would collapse completely if one of the other three men were executed first, so he was chosen to head the death march."[2242]

This was the last quadruple execution in Tennessee. The fact that the Christmas Killers asserted their innocence as death neared, blighted any prospect that the governor would commute the sentence of Maurice Mays, black, also from East Tennessee. Mays had proclaimed his innocence from the first. If the governor had commuted Mays, he would have had to commute the Christmas Killers as well, and visa versa. It was a political decision the governor could not afford to make in an election year. He lost the election anyway.

Maurice Mays, black, age 32/34. *Murder.*

Maurice (pronounced Morris) Mays is the only person in Tennessee thought to have been wrongly executed by more than one death penalty researcher. He was declared innocent ("wrong man") by sociologists Hugo Adam Bedau and Michael L. Radelet in a famous study in 1987.[2243] Writer John Edgerton had reached the same conclusion in 1983 by emphasizing the racially prejudiced nature of Mays's two trials.[2244] By 2000, it had become accepted truth that Mays was innocent ("wrong man") or if not, was "wrongly convicted," according to an historian, Matthew Lakin, who wrote about Mays's trials in the context of the race riot that occurred the day after he was arrested for the crime that ultimately sent him to the electric chair.[2245] Finally, in 2006 a well-known scholar of Tennessee evidence and legal history, Don Paine, argued that Mays was "wrongfully convicted" by arguing he had no motive for the purported sexual assault and incidental killing.[2246]

However, none of these writers has come forward with any scientific or testimonial evidence exonerating Mays. Instead, each approached the case by emphasizing certain facts which suggest to them Mays was "wrongly convicted." For example, Bedau and Radelet emphasized a police officer's animus toward Mays, coupled with the confession of a woman five years later that she had dressed up like a black man and killed Mays's victim because she thought she was having an affair with her husband.[2247]

Journalist Edgerton described the policeman's animus in detail as well. He mentioned the belated confession and explained why the authorities failed to accredit it, then described his own search for the purported confessor fifty-five years later.[2248] Historian Lakin discussed no details of Mays's conviction, but mentioned several letters from notables such as state Supreme Court justices, which urged clemency.[2249] Legal writer Paine highlighted "unethical police investigation and police perjury" and continuing racial prejudice in the aftermath of the race riot.[2250]

Who Was Maurice Mays?

According to Paine, "Maurice Mays was born on May 8, 1887, to Ella Walker. She was a mulatto maid in the household of prominent white politician and banker John McMillan. McMillan was the father, so Maurice Mays was a quadroon. At about age six months he became the foster child of William Mays and wife Frances. His natural father supported him as needed."[2251] At no time in either of Mays's trials was his parentage discussed. Rather, William Mays (sometimes called Uncle William), black, then age thirty-three, was always referred to as Mays's father. On the stand, Uncle William, then sixty-five, apparently belied the truth. "Q: Uncle William, are you Maurice Mays' father? A: Supposed to be."[2252]

Paine explains, "In August 1904 at age seventeen Mays got into trouble. While helping police break up a craps game, he shot John Boyd. Despite his claim of self-defense he was convicted and sentenced to two years in prison. Governor Cox immediately signed a pardon. No wonder, because letters came from the trial judge and prosecutors and all 12 jurors. Why he was tried is mysterious."[2253]

Paine continues, "Maurice Mays married Mattie Douglass on July 1, 1917. They soon separated and she moved up north. Mays went back to consorting with women of all colors — black and white and in between."[2254] According to Paine, Mays had run an establishment in Knoxville called Stroller's Café located in Knoxville's red-light district. "Various sins were committed and tolerated there."[2255]

Historian Lakin explains, "On a typical night, Mays could be found at a table in his café, surrounded by adoring women of both races. Popularly described in the black community as 'so white he wouldn't eat a black hen's egg or drink a black cow's milk,' he was known to have a fondness for white women and had been forced to leap from a window to escape an angry husband."[2256] Lakin continues, "These adventures, together with a brief career as a deputy sheriff and the killings of two men, both black, had made him well known to law enforcement officials over the years. Several times he had been arrested on charges that ranged from carrying a concealed weapon to operating a gambling house but, apart from a manslaughter conviction as a teenager, was rarely prosecuted."[2257]

Mays had served as a deputy sheriff from September 1 until October 15, 1916, stating he found the office "a very disagreeable one" and had resigned to become an agent for a local bonding company.[2258]

Maurice Mays also had three criminal charges pending against him at the time of the killing on August 30, 1919. He had been arrested for peeping into a woman's window (trespass) and when arrested was found in possession of a pistol. He was also under indictment for a gambling charge.[2259] He acknowledged the charges in court, but insisted he "had never been indicted on but [these] three charges." When cross-examined about whether he had been indicted for murder and convicted of manslaughter and sent to the penitentiary, he replied, "No, I never went to the penitentiary for murder. I was indicted and convicted by the jury and the Governor pardoned me."[2260]

Politics and a Crime Wave in Knoxville in 1919

The presumed reason for Mays's favored status at the time of the killing which sent him to the electric chair was his close relationship with his purported father, Mayor John E. McMillan, a Democrat who was elected in 1915 with support from the city's black population. Mays and Uncle William had spent all day on August 29, 1919, canvassing on foot and in a buggy by handing out blank poll tax receipts (needed to gain access to the voting). The hotly contested mayoral election was set for September 6, 1919.

Knoxville faced another problem at the time of the killing. According to Lakin, "An unprecedented crime wave gripped the city as 'Pants,' a mysterious prowler, began burglarizing homes in the working class districts and attacking white women, most of whom described their assailant as a light-skinned Negro."[2261] Lakin explained, "Police appeared baffled as the attacks continued, and many whites soon began to suspect that authorities were content to let Pants run wild, so long has he confined his assaults to working people."[2262] One of those baffled policemen was Andy White (who was white) who had a longstanding grudge against Mays. Whether it arose out of competition for the same white woman, as some alleged, or whether it arose out of Mays's interference with an arrest (as White testified), White had enlisted the help of other white cops in a "relentless campaign of harassment against his enemy, arresting Mays on an almost weekly basis, particularly in the wake of the recent midnight assaults."[2263]

Numerous people testified they saw or spoke with Mays throughout the day and he was dropped off at his house about 12:30 A.M. His alibi was that he was at home asleep when the crime was committed about 2:30 A.M. that night, August 30, 1919. Mays lived alone in a house four blocks from his father's. He occupied two front rooms in the house; the two back rooms (separated by a door locked from Mays's side) were occupied by a black couple. They were unable to testify when Mays came home. It had rained about 2:00 P.M. on the 29th and the grass surrounding the victim's home was still wet at the time the crime was committed.

The Death of Mrs. Bertie Lindsey[2264]

The crime was committed at the three-room wood-frame home occupied by Mrs. Bertie Lindsey, white, age 27, at 1215 Eighth Avenue in a working-class section of north Knoxville. Bertie (variously Birdie) worked at the nearby Standard Knitting Mills. Her husband, Daniel Lindsey, was working as a carpenter in Akron, Ohio, and she planned to join him. Meanwhile, she had asked her cousin, Ora Smyth (sometimes spelled Smith), white, age 21, who lived with her parents in the country, to stay with her. The women, both dressed in white nightgowns, had gone to bed about 10:30 P.M. and were sleeping in the same double bed.

Mays entered the room where the women were sleeping by cutting and enlarging a hole in the screen door and unfastening the latch. He carried a .38 Smith & Wesson pistol and a flashlight. He entered the room where the women were sleeping and as he approached the bed he awakened Mrs. Lindsey. She arose in the bed, grabbed the arm of Ora Smyth, and called her name twice: "Ora! Ora!" Mays told her to keep still and lie down. Ora Smith was awakened but did not move.[2265]

Here is what happened next:

> Mrs. Lindsey jumped to her feet in the bed and got over next to the wall on the opposite side of Miss Smith, but still on the bed, standing up; that the defendant continued to throw the flash-

> light on her and to hold the pistol on her and commanded her to lie down, which she did; that she jumped up a second time on the bed and got over next to the wall, that the defendant continued to throw the flashlight and present the pistol to her and by means of threats and oaths commanded her to lie down the second time, which she did; that Miss Smith continued to remain still in the bed; that Mrs. Lindsey jumped up the third time and jumped out of the bed onto the floor at the foot of the bed and looked out of the window; that the defendant continued to throw the flashlight on her and to present the pistol to her and to curse her, and commanded her to get back in the bed and lie down, telling her he would kill her if she did not do so. That then Mrs. Lindsey made one step towards the door, whereupon the defendant fired, the ball entering to the right of the spine between the first and second ribs, ranging downward and across the body some 18 inches, where it was later extracted just beneath the skin, and which produced instant death.[2266]

Ora Smyth (at the time of the second trial she was Ora Smyth Parsons) testified "that from what Mays said to her that night, she thought he was there for the purpose of assaulting a woman and not for the purpose of robbery."[2267] Ora's testimony included the following exchange:

> "The shot caused her to fall; after he killed Mrs. Lindsey, he went half way to the door and then he came back to the bed and that was when he put his hands on my person." She was asked, "What did he say he would do to you when he came back to the bed and put his hands on your person?" and replied, "I do not care to repeat it." Was pressed to tell what he said and she said, "I do not care to repeat it," but that it was vulgar. "After he made this vulgar remark, he said he had a notion to kill me now. I told him to spare my life and take my money; I told him where my money was; I told him it was on the dresser; that it was there in a vase, that Mrs. Lindsey had some money there also in a pocketbook. He went over there in the direction of where the money was. He did not get my money; he got Mrs. Lindsey's; hers was in a pocketbook; took the pocketbook and money."[2268]

The first challenge to Mays's guilt offered by Bedau and Radelet in their 1987 article was criticism of "the testimony of an eyewitness who never got a clear look at the killer."[2269]

Ora Smyth Parsons explained why she saw Mays clearly. A dressing table with a mirror had been placed diagonally to the bed. "The refection of the flashlight in the mirror at the corner of the room aided in lighting up the room."[2270] Moreover, everything in the room seemed to reflect light, "The color of the bed-clothing was white, a white counterpane was on the bed; the gowns we had on were white; the pillow-slips were white."[2271]

Ora Smyth Parsons explained what she saw:

> In changing the flashlight from one hand to another, he flashed the light in his own face and when Mrs. Lindsey got on the foot of the bed, he threw the light on her and that gave me a good view of him; it was a very clear view. At the time he fired the shot, he was standing there at the corner; at that time he threw the flashlight off of me at the head of the bed and threw it in the corner and then I got a good view of him. He took the flashlight off of me and turned it on Mrs. Lindsey; he changed it about two or three times, and gave me a good view of his face. Every time she would stand up, he would throw the flashlight on her and command her to lay down, and I would get a good view of him; I could clearly see his face. The flashlight was thrown off of me so I could see him two or three times; he changed it from one hand to another at least that many times.[2272]

Ora Smyth Parsons was adamant, "While he was standing there, making this motion and threatening, I got a clear view of his face and there is no doubt about the man being Mays."[2273]

Knoxville chief of police Edward M. Haynes made a personal investigation with other officers three days after the killing and testified:

> We took a flash light about the size that was claimed that this man used and flashed the light around in the room to see if we could see anybody in there. Then we placed Miss Smyth in the bed the way she claimed she was in the bed and had the flashlight run over her and then we turned it back over on the wall, back in the corner, here, about the dresser, and there was no question about seeing anybody in the room with the flashlight on.[2274]

Explained chief Haynes:

> You could see very plainly in there. The wallpaper was white and the bed had a white spread and white pillowcases. You could tell a white man from a colored man in the room. We could tell a white man from a mulatto. With a flashlight with a bell top on it or funnel shape top on it flashed about in the room you could see to pick up a pin. It makes a reflection on the wall about eight feet in diameter and there is no question about seeing and identifying anybody in the room.

His testimony was recounted by the state's brief:

> Said the mirror was sitting catty-cornered across the room and reflected light also. Said that anyone on the bed could see from the head of the bed to the foot when the flashlight was turned

> on one from the foot of the bed at the place where she was killed. The first experiment we made with it was on the left hand side of the bed. I turned it over to Mr. Fogerty and I got against the wall at the window on the left hand side of the bed and flashed the light around there and has Miss Smyth lying down on the bed and that threw me with my face towards the dresser, and when Fogerty flashed the light around, I could see plainly in there.[2275]

The Bedau and Radelet assertion that Ora Smyth Parsons "never got a clear look at the killer" runs counter to what the Tennessee Supreme Court said:

> We have further evidence that some time after the commission of the murder Chief of Police Haynes and other officers of the city of Knoxville went to the Lindsay home and made an experiment with an ordinary flashlight at night, and at a time when Mrs. Parsons was present, and after she had arranged the furniture in the room where the murder was committed in the same way that it was arranged on the night of the murder; the room being decorated with very light paper, as it was on the night of the homicide. This experiment showed that a person could be easily seen in the room; his color distinguished; his form, general appearance, size, and features observed and noted. Some of the officers say that it was almost light enough in the room to enable one to see a pin on the floor. This evidence is uncontradicted, and strongly corroborates Mrs. Parsons in her statement that she was able to see and observe the intruder who shot Mrs. Lindsay in the same room on the night of August 29, 1919.[2276]

The Apprehension of Maurice Mays

Ora Smyth dashed from the house and ran next door to the home of Emmett Dyer and his wife Gertrude, waking the wife and falling into her arms. Dyer was soon awakened. He was a four-year member of the Knoxville Police Department. He went to the Lindsey home, discovered the body, made a quick look for the mode of entry and telephoned a report to police headquarters that was taken by desk sergeant A.J. Watkins.[2277]

Watkins telephoned several officers including Andy White, who testified, "He ordered me to go to Eighth Street and Gainger with the patrol wagon as soon as I could get there; myself and the patrol driver. No one else went with me there. The others had gone before. It took me ten minutes to get there."[2278]

Officer Andy White testified: "I immediately went into the house and saw the lady lying there. I looked at her and stood there a minute and walked out: walked around the house and went down the street and out the alley, down towards the Crystal Ice Factory and came back into the yard again and Captain Wilson was questioning this young lady that was in there and I stayed there and listened to that a few minutes. Captain Wilson, in pursuance to that talk with Miss Smyth, directed me to go to Maurice Mays's house and see if he was at home, and if so, what was his condition."[2279]

Jim Smith, black, drove the patrol wagon that carried officers White, Kirby and Hatcher.[2280] It first went to the home of William Mays[2281] (Maurice's father) and the officers asked if Maurice was present. Told no, they went to Maurice's house four blocks away on Hume Street.

Andy White testified, "We went to the door and took one of the boy's sticks and knocked on the door. Took hold of the door and shook it and we got no answer and we called him and got no answer. We made so much noise that we waked up the man that lived next door. White,[2282] Robert Brown and I went over there and asked him if Mays lived there and he said he did. I said, "Is he at home?" and he said, "I don't know." He said somebody went in there something like an hour ago."[2283]

Andy White continued:

> I came back again to the side window on the north side of the house. The house sits east and west on the north side of the house and I prized up a little piece of screen and took the policeman's billy and pushed the curtains back and I could see his clothes on the bed but could not see him, for the foot of the bed. The bed was sitting diagonally across the room. We went around the house on the south side and pushed the curtain back and you could see a man in bed, and I said, "He is lying in bed," and Tom Kirby was in front. His head was towards the foot of the bed and his feet towards the head of the bed: that would make his head three feet from the door that we had been knocking at. We made enough noise to wake the man up next door. Said we knocked hard and loud on the door and made an impression on the door with the policeman's billy.[2284]

While the police were shouting for Mays to open the door and beating on it, Mays's father arrived and "hallooed for him several times in a loud voice" but he still did not answer the door, explained officer John Hatcher, until after "Mr. White had one of those big lights and we threw that in the window next the house that we had knocked at and we could see his hat and clothes and we went around to the side window on the opposite side of the house, on the south side, and threw the light in that window and could see him laying in the bed."[2285]

Andy White continued, "Tom Kirby said, 'Maurice, open the door!' He used a pretty harsh tone of voice, and had a strong voice. He opened it right then. His reason for not opening the door was that he said he never turned anybody in his house after night."[2286]

The officers entered the house and found that Mays had placed the top of his trousers under the mattress with the legs hanging down. White testified that the pants legs were "damp, wet."[2287] Hatcher saw them but did not touch them. White testified, "I saw his shoes there. They were under the side of the bed over towards the foot. I picked up the shoes and scratched the bottoms this way (indicating) with my thumb nail and there was red mud on them with cinders in it. There was red mud and cinders around the edges of the sole. There were signs of red mud stains and tracks on the carpet of the floor of his room. These tracks were very plain. There was not as much mud as cinders. The tracks went to the center of the room."[2288]

Officer Kirby felt the pants and concluded they were wet. He saw White examine the shoes and saw the red mud and cinders on both the shoes and the carpet.[2289]

The officers asked for Mays's flashlight. Initially, he claimed not to have one, but at trial said it had been loaned to Mr. Ethel King two or three months before and never returned. King did not testify.[2290]

Andy White asked to see Maurice Mays's pistol and was told it was in the dresser drawer. Andy White testified, "We took the pistol and broke it down and looked into it and smelled it. It had a fresh smell of powder. It had been shot recently. There was one bright cartridge and four that were corroded, showing that they had been there some time. I called the attention of the other officers to the smell of the pistol, to see if they smelled powder in it as I did. They both smelled it. They both looked at the pistol after it was broken down."

The other officers testified they smelled burnt powder on the pistol. Hatcher testified, "His pistol was in the dresser drawer. I examined it. Three of us examined it, Kirby, White and myself. We smelled gunpowder. It smelled fresh. I examined the new cartridge and the old cartridges. It had four tarnished cartridges with black spots on them like they had been in there quite a while. One particular, new looking as if it had been carried in the pocket. It showed up bright and shiny looking."[2291]

Neither side offered any ballistic evidence. The concept was relatively new, but had been used to free Charles E. Stielow, a New York man who was actually strapped into the electric chair in 1915 when he received his last stay of execution and was ultimately exonerated when another man confessed to the killing in 1918.[2292] Ballistic evidence was used to prove the guilt of Sacco and Vanzetti in 1921 (the deadly bullet had come from Sacco's pistol; whether Vanzetti was present is another matter altogether).

On appeal, Mays's lawyers asserted a fact conflict: "White and the other officers say that the pistol had a "faint smell" of burnt powder."[2293] Against this testimony, they asserted, "William Mays smelt the pistol and says there was no such smell. Dave Sanders, policeman, smelt the pistol and says there was no odor about it."[2294] But the key testimony, according to Mays's appellate brief was this, "Jim Smith says the officers kept smelling the pistol as if they were dissatisfied about it and he smelt the pistol and there was no trace of powder smell — not one bit."[2295]

Mays's appellate brief language was partially true. Mays's father was allowed inside the house: "They held it to my nose and asked me to smell it and I smelled it and they asked me if I smelled powder and I said no."[2296] However, Jim Smith did not smell the pistol when it was first discovered. He remained in the patrol wagon and did not enter the house when Mays was arrested.

The jury simply found that the pistol, which belonged to Mays, had been recently fired. The Tennessee Supreme Court affirmed the evidence as supporting Mays's guilt.

The Identification of Maurice Mays

Patrol wagon driver James Smith, black, had stayed in the vehicle while Mays was being arrested. He drove officers White, Kirby and Hatcher (along with Mays, who was now wearing the gray suit with the wet pants and the clay and cinder-dirtied shoes) back to the corner of Gillespie and 8th Street, the nearest intersection with a streetlight, closest to the Lindsey home. According to White, Mays was not told of the reason for taking him to this location, but Mays exclaimed as they went, "You're going to take me out there and get me lynched!" Hatcher testified that Mays made the statement before he was informed that he was being taken to be identified because a woman had been shot, but he did not say the woman "was dead or anything of that kind."[2297] Said Hatcher, "He did not give any reason why he thought we were going to get him lynched."[2298]

The streetlight was about 175 feet from the Lindsey house. Hatcher stayed in the patrol wagon with Mays while White and Kirby walked to the Lindsey house. They returned with Ora Smyth, White holding her arm, followed in the darkness by Kirby and Mrs. Dyer. The latter two walked in the street, while White and Ora Smyth walked on the sidewalk.

Mays was taken from the wagon and placed under the 5,000-candlepower streetlight.

She identified Mays without hesitation, and said, "If I had a pistol I would shoot you!" "She looked at him twice, two different times. After she looked and started away, the defendant said to her, "Come back here, woman, and tell them I am not the man!"[2299] White snapped, "Damn you, she has seen you all she wants to!" according to James Smith at the second trial.[2300]

White was not asked about his remark. He testified: "She did not come back. She had already come back once and looked at him. He wanted her to return the second time and made the above remark to her. I took her back to the house. I did not, at any time, either directly or by insinuation or in any other way, suggest to this young woman to identify this man as the man who did the killing. No one in my presence suggested to her that she identify Mays as the man who did the killing."[2301]

White took Mays to the city jail, where he stayed until he was taken to the county jail about 8:30 A.M.[2302] Mays was "charged out at 11:00 o'clock," and made it a point to tell the sheriff that there was no mud on his shoes at that time.[2303]

About an hour later, the afternoon edition of the *Knoxville Sentinel* hit the street with front-page stories of the killing and Mays's arrest. The sheriff had already gotten permission to take Mays to Chattanooga for his safety. By 6:00 P.M. a mob was threatening the jail and demanding Mays. By 8:30 P.M. the mob had gained entry to the jail. Finding Mays gone, it splurged on confiscated whiskey and began looting businesses for firearms and assaulting African Americans. The disorder, known as the Knoxville Race Riot of 1919, continued until at least 3:00 A.M. the next day. Two were confirmed dead: a black man and a white National Guard officer, accidentally shot by his own men.

Mays was put on trial for the murder of Mrs. Bertie Lindsey on October 1, 1919, only thirty-five days after her death. He was quickly convicted on October 4, 1919, and on October 18, Judge T.A.R. Nelson, giving the verdict his "hearty approval," sentenced Mays to death. The conviction was appealed and overturned. The newly reinstated death penalty had provided for *jury sentencing*, not judge sentencing, as had been the law in Tennessee since 1858. Mays was given a new trial.[2304]

It was Mays's second trial — which featured the testimony of James Smith, the Negro patrol wagon driver who was now a defense witness — that sent Mays to the Tennessee electric chair on March 15, 1922. (The testimony cited here was from his second trial.)

The Physical Evidence Against Maurice Mays

When the police officers arrived at the Lindsey house after being summoned by officer Dyer's call, they walked around the house, the adjoining streets and an alley, and quickly discovered that Mays had originally run past the house into some chicken wire and had dropped the victim's pocketbook. Retracing his steps, he had apparently run around the house between it and the Dyer house, then down an alley.[2305]

Mrs. Dyer testified she had seen a man run past her house after she heard the shot. "I have seen the defendant Maurice Mays. I testified in the case below. I saw him that night on Gillespie Street under the streetlight. I also saw him before that. He passed my house. To my best knowledge he is the man that went across the street and went down into the alley. He had on a dingy gray suit that night."[2306] On cross-examination she admitted, "I saw the [flash]light but did not see him. Just saw the light as I opened the door [to allow Ora inside] but did not see him."[2307]

The officers, aided by the searchlight carried by Andy White, soon discovered fresh tracks in the muddy cinder-ridden alley. The tracks were distinct. Explained Detective A.L. Wells, "The right track was a rubber heel and showed it was half-soled. It showed that the rubber heel was pretty well preserved and in good condition. It also showed the half-sole up; showed it plainly. That was the right track. The left track did not show the heel. It showed that the outside of the heel did not touch or did not leave the impression like the right track did, and it didn't show whether it was half-soled or not on account of the slope. The ground was harder there."[2308] "He said that it was a rubber heel on the shoe because the impression made in the dirt showed there were little holes in the heel. Said that the right track showed the heel to be in good shape and heels square, and that the left heel showed to be worn off on the right side."[2309]

Wells's testimony was inconsistent from the first trial to the second, emphasized Mays's appellate brief. In the first trial, Wells had said there were "dents" in the heels, in the second he used the word "holes," meaning holes that were left by shoe nails being driven into them. Mays's lawyers had driven the point home by showing sample heels and had Wells acknowledge the difference between "dents" and "holes."[2310] Moreover, the defense offered the testimony of cobbler "L. Trobe," identified as "a Jew from Poland," who had put the heels on the shoes two months before the killing, in part to explain the difference between "dents" and "holes," but also to show, "The heels on Mays's shoes show that they were not new or in good condition."[2311]

Mays's shoes were an exhibit to his testimony, his appellate brief stating they had not been in his possession since the first trial.[2312] What they show cannot be determined at this time. They are no longer part of the court file.

The Animus of Officer Andy White

The fact most cited by persons asserting Mays was either the wrong man or wrongly convicted was the personal animus of officer Andy White. They argue that White's dislike of Mays animated the arrest and the show-up identification, which tainted the prosecution unfairly against Mays.

White's chief accuser was James Smith, the black patrol wagon driver. He testified briefly at the first trial, but was not asked about White's statements. However, at the second trial his testimony was clear. He had heard White say he was going to "get that black son of a bitch" and put him in the penitentiary. While the pair was driving to the murder scene, White said that that "God damn Maurice Mays killed that woman."[2313]

Mays's lawyers framed their case on racial lines. They attempted to show Smith was a worthy black man, one who regularly ate his meals with White[2314] (an early 20th century sign of racial acceptance), and attempted to prove that several important political figures had served as pallbearers at the funeral of Smith's father thirty-five years earlier.[2315] One of these was Gov. Robert L. Taylor.[2316] The court barred testimony regarding funeral attendees.[2317] On appeal, the Tennessee Supreme Court said this was proper.[2318]

Observed Mays's brief: "Is it not worth something to James Smith to be the son of that kind of man? Lineage tells in men as well as in stock and we submit that the jury had a right to that evidence. It would have introduced him to the jury and the jury could have better weighed his testimony, knowing him, where it came in conflict with that of White."[2319]

Mays's ninety-page printed brief (the state's was merely typewritten) quoted long passages from legal and scholarly treatises suggesting that White lacked "free will" in asserting that Mays was the culprit, but was "acting under a necessity."[2320] (Mays's brief was filed long after it was due. The State was compelled to file its brief based on the motion for a new trial; the defendant's brief was filed later, out of order.)

In rebuttal, the state summarized White's testimony.

> He had no bad feelings towards Mays, and felt towards him like he did toward other people. He looked like any other man; that he had not cursed him on Vine Street or at any other time; that he had not cursed him on the street for some time before the killing.[2321] He denied that he had cursed Mays to his face at all that night; denied that at different times down at the city jail where the boys were accustomed to meet that if Mays's name should be mentioned by anyone, that he had cursed him, and denied using any profane language with respect to Mays more than he ordinarily used with respect to other people.[2322] He said it was not a fact that on the way out there when [White] had only heard that a woman had been killed, and when he did not know any of the details, that he said to Jim Smith that Maurice Mays, or that damned Maurice Mays, was the man who committed the crime. He denied this statement.[2323]

The state's brief continued recounting White's testimony: He denied that he ever said about Maurice Mays that he would catch that damned little s.o.b. sometime and send him to the penitentiary. Said he told him up there one night after he had butted in and run a fellow off, that if he didn't change and quit harboring criminals [at his restaurant] that he would be sent to the penitentiary. I told him he would land in the penitentiary from the pace that he was running there unless he stopped that kind of business.[2324]

The Tennessee Supreme Court sifted the testimony of White and Smith. Regarding the wrongful show-up, it opined, "It is said for the defense that a suggestion was made to Mrs. Parsons by Officer White, while on the way with her from the Dyer home to the point where she identified Mays, that he was the guilty man, and that it was upon the suggestion of White that she made her identification."[2325]

The Supreme Court rejected this argument: "There is no evidence in the record of any such suggestion having been made by Officer White. Mrs. Dyer, Officer Kirby, and Officer White all say that no such suggestion was made at any time; in fact, they say that no suggestion was made to Mrs. Parsons whatever as to who was guilty of the murder of Mrs. Lindsey. Mrs. Parsons says no such suggestion was made to her."[2326]

The Tennessee Supreme Court also addressed the issue of White's animus toward Mays: "The defense did offer the testimony of Jim Smith, the colored driver of the patrol wagon, who accompanied Officer White to the scene of the murder from the police station, to the effect that White said to him on the way to the scene of the murder that he would bet that "G — D — Maurice Mays killed that woman." Officer White emphatically denied that he made any suggestion or statement to Jim Smith, or to any other person."[2327]

Regarding this issue, the court explained: "The jury evidently discredited the statement of Smith on this point, and, we think, rightly so. It does not appear from the evidence that White knew anything about the particulars of the murder at the time he and Smith left the police station with the patrol wagon. The desk sergeant at the police station had only informed him that Mrs. Lindsay had been killed. It is utterly unreasonable that he would have made any such suggestion or statement to Jim Smith on the way to the Lindsey home when it is not shown he had any information whatever as to who had killed Mrs. Lindsay."[2328]

The court said, "Furthermore, we think that Smith's testimony shows that he is very much biased in behalf of Mays, and his testimony is not entitled to credit."[2329]

The court concluded:

> We do not think there is anything in the record which reflects on the integrity of Officer White. Some evidence was offered by the defense tending to show that he entertained a feeling of animosity towards Mays. This White denies. He does say that Mays had sought to interfere with him in the discharge of his official duties on more than one occasion, and that he told Mays on one occasion, at least, that he would go to the penitentiary if he did not quit his ways, and he (White) would break his head if he continued to interfere with him in the discharge of his duties. We gather from White's testimony that he probably had a contempt for Mays's previous conduct. He denies, however, that he entertained a feeling of animosity or hatred towards him; but if it be conceded that he did entertain a feeling of animosity towards Mays, this is immaterial, because it is not shown that he made any suggestion to Mrs. Parsons or in any way aided her in the identification.[2330]

In addition to citing White's animus, commentators suggest racial animosity tainted the entire second trial and cite a line of questions offered by the state: "Q: How many pictures of white women did you have in your room? A: None that I know of. Q: How many in your trunk? A: None that I know of. Q: Do you deny there were any in there? A: No white women. Q: Do you deny there was a picture of some white women in your room? A: No white women's picture that I know anything about. Q: Do you deny there were any there? A: Yes, sir, the only white person's picture in my house was that of Mayor McMillan."[2331] Neither side raised any other race-related issues.

Evidence of Crimes by Others

Aside from asserting that the prosecution was animated by White's dislike for Mays, the chief defense was simply "wrong man." Precisely, the defense offered the testimony of twelve women whose houses had been entered by someone in the nighttime and either assaults or attempted assaults made upon females.

The Court barred this evidence from the jury's consideration.[2332] There were eight reasons, explained the state. 1. In each and all of the cases there was no effort made to identify any individual as the author of the crime, which it is proven that he either committed or attempted to commit. 2. Some of the witnesses testified they could not tell whether the man was a white man or a Negro. 3. Other of the witnesses testified that the man was a Negro, while still others testified that he was white. 4. Some of the witnesses testified that the man was a low, heavy-set man, while others testified that he was a man from six to six and half feet in height. 4. In some of the instances given by the witnesses the man had a flashlight, and in others he did not. 6. In some instances he attempted to commit the crime or rape and assault, and in others he did not. 7. In some instances he was guilty of robbery, and in others he was not. 8. Finally, there was no connection whatever shown by any fact or circumstance between any one of these separate and distinct crimes and the one under investigation here.[2333]

The "wrong man" defense, namely that the crime was committed by someone else, was a valid defense in certain cases, agreed the state.[2334] The state said:

> This rule, however, cannot be invoked in this case, because there is nothing whatever in any of this proof which proves or even tends to prove that any other person had committed this particular crime of killing Mrs. Lindsey. There is no proof of identity of any person in the commission of any one of these crimes. So that the proof offered by these twelve women, while it did show that houses had been entered and assaults either threatened or made or burglaries committed by parties unknown, yet none of it tends to establish that a person other than defendant committed this particular crime. So that

> this line of cases cannot be invoked to put the lower Court in error in excluding all of this testimony.[2335]

The state's brief explained, "It is the general rule that the defendant cannot prove against the State a crime alleged in the indictment by a third party, either as the foundation for his acquittal, or in aiding the proof of his innocence, and especially is this true when the person committing the alleged independent crime is unknown."[2336] But there are five exceptions to this general rule that separate crimes cannot be proven either to fix guilt or to exonerate or show innocence.[2337] They are allowed when the testimony tends to establish: 1. Motive; 2. Intent; 3. The absence of mistake or accident; 4. A common scheme or plan embracing the commission of two or more crimes so related to each other that proof of one tends to establish the other; 5. The identity of the person charged with the commission of the crime on trial.[2338]

The state's brief applied each one of the exceptions to the present case:

> 1. The motive of this defendant is shown to be both that of assault or rape as well as burglary; and none of these twelve witnesses identify any man as having the same motive, and therefore, proof as to unknown parties on the subject of motive was incompetent.[2339]
>
> 2. Intent. It is true that the intent of each of these cases was the same as that of the defendant; but no individual is pointed out or identified as having this same intent, which prompted the defendant; and therefore, the proof is incompetent.
>
> 3. The absence of mistake or accident. The fact that the homes of these twelve women were entered, some of them by white men, some of them by Negroes, some of them by persons where the parties were unable to tell whether they were white or black, and some of them being large men and some small men, does not tend to disclose that Miss Smith made any mistake in this identification of this particular individual. There is nothing in the testimony of either one of these witnesses that would clear up or elucidate or explain the positive identification of this man by Miss Smith; nor is there anything in the testimony of either one of them that would contradict or impeach this clear and unmistakable identification of this defendant.[2340]
>
> 4. As to common design and purpose. It is submitted that there is nothing in this proof that shows a common design or purpose except and only that the purpose of these unknown parties was either rape or burglary, or both, just as was the purpose of the defendant. That fact that an unknown party or parties had at different times, both before and after this crime, entered houses for the purpose of rape or burglary, or both, was insufficient, and incompetent to shed any light upon the guilt or innocence of this particular defendant after his complete identification.[2341]
>
> 5. What has been said heretofore with respect to mistake and accident applies equally to the fifth exception, which is where the identity of the defendant is in question. None of these women who had been assaulted or who were present, so far as the record shows, ever saw this defendant, nor were any of them able to identify the man in their respective houses.[2342]

The state's brief explained, "Cases in Tennessee dealing with these rules are very numerous,"[2343] and cited an elaborate annotation involving a New York case (Molineaux, 62 L.R.A. 193). Citing the transcript, the state showed the trial court had considered the case law and the annotation. Here is what the trial court said in rejecting the proffered testimony:

> Now, this is a case of circumstantial evidence largely that we are engaged in trying, and in a case of that kind the defendant has a right to show that somebody else committed this offense, and the State must show that he is the guilty party. Now, in the effort to show that somebody else did this, it is proposed to show that at different times, both before and since the Lindsey occurrence and murder, that similar offenses have been committed in the city, and it is insisted that the defendant ought to have the right to show that because there are certain circumstances connected with the Lindsey killing that are similar and peculiar to the circumstances connected with the other matters; and it is insisted that the circumstances proposed to be shown are these: that the assaults were all upon women, all were for the purpose of rape, and they were all committed by the use of pistols and flashlights; and it is insisted that this evidence ought to go to the jury. I am of opinion that the evidence is incompetent, for this reason: that while there is similarity in the evidence introduced in this case and the evidence proposed to be shown, yet there is nothing about the evidence proposed to be shown that I can see that bears a relation to this particular matter that we have in hand. It is evidence that usually attends all case where there are assaults of this kind; that is, all such cases are usually committed after night, and in practically all cases it is inflicted by means of a pistol and flashlight; and if there was anything in the testimony whereby one assault related to the other; that is, if the pistol which, for instance, is identified at one place, is identified as being at the other place, then we would have a case where it might go to the jury; or if there was some identification of some particular matter at one place that existed at the other. And I will state further in this connection, I am

> especially satisfied that this would be improper testimony as to the matter that happened after the Lindsey killing.[2344]

The Tennessee Supreme Court agreed that the testimony about other crimes — including those that were committed while Mays was in jail awaiting trial — was inadmissible. The court's opinion tracked the state's explanation of the law, including citation to the state's leading cases and the Molineaux annotation.[2345]

The Low Heavy-Set Man in Overalls

A defense argument at the second trial attempted to fix blame on a "short, heavy-set black man wearing overalls."[2346] Clearly, this description did not fit Maurice Mays, who was considered tall (5' 8") and thin (127 pounds),[2347] and was, according to his own lawyer, a "light mulattoe." The existence of the "low black man in overalls" was first mentioned by black policeman Dave Sanders at the second trial. But it was disallowed as hearsay.

According to standard police procedure, each officer was required to call in every hour and report to desk sergeant O.J. Watkins. Sanders was put on the stand by the defense (out of the jury's presence) and explained what he had been told by Watkins, namely, "That a woman had been killed on Eighth Avenue. That the man who killed the woman was a low black man and wore overalls."[2348] Sanders and another policeman went in the direction of the home and on the way were met by two men, both white, dressed in overalls. They said they were hoboes, were lost and were looking for the train station. About this time, Officers White and Hatcher arrived on the scene. Hatcher got out of the patrol wagon, spoke to the men with Sanders, and the men were sent on their way.[2349]

Sanders was allowed to testify about what he saw and said to the white men in overalls, but was not allowed to repeat the hearsay from officer Watkins. In the defendant's brief, this failure was assigned as error. But the Tennessee Supreme Court did not discuss the issue. The state's brief explained why Sanders was not allowed to speak about what Watkins said: "It was purely hearsay evidence — and which, of course, is the truth about it." Said the state, "There was no effort made to show how Watkins, desk sergeant, got his information. It was purely a conversation between third parties, neither of who had any connection, either directly or indirectly, with this killing, and wherein it was not shown from what source Watkins received this information."[2350]

Throughout Mays's struggle for a commutation, his lawyers mentioned the issue of "a low black man in overalls" frequently.[2351]

The "True" Killer Comes Forward

The centerpiece of the Bedau and Radelet argument that Mays was the "wrong man" was the fact that on August 18, 1927 — five years after Mays was executed — a woman came into the police station of Norton, Virginia (130 miles northeast of Knoxville), and confessed to killing Mrs. Bertie Lindsey.[2352] The story made front-page news in the *Nashville Tennessean*, which reported the headline of another famous case: Sacco and Vanzetti had lost their appeal.[2353]

The confessor was Sadie Mendil. She said she had blackened her face to appear as a Negro, wore men's clothing, and had killed Bertie because she suspected Bertie was having an affair with her then husband, John Roddy. She made a signed confession in the form of an affidavit.

This Sadie Mendil confession was not mentioned or accredited by journalist Edgerton, historian Lakin or legal writer Paine.[2354] Justice Department lawyers Stephen J. Markman and Paul G. Cassell wholly rejected it.[2355] The document has not been located.

The Knoxville police chief ridiculed the so-called confession and insisted it contained discrepancies. He never brought Sadie Mendil to Knoxville and told the newspaper she should be released.

Within days, a man identifying himself as Sadie's husband (Mark or Mack Mendil) appeared at the Norton jail and said his wife was "temporarily demented from brooding" over her two-year-old son who was being cared for by another family. The pair traveled the country performing magic tricks.

Enter the National Association for the Advancement of Colored People

The National Association for the Advancement of Colored People sent a white investigator to interview Sadie Mendil. Since its beginning in 1909, the NAACP had become an influential force in the lives of black Americans, due to the editorial work of W.E.B. DuBois, who edited its monthly magazine, *The Crisis*, and its energetic leader (and author) James Weldon Johnson. *The Crisis* had carried stories about Mays, including the report of his execution and his claim of innocence.

The investigator found that Sadie Mendil was only thirteen years old at the time of the killing, and her confession (affidavit) placed the killing in 1922 instead of 1919. Said the report, "In July 1927 she married Mack Mendil. He is a palmist and fortuneteller, and travels around the country. On August 18, 1927, they were in Norton, Virginia. She claims that her husband was very drunk and frightened her so that she had a brainstorm. After he left her, she went to the police and gave herself up, making the confession which they have."[2356]

The report continues, "This story, in connection with her appearance and apparent youthfulness, is quite convincing. It is possible that she knows something about the murder. But she has now been frightened into silence. Her husband is a tall, dark-haired man, with broad shoulders but not heavy set. He has rather intense blue eyes and claims to be clairvoyant. Of the two, he is far less sane in appearance. If real detective work could be done it might be worthwhile to look up this man's history, as well as the man Roddy. I feel sure that there is nothing in this confession, but I am not satisfied with Mrs. Mendil's explanation as to why she made it."[2357]

In her transmittal letter to James Weldon Johnson, investigator Boardman said, "The Knoxville trip turned out to be a wild goose chase, and I am sorry that it commanded such time. I do not, however, feel that it was a mistake to go, for of course it is only by following up every clue that the truth will be learned. I enclose a report of my investigation. I did not try to verify the facts given me by Mrs. Mendil, as they were obviously true. She has a very low-grade and unstable mentality and would be incapable of carrying such a plan through even if she had the physical strength."[2358]

Maurice Mays's "Dream Team" of Lawyers

Easily overlooked in discussing the Mays case were his lawyers. It was a veritable "dream team" of the Knoxville defense bar. It was led by former prosecutor Reuben L. Cate, white, and the chief prosecutor's father, Lincoln C. Houk, white (long a prominent political family). Also serving as co-counsel was William F. Yardley (1844–1924), the dean of the African American bar in Knoxville, and a young black lawyer, John A. Huff. Yardley was clearly past his prime, but had been the foremost black Knoxvillian of his time. He was the first African American to run for governor of Tennessee (1876), held several local offices and consistently defended the rights of black people. Frederick Douglass called him "one of the most remarkable men that I have met."[2359] Also assisting was James A. Fowler, white. He was the Republican candidate for governor in 1898, was one of the city's best-known public figures, and had served in the Justice Department under Presidents Roosevelt and Taft from 1908 to 1913. The names of all five lawyers appear on Mays's printed brief to the Tennessee Supreme Court. Of them, Governor Taylor said, "Maurice Mays had among the ablest lawyers at the bar to defend him, and knowing that the case turned upon the testimony of Ora Parsons, if her testimony could have been weakened by an assault upon her moral character, or by regular impeachment, this would unquestionably have been done."[2360]

Ora Smyth Parsons's Eyewitness Testimony Regarding Maurice Mays

When Governor Alfred A. Taylor refused to commute Mays's death sentence on March 14, 1922, he said, "The case turned on the testimony of Ora Parsons" and the defense had been unable to discredit her. "Therefore," he said, "she stands in the case unimpeached and unimpeachable."[2361]

In reaching this conclusion, the governor was aided by the certainty expressed on this issue by the Tennessee Supreme Court:

> Furthermore, the testimony of Mrs. Parsons inspires confidence. She is careful in her statement of the facts, and there is nothing in her testimony to indicate that it should not be given full credence. She was the only person present except the victim of the intruder, and the record shows that she exercised remarkable coolness and caution in meeting the trying situation in which she was placed. It is true she had never seen [defendant] before, but she heard his voice on the night of the murder, quite a little conversation having occurred between them; she observed his form, face, and clothing while in the room; and within less than an hour after the murder she described him to Capt. Wilson of the police force of the city of Knoxville as the man who shot Mrs. Lindsay with such detail that Capt. Wilson, who knew Mays well, ordered the officers under him to go and arrest Mays. When Mays was brought into the presence of Mrs. Parsons a few minutes later, at the corner of Eighth and Gillespie avenues, and while he was standing under or near a strong electric light at said corner, Mrs. Parsons promptly and positively identified him as the man who had killed Mrs. Lindsay.[2362]

On the identification issue, the Tennessee Supreme Court said: "As an illustration of her cautiousness and an honest desire on her part not to make any mistake as to her identification of the intruder who killed Mrs. Lindsay, on the following morning she requested the officers that she be allowed to see Mays again, and upon his being brought into her presence at the city jail she, without hesitation, positively identified him again as being the man who shot and killed Mrs. Lindsay, and has remained positive in her identification of him ever since."[2363] On this issue the court concluded: "We are wholly unable to see any motive which Mrs. Parsons could possibly have in identifying Mays as the man who killed Mrs. Lindsay, except to speak the truth. It is shown that she had no previous acquaintance with him, and it does not appear that she could possibly have had any ulterior motive in her identification of Mays as the perpetrator of the murder."[2364]

The Struggle for a Commutation

The Tennessee Supreme Court affirmed Mays's conviction on October 29, 1921, and ordered his execution on December 15, 1921. The governor was besieged with letters and petitions urging mercy as well as counterpetitions. Mays wrote several letters to the governor.[2365] His strategy was to write letters to influential people and ask them to contact the governor. Many did so and included Mays's handwritten letters with them. In each letter, his return address was "Death Chamber, Tennessee State Prison, Nashville."

The great bulk of letters on Mays's behalf came prior to December 14, 1921. For example, the principal of Knoxville Colored High School, Charles W. Cansler, a mathematical savant and important voice in the Knoxville black community, wrote there was "at least a reasonable doubt of his guilt," and made an argument that would ultimately give Mays more time, namely, "It is yet possible that the murderer of Mrs. Lindsay may be found in the apprehension of the midnight marauder who is committing so many similar crimes in similar fashion in the vicinity of Knoxville."[2366]

The sentiment was echoed in former mayor John E. McMillan's letter. He recounted that Mays had come to him complaining about officer White's threat to put Mays in prison even before the murder. "Officer White's threats have been realized and since Mays has been sentenced to die, White by his demeanor and actions among his associates is proud and happy in his accomplishment."[2367] He explained, "Our city is most unfortunate in having these murders of women continuing over a period of two years even up to within the past few nights, each and every one identical in detail and plan. I have a feeling that some day in the future these many identical murders will be cleared up and the real guilty party will be convicted with unquestionable evidence."[2368] He asked for commutation to a life sentence: "Life imprisonment is all that is asked, but it holds out hope for the future where doubt exists — yet it punishes severely and hard indeed."[2369] McMillan's letter was no more emotional or personal than any others. "May I assure you that if you commute this sentence your action will meet with the approval of thousands of our very best citizens," wrote McMillan, the cashier of the Third National Bank in Knoxville, and a Democrat.

The most powerful arguments for clemency came from the Attorney General of Tennessee, L.D. Smith. He had been a special judge on the Supreme Court, which heard Mays's first appeal, but recused himself because he had determined to his satisfaction that Mays was factually innocent. Although his office had handled the second appeal and Mays "has had a fair and legal trial according to the rules of law," nevertheless, "It is true that many times evidence which cannot be received in court may be properly considered as causing serious doubt upon the guilt of the accused and properly cognizable by one in your position."[2370] He wrote on December 13, 1921, and his summary of the issues favoring Mays identified six issues. These were the problem of eyewitness identification, the revengeful spirit of the officers, the fact that the officers were discredited on the issue of whether the initial pistol had actually been fired, the fact the officers had a grudge against Mays, the subsequent crimes similar in nature, and the "large sentiment existing in the minds of the intelligent people of Knoxville that a serious mistake has been committed."[2371]

Other notables who wrote on Mays's behalf included William Jasper Hale, the president of the state's public black college, Tennessee Agricultural and Industrial State Normal School. His letter consisted of sending to the governor a letter from an important black churchman in Knoxville. Hale wrote, "His letter is self explanatory. If thru justice or mercy you can do anything for the young man, same will be appreciated by our people."[2372] Another letter came from Nahum D. Brascher, editor-in-chief of the *Associated Negro Press*, headquartered in Chicago. "The people of my Race, throughout the United States, are interested in this unfortunate case. I should have been haunted the rest of my life by the spirit of Mays, should he be put to death, and I had failed to write this letter to you after seeing the one written by him from his Death Chamber."[2373]

Robert R. Church, the foremost black leader of Memphis and a nationally-known Republican, wrote asking for a commutation: "Under no circumstances would I request you to do this if I did not believe the man innocent of the crime and believe sincerely that, if this sentence is commuted, those guilty of this crime will be apprehended."[2374]

Not everyone endorsed clemency for Maurice Mays. The most notable opponent was prosecutor S.G. Heiskell, former mayor of Knoxville. Ironically, on July 14, 1915, he had written a letter of recommendation on Mays's behalf saying he had known him since he was a boy. "I can say in his behalf that he has always borne the reputation of being a young colored man of integrity, intelligence and good character, and that he is so considered in this community."[2375] By December 8, 1921, the former mayor had changed his mind. He telegraphed the governor, "Maurice Mays assassinated Mrs. Lindsay because she objected to his raping her. One grand jury, two trial juries, two trial judges, five Supreme Judges, forty-three in all, said he was guilty. Leniency would disgrace Tennessee and increase rapings of women so common in Knox County and Knoxville."[2376]

The American Legion, a new and powerful force in public opinion, urged the law be carried out "in the interest of law and order."[2377] One man wrote to explain how his wife, who was the bookkeeper and cashier of his auto repair shop, had gone home and was confronted by Mays attempting to come in her back door with a knife in his hand. At that moment, the woman's adult son began singing in the bathtub upstairs and Mays bolted. She did not know who Mays was until his trial.[2378]

One letter illustrates the governor's dilemma succinctly. Knox County Trustee W.L. Clapp wrote Governor Taylor of his own volition on November 22, 1921. His letter explained, "I have known this Negro ever since I have been in politics, a period of near fifteen years, and I want to say that I have absolutely no respect for him as a citizen and I think he is a crook if not a criminal. I am satisfied that a life term in the penitentiary is what he ought to have on general principles."[2379]

Trustee Clapp continued, "I am familiar with the evidence in the case where he was tried for the crime of killing the Lindsay woman; heard most of the proof and am satisfied that the evidence was conclusive and that the Court could do nothing but give him the death penalty; but at the same time there has always been in my mind a doubt as to his guilt, in view of the fact that so many similar crimes have been committed in this city, and two other Negroes barely escaped when they were beyond a doubt innocent. If I were Governor I would commute this Negro's sentence to life imprisonment."[2380]

Governor Taylor was conflicted about what to do. On December 5, 1921, he wrote confidential letters to the editors of both Knoxville newspapers. "I want your opinion in the Maurice Mays case. That opinion should be kept secret if you so desire. One group of good citizens there express serious doubt as to his guilt, another group wishes the execution to proceed in order that he may be put out of the way on general principles, still another group, evidently the minority, think he is guilty and demand his execution. The first group appeal to me to commute to life imprisonment. I want your deliberate judgment."[2381] Earlier, the reporter who had covered the case for the *Knoxville Sentinel* (but was now a reporter for the *Journal and Tribune*) had written a strong letter in support of Mays. He challenged the eyewitness testimony as too greatly influenced by Officer White.[2382]

But the reporter's boss, William Rule, a former mayor of Knoxville, and editor of the *Journal and Tribune*, was not helpful:

> I have made such investigation as I could in the matter referred to in your letter, but find little in the way of light in the case. I find there is here a divided opinion on the part of those who know more about it than I know. Without ever mentioning your name directly or indirectly I find those who profess to know the facts, some of them, who assume to know the facts, who say the jury before which Maurice Mays was tried acted upon the evidence, but claim mitigating circumstances, the nature of which I have not heard explained. I wish I could help you, but I know whatever you may do, you will do what you believe to be right.[2383]

On December 14, 1921, Governor Alfred Taylor decided on a half-measure of mercy for Maurice Mays. He granted him a 90-day reprieve, which stated Mays would be executed on March 15, 1922.[2384] The governor explained that this time would give those who supported Mays's innocence the opportunity to come forward with evidence exonerating him. That is, the black community of Knoxville was expected to identify the real killer. The governor (and most white people) thought that once it was clear that he would entertain evidence incriminating another man (whom it was assumed the black community was protecting), the real culprit would be identified by members of Mays's race.

Meanwhile, the governor offered Mays another "escape" from death. He appointed a five-member Board of Mental Examiners to examine Mays. The board included the superintendent of Central State Hospital (for the insane) and his chief assistant physician. On February 24, 1922, the Board wrote the governor, "We feel so strongly that Maurice

Mays (col.) condemned to die March 15th is definitely insane that we urgently petition that his execution be postponed and that he be placed in one of the Institutions of the State for observation to determine definitely whether or not this impression is correct."[2385]

Brushing aside this strategy to buy time, which may have saved his life, Mays would have none of it: "I humbly beg to deny that I am insane, as was published in Saturday's Evening Banner of Feb. 25th which was said to be a report of Mental Examiners headed by Dr. Farmer. I beg to say I really don't think I am insane and neither does any one else who is acquainted with me, and in the Examiner's report I feel that I am again mistakenly accused. I am 31 years of age, born and reared in Knoxville, Tenn, and during all the 31 years of my life this is the first time it has been reported or even intimated that I was insane. My defense was *not* insanity. My defense was an absolute Mistaken Identification."[2386]

Mays persisted, "God knows I am innocent of the charge for which I stand a convicted and I appeal and pray for clemency upon the firm belief that the unknown guilty party who killed Mrs. Lindsey will be hereafter captured."[2387]

As his execution date approached, Mays both beseeched the governor and blasted him. On March 9, 1922, he wrote what was apparently his last letter, again explaining he was home at the time of the crime and begging for commutation to life imprisonment.[2388]

The next day, Judge Grafton Green, the most respected member of the Tennessee Supreme Court, wrote the governor suggesting a second respite. He explained:

> Since the case of Maurice Mays has been out of our Court, I have been informed of several matters which did not appear in this transcript and some of them possibly could not have been brought into the Court files under the rules of evidence. These things throw some doubt on the sufficiency of the identification of Mays as the author of the crime for which he has been sentenced. All these matters will no doubt be brought to your attention and you, I know, will be glad to give them full consideration. May I, therefore, join in the request made on his behalf that you grant Mays a considerable respite to permit a further investigation of later developments. Of course, all of us would deplore a mistake. I am writing merely as a citizen and this is purely an individual expression.[2389]

On March 14, 1922, literally the day before Mays was scheduled to die, another letter came from two more Tennessee Supreme Court judges, Nathan Bachman and Colin P. McKinney, urging another respite while the matter was more fully investigated.[2390] The letter was hand-delivered to the governor by Ben Carr, a black Republican leader in Nashville.

The "New" Information Tending to Exonerate Mays

To the last, two of Mays's lawyers, Reuben L. Cates and James A. Fowler, sought a commutation. Fowler wrote a 17-page single-spaced letter on February 28, 1922, recounting the purported evidence against him, emphasizing the wrongful nature of the show-up, the confusing testimony regarding whether the pistol had been fired, and White's animus toward Mays. But Fowler offered a new factual issue.

On January 31, 1922, a white man named Benjamin Franklin Peters made an affidavit that impeached Ora Smyth Parsons's testimony. Plainly stated, on the day after the killing he heard Ora say that a stranger had come to her house twice on the murder day and sought to spend the night.[2391] Putting the evidence most strongly in Mays's favor, he wrote:

> He resided on Mitchell Street in Knoxville and from his home he could see the house of Mrs. Lindsay, and that he knew Mrs. Lindsay, becoming acquainted with her in pasturing their cows together; that he heard of the killing the next morning after it occurred and then he went to her home; that people were coming and going from the place of the murder; that he knows Ora Smythe; that when at Mrs. Lindsay's home that morning he saw Miss Smythe on the walk or pavement about midway between the Lindsay home and the Dyer home; that he heard her state that about sundown the previous day a man came to the Lindsay home and asked to spend the night; that she and Mrs. Lindsay were the only ones there and they refused to give him permission to stay; that the man went away and sometime after that, in the early part of the night, he returned and again asked permission to spend the night and was again refused, and that he went away after the second visit; that she described the man as of medium size and, as she remembered, was wearing a dark gray coat, and she said that he was a white man; that he heard that statement made to a number of people on the walk at that time; that she was not speaking directly to him, but he was listening to her talking with those about her, and that there was still considerable excitement in the neighborhood, and, as stated, the people were coming and going and standing around the Lindsay home. The affiant is a minister of the gospel of the

> Church of Christ, and he states in what parts of the city he at times preaches, and states that he did not bring the information to the attention of the attorneys for the defense before the trial of the case because he did not desire to be called as a witness, but that he has talked with his wife about the matter a number of times.[2392]

Counsel Fowler, who was a Justice Department employee at the time he wrote the letter, continued: "He never met General Reuben Cates before he met him in his office when his affidavit was given; and how he happened to make the affidavit was that he had told Charlie Johnson, a colored janitor at the City Hall about it, and he had given the information to Maurice Mays's father, who communicated it to General Cates."[2393]

Fowler concluded his discussion of the "new" evidence by underlining his point: "Miss Smythe was making these statements some time after she had pretended to identify Maurice Mays as the man who had shot Mrs. Lindsay and yet manifestly she was telling about this man twice coming to the Lindsay house and requesting to be permitted to stay there as a most likely clue to the solution of the crime, and she apparently believed at that time that the man who made that request was the one who returned in the night and shot Mrs. Lindsay."[2394]

By this time, however, Fowler had painted himself and Mays into a corner. Fowler had met personally with the governor in late November 1921, and wrote a letter on December 1, 1921, in which he stated, "I do not criticize the Supreme Court for affirming the judgment, because Mays has had two trials and had been convicted by two juries whose verdicts had not been set aside by the trial courts, and the Supreme Court under well recognized precedents, felt that I should give the fullest weight to those verdicts."[2395]

If the governor remained unmoved by the "new" evidence, Mays was doomed.

Apparently the last letter to the governor by any of Mays's lawyers was written on March 6, 1922, when Reuben L. Cates sent him a three-and-one-half-page single-spaced letter.[2396] He explained that under Tennessee law (and the law generally) an admission by another person made to a witness that the other person told him he had done the killing, was not competent evidence.[2397] Still, such evidence could be considered by the governor — and it should be, argued Cates, because the testimony showed the killing *was committed* by someone other than Mays. That is, the testimony of two white women who were assaulted by a black man *after* Mays was in jail, and who threatened to kill them just as he had done Mrs. Lindsay, constituted proof that Mays was *not* the killer.[2398]

Cates told the governor that the women's hearsay evidence was actually the most credible evidence the governor would hear. He wrote, "We cannot bring the murderer before you, that is an impossibility, but here are his statements."[2399] Cates argued that other governors had pardoned based on hearsay statements and included a newspaper clipping from Wisconsin, where the governor had released a man based on hearsay evidence from a relative. Cates wrote, "If the murderer of Bertie Lindsay on his deathbed had confessed the crime to one in whom you have confidence, and on the trial of Mays we had offered to prove that fact, such testimony would have been excluded as hearsay."[2400] In short, deathbed confessions are truly credible, after all, argued Cates, despite their hearsay status. Cates closed his letter by reminding the governor that the police initially said the culprit was "a short, heavy-set black man, and wore overalls."[2401]

By the time Cates's last letter reached the governor, the letters in support of Mays were largely anecdotal. John A. Brownlow, grandson of the first Republican governor of Tennessee, William G. Brownlow, said he had explained to Mays's father, "I told the old man that his son had had such a bad reputation since his boyhood as to justify the public in believing that his boy was capable of having committed the crime of which he was convicted. To this the old man assented."[2402]

Brownlow explained that when Lucius Q.C. Lamar Sr. was a trial judge in Georgia he sentenced a man to death. When the governor wrote asking if the man's life should be spared because all the jurors had urged such action, the judge said no. Two years later it was shown that the man was innocent. This sent Judge Lamar into despair and he committed suicide. When his son, Lucius Q.C. Lamar, Jr., later United States Senator and member of the United States Supreme Court, was asked many years later why he always seemed so gloomy, he replied that the thought of his father's suicide was the cause. Brownlow's letter did not actually ask for a commutation for Mays, only implied it.

Another anecdotal letter came from J. Kelly Giffen, white, the president of black Knoxville College. He said he did not know Mays but questioned the wisdom of the conviction based on only one witness. He invoked scripture: "At the mouth of two witnesses, or three witnesses, shall he that is worthy of death be put to death; but at the mouth of one witness he shall not be put to death," citing Deut. 17:6.[2403]

But the governor also received a letter from A.R. Smith, the victim's brother (and Ora's cousin). He had earlier visited the governor in person and reminded the governor he had asked him to write again before the 90 days was up. He did so on February 10, 1922. He reminded the governor they were both Masons and "because if a brother was ever favored I think it should be in this particular case."[2404] He continued, "His side will ask for another reprieve and do all they can to keep him from being electrocuted."[2405]

Brother Smith closed his letter in the fashion of victims' families: "Suppose in this case it had been a sister of yours, don't you believe he would have been put to death some time ago with the same evidence that has been produced?"[2406]

Time Runs Out for Maurice Mays

The governor's tactic of signaling his willingness to hear new evidence for a ninety-day period took the momentum out of the drive to commute Mays's death sentence. Everyone simply waited and hoped that such evidence would be forthcoming. Commutation letters for Mays fell off dramatically, but mercy requests for the Christmas Killers — four white men from Anderson County, scheduled to die a week before Mays, continued to arrive.

The four, led by Tom Christmas, had slashed the throat of an innocent passenger in a touring car they commandeered to use in a bank robbery.[2407] Captured immediately after the May 20, 1921, killing, they incriminated each other, but by the time of their executions were insisting they too (like Mays) were innocent. One (McClure) remarked about the governor, "It does look like Governor Taylor would give us a little time. He gave Maurice Mays, the Negro up the hall, 90 days. Don't you think we deserve that much consideration?"[2408] Like Mays, he insisted, "I killed no one."[2409] Fellow killer Charles Petree said he was being executed for "politics' sake," and asserted, "And I can say before my God that I am innocent, and that is more than a lot of the public can say now."[2410]

Because some mercy petitions for the Christmas Killers invoked Mays's name, they ended up in his file. This was especially true for the only one who might have been the subject of executive clemency, Charles Petree, white, who was of very low intelligence. Public sentiment was overwhelmingly against mercy for the Christmas Killers and it overlapped Mays's clemency appeals badly. A lawyer not involved in the case wrote, "Public sentiment in Anderson and adjoining counties demands a full penalty of the law in this case."[2411]

At 1:30 P.M. on March 14, 1922, the governor announced his decision. After explaining that two juries had found him guilty and the strongest evidence was "the positive testimony of Ora Smythe Parsons, who unequivocally, and positively identified Mays as the man who killed Mrs. Lindsey," he dismissed the "new" evidence.

Said Governor Taylor, "Numerous theories have been advanced — one that a low, heavy-set Negro wearing overalls, seen coming from the Lindsey home, may have been the man who killed Mrs. Lindsey. Another theory is that a man who called twice at the Lindsey home, asked to stay all night, and who was refused, may have been the man who killed her. All hearsay evidence and all theories must fall before positive testimony."[2412] He concluded, "The responsibility for the fate of Maurice Mays rests with the courts and juries of Tennessee and not upon me."[2413]

Maurice Mays's upcoming execution did not take place in a vacuum. John Green, white, a Washington County murderer who did not appeal his sentence but also sought mercy, was executed on February 17, 1922. Asbury Fields, white, who killed a fellow moonshiner with hammer blows to the head, but maintained his innocence to the end, was electrocuted on February 18, 1922. His wife had made a tearful appeal to the governor on behalf of their small son. She shared his last meal at the "death house" at the prison. After she left, Fields complained it was too cold. The guards put more coal in the stove.

The four Christmas Killers were put to death on March 1, 1922. The next day, speaking from Chattanooga, the governor announced he had gotten his first good night's sleep in two weeks. A large number of women had become interested in the Christmas Killers case and had come to Nashville on their behalf, especially the weak-minded Petree, who supposedly had been exonerated by an affidavit from McClure. However, McClure had disavowed the affidavit "with practically his dying breath."[2414]

The governor said, "It is a hard position for a governor, this thing of determining himself whether a man should live or die. And it is even more difficult when the lives of four men are immediately in the governor's hands with a fifth approaching the day whether he must die unless some reason develops for interference with the laws of the regular courts." He said, "It is wrong. No one man should have the power, and no one man should face the duty of determining matters of life and death. But it is our law and I have endeavored to face the responsibility without flinching or evading."[2415]

Mays was executed as scheduled on March 15, 1922, but his death was a normal part of the criminal justice system at work. Wife killer Granville Bunch, white, followed him on April 11, 1922. William Dwight, black, who shot a store owner, soon confessed, but sought mercy by claiming he was not the actual shooter, was executed on July 25, 1922. James McElroy, white, who killed a store owner, went home and got a Bible and offered fervent prayer over the body, was electrocuted on August 15, 1922.

On the day before his death, when the governor announced his decision not to commute Mays's sentence, Mays exploded in anger at the governor. "I am to die to satisfy a few Republican politicians," he told friends a few hours before his execution.[2416] "The Governor hasn't man enough in him. You might as well talk to a rock. Some Republicans told him he'd lose 20,000 votes if he helped me."[2417]

Mays declared, "With my dying breath, I appeal to the Negro voters of Tennessee to vindicate my death by aiding forever removing from political life this fox hunting governor who with 'Ole Limber' is chasing the Negro Republicans to seek protection under a future Democratic administration."[2418] Mays was prescient.

Gov. Alfred A. Taylor was seventy-two years old when elected governor on November 2, 1920, taking advantage of a split in the Democratic Party and unseating an unpopular Democrat governor, Albert H. Roberts, who had only been elected in 1918. (Governors served two-year terms at the time.)

"Uncle Alf" Taylor had been the Republican gubernatorial nominee in 1886 in an unusual election where his brother "Bob" Taylor was the Democratic nominee. They traveled the state together telling stories and playing the fiddle. He had remained the grand old man of the Republican Party and had campaigned in 1920 in similar manner, telling stories, which frequently involved his dog, "Ole Limber."

Although woman suffrage was passed during Gov. Roberts's tenure, women did not favor him. They felt more comfortable with the folksy "Uncle Alf" and the photogenic Warren G. Harding, leading to a Republican sweep which put Harding in the White House. Taylor got fifty-five percent of the vote: 229,143 to 185,890.

In the election of November 7, 1922, the tables were reversed, and most people (including women) simply stayed home. The popular Austin Peay, a Democrat, won by a margin of 141,002 to 102,586. In time, he became known as "The Pardoning Governor," and complained that the strain of hearing commutation requests would bring him an early death when he retired as governor. In fact, he died of a stroke in office on October 2, 1927. His successor, Gov. Henry Horton, complained to the General Assembly that half his time was spent hearing requests for commutation.[2419] Still, "Uncle Alf" Taylor was the last Republican elected governor until 1970 as African Americans moved away from the G.O.P.

The Last Hours of Maurice Mays

Twenty-four hours before his death, Mays was baptized in the African Methodist Episcopal church, and declared he was now free from sin and was bound for heaven. Three female inmates were allowed to sing and pray outside his cell and he broke down crying twice, but was comforted by two black ministers. He continued to assert his innocence and condemn the governor, but at one point asked if the execution could be moved up instead of waiting for the next day.

Mays, like most, ate little of his large "last meal" except for the dessert. At 6:15 on the morning of March 15, 1922, he was seated in the electric chair. "I am as innocent as the sun that shines," he said.[2420] His father took his body back to Knoxville. Some two thousand of the city's twelve thousand African Americans filed by to see it before he was buried in an unmarked grave in a black cemetery.

Granville Bunch, white, age 36. *Murder.*

The crime was committed on the afternoon of April 12, 1921, near the home of Joe Dougherty, the victim's father, in a rural part of Anderson County. The victim was Barzilla Daugherty Bunch, white, age thirty-two. The killer, angry that his wife would not return to him, shot her in the back. The killing was seen by several witnesses, including the victim's father and her children. After shooting his wife Bunch attempted to shoot himself in the left breast.[2421] Barzilla was visibly pregnant.

Both Granville and Barzilla had been previously married. Granville had three children by his former wife; Barzilla had two by her first husband. They had been married only a year, first living with her father, Joe Dougherty, then moving to Petros. Barzilla left Granville in Petros because he mistreated her, and moved back in with her father.

On April 5, 1921, Granville came to the father's house and asked Barzilla to return. She refused. He demanded she return a ring and lavalier which he had given her. Later he returned and demanded return of the clothing he had purchased for her. She complied. Then he demanded she give him the dress she was wearing because he had given it to her. Barzilla went into the house, took off the dress and put on a dress that had belonged to her mother. She gave Granville the dress and he put the clothing in a pile and set them on fire, while standing over the fire with a pistol. Barzilla's mother told Granville that he could be arrested for this conduct, and he replied, with an oath, "No man could arrest him."[2422] Later that day, Bunch traveled to the coal mine where the father worked and struck him with a pistol.

Shortly thereafter, Granville went to the home of another of his wife's relatives, William Dougherty. There he spoke to his reluctant wife, at least one time entering the house after being told she did not want to talk to him. He was told that his wife's pregnancy was a reason not to upset her. He responded by laughing, but said nothing.[2423]

Here is what happened next, according to the Tennessee Supreme Court's opinion:

> In the afternoon Barzilla, in company with William Dougherty, Mrs. Duncan and Barzilla's children, left the house, Dougherty intending to cross the mountain, and the women on their way to their respective homes. Upon reaching a point at the ford or crossing of the river, some four or five hundred yards from the Dougherty home, the defendant was seen sitting near the forks of the road, and upon their coming up, joined and went along with them. After they had proceeded for some little distance the defendant was heard to request his wife to step back and talk with him; no reply was made by her and the defendant renewed the request, to which she replied that she did not care to do so. After proceeding only a short distance the defendant, with the statement, "Barzilla, don't treat me that way," shot her in the back, and then turned the pistol on himself, inflicting a wound in his left breast. Barzilla died almost immediately from the effect of the shooting.[2424]

The court said the defendant's details of the killing did not differ in any material regard with those of the state, and Granville offered no explanation or justification for his action. He said he knew his wife was pregnant and one of the things he wanted to talk to her about was his arrangements for a physician to attend her.[2425]

His chief defense was insanity, but despite a few relatives testifying about his prior erratic and unusual conduct, no one opined that he was insane. Rather he was a "high tempered, irascible man."[2426] His counsel sought to show he was also of low mentality and the killing was not premeditated. The court said that the facts showed he had waited for his wife at the fork in the road and shot her in the back.

Bunch asserted that the district attorney's argument was improper. He said, "Gentlemen of the jury, if you convict this man and send him to the penitentiary of the State for a lifetime, Mr. Byrge and Mr. Burnett, counsel for the defendant, will be after you in less than a year to sign a petition to get him out of the penitentiary. I hate to talk about the Bunch family, but it appears that the whole Bunch family are criminals." The court said the statement was not included in the bill of exceptions and technically it could not pass on it, but concluded the statement was not prejudicial.[2427] The court ordered the execution on April 11, 1922. He was electrocuted that day.

At the prison, Bunch insisted that he could not remember the killing itself or any of its details. He ate a hearty last meal, but told the ministers who came to pray in front of him that he did not believe in a deity or anything in the Bible, and maintained this to the end. He left a letter with one of the ministers saying that a bad woman was the cause of his trouble. The letter said he did not care that no one visited him, including his family that publicly disowned him. Because no one claimed his body, it was buried on the prison grounds.[2428]

William Dwight, black, age 18. *Murder.*

The crime was committed on the night of April 14, 1921, on East Ninth Street in the store owned by George Stoner, in Chattanooga, in Hamilton County. The victim, George Stoner, white, age sixty-one, was alone in the store, a customer having just left.

The facts were described by the Tennessee Supreme Court, "On the night of April 14, 1921, three negroes, the defendant, T.R. Curtis, alias Jesse James, and Will Hall, alias Tootsie, met in a pool room on East Ninth Street in the city of Chattanooga and 'planned to go out and hold up somebody and get some money.' Armed with a pistol, and in furtherance of their joint design, they visited three or four stores in the neighborhood of East End Avenue, but finding them crowded with too many people, proceeded up Magnolia Street to East Ninth, where they turned and passed the store of George Stoner. After going two or three blocks they determined to turn back and rob him, as expressed by them 'to get them few dollars what that old man has got.' It was agreed that Dwight and Curtis would enter the store and hold up Mr. Stoner while Hall remained outside to watch."

The court continued, "Pursuant to this plan, after peering through a window and seeing only the deceased, a woman customer and her child in the building, the two named suddenly entered and called to Stoner to throw up his hands. In reply to this demand the latter replied, 'Boys, you will have to shoot,' whereupon he was immediately shot through or near the heart, and staggering through the building and out upon the sidewalk, died. The participants in the murder fled, were apprehended by the authorities within a few days and severally made confessions embodying the facts above narrated."

The courts said, "Their confessions, as is often the case among conspirators, are not in entire accord; Dwight maintaining that Hall was the owner of the pistol and that Curtis fired the shot which killed Stoner; while his associates assert that Dwight was the owner of the weapon and used the same in the murder."[2429]

Because no bill of exceptions was filed with the appeal, the court could not pass on the issue of whether the grand jury foreman was properly seated. The court said, "It could little avail Dwight in view of his admitted guilt."[2430] The court said, "This murder was bold, brutal and without the claim of excuse." The court set Dwight's execution for July 25, 1922.[2431] The black ministers of Chattanooga urged Curtis to admit being the shooter, based on their belief that this would result in a commutation of Dwight's sentence. He did not.[2432] William Dwight met death on the appointed day in the electric chair of the Main Prison in Nashville. The co-defendants had received life sentences.[2433] Dwight ate a hearty chicken dinner the night before his execution. His last actions and words were not reported.[2434]

Austin Harris, black, age 41. *Murder.*

The crime was committed at 10:00 P.M. on November 27, 1921, on a rural farm in Madison County, in the cabin shared by the killer and his victim. Both were tenant farmers on land owned by Thomas C. Long, age sixty-three. The victim was Ellis Robinson, black, age thirty. Harris had been paroled from the prison in Nashville on June 20, 1921, after serving three years of a ten-year sentence for larceny. Long was known to accept parolees for work in the country, where they could "stay away from trouble." Born in Mississippi, Harris had several scars on his head, neck, arms, buttocks and heel.

Harris killed his housemate because Robinson had apparently taken a place of favor Harris wanted with a neighbor woman. The day of the murder, Harris saw Robinson with the woman in Long's barn, and saw the place where they had been lying on the ground. Harris raged at the woman. He returned to the cabin and brooded while sitting by the fireplace shaving pieces of kindling. He had an ax between his legs. Later, Robinson returned to the cabin and went straight to bed without talking to Harris. Unable to control his anger, Harris twice struck Robinson's head with the ax. A few minutes later he went to Long's house and told him and his adult son what he had done.[2435]

At trial, Harris told a different story. He said he was sitting at the fireplace. Robinson came in and began striking him with a poker taken from the fire. He threw up his arm to protect himself. He "tapped Ellis with the ax."[2436] The murder scene did not support this scenario. The cabin did not show any evidence of a struggle when the Longs visited it immediately after Harris came to them. Robinson was clearly undressed and in bed when he was struck. There was no blood anywhere but on the bed where the body lay. The Tennessee Supreme Court said Harris's version was a fabrication.[2437]

No one else testified on the defendant's behalf. After the trial, a number of affidavits of family members and a doctor from New Orleans (where Harris was reared) were offered the trial court, supporting the notion that Harris was so weak-minded that he did not know right from wrong. The affiants attached much credit to the story of Harris's birth: "His mother attended a circus just before he was born and saw a hippopotamus and got frightened and this circumstance had impaired Harris's mind from his birth."[2438] The Supreme Court was unimpressed with this evidence, explaining that the killer's actions in coming to the Long house and confecting the self-defense story belied his ability to tell right from wrong.[2439]

Austin Harris was executed on the morning of August 15, 1922. He was followed by Jim McElroy. Harris's last words were, "Good-bye, everybody."[2440] Because no one had made arrangements for his body, he was buried on the prison grounds.

James McElroy (aka Jim McElroy), white, age 38. *Murder.*

The crime was committed at 6:30 A.M. June 30, 1921, in front of the store (commissary) of the Roane Iron Company, on Chamberlain Street in Kingston, in Roane County. The killer was a miner and part-time preacher in an evangelical sect whose exuberant religious services caused them to be called "Holy Rollers" by other denominations. His home was near the store. The victim was store manager Edward L. Bennecker, white, age thirty-two.

McElroy had a wife and five children, and was

among those put on short hours by the mining company because of a drop in iron ore prices. He had worked for the company since he was fourteen years old. The store was the company store, where employees normally bought on credit. Bennecker had been told not to sell more goods on credit to McElroy. On the morning of the killing, McElroy was the first adult to approach the store, following Bennecker. Just ahead of him was a little girl, Winnie Griffith. McElroy was carrying a shotgun.

McElroy pushed the girl out of the way, saying, "Get out of my way, little girl, I am going to shoot Bennecker," who responded that he hadn't done anything to deserve shooting. Without hesitation, McElroy fired one shot and Bennecker fell "kinder on his side."[2441]

Following the shooting, McElroy went home immediately and "returned with a Bible and prayed and preached over the deceased until he was placed under arrest by the officer."[2442] "He began praying for the Lord to save the soul of the dead man."[2443] McElroy told witnesses, "He had been directed by the Spirit to kill Bennecker; that the Lord told him to kill this man; that he had seen a vision, and saw it in a rainbow."[2444] The newspaper attributed the killing to the refusal to extend more credit and to the "Bolshevic literature and socialistic tendencies which the man always had."[2445]

McElroy's defense was temporary insanity. His chief medical witness, Dr. John Roberts, a general practitioner and county physician,[2446] was not allowed to testify because he said he was not an expert in psychiatry (he used the word "alienist") although he had seen from fifteen to twenty cases of insanity and sent them to an asylum.[2447] Precisely, McElroy's mental condition was paranoia. The morning of the shooting he saw a vision in the sky and the Lord told him to do it and "the table was swept clean." McElroy said he had only done what "many other men would do in this country, and now since he had killed Bennecker work would start up for everybody."[2448]

To show McElroy's state of mind, his mother was placed on the stand. She explained that as a four-year-old he fell into the fire and all the hair and flesh sloughed off the left side of his head, exposing the skull. He did not get over this trauma until he was about fourteen years old. He was later struck in the head with a rock, kicked in the head by a mule, received head injuries from falling slate in the mine, and received a fractured skull when hit by a club. His mother said he was "crazy on religion" and his mind had been unsound for the past four years.[2449]

The Tennessee Supreme Court said that McElroy's claim that God had told him to kill Bennecker was not a defense because other evidence showed he knew right from wrong. He was able to attend to his work, begat five children, and had served in higher than wage jobs at the mine.[2450]

When placed on the stand by his own lawyer he remained mute, but when the lawyer asked him to show his head to his mother and sister, he complied. There was nothing wrong with McElroy except, in the words of his brother-in-law, he was "just kinder cracked on religion."[2451] It was not error for the court to refuse to hear the doctor because he said he did not treat mental illness; he only sent people to the asylum. The decision to allow the doctor to testify was a matter for the court's discretion.[2452] The court ordered McElroy executed on August 15, 1922, and he met death that day.

Sullen and quick-tempered, McElroy refused to talk about his crime. The newspaper reported, "No plea for mercy came from him or his family. It was murder in cold blood, and his wife, when she wrote asking for his body, entered no plea for clemency."[2453] McElroy was the second person executed on August 15, 1922. He was preceded by Austin Harris.

1925

Ben Burchfield, white, age 44. *Murder.*

The crime was committed in the early morning hours of Sunday, November 25, 1922, at the grocery store owned by James W. Smith, white, age fifty, and his wife, Mary E. Smith, white, age thirty-nine, in the city of Bristol, in Sullivan County. Mary Smith was the aunt of the killer's wife, Delia Burchfield, white, age twenty-eight. The victims were Delia Burchfield, her son (the killer's stepson) Charley, white, age eight, and both of the Smiths, along with their daughter, Rubie, white, age three.

Burchfield had entered the store and smashed the victims' skulls as they were sleeping. Mrs. Burchfield and Charley were in one bed, the Smiths and Rubie in another. The sleeping quarters were in the back of the Smith grocery store. Burchfield set fire to the store to mask the killings. The fire was spotted between 3 and 4 o'clock in the morning. The building was fully involved in flames, but the charred bodies showed obvious signs of crushed skulls. Burchfield was tried only for the death of his wife, for which he received the death penalty.

This remains the largest multiple-death homicide by a single killer in Tennessee history to result in the death penalty imposed by a Tennessee jury — Champ Ferguson was tried by a military commission.

Burchfield, described by the Tennessee Supreme Court as "thriftless, worthless, illiterate and devoid of moral perception,"[2454] denied killing any of the five victims. No murder weapon was found and he provided a reason for every piece of evidence the state offered.

Burchfield was arrested the day of the killings (Sunday morning) and a clot of blood or flesh the size of a pea was found on his collar, and some blood was found on a stickpin on his tie, as well as on his sleeve.[2455] Burchfield said the blood may have gotten there when he broke up a fight the night before at a dance he had attended. But proof showed there was no fight.[2456] Then he said it might have gotten there from handling meat at the restaurant where he worked the night before. But the proof showed he had never handled raw meat at the restaurant. Then he said it might have gotten there when he dressed rabbits at the restaurant. But the proof showed that no rabbits were dressed that day, and when they were, it was done in the kitchen, not in the restaurant proper, where Burchfield worked.[2457]

The killing of Mrs. Burchfield was prompted by her husband's need for money and his anger that she was divorcing him. The marriage was turbulent and the couple, married four years, had lived apart for several months. Delia and Charley had gone to live with the Smiths while the estranged husband took jobs in mines in West Virginia, always returning after a few weeks to insist Delia return to him. About a week before the killings, Burchfield asked his wife for twenty dollars, but she only had ten. Mrs. Smith loaned her the rest, with the understanding that Burchfield was going to return to Virginia and leave his wife alone. Instead, Burchfield promptly spent some of the money on new corduroy pants and leather leggings at a store in Bristol.

That same day he got a job at the Heirs & McMillan restaurant in Bristol, being paid room and board and $4.00 a week. He seems to have been fired on Saturday, November 25, 1922. During this week he told several people that his wife could get a divorce but "it would never do her any good."[2458] Several witnesses recounted Mrs. Burchfield's fears of her husband, including one who saw him beat her. Witness Rose Shell testified she had stayed with the Smiths one night because Mrs. Smith said she was afraid of Burchfield.[2459] He lurked around outside the Smith store, and said the couple were responsible for Delia's remaining away from him.

A factor in Burchfield's need for money was the fact that a man in Johnson City had filed a police report that Burchfield had stolen some copper pipe from him. However, a brother of Mr. Smith had intervened and relayed the message that the complainant would abandon the charge if he were paid the value of the pipe, some $25.[2460] On the night of the killings, Burchfield received his $3.65 pay, packed his suitcase, ate supper at the restaurant after it closed at 7:00 P.M. and complained to everyone that he had no money because his wife had been entrusted with $1,800 and had "run away" with it.[2461]

After eating, Burchfield went to a country dance at a home in the outskirts of Bristol. He paid the same cab driver to take and return him. At the dance he bought some whiskey and "associated" with a woman there, giving her three dollars.[2462] Returning to the Smith store about 11:30 P.M. he found the lights were still on and he called to his wife and asked for twenty dollars to pay the man at Johnson City, saying that police officers were present in the waiting car. Mrs. Burchfield was not deceived by this, although she gave him one dollar for the cab fare and Burchfield entered the building.[2463] He was wearing his new corduroy pants and leather leggings.

What happened next is unknown. The best conclusion is that Burchfield killed the victims between that time and when the fire was discovered. The Smith store usually had between twenty-five and thirty-five dollars on hand at the end of the week.

Burchfield testified that he came back to the restaurant about one o'clock in the morning, talked with the counter boy, and put his corduroy pants in his suitcase, with the leggings tied to the side. He said he had asked the restaurant owner to allow him to stay overnight before he left for Virginia. He said he put on a new pair of green pants which he had bought a few days earlier at Watson Salvage Store in Bristol.

He said he had made arrangements with cab driver Wampler to take him from Bristol to Johnson City in order to pay the criminal complainant. He said the thirty-five dollars in his possession had been given to him by his brother. He explained that the cab was to take him to Johnson City and return him by 8:30 A.M. so that he could take the train to Virginia at that time. According to Burchfield, the cab had three flat tires on the way to Johnson City. The driver abandoned the trip, returning and not charging him anything for the partial trip. Burchfield said he walked to Johnson City, where he was ultimately arrested.

Except for the assertion that the cab driver was asked to be ready to take him to Johnson City, nothing Burchfield said could be proven, in fact, it was largely disproved. The restaurant owner said Burchfield never returned after leaving (although he had said he wanted to spend the night), the counter boy was not produced as a witness, and the new green pants were actually purchased by Mrs. Smith at a different store; the clerk at Watson Salvage said they did not sell that type of pants. His brother did not testify. He could not identify the cab driver who had so much tire trouble.

Blood was found on the new green pants he was found wearing.[2464] According to the state's theory, blood had gotten on them when he disposed of the corduroy pants and leggings. The court said, "Ida Mitchell, a negro woman, who lived two or three blocks from the Smith home, found a pair of corduroy pants and leather leggings stuffed under the sidewalk near her home."[2465] They were bloody. The store clerk who sold them to Burchfield identified them. A jail inmate testified that Burchfield told him following his arrest that if he could find someone to swear that he drove Burchfield to Johnson City the night of the killings, "it would be worth $50.00."[2466]

The Tennessee Supreme Court summarized the case as follows: "Brooding over being separated from his wife and child; facing a criminal prosecution unless $25.00 were paid the next day, and having no funds at midnight, but having $36.00 when arrested the next morning, and leaving shortly after midnight for Johnson City without occupying the room or waiting for the conveyance he had hired; having blood on his pin, collar, shirt and clothes, and on the pocket of the new green pants; having on the green pants when arrested which Mrs. Smith had purchased that night; the finding of his corduroy trousers under the walk with blood on them, as well as other circumstances referred to above, present a state of facts that are irresistible, and not only consistent with his guilt but are inconsistent with his innocence."[2467] Affirming the trial court, the Supreme Court set the execution date for January 14, 1925.

Governor Austin Peay was unwilling to believe that a man who killed five people would continue to assert his innocence. Therefore, he spent sixteen straight hours examining the record and talking with Burchfield's lawyers.[2468] He had earlier gone to the prison and talked to Burchfield. Following the interview, he ordered physicians to examine the man. They reported that Burchfield was sane and was "shamming" insanity, just as he had done when the Supreme Court had ordered an evaluation a year earlier.[2469] Burchfield was electrocuted at the Main Prison in Nashville on the scheduled day.

Burchfield was attended by prison Chaplain R.E. Travis, Burchfield's father and a sister, who prayed on their knees in front of his cell. He knelt facing them. The warden's wife had prepared a large breakfast which Burchfield largely ignored.[2470] Burchfield told everyone that he was prepared to meet God.

Warden A.A. McCorkle, an outspoken opponent of the death penalty, was discomforted by his duty to carry out executions. McCorkle barred the media from interviewing Burchfield, saying he was "as religious as a human can possibly be." The warden continued, "He is not an idiot, but has the mind of a seven- or eight-year-old child—just a lank, ignorant mountaineer."[2471] Burchfield said nothing on his way to the chair and nothing while seated in it.

Robert Tate, white, age 29. *Murder.*

The crime was committed on the evening of January 2, 1925, in rural Cedar Springs, at the barn on the property of the victim, in rural Marion County. The victim, Adley W. "Ed" Condra, white, age forty-nine, was a merchant and station agent killed during a robbery.

Robert Tate and R.T. Waters, white, age nineteen, had decided to rob Condra. Tate was the designated shooter because Condra did not know him. Condra had locked his little store and gone to his nearby barn to tend to some livestock. He left the barn carrying a satchel assumed by Tate and Waters to contain a large amount of money. It contained $300, mostly in checks. Tate, with a kerchief on his face, barked, "Put up your hands!" As he started to do so, Tate suddenly fired, grabbed the satchel and ran away. Hearing the gunshot, Condra's wife and small daughters came running from the house nearby. Condra described the shooter's clothing, mask and hat. He died two hours later.

Another man who had been asked by Tate to help rob Condra told the sheriff about the request and R.T. Waters was arrested the day after the shooting. A few days later Tate was arrested in Sequatchie County, where he was discovered hiding in a barn. Held in the jail at Jasper, Tate confessed to the Marion County sheriff, but repudiated his confession at trial. Tate's and Waters's trials were separate; Tate was tried first. Tate insisted Waters was the shooter.

Waters testified that the two hid near the barn and Tate pulled the trigger. Then the pair ran to their hidden horse and mule and escaped to a mountain hideout. The guns were hidden behind a rock. The pair burned papers and checks found in the satchel, and returned to Waters's house about midnight. Waters said he refused a cut of the money found in the satchel, namely ten dollars. The jury also heard testimony that after his arrest, Waters took law officers to where the guns were hidden, finding Tate's hat there also.

Tate testified he confessed because he was fearful of a lynching. He denied any involvement in the case. However, a witness, Albert Dempsey, said Tate had tried to get him to rob Condra a year earlier. George Bryant testified that the morning after the killing he picked Tate up in his car and Tate blurted out that he had killed Condra after Bryant mentioned he had been shot.[2472]

Tate admitted his hat was found behind the rock on the mountain. This was because he and Waters had exchanged caps. "He is wholly unable, however, to give any reason why Waters wanted to exchange his cap for the defendant's hat."[2473] Waters said the reason for hiding the hat was fear that Condra, if alive, might recognize it.[2474]

The Tennessee Supreme Court affirmed the conviction and ordered Tate executed on September 3, 1925.[2475] Waters was convicted and he received a thirty-year sentence. Robert Tate was electrocuted at the Main Prison in Nashville on November 5, 1925, after Gov. Peay, who said he personally opposed capital punishment, refused to intervene.

Only Tate's brothers visited him the night before his execution. Tate cried as his brothers left at 9:00 P.M.[2476] He spent the rest of the night awake, smoking, bantering and joking with the guards. He ate nothing. He rolled his trouser legs up himself. Tate had earlier boasted he would escape from the penitentiary. In response, Warden A.A. McCorkle put a chain around his locked prison door.

Tate was visited by the prison chaplain and another minister. As the ministers prayed in front of him on their knees, Tate sat unbent. However, he did repeat the Lord's Prayer with them. Tate made no confession of faith but told the newspapers that he had received the holy sacraments some time before, had read the Bible frequently and said he had no fear of passing to the great beyond. He spent the last hour of life joking and boasting with the guards.

Prison Chaplain R.E. Travis asked Tate, seated in the electric chair, "Robert, you are facing death, and there is one question I want to ask you before you die — are you guilty?" "No," said Tate, just before the black hood was placed over his head.[2477] He then asked that the electric headpiece be adjusted in order that it might be more comfortable; it was. Tate was survived by his wife and three children, both parents and two brothers.

1926

Charles Barr (aka "Black Panther"), black, age 26. *Murder.*

The crime was committed on the night of May 24, 1923, on Highland Boulevard in Memphis, in Shelby County. The killer had come to Memphis at the age of sixteen, and had served briefly as the personal chauffeur to Memphis political leader Ed "Boss" Crump. The victim was William Obe Spencer, white, age twenty-four, a grocery store manager.

Spencer and his date, Miss Laura Wheaton Johnson, white, age twenty-four, a public school teacher, had been to a movie and were on their way to her home to the suburbs in his car. He was teaching her how to drive. She stopped the car to give him the wheel. As the car sat parked, Barr came up behind the car and shot a small caliber pistol through the back window.[2478] Four shots hit Spencer, who died within minutes; one shot hit Miss Johnson in the head, but she survived. Barr took Spencer's wallet and Johnson's wristwatch and rings.

The killing terrorized the city because on January 27, 1923, a virtually identical crime had occurred in a secluded street in Berclair, a Memphis suburb. Duncan Waller, white, age eighteen, and Mrs. Ruby McElwain Tucker, white, age twenty, had been shot through the back window of their parked car. Their bodies had been robbed of money and jewelry. This was the first, but not the last, of the crimes committed by someone the media soon called the "Petting Party Bandit."

Approximately a year after the Spencer shooting, Miss Johnson's watch was pawned by Mrs. Luada Barr, the wife of Charles Barr. After he was arrested on July 16, 1924, a ring belonging to Mrs. Tucker was located and traced to him. Two days later, Barr made a partial confession after agreeing to be taken to the Spencer crime scene. Within two days he had made several confessions to different people, including some in writing.[2479]

Barr went to trial on October 24, 1924, and was charged with two capital offenses for Spencer's death, namely, premeditated murder and murder during an armed robbery. Seven panels of veniremen, consisting of one thousand five hundred people in all, were exhausted before a jury was seated. Barr repudiated his confessions and strenuously argued that he had been repeatedly beaten by law enforcement officers. In what is considered to be one of the most hard-fought criminal cases in Memphis memory to that time, the public defender worked exhaustively on Barr's behalf, but he was convicted on October 27, 1924. The Tennessee Supreme Court said the evidence clearly supported the conviction, explaining that Barr gave three different versions of how he got Johnson's watch, finally saying it came from a man who did not come to testify.

Barr's lawyers argued that the confessions were the result of torture, insisting that he had been stripped naked with his hands tied behind his back and had been forced to stand on two chairs as he was lifted by the arms. The court rejected his claims, explaining that many people, including newspaper reporters, were in and out of the room and no one saw any evidence of physical violence. Furthermore, he was not denied food and water. For example, there was running water in his cell. The court remarked that someone had sent a part-time judge to his cell to tell him not to talk to the police.[2480]

Governor Austin Peay said he would not commute Barr's sentence because of the myriad of confessions, and said, "To interfere in this case would be to say that I will not permit the death penalty while governor."[2481] He also told the media, regarding the appeals for executive clemency in capital cases, "In five years, when I go to my home for peace, these things will be the nightmares of my existence."[2482]

In August 1925, the public defender filed a writ of habeas corpus in Nashville federal court which was denied on September 5, 1925. Counsel sought relief in the United States Supreme Court, but it was denied on January 16, 1926. Finally, on April 12, 1926, Barr's last federal appeal was denied, and he was ordered executed on August 20, 1926. He met death that day in the electric chair at the main prison in Nashville.

Barr was given an elaborate last meal which he did not eat. Two separate quartets, one called the Warden's Quartet, and the other called the Prison Quartet, sang hymns and spirituals on the night before he was executed. Four ministers, including Prison Chaplain R.E. Travis, and two black ministers, spoke and prayed with Barr in his last hours. He was comforted by his mother, "Aunt Ella" Barr, whom he referred to as his "Mammy," but his father, a Baptist minister, did not come to say goodbye.

Because Barr steadfastly denied the crime, and insisted that his confessions were coerced, the newspapers were especially interested in his last words. "I don't want to say nothing else about this case. I don't want to say whether I'm guilty or not. I just don't want to talk about it anymore."[2483] But his last request was honored. Seated in the electric chair, he complained that the straps around his body were too tight and he wanted to be comfortable before his death.[2484]

1927

John Franklin Webb (aka "Kiddo"), black, age 21. *Rape.*

The crime was committed on November 1, 1926, in Memphis, in Shelby County. The precise location is unknown. Webb, along with Charles Harrison, black, age twenty-six, held up a parked car containing two white couples. The car was driven by Byron B. Hughes, age seventeen; his front-seat passenger was Miss Lucille Dutton, age seventeen. In the back were Hughes's roommate Reuben Parsons and May Belle Phipps, ages unknown.

Both Webb and Harrison brandished pistols and only a robbery was planned. Harrison took Byron's wristwatch but referred to Webb by his nickname. Following the robbery, Webb pulled Miss Dutton from the car and raped her. Hughes attempted a rescue and was shot and badly wounded by Harrison. Because of his light skin tone, Harrison, who testified against Webb, bore the nickname "Yellow Boy."

Ruben Parsons was an employee of Bee Line Taxi and the cab drivers in Memphis helped locate known criminals meeting the pair's description, including the nickname "Kiddo." They were arrested two days after the robbery-rape. They boarded with a family named Carter. The family was subpoenaed to appear before the grand jury, but did not actually appear. Instead, they gave statements. Harrison quickly named Webb as the rapist and Webb made incriminating statements to several police officers and newspaper reporters.

At trial, the car occupants named Webb as the rapist, as did Harrison. Webb received the death penalty; Harrison was sentenced to five years for attempt to commit a felony. Later, he was convicted of highway robbery but his sentence is unknown.

Webb's attorney raised two issues at the trial court and on appeal. First, although nine hundred names were entered in the jury pool, none selected by the blindfolded man was African American.[2485] The state responded that the jury pool was selected from "the Poll List and Tax Book and the Telephone Book" of Shelby County in accordance with statute and no effort was made to exclude anyone on the basis of race or color. Furthermore, Webb's lawyer had been provided a list of the jury pool ten days before the trial, as mandated by statute. Next, Webb's lawyer demanded a change of venue which was denied.[2486] Both contentions were rejected by the trial court before and after trial.

Webb's case was appealed to the Tennessee Supreme Court but the opinion cannot be located. It ordered Webb executed on September 3, 1926.[2487]

Governor Austin Peay, known for his painstaking review of death penalty cases, came to the prison and interviewed Webb and Paul Record, scheduled to die the same day. He commuted Record's sentence at the request of ten of the twelve jurors. Peay said the evidence in Webb's case, especially the three confessions given to three different people, was compelling and would not be disturbed, although he did not think the death penalty was a deterrent.[2488] John Franklin Webb was electrocuted at the Main Prison on May 20, 1927.

"They've got the wrong man," is all Webb would say to the newspapers. He was attended by several ministers, three black, including an evangelist. He heard the prison quartet sing "Death Is Only a Dream" and "Coming Home to Jesus." His hands were noticeably trembling as he was taken from his cell to the electric chair. No relatives had visited prior to his execution. Webb explained that his parents "ain't got much money," but expressed dismay that his aunt had not come from Memphis. "She told me she would come."[2489]

John Henry Wallace, black, age 21. *Murder.*

The crime was committed about midnight on April 16, 1925, in the farm home of Mr. and Mrs. Everett Hedgecoth near Lewisburg in rural Marshall County. The killer was a farm hand on the farm of Luther McDaniel, white, which was located one-half mile from the victim's house. Wallace lived in a room in the McDaniel house and was treated as a family member, having free access to the McDaniel automobile and weapons. The second killer, Riley Jackson, black, age fifty-five, also lived on the McDaniel farm in a separate cabin. The victim was Everett Hedgecoth, white, age thirty-four, who knew the killers.

The day before the killing, Wallace bought two blue shotgun shells from a store in Cornersville. The day of the killing he went to the victim's home carrying McDaniel's shotgun and asked Mrs. Hedgecoth if she could shoot a gun. That night, Wallace and Jackson met behind the McDaniels' barn and went to the Hedgecoth home, entering through an unlocked door. The couple were in the bedroom. The noise from the door closing prompted Everett Hedgecoth to strike a match to light a kerosene lamp. At that moment, Wallace fired a shot which hit him in the arm. He exclaimed, "Oh, John, don't do that!" causing Wallace to accidentally fire a second shot.

Hedgecoth stumbled after Wallace into the yard. Accounts differ as to what happened next. Wallace testified that Jackson took the gun from his hand, put two red shells in it and fired a shot at Hedgecoth. By this time Mrs. Hedgecoth came to care for her husband. She saw him crumple with the third shot. According to Wallace, Jackson shot her too. Four expended shells were found in the yard, the two blue ones and two red ones brought by Jackson.[2490] Jackson insisted that all the shooting was done by Wallace. Jackson was convicted and received a twenty-one-year sentence. Nothing was taken in the robbery-murder.

Wallace testified that he needed money because he had gotten a girl in trouble and needed to get away. He insisted that Jackson had been badgering him for some time to rob the Hedgecoth home because a large amount of money was kept in the house.

After the shooting, Mrs. Hedgecoth was able to return to the house, where she called neighbor McDaniel. He came running toward the house and met the defendant Wallace heading to his house. (This was admitted by Wallace.) Wallace was found the next day in bed at the Jackson cabin. His shoes, clothes and bedding had blood on them, which he insisted had come from a pinched finger sustained the night before in putting a tire on the McDaniel car. Arrested that day, he was brought to the Nashville jail for safekeeping.

At the Nashville jail the Marshall County sheriff interviewed him, saying, "It looks like you are guilty, you might just as well acknowledge it." Wallace then confessed, and signed the confession before a notary. Regarding the confession, the defendant did not insist that any "third degree methods were resorted to, or that the sheriff induced him to make the confession 'by flattery of hope or the torture of fear,'" said the Tennessee Supreme Court.[2491] Wallace's trial was moved to Rutherford County and he was given the death penalty, but the Supreme Court reversed. The opinion cannot be located. He was likewise given the death penalty by the second jury. John Henry Wallace was electrocuted at the Main Prison on May 25, 1927.

The day before his execution, Wallace slashed his throat with a safety razor he said he had found in his cell while sweeping it. The wound was sutured and Wallace could barely talk that night and the next day. His aged mother visited him. Upon leaving she said, "God, I cannot leave him," swooned and fell at the death-house steps.[2492]

Wallace was attended by Prison Chaplain R.E. Travis and three other ministers, one black, and the prison quartet. Wallace confessed the crime to the chaplain, who announced that Wallace was "ready to go on."[2493] The warden's wife prepared an elaborate last meal, but Wallace was only interested in chocolate cake and large quantities of ice cream. The next day an eight-member choir sang "Coming Home," "Swing Low, Sweet Chariot," and "Too Late." They also sang "Steal Away," and the hymn which had become a gallows standard, "Death Is Only a Dream."

Wallace said nothing on his way to the chair or while seated. His mother had left the prison by this time. The only interested person who stayed through the execution was Mrs. Hedgecoth. She had come to the prison hoping to talk to Wallace because she was unsatisfied that the reason for the killing was robbery; however, Wallace refused to talk to her.[2494]

Herman Coggins, white, age 31. *Rape.*

The crime was committed on January 21, 1926, in the defendant's home located in North Nashville. Coggins stayed home from his waiter's job at Tony, The Chili King. His wife was away. He placed one of his children, an infant, on the porch because she was crying. Coggins was a World War I veteran.

The victim was Margaret Catherine Weis, white, age ten. She was a neighbor who saw and heard the child on the porch. Because she sometimes babysat for the family, she came across the street to tend the child. Coggins took the girl into the bedroom and raped her. He told her not to tell anyone or he would kill her. The girl did not tell anyone of the crime until a few days later when she became sick and was taken to a doctor. Word of the doctor's examination reached Coggins, who fled to Cincinnati. By the time of trial, the girl had fulminate gonorrhea. She was brought to the trial on a cot.

Coggins did not deny the crime (he pled guilty) or take the stand. His defense was insanity, in particular, that he was suffering from "shell shock," the term then used to describe post-traumatic stress disorder. His witnesses said he had the mind of a child, was a sexual deviant, had syphilis, and needed care in a mental institution. The trial was dominated by sexual themes. Coggins's wife said he was unable to reach orgasm with her and frequently masturbated in front of her. One of his experts said that masturbation brought on insanity. The little girl's mother blurted out that Coggins's reason for wanting sex with the girl was the notion that sex with a virgin would cure gonorrhea. The court ordered the jury to disregard her comment.

The Tennessee Supreme Court said the only issue before it was whether it should recommend to the governor a commutation of punishment from death to life imprisonment. The court said, "While the medical profession differs as to whether or not masturbation produces insanity, we have no evidence here that the mind of plaintiff in error was affected by this practice, if it be conceded that he engaged in it, which may well be doubted, in view of the expert testimony referred to. In view of the fact that the plaintiff in error was not examined as to his mentality, and the further fact that he did not take the stand so that his mental status might be tested by cross examination, there is really no evidence upon which this court could recommend clemency."

The court continued, "In a sense every person who commits a crime is abnormal, and if that were made the basis of judicial recommendation for commutation it would practically result in the abolition of capital punishment. Barring these suggestions of abnormality, which were insufficient, there is nothing upon which a recommendation for commutation can be based."[2495]

Coggins's counsel, John W. Hilldrop, worked strenuously on his behalf, filing a petition to rehear, and when that failed, a habeas corpus petition in federal court, and finally persuaded the county court to appoint a commission to determine Coggins's sanity. It found him sane.

On the petition to rehear, the court said, "The petition presents no judicial question for our determination. In a few instances this Court has recommended a commutation of sentence where from the record it appears that the punishment imposed was excessive; but there is no precedent for the

Court to take or consider extraneous testimony with a view of recommending to the Governor a reduction of sentence, and it would be unwise to establish such a precedent. Furthermore, since the matter is not of justifiable nature, it is more properly one to be exercised by the Chief Executive of the State based upon such evidence as may be submitted to him, and upon such independent investigation as he may see proper to make."[2496]

Governor Austin Peay died while Coggins's plea for clemency was pending. His successor, Henry Horton, declined to intervene. Herman Coggins was electrocuted at the Main Prison in Nashville on November 10, 1927.

To the last, Coggins remained in good humor, joking and exchanging war stories with his guards. Coggins had served in the Thirtieth Division, 115th machine gun battalion, while his chief guard had served in the 117th infantry. Coggins spoke repeatedly about his mother, who had died five years before, and told everyone that he expected to meet her in heaven. "She was the best friend I ever had," he said. He was attended by the Rev. Pickens Johnson, "of the Vanderbilt School of Theology, who is interested in prison work."[2497] He had asked a member of the Salvation Army to come and sing his favorite hymn, "Tell Mother I'll Be There."

Coggins did not dispute his crime, but asserted he had not gotten a "square deal" at his trial because "it never was all told." Coggins puffed a cigar while talking to his family. But his wife had left their two children, a boy, age five, and a girl, age two, at home. His lawyer explained to the newspapers that Coggins should not be executed because he was "extremely weak-minded and a moral degenerate and pervert." Meanwhile, Coggins named the persons he wanted as pallbearers.[2498]

He was attended by the prison chaplain, Salvation Army officers, and another minister, who sang several hymns including "Rock of Ages," and they all prayed the Twenty-Third Psalm. He gave the warden two written notes. One was officially withheld; the other said, "My last request is for my wife and two children to stay with my father until his death. Yours truly, Herman Coggins."

According to the account by *Banner* reporter Brainerd Cheney (later a novelist): "A few minutes later, a tiny flicker of all lights in the penitentiary due to the release of the heavy current told that the fate of Herman Coggins was fulfilled."[2499] Cheney reminded readers the execution occurred only a day before Armistice Day. The *Tennessean* reported, "So far as records show he is the first white man convicted in this county to pay the supreme penalty."[2500] Actually, he was the first Davidson County man to be electrocuted.

1928

Ben "Two Gun" Fowler, white, age 35. *Murder.*

The crime was committed on the evening of March 5, 1927, in the high school auditorium of Robbins, in Scott County. Ben "Two Gun" Fowler, a deputy sheriff, was seated in a large crowd that had come to the school to see a moving picture show, a regular event because the town did not have a theater. Fowler came to the movie clearly wearing his customary two pistols, but was also wearing a bulletproof "steel jacket" under his clothing. He claimed he had come to the movie to serve a civil warrant on a man he anticipated seeing there, but also to keep order and enjoy the movie, a comedy.

As the movie began Fowler became enraged because the children were noisy. He threatened to arrest the children, but this prompted more laughter. Under the influence of whiskey confiscated in a moonshine raid, Fowler turned his anger on Dr. Wylie W. Foust, who was also laughing, and said to the doctor, "This means you, too, big boy!" Dr. Foust, white, age fifty-four, a well-known town doctor, was seated next to his wife. Dr. Foust gave a soft reply. Fowler threatened to arrest him. The doctor said, "You won't do that." Fowler then struck the doctor in the face with a pistol and as the doctor fell, shot two or three times into his face and head.[2501]

Dr. Foust's adult son, attorney Wiley W. Foust, Jr., age twenty-six, was seated behind his father. When the shooting began, the son pulled a pistol and shot Fowler, but the bullet harmlessly struck the steel jacket. Fowler began shooting at young Foust. At least two bullets struck an innocent member of the audience. John Wesley West, white, age fifty-three, a deputy sheriff, died later in a hospital.

After the shooting, Fowler stalked around the schoolhouse claiming he did not know who did the shooting, with his pistols drawn, terrorizing the people who remained. According to the Tennessee Supreme Court opinion, "He ordered Mrs. Foust to cut out her crying and generally conducted himself in a violent manner."[2502] Fowler was indicted the Monday after the Saturday killings and his trial began on Thursday. The case was given to the jury the next Monday. It convicted Fowler in two minutes. His defense was drunkenness, which he asserted mitigated the crime to second-degree murder. Fowler testified he was so intoxicated on moonshine that he remembered nothing of the incident until the bullet from Wiley Foust's pistol struck his steel jacket.

The Supreme Court noted that neither Fowler nor any other witness testified as to the amount of whiskey consumed. The county judge, who had seen Fowler the afternoon before the killing, testified he had admonished Fowler not to attend the movie because he was clearly under the influence, but was not drunk. But the deputy who arrested Fowler testified that he was clearly drunk.

Several prosecution witnesses said Fowler did not appear drunk prior to the shooting. The most notable was his boarding house landlady, who said she saw nothing wrong with Fowler in her house some fifteen to twenty minutes prior to his going to the movie.

The Supreme Court, citing authority, recited that a drunken man may be guilty of first-degree murder if the drunkenness "be not to such an extent as to render his mind incapable of deliberation and premeditation."[2503] The court said, "The proof shows that liquor or something else made Fowler quite malignant, but his actions do not appear to be those of a man who did not know what he was doing. When Fowler got to the show he noticed the laughter of the children and threatened them. He noticed the laughter of Dr. Foust and threatened him and killed him when the latter gently remonstrated. He noticed the tears of Mrs. Foust and ordered her to stop crying. It thus seems that Fowler was observant of everything around him, and when irritated by anything observed, took steps to remove the cause of his irritation. He does not appear to have been confused in his mental processes but to have been purposeful and deadly. His frame of mind was that of a killer rather than that of irresponsible drunkenness."[2504]

Fowler caught the fancy of a cub reporter for the *Tennessean,* Brainard Cheney, who later became a novelist. Cheney began polishing his writing skills by describing the "giant of mountaineer, who smiles philosophically at his scheduled death."[2505] Cheney described in lyric detail Fowler's last day and hours as the condemned man alternately told anecdotes of his moonshine raids and tried on the new shirt and suit in which he was to be buried. Fowler comforted his weeping father and younger brother, and solemnly gave them a letter to his mother. Cheney dutifully recorded Fowler's dialect, "Man, I've waded acrost one mountain to 'nother, chargin' a still, while them moonshiners stood all about behind trees and took pot shots at me. That old steel vest of mine saved my life many time."[2506]

Fowler's chief qualification to serve as deputy sheriff was his immense size and threatening manner, plus the fact that he had served overseas in World War I, spending most of his time in the hospital, battling influenza. Fowler and another deputy had been charged in the past with killing a moonshiner named Roosevelt Jones, and another man; however, they were acquitted. He claimed to have broken up 200 moonshine stills in the three years he was a deputy.

A week before his execution, Fowler was baptized in the Methodist faith at the prison.[2507] The governor had granted him a stay of execution for this purpose and allowed his father to come visit him from Albany, Kentucky. But Fowler maintained his innocence and steadfastly denied shooting Deputy West, for which he was not charged.[2508] Fowler was electrocuted at the Main Prison on January 25, 1928.

Wiley W. Foust, Jr., was barred by the warden from seeing Fowler executed. He stayed at the Maxwell House Hotel and complained to the newspaper, "There's no use in my going out there if I can't see the juice put to him."[2509] Fowler walked steadily and unassisted to the chair and said nothing as he helped the guards adjust the straps. Unlike prior killers who were executed in their new clothes, Fowler left instructions that his new clothes be placed on him after death.

Will Terrill, black, age 21. *Rape.*

The crime was committed about noon on January 17, 1927, on Vaughn's Gap Road, in a suburban area of Nashville, in Davidson County. The rapist was a groundsman at the fashionable Belle Meade Country Club, located in the area. He had gone to work that morning to say he would not be working that day and left by way of Vaughn's Gap Road, going out of town. The victim, Miss Emma Porter, white, age fifty-three, lived in a small cabin inside the city of Belle Meade, still largely undeveloped, with her blind sister, Miss Susie Porter, white, age seventy-two. The couple lived in poverty, existing on the charity of their prosperous neighbors, who were building fine homes on large tracts of land.[2510]

The Tennessee Supreme Court described the facts of the case. "About noon on January 17, 1927, while Miss Emma Porter, age fifty, and her blind sister, age seventy, were walking along the Vaughn's

Gap Road on their way to a store, Will Terrill passed them and spoke in passing. After going beyond them about seventy-five steps he turned and overtook them. When he did so he announced to Miss Emma Porter that his purpose was to have carnal intercourse with her and threw her upon the ground.[2511] When her blind sister commenced to screaming, he arose and knocked her down and kicked her, and returned to his assault upon the other woman, and by force had intercourse with her."[2512]

Miss Emma Porter described her assailant to those who soon came to her assistance and this description led to his arrest about two o'clock. He was taken to the Nashville Police Station, where Miss Porter identified him among a number of other Negroes. Her testimony as to the character of the assault and the accomplishment of the crime was corroborated by Miss Susie Porter, the blind sister, by physicians who examined Miss Emma Porter after the assault, and by citizens who came upon the scene soon after the crime was committed.[2513]

On Terrill's first night at the jail (his first imprisonment), a fellow prisoner called the jailer and told him Terrill wanted to talk about his case. Terrill admitted to him that he had raped Miss Porter. Later Terrill repeated this statement to Thomas Little, a reporter for a Nashville newspaper. "The statement by Terrill, as appears in the record, was unattended by any of the crass police methods sometimes resorted to as a means of discovering a crime, or at least of finding a victim. Nothing in the record indicates that Terrill's statement was not voluntary and freely made. The accused did not testify."[2514]

Terrill pled not guilty and his counsel attempted to show that he was insane. His parents said that as a youngster he would disappear from time to time and could not tell them where he had been. He complained that things crawled inside of him, and people with whom they lived and worked objected to their son being around because of his peculiar conduct. There was no expert testimony on the issue of his sanity. The court said the meager proof did not show that Terrill could not distinguish between right and wrong at the time of the crime.[2515]

An objection was raised that the rubber boots he was wearing when arrested were taken from him and compared to footprints at the scene of the crime and footprints left when he walked across a field to catch a streetcar. This did not amount to compelled self-incrimination, said the court.[2516] Error was also asserted in the jury argument of the district attorney, who said, "If I were in the jury box, I...." But the court said that because the judge cut off this line of argument, there was no error.[2517] Terrill was ordered executed on April 18, 1928. He was electrocuted at the Main Prison in Nashville on June 19, 1928. Following the Supreme Court's decision, Terrill received a psychiatric evaluation and was found sane, but not "mentality developed comparable with his age."[2518]

Terrill had long denied he struck and kicked the blind sister, but as his execution approached he began to deny the rape as well. Reminded of his jailhouse confession, he maintained his innocence. He was attended by a black minister as well as prison chaplain R.E. Travis, and the Negro quartet sang spirituals for him. For his last meal he asked for a wiener sandwich, but fell asleep before it came. His parents visited him and because they were late, they were given extra time with him.[2519] The newspapers ignored his last words, if any.

Henry Brown, black, age 37. *Rape.*

The crime was committed at 11:00 A.M. on February 28, 1928, at the home of Mr. and Mrs. Charles T. Moss on Clees Ferry Road six miles from Nashville, in Davidson County. The victim was Mrs. Annie Lee Moss, white, age forty-eight. Brown was a parole violator from Cowan.[2520] He rode to the end of the Charlotte Pike streetcar line and was walking around the neighborhood trying to enter homes to steal money.

Brown came to the back door of the Moss house and when Mrs. Moss answered he asked if she needed any work done. She said no and he asked for a match to light a cigarette. When she said she didn't have any, he pushed his way into the house. A struggle ensued. They fought in the kitchen and he pushed her into a bedroom and threw her onto a bed. She screamed and begged him to leave her alone, offering him the rings she wore. He held a knife to her throat and put his mouth over hers, saying, "Kiss me, honey, it won't be long until it's all over."[2521] He then raped her.

After the rape, Mrs. Moss began fighting more. The pair ended up on the ground in the back yard until Brown pulled away and ran. From the time Brown entered the house until he left, Mrs. Moss's terrier bit at his heels and legs and barked continually.

Mrs. Moss called her husband at work, neighbors, and police. She was bruised and muddy, had a scratch on her neck and her mouth was bleeding. She was able to describe her assailant's clothing: white sweater with a purple collar, gray cap, blue trousers. His upper teeth were bad.[2522]

That evening, James "Goldie" Amos, who ran a pressing shop, dealt with Brown. Asked why his shoes and trousers needed cleaning, Brown replied "he had some trouble with a white woman and a dog." Brown was arrested later that evening. He gave several statements to police and the assistant district attorney. He admitted attempting to rape her, but said he was unsuccessful in getting his "tool" inside her. That was his contention at trial.[2523]

Here is the entire Tennessee Supreme Court opinion in the case:

> Henry Brown, referred to hereinafter as the defendant, was indicted and convicted of the crime of rape, and the jury fixed his punishment at death by electrocution. The assignments of error are limited to one question of fact; that is, whether the defendant accomplished his attempt. The defendant admits that he entered the home of Mrs. Moss, when she was alone, for the purpose of robbery; that she tried to eject him; that during the scuffle he threw her across a bed and undertook to ravish her, but that she fought so hard that he desisted and got up off of the bed, and that Mrs. Moss fought him out through the kitchen and into the back yard. Mrs. Moss testified positively that the defendant did accomplish his purpose, and it is unreasonable to believe a white woman would testify that she had been ravished by a negro if it were not true.
>
> The defendant was arrested on the day of the crime and lodged in jail, and two days thereafter confessed to Sheriff Briley, and other reputable persons present, that he did accomplish his purpose. There is no claim on the part of the defendant that this confession was not freely and voluntarily made. He simply denied having made the confession to the extent testified to by the witnesses. Counsel representing the defendant insist that there is enough doubt about the matter for this court to recommend a commutation to life imprisonment, and this contention is based upon the testimony of Mrs. Moss that she frightened the defendant away, and so stated to Mr. Liggett, the first witness who arrived on the scene after the commission of the crime.
>
> From the testimony of Mrs. Moss it plainly appears that she did everything within her power to get the defendant to leave both before and after the commission of the offense, and she was evidently apprehensive that his beastly desires were such that he would likely attempt to repeat his assault upon her. In view of the admissions made by the defendant on the witness stand, we entertain no doubt whatsoever as to his guilt, and, therefore, affirm the judgment of the trial court. The Marshal of this court will deliver the defendant, Henry Brown, to the Warden of the State Penitentiary at Nashville, who will safely keep him until Wednesday, August 22, 1928, when, in the manner prescribed by law, he will be put to death by electrocution.[2524]

Henry Brown was executed that day.

Brown ate a hearty meal the night before his execution. Prison Chaplain R.E. Travis led in prayer and the black prison quartet sang hymns and Negro spirituals, with Brown joining the singing.[2525] His only visitor was a half-brother he had not seen since childhood. "Brown maintained a dull sort of composure throughout the ordeal and went to the chair without any show of feeling."[2526]

1930

John Jones, black, age 22. *Murder.*

The crime was committed on September 12, 1928, in the yards of the Southern Railway, in Rockwood, in Roane County. The killers were John Jones; Oliver Stephenson, black, age twenty-four; and Rufus Witherspoon, black, age seventeen. They were hoboes riding on the train as it went north from Chattanooga towards Cincinnati. The victim was Tom E. Sartin, white, age twenty-six, son of the Rockwood Chief of Police. The son was assisting his father arresting the trio when he was shot by John Jones. The other two were given life sentences.

The three were riding in a gondola car, which has sides three to four feet high. They had held up and robbed other hoboes in Chattanooga and a telegram had been sent to James L. Sartin, Rockwood police chief (also a county deputy sheriff), to intercept the men when the train made a scheduled stop in Rockwood. Tom Sartin, the son, was authorized to assist his father, and was carrying his father's shotgun when the killing occurred.

The Tennessee Supreme Court described the facts:

> The [officers] proceeded to a point near the railroad station, and upon the arrival of the train, after dark and about 8:30 o'clock, Tom Sartin climbed up on the gondola car at the north end, armed with the shotgun and, seeing the three men therein, exclaimed, "Here they are!" and, addressing himself to them, used the familiar expression, "Stick 'em up." The father of Tom Sartin was standing by the side of the car, and, in response to this order, a volley of shots was fired from the car toward the north end of the

> car and the young man fell to the ground, his gun falling into the car. He says that the men on the inside of the car continued firing, shooting both at the fallen man and at the father who returned fire; that one of the men, who proved to be Witherspoon, was shot by him as he was climbing or jumping from the car. He says that he could see the fire coming from guns in three different parts of the car at the time they shot at young Sartin, and also as they continued to shoot over the side of the car at him. He saw three negroes coming out of the car, but could not say in just what order they escaped."[2527]

The younger Sartin was instantly killed. All of the men were quickly captured. J.L. Sartin was quite positive that the three men in the car were all shooting both at his son, and also, later, at him.[2528]

At trial, Jones admitted he was armed and fired at the younger Sartin. He insisted that he did not know that Sartin was an officer and that when ordered to "Throw 'em up," or "Stick 'em up," Sartin "did not say that he was any law." Jones said that he started to go towards the other end of the car when Sartin said, "If you move, I'll kill you." Jones said, "I throwed my left hand. With my right hand I pulled my pistol out of my shirt and leveled, or aimed at over my left arm, and shot at the man on the end of the car, the man who had the shotgun; that at the time I shot I did not know who the man was, or what he was doing, but I did not know but what he intended to kill me." He further said that he did not know how many shots he fired. He testified that at the same time, Stevenson and Witherspoon started to shoot at this man; that all three had pistols and all three began shooting at about the same time. He did not know which one killed him, since all three were shooting at him, and he said that all three also shot at the officer standing on the ground.[2529]

Witherspoon testified that he had no gun and did not shoot at all, but he testified that he recognized Sartin as a law officer. Stevenson also denied having a pistol or shooting, and confirmed that Witherspoon was not armed. The court concluded that these two testified falsely because several other witnesses said that shots were fired from several weapons in different locations in the gondola. The court concluded that these two were active participants in the shooting and their life sentences were proper.[2530]

The court said the real issue before it was "whether or not one or all of these men were justified in shooting at the deceased by apprehension of death or great bodily harm from the deceased and in ignorance of his purpose to arrest them."[2531] The court said, given the "violent and felonious conduct" of the trio, they had a reasonable expectation that law officers would arrest them at the first opportunity. Next, when a white man climbed on the car and said, "Here they are!" and "There they are!" they knew they had been discovered and that their arrest was imminent. This, followed by "Stick 'em up," which is "so commonly used by officers in the arrest of persons who are known to be armed, we think the circumstances were clearly suggestive that the white man giving the order was one with legal authority."[2532]

The court explained, "It is not plausible to assume that these men could reasonably have concluded, under all these circumstances, that this was an assault in the nature of a hold up for illegitimate purposes."[2533] One of the reasons Jones could not think this was a robbery was his stated belief that the man was a railroad special agent, namely someone with authority on that train and with the right to eject him, and was not justified in shooting him.[2534]

The court said that although Jones saw the shotgun, it was never "presented" nor did Sartin make an attempt to use it, especially since it fell from Sartin's hand into the car. The court said premeditation was present because the "premeditation necessary to constitute murder in the first degree may be conceived a moment before the fatal shot is fired."[2535] Here, Jones knew that the young Sartin was speaking to someone else (his father and an officer on the other side of the car) and that Jones had time to deliberately draw his pistol and take aim over his left arm.[2536]

The court declined to adopt a rule that police officers have a duty to inform such defendants of their identity. It said this was a "proper and prudent" thing to do, but the issue becomes material only bearing on the state of mind of the defendants at the moment. Because they had reason to think that Sartin was a law officer, his failure to say in as many words that he was, did not excuse the slaying.[2537]

Jones's assertion that he thought he was being threatened by a holdup was "unreasonable" and was rejected. Said the court, "Here we have three negro hoboes stealing a ride on a freight train, and it is inconceivable that they should have been under the impression that in the heart of the City of Rockwood at this early hour in the evening this young man would have climbed up on the train in the presence of others, of whose presence these defendants had ample opportunity to know, and made an assault on them for the purpose of holding them up."[2538] Jones's execution was set for January 31,

1930, and he was electrocuted at the Main Prison in Nashville on February 14, 1930.

Governor Henry Horton visited Jones at the penitentiary but could find no reason to commute his sentence.[2539] As Jones sat in Cell 1, the death row cell closest to the electric chair, he sipped coffee, read his Bible, listened to ministers, and told them he had made peace with his Maker.[2540] Jones told the three ministers (one black) that he was guilty, "confessed a belief in religion, that he was saved, and stated his readiness to die."[2541] The quartet sang "Pass Me Not, O Gentle Savior," "Swing Low, Sweet Chariot," and "Death Is Only a Dream," the latter bringing a groan from Jones. None of Jones's relatives visited him in prison. His mother sent a telegram.[2542]

Carey Gunn, black, age 20. *Rape.*

The crime was committed on the afternoon of December 5, 1929, near the village of Middleton, in Hardeman County. The victim was a white fifteen-year-old girl, Ada Cornelius. She was walking home from school. She testified, "He was ahead of me when I first saw him. I was walking home from school. After I turned off on a side path to home, crossed over a wire fence and entered a little wood he ran up to me, threw me to the ground and cut my clothes with his knife. Then he cut my throat."[2543] A doctor's testimony confirmed the rape.

Gunn was scared off by the appearance of two white men whose attention was caught by Ada's scream when her throat was cut. A posse found him five hours later. The sheriff held off an angry crowd until Gunn could be spirited to the Shelby County jail. The one-day trial on January 29, 1930, was conducted with about seventy-five armed National Guard soldiers surrounding the courthouse. "Gunn dozed through a part of the proceedings and laughed when Mr. Carter [his lawyer] sought to involve another negro."[2544]

Gunn was convicted on January 29, 1930, and there was no appeal.[2545] Following his conviction, Gunn explained, "I have never been in any trouble before. I was arrested only one time before. I was arrested for shooting craps. I didn't even know this girl and can't remember having seen her before. I had been drinking for about a week and that liquor caused me to do what I did."[2546]

Gunn said he was glad he "faced the music and didn't make any attempt to escape." "I stood a good chance of getting away. When they first came to arrest me I saw them coming with guns and knew I was the one they wanted. I was out chopping wood and could have made a run for it, but I didn't want to." He explained, "If I had got away, I would have had to hide from people all my life. When I was 18, I decided I wanted to run away. I came down to Millington to work for a man and the first day I was away, I got so homesick I just knew I had to go back home. I stuck it out a week and then I went back."[2547]

Gunn was brought to the prison in Nashville the day before his execution. He was taken to the death house at 7:00 P.M. and went to bed at 11:30 P.M. He was awakened at 4:30 A.M. and participated in a service performed by three ministers, including the prison chaplain, the Rev. Pickens Johnson. Gunn told prison officials he had made peace with his Maker and was ready to die.[2548] He was executed at 5:21 A.M. on March 14, 1930, following a visit by the prison quartet, which sang hymns.

1931

Theodore James Harris, black, age 22. *Murder.*

The crime was committed on the evening of December 24, 1929, in the fashionable home of Dr. and Mrs. Barclay J. Jones on Armstrong Ferry Pike in Knoxville, in Knox County. The killer was the family houseboy. The victims were Dr. Barclay J. Jones, white, age fifty-six; his pretty wife, Lena Buffalow Jones, white, age forty-two; and her nephew, George Lane, white, age fourteen. Harris killed all three but was tried only for the murder of Dr. Jones, who was killed last.

The facts of the case are presented in the Tennessee Supreme Court's opinion: "Theodore James Harris was convicted of murder in the first degree for killing Dr. Barclay J. Jones, and his punishment was fixed at death by electrocution. The defense interposed was that of insanity. The accused is about twenty-two years of age and was employed by deceased as a house boy. Dr. Jones was a practicing physician in Knoxville, and lived on Armstrong Ferry Pike, about a mile east of the corporate limits. His household consisted of himself, wife and George Lane, a fourteen-year-old boy, who was nephew of his wife."

The court continued:

> Late on the afternoon of December 24, 1929, the accused and young Lane had a quarrel in the basement of the Jones home, whereupon the former picked up an iron pipe and struck the latter over the head, inflicting a mortal wound.[2549] Re-

alizing the enormity of his act, and conscious of the fact that Mrs. Jones would be a witness against him, he went upstairs, dragged her to the basement and killed her with an ax. He then took $12.00 from Mrs. Jones' purse, gathered up numerous other articles and put them in his suitcase, placed papers over the basement windows, turned off the lights, locked the house, throwing away the key, and with an ax entered the garage to await the arrival of Dr. Jones. When he drove in and alighted from his car the accused killed him with an ax, dragged his body into the garage, took his pocket book, closed the door, and left. After going a short distance and removing the money he threw the pocket book in a manhole, where it was later found. He then purchased a large pistol and two boxes of cartridges, and after going to the home of some colored friends, with whom he had lived, and giving them some Christmas presents, he went to the home of William Morrison, father of the girl he was in love with, where he remained until the morning of December 26th. That morning, accompanied by Morrison, he went to the office of the county court clerk and procured a marriage license and was married that day. Friday morning at one-thirty the officers came to the Morrison home and found the accused in bed with his wife, and the pistol and cartridges beside him. He positively denied his guilt then and when taken to jail, but later made a full confession.

There is practically no direct testimony that the accused is insane, but there is evidence of insanity in his family, of a tendency on his part to have violent headaches and a disposition to shed tears over trivial matters. The evidence shows that the accused is afflicted with syphilis, but it is not of the cerebral form; that is, the kind that affects the mind. On the other hand, numerous parties for whom the accused had been working during the year he had been in Knoxville, as well as those of his own race with whom he lived and associated, testified to his sanity. He could be insane, however, and still be amenable to our criminal laws. The test adopted in this State, and in most jurisdictions, is as follows, "The general rule is that if a defendant has capacity and reason to enable him to distinguish the difference between right and wrong as to the particular act he is then doing, he is criminally responsible for such act." *Davis v. State*, 161 Tenn. 506.

Neither experts nor laymen undertake to testify that accused is incapable of distinguishing between right and wrong. In fact, the circumstances detailed above convince us that he was conscious of committing an unlawful act when he tried to cover up his first crime by doing away with the most likely evidence against him, and by attempting to shut from view the place where two of his victims are stilled in death. His denial of guilt was another evidence of conscious wrongdoing. We are satisfied that the accused is a person of low mentality, possessing propensities of the brute, so that when, through anger, he committed the first crime he did not hesitate to do any act, howsoever cruel and inhuman, in order, as he thought, to prevent detection.

The accused is the eighth of nine children, and it is only claimed that three of that number, including accused, showed any signs of abnormality. In fact, one of his brothers testified in his behalf, and appeared to be altogether normal. While Gertrude Kelly, with whom the accused boarded, testified that he cried on occasion when she chided him for not "setting her up" at a church festival, she says that he is sane. All of his employers say that he is sane, and William Morrison and wife were of the same opinion, and consented to the marriage of their daughter to him after they had been associating together for about a year.

It further appears that every one who came in contact with accused after he committed these crimes says that he is sane. It its final analysis, the substance of the testimony offered on behalf of the accused is to the effect that the mother and an uncle of the accused were insane, and that there was something wrong with two of his brothers. This, of course, even if true, was not sufficient to justify the jury in finding that accused was unable to distinguish right from wrong, and that he was unconscious of having committed a crime.

The court concluded, "After carefully considering and weighing the evidence, we find that the verdict of the jury is abundantly sustained."[2550] The court ordered Harris executed on January 27, 1931, and he was executed that day by electrocution at the Main Prison in Nashville.

As his execution date approached, Harris "jeered and laughed at death and performed strange antics behind bars."[2551] He regaled the newspapers with details of the crime, explaining that Mrs. Jones was clad in her underwear and begged for her life. When asked why he had done it, he said he "felt killing in his mind," and could not get rid of it. "I killed them. I had nothing against them."[2552] Harris insisted that he did not rape Mrs. Jones, "I just had killing on my mind."[2553]

Harris could not stop talking. "I'm not afraid of your old electric chair. Now I will 'Ride Ole Dan' for you," at which point he performed an impromptu dance mimicking an old horse shuffling along a country road. He performed what he called the half-hour test, namely holding a brimming cup of water straight out without spilling a drop. "There just ain't a spot of weakness in me," he boasted. When offered a cigarette, he quipped, "Some folks smoke 'em as long as they can, I smoke 'em short as I can."[2554]

The prison quintet sang a hymn commonly heard at executions, "Marching Home to Glory," and Harris sang with them. His final words were lengthy. He quoted scripture: "Now the days of David drew nigh that he should die; and he charged Solomon his son, saying, I am going the way of all the earth. Be thou strong therefore, and show thyself a man."

Seated in the electric chair, he spoke loudly: "Tell 'em, tell 'em all, I made fun of this old electric chair. I had rather be electrocuted a thousand times than be hanged. They told me thirty-nine have been in that chair, I'll make it an even number, forty. Let it stay that way until the end of the world."[2555]

1933

John Thomas Shaw, black, age 30. *Murder.*

The crime was committed on December 9, 1931, at about 2:30 P.M. in a small house that fronted an alley between Seventh Avenue and Eighth Avenue, North, just north of Lea Avenue, in Nashville, in Davidson County. The killer and victim knew each other. The victim was Mary Lee Foster, black, age twelve, a schoolgirl. She was raped and murdered in her home after school. Shaw was only tried on the murder charge.

On November 27, 1923, Helen Hager Whelchel, white, age twenty-two, was murdered at Indianapolis, Indiana. She had been forcibly abducted from a public sidewalk. Her body was found the next day with its head knocked in. It had been picked clean of valuables and thrown off a bridge onto railroad tracks that ran under the bridge, apparently with the intent that a passing train would destroy evidence of foul play. The victim's jewelry was recovered from pawnshops and traced to Shaw. He was sentenced to death but the Indiana Supreme Court ordered a new trial and a change of venue. A mistrial ensued. Tried a third time, Shaw was acquitted on the theory that a jealous lover had killed the woman and Shaw had acquired the jewelry by mischance. At the Indiana trials he kept saying, "You've got me wrong; you've got me wrong!"[2556]

Mary Lee's mother was employed during the day and the child attended public school. On the day of her death, Mary Lee Foster was dismissed from school at the regular hour, and reached the home of her aunt about two o'clock in the afternoon. About two-thirty o'clock she received permission from her aunt to go to her own home to get something to eat. The aunt, Fannie Mays, testified that she became uneasy about the child in about thirty minutes and went to look for her. She undertook to enter the house in which Mary Lee Foster lived, and was prevented from entering by a man who escaped through a window at the side of the house. The body of the child was then found on the bed in the front room of the house. She had been ravished and strangled.[2557]

Shaw never admitted he committed the crime. In the hours before his death he insisted, "I did not do it. A pal of mine did it, and I watched."[2558] Shaw had spent the hours immediately preceding 2:00 P.M. at the home of Joe Erskin. The exact location of Erskin's place was not shown, but was in the same section of Nashville as the victim's. Shaw left Joe Erskin about 2:00 P.M. The latter testified that Shaw was not drunk, but he had consumed a considerable quantity of whiskey during the morning, and was under the influence of whiskey at the time.

Shaw returned to Joe Erskin's about 4:00 P.M., where he learned the police were seeking him for the death of Mary Lee Foster. He made an attempt to have Erskin testify that he had been at Erskin's house during the entire afternoon. He then decided to report to the police station. But when his wife refused to accompany him, he abandoned that purpose, and went to his former home in Tullahoma, where he was arrested.[2559]

Ethel Johnson, black, testified that she lived on Eighth Avenue, about a block and a half from Mary Lee Foster's home, near the intersection of Lea Avenue and Eighth Avenue. Between two and three o'clock on the day of the homicide she saw Shaw at the corner of Eighth Avenue and Lea Avenue, and he was wearing a red raincoat; that at this time he was talking to Mary Lee Foster. Johnson testified that a short while before this she had seen Mary Lee Foster enter the home of her aunt, Fannie Mays. On cross-examination she testified that Shaw had formerly lived in the same building with her, at which time Shaw's son had played with Mary Lee. Said the court, "From this it appears, not only that [Johnson] was well acquainted with Shaw, but that the latter was well acquainted with the deceased."[2560]

The red raincoat which Shaw was wearing fixed blame on him. Fannie Mays testified that when she was denied entrance into the girl's home, she walked to the end of the porch and saw a man wearing a red raincoat raising the window of the back room. Viola Franklin, who was passing, also testified that she saw a man wearing a red raincoat raising the window of this room, while Fannie Mays was standing at the corner of the building. Fannie Mays further testified: "About the time Viola Franklin passed out of the alley, John Thomas Shaw raised the window again and jumped out of the window in the rear room into the alley and run across the lot south toward Lea Avenue. He was wearing a red raincoat."[2561]

Shaw's wife testified that she saw her husband on Twelfth Avenue about 2:30 P.M., coming from the direction of his own home, and he was then carrying a red raincoat on his arm. Said the court, "It does not appear clearly, but it seems likely that this was just before Shaw met the deceased at the corner of Eighth Avenue and Lea Avenue."[2562]

When Shaw was arrested and brought to the police station he was examined. The result of this examination was introduced by the state in the form of questions and answers.[2563] Shaw stated that he left the home of Joe Erskin about noon and went to his own home, where he ate dinner. He then returned to Joe Erskin's about one o'clock and remained until three or three-thirty. He then started home and met a Negro called John or Rock (sometimes "John the Rock") at the corner of Twelfth and Division Street. He went with this man to the corner of Eighth and Lea Avenue to get some whiskey. They entered the alley and the man went into the house where the homicide was committed, while he waited outside. He denied that he met Mary Lee on the street. He admitted that he was wearing a red raincoat, which he said belonged to his sister-in-law.[2564]

According to Shaw, after he had waited outside the house for ten minutes, he knocked on the door and his friend jumped out the window. He entered the room and found the child dead on the floor. He picked her up and placed her on the bed, and just at this time Fannie Mays knocked at the door, as she testified. "He admitted that he refused to let her enter, giving as a reason that he was alone and feared discovery. He left the house as related by Fannie Mays and overtook the man named Rock, who threatened to kill him if he disclosed what had occurred."[2565]

The court ruled that Shaw's statements were in the nature of a self-serving declaration, intended to explain his presence in the room, soon after the homicide. It was competent in evidence only in so far as it was an admission against interest, of the fact of his presence and escape. "The self-serving declarations contained therein cannot be treated as evidence of the facts so stated."[2566]

The court said Shaw's statements were inherently incriminating because he did not explain his meeting and conversation with the girl at the corner of Lea Avenue and Eighth Avenue, but denied that he saw her at that point. There was no evidence contradicting the testimony of Ethel Johnson that he did meet and talk to the girl at that point. "Strangely enough, the plaintiff in error, in his statement, fixed that point as the place where he met the man named Rock."[2567]

The court said, "We are unable to give any credence whatever to the argument that Shaw did meet such a man, and that such a man was guilty of the murder of the child. As stated, there is no evidence in the record to that effect, but even if Shaw's statement to the police had been repeated by him on the witness stand, the jury would have been almost required by the other proof to disregard it as a pure fabrication."[2568]

The court explained, "Shaw had been drinking whiskey throughout the day, when he met the deceased on the corner of Eighth Avenue and Lea Avenue; that he there had a conversation with her, and within thirty minutes later was in the room of her home with her dead body, from which he escaped after denying admittance to the woman who had come to look for the child. During the afternoon he made a statement, while very drunk, that he had killed the deceased with an ice pick, a statement which was false as to the method or means of the homicide."[2569]

The court concluded, "The proof of guilt is direct and not merely circumstantial. The presence of Shaw in the room with the girl, following his meeting with her at the corner, and his refusal to permit the aunt of the girl to enter the room, until he had made his escape, are facts so closely related to the violence with which death was inflicted as to constitute direct evidence of guilt and not mere circumstances within the contemplation of the circumstantial evidence rule. In support of this ruling we cite the discussion in *Barnards v. State*, 88 Tenn. 183, 236–238."[2570]

Finally, there was no error in the jury charge that the state's theory of the case was that the defendant's motive was rape as well as murder, because this case came within the felony murder rule.[2571] Shaw was ordered executed on May 3, 1933. He was electrocuted at the Main Prison on July 3, 1933. The conviction that led to Shaw's execution was actually his second trial. The trial court had granted a new trial following his first conviction (and death penalty) because his lawyers contended they had been denied time to prepare for trial.[2572]

The night before the execution, Shaw slashed his wrists and inflicted slight gashes on his chest and neck with a piece of wire twisted off his bed springs. He was immediately attended by two physicians who happened to be visiting the prison.[2573] That night Shaw ate little, listened to the quartet singing spirituals and attempted to gain more time. Described as "cold and calculating," he sought a delay of five days in order to tell police about other unspecified crimes, saying, "I could tell plenty in five more days. You won't give me any more time, I won't tell you what I know." Reporters asked him about the Indianapolis case of Helen Whelchel. Shaw said, "I was involved in that case. I was being paid to keep quiet."[2574]

While seated in the electric chair, Shaw asked for a drink of water, which he was given, and he asked the quartet to sing for him again. His last words, made in reference to the electric chair, were, "I hope there is enough of it."[2575]

Andrew Wilcoxen, black, age 26. *Rape.*
Oscar Bevins, black, age 25. *Rape.*

The crime was committed between three and four o'clock in the morning on Sunday, March 27, 1932, near the intersection of 23rd and Baldwin Streets, in Chattanooga, in Hamilton County. The victim was Mae Brown, white, age eighteen.

The Tennessee Supreme Court described the facts: "Early on Sunday morning, March 27, 1932, Miss Mae Brown was brutally assaulted and raped by two strange men. The fact of the rape is conclusively shown by the record and is admitted by counsel, but they say it was not done by the defendants. The only question was one of identity." The court said:

> After Miss Brown, accompanied by Millard Prince, left the home of a sick friend, they were assaulted by two negro men. The assault occurred between three and four o'clock in the morning of Sunday, March 27, 1932, near the intersection of 23rd and Baldwin Streets, Chattanooga. Miss Brown testified that in dodging about to evade bricks hurled by their assailants, she and Prince became separated. One of the negroes followed up the attack on Prince and drove him away, the other caught and dragged Miss Brown into a vacant lot, where the other soon joined him. The two forcibly carried her some distance into a field near the mouth of a large manhole or sewer entrance, where they detained her for an hour or more, and both made and accomplished repeated criminal assaults and each, by the aid of the other, forcibly had carnal knowledge of her.
>
> That the rape was accomplished is established by the testimony of Miss Brown, corroborated by Dr. Zimmerman, who examined her when carried by the officers to the hospital, and by her condition when she was found by the officers at the scene of the crime. Millard Prince testified that because of his physical weakness he was not able to repel the man who assaulted him, and he ran from house to house seeking aid, and at last reached a telephone, where he called the police.
>
> When Police Captain Gorman received the call about four A.M. he detailed officers who went to 23rd and Baldwin Streets. Nearby the ground showed evidence of a scuffle. A little further on they found a man's right shoe that had just fallen off, and later Miss Brown's purse. Upon further search the officers came upon Miss Brown, some distance away. She was found at the place where the assault was committed. She was crying, her hands and arms were bleeding, and her garments torn and disarranged. The officers sent her to the hospital and commenced a search for her assailants.
>
> Within an hour Officers Gouldy and Tinsely came upon Andrew Wilcoxen. He was about four blocks distant from the place of assault, crossing a railroad bridge. They knew about the shoe found at the scene of the assault and by their flashlights saw that Wilcoxen wore mismatched shoes. They arrested him. Prince came up in a very little while and immediately identified Wilcoxen as one of the assailants. Some days after the assault Miss Brown identified Wilcoxen as one of her assailants in a group of colored men at the jail. At the trial she testified that he was the one who caught her while the other was assaulting Prince with bricks. Bevins was arrested a week later. The chain of circumstances connected with the crime led to his arrest.
>
> Miss Brown and Prince had not seen either of their assailants before the night of the arrest. Miss Brown recalled, after the assault, and stated to the officers, that one of them called the other "Skin." Constable Roy Clinton knew that Bevins sometimes bore that name, and knew that he had formerly associated with a negro woman in Chattanooga, Ada Carson by name. Mr. Clinton went to Ada Carson's. Her testimony, which is in the record, shows that she informed Clinton that she found Bevins hiding at her home Sunday sometime during the day upon her return from a visit. She did not fix the hour. He was wearing overalls and one shoe and one slipper. Soon afterwards Hattie Mae Glenn brought Bevins some tennis shoes and trousers which he put on and wore away when he left Ada Carson's. He left the slipper at her house but carried the shoe away. She delivered the slipper to Mr. Clinton. Ada Carson testified that Bevins stayed at her house Sunday night and early next morning when she learned that City

Detective Sims was looking for him she returned to her home and told Bevins to leave or she would call the officers. In response to her inquiry as to why he was hiding, the Carson woman testified that Bevins said he was scared Andrew Wilcoxen had told on him.

R.C. Hunt, a colored man and brother of a colored deputy sheriff, testified that he accidentally came upon Bevins while over on the river and asked him why he was there and testified that Bevins replied that he had grabbed a white woman on 23rd Street Sunday morning and was scouting from the law and intended to leave town after hiding a few days. Hunt was well acquainted with Mr. Clinton and knew that Clinton suspected Bevins and was hunting for him, so Hunt informed Clinton of Bevins' whereabouts and of his statement in explanation of his presence on the river. Will Talley, a dealer in junk and old paper, testified that Bevins, nicknamed "Skin," came to his house about ten o'clock in the night of March 28, Monday, and asked leave to stay. In explanation, he said that "some woman had got hit up yonder on the street and they think I done it.

Paul Fennell, an employee of Talley, testified that while Bevins was staying at Talley's he asked him what was the matter, and Bevins told him that he had got drunk and got in trouble on the Sunday morning before but did not tell Fennell what the trouble was. Bevins stayed at Talley's several days and until arrested by Hunt and C. Evans, colored. While there he would not leave the house or the paper warehouse in the daytime. According to Fennell, he was concealing himself.

Constable Clinton did not attempt to arrest Bevins but sent R.C. Hunt, a brother of the deputy sheriff, and C. Evans, colored. After they handcuffed Bevins and put him in the car, he remarked, "If anybody told about him grabbing that white woman, he would kill them when he got out." Hunt and Evans both testified to that fact and say that they had made no statement to Bevins of the cause of his arrest. After the arrest, Clinton joined the two colored officers and with Bevins handcuffed to one of them they went to the home of Miss Brown. She was not acquainted with either Hunt or Evans. Upon their appearance Miss Brown immediately pointed out Bevins as one of her assailants. After Bevins was arrested, Prince went to the jail where he was confined, and, unaided by suggestions from anyone, identified Bevins among several negroes as one of the assailants.

Miss Brown and Prince both testified positively to the identity of Wilcoxen and Bevins. They explained that they saw them plainly as they came under the street light before the assault was commenced with bricks, and that they knew how they were dressed and could identify them. Miss Brown further testified that they had her an hour or more and it was getting light enough in the east to enable her to distinguish the features of each of the men before they released her. The shoes presented by the evidence supply a circumstance to corroborate the testimony of Prince and Miss Brown. These shoes are called in the evidence slippers. The shoe found at the scene of the assault was a man's right shoe. When arrested an hour after the assault, Wilcoxen wore the mate of that shoe on his left foot. The odd shoe on his right foot matched the shoe left at Ada Carson's by defendant Bevins. When arrested Wilcoxen's sock and foot were muddy. The left shoe was muddy but the sock and foot were dry. The left shoe worn by Wilcoxen, it seems, matched the shoe found at the scene of the assault. Against this array of facts and circumstances we have only the denial of the defendants and their unsupported alibi.[2576]

The Tennessee Supreme Court's discussed the alibis offered by the pair and said, "There is no evidence to support either alibi."[2577]

The other evidence offered by the pair was designed to show that Miss Brown and Prince were mistaken in identifying them, yet each person who gave testimony was vague on important points, such as whether the woman seen being dragged up the street was white or black. The issue of the mismatched shoes was apparently not addressed by the defendants or their witnesses. The court found the alibi weak and did not overcome the evidence of guilt "which so strongly supports the verdict against both defendants."[2578]

The court continued, "It is complained that the trial was surrounded by an atmosphere of hostility. That does not appear from the record. On the contrary, it seems to have been an orderly trial, stripped of racial feelings. Two reputable negroes arrested Bevins, after one of them had revealed his hiding place. Some of the strongest circumstances were disclosed voluntarily by people of defendants' own race."[2579]

The court concluded its discussion of the important issues raised by the appeal. It said, "There is no merit in the complaint that the trial judge erred in his lecture to bystanders and veniremen on the scruples against capital punishment which had been expressed by some of those excused after examination. The lecture was not delivered in the presence of the jurors. The men already accepted on the jury were ordered into the jury room and out of hearing of anything that the judge said. The venire had been exhausted. Many had been disqualified by declaring their scruples against capital punishment and a new panel had been summoned.

The judge explained the law and declared it the duty of those qualified for jury service to be willing to enforce it without declaring or asserting their objection to capital punishment. Such lectures are useless and ordinarily ill-timed. They are improper because calculated to impress the defense with the idea that the trial judge acts from a vindictive spirit. But nothing on the record was actuated by any such motive, and his statement to the bystanders could not have prejudiced the defendants.[2580]

The pair were ordered executed on September 7, 1933, and died that day by electrocution at the Main Prison in Nashville. The governor had read the transcript of the trial and talked with them personally. The night before the execution, Wilcoxen confessed to the crime, but Bevins only "partially confessed" to deputy warden Ed Connors, maintaining he was not guilty of the crime for which he was convicted. The pair took no food as a last meal, just coffee. They sang spirituals along with a prison quartet. Wilcoxen, executed first, continued to sing while sitting in the electric chair. Bevins had stopped by that time.[2581]

Willie Jones, black, age 24. *Murder.*

The crime was committed on the night of November 26, 1932, on the outskirts of Memphis, in Shelby County. The killer had worked for the victim in the past. The victim, Granville Garner, white, age thirty-five, was the owner of an automobile junkyard. He lived by himself in a house on the premises. On the night in question, his brother who lived in Alabama was visiting, and because the victim was not feeling well, both retired early, sleeping in the same bed.

About eleven o'clock that night the phone rang and the victim spoke in monosyllables. What happened next was contained in the Tennessee Supreme Court's opinion:

> Deceased's brother said that during the night he was aroused by a crash, a blinding light in his face, and the report of a gun. The brother rolled out of his side of the bed, saying he was trying to get to a pistol which the deceased kept in the room, and as the brother went across the room another shot was fired at him, which missed him and made a large hole in the wall of the room, opposite the window through which it was fired. The assassin had broken the glass out of a window near the bed, turned his flashlight through the window, and fired a shotgun at Granville Garner, killing him almost instantly.[2582]
>
> The surviving brother called the police station promptly to report the murder and the records of the police station show that the call came in at 2:24 A.M. About daylight that morning police officers noticed the defendant and his wife in a car at a filling station further into the city. The car did not bear a Shelby County license and the defendant was asleep. The car and its occupants looked suspicious to the officers and they woke up the defendant and began to interrogate him. He told them that the car belonged to his uncle. While they were talking to him, the officers noticed some movements of his hand indicating that he was trying to conceal something in his coat and they searched him and found a pistol. He was arrested on the charge of carrying a pistol, and his wife was picked up, and they were taken to the police station. The automobile was taken to the place were stolen cars are kept.
>
> Proof very clearly showed that the car was the property of the deceased Garner and had been on his premises the night of the murder. The identification was unmistakable. Defendant was not suspected of killing Garner when first arrested. He was taken to the police station in Memphis. This was a Sunday morning and he remained at the police station until Monday afternoon. It is not claimed that he was subjected to any examination or mistreatment while he was at the police station.
>
> On Monday afternoon, for the reason that the car had by that time been identified, defendant was taken to the Shelby County jail on a charge of murdering Garner, and sometime in early evening he made a confession that he had killed Garner. It is undisputed on the record that defendant had previously worked for Garner and had been discharged by Garner. Defendant said that Garner had beaten him up and threatened him. The murder was evidently committed by someone familiar with the premises. The man who fired the shot through the window stood on half of a barrel, which was left by the window. Garner kept some stock on his place and had two half barrels, placed in his lot, out of which he watered the animals. It was one of these half barrels that was taken to the window. The murderer also must have known exactly where Garner slept since, according to the testimony of the brother, the crash of the glass, the flash of the searchlight, and the report of the gun came right along together.
>
> The deputy sheriff who obtained defendant's confession testified that he asked defendant if he owned a shotgun, which defendant denied. A search of defendant's home was made and the shotgun there found, broken in two. Evidence was not introduced as to the condition of the shotgun, showing whether it had been recently fired. There was evidence, however, that there were scratches on the barrel of the gun, which might have been made by contact with broken glass. On the trial of the case, while admitting that he had previously worked for Garner, and his discharge by Garner, and claiming that Garner had beaten him up, defendant denied that

he had killed Garner or that he knew anything about Garner's having been killed until he [defendant] got the news in jail.

Asked about his possession of the automobile, defendant told a story to the effect that he was out late that night and that he met two white men in the automobile. That one of the white men gave him [defendant] five dollars and asked him to take the automobile to a filling station and get some gas. Defendant said the white man rode with him part of the way but did not go all the way to the filling station. That he told the white man that he [defendant] would not take the car to the filling station unless he could get his wife, and that he thereupon got his wife. Defendant claimed that the gas in the car ran out and he had to wake up his brother and get the latter to pull the automobile to the filling station with two mules. Defendant did not know who the white man was and neither did defendant's brother, nor his wife, who were introduced to corroborate defendant's testimony.

Other proof was introduced in behalf of defendant tending to show his whereabouts on the night of the killing. Only one of the witnesses saw the defendant that night later than twelve o'clock. One witness said that he saw defendant as late as 2:05 that night. There is no proof as to the distances between the several points at which defendant was seen on the night of the homicide and the premises of the deceased. We assume that all these places were in the same neighborhood, and even if defendant were elsewhere and seen as late as 2:05, he doubtless had an opportunity to get to the premises of the deceased by the time of the murder. The murder was committed only a few minutes before the brother's call to the police station and that came at 2:40.

The testimony of the defendant as to his acquisition of deceased's car is hazy, improbable, and rather plainly fictitious. He was vague, uncommunicative, and forgetful as to all his movements in connection with the automobile. Deceased's brother did not hear the automobile taken off the premises of the former. Possibly it was so taken before the shot was fired. A deputy sheriff named Key testified that he went down to the jail when defendant was first taken over there from the police station and that he saw defendant in the bull pen, with bars between them, and asked defendant if he killed Garner. Key said that defendant replied that he did and that he did it because Garner was going to kill him [defendant].

Later defendant was taken to a private room in the jail and examined by Deputy Sheriff Friddle. He there made a detailed confession, stating that he had killed Garner. He said he went to Garner's place, pushed the car out in the road, took his shotgun and went to Garner's window. That he broke out a windowpane and shot one time. After he shot once, he said he saw a man get out of bed and shoot at him. That he then went to the car, pushed out in front of the place, and went off. He gives some other details of his movements on that night, which are not material. The defendant stated in his confession that he killed Garner because Garner said if he ever caught him [defendant] at the place, he was going to kill him. Defendant further stated that he had used a flashlight, after he had broken the window, to see inside. It was otherwise proven in the record that he had bought flashlight batteries from a hardware store on the day of the killing.

Defendant claimed that Friddle struck him twice with his fists and kicked him. That the other officer also hit him. That he made his confession to avoid punishment. Friddle and the other officer both denied mistreatment of the defendant. Sheriff Bacon testified he was in and out of the room while defendant was being interrogated and that he saw no mistreatment of the latter. A newspaper reporter was called in to type defendant's confession and he testified that defendant suffered no mistreatment while he was present; that he also examined defendant and saw no bruises on the body of the defendant.

Certainly, the defendant was not mistreated for any great length of time, if at all. His first statement to Officer Key was made in the bull pen, before he had been privately examined at all, and before there was any opportunity for mistreatment. We are accordingly of opinion that the confession was properly admitted and the evidence preponderates against the contention of the defendant that it was obtained by threats or force.

The defendant had the motive to induce this murder, according to his own testimony. By reason of his previous employment, he had knowledge of the premises of the deceased which permitted the commission of the murder in the expeditious manner it was carried through. Evidently he stole deceased's automobile, got his own wife, and it seemed that the two had started to make a getaway. Defendant's denial of the ownership of the shotgun when first examined and the subsequent finding of the shotgun at his home, broken down, and put away, with scratches on the barrels, is another strong circumstance against him.

The court concluded, "On the whole case we cannot escape the conclusion that the defendant was guilty of this murder. That the crime was a brutal assassination deserving the extreme penalty of the law cannot be questioned. The judgment of the lower court is accordingly affirmed and the sentence will be executed on Thursday, August 31, 1933."[2583]

As was his custom, Warden A.W. Neely tried to get Jones to discuss his crime and confess. The warden said, "He was sullen and wouldn't say a word. I told him he could have anything to eat that he wanted, but he wouldn't answer me." In the morning, Jones drank some coffee and listened to songs and prayers, having cried some during the night. After he was placed in the chair, he was asked again to talk. Jones replied, "I didn't kill him. I ain't going to talk no more."[2584]

1934

Jim Allen, black, age 23. *Murder.*

The crime was committed at eight o'clock at night on Fifth Avenue, near Morgan Street on March 27 (Easter Sunday), 1932, in Knoxville, Knox County. The killer had worked for the victim's brother. The victim was Roy Painter, white, age thirty-seven, a cigar store owner, who was walking to his mother's house. Shot by Allen in a street robbery, he died eight days later.

It was dark and had been raining. A young couple was seated in a car on Morgan Street, about seventy-five feet from the shooting. The couple testified they saw a black man come from the direction of Hudson Alley, which entered Morgan Street further away, pass them going toward the point where the shooting took place. They heard a shot, but did not see the shooting. They saw the man run out into the street and fire a second shot. It was this second shot which caused Painter's death.

Hearing shots, a woman who lived in an adjoining house ran out into the street and found Painter lying partially on the sidewalk and partially on a bank of the adjoining lot. She asked what happened and he said, "A Negro who used to work for my brother shot me." A few moments later, as the woman was telephoning the police, a man came out on the sidewalk, and Painter said the same thing.[2585]

A moment later the couple saw a black man come back down Morgan Street toward the alley. They became frightened and feared the man would see them. They crouched down in the car and did not see him go up the alley, but they heard his footsteps as he walked up the graveled alley. The defendant, Jim Allen, made his headquarters in this alley.[2586] Police immediately suspected Allen, a police figure, was the shooter. Forty minutes later, they found Allen in his Hudson Alley house, in bed with his paramour.

Allen's clothes were wet and he was searched but the pistol was not found. Allen was taken to the hospital and said to the victim, "What is the matter with you, Mr. Painter?" The testimony of the officers and Dr. Elder and another witness was that Mr. Painter at once said to him, "You know what's the matter, and why did you do me this way?" Both the officers and Dr. Elder said that Painter told them Allen was his shooter. Dr. Elder and Dr. Cain both testified that Painter was entirely rational and understood fully what he was saying.[2587]

A bullet from a thirty-two caliber pistol was taken from Painter's body. When taken to the jail, a few minutes after being identified at the hospital, Allen was searched and in his trousers pocket were found two empty pistol cartridges from which thirty-two caliber bullets had been discharged. Two officers testified the cartridges had been recently fired because of the strong smell of powder. The murder weapon was never found.

At least three witnesses testified to having been held up within the preceding few weeks near the point where the killing took place. All identified Allen as their assailant. Allen's defense was an alibi offered by his girlfriend, but the Tennessee Supreme Court said this could have been rejected by the jury because it was possible for Allen to get to his house within five minutes of the shooting.

Said the court, "It would seem almost impossible that Mr. Painter could have been mistaken. It is significant to our minds that, while Allen did make some remark evidently intended to carry the impression of surprise, when taken into the room of the deceased, nevertheless, when directly accused by the deceased, it does not appear that he entered any protest."[2588]

The positive identification, the recently spent shells, the sighting by the young couple, the proximity of Allen's home to the shooting scene, and the experience of other holdup victims, "presents a case from which there can be no escape."[2589] The court ordered Allen executed on January 5, 1934, and he was electrocuted that day.

Because Allen maintained his innocence to the end, Gov. Hill McAlister visited him at the penitentiary. Allen asked that his last meal come from the guards' table and this was granted. Although he was executed at 5:12 A.M., Allen "took a nap before going to the chair," according to the newspaper. The deputy warden said the impending execution "didn't seem to bother him much."[2590] The newspaper reported no last words.[2591]

Joe Emory, black, age 39. *Murder.*

The crime was committed on the morning of October 31, 1932, in a fashionable section of

Knoxville called Lindbergh Forest, behind the home of Dr. Brashear on Chamberlain Drive. The victim was Marion Arthur, black, age twenty-eight, variously described as Joe Emory's wife, although they had lived together only briefly a few years before and she still went by her first husband's name.

Marion Arthur was a domestic servant in the home of W.P. Haynes next door to the Brashear residence. She lived outside the city with the children of her dead sister. Emory lived in a boarding house operated by Pearl Jones, a mile from the murder scene. Marion's mother said Emory had threatened to kill Marion in 1928 because she would not live with him. Apparently, they had gotten married on a trip to St. Louis, but she had successfully avoided him until a year before the killing.

The night before the killing, Emory had gone to Marion's home, where a fourteen-year-old niece had heard him say, "If you don't meet me tomorrow it is going to be too bad for your life."[2592] The confrontation leading up to the killing was witnessed by Pearline Smith, a seventeen-year-old black domestic in the Mynatt home next door to the Brashear residence. She saw the two quarreling, with Emory insisting she leave with him. Marion dropped a saucer and some clothing she was carrying and ran around the house just as a shot rang out.[2593] (Smith did not see the actual shooting.) Marion ran up the back steps of the Brashear home and when she reached his door, and was within one and a half feet of Dr. Brashear, Emory appeared at the top of the steps with a smoking revolver in his hand.

Dr. Brashear jumped back, slammed and locked the door to keep from being shot, and just as he did, the second shot was fired into the victim's head. No one actually saw the shooting, but Dr. and Mrs. Brashear and Mrs. Mynatt saw Emory standing in the driveway after the second shot. An upstairs house guest of the Brashears also saw Emory underneath the window at the time of the shooting. Several people saw him run into the woods. Emory flatly denied the killing, claiming he was at his boarding house at the time of the shooting. He offered the testimony of the small children of Pearl Jones, who said as much, but on cross-examination it became clear that the children were utterly confused about when they saw Emory.

Emory's actions after the killing pointed to his guilt. He insisted he went to the funeral home to view the body, but this was shown not to be true. He spent the next day in his brother's home, but forgot to mention that his wife was dead. After spending a few days with his brother, he hopped a freight train but was identified by the brakeman and arrested in Morristown on November 5, 1932.

The Supreme Court said:

> The defendant was in love with this woman and probably jealous of her. He evidently wanted her to live with him and she rejected his overtures. On the night before her death he concluded his interview with her by a threat that unless she came to him the next day he would take her life. It is inferable that he made up his mind that if he could not enjoy her favors no one else should. Arming himself with a pistol, he spent the night out in the open, and was on the ground where he knew she would appear the next morning, and when she did appear, and when she declined to go with him, he put his threat into execution. Every ingredient of first-degree murder was present. This was a most cruel and brutal murder, and the jury very properly meted out the extreme penalty of the law.[2594]

Emory had served sixteen months overseas in the 802nd Pioneer infantry, and both the black and white American Legion attempted to have his sentence commuted to life imprisonment. A few days before the execution, Emory was baptized in the Methodist faith and confessed to the killing.[2595] Emory's last wish was to talk to his "mammy" and this was granted when he was allowed to talk to his mother by long-distance telephone the night before his death.[2596] He was electrocuted at the Main Prison in Nashville on February 5, 1934, a few minutes before the execution of James Swann.

James Swann, black, age 20. *Murder.*

The crime was committed on December 24, 1932, on a road about two miles from Dandridge, near the county poor farm home in Jefferson County. The victim, Miss Sarah Abbie Rainwater, white, age fifty-six, was carrying a box of candy. She was walking down the road when Swann leaped upon her out of hiding and overpowered her. She was brutally raped. Swann, who was six foot three inches tall and weighed one hundred and eighty pounds, then twisted her head, breaking her neck.

Abbie had been walking along the road and had stopped at various houses to get out of the rain. One was the home of Bill Swann, the killer's father-in-law, where she was seen with the candy. James Swann said he killed Abbie to keep her silent after the candy theft. In jail, Dock Swann (Bill's twelve-year-old son) admitted he had helped hide the body after James came to his house and said he'd killed somebody and "I'm on my way to the electric chair." Miss Abbie lived with her widowed brother, Lockie Rainwater, white, age fifty-three, and his children Dewy, age twenty-two, and Alice, age nineteen, although she generally lived at the county poor farm.[2597] Swann was convicted by a jury in Dandridge on March 30, 1933, and sentenced to die on May 1, 1933.[2598]

The Tennessee Supreme Court upheld the conviction, but an opinion cannot be located. Swann, a former reform school and prison inmate, maintained his innocence at trial and in prison. Swann and Joe Emory, scheduled to die on the same day, had been baptized in a pool on the prison grounds a few days before their executions, each emerging from the water shouting, "Hallelujah!" Several ministers visited him in the days and hours before his death but Swann refused to discuss his crime. Three minutes before he was taken to the electric chair, Swann suddenly confessed to killing Rainwater for "fear she might tell."[2599] As he sat in the chair, he said, "Gentlemen, I want to tell you I killed that white woman. I want the whole world to know I killed her."[2600] The executions took place on February 5, 1934. Emory was first, then Swann.

Louis Fain, black, age 28. *Murder.*

The crime was committed about 6:30 P.M. on November 28, 1932, in the victim's rooming house apartment on 614 Church Street in downtown Knoxville. The victim, Louise "Carrie" Allen, white, age nineteen, was a cashier in a downtown cafeteria, as was her roommate, Viva Robinson.

Carrie Allen was off work that day, which was payday. Robinson brought Carrie's pay, in cash, to their room shortly after 2:00 P.M., placing it in a box. Carrie was not home. Her pay consisted of a five-dollar bill, three one-dollar bills, a fifty-cent piece and a quarter. Robinson left about 4:00 P.M. to return to work. She worked at the cafeteria until it closed at 8:00 P.M., returning to the apartment shortly thereafter. She found Carrie bleeding from a jagged throat wound. Carrie had been outraged.[2601] She died at the hospital.

The rooming house was conducted by Mrs. Millie Schubert, who lived on the ground floor. She testified she heard Miss Allen return before 6:00 P.M. and specifically heard her walking around in the upstairs apartment at 6:20, shortly before Mrs. Schubert left to catch a 6:30 streetcar.

Fain had been playing poker at a house about 125 yards from the victim's apartment. He had gambled with Harmon Hale, black, the key state's witness. According to Hale, the game broke up at 6:00 P.M. and both he and Fain "went broke" at the game. Hale testified he left Fain at the corner of Broadway and Cumberland Street after the game, and that he (Hale) went directly to Fain's house, five blocks away. Hale had supper with the Fain family, but Fain did not join them until the meal was over. When Fain arrived, he motioned Hale to come to a bathroom adjacent the kitchen. He displayed a five-dollar bill, three ones and some silver, a ring and a white gold lady's wristwatch. Hale testified that Fain told him he had robbed a lady and had to kill her to keep her from identifying him.

Later that evening, about the time Allen's body was discovered, Hale, Fain and two young women attended a Negro dance hall. There was conflict about who paid the admission and beverages. Hale testified Fain had paid. Fain said Hale had done so. The partygoers returned to the Fain house about 11:00 P.M. Hale spent the night. He and Fain slept in the same bed. The day after the killing, Fain went to the country to visit his estranged wife and mother-in-law. The latter testified that Fain had asked how to get away if the law came after him.

Arrested on December 30, 1932, Fain was spirited away to the Chattanooga jail after a three-hundred-member mob of drunken revelers appeared at the jail to lynch him the next evening.

At trial on February 15, 1933, Fain vigorously denied any involvement with the crime, insisting there had been no discussion in the bathroom, and that he was home about 6:30 P.M. His sister supported his story, but the court said she was not credible. Fain and his sister's testimony seemed to implicate Hale as the killer. Heavy police presence was obvious both inside and outside the courthouse with state troopers carrying Thompson submachine guns.

A police search of the Fain home discovered a flashlight with blood on it, and burglary tools which exactly fit the marks on the door and window that had been prized open at the rooming house. These tools were found in the coal stove grate/screen at the Fain house. Said the Tennessee Supreme Court, "The unfortunate girl's throat was cut with a dull edged implement similar to the screw driver or coal chisel found in the grate in the Fain house."[2602]

The defendant's father, Walter Fain, was "picked up by officers and examined."[2603] (There was no explanation why.) He ultimately took them to a point near the house where jewelry had been buried by the father at the son's request. Among the jewelry was a ring that belonged to the victim.[2604] Allen's fiancé identified the ring, which he had given her, as did Miss Robinson, based on its unusual sizing and setting. Fain initially offered no explanation for the ring, according to the Supreme Court's opinion, but attempted to shift responsibility to Hale by saying he had access to Fain's trunk, were he kept his possessions. Fain insisted the jewelry had been proceeds of his selling bootleg liquor, but the named buyers denied this in court.

Fain contested everything Hale asserted, including whether the two had "gone broke," and the statement about killing Carrie Allen. Fain's sister Juanita's testimony tended to track his denials, but both his father (Walter) and brother Jasper Fain's testimony incriminated him, especially their testimony regarding the jewelry.[2605] Jasper testified that when he visited Louis in jail, he said that if he got the death penalty their father would be responsible for it.[2606]

Fain had been sent to reform school as a youth and assigned error because this issue was raised by the prosecution. But Fain was allowed to testify at length about the guilty plea that sent him to reform school. Hence, there was no error in this line of questioning.[2607] The court concluded that Fain had likely entered the house for the purpose of burglary and killed Carrie Allen to prevent her from identifying him.[2608]

Louis Fain continued to assert his innocence until the night before his execution. He then prepared a five-hundred-word confession titled "The Wages of Sin is Death," in which he fully confessed. Fain said that Carrie Allen had hit him in the back with a shoe or something like it after he raped her and this caused him to return and cut her throat.[2609] Fain was electrocuted on February 26, 1934. His last words were, "Just tell my dear family and friends that I died like a soldier."[2610]

On November 4, 1931, Mrs. Maude Messner, white, age thirty, had been bludgeoned to death at her home in the Glencoe Apartments not far from Carrie Allen's rooming house. She was a widow who lived alone. Then on November 13, 1931, Vincent Hodge, black, age twenty-five, was found with a bullet hole in his skull. He was in a bed at the Fain home. It was deemed a suicide. At the time Fain was arrested, police began investigating his involvement with these cases, but he was never charged. It is not known whether his last confession mentioned these crimes.

Percy Smith, black, age 25. *Rape.*

The crime was committed on the morning of November 3, 1933, in the farm home of Mr. and Mrs. Rufus Lytle Hartsfield near the town of Bartlett, in Shelby County. The victim was Mrs. Theresa Newman Hartsfield, white, age forty-four, a housewife. She was home with her partially paralyzed sister, Miss Rose Newman, white, age fifty-three.

Smith had done yard and garden work for the family under the husband's supervision. At 7:00 A.M. he went to the barn, where he put on a brown coat and put a handkerchief over his face. He entered the house and hid behind a door. Brandishing a pistol, he ordered both women into a closet. He searched the house and gathered the women's jewelry and money. He then went to the closet and ordered Mrs. Hartsfield to come out. She begged him not to hurt her and promised not to tell anyone that he had been there if he left them alone.

Because of continuing threats, Mrs. Hartsfield came out. He raped her. "The other woman was praying in the closet but that didn't scare me," he later explained.[2611] After the rape, he ordered the victim back inside the closet. He fixed himself a large breakfast, ate it leisurely, and played phonograph records. About 10:30 someone knocked at the door. Smith asked Mrs. Hartsfield who it was. She said it was her husband. It was a man delivering laundry. When Smith stepped into a back room, Mrs. Hartsfield ran from the closet to the front door and outside. She began screaming. Hearing this, Smith ran out the back door and made his way to downtown Memphis.

When word of the crime spread, every deputy sheriff and many others formed a posse numbering at least sixty men, some with tracking dogs, and scoured the Bartlett area. The sheriff asked the radio stations to broadcast a description of the assailant. "About 25 years old, about five foot three inches tall, is quite black, with kinky oily hair and small ears. He was wearing a short army coat, blue trousers, a gray cap and black shoes."[2612]

Within hours Smith was the prime suspect, in part because he lived in the area. It was learned that his girlfriend was Frances Fizer. A domestic, she was arrested and found in possession of the pistol Smith had used. She had stolen it from a family for whom she worked. She apparently told police where to find Smith. Fearful of the size of the posse, Smith eagerly surrendered to police and quickly admitted the details of the crime.[2613] His trial began on November 21, 1933, and he was promptly convicted. The Tennessee Supreme Court affirmed the conviction on February 24, 1934, but the opinion cannot be located.

Smith had maintained his innocence until a few days before the execution. "Until I confessed, I felt terrible. I had chills and it was a mighty funny thing — knowing that I was going to die. But since

I told the truth I feel fine." Smith said he was "certainly sorry" for his crime and added, "I've told the truth to these men and the Lord, and I ain't afraid of anything. There's nothing to be afraid of when the Lord is on your side. I'm ready to go. We all have to go sometime."[2614]

Along with Jasper Graham and Frank Mays, he was given a huge meal around midnight. An inmate quartet sang spirituals to the men during the night. Smith had been given a new suit of clothes the day before his execution and died in them. The order of executions had been decided several weeks earlier and Percy Smith was the first to die on April 4, 1934. The system short-circuited after his death, giving Graham and Mays an extra hour of life while it was being repaired. Rufus L. Hartsfield died of cancer the next month.

Jasper Graham, black, age 29. *Rape.*
Frank Mays, black, age 30. *Rape.*

The crime was committed on the evening of September 28, 1932, beside a street in North Memphis, "in an exclusive Negro settlement," within a few blocks of a Negro park. The victim was Miss Mary Louise Johnson, white, age seventeen. She and Archibald Hollis, white, age nineteen, apparently stopped the car in the unlit area to engage in petting.

Here is the Tennessee Supreme Court's opinion in the case:

> This is a conviction of rape upon Mary Louise Johnson. Various assignments of error are presented, the first two raising the question of the preponderance of the evidence. This young white woman, seventeen years of age, and a companion, Archibald Hollis, age nineteen, were out driving together in an automobile on the night of September 28, 1932, and, between eleven and twelve o'clock, stopped their car on a street in North Memphis, in an exclusive Negro settlement, and parked it on the roadside within a few blocks of a Negro park. There was no street light in the vicinity, and, while a clear, starlit night, there was no moon.
>
> Shortly after they stopped, two Negroes approached the car and stepped on the running board and demanded money, and then forced Hollis, who was under the wheel, to drive the car perhaps half a mile up the street and into a nearby field, where they forced the occupants to alight and searched them both. One of the Negroes then held a pistol on Hollis, while the other Negro committed a criminal assault on the young woman. Hollis attempted to resist and assist the woman, and was shot in the abdomen by one of the Negroes and rendered helpless.
>
> Thereafter, the other Negro committed a like assault. The Negroes then left, and the young woman succeeded in getting her wounded companion into the car and conveyed him to a nearby filling station and from that point procured an ambulance and Hollis was carried to a hospital. She accompanied him and was there examined by the nurse, who, however, does not testify. The young man was seriously wounded and confined for a number of weeks, but finally recovered.
>
> After some seven or eight weeks defendants were arrested and charged with other holdups and robberies which the record shows had been committed in that immediate neighborhood, along about the time of this particular assault.
>
> On the trial of the case, both Miss Johnson and Hollis identified defendants positively and definitely as their assailants. Also, several other parties identified the plaintiffs-in-error as the parties who had held them up for the purpose of robbery. Elaborate confessions in writing were produced on the trial to which the names of these defendants were affixed by one of the officers and their acknowledgments taken before a notary public. The proof shows that these Negroes were illiterate and could neither read nor write and could not sign their names. These confessions went into considerable detail, not only as to this particular offense, but as to the like offenses to which reference has been made. Moreover, independent of these written confessions, proof was made of various incriminating statements made by defendants following their arrest connecting them with this and other crimes mentioned. For illustration, unimpeached evidence was given that when returning in an automobile from a visit to the home of Hollis, where defendants had been carried by the officers to be identified by him, he being at the time confined by his wound, one of the Negroes commented to the other upon the fact that Hollis was still alive, with the statement that they had supposed him to have been killed. Another time, one of them stated in the presence of the testifying officer that, while he had taken part in the holdup, anyone who said that he had ravished the young woman was telling a lie.
>
> We think it unnecessary to review in greater detail the evidence in the case, as we can see no basis for the insistence that the evidence sustaining identification of these parties, preponderates against their guilt. It is argued that the evidence does not go so far as to establish that the offense of rape was consummated, the reasoning in part being that if this had been true the young woman would not have been able to render the assistance she did render to her companion and would also have taken certain medical precautions which it does not affirmatively appear were taken. We think the definite testimony of the young woman herself is conclusive of this question.

It is insisted that the Court erred in admitting testimony of confessions and statements made by the parties because they were not made freely and voluntarily. The trial Judge went into this matter fully, in the absence of the jury, and found that there was no evidence to sustain the insistence. It is true that both Negroes testified to having been beaten while in confinement with a rubber hose, but this was emphatically denied by the police officers, and there is nothing further than their bare statements to support the insistence. Moreover, many of the incriminating statements were apparently made independently of and wholly apart from the alleged mistreatment.

It is objected that the Court erroneously permitted introduction of statements with respect to the other crimes to which reference has been made. Quite clearly, proof of these similar offenses, committed under like conditions in the same vicinity, all within a brief space of time and within a short time of the commission of this particular offense, was competent and material as tending to support the evidence of identification.

It is insisted by other assignments that the Court erred in restricting counsel for the defendants in his reference to news articles and editorials in newspapers touching the reputation of the police department for use of the third degree. We have examined the record carefully, and we do not think the trial Judge abused his discretion in thus limiting the argument. We are satisfied that diligent counsel got before the jury all that could be of value in this regard. Objection is also made to statements made by the Court in the course of the argument as to the question of the reputation and conduct of the police department, but we do not find that prejudicial error was committed in this regard. As we read this record, the case is so clearly made out against the defendants that the result reached by the jury could not possibly have been materially affected by these incidents occurring in the course of the argument. The same is true of the complaint made of the argument of the Attorney-General. Counsel for the defendants had a right to comment upon the peculiar situation presented by the conduct of these young people in parking their car at the time and place indicated, but the Attorney-General also was within his rights in repudiating any charge or innuendo reflecting upon the character of the young woman. None of these matters can be properly said to have affected the result, and the assignments directed thereto must be overruled.

Finally, it is insisted that the Court erred in over-ruling the motion for a new trial based on the ground of newly discovered evidence. This consisted mainly of the testimony of a Negro woman that Graham spent the night on which this assault was committed at her home with her, corroborated by another Negro woman. In the first place, we are satisfied, again, that the introduction of this evidence, if produced on the original trial, would not have affected the result. Proof of an alibi is a defense too easily concocted and made by interested parties and is always looked upon with suspicion. And, in the second place, we do not think that a sufficient showing is made under the rule of an excuse for failure to introduce this evidence at trial. Certainly, defendant must have known, or been able to ascertain, where he was at the time. Moreover, this is a matter largely in the discretion of the trial Judge, and we cannot see that his discretion was abused.

The court concluded, "On the whole case, we find no reversible error, and the judgment must be affirmed and plaintiffs-in-error will be delivered to the keeper of the State Penitentiary, where they will be held until the 23rd day of March 1934, and on that day, between the hours fixed by law, they will be put to death by electrocution."[2615]

On the day of the execution both Mary Louise (along with her husband, whom she married after the rape) and Archibald Hollis were allowed to come to the prison and confront the condemned. "Do you deny that you confessed in Memphis?" asked the woman. When the criminals maintained their innocence, the woman said, "They are the men, just the same," in front of a Memphis detective who had accompanied her to the prison.

Hollis was especially eager the rapist-shooters affirm their prior confessions, explaining that he had been hospitalized for months and doctors at one time where so sure of his impending death that the family had made funeral arrangements. The victims wanted to see the actual executions but were barred; the warden informed her that the law imposed a five-hundred-dollar fine for allowing anyone to see an execution, other than duly appointed officers and witnesses.

The Rev. Pickens Johnson confirmed the two refused to admit their crime, although Percy Smith, scheduled to die the same day for an identical crime, had confessed, after insisting he was innocent. All three were given a hearty last meal at their request, served about midnight. Warden A.W. Neely gave them cigarettes and cigars.[2616] A black quartet sang spirituals, including "Going Home."

The pair was executed on April 4, 1934, but lived one hour longer than expected. Percy Smith was the first person executed that morning, but a short circuit in the high-powered wires of the system had to be repaired before Graham and Mays could meet their deaths.[2617] Graham was executed first. Graham said the night before his execution, "I'm an innocent man. The Lord knows I am and they are killing me for something I never did. They identified the wrong man."[2618] By this time Mays insisted he was innocent too.[2619]

John Deal, black, age 30. *Murder.*

The crime was committed on the afternoon of May 20, 1933, at 1370 Union Avenue, a rooming house operated by William Gaston, in Memphis, in Shelby County. The killer had been a cook at the boarding house for about six weeks. The victim was Mrs. Elizabeth Sangster Summerfield, white, age sixty. She and her adult son, Herman Summerfield, lived at the rooming house.[2620] Formerly prosperous because of her husband's mercantile business, the widow was "practically destitute at the date of her death."[2621] According to Deal, Gaston had told him that the victim had $1,800 in a purse which she kept fastened around her waist. The newspaper called it a money belt.[2622]

Said the Tennessee Supreme Court:

> Mrs. Summerfield was last seen alive about 1:40 P.M., seated at the window of her bedroom. Two ladies, Mrs. Foltz and Mrs. Lerner, one of whom was a niece or cousin of the deceased, passed her house at that hour and noticed Mrs. Summerfield at her window. Shortly after 3:00 P.M. the attention of the occupants of the house was challenged by the falling of plaster and the dripping of water, in the lower floor. They discovered that the door to the bathroom in Mrs. Summerfield's apartment was locked, and the key removed. Opening the door with another key, they discovered Mrs. Summerfield's body in the bathtub, with her head under water. A piece of jewelry was found on the floor, which the proof shows the woman had kept in her purse. There was also found on the floor of the bathroom a towel, made from a sugar sack, of the kind usually used as a dish towel in a kitchen. An examination disclosed no water in the lungs of the woman, which excluded the idea that her death was caused by drowning. There was a bruise and a scratch on the side of her nose, and there were bruises about her throat. She had been bleeding at one of her ears. Evidence submitted by the trial court expert testimony, without objection, characterized her death as having been caused by smothering or choking.
>
> Herman Summerfield, a son of the deceased, employed at an automobile sales agency in Memphis, was notified of the death of his mother, and soon after his arrival examined the purse which was taken from the body. An envelope in which articles of jewelry were kept was found to have been torn open. A piece of the envelope was found on the floor of the bedroom. No money was found in the purse. Summerfied testified that his mother had in her possession the sum of $40, which represented her entire capital. Gaston and his wife and Deal were taken to the police station and questioned. Deal undertook to throw suspicion on Gaston from the beginning. He told police that Mr. and Mrs. Gaston were living together without having been married, and told Mr. Weinstein, a local lawyer whose wife was a relative of the deceased, that he had seen Gaston go upstairs shortly after lunch. Gaston had a police record, as a petty thief, and was held in the police station overnight. Deal was released.
>
> On the next day, which was Sunday, Deal directly accused Gaston, and told the police that he could show them where Gaston had concealed the towel with which he had smothered Mrs. Summerfield. The police accompanied him to the house, and, in the presence of other witnesses, Deal took a towel from a hand bag, located in the kitchen or breakfast room. On this occasion Deal made the remarkable statement to Herman Summerfield that Gaston told him what he had done and asked him to go upstairs and push her further under the water, which he did.
>
> Deal was taken back to the police station and in a short while told the police that he could show them where Gaston had concealed the money taken from the deceased. He was again returned to the house, and, in the presence of witnesses, asked that they look under the linoleum in the breakfast room or dining room. This was done and there were found a twenty-dollar bill, a ten-dollar bill, and five one-dollar bills. At this stage in the investigation Deal was charging Gaston with having killed Mrs. Summerfield shortly after lunch, which was concluded about 12:30 P.M. It was very conclusively shown by the testimony of the other boarders that Gaston and his wife had left the boarding house prior to one-thirty, to go to the "curb market," and that they did not return until shortly before three o'clock. The location of the curb market is not disclosed by the record, but it is shown that it was far enough from the house to require the use of a street car.
>
> When Deal was returned to the police station, after having located the money under the linoleum, he was notified that Mrs. Summerfield had been seen at her window after 1:30 P.M., as above related, which was after Gaston had gone to the curb market. Upon receiving this information Deal, according to the testimony of Inspector Griffin, confessed that he alone had committed the murder. He made a written confession in which he said that he first went to Mrs. Summerfield's room to perpetrate the robbery and that his nerve failed; that he asked Mrs. Summerfield for some aspirin, and when she had given him two tablets, he left; that he

returned to the room with a piece of paper which he pretended was a notice of eviction, requiring the Gastons to vacate the house; that when Mrs. Summerfield approached him to see the paper, he threw the towel over her face and forced her into the bathroom, and upon discovering that life had departed, placed her in the tub, where she was found. In his confession he also said that he had taken a twenty-dollar bill and two ten-dollar bills from the purse; that he had taken one of the ten-dollar bills to a restaurant and had it changed on Saturday night, and on Sunday morning he placed five one-dollar bills with the twenty and ten under the linoleum.

In addition to the circumstances hereinabove recounted, the confession of Deal is corroborated by the testimony of Mrs. R.V. Rowland, a boarder at the house, that between one-thirty and two o'clock she started upstairs to get her baby, who had awakened from his nap, and met the plaintiff in error coming down the stairs, with two aspirin tablets in his hand. In his testimony before the jury, Deal denied that he got the aspirin from Mrs. Summerfield, and denied that Mrs. Rowland met him coming down the stairs. He said that he had two aspirin tablets, which he had gotten from a downstairs room, and that Mrs. Rowland saw him with them in the hall, at the foot of the stairs. He had, however, no explanation of his presence at the foot of the stairs. The confession was further corroborated by an employee of the restaurant to which Deal had referred, who said that he had changed a ten-dollar bill for the him after midnight on the Saturday night in question.

The testimony of Deal is that after the body of Mrs. Summerfield had been discovered, and while he was preparing supper, Gaston thrust the ten-dollar bill in his pocket, telling him to say nothing about it, and that he then saw Gaston place the rest of the money under the linoleum; that he did get the ten-dollar bill changed in the manner already stated, and that he put five one-dollar bills with the money which he had seen Gaston conceal.

It is our opinion that the evidence is sufficient to sustain the verdict of conviction without reference to the confession. The very clear weight of the evidence is that Mrs. Summerfield was killed while Gaston and his wife were away from the house, on their trip to the curb market. Deal's knowledge of the place of concealment of the money taken from the deceased, and his admission that he had gone upstairs and had pushed the body further under the water, together with the fact that he was seen by Mrs. Rowland coming downstairs, and was in fact the only person who had opportunity to commit the murder, would have supported the conviction. The testimony of Deal implicates him in the crime, and since his alleged confederate, Gaston, is shown to have been away from the house, his testimony, in connection with the circumstances related, seems conclusive of his guilt as found by the jury.

However, the record affords no justification for repudiation of the confession. It is shown to have been made following the information that Mrs. Summerfield had been seen alive after Gaston had left the house, and after the hour at which Deal had said she was killed by Gaston. Mr. Harris and Mr. Brassell, reporters for the *Commercial Appeal*, were present when the written statement was made, and testified that they observed no evidence of coercion or intimidation. Subsequently, Deal repeated his confession to Mr. Nat Summerfield, and on Monday morning repeated it in a routine examination conducted by the police department. He testified, as will be noticed more particularly, that he made the confessions as the result of physical torture administered by Detective Officer Quianthy, but his unsupported statement is, we think, clearly overthrown on the record. It results that we find no merit in the assignment of error that the weight of the evidence is against the verdict.

It was a part of the testimony of Deal that Gaston borrowed a shirt from him, and that he wore that shirt when he went upstairs to rob and kill the deceased; that following the crime, Gaston concealed the shirt underneath the steam radiator in the kitchen. During the progress of the trial such a shirt was found at the place indicated, and the witness who discovered it offered to testify that the shirt was stained. The significance of this testimony seems to be that the stain came from the purple robe which the deceased was wearing at the time of her death; and it is assigned as error that the trial judge refused to permit the witness to testify about the stain. The shirt was filed as an exhibit to the testimony, and the ruling of the trial judge was that the jury could examine the shirt for stains as well as the witness. This seems to us to be an obviously correct ruling, but it appears further that the trial judge did permit the witness to point out to the jury, during his testimony, the only stain which he said he could find on the shirt.

It seems to us that this assignment of error is wholly without merit. The finding of the shirt could not possibly have any probative effect in supporting the testimony of Deal. It was admittedly his own shirt, and it is only by his own testimony that it is in any way connected with Gaston. It is our opinion that Deal merely disclosed the whereabouts of the shirt which he himself wore at the time of the homicide, and which he had concealed because he had stained it in handling the body of his victim.

The only other assignment of error which is pressed is one which has given the Court, as it did the trial judge, much concern. During the

> cross-examination of Deal with regard to his confession, he pointed out Mr. Quianthy in the court room and said that Quianthy had seized him and tortured him, which caused him to confess to the crime. Mr. Quianthy at once arose and stepped forward, saying: "You G__ d___ liar." The trial judge said: "Shut up, Mr. Quianthy," and directed an officer to remove him from the court room, which was done. The scene caused considerable disturbance and the court ordered a recess. When the proceedings were resumed the court instructed the jury not to let the disturbance influence them, and overruled an application for a mistrial.
>
> Mr. Quianthy is a police officer of long standing, and his conduct was most reprehensible, as an affront to the court in which the trial was being held. The record is silent as to whether the trial judge at any time undertook to reprimand or punish him for his action. On the hearing of the motion for a new trial, the court indicated his opinion that the incident injured the State rather than Deal, but stated that he had asked the jury if they would be influenced by the incident, and the jury had replied in the negative. If the merits of the prosecution were in any way doubtful, we should not hesitate to order a reversal under this assignment of error, but whatever may be our opinion as to the conduct of Mr. Quianthy, we have not been able to reach the conclusion that his conduct had anything to do with the verdict, and that being true, we cannot find reversible error in the incident.

The court concluded, "If we should reverse the conviction, it would only be because the trial judge failed, in so far as the record shows, to administer adequate reprimand or punishment upon the disturber. And except insofar as such a disturbance could be said to have affected the result of the trial, the preservation of order and decorum of a trial court is within the sound discretion of the presiding judge. It results that we find no reversible error on the record, and the judgment of the criminal court will be affirmed. The judgment to be entered will fix August 15, 1934, as the date of execution."[2623]

As the date neared, the governor granted a thirty-day reprieve to review the records but finally denied a commutation. Deal was electrocuted at the Main Prison in Nashville on September 15, 1934.

Deal and fellow death row inmate James Pillow refused a last meal, taking only coffee, according to one newspaper. Another said they had roast beef dinners.[2624] The pair listened to a prison quartet sing spirituals virtually all night, with Deal's voice heard above them singing.

The night before the execution Deal admitted to prison chaplain the Rev. Pickens Johnson that he alone killed the woman, saying he would now die without "any lie on my soul." Deal sang verses from spirituals as he was led to the chair, and while seated sang, "Never passes away, never passes away," until the hood was placed over his head.[2625] James Pillow was executed fifteen minutes later.

Two Memphis men pulled the switch in the electrocutions. One of them was W.E. Goswick, a prison guard who had served nineteen years as a deputy sheriff in Memphis. The other was I.B. Stewart, also a prison guard. As the quartet walked slowly away it repeated the refrain, "Won't be trouble no mo', Won't be trouble no mo'."[2626]

James Pillow, age 23, black. *Murder.*

The crime was committed on March 12, 1933, at the victim's store at Mt. Olive and Warford Road, outside Memphis in Shelby County. The victim was a Chinese grocery man, Sam K. Lum, age forty-eight, shot with a pistol during a robbery at the store. Lum and his wife lived in the back of the store.

Here is the entire Tennessee Supreme Court opinion:

> The only matter submitted in this Court by counsel for defendant, a Negro man twenty-one years of age, convicted on his own admission of murder in commission of robbery, is a plea that the Court recommend commutation of his sentence from death to life imprisonment. Guilt is clear and the record brief, and this Court finds no reasonable ground for making such recommendation. This is a matter for the consideration and action of the Governor to whom application may be made, accompanied by a showing of facts, if any, outside the record which may support an appeal for clemency. Affirmed. August 15, 1934, is fixed as the day of electrocution.[2627]

Pillow was executed at the Main Prison in Nashville on September 15, 1934, a few minutes after the execution of John Deal. Both had become very religious while on death row and sang along with a prison quartet that sang spirituals for them during their last night.

Unlike Deal, who finally confessed to a murder he had long denied, Pillow maintained his innocence. Asked if he was afraid to die, he smiled wanly and replied, "I'm a little nervous. There are times when all of us are afraid." Becoming solemn, he remarked, "I am not guilty, but I am going to yield myself to the grace of Jesus Christ."[2628] Unlike Deal, Pillow did not sing a spiritual on his walk to the chair. He was silent.

1936

William Lee, white, age 24. *Murder.*

The crime was committed at 9:30 P.M. on February 23, 1933, in the cabin of Mr. and Mrs. Jasper Shaw in the rural community of Tellico Plains in Monroe County. The killer was the victims' grandson, recently dismissed from the Navy. The victims were Jasper Shaw, white, age sixty-four; and his wife, Nellie Shaw, white, age sixty-two. Also killed was a house guest, Matthew Hensley, white, age sixty. Lee was prosecuted only for the murder of grandmother Shaw.[2629]

Granny Shaw, her grandson Howard Shaw, age twelve, and Hensley had gone to bed in the cabin, the beds in the same room. Howard was in the same bed as his grandmother. Lee had gotten in bed with Hensley, while grandfather sat by the fireplace warming his feet. After grandfather put out the kerosene lamp and went to bed, Lee took down a shotgun hanging on the wall. He told grandfather to give him his money.

Hensley admonished Lee, who turned and fired, killing Hensley in his bed. The grandfather came toward Lee and was shot, falling to the floor. Grandmother ran into the kitchen and the boy scrambled under the bed. Lee told grandmother to come back or he would kill her unless she gave him her pocketbook. She did, but he bludgeoned her with a pistol and she fell on the bed.

Lee took money out of a dresser drawer and took twenty-five dollars from his grandfather's body. He took a couple of weapons and left in grandfather's car.[2630] After the shooting, Howard Shaw ran to a relative's house. He was the chief prosecution witness.

Lee claimed that all the adults had been drinking heavily for several days and the grandparents got into a quarrel because the grandfather was seeing a woman in Tellico Plains. The elder man went for the shotgun. As Lee pulled it from him it went off, killing Hensley. As the two scuffled, the gun went off once or twice. The gun broke as he was swinging it. But he did not know how, saying, "I never did hit at her and I did not want to hurt her. If she was hit by me it was accidentally in the scuffle with Pap."[2631] Lee testified that the reason he ran away was that he feared the extended Shaw family would kill him. He took the money to make a getaway. He denied threatening Howard: "I never threatened Howard or tried to hurt him. He is little and I could have killed him easily if I had wanted to."[2632]

Wakeman O. Shaw had been at the house the day before for the evening meal. He testified that no one was drinking. He testified that Lee had said, "The old man has a roll of money and I am going to get it."[2633] He was among the first to visit the cabin and saw Hensley's body partially covered with a blanket which had been hit before the blast entered his body. Wakeman found Jasper Shaw with a shotgun blast to the heart, and an apparent blast in the direction of the wife. The blast had come from the direction of her feet and ranged along the wall towards her head, but it had not hit her. She was bludgeoned. There were scars on the kitchen floor indicating that they were made by an instrument the size of a shotgun.

The undertaker who retrieved the bodies said there was no odor of alcohol, nor was there any alcohol smell in the house. Twelve-year-old Howard Shaw said there was no drinking on the murder night. Lee also denied telling various police officials conflicting stories of what happened. He couldn't explain why a shot went toward the head of the woman's bed from the foot. He admitted that when arrested in North Carolina, after linking up with two men in a stolen car, he was dressed in women's clothes.[2634]

The Tennessee Supreme Court said there was ample evidence to show that Lee had planned to rob the old man, and when he resisted, shot him and the others. The jury was within its power to disregard the notion that these people were killed when Lee tried to disarm the old man. It set the execution date for January 21, 1936.[2635] William Lee was electrocuted at the Main Prison in Nashville on that day.

Lee had been in the Navy and constantly spoke about his adventures and himself. "I am ready. My heart is right with God. I've prayed day after day," he said. "I've been here seven months, but it seems like it's just a day. I've gotten a letter from my wife. She's awful sorry about all this, but I may come out of it all right. If I do go, I won't have to eat any more beans, because I'm going to heaven, and they don't have beans there."[2636] Lee maintained his innocence, saying he was praying for those "who have dipped their hands in blood," and "testified falsely against me."[2637]

Lee listened attentively as two ministers, including the Rev. Pickens Johnson, spoke to those waiting execution and prayed for them. As a black quartet lined up to sing for him (and two others waiting death, Kennedy and Willis), he said, "Hello, boys. I'm going to try to do this right in the morning, but it's a little bit new to me, you know," attempting humor. He talked about his last meal, "Boy, I had sausage and bacon and eggs and peaches and a lot of things. I asked for frog legs, but they couldn't find me any of them."[2638]

At the time of his execution, Lee was the father of a seventeen-month-old girl. He maintained he was innocent, "There wasn't any use of them lying about it. They lied a lot of things about me."[2639] When the sheriff of Monroe County arrived to watch his execution, Lee jokingly said, "I wish you'd kept me up there in jail a little longer." The sheriff remarked, "Probably a good thing I didn't. They might not have let you stay there."[2640] This brought a laugh from Lee. He was executed first, Walter Kennedy a few minutes later.

Walter Kennedy, white, age 22. *Murder.*

The crime was committed on August 24, 1934, in a rural area called New River, in Anderson County. The killers were Walter Kennedy; Elmer Bunch, age eighteen; and Wilse Bray, age thirty-two. All were white. The victims were John H. Lytle, white, age sixty-seven, and Joseph M. Gordy, white, age twenty-one.

Here is how the Tennessee Supreme Court described the killing:

> The deceased, John Lytle, also known as Dr. Lytle, lived in Knoxville; he manufactured a patent or herb medicine, and traveled from place to place in East Tennessee, selling his product. On Friday night, August 24, 1934, he was in Anderson County, in the Tenth Civil District, in the New River neighborhood. He was accompanied by a young man by the name of Gordy. Dr. Lytle had a Dodge automobile, to which was attached a trailer; the trailer was equipped for sleeping quarters at night. At night the car and trailer were parked on the roadside, and Dr. Lytle and Mr. Gordy slept in the trailer.
>
> On the night mentioned, Dr. Lytle and Mr. Gordy were forced out of the trailer, robbed, and were marched a distance of 1200 or 1500 feet from the highway and where the car was parked, to a secluded and lonely spot in what is known as Tiger Hollow, and were there murdered. Both were shot with a shotgun. Mr. Gordy, who was younger of the two, being shot first, and Dr. Lytle was murdered while in the act of praying. It appears the bodies were searched and robbed after the murder. It seems the robbers got only a watch and about ninety cents in money. It was a deliberate, cold-blooded, brutal murder, and if plaintiffs in error are guilty, they well merit the punishment pronounced.[2641]

The primary issue on appeal was who actually shot the victims.[2642] Elmer Bunch, a codefendant, testified that Kennedy fired the first shot, killing Gordy, and that Bray fired the second shot that killed Dr. Lytle. Kennedy testified that Bunch killed both Gordy and Dr. Lytle. Kennedy's own testimony showed his guilt, regardless of whether he was a shooter, because he testified that he helped march the men to their deaths, and provided details such as Dr. Lytle's asking to stop and drink water from a spring. The court said it was clear that Kennedy aided and abetted in the murder of Dr. Lytle, whether he actually fired the fatal shot.[2643]

The guilt of Wilse Bray, said the court, was "not so easily determined."[2644] Elmer Brunch's defense was that he was an unwilling participant in the crimes and that he was "marched" along with the victims (slightly behind them). His mother saw him from the window of the home they shared and summoned him home. She said she heard Bray threaten to blow her son's brains out if he left. This testimony put Bray at the scene, armed with one of the shotguns used to kill the victims. However, Bray offered a general denial. He testified he had nothing to do with either the robbery or the killing, that he spent the evening drinking, going from one friend's house to another, finally ending up sleeping on his uncle's porch.[2645] However, Mrs. Bunch saw Bray in the Dodge after the killings along with Elmer Bunch (who had driven it off the road).

To counter this, Bray said he was there at that time because he happened to be walking along, saw Kennedy and Bunch in the car and paid them a quarter for a ride.[2646] To buttress his alibi that he was nowhere near the killing ground, he insisted that he and Kennedy had argued and were not together the night of the shooting. However, a Bunch relative, Clarence Bunch, testified that on the night of the killing, Bray had come by his house to borrow a pistol (which was refused), but ten minutes later Kennedy came with the same request, and he saw the two walk down toward the creek together.[2647] Likewise, another witness (Marshall Bunch) saw the two walking together.

Bray's only alibi witness, Ernest Daugherty, "did not tell a reasonable or connected story" of Bray's whereabouts.[2648] On the other hand, the testimony of Elmer Bunch and others put Bray in the presence of Kennedy, carrying a shotgun.[2649] In short, the jury was correct to conclude that Bray was a shooter, or at least a willing participant. The court ordered Kennedy and Bray executed on January 21, 1936. Three days before the date of the execution, Governor McAlister commuted Bray's sentence to ninety-nine years. The reason he gave was that two justices of the Tennessee Supreme Court had recommended it.

The day before his execution, Kennedy's last act was an attempt to exonerate Bray. In the presence of Warden Neely, newspaper reporters, and a prison secretary, he read and signed a statement which said, "To Whom It May Concern: As I go to my death in the electric chair I wish to make this statement: Wilse Bray was not connected with my crime in any way."[2650] The statement was given little credence because Kennedy still insisted he was innocent of murder. And Bray had killed before. His 99-year sentence was actually his second murder conviction.[2651]

Walter Kennedy was executed on January 21, 1936, a few minutes after the execution of William Lee. He complained that he had gotten a "dirty deal." Commenting on the sentences of the others, he said, "If we all did the same thing, I don't see why I've got to die and the rest don't." He described his time on death row: "I've read the Bible a good deal lately. I never read it much until they sent me down here, and it's interesting." He continued, "I also read *True Stories* and love stories, but most of the time I just sit and think."[2652]

Seated in the electric chair, he said, "I am satisfied I am right with God," having been baptized three days earlier, at which time he said, "I have confessed my sins to God and I don't need to [confess to] man."[2653] Kennedy's father, age fifty, had driven his truck from East Tennessee and in the back was a large wooden box, not a true coffin. At the time his son was taken to the electric chair, the father was sleeping on a bench inside the prison. Officials decided not to awaken him. He carried his son's body back home in the box.[2654]

Lewis Willis, black, age 27. *Murder.*

The crime was committed on the afternoon of September 15, 1933, inside the Main Prison on the outskirts of Nashville, in Davidson County. Willis was an inmate and along with five others made a break for freedom by overpowering a guard and taking his pistol. The victim was Edward Lowery, white, age sixty-five, an inmate trusty on gate duty. With a pistol in his face, Lowery opened the gate. He begged for his life. Willis shot him. Lowery died several days later.

The prison break was led by Lonnie Taylor, white. He and Edgar McChriston, black, got over the walls and made an escape to the free world. Taylor was later recaptured in Tennessee. McChriston made it to Portland, Oregon, where he was killed in a gun battle with police. Willis and William O'Day, Ernest Cassilas, and Bernard Tassen were captured inside the walls. All of the escapees were tried together and the latter three given twenty-one-year sentences, Taylor a ninety-nine year sentence. Willis, the shooter, received the death penalty.

Because Willis was captured within minutes of the shooting, he was brought back to face the man he shot. Lowery named him as the shooter. Said the Tennessee Supreme Court, "The evidence put before the jury was overwhelming that Willis fired into the body of the deceased while his hands were in the air and while he was begging for his life."[2655]

Before the Tennessee Supreme Court, counsel for Willis raised several issues. First, it was error to charge Willis with premeditated murder because the killing was not "deliberate and cool." The court said otherwise, saying that Willis showed deliberate persistence in shooting a man who was offering no resistence.[2656] Next, Willis's comments to the warden "in the nature of a confession," were not coerced merely because they were spoken to Neely, the warden, in the course of investigating the prison break. Likewise, Neely had asked Willis, in the presence of the wounded Lowery, why he had shot him, and Willis's answer, "He was fixing to grab me," was properly allowed because it was an admission that Willis had done the shooting.[2657]

The chief issue before the court was whether it was error to allow the statements of the other co-defendants to be heard by the jury because it was testimony of felons rendered inadmissable under a statute.[2658] Here the testimony was not prejudicial because it was corroborated by non-felons. For example, prison guard Lee testified that he saw the shooting and heard Lowery say, "Don't shoot me! Don't shoot me!"[2659] Thus, although the statute did not specifically allow felons to testify in capital cases, it removed the disability in several other kinds of cases, and the use of this testimony was not prejudicial.[2660]

Finally, while it was improper for counsel for one of the other defendants to have asked Willis if he was in prison for kidnapping a little girl in Chattanooga, this was cured by a timely instruction from the court to disregard the question. Willis had been sent to prison in 1927 for a robbery and the kidnapping of a Chattanooga girl in which he had received $3,333 in shared ransom proceeds. He received a fifteen- to twenty-five-year sentence.[2661]

On December 29, 1935, a month before his scheduled execution, as Willis was being taken from his cell for a bath, he attacked a guard with an iron bar. He was overpowered and this escape attempt was foiled too. Willis told the media, "Money was my trouble before I got into prison, and then it was a desire for freedom. I wanted money and I kidnaped a little girl in Chattanooga. They put me in here and then I wanted freedom. All the trouble I ever gave them here was trying to get out. But I guess that was trouble enough."[2662] He was electrocuted on January 28, 1936, at the Main Prison in Nashville.

At the time of his execution, Willis had become somewhat Afrocentric, in part because of the war between Ethiopia and Italy. He had put a map of Ethiopia on the wall of his cell. He said, "It's because of things over there that I ain't got much faith anymore. I used to read the Bible a lot, but I don't now. I read of the all suffering in Ethiopia, and I know they are praying for things to get better, and it looks like it don't do them any good. So I figure, if God won't do anything for a whole nation like that, he ain't going to hear me — a poor boy on death row."[2663] Willis asserted that Emperor Haile Salassie was one of the greatest of the world's kings and that he was still hoping that Ethiopia would prevail. The newspaper reported no details of Willis's last meal or words other than to report that he was the fiftieth man executed in the Tennessee electric chair.[2664]

Ernest Womack, Jr., black, age 18. *Murder.*

The crime occurred about eight o'clock in the evening of April 16, 1935, on a rural road a few miles from McMinnville in Warren County. The killer was seventeen years old at the time. The victim, Paul Cunningham, white, age forty-four, was a taxicab driver and was killed for the money he carried.

The Tennessee Supreme Court described the facts:

> The crime was committed on a highway a few miles from McMinnville, on what is known as the Faulkner Springs Road. Womack engaged Cunningham to drive him out on this highway, telling Cunningham that he had some whiskey hidden, and wanted to go and get it. In fact, Womack had previously procured and concealed just off the highway the twelve-gauge shotgun with which he shot Cunningham. Cunningham accepted the employment and drove Womack to the spot were Womack told him to stop. At the time the automobile stopped at the direction of Womack, another car was approaching. Womack told Cunningham to go on up the road, turn around, and come back, and he (Womack) would get in the car as it returned.[2665]

Womack got out of the taxi, Cunningham drove away and turned around, during which time Womack got his concealed weapon, and when Cunningham returned and stopped, Womack shot him without warning. Womack then dragged Cunningham's body out of the car into the weeds and honeysuckle vines, some twelve or fifteen feet from the highway. The robbery netted Womack eighteen dollars. The victim's trousers and shoes were removed.

Pools of blood marked the route over which the body was dragged, and the seat of the automobile was soaked in blood. Womack threw the shotgun into a nearby pond, from which it was later recovered. Following the murder, Womack fled to Nashville and was apprehended there.

The Tennessee Supreme Court said, "Womack made a written, signed, and sworn confession to captors, admitting his guilt, and giving the details of the crime. This confession is in proof, but it is not relied upon by the State as alone establishing the guilt of the accused; other witnesses and proof were adduced before the court and jury, which clearly establish the guilt of the plaintiff in error, regardless of the confession."[2666]

Womack initially pled guilty, but the court said it did not have the power to allow such a plea, with the jury deciding only the punishment. The trial went forward with the jury hearing both guilt and punishment.

The crucial issue on appeal was whether blacks were systematically excluded from both the grand and petit jury. Womack's counsel asserted the recent cases of the Scottsboro boys, which forbade such practice.[2667] The Tennessee Supreme Court brushed this issue aside, saying there was no proof that Tennessee "officers consistently and habitually excluded negroes from jury service, because of their race or color."[2668] The court characterized Womack's argument as a demand to have "one or more negroes on the grand jury which indicted him, and on the jury which tried him."[2669] The court said, "But this is not the law," citing case law.[2670]

The court also ruled that his complaint about the complexion of the grand jury (and later the petit jury itself) was waived because of his guilty plea.[2671] The court also turned aside objections raised because Mrs. Cunningham had begun crying during the trial while holding a baby. Likewise, it was not error that some courtroom observers laughed during a portion of the testimony.[2672]

Womack sought a new trial because "the punishment insisted upon by the jury was cruel and excessive and against the spirit and language of the State and Federal Constitutions against cruel and excessive punishment as he is a mere lad of seventeen years of age, a member of a benighted race oppressed throughout the centuries and this coupled with the laws of heredity and environment, should have mitigated his punishment from death to life imprisonment."[2673]

The Tennessee Supreme Court ruled: "We are satisfied that no right of the prisoner has been violated, and that he has suffered no injustice. We observe that the trial court extended every courtesy and consideration to the accused, and granted every request which his counsel asked to have included in the charge, even though such requests were, at least in some instances, not strictly accurate, but they were favorable to the prisoner."[2674]

Womack was electrocuted at the Main Prison in Nashville on April 10, 1936. He told the newspaper, "I know I am going to die and haven't expected any reprieve, so I'm ready to go."

Warden A.W. Neely said that Womack did not want to talk about his crime, but that two preachers talked and prayed with him before he walked to the chair. "He was one of the coolest customers we've seen in a long time," said Neely.[2675]

Ernest K. Harris, black, age 23. *Rape.*

The crime was committed near Shelbyville, in Bedford County on the early afternoon of November 19, 1934, some seventy-five feet from the rear of Fall Creek schoolhouse, near the girls' outhouse toilet. The victim was Lillian Gibson, white, age fourteen, a student at the school. Harris was a farm hand, employed by Moody Shell, whose dairy farm was near the school. Lillian recognized Harris, who had also worked for a Mr. Dunnaway in the vicinity of her father's home.

Lillian testified that Harris seized her at the toilet and dragged her into the woods, choked her, threatened her life if she made an outcry, removed some of her clothing, threw her upon the ground and raped her. When Harris ran off, she returned to the schoolhouse. Her teacher, Miss Lorraine Scales, first saw her at the door. Miss Scales testified that when the girl returned there was an expression of agony on her face, and she was holding her hands to her throat on which there were marks. She was almost exhausted, her clothing was torn and disarranged, and there was trash in her hair. She tried to tell Miss Scales what occurred but her speech was incoherent; her mouth was bleeding and swollen. She exclaimed, "I am going to have a baby!"[2676]

The case went to trial on December 19, 1934, amid extreme emotion in the Shelbyville community. As the trial got underway, a mob formed to lynch Harris. The mob stormed the jail, which was attached to the courthouse, and was dispersed only after National Guard troops fired into their ranks after the use of tear gas failed. Shortly thereafter, the mob attacked the jail and courthouse again, burned it to the ground (thinking Harris was still inside), and destroyed four National Guard trucks. In all, at least four people died in the rioting.[2677] Harris had been brought to Nashville for his safety.

Harris was tried in Nashville in a courthouse that was surrounded by armed National Guard troops. Throngs from Bedford County came to Nashville for the trial. They were barred from entering the courthouse by a cordon of National Guard troops and police.

Harris was represented by "able counsel," according to the Tennessee Supreme Court, which affirmed his conviction. Aside from Lillian and the teacher's testimony, a woman who lived two hundred yards from the school, Mrs. Sam Osborne, said that she had seen a Negro who looked like Harris cross the road about noon that day. The clothes he wore resembled those worn by Harris, but Mrs. Osborne said she did not see Harris's face. She was asked if the person she saw was Harris, she said, "I think it was. I remember the way he walked and looked." She was emphatic that she was not positive that Harris was the person she saw.[2678]

Two policemen who took Harris out of the county for safety said he told them he had "tried to rape the girl, and dragged her from the toilet and had her on the ground but didn't have her but three minutes and she hollered so he got up and ran off."[2679]

Harris testified on his own behalf. He denied being at the scene of the rape. He said he had worked for Mr. Shell on the truck gathering milk cans that morning and returned to Shell's house about four o'clock. After that, he walked to Shelbyville, loafed around a pool hall until after four o'clock, and then went to his brother's home where he remained until dark and started walking back to Shell's place. On the way he met Mr. Shell driving his car toward Shelbyville and returned there in Shell's car. Harris admitted he had a sister who lived near the schoolhouse.

Moody Shell testified that Harris did not work for him on the day of the assault and did not eat dinner (lunch) at his home. He said Harris worked for him the week before but was not present Monday when Moody left with the milk truck. He first saw Harris as he was driving his car to Shelbyville. It was about 7:00 P.M. that night and Shell let him ride back to Shelbyville, intending to bring him home that night. At the time, he had not heard of the assault. Harris was sitting in Shell's car when the police arrested him.[2680]

Before the Tennessee Supreme Court, Harris said the jury was contaminated by the angry citizens outside the courthouse. During those times the jurors were allowed to leave the Nashville courthouse, they encountered a large hostile crowd that had to be held back by ropes, and soldiers on foot and on horses. The Tennessee Supreme Court said there was no contact by jurors with the crowd. Said the court, "It may be unfortunate that no means are possibly available to prevent the psychological effect of such situations upon the jury but it is an impotence that is inherent in the people in our institutions. A secret trial would not be countenanced and could not be made available under our system."[2681]

Likewise, it was not error for the jury to hear the testimony, offered in rebuttal by the state, from the two police officers. There was no evidence to show that Harris's statements were made because of violence or the hope of reward to induce the statement.[2682]

Harris insisted he was guilty only of assault with intent to commit rape. His reason was there had been no penetration. Dr. Moody had seen Lillian about four o'clock after the assault. He testified that the external genital organs were bruised. There was soreness and she flinched under examination. He stated that he found no evidence of penetration of the organs but added that would depend on what is meant by penetration. He then explained that he found no evidence of complete penetration but observed that the immediate entrance to the vagina was bruised, discolored and swollen.[2683] This was enough, said the Tennessee Supreme Court: "The testimony of Dr. Moody, which negatives complete penetration, a fact not required by the statute, affirmatively supports the girl's charge of rape, which, says our statute, is accomplished by the commencement of a sexual connection."[2684]

The court said the judge had been correct in refusing a defense instruction which said the rape was not complete unless Harris "caused his private parts to penetrate the lips of her female organ." This is because the statute said, "Rape is the unlawful carnal knowledge of a woman, forcibly and against her will. Carnal knowledge is accomplished by the commencement of sexual connection, and proof of emission is not required."[2685]

The court said the instruction that included the following was correct: "Carnal knowledge within the meaning of the statute, rape, is sexual bodily connection or intercourse between a male and female, that is, the actual contact of the sexual organs and the penetration of the sexual organ of the male through or into the sexual organ of the female. However slight such penetration is not required under our statute, but only the commencement of sexual connection."[2686] In simple terms, the court said, quoting a legal treatise, "The private parts of the male entered at least some extent in those of the female."[2687]

The Supreme Court set Harris's execution for May 22, 1936, and he was executed that day. Twelve hours before he was executed, Harris was baptized by a black minister (himself a prison inmate) and the temporary baptismal pool was surrounded by other inmates who assured Harris that he was "all right." Harris had "confessed his sins," but still maintained that he had not actually raped the victim because there was no penetration. The Rev. Pickens Johnson, the prison chaplain, said he had talked to Harris before and after the baptism and said Harris seemed slightly melancholy.[2688]

Carl H. "Curly" Ballard, black, age 46. *Murder.*

The crime was committed about 10:00 P.M. April 3, 1936, on Holston Street near Bristol in Sullivan County. The victim was Willie Green, black, age seventeen. The killer operated a pool room in Kingsport and Green worked for him. Ballard took him to a movie theater in Bristol and when the movie was over they drove back to Kingsport. In the car was Rosa Ballard, black, the killer's daughter-in-law. Ballard pretended the car had a flat tire. As Green bent down to examine it, Ballard struck him repeatedly with a large hammer around which he had wrapped some cloth.

Ballard pushed Green to the side of the road to make it look like he had been struck by a car. The killing was done to collect on a life insurance policy amounting to $192. This type of policy only paid if the insured died by accidental means.[2689] No physical exam was required to obtain it.[2690] Green was discovered unconscious the next day and died without regaining consciousness.[2691]

Ballard became the chief suspect when a receipt for the insurance was found in Green's pocket. An investigation showed Ballard had insured at least eighteen other black youths in the Sullivan County area. Rosa Ballard was charged as an accessory and was tried with the killer. She turned state's evidence. She testified she had nothing to do with the killing and the first she knew about it was Ballard's statement, when he got back in the car, "He's out of the way."[2692] Curly Ballard's wife, two sons and stepdaughter-in-law also testified against him, saying he had threatened to kill them if they went to the police.

At the close of the state's evidence, the charges

against Rosa were dismissed. Curly Ballard was convicted and sentenced to the electric chair on May 22, 1936.[2693] There was no appeal. To the last, Ballard insisted he was innocent of the killing, but admitted he was present. The governor had asked physicians to determine whether he was sane. The doctors examined him on June 20, 1936, July 11, 1936, and August 11, 1936. They found him to be of "a low order of mentality but not medically insane at the present time, and we think today that he is malingering, and covering up a lot of things that he really knows."[2694]

Curly Ballard was executed on the morning of August 14, 1936. Ballard, a peg-leg, walked to the chair using his customary crutch. After him, James Smith and James Clarke were executed. Ballard and the others had "talked to the preacher," namely Prison Chaplain the Rev. Pickens Johnson, and declared they were "not worried." The warden explained to a newspaper reporter it was his decision who died first. He explained the first to die was the one who was the most "nervous." Said he, "The one who is the most nervous will be taken first, in order to have the least excitement."[2695] The three executions took sixteen minutes. Although Ballard was married, his wife declined to claim his body. Anticipating this, he had decided to donate his body to Vanderbilt Medical School. Whether the school accepted is unknown.

James Smith, black, age 27. *Murder.*
Anderson Berry, black, age 26. *Murder.*

The killing was done on the late afternoon of October 31, 1935, just outside Fayetteville, in Lincoln County. The victim was Hugh Matlock, white, age sixty, a stonecutter and farmer. He was reputed to carry all his money, variously nine hundred to fifteen hundred dollars, on his person.

The killers walked out of town to buy some liquor from a bootlegger and on the way back decided to wait near a railroad track, which paralleled a road which Matlock frequently took, and rob him. Placing himself in front of Matlock, Berry distracted the old man by pointing to the sky and remarking on wild geese going over. Matlock responded, "Boys, I can't see very well." Smith was holding a pistol to Matlock's back, but suddenly struck Matlock from behind with a homemade blackjack. Berry testified he said to Smith, "Nigger, what do you want to do that for? You oughtn't to kill that old man." Berry said that Smith replied, "God damn you, you hush or I'll kill you the same way."

The first blow did not fell Matlock, who implored the two to search him for money but not kill him. Smith struck again, sending Matlock to the ground. He used a rock to smash the old man's skull. Smith then grabbed a leg and dragged the body about fifteen feet and threw it under some honeysuckle vines. According to Berry, Smith looked at the victim and said, "That old man ain't dead, watch him kick," and opening a pocket knife, went down into the ditch and cut Matlock's jugular vein and covered the body with more honeysuckle vines.

There were no eyewitnesses, but several witnesses saw Berry and Smith on their way to get the liquor. The testimony of Berry implicated Smith in other ways. For example, the pistol was found under a rock at a place near the railroad tracks where Berry said Smith had told him it could be found. Witnesses testified that Smith had tried to sell the pistol the day after the murder. Other witnesses confirmed the knife found near the body was owned by Smith, who had won it in a craps game. Another witness confirmed that the homemade blackjack belonged to Berry. The sheriff and the city police chief testified about what Smith and Berry said shortly after arrest, when in the presence of each other, they laid the blame for the actual killing on each other. At trial, however, Smith did not take the stand and offered no proof.

On appeal, Smith found fault with the court's ruling that the sheriff and police chief could testify, but the Tennessee Supreme Court ruled that no trial court objection had been made. During deliberations, the foreman had asked the court to explain exactly the number of years Smith would have to serve if given a life sentence or a term of ninety-nine years. The trial court replied in writing that a life sentence, under the parole system, would be the equivalent of thirteen years and seven months, and ninety-nine years would be the equivalent of fifty years. The Supreme Court said there was no reversible error in the trial court's action. The court affirmed Smith's conviction on May 28, 1936, and ordered him to die on June 15, 1936.[2696]

Berry was tried after Smith. The same witnesses testified against him. The jury returned the following verdict: "We, the jury, find the defendant guilty of murder in the first degree without mitigating circumstances, and if the law says he must have the death sentence, then we fix that." Upon receiving the verdict, the trial judge restated the verdict as follows, "Your foreman reports that your verdict is that you find the defendant, Anderson Berry, guilty of murder in the first degree, without mitigating circumstances and fix his punishment at death by electrocution as now provided by law. So say you all?" The jurors then nodded their assent.

The Tennessee Supreme Court reversed the conviction, saying that the jury's original verdict was an attempt to shift to the Court the responsibility of fixing the punishment, and amounted to an "evasion of the express duty imposed by the statute upon the jury." The court stated, "A judgment of death must be predicated upon a verdict unequivocally fixing death as the punishment." The court said that the action of the trial judge in stating to the jury, when the verdict was returned, what would have amounted to a valid verdict if found by the jury in its verdict, and asking, "So say you all," could not be considered as the verdict of the jury. This was the law despite all the jurors' nodding their heads, as the record disclosed they did.[2697] The opinion in Berry's case was rendered on May 2, 1936, prior to the opinion in Smith's, May 28, 1936.

Berry's second trial was moved to Franklin County and there were no new witnesses for either side. Smith was awaiting execution at the time of Berry's second trial, but was not brought to testify by the state. Berry's statement to the sheriff and chief of police, "Me and Big Jim did it," together with the prior evidence regarding their having been seen together shortly before the killing and Berry's saying to Smith, "Why in the hell don't you come on?" shortly before they left to get the liquor, were accredited by the Winchester jury. A witness at both trials was John Grant, who had been in jail with Berry and Smith at the time they were arrested. He said that each blamed the other for the crime. Berry did not take the stand and no evidence was offered by the defense. On June 19, 1936, Berry was convicted again and given an unequivocal death sentence. The delay in convicting Berry had kept Smith alive until August 14, 1936.

Berry's second appeal focused on the lack of evidence that he wanted to kill Matlock or played any role in his death. Rather, he raised a protest when he saw that Smith was going to kill the old man. The Supreme Court's opinion said, "But his protest came too late. Having entered into the agreement to rob and place deceased at the mercy of Smith, he cannot escape the consequences of his act by asserting that in furtherance of the design more force was used than he intended or authorized. Berry was present aiding and abetting in the attempted robbery and, under the statute, is just as guilty as Smith."[2698] The Supreme Court affirmed the conviction and set March 17, 1937, as the execution date.

Smith "talked to the preacher" and told reporters he was "not worried" about death. Smith explained that he expected to be the first to go on August 14, 1936. Two others were scheduled for death on the same day, James Clarke and C.H. "Curly" Ballard. But he was bitter about having been "pushed up front all during the trial and I might as well be the first to die." He denied guilt and insisted that he had been "framed" by Berry.[2699] Warden A.W. Neely decided that the most "nervous" person would be executed first. This was Ballard, followed by Smith and Clarke. At the time of Smith's execution, Berry was being held in the state prison.

Berry was electrocuted as scheduled on March 17, 1937. This was the first execution under the direction of a new warden, Joe Pope, but the old warden (Neely) had remained on staff for a thirty-day transition. Before the execution Berry told Neely and Pope that he was present when Smith crushed Matlock's head with a rock.[2700] The evening before, he had eaten a last meal of chicken, pork chops, several vegetables, hot biscuits and coffee.[2701]

James Clarke (aka James Foster, Henry Johnson, Pepper-Head), black, age 23. *Murder.*

The crime was committed at 4:00 A.M. on August 7, 1935, at a house on 1605 Waverly Place in Memphis, Shelby County. The killer had served a term in the county workhouse for burglary and a prison term for shooting another black man. On the night of the killing, he and L.C. Smith, known as "Railhead," had stolen a car and a pistol and had been driving around looking for a place to burglarize. They chose the victim's house because it had a red light burning in the living room. The victim was Richard Thomas Sheehan, white, age twenty-seven, who lived in the house.

While Railhead stayed outside on the porch, Clarke entered the house by removing the screen on a large window. He walked about the darkened house, found two purses and was leaving when he heard a noise. A man's voice said, "Hey! Hey, get out of here!" The voice scared Clarke and he wheeled around and fired a shot.[2702] Sheehan began screaming after he was hit and died later that day.

Clarke was arrested the next day, having been implicated by Railhead. He was found at home hiding under a bed. He gave a lengthy statement (confession) which was transcribed. In it he admitted several burglaries and auto thefts in the weeks prior to the shooting. Clarke insisted throughout the trial that he had no intention of killing anyone when he entered the house. He said repeatedly he had fired the shot towards the floor and did not intend to shoot Sheehan and did not know he had hit anyone. He begged the jury for mercy.[2703] His case was appealed to the Tennessee Supreme Court but the opinion cannot be located.

James Clarke was executed at the Main Prison in Nashville on August 14, 1936. He was the third person electrocuted that day. C.H. "Curly" Ballard was executed first, then James Smith. The criteria used to determine who would be executed first was determined by warden A.W. Neely, saying, "The one who is the most nervous will be taken first, in order to have the least excitement."[2704] By the time of his execution, Clarke stopped maintaining he was innocent because he did not intend to kill Sheehan. He spent the last hour of his life writhing on his bunk, weeping into his pillow.

Like the others, Clarke had "talked to the preacher," namely prison chaplain the Rev. Pickens Johnson, and said they were "not worried," and their only requests were for cold water to drink during the hot summer day.

Elmer "Moon Pie" Barrett, black, age 22. *Murder.*

The crime was committed in the night of May 21, 1935, in the store of William M. Hardwick, black, age fifty-three, in Knoxville, Knox County. Barrett, along with two others, Will Turner and W.D. McAlister, were burglarizing the store and did not know Hardwick was present. A fight ensued in which Hardwick was shot by Barrett.

The details of the trial are unknown except that Turner and McAlister testified against Barrett in exchange for five-year sentences. Following a three-day trial, Barrett was convicted of felony murder on September 26, 1935. His counsel told the court there were no funds to prepare the bill of exceptions (transcript) and the court allowed the appeal to go forward on the technical record.

The Tennessee Supreme Court said this was improper, citing case law.[2705] Nevertheless, it allowed the appeal on the technical record and affirmed with these words: "There is no error apparent on the record. The killing was done in the act of burglary and is murder in the first degree. The judgment of the trial court must be affirmed."[2706]

The Supreme Court set the execution for September 4, 1936, but the governor granted three reprieves while Barrett's lawyers attempted to gather evidence of his insanity. Part of the governor's reluctance to become involved was Barrett's record. A career criminal despite his youth, Barrett had previously served a short sentence for manslaughter.

At the time of Barrett's execution, the newspapers were still placing quotation marks around the term "death row" and reporting the newsworthy aspects of a killer's last twenty-four hours such as his last meal, his last words, and whether he admitted his crime. Barrett refused to discuss his crime. He asked to see the electric chair the day before his execution. This was denied. He ate a massive last meal of six eggs, fried chicken and pork chops. He said, "An' I wants a bottle of champagne. Not the beer, but the real stuff." This was denied.

Barrett was attended by both a Catholic priest and the Rev. Pickens Johnson, the prison chaplain. He explained, "I ain't got nobody to worry 'bout me 'cept my mother and I know the good Lawd'll let us meet again in Heaven. When you got the Lawd on yo' side, cain't nobody hurt you."[2707] Barrett was executed on the morning of November 18, 1936. At the time the electric current was administered he was singing a song, "There's Something on My Mind That's Worryin' Me."[2708]

1937

James Turner, black, age 24. *Murder.*

The crime was committed on February 20, 1936, in downtown Memphis, in Shelby County. The killers were James Turner and his nephew Earl Brevard, black, age eighteen. They had robbed a streetcar motorman, B.E. Lytle, of $4.09. Turning to run, they stumbled into the face of a city policeman, Roy A. Scott, white, age thirty-two. Turner shot him in the abdomen.

Brevard testified against Turner, was tried separately and given a two- to ten-year sentence. After the state's proof was made, Turner changed his plea to guilty. His lawyer guided him through a series of leading questions designed to show the killing lacked premeditation because Turner was surprised. Turner said he fired the pistol out of "fright." The jury voted three times on the death penalty. The first vote was eight to four in favor of electrocution. The second was nine to three. The third was unanimous.[2709]

Turner's lawyer sought a new trial asserting the proof did not show that officer Scott knew a robbery had been committed when he tried to arrest Turner. In short, the attempted arrest was improper.[2710] The trial judge rejected the plea. The Tennessee Supreme Court affirmed the verdict but the opinion cannot be located.[2711] Turner was electrocuted on March 5, 1937.

Turner ate a hearty meal during the night, but barely touched his breakfast. Shortly before he walked to the electric chair he knelt before his cot in prayer. The night before the execution Earl Brevard was allowed to visit Turner, and he led the prison quartet in singing spirituals. According to the newspaper, "No other relatives of the Negro visited the prison during the time he was on 'death row.'"[2712] Turner maintained he was innocent. He discussed the robbery with prison officials in detail, but denied he shot the officer.[2713]

James Taylor, black, age 25. *Rape.*

The crime occurred in the home of Denver and Virginia Perry, in a residential area near Nashville called Donelson in the Bluefields subdivision. This was a white area of town and the victim, Mrs. Virginia Perry, white, was a twenty-five-year-old housewife. Mrs. Perry had recently spent some time in Florida and while she was away her husband had hired Taylor as a houseboy.[2714] She returned on February 14 and the crime occurred in her home on February 18, 1936.

The Tennessee Supreme Court explained what happened:

> Mrs. Perry testified that after her husband left and about eleven o'clock in the morning she was sitting in the living room reading a magazine — that the defendant was engaged in his duties in the kitchen and the basement. While thus reading, and unaware of the approach of anyone, Mrs. Perry said that she was struck in the head, the blow coming from the rear, and rendering her unconscious. She was clad in pajamas and her husband's dressing gown over the pajamas. Just what happened immediately after this blow, she does not know. She came to herself in the bathroom, lying on the floor, with defendant standing over her, an ax in his hand. He addressed some language to her, hereinafter mentioned, and undertook to remove the trousers of Mrs. Perry's pajama suit. She remembered fighting and struggling with him in an effort to prevent this and she heard what he said. She lapsed into unconsciousness again. She was evidently struck with the ax again in the bathroom. One of her wounds was a cut by the side of the nose, through the roof of the mouth. Later one of her knocked-out teeth was found in the bathroom."[2715]

The opinion continued: "Sometime later Mrs. Perry again recovered consciousness, lying on the floor in her bedroom, which opens into a short hall leading into the bathroom. When she again regained consciousness in her bedroom, the bathrobe had been thrown over her head, a sheet thrown over her body, but she was naked from the waist down."[2716] Taylor took a car which was in the driveway, but abandoned it when it ran out of gas, taking some $25 from the glove compartment. He took a bus to town, where he spent the money on clothing. He was captured the next evening in his grandmother's house, hiding under a bed.

Mrs. Perry managed to phone a neighbor, who thought Mrs. Perry was dead when she arrived, but called an ambulance.[2717] At the hospital, her condition was described by a doctor as follows: "She was in very serious condition. There was a large wound across the head and a flap of the scalp torn from it. There was another large wound on the side of the head. She was bleeding from the mouth and nose. She was unconscious. There was a large wound in the base of the nose which went through into the nasal cavity. There was a wound in the mouth. Two front teeth were almost knocked out. Both hands were attached to the arm only by the soft tissues of her arm. She was in profound shock."[2718] The doctor went on to say that she was so bloodless it was difficult to get enough blood to make a test preliminary to a blood transfusion. Said the doctor, "Both hands were swinging by the soft tissues and the left was almost entirely severed off, and the right one was not quite so bad."[2719]

The important question on appeal was whether Mrs. Perry had been raped.[2720] She initially testified that she could not remember, and the doctor said he could not tell from an examination. Under direct examination, she was asked, "Mrs. Perry, when you were lying on the floor fighting the defendant James Taylor when he was trying to remove your pajamas, what did you say?" She answered, "You're are not going to fuck me, are you?"[2721] Taylor made two separate confessions, including one to the district attorney, who took the witness stand to say that Taylor had admitted raping Mrs. Perry.[2722]

Taylor's defense was that he had not raped her. He took the stand to give his account, which the Tennessee Supreme Court described as "disconnected and incredible." According to him, he struck her with the hatchet after she had called him a damn black bastard and a son of a bitch. Her hands were injured because she threw them up to protect herself, and that after he had done this he felt sorry for her and picked her up and sat her on the davenette and got some towels and handed them to her. He insisted that he left her there, but could not account for the blood in the bathroom, nor why there were bloody towels in the kitchen as if someone had tried to wipe blood from their clothing. He also detailed other unspecified conversations between the two.

The Supreme Court said, "Of course, it was utterly impossible for a woman, mutilated as she was, to have said and done the things that defendant ascribed to her. There is no attempt on his part to explain the assault in the bathroom and we are satisfied there is no truth whatever in any of his story."[2723]

Taylor's court-appointed attorney (whom the Supreme Court said had done a good job) had argued that independent evidence of the crime had to be presented to the jury prior to evidence of the confession, but the Supreme Court said this was not the law, citing authority. Likewise, there was no proof that Taylor was not advised that any statements he made could be used against him. In fact, the sheriff testified that he had been so advised.

Mrs. Perry, heavily bandaged, was able to testify in a trial that began on April 20, 1936. The trial began in the morning and the jury was sent to deliberate shortly after noon. It returned a verdict in seven minutes.[2724] Taylor denied to the last that he had raped Mrs. Perry, although he admitted in his last hours that he had hacked her repeatedly and thought she was dead when he left. He was electrocuted on March 15, 1937.

Taylor also explained to prison officials the details of how another inmate, Frank Haynie, Jr., black, age nineteen, had managed to gain a prison-made knife and stab and kill a prison guard, J.L. Simms, white, age sixty. This happened minutes before Frank Haynie, Jr., was shot and killed by a guard in an escape attempt (see Tom Franklin, below). The knife had been given to him by Gus McCoig, white, age twenty-three, who was later executed for an unrelated crime.[2725]

Tom Franklin, black, age 20. *Murder.*

The crime was committed at 9:45 P.M. May 25, 1936, inside a small café called a pie wagon at 204 Shelby Avenue in Nashville, in Davidson County. The pie wagon was named Davidson's Quick Lunch Room. The killers were Tom Franklin and Frank Haynie, Jr., black, age nineteen. The victim was James Brandon Scott, white, age thirty.[2726]

The pair was in the process of holding up the pie wagon when a soft drink salesman, James Brandon Scott, making a delivery, came in the front door, surprising the pair. He was ordered into the café, where he said, "Take what you want. I haven't done anything." Haynie responded, "By God, I'll kill you!" Haynie shot him in the stomach with a pistol. When he attempted to rise up off the floor, Haynie shot him in the back. Then Haynie shot the waiter, Harvey King, white, age twenty-four, in the neck. He was paralyzed and died of his wound several months after the holdup. The shootings were witnessed by two black women diners; both testified at trail.[2727]

Within minutes of the shooting, police officer Ed Pugh was on the scene with bloodhounds. Canvassing the area, they went to a "negro eat joint."[2728] According to Pugh, someone gave him a tip that the pair he was looking for were Franklin and Haynie and to look at the house of Willie Mae Jackson, located at 437½ 7th Avenue North. There he found two pistols and some bullets. Pugh knew one of the suspects, Franklin, had a brother in the workhouse (jail). He told a jailer to watch for them. The next day, when the pair came to the workhouse to visit the brother, they were arrested.[2729]

Franklin confessed promptly, shifting the blame for the shooting to Haynie. The detailed confessions of both yielded the hiding places of the clothing they had worn. Examination of Franklin's pistol showed it had not been fired. The pair were tried only for the Scott killing and received the death penalty. An issue was whether Franklin had fired any of the shots. He insisted that Haynie had done all the shooting, and he deserved mercy for that reason. The Tennessee Supreme Court affirmed the convictions on January 30, 1937, but the opinion cannot be located.

Haynie cheated the executioner. On March 12, six days before he was to be executed, Haynie sprung from his cell as he was being given his food by guard Joseph L. Simms, white, age forty-five, and he stabbed Simms with a homemade knife. The shoulder wound struck an artery and Simms died in the prison infirmary before he could be taken to the hospital. Haynie made a dash for freedom inside the cell block The stabbing was witnessed by another guard, who shot Haynie twice in the head, killing him instantly.

The origin of the knife remained a mystery until shortly before James Taylor was executed on March 17, 1937. He said the knife had come from another inmate, who gave it to Gus McCoig, who passed it to Haynie. Both were questioned about the matter and denied any involvement. Because Taylor provided so much detail about how the knife got to Haynie, Neely said he was satisfied that Taylor told the truth. Supposedly, Haynie said he wanted to use it to kill himself and it was given to him in a piece of bread.[2730]

Tom Franklin was executed on the morning of March 18, 1937. According to former warden Neely, Franklin was not bitter about the punishment meted out to him. "He seems to understand that the law holds him liable just the same as Haynie even if he didn't do any shooting."[2731]

Franklin had consumed a large "last meal" the night before consisting of a double order of pork chops, eggs, bread, butter and coffee, but barely touched his breakfast. Franklin carefully examined the chair before he sat down and helped adjust the death helmet. After it was fitted, he asked that it be removed for a moment so that he could see the prison chaplain, the Rev. Pickens Johnson, during a final prayer offered for him. This was done.[2732]

Gus McCoig, age 25, white. *Murder.*

The crime was committed in the afternoon of December 6, 1935, on Highway 33 on the Clinch River bridge in Union County. The killers were Gus McCoig, Crawford (Pete) Dean and Frank Hopson. The trio had just robbed the New Tazewell bank. McCoig brandished a pistol, Hopson a single-barreled shotgun. Dean carried a bag. They got all the available cash. Within minutes, the robbery was broadcast to neighboring counties. One of those notified was the victim, the sheriff of Union County, Louis B. Hutchinson, white, age fifty-one. Within minutes, Hutchison drove his car in their direction.

Seeing the sheriff's car approaching them, the robbers sped ahead, but the sheriff turned his car around and attempted to catch up with them. When the robbers reached the south end of the bridge they stopped their car and parked it at a forty-five-degree angle, blocking traffic.

As the car containing the sheriff and part-time deputy Austin Matthews came to a stop, here is what happened, according to the Tennessee Supreme Court's opinion:

> After stopping, Dean remained in the car, while McCoig and Hopson, each with a pistol, one of which they had taken from the bank, jumped from their car and confronted the sheriff's car. As the sheriff opened the car door a shot from McCoig's pistol shattered the window and as the sheriff was in the act of leaving the car a second shot fired by McCoig struck him in the head and produced death. After the sheriff was shot down, McCoig and Hopson forced Matthews to surrender his pistol and then fired into the radiator of the sheriff's car. After that they returned to the place where Dean was waiting in the car and all three drove away.[2733]

Gus McCoig already had a reputation as a bandit and "bad man" of East Tennessee. On December 1, 1935, he and Dean were inmates at the Nashville prison. By using a dummy wooden pistol they threatened the deputy warden, forced him into his automobile and escaped. They released him but drove away in his car.[2734] By the day of the shooting, McCoig was seen in his home county, Claiborne, where his criminal career was well known.

After the killing, the trio abandoned the car and were sleeping in a field when Hopson sneaked away and went to his home at three o'clock in the morning, telling his father what had happened. Hopson was arrested and gave the details of the crime. Dean was arrested in Jackson County on February 3, 1936. McCoig was arrested at a filling station in Crossville, Cumberland County, on February 17, 1936. Promptly indicted, they were put on trial on February 25, 1936.

Hopson became the state's chief witness, followed by Dean. Both insisted that McCoig had done the shooting and that Hopson was a participant only because he was fearful of McCoig. The trio was convicted of first-degree murder and all three were sentenced to the electric chair.

The testimony of bank employees and Deputy Matthews proved all elements of first-degree murder justifying the death penalty, said the Tennessee Supreme Court, with the only serious issue remaining whether Hopson and Dean were insane.[2735] Several doctors from Eastern State Asylum testified they were sane. Sixteen lay witnesses testified that Dean was insane, but the court reviewed the testimony and said it indicated "no more than a boy's exaggerated and unrestrained egotism."[2736] The court also said there was no evidence that Hopson was under such duress as to absolve him of any responsibility for the crime, and the death verdict was upheld.

However, the court said that it found some mitigating circumstances in favor of Dean and Hopson, saying, "There is evidence that Hopson is mentally subnormal although not insane, and it appears that he was an easy subject of McCoig's influence and was in fear of McCoig."[2737] The court continued, "Dean did not participate in the shooting. He sat in the car and, though present and associated in the criminal enterprise, including the shooting of the sheriff, he took no part in the assault by which the sheriff was killed."[2738] Invoking a statute that allowed the court to suggest that mitigating circumstances could be suggested as factors in asking the Governor to commute sentences, it recommended that Dean and Hopson receive life sentences.[2739] The governor agreed.

At the prison, fellow inmates called McCoig "Smilin' Gus," and his last words were, "I knew I'd be caught sooner or later. I'm twenty-five now, and I started wrong when I robbed a store at the age of eighteen. It doesn't get you anywhere." He cautioned other young men not to follow his path, but to "go straight and lay off the liquor."[2740] McCoig was executed at the Main Prison on April 8, 1937.

The new warden allowed Mrs. Hutchison and her adult children to come from Maynardsville and speak to McCoig the day before the execution. McCoig did not recognize the widow and when told who she was, said, "I am really sorry it happened. I am sorry of the whole thing. It didn't happen because I had it in for him. It's sad." He continued, "I am not sorry just because I got the chair. I am sorry because he's gone. I really hate it. I hate it in my heart. I never intended to kill anyone."[2741]

Mrs. Hutchison had served out her husband's term as sheriff but chose not to run for the post herself because it was a man's job, she said. When informed that she would have been allowed to see the actual execution if she were the sheriff, she said she regretted not running for reelection. She also said that Dean and Hopson would be executed if she had her way. She and the family were allowed to look at McCoig's body as it lay in the prison infirmary after the execution. They said nothing.

McCoig's statement that he didn't want to kill sheriff Hutchison had a hollow ring. On March 12, 1937, inmate Frank Haynie, black, age nineteen, awaiting execution for a double slaying committed with Tom Franklin, burst from his cell as he was being served his food. Using a homemade knife, he stabbed prison guard J.L. Simms, severing an artery just below the shoulder. Simms died in the prison infirmary within a half-hour. The stabbing was witnessed by another guard, H.B. Harris, white, age forty-six. As Haynie bolted fifteen feet in a frantic attempt to escape, he was shot twice in the head by Harris and died immediately.

The question remained: How had Haynie gotten the knife? It was answered on March 15, 1937, when shortly before his own execution, James Taylor said the knife had originally come from inmate Charlie Murphey, who gave it to McCoig, who gave it to Haynie. The latter had said he wanted the knife to kill himself. Warden Neely said that both McCoig and Murphey denied giving Haynie the knife, but that he was satisfied that Franklin was telling the truth because of the detail he provided regarding the knife.[2742]

Roy W. Eatmon (aka Roy Wallace Evans), white, age 23. *Murder.*

The crime was committed about 3:45 A.M. May 17, 1936, at Groome's Filling Station at 2265 Lamar Avenue, in Memphis, in Shelby County. The victim was Griffith C. Thomasson, white, age forty, killed by Eatmon in a robbery.

Eatmon and two acquaintances, Cecil C. Causie and Melvin D. Gilbert, both white, had taken three young women for a night of boating and skylarking. The women were taken home. Eatmon asked the driver, Gilbert, to stop at his house to get some money. When Eatmon's wife refused to give him any money, he took a pistol from the one-room apartment.

Telling the other two to stop the car some distance from the gas station, he went on foot as they waited in the car. Causie said he was asleep from the time the car left Eatmon's house until Eatmon returned from the gas station. When Eatmon appeared, running at full speed, he told them he had shot someone and kept running. "Gilbert then drove back to the city, and neither he nor Causie disclosed to anyone what had happened until after their arrest."[2743] Eatmon had also seriously wounded a night watchman, Bonnie M. Bennett, who gave a description.

According to Bennett's testimony, Eatmon walked up to the station and encountered him and Thomasson sitting on a bench. Eatmon asked for a match, said he had had too much to drink and went to the bathroom. Emerging, he said, "Put 'em up or I'll blow you down." Bennett went for his pistol and Eatmon shot it out of his hand. Eatmon then shot Bennett in the chest. Bennett fell and blacked out. When he came to, he saw Thomasson face down on the floor.[2744]

Eatmon testified that when he came out of the bathroom, Thomasson was standing behind a chair and Bennett was behind him. He fired four shots randomly. "I didn't intend to hurt anybody, but I had to shoot to save my own life because I was hemmed up and the watchman had a gun," he said.[2745] Eatmon's defense was intoxication. His lawyer was allowed to offer leading questions which Eatmon followed and insisted he was so intoxicated he didn't know what he was doing.

He was asked: "Q: What was the state of your mind? Was it baffled and muddled or functioning clear and perfect? A: Well, I know part of the things I did and part of the things I didn't. I was drunk enough that I never realized what I was doing. Q: Was your mind in a clear state or muddled state? A: I guess it was what you might call muddled. A: Would you say you were in a sort of haze or daze, would you describe it that way? A: Yes, sir."[2746] The court said the testimony did not support a conclusion that he did not know right from wrong.

The case went to trial on June 15, 1936, and the

verdict was reached three days later. Eatmon's wife, tending to a newborn and a seventeen-month-old, sat in the courtroom sobbing throughout the trial.[2747] So did Mrs. Thomasson. The jury also heard that he had been in prison for robbery and had robbed several other gas stations in the Memphis area.[2748] Codefendants Causie and Gilbert insisted they knew nothing about an impending robbery. They had only known Eatmon about two weeks. Their convictions for involuntary manslaughter were overturned on appeal while Eatmon's was affirmed.

Roy W. Eatmon was executed at the Main Prison in Nashville on April 16, 1937. He was the first white man from Shelby County to be electrocuted. Five other whites had received death sentences but had received commutations. Waiting to claim his body were his wife and infant son, Roy Gene (born a week after the Thomasson killing) and Eatmon's brother.[2749]

Howard Dunn, white, age 22. *Murder.*
William Farmer, white, age 21. *Murder.*

The crime was committed about 5:00 P.M. on March 16, 1936, on a rural road called Nine Mile Hill, in a suburb of Nashville called Green Hills, in Davidson County. The killers had long records despite their ages. They had met at the state's juvenile reformatory called the State Training and Agricultural School, five miles from Nashville.[2750] Both were from Knoxville. Farmer, under the name Clyde Lester, had been serving a four-year sentence for larceny for looting a Knoxville department store, after he and several other inmates tunneled their way out of a coal mine at Brushy Mountain Prison on January 19, 1936. He had simply gone to his parents' home in Knoxville. Police made no effort to capture him. The victim was Jasper K. Milliken, white, age forty-seven. He was assistant deputy of marketing with the state Department of Agriculture. The affable Milliken was well-known because of his daily radio broadcast of stock and crop prices.

The crime frolic that led to Milliken's death began in Knoxville where the pair lived. They stole a car and drove to Nashville. On the way, they sped away from a Murfreesboro gas station without paying. They drove to the reformatory looking for a way to free two friends held there. Suspicious guards notified the sheriff's office and two deputies attempted to flag down the car. It sped off, crashing five miles away. The officers chased the pair into the woods, firing warning shots to flush them out, but the two escaped. They walked to downtown Nashville looking for someone prosperous with a car.

As Milliken came out of his office near the state capitol, Dunn pulled a pistol. Milliken was placed in the front seat between Farmer, who drove, and Dunn holding the weapon. They drove aimlessly looking for a rural spot. They found one at Nine Mile Hill, where they ordered Milliken out of the car.

Milliken begged for a "square deal" saying, "Take my money and my car, if you want to, boys, but don't kill me!" While he was still pleading, Farmer shot him in the back of the head. Milliken fell on his face. After he fell, Farmer gave the pistol to Dunn to get him to "do his part," and Dunn shot him in the back. They turned the body over, and Farmer shot him in the heart.

Milliken was relieved of all his money, $14, a diamond stickpin, his watch, his hat, some shirts he had in the back seat of the car, and his shoes. He had just purchased new shoes, which were still in the car. The killers took the shoes from his feet as well as the new pair. They found in his pocket a credit card and tore it up. Continuing down the road, the killers found it was a dead end. As they were retracing their route, their car was seen by a distant neighbor.

Milliken's body was found two days later by a farm woman who was looking for her lost mule. By this time, the killers had made their way to Florida, where they planned to rob banks. Before leaving Nashville they came back downtown. Pulling the car to a stop at 8th Avenue North and Church Street, they asked a pedestrian the best way to Chattanooga. They asked him to confirm it was the best way to get to Florida. Making a U-turn, the car sped away.

Police investigators quickly found the torn credit card (made of paper) and pieced it together, identifying Milliken as the victim. Telegrams were sent to police departments on the main roads to Florida identifying the car, a 1936 blue Plymouth sedan bearing Tennessee license plate 1-16893.

On the night of March 18, the pair held up a pawnshop in a small Florida town, getting only three dollars. Two days later, they were spotted by a Lake City, Florida, police officer as they attempted to remove a license plate from a Florida car. Giving foot chase, he captured one of the pair, who identified himself as Dick Sloan. The other escaped by jumping into the blue Plymouth and speeding away. The Lake City police kept "Dick Sloan" in custody after hearing about the pawnshop holdup, and contacted Chattanooga police, where Sloan said he lived. The Chattanooga police told him to contact the Nashville police. They asked if the suspect was wearing new Florsheim shoes, size 9½. When it turned out he was, it became clear that Sloan was actually Howard Dunn.

Dunn confessed in a boastful manner, admitting the details of a series of crimes, including the killing of Milliken, although asserting that Farmer had done the shooting. He signed a written confession.

Notified of the arrest, police officers and newspaper reporter (later novelist) Brainerd Cheney left by car to pick up Dunn. Near Murfreesboro, their car collided with an oncoming truck, killing the driver, city detective Albert Foster. Others seriously injured included a police investigator, assistant district attorney (later mayor) Ben West, and Cheney. Investigator Aldred and deputy sheriff Corcoran were also injured, less seriously.

Another team of detectives was dispatched. In the car was newspaper reporter Francis "Red" O'Donnell, who was present when both Dunn and Farmer were interrogated by Nashville lawmen.

At the town of Brookeville, thirty miles south of Lake City, a policeman noticed two young men suspiciously examining a car. When he hailed them for questioning, they jumped into the car and sped away. Giving chase, the police attempted to shoot the car's tires, but found themselves under gunfire from the car. As they approached the town of Inverness, city police joined the chase, which ended in a dead-end street near a small lake. One youth jumped into the lake to swim away but was dragged from the water. The other, William Farmer, seemed to have disappeared. Puzzled lawmen finally found him hiding underneath the car.

Full of bravado, Farmer identified himself as Larry Miller and said he was from Chattanooga. A piece of paper was found in his pocket. It read, "In case I'm killed, please send my body to my father, W.H. Farmer." It bore a Knoxville address.[2751]

Back in Nashville, the pair gave verbal confessions to the district attorney. Farmer initially pled guilty to escape the death penalty; Dunn tried the same by asserting that Farmer had done the shooting. He insisted that Milliken was dead when he shot him.

The trial began on April 8, 1936, and the pair was vigorously defended by two able lawyers, Seymour Samuels and George Smith. The killers smirked, joked, acted impassive and at times nonchalant as the testimony from police and others was offered. Neither took the stand. Mrs. Milliken identified the stickpin and the shoes.[2752] Reporter O'Donnell took the stand to say the pair gave voluntary statements to him and both knew he was a newspaper reporter.

The defense was that both Dunn and Farmer were insane. Dunn's father said that his son's problems began in 1933 when he sustained a head injury in a motorcycle accident and was briefly committed to a mental health home in Knox County. Since coming home, he had acted silly, impulsive, and paranoid, and had engaged in criminal behavior as far away as Dallas, Texas. The father said he was unable to place his son in Eastern State Mental Hospital because he could not afford it. Howard Dunn was the eldest of five children.

Other family members and friends recounted anecdotes of bizarre behavior such as strange laughter and twisting his body from side to side in a series of contortions, and his brandishing knives on them. Dunn had told everyone that his father was trying to "frame" him. Most of this testimony was offered by way of depositions, some twenty in all. Each said they thought Dunn was insane.[2753] However, the doctor who saw him at the mental health home testified that while he had a mental problem he was not insane and knew right from wrong.

Farmer's family likewise testified he was insane and attributed this, in part, to the fact that he had two grandparents who were insane, and that he had epileptic fits.[2754] The father said his son was hardly ever able to carry on an intelligent conversation and seemed to be unconcerned about the trouble which he would find himself in as a result of his various thefts. His son never seemed to show the slightest bit of remorse. Asked if his son was insane, he said, "I would not say his mind would be right."[2755] Guards from the reformatory were called and testified that Farmer was sane towards them.

No Nashville doctors offered testimony about the insanity of the two, a fact that was brought to the jury's attention in closing argument. During the trial the pair acted bored and unconcerned, told inside jokes to each other, and laughed at inappropriate times.[2756] When the jury returned a guilty verdict, the pair laughed and asked bizarre questions. Dunn remarked, "It must be a frame-up," and Farmer said, "Yeah, they got the wrong guys this time."[2757]

The convictions were upheld by the Tennessee Supreme Court. It found no error in allowing a police detective and a deputy sheriff who went to Florida to get the defendants to testify about what they had said to them.[2758] The court said the testimony showed they were rude, indifferent to the opinion of others, idiosyncratic, unmanageable, and threatening to their families and everyone they met. But they were not insane in the sense that they did not know right from wrong.[2759] The pair was ordered executed on April 30, 1937, and died that day at the Main Prison.

As the execution date neared, the pair dropped most of their jocular bravado and declared they were "saved." Dunn said, "Why should I be afraid to die? It's nothing to be afraid of. I'm going to walk in there and take it like a soldier. Anyway, the world is liable to come to an end before then."[2760] By this time, they were blaming the murder on liquor. Farmer asserted he and Dunn "had been drunk for three days before the Milliken trouble."[2761] He also claimed he had not gotten a fair trial because no Nashville doctor could be found to examine him, saying, "Yes, I suppose I was guilty under some circumstances, but not the way they got it."[2762]

During the evening before their deaths, they heard spirituals from a white prison quartet and ate large meals. Neither cared who was executed first. Warden Joe Pope selected Dunn, the smaller of the two, but slightly older, in part because he was becoming very nervous. As he walked to the chair he turned to Farmer and said, "Good-bye, I'll see you in another world."

When his cell was opened, Farmer seemed to jump toward the electric chair "like a long-distance runner." He made no last words on the way, but earlier had said, "I hope Mrs. Milliken's got no grudge against me. I hope she's forgiven me just like I've forgiven people that have done things to me." On the wall of his whitewashed cell he had written, "William Farmer 28587. Died in the Chair. April 30, 1937, born January 18, 1917."[2763]

Jimmy Lee Parrish, black, age 35. *Rape of child under twelve.*

The crime was committed at 10:00 A.M. on December 16, 1936, at a home on Caldwell Lane in a fashionable neighborhood of Nashville, Davidson County. Parrish was a yard man who worked for a family on the street. Homes in the area contained servants' quarters in the basement which included a separate bathroom and a cot for sleeping or a separate garage with a bathroom. The victim was Helen Dunn, white, age six, who lived with her parents next door.

Parrish pulled down Helen's panties, and raped her by putting her in his lap. Helen immediately ran to her mother explaining that Parrish had "played wee-wee" with her. The hysterical mother called her husband. When he arrived he called police and Dr. T.B. Zerfoss. The doctor examined Helen and took vagina smears which the laboratory confirmed to be gonorrhea.

Parrish was taken to jail and examined by Dr. Thaxton Parker. He found Parrish to have an active case of gonorrhea. Assistant Attorney General Ben West (later mayor of Nashville) questioned Parrish, who confessed to having digitally penetrated Helen several times two or three weeks earlier. Parrish later admitted:

> On yesterday, Tuesday morning, on the platform of the steps going down into the basement I gave her cake and some peanut candy. I sat her on my lap straddle of me and put my thing between her legs and tried to put it in her. It wouldn't go in. I tried for about twenty minutes. She said, "Stop, I don't want to do that." She told me to turn her loose and let her go. She said she was going to tell her mother and I had some peanut candy in my pocket and gave her some and she promised not to tell. I pushed her privates apart with my fingers and put the end of mine up into as far as I could and it was then that she hollered and I stopped.

Parrish's transcribed statement was notarized and offered as proof at trial.[2764]

Helen Dunn testified at trial along with her father and the two doctors. Dr. Zerfoss found the girl to be in a highly nervous condition, but did not find abrasions and lacerations on her private parts. Parrish testified that he had only helped the girl button and unbutton her clothes and that he had given her candy and peanuts, but when he refused to give her more she went home crying. He denied the crime and repudiated his confession.

On cross-examination, Parrish admitted that he had served seven years in the Tennessee penitentiary for assault with intent to rape.[2765] He had pled guilty to the charge in 1923 but asked the jury to assess his punishment. It gave him a 10- to 21-year sentence. Because he had been "one of the splendid workers in the prison," he was paroled in 1934. At the time of the Dunn rape he was a parole violator, having changed his place of employment without telling his parole officer.[2766]

The Tennessee Supreme Court recounted the facts and dealt with the only issue before it, i.e., whether the corpus delicti had been proven. Acknowledging that the corpus delicti cannot be established by confession alone, other evidence, direct or circumstantial, corroborating it could prove the crime. Here, the testimony of Helen, her father, and the doctor were sufficient, especially since Parrish had admitted on the stand having buttoned and unbuttoned her clothes, having given her candy, and having committed his prior crime.[2767] Jimmie Lee Parrish was electrocuted at the Main Prison in Nashville on August 9, 1937.

On the morning of his execution, Parrish was visited by the prison chaplain, the warden, a Catholic layman and a black minister. Under repeated questioning, Parrish maintained his innocence, insisting that the reason for his arrest was simply to bring him back to prison and that he was being punished too harshly.[2768] Said the chaplain, "Now, I think you should tell the truth about it. As a chaplain I wouldn't want you to die with a lie on your lips. You know you played with her." Parrish responded, "I didn't do anything but play with her. They kept me over there and framed up on me, they didn't arrest me to be tried, they just did it to bring me back here."[2769]

After the others left the interview, the chaplain continued to talk to Parrish. The chaplain added to Parrish's statement, "He said he did take her underwear down at the back of the garage. He first said he wasn't there, then he said he took down her underwear so she could pee-pee."[2770] It was reported that Parrish had made of full confession of his crime.[2771] Another newspaper account said, "Parrish did not make a full confession of the crime for which he paid the supreme penalty, [Warden] Pope said, although he partially admitted his guilt."[2772]

Fred Richie (aka Fred Ritchie), white, age 34. *Murder.*

The crime was committed at 10:10 P.M. on August 10, 1936, at the Rock City Paper Box Company located at Twelfth Avenue South and Harrison Street in Nashville, in Davidson County. The victim was the killer's wife, Elsie Mae O'Brien Richie, white, age thirty. She had recently told him not to return to their home.

Elsie worked the night shift and Fred Richie came to her work. Said a co-worker, "I looked around and he had his left arm holding her head and his right arm round her throat, and she was screaming."[2773] "Save me, he is killing me!" she screamed. Richie held her down with his knees while he stabbed her eight times. "God damn you, I told you I would kill you," he said.[2774] A co-worker struck Ritchie with a wrench and he fell away. Elsie ran to the office and spoke her last words, "Please do something for me."[2775] She died later that night at the hospital.

Richie's chief defense was intoxication. He had injured a leg as a boy and had undergone surgery. It hurt from time to time and he used whiskey to numb the pain. He insisted he did not remember anything about the killing because he was intoxicated. Several people who saw him that day said he smelled like alcohol but was not intoxicated.

One of his witnesses was his brother, Joe Richie, who was asked if he knew whether his brother's wife was a good woman. He said, "As far as I know, yes, sir." He was asked, "Have you ever heard him say anything against her?" He answered, "No, sir."[2776] The Tennessee Supreme Court affirmed the conviction on June 17, 1937, but the opinion cannot be located. It set Richie's execution for August 10, 1937, and he was electrocuted that day. He was apparently the first man executed in the "humanized" electric chair. Welfare Commissioner George Cate, a reformer, had ordered three new switches added to the existing one, requiring four men to throw them, with only one actually carrying electricity.[2777]

Richie declined to discuss the killing but insisted, "I'm going to die like a man." He declined any special last meal, saying, "Just bring what the rest of the men will have. I don't want to put anybody to any trouble."[2778] Nevertheless, around midnight he was brought a large meal of steak, eggs, milk and coffee, which he ate. He declined any breakfast, saying, "Not a thing. Don't suppose I'll be hungry anymore."[2779] Richie's last words were, "If a person walks the straight and narrow path he'll never be brought to a place where I am now. Don't let anything break up your home. I killed a good woman because I was full of liquor."[2780] Richie, one of thirteen children, said he had never been to school.

One person who did not heed Fred Richie's words was his brother Joe Richie. On July 31, 1938, hardly a year after his brother's execution, Joe Richie, white, age thirty-seven, shot to death his wife, Mary Elizabeth Richie, white, age twenty-five, in their home at 6018 Pennsylvania Avenue in Nashville.

Joe told police that he killed Mary because she and her mother, Mrs. Eva Barnes, had accused him of seeing a former wife, Mrs. Sally Richie Harper, whom he had divorced five years earlier. "I married Mary after Sally and I were divorced. We got along all right for a while and then she started doing things she should not have done."[2781] Using a pistol taken from a friend's house, Joe Richie went to his home about 8:00 o'clock in the morning and shot Mary five times as she was preparing to attend church. Hearing the shots, her parents, Mr. and Mrs. Barnes, came from another room and were fired upon by Richie. The bullets missed and they rushed him and were sitting on him when police arrived.

Longtime police investigator for the district attorney, R.L. Tarkington, told the newspaper that Joe Richie had a history of threatening his wife, and according to a witness, "One time Richie said that he was going to go just where Fred, his brother, went."[2782] Joe Richie pled not guilty but the jury sentenced him to ninety-nine years, although the prison records say this was revised to life imprisonment. Joe was found to have an active case of syphilis when he arrived at the prison on October 14, 1938. Joe told prison officials he had no recollection of the shooting, but had been hit on the head by his wife. He was paroled on October 25, 1956.[2783]

1938

Gus McKinney, black, age 19. *Murder.*

The crime was committed about 8:00 P.M. March 26, 1937, at the store of P.J. Agnew at 102 West Colorado in Memphis, in Shelby County. McKinney and codefendants Harry James and Bennie Hyler, both black, had entered the store with guns drawn. They robbed the store and its employees of forty dollars and cigarettes. As they were leaving, John Russell, black, age twenty-six, entered the store and said something to McKinney. This made McKinney think Russell knew him. He escorted Russell outside, took him behind the store, and shot him. "I didn't want him to tell on me," McKinney told the jury.[2784] Earlier, he had told police the shooting was to prevent Russell from "squawking," to use McKinney's words.

Tried together, McKinney received the death sentence, the others life sentences. They were convicted on April 23, 1937. The Tennessee Supreme Court affirmed the conviction in an opinion issued in January 1938, but the opinion cannot be located.

On February 28, 1938, the day before his scheduled execution, McKinney attempted suicide by cutting his throat and left arm with a sharp piece of tin. The same day, Governor Gordon Browning granted him a 30-day reprieve so that his mother could talk to the trial judge, who at the time was ill.

McKinney's execution was reset for March 28, but when it became apparent that the head electrician at the prison was ill and could not participate in the execution, the date was reset for April 15, 1938, and was carried out that day. Because of the suicide attempt, McKinney was watched closely.[2785] McKinney asked for no special last meal and was given a regular dinner consisting of steak, pie and sweet milk. He spent most of the night before his death listening to a prison quartet sing spirituals. Asked by a guard if he wanted the singing stopped so he could get some sleep, he said, "I have more time than anything else." Later during the night he asked for several pieces of chocolate pie, which he ate heartily.

Just before he was led to the chair, Warden Joe Pope asked McKinney if he thought he got justice. "Yes," he replied, "I'm guilty and ought to suffer." As he sat in the electric chair, guards wiped McKinney's face with a towel because he was crying. His last word was "Good-bye."[2786]

Arthur Mosby, black, age 17. *Rape.*

The crime was committed at 5:30 P.M. November 5, 1937, near Trezevant and South Parkway in Memphis, in Shelby County. The victim was Mrs. Mantye E. Hood, white, age thirty-eight. She had been to the grocery store operated by her husband located at Trezevant and Lamar. She was walking to her home located at 1039 Bruce Street. Accompanying her was Fred Hood, Jr., her ten-year-old son. Mosby came from behind and dragged her to a field nearby and raped her. The boy ran for help. Mosby's hat came off in the struggle and he left quickly. When police arrived they found the hat. In it was a part of a club plan purchase receipt through which he was identified.[2787] The rape was confirmed by a doctor and a nurse at John Gaston Hospital.

Mrs. Hood also identified Mosby because of a bite mark she left on his finger. It was still visible at his January 19, 1938, trial. Mosby claimed he had loaned Mrs. Hood ten dollars and simply came up to her to ask for his money when she began screaming. This caused him to run away. He insisted he did not rape her. Five witnesses, including two newspaper reporters, testified he had confessed the rape when arrested two days after the crime.[2788]

The Tennessee Supreme Court affirmed the conviction in May 1938, but the opinion cannot be located. Several days before his execution he was examined by physicians and pronounced sane, a question of his sanity having been raised by prison officials. Mosby paced his cell in the little brick "death house" inside the walls where the electric chair was located.[2789] Mosby declined any food in his last hours. According to Warden Joe Pope, Mosby refused to discuss his case, either to confirm or deny his guilt. He was electrocuted on July 25, 1938.[2790]

1939

Ernest Stanley, black, age 27. *Murder.*

The crime was committed about five o'clock in the morning of October 20, 1937, near the grounds of Brushy Mountain Prison in rural Morgan County. The victim was Glenn Johnson, white, age thirty-three, a guard at the prison. He was to bring Stanley, a recent escapee, back to the prison. Two days before, six inmates being led to the coal mine escaped. The others were recaptured the same day, but Stanley broke into a commissary, stole a pistol, and returned. It was the state's contention that he had returned in order to free another inmate, James Jackson. Stanley asserted that he shot Johnson in self-defense.

The Tennessee Supreme Court said, "Ernest Stanley was convicted of murder in the first degree, his punishment being fixed at death by electrocution. He has appealed to this court, and the only errors assigned question the sufficiency of the evidence to sustain the conviction. On the morning of October 20, 1937, the defendant inflicted wounds with a pistol upon the body of Glenn Johnson from which he died the next day."

Said the court, "The defendant, a twenty-seven-year-old negro, who had escaped with five other prisoners from the Brushy Mountain Penitentiary, on October 18, 1937, shot Glenn Johnson, who was a guard at the penitentiary, while the latter was attempting to arrest and return him to the prison. The shooting occurred between five and six o'clock in the morning at the bottom of the incline, about 500 yards from the main prison, where the prisoners are assembled to be conveyed up the mountain to the mine where they work. We quote the defendant's testimony in full, which is as follows:

> I am 27 years old, and am in the penitentiary at Petros for housebreaking. I have been here about three years and I got out in October the 18th. Five except myself got out. I got out in the mountain and got lost. I came upon the Commissary and broke in in order to get some clothes so I could change and get rid of my prison clothes. I got some clothes and put them on. I saw a pistol and got it, a hat, shoes, and socks. Someone got after me and chased me away from the store and I was still lost and wandered around in the mountain and had been walking two days when I came back in sight of Petros. I didn't know where I was, didn't know it was the prison. I had worked in No. 3 mine, we go up the manway to get to the mine. I was lost and thought I was at Oliver Springs. When I saw the prisoners coming, I found out where I was. I saw Glenn Johnson coming toward me and behind me. I went to the Rice house to make out like I was a Trusty. He called to Sam Wilson, and said, "Who is that boy?" They come up. I said I was looking for a fellow named James Jackson. I didn't go there to rescue James Jackson. I just barely knew him. When I knocked on Rice's door, a boy came to the door and ask me what I wanted. The first name that popped in my mind was James Jackson, so I ask him if he had seen James Jackson. I set down on the porch, when presently Glenn Johnson and Sam Wilson came up to where I was and ask what I was doing there. I said I was looking for James Jackson. Johnson said, "I'll have to take you to the prison," and he went out of the Rice yard and when he reached the road he started down the road toward the power house and had gone only a few steps when Johnson fired. He turned around and commenced shooting at me, and I turned around and began firing at him. I fired four shots. I fired two shots as I came across the mountain to a tree to see if the gun would shoot. I did not know Johnson; I was trying to make my escape when he began shooting at me. I took the pistol and knives out of the store for the purpose of selling them to get something to eat. I have been in the penitentiary two times before. Three times in all. I was never a trusty, and I did not know anything about the country around the prison. I knew where Mr. Rice lived. I could see his house from the main prison. I had no reason to inquire for James Jackson, but mentioned his name because it was the first one I thought of. I did not get the pistol and return to the prison for the purpose of rescuing Jackson. I was lost and didn't know where I was until I saw the prison.

The court said:

> The testimony shows that deceased had been a guard at the prison for three months, and that one of his duties was to bring the prisoners who worked in the mine to the incline each morning. The defendant worked regularly in the mine and must have known the deceased. Defendant testified, as quoted hereinbefore, that when he saw the prisoners coming he knew where he was; and at that time, "I saw Glenn Johnson coming toward me," and that Johnson said, "I'll have to take you to the prison." And further, "I was trying to make my escape when he began shooting at me." From the foregoing we think the jury was justified in finding that defendant knew deceased, knew what he was arresting him for, and killed him to avoid being returned to the penitentiary. There is nothing in the record to show that deceased did not inform defendant of his authority and the cause of the arrest. Defendant did not testify that he received no such information.

With respect to the claim of self-defense, the unreasonableness of defendant's version of the shooting, his flight thereafter, the dying declaration of deceased are sufficient to overcome this contention. With respect to the element of premeditation, we will briefly refer to the other testimony in the record. Robert Rice testified that defendant came to his home that morning; that shortly after arriving there deceased came up and said something to defendant that he did not understand; that they both left the porch going out through the yard gate. "I heard Glenn Johnson say, I will go and take him to prison. Johnson asked him to get in front of him and go up the road, he pointed up toward the prison. The defendant had his hand in his pocket and started to pull it out. I could see both pistols, and they fired several shots at each other, but I do not know which fired first."

Sam Wilson, a trusty at the prison, was present and gave substantially the same testimony as Rice. Dr. Mathis testified that deceased was shot in the hand and the hip, the bullet entering the hip and lodging against the spine, causing the death of deceased a day and a half later. The deceased made the following dying declaration to his father, Jack Johnson: "I saw the negro down on the porch dressed in civilian clothes, that attracted my attention. I went to the negro and told him I would have to take him to the prison and told him to get in front of me and go on to the prison, but instead of doing so, the negro started in the opposite direction, and I called to him to halt, and immediately the negro turned around and began firing at me. I returned the fire until I got shot in the hand."

And further: "The negro got me; I was going to take him in without shooting him, but he got me first; he shot my hand and I was unable to do much." The probability is that the negro got the drop on deceased because the latter did not suspect that he was armed. In *Lewis v. State*, 40 Tenn (3 Head), 127, 148, the court said: "Premeditation involves a previously formed design, or actual intention to kill. But such design, or intention, may be conceived, and deliberately formed, in an instant. It is not necessary that it should have been conceived, or have pre-existed in the mind, any definite period of time anterior to its execution. It is sufficient that it preceded the assault, however short the interval. The length of time is not the essence of this constituent of the offense. The purpose to kill is no less premeditated, in the legal sense of the term, if it were deliberately formed but a moment preceding the act by which the death is produced, than if it had been formed an hour before. The mental state of the assailant at the moment, rather than the length of time the act may have been premeditated, is the material point to be considered. The mental process, in the formation of the purpose to kill, may have been instantaneous; and the question of vital importance is — was the mind, at that moment, so far free from the influence of excitement, or passion, as to be capable of reflecting and acting with a sufficient degree of coolness and deliberation of purpose; was the death of the person assaulted, the object sought to be accomplished — the end determined upon."

This principle of law was reaffirmed in *Galvin v. State*, 46 Tenn. (6 Cold.) 283, and has been adhered to ever since. In both of those cases the accused were convicted of murder in the first degree for killing officers who were attempting to place them under arrest. A stronger case of premeditated homicide is presented in the record before us in the present case as a most cruel, inhuman, and unnecessary crime that fully warranted the jury in meting out to the defendant the severest penalty of the law. For the reasons set forth herein the judgment of the trial court is affirmed, and the date of execution is set for Tuesday, January 10, 1939.[2791]

Ernest Stanley met death that day. "I never saw anyone any more calm than Stanley was just before he was executed," said Deputy Warden Glenn Swafford. "He ate a good breakfast and then went to the chair without a word."[2792]

White Miller Tollett (aka Miller Tollett), white, age 31. *Murder.*

The crime was committed at 2:00 A.M. on January 7, 1938, at the home of Harmon and Evelyn Gouge, in the small town of Hampton, in Carter County. The killers were White Miller Tollett and Church Calvin Lester, aided by Thomas Lee Walker and Alva Ulysses Wallin.[2793] The victims were the Gouge children, Sonia June, white, age nine; Luena, white, age seven; and Roma Jean, white, age six. The defendants were only prosecuted for the death of Roma Jean, for which Tollett and Lester received the death penalty.

The four had driven from Pikeville in Bledsoe County on January 6. While Walker stayed in the car and Wallin stood as a lookout, Miller Tollett (as he was known) and Lester made their way in silence to the house. There they placed three sticks of dynamite in a basement vent, virtually underneath the bedroom where the adults were thought to be sleeping. Two thirty-foot long fuses, which burned at the rate of a foot a minute, were attached to each end of the dynamite, giving the group time for a getaway.[2794]

The explosion virtually demolished the house and was heard three miles away. Jolted from sleep in his house next door, Harmon's brother stumbled through the wreckage and found his sister-in-law

Evelyn badly injured, and soon discovered the bodies of the three girls. They had been sleeping in the same room as the mother, one in the same bed. They had been killed by the concussion. The youngest was also struck by the falling ceiling as she lay beside her mother. Fearful that the family car might be rigged with dynamite, Mrs. Gouge was taken to the hospital by a neighbor. Onlookers were convinced she would die, but she made a complete recovery. Mr. Gouge, the intended target, was not hurt because he had been staying at a hotel in Johnson City.

This case attracted national attention because of the deaths of three innocent girls against the backdrop of decades of feuding in the Tennessee mountains, in this case, Bledsoe County.[2795] A history of the feud provides insight into how a triple murder came to a quiet hamlet some two hundred and twenty winding miles away.

The largest families in Bledsoe County were the Tolletts, Swaffords, Walkers and Wallins, whose quarreling and shifting alliances dominated the county in both law and disorder. Fighting between the Tolletts and Swaffords began in 1886 when one shot another following a wrestling match. By 1932 at least seven were dead and many more wounded. On October 9, 1932, the sheriff, Thomas J. Swafford, had been shot by someone in hiding, but the crime went unsolved.

In September 1935, J. Calhoun Swafford and Coleman Johnson had been shot by Church Lester. He claimed they had reached for weapons and he shot them in self-defense after they had forced "unwelcome attentions" on two mountain girls, and Lester had reprimanded them for it. Lester, thus allied with the Tolletts and Wallings, was acquitted on a manslaughter charge. Church Lester was the youngest child of a minister who had raised his children in virtual isolation on Waldon's Ridge. He bore the unusual first name because he had made an unanticipated entry into the world while his mother was attending a church service.

The immediate cause of the bombing was the death of Arnold Lester, Church's brother. He had been in business with Harmon Gouge at a roadhouse called Hi-Cliff Camp, in Carter County, but the failing venture brought conflict between the two. Arnold Lester was especially distressed over the lack of money, particularly because his wife was due to give birth and was taken to the hospital. On January 29, 1937, the two met at a gas station in a place called Ash Fork, where an argument ensued. Gouge claimed that Tollett went for a gun in his back pocket and Gouge pulled a pistol and fired two shots into Arnold's abdomen. He was brought to the same hospital where his wife was confined. An hour later she delivered a girl. A week later he died in the hospital.

Gouge was charged with murder and the Tollett clan came to Carter County to witness the trial. However, it was continued three times over nearly a year, and the Tolletts came to believe that Gouge would never be tried because he was well-connected with the ruling families of Carter County.[2796] Out of this frustration came the plan to kill Gouge.

The first attempt was a bitter failure. A dynamite bomb had been placed in Harmon Gouge's car, designed to explode when ignited by the heated exhaust pipe. However, the bomb exploded a minute after Gouge left the car, causing no injury. Since that time, he had avoided any contact with the Tolletts and their allies, and had stayed in Johnson City at a hotel while he tended his businesses in that town and Elizabethton. His wife was fearful of another attack on him and had urged him to stay away.

The day after the home dynamiting, special investigators from the fire marshal's office in Nashville, together with a special investigator from an insurance association, were working with the Carter County sheriff and a clue was found. The four had thrown the extra fuse cord off the bridge over the Roe River, but a sticker, giving the name of a Chattanooga hardware store, did not fall into the river, but stuck on the bridge. Shortly thereafter, the fuse itself was found stuck on a branch in the river within sight of the bridge. The clerk at the store said he could not identify the person who bought the fuse (nor recognize him), but investigators concluded from the description that the buyer was Miller Tollett.

In order to build a case against Miller Tollett, the fire marshal and others sought to determine who was seen with Tollett on the day before the bombing, and at the earlier continued hearings on Harmon Gouge. Lee Walker, a Bledsoe County deputy sheriff, was identified by several people, along with Cave Tollett, another deputy. Walker (and later Miller Tollett) insisted that they had been visiting Tollett's girlfriend on the night in question, but had left that evening and spent the night in a hotel room of a friend in Pikeville. They and the male friend had all slept in the same bed, they insisted.[2797] The bed was a three-quarter-size bed, so this alibi seemed unlikely, concluded the officers. Walker was taken to a hotel in Elizabethton and confronted with the inconsistencies in his alibi. Within a few hours he gave a statement telling the facts of the bombing.[2798] Shortly thereafter, Ulysses Wallin was brought to the hotel. Confronted with Walker's statement, he gave a similar one. When confronted with the Walker and Wallin statements, Tollett said nothing.[2799]

Carter County sheriff Moreland's approach to solving the case involved arresting as many Tolletts and their allies as he could and holding them as long as possible, in order to show that the law would be vindicated. When it became clear that an alibi provided by a young couple for the benefit of Lee Walker may have been influenced by Bledsoe County sheriff Walter E. Walling, the Carter County sheriff arrested him as well. He was charged as an accessory but acquitted.[2800]

Three people who offered alibis for Tollett or Walker, which were found to be untrue, were indicted as accessories after the fact. They appealed, contending that since their actions had taken place in Bledsoe County, not Carter County, they should have been indicted there. The Tennessee Supreme Court agreed.[2801]

Six thousand people viewed the children's bodies as they lay in the funeral home, and the trial was the largest attended case in the county's history, with hundreds waiting outside the courthouse.

The case against Miller Tollett, Church Lester and Crave Leonard Tollett was based on the testimony of codefendants Lee Walker and Ulysses Wallin. The jury exonerated Crave Tollett,[2802] but found against Walker and Wallin and gave them twenty-year sentences. Miller Tollett and Church Lester were given death sentences.

While Church Lester was being held in the Carter County jail he became despondent that no one visited him or sent him mail. He had counted on the friendship of the Tollett clan to provide him emotional support. Realizing that he had dishonored his family, Lester hanged himself with his leather belt, choking to death with his feet barely an inch off the floor. The photograph of Lester hanging in his cell with the coroner reading his suicide note became an image of the case that was widely published.[2803]

White Miller Tollett's appeal to the Tennessee Supreme Court emphasized the wrongfulness of using the statements of codefendants Walker and Wallin to convict, because they were principals in the crime.[2804] The court noted that Tollett could not be convicted on their testimony alone, but found several instances of corroboration. For example, at least two people put Tollett in the car shortly before the killings, including two people who had been given rides in the car because they were friends of at least one of the defendants. Tollett had not taken the stand in his own defense, and no witnesses testified on his behalf, said the Supreme Court, except Church Lester.[2805] Although Tollett was never identified by the store clerk, witnesses did place him in the vicinity of the store the day the dynamite fuse was purchased, and Tollett had a motive. Said the Supreme Court, "This record clearly shows that these kinsmen of the Tollett brother who had been slain by Gouge were roused and angry and resentful of the law's delays and entertained intense animosity toward Gouge."[2806]

The court also turned aside the contention that unless the state showed that Tollett had particularized malice toward the actual victims (the girls) he could only be convicted of second-degree murder. The court said this was not the law.[2807] The execution was set for January 11, 1939, and was carried out that day at the Main Prison in Nashville.

Miller Tollett maintained his innocence to the end, hoping for executive clemency as the Tollett clan and their allies besieged the governor's office seeking commutation.[2808] "If I were guilty it would be different, but I pleaded not guilty at the trial and I am innocent. The man who got me into this is here now."[2809]

Surrounded by family on his last full day of life, Miller Tollett solemnly gave his pocket watch to his brother, Thompson Tollett, saying, "Thompson, here's the watch that came from Arnold down to me. It's got a little string on it. Somebody show him how to loop it on his belt. Maybe you ought to get a chain for it, Thompson."[2810]

The last hours were especially dramatic, as he was given a sheet of paper to write a letter to be hand-carried to his mother. He was allowed to shake the hand of his elderly father, and said, "I want you to be ready to meet me up there. Dad, I want you to brace up. I know it's goin' to be hard, but maybe we'll all meet up there someday. That's the reason I can take it."[2811]

Among the last to visit Miller Tollett was the former sheriff, W.L. Walling, who had refused to arrest him when asked to do so by the Carter County sheriff. Said Walling, "I never thought you were guilty. I don't think so yet."[2812]

The prison official most affected by Miller Tollett's execution was Warden Pope, who explained with tear-filled eyes that he had known the man since he was a toddler. The person usually in charge of the execution was the person most likely to get a last-minute confession. He had received such confessions in the past and would continue to do so in the future. However, Deputy Warden Glenn

Swafford, of Bledsoe County, took no part in the execution.

Frank Murray (aka James Robertson), black, age 19. *Murder.*

Hyman Johnson (aka Hyman Bostic), black, age 21. *Murder*

The crime was committed at 7:30 P.M. on January 26, 1938, at 621 Fern Street in south Nashville in Davidson County. Murray had been convicted of thievery at age nine and had spent almost four years at the state's reform school. Johnson had a string of small convictions for assault and had served over a year at the reform school. That is where they met.

The victim, Isaac Gordon, white, age thirty-eight, was an insurance collector. The "sick and accident" policies that he sold were targeted at poor people, and a collector (called "the debit man") literally made calls on policyholders' homes on a weekly basis to collect the premiums. This meant that Gordon could be expected to have some money on his person. He carried $22 at the time of his murder.

Using a stolen car, the pair were looking for someone to rob when they came across Gordon, who was unknown to them. He entered the Fern Street house and Murray got into the back seat of his car as Johnson stood lookout. As Murray held a gun on Gordon, Johnson took the wheel. Murray drank from a whiskey bottle and smoked hand-rolled cigarettes, Johnson drove the car across town to a remote factory. Murray fired two shots, one piercing Gordon's hat, the other striking him behind the left ear. The pair threw Gordon's body from the car, taking his wallet and the record book he carried. The whiskey bottle was thrown nearby. The wallet and record book were thrown in a weed-filled field as the two walked away from the body and the car. Johnson took the hat but threw it into a yard nearby. A woman living there threw it onto the sidewalk a few days later. It was picked up by a man who concluded it belonged to the dead man, having read about the case in the newspaper. He turned it over to police, who found the empty wallet and record book. Using the record book, police went to the last address where Gordon had stopped, Fern Street.[2813]

Johnson and Murray became prime suspects in the case when a witness came forward and described them as having loitered near the Fern Street address, and they were suspects in a series of armed robberies of stores. On February 9, 1938, a policeman was called to the scene of an ongoing store robbery and was fired on by Murray. He got off one shot which wounded Murray in the thigh. Two days later, the pair was apprehended in the course of an armed robbery of another store. Fingerprints on the whiskey bottle matched Murray's. Confronted with the witness statement and the fingerprints, plus the unique tobacco and papers used by Murray, the pair quickly confessed. Each named the other as the shooter.

The trial was one of the briefest capital murder cases in Nashville. Evidence began in the morning and the jury retired to reach a verdict late that afternoon. The only contested issue was who was the shooter. The killers named each other.

The Tennessee Supreme Court rejected the plea that no corpus delicti was proven. Identification of Gordon's hat by his wife was sufficient. Moreover, there was no issue or controversy about the victim's identity. The trial court had not erred in refusing a severance. "It was wholly immaterial" who was the actual shooter, ruled the court. "Both defendants planned the robbery, perhaps the murder, both were present and divided the proceeds of the robbery. Both are equally guilty of the murder committed to accomplish the robbery. It is, of course, elementary law."[2814] The pair were ordered executed on March 28, 1939, and died by electrocution at the Main Prison in Nashville on that day.[2815]

The pair sought spiritual salvation shortly before their execution and relatives were allowed to visit and sing funeral spirituals. Johnson remarked, "We all got to die some time and this is the jumping off place for us. It's hard, but if we hadn't had time to think about dying like we have then we would not have had the chance to get ourselves right with God. We've got a longer time to be dead than we have to live, and if this hadn't happened we would have gone to hell, maybe."[2816] He continued, "If we had kept on we might have got killed without time to make our way to get to Heaven. That's why we are telling the truth about it now, so God couldn't hold anything against us."[2817] Because the pair spent their last hours in spiritual matters, they declined a last meal, taking only milk and soft drinks. Mrs. Gordon was refused permission to see the execution, since state law forbade it, said prison officials.

The warden declined to tell the pair which would be executed first, but explained to the newspapers, "If we take Johnson first we will have to carry Murray to the chair because he is breaking fast."[2818] That was the reason Murray was executed first. Acting Deputy Warden Glenn Swafford said Murray told him he had fired the shot that killed Gordon.

Hubert Harris, black, age 22. *Murder.*

The crime was committed at 2:00 P.M. on February 24, 1938, in a rural area of Davidson County called Bellevue near Newsom Station. The killers, Hubert Harris and Jimmy Thompson, black, age fourteen, were neighbors of the victim, Mike Finnegan, white, age seventy-one. Finnegan lived alone in his farmhouse and was an "eccentric elderly recluse," and a "solid and substantial citizen of the community and was well liked and respected by all of his neighbors."[2819]

Harris testified, "He had been arrested and convicted on a number of occasions; that he had been convicted of breaking into a boxcar and confined to the penitentiary, and had been convicted on a charge of housebreaking and larceny and given a workhouse sentence. Also, he had served time on the county road on a whiskey charge, and had stolen an automobile and had been sent to [a center for youthful offenders] and had only gotten out in November 1937."[2820]

Harris said that he was at Thompson's home the night before the killing and the teen-ager urged him to go to Finnegan's house and look for money because the old man was said to keep large amounts in a sack in the house or on his person. Harris insisted that Thompson prodded him to go along and thrust into his hand a stick of wood from the wood pile, Thompson taking a larger piece. After they crept into the man's house, Thompson repeatedly bludgeoned Finnegan's head, continuing the beating when the man was on the floor flailing his hands. According to Harris, they took $26 from the man's pocket, along with some of his socks, a knife, and a razor. These were put in a cloth sack.[2821]

Leaving the house, they threw everything into some bushes near the house, except the money. They went to Thompson's house, later bought beer, and played cards until the early morning hours when they saw flashlights coming through the yard. Harris ran out the back door and was tracked by hounds. The pair was arrested.

Thompson's testimony was identical to Harris's except for two notable differences. It was Harris who planned the robbery and Harris who bludgeoned the man. He was told by Jimmy Thompson, "Hubert, you better quit hitting him." To this Harris replied, "I am going to kill the old son of a bitch, because he will jump up here in a minute and will kill all of us."[2822]

Finnegan staggered to a neighbor's house but was unable to talk. His head was badly crushed and blood was flowing freely from his head and gushing from his nose and mouth. He was taken to a hospital and died about ten o'clock that night without making a statement. Because bloodhounds were quickly brought to the crime scene, the discarded cloth sack and socks were found immediately. The dogs led the police to Thompson's house that night.[2823]

The Supreme Court said that while each defendant blamed the other for the actual killing, both were equally responsible. It said, "However, we think it unreasonable to say that the defendant, James Thompson, fourteen years of age and without a criminal record, induced the defendant, Hubert Harris, an habitual criminal twenty-two years of age, to enter the plan to rob the deceased."[2824] Affirming the convictions, the court urged the governor to commute Thompson's sentence to life imprisonment, which the governor did.[2825]

Harris was ordered executed on April 4, 1939, and died that day. The night before, he asked for pork chop and egg sandwiches. A few minutes before his electrocution, Harris told Deputy Warden Glenn Swafford that he alone had killed Finnegan.[2826]

James Otha Martin, white, age 42. *Murder.*
Joe McKay, black, age 40. *Murder.*
James Willis Smith, black, age 38. *Murder.*

The crime was committed at 6:28 P.M. February 17, 1938, at the Sinclair gas station located on 373 Front Street in downtown Memphis, in Shelby County. The station was owned by James Otha Martin, who conspired with Joe McKay and James Willis Smith. The victim was Oliver James George, white, age twenty-two, known as Shorty because he was five feet, three inches tall. He was a handyman at the station. The shooter was James Willis Smith.

According to a plan scripted by McKay (and instigated by Martin), Smith came to the station just as the lights over the pump were turned out, walked to a point were he was between Martin and the victim, and said, "Stick 'em up!" He fired two pistol shots, one hitting the victim in the forehead. The shooter ran away. Martin claimed he was standing in the door of the gas station when the shooting occurred. This meant the shooter had his back to Martin. The police, who were on the scene within twenty minutes, became suspicious because robbery was obviously not a motive for killing George.[2827]

In a search of George's rooming house (he was separated from his wife), police found an envelope in a wastebasket which contained the following writing, "I wish to inform you that ... and I object to anybody buying any more insurance policies on my life." The writing was deemed to be the draft of a letter George had composed.[2828] The writing prompted the police to return to the gas station to question Martin. He was not present and they opened a roll-top desk and discovered several double indemnity insurance policies on George's life, with Martin the beneficiary or assignee on two. In all, there was about $13,000 in insurance on George's life, with the annual premiums totaling $215.54 per year. All of the policies had been purchased at Martin's insistence, and were about ten times the amount a person of George's income would normally have, since he earned from eighty-five cents to three dollars a day. He was not paid regular wages, but received a percentage for washing cars and fixing tires.[2829]

Martin was taken to police headquarters and within hours had signed a typed confession in which he said he had hired someone to kill George, but did not know the shooter's name. He showed police the name of the go-between, McKay, in the telephone book. McKay was promptly arrested and vigorously protested his innocence, but several hours later he named Willie Smith as the shooter.

When Smith was brought in he gave a complete account of the shooting. Martin had induced McKay to get Smith to shoot George (whom he did not know) in return for $500 of a $1,250 insurance policy on George's life. McKay was to get the balance. Smith testified against the other two at the joint trial, hoping the jury or a court would grant him mercy, in part because he claimed he was threatened by McKay if he failed to carry out the plan.

At trial, both Martin and McKay asserted their innocence. Martin insisted he bought the policies because George owed him money, about $200, and he wanted the policies "for protection."

He maintained that the shooting was a robbery gone bad and he had no role in it. McKay admitted he knew Smith for eight years because they had repaired cars in McKay's back yard. He admitted taking Smith to a spot near the gas station on the night of the killing but said it was for the purpose of buying a flashlight. McKay said that when he went to his employer's place of business on the night of the killing to get his mail, he discovered Smith sitting in his car. He said Smith blurted out that he had just killed a man and McKay asked him to get out of the car. He did not force Smith to get out of the car because he was afraid that Smith might shoot him.[2830] They drove to the Peabody Hotel, picked up a woman who worked there and went home.

The key issue on appeal was whether the written confessions of Martin and McKay were properly introduced, Martin claiming he had been roughed up by the police, who shined a light in his eyes, and he was in a "daze" when he signed his confession. The Tennessee Supreme Court concluded there was no evidence of brutal behavior for several reasons. First, the men were given a bath and photographed naked, then examined by two physicians, who found no bruising. Second, Martin was allowed to walk freely around the police office and corridor, was free to ask for food and water and sought none. Third, several people, such as the newspaper reporter who was present when the confession was taken, testified that Martin did not seem unduly stressed when he saw him, although Martin recanted the confession when the reporter visited him in the jail three days later.[2831]

McKay's attempt to repudiate his confession was based on his fear of being beaten by a policeman who said, "I want to have you by myself, when I have you in a room, when you come back you will be glad to make a statement like the white man did."[2832] McKay testified that he was not physically hurt by any policemen, but his confession was the result of fear.

The Supreme Court said the confessions were not produced by brutality or fear, and there was full evidence to convict. First, there was evidence that Martin had attempted to buy insurance on a former employee, going so far as to arrange an imposter to take the physical exam, since it was clear that the employee had advanced tuberculosis and died several months later. (It seems that Martin had made no effort to claim the benefits of that policy, which the company denied.)

Second, several insurance agents testified they were unable to sell insurance on George with Martin as the beneficiary because he was not related to George.[2833] Third, although McKay did not testify that Martin had gotten him to arrange the killing, there was no way the police could have found McKay without Martin's having given him the name. Martin testified that he only knew McKay because he traded at the station. This was directly contradicted by his statement at the police station: "You send out and get this boy, and he will tell you who killed George."[2834] Finally, the murder weapon was recovered from the possession of Smith's cousin, who testified Smith had returned it to him a few days after the killing. Ballistics testing, and the fact that two bullets were missing, showed it was the murder weapon.[2835]

The Supreme Court said, "The brief filed on behalf of the defendant Smith is nothing more than a plea for mercy. He was the actual perpetrator of the murder. His position is that he acted under coercion and fear of McKay and Martin. The answer to this is that he could have gone to the sheriff or police at any time and exposed the plot to kill George."[2836] The court set the executions for April 10, 1939, and all were executed that day.

By the time of the execution, Martin asserted that the killing was a "joke" gone bad, that he had said he would pay McKay half the insurance money to "throw George in the river," but never meant it should happen. "I just made this remark as a joke and this is the truth as I want to meet God, and I know I could not hope to do this with a lie on my lips."[2837] From a nearby cell, McKay told Martin, "Cut it out." He said, "You know you kept after me to get someone to kill Mr. George before he could join the Navy." Later that evening, when it appeared that Martin was about to confess, his wife declared hysterically, "All these stories of Smith and McKay are lies. Otho is telling me the same story he has told me all the time." She did not want him to confess.

A few hours before his execution, McKay did confess. He admitted what he had denied all along, namely, that he had hired Smith to kill George, having been induced by Martin.[2838] None asked for a special last meal. They were served regular prison food on trays but ate little.

Martin was executed first; his last words while seated in the chair, were, "Chaplain, they tell me there is not any pain."[2839] McKay and Smith had spent their last several hours in fervent verbal prayer, each speaking when the other became tearful and could not continue. McKay and Smith had no last words and were executed in that order. Because no one claimed their bodies, they were buried in the prison graveyard.

Mrs. Lela George sued to collect on the life insurance policies on her husband. The court ruled that the policies were induced by fraud and were unenforceable. She collected nothing.[2840]

Willie Williams (aka William Henry Williams), age 33, black. *Murder.*

The crime was committed about 9:30 P.M. on June 8, 1937, in a black area of Nashville, 26th Avenue North and Heiman Street, behind a dance hall called the Silver Streak Cotton Club, which catered to blacks, served as a nightclub and center for numbers running and small-time gambling.[2841] The victim was William "Cap" James, Jr., black, age sixty-seven, owner of the business.

William James, aided by George Crite and L.D. McKnight, were transferring about eighteen hundred dollars from the rear of the club to be put in a safe at a nearby filling station.[2842] The automobile stood just a few feet from the rear door of the building. McKnight was just behind Crite with a bucket of money that had been handed him by the victim, who followed. Voices from behind or near an old piano box ordered "Hands up!" and the men beside the piano box began shooting into the ground.

James called to a woman inside the building to hand out his pistol. While he was waiting for it, he was shot in the side and died several hours later. Crite entered the automobile when the shooting began. McKnight ran behind the automobile and circled to the front of the building. William Brown, who was inside the dance hall, heard the shooting and ran to the rear. He came upon the woman with the pistol, took it, and retraced his steps to the front door. He ran around to the rear of the building where gunfire was underway. He fired four shots, ran back to his room inside to get another pistol, and returned to the rear, firing more shots.[2843] Brown shot at the fleeing men. One dropped the bucket of money he was carrying.[2844]

Willie Williams was the robber who was shot running away. He was positively identified by Crite and McKnight as one of the two robbers they recognized, the third being obscured by a shadow, but thought to be Buford Fishback. They were able to see because the area was illuminated by a floodlight. Brown offered confused testimony. He identified Williams, but said that codefendant Henry Crockett was a man he saw "running away and at a distance of fifty or seventy-five feet because it was a bright moonlight night."[2845] Brown was clearly wrong, confusing Fishback with Crockett. The defense offered an expert witness, a government meteorologist, R.M. Williamson, who said there was no moon that night.[2846]

Fishback, originally a codefendant, whose case was severed from that of Williams and Crockett, had fingered Crockett by implication. Fishback said that Williams had told him he was "going after the Silver Streak and left saying that he was going to Crockett's."[2847] Said the court, "No other circumstance implicates Crockett, who introduced evidence of an alibi that is not contradicted."[2848] The court ordered a new trial for Crockett. Several people testified Williams had told them he was "going after the Silver Streak." Later, he told some witnesses he had robbed the place the night before.

The chief evidence against Williams was his own arm. A female witness, one of two who slept with Williams the night after the shooting, saw the wound and saw him put soot on it to stop the blood. Another said it looked like a bullet hole.

In mid–June, Williams went to a doctor who treated the infected wound and said it looked like a bullet hole because it was a through-and-through wound.[2849] Williams explained he had punctured his arm on a nail in a barn, demonstrating for the jury how it happened. The Supreme Court affirmed the conviction and ordered him executed on March 15, 1939. Willie Williams was electrocuted at the Main Prison on April 15, 1939.

Williams walked his "last mile" after eating a last meal of sandwiches and soft drinks.[2850] Eager to draw attention to his plight, Williams staged a hunger strike until it was clear that Governor Cooper was not going to hear his plea for mercy.[2851] Williams's last statement, one of the few written statements from a Tennessee death row inmate about to be executed, said:

> To Whom It May Concern:
>
> I wish to warn all young boys and girls, and older folks too to stay out of bad company and go to church and live right. We don't know when sin will trip us up. I am not guilty of the charge of which I am to pay with my life, but I was framed by my so called friends. One of them pretended to be a preacher, but I pray that God will have mercy on him. I am sorry that the son of the man I am accused of killing made his boast that he brought me the chair. God have mercy on him and his soul in the judgement. I have never been able to understand how he was able to have this done as I was never in his father's place of business in my life, and God knows that I am telling the truth, as I would not dare tell anything else in an hour like this, as I know I am to pay with my life.
>
> I want to thank all the guards and all who came and spoke kind words to me while I have been in prison.
>
> The cause of all this was because of an old grudge, but I am going to a place where there is justice by a judge that does all things well. In my last statement I wish to say that I am innocent.
>
> Signed: Willie Williams.[2852]

After giving the statement and promising it would be given to the newspapers, Williams told Deputy Warden Glenn Swafford what happened. Williams said that he drove the getaway car, and the shooter came running back and jumped in the car. This person (unnamed) gave him $125 as they drove away and kept the rest, which Williams believed to be about $500.[2853] This story differed significantly from court testimony which showed the robbers made off with an iron box containing paper money and two buckets of coins, one of which was recovered in the field, where Williams dropped it when he was shot.[2854]

Harley Evans, white, age 26. *Murder.*

The crime was committed at 8:30 P.M. on March 15, 1938, in the business section of Jamestown, in largely rural Fentress County. The victims were town constable Oder Fowler, white, age thirty-six, and Ross Phillips, white, age fifty.

Evans had spent most of the day in a beer tavern and was intoxicated. He pulled a pistol and fired a shot into a wall. The sheriff was notified and a warrant was sworn out for Evans. Deputy Sheriff Robins and Constable Oder Fowler went looking for Evans to serve the warrant. Evans was seen driving his car around the town and the officers blew a whistle to stop him as he drove by. He ignored them.

When Evans finally returned to the business section he was confronted by the two lawmen. Told he was being arrested, Evans asked why. The officers took him under a street light to read the warrant to him. As Robins was reading the warrant, Fowler came up behind him as a backup. Without saying a word, Evans suddenly pulled out his pistol, reached around Robins, and fired one shot at close range. Fowler fell to the ground, writhing in pain.

Robins and Evans began to struggle. Evans shot Robins in the neck, but not seriously injuring him. As this was happening, Ross Phillips, a surveyor, came out of the tavern and rushed to cradle Fowler's head. Evans became enraged and told Phillips to get away and fired a warning shot in the air. The command was repeated and again ignored. Without giving Phillips further opportunity to get away, Evans shot and killed him instantly. When word got out about the killings, a mob formed and Evans was taken to the jail in Crossville for his safety.

Evans was indicted for the murder of both men, but went to trial first in the Fowler killing. The jury found him guilty and sentenced him to ninety-nine years, and he was immediately sent to prison. At his lawyer's request, the second trial was several times postponed, but he finally went to trial in January 1939. An issue on appeal was whether the delay was unreasonable, denying him a speedy trial. The Tennessee Supreme Court ruled it was not.[2855]

Evans claimed he lacked intent necessary to support a first-degree murder conviction because he was highly intoxicated. The Supreme Court said, "The great weight of the testimony is that he was drinking rather than drunk."[2856] He was sufficiently sober to drive his car, asked why he was being arrested, and after the shooting made statements to several witnesses that he had malice toward Fowler and other law officers in the Jamestown area. Moreover, he knew Phillips and was friendly enough with him to fire a warning shot before killing him without provocation. The killings were seen by witnesses who affirmed that Evans had consumed a "considerable amount of whiskey," but none described him as drunk.

Harley Evans was electrocuted on August 28, 1939. On that day, he was asked by the longtime prison chaplain the Rev. Pickens Johnson if he had anything he wanted to say to the boys in prison. Evans replied, "Tell 'em to do the best they can. Eff a man tries to kill 'em, kill him." When asked if he had anything against Fowler to justify killing him, Evans answered, "Oder Fowler was my best friend. I didn't have anything agin' him. He pecked my head [blackjacked him] an' took my pint. But I took his life."[2857] As his death neared, the young mountain man expressed confidence in his religious "conversion," admitting, "If I hadn't been charged, I'd a done hit agin," in his mountain vernacular.[2858]

As the death house was cleared, Evans told those leaving, including his weeping parents, "So long, I hope to meet you in the best place."[2859] However, as he sat in the electric chair, Evans noticed several men outside a window looking at him. He grinned and said, "You boys ain't doin' no good, are you?"[2860]

1940

Clyde Wills (aka Clyde Willis), white, age 29. *Rape.*

The crime was committed on the night of December 6, 1938, in South Knoxville, on Sherrod Road, in Knox County. The victim was Miss Elizabeth Merchant, white, age twenty-five. She was a nurse. Wills had a long criminal record for larceny, robbery and housebreaking. At the time he committed the crime, he was an escapee from the Main Prison in Nashville.[2861]

He was captured the day after the crime and quickly confessed.[2862] He was convicted on January 7, 1939. This conviction marked the first capital case his lawyer, noted defense counsel Arthur Atchley of Knoxville, had lost.

The Tennessee Supreme Court's opinion said: "In presenting the case at the bar of the court counsel stated very frankly that the defendant is clearly guilty, but earnestly appealed to the court to recommend a commutation to life imprisonment in the penitentiary on account of his mental deficiency."

The court said:

> On the night of December 6, 1938, Elizabeth Merchant, aged twenty-five years, her friend, Hope Miller, and two young men friends, Frank Pickens and Bill Pickens, were driving around the city of Knoxville in Miss Merchant's car. The moon was shining. They drove to South Knoxville and stopped the car on Sherrod Road, engaged in conversation, and observed the lights of the city. While the car was thus parked the defendant came down the bank with a drawn pistol, informed them that this was a holdup, and ordered them out of the car. When they got out he took fifty-one cents from one of the men and a wrist watch from the other one. He then had the two young ladies tie the hands of the men, and after this was done he made Miss Merchant tie the hands of Miss Miller. Thereupon he ordered them all back into the car, and entered it himself under the steering wheel with his pistol in his right hand and his left hand on the steering wheel. He drove them to a thicket on Brown's Mountain, in Knox County, stopped the car, and made them all get out and turn their backs to him.
>
> He then forced Miss Merchant to accompany him some 15 or 20 feet where, holding his pistol with one hand around her neck and raising her dress with the other hand, he had sexual intercourse with her, notwithstanding her bitter protest and weeping. He then drove the four back to the city, pointing out to them a house in which he said he lived. But he did not live there and evidently did that to throw them off his track. When the parties were discharged they went to a near-by dwelling, telephoned to friends to come after them, and upon their arrival Miss Merchant was driven to the office of a physician who administered to her. She had not fully recovered from her injury and shock when the case was tried a month later, and had only been able to engage in her work as a trained nurse a part of the time. Miss Merchant testified in detail as to the assault; her three companions fully corroborate her in every particular; and the physicians who examined and treated her testified that she had been ravished, and there is no testimony to the contrary.
>
> All four of the parties positively identify the defendant as the perpetrator of the crime. From pictures of criminals, including one of defendant which the officers exhibited to these parties, they all selected the one of defendant. When the officers went to the home of defendant's mother the next morning they found him hid in a clothes press. In the same place they also found the fifty-one cents and the wrist watch. They also recovered the pistol used the night before which defendant had taken from an officer.
>
> The defendant did not testify on the trial, and introduced no testimony tending to contradict that of the State as to his identity or as to the

commission of the crime. At the time of this offense the defendant was an escaped convict from the penitentiary in Nashville. He was serving his third term in that institution. He stated to Doctor Hill that he had been incarcerated three times for larceny, robbery, and housebreaking.

Hubert Lytz, a state parole officer, testified that a few days before defendant committed the assault upon Miss Merchant he arrested him in the L & N Yards in Knoxville on a charge of trespass; that he was looking for defendant but he gave him another name; that while taking defendant to his home, 706 West Cumberland Avenue, to be identified, defendant attacked him, whereupon he drew his pistol which defendant took away from him and made his escape. This is the same pistol which the officers obtained when they arrested defendant the morning after he assaulted Miss Merchant.

James Wright testified that he is a switchman at the L & N Yards, and while on duty about a week before defendant's attack upon Miss Merchant he held him up at the point of a pistol and robbed him. The record does not show the age of defendant. His brother, who is twenty-two years old, testified that defendant was the older. His counsel stated at bar that he was twenty-nine years old. He has a wife and a child. From the foregoing it will be seen that defendant is an habitual criminal and a menace to society. The record rather indicates that he is also a sex pervert.

The test in this state as to one's responsibility for crime is his ability to distinguish right from wrong and to realize the consequences of his act. *Davis v. State*, 161 Tenn. 23; *McElroy v. State*, 146 Tenn. 442; *Watson v. State*, 133 Tenn. 198; *Bond v. State*, 129 Tenn. 75; *Wilcox v. State*, 94 Tenn. 106. Applying this test in the present case, the overwhelming weight of the testimony is to the effect that defendant knows right from wrong.

Dr. Jesse Hill, a psychiatrist who has specialized in mental and nervous diseases for twenty-three years, and who was psychiatrist at the Eastern State Hospital near Knoxville for seventeen years, examined defendant on two occasions, giving him every known test in order to determine his mental condition, and concluded by saying:

> Well, as to his early habits they were normal and diseases of childhood, ordinary, and diseases of later life, colds, flu and he has gonorrhea at the present time. He knows where he is, and knows the time of day and realizes he is in a bad situation, his judgment at the present time is good, his memory is good for both recent and remote times, he has no hallucinations or delusions except two or three about his rupture and stomach, that is, he thinks that the rupture causes pain in his stomach, that is what you would call hypochondrial.

Dr. Hill was asked this question:

> Q: And I desire to ask you, doctor, from all your investigations and examinations and the questions that he answered for you, would you say he knew right from wrong?
>
> A: I would say that he does know right from wrong, and he did know.

Dr. R.R. Wood, another psychiatrist, examined defendant the day after he assaulted the prosecutrix, and testified as follows:

> Q: State whether or not in your opinion, from his actions and conduct and demeanor, is he sane or insane?
>
> A: I would consider him a sane man.
>
> Q: Did or not in your opinion, did he know and understand right from wrong?
>
> A: I think so.

Dr. Smith, the jail physician, who was present during a portion of Dr. Hill's observation of defendant, testifies that in his opinion defendant knows right from wrong.

The trial court had Dr. Sam H. Hodge of Knoxville, who has been engaged in the general practice of medicine for thirty-two years, to examine the defendant, and this physician stated that he was a moron, and defined a moron as one "whose mentality is not up to the average person."

Dr. Hodge testified that he had considerable experience with mental cases, and while he did not consider himself an expert on insanity he believed his training would permit him to testify above the average physician. He further testified that in his opinion defendant knows right from wrong. This witness made the further statement that "from this man's physical condition and his development of the brain, he might have what we call a sex urge, that is common to all animals and he, his intelligence being taken into consideration, while he knows right from wrong he has not the ability to confine his acts as easily as a man who has intelligence and coupled along with strength, and this therefore leaves him handicapped in his condition to where a normal intelligent man would more easily meet the circumstances, I think that is in the interest of justice and I think entirely proper to say." Quite a number of lay witnesses who have talked to and observed defendant gave it as their opinion that he knows right from wrong.

Opposed to the foregoing testimony is that of the father, mother, brother, sister, and brother-in-law of defendant[, who say he] does not know right from wrong. Some of them testify as to injuries defendant received as a child, as to his inability to learn at school, and as to peculiarities which he exhibited. It does not appear, however, that he was ever treated for any mental troubles; that any effort was ever made to have him placed in an institution for one so afflicted, or to have him confined so as to restrain him from committing wrongs against society. Neither do these relatives show that when he was tried for his other crimes that any effort was made to prove that he was not mentally responsible for his act.

There are several incidents appearing in the record from which counsel for defendant argue that he is insane. On the other hand, counsel for the state refers to a number of circumstances which he states demonstrate the sanity of defendant. These contentions offset each other and are not of enough importance to merit a detailed discussion. Upon the important question of criminal responsibility, we can but repeat that the evidence preponderates in favor on the verdict. That, primarily, is a matter for the determination of the jury and the judge.

The defendant was accorded a fair trial by an impartial jury. In addition to the evidence introduced on behalf of the state and the defendant, the trial judge, in order to fully satisfy himself as to the mental status of the defendant, had an able, conscientious, and unbiased physician to examine the defendant; and his testimony most likely impressed the trial judge as it has the members of this court, the substance of which is that while the mentality of the defendant is below that of the average person, he nevertheless knows right from wrong. According to the testimony of Dr. Hill, the defendant realizes that he has committed a horrible crime, and stated that he expected to escape the consequences thereof by pleading insanity. Criminals of this class are usually below the average person in intelligence.

The court concluded, "The defendant was represented by able counsel who have made a strong appeal to this court for recommendation or commutation or punishment, but, after carefully reading the testimony and giving it thoughtful consideration, we are unable to accede to this request. There is no error in the record; the assignments of error are overruled; the judgment of the trial court is affirmed; and the date of execution fixed for Wednesday, January 10, 1940."[2863]

Wills was electrocuted on the assigned day. He maintained his innocence to the last. Baptized a Catholic a few days before his execution, Wills told prison officials to tell young people "to read the Bible and do as it says." He said, "If I had read the Bible, I wouldn't be here now."[2864] His final request was that a prison quartet sing hymns as he was taken to the electric chair. It was granted.

Asa Caldwell Mobley (aka A.C. Mobley), black, age 33. *Rape.*

The crime was committed in the late evening of September 1, 1938, on Lakeview Boulevard, outside of Riverside Park in Shelby County. The victim was Miss Eloise Brown, white, age twenty. Mobley, very light-skinned, was generally called a mulatto. He had a distinctive appearance because his right eyelid drooped, virtually covering the eye. Married with three children, he could not write his name at the time he was brought to the prison on February 2, 1940.[2865] At trial, Mobley strongly denied raping the woman. He admitted robbing her and shooting her companion.

Here is the Tennessee Supreme Court opinion:

A.C. Mobley was charged by indictment with having carnal knowledge of Eloise Brown forcibly and against her will. The evidence shows that on the evening of September 1, 1938, Miss Eloise Brown and Forrest Darnell were returning about 11:00 P.M. from Riverside Park, just south of the City of Memphis, where they had been to eat a watermelon, and after turning the automobile coupe in which they were riding into Lakewood Boulevard, and while traveling at a slow rate of speed, a man armed with a pistol, with a flashlight, and with a handkerchief over his face, from the nose down, jumped on the left running board of the car and ordered Darnell, who was driving, to pull over to the side of the road, which he did. After robbing Darnell of ten cents (all the money he had with him) and robbing Miss Brown of her purse, wrist watch, and two rings, and searching the car, he proceeded to rape Miss Brown, according to the testimony of Miss Brown and Mr. Darnell. The testimony of Miss Brown establishes the facts necessary to constitute the crime of rape.

Mr. Darnell, notwithstanding this man menaced him with the cocked pistol and threatened him with death, got a pair of pliers out of the car while this man was taking a cushion out of the car, and struck at him with the pliers while he was in the act of raping Miss Brown, and grabbed him and they fell to fighting in the ditch and this man shot Darnell three times, once through the left side of the neck, under the ear, the bullet passing through the neck and coming out under the chin, once in the shoulder and once in the leg, and then walked fast down the road. He had stolen the keys of the car, so that it could not be operated. Mr. Darnell was bleeding and Miss Brown thought he was dying. They cut across a field and went to the house of a negro, who took them to the home of another negro, who got his shotgun and took them to a place down the road to the nearest telephone and they called Miss Brown's brother-in-law, who came and took them to a hospital. It does not appear that Miss Brown was examined by a physician.

Miss Brown testified that the only way she could tell that her assailant was a negro was that he smelled like a negro and talked like one. Both she and Mr. Darnell described this man as about six feet tall, weight about 180 or 190 pounds, wearing dark trousers, a light colored hunting coat and a cap with a bill. Miss Brown says he was a light complected negro. She pointed out defendant, on the trial as the man she saw that night. Mr. Darnell says he was about twenty-six or twenty-seven years old and was of a similar type of man as defendant; that defendant looks like the man out there that night and resembles him very much, but could not be sure of his identification.

Defendant testified in his own behalf and admitted that he was the man who robbed Miss Brown and Mr. Darnell on the night in question, but denied the rape. But, outside of his admission of the crime of highway robbery, there is abundant proof that he is the man who held up this automobile.

Later, on the night in question, Miss Brown accompanied certain officers to the scene of the crime, and the officers found the assailant's cap and flashlight. They took this cap and talked to the different people in the neighborhood to ascertain if they had seen a negro wearing it. From a description of the man wearing the cap, the officers knew it was the defendant, Mobley, and began looking for him. They first went to the neighborhood where he lived and ascertained that he had not been home. They then went to defendant's house and searched the house, and in the wood shed, about twenty feet behind the house, they found under a big pile of wood, a hunting coat buried in the ground, and in the pocket of that coat a beaded bag. On the trial, Miss Brown identified this bag as the purse forcibly taken from her in the robbery. Likewise, Mr. Darnell identified the purse. The officers also found at defendant's house a pair of blue corduroy trousers, patched on the knees, hanging on the wash line in the yard; they had been washed. The witness, Mary Brown, colored, identified these trousers as the ones worn by defendant on the afternoon of the day in question.

The officers set about looking for defendant, and he was finally apprehended at the home of his cousins, near Marks, Mississippi, by the sheriff of that county. In making the arrest, defendant was shot as he came out of the back door of the house and, when called on to stop, fired one shot at the officers. The sheriff recovered from the house a lumber jacket and some cartridges belonging to defendant, also a homemade pistol scabbard. In the pocket of the jacket, or coat, the sheriff found some jewelry, wrapped in a piece of white tissue paper. This jewelry consisted of a wrist watch and two rings. Both Miss Brown and Mr. Darnell identified this jewelry as having been taken from Miss Brown by their assailant on the night in question.

Certain witnesses (colored) testified that they had seen defendant, on the afternoon of the day the crime was committed, in the general locality, or no great distance, from the scene of the crime. When seen by these witnesses, defendant was wearing an old straw hat.

As before stated, defendant in both a written confession and while testifying in the case freely admitted holding up this automobile and robbing these parties. However, he denied raping Miss Brown. He admitted shooting Mr. Darnell. He says that Mr. Darnell "grabbed" him and jabbed him in the face with some pliers and that they struggled in the ditch and that is why he shot Mr. Darnell. The jury could have found it was highly improbable that Mr. Darnell would attack this armed negro for no other reason than that a negro had robbed him of ten cents and had robbed Miss Brown of a little jewelry. The good character and reputation of Miss Brown and Mr. Darnell stands unquestioned.

No reason is suggested, or can be reasonably imagined why these parties would frame up a story of rape, when none took place. The narration of the facts of this shocking crime, by Miss Brown and Mr. Darnell is too much in detail and too convincing to admit the suggestion of fabrication. The jury saw and heard these parties testify and could judge of their credibility. The trial judge approved the verdict. By no stretch of the imagination could it be said that the evidence preponderates in favor of defendant. The defendant had a fair trial before an impartial jury and judge. He was represented by the public defender, an able lawyer. All of the assignments of error must be overruled and the judgment of the trial court affirmed. The judgment of this court is that defendant, A.C. Mobley, be put to death by electrocution in the manner provided by law on Friday, March 15, 1940, A.D.[2866]

Mobley was executed on the day set. As the hour of his death neared, Mobley dictated a confession which was written down by Deputy Warden Glenn Swafford. It said, "As the man and woman drove beside a hedge and stopped, I crawled behind the hedge and when the man got out of the car I searched him and found one nickel. I then removed the front seat of the car and found two rings and a wrist watch."[2867]

Mobley's confession said that he attempted to rape the woman, but failed when her companion struck him and "we rolled down the dump." He continued, "I shot him somewhere in the shoulder or neck one time and then jumped up and ran. I don't know what was wrong with me to make me want to ravage the woman. At first I just meant to rob them. I didn't have any job and was out to pick up someone."[2868] The newspaper reported that Mobley's execution "emptied" death row.[2869]

William Henry (aka Clay Nelson), white, age 44. *Murder.*

The crime was committed about 5:30 P.M. on December 8, 1939, in a rural part of Dyer County, near the unincorporated town of Chic, which is situated on the Mississippi River. The killer, known to his neighbors as Clay Nelson, was a cotton tenant farmer whose land abutted that of the victim, Frank Boyd, white, age fifty-four, another tenant farmer. The two had argued over the ownership of some pecan trees which bordered their property. A week before the shooting, the landowner had asked two men to run a line marking the boundary. It showed the trees were on the Boyd property. At the time of the killing, the victim had sworn out a criminal trespass warrant on the killer, but the warrant had not been served. There was a dispute at trial over whether the defendant knew about the existence of the warrant.

The victim was in his tenant farmhouse with his two daughters, Juanita, age sixteen, and Helen, age fourteen. According to one of them, the defendant appeared outside in the yard and began calling for the victim, and demanded that he come outside. The only distinct words the girls heard were, "Have you got your burial paid up with Curry?"[2870] Three to five pistol shots rang out. When the girls found their father on the ground and carried him into the house, he had been hit in the chest with three bullets and was dead within minutes. The killer ran off toward the river.

The initial investigation cast suspicion on a neighbor named Elliot,[2871] who was seen drunk and angry at Boyd on the day and evening of the killing because Boyd had refused to allow Elliot to come courting Juanita. The investigation also turned to Nesbitt,[2872] who admitted he had owned a .38 caliber pistol, the size bullet that had killed Boyd. Nesbitt's alleged motive was that Boyd had attempted to be too friendly with Nesbitt's wife in the year since Mrs. Boyd had died.

Tracking the killer became confused because the sheriff's posse had seen two boats (skiffs) at various times on the river bank, but at times only one was present. One of the boats was known to belong to Elliot, and at various times both men said they had helped Henry to cross the river. But the times conflicted with each other and were prior to the killing, which would have cleared Henry of the killing.

Detailed questioning of the neighbors raised the suspicion that Boyd had made amorous advances to Elliot's wife and to Mrs. Nesbitt. This, plus the discovery of the warrant, turned suspicion on Henry, who had disappeared. With Elliot and Nesbit in jail, the sheriff had another inmate watch for any unusual mail addressed to one of them. When a letter from "Joe Cox," postmarked Hornersville, Missouri, a short distance across the river, arrived for one of the men, the sheriff was alerted. The sheriff went to Hornersville and watched the post office and arrested William Henry. Confronted with the evidence so far, Elliot and Nesbitt eagerly gave statements that Henry had threatened to kill Boyd, citing the pecan tree dispute, and the outstanding warrant. According to one of the men, Henry said, "I am going over there and see him about this. These fellows just try to run things to suit themselves, and I am going over there to see him. If he has a warrant out for me, I will kill him sure as paper, I mean, powder will burn."[2873]

The trial began in Dyersburg on February 14, 1940, and ended ten days later. Henry steadfastly denied any involvement until the trial, when he asserted that the reason he shot the victim was that Boyd had made advances towards his wife. She testified that Boyd had come over to her house when her husband was gone and propositioned her, and at one time tried to kiss her and tore her dress.[2874] Mrs. Nelson could not say for sure when this had happened ("sometime when the water was up," meaning spring 1939), and claimed she told her husband about this for the first time on the afternoon of the shooting. Another neighbor, Mary Tye, was present when the words were spoken, but on the witness stand she collapsed under cross-examination, "Lord, I'm going to faint. I know I am. I am sick." She fainted. She was excused after a doctor said she was having a hemorrhage and threatened miscarriage.[2875]

Other neighbors testified about Henry's threats to kill Boyd because of trouble over the pecan trees, and several heard Henry talk about or show them the pistol (the murder weapon) that was found in a phonograph record box hidden underneath Henry's house.

Henry asserted on the stand that the reason he shot Boyd was that he was angry about his advances on his wife, that there was no dispute about pecan trees, that he never threatened Boyd and did not know about a warrant.[2876] Henry described the last confrontation in terms of self-defense. He said that Boyd had bent down coming off the porch and came up with his hand behind him and was advancing in a threatening manner. Henry was retreating and said, "Don't follow me," after which Boyd said, "I will get you now." At this point, "I turned and shot him," as Boyd was advancing, shooting five shots. Asked why he shot him, Henry answered, "Because of the way he talked to my wife." Henry then described an unspecified mental condition: "I suffer a lot of times, I had a busted skull."[2877]

The chief issue on appeal was whether the jury instruction, which used the term "mental attitude," fairly allowed the jury to consider whether the killing was made with "heated blood," which would have allowed conviction for a lesser degree of homicide. The court found that the trial court had actually granted a special request on the issue of Henry's state of mind after hearing the "insulting remarks and conduct" of the victim, and there was no error.[2878] The court observed that defendant had served a sentence in prison for larceny and that Boyd had a "good reputation for peace and quietitude."[2879]

William Henry went to the electric chair on the morning of September 4, 1940. The night before, he and James "Trigger Slim" Goodin, had to choose between roast beef and fried chicken for their last meal. They chose chicken. Henry was executed first.[2880]

James "Trigger Slim" Goodin, black, age 22. *Murder.*

The crime was committed on October 30, 1939, at a liquor store at 1286 Florida Street in Memphis, Shelby County. The victim was Raymond J. Payne, white, age forty-nine, who was variously described as a "village blacksmith" and an employee of the liquor store.[2881] Goodin, who had an extensive criminal record, began the day by holding up a liquor store at Arkansas Street and Virginia Avenue that morning. The owner's daughter, Kay Rutsky, had smashed a wine bottle on his free hand as he reached toward the cash register. With a bloodied hand, Goodin ran outside. Two truck drivers gave chase. He fired two shots from his pistol and escaped.

Later that afternoon, Goodin came to the Florida Street liquor store and pulled his pistol on clerk Morris Gerber. After taking $18 from the cash register, Goodin robbed two customers who walked into the store at that moment. He struck one in the face, sending him to the floor in a pool of blood. Gerber was ordered to pick out a pack of cigarettes and give them to Goodin, who told him, "If I don't like the brand, I'll gut shoot you." Liking the cigarettes, Goodin made the same demand regarding a half pint of whiskey, saying, "Drink it down. Every drop or I'll gut shoot you."[2882] Gerber complied.

At this moment, store owner Bob Cartmell and his friend Ray Payne appeared at the store entrance, having been alerted that a holdup was underway. Goodin raced toward the much larger Payne and struck him in the face with the pistol. But the burly blacksmith did not fall. Pushing him aside, Goodin dashed to the street, saying, "Out of the way, I've killed bigger ones than you!"[2883] Payne gave chase and was shot in the abdomen, falling to the sidewalk. He died the next morning. Payne gave police a description of Goodin, a slight, very light-skinned black man. Police thought the shooter might be a white man who may have put walnut stain on his face to appear as a Negro.

Two nights before the killing, three black men had fired their weapons into the air after robbing the patrons of the Willow Grove, a black nightclub. Police were on the lookout for two, one whose nickname was "Stack the Dollars," and the other "Draper." When finally arrested, they identified the third robber by his nickname, "Trigger Slim." They claimed not to know his real name, but they told police he bragged about hiding out on President's Island. Police went there and were told that "Trigger Slim's" last name was Goodin and his family's home was on Indiana Street in Memphis.

About two weeks later, a man meeting the description of "Trigger Slim" held up another liquor store on Georgia Street, but was thwarted because the owners had a hidden guard who followed Goodin out into the street and fired a shotgun at him, causing him to drop the money.

Ten days later, a stakeout on the Goodin family house spotted Goodin walk by the house but proceed on toward Beale Street's Palace Theater. Goodin went in and was watching the gangster movie *Dark Manhattan* for the second time when he was surrounded by four detectives.[2884] Goodin had told friends he would never be taken alive. Police snatched a pistol he was holding in his lap.[2885]

The Tennessee Supreme Court's opinion said:

> [Goodin] appeals from a conviction of murder with sentence of death. He admits the killing of Raymond Payne, an employee of a liquor store in Memphis, on the night of October 30, 1939, while escaping from this store after a holdup and robbery of the man in charge. Several witnesses positively identify him as the robber and murderer. There is no dispute about the facts. The plaintiff-in-error had a bad criminal record and is quite evidently a desperado. We find no reason for suggesting commutation of his sentence.
>
> One or two questions are raised in his behalf, mainly that his rights were invaded in receiving

> and failing to set aside his plea of guilty. In the first place, it is shown that he had counsel and acted voluntarily; and, in the second place, was later put to trial before a jury he was permitted to enter a plea of not guilty. In no manner or event was he prejudiced. We find no error in the charge of the Court. The proof showed that the robbery had been completed in the store and the accused was escaping when he shot Payne, who was attempting to intercept him, but this does not excuse or reduce the offense for murder in the first degree, and the Court properly so charged.

The court concluded, "There is no error and the judgment is affirmed. James Goodin, alias Goodman, alias Trigger Slim, will be committed to the State Prison and there be confined until Friday, the 2nd day of August 1940, when he will be put to death between legal hours by the State Warden in the manner provided by law."[2886]

Goodin and William Henry (Clay Nelson), white, also of west Tennessee, were executed on the same day, September 4, 1940, after the governor had given them each three reprieves in order to study their cases. "They seemed resigned to their fate and both professed religion," said Warden Thomas P. Gore. The two could not make up their minds about a last meal, whether roast beef or chicken, and finally chose the latter.[2887] Goodin was executed second.

1941

Van Gilmore (aka Van "Circus" Gilmore), black, age 32. *Rape.*

The crime was committed at 10:30 P.M. April 17, 1940, on Huguenot Street in Memphis, Shelby County. It was raining heavily. Mrs. Grace Manley, white, age twenty-five, was driving her car, and her husband's nephew, Pat Manley, age unknown, was the passenger. When she stopped the car at some railroad tracks it stalled and could not be restarted. As she was attempting to get it started, Gilmore suddenly appeared. Brandishing what appeared to be a gun, he opened the passenger door and ordered Pat Manley out of the car, saying, "Stick them up!" Pat gave him his money. Gilmore then came around to Mrs. Manley's side, pulled her out of the car, took her to a nearby field and raped her.[2888] During the struggle her arm was broken. Gilmore ran away.

Pat Manley ran to summon police and they arrived promptly. Mrs. Manley was taken to a hospital where the rape was confirmed. The police immediately suspected Gilmore. He had been indicted for rape on August 19, 1939, and was a suspect in several other rapes on both white and black women.

Police went to his home and arrested him at 3:00 A.M. on April 18 and he was taken to the police station. Later, he was placed in two lineups and was identified by both the Manleys. He began confessing, gave several confessions, including one taken by a stenographer and signed by three witnesses. He denied any penetration, a defense he maintained throughout the trial. In his confessions he said no pistol was brandished, only a monkey wrench. He took police to where he had thrown the wrench and it was recovered. He told the police where his cap was hidden. It was found still wet. Gilmore went to trial on May 7, 1940.

On the witness stand, Gilmore admitted taking Mrs. Manley to the field for the purpose of "using" her (his words), but denied any penetration. On cross-examination he admitted penetration, at least to the extent of penile contact with her labia.[2889]

He was cross-examined about other rapes. When asked how many women he had raped since the prior spring, he replied, "Just only five."[2890] He admitted being indicted for raping Mrs. Viola L. League, white, age forty-three. She was in the courtroom and was asked to stand up. Gilmore identified her and admitted raping and robbing her. A black woman was asked to stand up. Gilmore said, "She gave it to me."[2891] He could not remember the names of the other two black women he had raped. The jury took eight minutes to decide his fate.[2892]

The cross-examination was challenged on appeal. The Tennessee Supreme Court said that when a defendant takes the stand he can be impeached in the same manner as any other witness and be "questioned about special acts of moral turpitude."[2893] He can invoke the privilege of refusing to answer when the matters involve self-incrimination. "It was not error to permit defendant to be interrogated as to other crimes involving moral turpitude."[2894]

The court ordered him executed on April 18, 1941. This was a year and a day after the crime and he was executed that day. The newspaper did not report any details about his last meal or words.[2895] Prison records indicate that Gilmore had willed his body to Vanderbilt Medical School.[2896]

Walter Reed, black, age 55. *Murder.*

The crime was committed about noon on April 12, 1941, in the home Mrs. Jane Fowler Cathey, white, age thirty-five, shared with her husband, at 1413 Hixon Pike, in a residential section north of Chattanooga, in Hamilton County. The victim was Mrs. Cathey, a housewife, who was alone. Reed had worked as a yard man for the couple, but had been terminated by the husband, superintendent of the Chattanooga Traction Company, who nevertheless offered him a ride to town when he appeared at the home that morning. Mrs. Cathey did not expect to see Reed when he returned to the home about noon. Reed had been convicted of the first-degree murder of his wife and was imprisoned in Georgia from September 19, 1919, to March 23, 1932, when he finished his sentence. He had also killed a schoolmate as a youngster but was acquitted. Reed was described as a "slight, small inoffensive looking Negro."[2897]

Reed came to the back door. According to his confession, he was under the influence of alcohol and flew into a rage when the victim "fussed" at him because of the alcohol. He picked up a miniature baseball bat on the back porch which belonged to the couple's twelve-year-old daughter. He struck Mrs. Cathey on the back of the head, she ran, he struck her several more times. The room was covered in blood, his fingerprints were found in the room, including a blood-spattered drinking glass she had offered him before the killing. Photographs of her battered and partially clad body were shown the jury. Reed did not take the stand. Several witnesses saw him near the house before and after the killing and blood was found on his shirt and pants when captured.

Reed was caught walking down a Georgia road three days later. He never denied the killing but maintained he could not remember committing it because he was, in his words, "crazy drunk" at the time.[2898] At trial, his court-appointed lawyers could not find a doctor to testify that Reed could not tell right from wrong at the time of the killing, but a doctor testified that Reed was a "lepto-cephalic," meaning he had a small, flat, elongated and egg-shaped head whose bone structure prevented the proper development of brain cells. The defense theory was that Reed was a man of limited intelligence who could not be held criminally responsible "if his mind was inflamed by liquor at the time of the crime."[2899]

His trial began on May 14 and lasted three days. The jury took nineteen minutes to convict Reed, who did not appeal his case. Reed declined to talk to the newspapers. Speaking only to prison officials, he said he was "ready to go," and he was electrocuted July 18, 1941.[2900]

Lee Willie Porter, black, age 21. *Murder.*
Carl Leonard Cole, black, age 23. *Murder.*

The crime was committed on the night of August 9, 1940, at the Jackson Bottling Company, in Jackson, Madison County. The company was a Coca-Cola bottler. Cole worked at the plant. The victim, Grant Vernon, white, age fifty-seven, was the night watchman. As the pair was attempting to burglarize the building, they were caught by Vernon. A struggle ensued and Vernon was bludgeoned to death so that he could not identify the pair, especially Cole.

Deliverymen who returned in the late afternoon or early evening turned their proceeds over to Vernon, who put them into a cash drawer. It was kept locked but Vernon had a key. The killers climbed over an eight-foot fence, hid in the garage and waited for Vernon. Just after he arrived, they struck him on the head twice with an iron bar, took his keys and pistol, removed three hundred dollars from the cash drawer and dashed away. Among the money taken were two rolls of nickels stamped with the name of the bottler.

Porter and his wife lived near the bottling works and suspicion fell on him because she began spending money, "much more than her economic condition would justify."[2901] Arrested the day after the killing, Porter was interrogated from ten-thirty that night and "continuing intermittently until four o'clock the next morning."[2902] At this point, Porter said he had seen Cole near the bottling works with some money sacks and Cole had given him ten dollars not to tell on him.

Porter took police to his home and showed them where he had hidden thirty-eight dollars, including the rolls of nickels. He also showed them the pistol taken from Vernon and where the iron bar could be found. "Porter was born out of wedlock, his reputed father died in the penitentiary. He only attended school a few months and was considered a backward pupil. One witness testified that he was a waif upon the streets of Jackson."[2903] Porter had served a year in reform school when he was fifteen. He had swung the iron bar.

Cole vigorously denied guilt until confronted with Porter's written confession. He then confessed. Each insisted the other had struck the fatal blows. The Tennessee Supreme Court found no errors in the trial including the refusal of the judge to answer a jury question about whether the defendants, if sentenced to ninety-nine years, could be pardoned in ten or fifteen years.[2904] The Supreme Court called the killing "one of the most brutal that we have been called upon to consider," and ordered the pair executed on July 24, 1941.[2905] Both died at the Main Prison in Nashville that day.[2906]

Porter, who was executed first, attempted to exonerate Cole, doing so while seated in the electric chair. The pair had agreed that whoever went first (neither knowing until the morning of the execution) would attempt to take entire blame for the killing, in order to buy time for a possible commutation.

Lawrence West, black, age 16. *Murder.*

The crime was committed shortly after dark on February 4, 1941, on the rural farm of Mr. and Mrs. Robert Davidson in Montgomery County. The victims were Robert Davidson, white, age seventy-six, and his wife, Adeline "Addie" Davidson, white, age seventy-four. The killer was "sixteen or seventeen years" old, according to the Tennessee Supreme Court's opinion, and was known to the couple because he and his father had previously cut wood and performed other chores for them.[2907] The West family lived on a neighboring farm.

On the afternoon of the shooting, the couple's daughter, Elizabeth "Etha" Davidson, white, age twenty-seven, had come home in the afternoon from her job working at a doctor's office and found West sitting in the house talking to her mother, Addie Davidson. He had brought a jar of molasses to trade for a half gallon of pickles. When the mother went outside, West sexually propositioned Etha, who told him, "The best thing for you to do is to get up and go home."[2908] West asked when did the father come home and from which direction did he come, saying, "I don't want to meet him." When the mother returned with the pickles, Etha told West, "Don't you ever come back here anymore."[2909]

About seven that evening, Mrs. Davidson went outside to the henhouse and a shot rang out. Mrs. Davidson called out, "Lawrence has shot me from behind the smokehouse where he was hid." Mr. Davidson ran outside and started to lift his wife, saying, "Don't shoot no more. You have already killed the old lady!"[2910] West shot the father. By this time, Etha came from the house and saw West standing by a post near the smokehouse. He ran up the road.

Etha assisted her parents into the house, where her father fell across a bed. Within minutes, West appeared on the front porch, broke out a windowpane, and shot at Etha through the window. He pushed the door open, holding the gun behind him as she begged him to leave.

West said, "Hush, so damn much hallooing," and threatened to shoot again. Then he said, "Come over here, sweetheart, and hug and kiss me and I won't shoot no more." The father said, "Who is that?" Etha said it was Lawrence. The father said, "Lawrence, what made you do it?" Lawrence gave no answer and left.[2911]

The couple had been shot with West's .22 rifle. Mrs. Davidson had been hit in the hip but the bullet had penetrated her bladder. It was not until the next morning that Etha was allowed by her parents to call the police or a doctor. When Dr. R.L. Morris arrived he found the victims in beds, but Mrs. Davidson refused to be taken to a hospital. Attended by her daughter, she died at home about three o'clock on the morning of February 6, 1941. Mr. Davidson had been shot through the biceps with the bullet entering about an inch below his heart. He died in the hospital.[2912]

The morning after the shooting, Joe West, the boy's father, appeared at the Davidson house saying he was ready to cut wood, and was surprised to learn that his son, who was missing, had shot the family. He was the person sent to get the doctor. In court, he said that while on his way to a daughter's house, he found the murder weapon beside railroad tracks and turned it over to the sheriff.

Lawrence West was arrested on February 6, 1941, in Erin. He told different accounts to several different law officers. His primary reason for shooting Mr. Davidson was that he owed him $1.20 and was being "crowded" by him for it. To another, he implied that shooting the man was self-defense because Mr. Davidson was going back into the house to get his shotgun. He denied breaking the window and shooting into the house. (One of the panes was recently broken, according to the sheriff.).

West never gave any reason for shooting Mrs. Davidson, and the conviction that resulted in his death penalty involved only her murder. He was never tried for killing the husband.

Two issues permeated the trial. Etha had an out-of-wedlock son, age six, who was present but did not see the shooting. Several witnesses were asked if they had heard any "talk" of a relationship between West and Etha. The questioning backfired as both the doctor and a deputy sheriff said no. The doctor said he had heard that West attempted to assault a white girl a year or so before, and the deputy said he had arrested West on an attempted assault charge involving a white girl named Turner. The case was dropped on payment of the costs.[2913] Etha insisted that no relationship ever existed, and that West made no attempt to touch or harm her, aside from propositioning her.

The second issue was Lawrence West's age. The father testified that he could find no birth certificate for his son, but had recorded the birth dates of his children on a piece of paper (which he forgot to bring to court). He said Lawrence was born September 24, 1924, making him sixteen years and four months old at the time of the shootings. The elderly black midwife who attended the birth said that her birth record book had been destroyed in a fire in her home, but she offered a piece of tablet leaf with the September 24, 1924, date on it, saying that was Lawrence's birthday. Public school records showed him born in various years, ranging from 1923 to 1925. Etha said she had heard West tell others that he was nineteen shortly before the shooting.

West did not testify on his own behalf, and his lawyers urged compassion, by stressing the young man's age. The issue of West's age was not raised on appeal, except in a mercy plea to the Tennessee Supreme Court.

The court was unmoved. It said:

> In the present case the defendant went to the home of the deceased with a deadly weapon. The language used before the killing in the presence of and addressed to Miss Etha Davidson clearly showed his motives. He later returns to a point near the house and there lies in wait until Mrs. Davidson goes to her yard in the nighttime and then in a concealed place and while so lying in wait shot her and this wound resulted in her death. He had expressed malice towards her father and he had also used very reprehensible language toward Miss Davidson, and there was no doubt of his purpose to take the life of Mrs. Davidson and also Mr. Davidson to the end that he might effectuate his purposes on Miss Davidson.[2914]

The execution was set for July 30, 1941.

On July 8, 1941, prison warden Thomas P. Gore wrote Governor Prentice Cooper, urging him to commute the sentence to life imprisonment. Gore had asked the Attorney General's office to see if there was a birth certificate on file for West and there was. It showed he was born on October 25, 1924, and was therefore sixteen years old. Gore, a lawyer, explained that the prison held another inmate whose sentence was commuted by the Tennessee Supreme Court, quoting the opinion:

> We are disinclined, however, to affirm these death sentences owing to the extreme youth of the plaintiffs in error. The record shows that Edwards was seventeen years old at the time of the murder, and Coleman was seventeen years old. Lott who was doubtless in front and did not participate in the actual shooting was two years older, or nineteen at the time of the shooting. A judgment of this Court directing that all these young boys be put to death would smack too much of an order of King Herod. The execution of such youthful offenders tends to shock the sensibilities, and in our opinion would not be calculated to promote respect for the law.[2915]

Gore continued, "The opinion was written by Chief Justice Grafton Green in the case of *State v. Kissiah Edwards, et al.* Having the respect I do for any opinion written by Judge Green, I thought you would not object to my calling this to your attention in this particular case."[2916] The warden concluded, "In the absence of any instructions from you, this prisoner will be electrocuted July 30, 1941."[2917]

Governor Prentice Cooper visited West a week before the July 30, 1941, execution and said he found no reason for extending clemency. The newspaper reported that West was seventeen years old, but did not feature that issue, nor did it say anything about his last meal or words, other than he admitted the slayings.[2918]

1942

Roy Walden, white, age 36. *Rape of a child under age of twelve.*

The crime was committed at 3:40 A.M. on September 9, 1940, at a home located at 4424 Kingston Pike, about one and one-half miles west of the city of Knoxville, in the community of Bearden, in Knox County. The rapist was known to the victim's parents because he delivered baked goods to their business, the Canary Café, located about one thousand feet from their home.[2919] The victim was the daughter of Mr. and Mrs. Wesley Sorrell, lunchroom owners. She was Nancy Ruth Sorrell, white, age eight and one-half.

The rapist lived with his father in a house at 4514 Kingston Pike, two blocks from the Sorrell home. He was divorced, and his former wife and children lived in Cincinnati. He had known the Sorrell family for several years and was familiar with their habits.

At eight-thirty at night on September 8, 1940, a café employee walked Nancy Ruth to her parents' home and put her to bed. She was left alone in the house. Walden arrived at the café about ten minutes before it closed at 2:00 A.M. Between then and 3:10 A.M. he drank three bottles of beer and was deemed "perfectly sober," in part, because Nancy Ruth's father had helped jump-start his car. He was sitting in the car with the engine running when the parents, the employee and another man went to downtown Knoxville to eat oysters.

When the parents and the other two returned together to the Sorrell home at 4:20 A.M., Nancy Ruth was missing. The sheriff was notified and a search begun. About noon a dazed Nancy Ruth wandered into her yard. She was covered with scratches, her legs were bleeding, her dress was muddy and her hair was matted and filled with beggar's-lice. She was taken to a doctor who confirmed she had been raped.

Nancy Ruth was able to identify Walden as her attacker from photos and a police lineup at the jail. She also knew him by appearance, but not name, because he had delivered doughnuts to the Canary. Said the Tennessee Supreme Court, "There is no insistence that she was not raped. Neither is it sincerely contended that the defendant is not the perpetrator of the crime."[2920]

Nancy Ruth testified that Walden came to her house alone and told her that her parents wanted her to come to Bearden. She got dressed except for her shoes. When they got outside, Walden carried her into the woods and raped her two or three times.[2921]

Walden's defense was intoxication. In particular, due to prior injuries, he routinely took Veronal and Luminal and "considerable quantities of whiskey and beer."[2922] He insisted that he had taken two of the tablets and some whiskey the morning of the rape. He asserted he drank seven or eight bottles of beer while at the Canary, drove home but could not get the car into the garage, drove five miles to the rear of the post office, drank more whiskey, and went to sleep in the front seat of his car. He said he was "unconscious until he woke up in the woods several hours later."[2923]

The Tennessee Supreme Court said intoxication was a jury question, and the jury was not wrong in concluding he was not intoxicated. Rather, he was sober enough to know Nancy Ruth was alone, concoct the story about taking her to Bearden, change his muddy clothes after the rape, and mislead the police about where he had spent the night. Furthermore, said the court, "The defendant's testimony, as to his whereabouts and conduct during the preceding week is coherent, connected and free from any mental aberration."[2924]

The court also ruled there was no evidence of insanity (although family members testified he acted in a peculiar manner from time to time), in part because a doctor introduced on his behalf at trial said he was sane and able to distinguish right from wrong.[2925] Walden's execution was ordered for January 15, 1942.

Roy Walden was executed at the main prison in Nashville on February 13, 1942. Walden, who had served twenty months in a Florida prison in 1933 for forgery, was survived by his parents and several adult siblings.[2926]

"I'm suffering death for another person's crime. Oh, God, if I could only get them to tell the truth!" Walden wailed from his death row cell. His mother and two sisters visited him the afternoon before his execution. They saw his shaven head and bade him a tearful good-bye.[2927]

Ernest Dixon, white, age 22. *Rape.*
John Dockery, white, age 19. *Rape.*

The crime was committed about midnight on June 4, 1940, at an old sawmill plant twelve miles from Knoxville, in Knox County. Dixon had a criminal record, having spent time in both reform school and prison. The victim was Susan Leeper, white, age twenty-two. She was a deaf-mute, as was her male companion, Floyd Carr. Both were students at the State Institution for the Deaf in Knoxville.

The young couple stopped their car in Chilhowee Park for a short time about eight o'clock and then drove out on the highways and stopped. Dixon and Dockery drove by and parked their car some little distance away. They returned, each with a pistol in hand, and approached the car, robbing the couple and forcing them into the back seat. The pair drove the couple's car around for about three hours, stopping at one point and taking the girl out of the car to rape her. The pair took the couple to the sawmill where she was raped again.

In some manner, the rapists used handkerchiefs to assist in the rapes; these were found at the two places the car had stopped, including the sawmill.[2928] These were vital clues to catching the rapists. Earlier in the afternoon, the pair had picked up a hitchhiker named Kennedy and robbed him of his clothing; he had no money. The handkerchiefs belonged to Kennedy and he identified them later.

Both Dixon and Dockery admitted on the witness stand they had robbed the pair, but vigorously denied raping Miss Leeper. This was the only issue of fact in the record that was contested. Dixon insisted that at the first stop there was no rape because of light cast by an oncoming car's headlights. The court noted that the proof showed the time Dixon was alone with the girl was enough time to rape her, and she testified that he was struggling with her on the ground when the headlights appeared. Dockery, she said, raped her at the sawmill.

On this issue, the court said:

> With respect to this issue of criminal forced intercourse, we find not only no preponderance against the finding of the jury, but that the great weight of the evidence sustains the charge that both of these boys, by force and violence, had criminal intercourse with this young woman, in a most brutal fashion. Her testimony is clear and convincing, and that of her companion, Carr, is strongly corroborative, although he could not testify as to penetration, of course. But of this there was abundant other evidence besides her own testimony, she having been taken to the hospital that night and there examined by the attendants and physicians, and her clothes and physical condition altogether offered convincing evidence of the commission of this crime.[2929]

The defendants also insisted that the couple were having sex when they came to the car to rob them. Furthermore, neither made any attempt to run away or cry out when the car stopped once for gas, and another time for soft drinks. Said the court, "This is explained by young Carr and Miss Leeper, who stated that pistols were continually held on them with the threat that they would be shot if they made any outcry, and in each instance the driver of the car, usually Dockery, took pains to stop it at some little distance and in such position that the attendant would not readily discover who the occupants were."[2930] Regarding the first allegation, the Supreme Court did not address the issue directly, saying instead, "Both [Leeper and Carr] bore excellent reputations so far as this record shows. Indeed, there is affirmative proof showing in the record of an unusually good reputation as to the young woman."[2931]

The trial which resulted in these convictions was actually the second trial, the first having resulted in a hung jury. The defendants raised the bar of double jeopardy, but the Supreme Court ruled that the minutes showed that the jury had not reached a verdict as to punishment, although it had decided the pair were guilty of the crimes, when the judge ordered a new trial, the jury having deliberated three days.[2932]

The court also said, "The next assignment complains of the examination by the prosecuting attorney of jurors, particularly inquires as to their views touching the infliction of the death penalty. In *Ray v. State*, 108 Tenn. 282, this practice was approved. It does not appear that what was done in this case resulted in prejudice to the accused; there being no showing that a fair and impartial jury was not selected. It is well settled that this Court will not reverse merely because the accused failed to secure other jurors when it appears that the jurors selected were fair and impartial. *Mahon v. State*, 127 Tenn. 535, 548."[2933]

Another issue before the court was whether the prosecutor erred in responding to a comment by Dixon: "You seem to think I done it in the first place," to which the prosecutor replied that he was of such opinion. The trial court instructed the jury to disregard the prosecutor's remark. Said the court, "This was all that was necessary. Moreover, we know of no rule that requires the prosecutor to exercise care in his examination of a defendant to avoid the implication that he suspects the defendants of being guilty, or so believes."[2934]

A final important issue on appeal was this: "Complaint is made of language in the charge to the effect that violations of the law must be tried according to our statutes and not according to the scriptures. This reference indicates that scriptural texts had been used in argument, and in this view the language in the charge was proper. Moreover, we are unable to see how any prejudice could have resulted from this obviously proper statement in the charge."[2935]

The court ordered the pair executed on January 16, 1942, and this occurred on February 14, 1942. The pair had simple meals the night before their deaths and maintained their innocence, especially Dixon, the older, who was executed first. Dockery was seated in the electric chair when he blurted out that he was guilty of raping Leeper. When asked if Dixon was guilty, he said, "I guess Dixon was as guilty as I am — he did about the same thing as I did."[2936]

Clarence May, white, age 33. *Murder.*

The crime was committed on March 2, 1941, near the farm home of the killer and his wife, located in the Cumberland Mountains, in tiny Sequatchie County. The victim, white, age thirty-two, was the killer's wife, Annie Savage May.

Here is the Tennessee Supreme Court's opinion:

> Clarence May shot and killed his wife, the mother of his five children, at their home in the Cumberland Mountains, on Sunday afternoon, March 2, 1941, in the presence of his oldest child, a girl named Ruby, then twelve or thirteen years old, and his son, Robert, at the time about eight years old.[2937] There is no doubt on this record that May did the shooting, and wholly without provocation. Indeed, there is no at-

tempt to dispute this, the theory of defense advanced being that May was so intoxicated as the result of the drinking of a large quantity of whiskey that he was wholly unaware of what he was doing and therefore unaccountable. These two children were put upon the stand by the State and told of the tragic event in a way so simple and frank, their accounts being supported by incidental and unsuggested corroborative remarks, that no question of doubt arises as to the truthfulness of the story they tell.

May had been drinking rather heavily for two or three days. On this Sunday morning he planned to kill and dress a hog. He first went some two miles distant to the home of Lizzie Roberts, who will be later referred to, and her husband, hoping to get this man to assist him, but did not find him at home. He returned and arranged to proceed with the killing and dressing of the hog with the aid of his wife. He took a twenty-two caliber rifle to the hog pen and there shot the hog, hitting the animal directly between the eyes and killing it with one shot. He then put the two hundred pound hog into a wheel barrow and carried it some two hundred yards to a point just below the house where there was a spring. It appears that he was displeased at that time because his wife had not kept the fire up under the large tin barrel used for heating the water. He first abused her, striking her. She climbed over a nearby fence to get wood and while she was in the act of doing so, he called to his small son, Robert, telling him to bring the rifle with which he had killed the hog. After the killing of the hog, this rifle had been re-hung on the wall in the cabin.

The little boy got the gun and carried it to the father. He testifies that he did not know what his father wanted with the gun, but hearing his mother beg his father not to kill her, he went back into the house. He is pressed to say why, but child-like, could not express the feelings of apprehension which doubtless influenced him. Shortly afterwards he and his sister both saw the killing, or at least so much of it as to be convincing of the fact. The little girl says she saw her father through the window point the gun at her mother; but then she looked away, not wanting to see her mother killed. Both children heard the shot. They say that, when handed the gun, the father sat down on a log and deliberately took aim at his wife, who was calling on him not to shoot, and shot her just above one eye, near the middle of the forehead. She died practically instantly.

She lay on the ground until the next morning. About four o'clock, just before day, May sent the children, carrying a lantern, to the home of Lizzie Roberts, with instructions to report that their mother was dead and to tell that she had killed herself if asked about it. The children went and roused the people and obeyed their father's instructions, testifying that he had threatened to whip them if they did otherwise.

Later, the sheriff and others arrived and found Clarence May sitting on a log outdoors near his wife's body, the rifle lying on the wet ground nearby. They say he gave evidences of drink at that time and of probable continued drinking. He was more or less soiled and, as one witness says, hollow-eyed. Interrogated as to what had happened, he told the sheriff that his wife had started to the house with his gun and had been accidentally shot. However, he first carried the sheriff to one point and then to another, places at which he said the shooting had occurred. However, the sheriff observed and called his attention to the fact that the ground was soft and wet and there were no tracks whatever supporting these statements. He was carried to the jail and discussed various matters about his stock on the way. The opinion of the sheriff and others about him is that he was rational, although giving signs of having been drinking heavily. He took the stand and disclaimed entirely and absolutely any knowledge whatever of what took place at or about his home from some time Saturday until the sheriff's party showed up there Monday morning. To all questions he would consistently reply that he did not know. He said that he did not deny having killed his wife, but simply did not know anything about it. He said he loved his children and did not question their truthfulness. His whole defense was based upon the proposition that he did not know at the time what he was doing and had no recollection of it whatever.

Now the State met this theory first by proof of various details of the commission of the tragedy, some of which have been mentioned, such as his conduct on that day, which seems utterly inconsistent with any theory of drunkenness to the extent now undertaken to be relied on. There is proof that he had drunk a great deal of whiskey in the preceding few days, but it is inconceivable that a man could be blindly drunk and yet able to handle a rifle as this man did and to handle a two hundred pound hog as he did, or otherwise act as the proof shows he did. But, in the second place, the testimony of these children shows that he had a full appreciation and recollection of what he had done when he sent for neighbors before day the next morning. His instructions to these children indicate a clear comprehension, not only of what he had done, but of the wrongfulness of his conduct and a disposition to conceal it. In the next place, his statements made to the sheriff and his associates again indicates a disposition to conceal the truth and mislead.

In addition to all this, the State put upon the stand a woman heretofore mentioned, a neighbor, one Lizzie Roberts, who testified that she had been sent for by Mays and had had a conversation with him in the jail, at which time Mays told her circumstantially about his killing his wife and added details which the children had not mentioned, for example, that after she fell he had taken her by the hair and dragged her body some distance across the ground to the point where it was found the next day. He also told this woman that he intended to kill his wife for some four years. This woman's testimony was vigorously attacked by cross-examination, but she quite apparently held her own. It developed in the course of the cross-examination that Attorney Joe Bean had given the woman a glass of beer the day before, and a good deal of the cross-examination was devoted to the circumstances and whether or not she was at that time intoxicated. It was brought out that she had been involved in several difficulties and had killed one man, as she insisted, justifiably. We think it quite apparent that she is a rough and violent character. Indeed, she says that he told her he sent for her to talk with her about his case and desperate situation because she had herself been in trouble and had had experience. He admits sending for her and talking with her, but says he sent for her to get her to care for the stock, etc., and denies having told her this story of the killing.

Now, if this woman's testimony is to be accepted, it is quite apparent that his testimony on the stand is fabricated. He was doubtless aware that he had no other avenue of escape and he pursued this one consistently. The woman is not impeached. The fact that she has been engaged in different brawls and personal difficulties and has been guilty of crimes of violence does not necessarily impeach her. In the recent Model Penal Code promulgated by the American Institute of Law, a distinction has been taken between impeachment because of crimes of dishonesty, etc., and those of mere physical violence, upon the theory supported by experience that many men who commit deeds of violence, even manslaughter, will tell the truth to the letter. Moreover, applying the well settled rule that the question of credibility is for the jury, the jury in this case heard this woman's story and has decided in her favor on the issue.

It is argued that the facts of this case present only a case of manslaughter; that all the circumstances indicate that this man was so much intoxicated that he was not responsible for his crime, and that at least his sentence should be commuted to imprisonment. The jury and trial judge saw and heard him and all the witnesses in the case, and we find nothing on this record which demands either a reversal of the case because the conviction is of first-degree murder, or a recommendation to the governor of a commutation of the sentence.

A motion appears to have been made for a change of venue, but the transcript does not contain the evidence introduced on this question, and we cannot therefore consider this matter. Reliance is made upon an assignment challenging the action of the trial judge in overruling the motion for a new trial, upon the ground of newly discovered evidence. We find no error here. The affidavits are wholly insufficient. In the first place, we are not satisfied with the showing made of the exercise of due diligence, particularly, an affirmative showing that the matters set up in the affidavits produced could not have been known and brought before the court on the trial. In the second place, these affidavits are chiefly directed to an attempt to impeach the testimony of witnesses, and it is well established that a new trial will not be granted for this purpose. We may observe in this connection that several of these affidavits are not shown to have been sworn to, as far as the transcript now shows.

It is argued, by way of appeal to this Court, that one of the counsel representing the defendant was at the time under great mental strain because of proceedings at that time pending to disbar him, and that he was therefore unable to do justice to the case. We find nothing on the record to support this theory.

The court concluded: "In conclusion, attention is called to an unusually exhaustive review of the facts and discussion of the law applicable on the brief of learned counsel for the State, which we adopt. On the whole, we find no reversible error and the judgment is affirmed, and plaintiff-in-error, Clarence May, will be delivered into the custody of the warden of the state prison and put to death according to law on the 20th day of March 1942."[2938]

Clarence met death in the electric chair at the Main Prison in Nashville on the appointed day.

The newspaper did not report any facts about May's last meal, but prison officials said that he admitted while seated in the electric chair that he had killed his wife. He was executed first that day. The chair's next occupant was John Henry Goode of Memphis.[2939]

John Henry Goode, black, age 31. *Murder.*

The crime was committed at the corner of Vance and Lauderdale Streets in Memphis, in Shelby County on March 16, 1941. The victim was Clyde Othel Miller, black, age thirty.

Here is the complete Tennessee Supreme Court opinion:

Just after midnight on Sunday morning, March 16, 1941, as Clyde Othel Miller, accompanied by Grace Evelyn Edwards, reached the corner of Vance and Lauderdale Streets in the city of Memphis he was fired upon three times with a pistol by someone in waiting, one shot entering his back inflicting a wound from which he died within a few seconds. On the following day John Henry Goode was arrested as the perpetrator of the crime, was indicted, tried, and found guilty of murder in the first degree, his punishment being fixed at death by electrocution. It is the insistence of the accused that he was in West Memphis at the time, and hence could not have killed the deceased.

> The accused, the deceased, and practically all of the material witnesses are negroes. Goode is thirty-one years of age and came from Arkansas to Memphis about two years prior to this homicide, after serving a term in the penitentiary in that state upon a conviction for highway robbery. Grace Evelyn Edwards also came to Memphis from Arkansas, after having served a term in the penitentiary for murder, and sometime in November or December 1940, became the paramour of Goode. Sometime in January 1941, she removed from the home of Goode and began going with the deceased. She testified that two days before the killing Goode came to her home and "jumped on her" because she was with Miller. Elmer McGee, who lived in the house with Goode, testified that he and Goode on one occasion visited the home of Grace and found Miller there. It is rather inferable from the record that Goode was jealous because this woman left his home and began keeping company with Miller. That furnishes a motive for the slaying.

> Sometime after Grace left the home of Goode a woman by the name of Gladys Wheeler became an inmate of the home of Goode as his paramour. On the afternoon of March 15, 1941, Goode procured his cousin, Robin Hobson, and his wife, Geneva Hobson, to drive him and Gladys Wheeler to Marion, Arkansas, where they were to be married. They were married about seven-thirty or eight o'clock that evening and then drove back to West Memphis. Upon arriving at that place Goode purchased and delivered to the occupants of the car a quart of whiskey. He testified the he did not drink any whiskey himself for the reason that he was going to gamble. He left the three named persons in the automobile about ten o'clock. They waited for him until one-thirty, but he never showed up, so they drove across the bridge spanning the Mississippi River to Memphis.

> The accused, in support of his alibi, introduced four witnesses, habitues of the gambling establishments in West Memphis, the first being Everett Gates, who works with him and who testified that he saw him in West Memphis on the night in question at about eleven and twelve-thirty o'clock, and that on both occasions he was shooting dice at the Club House. This witness had no watch and, on cross-examination, was unable to account for his whereabouts or actions on any other night shortly before or after the night of the fifteenth, and had no particular reason for impressing his mind with the exact time that he saw Goode on this occasion.

> Walter Grant testified to having seen Goode in West Memphis at about one o'clock on the morning of March 16th. Willie Greyson and Lee Cox testified that shortly after one o'clock they picked up Goode in West Memphis and discharged him in Memphis at ten minutes to two. It will thus be noted that since the crime was committed around midnight Goode could have easily returned to West Memphis by one o'clock. So that from ten to one o'clock on the night in question no one claims to have seen Goode in West Memphis with the single exception of his colaborer, Everett Gates.

> Sanders Williams, who operates a barber shop in the basement at the corner of Vance and Lauderdale Streets in Memphis, had just come out of his shop and started to a café in the adjoining building on Lauderdale Street to purchase a cigar when Goode passed him and shot Miller as he came around the corner. There was an electric light at this corner, and Goode after shooting Miller turned north on Lauderdale Street and passed within one and one-half feet of Williams, so that he had a good look at him. A few days later Williams was called to the county jail and out of a line of nine or ten prisoners very readily picked Goode as the one who shot the deceased. Williams was not acquainted with any of the parties, is positive in his identification, and his character is in no wise attacked. Goode is also positively identified by Grace Evelyn Edwards as the one who shot Miller, notwithstanding the fact that after the homicide, on the same night, he sent for Grace and requested her not to say anything about it.

The court concluded:

> In addition to the foregoing, Goode on the night of the slaying admitted that he shot the deceased to the following persons: Elmer McGee, Geneva Hobson, Quinton Harris, Hattie Harris, and Gladys May Goode, his wife. The surrounding facts and circumstances point strongly to Goode as the perpetrator of this crime, and there is nothing in the record to suggest any motive or reason for any person to have taken the life of Miller. We have read the record very carefully, are thoroughly convinced of the guilt of the accused, and find the verdict amply supported by the testimony. Finding no reversible error in the record, it results that the judgment of the trial court will be affirmed, and the date of execution fixed for Tuesday, March 3, 1942.[2940]

On March 2, 1942, the governor granted Goode a reprieve to study the case, but decided not to intervene. Goode was electrocuted on March 20,

1942. Clarence May was executed the same day as Goode, who was executed about ten minutes later.[2941] The newspaper noted, "Until the last, attendants said, he declared he was innocent of the crime for which he was sentenced to death."[2942]

1943

William Hedden, white, age 44. *Murder.*

The crime was committed at 6:30 P.M. November 18, 1941, in a mountain section of Polk County called Archville, a rural area at the forks of Greasy Creek Road and the Kimsey Highway. The killings took place in the sixteen by sixteen foot cabin occupied by Jack Hedden and his pregnant wife Lecie Mae Chastain Hedden, white, age twenty; their son, Ernest, age one; Mrs. Arlene Dillard, white, age twenty-one; and her son, Steve, age fourteen months. The women were best friends. Because Mrs. Dillard did not plan to live with her husband, who had found work in Detroit, she had come to live with the Heddens, at least until Lecie gave birth.[2943]

The killer, William Hedden, was a constable who had once served as a deputy sheriff.[2944] He was a cousin of Jack Hedden. Constable Hedden's stern manner and sometimes fiery temper was "usually enough to cower a rough mob of miners and quarrelsome, drinking dam workers without having to resort to force. To gentle the worst of them, it generally was sufficient for him to stride into a tavern and rasp out an order for quiet."[2945] According to one account, "The tough constable was not slow to use his fists, or his gun, to enforce his rule. He was feared throughout the district."[2946] A week before the killings, he had been indicted by the grand jury for assault with intent to murder growing out of his effort to control a fight. In 1924, William had also killed his father, Riley Hedden, but the action was deemed justified and no charges were pressed.[2947]

Because William Hedden maintained his innocence to the end, the facts of the crime came largely from the testimony of Julius Goforth, and the physical evidence, notably the fact that the FBI laboratory concluded that the .38 caliber pistol taken from Hedden's holster upon his arrest was the murder weapon.

Mrs. Dillard's beauty and agreeable nature had immediately attracted the attention of several young men who called on her day and night. Hedden wanted her too and had bought her a bracelet, but on the day of the killing he had stayed around the house until midafternoon for the purpose of sending potential suitors away. Among these was Lawrence Breeden, who along with another man[2948] was changing a flat tire on the road near the house. Hedden had told him to leave, brandishing both a .38 and a .32 caliber pistol. Breeden said he was simply going to the house to get a drink of water, which Hedden disputed.[2949] Breeden also claimed that as he continued walking he came upon Julius Goforth sitting in Hedden's car, but only said hello to him.[2950]

At 6:15 the evening of the killings, Hedden came to the house in his car, driven by Julius Goforth, who roomed at his home. While Goforth stayed in the car chewing his customary match sticks and throwing them on the ground, Hedden went inside. Within minutes Goforth heard the only recognizable words spoken, "It's my house and I'll go to bed when I get ready!"—said by Lecie Hedden, who also told him to leave or she would call the sheriff.[2951]

Within minutes, shooting began and the women "hollered two or three times." Hedden got back into the car with a pistol in each hand and said, "There wasn't anybody left to tell the tale."[2952] The sequence of shooting is unknown, but from the location of the bodies it appeared that he shot Mrs. Hedden first; her body was found in the doorway, feet toward the door. She had been shot perpendicular, probably having been pushed down by Hedden. Next, he went to the bedroom where Mrs. Dillard was in bed and shot her in like manner. Both women were found fully dressed with no signs of sexual assault. Mrs. Hedden's shirt was pulled up over her head, as if the killer had examined her wounds. Hedden then shot baby Steven. It was the first triple slaying in Polk County.

Jack Hedden came home from his welding job at a TVA site about 11:30 P.M. and stumbled over his wife's body. The house was dark because William Hedden and Goforth had returned to the house within an hour of the killings, at which time Hedden went inside, took six dollars from his sister-in-law's purse to make it look like a robbery-murder, and blew out a kerosene lamp that had been left burning.[2953] A few hours later, after driving around, the pair went to Hedden's house and went to sleep.

When Jack Hedden came into the house and saw the bodies, he found his son Ernest unharmed, but sleeping in a bundle of bedclothes next to Mrs. Dillard's body. Both she and Mrs. Hedden had received numerous bullet wounds, including shots in the middle of their foreheads. Investigators found .38 caliber bullets in Mrs. Hedden, including two slugs that had passed through her body; but .32 caliber bullets were found in the other woman. Lawmen later concluded that Hedden had used two pistols to make it appear that the shootings had been done by two gunmen, but the .32 caliber weapon was never found. Russell Hedden, one of William's brothers, testified that in midafternoon of the day of the shooting he saw William carrying both a .38 in its holster and a .32 under his belt.[2954] A store clerk said he had sold .32 caliber bullets to William Hedden the day before the shootings.[2955]

In shock, Jack Hedden ran to a neighbor's house carrying his son, and Sheriff Broughton Biggs and deputies were soon on the scene. Three significant clues were soon identified, namely the bullets, the match sticks, and the distinctive tire tread from a car which had recently pulled up next to the house. While it was possible to drive from the road to the house, few people did so, preferring to park by the road and walk thirty feet to the house, which was on a low hill.

As word spread, neighbors came to observe, and these included William Hedden. Offering his services, he said with clenched fists, "If I find the devil who did this, I'll tear him apart!"[2956] He was asked by the sheriff to go to Brushy Mountain Prison to get bloodhounds, but he begged off, saying he needed to inform his sister-in-law's parents and other kin of the shooting, but that he had already talked to the closest neighbor, Noah Bates, who told him he had not heard any shots.[2957]

As the sheriff pressed the investigation, he was told by William Hedden that two men had been near the house that afternoon changing a flat tire on a car in the road — or pretending to do so — but he thought they were stalling until Hedden left the house because he knew they were interested in courting Mrs. Dillard. Hedden said that he knew that one owned a .38 pistol. A day or so later, the gun owner was rousted from bed and asked whether he owned such a pistol. He denied it, but gave permission to search his home. Under a pile of magazines, a .38 pistol was found, and he was arrested for the murders. Likewise, the other man seen changing the tire was known to own a .32 pistol, according to William Hedden. Again, such a weapon was found in that man's house, and he too was arrested.[2958]

William Hedden's assertion about the .32 pistol puzzled the sheriff because no one had been told that two weapons had been used. He began checking out Hedden's statements and quickly discovered that Hedden had not notified his sister-in-law's relatives, nor had he questioned Noah Bates. When the sheriff finally talked to Bates, it became clear that he greatly feared Hedden. Bates had heard the gunshots between 6:15 and 6:30, along with a voice that sounded like Hedden's, and had seen a recent-model sedan with two taillights in dark outline near the house at the time of the shooting. He also saw what he thought was the same car return to the house a short while after the shooting.[2959]

When it became clear that Jack Hedden was at work and Mr. Dillard was in Detroit at the time of the slayings, the sheriff asked William Hedden where he was at that time. He asserted, and his wife confirmed, that he had returned home about 5:00 P.M. (before the killings) and had gone to bed because he was not feeling well. His wife said he never left the house, nor did Goforth, who talked to her some time before going to sleep on the couch with his clothes on.

With the tire-changing "killers" in custody, the sheriff asked Hedden to come to the courthouse and confronted him with his inconsistent statements, taking his weapon in full view of other deputies. Within hours of Hedden's arrest, Goforth explained the details of the killings. He said he had been threatened by Hedden if he told the truth. He became the state's star witness, although Hedden attempted to show that it was possible that Goforth may have left the house, taken the car, and killed the women and child, returning without anyone in the Hedden household knowing about it. This was rebutted, in part, because Goforth had actually served as a member of the coroner's jury summoned to view the crime scene on the night of the murder.[2960] He had been told to do this by Hedden, he explained. The tire tracks matched Hedden's car.

The FBI laboratory in Washington concluded that the pistols taken from the tire-changing men had not been fired in months and that Hedden's pistol was one of the murder weapons. A ballistics expert, Donald J. Parsons from the Bureau, testified.

Indicted on November 24, 1941, William Hedden went to trial on December 3 in front of a packed courthouse, drawn to the trial because both Jack and Russell Hedden were shown on the indictment as witnesses against their cousin and brother. Three days later the jury took forty minutes to find William Hedden guilty of first-degree murder without a recommendation for mercy. He had also been indicted for the murder of Mrs. Hedden and Mrs. Dillard's son, but the charges were continued at trial, and not pressed after his conviction.

The Supreme Court's thirty-seven page opinion, one of the longest up to that time, included extensive quotations from the transcript, showing both the testimony that implicated Hedden, notably that of Bates, and the testimony the defense asserted showed Bates could not have seen or heard what he did because of the distance between the houses, hammering the point that it was not possible to see Bates's house from the porch of the Hedden house. This was true, wrote the court, but it was beside the point because no one had testified that Hedden was on the porch.[2961]

The court said, "According to the testimony of Julius Goforth, defendant is guilty of the murder of Arlene Dillard. However, he [Goforth] occupies the status of accessory after the fact in this murder. It is necessary, therefore, that he be corroborated by other evidence. We think the jury could well have found from the evidence that the testimony of Goforth to the effect that defendant fired a number of shots into the house of Jack Hedden on the night in question, was corroborated by the testimony of Noah Bates."[2962] Goforth explained that Hedden had told his sister-in-law to go to bed (prompting her negative response) because he wanted Mrs. Dillard to get in the car with them.[2963]

William Hedden was electrocuted at the Main Prison in Nashville on March 30, 1943.

Hedden vehemently denied the killings. "Their lies put me here. They are going to put me to death in the morning for a crime I know nothing about."[2964] Hedden had embraced the Catholic faith while in prison, as did Robert Cannon, who was also executed with him for a Shelby County murder. The newspapers ignored the issue of what the men had for their last meal. Hedden was executed first.[2965]

Robert Cannon, black, age 28. *Murder.*

The crime was committed at a gas station about midnight on May 9, 1942, in Memphis, Shelby County. Cannon had just robbed the attendant, whom he had locked in a storage closet. He was leaving when a car containing the victim, Roy Eldridge Woods, white, age twenty-one, drove up. John Arnold was the driver. Woods remained in the back seat and two female passengers went to the rest room. They encountered the gun-wielding Cannon. They screamed and ran away.

Cannon emerged from the station and went to the car. He said he told Woods to stay where he was. Instead, Woods came out of the car, told him to drop his pistol and advanced. Cannon said he fired one shot in the ground to stop him, but Woods continued to threaten him.[2966] He shot Woods in the abdomen. With Woods down, Cannon demanded Arnold's wallet. Arnold replied he had no wallet. Cannon demanded the contents of his pockets. Arnold reached into his pocket and threw a handful of change in Cannon's direction. Some of this money was found by police when they arrived.

Arnold testified that Cannon simply shot Woods as he was getting out of the car. One slug missed and went through the side of the car. The other struck Woods, causing his death within an hour. Cannon fled on foot. Arnold went into the station and freed the attendant, who called police. A roving squad car spotted Cannon eight minutes later. He was taken to the police station where he promptly confessed and told the committing magistrate, "I just don't know why I shot that boy, but I did. I guess they will give me the hot seat for it."[2967] At trial, he insisted he shot in self-defense. Cannon had served three years (1935–37) in prison for grand larceny.

The Tennessee Supreme Court ruled these facts warranted the jury's finding of first-degree murder, namely felony murder, a killing in the act of robbery.[2968] The court was again confronted with the unusual language of the Tennessee Constitution: "And in all indictments for libel the jury shall have the right to determine the law and the facts under the direction of the court, as in other criminal cases."[2969] This was the chief legal issue raised on appeal, but the opinion does not say how Cannon's lawyers felt his rights under this section had been violated.

"This section of the Constitution has been under discussion of this Court on many occasions and the interpretations which the Court has given it are not always in harmony," said Chief Justice Green's opinion.[2970] The court said the provision had been extensively discussed in *Ford v. State*[2971] and was as follows: The duty of the judge was to declare the law, the duty of the jury was to decide the facts and apply them to the law. The jury was to assume the law was correct, and "not assume to set up any knowledge of their own as against his."[2972] In practice, this means that defendant's counsel has the right to argue both the law and the facts to the jury and to insist on a proper jury instruction if the judge's charge is wrong.[2973] Finding nothing in the record indicating an improper instruction, the conviction was affirmed and Cannon was ordered electrocuted on March 30, 1943.[2974]

Cannon met death on the appointed day. He had embraced Catholicism in prison and freely admitted his guilt. He told the newspaper, "I have no dread. I am ready to go."[2975] His appointment with death was delayed fifteen minutes because Warden Thomas P. Gore decided that William Hedden would be executed first that day.

James Felix Tucker (aka Jimmy Tucker), white, age 29. *Murder.*

The crime was committed on May 21, 1942, at the victim's apartment which she shared with her husband at 411 Trinity Lane in suburban Nashville, in Davidson County.[2976] The victim was the killer's wife, Minnie Margaret Tucker, white, age nineteen.

The couple moved into the house about a month before the killing and had an eleven-month-old daughter. Minnie was a housewife and Tucker, unemployed, was taking classes in electrical welding at Central High School in Nashville.

Jimmy Tucker burst from the house about 6:30 P.M. on May 21, 1942, clutching the baby and screaming, "My wife's been murdered! My wife's been murdered!"[2977] When police arrived, Tucker seemed dazed and had trouble talking clearly but explained that his classes ended at 5:00 P.M. and he went straight home but had stopped to talk to George Samples, a clerk in a Dickerson Road store, a friend with whom he had planned a fishing trip.

The police found Minnie Tucker dead in the bedroom. She was fully dressed and wearing a light topcoat and held the baby's knitted hat in her left hand. She was lying on her left side and had been stabbed in the back. The murder weapon, a large homemade knife, was lodged in her spine and was protruding from her back. The knife showed no fingerprints, only smudges. The weapon was shown to Tucker, who said that he had made it in one of his classes and the knife was usually kept in the cupboard drawer with other utensils.

The bedroom indicated that Minnie was preparing to leave because a small suitcase was open and slightly packed and the closet door was open. Minnie's handbag and gloves were placed near the suitcase. Tucker was asked about this and explained that Minnie was planning to spend a few days with her mother and he was using the opportunity to go fishing with Samples.

Based on the condition of the body and bloodstains, the coroner said Minnie had been killed between four and four-thirty. The only other clue was a deep shoe print in the back yard left by someone who had left the house in haste. A moulage was made of it. Store clerk Samples confirmed that Tucker had come by the store shortly before six o'clock and they had discussed a fishing trip. Neighbors across the street confirmed seeing Tucker enter the house shortly after six o'clock.

Extensive questioning of neighbors revealed that two men were known to visit Minnie while her husband was away. One was a middle-aged man who sometimes sat on the porch with her and took her and the baby away in his car, always returning before Tucker came home. The other was a household goods salesman who seemed to visit Minnie on an almost daily basis, and had come to the house and stayed most of the afternoon the day she was killed.

When the salesman's name was given to Tucker he acknowledged knowing him and knew that his wife had bought items from him. The salesman drove a truck which he customarily parked in the alley, which meant it was easier for him to enter the back door, closest to the kitchen. The older man was questioned and he was found to be Minnie's brother, who explained the couple had financial problems since Tucker had lost his job two years earlier and the family was offering support, including his schooling. He knew the salesman as well.

The investigation showed that the salesman had known Minnie before she married Jimmy Tucker and was deeply smitten with her. He called many times after her marriage and she had tried to get him to stop calling out of fear that it would cause Jimmy to become angry. He had left town on the evening of the murder. Located in Birmingham and arrested for Minnie's murder, he was brought back to Nashville and grilled intensely.

The salesman admitted he had visited Minnie the day of her murder, and had left town because he was fearful of being implicated. He admitted that he was in love with Minnie. He said she was crying when he saw her because Jimmy had beaten her the day before, after accusing her of flirting with other men. He had offered to take her to her mother's house but she refused, wanting to wait for her husband to arrive around six o'clock.

The salesman said that he had left the house about four o'clock and parked his truck where it could not be seen by Jimmy Tucker on arriving home. The salesman was surprised to see Jimmy walking down the alley towards the house at about four-thirty and enter the house from the rear door. Within minutes he saw Tucker leave the house and walk down Trinity Lane. Later, when police arrived at the house, the salesman stayed at the edge of the crowd to find out what happened. He left town when he learned Minnie had been murdered. He also said that Jimmy was very jealous of Minnie and that morning had threatened her because she was leaving, possibly for good, to live with her mother.

Neighbors confirmed the violent nature of the Tucker household, including Minnie's begging Jimmy not to beat her. Tucker was again questioned and admitted that the salesman was a problem because he would not leave Minnie alone. But he insisted he was not jealous. He suggested the salesman may have killed Minnie when she would not leave with him.[2978]

In a dramatic confrontation, the salesman was brought into the same room as Tucker. The police explained to Tucker what the salesman said. They asked both men to put forward a shoe in order to compare it with the plaster mold of the footprint. It fit Tucker's shoe exactly.

He immediately confessed, saying he had killed Minnie in a fit of rage when she said that she was leaving him and that the salesman had offered to take her to her mother's house. A stenographer took his words down verbatim, which he later signed. (The confession was not offered at trial.) He had come home early, killed Minnie, backtracked down the alley and calmly waited until after 6:00 P.M. to talk with George Samples. He did not see the salesman or his truck. Tucker went to trial on November 29, 1942. His defense was temporary insanity, which was rejected by the jury.

Awaiting death, Tucker insisted he was innocent of first-degree murder and his punishment was unjust. He explained, "I do say that, according to the statutes of Tennessee, I haven't received justice. To carry capital punishment, a crime has to be premeditated. My act was not done with premeditation. It was done in a fit of passion. How the state proved premeditation, I don't know. There was nobody there but us. Nobody knew anything about it until I called the police to come after me."[2979]

At trial, Tucker's explanation of the killing (before an all-male jury) began with Minnie's admitting that morning that she had been intimate with the salesman. She taunted him by saying, "What are you going to do about it?" He slapped her, and her red, bruised face was seen by others that day. According to Tucker, he went to the store with his landlord, who said that Minnie and the salesman were misbehaving. Returning from the store, Tucker went into the bedroom and found his wife gone, but the baby was on the bed. Tucker said he got the homemade butcher knife for self-defense because he thought Minnie was away telling one of her brothers that Tucker had abused her. The brother had threatened Tucker if he hurt Minnie again. Tucker lay down on the bed with the baby.

Minnie came into the bedroom and began cursing him and assaulted him, but he threw up his knees for protection. At this point, "his mind went blank and he remembered nothing else until later when he found himself holding the baby in his arms."[2980] The court said the jury was justified in concluding that Tucker's claim that his wife had been unfaithful was a fabrication. The landlord said there had been no such conversation and the neighbors all said that the salesman only sat on the porch with Minnie. They all said she was afraid of Jimmy, who beat her because of his jealousy. Tucker's claim of temporary insanity was unsupported by any expert testimony. All the doctors who testified said he knew right from wrong at the time of the killing and some said he was malingering.[2981] The court ordered him executed on July 15, 1943, and he met death that day.

The night before the execution, Tucker's visiting family members were overcome with emotion. He said, "Another thing I want you to put in the papers is that I feel no ill will against anybody." Shortly before the execution, Tucker bowed his head in prayer led by prison chaplain the Rev. Pickens Johnson. Tucker was executed at 5:25 A.M. and Marshall Spigener was executed fifteen minutes later. The Tucker murder case is one of the few Tennessee cases where a published photograph of the dead victim in situ can be found.

Marshall F. Spigener (aka Marshall Spigner), white, age 45. *Murder.*

The crime was committed on the night of August 8, 1942, in room 1011 of the Claridge Hotel in downtown Memphis, in Shelby County. The victim was a widow, Mrs. Jewel Talley Roberts, white, age twenty-seven, a waitress.

Registering under the name "Mr. and Mrs. Joe Thomas, Los Angeles, California" but carrying no luggage, the couple rented the room on the night of August 7, 1942, paying cash. Accounts from bellmen and elevator operators differed, but some said Roberts appeared fearful about being with Spigener. No one heard any sounds from the room, although there were conflicting accounts about whether another couple had been to the room. Roberts's body was found the next afternoon by the maid.

The room was in disarray, with Roberts's clothing thrown about. Her body, clad only in a slip, was found on the bed and she had been strangled. She had some bruising on her arms and one leg. A false fingernail had broken off and was in the bed. Accounts differ, most suggesting she had recently had sex, but there was no evidence of rape. Shoe prints showed on the bed linen.

The killer, Marshall Spigener, had served in World War I and was discharged in 1919. He had been in trouble with the law since. He served prison time in Mississippi and Arkansas for grand larceny and had escaped from the Arkansas prison. On January 8, 1927, he shot and killed his Memphis girlfriend, Grace Elizabeth Bennett, white, age twenty-eight, on the front porch of her home after a quarrel. According to one account, Spigener expressed extreme remorse. Weeping on the witness stand, he begged the jury to sentence him to the electric chair.[2982] He received a life sentence but was released on parole in 1940, and was returned to the Arkansas prison. He was released on September 1941 and came to Memphis, where his brother and sister lived.

Spigener continued his life as a career criminal. On May 31, 1942, several gunmen robbed a movie theater office at gunpoint, taking $2,500. The cash was bound in custom-printed money bands, and one of the bands was found in the hotel room by the police.[2983] This clue helped turn attention to Spigener, because the police concluded that the killer was someone with a criminal history in Memphis.

After talking with Roberts's mother, police went to the café where she worked and Spigener became the prime suspect. Spigener knew Roberts because he ate at the café. Café patrons and another waitress did not know Spigener personally, but several recalled Roberts calling him by his first name, which they found unusual because she typically referred to men as "Mr."

On the day of her death, Roberts was wearing three diamond rings.[2984] One was an engagement ring costing $125 that she had received from her fiancé, who was in the Army, and was scheduled to marry her in September. Police examined their own records, including handwriting exemplars, which matched the hotel registration card. Spigener was arrested on August 10. He gave a false name, but clearly had a scratch on his neck. The waitress and patrons identified Spigener in a lineup as the person they had seen Roberts dining with the night she was killed.[2985] Women tended to remember Spigener because of his distinctive pale blue eyes.

Spigener denied knowing Roberts, but when confronted with the hotel registration card showing his unique handwriting, he admitted having met her in the room. As Spigener sat in jail, his girlfriend was located and she was found in possession of the three rings.[2986] The police strongly suggested she might be implicated in the crime, in order to seek her cooperation. She was brought to Spigener and confronted him.

After the girlfriend confirmed Spigener as the source of the rings, Spigener admitted he was overcome by a sudden urge to kill Roberts after she had taken off her clothing. He told police that he placed his belt around her neck, strangling her, as she struggled. He then removed her rings, took seventy-five dollars from her purse, and removed her identification.[2987]

One version of the crime says that Spigener had arranged a meeting between Roberts and an elderly man at the hotel in which Roberts was to pay $4,000 cash for a house the man had for sale. When Spigener discovered Roberts had not brought the money, he demanded sex. When she refused and slapped him, he flew into a rage and strangled her.[2988]

Spigener was charged with murder in the commission of a felony (robbery). He went to trial on November 18, 1942, and repudiated his confession, giving an alibi that he was with his brother.

The alibi was challenged because the brother had given the police a written statement that he thought Marshall "had been in on the killing if he had not actually killed Jewel Roberts."[2989] The alibi was also challenged because Spigener insisted that he was in a barbershop with his brother the Sunday after the killing, but the brother could not confirm this.

A second defense was insanity, several family members testifying that Spigener was of "low mentality and is not really responsible for his actions."[2990] No medical testimony was offered that Spigener was insane, but a doctor who observed him from November 6 to November 15, 1942, said that he was sane.[2991]

The state's theory of the crime was that Spigener killed Roberts after forming the intent to rob her. It posed the theory that he was fully dressed at the time, and came upon the bed of the (probably) intoxicated Roberts in order to steal her rings.[2992] When she struggled, he strangled her, holding her arms down by kneeling on them, leaving shoe prints on the sheets.[2993]

A few minutes before he was executed, Spigener said the following to the prison warden: "Jewel kept trying to get out of the room. I knocked her unconscious and put her on the bed. I held her until she began moving. Then I left her long enough to tear some strips from the bathroom curtains. I put them around her neck and pulled them tighter and tighter until she was dead. Then I took her rings and money, wiped off all fingerprints and left."[2994]

Spigener was electrocuted on the morning of July 15, 1943, a few minutes after the execution of Jimmy Tucker. Having become a Catholic, he asserted he was not afraid to die. His message to his unnamed girlfriend was, "God bless you. May God have mercy on your soul. I'm more than sorry that it had to come to this but under the circumstances I wasn't responsible. So good-bye to the one I always loved. Remember me in your prayers." To his sobbing brother, he said, "Don't feel bad about it, everything is all right. When they get my body back home in Memphis, I don't want anybody crying. I want you all to just stand there and laugh at me. I want you to go ahead and join the Army and make a good soldier."[2995]

The frightening story of the betrothed woman who was lured to a hotel room by a compelling near-stranger who picked her up at work has made the Roberts murder an enduring feature of true crime reporting, having been retold in 1964, 1980, 1992 and 2000.[2996]

Clyde Arwood, white, age 46. *Murder.*

The crime was committed in the afternoon of November 21, 1941, outside the village of Halls, in Lauderdale County. Arwood, a former Lauderdale County barber, was being questioned in a moonshine investigation that day by federal revenue agents. United States Alcohol Tax Agent William Milton Pugh, white, age forty-nine, had twice visited the rural home of Arwood's mother and had discovered an underground still in the woods. The agents had destroyed the still, but evidence such as a watch and recently cut firewood (some of which was found in a shed near the house) suggested Arwood's involvement.

Agent Pugh, with agents Howes and Rossner (who remained in the car) chatted amicably with Arwood, who took them to the shed, then into the house, as the officers asked Arwood about a padlock they had taken from the door to the still. As the agents continued walking around and asking questions, they came upon more incriminating evidence such as a copper coil in the shed and bags of sugar in the chicken house. The questioning proceeded without rancor as Arwood agreed to tell the agents the whole truth. He said, "I'm going in the house to see my mother a minute." Because the house was on stilts, agent Howes was able to stoop low and walk under the crawl space, where he discovered a thermos jug. Agent Pugh was standing beside the house using the padlock to idly crack pecans.

Without speaking, Arwood fired a shotgun from inside the house, hitting Pugh in the lower face. Arwood then went to the front door and fired two times at Rossner, missing. Pugh was able to walk to the car. He was driven to a Dyersburg hospital where he died in thirty minutes.

Arwood was tried in the federal district court in Memphis and found guilty of murder of a federal officer, a capital offense.[2997] Through the testimony of his parents and his girlfriend, Arwood attempted to show that he was of "low and irresponsible mentality" and was drunk at the time of the shooting. The case was uneventful except for Arwood's mother, age seventy, fainting on the witness stand, which brought Arwood to tears.

Arwood's intoxication defense backfired when he was confronted with his past. He had used that defense in other crimes, including his killing of Deputy Sheriff John Wyde Lunsford, white, age sixty-two, in Ripley, Tennessee, on June 28, 1932. He was convicted of second-degree murder and sentenced to twenty-one years. On August 24, 1938, his sentence was commuted by Gov. Browning, which allowed the model prisoner to be paroled that day. He returned as a parole violator in 1939 and was released on February 16, 1940.

On appeal, Arwood argued that the jury should have been specifically instructed that when an officer lacking a search warrant is killed, the jury, in its discretion, could impose life imprisonment. Likewise, Arwood argued that it was improper for the trial court to have allowed into evidence reports written by Pugh to his supervisor describing the investigation and mentioning "the Clyde Arwood still." These arguments were rejected by the Sixth Circuit Court of Appeals, and the Supreme Court refused to hear the case.[2998] President and Mrs. Roosevelt declined to answer the letters they received from Arwood, his parents and brothers and sisters.

Clyde Arwood was the only person executed in Tennessee under federal government authority in the twentieth century. He was electrocuted at the prison in Nashville on August 14, 1943.

His only words as he was strapped into the chair were, "Good-bye, friends." Immediately asked by the warden if he wanted to make a last statement, he replied, "That's all."[2999]

Robert Hall, black, age 52. *Murder.*

The crime was committed on the night of October 24, 1942, near a home in a black neighborhood in Chattanooga, Hamilton County. The victim was Arlie Emerson "Toby" Carr, white, age thirty-one, a uniformed police officer with the

Chattanooga Police Department. Carr and his police partner were answering a domestic disturbance involving Hall and his wife, when Hall suddenly turned a gun on Carr.

Here is the entire Tennessee Supreme Court opinion:

> The defendant below, Robert Hall, a colored man, was convicted for the unlawful killing of A.E. Carr, a white man and policeman. He was convicted of murder in the first degree and his punishment fixed at death by electrocution. The defendant is a negro of middle age and some years ago had a fight with another negro in which his opponent stuck an ice pick in his head. The proof shows that since that time the defendant had complained of headaches at times and had carried medicine for relief. The evidence shows that when the defendant is sober he is entirely normal but when he is drinking he is inclined to be mean. The deceased, A.E. Carr, was a police officer of the City of Chattanooga and at the time he was killed was in full uniform.
>
> The homicide occurred between eight-thirty and nine o'clock on the night of October 24, 1942. On that night the defendant ran his wife away from home and threatened to kill her. She went to the home of a sister who lived nearby. The defendant armed himself with a rifle, described by his wife as a "war gun," and followed his wife to the home of her sister and undertook to gain entrance to the house by saying that he was going to kill her. The sister refused to let him in, barring the door against him, and turned on a 60-watt porch light so that she might see the identity of the defendant. It seems that in the meantime the wife of defendant slipped out through the back door to a nearby grocery, had the grocer call the Police Department and notify them of trouble. The record indicates that the wife of the defendant notified the grocer that this man was armed with a rifle, but it does not indicate whether the grocer advised the Police Department of that fact.
>
> The communication seems to have been broadcast upon the police radio. Deceased and his partner, Mr. Sheridan, were cruising in a squad car and picked up this information and drove to the home of the sister of defendant's wife, where they parked the car near the porch. The proof shows that this car contained the insignia of the Chattanooga Police Department. Three of the officers testify that after the defendant's conversation with the occupants of the house, the defendant said in substance, "Let the God damn police come on, I will take them on one at a time."
>
> Sheridan, the companion of the deceased, seems to have been driving this squad car and the deceased was riding on the right-hand side and the side next to the house on the porch of which defendant was sitting. According to those where were present, the deceased said to the defendant, "What is going on here?" and began to open the right-hand door of this car preparatory to getting out, and as Carr was getting out of the car the others noticed that the defendant was armed with a gun and called out to the deceased to that effect.
>
> The defendant seems to have been standing with his back somewhat toward the car in which the deceased was riding and according to the testimony, as soon as the deceased asked the defendant what was the matter, the defendant whirled and fired one shot, it striking the ventilator on the car. Then the defendant shot the deceased and he died in two or three days.
>
> It is insisted that the defendant is of low mentality and is not well, and at most he is not guilty of murder in the first degree. We are unable to agree to this contention. The record discloses that the defendant has been repeatedly in trouble, that on the night of the killing he ran his wife away from home, that he followed her to the home of her sister and undertook to gain entrance, that his wife slipped out through the back door to a grocery and had the grocer call the Police Department, and that when he was being talked to by the inmates of the house uttered these deadly threats against the deceased.
>
> We think all the elements that go to make up murder in the first degree appear in this case. An innocent man, a policeman of the City of Chattanooga, was going about his duties trying to maintain the peace and to enforce law and order when this murderous attack was made upon him by the defendant without any justification whatever. The jury saw and heard the witnesses testify and they have exacted the most severe penalty prescribed by law. Nothing appears in the record that would justify us in changing their verdict. It results that the judgment of the lower court is affirmed, and the date of the execution is set for Thursday, December 2, 1943.[3000]

Just after midnight on the day set for his execution, Hall was given a fourteen-day reprieve by Governor Prentice Cooper, to give Hall's attorneys time to prepare what the newspaper called new materials which the lawyers asserted would serve as a basis to commute his sentence.

Actually, the lawyers had filed a petition to rehear with the Tennessee Supreme Court, asserting that Hall was "so drunk at the time of the shooting that it couldn't have been a case of premeditated murder."[3001] The court granted the motion and made a recommendation to the governor that Hall's sentence be commuted to life imprisonment, but this order/opinion cannot be located.

Chattanooga police officials protested, asserting that "abundant testimony in the records refutes the claims" of Hall's insensibility, and urging the death sentence be allowed to stand. Mrs. Carr and her brother came to the governor's office with her two children, Janice, age six, and Joan, age four, and pled with the governor to disregard the court's recommendation. Mrs. Carr, with tearful eyes, said, "I simply want to see justice done."[3002] According to a Chattanooga newspaper, this was supposedly the first time a governor disregarded a clemency recommendation from the Tennessee Supreme Court.[3003] Robert Hall met death in the electric chair on December 15, 1943.

Deputy Warden Glenn Swafford told the newspapers that the night before the execution Hall talked about the killing and also admitted that he had stabbed to death another Negro some time before.[3004] Swafford said that the customary "last meal" for which condemned men are allowed to choose whatever they want was offered, but "condemned men rarely ever eat very much the night before the execution."[3005] The newspaper also reported, "A strange custom at the state prison is that condemned men are given a new pair of shoes the day preceding the execution."[3006] Hall walked calmly to the electric chair, had no last words, and made a short silent prayer while seated.[3007]

1945

George Mansfield Hambrick, black, age 26. *Murder.*

The crime was committed about 3:30 P.M. October 16, 1943, on Charlotte Pike near Richland School in Nashville, in Davidson County. Hambrick was a workhouse inmate serving a three-year term for housebreaking and larceny.[3008] The victim was Robert P. McGrew, white, age sixty-eight, the officer in charge of the work detail. Hambrick had broken his leg shackles earlier in the day but wired them together to look as if they were secure. When McGrew's back was turned, Hambrick hit him on the head with a pick ax. McGrew died three days later.[3009]

Hambrick had a long record of carrying a pistol, housebreaking, and larceny. He had escaped from the road crew on three previous occasions. This time he took a pistol and a shotgun from the fallen McGrew, fired a pistol shot at another guard, and made his escape in a county truck. Near the Main Prison he encountered three teen-age boys (sons of prison guards) and held two at gunpoint, ordering the third to bring him suitable clothes to make his escape. This done, Hambrick hid near the Cumberland River, but a 35-man posse of city and county police officers captured him the same day as the killing.

Hambrick said that McGrew had hit him with a stick and cursed him a few days before. He said McGrew hit him with a stick shortly before the killing. He claimed the killing was an impulsive gesture because, "the next thing I knew I was standing over him with his pistol and shotgun in my hand."[3010] He insisted the crime "was committed in passion and without premeditation and while in a brain storm."[3011] He said he was not "mad" at McGrew when he killed him. Hambrick had been arrested a few years earlier for shooting an East Nashville grocer when the latter surprised him attempting to loot his store.

The state's case was prosecuted by assistant district attorney (later mayor) Ben West, who offered testimony of both a deputy and a cell mate that McGrew's death was planned for some days, satisfying the requirement that the killing was premeditated.

The Tennessee Supreme Court upheld the verdict. It turned aside the contention that it was wrong for the judge to refuse the testimony of prison inmates offered by the defense to show the pattern of brutality at the county jail and workhouse.[3012] An unusual opinion on a petition to rehear withdrew a portion of the opinion, but affirmed the conviction.[3013] The execution was set for August 18, 1944, but was delayed while Hambrick's lawyers attempted an appeal to the United States Supreme Court.[3014]

Hambrick's last meal consisted of ham and egg sandwiches and several soft drinks, but he spent most of the night before his execution talking to family, including his parents. Prison chaplain the Rev. Pickens Johnson said that Hambrick told him, "I've made my peace with God. Pray for me."[3015] George Hambrick was electrocuted at the Main Prison in Nashville on April 24, 1945.[3016]

Billy Leon Dixon (aka Billy Dixon Hickman), black, age 26. *Rape.*

The crime was committed near the Round Pond community in a rural section of Montgomery County on the evening of November 25, 1944. The victim was Mrs. Maggie Jones, white, age twenty, who was obviously pregnant. Dixon went to trial on January 12, 1945, and one hundred and seventy prospective jurors were summoned before a jury was selected.[3017]

Here is the entire Tennessee Supreme Court opinion:

> The defendant has been convicted of rape on the body of a young married woman named Maggie Jones and sentenced to death. He has appealed in error to this Court. Mrs. Jones and her husband lived in a rural section of Montgomery County. At the time of the assault her husband was sick in bed and she was working in Clarksville. She left Clarksville in a bus on the late afternoon of Saturday, November 24, 1944, and alighted at a point within a mile or so of a brother's house where her husband was at the time. She started down the road toward her brother's house and heard a man approaching from the rear, to whom she paid no particular attention until he walked in front of her and stopped her. This man, a negro, drew a pistol on her and demanded that she yield to his sexual desires. She protested, offering him money to let her alone. He refused, and then with a drawn pistol dragged her through the bushes off to a side of the road. He forced her to the ground, threatening to shoot her if she resisted, and with this threat overcame her, removed some of her clothing and fully accomplished his purpose.[3018]
>
> When she was allowed to get up the negro followed her to the road and threatened to kill her there. She again offered him money not to kill her. He refused the money but finally let her go, telling her that he would kill her if she told of the assault. She made her way to the house of people nearby whom she knew and according to their testimony arrived in a highly nervous condition and told them of the occurrence. She gave a detailed description of the negro and his clothing. The gentleman got out of his car and he and his wife took Mrs. Jones to her brother's house where she was put to bed. The incident was reported to the sheriff, he came to see Mrs. Jones, and she described the assault and described the negro and his attire. The place of the assault was visited by officers and others and their testimony as to the tracks in the road and broken bushes evidenced a struggle such as the woman had related and also there was evidence of her having been dragged.
>
> The State's proof shows that this negro Dixon and two other negroes had boarded a bus at Clarksville on that afternoon and got off at the place where Mrs. Jones alighted. Neither of the other two negroes figured in the assault. From the description given by Mrs. Jones of her assailant and perhaps other information, city officers in Clarksville arrested Dixon at a picture show at that place three or four days later. When they found him in the picture show he had on a woman's coat and paper in his mouth between his lips and his teeth, evidently trying to disguise his identity. Clothes exactly like those which Mrs. Jones said her assailant wore were found in Dixon's possession, including a pair of boots which she said she was wearing at the time he assaulted her.
>
> After Dixon was arrested he made a full confession of the assault to the sheriff and an earlier confession of the assault to the chief of police at Clarksville. There is no suggestion on the record that either of these confessions were procured by undue means. No exceptions were taken to either of them, although four able counsel were appointed by the court to represent the defendant. The confessions gave the details of the rape just about as they were given by Mrs. Jones.
>
> Dixon did not take the witness stand in his own behalf. The only error assigned in this Court as a ground for reversal is with respect to the court's charge. Evidently, in inadvertence, in giving his instructions to the jury the court embodied the customary language, "When the defendant testified in his own behalf, his testimony is to be weighed by the same rules that the testimony of the other witnesses is weighed."

But later the court told the jury, "However, the defendant did not testify in this case and this cannot be taken against him for the law presumes that he is innocent until he is proven guilty." After the regular charge was given, upon the request of counsel, the court gave this additional instruction: "I charge you that the defendant's failure to take the stand in his own defense shall not be construed by you as an admission of guilt. He may or may not take the stand in his own defense, without prejudice to him or without prejudice to the issues that are before you for determination."

Said the court, "Counsel argue, but without support of authority, or without, we think, any good reason, that the portion of the court's original charge quoted above was error and resulted in great prejudice to the rights of defendant. We do not see this at all. Certainly the requested instruction given by the court met the situation and made the legal rights of the defendant perfectly clear."

The court concluded, "This was an atrocious crime committed upon a young woman who was at the time an expectant mother. She informed the defendant of this fact when she was begging to be let off but he told her that made no difference and proceeded in his brutal lust. We see no reason to interfere with the verdict and judgment below and that judgment be affirmed. The date of execution is set for July 16, 1945."

Billy Dixon was executed on July 16, 1945, and the newspapers reported nothing of his last meal or words.[3019]

1946

Johnnie Outlow (aka Johnnie Outlaw), black, age 27. *Murder.*

Thomas Walker, black, age 35. *Murder.*

The crime was committed on April 21, 1945, in the outskirts of Memphis, in Shelby County. The victim was Andrew Jackson Mitchison, white, age thirty-four, a civilian employee of the Army Air Corp depot, and his white female companion, Irene R. Duffy, age unknown. He and the woman were petting in his parked car. Already at the spot were Outlow and Walker, who had arrived in a car with two black women. Outlow had a record of violent crime, including putting a woman's eye out and knifing her husband. The Mitchison car drove slowly by and stopped. In a few minutes Outlow said he was going to get some money, implying that he knew the occupants of the Mitchison car. Walker followed. Outlow pulled Mitchison from his car.

A struggle ensued and Outlow cut Mitchison's throat, nearly severing the head from the body. While Walker held the woman and served as a lookout, Outlow repeatedly raped her.[3020] The evidence was conflicting whether Walker raped her as well. He maintained he did not. His detailed motion for a severance fixed all the criminal activities on Outlow. Walker's argument suggested he was only an observer.[3021] But he held the woman while Outlow took Mitchison's body and dumped it in a nearby river. After the murder and rape, the attackers told the woman not to leave the site of the crime for at least half an hour. Returning to their car, they found it gone.[3022]

Here is the entire Tennessee Supreme Court opinion in the case:

> The accused were convicted of first degree murder of A.J. Mitchison, with death sentences. It is clearly established that the crime was committed after night in the outskirts of Memphis, Shelby County, where the defendants pulled the deceased and his female companion from their car, Outlow cutting the throat of deceased while Walker held his companion; that it was thus committed in the course of robbery of the person and attempted rape of the female companion of the deceased; that both parties actively participated in the crime and that it was a crime of unusual brutality.[3023]
>
> The assignments filed for Outlow challenge only sufficiency of the evidence and are obviously without support on the record and need not be considered further than to note that identification is clear and without conflict and the facts briefly summarized above are testified to by State's witnesses without contradiction.
>
> Assignments filed for Walker by the Shelby County Public Defender question the refusal of a severance and rejection of testimony as to the brutal and dangerous character of Outlow, offered in support of his plea that he was coerced by Outlow. These matters are discussed by the Attorney General in his brief, and we agree with his disposition of them. We deem further consideration of them unnecessary, since, on the argument in this Court we understand counsel to press only a plea for a recommendation by this Court to the Governor that Walker be relieved of the sentence of death.
>
> We have given serious consideration to this plea. While the record does indicate that Outlow was, perhaps, the primary and dominant mover in the commission of the crime, we find nothing convincing to the effect that Walker did not enter freely into the attack, robbery, of which he shared the fruits, and the murder of deceased. And while he did not attempt for himself to commit rape on the woman companion, there is proof that he dragged her and restrained her outcries and thus rendered assistance to Outlow in this regard also. He had held the woman, as before stated, and when she sought to assist the deceased in resisting Outlow, and thereafter continued to render assistance to Outlow.

The court concluded:

> We think it only too clear that Walker might have easily, if he had desired, fled from the scene at any time, both before and during the attack. He appears to have rather elected to participate in it. We are unable to say that one so implicated in a crime so brutal and inexcusable is deserving of consideration. Granting that he was somewhat less responsible, as argued, than Outlow, his offense nevertheless calls for the extremest punishment which the law provides. Outlow is deserving on this record of greater punishment than man made laws can inflict. Even if Walker's crime is of a degree somewhat less reprehensible, it is still of such quality to demand, in justice, the extreme penalty of the law. The judgment is affirmed, and the defendants will be delivered to the State Prison and the authorized official thereof will execute the sentences on the 1st day of March 1946.

One death penalty researcher has accredited Walker's position that he was a near hostage of Outlow's.[3024]

The pair was electrocuted on the day set. The newspapers published nothing about their last meals or words. Outlow was executed first, Walker fifteen minutes later.[3025]

George Douglass, black, age 20. *Rape.*

The crime was committed at 10:00 P.M. on March 23, 1945, near the intersection of Hollywood and Summer Street, in Memphis, Shelby County. Douglass, married, worked for a wood products company. He had been at the Paradise Grill, about a mile a way, but was seen leaving on a bicycle with a mounted wicker basket. The victim was Charlene Holste, white, age seventeen, a schoolgirl.

Charlene had been visiting school friend Imogene Barkley when the two left Imogene's house at 9:30 P.M. and walked together to the intersection of Hollywood and Broad. Imogene returned home and Charlene continued alone. As she continued walking, Charlene became aware of someone behind her on a bicycle. She quickened her step but heard someone dismount and drop the bicycle. Douglass came up behind her and with gloved hands put a hand over her mouth and another around her neck.[3026]

Douglass walked Charlene about a half-block to a dark area between two buildings. When she refused to take off her clothes and lie on the ground, he threw her to the ground and pulled off her jeans and panties and raped her. During the struggle her nose began bleeding. When finished, he told her to come to a nearby movie theater the next afternoon and bring two other girls with her.

Charlene ran to her sister's house, wetting her pants as she ran. The sister administered a hot-water douche. Charlene was taken to the hospital and a doctor confirmed the physical signs of rape. Her hymen had been broken and she was bleeding. An issue that was not raised until after the trial was whether the hymen was broken by the rape or by the douche.[3027]

That evening the police went house to house asking if anyone had seen a man on a bicycle. Fred Cartwright, black, who worked at the same woodworking plant, said he had seen someone riding a bicycle with a wicker basket and heard a woman's scream about the time of the rape. Cartwright did not know Douglass's name from work, only that he pushed a wheelbarrow.[3028]

Police summoned officials of the woodworking plant. From the company files they got several names and addresses. Taking Cartwright along, the police finally got to Douglass's house, where he was summoned to the door in his underwear. Cartwright identified Douglass and a search of the house revealed his trousers with both blood and mud on them, along with leather gloves. One glove showed both blood and lipstick. Blood was also found on his shirttail and underwear.

Douglass was taken to the hospital and Charlene identified him. It was here, in the presence of Charlene and the police, that he admitted telling her to come to the movie theater the next day and bring two friends.

Taken to police headquarters, Douglass quickly confessed, taking the police to the scene of the rape and the location of the bicycle. He said he had raped several other women, all black.

At trial, he repudiated his confession, insisting he had been tortured. He said the detective had ordered him to stand on two chairs, handcuffed in the back, and suspended him from a chain attached to the ceiling. At trial, he had an explanation for most of the physical evidence. The blood was from having sex with his wife, who was menstruating. It was not lipstick but a red crayon on his glove, used to mark lumber. He was unable to explain how the blood had gotten on the glove or his trousers. The blood type on the gloves and his clothing did not match his wife's. It matched Charlene's.

The case was appealed to the Tennessee Supreme Court, which said there was no evidence to support the torture story because Douglass had been examined by a doctor after the questioning. The doctor found nothing wrong with him and Douglass told him he had not been mistreated by the officers.[3029] Douglass was first asked about the "date" for the movie by Charlene when Douglass was taken to her in the hospital; the officers had not been told of this demand.[3030] His alibi witnesses, which included two of his cousins, all stated that he was gone from the Paradise Grill from about 8:30 to 10:45 and that he left and returned on the bicycle owned by a cousin.[3031]

Douglass was ordered executed on March 15, 1946. An attempt was made to have the United States Supreme Court hear the case, but it was rejected. Governor Jim McCord studied the record and allowed the execution to go forward on July 5, 1946.[3032] Douglas declined to discuss the crime and went calmly to his death in the electric chair at the appointed time.[3033]

John Luffman, white, age 46. *Murder.*
Alvin Hicks, white, age 23. *Murder.*

The crime was committed on the morning of August 15, 1943, in the home of Newton K. "Jink" Herndon near the town of Tharpe, north of Dover, in Stewart County. Herndon was a prominent local farmer and a former deputy sheriff. Herndon and his wife had left their home for the day on August 14, 1943. He asked his niece Ruphine Wallace Cherry, white, age twenty-two, and her husband

Grady W. "Cotton" Cherry, white, age twenty-six, to watch the house while the couple was gone.

John Luffman was a farmhand who worked on Herndon's farm. Grady Cherry was a ladies' man known to offer young women rides in his mail delivery truck while on his rural delivery route. Because Luffman had an incestuous relationship with his fifteen-year-old daughter Ophie, he objected to Cherry's offering her rides into town and giving her the opportunity to meet other men.[3034]

Alvin Hicks had made repeated advances towards Ruphine before and after her marriage to Grady.[3035] The couple had been married five years and in May she had given birth to a daughter, who died two weeks later. On the Saturday night before the murders, Hicks and Luffman met and planned to kill Grady Cherry. Each man had a different motive. Luffman wanted to keep him away from Ophie. Hicks later said that Luffman had offered him one hundred dollars to assist in the killing.[3036] Hicks was aware of Luffman's incest and later claimed that Luffman promised him he would also enjoy the daughter's physicality if he helped with the murder.

The murder weapon, a .32 caliber pistol, was owned by Herndon and had been stolen from his home a few weeks before.[3037] Luffman, carrying the pistol, and Hicks quietly entered the home. According to both men's written confessions, Luffman shot and killed Grady Cherry while he was sleeping on the couch. Using a different pistol, Hicks shot and killed Ruphine Cherry, who was sleeping on a mat on the floor beside her husband. The first shot awakened her and she began to scream.[3038] The Supreme Court opinion says both were shot while in bed.[3039]

After the murders, one of the men had sex with the dead body of Ruphine Cherry, although both men denied doing so in their written confessions. Each said the other had remained behind for this purpose.

After killing the couple, Hicks wrote on a scrap of a Mother's Day card, "To Deputy Sheriff Herndon: Here's your gun, also your niece. I owe you and Trinkle a debt and I'm paying them. I will visit him later. Take good care of the gun. I may want to borrow it again sometime." The message was signed, "The Gang."[3040] The note was designed to make the murders look like a revenge killing against Herndon and the current sheriff, Clyde C. Trinkle. But for the note, the deaths may have been considered a murder/suicide because the pistol was found between Ruphine's breast and arm.

Luffman was the first person to notify neighbors of the deaths. He claimed he came by to deliver corn and when no one opened the door he looked in the window and saw Ruphine's body on the floor. According to one account, suspicion focused on him when the sheriff's daughter (also a deputy) pointed out that Luffman had said he saw two bodies when he looked in the window, but in recreating the scene, only one could be observed.[3041]

Unable to proceed, the sheriff and Herndon hired a private detective, Park Summer, from Memphis. He canvassed the neighborhood posing as a salesman, and soon learned that Hicks had told several people before the killing that he wanted to have Ruphine run away with him, and if she refused, he would kill her. He also found two witnesses who heard gunshots at the time of the killings and could place both Hicks and Luffman nearby. (By this time Luffman was in prison for committing incest with his daughter.) Hicks had left town and was working in Evansville, Indiana.

Sheriff Trinkle and the private detective went to Evansville and took Hicks to a fine hotel for a meal. The sheriff asked him to come back to Stewart County and serve as a special deputy sheriff in order to find the killer. As an inducement, the sheriff gave Hicks an "official" pistol to carry. Hicks was flattered and wrote in longhand an application for a commission as deputy. As dictated by the sheriff, he wrote, "Sheriff Clyde Trinkle: I am herewith making application to you as deputy sheriff on your force while I am working on this thing and trying to catch the gang who killed Herndon's niece and son-in-law. I am here to visit my father and will work until I return home later. I will thank you to borrow your gun and will return it again. Until this debt is better paid, I am sincerely yours, Alvin Hicks."

The "application" contained several words used in the death scene note, such as "gang," "niece," "debt," "borrow," and "visit." A handwriting expert in the Memphis police department concluded the writing in both documents were the same because the "t" was written in a distinctive "fishhook" manner.[3042]

Hicks was confronted with the evidence and promptly made a written confession.[3043] When it was shown to Luffman in prison, he quickly confessed and said Hicks had killed and sexually assaulted Ruphine.[3044] Hicks had earlier served a brief jail term for assaulting a schoolgirl.[3045]

According to the Supreme Court, "While he was in jail awaiting trial, Hicks continued to admit his guilt and made confessions to the sheriff, to the sheriff's wife, to his own wife, and to members of the grand jury when the latter were inspecting the jail."[3046] However, at trial Hicks claimed innocence.

At trial, the defendants were visibly angry at each other and had to be kept separate at all times. Hicks told the jury that his confession was false, part of his plan to lull the real killer into a false sense of security, and was convinced his alibi that he was with his family would clear him. Luffman also initially pled not guilty, but after the prosecution made its case he changed his plea and begged for mercy.[3047] When sentences were pronounced, Luffman said nothing, but Hicks said the penalty was "a little too much."[3048]

Hicks's family alibi involved his presence at a birthday party, but the state offered evidence that hunters had seen Hicks and Luffman on the morning of the killings near the Herndon house, and Hicks was seen at Luffman's house the evening before the crime, when Luffman said it was planned. Said the Supreme Court, "If, therefore, the alibi was false in part, the jury was justified in disbelieving it entirely."[3049]

The court also rejected a claim that the experts who testified about the similarity in the notes had not been properly qualified as expert witnesses, saying this was a matter for the discretion of the trial court.[3050]

The court also rejected the claim of newly discovered evidence in the form of an affidavit from a Baptist minister who said that a Sunday school had been held on the afternoon of August 15, "although other members of the congregation had testified that no such service was held."[3051] What this evidence was supposed to mean cannot be determined from the opinion, which states, "He, of course, would not testify that the defendant Hicks had been in attendance. The fact of the attendance or non-attendance at Sunday school some hours after the crime had been committed was, we think, only an incident of the alibi and immaterial."[3052]

The court said the pair had received a fair trial. "The eighteen months which elapsed between the crime and the trial dimmed to some extent, the clarity of the testimony, but that passage of time served to the advantage of the defendants to dim also the passions of the community against the defendants for their hideous and revolting crime."[3053]

While the case was on appeal the Supreme Court sent the pair for observation at Central State Hospital for the Insane where the doctors pronounced them both "criminally responsible."[3054] Hicks offered a last affidavit to the court which was also meant to support his bid for a commutation. The killings were instigated by Jink Herndon, who said he would rather see his niece dead than see her "dragged all over the country from one Army camp to another," because the worthless Grady was soon to be drafted.

Hicks told an elaborate story of how Herndon had gotten Lewis Aaron, who was Luffman's son-in-law, to arrange the killings. Hicks's last affidavit portrayed him as a passive participant who wrote a note he did not understand, went along with Luffman and Aaron to the house unaware of what was to happen, but willing to go along because Luffman had offered Ophie's favors if he helped. At the house, Luffman and Aaron shot the pair while "I was standing in the hallway looking into the room with my right hand on the door facing."[3055] Hicks further explained that after the killings, he was prevented from seeing Ophie by Lewis Aaron, who drew a shotgun on him.

Following two reprieves, both men were executed on the morning of August 30, 1946. Luffman was executed first. Seated in the electric chair, he said, "Hicks killed the woman. I had nothing to do with the woman."[3056]

Hicks continued to assert his innocence, persisting that by doing so he would receive a commutation. As he was taken to the electric chair, he said, "I ain't got no statement to make. I just hope to meet you all in heaven."[3057] Two days before, he had embraced Catholicism.[3058]

1947

Albert "Bantam" Duboise, white, age 37. *Murder.*

The crime was committed on February 20, 1946, about ten o'clock in the morning in a taxicab office in Murfreesboro, in Rutherford County. The office was known as "797," and the victim was Albert Willis, white, age thirty, a cab driver. The cab office was a nine-foot-by-twelve-foot building which had only one door, two chairs and a couch.

About a week before the killing, Duboise, a town bully, morphine addict, and bootlegger, had been sleeping on the couch in the office when he was awakened by a city policeman at 3:30 A.M. and told to go home.[3059] Duboise became angry and began asking the police and everyone who had anything to do with the cab company, whether it was Willis who had called the police. Duboise used the phrase "turned him up" to describe the act of calling the police.[3060]

In the days that followed, Duboise's anger at Willis seemed to increase. To one person he said Willis was a coward who would not fight him. To another he said he planned to kill Willis and brandished a ten-inch knife. The night before the killing, Duboise had returned from Nashville by bus, where he had picked up seven half pints of whiskey and had garnered some morphine. Both he and codefendant Claude Higdon were morphine users. When arrested, Higdon was carrying a hypodermic syringe which was shown to the jury. At trial, Duboise freely admitted he was a ten-year morphine addict, using from two to six grains a day.[3061]

On the afternoon before the killing, Duboise had come to the cab office and showed cab company co-owner "Rooster" Messick a ten-inch knife (the murder weapon) and said, "I bought this knife for the somebody that turned me in." Messick remarked that Duboise should take the knife home to his wife "to cut meat with, or you will get killed with it." To this Duboise responded, "I will never get killed. When I get ready to kill a man, it will be just 'dear John,' and he will never know anything about it, and it will be 'dear John.'" As he said this, he pretended to stab Messick in the shoulder.[3062] Duboise said that he had killed three men and cut another twenty-seven and had never served much time. He also said, "When I kill a man, I just sit in jail and say my story over so many times until it would be just that way."[3063] In 1936, Duboise had been convicted of manslaughter in the knife slaying of restaurant owner George G. Snow, white, age thirty-two. Sentenced to ten years, he had been paroled after only fourteen months.[3064]

On the morning of the killing, Duboise and his two longtime fellow petty criminals, Claude Higdon and James "Wren" Miller, had been drinking whiskey but were not intoxicated. They left a combination pool room/barbershop and, led by Duboise, went to the cab office. Duboise made it clear that he was going to confront Willis about the earlier incident. Present in the office was Buck Climer, a cab driver; Smithson, a teen-ager who served as dispatcher; and Willis, who was seated in a cane-bottom chair. Shortly after the trio entered and Duboise began haranguing Willis, Messick arrived.

Willis was sitting in the chair backwards. That is, he was facing the back of the chair straddling it, with his arms crossed over the back of the chair. Each time Duboise angrily accused Willis of turning him in, Willis calmly denied having done so, and said that he was going home and didn't want any trouble. Both Miller and Higdon chimed in with remarks that taunted Willis or goaded Duboise. Miller said, "If a man were to tell me I told a lie, I would kill the son-of-a-bitch." He also said, "Duboise, we are behind you, ain't we, Claudie?" to which Hidgon, said, "Yeah."[3065]

As Willis began to rise, Duboise stepped forward and cut him on the top of the head with the knife. Willis fell backward and Duboise stabbed him in the shoulder. Climer and Messick carried Willis to the hospital, where he died shortly thereafter. Duboise fled to Jasper, in East Tennessee, where he was arrested when he came to a doctor's office begging for morphine. He said he would surrender if the doctor gave him the drug. The other two were found locally, inebriated.

At trial, Duboise and codefendants insisted that Willis had come forward in a threatening manner and the stabbing was in self-defense. The other witnesses soundly contradicted that contention, and defense counsel argued that Duboise's drug addiction, plus the amount of alcohol he had imbibed, vitiated the element of premeditation needed for first-degree murder. Miller and Higdon asserted they were little more than bystanders. The jury gave Duboise the death penalty and the others received twenty years and a day.

The Tennessee Supreme Court rejected the defenses factually as well as legally, saying, "The conduct of the defendants, their movements as described by persons who observed them, their words of encouragement to Duboise at and before the time he struck the fatal blow, all show that the killing was the result of a wilful, deliberate, and premeditated design among them."[3066]

Duboise asserted it was error for the prosecutor to argue, "One who would commit such a crime in such a manner is not worthy to trod the soil or earth of a penitentiary ground. If he is sent to the penitentiary and were pardoned or were to escape, you, Gentlemen of the Jury, and everybody else connected with or interested in the prosecution, would be in danger. Even your life and mine would be unsafe." This was not improper argument, concluded the Supreme Court, saying the prosecutor may argue that the "accused has no right to live, and that he is a menace to society even when confined within prison walls."[3067] Duboise's execution was scheduled for March 13, 1947, but was carried out on April 11, 1947, because the governor had asked for a sanity hearing.

Members of the Duboise family haunted the governor's office the day before the execution and his wife was allowed to hold his hand through the prison bars the night before the execution. Duboise had been baptized by prison chaplain the Rev. Pickens Johnson a week before the execution, and the condemned man spent much time in Bible reading. Said to be extremely nervous, he made no request for a last meal and was given sandwiches. He accepted a new suit of clothes, apparently reviving a so-called tradition that had not been followed in many years.[3068]

He took sole responsibility for the killing, saying about Miller and Higdon, "They had absolutely nothing to do with the killing. I killed Albert Willis myself in an argument over a cab." During the time the three were incarcerated, neither Miller nor Higdon ever spoke with Duboise, nor sent him a message prior to his execution.

Duboise was placed in the electric chair at 5:26 A.M. to be executed in two minutes. After he was strapped in the chair a wire that carried current was found broken. He remained bound in the chair while the prison electrician worked feverishly to fix the problem. The chair had not been tested prior to its use that morning. The switch was finally thrown at 5:42 A.M.[3069]

John Hodge, Jr., age 28, black. *Rape.*

The crime was committed in the afternoon of April 27, 1946. The victim was Mrs. Erma Beake, white, age twenty-two. She was a housewife; her husband was a tenant farmer on land owned by Vernon Peters, near Ripley, in Lauderdale County.[3070]

Hodge was a trusty at the Fort Pillow Prison Farm in west Tennessee. He was serving a ten-year term for burglary and larceny. He simply walked away from the dairy barn where he worked, carrying an ice pick used in his work. He walked to the victim's house on a neighboring farm. He threatened Erma with the ice pick and a rifle he found at the house before gagging and raping her in front of her infant child. Erma's husband came to the house a few minutes after the rape and Hodge ran away in the direction of the prison farm.

The entire prison farm was called to stand in line and Erma immediately identified Hodge. Within hours he signed a written confession and led law enforcement officers to the location of the stolen rifle and ammunition. News of the crime caused great excitement in the Ripley area and Hodge was taken to Memphis and jailed. The same was done after his conviction. His conviction was affirmed by the Tennessee Supreme Court on May 3, 1947, but the opinion cannot be located. Hodge, from Nashville, was electrocuted at the Main Prison in Nashville on June 19, 1947.[3071] "I've made peace with my Lord," he said a short time before his execution, "I'm ready to go."[3072]

Fred Jackson, black, age 18. *Murder.*

The crime was committed on January 8, 1946, at the home of Mr. and Mrs. I.T. Goss. The family lived in a small four-room house about five miles outside of Memphis, near White Station, in Shelby County. Mr. Goss, white, had gone to work, leaving his wife Hazel, white, age thirty-three, to care for their two youngest children, Freddie J. Goss, age three, and Sammie M. Goss, fourteen months. The other four children were at school. Freddie and Sammie were the victims.

Fred Jackson, age sixteen, was a neighbor. He had staked out the house because tracks from his boots led to a chicken coop about seventy-five feet from the house. He waited there until Mr. Goss and the schoolchildren had gone. He approached the house from the back gate, stating he was there to pay for rifle cartridges he had borrowed from Mrs. Goss's son while hunting with him. Using this story to distract her, he gained entry into the house as she looked in another room to make change for a silver dollar he offered as payment.[3073]

Once inside the house, Jackson propositioned Mrs. Goss. Angered by his approach, she told him to leave, telling him that he would be in a great deal of trouble. Jackson then attacked her. She reached for the family pistol in a nearby drawer. But the pistol was broken and did not fire. Jackson attacked her with a kitchen knife, causing severe damage to one of her hands as she tried to protect herself. She was ravished by Jackson.[3074] He then clubbed her and her two crying children with a blunt pipe and set the house on fire. Because it had rained the night before, Jackson doused the house with both gasoline and kerosene, inside and out. The house smoldered for about thirty minutes and within two hours burned to the ground.[3075]

Police were called when neighbors reported a fire at the Goss home. Upon arrival, they found the three victims lying unconscious outside the burning ruins of the home. Hazel Goss had regained consciousness and had been able to carry her children out of the burning house before it collapsed. All received serious burn injuries. Freddie died in the hospital that night, Sammie the next day.

Mrs. Goss went in and out of consciousness over the next two days, but was able to name Jackson as her assailant. The police arrested him immediately and he was found with a fresh cut on his hand. Jackson told the police the injury was caused while cutting fat meat to make lard a week earlier. When confronted that the wound was too fresh, Jackson changed his story and said that it had happened on Saturday (the day after the assault) while cutting spare ribs in a smokehouse. This prompted the police to ask him to show them where the injury occurred. Jackson directed them to his home. There, Jackson's father, whose name was Young Jackson, gave permission to search the property.

According to the Tennessee Supreme Court, "The officers searched and found a pair of brown pants, a leather jacket and a shirt, and all of these garments appeared to have blood stains on them. These garments were exhibited to Mrs. Goss during the course of the trial and she identified them as being those worn by Jackson on the morning she was assaulted and her children were killed. When the pants were found they were wet. They were in a closet stuffed behind the brick chimney."[3076] Boots found at the Jackson home fit the footprint casts made at the chicken coop.[3077]

Hazel Goss identified Jackson from her hospital bed the second time he was brought to her. The first time she could not because her eyes were swollen shut.

Jackson made a written confession to the police and a newspaper reporter after being identified by Mrs. Goss. He said, "I grabbed a butcher knife and cut her. Then I got hold of that pipe. Then I hit the two small kids and set the house on fire to make it look like an accident."[3078]

At trial in March 1946, Jackson denied any involvement, and sought to fix blame on two acquaintances, Frank Dean and Bo Garret. But during the police investigation when he implicated them, Garret insisted on being taken to be seen by Mrs. Goss. Dean was able to show an alibi by the testimony of Albert Jackson, the defendant's uncle, as well as Garret. Jackson's written confession was produced after he implicated Garret and Dean. He could not explain why it did not mention the pair. The policeman who took the written confession also testified that after doing so, Jackson told him where to find the pistol that did not shoot.

Fred Jackson was nearly seventeen years old at the time of the crime, but was only in the eighth grade. The Tennessee Supreme Court described him as "bright in his work and very well liked by his companions."[3079] By the time of his execution on August 11, 1947, Jackson was eighteen years old, but the court refused to consider clemency because of the nature of the crime. During the appeal, Jackson admitted the sexual assault on Mrs. Goss. He had only been charged with the murder of three-year-old Freddie Goss, for which he was sentenced to death.[3080]

Fred Jackson ate a large dinner the night before his execution but skipped breakfast. Described as calm and "Sphinx-like" to the very end, he had been counseled by the Rev. Pickens Johnson, the prison chaplain. Strapped in the electric chair at 5:30 A.M., Jackson was pronounced dead four minutes later. The Rev. Johnson declined to discuss Jackson's last words with him, but did not deny that Jackson had admitted his guilt in raping Mrs. Goss.[3081]

1948

James D. Sandusky, white, age 20. *Murder.*
John T. Kelley, white, age 19. *Murder.*

The crime was committed on January 6, 1947, in rural Hickman County about seven miles from Centerville. The victim was James Edward Sprouse, white, age thirty-six, an executive with the Tennessee Burley Tobacco Growers' Association. He had been a lieutenant in the Army serving overseas during World War II.

The killers had met while confined to a Navy disciplinary barracks in Boston a few months before the killing, just prior to their respective dishonorable discharges from the Marines. Kelley was from Marion, Illinois. Sandusky had grown up in Nashville. Kelley came to Nashville shortly before the murder and the two had agreed to stage a robbery in order to pay for a trip to Florida, where they intended to find jobs. On Sunday, January 5, Kelley bought a .22 pistol in Nashville from a friend of Sandusky.

The day of the killing, the men were hitchhiking "on Hillsboro Road just beyond the Tennessee Central overpass," in the outskirts of Nashville.[3082] They were picked up by a man named Byrne, who became uneasy about them when it appeared that Sandusky was carrying a pistol. Byrne explained he needed to stop at a gas station in the Green Hills area and the killers asked to be let out of the car. They walked on ahead. When Byrne came upon them again they assumed he was going to pick them up and stepped near his car. He swerved to avoid them and continued home.

As the pair continued walking along Hillsboro Road, Sprouse came along in his green 1942 Ford Sedan and gave them a ride. Sprouse was from Clarksville and his car bore Montgomery County license plates. He was on his way to Columbia for an evening meeting of the tobacco growers and was headed by way of Franklin. Sprouse stopped at a gas station in Brentwood and the pair was seen in the car. Kelley had distinctive bushy hair and Sandusky's hair was very long and tended to fall over his forehead "like Hitler."[3083]

The pair overcame Sprouse as the car neared Columbia and took Highway 50 toward Centerville, where they turned off onto a small road. Here they tied Sprouse to a tree using his necktie and overcoat belt. They got back in the car and drove some distance when Sandusky became concerned that Sprouse had not been bound firmly enough.

At trial, Kelly insisted that he stayed in the car and "had no knowledge of Sandusky's purpose when the latter committed the homicide."[3084] According to the Supreme Court, "At any rate, with the deceased thus tied and pleading for his life, Sandusky, who had received a rating as a Marksman during his service in the Marines, shot the deceased six times."[3085] According to one account, Sandusky said, "Before I pulled the trigger he looked at me and said, 'Please don't harm me,' but I shot anyway. He slumped over but didn't cry out. I shot him seven times and I hit him close to the heart."[3086] The killers drove to Centerville and bought gas and cigarettes. They concluded the body was too close to the road. They returned and untied the body and dragged it into the woods. Later, they threw Sprouse's belongings into the Duck River.

At about 8:00 P.M. the car pulled into a combination service station and general store near Centerville and the two jumped out, but quickly got back into their car (Sprouse's) and sped away when another customer drove up. The feckless killers decided not to proceed to Florida but returned to Sandusky's home in Nashville and spent the night.

About the same time, Mrs. Sprouse called the Tennessee Highway Patrol deeply concerned about her husband's disappearance. He always called her when he was late, but was past the time he was due home, and he had missed the 4:00 P.M. meeting in Columbia. She said he carried about twenty dollars in his wallet. The family was among the wealthiest in Montgomery County and a kidnapping was possible. Three hours later, the patrol sent a radio alert to its branches to watch for Sprouse's car. A reporter present at headquarters was told of the disappearance and the next day's *Tennessean* newspaper contained a photograph of Sprouse, explaining he was missing.[3087]

Taking the road the next day, Sandusky and Kelley held up a gas station in Pulaski, Tennessee. Within minutes, a description of the car and the robbers was broadcast over the Tennessee Highway Patrol radio network and lawmen began converging on Pulaski and southward. In Athens, Alabama, the two attempted to rob another service station, without success, and by now the Athens police were alerted and the car spotted.

The city lawmen gave chase, and the cars sped for miles, exchanging gunfire. Kelley knocked out the back window of their car and fired shots at the police cruiser. Apparently losing control of the car, the killers got out and ran into a densely wooded area where a dozen lawmen found them. The pair gave up without a struggle.

In custody, the killers said they had let Sprouse out of the car unharmed. Highway Patrol commissioner Lynn Bomar, in charge of the interrogation, did not know of Sprouse's death or his location, but barked to the killers who insisted he was still alive, "You better come up with something better than that. We found his body this afternoon, just this side of Centerville."[3088]

Kelley said, "We'd better tell it all, Sandy. It's the only way we'll get a break."[3089] The duo confessed the details of the killing and led police to the body. During this time, Sandusky was asked how he felt about killing Sprouse and he answered, "It was just like wringing the neck of a chicken."[3090]

The pair maintained an attitude of bravado, almost mirth, and were photographed the next day joking and eating ice cream cones while in custody. They were tried in Hickman County on January 30, 1947, and the judge sentenced them to death.[3091]

Sandusky's chief issue on appeal was whether he was so intoxicated by the half pint of whiskey he had shared with Kelley that he lacked requisite intent to commit first-degree murder. The court recited the facts and said there was no proof as to Sandusky's intoxication, and the burden of proof on this issue was on Sandusky.[3092] Kelley tried to argue that because he sat in the car while Sandusky did the shooting, he was guilty only of participating in a robbery. The court recited the felony murder doctrine, stressing that the doctrine does not require express intent to kill in carrying out the predicate felony, here robbery and larceny.[3093]

The Tennessee Supreme Court said, "This appeal largely addresses itself to a plea for mercy for these boys. How can we have any feeling of mercy when Sandusky describes his feeling in killing Sprouse: 'Just like you would feel killing a chicken.'" At trial he said, "I don't have a funny feeling. I do feel kinder bad over it so I am ready to take it and get it over with quick."[3094] The court concluded, "This killing shows that it was a malicious, deliberate, sadistic thing. These boys took this automobile from Sprouse, and our conclusion is, then deliberately killed him to silence him. It was clearly a case of purposeful killing."[3095]

April 22, 1948, was the date the Supreme Court set for the execution. The night before, the governor commuted the death sentences of Daniel Budzynski and Richard Reilly to ninety-nine years, but refused to consider clemency for Sandusky and Kelley. "They were just lucky," commented Kelley.[3096] The pair put up a "bold front," to the last, reported the newspaper, talking about boxing, football and baseball, and expressing no anxiety about their fates, even encouraging well-wishers not to mourn. When they were shaving Sandusky's head, Kelley joked that he wished Sandusky's girlfriend could see him.

Sandusky had been baptized by two students from Free Will Baptist College. Prison chaplain Pickens Johnson said, "Kelley just seems to be a little mixed up on what he believes."[3097] The two were denied their last wish, namely the privilege of playing poker all night before their execution. Sandusky said, "I've been playing solitaire for fifteen months and I haven't beaten Sol yet. It doesn't look like I'll ever get to."[3098]

The pair asked the newspaper to explain "we're going like men," and when asked to tell how others could avoid their fate, Kelley said, "I don't see how I can. Looks like people can't learn. They've got to be shown." Sandusky agreed, saying, "Just tell them to keep out of trouble all the way."[3099]

On the issue of who was to die first, Sandusky had wanted to cut a deck of cards to decide, but Kelley refused, leaving the decision up to the warden, who ordered Sandusky's death first.

A few days before the execution, the pair had offered their corneas for possible transplant, a then new procedure which required the tissue be harvested and sent to New York City. However, no doctor could be found to volunteer this service, especially in light of the fact that the tissue was likely unusable due to the temperature caused by the 2,300 volt charges.[3100]

James M. Scribner, black, age 25. *Rape.*
William J.C. Turner, black, age 21. *Rape.*
Thomas H. Taylor, black, age 33. *Rape.*

The crime was committed at 11:00 P.M. August 7, 1947, on the north side of the Capitol building, near a railroad underpass in Nashville, in Davidson County. The victims were Mae Pullum, white, age nineteen, and Wanda Poston, white, age twenty. Both young women had come to Nashville to attend a business college. Pullum's cousin, Dillard "Steve" Morris, white, age twenty, was also a student at the college.

The trio had gone to a movie, gotten soft drinks, and went to the Capitol to see the city lights.[3101] As they sat, they noticed a Negro with two-tone shoes pass them. A few minutes later, they were surrounded by Scribner, Turner and Taylor, holding pistols. The trio took the girls' watches, rings, and money, and took the wallet of Morris.

The victims were taken to the railroad underpass. A gun was held on Morris. Mae Pullum was raped by Turner and Taylor. Wanda Poston was raped by Scribner. When the rapists ran away, the females hailed a cab and went to their boarding house. "Miss Pullum was taken to a hospital on this same night and examined by a physician who testified to finding physical circumstances very definitely indicating that she had been the victim of penetration and that she was a virgin prior thereto."[3102] The trio was prosecuted only for the rape of Pullum.

The trio's arrest came about in an unusual manner. Court officer Robert Justice was patrolling Crawford Street about three blocks from the Capitol about midnight on August 19.[3103] He happened to see a Negro (who turned out to be Turner) walking across the street wearing a bandana mask over his lower face. Following on foot, he ordered Turner to stop and come out from a darkened building. When Turner flashed a pistol, the officer hit him with a baton, knocking him to the street.[3104] Officer Justice took Turner to a police call box at Fifth Avenue and Jo Johnson. Several bystanders saw Turner's bleeding head.

A patrol car arrived and Turner was placed in the back seat. Officer Justice told the other officers he thought Turner met the description of one of the rapists. Turner blurted out that he had been present, but he was only there because the other two held him at gunpoint. He denied any part in the rapes. At the police station, he was identified by Pullum, in part because of an unusual ring he wore. The watch taken from Poston was later found in the possession of a woman who said she was given it by Taylor.

Turner named the other two. He took police to their homes and they were arrested. At the police station their verbatim confessions, offered at trial, fixed blame on each other, each disclaiming any rape activity. Turner said he was wearing the handkerchief mask to conceal his identity from an enemy with whom he had gotten into a fight the evening before. He admitted carrying the pistol. It was also discovered that Turner had returned to the Capitol a week after the Pullum/Poston rapes with two other young men. They bumped into some undercover police; two identified him at the time of his arrest.

The trio had committed six other rape/robberies at the Capitol location but the victims had been too scared or ashamed to report the crimes. They did so after news of arrests in this crime was reported in the newspapers.

At trial, the trio repudiated their confessions, insisting they had been coerced. Turner said he had been taken to the city garbage dump and beaten by Officer Justice before he was taken to the police station. Scribner said he was left in a sitting position on the floor of the police station and each time a policeman came by the officer pushed his head against the concrete wall. The beatings were not accredited by the court because no one saw any bruises on any of them, except Turner, and the officer's arrest story explained the injuries.

The primary defense was alibi. Turner said he was home with his family, including his wife. But he insisted he was arrested on August 12 (Scribner said August 13), when they had been arrested on the nineteenth and twentieth. The family members insisted they remembered the earlier day because they talked about a joint birthday gift for Turner's mother-in-law, whose birthday was the thirteenth. All agreed there was a joint birthday gift. However, one said it was just a card, another said it was a mirror and comb set, another said it was hosiery.[3105]

Scribner's alibi said he was at home eating peaches and left with a few to eat. His mother supported the alibi, but added that a delivery boy for a local drug store had come and gotten her son. The delivery boy said he had come later than Scribner and his mother said, and the wrapped package was much larger and different in shape than some peaches. It looked and smelled like a large smoked sausage. Because Scribner was very deaf, he also had a distinctive speech pattern.

Taylor's alibi was supported by the woman he lived with, who said they played cards that night with another couple. This couple was not named and did not testify. Taylor's identification was made easier because he had three missing bottom teeth.

The Tennessee Supreme Court said the proof showed Taylor's ring linked him to the crime, as did Poston's watch.[3106] The various sworn statements were admissible because there was no evidence of coercion and the statements were internally consistent: all the defendants admitted they were present, but each insisted he was terrorized and intimidated by the others.[3107] The court said the jury did not believe the alibi witnesses. "There were many discrepancies and contradictions in the details of the stories of the several witnesses.[3108]

A petition to rehear rejected Turner's objection that the use of his confession was improper. Turner asserted that he was not told that his confession could be used against him. The court said that this warning was not the law in Tennessee, but the assistant district attorney who took the statement had told Turner that he did not have to make a statement and he could have a lawyer if he wanted one.[3109] Turner also contended the Supreme Court failed to consider evidence of his alibi. Here the court said the defendant's witnesses regarding his whereabouts were so confusing and contradictory that the jury was justified in concluding it was a fabrication.[3110]

An identical charge was pending against the trio for the rape of Poston at the time they were executed on August 31, 1948. No details of their last day or last words were reported in the newspapers. Turner died first; Taylor was last.[3111] This was the last triple execution in Tennessee.

1949

Barney Thompson (aka Bonnie Thompson), black, age 31. *Murder.*

The crime was committed at 9:00 P.M. on Saturday, November 29, 1947, in "a negro restaurant and beer hall" called the Manhattan Café in downtown Cleveland, in Bradley County.[3112] Thompson had lived with the victim, Maggie Ashmore, black, age thirty-three, who was separated from her husband. She had five children, but the record is not clear whether any were fathered by Thompson.

Maggie ended the relationship and forced Thompson to move out but he persisted in seeking her affection. Several weeks before the killing she had gotten a peace warrant against him. Technically, it had been withdrawn, but she thought it was still in force.

Thompson had been drinking all day and went to the beer hall knowing Maggie would be there. She was sitting in a booth with Arthur Kennedy and another woman. Kennedy had been "running after Maggie for some time," according to Thompson, and when he appeared, Maggie grabbed and hugged Kennedy in a manner that enraged Thompson. He testified, "I asked if she thought that was nice, hugging a married man." He left in anger, returned and ordered a beer. He said, "I went outside and came back in and her and Arthur was in a booth. I don't remember what happened."[3113]

Thompson told Maggie to come to him. She refused and he pulled an eight-inch knife out of his pocket and began stabbing her. She tried to escape but he blocked her exit. She then turned toward the kitchen and fell to the floor. While she was lying on the floor, he stabbed her several more times in the back. Thompson left the beer hall and shortly surrendered to the sheriff at the jail.

Thompson claimed that he was so drunk he lacked requisite intent to commit first-degree murder. He had been drinking all day and that morning had called the police chief asking that Maggie and her sister be put in jail. The chief told him to leave the women alone, to which Thompson replied that he would kill both if they did not watch out. Thompson denied making the statement and said the chief misunderstood him.[3114]

All witnesses said Thompson had been drinking but was not drunk. He maintained that he did not intend to kill her but still loved her at the time of the stabbing. The court said, "Clearly his act of giving himself up to the sheriff immediately after committing this crime did not indicate drunkenness to the point necessary to excuse a mind capable of premeditation. The acid test in such cases is: was the accused so stupefied as to be incapable of premeditation.[3115]

The court said:

> The evidence is clear that Thompson entered this restaurant and seeing the deceased with another left the restaurant and when she refused to talk to him and shortly thereafter returned and started stabbing her until she was killed. The jury were clearly entitled to infer that the defendant considered these acts of the deceased as an affront to his pride and brooding over this he possessed himself of this knife or dagger for the purpose of this homicide during the interval of his absence from the restaurant even though he claims to have had it all the time. It is certain that when she refused to come to him on his return to the restaurant, he immediately began his onslaught on her. From these acts of the defendant the jury might well infer premeditation or a preconceived purpose to kill by the immediate reaction of defendant to this refusal of the deceased to talk to him. The very barbarity of the homicide (cutting and stabbing the deceased with this large knife or dagger even after she lay helpless on the floor) justifies an inference that it had been thought over and the determination reached to this end.[3116]

Thompson was tried by an all-white jury. He asserted that the majority of the Negroes in the community were prejudiced against him, and that this influenced the white jurors against him, but the court said there was no evidence of this prejudice. The court said, "It is common knowledge that normally and ordinarily the white people of this State do not get overly excited or prejudicial over a killing of the kind here committed by members of the minority race to one of its members."[3117] The court said appointed counsel had acted "ably, energetically and efficiently," and "we gladly give them our commendation for their faithful service."[3118] Thompson's execution was set for February 17, 1949. Governor Browning declined to intervene and Thompson was executed at the Main Prison in Nashville that day. The details of his last meal and last words were not reported by the newspapers.[3119]

Bruce Edward Watson, black, age 24. *Rape.*

The crime was committed on October 6, 1947, at 3780 Allen Road in an area called Raleigh, a suburb of Memphis, in Shelby County. This was the victim's home. The victim, Mrs. Edith Comer, white, age fifty, divorced, lived alone in the small house. Bruce Watson lived in the same neighborhood.

Mrs. Comer had gone to bed about midnight and she was raped by Watson between 1:45 A.M. and 2:00 A.M. She put up a vigorous struggle and sustained severe bruises, including a mouth injury caused by Watson's stuffing her underwear into her mouth.

Watson had gained access to the house by prizing open a small window in the kitchen. His fingerprints were found on the refrigerator beneath the window and other places in the house. His car was seen parked off the road a short distance from her house. Watson left his hat in Mrs. Comer's bedroom; it had come off in the struggle and he failed to retrieve it.

Watson was arrested on a Saturday, the day after the rape, but released. He was re-arrested on Sunday, and was questioned from 2:00 P.M. to 10:00 P.M. on Monday, when he finally gave a written confession. His appeal was concerned largely with the circumstances of the confession.

In 1944, the United States Supreme Court held inadmissible a confession garnered by the Memphis police department because it used what had been called Gestapo tactics, namely, near-continuous questioning under a bright light by relays of detectives and investigators.[3120]

Watson contended that his questioning fell within the Ashcraft rule, but the Tennessee Supreme Court said the facts were different. "We think the guilt of the defendant is conclusively shown independently of any alleged confession. This was not true in the Ashcraft case, where guilt was based solely upon circumstantial evidence. Moreover, it appears in the Ashcraft case that he was questioned continuously by officers in relays for more than thirty hours, as he sat under a glaring electric light; not so in the instant case. While the officers questioned Watson for several hours, he suffered no discomfort other than to be asked questions. He made no complaint as to the manner of questioning except to say that he was slapped twice."[3121]

Watson maintained that he had been slapped twice. He said he was told that his family, who had come to see him, would not be allowed to leave the jail until he signed the confession. The court ruled that the slapping, if it happened at all, occurred after he had given the confession, by his own testimony on the witness stand.[3122] Further, no one in his family felt they were being kept unreasonably long in the courthouse; in fact, they were provided with at least one large meal.[3123]

Watson's appeal points were confusing. He contended it was error for the trial court not to allow the jury to see the "dry cell," a special cell used for incorrigible or insane prisoners, where he had been held overnight on Sunday. But the Supreme Court said it was unable to see what was wrong in the court failing to allow this visit, in part because Watson did not explain clearly what was wrong with the cell.

The Court ruled the evidence such as fingerprints, the location of his car, and his hat, showed overwhelming guilt.[3124] It turned aside an argument that the state took too long to present Watson for arraignment, flatly rejecting his constitutional claim under *McNabb v. United States*,[3125] by saying that the doctrine was not the law in Tennessee.[3126]

Watson also alleged error in the district attorney's using a yardstick to point at evidence and said it was error for the district attorney to ask questions that were "confusing the witness," namely, Watson. No error was found here, nor in the district attorney's restating evidence over which Watson's counsel had objected.[3127]

While the opinion does not make it clear, Watson's actual defense was that he had entered the house for the purpose of stealing whiskey and although he had scuffled with Mrs. Comer, he had not actually raped her. The Tennessee Supreme Court did not deal with the last assertion, but said, "This is unquestionably a pure fabrication, because she had no whiskey in the house and no one had any information that she had."[3128]

Watson was executed at the Main Prison in Nashville on June 10, 1949. He maintained his innocence to the end. He said he was innocent because he had only attempted to rape Mrs. Comer, but had not actually done so.[3129]

Two death penalty opponents wrote in 2001, "There was substantial evidence against Watson: his hat and fingerprints were found in the victim's home, and she identified him as her attacker."[3130]

Paul Lacy, black, age 35. *Murder.*

The crime was committed about 6:30 P.M. September 21, 1949, on the farm of Mrs. Susan Brown, located on Brown Hollow Road in the Nebo community near Columbia, in Maury County. The victim, Mrs. Brown, white, age sixty-seven, was a widow who lived alone in the farmhouse. When she failed to answer the phone at 7:00 P.M., the time her adult daughter customarily called her, the daughter became concerned and called a neighbor, Stockard McBride, who agreed to look for her.

After looking for an hour, McBride told the daughter that Mrs. Brown was not home. The daughter beseeched McBride, soon accompanied by John Cook, to look more. At 11:00 P.M. they found Mrs. Brown's body about a hundred yards behind a stock barn at the bottom of a steep ravine.[3131] Mrs. Brown had been struck on the back of the head and face by a heavy object and her neck and body had been savagely scratched. She had been raped and vaginally penetrated with a foreign object. She was wearing no underwear.

Investigation that night and the next morning showed she had been attacked in the barn where she customarily milked the cows, which she usually started around 5:30 P.M. Her false teeth and glasses had been knocked away by the blows. She had put up a fierce struggle. But she had not scratched her assailant. A stick three feet long and two inches in diameter with congealed blood at one end, and a bloody rock with some of Mrs. Brown's hair adhering to it, were found a few hours later between the barn and the ravine.

The next day, the sheriff called a former Maury County policeman who now worked at the Criminal Identification Bureau in Nashville asking for suggestions. The investigator, Gerald Holcomb, immediately suggested Paul Lacy, because he was the prime suspect in a robbery and violent rape of a local girl thirteen years before. He had not been charged because the girl could not make a positive identification.[3132]

Lacy was arrested at his home in the neighborhood. Mrs. Brown's farm hand, who had been paid four dollars the same day she was killed, was missing, and when located he was also arrested. Also taken into custody was a white man who had committed a series of burglaries in Maury County twenty years earlier, because he specialized in preying on women who lived alone.

When Lacy was arrested, bloodstained overalls he had been wearing were found in his home, a house he shared with an elderly white man. The man said that Lacy had been home the entire evening of Mrs. Brown's murder. Lacy said the blood was chicken blood and initial tests proved this true.

Another suspect, a young white farmhand, was arrested and during questioning explained that he had been with the *same* elderly white man in Franklin at the time of the murder. With two men naming the same person to support their alibi at different locations, police returned to question the elderly man. He quickly admitted his previous lie and explained he was attempting to protect Lacy, who had come home at 7:30 P.M. the night of the killing. Lacy appeared very nervous and explained that someone had killed Mrs. Brown and he was fearful he would be accused because of the similar crime thirteen years earlier.[3133]

Under intense questioning, Lacy steadfastly maintained his innocence, even when confronted with a question about how he knew at 7:30 P.M. that Mrs. Brown was dead when her body was not found until hours later. Investigators took samples of tissue from underneath Lacy's fingernails and cut off portions of the nails. Within hours tests confirmed Mrs. Brown's blood type in the samples.

Confronted with this finding, Lacy promptly confessed. He had only intended to knock her out and search the house for reputed hidden wealth. But after killing her, he became frightened and hid her body, and never entered the house. This was apparently true. Her purse containing money was in plain view in her bedroom. The confession was typed by a newspaper reporter, read to Lacy several times, and his photograph was taken with the written confession in his hand.

An angry mob soon appeared at the jail and Lacy was taken by car to the Nashville jail, and the other suspects were also taken in separate cars in different directions, as decoys. Law enforcement officers, notably the Highway Patrol, were determined that no race-related violence occur because the notorious "Mink Slide" riot had occurred only three years before.[3134]

On October 21, 1949, exactly one month after the killing, Lacy went on trial. He disavowed his confession, asserting it was given under fear of the mob. His brother's wife and a nephew said he was at their home at the time of the crime. However, his brother testified that Lacy had hidden Mrs. Brown's underwear at the brother's home. The courtroom was cleared before the bloody garment was presented as evidence. Further tests of the overalls showed the presence of Mrs. Brown's blood and pubic hair. Chicken blood had been rubbed on top of it.

Lacy had three court-appointed lawyers. Each gave a closing argument, emphasizing different aspects of the case. The last argument, given by Marine W. Bledsoe, quoted the Bible and recited William Cullen Bryant's "To a Waterfowl."[3135]

When the jury returned a guilty verdict in fifteen minutes and the judge imposed the death sentence, Lacy's court-appointed lawyers promptly rose and said there would be no appeal. This gesture was intended to cool passions in the crowd both inside and outside the courtroom. Forty-eight armed Highway Patrol troopers had protected Lacy and the courthouse during and after the trial because one of the Mrs. Brown's sons had lunged at him with a pistol as he was brought down a hall on the first day of trial.

Lacy was taken to the prison in Nashville. No appeal was filed and he was executed as scheduled on November 25, 1949. Lacy maintained his innocence to the end. He complained that Mrs. Brown's blood had been placed on the overalls at the Nashville jail. He complained that bloodhounds were never brought to search the Brown farm and that he was at home during the killing.

Warden Glenn Swafford explained his experience with condemned men who assert their innocence: "They will sit there all night long denying their crime, some of them confess just before they are put in the chair, others wait until they are strapped in before they blurt out their confession."[3136] Said Swafford, "If he doesn't confess the entire crime by the time he is placed in the chair in the morning, he will be the third man not to confess out of the thirty-nine I have seen die. One of the other two was described 'as guilty as I am,' by the man who died with him for the same crime."[3137]

The doe-eyed, sleepy-faced Lacy refused to answer specific questions put to him by Swafford about the crime.[3138] He asserted, "It's pretty hard, but I'll make it all right, with God." Mrs. Brown's adult sons were present inside the prison at the time of Lacy's execution, but were prohibited by law from witnessing the death.

An unusual coincidence followed the Lacy case. On the same day he was convicted, the trial judge refused to grant a new trial to Arthur Leonard Bass, white, age forty-six, who had been convicted of killing his cousin Ranier Bass following a poker game on April 22, 1949.[3139] Arthur had received the death penalty in a July 1949 trial and was ordered executed on the same day as Lacy, November 25, 1949.

The two death sentences were the first in modern memory in Maury County. Several weeks after his conviction, Bass was publicly baptized in Bear Creek in a ceremony witnessed by four thousand people as part of a religious revival. Both murder victims were buried in the same cemetery, the Mt. Nebo Cemetery. However, Arthur L. Bass's conviction was overturned by the Tennessee Supreme Court.

1950

Clyde Steele, black, age 21. *Rape.*

The crime was committed about 9:30 P.M. on March 28, 1948, near the victim's home, which "seems to have been in a section of Knoxville largely populated by Negroes."[3140] The victim was Mrs. Annie Kennedy, white, age fifty-eight, a grandmother who lived in the neighborhood. She was walking her five-year-old granddaughter from a neighborhood movie theater when "she was confronted by some Negro who announced that he wanted to walk home with her."[3141] The Supreme Court continued, "She indignantly repulsed his advances, went a short distance to a street light, stood there five or ten minutes, then thinking that she could proceed safely, started on her way home."[3142]

A short distance away she was accosted by two black males, one tall and heavyset and the other somewhat taller. The larger man dragged her from the street over a vacant field near a pigpen and raped her while the other held her granddaughter. After the first rape, she was raped a second time by the other black man. The victim and granddaughter ran home and summoned police.

The Supreme Court described what happened next:

> As a result of much investigation, a Negro cab driver, Columbus Stevens, and another Negro by the name of James Simpson were questioned by the officers. It seems that Stevens had driven Simpson to a point near the place of the assault and there he saw the defendant Herbert Bearden. Simpson was employed by the Southern Railway, and he testified that on the night of the assault he had driven to this corner near the scene of the assault and there saw the defendant [Steele], that he got a match from one of them, that around this time he saw a woman and a little girl going down the street, and that defendant Bearden made a remark to him disclosing his intention to have carnal knowledge of this woman. Simpson further testified that both defendants appeared to have been drinking, and that he asked Bearden if he was not drunk, following this remark about his intention.[3143]

Bearden was arrested; and after being confronted by Stevens he confessed to raping the victim. Steele was arrested and confronted with Bearden's confession. He became nervous and started "slobbering."[3144]

Clyde Steele and Herbert Bearden were given the death penalty. The trial was unusual because the judge who tried the case was called as a witness. He said the two had actually pled guilty at their arraignment (much to his surprise), before he appointed counsel for them. The Supreme Court held this was reversible error and ordered a new trial. It also found error in the district attorney's argument that the death penalty was necessary as a moral justification for Mrs. Kennedy's son's death at Okinawa during World War II. The opinion addressed an issue that would arise following the second trial: "It is insisted that following the verdict they [the lawyers] were advised for the first time that these boys had been beaten and otherwise mistreated by the [police] officers."[3145]

As before, neither took the stand at the second trial, but introduced evidence that they had been drinking and introduced testimony as to their good reputations. Neither had been in any prior trouble with the law. At the second trial, the key evidence came from Stevens and Simpson as before, because the central issue was whether Steele had been beaten in the face and head with a rubber hose by one of the deputies in the afternoon before he confessed, namely at 5:30 P.M. the day he was arrested. The court said there was no evidence of a beating, including lack of such shown in a photograph taken two days later.[3146]

The court ruled the confessions were properly admitted, especially Bearden's, who took the officers to the spot where the rape occurred. Intoxication was not a mitigating factor because no specific intent to commit the crime of rape is necessary, because "no intent is requisite other than evidenced by the doing of the act constituting the offense."[3147] There was no error in allowing an investigator with the district attorney's office to testify in violation of the rule of sequestration of witnesses.[3148]

There was no error in the court's not permitting the jury to hear all the witnesses "with reference to the circumstances under which the confessions were made.[3149] This was because the court had held a hearing on the admissibility of the confessions and the defendants had not cross-examined the witnesses with reference to the circumstances of the confessions.[3150] Finally, it was not error for the trial court to wait until after indictment and arraignment to appoint counsel. The Supreme Court ordered the defendants executed on January 24, 1950. Clyde Steele was electrocuted at the Main Prison in Nashville on that day.

Herbert Bearden cheated the executioner. On January 20, 1950, he provoked a fight with prison guards, severely stabbing two with a hand-made knife, and he made a dash for freedom. He was shot inside the prison and died within minutes. The newspaper offered no details of Steele's last day or execution.[3151]

1955

Samuel L. Voss, black, age 31. *Murder.*

One of the crimes for which Sammy Voss was executed occurred about 11:30 P.M. on August 27, 1953.[3152] The victim, Louis Hutchison, white, age fifty-three, was the clerk at the Southerner Liquor Store at 1604 Church Street in downtown Nashville, Davidson County.

Codefendant Alice Jones entered the store wearing overalls and served as a lookout/decoy by asking to use the telephone.[3153] As she did so, Voss entered the store brandishing a sawed-off shotgun. He ordered Hutchison to open the safe, which he did. Accounts differ on what happened next. Jones testified she was forced by Voss to lie down on the floor and that she left after Voss had taken the money.[3154] Voss said he shot Hutchison in the face because the clerk refused to stay on the floor and peeked around the corner of the counter to get a better look at him.[3155]

Somehow a large glass ashtray fell to the floor and shattered. The startled Hutchison had apparently dropped it when the holdup began. The telephone was on the floor. The crime occurred on what was the busiest commercial street in Nashville but there were no witnesses or passers-by to offer any clues. Voss had taken Hutchison's wallet and $546 from the store. The only clue puzzled detectives. It was one bloody shoe print left by a woman's shoe.

In spring 1953, Nashville was beset by ten robberies carried out by a heavyset black man wearing a kerchief mask over the bottom half of his face and brandishing a sawed-off shotgun. The robberies focused on gas stations and auto shops in the same Church Street and Charlotte Avenue area, most netting less than one hundred dollars. But the gunman loudly cursed his victims and was very threatening. In one of the robberies the gunman's hat came off, revealing long black curly hair. The newspapers soon began referring to the "Curly-Top" robber.

Considerable police resources were spent tracking the robber. Police were dressed in workingmen's clothes and walked the streets. Apparently, this prevented any Curly-Top robberies until August 9, 1953, when he struck a gas station at 1038 Charlotte Avenue at 3:30 A.M. The robber became furious when the attendant gave him all the money in the cash register, only eight dollars. The screaming robber threatened to kill him. The attendant dashed for the door, which was hit by a shotgun blast. The robber came outside, confronted a passer-by and fired from the hip, narrowly missing him. A black 1938 Ford sedan drove up and the robber got away. Neither man got a look at the driver.[3156] Five days later, another gas station was robbed by Curly-Top, accompanied by a younger, smaller companion. They escaped in a black 1938 Ford sedan. By the time of Hutchison's killing, Curly-Top was the prime suspect in fifteen robberies and two attempted murders.

Early in the morning of September 19, 1953, motorists discovered the body of gas station attendant James Buchanan Cox, white, age forty-six, next to a wall on Centennial Boulevard near the Tennessee State University campus. The place of death suggested that Cox had been hit with shotgun pellets trying to run away. He had been shot in the leg and trailed blood fifty feet. A second shot had hit his face. Cox had apparently been taken there from his Red Ace gas station in downtown Nashville on Fifth Avenue across from the Sulphur Dell baseball park. The cash register was found empty.

A night watchman at the ballpark said he heard a gunshot at about one in the morning and said he saw an orange panel truck pull away. The truck had some sort of writing on the side, such as the name of a store. The next day, an orange Resha Produce panel truck, parked at the business, was found with blood inside, although an attempt had been made to clean it.

The truck had been stolen the night of Cox's death from behind the Resha wholesale grocery company. The back door to the business had been smashed but nothing was gone except the keys to the truck. Resha told police that a former employee, Eddie Snell, had come by that morning asking to borrow five dollars and had been chased away. Questioning of Snell's family revealed he was living somewhere on 9th Avenue North with a man named Voss.[3157]

Police walked by every house on the street until 9:30 P.M., when they came to a house at 406 9th Avenue North which appeared dark except for a poorly-lit living room. Officers entered the house without warrants and quickly arrested Edward Lewis Snell, black, age twenty-one; Alice Jones, black, age thirty-five; and Sammy Voss. The trio was taken to the police station for questioning and police immediately returned to the house.

In a detached garage they found a black 1938 Ford sedan. In the house they found a double-barreled shotgun taken in a gas station robbery, blood-stained clothing fitting both Snell and Voss, and other crime-related items, notably an olive drab money bag stamped "Southerner Liquor Stores." The key to the Resha delivery truck was found tucked in the hat Snell was wearing at the police station.

Confronted with the evidence, Snell began confessing and implicated Voss and Jones. Cox had been shot in the leg at the gas station, Snell explained, and Voss ordered him into the truck, thinking he was withholding money. Cox, bleeding in the vehicle, had been taken to the Centennial Boulevard site and robbed of his wallet. When he suddenly bolted, Voss fired a blast which missed, then a second which killed him. The pair discovered blood inside the panel truck and stopped at a gas station to wash it.

Confronted with Snell's confession, Voss admitted killing both Cox and Hutchison, insisting he had acted alone in the latter. A key piece of evidence became a letter Voss wrote to Alice Jones while both were in jail. He said he would assume blame for the Hutchison shooting, but would act crazy so that he would not be put to death.

Voss and Snell went to trial on November 16, 1953, for the Cox murder. Sammie Voss's partial insanity defense was predicated, in part, on his life history. According to the state's brief:

> His father had killed his mother when he was 8 or 9 years old. He only went to the third grade in school and had considerable difficulty in passing. When he was 15 or 16 years old he was sent to Reform School for housebreaking. When he reached manhood he joined the Navy and served in a combat area. He testified that while in the Navy he was frequently punished for fighting and arguing. He went AWOL and for this offense served two years in a Naval Prison. He had been incarcerated in the State of Michigan for attempted breaking and entering. He testified that he had no remorse or feeling about the crime he had committed and that he didn't know why he killed Cox. Some months before the trial he had tried to commit suicide by slashing his wrists. He stated that he believed in hexes and voodoo.[3158]

A defense expert witness, Dr. Otto Billig, from Vanderbilt University, said Voss could not control his actions. He expressed doubt that Voss was able to be cool and calculated at the time of the killing. "It was Billig's opinion that Voss could not show affection or love and that he could not learn by experience."[3159] Another expert said that tests showed Voss to have an I.Q. of seventy-four and a mental age of an average eleven-and-one-half-year-old.[3160] Snell was convicted of second-degree murder and sentenced to twenty-one years in prison. Voss received the death penalty.

The Tennessee Supreme Court said the "murder was one of the most atrocious in the annals of Davidson County."[3161] It explained that Voss admitted the killing and asserted an insanity defense. It was supported by Dr. Billig, who explained that Voss suffered from "panic reaction," and was unable to be "cool and calculating at the moment of committing this crime and that in all probability was not a person of sound discretion."[3162] But Voss was able to decide between right and wrong and wrote to his girlfriend, "I'll play crazy and go back to Central [State Mental Hospital]."[3163] The only issue on appeal was whether the court erred in not individually polling the jurors. It was not reversible error because the court said to the jury, "So say you all, Gentlemen of the Jury?" and the trial judge was entirely satisfied with the verdict.[3164] The court ordered Voss executed on September 10, 1954.[3165]

Sammy Voss and Alice Jones were tried later for the Hutchison killing. Jones was convicted of second-degree murder in the killing of Hutchison and received a twenty-year sentence. Voss was again ordered executed and became the first man in Tennessee history to receive the death penalty twice for two separate murders.[3166]

Voss's appeal in the Hutchison case insisted the warrantless search of the house following his and Jones's arrest was illegal. The Supreme Court ruled otherwise, saying the search was still incident to a lawful arrest because only a short time had passed between the arrest and reentry of the house.[3167] Also, the court noted that Voss had actually confessed to police of killing Hutchison.

Voss again raised an insanity defense at trial. Although Dr. Billing said Voss was a psychopath who suffered from a panic reaction at the time he killed Hutchison, this did not support a finding of insanity because Billig said Voss knew right from wrong at the time.[3168] The Tennessee Supreme Court ordered Voss executed on April 15, 1955. On March 14, 1955, the United States Supreme Court denied a petition for certiorari in (apparently) the Cox killing, and Voss was executed on April 15, 1955.

Voss embraced the Roman Catholic faith in prison, admitted his killings, and declared he was saved. His last words were, "I am sorry for my crime." Earlier, he had told the newspapers that he was resigned to death, and said the electric chair would be no different from "sitting down in a barber chair."[3169] Voss's arms contained two tattoos. One was of a nude woman and the words, "True Love." The other was a heart with the name "Beatrice." His wife, Elizabeth Voss, refused to claim his body. It was taken by his father.

Harry Kirkendoll (aka Henry Kirkendall), black, age 34. *Murder.*
Charlie Sullins, white, age 38. *Murder.*

The crime was committed about 11:30 P.M. on March 4, 1953, on East Main Street at the tiny one-man Thoni gas station in the city of Lebanon, in Wilson County. The killers were farmers who wanted the victim's money. The victim was gas station attendant Edward Martin Collier, white, age sixty-two, a former prison guard known to assist the sheriff on a voluntary basis. At the time he was killed, Collier wore an honorary sheriff's deputy badge on his shirt pocket.

The crime was planned by Sullins, a farmer, who convinced Kirkendoll, a farmhand for others, that Collier was a good candidate for robbery because he was known to carry large amounts of money in his wallet. Sullins was respected in his community. He had been elected constable.[3170]

Sullins picked up Kirkendoll in his car and gave him the murder weapon, a .22 rifle, and parked about three hundred feet away from the gas station, sending Kirkendoll off alone. (Sullins would later insist that only a robbery was contemplated.) Kirkendoll crept within one hundred and fifty feet, crouched on one knee and fired one shot at Collier, who seemed to be looking straight at him. The bullet struck Collier in the heart. According to Kirkendoll's confession, "Just as I pulled the trigger, he jumped straight up and tried to holler. He couldn't holler, he just made a sound."[3171] Kirkendoll took a pistol from Collier's body, along with his wallet and the money pouch on his belt. The crime garnered six hundred dollars, which the two men split, including several one-hundred-dollar bills. They had anticipated getting four or five thousand dollars.[3172]

Because it was raining at the time of the killing and thereafter, the crime scene yielded no evidence. In the weeks following, numerous people such as out-of-town motorists, boastful teenagers, and traveling salesmen were investigated. Many people came forward to offer help to town mayor William Baird, who took charge of the case. One of these was constable Charlie Sullins, who vowed not to rest until the killer was found.

Accounts differ, but according to one it was Sullins who suggested that police talk to Collier's middle-aged girlfriend. She provided information unknown to everyone (including Sullins) up to that time. She said that Collier had converted his earnings into one-hundred-dollar bills. But as an aid in keeping track of his money, he routinely asked her to record the serial numbers in a memorandum book which she kept. It carried a notation of two such bills he had asked her to enter on the day of his murder. Mayor Baird quietly asked bankers and large businesses to be on the lookout for hundred-dollar bills.

On May 12, 1953, a businessman came forward with a torn and crumpled one-hundred-dollar bill with a serial number shown in the memorandum book. The businessman had gotten it from a grocer-cattle merchant. He, in turn, explained he had gotten it from Charlie Sullins who bought a calf for seventy dollars, taking thirty in change.

Sullins was questioned and confronted with the evidence. He promptly confessed, hoping to shift the blame to Kirkendoll. Confronted with Sullins's detailed written confession, Kirkendoll also confessed. Each man gave at least two written confessions, including ones given at the Murfreesboro jail where they were taken for their safety. The confessions were also tape-recorded and these were played for the jury. The confessions, especially Kirkendoll's, told where the rifle, the wallet and pouch, and even some other money could be found. These items were recovered.

Kirkendoll was represented by appointed counsel, Z. Alexander Looby, the dean of the Negro bar in

Tennessee, and his young black associate, Avon Williams, Jr., who became the foremost civil rights lawyer in Tennessee. Sullins's counsel was white. The Supreme Court's opinion began by complimenting the three lawyers for their "masterly work" in the case, since counsel "had nothing to go upon in defending these parties except to try in every human way — far beyond the call of duty — to try to minimize the sentence that the defendants would receive."[3173]

A dozen assignments of error were raised. The twenty-four-page opinion was among the longest death penalty decisions to date. First, Sullins's confession had been shown to the jury; this was wrong, said Kirkendoll. But the result was proper, said the Supreme Court, because the trial court had instructed the jury not to consider it against Kirkendoll, who had made no motion for a severance.[3174] The use of Kirkendoll's tape recording was likewise proper.[3175] Kirkendoll's unsupported (by affidavit or otherwise) motion for a sanity hearing was properly denied. It was not error to allow Sullins to use his peremptory challenges to strike the only two Negro jurors because "a Negro defendant has no constitutional right to a mixed racial jury."[3176] Furthermore, Kirkendoll himself had peremptorily challenged a Negro juror.[3177] It was not error to allow an illiterate juror to serve.[3178] Allegations that two jurors had made up their minds about guilt and punishment before the trial were not supported by credible evidence and were strongly refuted by the jurors themselves.[3179]

The confessions of Sullins, whom the court described as "a rather ignorant tenant farmer and a constable in his district" was the most compelling evidence of guilt.[3180] The court described Sullins's interrogation:

> To begin with and for some time he denied knowing anything about the crime and denied that he had ever had a $100 bill in his life when he was finally advised by the officers that he had presented such a bill to the merchant. Sullins denied this and the merchant was sent for. While they were asking for the merchant, Sullins asked the Mayor if it would be any easier on him (Sullins) if he told about it, and was advised by the Mayor, that no promises would be made. Sullins thereupon stated that he had to tell it anyway because he had not been able to sleep at night and that his hair was turning gray. He gave a written statement telling about how the crime was committed.[3181]

The day before execution Sullins was visited by his wife and some relatives. Kirkendoll said goodbye to his wife and some of his six children, all boys and all under the age of thirteen. Both men ate a hearty last meal.[3182] That day Governor Clement refused to grant the men clemency, but did so to child rapist John Arthur Hale, black, age nineteen, because his death sentence had been upheld by a 3–2 majority.[3183]

The media still put the term "death row" in quotation marks at this time, and reported that for the first time the condemned men were allowed to walk to the electric chair without handcuffs, which was one of Sullins's last requests, granted by Governor Clement.[3184] The pair were executed on August 1, 1955.

Sullins walked calmly to the chair and said, "I am ready to meet God. I have no ill will or hard feelings toward any man. Gov. Clement has been a Christian gentleman in every way. I hope and pray that this will not be held against my family. If killing me would bring back Mr. Ed Collier, I'd be more than glad to die. The prison personnel have treated me fairly and kindly."[3185]

What happened next had been planned with the aid of prison minister the Rev. Eugene Parks. After Sullins sat briefly in the electric chair, he said, "Wait a minute." He was allowed to step from the chair. He knelt down in front of it, prayed briefly, and calmly sat down in it.[3186] He was executed without saying more. Kirkendoll was executed next without saying anything or making any prayerful gestures. Their wives claimed the bodies.

Robert L. "Hambone" Crenshaw, black, age 43. *Rape.*

The crime was committed at 11:30 P.M. on September 1, 1954, beside an embankment on the Victory Memorial Bridge on the east side of the river in downtown Nashville, in Davidson County. The victim, whose name is unavailable in any existing court records or newspaper accounts in order to protect her identify, was a white woman, age unknown. She was the wife of a policeman, a fact known to Crenshaw. The victim worked until eleven o'clock P.M. at a downtown hotel. She had walked across the bridge and was only two blocks from her home when she was accosted by Crenshaw. He threatened her with a knife, beat and dragged her down the embankment to a lot filled with scrap lumber, barbed wire and tall grass. He raped her twice.

"Having accomplished his purpose he refused to let her go and told her he couldn't because she would have every cop in Nashville after him," said the Tennessee Supreme Court.[3187] It explained, "He told her he would have to kill her and he was going to call a cab and take her to his house but she managed to escape from him when they went back upon the street. She then managed to get to the front door of her home where she fainted and was taken into the house by her father-in-law."[3188]

Crenshaw was arrested almost immediately and the victim identified him in a lineup. "He was also identified by the fact that his eyeglasses were found at the scene of the crime and were identified as belonging to him by the optician who ground the lenses."[3189]

As trial was about to begin, Crenshaw's lawyer announced a change of plea to guilty in order to receive a 99-year sentence and avoid the death penalty. Crenshaw was to offer his mother and pastor as witnesses. During the colloquy with the jury present, Crenshaw's lawyer explained, "We have tried to settle this matter by agreement, but we were unable to do it."[3190]

The court turned to the district attorney and restated the court's understanding of what Crenshaw was attempting. The court then asked what sort of opening statement the district attorney was going to make, an obvious attempt to get the state to agree to a plea. Turning to defense counsel, the district attorney then said, "Does counsel, by making that statement, agree also as to this defendant's past record?" Crenshaw's attorney interrupted, "Just a minute, I think the...." Here the district attorney cut him off, saying, "That is part of the proof, and we intend to prove it, therefore I will just choose to put the proof on."[3191]

At this point the jury was abruptly excused for lunch with a strong admonition not discuss the case. Crenshaw's lawyer then asked for a mistrial, which was denied. Further colloquy with the court indicated that Crenshaw's lawyer had not made it clear earlier that he was not going to put Crenshaw on the stand.

The district attorney did not introduce evidence of Crenshaw's criminal record. He had served three prison terms for three prior sexual assault crimes.[3192] However, when the victim testified about the crime, she quoted Crenshaw as saying, "I can't let you go; you're not the first and you won't be the last."[3193] The combination of the district attorney's comment plus the victim's testimony were reversible error, argued Crenshaw, and were responsible for the jury's death sentence.

The Supreme Court said otherwise: "We are unable to see how, under the circumstances, the jury could have been affected to any extent by one brief reference to his past record. There was not a scintilla of evidence before the jury with reference to whether his past record was good or bad, or if bad, in what way."[3194] The victim's statements quoting Crenshaw were part of the res gestae, and were likely more damaging than the district attorney's brief statement.

The court thanked appointed counsel for the "earnest and capable effort" made on Crenshaw's behalf, but affirmed the sentence and ordered him executed on September 15, 1955, which was carried out that day.[3195]

In the weeks before his electrocution, Crenshaw was baptized in the Church of Christ. A few days before his execution Crenshaw was visited by Governor Clement. True to his nickname, Crenshaw ate a hearty meal of country ham the night before. He was asked if he had any last words. He replied, "No, I'm ready to go."[3196] His body was claimed by relatives.

1957

Jimmy Allen, black, age 38. *Murder.*

The crime was committed on June 26, 1955, in Nashville. The victim, Jeanette Patricia Allen, black, was the nineteen-month-old stepdaughter of the killer. The child's mother and Allen had married on March 21, 1955, and within weeks Allen had purchased three life insurance policies on the girl's life. The total amount was $3,245. Allen said he was an interior decorator.

The day of the killing, Allen told the child's mother he was going to the doctor to get an injection of penicillin and would also try to sell a pistol he owned in preparation for a Florida trip they had planned to take. Returning three hours later, he parked the car in an unusual location and did not bring the infant inside with him. The mother rushed to the car, found the infant in the back seat with its face turned toward the back of the seat and a white frothy substance coming from its mouth. It was then Allen said the girl had swallowed two pistol cartridges and urged she be taken to a hospital. Despite the fact that the Allen home was only a few blocks from Vanderbilt Hospital, the defendant insisted the girl be taken to the Meharry Hubbard Hospital.

At the hospital, a city detective who happened to be present on other business became suspicious and began to investigate. Allen was immediately arrested for questioning. Although he said nothing incriminating at the time, further investigation (and the autopsy) suggested culpability.

Allen's nine-year-old son Jimmy had died under mysterious circumstances in Nashville on July 10, 1952. So had his divorced former wife, Annie Sue Mosely Allen, on April 12, 1955. Another stepson, Reginald Allen, age three, had been strangled to death in Miami on April 8, 1953. No charges had been placed against Allen in these deaths and he challenged police investigators to prove his guilt in killing the little girl because he had passed two lie detector tests demanded by insurance investigators in the earlier cases.[3197]

The autopsy showed the two cartridges were found in the infant's stomach, and could not have played a part in the infant's death, concluded the pathologist. Rather, the child had died of strangulation from a cord similar to that used as a trotline. The marks were plainly visible and were shown to the jury in photographs.

Said the Tennessee Supreme Court: "This is a case of circumstantial evidence but the circumstances seem to us to be very compelling. This child was in the exclusive custody of the defendant for three hours, was in sound health except for a slight cold, at the time she and the defendant left their home, but was dead upon arrival back at the home three hours later. It is established by the photographs in the record and by the testimony of the doctors that this child undoubtedly was strangled to death by a ribbed type of cord and that she could not have been strangled by her own clothing."[3198]

The court ruled that the existence of the three insurance policies showed Allen had a motive for the killing. The opinion makes no reference to testimony regarding the three other mysterious deaths. The key issue on appeal was whether it was error for the district attorney to question Allen about having served two years in the state prison for "highway robbery" after Allen admitted having been sentenced for assault and battery. The court said this was not error.[3199] The court also said it was not error for the jury to see the photographs which had been taken by detectives.[3200]

Allen protested his sentence, declaring to relatives who visited him, "It's God's will for me to go, but I'm dying an innocent man." He had refused the proffered "last meal," but had been visited by the prison choral group, The Prisonaires, who sang spirituals.

Jimmy Allen was electrocuted on March 16, 1957, at the Main Prison. A few moments after being seated in the electric chair Allen blurted out that he had killed the girl, and added, "She was as guilty as I was," an apparent reference to the infant's mother.[3201]

Billy Thomas Gibbs, white, age 23. *Murder.*

The crime was committed on March 23, 1955, at a farm in the Rowland's Station community about seven miles outside of McMinnville, in Warren County. Gibbs, a Korean War veteran, was unemployed but had performed farm work for various people, including one of the victims, Henry Bratcher, white, age forty-four. Gibbs was well-known to the family and was a boyhood friend of Charlie Bratcher, Henry's son, who was Gibbs's age. Gibbs had also been a car salesman briefly and was married. His wife gave birth to twin girls on the morning of March 23, and Gibbs was in debt and extremely anxious about money. Henry Bratcher was known to carry several hundred dollars in his wallet.

At about 9:00 A.M. Gibbs arrived at the Bratcher farm, where he encountered Henry's wife, Cassie Fields Bratcher, white, age forty-two, who was also caring for her granddaughter, Charlotte Ann Bratcher, white, age twenty months. Also living there, but at school, was Lily May Bratcher, white, age ten. Lily May was Henry and Vassie's daughter; the family was caring for Charlotte Ann because her mother had died about a year earlier. The baby's father, their son Charlie Bratcher, lived and worked at a sawmill in town and could not care for the infant by himself. He saw the baby on weekends.

Gibbs's initial confession said that he had gone fishing with Henry Bratcher in a pond near the farm when the two got into an argument. Gibbs sought to borrow money, but Henry cursed him saying it was time he got a job and acted like a man, and that Gibbs was crazy if he thought Henry would loan him money. Gibbs became enraged at being called crazy and Henry responded in kind by pushing him off a stump. As Henry ran away, Gibbs shot him with a .22 rifle, the bullet piercing his neck.[3202] Gibbs said he meant to shoot him in the leg. When he found that Henry was hit in the neck, he shot him in the head.[3203]

Gibbs dragged the body to Henry Bratcher's sorghum mill nearby, buried the body in a shallow grave, and covered it with sorghum pomace. Midway though the burial, Gibbs remembered Henry's wallet. He dug through the dirt and retrieved it, taking about two hundred dollars.

Hearing the gunfire, Cassie Bratcher came running toward Gibbs, and as she was doing so, she picked up baby Charlotte Ann, who was crawling in the yard near the house. Gibbs held the gun on

Cassie and walked her to an abandoned cistern in an outbuilding. He ordered her to drop the baby into the brackish water. Accounts differ whether she dropped the baby or whether it was snatched from her and thrown by Gibbs. The gurgling sound of the drowning child caused Cassie (and Gibbs as well) to become hysterical. To silence the screaming woman, Gibbs shot her in the breast, killing her at once. Her arms were outstretched over her head, and she fell that way. At this point, the family dog, a collie named Laddie, began snarling at Gibbs, who shot it in the head.

Gibbs loaded a sow and its litter, along with two mules, into Henry Bratcher's truck. He drove to town, where he sold the animals to two livestock dealers, getting about $145. Later that day, he also sold to a grocer some hams he had stolen from the Bratcher farm, and sold the murder weapon to a young man on the street in McMinnville for $17.50.[3204]

Accounts differ, but apparently at this time Gibbs realized it was nearing time for Lily May to return from school. He returned to the farm and waited on the porch. He struck the girl with a claw hammer, but she staggered into the kitchen. There he battered her head until she was dead. He carried her body about a quarter mile away and dropped it into a sinkhole, where he had thrown her mother's body. When her body was found, the mother's hands were still outstretched. To allay suspicion regarding the disappearance of the Bratcher family, Gibbs left a note on the front door which read, "Charlie. Baby in Nashville Hospital."

The killings occurred on a Wednesday, but were not discovered until Sunday. On Friday night Charlie Bratcher went to his parents' house and saw the note and the dead dog in the yard. He left and began calling hospitals in Nashville, and when they all denied having the baby, he went to the sheriff's office. The sheriff did not suspect foul play, thinking that the child had been bitten by the dog (which may have acted rabid) or a snake.

At dawn the next day the sheriff and deputies, accompanied by Charlie, entered the house and found dried blood in the kitchen. Initially, it was thought that the blood was the dog's, but by the next day it was confirmed as human. Charlie Bratcher noticed the animals were missing, as was his father's truck. Mrs. Bratcher's purse was still there, but it contained no money, and the cookie jar that contained money was empty.

Sheriff's deputies began questioning livestock dealers and two explained they had bought the animals from Billy Gibbs, who signed a receipt for the cash he took for them. Bratcher's truck was found in a parking lot in town. Inside was some blood. That day Gibbs had gone to a used car lot and paid $120 cash for a 1940 Buick. Gibbs became an immediate suspect because the "B" in "Baby" was identical to that in "Billy" on the receipt.

Gibbs was arrested late Saturday night.[3205] He expressed his fondness for the Bratcher family and explained that he had been asked by Henry Bratcher to take the truck to town and sell the animals for him. He said he had seen the note when he returned to give Henry the money. He said he had returned the next day, Thursday, and saw the dead dog, but was perplexed and drove back to town. The sheriff held Gibbs on a charge of vehicle theft and obtaining money under false pretenses.

The next day, a swarm of deputies and others (some fifty in all) began searching the Bratcher farm and discovered the bodies, starting with the baby, then Lily May and her mother, and finally Henry Bratcher. Gibbs, in the sheriff's custody by this time, became very agitated, especially when the sheriff indicated he wanted to take Gibbs to the funeral home to officially identify the bodies. This did not occur.

As a crowd began to surround the McMinnville jail and some called out for Gibbs, a rock was thrown through a window. Gibbs panicked, fearing a lynching, and suddenly exclaimed, "Get me outta here! I killed 'em!" Gibbs was secretly taken to the jail in Tullahoma. There he gave a written confession to an agent of the Tennessee Bureau of Investigation.[3206] During some of the time Billy was being questioned, his father was present.

Gibbs's lawyers entered a "not guilty for the present" plea, and the judge sent him to the state mental hospital, where he was found sane and capable of assisting at trial. The difficulty of seating a jury in McMinnville prompted the judge to move Gibbs's first trial to Manchester, in a neighboring county. He was charged with killing Lily May and, following a mistrial, was convicted in August 1956 and sentenced to death. Gibbs's wife attended a portion of the first trial, throughout which Gibbs feverishly chewed gum. He was later charged with killing the adults and the baby, convicted, and given two 99-year sentences, and a 20-year sentence for killing Henry Bratcher. The jury deadlocked on a second death penalty.

Sometime in the case(s) he raised the defense that he had been under the influence of a nasal antihistamine which had thrown him into a frenzy. The small nasal device, which was carried in one's pocket and was the size of lipstick, had been introduced to the armed forces during the Korean War. The notion that these devices caused mental problems was a popular defense in criminal cases in this era. It did not influence the governor, however.[3207]

Gibbs was supposed to be executed on December 7, 1956, but last-minute appeals caused the Supreme Court to waive some of its procedural rules and his appeal went forward. The court said his transcribed statement about killing Cassie was proper evidence against him for killing Henry because it was part of the res gestae.[3208]

Gibbs raised an intoxication defense on appeal. The court said, "One minor insistence made on this appeal is that the defendant committed these acts due to his intoxication." The defense was rejected because he "went out with a loaded rifle and we think this being true that even though the killing of these people was not intended this would amount to murder anyhow."[3209] Gibbs had not taken the stand or offered "any other evidence as to his condition in an effort to mitigate this crime if he could have done so."[3210] The court ordered his execution on May 6, 1957, and he met death that day.

Gibbs was baptized in the Church of Christ on Good Friday before his execution. Gibbs ate a hearty last meal the night before his execution and was given a large breakfast the next morning.

Gibbs had two last requests. First, he asked that the four ministers who attended him pray for the jury that sentenced him to death and for the prison officials who handled the execution. He also wrote a letter to his mother, which, under prison rules of the time, was required to be opened and read by prison officials. But the letter was given unopened to Gibbs's father, who claimed his body and buried it the same day in the local cemetery. Gibbs's body featured several tattoos. One was the names of his sisters, another said "Dad & Love," another was "Bill, G.H.G. [his wife's initials] & Love," another was of a nude woman, and another was "Mom."[3211]

Billy Gibbs went to the electric chair "fully dependent on the Lord," said prison chaplain C.E. Hall, who explained, "He had no question about his soul's salvation."[3212] Gibbs was reciting a prayer in a barely audible voice when the electricity was applied because, said the chaplain, "He expected to come into the presence of the Lord immediately."[3213]

According to the newspaper, one of the twins died of natural causes a year before the execution, the survivor was in the care of relatives, and "Mrs. Gibbs's whereabouts is unknown."[3214]

1959

Tom Rutledge, white, age 33. *Murder.*

The crime was committed on June 14, 1958, in a rural area outside the village of Campaign, near McMinnville, in Warren County. The killer, married with three children, was a sometime chicken trader/sawmill worker. Rutledge could neither read nor write and was frequently seen intoxicated. The victim was his second cousin, Treva Joyce Raper, white, age twelve.

Treva left home about 9:00 A.M. to walk to her grandmother's house a mile away, a route which ran near a railroad track through a swampy area filled with honeysuckle and other vines. When she did not return, a search was begun that night. One of the many people who assisted in the search was Tom Rutledge.

Suspicion turned to Rutledge because of his odd behavior with Treva's mother. About 10:30 A.M. the morning of Treva's death, he appeared at the mother's house and asked where the girl was, explaining he had not seen her in "I can't tell you when."[3215] Later, when the search was underway, the mother said out loud that she feared Treva's body had been hidden in the dense vines, Rutledge replied, "You need not look in the damn thicket. She ain't there."[3216] After midnight, the defendant again appeared at the house, clearly intoxicated.

Treva's body was found in the thicket the next morning. It bore no obvious signs of homicide or a struggle. The girl's glasses were still on her face. At first, the sheriff and the parents treated it as a natural death of unknown cause, in part because Treva had suffered from cerebral palsy since infancy and had been known to faint. The body was embalmed and readied for funeral.

The sheriff went to the funeral to persuade the parents to allow an autopsy, convinced that someone had killed Treva because it would have been nearly impossible for her to have climbed over a barbed wire fence to the place where her body was found without scratching herself.[3217] The sheriff insisted that Treva had been killed by someone she knew and trusted. The hearse that bore her body was directed away from the cemetery to Nashville. An autopsy was performed by the chief medical examiner for the Tennessee Bureau of Identification. He concluded Treva had been manually strangled. Sperm was found inside her vagina, which had received a half-inch tear.[3218]

Sheriff's investigators began questioning people

who had seen Treva the morning of her death, and several said they had seen her walking with "Uncle Tom," the defendant whom she knew and trusted. Rutledge vigorously denied any involvement with the crime, but the fact that he had clearly lied to the mother about seeing her focused attention on him. He was taken to TBI headquarters in Nashville and given a lie detector test. He badly failed the test.

Confronted with the test results and the sheriff's findings, Rutledge told several versions of events leading to Treva's death. First, he said she had voluntary sexual intercourse with him but "got sick and died." Another time he said he had asked her for sex, she refused and began screaming. He cupped his hand over her mouth and she "had a spell" and became unconscious. He slapped her to bring her to consciousness but she died. In court, his primary defense was intoxication, in order to mitigate the first-degree murder charge. However, several friends and acquaintances who saw him that morning strongly disputed this, and the mother asserted he was not intoxicated when she talked to him the morning of Treva's death. Rutledge was convicted of homicide committed in the perpetuation of rape.[3219]

The issue on appeal was whether a juror who was of unsound mind who had recently been committed to the public mental hospital had been improperly seated. The Supreme Court ruled that juror incapacity serves as a basis for a new trial only if prejudice or bias is shown. Here, some fellow jurors gave affidavits that this juror "was inclined to do what the other members of the jury wanted to do without disposing of the case and that he did not appear to comprehend the gravity of the charge."[3220]

The court said this did not show prejudice. "The observation of the writer[3221] is that usually when one juror is obstinate in not agreeing with the others, the impression arises that the lone juror ought to be in some mental institution instead of in the courtroom."[3222] The court concluded, "We are unable to see any evidence of prejudice in the mere fact that this juror was willing to go along with the others."[3223] The court found no mitigating circumstances and affirmed the conviction, thanking appointed counsel for their services. Governor Buford Ellington came to the prison the night before the execution but told the press he could not find a reason to stay the execution.[3224]

As mandated by the Supreme Court's opinion, Rutledge was executed on June 15, 1959. He declined a ritual last meal and spoke with his siblings until 3:30 A.M. He was then attended by three ministers.

Rutledge was the first man executed in the new death house located just inside the prison. Billy Gibbs, also of Warren County, was the last man executed in the old corner chamber. Rutledge was calm and walked to the electric chair with his arm around the warden's shoulder. Warden Bomar said that Rutledge told him he was "sorry for the bad thing," and asserted, "I have made peace with the Lord."[3225]

Rutledge faced the traditional inmate hostility other inmates show for child rapists, and was kept separate from other inmates, including others facing the death penalty. Few spoke to him. Other inmates publicly denounced him; one said he would enjoy pulling the switch.

To taunt Rutledge as he was taken to the electric chair, another inmate began singing to the tune of a ballad "Tom Dooley," revising the words with Rutledge's name. He was joined in the song by other inmates.

1960

William James Tines, black, age 37. *Rape.*

The crime was committed at 9:00 A.M. on April 24, 1957, in the home of Luther and Margaret Nichols on a rural stretch of Highway 61 in Roane County. The rapist was a lifelong criminal whose first brush with the law came at age eleven. He had been sent to the state reformatory three times. On January 22, 1945, Tines and four other black men had been gambling in Knoxville when two of them left in a car. John Lewis Johnson, age thirty, and Marshall Kyle, age twenty-seven, were pursued by a car carrying Tines. Their car was forced to a curb and Tines emptied two pistols into the men. Tines admitted the shootings and pled guilty, receiving two life sentences for the murders. Tines was a Brushy Mountain prison inmate on outside trusty duty cutting wood on the morning of the rape. He and two other inmates ran away from the work duty.

Within two hours, Tines was seen approaching the Nichols family front door carrying his shoes, wearing his prison clothes.[3226] The victim was Mrs. Bertha Riggs, white, age forty-five, a widow. She was a housekeeper for the Nichols family. No one else was home. Tines was making his way toward Knoxville and was looking for food and money. He did not know Bertha was present. Surprised by

Tines while ironing clothes, she reached for the phone as he began hitting her, the receiver falling to the floor.

Tines beat Bertha Riggs severely; a blow to her nose produced a laceration that bled profusely. She had an injury behind her ear when she was knocked to the floor. She had a friction burn on her back from being raped. Sperm was found in her vaginal canal.[3227] Taken to the hospital, she was unable to see from one eye because of the swelling. The house had blood on the floor and walls.

The fallen telephone was connected to a party line and numerous people heard her screaming both during and after the rape. By the time the Nichols family returned at 10:30 A.M. about twenty people had gathered at the house, having heard the screams over the telephone. Tines, still carrying his shoes, was spotted by a state trooper within the hour and gave up without a struggle. He was immediately taken back to the prison. On the way, he told the trooper he had not meant to hit Bertha so hard. The next day, he signed a confession admitting the rape, including the statement he tore her panties.

Bertha testified she had been raped because she felt the penetration and saw and felt the seminal discharge from her vagina.[3228] She could not positively identify Tines because she had been struck so quickly and stunned by the assault. Tines said he also could not recall the incident, attributing the failure to his epilepsy, although prison medical records made no mention of this condition.

At trial, Tines repeatedly denied raping Bertha and repudiated his confession, saying he thought he was signing a document that allowed him to ask for legal counsel. The Tennessee Supreme Court said the confession was given voluntarily. But the confession was unnecessary to convict because considerable other evidence supported the corpus delicti, including the fresh injury to his finger caused by Bertha's biting him.[3229]

William Tines had a second team of lawyers who sought habeas corpus relief and a second appeal to the Tennessee Supreme Court.[3230] Their attempt to have the United States Supreme Court hear the case also failed, but these appeals gave Tines an extra three years of life on what the newspaper now called "death row," with the term in quotation marks.[3231]

Tines ate little of his last meal but spoke with his mother and stepbrother until a few hours before his electrocution. "He acted as if he was ready," said his stepbrother. His mother, Lucille Neal, whom he had seldom seen during his life, in part because she had been married two or three times, insisted he had not been given justice. She said he could not read the confession and had been given "crazy pills" before he gave the confession. Weeks before, prison officials, including Warden Bomar, said Tines had confessed to the rape.[3232]

William Tines was electrocuted at the Main Prison in Nashville in the new "death house" built for that purpose. Because it took thirteen steps to reach the electric chair from the death-house door, that term became a popular way of referring to an execution. Strapped in the chair, his last words were, "Pray for me." He was electrocuted at 5:05 A.M. on November 7, 1960. His death was little noticed because it was Election Day and the evening newspaper, the *Nashville Banner*, devoted its coverage to the close race between Sen. John F. Kennedy and Vice-President Richard M. Nixon. The execution was not mentioned in the morning newspaper, the *Tennessean*.

No one knew it at the time, but William Tines, the one hundred and twenty-fifth person to die in the Tennessee electric chair, would be its last.[3233] The Rev. Pickens Johnson, who retired as prison chaplain in 1959, had been present for sixty executions.[3234] He had given spiritual comfort to all but one of the men. He had said earlier, "Before a man goes to the electric chair, I've sometimes held his hand and felt his flesh quivering like that of a high-spirited horse on the edge of a precipice."[3235] The Rev. Johnson opposed capital punishment.

Executions in 2000 and the Twenty-First Century

Few would have predicted in 1960 that Tennessee would not have another legal execution until 2000. In the intervening time, much happened regarding the penalty of death.

As the 1960s began, both law and politics seemed to turn against capital punishment in the nation, including Tennessee. A bill was introduced in 1963 to abolish the death penalty.[3236] Gov. Frank Clement personally addressed the state House asking for repeal in 1965.[3237] When the measure failed, he promptly commuted the sentences of the five men on death row.[3238] Counsel for capital defendants began working together during this era, getting stays of execution by invoking other pending cases.[3239] There were no executions nationwide in 1968, the first year since statistics had been kept; most commentators called this a de facto abolishment of the penalty.[3240] That year a Congressional committee held a hearing on abolishing the federal death penalty.[3241] Meanwhile, in 1967, a new procedure called Post-Conviction Relief allowed challenges in cases where the normal appellate process was complete.[3242] Finally, in 1972, the United States Supreme Court banned the death penalty as it existed at the time because state statutes did not contain standards for juries to follow.[3243] This prompted Governor Winfield Dunn to commute twenty-one death sentences on July 18, 1972.[3244] By 1977, there were thirty-five men on death row when the Tennessee Supreme Court found a 1974 statute unconstitutional.[3245] Governor Ray Blanton commuted their sentences.[3246] The Tennessee electric chair was literally removed from the Main Prison.[3247]

However, in 1976 the United States Supreme Court ruled that modern revised statutes which incorporated standards were constitutional.[3248] Many changes came to death penalty law between then and the present, several of which would have affected Tennesseans executed in earlier times.[3249]

Rape of an adult woman was no longer death eligible.[3250] Death may not be visited on aiders and abetters who do not kill, attempt to kill, or intend to kill.[3251] Death must await only the "worst of the worst," which usually does not include the typical wife-killer.[3252] Minors may not be executed[3253] nor the mentally retarded.[3254] Lethal injection, using three drugs, replaced electrocution for persons convicted after 1999.[3255] Finally, death sentences can be overturned where it is shown the killer did not have an effective lawyer.[3256]

The Exoneration Movement

In 1989, a movement began utilizing DNA evidence to exonerate wrongly convicted prisoners and by 2004 some twelve death row inmates had been set free nationwide. By 2004, an "innocence revolution" was underway.[3257] Responding to this trend, the legislature allowed for otherwise time-barred post-conviction petitions where the defendant offered scientific evidence to show actual innocence.[3258] The innocence revolution has continued unabated since 2004.[3259]

Exonerations were seen in noncapital cases earlier and during this time. Douglas Forbes, white, was convicted of two counts of rape and served five years before another man was caught following a similar rape and admitted guilt in Forbes's crimes in 1980.[3260] Forbes was given a pardon based on innocence. Clark McMillan, black, had spent twenty-two years in prison in a noncapital rape conviction before he was freed by DNA evidence in 2002. Michael L. McCormick, white, who had served twenty years in prison, including fifteen years on death row for murder, was given a new trial based on DNA evidence. He was acquitted at a second trial in 2007. In 2009, charges were dropped against former death row inmate Paul Gregory House, white, who had been convicted of murder following the rape of a woman in Union County in 1986.[3261] House had convinced the United States Supreme Court to overlook time-barred habeas corpus relief when it concluded that he had made a good claim of actual innocence.[3262]

As shown below, five of the six men executed in Tennessee since 2000 have claimed innocence. By this time, death row inmates had at least five methods of challenging their convictions: direct appeal (Court of Criminal Appeals and Supreme Court)[3263]; post-conviction relief; writ of error coram nobis[3264]; writ of habeas corpus (usually in federal court); and less promising, a civil rights suit invoking federal statutes.[3265]

Tennessee reenacted a "guided discretion" death penalty in 1977.[3266] Tennessee's death row began to fill again. Inevitably, someone would be executed. Here are the persons executed in Tennessee since the penalty returned to the state.

2000

Robert Glen Coe, white, age 24. *Murder.*

The crime was committed in the woods near the community of Greenfield in rural Weakley County.[3267] On September 1, 1979, Coe, a part-time auto body worker, married with an infant child, lived in McKenzie, Tennessee. Coe enjoyed flashing women, and when he could not find any victims, he drove his car until he came to a church parking lot in tiny Greenfield. Riding their bikes in the lot were Cary Ann Medlin, white, age eight, and her stepbrother, Michael Stout, age eight. Coe told the girl he needed her help to find her father; he asked Michael to hold the bikes while they were gone.[3268] Taking her to a secluded spot about five miles from town, he raped and sodomized her in his car.[3269] During this, Cary told Coe that God loved him and that Jesus loved him. This propelled him into a rage and he attempted to strangle her. Having some difficulty, he drew a pocketknife and stabbed her neck, remarking later that her blood began to pour from her neck "like turning on a water hose."[3270] He carried her body into some overgrowth on a field road. He placed her shoes beside her feet. There was blood on her shorts and panties.

Coe returned home to his wife and child and told her and two friends that he was in trouble with the law for stabbing a state trooper in the throat. His wife and her friend helped dye his dirty-blond hair black. The next day, Coe traded the murder vehicle for another car at the dealership where he had bought the murder vehicle. Michael Stout and his grandmother were taken to view the murder car at the dealership and recognized it. An official at the dealership recognized Coe from his earlier purchase and noted the hair dye had left black smudge marks on his forehead.

Governor Lamar Alexander offered a five-thousand-dollar reward for information about the case. The person who accompanied Coe to trade in his car, and helped him purchase a bus ticket from Huntington to Marietta, Georgia, was present when Coe was arrested at the bus station. This was September 4, 1979.

Coe was taken from Huntington to the Weakley County jail by two officers. Fecal matter was found under the foreskin of his penis. One of the officers was Tennessee Bureau of Identification agent Alvin Daniel. To him, Coe promptly began confessing. At least one of his confessions was tape recorded and played at his trial. Asked why Cary's statement that God loved him made him kill her, he replied, "Because it ain't true." He was kept at Fort Pillow Prison Farm pending trial, and during several trips for hearings fully admitted the crime.[3271]

After several venue changes, he was charged with aggravated kidnapping, aggravated rape and first-degree murder in a trial in February 1981 in Shelby County. Coe did not take the stand.[3272] Coe repudiated his confessions, but several witnesses placed Coe in the murder car at the time of the killing. Some jurors cried when his tape-recorded confession was played.[3273] The jury heard conflicting testimony regarding Coe's sanity. He had a long history of mental treatment and arrests for indecent exhibitionism and attempted rape.[3274] But his wife and friends said he appeared normal when he returned home after the killing. After sentencing, Coe said he wanted an immediate execution and did not want to appeal.[3275]

Coe's numerous appeals raised the issue of his sanity, both at the time of the killing and as his execution day approached. By 1999 Coe had seemingly exhausted his normal appeals, but when the state asked the Tennessee Supreme Court to set an execution date, Coe demanded a competency hearing, which was ordered.[3276]

During a competency hearing in Shelby County in January 2000, he yelled, banged on his chair, spit and screamed obscenities. He was removed from the courtroom and watched the hearing on closed-circuit television.[3277] The trial judge said Coe met the test for sanity, namely that he understood that he was found guilty of murder and was sentenced to die.[3278] By this time, Coe's lawyers were claiming both due process violations relating to his sanity and that he was factually innocent. They attempted to fix blame on another man who was an early suspect in the case and was imprisoned for an unrelated charge. Five days before his execution, scheduled for March 23, Coe's lawyers filed a clemency petition which was quickly denied by the Board of Probation and Parole and the governor.[3279] Earlier, the Tennessee Supreme Court had refused clemency.[3280] The court set his new execution date for April 5, 2000, and later for April 19.[3281]

Robert Glen Coe's clemency petition emphasized his childhood marked by poverty, violence toward him by his father and lack of sexual boundaries by both parents.[3282] His father, Willie, used his disability check to purchase and consume two cases of beer in quart bottles each weekend. Robert was the fourth of five children: Jimmy (deaf, spent most of his youth at the Tennessee School for the Deaf), Anna May (born prematurely and died at seven months), Bonnie, Robert (he was born at home), and Billie Jean. When Robert was eight, his father shot him in the leg when he ran to escape a beating. Robert had seizures until he was twelve. These happened about once a week and more frequently when he was around other children. Because he would flop or "flubber" around, he got the nickname "Flubby." The family slept in one room. Bonnie was repeatedly fondled by her father at night. When she was fourteen, her father forcibly raped her and forced Robert and Billie Jean to watch. Shortly thereafter, the father was committed to Western State Mental Hospital, where he stayed for about three years. The mother, Anna Belle Coe, was sexually promiscuous in front of the children, and both parents said Robert was conceived during one of Anna Belle's liaisons with the landlord. The parents divorced when Robert was fourteen.

The clemency petition included voluminous medical records. When Robert was eighteen his forty-three-year-old mother married a twenty-two-year-old and moved to Florida. Robert went too. On January 31, 1975, still eighteen, Coe entered the mobile home of a forty-year-old neighbor and propositioned her. When she laughed at him, he tried to rape her and when she screamed he stabbed her with a paring knife. He now went in and out of jail and the Florida State Hospital, a mental hospital. There he exposed himself to female employees, and progress reports for the two and one-half years repeatedly called him a menace to society for this activity.

Doctors' reports said hospitalization was doing no good and predicted Coe would engage in sex-related crime after release. In 1978 it was determined that because his mother and stepfather were moving back to West Tennessee, Coe could continue treatment at a Memphis program for sex offenders. He sought no treatment. On March 7, 1978, he was arrested for flashing a woman in Dresden and put on ninety days' probation. On October 31, 1978, he flashed a woman in Obion County and checked into Western State Hospital in a plea to avoid jail. He stayed there a month. During a hospitalization he said his exhibitionism was prompted, in part, due to his wife Tammy's pregnancy. The clemency petition did not assert innocence.

In the weeks before his execution, Coe received the federal court's permission to have his counsel present to witness the execution, supposedly a matter of first impression in the nation.[3283] Finally, the day before his execution, Coe sought and received an order from a Davidson County judge staying his execution because of challenges to the execution protocol. The Tennessee Supreme Court overturned the order in the very early morning of April 19, 2000.[3284]

Coe was placed on the death watch on April 17, 2000, at a special unit (Unit 2) at the new Riverbend Maximum Security Prison in Nashville. Earlier, he had chosen death by lethal injection under a statute that allowed persons given the death penalty before January 1, 1999, to choose this or electrocution. His requested last meal was catfish, French fries, cole slaw, white beans, pecan pie and sweet tea.[3285] Coe was forty-three years old when he was strapped to a gurney and moved fifty feet to the execution room. Under an established procedure, a catheter was placed in each arm and an overhead microphone allowed his last words to be heard by official visitors and the victim's family.[3286] Coe had embraced Christianity in the months before his death, and his manner was calm in the days before his execution.

Robert Glen Coe's execution procedure began at 1:00 A.M. on April 19, 2000, and he was pronounced dead at 1:37 A.M. His final statement said, "I forgive the state of Tennessee for murdering me for something I didn't do. I am not guilty of this crime and that's the God's truth. I'll see you all in heaven." Then he said, "Charlotte Stout, I forgive you, too, for helping the state murder me." He recited the Lord's Prayer with the prison chaplain. As the injection was being given, he said, "Forgive everybody. God loves you. I'm gone. I'll see you in heaven. Bye-bye."[3287] His body was claimed by two sisters and a brother who had helped him plan his funeral. His body was cremated.

The victim's family waiting room allowed them to see Coe on the gurney both before and after the execution, by closed-circuit television. Present were the now grown Michael Stout and Cary's father Jerry Medlin. Also present were Mickey Stout, husband of Charlotte Stout, Cary's mother. For twenty years Charlotte had attended most of the hearings in Coe's many appeals. At the time of Cary's death she was eight months pregnant with son Joshua and later had another son, Jesse.

2006

Sedley Alley, white, age 29. *Murder.*

The crime was committed at 10:30 P.M. on July 11, 1985, on Navy Road on the Millington Naval Base, in Shelby County. The victim was Suzanne Marie Collins, white, age nineteen. She was a lance corporal in the Marines and was stationed at the base taking a course in avionics. The killer's wife was also in the military and the couple lived on the base. Wearing a red Marine T-shirt and red Marine shorts, Collins had left her barracks about 10:00

P.M. to go jogging on the base. Collins was last seen alive by a Navy officer and two other male Marine joggers. Meanwhile, Alley had driven his car, a 1972 dark green Mercury station wagon with wood grain paneling and Kentucky plates, to a place on Navy Road where he encountered the jogging victim. The car was seen by the two male joggers, with a white man standing beside it. In a matter of minutes, the two heard a female voice screaming in distress, "Don't touch me," "Leave me alone." The joggers returned in the direction of the screaming, suspecting a kidnapping, and saw the station wagon, which had been on the wrong side of the road, drive off toward the main gate. The car had a loud, faulty muffler. The joggers went immediately to the gate and reported a suspected kidnapping. Within two hours, Alley (and his wife) were questioned by the military police and released. This was due, in part, to the failure of the two male joggers to identify Alley. However, as Alley and his wife left in the station wagon, the joggers heard the distinctive muffler sound. Returning to the security checkpoint, they insisted it was the same car they had seen and heard earlier.

At 6:00 A.M. on July 12, 1985, Collins's nude body was found in Orgill Park, which adjoins the base, north of Navy Road. Her face was mutilated beyond recognition. That morning Alley was arrested by military police. After he was advised of his rights, he confessed to having accidentally struck her with his car as she jogged, and taking her into the car, intending to take her to a hospital. His tape-recorded statement was lengthy and explained that she cursed him in the car and threatened to get him in trouble, in part, because he was drunk. He said he had stuck a screwdriver in her head (this was shown false), hit her a few times and held her on the ground. After she collapsed, he decided to make it look as if she had been raped and killed by a maniac. He insisted he had not raped her.[3288] He took off all her clothes and dragged her by the feet to a tree. There he broke off a tree limb and pushed it into her vagina. After giving the statement, he voluntarily took officers to the place her body had been found earlier that day and pointed out the tree from which he had broken the limb. His transcribed statements comprised sixteen single-spaced pages upon which he had made corrections and signed each page.

By the time of trial in March 1987, it was clear that Alley's defense was insanity, specifically that he had multiple personalities, namely Sedley (his normal self), and two others, "Death," and "Billie." "Death" wore a black cape and rode a white horse. He maintained he could not remember the killing and was under the influence of one of these personalities, Death, and therefore did not know right from wrong. Alley recalled that he was under the influence of alcohol and amphetamines at the time. He was shown to have a violent personality (he beat both of his wives) and frequently used vulgar language. At the time Collins was killed, he worked as an air conditioning technician. Earlier in the day, while repairing an officer's unit, he had taken some items from the yard which were found at Alley's home.

At trial, a pathologist said Collins died of multiple injuries, several of which could have caused death. There were strangulation bruises on her neck. She had about one hundred bruises and abrasions over her entire body, front and back. The skull injuries came from being struck from the rounded end of a screwdriver (not the point) that was found near the scene. He said the tree branch had been inserted into her body more than once, to the depth of twenty inches, causing severe injuries and hemorrhaging. He said she was alive when the tree limb was inserted.[3289] Photographs of her body suggested that one of her breasts had been chewed.

Two defense doctors confirmed the existence of multiple personality disorder, but could not say which was in play at the time of the murder. One agreed that Alley's detailed statement the day after the killing was inconsistent with his later claim of amnesia regarding the killing. At least five doctors and psychologists who had examined Alley said he did not have multiple personality disorder, that he was malingering, but had a borderline personality disorder. Many lay witnesses were offered to show he was normal at the initial questioning on the night of July 11 and at other times.

On appeal, a dozen errors were raised. These ranged from whether it was proper to display a large photograph of Collins in the first day of trial, to whether it was wrong for the jury to see photographs of her battered body, including the stick protruding from her vagina. They included challenges to the qualifications of some master's degree-trained psychologists and whether it was proper to cross-examine Alley's brother, a professing Christian, about a Bible passage, "He that smiteth a man, so that he die, shall be surely put to death." The Supreme Court said it was clearly wrong ("reprehensible") for the prosecutor to have asked the brother about an assault charge against the defendant in Michigan, when he knew no charge had been brought, but this did not warrant a new trial. The court said, "Defendant's guilt in this case was established at the level of absolute certainty."[3290] He was ordered executed on May 2, 1990.

With new counsel, Alley had a post-conviction hearing which ended on April 29, 1991. The chief issues were incompetence of counsel, and on appeal, whether the judge showed bias toward Alley in making rulings regarding offered testimony. Alley's strategy was to show his former counsel were ineffective because they had failed to meet with one of his expert witnesses to clarify his testimony regarding whether he could testify as to Alley's sanity. The judge refused to allow the doctor to testify ("make a record"). Post-conviction relief was denied by the judge. On appeal, the Court of Criminal Appeals said it was error to refuse to allow the testimony. Further, during the hearing the judge made remarks which, when viewed objectively, showed the appearance of bias. Alley was granted another post-conviction hearing before a new judge.[3291]

At the second post-conviction hearing, Alley raised several issues he said showed ineffective assistance of counsel. In particular, there was a failure to emphasize that as a youngster Alley had undergone a painful dilation of the urethra, which should have been linked to the victim's vaginal penetration caused by "Death." In addition, a similar dilation instrument should have been shown to the jury. The prior attorneys were faulted for failing to understand that their defense witness, Dr. Battle, was going to testify that he could not say whether Alley was sane at the time of the killing, only that he had multiple personality disorder. About ten other issues were raised, going to the fairness of the trial, such as whether the judge should have shared with defense counsel a letter the victim's family had written to the judge, and whether it was proper for the judge's wife to sit with the parents. The post-conviction judge denied relief.

On appeal, the Court of Criminal Appeals affirmed the denial.[3292] Virtually all of the medical witnesses said prior counsel had spent considerable time with them, that use of an exemplar instrument was a tactical matter, that it was not error for the lawyers to fail to rehabilitate Dr. Battle, in part because his colleague, Dr. Marshall, had opined that Alley was insane at the time of the killing. Other issues, such as a birth defect (spina bifida), Alley's not wanting to play with other children, and the mental abuse he suffered from his father, were properly raised at trial.

Alley turned to the federal court seeking habeas corpus relief. The federal judge said the trial judge was not biased during the trial, there was no improper argument by the prosecutor, it was harmless error to allow the victim's father to testify during the sentencing phase, and there was no showing of ineffectiveness of counsel.[3293]

An issue throughout the various appeals was whether it was error for the trial judge to refuse to admit videotapes of some sessions with Alley's doctors. This issue was raised again in federal court, but on appeal to the Sixth Circuit, was found groundless, along with his other arguments, notably the ineffective assistance of counsel claim.[3294] The United States Supreme Court denied his appeal and the Tennessee Supreme Court set his execution date for June 3, 2004.

A month before the execution date, Alley asked the trial court to order post-conviction relief in the form of allowing DNA testing of vaginal and leg swabs, head hairs found on the victim's socks, various body hairs found on the victim, hair found on the stick, and blood and hair samples from the victim. Seminal fluid (but no sperm) had been found in Suzanne's vagina and on her legs; Alley's statement had denied raping her. Alley's purpose in seeking the DNA testing was to show that someone else may have killed Suzanne Collins. On May 17, 2004, the trial court ruled these tests would have no probative value and their results would not have changed the outcome of the trial. This was affirmed on appeal.[3295]

On May 19, 2004, a federal judge stayed his execution and declined to rule on whether it should hear a second habeas petition until the resolution of another case then pending in the Sixth Circuit. After that decision, the Sixth Circuit ordered the federal judge to decide whether to entertain Alley's latest petition.[3296] The federal judge rejected his petition on procedural grounds on November 25, 2005, and rejected an appeal made to have the judge alter or amend her prior decision. On March 29, 2006, the Tennessee Supreme Court set a date for Alley's execution. The next day he informed prison officials that he objected to the state's lethal injection protocol, and on April 11, 2006, he filed suit in Nashville federal court challenging the protocol.[3297] The same day, he filed a civil rights suit in Memphis federal court demanding the samples for use in DNA sampling. Nine days later the federal judge ruled he did not have jurisdiction to rule on these matters.[3298]

The Memphis federal judge's decision was affirmed by the Sixth Circuit Court of Appeals on May 9, 2006, but left open a decision on his Nashville civil rights suit.[3299] The federal judge dismissed this suit on May 11, 2006, and this was affirmed three days later.[3300]

Earlier, Alley had asked the Board of Probation and Parole to recommend a reprieve so he could petition a court for more samples for DNA testing. It voted 4–3 in his favor and the governor agreed, but only to a fifteen-day reprieve.[3301]

During this time, Alley filed a petition in state court demanding more samples, including materials found on a pair of men's underwear found near the body and fingernail scrapings. In this petition, Alley suggested the real killer was Collins's civilian boyfriend (who had admitted he was with her earlier in the evening), because he more closely resembled the initial description of the suspect.[3302] Also raised was a discrepancy between tire prints and his shoe prints. The trial court denied any relief and the Court of Criminal Appeals affirmed on June 22, 2006.[3303] Both the Tennessee Supreme Court and the United States Supreme Court declined to hear the case. Following this, on June 27, 2006, the governor declined clemency for Alley, who had previously been scheduled for execution on June 28, 2006.

Sedley Alley's clemency petition, filed by the Innocence Project, asserted, "The jury convicted the wrong man," explaining that Suzanne's civilian boyfriend better fit the description originally given as the man with her.[3304] It further asserted he had a motive for killing her. He thought he had an exclusive relationship with her, said an affidavit from a private investigator.[3305] The petition argued that further DNA testing would exonerate Alley and help find her real killer. It argued the case was nearly identical to a New Jersey case involving a woman whose vagina was penetrated by a stick but the conviction was overturned by DNA testing. The Innocence Project would pay for the testing.[3306]

Alley filed another petition in Nashville federal court on June 27. A judge of the Sixth Circuit granted a stay at 11:00 P.M. but a panel of Sixth Circuit judges rejected both the stay and the petition at 1:10 A.M. on June 28.[3307]

On June 27, Alley and another man scheduled to die the next day were already in the special death unit.[3308] Alley, age fifty-one, conversed with his adult daughter, who said that he had maintained his innocence to her. Suzanne's parents and brother did not attend the execution, but a victim advocate observed on their behalf. At 2:00 A.M. on June 28, 2006, Alley, on a gurney, was taken to the execution room. The warden asked if he had anything to say. He replied, "Yes, to my children." His two adult children were in the next room, with their hands against the glass separating the room. Alley said, "April, David, can you hear me? I love you. Stay strong." He thanked the prison chaplain. Then he said, "I love you, David. I love you, April. Be good and stay together. Stay strong."[3309] Two minutes later the drugs were injected into the catheters. Alley exhaled twice and turned pale. He was pronounced dead at 2:12 A.M. His children claimed his body.

2007

Philip Ray Workman, white, age 27. *Murder.*

The crime was committed about 10:30 P.M. on August 5, 1981, outside a Wendy's restaurant at 3275 Danny Thomas Boulevard, in Memphis, Shelby County. Workman, a drifter, was a drug addict under the influence of cocaine and amphetamines. He had been convicted of burglary and two drug charges were pending against him in Florida. He had been hitchhiking and was dropped off at an interstate exit near the Wendy's. He entered the restaurant just before closing time and dawdled until closing was announced. He pulled out a .45 caliber semi-automatic pistol and herded the staff into the manager's office. He told the employees that he had an accomplice who was not as "cool" as he was and this person would shoot anyone who disregarded his orders. He took an employee's car keys, ordered everyone to stay in the office, locked the door and left. He started to leave the restaurant with a thousand dollars in a bag when he encountered the victim, Ronald Oliver, white, age thirty-two, a lieutenant in the Memphis police department. What happened next is unclear, but as Oliver attempted to hold him, Workman broke away and ran. Failing to stop, Workman was grabbed by Oliver and fellow police officer Aubrey Stoddard. Breaking free, Workman shot Oliver in the chest, hit Stoddard with a bullet to the arm, and fired at least one more shot at another police officer who had arrived. A police dog found him hiding in underbrush near another store. He had cuts and scratches and dog bites. He told police he needed the money to leave town and gave a false name.[3310]

At trial, he attributed the shooting to the influence of drugs and said he was trying to give up when he was "hit or grabbed" by the officers, which caused him to shoot. He said he could only remember "bits" and "pieces" of the events that evening.

He testified he could not recall shooting Oliver, but that he had his hand around the pistol and pulled the trigger, shooting all the bullets in the clip. He was convicted of felony murder with aggravated circumstances and sentenced to death. Numerous issues raised on appeal, dealing with issues such as a challenge to a scrupled juror and admission of evidence, were rejected by the Tennessee Supreme Court. Its opinion did not mention Harold Davis, black, who claimed he drove up to the Wendy's as the shooting began and saw Officer Oliver go down. He recognized Workman when police gave him photographs the next day. The opinion did not mention the testimony of Vivian Porter, who testified she was in the Davis car when it pulled into the Wendy's. It did not mention that no ballistics testing was made regarding Workman's gun. Philip Workman's execution was set for May 29, 1984.[3311]

Philip Workman's first post-conviction hearing was set for January 1986. During transport to Memphis, Workman pulled a pistol on the two correctional officers in the front seat. He said, "You people seem like real nice people. If you don't do what I say, I'm going to kill you, I'd hate to have to do that."[3312] The male driver signaled to a chase car that something was amiss by tapping on the brake and driving erratically. The female correctional officer in the passenger seat began loudly complaining she was getting sick from a diabetic attack. The driver slowed the car and drove off the road. Both officers rolled from the moving car. One emptied his revolver at the car while Workman struggled to free himself. At that moment a Highway Patrol car drove up. Workman had managed to escape his handcuffs by using petroleum jelly that had been bound up in an Ace bandage on his arm. He was found with a knife. The report of this incident was presented to the Parole Board during Workman's first clemency hearing and remained in his file.

At his first post-conviction hearing in 1986, Workman raised several issues which were rejected and the Court of Criminal Appeals concurred.[3313] In a second post-conviction hearing in 1991, he raised for the first time the notion that Oliver may have been hit by "friendly fire," that is, a bullet fired from a fellow officer's pistol. This issue was known at the time of his trial, ruled the appellate court, which again rejected his claims.[3314] The issue was important because the law at the time said that the death penalty was allowed only for shooters and accomplices.[3315]

In 1994, Workman sought habeas corpus relief in a Memphis federal court. He subpoenaed numerous documents, including an X-ray of Oliver's body. The state responded it could not find the X-ray. The habeas corpus petition was denied. The Sixth Circuit concurred, but recounted Workman's theory of the case. First, the Georgia medical examiner offered an affidavit that the exit wound was inconsistent with a .45 caliber wound because it was too small. Next, witness Davis was actually not present at the shooting, and was planted by the police. Further, the prosecution withheld evidence that officer Parker had fired a shotgun during the incident. Finally, the prosecution withheld evidence that Workman was bludgeoned by Officer Stoddard with a flashlight. In short, officers Stoddard and Parker had committed perjury. The appellate court refused to accredit the medical examiner's affidavit and found there was no evidence of perjury.[3316]

In 2000, Workman sought clemency from the governor in a proceeding before the Parole Board. At the hearing, Workman testified he involuntarily fired two shots. (His lawyer told the Board Workman had fired four shots.) During preparation it became clear that the Shelby County medical examiner had recently examined an X-ray of Officer Oliver's body. This new evidence was crucial because it served as the basis for the Georgia medical examiner to testify at the clemency hearing that Workman's gun had not fired the death bullet; rather, it was a smaller caliber bullet fired by a fellow officer. The Board refused to recommend clemency.[3317] Workman asked the Tennessee Supreme Court to recommend clemency under a statute dating from 1838 giving it that power. It refused.[3318]

In March 2000, Workman sought a second habeas petition and the Sixth Circuit ordered a rare en banc hearing on his various motions.[3319] In September 2000, the court ruled 7–7, which meant it denied Workman habeas relief.[3320] He filed a motion to rehear the matter, which the Sixth Circuit also denied on March 23, 2001.[3321] Four days later, the governor denied Workman's clemency request.[3322] His civil rights suit filed that day charged a variety of state officials had conspired to present false evidence at the clemency hearing. A Nashville federal judge dismissed the suit, which was affirmed on appeal.[3323]

Meanwhile, by a 6–3 vote, the United States Supreme Court affirmed the Sixth Circuit's 7–7 denial of relief on March 29, 2001.[3324] This meant the state could go forward with Workman's execution scheduled for the next day.[3325] However, at 12:11 A.M. the next day, forty-nine minutes before he was scheduled to receive the lethal dose, the Tennessee

Supreme Court issued a stay and ordered a hearing on Workman's various claims, notably that Davis had recanted his testimony and the withholding of the X-ray.[3326]

The hearing on a petition for coram nobis, conducted in Memphis by Judge John Colton, began in August and was carried over during October and November, for a six-day period. Workman was present in the courtroom but was not placed on the stand. Proof showed Harold Davis had been located by defense counsel in an Arizona prison in 1999 and gave a videotape recantation of his 1985 testimony at that time. However, he was high on drugs and was pressured by Workman's lawyers, he said. Davis, age forty-six, now testified that he had been a drug user for the last twenty years and lived largely on the street. He had been brought from a Florida jail where he was being held on a shoplifting charge. Davis admitted he had lied in 1985 about seeing Workman shoot Oliver. He said his other testimony about seeing Oliver on the ground attempting to shoot, and testimony about seeing the pistol in Workman's hand pointed at Oliver, was false. However, when asked what he presently remembered about the night, he testified he could not remember because of his history of drug use and a possible series of small strokes. "Some things I remember and some things I don't," he said.[3327] He denied that Vivian Porter was with him in his car.[3328] Vivian Porter, who now operated a transitional house for battered women and had been clean and sober for nine years, testified their car simply drove past the Wendy's while the shooting was underway. She also had no present recollection of the events relating to the shooting. Medical examiner Wecht repeated his clemency hearing testimony that he did not think the bullet that killed Oliver came from Workman's gun, but he could not state with "absolute medical certainty" that his opinion was accurate.[3329] The state offered no proof, although former Officer Stoddard was present in the courtroom and told reporters, "All the shots came from right there. I didn't see 'em because I got knocked down, but I know all the shots came from where he was."[3330]

On January 7, 2002, Judge Colton released his decision. Because the corum nobis procedure was designed primarily to review "new" evidence, Workman had not carried his burden that the Davis and Porter testimony met that standard. Rather, even if they had told the truth in 1985 it would have made no difference. Further, he ruled that the confusing Davis testimony, taken as a whole, was not a true recantation. Likewise, the X-ray evidence and Wecht's testimony could have been elicited prior to the 1985 trial. Judge Colton's opinion was upheld by the Court of Criminal Appeals.[3331] The Tennessee Supreme Court declined to review the case, ending his state remedies, and ordered Workman executed on September 24, 2003.

On August 12, 2003, a clemency petition was presented to the governor, who declined to act.[3332] It raised all the issues that had been addressed by the courts, notably the caliber of the bullet and the Davis recantation. Clemency was urged by ninety-one professionals and professors of criminal justice around the nation.[3333] The Memphis district attorney filed a counterpetition. Drawing from the trial transcript, it explained, "Neither Stoddard nor Parker ever fired a shot."[3334] It explained that Workman only raised the issue of his not actually shooting Oliver in 1991, ten years after his conviction, and after having testified several times that he shot Oliver. The Atlanta forensic examiner's affidavit was defective because it failed to state that Workman's weapon and ammunition could not have fired the fatal shot.[3335]

Twenty days before his execution date, Workman filed a motion in Memphis federal court asking it to reopen his 1994 habeas petition. The federal judge granted a stay, pending the outcome of a case pending before the Sixth Circuit, regarding the proper way to treat motions which are arguably second motions and thus not allowed.

Meanwhile, on September 15, 2003, Governor Bredesen had granted a reprieve until January 15, 2004, later extended to April 15, 2004, in light of a pending federal investigation regarding the medical examiner who had testified at the 1985 trial.[3336] The Tennessee Supreme Court set a new execution date for September 22, 2004. The Memphis federal judge had granted a stay on September 13, 2004. On December 13, 2004, the Sixth Circuit announced its decision in the other case, but the Memphis federal judge took no action while the other case went to the United States Supreme Court. This came in 2005.

Relying on the Supreme Court's decision, the Memphis federal judge denied Workman's various motions pending before her, the last decision coming on December 12, 2006. On January 17, 2007, the Tennessee Supreme Court set Workman's execution for May 9, 2007. However, in April 2007, the Memphis federal judge allowed Workman to appeal her earlier orders. This was rejected by the Sixth Circuit on May 7, 2007.[3337] Meanwhile, on May 4, 2007, a Nashville federal judge halted the execution, ruling that the state's three-drug protocol raised an issue of whether persons executed might suffer unduly. The Sixth Circuit rejected the ruling three days later.[3338]

On May 8, 2007, the day before his execution, Workman filed stay motions before the United States Supreme Court which were immediately denied.

By May 8, 2007, Philip Workman had received at least seven stays and this was his fourth time on death watch, the seventy-two-hour period leading to his death, in a cell next to the execution chamber. During his time on death row, Workman had become a born-again Christian, and commonly wore a baseball hat bearing a cross and a scriptural verse. One of his closest friends was the Rev. Joe Ingle, who had counseled him for seventeen years. The day before the execution Ingle sat for two hours in a chair outside Workman's cell. They held hands through the bars and leaned forward so their heads touched as they prayed: "I could feel his tears and my tears running off our faces and dripping onto our hands."[3339] Workman's last meal request the night before his execution was vegetarian pizza, but he asked that it be delivered to the homeless. The request was denied. After the news media announced the last request, citizens sent the Nashville Union Rescue Mission a total of 170 pizzas.[3340]

Placed on a gurney and taken to the death chamber at 1:00 A.M. on May 9, 2007, Workman, age fifty-three, was asked by the warden if he had any last words at 1:21 A.M.[3341] Workman, staring at the ceiling, said, "I have prayed to the Lord Jesus Christ not to lay charge of my death to any man." The lethal dose was started. Workman loudly proclaimed, "I commend my spirit into your hands, Lord Jesus Christ." He exhaled, blinked, his head tilted slightly to the left and he did not move. A few minutes later his face turned blue, then ashen. Seventeen minutes later the warden closed the blinds. A voice came over the speaker, "This concludes the execution of Philip Workman. Time of death, 1:38 A.M."[3342] Workman's brother claimed the body and insisted, "The state of Tennessee killed a man that did not commit the crime they say he did."[3343] In 2000, Officer Oliver's daughter, Paula Dodillet, said in a film about the case, *Philip Workman: A Case for Clemency*, "My belief and my feelings are that Mr. Workman did not kill my father, and if so, he did not do it intentionally."[3344] She had urged clemency.

Daryl Keith Holton, white, age 36. *Murder.*

The crime was committed about 7:30 P.M. on November 30, 1997, in the back bay area of Holton's Wrecker Service and Garage in Shelbyville, in Bedford County. The victims were the killer's children, Stephen Holton, white, age twelve; Brent Holton, white, age ten; Eric Holton, white, age six; and Kayla Holton, black, age four.[3345] The defendant, formerly a career Army enlisted man, had obtained a hardship discharge in 1992 in order to return to the United States to care for his children. He divorced the children's mother, Crystal, in June 1992 and obtained custody of his three children, all boys. On June 23, 1993, his former wife gave birth to Kayla Marie, fathered by a black man. The couple resumed living together but did not remarry, and Kayla was given Holton's name. After living with Holton two years, the mother moved to Murfreesboro, taking the children with her. Holton saw the children on weekends. During a return on Sunday night in 1995, he threatened that unless she got into the car with him, "You are going to regret it." He drove off with the children, but later turned them over to police. About this time, the state took brief legal custody of the children with the mother retaining physical custody. On February 27, 1996, a Bedford County court granted full custody to the mother, leaving to her discretion when he could visit them. In 1997, she moved in with another man in Spring Hill, Tennessee. At trial, the children's mother admitted the marriage was "up and down," that she drank frequently from pint-size bottles of liquor and was a poor housekeeper, and that Holton had hit her during their marriage, blaming it on her drinking. Holton frequently complained of the safety and wholesomeness of the various places she lived, notably public housing in Murfreesboro. At this time, he lived in his uncle's garage, in an area cordoned off by a tarpaulin, heated by a portable propane gas heater.

On Thanksgiving Day, 1997, Holton learned that his wife had moved in with the other man and became angry as he did not want his children calling the man "Dad." On November 30, 1997, he picked the four children up at 3:00 P.M., telling them he had a surprise for them, variously that they were going Christmas shopping or that he had a dog at the garage he wanted them to see. After taking them to Wal-Mart and Funland, he took them to the garage. Distracting the young children, Holton took the older boys into another part of the garage. Telling them "Don't peek," he told them to put their hands over their eyes. He ordered Stephen to stand in front of Brent. He put an SKS semi-automatic military rifle into position so that it was touching Brent's back, and fired one shot designed to pierce both boys' hearts. When they fell, he shot each one again. He put the bodies under a tarpaulin. Then he brought the younger children to the same spot, told Eric to stand in front of Kayla, and again from a kneeling position fired the same rifle with one shot striking the children's hearts. Then he fired a second shot at Kayla and placed the bodies on top of their siblings. He left the rifle near the scene.

At 9:45 that night, Holton walked into the Shelbyville Police Department and calmly announced he wanted to report a "homicide times four." He said he had killed his four children, explained where the bodies could be found, and in two statements given to police explained his motive. He did not want their mother to keep them because they "had been taken away from me and given back to me, taken away from me and given back to me enough." He explained that when he picked the children up his former wife "was dressed nicely." "She was wearing makeup. She said she was happy. And that did not make me happy." He told the police there were homemade explosive devices at the garage. Holton explained his plan was to kill their mother, but he ran out of time and returned to the garage. He said, "I had done what I wanted to do. I wanted to shock Crystal to death." He decided not to kill himself because someone who "was involved" should be left alive to help people "have a chance of understanding this." He professed love for his children, but told police he had no regret or remorse for killing them.

At trial, Holton did not take the stand. Expert testimony was offered that carbon monoxide from the propane heater may have triggered his depression, psychosis and neurologic deficit. There was expert testimony to the opposite, including testimony that the heater worked properly. A defense psychiatrist emphasized the killing was related to the fact that Holton loved his children too much, that he fit the profile of a man who kills his children. Holton was severely depressed, he explained, because he exhibited symptoms. He worked seven days a week except when he saw his children, he had lost interest in other activities, he had difficulty thinking and concentrating, he spoke slowly and stared into space, he had lost weight and withdrawn from human contact, had been found lying on the floor for no reason and had expressed a desire to kill himself. The psychiatrist conceded that a person in Holton's mental condition knew right from wrong, but thought the killing was "done for almost the right reasons." The state offered a forensic neuropsychologist who explained that Holton had a history of depression, had been suffering from major depression, and had a passive-aggressive personality disorder and a schizoid personality. But he knew right from wrong. Holton offered no evidence during the punishment phase of the trial except testimony from the jailer, who said he had been a good prisoner. The jury convicted him of four counts of premeditated murder.

Numerous legal issues were raised on appeal, including whether the acoustics in the courtroom were so poor the jury could not hear witnesses. The Tennessee Supreme Court turned aside claims that the statutory insanity defense was improper law, and that there was sufficient "residual doubt" to warrant a punishment less than death. On this issue, the court declined to second-guess the jury, observing that Holton had made a voluntary, knowing and intelligent decision not to put on any mitigating evidence. The court upheld the death penalty generally and in this case, saying it compared to other cases where children had been killed.[3346] Proof showed Holton was highly intelligent (he had an I.Q. of 120) and was thirty-six years old. These were meticulously planned and carefully premeditated murders, the court said. It ruled that requiring a defendant to prove insanity by clear and convincing evidence was not unconstitutional. The Tennessee Supreme Court ordered Daryl Holton executed on June 2, 2004, which was later set for June 8, 2005.

Holton sought post-conviction relief on April 29, 2005, but the petition was obviously defective because it was outside the one-year limitation period and Holton had not signed the petition. Because the petition, which was filed on Holton's behalf by the post-conviction defender as "next friend," focused on Holton's mental health, the trial court ordered Holton to meet personally with the defender and a court-designated mental health expert. The state appealed. While this was underway, a Knoxville federal judge appointed the federal public defender to Holton's case, who filed a habeas corpus petition in his name on September 30, 2005.

On May 4, 2006, the Tennessee Supreme Court rejected the post-conviction public defender's petition, saying there was no statutory basis for filing it and that it had not been signed by Holton. However, it explained that Holton could petition for a mental competency hearing.[3347]

A new execution date of September 19, 2006, was set.

Meanwhile, the Knoxville federal judge had ordered a hearing on whether Holton had authorized the habeas petition, during which Holton said he had not. The judge ordered a psychiatric evaluation. That report said that Holton was competent and had rationally decided not to pursue the appeal. The judge dismissed the petition on September 6, 2006. The Sixth Circuit Court of Appeals granted a stay on September 18, 2006, also noting that Holton had filed his own habeas corpus petition directly with the United States Supreme Court. Three days later, Holton sent the Sixth Circuit a letter explaining he did not want either his appeal or the Supreme Court matter to go forward. On January 7, 2007, the Sixth Circuit Court of Appeals dismissed Holton's appeal.

When the state asked the Tennessee Supreme Court for a new execution date, Holton wrote the court saying he did not oppose the setting of a new date, which the court set for February 28, 2007.

However, the next day the governor granted a reprieve of all executions until May 2, 2007, to give the Commissioner of Corrections time to conduct a review of the state's execution process, lethal injection. This was accomplished on April 30, 2007. On May 22, the Tennessee Supreme Court set a new execution date for September 12, 2007. Holton had earlier chosen electrocution as his method of execution. Previously, a group of seventy-eight Tennessee lawyers had asked the Tennessee Supreme Court to withdraw its electrocution order. The court declined on September 11, 2007.

Daryl Keith Holton was electrocuted at Riverbend Maximum Security Prison at 1:16 A.M. on September 12, 2007. Because this was the first electrocution since 1960, there was concern about whether the chair would work properly. The two men who had built it had stated that the state's use of only 1750 volts, not the 2,640 volts it was designed for, might not actually kill on the first shock.[3348] The pair had built the chair in 1989, supposedly using some pieces from the old chair. The chair was normally kept along with the death gurney in the execution room, and removed when the gurney was to be used. Now it had to be bolted to the floor and connected to wires. The state execution manual called for two shocks.

A special extraction team of eight guards took Holton from his holding cell, using a body belt, leg irons and plastic handcuffs. Holton walked unassisted to the execution room. "He had a certain dignity about him and was clearly resigned to his fate," wrote his lawyer. After the other restraints were removed, the guards placed the leather straps and belts around his body and electrodes were attached to his feet and moist sponges to places of contact. The process of strapping him in the chair took about ten minutes. (Nothing was said about a shaved head.) During this time Holton began hyperventilating and by the time the charge was given, he looked sleepy and sedated. His bobbing head, yawning, droopy eyelids and slurred speech were attributed to that.[3349] A saline-soaked sponge was placed on his head, followed by the headpiece, which looked like an old-fashioned football helmet. Water from the sponge dripped onto his face, prompting the guard to apologize and Holton to remark, "Didn't matter." The Warden approached Holton and asked if he had any last words. Holton replied, "I do." But he said nothing. The Warden asked if he had anything more to say, and Holton replied in a such a low voice it could not be heard, but his lawyer thinks Holton actually replied in the negative. Asked if he wanted a blindfold, Holton said yes. A large black shroud was affixed to the headpiece.[3350]

At this point, the visitors (which included his lawyer) were asked to leave the room and go to a windowed room to watch the execution. An exhaust fan was turned on and five seconds later the current was applied. Holton's hands gripped the chair arms and his body convulsed, pinning him in the chair for fifteen seconds. He slumped over. Another shock lasting twenty seconds was given and he convulsed again. The body was turned over to the county medical examiner, who said that Holton had suffered some first- and second-degree burns, akin to sunburn, and that his heart had stopped with the first charge.[3351] The body was claimed by family. A short film called *Robert Blecker Wants Me Dead*, about Holton's relationship with a pro-death penalty law professor, had been filmed earlier.

2009

Steve Henley, white, age 30. *Murder.*

The crime was committed in the afternoon of July 24, 1985, on Pine Creek Road in Jackson County. The killers were Steve Henley and Terry Flatt, white, age thirty. Henley, a high school dropout, had married at eighteen, but was now divorced with two small children. The victims were Fred Stafford, white, age sixty-seven, and his wife Edna Stafford, white, age sixty-four. The Stafford home was a short distance from the farm that had been owned by Steve's grandfather. Steve had been raised by his grandparents and his grandmother still lived there. Henley, accompanied by Flatt, had gone to the grandmother's house earlier in the day. The pair had been driving around in Henley's truck drinking beer and taking Dilaudid. As the truck passed the Stafford home, Henley said, "There was some people that lived on that road that owed his grandmother and grandfather some money and they done him wrong, his grandparents wrong years before, and he was going to stop and see about collecting some money."[3352] They drove to the grandmother's house (Henley let Flatt out shortly before reaching the house) and returned with a .22 rifle. Henley stopped the truck about seventy-five yards away and loaded the rifle. He also filled a plastic jug with gasoline from a five-gallon can he had in the back of the truck.

They proceeded to the Stafford house. They found the couple standing beside the road. Henley stopped the truck, jumped out and told them, "I want your money, if you don't give it to me this man in the truck here, he's going to kill me." He told them to go to the house. Mr. Stafford said, "Steve, if you want money or something, I got $80, maybe $100, you can have it." He forced them to the house at gunpoint (a pistol). Henley followed the couple; he told Flatt to bring him the .22 rifle. When they got within 20 or 30 feet of the house, Henley told Flatt to give him the rifle and return to the truck for the jug of gasoline. Flatt complied. As Flatt approached the porch he saw Henley begin to shoot the rifle. He first shot Mr. Stafford, then turned and shot Mrs. Stafford twice. While she was lying on the floor moaning and groaning, Henley threw the rifle to Flatt, took out his pistol and shot her again. He told Flatt to pour out some gasoline, but when he only poured out a small amount, Henley took the container and emptied it. Henley told Flatt to light the gasoline. When Flatt replied he could not, Henley struck the match and as the flames went up they ran to the truck. The house burned to the ground. The bodies were badly burned, but the county medical examiner said Mr. Stafford had been killed with a shot to the heart. Mrs. Stafford died from burns and smoke inhalation. Henley threw the guns out of the truck and they were located two days later by the sheriff.

Trial began on February 19, 1986. Henley was taking prescription codeine and Xanax. The testimony against Henley came from Flatt, who admitted in court that he had received a plea bargain on two counts of second-degree murder, armed robbery and arson. Flatt had known Henley only three months and said he was afraid of him. Flatt was a Dilaudid addict with a bad heart. As soon as he was picked up and was taken for a polygraph exam, he told the sheriff what had happened.

Henley steadfastly testified at trial that he had no role in the couple's death. He gave conflicting accounts of his whereabouts prior to the house burning. He said he knew nothing about the house burning until the next day, but had pointed a sheriff's deputy toward it after having been told there was report of a fire there.[3353] A neighbor saw him drive past in his truck with smoke coming from the direction of the Stafford home. Henley had financial difficulties. He denied any use of alcohol or drugs on the day of the killing or before. He had lost his grandfather's farm, had filed for bankruptcy, worked irregularly, drank and drove with Flatt. The day after the killing he appeared in court on an unrelated debt matter. The jury heard he had received a suspended sentence for stealing a tractor, and had been charged with public drunkenness and a worthless check charge. Directly contradicting a friend's testimony, Henley said he had no animosity toward the Staffords. Each side had accused the other of causing a head-on collision a few years before. The jury found for neither. A Stafford neighbor said Henley drove his tractor through the Staffords' fields.

During the mitigation phase, Henley's mother, who had little contact with him, appeared in the courtroom. Henley's counsel called her to the stand. She said, "I'd like to talk to you first, Mr. Reneau," in front of the jury. They left the room together. She never testified. Other than his grandmother's testimony, no mitigating factors were offered the jury during the sentencing phase.

Henley sought post-conviction relief in 1990, and the Court of Criminal Appeals ruled he was entitled to relief based on ineffectiveness of counsel. Three criticisms were: (1) his lawyer should have spoken to the mother prior to trial; (2) his lawyer should have contacted siblings, friends, and even Henley's children, to testify; (3) his lawyer should have accumulated information about his background and mental status and presented it during the mitigation phase. The Tennessee Supreme Court rejected these reasons in 1997.[3354] The facts showed the mother had little contact with him in the years before the killing, that she did not refuse to testify in front of the jury, she only demanded to talk to the lawyer. For unknown reasons, she was not put on the stand. Regarding siblings and ex-wives, their testimony would have been very general (probably not as compelling as the grandmother's) and all would have testified that Henley used both alcohol and marijuana prior to the time of the killings. The testimony of his children, son Greg, age twelve, and daughter Leanne, age ten, was problematic. The psychiatric testimony would not have helped because it showed he was "self-medicating" with drugs and alcohol at the time of the killings.

Sometime after 1991, Henley raised an issue that had not been raised before, namely, the prosecutor allowed Flatt to lie that he had made no deal regarding sentencing. Henley's new proof showed that Flatt had been given parole after only five years in prison, without objection from the prosecutor. However, no specific proof was offered regarding the deal. Flatt refused to cooperate.

Henley was denied habeas corpus review in 2007.[3355] The Sixth Circuit said he did not have legal grounds to complain, because he was a man, that no woman had ever served as grand jury foreman. It ruled there was no ineffective assistance of counsel regarding the sibling, ex-wives, and children's testimony, nor would the psychiatric testimony have made any difference. Regarding the issue of Flatt's special treatment, Henley had simply waited too long to raise this issue.

When the state asked the Tennessee Supreme Court to set a new execution date, Henley responded by arguing that more state appellate judges had ruled in his favor (three judges of the Court of Criminal Appeals and two Supreme Court judges) than had ruled against him (three Supreme Court judges). He asked the court to modify his sentence or ask the governor to do so. The chief reason was the failure of Henley's lawyer to prepare his mother to testify. The court must act *in favorem vitae* (in favor of life), he argued.[3356] The court refused.[3357]

Two months before his execution, Henley asked for a stay while the United States Supreme Court considered whether federal public defenders could file state clemency petitions.[3358] The stay was denied, but a last-minute clemency petition was filed. Seventy days before his execution, Henley filed a civil rights suit in Nashville federal court challenging the three-drug cocktail. The judge dismissed the suit on January 26, 2009, and a feverish attempt to get the Sixth Circuit to grant a stay before his March 5, 2009, execution proved fruitless.

Steve Henley's clemency petition was actually a request for a reprieve so that one of his lawyers could present a formal petition for clemency. It assumed Henley would have some kind of hearing in which two former Supreme Court judges and a former court of criminal appeals judge would be asked to appear. The request said that Terry Flatt was "90 percent sure" that he had an agreement with prosecutors not to object to his early release on parole. It further criticized counsel Reneau on the issue of Henley's mother's court appearance. It said that Reneau had never before handled a capital case.[3359] The petition did not assert that Henley was factually innocent, only that with a proper trial he would not have been sentenced to death.

During his time on death row, Henley was visited frequently by a sister and his children. They were with him the day before his execution. He was placed on death watch seventy-two hours before the execution and met with his spiritual advisor.

He was wheeled to the execution chamber on a gurney at 1:05 A.M. on March 5, 2009, and the blinds covering the window separating him from the press and family were withdrawn at 1:17 A.M. Henley raised his head, turned to see his family, smiled and stuck out his tongue. He tried to blow a kiss to them. As the microphone was lowered he said, "I would like to say that I hope this gives Fred and Edna's family some peace. In my experience in life, it won't. The death of a family member never brings anything but pain. I wish them the best."[3360] He continued, "I'm sorry for what Fred and Edna had to go through, what they went through." He said, "As I've said, ever since this happened, I did not kill them." He told his family he loved them and again said he was innocent. The warden gave the order to proceed. Seeing his family crying, he said, "You're a pitiful bunch. I'll see you on the other side."[3361] He told them and his pastor, "Never quit." Then he said, "Let's go to Pine Lick Road." In a few moments he shouted, "I feel it coming!" He snored a few times and stopped moving. Henley's sister, with his sobbing family, turned to the news media spectators and said, "Not a tear in anyone's eye back there. Don't human life mean nothing to you? You're like a pack of dogs."[3362] The family claimed his body.

Cecil C. Johnson, Jr., black, age 24. *Murder*

The crime was committed on July 5, 1980, at Bob Bell's Market, 2312 12th Avenue South, in Nashville, in Davidson County. The killer, married with a two-year-old daughter and a newborn son, was a dishwasher and cook at Vanderbilt University. He had spent the day skylarking with Victor Davis, black, age nineteen, and they returned from a neighboring town to the market about 9:25 P.M. Johnson got out of the car, saying he was going to rob the market and going to "try not to leave any witnesses."[3363] In the store were Bob Bell, Jr., white, age forty; his son, Robby Bell, white, age twelve; and Louis Smith, white, age fifty. Robby was behind the cash register, the other men were tending to a motor they were trying to repair. Brandishing a pistol, Johnson ordered the men to join Robby behind the counter. A customer, Debra Ann Smith, black, entered the store, made a quick purchase and left. She testified that she thought a robbery was underway, but was acquainted with Johnson, and hurriedly left. She testified she did not want to get involved. About this time, Charles House entered the store and was ordered out by Johnson. The two were acquainted. House immediately left the store. Still behind the counter with the other three, Johnson put his arm around the elder Bell and said, "You sure make good barbeque." He told Robby to fill a sack with money. Robby was crying and filled the sack. Johnson began shooting; Robby was struck first, and died a few hours later. Louis Smith, not seeing how badly injured the boy was, threw himself between Johnson and the boy to protect him. He was shot in the neck and hand. The elder Bell, on the floor, was shot next. However, just as the shot was fired he put up his hands and the bullet hit his wrist. Johnson ran out the door, and Bell heard two more shots. When Bell came out of the store with a shotgun, he noticed a cab nearby. Inside were the cab driver, James E. Moore, black, age forty-one, and Charles H. House, black, age thirty-five, who had been ordered out of the store. Both had been shot in the head.

Bell told police he thought the gunman lived a block away on Gilmore and thought he recognized him because he had come to the store in his Vanderbilt clothing. The address on Gilmore was that of Johnson's father. Victor Davis testified that he drove Johnson to his father's and when Johnson got in the car he said, "I didn't mean to shoot that boy." Davis testified that Johnson threw the gun out the window, but Davis found it and sold to a friend the next day. At the father's house, Johnson opened the bag, which contained $200, and gave Davis $40. Johnson told his father they had won the money gambling that day.

Based on Bell's identification, Johnson was arrested the next day. But he wore hair curlers in his hair, and Smith, from his hospital bed, was not able to identify him in a picture array. Smith chose two men who were not Johnson in the array.

Trial began on March 4, 1981. Louis Smith and Debra Ann Smith testified they recognized Johnson as the shooter, in part because he had some modest facial hair. The elder Bell said he didn't notice because he focused on Johnson's eyes. Johnson testified that he had been with Davis earlier in the day but was not near the market at the time of the shooting. He was home with his father. The latter and a woman identified as Johnson's girlfriend supported his alibi.

Johnson was found guilty of three counts of murder, for which the jury gave him the death penalty. It also found him guilty of three counts of assault with intent to commit murder and one count of robbery.[3364] The judge presiding was A.A. Birch, Nashville's first African American criminal court judge, who in time would serve on the Tennessee Supreme Court. Birch sentenced Johnson to serve the noncapital sentences consecutively, which meant Johnson would have to serve 120 years in prison. Johnson's lawyer had provided Judge Birch with an affidavit from a juror which stated that she was confused about whether she could have voted for life, and that "deep down in her heart, she believes Cecil Johnson did not commit the crime." Judge Birch struck the affidavit and in denying a motion for new trial said Johnson showed neither remorse nor repentance.[3365] Taken immediately to death row at the Main Prison, Cecil Johnson maintained his innocence and the generally good demeanor he showed the rest of his life.[3366]

The chief issue on appeal to the Tennessee Supreme Court was whether prosecutors had acted unlawfully in convincing Davis to testify against Johnson, after Johnson's lawyer had indicated that Davis would be a witness for him. On January 9, 1981, Davis had been stopped with two other men on suspicion of robbery and booked at midnight on a charge of public drunkenness and carrying a pistol. Because the police knew the District Attorney's office wanted to talk to Davis before the trial, they contacted an assistant attorney general. He and others began questioning Davis at 1:00 A.M. Once Davis was assured he was only being questioned about the Johnson case, he gave a verbal statement and a written statement a few days later in the presence of his lawyer. Davis agreed to tell what happened in return for full immunity for his involvement in the killings. The scope of his immunity was addressed at trial. The Tennessee Supreme Court said there was no error in allowing Davis to testify.[3367] Johnson said it was wrong for the prosecutor to withhold the name of Debra Ann Smith until eleven days before the trial. The high court said this was proper. The court ruled that striking the affidavit was proper because settled law in Tennessee was that a new trial will not be granted upon the affidavit from a juror that he misunderstood the jury instructions.[3368]

On July 7, 1985, Johnson and another inmate attacked another death row inmate in the exercise yard of the prison. The pair repeatedly dropped two thirty-five pound dumbbells on the victim's head and chest, killing him. Tried together, they were convicted of second-degree murder. But because one of the jurors told the others she thought Johnson had killed her twelve-year-old cousin ten years earlier, the judge struck her from the jury just as it began to deliberate. The judge contacted an alternate juror at home who was summoned to the courthouse. The Tennessee Supreme Court ruled this was improper and granted Johnson a new trial.[3369] Johnson thereafter pled to voluntary manslaughter.

Judge Birch denied post-conviction relief in 1983, but in 1988 the Court of Criminal Appeals remanded the case for a new hearing on the first-degree murder sentences.[3370] The Tennessee Supreme Court said the Court of Criminal Appeals was wrong. There were no errors in the opening and closing arguments by the District Attorney which told the jury they were representing the reflective judgment of the people of Tennessee and the "jury is but one step in the process of determining what is the proper appropriate punishment for Cecil Johnson." The two sentences, taken in context of the whole opening and closing arguments were harmless. The Supreme Court appended the closing arguments to its opinion.[3371]

Johnson sought habeas corpus relief in Nashville federal court in 1991, but the case was put on hold while he filed another petition for post-conviction relief in state court. By now, Johnson had uncovered some police reports which indicated that witness Louis Smith had earlier told police that he could not recognize Johnson. The Court of Criminal Appeals ruled the documents were not important to Johnson's case.[3372]

Johnson's habeas corpus case ultimately went before the Sixth Circuit Court of Appeals.[3373] Like the courts below, it ruled that the police reports were not crucial, in particular because they were gotten from Smith while he was in distress in the hospital with gunshot wounds to his neck and hand. Moreover, Smith testified that by the time he identified Johnson in custody he had already seen his image on television, and admitted he was confused about the number and gender of the people who entered the store and the extent of Johnson's facial hair. The Sixth Circuit rejected issues that had been raised before, such as Davis's flipping. Now Johnson charged it was error for the District Attorney to mention that his daughter and Robby Bell had started first grade together and were in the same school. The District Attorney also said that anybody on the jury who was in the market that night might be dead. The Sixth Circuit said the argument was improper, but defense counsel had failed to object and the overall evidence showed Johnson's guilt. The issue of Debra Ann Smith's existence until shortly before trial was also rejected by the court. Finally, the court rejected the argument that Johnson's counsel was ineffective for failing to seek a continuance when it learned of Davis's flipping and Debra Ann Smith's existence. When a dissenting judge of the Sixth Circuit said the police reports showed that Bob Bell, Louis Smith and Debra Ann Smith had lied, another of the judges wrote a separate opinion saying the dissent was wrong.

The Sixth Circuit's opinion on April 29, 2008, was followed by an attempt to get the Tennessee Supreme Court to throw out Johnson's execution because of excessive delay in carrying out the sentence, namely twenty-nine years on death row. Seven days before his scheduled execution date, Johnson filed suit in Nashville federal court alleging the same argument. The court turned Johnson down on November 30, 2009, but allowed him to ask the Sixth Circuit Court of Appeals for relief. It declined on December 1, 2009. The governor had denied clemency a week earlier.

The day before his execution, the United States Supreme Court declined a stay and declined to pass on the issue of whether Johnson's years on death row were themselves unconstitutional.[3374]

Johnson's clemency petition said, "We are *not* asking [the governor] to make any finding of fact as to Cecil Johnson's guilt or innocence, or anything else."[3375] It sought a commutation to life imprisonment. However, several letters offered on his behalf asserted he was innocent.[3376]

The petition argued the evidence was flawed and pointed away from Johnson's guilt. It alleged several factors, notably the withheld police reports and mistakes by his inexperienced lawyers. They had agreed with the state that Louis Smith's pending charge of aggravated rape of a child would not be heard by the jury. "They did not even bother to make a closing argument and plead for Cecil Johnson's life in the sentencing phase of the trial."[3377] The petition sought clemency because of a "systematic breakdown" that pervaded his case. It argued there was a "residual doubt" that would have prevented the jury from imposing death.[3378] It argued the elder Bell was simply mistaken in fingering Johnson, and included a long report from an expert which described a process known as "unconscious transference" whereby Bell, having seen Johnson before, suffered from "different memory images [which] may become combined or confused with each other."[3379] It closed with this: "There is an intolerable risk that the State of Tennessee will be taking the life of an innocent man if Cecil Johnson's execution is allowed to go forward."[3380]

Johnson had been placed on death watch several days earlier. He refused a last meal and met with his spiritual adviser the night before his death. Cecil C. Johnson, Jr., age fifty-three, was brought to the execution chamber of Riverbend Maximum Security Prison at 1:00 A.M. on December 2, 2009. Lethal injection was begun. His brother David Johnson and daughter DeAngela Johnson were present and watched him mouth "I love you" to them. He made no last statement and was pronounced dead at 1:34 A.M. Cecil Johnson's son, James Johnson, age twenty-nine, sent a message that he forgave his father for not being there for him as he grew up. He said it was not the father's fault that he was in a West Tennessee prison serving a 23-year sentence for aggravated assault and aggravated robbery. The only victim's family member to attend the execution was Bob Bell, Jr.

Notes

Preface

1. Lewis L. Laska, "The Tennessee Death Penalty, 1870–1890," *Tennessee Historical Quarterly* 67 (Spring 2008): 23–35.

2. Lewis L. Laska, "Fact-Based Death Penalty Research," *Tennessee Journal of Law and Policy* 4 (2007): 103–112.

3. Sarah Kelley, "Death Row Lotto," *Nashville Scene*, February 28, 2008, pp. 14–20.

4. "Nine Killed," *Daily American*, July 13, 1887, p. 1. "Livid Lightning," *Daily American*, July 24, 1887, p. 1.

5. "Lightning—Associated Deaths—United States, 1980–1995," *MMWR Weekly* 47 (May 22, 1998): pp. 391–394. Ninety-eight were executed in 1999 (highest year since 1980), but from 1981 to 2008, the total was 1,143, or about 40 per year.

6. Dwight Aarons, "Adjudicating Claims of Innocence for the Capitally Condemned in Tennessee: Embracing a Truth Forum," *Tennessee Law Review* 76 (Spring 2009): 511, 554.

7. Larry J. Daniel, *Soldiering in the Army of Tennessee: A Portrait of Life in a Confederate Army* (Chapel Hill: University of North Carolina Press, 1991), p. 113. According to Daniel, sixteen executions can be documented for the Army of Tennessee under Gen. Braxton Bragg during his year-and-a-half tenure, with at least thirty-one executions for desertion at Dalton under Gen. Joseph Johnston; p. 188. He provides no reference for these data.

8. Jack A. Bunch, *Military Justice in the Confederate States* (Shippensburg, PA: White Mane Books, 2000); Jack A. Bunch, *Roster of Courts-Martial in the Confederate States Armies* (Shippensburg, PA: White Mane Books, 2001).

9. *Goodspeed's History of Tennessee* (Nashville: Goodspeed, 1886). The history did not include all of Tennessee's ninety-five counties.

10. Thomas P. Lowry and Lewis Laska, *Confederate Death Sentences: A Reference Guide* (Charleston, SC: Booksurge, 2008), 79 pp.

Persons Executed and Their Crimes

11. This is the proper spelling of his name. It was pronounced "macow."

12. John Allison, *Dropped Stitches in Tennessee History* (Nashville: Marshall & Bruce, 1897) p. 52; John Preston Arthur, *Western North Carolina: A History from 1730 to 1913* (Raleigh, NC: Edwards & Broughton, 1914), p. 374.

13. Washington County [North Carolina] Court of Pleas and Quarter Sessions, vol. 1, section 1, p. 161, 171, 172, 178 (WPA Transcription, April 21, 1938). The county court handled small cases. The Court of Oyer and Terminer had jurisdiction over felonies such as horse stealing and murder. Macay did not live in Washington County and was inconvenienced by having to come over the mountains for this court. His minutes are included in this document.

14. Ibid., p. 178. This was the last entry in the book.

15. Edward Scott, comp., *Laws of Tennessee* (Knoxville: Heiskell & Brown, 1821), vol. 1, pp. 156, 366.

16. Ruth Webb O'Dell, *Over the Misty Blue Hills: The Story of Cocke County, Tennessee* (Easley, SC: Southern Historical Press, 1982), p. 210.

17. Petition of William Evans to Tennessee General Assembly, Record Group 60, No. 5-2-1799-1. State Library and Archives. Sullivan County records prior to 1863 were destroyed in a courthouse fire that year.

18. The suit was styled William Evans v. Nathaniel Davis and James Charles, executors of James Allison. It was filed in the Superior Court for the District of Washington, according to Evans's petition. The case records cannot be located.

19. Petition of William Evans, p. 2.

20. Samuel Cole Williams, *History of the Lost State of Franklin* (Johnson City, TN: Watauga Press, 1924), p. 134, citing "Letter from the State of Franklin, April 24, 1787," in *Georgia State Gazette,* May 24th. Williams said, "This was the first legal execution in Franklin, or on what is now Tennessee soil, of which we have record." He was wrong. Later that year Judge Campbell (1750–1812) accepted a judgeship under the authority of the State of North Carolina, severely undercutting the Franklinite movement. President Washington appointed him a territorial judge and he served on the Superior Court of Law and Equity from 1797 to 1807.

21. *Knoxville Gazette,* August 25, 1792, p. 3, cited in Walter T. Durham, *Before Tennessee: The Southwest Territory, 1790–1796* (Piney Flats, TN: Rocky Mount Historical Association, 1990), p. 107. The town was called Jonesborough at the time.

22. Minutes of Superior Court of North Carolina Including Mero District, 1788–1803, Part 1 (1788–1798) (WPA Transcription, 1938), pp. 41, 42, 49. This is also known as Docket Book A, Mero District, North Carolina Superior Court of Law and Equity (Metro Nashville Archives). This court is referred to as "Mero District Superior Court" in Ely and Brown, eds., *Legal Papers of Andrew Jackson* (Knoxville: University of Tennessee Press, 1987), p. xxi–xxviii. They would cite the case as *State v. Aherrin,* MDSC Law Min. Bk., 1788–1803, p. 41 (1790).

23. *Ramsey's Annals of Tennessee* (Charleston, SC: Walker & James, 1853), pp. 594–595. The initial report said his wife and children also were killed, according to the *Knoxville Gazette,* July 31, 1794.

24. Ibid., p. 595.

25. See Chapter 10, "Terror and Violence Exchanged," in Walter T. Durham, *Before Tennessee: The Southwest Territory, 1790–1796, A Narrative History of the Territory of the United States South of the River Ohio* (Piney Flats, TN: Rocky Mount Historical Association, 1990), pp. 165–187, 173–174.

26. Clarence Edwin Carter, comp., *The Territorial Papers of the United States,* vol. IV: *The Territory South of the River Ohio, 1790–1796* (Washington, D.C.: GPO, 1936), p. 461.

27. John P. Brown, *Old Frontiers: The Story of the Cherokee Indians from Earliest Times to the Date of Their Removal to the West, 1838* (Kingsport, TN: Southern Publishers, 1938), p. 404.

28. Ibid., p. 405.

29. Ibid., p. 405.

30. Minutes, Knox County Oyer & Terminer Court, Hamilton District, 1793–1798 (WPA Transcription), pp. 245–246. This was a Superior Court conviction although recorded in these minutes. Records of Knox County, Superior Court Minutes, No. 3, 1793–1809 (WPA Transcription), pp. 106, 110. The same jury convicted a thief who stole six yards of gingham and four Spanish milled dollars and ordered him branded with a "T" on the brawn of the thumb; p. 250.

31. Minutes, U. S. District Court, Western District of Tennessee, pp. 247–249.

32. Ibid.

33. "Awful Murder," *Register* (Raleigh, North Carolina), September 22, 1801, p. 3.

34. Ibid.

35. "Diary of John Sevier," in S.G. Heiskell, *Andrew Jackson and Early Ten-*

nessee History, 2d ed (Nashville: Ambrose Printing, 1920), vol. 2, p. 583.

36. Although Article 2, Section 19 of the Tennessee Constitution (1796) gave the governor the power to grant pardons, some governors took the position they could not grant pardons to slaves.

37. Minutes of the [Knox County] Court of Pleas and Quarter Sessions, January 15, 1802, Minute Book 3, p. 321. This is considerably less than the forty-four dollars, eight and one third cents that it cost to hang Aaron Gist, white, on October 14, 1801.

38. House Journal, 1801, p. 38, in Robert H. White, ed., *Messages of the Governors of Tennessee, 1796–1821* (Nashville: Tennessee Historical Commission, 1952), vol. 1, p. 131.

39. Records of Knox County, Superior Court Minutes, No. 3, 1793–1809 (WPA Transcription, 1939), pp. 255, 257.

40. The County Court reimbursed sheriff Robert Houston forty-four dollars, eight and one third cents for executing Gist; payment made on January 15, 1802. Minute Book 3, Knox County Court of Pleas and Quarter Sessions, p. 321. The Espy list, apparently relying on this payment notation, wrongly asserts that Gist was hanged that day.

41. Minutes of the Superior Court of North Carolina Including Mero District, 1788–1803, pp. 487–488.

42. Ibid., p. 566.

43. Minutes of Superior Court of North Carolina Including Mero District, 1788–1803, Part II (WPA Transcription, 1938), pp. 614, 640. It is also called Docket Book A, Mero District, North Carolina Superior Court of Law and Equity (Metro Nashville Archives). Finally, it is known as "Mero District Superior Court" (MDSC) when cited by Ely and Brown, *The Legal Papers of Andrew Jackson* (1987). Hence, they cite these cases as *State v. Powel*; *State v. West*; *State v. Black*, MDSC Law Min. Bk., 1788–1803, p. 640.

44. Minutes of Superior Court of North Carolina Including Mero District, 1788–1803, Part II (WPA Transcription, 1938) pp. 620–621.

45. Ibid., note 1, pp. 620, 640.

46. Ibid., pp. 621, 640.

47. *Tennessee Gazette*, June 12, 1802, p. 2.

48. *State v. Samuel Inman*, Superior Court for Law and Equity, Mero District of Tennessee, Minutes, May 21, 1804, pp. 170–171.

49. "Item," *Tennessee Gazette*, April 6, 1803, p. 1.

50. *Tennessee Gazette*, April 27, 1803, p. 2.

51. "Item," *Tennessee Gazette*, April 6, 1803, p. 1; June 8, 1803, p. 2; October 19, 1803, p. 2.

52. Mary Sue Smith, abst., *Superior Court of Law & Equity, Mero District of Tennessee, 1803–1805* (Bowie, MD: Heritage Books, 2001), pp. 156, 157–158.

53. The court was composed of David Campbell, Hugh L. White, and John Overton.

54. Ibid., p. 196.

55. Order respiting Samuel Forrester, Papers of Gov. John Sevier, State Library and Archives, Box 1, file 2 (no date).

56. *State v. Morris*, 1 Tenn. 220, 221 (1806). The opinion is merely an abstract which only mentions Morris, saying the defendant, in receiving a continuance, was not required to disclose what his witnesses would swear. The Superior Court was composed of David Campbell, John Overton and Hugh L. White.

57. Knox County Superior Court Minutes, No. 3, 1793–1809 (WPA Transcription, 1939), pp. 449, 450, 451.

58. "Died," *Impartial Review and Cumberland Repository*, June 14, 1806, p. 2.

59. Minutes of Superior Court of Law and Equity, Docket Book B, Mero District, November Term, 1806, p. 271. On May 18, 1807, the sheriff was paid $62 for keeping and executing Clements; p. 325.

60. *Tennessee Gazette*, February 21, 1807, p. 2.

61. Minutes, County Court of Williamson County, Book 1 (February 28, 1807), p. 254.

62. Ursula Smith Beach, *Along the Warioto: A History of Montgomery County, Tennessee* (Nashville: McQuiddy Printing, 1964), p. 91; *Goodspeed's History of Montgomery County*, p. 784.

63. Petition of John R. McFarland and James M. Reynolds on behalf of Joseph Penrice, General Assembly, 1809, Box 21, file 1, State Library and Archives.

64. Knox County Superior Court Minutes, No. 3, 1793–1809 (WPA Transcription, 1939), pp. 479, 484, 541.

65. Jefferson County Court of Pleas and Quarter Sessions, Minute Book No. 4, 1807–1810, p. 125.

66. Jefferson County Court of Pleas and Quarter Sessions, Minute Book No. 4, 1807–1810, p. 126. His owner was ordered to pay the cost of prosecution.

67. Knox County Superior Court Minutes, No.3, 1793–1809 (WPA Transcription, 1939), pp. 558, 560; *Charleston* (South Carolina) *Courier*, October 27, 1809, p. 3. (Mentions his age.)

68. *Goodspeed's History of Tennessee* (Sumner), p. 809. Repeated without attribution in Sophie and Paul Crane, *Tennessee's Troubled Roots* (Old Hickory, TN: Earle-Shields, 1975), p. 95.

69. *Clarion*, March 21, 1811, p. 6; Dewey Edwards, *Execution of Murder: A Chronicle of Cases in Robertson County, Tennessee, 1810–1910* (Springfield, TN: The Author, 2005), p. 2; "Murder," *Charleston* (South Carolina) *Courier*, July 31, 1810, p. 3.

70. *Clarion*, July 13, 1811, p. 6.

71. Notice of sale: "Short History of the Life of Jacob Pickering Who Was Executed in the town of Nashville on the 13th day of July in the year of our Lord, 1811, for the Murder of Elijah Gardner, Also a Sketch of the Life of Stewart W. Thornton, who was executed at the same time for the same crime," *Carthage Gazette*, August 21, 1811, p. 1.

72. *The Clarion*, October 8, 1811, p. 4; Bledsoe County Circuit Execution Docket, 1810–1824 (WPA Transcription, 1938) includes *State v. John Cunningham* (James Hull, pros.), Case 45, P-19. No Bledsoe County circuit or county court records exist for the years 1807 through 1844.

73. *Records of Rutherford County, Tennessee, County Court Minutes, vol. G (1813–1814)* (Nashville: WPA, December 18, 1936), pp. 15–16. "It is ordered by the Court that Mathew McClanahan, Sheriff of Rutherford County be allowed the sum of twenty-nine dollars for his services rendered in taking a certain negro man Jess to Nashville Jail and from thence to Murfreesborough & executing said negro & that the same be paid out of any monies in the hands of the County trustee. It is ordered by the Court that William Nugent, James Miller and William Knight each be allowed the sum of two dollars for their attendance as a guard over a certain negro man Jess who was executed in Murfreesborough on the third of September 1813 — and that the same be paid out of any money in the hands of the County trustee." The Rutherford County courthouse was struck by a tornado in 1832 and no circuit or criminal court records exist for the period prior to 1849.

74. *Goodspeed's History of Tennessee, Including the Counties of Maury, Williamson, Rutherford, Wilson, Bedford & Marshall Counties of Tennessee* (Nashville: Goodspeed, 1886), pp. 820–821. Goodspeed explains the missing records: "A destruction of all the circuit and criminal court records during the war renders a detailed account of the transactions of these courts impossible"; p. 821.

75. Petition of George M. Sanders, Record Group 60, Legislative Petitions No. 30-2-1813-1, State Library and Archives.

76. Petition of George M. Sanders, Record Group 60, Legislative Petitions No. 24-3-1813-1. State Library and Archives.

77. Ibid.

78. Bill of Exceptions, *James Brice v. State*, Supreme Court, Eastern Section [n.d.], Box 227 State Library and Archives. Brice went to trial before circuit judge Archibald Roane and a jury. This is the earliest capital case for which appellate records exist.

79. Elizabeth Baugh, "Blount's 33 Sheriffs: Three Hangings," *Maryville-Alcoa Daily Times*, May 24, 1954, p. 3, 7.

80. Ibid., p. 3.

81. Tenn. Constitution, Article 10 and Schedule.

82. Chapter 73, Acts of 1807.

83. *Brice v. State*, 2 Tenn. 254 (1814). The case was decided in May 1814.

84. "Executions in Blount," *East Tennessee News*, July 23, 1883, p. 1.

85. *Roberts v. State*, 2 Tenn. 423 (1815). The case was decided in June 1815.

86. All information about these soldiers is taken from U.S. Army, Register of Enlistments, 1798–1914, Record Group 94, Adjutant General Office, National Archives series M233.

87. *The Democratic Clarion*, February 21, 1815, p. 3; "Waste of Human Blood," *Nashville Whig*, March 21, 1815, p. 3.

88. The Coffin Handbill is one of the most recognized documents in American politics. Marquis James, *The Life of Andrew Jackson* (Indianapolis: Bobbs-Merrill, 1938), p. 464.
89. Harold D. Moser, David R. Hoth, Sharon Macpherson, and John H. Reinbold, eds., *The Papers of Andrew Jackson,* Vol. III: 1814–1815 (Knoxville: University of Tennessee Press, 1991), pp. 166–168.
90. Reward Notice, *Nashville Whig,* February 22, 1814, p. 3. The notice also mentioned John Rush and Thomas Duff.
91. John S. Hare, "Military Punishments in the War of 1812," *Journal of the American Military Institute* 4(4) (Winter 1940): 225–239. In 1812 three were shot for desertion. In 1813 this number rose to 32. It climbed to 146 in 1814 and fell to 24 in 1815.
92. County Court Record of Sumner County, February 25, 1819, p. 77.
93. "Bridges' sentence for murdering a peddler in the upper end of Bedford County, one or two years ago, is also confirmed; his execution takes place some time in November," *The Clarion,* October 19, 1819, p. 2. Court records suggest this was Bledsoe County.
94. "Enrollment," *State v. Benjamin Bridges, State Library and Archives, Middle Tennessee Record Book,* vol. 1, 1817–1821, RG 191, Series V, p. 872–876. This book carries the spine notation, "Record Book D."
95. *Dula v. State,* 16 Tenn. 511, 513 (1835). See Chapter 10, section 1, Public Acts of 1820. Payment for jailor fees in Franklin County. The name is shown as Briges.
96. Ibid., note 2, supra. The reason for his execution in Giles County is unknown. Sam Houston prosecuted Bridges.
97. Circuit Court Records, Wilson County, 1817–1818, pp. 160, 162, 177–183, 230–234.
98. "Charles L. Bennett," *Nashville Whig,* Nov. 3, 1819, p. 2.
99. Ibid.
100. Ibid.
101. *The Clarion,* October 19, 1819, p. 2.
102. "Enrollment," *State v. Charles L. Bennett,* Supreme Court "Record Book," 1817–1820, State Library and Archives RG 191, Series V, vol. 1, p. 903–906.
103. Kenneth McKellar, *Tennessee Senators as Seen by One of Their Successors* (Kingsport, TN: Southern Publishers, 1942), p.184.
104. Ibid., p. 188. Why he was executed in Williamson County cannot be determined other than that it was done by the Supreme Court's order.
105. *Nashville Whig,* November 27, 1819, p. 2.
106. Gen. Thomas Overton was a Revolutionary War veteran and close friend of Jackson. He served as a second in Jackson's famous duel with John Dickinson.
107. Minutes, Circuit Court of Davidson County, November 10, 1819, p. 272.
108. Ibid., p. 273–274.
109. County Court Minutes, Davidson County, January Session, 1820, p. 285. "Thomas Hickman sheriff allowed $36.37 for whipping Gideon Tinsely and others and attending the trial and hanging of Negro Israel." "The negro convicted of the murder of Bryant was executed last week." *The Clarion* and *Tennessee Gazette,* November 30, 1819, p. 2.
110. Bill of Exceptions, State v. John Lusk, Supreme Court, Middle Section, no date [1820], State Library and Archives Box 22.
111. Ibid., Agreed statement, Bill of Exceptions, no page number.
112. *Cornwell v. State,* 8 Tenn. 142, 157–158 (1827).
113. "Enrollment," *State v. John Lusk,* Record Book, Middle Section, 1817–1821, State Library and Archives RG 191, Series V, p. 1103.
114. "Execution," *Nashville Whig,* July 3, 1820. "On Monday last, the awful sentence of death was executed on John Lusk, convicted of the crime of Rape, at the last November term of the Davidson circuit court. We understand that he maintained his innocence to the last"; p. 2.
115. With equal certitude, the governor's biographer insists he was a lifelong bachelor who lived with his mother, although he had an illegitimate son by a woman named Elizabeth Strong. Charles D. Rodenbough, *Governor Alexander Martin: Biography of a North Carolina Revolutionary War Statesman* (Jefferson, NC: McFarland, 2004).
116. "Executed," *Knoxville Register,* June 19, 1821. See also *Cahawba Press* and *Alabama State Intelligencer,* August 24, 1821.
117. Ibid., note 1.
118. Ibid.
119. Ibid.
120. See *State v. Delap,* 7 Tenn. 90 (1823) for the dispute over payment for costs of Delap's prosecution. His estate appeared inadequate to pay the $1,260 costs incurred by Hawkins County. Delap had earlier placed all his property in his wife's name. She remarried in 1823.
121. *The Watchman* (Clarksville), June 1, 1821, p. 3.
122. Ursula Smith Beach, *Along the Warioto: A History of Montgomery County, Tennessee* (Nashville: McQuiddy Press, 1978), p. 91.
123. Circuit Court of Williamson County, Loose Records, February 14, 1822, p. 54.
124. *The Gazette,* March 8, 1823, p. 4. (Sometimes called *Independent Gazette.*)
125. Loose Records of Williamson County, vol. 3, citing *The Gazette,* June 6, 1823, p. 60.
126. Will T. Hale and Dixon L. Merritt, *A History of Tennessee and Tennessean.* (Chicago: Lewis Publishers, 1913), vol. 3, p. 835; James Vaulx Drake, *History Notes of Henderson County* (unpublished manuscript), Miscellaneous Collection, Tennessee Historical Society, State Library and Archives, Box H, No. 78. No Henderson County Court records exist for the period 1821 through 1860, apparently due to a courthouse fire in 1896.
127. "James R. Bennett Murder Case," *Historic Maury* 23 (1987): 69–84, p. 75.
128. *Bennett v. State,* 8 Tenn. 134, 137 (1827).
129. Bill of Exceptions, *Bennett v. State,* Tennessee Supreme Court, Middle Section, n.d., p. 14, State Library and Archives Box 32.
130. Ibid., p. 16.
131. Ibid., note 1, p. 137.
132. "Memoirs of an Octogenarian," *Maury Democrat,* January 25, 1894, p. 4. The writer was the widow of A.O.P. Nicholson, a member of the Tennessee Supreme Court from 1870 until his death on March 23, 1876.
133. "Indignation Meeting," *Columbia Herald and Mail,* April 20, 1877, p. 1; "The Supreme Court of Tennessee," *Columbia Herald and Mail,* April 20, 1877, p. 2; "Thomason Escapes Death," *Columbia Herald and Mail,* May 4, 1877, p. 2. Thomason had been a "Jayhawker," a Union partisan, during the Civil War and had terrorized the vicinity.
134. Frank Ritter, "Executions: A Legacy of Doubt," *The Tennessean,* October 17, 1985, p. 1-A, 2-A. Ritter attributes his information to Watt Espy.
135. Bill of Exceptions, *State v. Burwell Cornwell,* Supreme Court, Middle Section [1826], State Library and Archives Box 32. McCallahan did not testify at Cornwell's trial.
136. Ibid., p. 7.
137. *Cornwell v. State,* 8 Tenn. 147, 153 (1827)
138. Ibid., p. 9.
139. This was a universal sign of comradeship in the 19th century. Later, a woman wearing a man's hat was a sign of their intimacy — particularly if she was a prostitute and the doomed man was one of her customers.
140. Ibid., p. 5.
141. Ibid., p. 7.
142. *Cornwell v. State,* 8 Tenn. 147, 157 (1827). On the day the court heard Cornwell's case it heard two other murder appeals, "two of whom may probably attribute his unnatural exit from this world to the immoderate use of ardent spirits"; p. 158.
143. Ibid., p. 161. The court had four members at this time: Peck, Whyte, Catron and Crabb. The latter delivered (wrote) the opinion.
144. Here is the newspaper's complete account of the execution: "On Monday last, agreeably to his sentence, Burwell Cornwell was executed near this place for the murder of Hughes." *Nashville Banner & Whig,* April 7, 1827, p. 1.
145. "Horrid Murder," *Jackson Gazette,* February 18, 1826, p. 4.
146. Ibid.
147. See Mrs. Otis Trentham, "Some Notes on Crime and Punishment in Madison," *Jackson Sun,* March 14, 1946, p. 3, for a garbled account of the case.
148. Minutes, Circuit Court, Madison County, p. 273. Richard Jameson,

whose relationship to Thomas is unknown, was indicted for misprision of murder but his case was nolled the day Thomas's trial began.

149. Minutes, Circuit Court, Madison County, p. 384–385; *Jackson Gazette*, January 27, 1827, p. 4.

150. "Item," *Jackson Gazette*, March 24, 1827, p. 4.

151. "Execution of Jameson and Randal," *Jackson Gazette*, May 5, 1827, p. 4.

152. Ibid. John Fisher, one of the people who had come to witness the execution, was running his horse around the racetrack near town and was thrown from his horse and killed. Another man, Hiram Harkins, of a neighboring town, was also thrown from his horse about seven miles from town and "his life is despaired of." The *Jackson Gazette* announced the publication of the "Confessions" of Jameson and Randal was available at its office but no copy has been located.

153. "Item," *Register and North Carolina Gazette* (Raleigh, NC), October 13, 1826, p. 1.

154. "Court News," *Village Messenger*, vol. 3, no. 25, October 18, 1826.

155. *Bonds v. State*, 8 Tenn. 494 (1827).

156. Ibid., p. 495.

157. Chapter 99, Public Acts of 1829, Sec. 2. Lincoln County was ordered to pay Davidson County.

158. Minutes, Circuit Court of Hardeman County, pp. 197, 294, 307, 420, 421; "Item," *Jackson Gazette*, August 30, 1828, p. 2.

159. Bill of Exceptions, *Henry Lunsford v. State*, Supreme Court, Eastern Section [n.d.], State Library and Archives Box 240. See Elizabeth Baugh, "Blount's 33 Sheriffs: Three Hangings," *Maryville-Alcoa Daily Times*, May 24, 1954, pp. 3, 7. This account says the victim's name was Arch Murphy and that he attended to his work for a month before his death.

160. Bill of Exceptions, *Henry Lunsford v. State*, Supreme Court, Eastern Section [n.d.]. The Tennessee Supreme Court was not required to render written opinions until 1829.

161. Elizabeth Baugh, "Blount's 33 Sheriffs: Three Hangings," *Maryville-Alcoa Daily Times*, May 24, 1954, pp. 3, 7; "Executions in Blount," *East Tennessee News*, July 23, 1883, p. 1.

162. Ibid.

163. Inez Burns, *History of Blount County, Tennessee: From War Trail to Landing Strip, 1795–1955* (Nashville: Mary Blount Chapter, Daughters of the American Revolution and Tennessee Historical Commission, 1957), p. 207.

164. "The First Murder and Execution in Fayetteville," *Fayetteville Observer*, October 16, 1884, in *Lincoln County Pioneers* 14, No. 1 (1985): p. 3–5; "Legal Hangings in Lincoln County," *Fayetteville Observer*, May 30, 1907, p. 2.

165. *McClure v. State*, 9 Tenn. 206, 220 (1829) per Catron.

166. "Every white male citizen, being a householder and arrived at the age of twenty-one years, shall be deemed and held legally qualified to act as a grand and petit juror; any law, custom or usage to the contrary, notwithstanding." Pub. Acts 1809, chapter 119.

167. Tenn. Constitution, Article 8, Section 2.

168. *McClure v. State*, 9 Tenn. 206, 224 (1829) per Peck.

169. Letter from Jacob Peck to Governor Samuel Houston, March 12, 1829, Petitions for Pardon, *Samuel McClure v. State*, Papers of Gov. Samuel Houston, State Library and Archives Box 8, file 10.

170. "The First Murder and Execution in Fayetteville," *Fayetteville Observer*, October 16, 1884, in Lincoln County Pioneers 14, No. 1 (1985): p. 5.

171. *Confession by James White of the Murder of George W. Brown, in the County of Marion, in December Last* (Knoxville: n.d.), 8 pages. This is one of the few 19th-century "confessions" that have survived. They were a popular method of spreading the Gospel and making money for the printers.

172. Ibid., p. 1.

173. Ibid., p. 1

174. Ibid., p. 3.

175. Ibid., p. 4.

176. The file in James White's case contains neither an opinion nor a bill of exceptions. *State v. James White*, Eastern Section, Tennessee Supreme Court, State Library and Archives Box 240.

177. Ibid., note 1, p. 5.

178. "Notes," *Knoxville Enquirer*, February 27, 1828, p. 2.

179. "Young's Confession," in *Confession by James White of the Murder of George W. Brown in the County of Marion, December Last* (Knoxville: n.d.), p. 8.

180. *Young v. State*, 10 Tenn. 292 (1829). See Young v. State, Eastern Section, State Library and Archives Box 239.

181. "Execution," *Jackson Gazette*, November 28, 1829, p. 3.

182. *History of Tennessee: From the Earliest Time to the Present: Together with an Historical and Biographical Sketch of Henderson, Chester, McNairy, Decatur, and Hardin Counties* (Nashville: Goodspeed, 1886), pp. 829, 841.

183. Ibid., note 1, p. 3.

184. Ibid.

185. W. Jerome D. Spence and David L. Spence, *A History of Hickman County, Tennessee* (Nashville: Gospel Advocate, 1900), pp. 66–67. Hickman County records relating to this case were destroyed when the courthouse burned in 1864.

186. W. Jerome D. Spence and David L. Spence, *A History of Hickman County, Tennessee* (Nashville: Gospel Advocate, 1900), p. 312.

187. John D. Templeton, "Great Storm of 1830," *Shelbyville Times-Gazette Sesqui-centennial, Historical Edition* (*Shelbyville Times-Gazette*, 1969), pp. 28–29. The execution was not covered in the Shelbyville newspaper (then known as the *Western Intelligencer*) because its editor was killed in the storm and the press wrecked, along with the courthouse and most buildings in the town. The Bedford County courthouses have been troubled. After the storm the courthouse was rebuilt but was occupied by federal troops during the Civil War and records were destroyed. The building burned again in 1877 and was destroyed by the riot attending the trial of E.K. Harris in 1934.

188. Jill Knight Garrett, *History of Humphreys County* (Columbia, TN: The Author, 1963), p. 17.

189. Ibid., p. 18.

190. County Court Records, Williamson County, Loose Records, p. 41–42.

191. County Court Minutes, Franklin County, August Term, 1833, p. 253.

192. Petition of George Gillespie, Record Group 60, Legislative Petition No. 58-1835-1, State Library and Archives.

193. Bill of Exceptions, *William Ford v. State*, Tennessee Supreme Court, Eastern Section, n.d. [1833], State Library and Archives Box 243.

194. Minutes, Circuit Court of Knox County, July Term, pp. 240, 241.

195. "Execution," *Knoxville Register*, August 21, 1833, p. 2. The newspaper said it was not going to discuss the execution because the case of Joel Clough, treated in a Philadelphia newspaper, was more interesting. It ran an extensive reprinted account from the paper.

196. *Western Weekly Review*, August 2, 1833, p. 4.

197. Louise G. Lynch, *Miscellaneous Records of Williamson County*, vol. 1, pp. 25–26.

198. *Ann, a slave, v. State*, 30 Tenn. 59 (1850)

199. Robert E. Corlew, "Some Aspects of Slavery in Dickson County," *Tennessee Historical Quarterly* 10 (September and December 1951): pp. 245, 355. Court records for this era were destroyed during the Civil War.

200. Bill of Exceptions, *State v. Bennett Dula*, Supreme Court, Middle Section, n.d., State Library and Archives Box 51A, p. 5, 31. Said a business partner, "William Patton was a man remarkable for his peaceable disposition and a pious member of the church"; p. 50. See also *State v. Bennett Dula*, Record Book, Supreme Court, Middle Section, August Term 1835, vol. 9, RG 191 Series V (1835–1836), pp. 268–282.

201. Ibid., p. 8, 34.

202. Ibid., p. 50.

203. Ibid., p. 24.

204. Ibid., p. 13.

205. *Dula v. State*, 16 Tenn. 511 (1835); Pat Thach, "The Murder of William Patton," *Sequachee Valley News*, March 5, 1934, p. 4.

206. *Nashville Republican Banner*, September 12, 1835, p. 2.

207. *Nashville Republican Banner*, September 26, 1835, p. 3.

208. A corner is the corner of a piece of land, usually marked in some way such as the blaze on a tree or a gathering of rocks.

209. *Mitchell v. State*, 16 Tenn. 514, 521 (1835).

210. *Mitchell v. State*, 13 Tenn. 340 (1833).

211. The judges were Green and Catron.

212. *Mitchell v. State*, 16 Tenn. 514, 541 (1835); United States Constitution, Section 10, according to Peck.
213. This execution has not been confirmed because there were no newspapers in the county at this time and courthouse records were destroyed when the courthouse burned in 1872. Prison records do not mention Jesse Mitchell.
214. Wilson County Circuit Court Minutes, Nov. 11, 1836, p. 351.
215. Wilson County Circuit Court Minutes, Nov. 14, 1836, p. 359.
216. Wilson County Circuit Court Minutes, Nov. 16, 1836, p. 371; County Court Minutes, Wilson County, March 6, 1837, p. 37, regarding payment to sheriff.
217. County Court Minutes, Wilson County, March 6, 1837, December 16, 1836, p. 14.
218. Wilson County Circuit Court Minutes, March 14, 1837, pp. 12–14.
219. *Goodspeed's History of Tennessee* (Nashville: Goodspeed, 1886), pp. 822–823.
220. County Court Minutes, Rutherford County, December 4, 1837, pp. 35–36.
221. *Goodspeed's*, pp. 822–823. Goodspeed provided no support for this statement.
222. "Trial of Julius, a Slave," *Tennessee Democrat* (Columbia, Tennessee), n.d.; Governor's Papers, Newton Cannon, GP 11, Box 2, folder 9 (1837).
223. Letter of A.O.P. Nicholson to Gov. Newton Cannon, February 2, 1837, Governor's Papers, Newton Cannon, GP 11, Box 2, folder 9 (1837).
224. "Trial of Julius, a Slave."
225. Letter of A.O.P. Nicholson to Governor Newton Cannon, February 2, 1837, p. 1.
226. Letter of A.O.P. Nicholson to Governor Newton Cannon, February 2, 1837, p. 2.
227. Petition of Citizens of Maury County, January 26, 1837, p. 2.
228. *The Union* (Nashville), March 7, 1837, p. 3.
229. Bill of Exceptions, *George Long v. State*, Supreme Court, Eastern Section, n.d., n.p., State Library and Archives Box No. 247.
230. Ibid., note 1.
231. *State v. Long*, 20 Tenn. 387 (1839), citing *McClure v. State*, 9 Tenn. 206 (1829) (per Catron)
232. Petition for Pardon, *George Long v. State*, Papers of Gov. Newton Cannon, State Library and Archives Box 3, file 1 (1839).
233. Ibid.
234. "Execution of Long," *Argus & Commercial Herald*, August 13, 1839, p. 4.
235. Ibid.
236. Inez E. Burns, *History of Blount County, Tennessee: From War Trail to Landing Strip, 1795–1955* (Nashville: Mary Blount Chapter, Daughters of the American Revolution and Tennessee Historical Commission, 1957), p. 206.
237. "Forty-Six Years Ago," *Maryville Watchman*, January 26, 1883, p. 1.
238. Ibid.
239. Bill of Exceptions, *State v. Bob & Jacob*, Tennessee Supreme Court, Middle Section, n.d. [1839], p. 2, State Library and Archives Box 62A.
240. Ibid., p. 36.
241. Ibid., p. 42.
242. Ibid., p. 45–46.
243. Ibid., p. 47.
244. *Bob & Jacob v. State*, Opinion, Tennessee Supreme Court, Middle Section, no date [1839], State Library and Archives Box 62A. The opinion, in the handwriting of Judge Nathan Green bears the notation in his hand, "Not to Be Published."
245. "To the Legislature," by "Howard," *Nashville Whig*, January 22, 1840, p. 2.
246. *The Southern Banner* (Athens, Georgia), December 10, 1841, p. 3.
247. County Court Minutes, McMinn County, December 6, 1841, n.p.
248. "Murder Most Foul!" *Jonesborough Whig*, December 1, 1841, p. 1.
249. Williamson County Circuit Court, Loose Records, July 21, 1842, p. 28.
250. *Jacob v. State*, 22 Tenn. 494, 495 (1842).
251. Ibid., p. 495.
252. Ibid., p. 522.
253. Ibid., p. 509.
254. "Execution," *Nashville Union*, January 31, 1843, p. 3.
255. Ibid.
256. "Grave Found," *Nashville Banner*, May 19, 1887, p. 3. He was now called Jake Bradford.
257. "Horrid Murder," *The Federal Union* (Milledgeville, Georgia), February 14, 1843, p. 2.
258. "Item," *Jonesborough Whig & Independent Journal*, March 15, 1843, p. 1.
259. *Kirby v. State*, 15 Tenn. 259, 262–264 (1834).
260. *Kirby v. State*, 17 Tenn. 382, 385–86. (1836).
261. *Lives and Confessions of Zebadiah Payne, the Murderer and Robber of William Coltart; Willis Green Carroll, the murderer and robber of Rev. Isaac Lindsey; and Archibald Kirby, the Pine Mountain Assassin and Murderer of Mrs. Polly Hunter Who Were Executed at Nashville on the 10th February, 1843* (Nashville: W.F. Bang, 1843), p. 35.
262. Ibid. p. 36.
263. *Kirby v. State*, 22 Tenn. 277, 278 (1842).
264. Ibid., p. 290.
265. Ibid., p. 290.
266. According to Kirby's account, he was accused of killing Mrs. Hunter for hire, induced to do so by her husband's son-in-law Matthew Wallis. The Supreme Court opinion does not suggest a motive. Ibid., note 3, p. 37. Wallis testified at trial that he had seen Kirby a few days before the shooting, as did another witness who saw Kirby at the Wallis home. Kirby steadfastly insisted he had not seen Wallis in several months. Bill of Exceptions, *State v. Archibald Kirby*, Supreme Court, Middle Section, n.d. [1843], State Library and Archives, Box 70, p. 17.
267. Death Notice, *Western Weekly Review*, May 27, 1842, p. 4.
268. Bill of Exceptions, *State v. Archibald Kirby*, Supreme Court, Middle Section, n.d. [1843], State Library and Archives, Box 70, p. 17.
269. "His mare had a hind foot of peculiar shape." Ibid., note 5, p. 299.
270. Ibid., p. 300.
271. Ibid., p. 301.
272. Ibid., p. 302.
273. Ibid., p. 303.
274. "Payne, Kirby and Carroll," *Nashville Union*, February 14, 1843, p. 2.
275. *Lives and Confessions of Zebadiah Payne*, et al., pp. 30–31.
276. Ibid., p. 33.
277. Sentence pronounced by Judge Green, *State v. Archibald Kirby*, Supreme Court, Middle Section, n.d. [1843], State Library and Archives Box 70.
278. Ibid.
279. The governor's proclamation was seen in East Tennessee, where it caused a constable named Eanes to arrest a man named Martin by mistake, thinking he was Payne. The Tennessee Supreme Court said that a criminal charge could be brought against Eanes for this. *Eanes v. State*, 25 Tenn. 53 (1845).
280. *Lives and Confessions of Zebadiah Payne*, et al., pp. 13–15. The account of the men's lives and crimes was written by Nashville lawyer Milton Haynes, who had represented Kirby in his last appeal.
281. Ibid., p. 18.
282. Payne v. State, 22 Tenn. 376, 377 (1842).
283. Hugh Walker, "The Day They Hanged 3 in Nashville," *Tennessean*, October 3, 1976, p. 3-B.
284. "Payne, Kirby and Carroll," *Nashville Union*, February 14, 1843, p. 2.
285. Ibid., note 1, p. 19–20.
286. John B. McFerrin, *History of Methodism in Tennessee* (Nashville: Southern Methodist Publishing House, 1875), vol. 2, pp. 152–156. See "Trial of Carroll," *Nashville Union*, March 17, 1842, p. 4. Carroll had four lawyers including Josephus C. Guild and William Trousdale.
287. *Carroll v. State*, 22 Tenn. 315, 319 (1842).
288. *Lives and Confessions of Zebadiah Payne*, et al., p. 22.
289. Ibid., p. 24.
290. Ibid., p. 24–25.
291. *Carroll v. State*, 22 Tenn. 315, 319 (1842).
292. Sentence pronounced by Judge Green, *State v. Archibald Kirby*, Supreme Court, Middle Section, n.d. [1843], State Library and Archives Box No. 70, p. 5–6. The three sentences were found in this file. "Sentence of the Murderers Payne, Carroll & Kirby," *The Federal Union* (Milledgeville, Georgia), February 14, 1843, p. 2.
293. Ibid., note 3, p. 21.
294. Hugh Walker, "The Day They Hanged 3 in Nashville," *Tennessean*, October 3, 1976, p. 3-B. And folklore it is. Contemporary accounts mention no woman screaming. Rather, the death procession passed in front of the house of Mrs. Nancy Taylor, age 46, on its way to the gallows. "The sight of the prisoners and the crowd passing her residence

brought on violent nervous excitement and congestion of the brain, of which she died on Sunday morning": "Payne, Kirby and Carroll," *Nashville Union*, February 14, 1843, p. 2.

295. Ibid., note 1, p. 157.

296. Minutes, Gibson County Court (June 6, 1842), p. 333. Report of N.D.K. Cole, coroner. "Shocking Outrage and Murder," *Nashville Union*, June 17, 1842, p. 2.

297. Minutes, Circuit Court of Gibson County, March 8, 1843, pp. 403, 404, 459, 470, 498.

298. Frederick M. Culp and Mrs. Robert E. Ross, *Gibson County, Past and Present: The First General History of One of West Tennessee's Pivotal Counties* (Trenton, TN: Gibson County Historical Society, 1961, rpt. 1996), p. 260. According to these authors, the sheriff was paid $12.50 for performing the execution.

299. Newton Cannon (1781–1841) was the first Whig governor of Tennessee (1835–1839). He was the first governor to suggest Tennessee abolish capital punishment. Robert H. White, comp., *Messages of the Governors of Tennessee, 1835–1845* (Nashville: Tennessee Historical Commission, 1954), vol. 3, pp. 1–2, 173.

300. Minutes, Circuit Court of Tipton County, 1843, pp. 16, 37, 48. Although Newton Cannon lived and died in Williamson County, it is not unusual that one of his slaves was living in Tipton County, which was a booming cotton producing county at the time.

301. Diary of Herndon Haralson, 1837–1847 (n.p.), State Library and Archives, Diaries (II-H-2. Box 1. ac. no. 37). Haralson, a Revolutionary War veteran, kept the diary for the last ten years of his long life, 1757–1847. This is the only available account of the case. Circuit court records are missing and newspapers in Memphis did not report the crime or the punishment.

302. "Murder," *Nashville Union*, June 13, 1843, p. 2. Here is the complete account: "The Brownsville Phoenix of the 1st inst. publishes the circumstances of the murder of Mr. Thomas Branch of Haywood County, while in bed asleep by four negroes belonging to his father. No motive is assigned but that the deceased had whipped or threatened to whip one of the murderers. One of the negroes has confessed the crime, and they have all been committed for trial at the next term of circuit court." See also "Another Murder," *Nashville Whig*, June 13, 1843, p. 2: "After the commission of the deed the body was removed to a neighboring cane brake where it was discovered horribly mangled."

303. Jonathan Kennon Thompson Smith, "Additional Gleanings from the *Southwestern Christian Advocate*," entry for May 10, 1844. According to Smith, the order book for the circuit court which describes the trial is missing. But minute book number two, pages 607 and 611, and the execution docket indicate that the execution was carried out on June 21, 1844. See Reported Deaths, *Southwestern Christian Advocate*, 1836–1946, published by Smith on the Internet at www.tngenweb.org.

304. Apparently, the muzzle-loading pistol had been loaded with two bullets, one pewter and the other lead; one was a cut bullet, smaller than the other. They entered the body about four inches apart and the wound produced by either was sufficient to cause death: *Jim, a slave v. State*, 24 Tenn. 145, 147 (1844).

305. *Jim, a slave v. State*, 24 Tenn. 145, 146 (1844).

306. *Jim, a slave v. State*, 24 Tenn. 145, 146 (1844). The fate of George is unknown.

307. *Jim, a slave v. State*, 23 Tenn. 289 (1843).

308. *Jim, a slave v. State*, 24 Tenn. 145, 148 (1844).

309. *Jim, a slave v. State*, 24 Tenn. 150. (1844).

310. John A. Fite, *Memoirs of Col. John A. Fite, 7th Tenn. Infantry, C.S.A.* "Short and Uninteresting History of a Small and Unimportant Man," Typescript, 1910. Manuscript Section, Tennessee State Library and Archives. Acc. No. 614 pp. 23–24.

311. Ibid., p. 23.

312. Ibid., p. 23

313. Ibid., pp. 23–24.

314. Ibid., p. 24.

315. *Jim, a slave v. State*, 24 Tenn. 145, 148 (1844). This case is considered one of the earliest to support a capital conviction based on circumstantial evidence.

316. Ibid., p. 151.

317. "An Old Letter," H.T. Meador, Dixon Springs, Tennessee, to Mr. J.B. Johnson, Redlands, California, June 11, 1925, published in *Macon County Times*, April 14, 1949. Transcribed by Pat Stubbs for rootsweb.com. Due to courthouse fires, no records exist for Macon County for this period.

318. *Bill, a slave v. State*, 24 Tenn. 155, 159 (1844). Bill was owned by Eli Moore who paid for his defense and offered affidavits on his behalf. *State v. Bill, a slave*, Middle Section, Tennessee Supreme Court, State Library and Archives Box 72.

319. *Heritage of Lincoln County* (Lincoln County Heritage Book Committee and Walsworth, 2005), p. 19.

320. Henry County Circuit Court Minutes, March 19, 1846, pp. 302, 324, 325.

321. Dewey Edwards, *Execution of Murder: A Chronicle of Murder Cases in Robertson County, Tennessee, 1810–1910* (Springfield, TN: The Author, 2005), pp. 10–11, citing circuit court records and several secondary sources. According to Edwards, this was the only legal execution in Robertson County during this period.

322. Minutes, Circuit Court of Franklin County, May Term, 1846, pp. 217, 225, 231, 237, 240, 242, 280.

323. Executive Order, Gov. Aaron V. Brown, Gov. Aaron V. Brown Papers, 1846–1847, State Library and Archives Box 1, folder 1.

324. "Item," *Academist* (Lawrenceburg, TN), July 1, 1846. County court minutes exist only from 1848; circuit court minutes exist from 1840, but the trial cannot be located in them. The venue may have been changed to a different county.

325. Petition of James P. Couch, Record Group 60, Legislative Petitions No. 250-1848-2, State Library and Archives.

326. *History of Tennessee from the Earliest Time to the Present: Together with an Historical and Biographical Sketch of Carroll, Henry and Benton Counties* (Nashville: Goodspeed, 1887), p. 805. The execution cannot be confirmed from existing records because the circuit court records were destroyed when the Carroll County courthouse burned in 1931. The county court records merely provide extra payment of $1.20 to Sheriff Jeremiah T. Rust for "ironing" Frank (no last name). Minutes of the County Court of Carroll County, vol. 4, 1843–1850, Part II (WPA, December 1941), p. 305 (July Term, 1847). The same minutes indicate the coroner's inquest report showing the day of Elizabeth's death was September 5, 1846, p. 241. There are no extant newspapers (copies of the *Tennessee Republican*) for the time of execution.

327. *Gilbert v. State*, 26 Tenn. 523, 528 (1847).

328. Ibid., p. 528.

329. Ibid., p. 527.

330. "Atrocious Murder," *Louisville Daily Journal*, March 21, 1848, p. 3.

331. Rutherford County Court Minutes, July Term, 1848, p. 84.

332. Minutes, Circuit Court of Washington County, October 24, 1848, pp. 181–184. Arrest Warrant, *State v. David, a man of color*, Washington County Circuit Court, September 8, 1848. Loose Records, Washington County.

333. "Robert Sims: First Man Executed in This County Since 1847," *The Comet* (Johnson City), November 8, 1897, p. 3. This account places the execution in 1847, not 1848.

334. At the time, the word grocery was used to describe a store that sold whiskey.

335. *Riley v. State*, 28 Tenn. 646, 650 (1849).

336. Ibid., p. 647.

337. Ibid., p. 648.

338. Under the statute, Public Acts of 1829, Chapter 23, Section 3 (Code Section 4598), if the killing was done by lying in wait, this shows evidence of malice to support a first-degree murder conviction.

339. "Murder Victim at Independence," *West Tennessee Whig*, May 4, 1849.

340. Death Notice, *Western Weekly Review*, June 29, 1849, p. 4.

341. Mrs. Otis Trentham, "Some Notes on Crime and Punishment in Madison," *Jackson Sun*, March 14, 1946, p. 4.

342. Ibid. Mrs. Trentham gave no reference to support this event. The murder occurred in Henderson, not Madison, County.

343. Emma Inman Williams, *Historic Madison: The Story of Jackson and Madison County, Tennessee, from the Prehistoric*

Moundbuilders to 1917 (Jackson, TN: Madison County Historical Society, 1946), p. 246.

344. "The Execution," *West Tennessee Whig*, June 15, 1849.

345. Ibid.

346. Ibid.

347. Bill of Exceptions, *State v. John Hill*, Supreme Court, Eastern Section [n.d.], p. 11, State Library and Archives Box No. 1855.

348. Ibid., p. 13.

349. Ibid., p. 15. These statutes made slave rape of a white woman a capital crime.

350. *State v. McCarn*, 30 Tenn. 493, 498 (1851). Also charged as an accessory after the fact was a white man who helped "harbor and conceal" McCarn, knowing of his involvement in the assault: *State v. Payne*, 31 Tenn. 383 (1852).

351. Hardin County Court Minutes, October 7, 1850; payment of $15 approved for hanging David, improperly described as payment for prosecuting him.

352. "The Tale of Hyde Godsey and John Morris," as told by Andy Godsey, October 7, 1959. TSLA Ms. Ac. No. 88-04; "A Man to Be Hanged," *Republican Banner and Nashville Whig*, April 2, 1850, p. 2.

353. Godsey had killed a man before and this was the reason Polly ran. He returned to the house to shoot the oldest child, about six, but changed his mind and looked for Polly.

354. "The Tale of Hyde Godsey and John Morris," as told by Andy Godsey, October 7, 1959.

355. "Stephen W. Rutledge: His Autobiography and Civil War Journal," *East Tennessee Roots* 6 (Fall 1989): p. 101.

356. Ibid., note 1.

357. County Court Minutes, Rutherford County, April Term, 1851, p. 332. In addition to the $12.50 payment to the sheriff for hanging Ransom, it cost $9.50 to build the gallows and purchase a shroud for his body. The cost of his prosecution, including witness and jailor fees, was $180.48, and had been paid earlier. Ibid., p. 290.

358. *Western Weekly Review* (Franklin, Tennessee), November 8, 1850, p. 2.

359. "Item," *New Orleans Picayune*, July 17, 1847, p. 4.

360. *Moses v. State*, 29 Tenn. 456 (1850). (Leading case.)

361. Haywood County Circuit Court minutes, November 7, 1850, p. 451.

362. *Moses v. State*, 30 Tenn. 232, 240 (1850).

363. Ibid.

364. *State v. Moses, a slave*, No. 846, Loose Records of Sumner County. Moses was visiting various females on neighboring farms and Lauderdale had given strict orders he was not to leave without permission.

365. Little Jim, the defendant's brother, said that a fight had ensued after the ox bow was broken and Lauderdale was "in the habit of whipping any of them when he wanted to when mad he would strike with most anything." Jim said it (the fight) was "life for life." Ibid.

366. Ibid., note 1, p. 241.

367. Moses was provided four appointed counsel. One was Josephus C. Guild. Minutes, Sumner County Circuit Court, September 19, 1849, p. 450.

368. "The Execution Yesterday," *Nashville Gazette*, February 22, 1851, p. 2.

369. "Public Executions," *The Review* (Nashville), February 28, 1851, p. 4.

370. "Gallows Speeches," *Nashville Daily Gazette*, February 27, 1851, p. 4.

371. *Henry v. State*, 30 Tenn. 224 (1850).

372. Ibid., p. 226.

373. Ibid., p. 226.

374. "The Execution Yesterday," *Nashville Daily Gazette*, February 22, 1851, p. 4.

375. Ellick v. State, 31 Tenn. 325–327 (1851). His last trial occurred in the May Term, 1851, and was appealed to the December Term of the Supreme Court. The bill of exceptions has not survived.

376. Supreme Court Clerk Records, Enrollments, vol. 10, 1850–1851, pp. 459–461. (December Term, 1851.) The court ordered him hanged on April 16, 1852. No opinion can be located and the bill of exceptions has not survived. Circuit court records of Rutherford County for the period March 16, 1851, through July 12, 1865, have not survived.

377. Supreme Court Clerk Records, Enrollments, vol. 10, 1850–1851, pp. 453–455. (December Term, 1851.) The court ordered him hanged at Nashville on April 16, 1852. No opinion can be located and the bill of exceptions has not survived. Circuit court records of Montgomery County for this era have not survived due to courthouse fires in 1878 and 1900.

378. "Execution of Yesterday," *Nashville Daily Union*, April 17, 1852, p. 2.

379. At the time he wrote his will (July 24, 1843), John Peck owned two lots in the town of Nashville and 1,400 acres in Weakley County. He owned three thousand dollars and had no debts. He owned sixteen horses, forty-eight cattle and twelve slaves in addition to Alfred and Anthony. Will of John Peck, County Court Record Book, 1834–1856, p. 320.

380. Weakley County Circuit Court Minutes, February 13, 1853, n.p.

381. Alfred and Anthony, 32 Tenn. 581, 583 (1853).

382. His name is shown as Isom in court records. Isom was owned by Elizabeth M. Gillespie, administrator of her husband George T. Gillespie's estate. Mary Riggs was described as a woman "of full age," and a widow. Bill of Exceptions, *State v. Isom*, a slave, Supreme Court, Eastern Section, n.d., State Library and Archives Box 1846.

383. Minutes, Circuit Court of Jefferson County, August 16, 1853, p. 606.

384. *Isaac v. State*, 33 Tenn. 111, 112 (1853). (Name misspelled.)

385. Ibid., p. 112.

386. Brief of State, *Isom, a slave v. State*, Tennessee Supreme Court, Eastern Section, n.d., State Library and Archives Box 1846. The issue of the confession cannot be understood from the state's brief, but the state argued that the judge had simply ordered Isom tried first on that day because he had been waiting in jail for a year. The issue of counsel's illness should have been raised in a motion for a new trial, said the state's brief.

387. Ibid., p. 111; Chapter 256, Public Acts of 1851–52.

388. Ibid., p. 115.

389. Ibid.

390. "Executions," *Daily Nashville Patriot and True Whig*, April 16, 1852, p. 2.

391. Bill of Exceptions, *Elias, a slave v. State*, Supreme Court, Middle Section, n.d., State Library and Archives Box 108. The bill of exceptions in this case is incomplete but it recited the appointment of lawyers N.B. Dudley and Thomas W. King for Elias. Minutes, Tennessee Supreme Court, Judgment, December Term 1854, no date, p. 40. State Library and Archives Record Group 191, reel 5.

392. Giles County Circuit Court Minutes, March 9, 1855, p. 477. There are no circuit court records for Marshall County for November 1853 through May 1865, apparently due to a courthouse fire in 1872 and another in 1927. Minutes, Marshall County Court, July Term, 1855, p. 461. (Payment of $12.50 to Thomas M. Stephens for executing the slave Martin.)

393. Minutes, Knox County Circuit Court, June 20, 1854, p. 392.

394. "Item," *The East Tennessean*, October 26, 1855, p. 2.

395. The initial account of the case described her as a free black woman, the account of Harbert's execution says she was a slave. "The Execution of Ben Harbert," *Clarksville Jeffersonian*, February 12, 1856, p. 3. The indictment charged Harbert with being both a slave and a free man of color. It described Hannah as a slave. Bill of Exceptions, *State v. Ben Harbert*, Tennessee Supreme Court, Middle Section, n.d., State Library and Archives Box 106 (first appeal), Box 109, p. 16–19.

396. "Atrocious Murder," *Clarksville Jeffersonian* (*New York Times*), March 4, 1853.

397. Bill of Exceptions, *State v. Ben Harbert*, Tennessee Supreme Court, Middle Section, n.d., State Library and Archives Box 109, p. 16–19.

398. Ursula Smith Beach, *Along the Warioto: A History of Montgomery County, Tennessee* (Nashville: McQuiddy, 1964), p. 92.

399. "Foul Murder," *Athens Post*, February 29, 1856, p. 2.

400. "Found Guilty and Sentenced," *Athens Post*, April 25, 1856, p. 2.

401. "Execution," *Athens Post*, June 27, 1856, p. 2.

402. Harvey Wish, "The Slave Insurrection Panic of 1856," *Journal of Southern History* 5 (May 1939): 206–222. Charles B. Dew, "Black Ironworkers and the Slave Insurrection Panic of 1856," *Journal of Southern History* 41 (August 1975): 321–338.

403. "An Excitement," *Clarksville Jeffersonian*, November 26, 1856, p. 3.

404. "To All Who May See This, the Undersigned Would Submit, Some of Us

of Our Own Knowledge, and Others According to Information Received, the Following Men," *Clarksville Jeffersonian*, Dec. 3, 1856, p. 3.

405. Most Tennessee counties had appointed patrollers (armed laymen) whose duty was to search for missing or out-of-place slaves. The number of patrollers was tripled in Stewart County on December 15, 1856. Stewart County Court Minutes, December 15, 1856, p. 236.

406. Ibid.

407. Ibid. The message was signed by thirty-four whites including the slave's owner. They reported, "Let everybody know then that J.N. Puckett, Esq., has done nothing wrong in this matter, but the act was just and highly honorable and is by us unanimously considered a blessing."

408. "Item," *Clarksville Jeffersonian*, Nov. 26, 1856, p. 3. The scheme was to sack Clarksville, rifle the banks and proceed north.

409. "The Proposed Negro Insurrection in Tennessee," *Milwaukee Daily Sentinel*, Jan. 6, 1857, p. 2. This is the only known listing of names of condemned.

410. "The Late Projected Negro Insurrection — Six Negroes Hung," *The Liberator* (Boston), January 16, 1857, p. 10.

411. "The Negro Excitement in Stewart County," *Nashville Dispatch*, Dec. 18, 1856, p. 3.

412. Ibid.

413. Harvey Wish, "The Slave Insurrection Panic of 1856," *Journal of Southern History* 5 (May 1939): 206, 212. "Sixty slaves belonging to Senator John Bell, then absent from the state, and employed in the Cumberland Iron Works were alleged to have been implicated; nine of these were hanged, four by court process and five by a mob." Support for this statement was a dispatch, dated December 16, in the *New York Tribune*, December 20, 1856. The newspaper reported, "The insurrectionary movement in Tennessee obtained more headway than is known to the public — important facts being suppressed in order to check the spread of the contagion." The story was repeated in the *Baltimore Sun*, December 24, 1856.

414. Betty Joe Wallace, *Between the Rivers: History of the Land Between the Lakes* (Clarksville: Austin Peay State University Press, 1992), p. 67. "Legend has it that at dusk, the Committee of Safety presented the heads of some of the rebel leaders impaled on spiked poles to the assembled blacks. The area was illuminated with pine torches and the lifeless heads of the black leaders were placed in front of the crowd. Committee members forced the blacks to stay all night without moving and watch the heads. The next morning the blacks were marched back to their homes." Wallace cites Stewart County records, Book 57, 11, 14, 22, 16–27; Book 58, 1–8, but your author cannot locate these documents.

415. Stewart County Court Minutes, January 6, 1857, pp. 246, 248

416. "Item," *Clarksville Jeffersonian*, Dec. 16, 1856, p. 3.

417. "Gallatin," *Nashville Dispatch*, December 21, 1856, p. 3.

418. *Kirkwood v. Miller*, 37 Tenn. 455, 459 (1858)

419. Ibid. Also in 1858 the Tennessee Supreme Court denounced lynching for the first time. In one of the earliest reported lynchings, a slave had been accused of raping and killing a white woman. A gang of whites took him from the jail and lynched him. The owner sued the ringleaders, but the jury awarded only nominal damages, one cent. Reversing, the Tennessee Supreme Court said, "No man, whether bond or free, is to be condemned or punished without a hearing — a fair and impartial trial. There is neither valor nor patriotism in deeds like these." *Polk, Wilson & Co. v. Fancher*, 38 Tenn. 336, 339 (1858). Commentators have long argued that Tennessee slave statutes and their interpretation were far less severe than those of other states. J.H. Henderson, "Slavery in Tennessee," Proceedings of the Bar Association of Tennessee (1903), pp. 163–178.

420. *Kirkwood v. Miller*, 37 Tenn. 455, 459 (1858).

421. Indictment and Loose Records, *State v. John, a Slave*, Hawkins County, Roll B-2357, State Library and Archives.

422. *John, a Slave v. State*, 38 Tenn. 49 (1858).

423. Indictment and Loose Records, *State v. John, a Slave*, Hawkins County, Roll B-2357, State Library and Archives.

424. Bill of Exceptions, *State v. William Holt*, Supreme Court, Eastern Section [n.d.], State Library and Archives Box 1837, p. 9–12. There are no circuit court records for this case because they were destroyed when the Marion County courthouse burned in 1922.

425. Ibid., p. 12.

426. Ibid., p. 22.

427. It reads: "By the Court — This is a clear case of murder in the first degree without mitigating circumstances, and there is no ground upon which the verdict can be set aside. Therefore the judgment be affirmed and the sentence of death pronounced and enforced. Carruthers." Ibid., cover page.

428. "Sentence of Holt," *Brownlow's Knoxville Whig*, October 15, 1859, p. 2. "The solemn sentence pronounced by Judge Carruthers made no impression upon him whatever. He received it with cold and stubborn indifference."

429. *Lewis v. State*, 40 Tenn. 126, 144–145 (1859).

430. The failure to get a warrant meant the sheriff was actually making a citizen's arrest.

431. Ibid., p. 150.

432. Ibid., p. 151.

433. In fact, it may be argued that Tennessee never had a mandatory death penalty because the condemned could claim "benefit of clergy," that is, ask for mercy and receive punishment less than death, albeit gruesome, such as branding, whipping and ear cropping. It has been argued that death was mandatory for slaves who killed their owners, but no Tennessee case law or statute can be found supporting this assertion.

434. "Sentence of Two Brothers," *Brownlow's Knoxville Whig*, October 22, 1859, p. 2.

435. "Execution of Two Brothers," *Brownlow's Knoxville Whig*, December 31, 1859, p. 1. The first brief report of the execution noted it was the same day as the John Brown conspirators, Cook, Coppie, Copeland and Green, and "justice demanded their execution, though it should make the "gallows as glorious as the cross." "Hanging Six Men," *Brownlow's Knoxville Whig*, December 24, 1859, p. 1.

436. Judgment, *State v. Joe, a Slave*, Roane County Circuit Court No. 2746, March 9, 1860.

437. Bill Waggoner, *Purdy and Her People, 1825–1891* (Selmer, TN: Banner, 1986), pp. 11–12.

438. Capt. T.M. Gates, "Murder of John H. Trice by His Negro Servant in 1860," reprinted from the *Jackson Sun*, circa 1912, in Jonathan Kennon Thompson Smith, *A Genealogical Miscellany, Henderson County, Tennessee*, vol. 3 (Bolivar, TN: The Author, 2001), pp. 11–15. Smith indicates the article was actually written by James W. Anderson, brother-in-law of the victim.

439. Ibid. The signers' names were then given.

440. "Murder, and Execution of the Murderer," *Daily Gazette* (Nashville), Dec. 21, 1860, p. 3. The same short article appeared in the *Daily Appeal*, Dec. 18, 1860, both originally published in the *McNairy Whig*.

441. Ibid., note 1, p. 12.

442. W. Jerome D. Spence and David L. Spence, *A History of Hickman County, Tennessee* (Nashville: Gospel Advocate, 1900), p. 67. Hickman County records relating to this case were destroyed when the courthouse burned in 1864.

443. "Legal Hangings in Lincoln County," *Fayetteville Observer*, May 30, 1907, p. 3.

444. "The Execution," *Fayetteville Observer*, March 7, 1861, p. 3.

445. Contemporary accounts assert that there was one lynching in 1851. An unnamed Negro was attempting to show his free papers to the city register, John K. Chester, who promptly declared them forged. The Negro drew a pistol and shot him in the head. Taken from the jail by a mob, he was hanged on a tree twenty yards away. The lynching was witnessed by twelve to fifteen hundred people. The individual who tied up the Negro was sued for money damages, which the jury set at one cent.

446. *Isaac, a Slave v. State*, 39 Tenn. 459 (1859).

447. "Execution of Murderers Moses and Isaac in Memphis," *Memphis Daily Appeal*, June 1, 1861, p. 3.

448. Ibid.

449. Ibid.

450. "Item," *Milwaukee Morning Sentinel*, May 17, 1861, p. 1.

451. Sheila Weems Johnston, *Murders in East Tennessee* (Rogersville, TN: The Author, 2004), p. 9, citing *Haynes Family History* (H.B. Stamps Library, Rogersville, TN). See also R. Donahue Bible, "The Murders of the Haynes and Kite

Families in 1861," in *From Persia to Piedmont: Life and Death in Vaughn's Brigade* (Mohawk, TN: Dodson Creek Publishers, 1995).

452. "Criminal Court," *Commercial Appeal*, June 26, 1860, p. 3; July 10, 1860, p. 3.

453. "The Condemned," *The Avalanche*, June 28, 1861, p. 3.

454. "The Execution Yesterday: Levi Stover Hung for the Murder of Aaron B. Stearnes," *The Avalanche* (Memphis), June 29, 1861, p. 3.

455. Ibid.

456. Ibid.

457. "The Execution Yesterday: Levi Stover Hung for the Murder of Aaron B. Stearnes," *The Avalanche* (Memphis), June 29, 1861, p. 3.

458. Ibid. Mrs. Stover died on September 21, 1878. Her son's fate is unknown.

459. Captain (later Colonel) Fry was captured and sentenced to death. He and several other prisoners escaped from the Atlanta Confederate Prison on the night of October 14, 1862, only hours before he was to be executed. He fought throughout the war only to be struck by a train and killed on September 19, 1872. Donahue Bible, "Tennessee Notes: Colonel David Fry Descendants Located," *Tennessee Historical Quarterly* 65 (2007): 371–373.

460. Charles F. Bryan, Jr., "'Tories' Amidst Rebels: Confederate Occupation of East Tennessee, 1861–1863," *East Tennessee Historical Society Proceedings* 60 (1988): 9–10.

461. William M. Robinson, Jr., *Justice in Grey: A History of the Judicial System of the Confederate States of America* (Cambridge: Harvard University Press, 1941), p. 275.

462. R. Donahue Bible, *A Short Sketch of the Tragedy at "Pottertown," November–December, 1861* (Greeneville, TN: Greene County Historical Trust, 2000), p. 9.

463. A general court-martial is the proper term for a "drumhead" court-martial, carried on without much legal formality. This action was taken upon the direct order of the Confederate Secretary of War.

464. Ibid. note 3 p. 274. Col. Leadbetter had recommended a suspended sentence for the teenager and this was commuted to imprisonment by President Davis.

465. David Madden, "Unionist Resistance to Confederate Occupation: The Bridge Burners of East Tennessee," *East Tennessee Historical Society Proceedings* 52 (1981–82): 22–39; 53 (1981): 22–39.

466. William G. Brownlow, *Sketches of the Rise, Progress, and Decline of Secession; with a Narrative of Personal Adventures Among the Rebels* (Philadelphia: George W. Childs, 1862), p. 311.

467. David Madden, "Unionist Resistance to Confederate Occupation: The Bridge-Burners of East Tennessee," *East Tennessee Historical Publications* 52 (1980): 42–52; 53 (1981): 22–39.

468. Donahue Bible, "Shattered Like Earthen Vessels: Five Tennessee Potters Pay a Dear Price for Their Loyalty to the Union," *Civil War Times Illustrated* 36 (December 1997): 48, 53.

469. William M. Robinson, Jr., *Justice in Grey: A History of the Judicial System of the Confederate States of America* (Cambridge: Harvard University Press, 1941), p. 276.

470. Official Records, War of the Rebellion, Series I, vol. 7, pp. 759–760, regarding martial law declared in the city of Knoxville and a distance of one mile from the city limits.

471. *Daily Gazette* (Nashville), December 13, 1861, citing *Knoxville Register*, December 11, 1861, p. 1.

472. W.G. Brownlow, *Sketches of the Rise, Progress, and Decline of Secession; with a Narrative of Personal Adventures Among the Rebels* (Philadelphia: George W. Childs, 1862), p. 312–313.

473. Ibid. 1, p. 7. The source is W.P.A. Civil War Records, vol. 1, p. 38–42.

474. W. Todd Groce, *Mountain Rebels: East Tennessee Confederates and the Civil War, 1860–1870* (Knoxville: University of Tennessee Press, 1999), p. 139.

475. R. Donahue Bible, *A Short Sketch of the Tragedy at "Pottertown," November–December, 1861* (Greeneville: Greene County Heritage Trust, 2000). p. 1–5. See also Donahue Bible, "Shattered Like Earthen Vessels: Five Tennessee Potters Pay Dearly for Their Loyalty to the Union," *Civil War Times Illustrated* 36 (December 1997), pp. 48–54.

476. Whether this was a legal fee or a method to prevent confiscation by the Confederate government is unclear. In 1867 widow Harmon asked Gen. Thomas to order the lawyer who took title, John Baxter, to return the land to her after he threatened foreclosure. It is not known what happened. See note 1, p. 12.

477. William M. Robinson, Jr., *Justice in Grey: A History of the Judicial System of the Confederate States of America* (Cambridge: Harvard University Press, 1941), p. 276. See also, Richard Nelson Current, *Lincoln's Loyalists* (Chicago: Northeastern University Press, 1992), pp. 2–59. The court-martial found Harrison Self guilty but recommended commutation of punishment, which was approved by President Davis.

478. Edward C. Johnson, et al., *All Were Not Heroes: A Study of "The List of U.S. Soldiers Executed by U.S. Military Authorities During the Late War"* (Gunnison, IL: The Author, 1997), pp. 29–30.

479. Robert I. Alotta, *Civil War Justice: Union Army Executions Under Lincoln* (Shippensburg, PA: White Mane, 1989), p. 53.

480. Jonathan A. Noyalas, "My Will Is Absolute Law," *A Biography of Union General Robert H. Milroy* (Jefferson, NC: McFarland, 2006) p. 146.

481. Ibid., p. 144.

482. Michael R. Bradley, *With Blood and Fire: Life Behind Union Lines in Middle Tennessee, 1863–1865* (Shippensburg, PA: Burd Street Press, 2003), p. 120; Michael Bradley and Milan Hill, "Shoot if You Can by Accident," *North & South* 3 (November 1999): pp. 33–46.

483. Benjamin F. Cooling, *Fort Donelson's Legacy: War and Society in Kentucky and Tennessee, 1862–1863* (Knoxville: University of Tennessee Press, 1997), p. 261.

484. Tom C. McKenney, *Jack Hinson's One-Man War* (Gretna, LA: Pelican, 2009), p. 322. He says the boys' heads were cut off and placed on the father's gateposts by the squad that had shot them; pp. 155–157.

485. "Affairs in West Tennessee," *Nashville Dispatch*, August 3, 1862, p. 2. The story was written by a *Chicago Tribune* correspondent on the day Beadle was captured and was reprinted from that paper. "Another Confederate Citizen Hung," *Fayetteville Observer*, August 11, 1862, p. 1.

486. Nothing has been discovered about Beadle's life other than that he was born in 1825 and married Mary Fite in Gibson County in 1847.

487. "A Base Scoundrel," *Nashville Daily Union*, March 5, 1863, p. 2. "He was a hired political bully and probably murdered his victim for pay." See *Kirk v. State*, 41 Tenn. 345 (1860).

488. Ibid.

489. "A Guerilla Brute," *Nashville Daily Union*, February 20, 1863, p. 2.

490. *Tennesseans in the Civil War*, Part 1, p. 96.

491. "We learn that the rebel guerrilla, L.M. Kirk, who was reported as having been shot a week ago, is on trial at Pulaski. The rumor of his being shot was erroneous." *Nashville Union*, August 1, 1865, p. 2.

492. Paul J. Welch, *History of West Point and Surrounding Territory* (Lawrenceburg, TN: P.J. Welch, 1962), p. 86.

493. *Linden Times*, March 4, 1880, p. 4.

494. "Guerillas," *Nashville Union*, January 10, 1865, p. 3; January 12, 1865, p. 3.

495. Kevin D. McCann, *Hurst's Wurst: Colonel Fielding Hurst and the Sixth Tennessee Cavalry, U.S.A.* (Dickson, TN: McCann, 2007), pp. 66–67, 90.

496. T. Vance Little, *Murder on the Wilson Pike* (Brentwood, TN: The Author, 1996), pp. 118, 120–121.

497. Private, Company H, 4th Tennessee Cavalry.

498. Sergeant, Company E, 4th Tennessee Cavalry.

499. Private, Company K, 1st Tennessee (Turney's) Regiment.

500. Military Commission Record No. MM1480 (Young C. Edmonson).

501. Jac Weller, "Nathan Bedford Forrest: An Analysis of Untutored Military Genius," *Tennessee Historical Quarterly* 18 (1959), pp. 213, 246. Like most aspects of his life, the episode regarding the color bearer is disputed. Jack Hurst, *Nathan Bedford Forrest: A Biography* (New York: Alfred A. Knopf, 1993), p. 239. Not shot, just thrashed.

502. Eddy W. Dawson and Daniel Foxx, *Nathan Bedford Forrest: In Search of the Enigma* (Gretna, LA: Pelican, 2007), p. 86. "If he did not personally execute this man, it was probably done on his orders."

503. Ibid., p. 107.
504. General Order No. 16, Army of Tennessee, December 15, 1862.
505. James Hall to father, December 22, 1862. James Hall Letters (Walter K. Hoover Collection), State Library and Archives MS. AC. 79-37. General Crittenton wrote his wife that he was shocked too.
506. The Asa Lewis incident figures prominently in accounts of the battle. Peter Cozzens, *No Better Place to Die: The Battle of Stones River* (Urbana: University of Illinois Press, 1990), pp. 41–42, 161–162; James Lee McDonough, *Stones River: Bloody Winter in Tennessee* (Knoxville: University of Tennessee Press, 1980), p. 54–55.
507. Kentuckians were called "orphans" because they could not easily return home since it was under Union Army control almost from the beginning of the war. William C. Davis, *The Orphan Brigade: The Kentucky Confederates Who Couldn't Go Home* (Garden City, NY: Doubleday, 1980), p. 160.
508. "Why Jeff Davis Visited Murfreesboro Last Winter," *Nashville Dispatch*, April 26, 1863, p. 1. "The visit of Jeff Davis to Murfreesboro in December 1862 was solely for the purpose of reconciling Bragg and Breckinridge and restoring order among the mutinous Kentucky troops. The cause of this mutiny and quarrel was the enforcement of the penalty in the case of a Kentucky deserter." See also "Execution," *Nashville Dispatch*, April 25, 1863, p. 2; this account says Lewis was hanged.
509. Bromfield L. Ridley, "Camp Scenes Around Dalton," *Confederate Veteran* 10 (February 1902): pp. 66, 68.
510. Larry J. Daniel, *Soldiering in the Army of Tennessee: A Portrait of Life in a Confederate Army* (Chapel Hill: University of North Carolina, 1991), p. 112.
511. James Lee McDonough, *Stones River*, note 1, p. 55.
512. Weymouth T. Jordan, Jr., comp., *North Carolina Troops, 1861–1865*, vol. 14 (1993), p. 555, citing Civil War Collection, Miscellaneous Records, box 70, folder 37, NCDAH.
513. The compiled service record of Asa Lewis says he was "killed in action at Stones River, 12/26/62." However, that battle did not begin until December 31, 1862. General Orders No. 22, Army of Tennessee, Polk's Corp, December 20, 1862 (Lewis, Norman, Phillips); General Orders No. 24, Army of Tennessee, Polk's Corp, December 22, 1862 (Litterell).
514. Peter Cozzens, *No Better Place to Die*, note 1, p. 42.
515. V.W. Cooper, "Some Experiences of Dr. V.W. Cooper in the Confederate Army," Miscellaneous Records, Reminiscences, etc., Box 70, Military Collection, Civil War, North Carolina State Archives.
516. "An Account of Two Very Different Scenes — A Ball and an Execution," *Nashville Dispatch*, January 10, 1863, p. 4.
517. Maxwell Elebash, "'When Shall Our Cup Be Full?' The Correspondence of Confederate Soldiers James T. and Reuben M. Searcy," *Alabama Heritage* 31, (1994): 28, 36.
518. General Orders No. 22, Army of Tennessee, Polk's Corp, December 20, 1862. Gray was described as a "Citizen of Tennessee, to be hanged on Friday, December 26, 1862, between the hours of 10:00 A.M. and 2:00 P.M. under the direction of the Provost Marshal General."
519. "Execution," *Nashville Dispatch*, January 26, 1863, p. 4.
520. "Military Executions," *The Appeal* (Memphis), January 5, 1863, p. 2. Story reprinted from the *Murfreesboro Rebel Banner*, December 27, 1863.
521. Ibid., note 2, supra, p. 160.
522. Ella Lonn, *Desertion During the Civil War* (New York: Century, 1928), p. 59; A Confederate (pseud.), *The Grayjackets and How They Lived, Fought, and Died for Dixie* (Richmond: Jones Brothers, 1867), p. 51.
523. General Order No. 12, Army of Tennessee.
524. Special Order No. 37; General Order No. 26, Army of Tennessee.
525. General Order No. 25, Army of Tennessee, December 22, 1862.
526. Jack A. Bunch, *Military Justice in the Confederate States Armies* (Shippensburg, PA: White Mane Books, 2000), p. 106, citing General Order No. 22 (February 5, 1863).
527. General Order No. 44, Army of Tennessee, March 5, 1863.
528. Ibid.
529. "Execution," *Nashville Dispatch*, May 2, 1863, p. 2.
530. General Orders No. 64, Department of the Cumberland, March 30, 1863. Welch pled guilty and asked for mercy. Court Martial Record No. MM33.
531. "Late News," *Nashville Daily Union*, April 8, 1863, p. 2.
532. General Orders No. 103, Head-Quarters Department of the Cumberland, Murfreesboro, Tenn., May 7, 1863; Court Martial File LL487. He was prosecuted under General Orders No. 55, Army of the Cumberland.
533. Court Martial File LL487, p. 6.
534. Ibid., p. 12.
535. Ibid., p. 14.
536. Ibid., p. 14.
537. Ibid., p. 18.
538. Ibid., He was ordered hanged under the direction of Brig. Gen. Crook on May 12, 1863.
539. General Orders No. 100, Army of the Cumberland, May 4, 1862. (Name shown as Mileka.) Milika was charged with desertion and violation of the 22nd Article of War: "No non-commissioned officer or soldier shall enlist himself in any other regiment, troop, or company, without a regular discharge from the regiment, troop, or company, in which he last served, on the penalty of being reputed a deserter, and suffering accordingly." *Revised Regulations for the Army of the United States, 1861* (Philadelphia: J.G.L. Brown, 1861), p. 503. Milika was convicted of both.
540. "Military Execution," *The Daily Press* (Nashville), May 16, 1863, p. 4. "Private Melika of the Tenth Michigan was shot yesterday, six bullets penetrating his body. There was a large crowd of persons present to witness the execution. The affair was conducted with great solemnity."
541. Edward C. Johnson, et al., *All Were Not Heroes: A Study of "The List of U.S. Soldiers Executed by U.S. Military Authorities During the Late War"* (Chicago: The Authors, 1997), pp. 57–58.
542. Diary of Cpl. Henry Carlton, provided to the author by George Wilkinson. Lionview @aol.com. Cpl. Carlton enlisted in the 18th Michigan Infantry on August 23, 1862, at Hudson, Michigan. He was twenty-eight years old. He was taken prisoner by the Confederates on September 24, 1864, at Athens, Alabama. Because the Union Army refused to exchange prisoners by that time, he languished in custody at Selma, Alabama, and died there on March 23, 1865.
543. "Execution," *Nashville Dispatch*, May 13, 1863, p. 2; "Milika," *Nashville Dispatch*, May 16, 1863, p. 4. The first was Michael Connel.
544. General Order No. 16, Hardee's Corp (May 29, 1863).
545. General Orders No. 123, Head-Quarters, Department of the Cumberland, May 30, 1863; (William A. Selkirk), Military Commission Record No. MM521; General Orders No. 142, Head-Quarters, Department of the Cumberland, June 13, 1863 (George Lyles, alias Mansfield Rhodes, and George W. Williams); Military Commission Record No. MM630 (Lyles), MM640 (Williams).
546. Military Commission Record No. MM521 (Selkirk) p. 25. To prevent the occupants from shooting, the robbers said the house was surrounded by a company of soldiers.
547. Military Commission Record, William A. Selkirk, No. MM521, p. 13. Selkirk said he was a federal soldier and that Favor Cason had told him Weaver had money. Weaver was wearing a federal overcoat and brown jeans pants; p. 36.
548. Ibid., p. 31.
549. Military Commission Record (Williams) No. MM640 p. 19.
550. Ibid., p. 14–15.
551. "I never shot at the old man at any time." Statement of George W. Williams (signed with an X). Military Commission Record (Lyles) File No. LL630, p. 3.
552. Military Commission Record (Selkirk) No. LL640, p. 24.
553. Ibid., p. 21.
554. Military Commission Record (Williams) No. MM640 p. 11.
555. Ibid., p. 40.
556. *Nashville Dispatch*, June 7, 1863, p. 2.
557. *Nashville Dispatch*, June 18, 1863, p. 2.
558. Wright's compiled service record says he was a member of the Army of Tennessee, Polk's Corp. The card dated January 10, 1864, says, "Shot at Shelbyville, Tennessee, for desertion, 8th June, 1863, by sentence of C.M."
559. Sam R. Watkins, "*Co. Aytch,*" *Maury Grays, First Tennessee Regiment; or, A Side Show of the Big Show* (Columbia, TN: The Author, 1882; rpt. Jackson, TN: McCowat-Mercer Press, 1952), pp. 99–100.

560. Ibid.
561. William Gilmore Beymer, "Williams, C.S.A.," *Harper's Monthly Magazine* 119 (September 1909): 498–510. This was apparently the first full-length account of the incident which had been mentioned in scores of newspaper accounts since the war. Williams's age has sometimes been given as forty, Peters's as twenty-five. See also J.L. Kirby, "Execution of Two Confederates," *Confederate Veteran* 15 (August 1907): 363–364.
562. "The Execution at Franklin (Tennessee)," *Franklin County Historical Review* 11 (1980): 113–117, from a verbatim account first published in the *Winchester Daily Bulletin*, June 1, 1863. The federal surgeon used only the initials "W.H." and was a member of the 85th Indiana.
563. William Gilmore Beymer, *Scouts and Spies of the Civil War* (Lincoln: University of Nebraska Press, rpt. 2003), p. 37.
564. Ibid., p. 39.
565. Ibid., note 2 p. 115.
566. Ibid., p. 45.
567. Ibid., p. 45.
568. "Williams, C.S.A." p. 508.
569. Ibid., p. 507, 509.
570. Ibid., note 2. p. 117.
571. It remains a favorite topic of Civil War lore. See John Bakeless, "Incident at Fort Granger," *Civil War Times* 8 (April 1969): pp. 10–16; James I. Robertson, "Military Executions," *Civil War Times* 5 (April 1966), p. 34.
572. "The Execution of Williams and Peters," *Harper's Weekly*, July 4, 1863, p. 1.
573. Ibid., note 10.
574. See note 1, Beymer, after page 506, for the stunning color image.
575. Stanley F .Horn, ed., *Tennessee's War, 1861–1865, Described by Participants* (Nashville: Tennessee Civil War Centennial Commission, 1965), p. 192, quoting Major Joseph Vaulx in an undated letter in the *Confederate Veteran*.
576. Capt. W.W. Carnes, "More Light on a War Mystery," *Confederate Veteran* 29 (August 1921): 287.
577. During the Civil War, officers were responsible for providing their own food.
578. Edward C. Johnson, et al., *All Were Not Heroes*, p. 64. This is file number LL 595. See General Orders No. 140, Department of the Cumberland, June 12, 1863.
579. Kenneth Noe, Jr., ed., *A Southern Boy in Blue: The Memoir of Marcus Woodcock, 9th Kentucky Infantry (U.S.A.)* (Knoxville: University of Tennessee Press, 1996), p. 166–167.
580. James M. Randall, Diary (1901), unpublished, entry for June 20, 1863. Available at eHistory at OSU.edu.
581. Edward C. Johnson, et al., *All Were Not Heroes*, p. 67. Court Martial Record No. LL634.
582. Ibid., pp. 67–68. General Orders No. 153, Department of the Cumberland, June 22, 1863. The testimony at his court-martial cannot be located; only the charges and the sentence. This summary was derived from his combined service record. Military Personnel Records, Record Group No.94; Court Martial Proceedings, Record Group No. 153. Combined Military Service Records.
583. Court-martial record of Joel T. Taylor, p. 18, in *Compiled Service Record*.
584. On November 16, 1862, Capt. John Q. Arnold shot and killed his superior officer, Major T.W. Adrien, as he was crossing the street. In overturning the court-martial ruling that Arnold be shot by musketry, the adjutant and inspector general ruled the military court had no jurisdiction because Adrien was not in the exercise of his duties. This was a matter for a civilian court in Kingston, Tennessee. General Order 68; A & I. G.O., May 27, 1863.
585. General Order No. 71, Western Department, June 14, 1862.
586. B.F. Schultz, "Lieut. A. H. Vaughan, Killed in the War," *Confederate Veteran* 8 (December 1900), p. 518.
587. Jack A. Bunch, *Military Justice in the Confederate States Armies* (Shippensburg, PA: White Mane, 2000), p. 106, citing General Order No. 141 (June 24, 1863); "Two Ohio Soldiers Hung," *Daily Cleveland Herald*, August 8, 1863, p. 1.
588. In most instances when men did this, they were seeking the bounty (enlistment) money.
589. "The Execution of Private William Whitehead, Company K, 2nd Regiment Tennessee Cavalry, C.S.A.," *Knoxville Daily Southern Chronicle*, July 19, 1863, p. 3.
590. Ibid.
591. Ibid.
592. Ibid.
593. General Orders No. 155, Department of the Cumberland, June 22, 1863. Court-Martial Record No. NN35, p. 10.
594. Ibid., p. 12.
595. Ibid.
596. Edward C. Johnson, et al., *All Were Not Heroes: A Study of "The List of U.S. Soldiers Executed by U.S. Military Authorities During the Late War"* (Chicago: The Authors: 1997), pp. 76–79 (Reynolds's Mexican War records and Navy records could not be located); Court-Martial Record No. NN188.
597. Ibid., p. 78.
598. "Private Reynolds Gains a Stay of Execution," *Nashville Daily Press*, August 15, 1863; General Orders No.188, Department of the Cumberland, August 11, 1863. Sets execution for August 17, 1863.
599. Ibid. note 1 p. 79.
600. "Soldier Hung," *Nashville Daily Press*, August 18, 1863, p. 4.
601. General Orders No. 105, Department of the Cumberland, May 9, 1863; Court-Martial Record LL526.
602. Edward C. Johnson, et al., *All Were Not Heroes: A Study of the "List of U.S. Soldiers Executed by U.S. Military Authorities During the Late War"* (Chicago: The Authors, 1999), pp. 79–80.
603. General Order No. 93, Army of Tennessee. No date.
604. General Order No. 174, Army of Tennessee, August 30, 1863.
605. Court-Martial, Capt. J.R. Rhodes, 1st Confederate Regiment, Chattanooga, Tenn., August 30, 1863; 8 pp.
606. "Letter," *Richmond* (Va.) *Examiner*, September 22, 1863, page unknown, contained in note 2, infra.
607. "Letter," *Augusta* (Ga.) *Daily Chronicle & Sentinel*, September 9, 1863, page unknown, contained in note 2, infra.
608. Edward S. Milligan, "A Civil War Officer Execution," *Military Collector and Historian* 53 (Spring 2001): 35–37, citing General Order No. 174, Department and Army of Tennessee, 30 August 1863. Adjutant and Inspector General Files, War Department, Confederate Records, Record Group 109, National Archives, vol. 198, p. 125. See also Compiled Service Record, Jabez R. Rhodes, Confederate Soldiers Who Served in Organizations Raised Directly by the Confederate Government, National Archives Microfilm Publication M-258, roll 57, 1st Confederate Infantry [1st Confederate Regiment, Georgia Volunteers] War Department Collection of Confederate Records, RG 109, National Archives.
609. "Execution of Captain J.R. Rhodes, 1st Confederate Infantry, Chattanooga," *OR*, Ser. I. Vol. 30, pt. III, p. 441, citing a report from Edward E. Potter, brigadier general and chief of staff.
610. General Order No.165, August 20, 1863; Jack A. Bunch, *Military Justice in the Confederate States Armies* (Shippensburg, PA: White Mane, 2000), pp. 111–112. Record Group 109 CSA Compiled Military Service Records. He was one of three unnamed Confederate deserters shot "near Chattanooga," according to a CSA officer's brief memoir. Col. A.J. McBride, "The Tenth Georgia in Atlanta; A Military Execution at Chattanooga," *Atlanta Journal*, March 23, 1901, p. 3. The triple execution may have been witnessed by Pvt. Watkins, although he saw only two die. Sam R. Watkins, *"Co. Aytch," Maury Grays, First Tennessee Regiment; or, A Side Show of the Big Show* (Columbia, TN: The Author, 1882; rpt. Jackson, TN: McCowat-Mercer Press, 1952), p. 87.
611. Thomas P. Lowry and Beverly A. Lowry, "Union Officers Sentenced to be Shot," *Military Collector and Historian* 54 (Winter 2002): 178–179.
612. General Order No. 49, Army of Tennessee, 1863; Bell I. Wiley, ed., W.W. Heartstill, *Fourteen Hundred and Ninety-One Days in the Confederate Army* (Jackson, TN: McCowat-Mercer Press, 1954), p. 163.
613. Gary W. Gallagher, ed., *Fighting for the Confederacy: The Personal Recollections of General Edward Porter Alexander* (Chapel Hill: University of North Carolina Press, 1989), p. 307.
614. *North Carolina Soldiers*, vol. 16, p. 373. Discussion of members of Company K, unspecified infantry regiment, Thomas's Legion.
615. Affidavit of D.H. Gallaher and A.J. Burum, February 5, 1866, in Pension Files of William R. Silvey, Abraham Hamilton and William Franklin Dabney, National Archives.

616. Edward C. Johnson, Gail R. Johnson, Melissa Johnson Williams, *All Were Not Heroes: A Study of the "List of U.S. Soldiers Executed by U.S. Military Authorities During the Late War"* (Chicago: The Author, 1997), pp. 119–120; Court-martial record number LL1173; Robert I. Alotta. *Civil War Justice: Union Army Executions Under Lincoln* (Shippensburg, PA: White Mane, 1989), p. 86. This may be true. According to Alotta, the staff at the Illinois Archives could find no record of a Union soldier from Illinois under any spelling of the name Daley.

617. Ibid., note 1, Johnson, p. 120–121. Court-martial record number unknown.

618. "Execution of Deserters," *Nashville Daily Press & Times,* November 23, 1863, p. 1.

619. Ibid.

620. This unit later changed its name to the 55th U.S.C.T. See Thomas P. Lowry, *Sexual Misbehavior in the Civil War* (Xlibris Corporation, for the Author, 2006), p. 151. His service record shows his name as Kemp. The court-martial records show it as Camp.

621. Edward C. Johnson, et al., *All Were Not Heroes: A Study of the "List of U.S. Soldiers Executed by U.S. Military Authorities During the Late War"* (Chicago: The Authors, 1997), pp. 121–122.

622. MM2819. Two other soldiers accused of raping other women near Pocahontas were acquitted. M1523, NN478.

623. The 6th Tennessee Cavalry Regiment, U.S.A., was also called the 1st West Tennessee Cavalry Regiment, and was drawn from west Tennessee unionists. It spent most of its time hunting guerrillas and bushwhackers in that part of the state. Despite its name, most of the soldiers did not have horses. It had repeatedly been given orders not to pillage or plunder, especially after members of the unit carried out depredations in Jackson, Tennessee, in the summer of 1863. In February 1864, Col. Hurst demanded the citizens of Jackson reimburse him and the government $5,139.25 which he had been assessed by federal authorities for the earlier rampage. The citizens produced the money. General Forrest sent a formal report about Hurst's activities, including the charge that prisoners had been murdered under his command, and demanded that Hurst be turned over to him. He further declared Hurst and his men to be war criminals "not entitled to be treated as prisoners of war falling into the hands of the forces of the Confederate States": *Tennesseans in the Civil War,* Part 1 (Civil War Centennial Commission: Nashville, 1964), pp. 333–335.

624. "Horrible Affair at Pocahontas. A Negro Commits a Brutal Outrage Upon a White Girl. He Is Tried, Convicted and Shot," *Memphis Bulletin,* November 21, 1863.

625. Ibid.

626. Edward John Harcourt, "'The Boys Will Have to Fight the Battles Without Me': The Making of Sam Davis, 'Boy Hero of the Confederacy,'" *Southern Cultures* (Fall 2006): pp. 30–54; S.A. Cunningham, "Sam Davis," *Confederate Veteran* 7 (December 1899): 31. Cunningham, the founder of *Confederate Veteran* magazine, was the driving force behind erection of the statue of Davis. The first published account of the Davis execution appeared in the *Pulaski Chanticleer,* December 1, 1863, the official newspaper of the "Left Wing of the 16th Army." The story was reported verbatim in the *Nashville American,* December 2, 1863, headlined "The Execution of a Rebel Spy," and in the *Daily Commercial* (Cincinnati), December 8, 1863. No copy of the *Pulaski Chanticleer* is known in any Tennessee library. For a book-length description of Davis and Coleman's scouts, including documents, see Edythe Johns Rucker Whitley, *Sam Davis, Hero of the Confederacy, 1842–1863: Coleman's Scouts* (Nashville: Blue and Gray Press, 1971).

627. Arkansas claims the title "Boy Hero of the Confederacy" for one of its own, David O. Dodd, who was hanged as a spy in Little Rock on January 8, 1864. Age seventeen, Dodd was a civilian found with encrypted information, written in his hand. Like Davis, he refused to tell the origin of the information, probably in order to protect his source, usually thought to have been a sixteen-year-old-girl. Jim Lair, *Boy Hero of the Confederacy: The Life, Legend and Execution of David Owen Dodd* (Springfield, MO: Oak Hill, 2001).

628. Sam Davis's enlistment and service are confusing. His compiled service record clearly states he enlisted in Company D, 1st (Feild's) Infantry at Camp Harris on May 10, 1861. (The misspelling is shown in the records.) This was a twelve-month enlistment. Later records show a two-year enlistment; the last shows for the duration of the war. On January 1, 1863, the 1st was consolidated with the 27th Regiment, now called the 1st and 27th Tennessee Infantry (Consolidated). Curiously, Special Orders No. 237, Army of Tennessee, September 3, 1863, order Davis and ten other members of the 1st Regiment "heretofore detailed will immediately rejoin their Regiment." Unclear is whether Davis knew about the orders at the time of his death.

629. This was the group's assumed name. It was headed by Captain Henry B. Shaw, alias "Captain Coleman." It was composed of forty to sixty men. Sam Davis was the oldest of nine children. A younger brother, John Davis, was also a member of Coleman's Scouts.

630. Stanley Horn, comp., *Tennessee's War, 1861–1865, Described by Participants* (Nashville: Tennessee Civil War Centennial Commission, 1965), p. 228. Horn quoted from the record, but did not specify its nature or origin.

631. "Pulled the Lever," *Nashville American,* February 5, 1899, p. 3.

632. Dr. H.M. Hamil, *Sam Davis: The Story of an Old-Fashioned Boy* (Griffin, Georgia, n.d.; rpt. Kennesaw, GA: Continental Book, 1959), p. 8.

633. Ibid.

634. General Orders No. 74 (Samuel Davis, Coleman's Scouts), November 25th, 1863.

635. Letter to Major R.M. Sawyer, Assistant Adjutant General from G.M. Dodge, Brig. Gen., Left Wing, 16th Army Corp., November 27, 1863.

636. The gallows was "upon the ridge east of town near the seminary": "Execution of Rebel Spy at Pulaski," *Memphis Daily Appeal,* December 31, 1863, p. 2. This is apparently the first article about the Davis execution published in a civilian Tennessee newspaper, although the paper was being produced in Atlanta at the time. It attributes the *Pulaski Chanticleer,* December 1, 1863.

637. "The Execution of a Rebel Spy," *Daily Commercial* (Cincinnati), December 8, 1863, p. 3.

638. This was the Battle of Missionary Ridge, in which thousands of Union troops crawled up the mountain and routed Bragg's Confederate forces, who had been spooked by a lunar eclipse two days before. Bob Womack, *Call Forth the Mighty Men* (Bessemer, AL: Colonial Press, 1987), pp. 308–316.

639. "Execution of Rebel Spy at Pulaski," *Memphis Daily Appeal,* December 31, 1863, p. 2.

640. Ibid.

641. Ibid.

642. Stanley Horn, comp., *Tennessee's War, 1861–1865, Described by Participants* (Nashville: Tennessee Civil War Centennial Commission, 1965), p. 230. Horn did not provide a reference for Naron's reminiscences.

643. Ibid.

644. Ibid.

645. Ibid.

646. Diary of Lt. George Bargus, 64th Illinois, entry for November 27 and 28, 1863; excerpts in "Eyewitness to Tragedy," *Civil War Times Illustrated* (February 1980): p. 44. See note 1, supra, for other accounts by diarists.

647. Ibid.

648. "Tribute of Respect," *Memphis Appeal,* April 6, 1864, p. 2.

649. Ibid.

650. "The Execution of a Rebel Spy," *Daily Commercial* (Cincinnati), December 8, 1863, p. 3.

651. "Pulled the Fatal Lever," *Nashville American,* February 5, 1899, p. 3. The soldier was C.B. Van Pelt, a private in the 81st Ohio. He was serving as a clerk to Captain W.F. Armstrong, the provost marshal. He tied the hangman's knot because Captain Armstrong did not know how.

652. John L. Jordan, "In Light of Military Law, Trial of Confederate Hero Mocked Ordinary Justice," *Nashville Tennessean,* November 21, 1937, p. 8.

653. General Orders No. 38, Department of the Ohio, April 13, 1863, in *OR,* Series 1, vol. 23, Part II, p. 237.

654. See note 1, supra. See S.A. Cunningham, "Sam Davis," *American Historical Magazine* 4 (1899): 195–209; Mabel G. Frantz, *Full Many a Name: The Story of Sam Davis, Scout and Spy, C.S.A.* (Jackson, TN: McCowat-Mercer, 1961); Paul Flowers, "Too Brave to Die: The

Sam Davis Spy Incident," *Civil War Times* 1 (August 1960): 15; John Bakeless, *Spies of the Confederacy* (1970; rpt. Mineola, NY: Dover Publications, 1997), 205–242.

655. Court-Martial Record No. NN1020, p. 6. General Orders No. 283, November 21, 1863.

656. Ibid. p. 6.

657. Larry J. Daniel, *Soldiering in the Army of Tennessee: A Portrait of Life in a Confederate Army* (Chapel Hill: University of North Carolina Press, 1991), p. 109. General Order No. 225, December 5, 1863, Army of Tennessee.

658. General Orders No. 3, Headquarters Department of the Ohio, January 5, 1864. Court-Martial Record No. LL1346.

659. "When turned over to Captain Rannel and he saw in my Diary where I was appointed Adjutant of a wagon train in his ignorance hastily thought that was proof that I was a Spy or the worst man he ever saw. As I told him I was a private, without any further comment": Statement of E.S. Dodd, no date. Court-Martial Record No. LL1346.

660. *OR*, Ser. III, Vol. 4, p. 54 states, "Inclosure No. 7 (here omitted) contains General Orders No. 3, Department of the Ohio, January 5, 1864, promulgating charges, findings, and sentence of death in the case of E.S. Dodd, Eighth Texas Cavalry, arrested and tried as a spy."

661. General Orders No. 3, Headquarters Department of the Ohio, January 5, 1864.

662. *Terry Texas Ranger Trilogy: Terry's Texas Rangers, Reminiscences of the Terry Rangers; Diary of Ephraim Shelby Dodd* (Austin, TX: State House Press, 1996), pp. 183–224.

663. Ibid., p. 22.

664. Statement of Dodd, Court-Martial Record, n.p.

665. Statement of Dodd, Court-Martial Record, n.p.

666. Daniel E. Sutherland, "Blind Justice," *Civil War Times* 35 (May 1996): 28, 32.

667. Court-Martial Record No. LL1346.

668. Ibid.

669. "Letter," *Confederate Veteran* 7 (August 1899): 361. The article says the letter was published in the *Louisville Journal* about the time of the execution.

670. Mentioned in note 9, supra, p. 35. Your author has been unable to identify these men.

671. Ibid.

672. Ibid.

673. Ibid., p. 33.

674. "Horrible Scene at an Execution," *Memphis Daily Appeal*, March 5, 1864, p. 2.

675. E.S. Dodd, p. 224.

676. "A Trip on the United States Military Railroad, Chattanooga to Nashville and the Execution of a Confederate Spy in Knoxville," *Boston Evening Transcript*, February 2, 1864.

677. Ibid.

678. J. H.M., "Singular and Tragical Coincidence," *Memphis Daily Appeal*, March 22, 1864, p. 1.

679. Ibid., note 5, p. 223.

680. Ibid., note 5, p. 190.

681. "From East Tennessee," *The Appeal* (Memphis), February 8, 1864, p. 2; Jack A. Bunch, *Roster of the Courts-Martial in the Confederate States Armies* (Shippensburg, PA: White Mane Books, 2001), p. 318. Says the trial was January 15, 1864, but could not confirm the execution.

682. Court-Martial Record (Joseph Cornell) No. LL1491 p. 4.

683. Court-Martial Record (Richard P. Carney and Wright B. Carney), No. MM1136, p. 9. When asked who owned the trap, a witness said, "Murphy the deceased and Mr. Pride always claimed the trap, until the past winter when it was claimed by the prisoner R.H. Carney. Murphy and Pride built the trap."

684. Richard Carney was a cousin of Lawson Murphy and had married a niece of Murphy's. Richard was angry that Murphy had filed a lawsuit in Chancery court to have the father's land sold, upon part of which Richard and his wife were living. Court-Martial Record, p. 18.

685. Court-Martial Record, p. 7.

686. Court-Martial Record, p. 8.

687. Court-Martial Record, p. 16.

688. Court-Martial Record, p. 12.

689. Court-Martial Record, p. 13.

690. Court-Martial Record, p. 13. "He heard that Carney was going to shoot his negroes at the trap."

691. Court-Martial Record, p. 19.

692. Ibid.

693. Ibid., p. 22.

694. Letter, Judge Advocate General Holt to His Excellency, The President, March 28, 1864, p. 2; Military Commission File No. MM1345.

695. Michael R. Bradley, *With Blood & Fire: Life Behind Union Lines in Middle Tennessee, 1863–1865* (Shippensburg, PA: Burd Street Press, 2003), pp. 6–7.

696. "Defense of John W. Johnson Against the Following Charges and Specifications," September 14, 1863, p. 1; Military Commission File No. MM1345.

697. Ibid., p. 3, 4.

698. "Defense of John W. Johnson Against the Following Charges and Specifications," September 13, 1863, p. 1; Military Commission File No. MM1345.

699. Ibid., p. 2.

700. Ibid., p. 4.

701. Ibid., p. 3.

702. Ibid., p. 8.

703. Letter, Advocate General Holt, To His Excellency, The President, March 29, 1864, p. 3; Military Commission File No. MM1345.

704. Ibid.

705. Ibid., p. 5, 6.

706. Edward C. Johnson, et al., *All Were Not Heroes: A Study of the "List of U.S. Soldiers Executed by U.S. Military Authorities During the Late War"* (Chicago: The Authors, 1997), pp. 181, 182. This is file number MM989, National Archives Record Group RG-94. General Orders No. 105, Department of the Cumberland, May 9, 1863. Meyers, a bachelor farmer, was born in Germany.

707. Ibid., p. 183.

708. Ibid., p. 183.

709. Ibid., p. 184.

710. "Hung from Same Gallows," *Columbia Herald*, December 10, 1897, p. 4.

711. Record, Thomas Martin Smith, Citizen, Proceedings of a Military Commission, Special Orders No. 37, Head-Quarters 16th Army Corp (April 21, 1864), Court-Martial File No. NN1611, p. 4.

712. Ibid., p. 55–58.

713. Ibid., p. 10.

714. Ibid., p. 12.

715. Ibid.

716. Ibid., p. 20.

717. Ibid., p. 26, citing "Benet, 243." The concept of "certain facts" is best understood by substituting the words "true facts."

718. Ibid., pp. 44–45.

719. General Orders No. 42, (Military Commission, Thomas Martin Smith, citizen). Head-Quarters 16th Army Corp, April 21, 1864, p. 2.

720. "Execution of T.M. Smith," *Memphis Bulletin*, April 30, 1864, p. 2.

721. *OR*, Series II, vol. 8, p. 421.

722. Navy Colt revolvers carried by cavalry troops.

723. "Hanging of Hugh Fraley," *Nashville Dispatch*, May 21, 1864, p. 2; *Nashville Daily Union*, May 21, 1864, p.2.

724. Ibid.

725. Diary of Cpl. Henry Carlton, provided the author by George Wilkinson. Lionview@aol.com. Cpl. Carlton enlisted in the 18th Michigan Infantry on August 23, 1862 at Hudson, Michigan. He was twenty-eight years old. He was taken prisoner by the Confederates on September 24, 1864 at Athens, Alabama. Because the Union Army refused to exchange prisoners by that time, he languished in custody at Selma, Alabama, and died there on March 23, 1865.

726. Transcript, Case of Abe, Colored Man, of Tennessee, Court-Martial Record No. NN1474, April 19, 1864, p. 3.

727. Ibid.

728. Ibid.

729. Ibid., p. 4.

730. Ibid., p. 15.

731. Ibid.

732. Ibid.

733. Ibid.

734. Head-Quarters, Dept. of the Ohio, Knoxville, May 20, 1864, General Orders No. 65; General Court-Martial Order No. 92, Judge Advocate General's Office, 1864.

735. Edward C. Johnson, et al., *All Were Not Heroes: A Study of the "List of U.S. Soldiers Executed by U.S. Military Authorities During the Late War"* (Chicago: The Authors, 1997), pp. 191, 192.

736. Ibid., p. 193.

737. Ibid., p. 194.

738. Ibid., p. 194. According to Alotta, they were hanged at Ft. Pickering on June 28, 1864, citing the *Memphis Bulletin*, date not given. Robert I. Alotta, *Civil War Justice: Union Army Executions Under Lincoln* (Shippensburg, PA: White Mane, 1989), pp. 114, 117.

739. Ibid., supra note 1, pp. 408–409.

740. The combined testimony and proceedings, although duplicative, comprise 258 pages. The case is: Cyrus Lee Cathey, William Lemmond, Jesse B. Neeren, Thomas R. West and Benjamin F. West, Court-Martial Record Number NN1368, National Archives Record Group No. 153, Court-Martial Proceedings. These are the spellings as shown in the transmittal document. The more accurate names are shown in the individual cases themselves. The cases are numbered individually. For example, Benjamin F. West's file contains 36 numbered and ten unnumbered pages which include the brief on his behalf, written by his lawyer, but signed with a mark by the illiterate West.

741. Benjamin F. West, p. 21.

742. Q: "When did [Cathie] leave the service of the so-called Confederate States?" A: "The last of October 1863." Q: "Has [Cathie] served in the service of the so-called Confederate States since October 1863?" A: No, sir. He has not been back. Q: "Have you heard him say that he had left the rebel army for good?" A: "He left on furlough and staid [*sic*] home." Cathie file, testimony of Alexander McAffee, p. 19.

743. Benjamin F. West, p. 31.

744. Benjamin F. West, p. 80. Testimony of Obadiah B. Edmondson, described as a citizen of Lincoln County, who also said he saw the commission.

745. Benjamin F. West, p. 12.

746. It remains unclear why White was referred to in the charges as a citizen. The proof showed he was dressed in a Union uniform when shot in his front yard.

747. Lemmons, p. 22. Tobe Edmondson was a member of this gang.

748. Culpability attaches to persons aiding and in company with others who violate the laws of war, wrote the advocate general in a written summation offered in each case. He cited Benet, *Military Law and Courts-Martial*, pp. 282, 297. Lemmons, p. 31.

749. Lemmons, p. 25.

750. Cyrus Eastland shot William White, according to former gang member Alexander McAffee. He was the government's star witness against all the defendants. Lemmons Court-Martial, p. 11; Court-martial record No. NN1368.

751. Neven, p. 30.

752. He was a member of Galbraith's Cavalry Regiment, U.S.: Neven, p. 19. The shooting was done at 8:00 P.M. according to Hyde's sister, who could only recognize Blackwell, Cook and Blakemore: Neven, pp. 22–23. Hyde's sister was Mrs. Mary Jane Blackwell. Her husband, William J. Blackwell, also testified for the prosecution: Neven, pp. 25–26; Cathie, p. 31; Lemmons, p. 12.

753. Cathie, p. 32. This was the testimony of Mrs. Mary Jane Blackwell, Hyde's sister. Miss Frances Hyde, another sister, was present and made similar testimony. Testimony in Lemmons's case said he was shot by Cyrus Eastman and Gary Talbot: Lemmons, p. 12.

754. Cathie, pp. 33–34. Testimony of Miss Frances Hyde. Blackwell personally took the boots off the dead man.

755. Cathie, p. 23.

756. Cathie, p. 38. Dogs had eaten his body by the time it was found. Cathie, p. 40.

757. Cathie, p. 43. Testimony of John S. Young, identified as a member of Forrest's cavalry.

758. Thomas West, p. 29.

759. Lemmons, p. 17.

760. The so-called statements or briefs were written in the first person, but none of the defendants actually testified in his own behalf or on behalf of others.

761. Brief of Neven, p. 10.

762. Neven, pp. 32–33, testimony of former gang member William H. Maulden.

763. Brief of Neven, p. 4.

764. Benjamin F. West, p. 14. Testimony of Alex McAffee. He said that Benjamin F. West was present when William White was killed: p. 19.

765. Benjamin F. West, p. 11.

766. The witness was Richard Layman. The advocate general cited the case of Lt. Love, U.S. Navy, Pensacola Harbor, 1839, from Benet p. 249.

767. Brief of Lemmons, in Lemmons file.

768. Thomas West, p. 30.

769. Brief of Neven, p. 7.

770. Letter of Transmittal, Major Gen. Slocum to E.M. Stanton, Secretary of War, March 30, 1864.

771. "Execution: Guerrillas Pay the Ultimate Price for Murder," *Nashville Union*, June 18, 1864, p. 1.

772. "The Execution of Five Rebels," *Nashville Union*, June 18, 1864, p. 1.

773. *OR*, Series II, Vol. 8, p. 421.

774. Ibid.

775. "Murder," *Nashville Daily Union*, February 8, 1863, p. 4. Report that Preston Pollock had murdered Jacob Pitt in Springfield over a horse.

776. "Notes," *Nashville Union*, December 25, 1863, p. 2. Naturally, Perkins had earlier been reported killed "by citizens who he had just robbed": *Nashville Union*, November 28, 1862. He was known as Captain Perkins.

777. Pollock's brother had brokered a deal in which for the payment of $500 the two would take the oath of allegiance before the United States Commissioner for Robertson County. The implication was that the payment would bring them some measure of protection. In re Preston Pollock, Court-Martial Record MM1384, pp. 139–141.

778. Court-Martial Record No. NN1476 (Gossett), p. 55; Special Field Orders No. 28; General Court-Martial Orders No. 11 [1864].

779. Ibid., pp. 21, 28.

780. Ibid., p. 20. When an animal has begun to decompose and is badly swollen it has become too dead to skin.

781. Ibid., p. 31.

782. Ibid., p. 68.

783. In re Preston Pollock, Court-Martial Record MM1384, pp. 149–150.

784. Letter, Adjutant General Holt to His Excellency, The President, April 20, 1864. Court Martial File No. NN1476 (Pollock).

785. Ibid., note 2. The president included a date, April 26, 1864.

786. The court found Gossett not guilty of killing B.F. Binkley, justice of the peace and commissioner authorized to administer oaths. Holt erred in saying Gossett had been convicted of killing Binkley: Court-Martial File No. NN1476 (Gossett).

787. "Notes," *Nashville Dispatch*, July 10, 1864, p. 2.

788. "Notes," *Nashville Daily Press*, August 5, 1864, p. 2.

789. Court-Martial File (O.C. Crossland) No. NN1477.

790. Ibid., p. 16.

791. Ibid., p. 21.

792. Ibid., p. 31.

793. Ibid., p. 37.

794. Ibid., p. 39.

795. Letter, Judge Advocate General Holt to His Excellency, The President, April 21, 1864, p. 3; Court-Martial File No. NN1477.

796. "Notes," *Nashville Dispatch*, July 10, 1864, p. 2.

797. "Notes," *Nashville Daily Press*, August 5, 1864, p. 2.

798. Court-Martial Record (Aaron) No. LL1700, p. 4.

799. Ibid., Letter from Judge Advocate Holt to the President, June 10, 1864.

800. Court-Martial Record (George Nelson) No. NN2168, p. 8; Thomas P. Lowry, *Sexual Behavior in the Civil War: A Compendium* (Woodbridge, VA: The Author, 2006), p. 151.

801. Ibid., p. 9.

802. Court-Martial Record (Daniel Tierce and Lewis Hardin) No. NN3007.

803. Q: "At the time these men were said to be killed, did I have any more command than the rest of the privates?" A: "No, sir, I don't think you did": Court-Martial Record (Jourdan Mosely) No. NN1820, p. 37. But the testimony was conflicting: Q: "Is not the prisoner a Lieutenant in Captain Elliot's company of Forrest's Scouts and recognized by Gen. Forrest?" A: "Yes, sir": p. 37.

804. "A Visit to the State Penitentiary in Nashville," in Elvira J. Powers, *Hospital Pencillings; Being A Diary While in Jefferson General Hospital, Jeffersonville, Ind., and Others at Nashville Tennessee, as Matron and Visitor* (Boston: Edward L. Mitchell, 1866), pp. 102–106.

805. Court-Martial Record (Jourdan Mosely) No. NN1820, p. 29.

806. These included Young C. Edmondson (Tobe Edmundson), p. 36–37. Jessie A. Broadway had been named as a shooter by others: pp. 39–40. He said that Mosely had been elected lieutenant under Captain Elliott. Edmondson's death sentence was commuted by Lincoln.

807. "The Execution of Confederate Guerilla Jourdan C. Mosely," *Nashville Union*, October 1, 1864, p 2.

808. "Escape of Confederate Guerilla Chief, Jourdan Mosely," *OR*, Ser. I, Vol. 32, pt. II, pp. 179–180.

809. Ibid.

810. Ibid.

811. "Guerilla Moseley," *Nashville Union*, March 27, 1864, p. 3; "Item," *Nashville Union*, April 1, 1864, p. 3.

812. "The Execution of Confederate Guerilla Jourdan C. Mosely," *Nashville Union*, October 1, 1864, p. 2.

813. Ibid.

814. Court-Martial Record (A. Vest) No. NN1712, p. 3. Special Orders No. 24, Head-Quarters, District of Memphis, February 20, 1864; General Court-Martial Orders No. 259, Adjutant General's Office, Washington, August 24, 1864. Wilks and Clark ordered returned to their company.

815. Ibid., p. 12.

816. Court-Martial Record No. NN1712; Court-Martial Record (Henry Irving) NN170.

817. The file contains the following notation from Adjutant General Holt, May 10, 1864: "Sentences of death awarded by General Courts Martial, in cases of Murder, Mutineers, Spies and Deserters, may be executed by the General Commanding the army in the field without submitting the record for the action of the President; but if for any reason it is desired that he should act on the case, the sentence being confirmed, its execution should be suspended (under the 89th Article of War) until his pleasure be made known."

818. Robert I. Alotta, *Civil War Justice: Union Army Executions Under Lincoln* (Shippensburg, PA: White Mane, 1989), pp. 138–39 (Alotta wrongly says Vess was given a drum-head court-martial); Edward C. Johnson, et al., *All Were Not Heroes: A Study of "The List of U.S. Soldiers Executed by U.S. Military Authorities During the Late War"* (Chicago: The Authors, 1999), p. 264 (The authors wrongly say no record exists for the Vess and Irving court-martial).

819. In re Dick Davis, alias J.W. Smith, Court-Martial Record No. LL2904, p. 45. Two other unnamed soldiers were also killed.

820. Ibid., p. 37.

821. Ibid., pp. 33–34.

822. Ibid., p. 36.

823. Ibid., p. 32–33. He had been a private in Company C, 113th Illinois, now discharged.

824. Ibid., pp. 42–43.

825. Ibid., p. 47.

826. Ibid., p. 13.

827. Ibid., p. 24.

828. Ibid., p. 57.

829. Ibid., pp. 125–127. The conviction was affirmed by Commanding General Dana and was not sent to Washington for approval.

830. Ibid., "Exhibit A."

831. Thomas S. Cogley, *History of the Seventh Indiana Cavalry Volunteers* (La Porte, IN: Herald, 1876), pp. 190–192.

832. Ibid., p. 192.

833. Ibid., p. 200.

834. Ibid., p. 201.

835. Sam Davis died in obscurity, Champ Ferguson in national view. "The Execution of Champ Ferguson," *Harper's Weekly*, November 11, 1865, p. 716. Ferguson appears with some frequency in books about famous executions. See August Mencken, *By the Neck: A Book of Hangings* (New York: Hastings House, 1942), pp. 120–126.

836. Thurman Sensing, *Champ Ferguson, Confederate Guerilla* (Nashville: Vanderbilt University Press, 1942, rpt. 1985), p. 1 (standard biography of Ferguson); Dr. Jonathon D. Hale, *Number Six: The Bloody Shirt* (Hale's Mills, TN: The Author, n.d. [1867], 57 pp. Dr. Hale had lost considerable property to Ferguson's depredations and seems to have taken his account from the verbatim newspaper coverage of the trial. Dr. Hale's "book" is available online from the Library of Congress.

837. One of Ferguson's lawyers was Josephus C. Guild, later a judge and dean of the Nashville bar. He vigorously defended Ferguson, but wrote nothing about the case in his memoirs except this: "October 20, 1865, Champ Ferguson was hung at the penitentiary on account of war operations. On the 20th of November William Heffran was dragged from his carriage and murdered by some ruffians belonging to the Federal army, who were subsequently apprehended, tried by a court-martial, convicted, and hung. The execution took place January 26, 1866." Josephus C. Guild, *Old Times in Tennessee* (Nashville: Tavel, Eastman & Howell, 1878), p. 496.

838. The massive file remains in the National Archives, Court-Martial Record (Champ Ferguson) No. MM2877.

839. Ibid., note 1, p. 83–84.

840. Ibid., note 1, p. 87.

841. Bromfield L. Ridley, "Champ Ferguson," *Confederate Veteran* 7 (October 1899): 442–443. Ridley served on Gen. A.P. Stewart's staff.

842. Bromfield L. Ridley, *Battles and Sketches of the Army of Tennessee* (Mexico, MO: Missouri Printing, 1906), p. 523.

843. Ibid., note 1, p. 29. This was the 5th Kentucky Colored Cavalry.

844. Thomas D. Mays, *The Saltville Massacre* (Abilene, TX: McWhiney Foundation Press, 1998), p. 58.

845. Ibid., p. 59.

846. Ibid., note 1, p. 177.

847. Thomas D. Mays, *The Saltville Massacre* (Abilene, TX: McWhiney Foundation Press, 1998) p. 63.

848. Bromfield L. Ridley, Battles *and Sketches of the Army of Tennessee* (Mexico, MO: Missouri Printing, 1906), p. 529.

849. Ibid., note 1, p. 188.

850. Ibid., note 1, pp. 208–216. At five feet, two inches tall, Wheeler was known as "Little Joe" Wheeler during the war, but became "Fighting Joe" thereafter. He was placed in command of the cavalry of the Army of Tennessee in 1862. Southrons saw his testimony at Ferguson's trial as a courageous gesture. By the time of the Spanish-American War, Wheeler "went over" to the Federal Army and was named a general, a largely symbolic gesture, but an important one.

851. "Ferguson's Execution," *Nashville Daily Press and Times*, October 21, 1865, p. 2.

852. Ibid.

853. "The Execution of Champ Ferguson," *Harper's Weekly*, November 11, 1865, p. 716.

854. "Champ Ferguson," *Daily American*, September 28, 1879, p. 2. In publishing the tale, the newspaper debunked it by saying that Ferguson was seen hanging by Henry Watterson, who wrote about it when he was a reporter for the *Republican Banner*, and was currently editor of the *Louisville Courier-Journal.*

855. "Fate of the Heffernan Murderers," *Nashville Union and American*, January 18, 1866, p. 1.

856. "Murder, Melancholy Progress of Highway Robbery in the State Capitol," *Republican Banner,* November 24, 1865, p. 2.

857. "Another Murderer Arrested," *Republican Banner,* Dec. 2, 1865, p. 1.

858. "Trial of Thomas Perry," *Republican Banner,* Dec. 3, 1865, p. 2.

859. "The Heffernan Murderers," *Nashville Union,* Jan. 18, 1866, p. 3; "Interview with the Hefferman Murderers," *Union and American,* Jan. 20, 1866, p. 3; General Orders No. 677, Department of the Cumberland.

860. "Talk with the Murderers of Heffernan," *Nashville Union,* Jan. 25, 1866, p. 2.

861. See *Pittsburgh Post* (Pittsburgh, PA), February 1, 1866.

862. "Execution of the Hufferman Murderers," *Nashville American,* January 27, 1866, p. 2.

863. Ex Parte Milligan, 71 U.S. (4 Wall.) 2 (1866).

864. "Highway Robberies on the Murfreesboro Pike," *Republican Banner,* December 10, 1865, p. 2; "Another Horrible Murder," *Republican Banner,* December 11, 1865, p. 3.

865. The indictment states the killing was committed on an unspecified day in "June 1864," but this is unlikely since German was known to be at Petersburg, Virginia, on June 1, 1864. The only known thorough account of the Lum German case (and his brother William) is John L. German, *Born Losers: The Untimely Endings of Lum and Bill German in Overton County, Tennessee* (unpublished manuscript, n.d.), 9 pp. The author is especially grateful to Mr. German, who is not descended from either Lum or William German, but is related to them because their mother was a sister of his great-great-grandfather, for allowing access and citation to this valuable document.

866. Newspaper accounts assert that Hays was a Union soldier, but this seems unlikely. John L. German identifies him as a Union sympathizer.

867. This indictment says the rape was committed on September 1, 1865, but this seems unlikely. Rather, this was the day Miss Osborn appeared before the Grand Jury; the rape was committed during wartime.

868. *Born Losers,* note 1 supra, citing *Nashville Dispatch,* September 10, 1865, p. 4.

869. *Born Losers,* note 1 supra, citing

Letter of C.C. German to Maj. Gen. Thomas, November 2, 1865, Union Provost Marshal Citizens File, War Department Collection of Confederate Records (Record Group 109), National Archives.

870. *Born Losers*, note 1, supra, citing *State of Tennessee v. Columbus C. German*, Overton County Circuit Court, January 23, 1866, Motion for Continuance. The illiterate German signed with a mark.

871. *Born Losers*, note 1, supra, "Up the Country," *Republican Banner*, June 24, 1866, p. 4.

872. Ibid.

873. *Born Losers*, note 1, citing Overton County Circuit Court minutes, June 16, 1865–September 18, 1869, pp. 71, 96, 188.

874. Robert L. and Mary Eldridge, *History of Overton County* (Livingston, TN: The Authors, 1976), pp. 64–65.

875. *Born Losers*, note 1 supra, citing, J.D. Eldridge, *Tales from Cracker Barrel News*, vol. 1, p. 7. Date and place of publication unknown.

876. "Notes," *Daily Avalanche*, January 16, 1869, p. 4; January 17, 1869, p. 4.

877. "Item," *Daily Appeal*, January 16, 1869, p. 2, cited by John L. German.

878. Judge A.A. Watson, "Hardin County History," *Savannah Courier*, June 30, 1933, p. 3.

879. See Alexander M. Beadle, (q.v.). To ensure outcomes in cases over which he presided, he sent the sheriff to summon jurors from lands owned or controlled by his extended family, lands in Chester and McNairy counties so extensive they were called "Hurst Nation." He died in 1882 and his grave was constantly desecrated. See Kevin D. McCann, *Hurst's Wurst: Colonel Fielding Hurst and the Sixth Tennessee Cavalry, U.S.A.* (Dickson, TN: McCann, 2007), 144 pp.

880. Bill of Exceptions, *State v. Joseph Huff*, Supreme Court, Eastern Section [n.d.] pp. 8, 9, State Library and Archives Box No. 1830.

881. Ibid., p. 9.

882. Ibid., p. 12.

883. *Joseph Huff v. State*, Minute Book (1865–1869) Supreme Court, Eastern Section, November 2, 1867, p. 419. Conviction affirmed and execution ordered for December 27, 1867.

884. Will R. McBath and E.W. Adkins, *The Life, Trial and Confessions of John Nance* (Knoxville: Brownlow & Haws, 1867), p. 4.

885. "Rebel-Killer's Last Chance Gone," *Republican Banner*, November 3, 1867, p. 1.

886. Ibid., note 1, p. 5.

887. *Tennesseans in the Civil War*, Part II. (Nashville: Civil War Centennial Commission, 1965), p. 549.

888. *Tennesseans in the Civil War*, Part I. (Nashville: Civil War Centennial Commission, 1965), p. 375.

889. Nance's confession merely mentions the earlier conviction but does not say anything about an appeal or punishment. The confession says 1866.

890. Ibid., note 1, pp. 10–11. The confession says December 1866.

891. Ibid.

892. Ibid., p. 4.

893. Ibid., p. 6.

894. Ibid., p. 11. The "confession" says, "He said at the time McBee was murdered, men were being killed in that section of the country almost daily. A reign of terror existed, brought about by the late civil war": p. 11.

895. Bill of Exceptions, *John Nance v. State*, Tennessee Supreme Court, Eastern Section, n.d., State Library and Archives Box 1829, p. 22.

896. Bill of Exceptions, *John Nance v. State*, Tennessee Supreme Court, Eastern Section, n.d., p. 25.

897. Ibid., p. 29.

898. Ibid., p. 38. Nance's father said, "He was always a bad boy."

899. *John Nance v. State*, Minute Book (1865–1869), Supreme Court, Eastern Section, November 2, 1867, pp. 418–419. Conviction affirmed and execution ordered on December 27, 1867.

900. Ibid., p. 11.

901. It is not known whether Nance's case was controlled by the Rankin decision or visa versa.

902. *State v. Rankin*, 44 Tenn. 145, 160–161 (1867). Your author has been unable to find the outcome of the case following remand.

903. William M. Wiecek, "The Great Writ and Reconstruction: The Habeas Corpus Act of 1867," *Journal of Southern History* 17 (1970): 530–548.

904. *Coleman v. State*, 2 Shannon's Cases 117, 122 (Tenn. 1876).

905. Jonathan A. Noyalas, *"My Will Is Absolute Law": A Biography of Union General Robert H. Milroy* (Jefferson, NC: McFarland, 2006), 212 pp; Michael R. Bradley, *With Blood and Fire: Life Behind Union Lines in Middle Tennessee, 1863–65* (Shippensburg, PA: Burd Street Press, 2003), 210 pp.

906. *Pearson v. State*, 1 Shannon's Cases 311, 316–317 (Tenn. 1874). Your author has been unable to find the outcome of the case after remand.

907. *Galvin v. State*, 46 Tenn. 283, 290 (1869).

908. Ibid.

909. Ibid.

910. Ibid., p. 291

911. Ibid.

912. Ibid., p. 295.

913. Ibid.

914. Ibid., p. 297. Throughout the next decades, the court would cite the case of *Lewis v. State*, 40 Tenn. 126 (1859) as support for this rule.

915. "The Gallows," *Memphis Daily Appeal*, August 21, 1869, p. 4.

916. "The Hanging," *Daily Avalanche*, August 21, 1869, p. 1.

917. Ibid.

918. "The Hanging," *Daily Avalanche*, August 21, 1869, p. 4.

919. Editorial, *Memphis Daily Appeal*, August 21, 1869, p. 4. "Moody declared his innocence on the scaffold. He did not fire the fatal shot, and so ignorantly supposes that he was not equally guilty as a principal with the man who did." Moody had been born a slave and lived his entire life in Memphis.

920. "The Hanging," *Daily Avalanche*, August 21, 1869, p. 4. This account says that Moody was executed in the jail following the execution of Galvin.

921. "Item," *Memphis Daily Appeal*, August 25, 1869, p. 1.

922. "The Gallows," *Memphis Daily Appeal*, August 21, 1869, p. 1. This account says that Moody was executed at Bartlett at the same time as Galvin.

923. "Item," *Memphis Daily Appeal*, August 25, 1869, p. 1.

924. *Williams v. State*, 50 Tenn. 37, 45 (1870).

925. Bill of Exceptions, *Andy Williams v. State*, Tennessee Supreme Court, Eastern Section, n.d., pp. 10–12. This is the first trial. The bill of exceptions for the second trial cannot be located. State Library and Archives Box 1822.

926. Ibid., p. 42.

927. Nelson died in a cholera epidemic in Knoxville on August 24, 1873. Albert D. Marks, "The Supreme Court of Tennessee," *Green Bag* 5 (May 1893): 225, 235.

928. "The Gallows," *Daily Avalanche*, February 3, 1872, p. 1; "Execution of Brute in Tennessee," *New York Herald*, February 7, 1872, p. 11.

929. The implication was that only a family member knew where she put these items after warm weather arrived.

930. *Robert Beatty v. State*, Opinion, Supreme Court, Middle Section, vol. 10 (1871–1872), pp. 162–167.

931. "The Gallows," *Republican Banner*, April 6, 1872, p. 4.

932. Ibid.

933. Ibid.

934. "Items," *Columbia Herald and Mail*, March 31, 1875, p. 4.

935. Ibid.

936. "Notes from Cal Logston Trial," *Fentress County Historical Society Newsletter* (Summer 2004), p. 31–35; "Identity of Witnesses at Logston Trial," *Fentress County Historical Society Newsletter* (Summer 2004), p. 36.

937. "A Whole Family Murdered in Fentress County," *Knoxville Daily Press and Herald*, December 5, 1868, p. 1. "It was generally known in the neighborhood that Mrs. Galloway had the day previous received some three hundred dollars, being the back pay and bounty on account of her husband who died in the service": "The Murder in Fentress County," *Knoxville Daily Press and Herald*, December 9, 1868, p. 1.

938. Lucinda Evens Galloway (July 2, 1815–November 19, 1868); Catharine Galloway (Dec. 29, 1842–November 19, 1868). The child's birthday is unknown. See "Samuel Galloway Bible," *Fentress County Historical Society Newsletter* (Spring 2003) pp. 9–11. Bill of Exceptions, State v. Calvin Logston, Scott County case, August 12, 1869. J.H. Storie, one of those who discovered the bodies and a member of the coroner's jury, said Catherine was "age about 26, W.B. about 4 years old and Lucy about 55 years."

939. *Calvin Logston v. State*, Memorandum opinion, Tennessee Supreme Court, Eastern Section, n.d., September

Term, 1869, pp. 135–136, discussed in *State v. Logston*, 50 Tenn. 277 (1871).

940. *Calvin Logston v. State*, Opinion, Supreme Court, Eastern Section, no date, unbound, found in Fentress County records, *State v. Logston*.

941. Bill of Exceptions, *State v. Logston*, Scott County trial, "Jane hit me," p. 29: State Library and Archives Box 1823; "Murder Will Out," *Knoxville Daily Press and Herald*, August 15, 1869, p. 1. Testimony at the Scott County trial.

942. *Logston v. State*, 50 Tenn. 413, 418 (1871).

943. Ibid.

944. Ibid.

945. Ibid., p. 420.

946. "Sentence of Death," *Republican Banner*, February 22, 1872, p. 1.

947. "The Gallows," *Republican Banner*, April 6, 1872, p. 1.

948. Ibid.

949. "The Condemned Criminals; Governor Brown Visits Logston in His Cell," *Republican Banner*, March 24, 1872, p. 1.

950. Ibid.

951. Lynwood Montell, *The Hanging of Calvin Logston* (research paper, Western Kentucky University, circa 1978), p. 2 in Venetia J. Newell, ed., *Folklore Studies in the 20th Century* (n.p., n.d.). Montell masked the party's names, changing Brown to Burr and Galloway to Outlaw, in order to protect the identities of living descendants. Among the other folklore is Logston's promise that if he were innocent the county would undergo a flood within three days. Supposedly, this happened. The story of the man who was tried for killing three people in three different counties and was hanged three times was later reported in the famous "Ripley's Believe It or Not."

952. The Rev. A.B. Wright, *Autobiography of Rev. A.B. Wright* (Cincinnati: Cranston & Curtis, 1896), p. 98.

953. "A Brutal, Horrible Execution," *Sweetwater Enterprise* (Monroe County), April 25, 1872, reprinted from the *Kingston East Tennessean*, no date. See also *Republican Banner*, April 6, 1872, p. 1.

954. A.R. Houge, *History of Fentress County* (Nashville: Williams Printing, 1916), p. 91.

955. *Presswood v. State*, 50 Tenn. 468, 474. (1871)

956. Ibid., p. 472.

957. Ibid., p. 472.

958. Ibid., p. 475.

959. Ibid.

960. "The Last Farewell," *Republican Banner*, April 19, 1872, p. 4. Presswood's petition for clemency included the statement from his father that his son had been feeble-minded since he was six years old due to an illness, and he needed to be constantly watched.

961. "Presswood Confesses," *Republican Banner*, April 21, 1872, p. 4.

962. Ibid.

963. "Presswood," *Republican Banner*, May 26, 1872, p. 4.

964. Ibid.

965. Ibid.

966. Ibid.

967. Ibid.

968. Ibid.

969. The Presswood execution was later described in the *Alexandria Times*, September 22, 1909, and the *Smithville Review*, May 20 and 27, 1948, and June 10, 1948.

970. Stuart Banner, *The Death Penalty: An American History* (Cambridge: Harvard University Press, 2002), pp. 150ff. Taken by one of the town physicians, the photograph is held by the Library of Congress.

971. Bill of Exceptions, *Professor Bryant v. State*, Tennessee Supreme Court, Middle Section [n.d.], p. 23. State Library and Archives Box 212.

972. Ibid., p. 33.

973. Ibid., p. 34.

974. *Bryant v. State*, 66 Tenn. 67, 69 (1872).

975. Bill of Exceptions, p. 29.

976. "Doomsday!" *The Pulaski Citizen*, April 13, 1874, p. 1.

977. Ibid.

978. Ibid.

979. Ibid.

980. Ibid.

981. Ibid.

982. *Kelly v. State*, 66 Tenn. 84, 86 (1872). (The published date is wrong.) The published opinion states that no brief was filed. This seems unlikely, but there is no file in Kelly's case at the State Library and Archives.

983. Ibid., p. 87.

984. "No Hope," *Nashville Union and American*, May 1, 1874, p. 4.

985. "The Gibbet," *Nashville Union and American*, May 9, 1874, p. 2.

986. "Kelley's Doom," *Nashville Union and American*, May 7, 1874, p. 2.

987. Ibid.

988. Ibid.

989. Ibid.

990. Ibid.

991. Ibid.

992. Ibid.

993. Ibid.

994. Ibid.

995. Ibid.

996. Ibid.

997. "Kelley's Resurrection," *Nashville Union and American*, May 13, 1874, p. 4.

998. "Execution in Tennessee," *New York Herald*, September 27, 1874, p. 11. Name shown as Robert Bascom.

999. Ibid. Baskin had been kept in the Memphis jail because of a report that armed Negroes were going to free him from the jail.

1000. "The Gallows and the Victim," *Bolivar Bulletin*, October 2, 1874, p. 2.

1001. "The Gallows and the Victim," *Bolivar Bulletin*, October 2, 1874, p. 2.

1002. Ibid.

1003. "The Gallows and the Victim," *Bolivar Bulletin*, October 2, 1874, p. 2. In this interview he denied telling a reporter for the *Memphis Avalanche* that a gang of armed Negroes said it was going to rescue him.

1004. "Execution in Tennessee," *New York Herald*, September 27, 1874 (quoting the *Memphis Avalanche*, no date).

1005. "Westmoreland's Confession," *Chattanooga Daily Commercial*, Nov. 20, 1874, p. 3.

1006. "Hanged by the Neck," *Nashville Union and American*, Nov. 21, 1874, p. 1. According to this report, Westmoreland moved back to the Hamilton County area, "living here and there, and making his living by questionable practices."

1007. "Westmoreland's Doom!" *Republican Banner*, Nov. 21, 1874, p. 2.

1008. "Hanged by the Neck," *Nashville Union and American*, Nov. 21, 1874, p. 1.

1009. *Shade Westmoreland v. State*, Opinions of Tennessee Supreme Court, Opinions 1874–1876 [no date], opinion number 21, pp. 27–33, p. 33.

1010. Ibid., pp. 30–31.

1011. Ibid., p. 31.

1012. Ibid., p. 32.

1013. Ibid., pp. 27–29.

1014. Fred Hixon, "Hamilton County Hangings — Legal, Otherwise," *Chattanooga Times*, Dec. 11, 1932, p. 4. See "Eight Legal Hangings Since the Civil War," *Chattanooga Times*, June 29, 1909, p. 5. These writers suggest that the hanging was so "scandalous" that it prompted the move for private executions, but contemporary accounts mention nothing unusual about the execution.

1015. "Westmoreland's Doom!" *Republican Banner*, Nov. 21, 1874, p. 2.

1016. Bill of Exceptions, *State v. William N. Berry*, Supreme Court, Eastern Section, State Library and Archives Box 1806, p. 53.

1017. "Black Friday, Three Executions in East Tennessee on the Same Day," *Nashville Banner*, August 14, 1875, p. 4.

1018. Ibid., note 1, p. 55.

1019. "Hangman's Day," *Knoxville Whig and Chronicle*, Aug. 18, 1875, p. 1.

1020. Ibid.

1021. Ibid.

1022. Ibid.

1023. Ibid.

1024. Ibid.

1025. Ibid.

1026. *Confession of Ananias Honeycutt Sentenced to Be Hung at Tazewell, Tennessee, August 13, 1875* [n.p., n.d.], pp. 3–5.

1027. Ibid., pp. 4–5. See "Hangman's Day," *Knoxville Whig and Chronicle*, August 18, 1875, p. 8.

1028. Ibid., note 1, p. 3.

1029. "Black Friday," *Nashville Banner*, August 12, 1875, p. 4.

1030. *Honeycutt v. State*, 67 Tenn. 371 (1875).

1031. Ibid., p. 507.

1032. "Hangman's Day," *Knoxville Whig and Chronicle*, Aug. 18, 1875, p. 8.

1033. Ibid., note 1, p. 2.

1034. Ibid.

1035. Ibid.

1036. Robert L. Kincaid, *The Wilderness Road* (Harrogate, TN: Lincoln Memorial University, 1955), pp. 292–296. Kincaid's authority for the handkerchief story is *Knoxville Daily Press and Herald*, Aug. 15, 1875, and *Knoxville Press and Messenger*, Aug. 18, 1875. However, neither of these newspapers on the dates shown is included in the microfilm collections at the Tennessee State Library and Archives nor the Knoxville Public Library. This author remains eager to see these newspapers.

1037. Jadom Gibson, "The Hanging of Ananias Honeycutt," *The Claiborne Progress*, Aug. 30, 1995, p. 10A; see also John Kivett, "Honeycutt Hanging Interviews," *The Claiborne Progress*, May 20, 1998, p. 11B; May 27, 1998, p. 8B. Transcript of 1967 interview with Nathan Smith, whose aunt Emily Smith had witnessed the hanging as a sixteen-year-old.

1038. "Execution," *Niles Weekly Register*, November 5, 1875, p. 149.

1039. The remnant of a newspaper article on this subject has been located in the vertical files of the Knoxville Public Library, bearing a handwritten notation that it was published in the *Knoxville Journal*, April 30, 1979. However, the microfilm of the *Knoxville Journal* at the Tennessee State Library and Archives notes this day was missing and not microfilmed.

1040. "Black Friday," *Republican Banner*, Aug. 14, 1875, p. 3. The same account of the crime appears in "John Webb," *Daily Press & Herald*, Aug. 13, 1875, p. 2.

1041. Ibid.

1042. Ibid.

1043. "What We Are Learning," *Daily Press and Herald*, Aug. 15, 1875, p. 2.

1044. Webb had deserted his wife four years prior to the killing and she had come to Knoxville from Missouri to claim his body, which was ultimately turned over to his brother.

1045. "Black Friday," *Republican Banner*, Aug. 14, 1875, p. 3. The reference to furniture was an insult to the sheriff, whose job also consists of levying on debtor's goods such as furniture and selling them at public auction to satisfy judgment creditors.

1046. Ibid.

1047. "Hangman's Day," *Daily Chronicle*, August 14, 1875, p. 2.

1048. "Only One White Man Hanged Here," *Knoxville Sentinel*, Feb. 3, 1908, p. 8: "Webb went upon the stand in the spirit of bravado, and never weakened in the slightest." The writer certainly meant since the Civil War.

1049. "O, Tempora! O, Mores!" *Daily Press and Herald*, Aug. 15, 1875, p. 2.

1050. "Hangman's Day," *Memphis Daily Appeal*, January 7, 1876, p. 8.

1051. *McLean v. State*, 3 Shannon's Tenn. Cases 478, 483 (Tenn. 1875).

1052. Ibid., p. 480.

1053. See, Terry Calvani, "The Early Legal Career of Howell Jackson," *Vanderbilt Law Review* 30 (1977): 39–72.

1054. *McLean v. State*, 3 Shannon's Tenn. Cases 478, 483 (Tenn. 1875).

1055. Ibid., p. 485.

1056. "Hangman's Day," *Memphis Daily Appeal*, January 7, 1876, p. 8.

1057. "The Gallows," *The Jackson Sun*, January 7, 1876, p. 4.

1058. Ibid.

1059. Ibid.

1060. "Scott and Williams," *Memphis Daily Appeal*, January 7, 1876, p. 8.

1061. Ibid.

1062. Ibid.

1063. Ibid.

1064. "Double Hanging!" *Public Ledger*, January 7, 1876, p. 3. This account says the Supreme Court overturned the first conviction. Another paper said the trial court itself had ordered a new trial.

1065. *Williams v. State*, 3 Shannon's Tenn. Cases 702, 704 (Tenn. 1875).

1066. Ibid., p. 703.

1067. Ibid., p. 705. Williams had been tried in the courthouse at Bartlett.

1068. Ibid.

1069. Ibid.

1070. "Scott and Williams," *Memphis Daily Appeal*, January 8, 1876, p. 1.

1071. Ibid.

1072. Ibid.

1073. Ibid.

1074. "Double Hanging!" *Public Ledger*, January 7, 1876, p. 3.

1075. "Scott and Williams," *Memphis Daily Appeal*, January 8, 1876, p. 1.

1076. *Frank Scott v. State*, Opinion, Supreme Court, Western Section, vol. 8. (1874–78), reel 97, pp. 229–230.

1077. Ibid., p. 229.

1078. Ibid., p. 229.

1079. Ibid., p. 330.

1080. "Double Hanging!" *Public Ledger*, January 7, 1876, p. 3.

1081. "The Gallows," *Memphis Daily Appeal*, January 7, 1876, p. 4.

1082. Ibid. This is supposedly the time Christ died.

1083. Ibid.

1084. "Scott and Williams," *Memphis Daily Appeal*, January 8, 1876, p. 1.

1085. Ibid.

1086. "The Gallows," *Memphis Daily Appeal*, January 7, 1876, p. 4.

1087. Ibid.

1088. Ibid.

1089. Ibid.

1090. Ibid.

1091. Kelly's role in the conviction remains unknown.

1092. *Beggarly v. State*, 67 Tenn. 520 (1875).

1093. "Life for Life," *Weekly American*, June 1, 1876, p. 1.

1094. Ibid.

1095. Ibid.

1096. Ibid.

1097. Ibid.

1098. Minutes, Fayette County Circuit Court, 1875–1876, pp. 379, 526, 535, 567. Among the persons named as potential witnesses against him, based on the grand jury report, were Mary Gaines, Rosamind Bridges, Lucy Davis, Charley Gaines, John Johnson, Smith Johnson, and Hawson Howell.

1099. *Clark v. State*, 67 Tenn. 592 (1875).

1100. Ibid., p. 595

1101. Ibid., p. 597.

1102. "Hawson Clark was hung in Somerville, Tennessee on the fifteenth instant, for the murder of his uncle": *Memphis Appeal*, December 24, 1876, p. 2. This was the entire article.

1103. "The Gallows at Dover," *Nashville Daily American*, May 26, 1877, p. 4.

1104. Ibid. See also Iris H. McClain, *History of Stewart County* (Columbia, TN: The Author, 1965), p. 79.

1105. According to Goodspeed, Mockbee was executed and Wilson was lynched: Goodspeed, *History of Stewart*, p. 908. The *Daily American* clearly shows Wilson as being executed and explains that Mockbee was lynched.

1106. Goodspeed, p. 908.

1107. "Jackson," *Nashville Weekly American*, July 19, 1877, p. 8.

1108. "Justice Is Terrible," *Tribune and Sun*, July 13, 1877, p. 4.

1109. Ibid.

1110. Ibid.

1111. *Min Wilson v. State*, Opinion, Supreme Court, Western Section, n.d. [1877–78], vol. 9, pp. 46–71.

1112. Mrs. Otis Trentham, "Some Notes on Crime and Punishment in Madison," *The Jackson Sun*, March 14, 1946, p. 4.

1113. "Justice Is Terrible," *Tribune and Sun*, July 13, 1877, p. 4.

1114. Actually, Andrew Jackson Hunt had *seventeen* surviving siblings. His father, George Washington Hunt (1811–1896), had ten children by his wife, Mary Caroline "Polly" Wilson Hunt (died 1899), from 1838 to 1860. During this same time (1843–1861), his mistress, Mary "Polly" McDaniel (died 1907), bore him thirteen children, of whom five lived to adulthood. He treated all his children (and their mothers) equally, but during his last illness was cared for by Polly McDaniel. Polly Hunt was buried at his side. Ruby Tidwell Hanicky, et al., *The Rev. William "Bucky" Hunt, 1793–1868* (n.p.: The Authors: 1998).

1115. "Jack Hunt," *Monroe Democrat*, December 20, 1877, p. 1.

1116. *Hunt v. State*, 2 Shannon's Tennessee Cases 295, 399 (Tenn. 1877).

1117. "Jack Hunt," *Monroe Democrat*, December 20, 1877, p. 1.

1118. Ibid.

1119. *Hunt v. State*, 2 Shannon's Tenn. Cases 395, 396 (Tenn. 1877).

1120. Ibid., p. 397.

1121. Ibid., p. 398.

1122. Ibid., p. 399.

1123. "Jack Hunt," *Monroe Democrat*, December 20, 1877, p. 1.

1124. "Jack Hunt," *Monroe Democrat*, December 20, 1877, p. 1.

1125. "Letter from Our Traveling Correspondent," *Maryville Times*, December 20, 1877, p.1.

1126. "Jack Hunt," *Monroe Democrat*, December 20, 1877, p. 1.

1127. Ibid.

1128. There is no record of his service, but he may have been in an irregular Home Guard unit that was attached to this regiment from time to time.

1129. Vann was a private in Company G of the 1st Tennessee Infantry Regiment. See *Tennesseans in the Civil War, Part II* (Nashville: Civil War Centennial Commission, 1965), p. 596.

1130. "Jake Harness," *Knoxville Daily Tribune*, December 30, 1877, p. 4.

1131. Ibid.
1132. *Jacob Harness v. State*, Opinion, Supreme Court, Eastern Section, n.d., vol. 1877–1879, pp. 149, 150.
1133. Ibid., p. 151.
1134. Ibid., p. 151.
1135. *Jacob Harness v. State*, Opinion, Supreme Court, Eastern Section, no date, vol. 1877–1879, pp. 149, 150.
1136. Ibid., p. 150.
1137. Ibid.
1138. Ibid., p. 151.
1139. Ibid., p. 151.
1140. Ibid., p. 151.
1141. Ibid., p. 152.
1142. "Jake Harness," *Knoxville Daily Tribune*, December 30, 1877, p. 4.
1143. "Hanging Harniss," *Nashville Daily American*, December 30, 1877, p. 1.
1144. "Jake Harness," *Knoxville Daily Tribune*, December 30, 1877, p. 4.
1145. "Jake Harness," *Knoxville Daily Tribune*, December 28, 1877, p. 4.
1146. "Jake Harness," *Knoxville Daily Tribune*, December 30, 1877, p. 4.
1147. Ibid., "The wagon passed out, leaving Harness dangling in the air.... Harness arose deliberately, threw off his coat, and stepped upon the platform, requesting William Hicks to hold him steady after swinging off."
1148. Ibid.
1149. *Coble v. State*, Supreme Court, Middle Section, January 26, 1878, vol. 18 (1878–1879), 567–569 (January 26, 1878).
1150. *Coble v. State*, Supreme Court, Middle Section, n.d., vol. 17 (1877), 1–3.
1151. *Coble v. State*, Middle Supreme Court, Middle Section, January 26, 1878), vol. 18 (1878–1879), 569.
1152. "Winchester's Hanging," *The Daily American*, March 15, 1878, p. 4.
1153. Ibid.
1154. Ibid.
1155. Ibid.
1156. Ibid.
1157. The case is the first Tennessee execution that was the subject of a book, which consists largely of reprints of contemporaneous newspaper articles, court records, the Tennessee Supreme Court decision, and contemporary newspaper accounts retelling the case. Donald E. Spurlock, *The Brassell Hangings of Putnam County, Tennessee* (Cookeville: Southland, 1981), 230 pp. It will be cited hereinafter as "Spurlock."
1158. Spurlock, pp. 19, 20. Spurlock's account of the crime came from "The Brassells Hung," *Weekly American*, March 28, 1878, p. 1. The same account appeared in the *Daily American* that day.
1159. The Brassells were suspects from the start: *Columbia Herald and Mail*, December 24, 1875, p. 1.
1160. His proper name was Samuel G. Brassell; his testimony did not provide an alibi for his brothers so much as it tried to show that the shooters were Johnson and Bates.
1161. Spurlock, p. 24. These words were somewhat more cautiously written by Spurlock.
1162. *Braswell v. State*, 2 Shannon's Tenn. Cases 595, 604–5.
1163. Spurlock, p. 186.
1164. The several accounts of the case spell the names differently, ranging from Brassell, to Brasswell, to Brazel, the latter the most likely phonetic pronunciation. The sister-in-law was known as Harriet Z. Braswell.
1165. Spurlock, p. 30.
1166. *Braswell v. State*, 2 Shannon's Tenn. Cases 595, 600 (Tenn. 1877).
1167. Ibid., p. 602. The Brassells later admitted they had been involved in a wide-spread counterfeiting ring.
1168. Ibid., p. 603.
1169. Spurlock, pp. 35–36, citing "The Braswell Hanging," *Cookeville Chronicle*, April 4, 1878.
1170. Spurlock, pp. 39–42.
1171. Ibid., p. 43.
1172. Spurlock, p. 44.
1173. Spurlock, p. 52.
1174. Spurlock, p. 52.
1175. Spurlock, p. 54.
1176. Spurlock, p. 56, citing "Putnam County Murders," *Nashville Daily American*, March 28, 1878, p. 4.
1177. Spurlock, p. 214, citing the *Cookeville Free Press* of January 25, 1894.
1178. "The Brassells Hung," *The Weekly American*, March 28, 1878, p. 1.
1179. See, Louise Davis, "Raw Oysters and Raw Whisky," *Tennessean Sunday Magazine*, July 21, 1946, p. 12 (Jesse: Tom Howard; Frank: Ben Woodson); Max York, "Frank James on Trial," *Tennessean Sunday Magazine*, February 28, 1971, p. 12. The botched Northfield bank robbery of September 6, 1876, had left several of the Younger-James Gang dead or seriously wounded, including Frank, with a bullet in his knee, and Jesse, with a bullet in his thigh. Making their way to the Nashville area following the Northfield debacle, the men lived peacefully, it is supposed. Jesse went by the name J.D. Howard and Frank went by B.J. Woodson. They turned their attention to train robbing and held up a train in Glendale, Missouri, in October 8, 1879, gaining six thousand dollars. Jesse James was assassinated by fellow gang member Robert Ford, who claimed a reward and a pardon in 1882. Frank James, perhaps enjoying the reflected glory of his brother, seemed immune to conviction by juries: "Frank James' Trial," *National Police Gazette*, September 22, 1883, p. 7. He died in his sleep in 1915.
1180. "A Hanged Murderer Resuscitated," *National Police Gazette*, May 18, 1878, p. 6. The source was an unnamed Nashville newspaper of May 7, 1878.
1181. "Howell's Confession," *Daily American*, September 6, 1878, p. 1.
1182. "The Gallows," *Knoxville Weekly Whig and Chronicle*, September 11, 1878, p. 2. See "The Howell Hanging," *Daily Constitution* (Atlanta), September 7, 1878, p. 1; "Negro Assassin Hanged," *National Police Gazette*, September 14, 1878, p. 10.
1183. Ibid.
1184. Ibid.
1185. *Griffee v. State*, 69 Tenn. 42, 43–44 (1878).
1186. At the time, the word "grocery" meant a store that sold liquor.
1187. *Griffee v. State*, 69 Tenn. 41, 43 (Tenn. 1878).
1188. Ibid., p. 44.
1189. Ibid., p. 44.
1190. The night before the execution he had made the same confession to his lawyer W.J. McQueen and the editor of a newspaper.
1191. "Griffee's Gallows," *Nashville Daily American*, November 23, 1878, p. 1.
1192. Ibid.
1193. "Griffee's Gallows," *Nashville Daily American*, November 23, 1879, p. 1.
1194. Ibid.
1195. "Public Executions," *Knoxville Daily Chronicle*, November 22, 1878, p. 2.
1196. "The Death Penalty," *Daily American*, March 29, 1879, p. 1.
1197. Ibid.
1198. "Knox Knocked Off," *National Police Gazette*, April 12, 1879, p. 13.
1199. "The Law's Vengeance," *Daily American*, March 28, 1879, p. 4.
1200. "The Death Penalty," *Daily American*, March 29, 1879, p. 1.
1201. Ibid.
1202. Ibid.
1203. Ibid.
1204. Ibid.
1205. "Conviction of Anthony Blair," *Morristown Gazette*, August 13, 1879, p. 1.
1206. Ibid., note 1. See also, "Conviction of Anthony Blair," *Morristown Daily Gazette-Mail*, November 4, 1956, p. 4.
1207. Ibid., note 1.
1208. Ibid.
1209. *Life and Confessions of Anthony Blair (Colored) Hanged at Morristown, Hamblen County, Tenn. September 26, 1879*, 8 pp.
1210. Howard L. Hill, "Faces and Places: Confession of Ant'ny Blair," *Morristown Daily Gazette Mail*, November 11, 1956, p. 4. The confessions are reprinted here.
1211. "Bric-a-Brac: Some Things He Saw on the Occasion of the 26th," *Morristown Gazette*, October 1, 1879, p. 2.
1212. Ibid.
1213. "Conviction of Anthony Blair," *Morristown Gazette*, August 13, 1879, p. 4.
1214. "Bric-a-Brac: Some Things He Saw on the Occasion of the 26th," *Morristown Gazette*, October 1, 1879, p. 2.
1215. Pugh's weapon was described as a "toy pistol," which at the time meant a small caliber weapon, not the typical Navy .40 caliber.
1216. *Hall v. State*, 71 Tenn. 552 (1879).
1217. "Paid the Penalty," *Fayetteville Observer*, March 4, 1909, p. 3. (Includes article, "Why Hangings Are Private.")
1218. "Hall-Smith," *Republican Banner*, February 26, 1880, p. 4.
1219. Act of March 22, 1883, Chapter 112, 1883 Tenn. Public Acts. For a discussion of the statutory history of the Tennessee death penalty, see Margaret Van-

diver and Michel Coconis, "'Sentenced to the Punishment of Death': Pre–*Furman* Capital Crimes and Executions in Shelby County, Tennessee," *University of Memphis Law Review* 31(2001): 861–918, pp. 867–878.

1220. "The Gallows," *Knoxville Daily Chronicle*, November 13, 1880, p. 1.

1221. Ruth Webb O'Dell, *Over the Misty Blue Hills: The Story of Cocke County, Tennessee* (Easley, SC: Southern Historical Press, 1982), pp. 210, 216.

1222. Ibid., p. 211.

1223. Ibid.

1224. Ibid.

1225. Ibid.

1226. Ibid., note 2, p. 218.

1227. Ibid.

1228. Charge of the Court, *State v. Ed Long, col'd*, Madison County Circuit Court, October Term, 1880 (Madison County Archives)

1229. "Ed Long Hanged for Murder of Another Negro," *Daily American*, December 19, 1880, p. 1. An account of the execution appears in the *Galveston Daily News*, December 22, 1880, p. 1.

1230. "The Johnsonville Othello," *Daily American*, March 29, 1881, p. 4.

1231. "Waverly's Hanging," *Daily American*, April 9, 1881, p. 3.

1232. Ibid.

1233. Ibid.

1234. Bill of Exceptions, *Andrew Saunders v. State*, Tennessee Supreme Court, Western Section, n.d., pp. 20–25. State Library and Archives Box 238.

1235. Ibid., p. 21.

1236. Ibid., p. 29.

1237. "Will He Swing?" *Memphis Daily Appeal*, August 26, 1881, p. 4.

1238. "Neat Necktie," *Memphis Daily Appeal*, August 27, 1881, p. 4.

1239. Ibid.

1240. Ibid.

1241. Ibid.

1242. Ibid.

1243. Ibid.

1244. Ibid.

1245. Ibid.

1246. Ibid.

1247. "The Hanging," *Chattanooga Daily Times*, September 3, 1881, p. 1.

1248. Lawson's lawyers were H.B. Case and Otto Fischer. The state was assisted by special prosecutor Lewis Shepherd, one of the city's leading lawyers. He later helped defend a black man accused of raping a white Chattanooga girl. The man was taken from the jail and lynched.

1249. "The Hanging," *Chattanooga Daily Times*, September 3, 1881, p. 1.

1250. Ibid.

1251. "The Hanging," *Chattanooga Daily News*, September 2, 1881, p. 4.

1252. Ibid.

1253. "The Hanging," *Chattanooga Daily News*, September 3, 1881, p. 4.

1254. Ibid.

1255. Ibid.

1256. Ibid.

1257. Ibid.

1258. Ibid.

1259. "Harris' Doom," *Knoxville Chronicle*, November 26, 1881, p. 1.

1260. *Harris v. State*, 75 Tenn. 538, 558 (Tenn. 1881).

1261. *Harris*, p. 542.

1262. *Harris*, p. 553.

1263. *Harris*, p. 555.

1264. "Harris' Doom," *Knoxville Daily Chronicle*, November 26, 1881, p. 1.

1265. Ibid.

1266. "Harris' Doom," *Knoxville Chronicle*, November 26, 1881, p. 1.

1267. Ibid.

1268. "Harris' Doom," *Knoxville Chronicle*, November 26, 1881, p. 1.

1269. *Rea v. State*, 76 Tenn. 357, 366 (1881).

1270. Ibid., p. 367.

1271. *Rea v. State*, p. 371.

1272. Ibid., p. 372.

1273. "Life for Life," *The Pulaski Citizen*, May 25, 1882, p. 1.

1274. Ibid.

1275. Ibid.

1276. *National Police Gazette*, April 1, 1882, page 6.

1277. "Goodrum's Murderer," *The Pulaski Citizen*, May 18, 1882, p. 4.

1278. "Life for Life," *The Pulaski Citizen*, May 25, 1882, p. 1.

1279. "Rea's Fate," *The Daily American*, May 20, 1882, p. 4.

1280. Ibid.

1281. Ibid.

1282. "The Awful Crime," *Memphis Daily Appeal*, June 1, 1882, p. 4.

1283. *Sandy Matthews v. State*, Opinion, Tennessee Supreme Court, Western Section, n.d., vol. 12 (1882–1883), pp. 88, 89.

1284. "The Awful Crime," *Memphis Daily Appeal*, June 1, 1882, p. 4.

1285. Ibid.

1286. Ibid., note 2, p. 90.

1287. Ibid., p. 91.

1288. Ibid., p. 89, 90.

1289. "Gone to Glory," *Daily Appeal*, June 3, 1882, p. 4.

1290. Ibid.

1291. "The Awful Crime," *Memphis Daily Appeal*, June 1, 1882, p. 4.

1292. "Double Execution," *Daily Chronicle* (Knoxville), November 11, 1882, p. 1.

1293. "The McFarland Murderers," *Daily Chronicle* (Knoxville), September 8, 1881, p. 2.

1294. "William Yardley," in C. Van West, ed., *The Tennessee Encyclopedia of History and Culture* (Nashville: Tennessee Historical Society, 1998), p. 1089. Frederick Douglass said Yardley, the first black man to run for governor of Tennessee, was the most extraordinary man he had ever met.

1295. *Milton and Samuel Hodge v. State*, Opinion, Supreme Court, Eastern Section, April Term, 1881, no date, p. 403–404.

1296. "Double Execution," *Daily Chronicle*, November 11, 1882, p. 1.

1297. Ibid.

1298. Ibid.

1299. "Double Execution," *Daily Chronicle* (Knoxville), November 11, 1882, p. 1.

1300. Ibid.

1301. *Robert Wilson v. State*, Opinion, Supreme Court, Western Section, May 29, 1883, vol. 13, Unpublished opinions (1883–1884), p. 505.

1302. Ibid., p. 506.

1303. Code 5042-3.

1304. Ibid., note 1, p. 507.

1305. Ibid., p. 507.

1306. Ibid., p. 508.

1307. "Black Friday," *Memphis Avalanche*, July 19, 1883, p. 4.

1308. "Wilson's Soul," *Memphis Avalanche*, July 21, 1883, p. 4.

1309. Ibid.

1310. Ibid.

1311. Ibid.

1312. Ibid.

1313. Ibid.

1314. "Bob's Bob," *Daily Appeal*, July 21, 1883, p. 4.

1315. "A Bloody Rescue," *Chicago Tribune*, September 15, 1882, p. 12.

1316. John Taylor, thirty years old, was an engineer on the steamer *Tellico* docked at Chattanooga. He and Capt. John W. Fletcher, the man who had recently installed the engine on the boat, got into an argument and Taylor ordered him off the boat. When he refused because an engineer had no authority to order anyone ashore, the argument escalated. Taylor visibly carried a pistol in his pocket. Capt. Fletcher approached him and said, "What's that you've got, you ____ _____ cowardly _____ ____ ____!" Taylor pulled the pistol and shot the captain. Outraged citizens persuaded the governor to offer a $250 reward and Taylor was soon captured: "Foul Murder," *Chattanooga Weekly Commercial*, February 27, 1881, p. 4; "Reward!" *Chattanooga Weekly Commercial*, March 6, 1881, p. 1.

1317. *Taylor v. State*, 79 Tenn. 708 (1883). This is one of the longest descriptions of a murder by the Tennessee Supreme Court to that time.

1318. "The Law's Vengeance," *Knoxville Daily Chronicle*, November 23, 1883, p. 1.

1319. "The Crimes of the Three Taylors," *National Police Gazette*, September 29, 1883, p. 3.

1320. "The Law's Vengeance," *Knoxville Daily Chronicle*, November 24, 1883, p. 1.

1321. Ibid.

1322. *Taylor v. State*, 79 Tenn. 708, 719 (1883).

1323. "Daring Taylor," *Knoxville Daily Chronicle*, November 23, 1883, p. 4.

1324. Ibid. "Blasphemy on the Gallows," *New York Times*, November 27, 1883, p. 8.

1325. Chapter 102, Public Acts of 1901.

1326. *Vowell v. State*, 178 S.W. 768 (Tenn. 1915).

1327. Ibid., p. 769. The court framed the issue in this way: Whether it is essential to jurisdiction in any case that the appellant in a criminal case shall be personally present during the argument, or at the decision of the case in the appellate court.

1328. "Hangman's Day," *Daily American*, July 12, 1884, p. 3.

1329. *Forrest v. State*, 81 Tenn. 103, 107 (1883). The court shows his name as Shin.
1330. Ibid., note 1.
1331. Ibid.
1332. Ibid.
1333. Ibid.
1334. "Hangman's Day," *Daily American*, July 12, 1884, p. 3
1335. Editorial, *Daily American*, August 2, 1884, p. 2: "The execution at Paris, some two weeks ago, was also in the presence of a gathered multitude. This merits a severe rebuke from the proper authority at the proper time."
1336. Bill of Exceptions, *State v. Charley Phillips*, Supreme Court, Eastern Section n.d., p. 34. State Library and Archives Box 305.
1337. Ibid., p. 23.
1338. Ibid.
1339. Ibid.
1340. Ibid., p. 25.
1341. Ibid., p. 22.
1342. Ibid., pp. 39, 40.
1343. Ibid., p. 36.
1344. "Huntington," *Daily American*, August 2, 1884, p. 1.
1345. "Editorial," *Daily American*, August 2, 1884, p. 2; "Huntington," *Daily American*, August 3, 1884, p. 1.
1346. "Paid the Penalty," *The Daily Chronicle* (Knoxville), November 1, 1884, p. 4.
1347. Bill of Exceptions, *Isaac Fain v. State*, Supreme Court, Eastern Section, State Library and Archives, Box 1671, p. 3.
1348. "Paid the Penalty," *The Daily Chronicle* (Knoxville), November 1, 1884, p. 4.
1349. Ibid.
1350. Ibid.
1351. "Joe Clark Executed," *Bolivar Bulletin*, June 5, 1885, p. 3: "The object of Clark in the murder was to get possession of the woman."
1352. Ibid.
1353. "The Doomed Man," *Clarksville Semi-Weekly Tobacco Leaf*, June 19, 1885, p. 1.
1354. "Bill Morrow," *Clarksville Weekly*, June 20, 1885, p. 3.
1355. *William Morrow v. State*, Memorandum opinion, Supreme Court, Middle Section, n.d., vol. 40 (1884–1885), pp. 606, 607: "It is not denied that these facts would make out a murder in the first degree."
1356. Ibid., p. 608.
1357. *Morrow and Bellamy v. State*, 82 Tenn. 475 (1885). The results of the later trials are unknown.
1358. "Bill Morrow," *Clarksville Weekly*, June 20, 1885, p. 3.
1359. Ibid. See also, "The Fall to Eternity," *Clarksville Semi-Weekly Tobacco Leaf*, June 23, 1885, p. 1.
1360. Ibid.
1361. Ibid.
1362. This was apparently John Long.
1363. The facts of the case were taken from the Tennessee Supreme Court opinion, reprinted in "McKeever Hanged," *Daily Appeal*, June 27, 1885, p. 4.
1364. *John McKeever v. State*, Opinion, Tennessee Supreme Court, May 9, 1885, vol. 14, pp. 401–407, at 406–407.
1365. "McKeever Admits," *Daily Appeal*, June 24, 1885, p. 4; "His Last Day," *Daily Appeal*, June 26, 1885, p. 4.
1366. "McKeever Hanged," *Daily Appeal*, June 27, 1885, p. 4.
1367. Ibid.
1368. Ibid.
1369. Ibid.
1370. The actual last words of many condemned men are a good-bye to the jailer.
1371. Ibid.
1372. "The Gallows," *Nashville Banner*, June 4, 1886, p. 1. There was no local newspaper in Lebanon at this time.
1373. *Baxter v. State*, 83 Tenn. 657, 658 (1885).
1374. Ibid., pp. 661–662.
1375. Ibid., p. 662.
1376. Ibid., pp. 660–661. The court relied on the authority of *Anthony v. State*, 19 Tenn. 265 (1838).
1377. "The Gallows," *Nashville Banner*, June 4, 1886, p. 1.
1378. Bill of Exceptions, *State v. Ben Brown*, Supreme Court, Middle Section, n.d. [1886], p. 61. State Library and Archives Box 676.
1379. Ibid., pp. 63, 64.
1380. Ibid., p. 65.
1381. *Brown v. State*, 85 Tenn. 439, 444 (1887).
1382. Ibid.
1383. Ibid., p.445
1384. A word used by the court.
1385. Ibid., pp. 445, 446.
1386. Ibid., p. 446. The implication was the court feared Brown would be lynched.
1387. "Ben Brown's War Record" (undated article), Bill of Exceptions, *State v. Ben Brown*, Supreme Court, Middle Section, n.d. [1886], p. 41. State Library and Archives Box 676.
1388. Ibid., p. 442.
1389. "To Die Tomorrow," *Nashville Banner*, April 14, 1887, p.4
1390. *Brown v. State*, 85 Tenn. 439, 448 (1887)
1391. "Scaffold Speeches," *Nashville Banner*, April 16, 1887, p. 2.
1392. "Expiated His Crime," *Nashville Banner*, April 20, 1888, p. 3.
1393. Ibid.
1394. Bill of Exceptions, *N.B. Lester v. State*, n.d., p. 26–27. State Library and Archives Box 1361.
1395. "N.B. Lester to Hang," *Nashville Banner*, April 19, 1888, p. 3.
1396. "Expiated His Crime" *Nashville Banner*, April 20, 1888, p. 3
1397. Ibid.
1398. "Dead! Dead! Dead!" *Knoxville Journal*, July 21, 1888, p.1.
1399. Ibid.
1400. "A Cruel Murder," *Knoxville Journal*, May 21, 1888, p. 1.
1401. "Dead! Dead! Dead!" *Knoxville Journal*, July 21, 1888, p. 1.
1402. Ibid.
1403. Ibid.
1404. "Hanged!" *Lebanon Democrat*, March 27, 1889, p. 4.
1405. "Hanged!" *Lebanon Democrat*, March 27, 1889, p. 1.
1406. Ibid.
1407. "Hanged!" *Lebanon Democrat*, March 27, 1889, p. 4.
1408. Ibid.
1409. Ibid.
1410. Ibid.
1411. "A Live Dead Man" *Memphis Appeal*, April 6, 1889, p. 1.
1412. "The Hangman's Rope," *Reporter and Falcon* (Somerville), July 17, 1889, p. 2.
1413. Bill of Exceptions, *State v. Thomas Jefferson*, Supreme Court, Western Section, December 8, 1888, p. 50. State Library and Archives Box 3891. Jack Walsh was the public undertaker.
1414. Ibid., p. 26. The landlord had seen a couple he did not recognize leaving the apartment together. Alice was apparently named as a co-defendant to prevent her from offering testimony favoring Jefferson. Initially, he claimed she was his wife.
1415. "The Doomed Man," *Memphis Appeal*, June 9, 1889, p. 2: "He has rehearsed the story so often that he evidently believes it himself."
1416. Ibid.
1417. Ibid.
1418. Ibid.
1419. "The Last Hope Gone," *Memphis Appeal*, July 12, 1889, p. 3.
1420. Ibid.
1421. Ibid.
1422. "'Twas Done Quickly," *Memphis Appeal*, July 14, 1889, p. 1.
1423. Ibid.
1424. Ibid.
1425. Ibid.
1426. Ibid. This is based on the notion that since the death warrant or opinion usually describes a time in which the execution must occur, it may not be done earlier or later. The customary latter time is 2:00 P.M.
1427. Vandiver describes Mrs. Riley as Condor's mother-in-law without explanation. Condor had been married to a daughter of the victim, but Mrs. Riley was not the girl's mother. Margaret Vandiver, *Lethal Punishment: Lynchings and Legal Executions in the South* (New Brunswick, NJ: Rutgers University Press, 2006), p. 43.
1428. Rebel C. Forrester and Betty Wood, eds., *I Had a Real Good Time: Memoir of James Brice* (Union City, TN: Lanzan, 1984), p. 142. James Brice was the founder and publisher of the *Troy News-Banner*. The newspapers have not survived.
1429. Ibid.
1430. Ibid.
1431. "Paid the Penalty," *Daily American*, August 14, 1889, p. 1.
1432. *Rea v. State*, 76 Tenn. 357 (1881); "Life for Life," *The Pulaski Citizen*, May 25, 1882, p. 1.
1433. Ibid., note 1, p. 1.
1434. Bill of Exceptions, *State v. Ed Carr*, Tennessee Supreme Court, Western Section [n.d.], p. 15. State Library and Archives Box No. 413.

1435. Ibid.
1436. Ibid., pp. 25, 30.
1437. "Law's Wrath," *Memphis Appeal*, June 25, 1890, p. 1.
1438. "Tomorrow's Execution," *Memphis Appeal*, June 23, 1890, p. 5.
1439. "Imitated Brenish," *Memphis Appeal*, August 19, 1889, p. 5.
1440. "Brenish-Harris Cases," *Memphis Appeal*, September 19, 1889, p. 5.
1441. "Brenish Convicted," *Memphis Appeal*, October 20, 1889, p. 10.
1442. "This Is Hangman's Day," *Memphis Appeal*, June 24, 1890, p. 5.
1443. "Law's Wrath," *Memphis Appeal*, June 25, 1890, p. 5.
1444. Ibid.
1445. Ibid.
1446. Bill of Exceptions, *State v. Hardy Ballard*, Supreme Court, Western Section, p. 32–41, State Library and Archives Box 411.
1447. "Law's Wrath," *Memphis Appeal*, June 25, 1890, p. 1.
1448. Ibid.
1449. Ibid.
1450. Bill of Exceptions, *State v. Frank Brenish*, Tennessee Supreme Court, Western Section, n.d., p. 3. State Library and Archives Box 411.
1451. "Law's Wrath," *Daily Appeal*, June 25, 1890, p. 1.
1452. "Brenish Convicted," *Memphis Appeal*, October 20, 1889, p. 10; "Says He Is Crazy," *Memphis Appeal*, August 27, 1889, p. 5.
1453. "Tomorrow's Hanging," *Memphis Appeal*, June 23, 1890, p. 5; "This Is Hangman's Day," *Memphis Appeal*, June 24, 1890, p. 5.
1454. "Law's Wrath," *Memphis Appeal*, June 25, 1890, p. 1.
1455. Ibid.
1456. Ibid.
1457. "Law's Wrath," *Memphis Appeal*, June 25, 1890, p. 1.
1458. "Brutally Assaulted," *Knoxville Daily Journal*, February 19, 1890, p. 1.
1459. "The Condemned Staples," *Knoxville Daily Journal*, November 19, 1890, p. 8.
1460. "The Execution," *Knoxville Daily Journal*, November 21, 1890, p. 5.
1461. "Staples Hanged," *Knoxville Daily Journal*, November 22, 1890, p. 1.
1462. Ibid.
1463. Ibid.
1464. Photograph (cabinet card) of Houston Kelly. The printed material on the back reads as follows: "Houston Kelly — His Life and Terrible Crime — The original of the picture opposite is the third party hanged in this county since the war. He is a bright mulatto, was born December 25, 1867 — 24 years old — three years married and has one child. He has always been regarded as a reckless, bold and defiant character, though quite intelligent. He was executed on Nov. 10, 1891 for the murder of Dan Charmichael, an industrious, well-behaved and respected mulatto bricklayer and plasterer, during a trivial melee at the house of George Cochraham, in the suburbs of Rogersville, in a locality known as "Guntown" during a festival and dance party on Christmas night, 1890. Will Christian and Henry Hounshell, the two other young colored men implicated in the murder, are now serving life sentences in the penitentiary. Four days previous to his execution Kelly expressed a desire to have his picture taken, and Sheriff Armstrong and his deputies accordingly escorted him to the photograph gallery of Nat W. Taylor, where his wish was gratified and this picture produced."
1465. Ibid.
1466. "Dead, Dead, Dead!" *Knoxville Daily Tribune*, November 11, 1891, p. 1.
1467. "Hanged! Houston Kelley Has Paid the Price," *Knoxville Journal*, November 11, 1891, p. 1.
1468. Ibid.
1469. Ibid.
1470. Ibid.
1471. Ibid.
1472. The minute order affirming the conviction can be found in Minutes, Supreme Court, Eastern Section, September Term, 1891, p. 76–77; Minutes, Supreme Court, Eastern Section, October 5, 1892, p. 118–120. Costs.
1473. Ibid.
1474. Ibid.
1475. Chattanooga Police Department. *Centurion II: A Commemorative Album of the Chattanooga Police Department* (Chattanooga: Police Department, 1989), p. 11. See also *Souvenir of the Chattanooga Police Department* (Chattanooga: Chattanooga City Police Department, 1899), p. 29.
1476. "Nerve," *Chattanooga Sunday Times*, January 3, 1892, p. 4.
1477. "He Professes Religion," Chattanooga Daily Times, October 23, 1891, p. 8.
1478. Ibid.
1479. Ibid.
1480. Ibid.
1481. "Hanged!" *Chattanooga News*, January 2, 1892, p. 1.
1482. Ibid., note 3.
1483. Ibid.
1484. Ibid.
1485. Ibid.
1486. Ibid.
1487. "Murderer Frierson," *Nashville Daily American*, January 2, 1892, p. 5.
1488. "Fearful Scene," *Chattanooga Daily Times*, January 2, 1892, p. 1.
1489. Ibid.
1490. "Nerve," *Sunday Chattanooga Times*, January 3, 1892, p. 4.
1491. *Lancaster v. State*, 91 Tenn. 269, 270 (1891).
1492. Ibid.
1493. Neither the opinion nor newspaper accounts mention anything about her husband.
1494. Ibid., p. 271.
1495. Ibid., p. 281.
1496. Ibid., pp. 281–284.
1497. Ibid., p. 272.
1498. Ibid., p. 274.
1499. Ibid., p. 274.
1500. Ibid., p. 275.
1501. Ibid., p. 278.
1502. Ibid., p. 282.
1503. Ibid., p. 283.
1504. Ibid., p. 288, citing Code (M & V) 6098; *Green v. State*, 3 Baxter 322; Lewis v. State, 3 Head 127, 150: "In the Lewis case, as in this, the trial Judge declined the commutation."
1505. "Died on the Gallows," *Nashville Banner*, April 19, 1892, p. 1.
1506. "Humor on the Scaffold," *Chattanooga Daily Times*, June 18, 1892, p. 4; "To Suffer the Penalty," *Nashville Banner*, June 17, 1892, p. 4. This account says the peddler's name was Henry Cote.
1507. "Hanging at Jasper," *Nashville American*, June 18, 1892, p. 4.
1508. "To Suffer the Penalty," *Nashville Banner*, June 17, 1892, p. 4.
1509. Humor on the Scaffold," *Chattanooga Daily Times*, June 18, 1892, p. 4.
1510. "Humor on the Gallows," *Chattanooga Daily Times*, June 18, 1892, p. 4.
1511. Bill of Exceptions, *State of Tennessee v. George Stone*, April 1, 1890. State Library and Archives Box 866.
1512. *Stone v. State*, Supreme Court, Western Section, n.d., vol. 25 (1887–1891), p. 486. Here the official court opinion is actually a newspaper account that has been pasted into the opinion book, comprising only one page of the book, namely page 486.
1513. "George Stone Hanged," *Nashville Banner*, July 8, 1892, p. 5. The Stone execution was mentioned in the newspaper account of Charles W. Baird's execution. See "Asserts His Innocence in the Shadow of Death," *Nashville Banner*, May 24, 1907, p. 12.
1514. *Lincoln County Heritage Book Committee & Lincoln County Heritage, Inc., Heritage of Lincoln County* (Waynesville, NC, 2005), p. 20; "Legal Hangings in Lincoln County," *Fayetteville Observer*, May 30, 1907, p. 3.
1515. "Two Hanged," *Chattanooga Daily Times*, February 17, 1893, p. 4.
1516. "Two Hanged," *Chattanooga Daily Times*, February 17, 1893, p. 4.
1517. Ibid.
1518. Bill of Exceptions, *State v. John Armstrong*, Supreme Court, Middle Section, n.d., pp. 18–20. State Library and Archives Box 1634.
1519. "Paid the Penalty," *Nashville Banner*, December 13, 1893, p. 1.
1520. Ibid.
1521. Ibid.
1522. See, Minutes, *State v. Cousan*, Supreme Court, Eastern Section, 1893–94, November 11, 1893, pp. 322–323.
1523. "By the Neck!" *Knoxville Tribune*, December 22, 1893, p. 11.
1524. "Cousan Ready to Die," *Knoxville Tribune*, December 21, 1893, p. 6.
1525. "By the Neck!" *Knoxville Tribune*, December 22, 1893, p. 1.
1526. Ibid., p. 11.
1527. Ibid., p. 11.
1528. Ibid., p. 11.
1529. Bill of Exceptions, *Lafayette Richie v. State*, Middle Section, Tennessee Supreme Court, State Library and Archives Box 1048, p. 43.
1530. Brief of State, *Lafayette Richie, v. State*, Middle Section, Tennessee Supreme Court, State Library and Archives Box 1048, p. 2.

1531. The undertakers had provided Richie new clothing which along with the coffin cost the county $15.95: County Court Minutes, Jackson County, July 2, 1894, p. 164.
1532. "Bennett's Last Day on Earth," *Memphis Commercial Appeal*, July 24, 1894, p. 5.
1533. Bill of Exceptions, *State v. Henry Bennett, Supreme Court*, Western Division, n.d. State Library and Archives Box 547.
1534. "Bennett to Hang at Noon," *Memphis Commercial Appeal*, July 25, 1894, p. 5.
1535. "Fearless to the End," *Memphis Commercial Appeal*, July 26, 1894, p. 5.
1536. "John, who is the only member of the trio who could read, had read the life of Jesse James to the confessor [General] and Josephus. They decided to organize as the 'Kennedy Boys.' John urged the organization of the band and this was perfected": "Strangled," *Chattanooga Daily Times*, December 18, 1894, p. 6.
1537. Ibid.
1538. Ibid.
1539. Ibid.
1540. It does seem she spent the night in his cell. Complained an editorial, "The public baptizing of the savages; the powwows in the court house ... the allowing of a loose woman to lodge with one of the wretches the night before he was 'worked off'—all this paraphernalia came as near making the tragedy a farce, as the actual hanging of the men would permit of": "Hangings—That at Jasper," *Chattanooga Daily Times*, December 19, 1894, p. 4.
1541. Ibid.
1542. "Strangled," *Chattanooga Daily Times*, December 18, 1894, p. 1.
1543. Ibid.
1544. "To Hang Today," *Chattanooga Daily Times*, December 17, 1894, p. 1. The author has been unable to locate a copy.
1545. "Strangled," *Chattanooga Daily Times*, December 18, 1894, p. 6.
1546. Vic Weals, "Home Folks," *Knoxville Journal*, April 3, 1951, p. 11-A. The paper contains a picture of the Snodderly couple.
1547. "Double Drop to Death," *Evening Sentinel*, December 22, 1894, p. 1.
1548. Ibid.
1549. Ibid., note 1.
1550. Ibid.
1551. "Ready for Their Death," *Knoxville Journal*, December 22, 1894, p. 1.
1552. The manuscript has never been located. Ben T. Cox, probably a relative of Clarence Cox, published a newspaper in Maynardville at this time. He produced a booklet that was sold at the execution, but your author has been unable to locate a copy. It was called *History of the Snodderly Murder on Hind's Creek, Union County, Tenn.*
1553. "Double Drop to Death," *Evening Sentinel*, December 22, 1894, p. 1.
1554. "Both Hanged," *Chattanooga Daily Times*, January 12, 1895, p. 6; "The Extreme Penalty," *Chattanooga Daily Times*, January 11, 1895, p. 6.
1555. Ibid.
1556. Ibid.
1557. Ibid.
1558. "Ghost of Buddie Wooten Very Busy at County Jail," *Chattanooga Times*, August 14, 1904, p. 5.
1559. "The Execution," *Maury Democrat*, April 25, 1895, p. 3.
1560. Ibid.
1561. Ibid.
1562. "The Execution," *Maury Democrat*, April 25, 1895, p. 3; "Matthew Calloway," *Columbia Herald*, April 26, 1895, p. 2: "These sensational reports sent abroad are alike untrue, unfounded and injurious to the community."
1563. "The Execution," *Maury Democrat*, April 25, 1895, p. 3.
1564. Ibid.
1565. "Hanged!" *Nashville Banner*, April 25, 1895, p. 5.
1566. "Bob Ford Hangs Today," *Nashville American*, April 25, 1895, p. 4.
1567. "Hanged!" *Nashville Banner*, April 25, 1895, p. 5.
1568. Ibid.
1569. Ibid.
1570. Ibid.
1571. Ibid.
1572. "Mike King Hanged," *Nashville American*, May 18, 1895, p. 1.
1573. Ibid.
1574. Ibid.
1575. H. Clay Smith, *Dusty Bits of the Forgotten Past* (Huntsville, TN: Scott County Historical Society, 1985), p. 437.
1576. "Mike King Hanged," *Nashville American*, May 18, 1895, p. 1.
1577. Ibid.
1578. *Green v. State*, 97 Tenn. 50, 55–56 (1896).
1579. Ibid., p. 59.
1580. Ibid.
1581. Ibid., p. 62.
1582. "Bart Green Is Hanged," *Nashville Banner*, July 29, 1896, p. 1.
1583. *Green v. State*, 97 Tenn. 50, 65 (1896).
1584. Ibid.
1585. Ibid., p. 70.
1586. "Executed in Somerville," *Commercial Appeal*, August 14, 1896, p. 8.
1587. "A Constable Murdered," *Commercial Appeal*, August 10, 1895, p. 1; "Constable Holliday's Funeral," *Commercial Appeal*, August 11, 1895, p. 8.
1588. Minutes, Circuit Court of Fayette County, January Term, 1896, January 25, 30, 1896, pp. 15, 41, 42.
1589. Minutes, Supreme Court, Eastern Section, June 13, 1896, pp. 368–369.
1590. "Executed in Somerville," *Commercial Appeal*, August 14, 1896, p. 8.
1591. "Will Hang Today," *Columbia Herald*, November 27, 1896, p. 1.
1592. Ibid.
1593. "Murderer Frank Johnson," *Columbia Herald*, December 4, 1896, p. 1.
1594. Ibid.
1595. Ibid.
1596. "Hatfield Hanged!" *Knoxville Journal*, December 17, 1896, p. 1.
1597. What appears to be the handwritten draft of an opinion, asserting the facts as shown above, mentions that Hatfield was a "young man, with less than ordinary intelligence." *State v. Maried Hatfield*, Memorandum, Tennessee Supreme Court, Eastern Section, n.d. State Library and Archives Box 1569.
1598. Ibid.
1599. Sheila Weems Johnston, *Murders in East Tennessee* (Rogersville, TN: The Author, 2004), pp. 75–76, citing *Hancock Courier*, June 10, 1896, p. 1.
1600. Ibid.
1601. "Maried Hatfield Hung at 1 O'Clock," *The Sentinel* (Knoxville), December 16, 1896, p. 1.
1602. Ibid.
1603. *DeBerry v. State*, 99 Tenn. 207, 42 S.W. 31 (1897).
1604. Ibid., p. 32.
1605. M & V Code Section 5366; "Has Paid the Penalty," *Commercial Appeal*, August 20, 1897, p. 5: "It is the first case of record in Shelby County where a legal hanging has been for the crime mentioned."
1606. "Has Paid the Penalty," *Commercial Appeal*, August 20, 1897, p. 5.
1607. The law at that time, according to the newspapers, required the execution to take place between 10:00 A.M. and 2:00 P.M.
1608. Ibid.
1609. Ibid.
1610. Ibid.
1611. Ibid.
1612. "Harvey DeBerry Dies Today," *Commercial Appeal*, August 19, 1897, p. 5.
1613. "Cold-Blooded Murder," *The Comet* (Johnson City), July 15, 1897, p. 2.
1614. "Robert Sims," *The Comet* (Johnson City), November 16, 1897, p. 2.
1615. Bill of Exceptions, *Robert Sims v. State*, Tennessee Supreme Court, Eastern Section, n.d. [1897], pp. 21–22. State Library and Archives Box 1564.
1616. Ibid., p. 22.
1617. Bill of Exceptions, p. 13.
1618. Ibid., note 1.
1619. Ibid.
1620. "Miss Effie Boring Dead," *The Comet* (Johnson City), August 5, 1897, p. 2.
1621. Ibid.
1622. "Will Mays Hanged in Blountville, Dying Game," *Chattanooga Times*, November 18, 1897, p. 3.
1623. Bill of Exceptions, *William Mays and Robert Cole v. State*, Tennessee Supreme Court, Eastern Section [1897], p. 13. State Library and Archives Box 1546.
1624. Ibid., p. 18.
1625. Ibid., p. 22.
1626. "William Mays Hanged," *The Comet* (Johnson City), November 18, 1897, p. 2.
1627. Ibid.
1628. *Leach v. State*, 99 Tenn. 584, 42 S.W. 195 (1897).
1629. Ibid., p. 197.
1630. Ibid.
1631. "Mynatt Leach Hanged," *Clinton Gazette*, December 8, 1897, p. 1.
1632. *Leach v. State*, 99 Tenn. 584, 42 S.W. 195, 198 (1897). Citations to cases involving the trial court's power to order sentence of death.

1633. Ibid.
1634. "Mynatt Leach Hanged," *Clinton Gazette*, December 8, 1897, p. 1.
1635. Ibid.
1636. "Assassinated," *Tipton Weekly Record*, August 6, 1897, p. 3.
1637. "Confesses," *Tipton Weekly Record*, August 13, 1897, p. 3.
1638. "Johnson to Be Hanged Today," *Commercial Appeal*, December 17, 1897, p. 5.
1639. "Tipton County's Event: The Negro Will Johnson Hanged for an Atrocious Murder," *Commercial Appeal*, December 18, 1897, p. 1.
1640. "Dan Harris Was Game to the Last," *Nashville Banner*, March 23, 1898, p. 2.
1641. *Harris v. State*, 100 Tenn. 287, 292 (1898).
1642. *Harris v. State*, 100 Tenn. 287, 293 (1898).
1643. Ibid.
1644. Ibid., p. 292.
1645. Ibid., p. 294.
1646. "Only One Day Is Left Him," *Nashville Banner*, March 22, 1898, p. 5.
1647. "Dan Harris Was Game to the Last," *Nashville Banner*, March 23, 1898, p. 2.
1648. Ibid., p. 1.
1649. Ibid., p. 1.
1650. Ibid.
1651. "A Negro Hanged at Jackson," *Nashville Banner*, June 18, 1898, p. 1.
1652. Bill of Exceptions, *George Pearson v. State*, Supreme Court, Western Section, October 31, 1898, p. 18. State Library and Archives Box 676.
1653. Ibid., p. 18.
1654. Ibid., p. 21.
1655. "Full Confession of Hiram Hall," in Helen Bullard and Joseph Marshall Krechniak, *Cumberland County's First Hundred Years* (Crossville, TN: Centennial Committee, 1956), pp. 108–110.
1656. Donald F. Paine, "Murdering Wifey to Please Mom?—The Trial of Hiram Hall," *Tenn. B. Jr.* 44 (March 2008), pp. 29–30.
1657. Ibid.
1658. "Paid the Penalty for His Crime," *Knoxville Journal and Tribune*, April 14, 1899, p. 3.
1659. "Murderer Hall Dies Gamely," *Nashville Banner*, April 13, 1899, p. 1.
1660. Ibid., p. 2.
1661. Ibid., note 2, p. 30.
1662. E.W. Crozier, *The White-Caps: A History of the Organization in Sevier County* (Knoxville, TN: Bean, Warters & Gaut, 1899; reprint, 1989). The White Caps should not be confused with the Ku Klux Klan, a wholly different organization with little influence in East Tennessee. Whitecapping has its own causes, origins and history. Usually related to economic frustration and dominance of the local economy by outside interests, its Tennessee origin can be traced to the Regulator movement in early North Carolina. Other examples of Tennessee whitecapping include the Reelfoot Night Riders and the Black Patch Wars.
1663. "Begged in Vain for Their Lives," *Knoxville Journal*, December 30, 1896, p. 1. The archives of the University of Tennessee at Knoxville contain substantial holdings about the case, gathered by legal historian Donald Paine.
1664. E.W. Crozier, *The White-Caps: A History of the Organization in Sevier County* (Knoxville, TN: Bean, Warters & Gaut, 1899; reprint, 1989), p. 70. The discussion of the case has been taken from this book.
1665. "Catlett Tipton and Pleas Wynn Hanged," *Knoxville Journal and Tribune*, July 6, 1899, p. 1.
1666. Sheriff Maples claimed self-defense when facing the drunken brother. He was indicted but the case outcome is unknown. E.W. Crozier, *The White-Caps: A History of the Organization in Sevier County* (Knoxville, TN: Bean, Warters & Gaut, 1899; reprint, 1989), pp. 104–105.
1667. Laura's mother was present and heard Laura tell Rou the story. The mother, fearing consequences, had told Laura to confront Catlett personally, not to involve Rou. Ibid., p. 72.
1668. Ibid., p. 72.
1669. "Hope Given Up, Are Ready to Die," *Knoxville Journal and Tribune*, July 4, 1899, p. 4.
1670. "Hanged," *Vindicator* (Sevierville, Tennessee), July 12, 1899, p. 1.
1671. The reason was the reward which had reached five thousand dollars.
1672. "Hanged," *Vindicator*, July 12, 1899, p. 1.
1673. Ibid.
1674. Ibid.
1675. Ibid.
1676. There is some question whether those present, possibly excluding the wives, thought the men's professions of faith were genuine because they remained aloof to discussion of the afterlife. Pleas Wynn's wife, leaving him at the jail, had said, "Heaven will be our meeting place," but he did not respond. Instead, he assumed the "cold, defiant demeanor which has been characteristic of him throughout the prosecution and trial of the Whaley case, and wore this expression to his death": "Pleas Wynn and Catlett Tipton Hung," *Knoxville Journal and Tribune*, July 5, 1899, p. 1.
1677. "Pleas Wynn and Catlett Tipton Hung," *Knoxville Journal and Tribune*, July 5, 1899, p.1.
1678. *Whaley v. Catlett*, 103 Tenn. 347 (1899).
1679. "Three Murderers! Watson, Crain and Brown," *McMinnville New Era*, April 26, 1900, p. 1.
1680. Ibid.
1681. "To Satisfy the Law of a Life for a Life," *Nashville American*, April 22, 1900, p. 20 (Special Sunday edition).
1682. Ibid.
1683. "Expiated," *Nashville American*, April 26, 1900, p. 8.
1684. "The Law's Heavy Hand," *McMinnville New Era*, date unknown, but found between papers dated April 26 and May 17, 1900.
1685. "Expiated," *Nashville American*, April 26, 1900, p. 1.
1686. "Expiated," *Nashville American*, April 26, 1900, p. 8.
1687. Ibid.
1688. "Three Murderers! Watson, Crain and Brown," *McMinnville New Era*, April 26, 1900, p. 1.
1689. "The Law's Heavy Hand," *McMinnville New Era*, date unknown, p. 1.
1690. "Expiated," *Nashville American*, April 26, 1900, p. 8.
1691. "Three Murderers, Watson, Crain and Brown," *McMinnville New Era*, April 26, 1900, p. 1.
1692. "The Law's Heavy Hand," *McMinnville New Era*, date unknown, but found between papers dated April 26 and May 17, 1900.
1693. Ibid.
1694. "Expiated," *Nashville American*, April 26, 1900, p. 8.
1695. Ibid., note 2.
1696. "Ends of Justice," *Commercial Appeal*, September 19, 1900, p. 5.
1697. "Paid the Penalty," *Woodbury Press*, September 28, 1900, p. 1.
1698. Ibid.
1699. Brief of State, *State v. Dillard Warren*, Supreme Court, Middle Section, Dec. 11, 1899, pp. 1–3. State Library and Archives Box 1398. Warren's shoes had some "peculiar marks about them." Also, he had greased his shoes the morning after the killing, a traditional method of confusing blood hounds.
1700. "Dillard Warren Was Strangled," *Nashville American*, September 28, 1900, p. 10.
1701. "Paid the Penalty," *Woodbury Press*, September 28, 1900, p. 1.
1702. Ibid.
1703. Ibid.
1704. Ibid.
1705. One source says it was committed on June 2, 1900. "Hanged," *Nashville American*, July 19, 1901, p. 10.
1706. "Three Murderers from One Scaffold," *Nashville Banner*, July 18, 1901, p. 1.
1707. "Three Men to Die," July 18, 1901, *Nashville Banner*, p. 4.
1708. Ibid.
1709. Ibid.
1710. Bill of Exceptions, *Andrew (alias Duser) Thompson v. State* and *Babe Battise v. State*, Supreme Court, Middle Section, December term, 1900 [n.d.], State Library and Archives Record Box 2748.
1711. Bill of Exceptions, *Andrew (alias Duser) Thompson vs. State* and *Babe Battise vs. State, Supreme Court*, Middle Section, n.d., December Term, 1900. State Library and Archives Box 2748.
1712. Minutes, Supreme Court, March 21, 1901, p. 472. The executions were set by the Supreme Court for May 1, 1901. The governor granted two reprieves and heard personal appeals from Battise's mother and sister. "Hanging Thursday," *Nashville American*, July 16, 1901, p. 10; "Three Men to Die," *Nashville American*, July 18, 1901, p. 2.
1713. Brief for Babe Battise, *Babe Battise and Andrew (alias Duser) Thompson v. State*, Supreme Court, Middle Sec-

tion, n.d. State Library and Archives Box 2748.

1714. "Three Murderers from One Scaffold," *Nashville Banner*, July 18, 1901, p. 1, 2. This was not true.

1715. "Hanged," *Nashville American*, July 19, 1901, p. 10. The newspaper said that this was the only execution that had occurred in Nashville in four years. The last was Dan Harris who was hanged from the same gallows.

1716. Bill of Exceptions, *Nathan Caruthers v. State*, Supreme Court, Western Section, n.d., pp. 22–23. State Library and Archives Box 793.

1717. Ibid., p. 29.

1718. "Paid Penalty Composedly," *Commercial Appeal*, August 7, 1901, pp. 1, 12.

1719. "Last Day on Earth," *Commercial Appeal*, August 6, 1901, p. 4.

1720. Ibid.

1721. Ibid.

1722. Ibid.

1723. Ibid.

1724. Ibid.

1725. Ibid.

1726. "Hensley Hanged This Afternoon," *Nashville Banner*, February 6, 1902, p. 2.

1727. Ibid.

1728. "Confessed and Died," *Commercial Appeal*, July 31, 1902, p. 7.

1729. Ibid.

1730. "Ready for Victim," *Commercial Appeal*, July 29, 1902, p. 7.

1731. Ibid.

1732. "Confessed and Died," Commercial Appeal, July 31, 1902, p. 7.

1733. Benjamin S. Bradford, *Gunshots & Ropes: Five Wasted Lives* (Hazel Park, MI: The Author, 2004). This 130-page account includes background information, trial testimony and photographs of the victims and killers.

1734. Bill of Exceptions, *Joe Delp v. State*, Supreme Court, Middle Section [n.d.] p. 102. State Library and Archives Box 189.

1735. *Joe Delp v. State*, Opinion, Supreme Court, Middle Section, March 12, 1904, p. 4.

1736. Ibid., note 1, pp. 115–116. His lengthy written confession was released after his death.

1737. "Will Hill Hanged," *Free Press* (Bolivar), July 29, 1904, p. 1.

1738. Ibid.

1739. "Murderer Hanged," *Commercial Appeal*, July 29, 1904, p. 8.

1740. "Will Hill Hanged," *Free Press* (Bolivar), July 29, 1904, p. 1.

1741. Ibid.

1742. "Law Avenges Brutal Crime," *Commercial Appeal*, July 29, 1904, p. 8.

1743. *Ben Springfield v. State*, Memorandum opinion, n.d. State Library and Archives File WT-885.

1744. Ibid., p. 2.

1745. Ibid., p. 2.

1746. Mrs. Otis Trentham, "Some Notes on Crime and Punishment in Madison," *The Jackson Sun*, March 14, 1946, p. 4.

1747. Ibid.

1748. "Mystery Solved," *Jackson Daily Whig*, July 31, 1904, p. 8.

1749. One account says Scudder was "born in slavery," and was fifty-eight years old.

1750. *Jim Scudder v. State*, Opinion, Supreme Court, Middle Section, February 13, 1904, 5 pp. State Library and Archives Box 1618.

1751. Bill of Exceptions, *Jim Scudder v. State*, Tennessee Supreme Court, Middle Section, n.d., p. 28. State Library and Archives Box 1618.

1752. Ibid., p. 20.

1753. Ibid., p. 43.

1754. Ibid., p. 34.

1755. "Without Flinching," *Nashville American*, April 6, 1905, p. 10.

1756. "Murder in the First Degree," *Nashville Banner*, January 13, 1904, p. 8.

1757. "Prosecutor Drunk," *Nashville American*, January 14, 1904, p. 10.

1758. *Andrew Hibbert v. State*, Order, Supreme Court, n.d., December Term, 1904.

1759. "Double Execution," *Nashville American*, April 5, 1905, p. 4.

1760. "Without Flinching," *Nashville American*, April 6, 1905, p. 4.

1761. *A.M. Miles v. State*, Memorandum opinion, Supreme Court, Western Section, n.d., p. 2.

1762. Ibid.

1763. Ibid., pp. 2–3.

1764. Ibid., p. 3.

1765. Ibid., p. 4.

1766. Ibid., p. 8.

1767. Ibid., p. 8.

1768. "Not Daunted by the Scaffold," *Commercial Appeal*, July 17, 1905, p. 4.

1769. "Miles Losing His Nerve," *Commercial Appeal*, July 18, 1905, p. 4.

1770. "Retributive Justice Calls for Three Human Lives," *Commercial Appeal*, July 19, 1905, p. 5.

1771. "Fatal Was the Fight," *Commercial Appeal*, August 28, 1904, p. 5.

1772. "Toots Taylor Must Hang," *Commercial Appeal*, October 6, 1904, p. 5.

1773. "Not Daunted by Scaffold," *Commercial Appeal*, July 17, 1905, p. 5.

1774. "Retributive Justice Calls for Three Human Lives," *Commercial Appeal*, July 19, 1905, p. 5. Taylor was convicted, executed and buried under the name Toots Taylor, but it is unlikely this was his first name.

1775. Bill of Exceptions, *State v. Major Mills*, Supreme Court, Western Section, p. 14. State Library and Archives Box No. 925.

1776. Gill told the policeman he did not have a pistol nor try to draw one. Ibid., p. 23.

1777. Ibid., pp. 14, 19.

1778. *Major Mills v. State*, Memorandum opinion, Supreme Court, Western Division [1905], pp. 2–3.

1779. Ibid., p. 3.

1780. Ibid., p. 3.

1781. "Not Daunted by Scaffold," *Commercial Appeal*, July 17, 1905, p. 4.

1782. "Retributive Justice Calls for Three Human Lives," *Commercial Appeal*, July 19, 1905, p. 5.

1783. Ibid.

1784. "Took Their Last Supper," *Commercial Appeal*, August 18, 1905, p. 4.

1785. "Three Expiate Their Crimes," *Commercial Appeal*, August 19, 1905, p. 4.

1786. "Three Expiate Their Crimes," *Commercial Appeal*, August 18, 1905, p. 4.

1787. Ibid.

1788. *General Boone v. State*, Opinion, Supreme Court, Western Section, April Term, 1905, p. 7.

1789. It is likely she was violated with an object after her death, a fact expressed in the following language: "He was charged with an even greater crime, a crime so rare, so fearful in its purpose, so morbid and diabolical, that the mere mention of it precludes any discussion of the subject": "Three Expiate Their Crimes," *Commercial Appeal*, August 19, 1905, p. 4.

1790. Ibid., p. 7.

1791. Ibid., p. 9.

1792. Ibid.

1793. Ibid.

1794. "Three Expiate Their Crimes," *Commercial Appeal*, August 19, 1905, p. 4.

1795. Ibid.

1796. "Hill Indicted," *Commercial Appeal*, July 20, 1904, p. 4.

1797. Ibid.

1798. "Assassination," *Commercial Appeal*, July 17, 1903, p. 1. Hill was named as the shooter from the first because of his prior threats to Sarah growing out of their pending divorce. *John Hill v. State*, Memorandum Opinion, Supreme Court, Western Section [1904], p. 2.

1799. Brief on Behalf of State, *John Hill v. State*, Supreme Court, Western Section, n.d., pp. 2–4. State Library and Archives Box 897.

1800. Ibid., p. 4.

1801. Ibid., p. 7.

1802. "John Hill Hangs at Covington," *Commercial Appeal*, October 11, 1905, p. 9.

1803. "John Hill Hangs at Covington," *Commercial Appeal*, October 10, 1905, p. 9.

1804. Bill of Exceptions, *Finley Preston v. State*, Supreme Court, Eastern Section, [n.d.], p. 15. State Library and Archives Box 1422.

1805. Judge L.D. Miller, "Riddle of the Red Purse," *True Detective* (September 1946), pp. 60, 108.

1806. Bill of Exceptions, *Finley Preston v. State*, Eastern Section [n.d.], p. 15–16. State Library and Archives Box 1422.

1807. Ibid., p. 16.

1808. Ibid., p. 15.

1809. Minutes, Supreme Court, Eastern Section, October 4, 1905, pp. 147–148.

1810. *Preston v. State*, 115 Tenn. 343, 90 S.W. 856 (Tenn. 1905)

1811. "Preston Dies on Scaffold,"

Knoxville Journal and Tribune, November 8, 1905, p. 4.

1812. Judge L.D. Miller, "Riddle of the Red Purse," *True Detective* (September 1946), pp. 60, 108.

1813. *John Mitchell v. State*, Memorandum opinion, Supreme Court, Western Section, July 16, 1906, p. 4.

1814. Ibid., pp. 4–5.

1815. "John Mitchell Hanged," Commercial Appeal, August 9, 1906, p. 6.

1816. "Execution of Two Negroes," *Knoxville Journal and Tribune*, December 20, 1906, p. 6. This paper says a full description of the crime can be found in last Monday's *Journal and Tribune*.

1817. Bill of Exceptions, *State v. Drew and Will Upton*, Supreme Court, Eastern Section [n.d.], p. 21. State Library and Archives Box No. 1373.

1818. *Drew Upton and Will Upton v. State*, Supreme Court, Eastern Section, Minute Book, 1906–1907 (November 10, 1906), p. 222. Convictions affirmed, executions ordered December 20, 1906.

1819. "Drew and Will Upton Hanged for a Murder," *Knoxville Journal and Tribune*, December 21, 1906, p. 11.

1820. Ibid. This was the second and last legal hanging in Monroe County history.

1821. "Killing Follows a Craps Game," *Knoxville Journal and Tribune*, July 22, 1906, p. 5.

1822. *John Thomas v. State*, Opinion, Supreme Court, Eastern Section, November 17, 1906; 3 pp.

1823. "Thomas Is to Die Today," *Knoxville Journal and Tribune*, January 10, 1907, p. 12.

1824. "John Thomas Is Hanged in Knox County Jail," *Knoxville Journal and Tribune*, January 11, 1907, p.1.

1825. Ibid.

1826. The wife's relatives brought suit in Nashville to prevent Baird from selling property jointly owned with his wife. The Davidson County chancery court granted an injunction and the matter was settled with an agreement to sell the property with a portion of the proceeds going to the daughters, with the bulk given in payment to the lawyers. In June 1906, Baird failed in a legal bid to have the daughters live with his sister; they remained with his wife's sister. "William Baird Is Executed," *The Fayetteville Observer*, May 30, 1907, p. 1.

1827. The reference is to J. Samuel McCue, mayor of Charlottesville, Virginia, who was executed there in February 1905 for uxoricide.

1828. Ruling on Motion for New Trial, Transcript, *C.W. Baird v. The State*, Supreme Court, Middle Section, February Term, 1906. State Library and Archives, Box 1756.

1829. Transcript, *C.W. Baird v. The State*, Supreme Court, Middle Section, February Term, 1906. State Library and Archives Box 1756.

1830. "Asserts His Innocence in the Shadow of Death," *Nashville Banner*, May 24, 1907, pp. 1, 12. The governor granted two reprieves as friends petitioned for commutation to life imprisonment. *The Banner*, reporting the case from the *Fayetteville Observer*, reported Baird was the first white man legally hanged in Lincoln County since about 1840.

1831. "William Baird Is Executed," *The Fayetteville Observer*, May 30, 1907, p. 1. When the state attorney general's office refused to pay the fees for keeping Baird in the Nashville jail, the city was forced to ask the Supreme Court to award these costs, which it did.

1832. "William Baird Is Executed," *Nashville Tennessean*, May 25, 1907, p. 1.

1833. The doctor said, "Baird, in a few moments you will be in eternity and if you are guilty tell it. If you expect to meet your God, don't die with a lie on your lips." "William Baird Is Executed," *The Fayetteville Observer*, May 30, 1907, p. 1.

1834. Bill of Exceptions, *State v. Mose Walds*, Supreme Court, Western Section [n.d.], p. 4. State Library and Archives Box 979.

1835. "Mose Walds Expiates Crime," *Commercial Appeal*, November 1, 1907, p. 5.

1836. Ibid.

1837. Bill of Exceptions, *Bulah McGee, Bob Henderson and Dave Sherman v. State*, Supreme Court, Eastern Section, January 13, 1907, p. 39. State Library and Archives Box 1359. James Hicks and Henry Cleage had left the house prior to the killing.

1838. "He said it was enough to run him through the winter": pp. 36, 49.

1839. Ibid., p. 42.

1840. Ibid., p. 42.

1841. Ibid., p. 44.

1842. Ibid., p. 43.

1843. Ibid., p. 44.

1844. "Lucy Jackson, an aged negress who lived about fifty feet from the house of Bob Henderson, testified that towards morning of that night she heard a lumbering noise and loud talking in the house of Bob Henderson, that she then heard licks like somebody was hit, and someone cried out, 'Oh,' which was repeated, but not so loud. That she then heard several passing her house and a man groaning as they passed by. She thought someone was being carried by." *Bulah McGee, Bob Henderson and Dave Shearman v. State*, Opinion, Supreme Court, Eastern Section, October 5, 1907, p. 2.

1845. Bill of Exceptions, pp. 31–32.

1846. Ibid., p. 34.

1847. "Making up" the mail means putting the outbound mail on a device so that the mail bag can be "caught" automatically by the passing train and passed inside the car to the mail clerks working in the mail car. "Hanged for Foul Murder," *Nashville Banner*, November 26, 1907, p. 3.

1848. Bill of Exceptions, pp. 17–18,

1849. Ibid., p. 21.

1850. Ibid., p. 27. Henderson said, "That's my fire shovel." The bloody blanket was also found in the house.

1851. Ibid., p. 22.

1852. Ibid., p. 24.

1853. "Athens Murderer Pays the Penalty," *Nashville Tennessean*, November 27, 1907, p. 6.

1854. Bill of Exceptions, p. 56.

1855. Ibid., p. 59.

1856. This is the court's spelling of his name.

1857. *Bulah McGee, Bob Henderson and Dave Shearman v. State*, Opinion, Supreme Court, Eastern Section, October 5, 1907, p. 5.

1858. *Bulah McGee, Bob Henderson and Dave Shearman v. State*, Opinion, Supreme Court, Eastern Section, October 5, 1907, pp. 6–12.

1859. Ibid., p. 13.

1860. Ibid.

1861. Hugo Adam Bedau and Michael L. Radelet, "Miscarriages of Justice in Potentially Capital Cases," Stanford Legal Review 40 (1987): 21, 160.

1862. Michael L. Radelet, Hugo Adam Bedau, Constance E. Putnam, *In Spite of Innocence: The Ordeal of 400 Americans Wrongly Convicted of Crimes Punishable by Death* (Boston: Northeastern University Press, 1992), p. 346. Notwithstanding nearly five years to discover there was an appeal, this statement of the case is identical to the original that appeared in the Stanford Law Review.

1863. "Murderer Hangs for His Crime," *Nashville American*, November 27, 1907, p. 4. See also, "Bula Magee Hanged," *Commercial Appeal*, November 27, 1907, p. 3.

1864. Prison Record Book, Reg. No. 4042, Bob Henderson. His age was 25. Prison Record Book, Reg. No. 4043, Sam Sherman. His age was 29. His actual name was Dave Sherman.

1865. Pardon of David Sherman, M.R. Patterson, Governor, January 13, 1911, Book of Pardons, 1911, p. 22. State Library and Archives, GP 35, Reel 12, Container 40, File No. 5.

1866. James Summerville, *The Carmack-Cooper Shooting: Tennessee Politics Turns Violent, November 9, 1908* (Jefferson, NC: McFarland, 1994); Paul Franklin Bumpus, *Carmack: The Edward Ward Carmack Story* (Nashville: Alpha Graphics, 1977).

1867. Act of May 1, 1909, Chapter 500, Section 1, 1909 Public Acts.

1868. "Turner to Be Hanged Today," *The Daily Journal and Tribune*, January 11, 1908, p. 1.

1869. "Peter Turner Hanged in Knox County Jail," *The Daily Journal and Tribune*, January 12, 1908, p. 1.

1870. *Turner v. State*, 119 Tenn. 663, 108 S.W. 1139,1140 (1908).

1871. Ibid., pp. 1140–1141.

1872. Ibid., p. 1141. The Supreme Court's opinion reads as if this were the in-court testimony of the defendant, but a close reading of the opinion reveals this version was taken from a 14-page written memoir of the event, prepared by the defendant after the shooting but before he was taken into custody. He told the same story to several policemen and newspaper reporters.

1873. Ibid., p. 1141.

1874. "Peter Turner Hanged in Knox County Jail," *The Daily Journal and Tribune*, Jan. 12, 1908, p. 1.

1875. Ibid.

1876. Ibid.
1877. Ibid., p. 1142.
1878. "Turner to Be Hanged Today," *The Daily Journal and Tribune*," January 11, 1908, p. 1.
1879. "Peter Turner Hanged in Knox County Jail," *The Daily Journal and Tribune*, January 12, 1908, p. 1.
1880. Ibid.
1881. Memorandum Brief for State. *Arthur Pearson v. State*, Supreme Court, Middle Section [n.d.], p. 3. State Library and Archives Box 1778.
1882. Before he appeared, she had met another man, Montie Colley, and told him the same thing. Apparently, he did nothing, although he testified about her condition at the trial. The bicyclist's name was Chap Grimes and he testified about her condition too.
1883. Memorandum Brief for State, p. 7.
1884. Ibid., p. 6.
1885. Ibid., p. 3.
1886. Pearson had worked on the steamboat previously, and his explanation for being on the steamboat was conflicting. He was not a crew member at this time and it was surmised that he had come aboard the boat sometime on Sunday and remained in hiding.
1887. "Arthur Pearson Pays the Death Penalty," *Clifton Times*, February 9, 1908, p. 1.
1888. State's Memorandum, p. 10.
1889. Ibid., p. 9
1890. Brief for Defendant, *State of Tennessee v. Arthur Pearson*, Supreme Court, Middle Section [n.d.], p. 6. State Library and Archives Box 1778.
1891. Ibid., pp. 6–7.
1892. Ibid., p. 4.
1893. Ibid., p. 15.
1894. "Crime Charged to Carmack," *Journal and Tribune* (Knoxville), June 22, 1906, p. 5.
1895. Some newspaper accounts call the victim Herbert Thompson, others called him John (or Henry) Ipson or Itter. Thomas's nickname was "Ipsom" after the last name of the family that had owned his parents during slavery. The parents died when he was very small and they raised him. Hence, he was sometimes referred to as "Ipsom's boy," or "Ipsom's Henry."
1896. *John Carmack v. State*, Memorandum opinion, Supreme Court, Eastern Section, December 5, 1907, p. 1.
1897. Bill of Exceptions, *State v. John Carmack*, Supreme Court, Eastern Section [n.d.], p. 31. State Library and Archives Box 1362.
1898. Ibid., pp. 13–14.
1899. Ibid., p. 17.
1900. Ibid., p. 41.
1901. Ibid., p. 18.
1902. Bill of Exceptions, *State v. John Carmack*, Tennessee Supreme Court, Eastern Section, [n.d.], p. 62. State Library and Archives Box 1362.
1903. Ibid., p. 46.
1904. Ibid., pp. 50, 56. *John Carmack v. State*, Memorandum opinion, Supreme Court, Eastern Section, December 5, 1907, p. 17.
1905. Ibid., p. 79.
1906. Ibid., p. 80. The officer denied giving him any liquor.
1907. This unclear sentence is taken directly from the Bill of Exceptions.
1908. Ibid., note 6, p. 101.
1909. Ibid., pp. 79–80, 86. He was a "brown skinned negro with a gold tooth": p. 89.
1910. Ibid., p. 75.
1911. *John Carmack v. State*, Memorandum opinion, Supreme Court, Eastern Section, December 5, 1907, pp. 9–10.
1912. Ibid.
1913. Minutes, Supreme Court, December 5, 1907, *John Carmack v. State*, East Tennessee Minute Book 1906–1907, p. 574. Some said 8:00 A.M. and 4:00 P.M.
1914. "Two Murderers Will Hang Today," *Nashville Tennessean*, February 27, 1908, p. 10.
1915. "Not a Tremor as He Faces Death," *Nashville Tennessean*, February 28, 1908, p. 1, 2.
1916. "Not a Tremor as He Faces Death," *Nashville Tennessean*, February 28, 1908, p. 1.
1917. *Ed Turner v. State*, Opinion, Supreme Court, Eastern Section, November 30, 1907, p. 13b.
1918. Ibid., p. 2.
1919. Because he admitted that letter was his, he was cross-examined about its contents, which included the statement, "I am staying at the Germania Hotel," and the statement, "Ed, this is a terrible life to live; I cannot stay here." Ibid., p. 13.
1920. Ibid., p. 3.
1921. Ibid., p. 4.
1922. Ibid., p. 10.
1923. Ibid., p. 4.
1924. Ibid., p. 13
1925. Ibid., p. 13.
1926. Ibid., p. 13d.
1927. Ibid., p. 13d.
1928. Ibid., p. 13e.
1929. Ibid., p. 4. A "sporting house" is a place of prostitution.
1930. Ibid., pp. 13, 18.
1931. "Hanging of Ed Turner Set for Tomorrow," *Chattanooga Star*, February 26, 1908, p. 1.
1932. "Not a Tremor as He Faces Death," *Nashville Tennessean*, February 28, 1908, p. 1.
1933. "Ed Turner's Execution," *Chattanooga Times*, February 28, 1908, p. 1.
1934. Mark Curriden and Leroy Phillips, Jr., *Contempt of Court* (New York: Faber & Faber, 1999).
1935. "Bloody Chapter in Local Criminal Annals," *Daily Journal and Tribune*, July 15, 1906, p. 1; "John M'Pherson Still at Large," *Daily Journal and Tribune*, July 17, 1906, p. 1; "M'Pherson Due to Be Hanged Today Unless Governor Again Intervenes," *Daily Journal and Tribune*, March 23, 1908, p. 1; "John M'Pherson Dies for Walker's Murder," *Daily Journal and Tribune*, March 24, 1908, p. 1.
1936. "John M'Pherson Pays Penalty," *Nashville Banner*, March 23, 1908, p. 8. "McPherson has always frequented the Bowery and had been arrested for many misdemeanors."
1937. *John McPherson v. State*, Opinion, Supreme Court, Eastern Section, October 19, 1907, p. 19.
1938. John McPherson said his father's buggy was standing still and was simply run into by Dr. Waddell. He said that when he pushed the horse back out of the way, Waddell hit him over the head with his whip. He admitted hitting Waddell with his pistol, but when he realized who it was, helped him back into his buggy. Ibid., p. 4.
1939. Ibid., p. 21.
1940. Ibid., p. 22.
1941. Ibid., pp. 25–27.
1942. "For Her Son's Life," *Nashville Tennessean*, March 23, 1908, p. 5.
1943. "John M'Pherson Pays the Penalty," *Nashville Banner*, March 23, 1908, p. 8. "John McPherson is the first white man that has been hanged in Knox County since 1875."
1944. "Thou Shalt Not Kill" (editorial), *Nashville Tennessean*, March 21, 1908, p. 4.
1945. Ibid.
1946. "His Composure Is Maintained," *Nashville Tennessean*, March 24, 1908, p. 3.
1947. "Henry Johnson to Pay Penalty," *Commercial Appeal*, August 8, 1908, p. 8.
1948. "Little Girl Is Assaulted," *Commercial Appeal*, October 10, 1907, p. 7.
1949. Ibid. Another version says the mother went looking for Ida May and saw her coming from the back room crying.
1950. "Hangs Man He Says Innocent," *Memphis News Scimitar*, August 9, 1908, p. 1.
1951. Ibid., note 2.
1952. In the Matter of Citation of R.H. Prescott, Affidavit of G.A. Griffith, June 4, 1908.
1953. Ibid.
1954. Margaret Vandiver, *Lethal Punishment: Lynchings and Legal Executions in the South* (New Brunswick, NJ: Rutgers University Press, 2006), pp. 65–67.
1955. "Henry Johnson Faces Trial," *Commercial Appeal*, October 19, 1907, p. 5.
1956. "Henry Johnson Found Guilty," *Commercial Appeal*, October 20, 1907, p. 8.
1957. *Henry Johnson v. State*, Memorandum Opinion, Supreme Court at Jackson, April Term, 1908, July 1, 1908, p. 2. The court issued an order on June 2, 1908, giving Prescott until June 6 to show cause why he should not be "punished for his dereliction of duty on behalf of his client, Henry Johnson." In the Matter of R. H. Prescott, Tennessee Supreme Court, Western Division, June 2, 1908. State Library and Archives, Western Division, Box 1033.
1958. Ibid., pp. 4–5.
1959. Ibid., 1.
1960. This has been referred to as "Substance of Testimony," by Vandiver, p. 223. She says that the appellate brief filed by Spraggins was "unusually thorough and detailed in comparison with the pleadings often filed in capital cases of the time": p. 67.
1961. "Substance of Testimony," pp. 2–3.

1962. "Substance of Testimony," p. 3.
1963. This included the father's two adult brothers, the grandfather, and two sons-in-law.
1964. Ibid., p. 4.
1965. Ibid., p. 5.
1966. Ibid., p. 6.
1967. Ibid., p. 6.
1968. Ibid., p. 13.
1969. "Johnson Will Hang Saturday," *Commercial Appeal*, August 6, 1908, p. 4.
1970. *State v. Henry Johnson*, Affidavit of R. H. Prescott, June 10, 1908, p. 1.
1971. Affidavit of G.A. Griffin, June 4, 1908, p. 1–2.
1972. Ibid.
1973. Petition to Re-Hear, no date, 6 pp.
1974. Brief and Argument on Behalf of the Petitioner, Henry Johnson, for a Re-Hearing, no date, 6 pp. "Any person who shall carnally know and abuse a female under the age of twelve years shall upon conviction, be punished as in the case of rape." Chapter 12, Public Acts of 1901.
1975. "Henry Johnson to Pay Penalty," *Commercial Appeal*, August 8, 1908, p. 6.
1976. Ibid.
1977. "Hangs Man He Says Innocent," *Memphis Press Scimitar*, August 9, 1908, p. 1.
1978. "Johnson Pays the Penalty," *Commercial Appeal*, August 9, 1908, p. 8.
1979. Ibid., note 6, p. 67.
1980. Ibid.
1981. Ibid., note 6, p. 67.
1982. Verdict, *State v. Henry Johnson*, Shelby Criminal Court, October 19, 1907.
1983. "Hangs Man He Says Innocent," *Memphis News Scimitar*, August 9, 1908, p. 1.
1984. "Affidavit of Frank L. Monteverde," June 28, 1908, p. 2.
1985. "Sheriff Monteverde Refuses to Enforce the Law," *Memphis News-Scimitar*, August 1, 1908 p. 5.
1986. Shannon's Code, Section 6455, Public Acts of 1893, Chapter 36: "Any person who shall carnally know and abuse a female under the age of twelve years shall on conviction be punished as in the case of rape."
1987. Shannon's Code, Section 6458, Public Acts of 1893, Chapter 129: "Any person who shall commit an assault and better upon a female under the age of ten years, with the intent to unlawfully and carnally know her, shall, on conviction, be punished as in case of rape."
1988. *DeBerry v. State*, 99 Tenn. 207, 42 S.W. 31 (1897). Leo Temples was also executed under this statute. *Temple v. State*, 127 Tenn. 429, 155 S.W. 388 (1913).
1989. "Little Girl Is Assaulted," *Commercial Appeal*, October 10, 1907, p. 7.
1990. *D.D. Edwards v. State*, Memorandum Opinion, Supreme Court, Eastern Section, October 31, 1908, pp. 1–2. State Library and Archives Box 1328.
1991. Ibid., pp. 4–5.
1992. Ibid., pp. 9–11.
1993. "Seven Weeks for Edwards," *Chattanooga Daily Times*, December 9, 1908, p. 7.
1994. "Happy Only When Eating," *Chattanooga Daily Times*, January 23, 1909, p. 1.
1995. "D.D. Edwards Is Executed," *Chattanooga Daily Times*, January 29, 1909, p. 5.
1996. "Execution for Edwards," *Chattanooga Daily Times*, January 28, 1909, p. 7.
1997. "D.D. Edwards Is Executed," *Chattanooga Daily Times*, January 29, 1909, p. 5.
1998. "Execution for Edwards," *Chattanooga Daily Times*, January 28, 1909, p. 7.
1999. "D.D. Edwards Is Executed," *Chattanooga Daily Times*, January 29, 1909, p. 5.
2000. Ibid.
2001. Fred Hixon, "Hamilton County Hangings — Legal, Otherwise," *Chattanooga Times*, Dec. 11, 1932, p. 4. It is unlikely that Edwards used the word "peas." This was likely a journalistic usage designed to protect readers' sensibilities.
2002. *State v. Frank Gilbreath*, col., Opinion, Supreme Court, Middle Section, January 23, 1909, p. 9. This opinion was written by B.D. Bell.
2003. She had earlier in the week given him a note to come to the cabin that night.
2004. Ibid., pp. 8–9.
2005. Emma Wright and Boyd Buchanan.
2006. Ibid., p. 10.
2007. Ibid., p. 16.
2008. "Paid the Penalty," *Fayetteville Observer*, March 4, 1909, p. 3.
2009. "Paid the Penalty," *Fayetteville Observer*, March 3, 1909, p. 3.
2010. Ibid.
2011. *State v. John Gilbreath*, Opinion, Supreme Court, Middle Section, July 26, 1901, pp. 5–9.
2012. Ibid., pp. 88. Judge Wilkes dissented, saying the lawyers had not time to prepare for the case and the proof did not "exclude the idea of an accidental killing beyond a reasonable doubt": p. 89.
2013. "Sentence Commuted," *Fayetteville Observer*, March 14, 1901, p. 2.
2014. *William Mitchell v. State*, Memorandum Opinion, Supreme Court, Middle Section, January 30, 1909, pp. 1–2.
2015. Hindman was very popular and with suspicion focusing immediately on the missing Mitchell, when he was arrested, a mob formed to lynch him.
2016. Section 64-39 of Shannon's Code.
2017. "Saw Sun for Last Time," *Nashville American*, October 1, 1909, p. 8.
2018. "No Faltering at Scaffold," *Nashville Banner*, October 1, 1909, p. 1.
2019. "Mitchell and Palmer Pay the Death Penalty," *Nashville Tennessean*, October 2, 1909, p. 1.
2020. The Rev. Nolen was not allowed to watch the execution because he was not an ordained minister.
2021. "No Faltering on Scaffold," *Nashville Banner*, October 1, 1909, p. 12.
2022. Ibid.
2023. Reply Brief for the State, *Cecil Palmer v. State*, Supreme Court, Middle Section [n.d.], p. 7; Bill of Exceptions, *Cecil Palmer v. State*, Supreme Court, Middle Section, October 14, 1908. State Library and Archives Box No. 1851.
2024. *Palmer v. State*, 121 Tenn. 465, 118 S.W.1022 (1908). This is apparently still the law today. The opinion did not discuss the facts of the case. A recently passed statute said the same. Acts of 1899, Chapter 383.
2025. Section 7253, Shannon's Code.
2026. Ibid.
2027. Ibid.
2028. The point of this argument was to insist that the case be carried over to the December 1909 term, giving Palmer a few more months of life.
2029. *Cecil Palmer v. State*, opinion, Supreme Court, December Term, 1908, July 27, 1909, p.3.
2030. "Saw Sun for Last Time," *Nashville American*, October 1, 1909, p. 8.
2031. "Virgil Lee Is Respited," *Nashville American*, September 30, 1909, p. 16.
2032. "Mitchell and Palmer Hang," *Nashville American*, October 2, 1909, p. 10; "Mitchell and Palmer Pay the Death Penalty," *Nashville Tennessean*, October 2, 1909, p. 1.
2033. "No Faltering on Scaffold," *Nashville Banner*, October 1, 1909, p. 12.
2034. "Item," *Decatur Herald*, August 6, 1909, p. 2; "Bryce McDonald, Col., Sentenced to Hang," *Decatur Herald*, November 5, 1909, p. 1.
2035. "Brice McDonald in Shadow of Gallows," *Nashville Tennessean and Nashville American*, October 2, 1910, p. 10.
2036. "Meets Death Without Fear," *Nashville Banner*, October 3, 1910, p. 1.
2037. "Brice M'Donald in Shadow of Gallows," *Nashville Tennessean and Nashville American*, October 2, 1910, p. 10.
2038. Ibid.
2039. "Negroes Shoot and Rob Victim," *Commercial Appeal*, December 18, 1908, p. 1.
2040. "Negro Witnessed Hold-Up," *Commercial Appeal*, December 20, 1908, p. 8.
2041. "Negro Suspect Arrested," *Commercial Appeal*, December 23, 1908, p. 4.
2042. "Collins and Casson Guilty," *Commercial Appeal*, November 25, 1909, p. 9.
2043. Judgment, *Mack Collins alias River George and John Casson v. State*, Tennessee Supreme Court, Western Division, June 25, 1910, p. 3.
2044. "Protests His Innocence," *Nashville American*, August 6, 1910, p. 6.
2045. "Triple Hanging Takes Place," *Nashville Banner*, November 9, 1910, p. 8.
2046. Brief for Plaintiff-in-Error, *M.B. Cook v. State*, Supreme Court, Western Section, April 10, 1910, p. 3. State Library and Archives Box 3001.
2047. Statement of the Case, Brief for Plaintiff-in-Error, *M.B. Cook v. State*, Western Section, April 10, 1910, p. 3.
2048. "Triple Hanging Takes Place," *Nashville Banner*, November 9, 1910.
2049. "Trio Paid the Last Penalty,"

Nashville Tennessean and Nashville American, Nov. 10, 1910, p. 2.
2050. Ibid., note 2.
2051. *Love Bond v. State*, Memorandum opinion, Supreme Court, Western Section, [n.d.], 17 pp. Found in Court of Appeals, 1910, I-D-5, Box 25, Folder 17. State Library and Archives.
2052. Ibid., p. 4.
2053. Ibid., p. 7.
2054. Ibid., p. 7.
2055. Ibid., p. 8.
2056. "Love Bond," *Bolivar Bulletin*, November 11, 1910, p. 2; "Love Bond to Die," *Hardeman Free Press*, November 10, 1910, p. 1.
2057. "Love Bond to Die," *Hardeman Free Press*, November 10, 1910, p. 1.
2058. "Triple Hanging Takes Place," *Nashville Banner*, November 9, 1910, p. 8.
2059. "Pays for Penalty for His Crime," *Nashville Banner*, March 15, 1922, p. 9.
2060. Bill of Exceptions, *State v. Napper (T.B.) Byrom*, Supreme Court, Middle Section, October 10, 1910. State Library and Archives Box 1899.
2061. *T.F. alias Naper Byrom v. State*, Opinion, Supreme Court, Middle Section, February 7, 1911, p. 4. The spelling is the supreme court's.
2062. Ibid., p. 5.
2063. Ibid., p. 18.
2064. Ibid., pp. 15–18.
2065. "'Napper' Byrom Hangs at Sunup," *Nashville Tennessean*, March 15, 1911, p. 1.
2066. "Pays Penalty for His Crime," *Nashville Banner*, March 15, 1911, p. 9.
2067. Ibid.
2068. "Upon the Gallows Negro Expiates Crime of Murder," *Nashville Tennessean*, November 17, 1911, p. 12.
2069. Brief for the State, *Robert Cooke v. State*, Supreme Court, Eastern Section, September 15, 1911, p. 2. State Library and Archives Box 1176.
2070. Ibid.
2071. "Negro's Fate Now in Governor's Hands," *Nashville Tennessean*, November 14, 1911, p. 7.
2072. "Robert Cook Hanged at State Prison," *Nashville Banner*, November 18, 1911, p. 2.
2073. One version says that he struck her with the ax when she chased him after the rape. The most likely sequence is that she was struck by the ax, raped, then managed to come outside and was found in the yard. "Outrage," *Tennessean*, October 9, 1911, p. 1.
2074. "Negro Hangs at State Prison," *Nashville Banner*, January 13, 1912, p. 1.
2075. Ibid.
2076. Steven V. Ash, comp., *Messages of the Governors of Tennessee, 1907–1921*, vol. 9 (Nashville: Tennessee Historical Commission, 1990), p. 478.
2077. "Negro Convicted of Rape of White Woman at Trenton," *Nashville Tennessean*, Dec. 10, 1911, p. 9.
2078. "Negro Rapist Swings for Crime at Dawn," *Nashville Tennessean*, January 13, 1912, p. 5.
2079. Stephen V. Ash, comp., *Messages of the Governors of Tennessee, 1907–1921*, vol. 9 (Nashville: Tennessee Historical Commission, 1990), p. 380–381. To frustrate lynchers, who took accused but untried criminals out of jails, the governor proposed a law which called for the summary removal of sheriffs who permit lynching of their prisoners "through cowardice, connivance or neglect."
2080. "Along the Color Line," *The Crisis* 3 (June 1912): 101.
2081. Ibid.
2082. Ibid.
2083. *George Shelton and John Bailey v. State*, Memorandum opinion, Supreme Court, Western Section, June 1, 1912, p. 2.
2084. Ibid., p. 5.
2085. Ibid., pp. 9–10.
2086. Ibid., p. 10
2087. Ibid., pp. 10–11.
2088. Petition for Clemency [n.d.], Papers of Governor Ben Hooper, State Library and Archives Box 24.
2089. Ibid.
2090. Letter to Gov. Hooper from N.B. Barkman, July 5, 1912, Papers of Governor Ben Hooper, State Library and Archives Box 24.
2091. "Governor Will Not Interfere," *Nashville Banner*, July 17, 1912, p. 1.
2092. "Condemned Men Pass to Eternity Without a Tremor," *Tennessean and Nashville American*, July 27, 1912, p. 9; "Two Men Pay Death Penalty on Scaffold at State Prison," *Nashville Banner*, July 26, 1912, p. 7; "Death Trap Sprung at Daybreak for Two Murderers," *Nashville American*, July 26, 1912, pp. 1, 19.
2093. "Along the Color Line," *The Crisis* 3 (June 1912): 101; "Along the Color Line," *The Crisis* 4 (September 1912): 221. Neither the NAACP nor DuBois opposed the death penalty in 1912.
2094. "Along the Color Line," 3 *The Crisis* (February 1912): 144.
2095. The length of her sentence is unknown. Bascom Miller was described as "demented," and Senter's punishment is unknown.
2096. "G.W. Rose Dies Upon Scaffold," *Nashville Banner*, August 26, 1912, p. 13.
2097. Ibid.
2098. "In Prison Attire, Relatives Follow Rose to Grave," *Nashville Tennessean*, August 26, 1912, p. 1.
2099. "G.W. Rose Dies Upon Scaffold," *Nashville Banner*, August 26, 1912, p. 1.
2100. Ibid.
2101. Ibid.
2102. "In Prison Attire, Relatives Follow Rose to Grave," *Nashville Tennessean*, August 27, 1912, p. 1.
2103. "Miss Mary Ewell of LaGrange Found Dead in Home," *Fayetteville Falcon*, March 15, 1912, p. 4.
2104. Ibid.
2105. "Dunlap Said He Was Guilty," *Nashville Banner*, September 4, 1912, p. 9.
2106. "Sid Dunlap Pays Penalty of Crime on Prison Gallows," *Nashville Tennessean*, September 5, 1912, p. 2.
2107. Ibid.
2108. "Temple Is Convicted; The Penalty Death," *Commercial Appeal*, September 23, 1912, p. 7. T.F. Queen, the father; Clara, the victim and her siblings Carl, Morris, Nora and Lenora Queen testified for the state.
2109. Ibid.
2110. Consensual sex with a minor is commonly known, in laymen's terms, as "statutory rape." According to W.E.B. DuBois, the age of consent was set very low in the South (age 12 in Tennessee and Mississippi, age 10 in Georgia, North Carolina and Florida) as a method of "damning the poor and helpless by making a distinction between 'chaste' and 'unchaste' children, the latter being given the least protection": "Along the Color Line," *The Crisis* 7 (July 1916): 165.
2111. Jury Instructions, *State of Tennessee v. Leo Temple*, Shelby County Circuit No. 2261.
2112. Affidavit of Defendant for a New Trial, *State of Tennessee v. Leo Temple*, Shelby County Circuit Court No. 2261. The file contains no bill of exceptions (transcript).
2113. Temple's trial and initial appeal was handled by P.M.D. Dowdall. The later appeal was handled by a young Nashville lawyer, J. Edward Moseley, who became interested in the case through the intervention of a minister.
2114. *Temple v. State*, 127 Tenn. 429, 155 S.W. 388 (1913).
2115. The father had retained a private prosecutor to press the case, a common practice in high profile cases well into the 1960s. Temple was sentenced on September 28, 1912.
2116. Ibid., note 5.
2117. "Hooper Refuses Mercy in Leo Temple Case," *Commercial Appeal*, December 18, 1912, p. 1.
2118. "Leo Temple, Negro Assaulter, Is Hanged," *Commercial Appeal*, December 20, 1912, p. 12.
2119. Ibid., note 7, p. 389. The statute was Shannon's Code Section 7217.
2120. Ibid., p. 389.
2121. Ibid.
2122. Ibid.
2123. "Brutal Murder Committed in Heart of City," *Nashville Tennessean*, August 7, 1909, p. 1.
2124. "State's Theory in Murder of Henning Develops in Trial," *Nashville Tennessean*, Jan. 10, 1912, p. 10.
2125. "Coils Tightening About Pat Malloy in Murder Trial," *Nashville Tennessean*, Jan. 11, 1912, p. 16.
2126. *Pat (alias Andrew) Malloy v. State*, Memorandum opinion, Supreme Court, Middle Section, March 8, 1913, p. 10.
2127. "Coils Tightening About Pat Malloy in Murder Trial," *Nashville Tennessean*, January 11, 1912, p. 16.
2128. Ibid., pp. 11, 12.
2129. "Pat Malloy Hangs for Henning Murder," *Nashville Tennessean*, May 9, 1913, p. 1.
2130. Ibid.
2131. Ibid.
2132. Robert L. Pigue, "Negro Dies in Electric Chair," *Nashville Banner*, July 13, 1916, p. 13.

2133. *State v. Julius Morgan*, Opinion, Supreme Court, Western Section, June 3, 1916. 3 pp.
2134. Ibid., p. 3, citing *Watson v. State*, 133 Tenn. 198 (1915).
2135. Ibid., p. 3.
2136. "Governor Visits Condemned Negro," *Nashville Banner*, July 10, 1916, p. 1.
2137. *State v. Julius Morgan*, Opinion, Supreme Court, Western Section, June 3, 1916, p. 3. The opinion was written by Judge Buchanon.
2138. "Death Chair's First Victim," *Nashville Tennessean*, July 13, 1916, p. 9.
2139. Robert L. Pigue, "Negro Dies in Electric Chair," *Nashville Banner*, July 13, 1916, p. 13.
2140. Ibid.
2141. "Charged with Foul Crime," *Pulaski Citizen*, September 6, 1917, p. 2.
2142. A type of brassiere.
2143. Brief for the State, *State v. J.D. Williams and Eddie Allsup*, Supreme Court, Middle Section, February 23, 1918, p. 3–4. State Library and Archives Box 2161.
2144. Ibid., p. 4.
2145. "Negroes Executed," *The Pulaski Citizen*, July 11, 1918, p. 4.
2146. Ibid., note 1, p. 6.
2147. Ibid., note 1, p. 8.
2148. "Negroes Executed," *The Pulaski Citizen*, July 11, 1918, p. 4.
2149. Ibid.
2150. "An Orderly Trial," *Pulaski Citizen*, October 25, 1907, p. 2.
2151. Assignments of Error, Brief and Argument for Defendants, *State of Tennessee v. J.D. Williams and Eddie James Allsup*, Supreme Court, Middle Section [n.d.], p. 11. State Library and Archives Box 2161.
2152. Ibid., note 2, p. 11.
2153. The compiled unpublished decisions of the Tennessee Supreme Court, Middle Section, for the December term 1918 have been missing for several years.
2154. "Negro Rapists Die in Chair," *Nashville Banner*, July 8, 1918, p. 4.
2155. Ibid.
2156. Bill of Exceptions, *State v. Frank Ewing*, Supreme Court, Middle Section, January 9, 1918, p. 18. State Library and Archives Box 2174.
2157. Brief of State, *Frank Ewing v. State*, Supreme Court, Middle Section, December Term, 1918, p. 4. State Library and Archives Box 2174.
2158. Affidavit of Mrs. J.M. Summers, 1919. Correspondence files of Governor A. H. Roberts, box 60, file 3. State Library and Archives.
2159. Margaret Vandiver, "More Than a Reasonable Doubt: The Trial and Execution of Frank Ewing," in Saundra D. Westervelt and John A. Humphrey, eds., *Wrongly Convicted: Perspectives on Failed Justice*. (New Brunswick, NJ: Rutgers University Press, 2001), pp. 135–153. Vandiver assumed Ewing came to the rape scene by car. By his admission, he came by the Tennessee Central Railroad, a commuter train, which closed in 1951. The rail bed is now largely obliterated by an Interstate highway.
2160. Bill of Exceptions, *State v. Frank Ewing*, Supreme Court, Middle Section, January 9, 1918, p.26. State Library and Archives Box 2174.
2161. Ibid.
2162. The term used at that time was "alienist."
2163. Letter from Thomas H. Harris, M.D., to Gov. A. H. Roberts, March 25, 1919. Roberts Papers 0038-0018-1738-1741. State Library and Archives.
2164. Message Re: Frank Ewing, n.d. Roberts Papers 0038-0018-1754-1755. State Library and Archives.
2165. "Frank Ewing Dies in Electric Chair," *Nashville Banner*, May 21, 1919, p. 6.
2166. *Winnifred Walker v. State*, Opinion, Supreme Court, Eastern Section, November 15, 1919, p. 4.
2167. Ibid.
2168. Ibid., p. 5.
2169. The statutory authority was Section 6455 of Shannon's Code.
2170. Chapter 36, Public Acts of 1919.
2171. "The offense of unlawfully and carnally abusing a female child under the prescribed age is not rape, but only punishable as rape." Citing *Hill v. State*, 3 Heisk, 319.
2172. Ibid., p. 7. This argument is not clear. Apparently, Walker's counsel was arguing that if the first count was *not* proven, then the second count failed because of the merger doctrine.
2173. Ibid.
2174. "Girl's Assailant Is Electrocuted," *Nashville Tennessean*, January 9, 1920, p. 13; "Negro Awaiting Chair Is Calm," *Nashville Tennessean*, January 8, 1920, p. 6.
2175. "Murder of Sergeant Brinkley Is Avenged," *Commercial Appeal*, September 4, 1920, p. 5.
2176. Ibid.
2177. *Taylor Neal and C.J. Jackson v. State*, Memorandum opinion, Supreme Court, Eastern Division, [n.d.] (1919–20), pp. 173–174.
2178. Ibid., p. 183.
2179. Ibid., p. 182.
2180. "Negroes Die in Electric Chair," *Evening Tennessean*, August 3, 1921, p. 4.
2181. "Everything Is 'Peaches' Say Negroes on Very Eve of Death," *Nashville Banner*, August 2, 1921, p. 2.
2182. "Two Negroes Pay Death Penalty at State Penitentiary," *Nashville Tennessean*, August 4, 1921, p. 1.
2183. "Negroes Die in Electric Chair," *Evening Tennessean*, August 3, 1921, p. 4.
2184. "Horrible Murder," *Savannah Courier*, April 30, 1920, p. 1.
2185. "Negroes Convicted," *Savannah Courier*, May 7, 1920, p. 1.
2186. "Justice Was Swift in '20s Brutal Murder," *The Courier* (Savannah), November 3, 1983, p. 4.
2187. "Knife Found in Cell of Gholson; Three Die Today," *Nashville Tennessean*, August 17, 1921, p. 1.
2188. "Waiting Death, Negroes Talk," *Nashville Banner*, August 16, 1921, p. 4.
2189. Ibid., p. 4.
2190. Ibid. See, "Negro Reported to Have Confessed," *Nashville Banner*, August 15, 1921, p. 1.
2191. "Hardin County Sheriff," *Nashville Tennessean*, August 17, 1921, p. 3.
2192. "Negroes Go to Chair Quietly," *Nashville Banner*, August 17, 1921, p. 1.
2193. "Waiting Death, Negroes Talk," *Nashville Banner*, August 16, 1921, p. 1.
2194. *Hamp Golhston, alias Will Brown v. State*, Opinion, Supreme Court, Western Section, March 21, 1921, p. 4. There is no consistent spelling of Gohlston's name, the Tennessee Supreme Court twice spelling it differently and the newspaper with its own spelling, Gholson.
2195. Acts of 1915, Chapter 181: "That the death penalty as punishment for crime be, and the same is hereby abolished, and in lieu thereof, and as a substitute therefor, shall be the punishment of life imprisonment in the State penitentiary; provided, that this act shall not interfere with the operation of statutes providing for the death penalty as punishment for the offense of rape; and provided further, that the provisions of this act shall not apply to convicts serving life terms in the State penitentiary who shall be convicted of any offense, now punishable under the law by death by electrocution."
2196. Acts of 1917, Chapter 14. The statute contained no caption and simply said, "That House Bill No. 94, chapter 181 of the Regular Session of 1915, be and the same is hereby repealed."
2197. Acts of 1919, Chapter 5, section 1. "When any person is convicted of the crime of murder in the first degree, or as an accessory before the fact of such a crime, it shall be the duty of the jury convicting him in their verdict to fix punishment, which punishment shall be death in the mode prescribed by law for the infliction of the death penalty in capital cases, or the jury may, if they are of the opinion that there are mitigating circumstances, fix the punishment at imprisonment in the penitentiary for life, or for some period over twenty years." Section 3 of this act also re-repealed the Bowers Act to cure the possible defect in the 1917 statute.
2198. *Gohlston v. State*, 143 Tenn. 126, 127 (1919).
2199. *Hamp Gohlston alias Will Brown v. State*, Opinion, Supreme Court, Western Section, March 21, 1921, pp. 5–7.
2200. "Negroes Go to Chair Quietly, Killed 6, Gholson Says," *Nashville Banner*, August 17, 1921, p. 1.
2201. Minutes, *State v. John Green*, Circuit Court, Washington County, December 23, 1921, pp. 138–140. There was no newspaper in Jonesboro at the time and no other newspapers in the area seem to have reported the trial.
2202. "Green, Murderer, Is Still at Large," *Kingsport Times*, July 22, 1921, p. 4.
2203. "Men Facing Chair Show Stoicism as Doom Draws Near," *Nashville Tennessean*, February 16, 1922, p. 1, 10.

2204. "John Green Dies in Electric Chair When Day Dawns," *Nashville Tennessean*, February 17, 1922, p. 1.
2205. Ibid., p. 1.
2206. "John Green Pays Penalty in Chair," *Nashville Banner*, February 17, 1922, p. 10.
2207. *Asbury Fields v. State*, Opinion, Supreme Court, Eastern Section, December 8, 1921, p. 10.
2208. Ibid.
2209. L.D. Miller, "Horror in the Grave Yard," *Expose Detective Magazine* (June 1944), pp. 30–33, 48.
2210. Ibid., pp. 4–5.
2211. Ibid., p. 6.
2212. Ibid., p. 9.
2213. Ibid., p. 12.
2214. "Asbury Fields, on Eve of Execution, Asserts Innocence," *Nashville Tennessean*, February 18, 1922, p. 1.
2215. "Fields Dies for Murder of Pierce," *Nashville Banner*, February 18, 1922, p. 1.
2216. Petree's parents lived in Clinton. Christmas was from Harriman. McClure, a barber, was from Columbus, Ohio, as was Stephens: "Bloody Tragedy," *Anderson County News*, June 21, 1921, p. 2.
2217. Christmas had a prior conviction for robbery; Stephens was the "town crook" of Oakdale, and went by the alias Harry Wilson.
2218. These "out in the country" rides were usually for the purpose of purchasing bootleg whiskey. Tennessee was a "dry" state even before Prohibition, and cab drivers liked to take along someone to help "avoid trouble" with bootleggers.
2219. "Executed: Four Men Pay Death Forfeit in Electric Chair," *Anderson County News*, March 4, 1922, p. 2.
2220. *Otto Stephens, Charles Petree, John McClure, Tom Christmas v. State*, Memorandum opinion, Supreme Court, Eastern Section, January 24, 1922, p. 8. This last sentence is one of the silliest ever found in a Tennessee Supreme Court opinion — if the wounds had been fatal, Crumley would not have been able to testify against the killers and they may never have been prosecuted!
2221. Ibid., p. 5.
2222. "Close of Evidence," *Anderson County News*, June 30, 1921, p. 1.
2223. *Otto Stephens, Charles Petree, John McClure, and Tom Christmas v. State*, Memorandum opinion, Supreme Court, Eastern Section, January 24, 1922, p. 8. A media account of the trial said a defense witness recounted that the injury produced a small scar, no doctor was called and Petree was soon laughing about the incident: "Close of Evidence," *Anderson County News*, June 30, 1921, p. 1.
2224. Ibid., p. 10.
2225. "Date of Electrocution," *Anderson County News*, July 30, 1921, p. 2.
2226. "Quartet Stoically Face Death Chair, Will Die at Dawn," *Nashville Tennessean*, March 1, 1922, p. 9.
2227. "Men Facing Death in Varying Moods; One Quotes Bible," *Nashville Tennessean*, February 28, 1922, p. 9.
2228. Ibid., p. 1. Christmas was a war veteran, unmarried, with a widowed mother.
2229. "Quartet Stoically Face Death Chair; Will Die at Dawn," *Nashville Tennessean*, March 1, 1922, p. 1, 9.
2230. "Men Facing Death in Varying Moods, One Quotes Bible," *Nashville Tennessean*, February 28, 1922, p. 1.
2231. Ibid., p. 9
2232. Ibid.
2233. Ibid.
2234. "Electric Chair Takes Its Toll," *Nashville Banner*, March 1, 1922, p. 6.
2235. Ibid.
2236. Ibid.
2237. "Four Men Die in Electric Chair," *Kingsport Times*, March 3, 1922, p. 2.
2238. "Electric Chair Takes Its Toll," *Nashville Banner*, March 1, 1922, p. 6.
2239. Ibid.
2240. "Executed: Four Men Pay Death Forfeit in Electric Chair," *Anderson County News*, March 4, 1922, p. 2.
2241. "Electric Chair Takes Its Toll," *Nashville Banner*, March 1, 1922, p. 1.
2242. "Executed: Four Men Pay Death Forfeit in Electric Chair," *Anderson County News*, March 4, 1922, p. 2.
2243. Hugo Adam Bedau and Michael L. Radelet, "Miscarriages of Justice in Potentially Capital Cases," Stanford Law Review (November 1987): 144–145.
2244. John Edgerton, "A Case of Prejudice: Maurice Mays and the Knoxville Riot of 1919," *Southern Exposure* (July/August 1983): 63; revised and expanded, "Maurice Mays and the Knoxville Race Riot of 1919," in John Edgerton, *Shades of Gray: Dispatches from the Modern South* (Baton Rouge: LSU Press, 1991), pp. 164–187.
2245. Matthew Lakin, "A Dark Night: The Knoxville Race Riot of 1919," *Journal of East Tennessee History* 72 (2000): 1–29.
2246. Donald F. Paine, "Race and Murder in Knoxville, 1919: The Trials of Maurice Mays," *Tennessee B. Journal* 7 (March 2007): 28–33.
2247. Michael L. Radelet, Hugo Adam Bedau, *In Spite of Innocence: Erroneous Convictions in Capital Cases* (Boston: Northeastern University Press, 1992), p. 332.
2248. John Edgerton, "Maurice Mays and the Knoxville Race Riot of 1919," pp. 183–187.
2249. Lakin, "A Dark Night," pp. 28–29.
2250. Paine, "Race and Murder in Knoxville," p. 33.
2251. Paine, p. 28. Neither Paine nor Lakin discuss the obvious: William and Frances Mays were African Americans. Paine is probably mistaken about the year of Mays's birth. In his numerous letters to the governor, Mays said he was thirty-one years old.
2252. *Maurice Mays v. State*, Criminal Court of Knox County, Transcript, p. 331, in *State v. Mays*, Supreme Court, Eastern Section, State Library and Archives Box 919. The case has drawn so much interest over the years that the massive file has been microfilmed. *State v. Mays*, microfilm No. 705, State Library and Archives.
2253. Paine, p. 28. At trial, Mays says he was fifteen when this happened.
2254. Ibid.
2255. Ibid.
2256. Lakin, p. 7. Lakin did not explain the second killing.
2257. Lakin, p. 7.
2258. Letter from Maurice F. Mays to John L. Galloway, Sheriff of Knox County, October 12, 1916. He wrote, "I owe you many thanks for the sincere friendship you have shown me, and I further advise you that I offer you my assistance free gratis in any way, shape or form to help make your administration a successful one."
2259. Original and Reply Brief for the State of Tennessee, *Maurice Mays v. State*, September 26, 1921, Supreme Court, Eastern Division., p. 6. State Library and Archives Box 919. Hereinafter, "State's Brief."
2260. Mays, Transcript, p. 460.
2261. Lakin, p. 4.
2262. Ibid.
2263. Lakin, p. 8.
2264. There is no consistent spelling of her name; various spellings were used in courts and newspapers. They are retained here. Likewise, Smyth was sometimes spelled Smythe.
2265. State's Brief, p. 7.
2266. Ibid.
2267. State's Brief, p. 27, citing Transcript, p. 82.
2268. State's Brief, p. 22, citing Transcript, pp. 60–62.
2269. Bedau and Radelet, p. 145
2270. State's Brief, pp., 23–24, citing Transcript, p. 65.
2271. State's Brief, p. 22, citing Transcript, p. 62.
2272. State's Brief, p. 23, citing Transcript, pp. 63–64.
2273. State's Brief, p. 23, citing Transcript, pp. 62–63.
2274. State's Brief, p. 32, citing Transcript, p. 110.
2275. State's Brief, p. 32, citing Transcript, pp. 111–112.
2276. Mays v. State, 145 Tenn. 118, 238 S.W. 1096, 1099–1100 (1921).
2277. State's Brief, p. 38, citing Transcript, p. 170–172.
2278. State's Brief, p. 41, citing Transcript, pp. 190–191.
2279. State's Brief, pp. 41–42, citing Transcript, pp. 190–191. City policeman John Hatcher was also directed to go with White to Mays's house by Captain Wilson. State's Brief, p. 51, citing Transcript, pp. 151–152.
2280. Thomas Kirby was a deputy sheriff; John Hatcher was a city policeman. The patrol wagon was actually a car.
2281. Spelled in Mays's second appeal brief as Mayes. Assignments of Error and Brief for Maurice Mayes, Plaintiff in Error, September 19, 1921, p. 18, citing Transcript, p. 333, 443.
2282. Clearly a transcription error, since the speaker was Andy White.
2283. State's Brief, p. 42, citing Transcript, pp. 194–195.

2284. Ibid.
2285. State's Brief, p. 52, citing Transcript, pp. 255–256.
2286. State's Brief, p. 43, citing Transcript, pp. 195–196.
2287. State's Brief, p. 44, citing Transcript, pp. 199–200.
2288. State's Brief, pp. 43–44, citing Transcript, pp. 197–198.
2289. State's Brief, p. 49, citing Transcript, p. 238.
2290. Transcript, p. 310.
2291. State's Brief, p. 53, citing Transcript, p. 259.
2292. Michael L. Radelet, Hugo Adam Bedau, Constance E. Putnam, *In Spite of Innocence: The Ordeal of 400 Americans Wrongly Convicted of Crimes Punishable by Death* (Boston: Northeastern University Press, 1992), pp. 308–309.
2293. Assignments of Error and Brief for Maurice Mays, Plaintiff in Error, *Maurice Mays v. State*, September 19, 1921, p. 18, citing Transcript, pp. 333, 443.
2294. Ibid. Sanders was apparently the only African American policeman on the case.
2295. Ibid., citing Transcript, pp. 386, 389.
2296. State's Brief, p. 67, citing Transcript, p. 332.
2297. State's Brief, p. 54 citing Transcript, p. 262.
2298. Ibid.
2299. State's Brief, p. 54, citing Transcript, p. 264.
2300. Matthew Lakin, "A Dark Night: The Knoxville Race Riot of 1919," *Journal of East Tennessee History* 72 (2000): pp. 1, 9.
2301. State's Brief, p. 45, citing Transcript, p. 204.
2302. Shortly after daylight, Detective Stouton took her to police headquarters, District Attorney general Mynatt's office and to the city jail. She saw Mays in the city jail and identified him. "They did not show her a picture of Mays, but that she asked to see him again and they brought him out." State's Brief, p. 27, citing Transcript, p. 82.
2303. State's Brief, p. 73, citing Transcript, p. 73 (Testimony of Sheriff W.T. Cate). The term "charged out" means he was discharged from the jail — in the custody of officers who took him to a train depot at Concord and thence to Chattanooga. It was on the way to Concord that he made the point regarding his shoes, said Cate.
2304. *State v. Mays*, 143 Tenn. 443. The decision was rendered on November 24, 1920. The new law had been construed in 1919 and it no longer contained the familiar language allowing juries to find guilt "with mitigating circumstances." This caused the trial judge in a Memphis case to tell the jury, "You have nothing to do with the penalty," a garbled statement of the law: *Gohlston v. State*, 143 Tenn. 126 (1919). Gohlston, like Mays, was convicted in a second trial and was electrocuted on August 17, 1921. For a good exposition of the history of death penalty law, see Original and Reply Brief of the State of Tennessee, *Maurice Mays v. State*, October 6, 1920, Supreme Court, Eastern Section, State Library and Archives Box 919; this is the state's brief in his first appeal.
2305. The police officers ultimately on the scene were Captain Wilson, Tom Kirby, John Hatcher, Andy White, Emmett Dyer, city detective A.L. Wells, "and another man whose name [Wells] had forgotten": State's Brief, p. 34, citing Transcript, p. 137.
2306. State's Brief, p. 29, citing Transcript, p. 94.
2307. State's Brief, p. 29, citing Transcript, p. 97.
2308. State's Brief, pp. 34–35, citing Transcript, pp. 140–141.
2309. Ibid., State's Brief, citing Transcript, p. 146.
2310. Defendant's Brief, p. 20. Detective Wells also testified that it would take 23 minutes to walk from the murder site to Mays's house walking at a normal gait.
2311. Defendant's Brief, p. 20.
2312. Ibid.
2313. State's Brief, p. 77, citing Transcript, p. 387.
2314. "That they had a kitchen down there at the Station and when they wanted anything to eat White would buy it and he would cook it and they would eat and do cooking down there at the Police Headquarters": State's Brief, p. 78, citing Transcript, p. 388.
2315. The jury was not allowed to hear this latter testimony. Defendant's Brief, pp. 55, citing Transcript, p. 466.
2316. Defendant's Brief, p. 55. The others were Gen. J.C.J. Williams, Judge J.F.J. Lewis, Col. Samuel B. McKinney, Judge James M. King, and Capt. Alex Allison.
2317. "I don't think this is competent, because the law presumes every witness is a man of good character, and I don't think it competent to go into details and pick out certain things in connection with a man's life that will show that he was a better man or worse man than the ordinary run of men, and especially when it has reference to his father and not him. For that reason, I don't think that that was proper to go to the jury": State's Brief, pp. 113–114, citing Transcript, p. 589.
2318. *Mays v. State*, 145 Tenn. 118, 238 S.W. 1096, 1103–1104. "We cannot see any error in the action of the court in excluding this evidence. It would not have shed any light on the credibility of witness Smith. The evidence shows the witness's father died and was buried some 34 years prior to the date said testimony was offered, and the question of who acted as pallbearers at his funeral would have shed no light whatever upon the witness's credibility."
2319. Ibid., p. 56.
2320. Defendant's Brief, pp. 65–75.
2321. State's Brief, p. 45, citing Transcript, p. 209.
2322. State's Brief, p. 46, citing Transcript, p. 210.
2323. State's Brief, p. 46, citing Transcript, pp. 210–211.
2324. State's Brief, p. 46, citing Transcript, p. 212.
2325. *Mays v. State*, 145 Tenn. 118, 238 S.W. 1096, 1100 (1921).
2326. Ibid.
2327. Ibid., p. 1100.
2328. Ibid., pp. 1100–1101.
2329. Ibid., p. 1101.
2330. Ibid.
2331. Transcript, p. 468. Mays's counsel objected to these questions after they were asked.
2332. State's Brief, p. 105.
2333. Ibid., pp. 106–107.
2334. Ibid., p. 107, citing *Hensley v. State*, 28 Tenn. 242; *Sibley v. State*, 50 Tenn. 139; *Susong v. Ellis*, 58 Tenn. 86; *Self v. State*, 65 Tenn. 248; *Peck v. State*, 86 Tenn. 267.
2335. Ibid., pp. 107–108.
2336. Ibid., p. 108.
2337. Ibid.
2338. Ibid., pp. 108–109.
2339. Ibid., p. 109.
2340. Ibid.
2341. Ibid., pp. 109–110.
2342. Ibid., p. 110.
2343. Ibid., citing *Boyer v. Pratt*, 20 Tenn. 91; *Britt v. State*, 20 Tenn. 30; *Outry v. Coffman*, 46 Tenn. 510; *Massengale v. Shadden*, 48 Tenn. 357; *DeFriese v. State*, 50 Tenn. 53; *Lawrence v. Hudson*, 59 Tenn. 672; *Summers v. Howland*, 61 Tenn. 406; *Guggenheim v. Rosenfeld*, 68 Tenn. 534; *Link v. State*, 81 Tenn. 701; *Rafferty v. State*, 91 Tenn. 655; *Boyd v. State*, 94 Tenn. 503; *Katzenberger v. Leedom*, 103 Tenn. 144; *Holder v. State*, 119 Tenn. 210; *Gardner v. State*, 121 Tenn. 709; *Parrish v. State*, 129 Tenn. 274.
2344. Ibid., p. 112, citing Transcript, pp. 477–479.
2345. *Mays v. State*, 145 Tenn. 118, 238 S.W. 1096, 1103 (1921), citing *Parrish v. State*, 129 Tenn. 274, 164 S.W. 1174; *Hensly v. State*, 9 Humph. 243; *Sible v. State*, 3 Heisk. 139; *People v. Molineax*, 168 N.Y. 264, 61 N.E. 286, 62 L.R.A. 193.
2346. Letter from J.A. Fowler to Hon. A.A. Taylor, February 28, 1922, p. 12.
2347. Mays said he was 5'8" and weighed 127 pounds. Transcript, p. 459.
2348. Defendant's Brief, p. 40, citing Transcript, p. 20.
2349. Defendant's Brief, pp. 41–43, citing Transcript, pp. 9, 40, 400, 438, 458.
2350. State's Brief, p. 104–105, citing Transcript, pp. 441–443, 458–459. The state's brief says the testimony was offered to contradict the contention that the killer was identified as wearing a gray suit.
2351. Letter from J.A. Fowler to Hon. A.A. Taylor, February 28, 1922, p. 12.
2352. "In 1926, the real killer confessed in a written statement which revealed that she was a white woman who had dressed up as a black man to kill the woman with whom her husband was having an affair. The authorities, however, never accepted the confession": Hugo Adam Bedau and Michael L. Radelet, "Miscarriages of Justice in Potentially Capital Cases," *Stanford Law Review* 40 (1987): pp. 21, 145.

2353. "Woman Confesses Murder for Which Negro Paid Life," *Nashville Tennessean*, August 19, 1927. Evening edition.
2354. See, notes 1–4, supra.
2355. Markman and Cassell attack Bedau and Radelet's own logic. "Despite their recognition that confessions of third parties are often 'false or dubious' and 'must be evaluated with extreme caution' (citing their article), the authors provide no justification for believing this bizarre confession to be true. Although they do note that the authorities never accepted it as true (citing their article), they fail to state the reasons for this official reaction: The woman's account of the murder contained serious discrepancies, and her husband explained to the police that she had confessed because she was temporarily demented. (citing Edgerton article)": Stephen J. Markman and Paul G. Cassell, "Protecting the Innocent: A Response to the Bedau-Radelet Study," Stanford Law Review (1988): 121, 140. They conclude: "Given these facts, as well as the confession's implausibility in light of evidence which convinced twenty-four jurors at two trials that Mays was guilty beyond a reasonable doubt, the woman's confession provides no sound basis for crediting the authors' claim that Mays was innocent."
2356. Letter to James Weldon Johnson and Report of Helen M. Boardman, October 3, 1927, NAACP Papers, Legal File, Library of Congress Manuscript Division, Box D-61.
2357. Ibid.
2358. Ibid.
2359. "William F. Yardley," Carroll Van West, ed., *The Tennessee Encyclopedia of History and Culture* (Nashville: Tennessee Historical Society, 1998), pp. 1089. Yardley was the son of a white woman and a black father and had been left on the doorstep of a home to be raised by the owners.
2360. "Supreme Court Judges Intercede with Governor on Behalf of Mays," *The East Tennessee News*, March 23, 1922, p. 4.
2361. John Edgerton, "A Case of Prejudice: Maurice Mays and the Knoxville Race Riot of 1919," *Southern Exposure* 11 (July–August 1983): 56, 63, citing *Nashville Tennessean*, March 14, 1922, p. 1.
2362. *Mays v. State*, 145 Tenn. 118, 238 S.W. 1096, 1100 (1921).
2363. Ibid.
2364. Ibid.
2365. Letter from Maurice F. Mays to Hon. A.A. Taylor, November 10, 1921; Letter from Maurice F. Mays to Hon. A.A. Taylor, November 28, 1921.
2366. Letter from Charles W. Cansler to Gov. A.A. Taylor, November 10, 1921. State Library and Archives, Governor's Pardons, Record Group 261, Box 21, folder 83.
2367. Letter from John E. McMillan to Hon. A.A. Taylor, November 29, 1921. State Library and Archives, Governor's Pardons, Record Group 261, Box 21, folder 83.
2368. Ibid.
2369. Ibid.
2370. Letter from L.D. Smith to Hon. A.A. Taylor, December 13, 1921. Smith's letterhead simply said, "Supreme Court, State of Tennessee," and listed the names of the judges.
2371. Ibid., p. 2.
2372. Letter from William J. Hale to Hon. A.A. Taylor, November 14, 1921.
2373. Letter from Nahum Daniel Brascher to Honorable Alfred Taylor, November 20, 1921.
2374. Letter from Robert R. Church to Hon. A.A. Taylor, November 25, 1921.
2375. Letter from S.G. Heiskell addressed To Whom It May Concern, July 14, 1915.
2376. Telegraph from S.G. Heiskell to Gov. A.A. Taylor, December 8, 1921.
2377. Telegram from Leroy Jones to Gov. A.A. Taylor, December 13, 1921.
2378. Letter from B.R. Stout to Hon. A.A. Taylor, December 8, 1921, enclosing Letter from E.J. McNew to Hon. A.A. Taylor, December 8, 1921.
2379. Letter from W.L. Clapp to Hon. A.A. Taylor, November 22, 1921.
2380. Ibid.
2381. Letter from Governor Alfred Taylor to William Rule, December 5, 1921; Letter from Governor Alfred Taylor to Wiley Morgan, December 5, 1921.
2382. Letter from C.W. Sanders to Governor Alfred Taylor, November 28, 1921.
2383. Letter from William Rule to Hon. A.A. Taylor, December 8, 1921. No letter from anyone at the *Knoxville Sentinel* has been located.
2384. Respite, Maurice Mays, December 14, 1921. The document read, "Maurice Mays is hereby granted a respite of 90 days — or until Wednesday, March 15, 1922, at which time during legal hours of said day he will be electrocuted according to law in obedience to the judgment of the courts. This action is taken in deference to the appeal of several hundred citizens of Knoxville and Knox County, both white and colored, representing every class of citizenship, who entertain a serious doubt as to the guilt of Maurice Mays, notwithstanding two juries have pronounced him guilty."
2385. Letter from S.S. Crockett, C.F. Thomason, A.W. Harris, George A. Hatcher, W.S. Farmer to Gov. A.A. Taylor, February 24, 1922.
2386. Letter from Maurice Mays to Hon. A.A. Taylor, February 27, 1922.
2387. Ibid.
2388. Letter from Maurice Mays to Hon. A.A. Taylor, March 9, 1922.
2389. Letter from Grafton Green to Hon. A.A. Taylor, March 10, 1922.
2390. Letter from Nathan Bachman and Colin P. McKinney to Hon. A.A. Taylor, March 14, 1922.
2391. Affidavit of Benjamin Franklin Peters, January 31, 1922. Tennessee Pardons and Paroles, 1840–1867; State Library and Archives Record Group 261, Box 21, folder 83.
2392. Letter from James A. Fowler to Hon. A.A. Taylor, February 28, 1922, pp. 14–15.
2393. Ibid.
2394. Ibid.
2395. Letter from J.A. Fowler to Hon. A.A. Taylor, December 1, 1921.
2396. Letter from Reuben L. Cates to Hon. A.A. Taylor, March 6, 1922.
2397. He cited *State v. Peck*, 86 Tenn. 267, 268. This is because unless the statement otherwise falls within some exception, it is hearsay. That is, the "confessor" must be brought into court to testify.
2398. Letter from Reuben L. Cates to Hon. A.A. Taylor, March 6, 1922, p. 2.
2399. Ibid., p. 3.
2400. Ibid., p. 2.
2401. Ibid., p. 4.
2402. Letter from John B. Brownlow to Governor Taylor, January 12, 1922.
2403. Letter from J. Kelly Giffen to Hon. Alfred A. Taylor, March 10, 1922.
2404. Letter from A.R. Smith to Hon. Alf Taylor, February 10, 1922.
2405. Ibid.
2406. Ibid.
2407. *Otto Stephens, Charles Petree, John McClure, Tom Christmas v. State*, Memorandum, Supreme Court, Eastern Section, January 24, 1922.
2408. "Men Facing Death in Varying Moods, One Quotes Bible," *Nashville Tennessean*, February 28, 1922, p. 1.
2409. Ibid., p. 9.
2410. Ibid., p. 6.
2411. Letter from John W. Staples to Hon. A.A. Taylor, February 2, 1922.
2412. "Supreme Court Judges Intercede with Governor on Behalf of Mays," *The East Tennessee News*, March 23, 1922, p. 4; "Maurice Mays, Near Death, Blames G.O.P. Politicians," *Nashville Tennessean*, March 5, 1922, pp. 1, 2.
2413. Ibid.
2414. "Taylor Discusses Four Executions," *Nashville Tennessean*, March 2, 1923, p. 8.
2415. Ibid.
2416. "Maurice Mays, Near Death, Blames G.O.P. Politicians," *Nashville Tennessean*, March 15, 1922, p. 1.
2417. Ibid.
2418. "Letter to the Editor," *The East Tennessee News*, March 23, 1922, p. 4. This was a black newspaper, Republican in politics. It did not survive the great shift of black voters to the Democratic Party with the coming of Franklin D. Roosevelt.
2419. "Our present system of hearing applications for pardons is unsatisfactory. At least half the time of the Chief Executive is consumed in hearing pleas for the release of prisoners." Steven V. Ash, ed., *Messages of the Governors of Tennessee, 1921–1933*, vol. 10 (Nashville: Tennessee Historical Commission, 1990), p. 333.
2420. "Maurice Mays Dies in Chair," *Nashville Banner*, March 15, 1922, p. 1, 3.
2421. This was described as a slight wound from which he soon recovered. "Death Sentence," *Anderson County News*, March 4, 1922, p. 1.
2422. *Granville Bunch v. State*, Memorandum opinion, Supreme Court, Eastern Section, July 28, 1922, p. 3.
2423. Ibid., p. 4.
2424. Ibid., p. 5.
2425. Ibid.
2426. Ibid.

2427. Ibid., pp. 1–2. He also complained that the district attorney's statement, "Gentlemen of the jury, we have got to tighten up on these murder cases," was improper, but the court said it was not.
2428. "Death Penalty Paid by Bunch," *Nashville Banner*, April 11, 1922, p. 1.
2429. *William Dwight v. State*, Memorandum opinion, Supreme Court, Eastern Section, June 12, 1922, p. 2. Curtis went by the name Jesse Curtis.
2430. Ibid., p. 2.
2431. Ibid., pp. 2–3.
2432. "Dwight to Die in Chair Today," *Chattanooga Daily Times*, July 22, 1922, p. 2.
2433. The newspaper reported that Dwight's cell was next to that of "Jesse Cantrell, who is serving a life sentence in connection with the same case." The name is wrong; it was Jesse Curtis. "Electrocute Negro Murderer at Pen," *Nashville Banner*, July 25, 1922, p. 1.
2434. Ibid.
2435. *Austin Harris v. State*, Opinion, Supreme Court, Western Section, July 5, 1922. p. 3.
2436. Ibid., p. 3.
2437. Ibid., pp. 3,4.
2438. Ibid., p. 4.
2439. Regarding the issue of sanity, the court said: "We have just discussed the principles of law applicable to a case like this in *Jim McElroy v. State of Tennessee*, and it is not necessary to go over this ground again": Ibid., p. 5.
2440. "Two Murderers Die in Chair," *Nashville Banner*, August 15, 1922, p. 4.
2441. *Jim McElroy v. State*, Brief of Appellant, Supreme Court, Middle Section, Filed February 9, 1922, p. 2. McElroy's motion for a new trial said the reason the doctor was not allowed to testify is because he would not say he was a expert, although he "had studied Neurology, nervous diseases, mental diseases while a student and had continued the studies of said diseases after graduation, that he was familiar with the symptoms and pathology of insanity": Motion for New Trial, *State v. McElroy*, No. 1278. State Library and Archives Box 926.
2442. Ibid.
2443. *McElroy v. State*, 242 S.W. 883, 146 Tenn. 442 (1922).
2444. Ibid.
2445. "Bennecker Shot Down in Cold Blood by Jim McElroy at Early Hour This Morning," *Rockwood Times*, June 30, 1921, p. 1. Bennecker was survived by his wife and five children.
2446. This is the person who treats patients at the jail or whom county officials call when care is needed, such as whether a person should be sent elsewhere for psychiatric treatment.
2447. *Jim McElroy v. State*, Brief of Appellant, Supreme Court, Middle Section, filed February 9, 1922, p. 3.
2448. Motion for New Trial, *State v. McElroy*, Tennessee Supreme Court Case No. 1278, p. 6.
2449. Ibid., pp. 6–8.
2450. *McElroy v. State*, 242 S.W.883, 884 (Tenn. 1922).
2451. Ibid.
2452. Ibid., p. 885.
2453. "Two Murderers Die in Chair," *Nashville Banner*, August 15, 1922, p. 4.
2454. *Ben Burchfield v. State*, Memorandum Opinion, Supreme Court, Eastern Section, December 1, 1924, p. 1.
2455. Ibid., p. 13.
2456. Ibid.
2457. Ibid., p. 14.
2458. *Ben Burchfield v. State*, Memorandum Opinion, Supreme Court, Eastern Section, December 17, 1924, p. 4.
2459. Ibid., p. 6.
2460. Ibid., p. 7.
2461. Ibid., p. 6.
2462. Ibid., p. 8. The implication here is that she was paid for the "association."
2463. Ibid., p. 9.
2464. "The defendant was unable to offer any explanation for the spot of blood on the new pants he was wearing when he was arrested." Ibid., p. 13.
2465. Ibid., pp. 11–12. This was a wooden sidewalk.
2466. Ibid., p. 14.
2467. Ibid.
2468. The governor worked on the case until 2:00 A.M. the morning Burchfield was executed. He disregarded a meeting with legislative leaders planning his inauguration, explaining he needed to spend time on the case.
2469. T.H. Alexander, "Burchfield Goes to Death Chair for Killing Five," *Nashville Tennessean*, January 14, 1925, p. 1.
2470. "Slayer of Five Goes to Chair," *Nashville Banner*, January 14, 1925, p. 3.
2471. "Conference to Decide Fate of Ben Burchfield," *Nashville Tennessean*, January 13, 1925, p. 1.
2472. *Robert Tate v. State*, Memorandum opinion, Supreme Court, Eastern Section, August 1, 1925, p. 4.
2473. Ibid., p. 10.
2474. Ibid.
2475. "Bob Tate, Convicted Slayer of Ed Condra, to Die September 3," *Sequatchie Valley News*, July 24, 1925, p. 1.
2476. "Governor Refuses to Extend Clemency to Condemned Man," *Sequatchie Valley News*, October 6, 1925, p. 1.
2477. Brainard Cheney, "Tate Dies in Electric Chair Denying Guilt," *Nashville Banner*, November 5, 1925, pp. 1, 2; "Tate Removed to Death House for Execution," *Nashville Tennessean*, November 5, 1925, p. 1.
2478. Her testimony was that the car had stopped briefly to change drivers. Few people believed that was true. Rather, the couple were attending to each other in the car.
2479. "Model Police Brief," *Journal of Criminal Law & Criminology* 19 (August 1928): 102–124 (Appendix). He confessed to the earlier killings apparently because the jewelry evidence linking him to those crimes was stronger than in the Spencer killing.
2480. *Charles Barr v. State*, Memorandum opinion, Supreme Court, Western Division, July 17, 1925, pp. 6–7.
2481. "Hard Fought Legal Battle for Barr Ends with Governor's Decision," *Nashville Banner*, August 20, 1926, p. 1.
2482. "Barr to Die in Electric Chair Here at Sunrise," *Nashville Banner*, August 20, 1926, p. 1. Governor Austin Peay died in office on October 2, 1927.
2483. Ibid.
2484. "Charles Barr's Body Sent to Mississippi," *Nashville Banner*, August 21, 1926, p. 1.
2485. Plea in Abatement, *State v. John Franklin Webb*, Shelby Criminal Court, Division II, No. 26351; Motion for a New Trial, *State v. John Franklin Webb*, Shelby Criminal Court, Division II, No 26351. Webb's lawyer also filed a lawsuit in Chancery Court challenging the adequacy of selecting the jury pool in Shelby County, but the details are unknown.
2486. Motion for Change of Venue, *State v. John Franklin Webb*, Shelby Criminal Court II, No. 26351.
2487. Your author speculates the delay between this date and the actual execution was caused by an attempt to have the United States Supreme Court hear the case. The file cannot be located.
2488. "Webb Is Doomed to Chair Today; Record to Live," *Nashville Tennessean*, May 20, 1927, p. 1; "Peay to Visit Death Cell to Decide on Fate of 2 Negroes," *Nashville Tennessean*, May 19, 1927, p. 1.
2489. "State Takes Negro's Life," *Nashville Tennessean*, May 20, 1927, p. 1. The front page of this day's paper showed a picture of Capt. Charles A. Lindbergh, with the caption, "The Flying Fool," announcing his takeoff from New York to Paris.
2490. *John Henry Wallace v. State*, Memorandum opinion, Supreme Court, Middle Section, April 9, 1927, pp. 2–3.
2491. Ibid., p. 10, citing *Deathridge v. State*, 33 Tenn. 79; *Self v. State*, 95 Tenn. 253.
2492. Brainard Cheney, "Wallace Pays Death Penalty," *Nashville Banner*, May 25, 1927, p. 1. Cheney, later a novelist, practiced his craft writing about executions, and the mother's wail was described as follows: "Her broken cries that ricocheted from the glarish white walls brought hard swallows to the jaw muscles of calloused prison guards to whom executions were a matter of routine duty": p. 5.
2493. "Negro, Doomed to Chair Today, Slashes Throat," *Nashville Tennessean*, May 25, 1927, p. 1.
2494. Brainard Cheney, "Wallace Pays Death Penalty," *Nashville Banner*, May 25, 1927, p. 5.
2495. *Herman Coggins v. State*, Memorandum, Supreme Court, Middle Section, June 25, 1927, p. 4.
2496. *Herman Coggins v. State*, Memorandum, Supreme Court, Middle Section, September 27, 1927, p. 2.
2497. "Coggins Selects His Pallbearers: Goes to His Death," *Nashville Tennessean*, November 10, 1927, p. 1.
2498. Ibid.
2499. Brainard Cheney, "State Takes Coggins' Life," *Nashville Banner*, November 10, 1927, p. 1.

2500. "Coggins Selects His Pallbearers; Goes to His Death," *Nashville Tennessean*, November 10, 1927, p. 1. Undoubtedly, the writer meant the first white man in Davidson County to be executed in the electric chair.
2501. "Fowler Goes to Electric Chair," *Scott County News,* March 18, 1927, p. 1.
2502. *Ben Fowler v. State*, Memorandum Opinion, Nov. 21, 1927, Supreme Court, Eastern Section, Knoxville, 1927, November 21, 1927, pp. 197, 200.
2503. Ibid., p. 201.
2504. Ibid., pp. 201–202.
2505. Brainard Cheney, "'Two-Gun' Fowler Goes to Death at Dawn; Composed," *Nashville Tennessean*, Jan. 25, 1928, p. 1; Brainard Cheney, "Fowler Meets Death in Chair," *Evening Tennessean,* Jan. 25, 1928, p. 1.
2506. Brainard Cheney, "Fowler Meets Death in Chair," *Evening Tennessean*, Jan. 25, 1928, p. 5.
2507. "Fowler, Facing Chair, Is Given Church Baptism," *Nashville Tennessean*, Jan. 24, 1928, p. 1.
2508. Tom Little, "Ben Fowler, Sentenced to Die Tuesday, Talks About Career," *Nashville Tennessean*, Jan. 3, 1928, p. 1.
2509. Brainard Cheney, "'Two-Gun' Fowler Goes to Death at Dawn; Composed," *Nashville Tennessean*, Jan. 25, 1928, p. 1.
2510. "Woman, 71, Beaten Sister Attacked; Negro Arrested," *Nashville Tennessean*, January 18, 1927, p. 1; "Negro Confesses Attacking Woman on Lonely Road," *Nashville Tennessean*, January 19, 1927, p. 1; "Doctors Examine Accused Negro," *Nashville Banner*, January 21, 1927, p. 17; "Negro to Face Trial for Assault Today," *Nashville Tennessean*, January 28, 1927, p. 6; "Jury Is Chosen in Terrill Case," *Nashville Banner*, January 28, 1927, p. 1; "Terrell Gets Death Penalty," *Nashville Banner*, February 1, 1927, p. 1.
2511. Although the opinion does not mention it, Terrill drew a knife on Miss Emma Porter, which he left at the scene.
2512. *Will Terrill v. State*, Memorandum Opinion, Supreme Court, Middle Section, March 12, 1928, p. 2.
2513. Ibid., p. 3.
2514. Ibid.
2515. Ibid., p. 4.
2516. Ibid., p. 5.
2517. Ibid., p. 6.
2518. "Terrell to Die Tuesday Morning," *Nashville Tennessean*, June 18, 1927, p. 2.
2519. "Terrell Dies in Electric Chair," *Nashville Banner*, June 19, 1928, p. 1.
2520. At the time, inmates could be paroled to an individual who "spoke up" for them. A farmer in Cowan had done so. Brown had worked for the farmer awhile and then wandered to Nashville.
2521. Bill of Exceptions, *State v. Henry Brown*, Supreme Court, Middle Section [n.d.], pp. 13–14. State Library and Archives Box 2697.
2522. Ibid. p. 14.
2523. Ibid., pp. 25–26.
2524. *Henry Brown v. State*, Memorandum opinion, Supreme Court, Middle Section, June 20, 1928, p. 1.
2525. "Negro Goes to Chair at Dawn," *Nashville Tennessean*, August 22, 1928, p. 5.
2526. "Henry Brown Dies in Electric Chair," *Nashville Banner*, August 22, 1928, p. 4.
2527. *John Jones, Oliver Stevenson, and Rufus Witherspoon v. State*, Memorandum Opinion, Supreme Court, Eastern Section, December 9, 1929, p. 2.
2528. Ibid.
2529. Ibid.
2530. Ibid., p. 3.
2531. Ibid.
2532. Ibid.
2533. Ibid., p. 4.
2534. Ibid.
2535. Ibid., p. 5.
2536. Ibid.
2537. Ibid.
2538. Ibid., p. 6.
2539. "No Respite to Be Granted in Case of Doomed Negro," *Nashville Tennessean*, February 13, 1930, p. 1.
2540. "Rockwood Slayer Doomed to Die at Dawn Today," *Nashville Tennessean*, February 14, 1930, p. 1.
2541. "Negro Slayer of Sartin Pays," *Nashville Banner*, February 14, 1930, p. 1.
2542. Ibid.
2543. "Jury Decrees Death for Attack of Girl," *Commercial Appeal*, January 29, 1930, pp. 1, 2.
2544. Ibid., p. 2.
2545. "Negro Doomed to Go to Chair Friday," *Nashville Banner*, March 13, 1930, p. 1.
2546. "Cary Gunn Talks of His Troubles," *Bolivar Bulletin*, Feb. 7, 1930, p. 2.
2547. Ibid.
2548. "Cary Gunn Dies in Electric Chair," *Bolivar Bulletin*, March 21, 1930, p.
2549. According to one account, the two were in the garage assembling model airplanes when Harris fumbled and broke two. This angered the boy, who called Harris a "nigger." Harris flew into a rage and hit the boy's head with a pipe, then continued striking him with an ax: Sheila Weems Johnston, *Murders in East Tennessee* (Rogersville, TN: The Author, 2004), p. 88, citing *Rogersville Herald*, January 1, 1930, p. 1.
2550. *Theodore James Harris v. State*, Memorandum opinion, Supreme Court, Eastern Section, December 15, 1930, p. 1–4.
2551. Walter Bruce, "Negro Laughs as Death Nears," *Nashville Banner*, January 27, 1931, p.1.
2552. Ibid.
2553. Ibid.
2554. Ibid., p. 15.
2555. Ibid.
2556. R.M. Johnson, "Payment Deferred: An Indiana Enigma," *Master Detective* (August 1937): p. 32, 74.
2557. *John Thomas Shaw v. State*, Memorandum Opinion, Supreme Court, Middle Section, March 18, 1933, p. 2.
2558. "John Thomas Shaw, Twice Sentenced to Death, Is Executed," *Nashville Banner*, July 3, 1933, p. 8.
2559. *John Thomas Shaw v. State*, Memorandum opinion, Supreme Court, Middle Section, March 18, 1933, p. 3.
2560. Ibid.
2561. Ibid., p. 4.
2562. Ibid., p. 5.
2563. Ibid. This means the defendant did not give a signed statement, rather, his statement was a transcript of the questioning.
2564. Ibid., p. 5.
2565. Ibid., p. 6.
2566. Ibid., p. 6. Shaw's counsel was apparently allowed to present the statement, although Shaw did not take the witness stand.
2567. Ibid., p. 6.
2568. Ibid., p. 7.
2569. Ibid.
2570. Ibid., p. 8.
2571. Ibid., pp. 11–12.
2572. "Negro Sentenced Second Time to Die," *Nashville Banner*, January 7, 1932, p. 5.
2573. "Condemned Negro Tries to Kill Self Before Execution," *Nashville Tennessean*, July 3, 1933, p. 1.
2574. "John Thomas Shaw, Twice Sentenced to Death, Is Executed," *Nashville Banner*, July 3, 1933, p. 8.
2575. Ibid.
2576. *Oscar Bevins and Andrew Wilcoxen v. State*, Memorandum Opinion, Supreme Court, Eastern Section, July 19, 1933, pp. 1–6.
2577. Ibid., p. 7.
2578. Ibid., p. 8.
2579. Ibid., 9.
2580. Ibid.
2581. "Two Negroes to Die in Chair Today for Criminal Assault," *Tennessean*, September 7, 1933, p. 1; "Negroes Go to Chair Singing Spirituals," *Nashville Banner*, September 7, 1933, p. 3; "2 Negroes Pay Life for Crime," *Chattanooga News*, September 7, 1933, p. 1.
2582. *Willie Jones v. State*, Memorandum Opinion, Supreme Court, Western Section, July 19, 1933, p. 2.
2583. *Willie Jones v. State*, Memorandum Opinion, Supreme Court, Western Section, July 19, 1933, pp. 2–8.
2584. "Execution This Morning," *Nashville Tennessean*, October 30, 1933, p. 1; "Negro Goes to Chair Claiming Innocence," *Nashville Banner*, October 30, 1933, p. 13.
2585. *Jim Allen v. State*, Memorandum opinion, Supreme Court, Eastern Section, November 18, 1933, p. 4. The court said these statements were part of the res gestae, citing *Garrison v. State*, 163 Tenn. 108, 40 S.W.2d 1009 (1931).
2586. In most Tennessee cities small houses (shacks) were built behind the main house, next to the alley. These were usually occupied by blacks who sometimes served as servants at the main house.
2587. Ibid., note 1, p. 5.
2588. Ibid., note 1, p. 6.
2589. Ibid., note 1, p. 7.
2590. "Condemned Negro Takes Nap Before Going to Chair," *Nashville Banner*, January 5, 1934, p. 8.
2591. "No Clemency for Negro,"

Nashville Tennessean, January 5, 1934, p. 1.

2592. *Joe Emory v. State*, Memorandum opinion, Supreme Court, Eastern Section, October 21, 1933, p. 219, 221.

2593. Bill of Exceptions, *Joe Emory v. State*, Tennessee Supreme Court, Eastern Section, n.d. [1933], pp. 37–40. State Library and Archives Box 522.

2594. Ibid., note 1, p. 226.

2595. "Two Negroes Confess Before Being Executed," *Tennessean*, Feb. 6, 1934, p. 12.

2596. "Pleas for Stay Being Made as Negro's Death Hour Approaches After He Has Talked to Mammy," *Tennessean*, Feb. 5, 1934, p. 1; "Negro, One of Pair to Die Here, to Be Ready as He Hears 'Mammy's' Voice Over Phone," *Evening Tennessean*, Feb. 4, 1934, p. 1.

2597. "Find Woman's Body in Weeds," *Knoxville News-Sentinel*, December 26, 1932, p. 1; "Woman Killed and Assaulted," *Knoxville News-Sentinel*, December 27, 1932, p. 7; "Find Tracks Where Woman Slain," *Knoxville News-Sentinel*, December 28, 1932, p. 2.

2598. Jefferson County Circuit Court minutes, vol. 3, pp. 301, 333, 337, 340 (May 1, 1933).

2599. "Two Negroes Confess Their Crimes as Electric Chair Death Draws Nearer," *Nashville Banner*, February 5, 1934, p. 8. Vivid account of impending executions—"A hearse, long, low, and black stood at the entrance, as if crouched for a getaway."

2600. "Swann and Emory Die in Chair After Confessing Two Murders," *Knoxville News-Sentinel*, February 5, 1934, pp. 1, 10.

2601. *Louis Fain v. State*, Memorandum opinion, Supreme Court, Eastern Section, January 13, 1934, p. 2. The opinion was written by the venerable Judge Grafton Green, who used the term "outraged." "Negro to Die, State Supreme Court Decides," *Nashville Banner*, January 13, 1934, p. 1.

2602. Ibid., p. 11.

2603. Ibid., p. 7.

2604. Kenneth L. Eagon, "Enigma of the Tennessee Beauty and the Phantom Killer," *Real Detective* (October 1937): pp. 44–49, 78.

2605. Ibid., p. 8.

2606. Ibid., p. 9.

2607. Ibid., p. 12.

2608. Ibid.

2609. "Negro Confesses to Crime Before Going to Chair Here Today," *Nashville Tennessean*, February 26, 1934, p. 1. The document has not survived.

2610. "Negro Confesses, Then Goes to His Death," *Nashville Banner*, February 26, 1934, p. 8.

2611. "Negro Attacker Is Jailed; Confesses," *Commercial Appeal*, November 5, 1933, p. 14.

2612. "Posse Takes Trail of Negro Attacker," *Commercial Appeal*, November 4, 1933, p. 8.

2613. Ibid., note 1.

2614. "Three Negroes Die for Two Attacks," *Commercial-Appeal*, April 4, 1934, p. 14.

2615. *Jasper Graham and Frank Mays v. State*, Memorandum opinion, Supreme Court, Western Section, February 26, 1934, 8 pp.

2616. "Negro Confesses on Eve of Death," *Commercial Appeal*, April 3, 1934, p. 12.

2617. "Three Negroes Die for Two Attacks," *Commercial Appeal*, April 4, 1934, p. 14.

2618. "Three Negroes Die for Two Attacks," *Commercial Appeal*, April 5, 1934, p. 15.

2619. See, Margaret Vandiver and Michel Coconis, "'Sentenced to the Punishment of Death': Pre–Furman Capital Crimes and Executions in Shelby County, Tennessee," *University of Memphis Law Review* 31 (Summer 2001): pp. 861–937, 912. Sympathetic account of Graham's guilt.

2620. William T. Griffin, "Horror in the Locked Room," *Master Detective* (May 1937), pp. 22–25, 64–67.

2621. *John Deal v. State*, Memorandum opinion, Supreme Court, Middle Section, June 23, 1934, p. 2.

2622. "Memphis Negroes Go to Execution Singing Spirituals," *Nashville Banner*, September 15, 1934, p. 7.

2623. *John Deal v. State*, Memorandum opinion, Supreme Court, Middle Section, June 23, 1934, pp. 2–11.

2624. "Condemned Negroes Eat Beef Dinners as They Await Death," *Nashville Tennessean*, September 15, 1934, p. 1.

2625. The name of the hymn is "God's Word Never Passes Away."

2626. "Memphis Negroes Go to Executions Singing Spirituals," *Nashville Banner*, September 15, 1934, p. 7.

2627. *James Pillow v. State*, Memorandum opinion, Supreme Court, Eastern Division, June 23, 1934.

2628. "Memphis Negroes Go to Execution Singing Spirituals," *Nashville Banner*, September 15, 1934, p. 7.

2629. R. Beecher Witt, "How We Solved Tennessee's Triple Death Riddle," *Startling Detective* (May 1936) p. 22; David Kent, "The Devil Wore a Dress," *Expose Detective* (August 1948); p. 17. When captured with two Kentucky prison escapees, Lee was disguised as a woman. Posing as a hitchhiker, the dress-clad Lee, wearing a wig and makeup, pulled a gun on a traveling salesman and forced him to stop and pick up the other two.

2630. *William Lee v. State*, Memorandum opinion, Supreme Court, Eastern Section, November 23, 1935, pp. 10–11.

2631. Ibid., p. 6.

2632. Ibid.

2633. Ibid., p. 8.

2634. Ibid., pp. 8–9.

2635. Ibid., p. 13.

2636. Rufus Jarman, "Trio on Death Row at Prison Face Chair with Varied Views," *Nashville Tennessean*, January 20, 1936, p. 1.

2637. Ibid.

2638. Rufus Jarman, "One Man Jokes, Other Is Silent as They Wait Dawn and Death," *Nashville Tennessean*, January 21, 1936, p. 1, 2.

2639. Richard Battle, "Two White Men, Convicted Murderers, Are Electrocuted Here, Denying Guilt," *Nashville Banner*, January 21, 1936, p. 11.

2640. Ibid. The implication was that Lee might have been taken from the jail and lynched.

2641. *Wilse Bray and Walter Kennedy v. State*, Memorandum opinion, Supreme Court, Eastern Section, November 23, 1935, p. 5. This opinion is very difficult to understand. Bunch was tried with Bray and Kennedy and was sentenced to twenty-one years. He did not appeal.

2642. The court did not explain why this was an important issue, but likely it was argued in order to lay a predicate for seeking commutation of the death penalty.

2643. Ibid., p. 7.

2644. Ibid.

2645. None of these people testified at the trial, but the court noted that it was unchallenged that Bray was found intoxicated on his uncle's porch the next morning.

2646. Ibid., p. 11.

2647. Ibid., p. 12.

2648. Ibid., p. 13.

2649. Ibid., pp. 12, 13.

2650. Richard Battle, "Two White Men, Convicted Murderers, Are Electrocuted Here, Denying Guilt," *Nashville Tennessean*, January 21, 1936, p. 11.

2651. On January 4, 1945, Bray was stabbed to death by another inmate.

2652. Rufus Jarman, "One Man Jokes, Other Is Silent as They Wait Dawn and Death," *Nashville Tennessean*, January 20, 1936, p. 1.

2653. "Anderson Youth Goes to Death in Electric Chair for Murder," *Clinton Courier*, January 23, 1936, p. 1.

2654. Richard Battle, "Two White Men, Convicted Murderers, Are Electrocuted Here, Denying Guilt," *Nashville Banner*, January 21, 1936, p. 11.

2655. *Lewis Willis, et al. v. State*, Memorandum Opinion, Supreme Court, Middle Section, February 23, 1935, p 2.

2656. Ibid., p. 2.

2657. Ibid.

2658. Ibid., p. 3. The statute had been passed in 1911 and was Section 12179 Code of Tennessee.

2659. Ibid., p. 5.

2660. Ibid., p. 5. The issue of inmate disability was presented in Willis's petition to have his case heard by the United States Supreme Court, which denied his application.

2661. "Lewis Negro Boy Confesses to Crime," *Sequatchie Valley News*, January 4, 1927, p. 2.

2662. Rufus Johnson, "Trio on Death Row at Prison Face Chair with Varied Views," *Nashville Tennessean*, January 20, 1936, p. 1.

2663. Ibid., p. 2.

2664. "Negro Kidnaper Dies Today for Slaying Trusty," *Nashville Tennessean*, January 28, 1936, p. 1; "Death Chair Claims Fiftieth Victim; Negro Executed for Killing Guard," *Nashville Banner*, January 28, 1936, p. 11.

2665. *Ernest Womack Jr. v. State*, Memorandum opinion, Supreme Court,

Middle Section, February 15, 1936, pp. 1–2.

2666. Ibid.

2667. *Norris v. Alabama*, 294 U.S. 587, 79 L. Ed. 1074 (1935); *Patterson v. Alabama*, 294 U.S. 600, 79 L. Ed. 1082 (1935).

2668. *Ernest Womack Jr. v. State*, Memorandum opinion, Supreme Court, Middle Section, February 15, 1936, p. 10.

2669. Ibid., p. 11.

2670. Ibid., p. 11. Citing *Virginia v. Rives*, 100 U.S. 313, 25 L. Ed. 667 (1880); *Thomas v. Texas*, 212 U.S. 278, 53 L. Ed. 512 (1909).

2671. Ibid., p. 12.

2672. Ibid., p. 13–15.

2673. Ibid., p. 15. This language came from the brief filed on his behalf.

2674. Ibid., p. 19. Womack was ordered executed on April 10, 1936.

2675. "Negro Murderer Is Electrocuted at State Prison," *Nashville Banner*, April 10, 1936, p. 5.

2676. *E.K. Harris v. State*, Memorandum opinion, Supreme Court, Middle Section, March 7, 1936. p. 7, 8.

2677. Phil Cooper, "Memory of 1934 Tragedy Lingers Today," *Shelbyville Times-Gazette Sesquicentennial, Historical Edition* (Shelbyville: Times-Gazette, 1969), pp. 256–257.

2678. Ibid., note 1, p.5.

2679. Ibid., p. 3.

2680. Ibid., p. 4.

2681. Ibid., p. 2.

2682. Ibid., p. 3.

2683. Ibid., p. 8.

2684. Ibid., p. 7.

2685. Code Section 10788 (1932)

2686. Ibid., p. 7.

2687. Ibid., p. 7. Quoting *Wharton's Criminal Law*, 10th ed., p. 515, Section 555. This book seems to be quoting "Williams, J.," which is apparently Samuel Cole Williams, who served briefly on the Tennessee Supreme Court.

2688. "Negro Who Pays State Life Confesses Sins, Is Baptized," *Nashville Tennessean*, May 22, 1936, p. 1.

2689. These low-value policies were marketed to poor whites and blacks to whom accidental death was a reality. The leading company, National Life and Accident Insurance Company, had devised a powerful method of reaching poor whites by sponsoring a radio show featuring music they liked—*The Grand Ole Opry*. The desire to collect on such a policy figured in the death sentences of James O. Martin, Joe McKay, and James Willis Smith in 1939 and Jimmy Allen in 1957.

2690. "Murder Evidence Shows New Angle," *Kingsport Times*, April 8, 1936, p. 3.

2691. "Ballard Arrested in Death of Youth," *Kingsport Times*, April 6, 1936, p. 3.

2692. "Ballard Murdered Negro Boy, Negress Testifies on Stand," *Kingsport Times*, April 7, 1936, p. 3. He also said, "That's one xxx that won't take anymore," according to the newspaper.

2693. "Owner Is Sentenced to Death for Hammer Slaying by Jury," *Kingsport Times*, May 22, 1936, p. 3.

2694. Inmate Record No. 28749 (Curley Ballard), no date, Tennessee Department of Corrections, Letter dated August 11, 1936, from W.S. Farmer and W.D. Martin to E.L. Pardue, Commissioner of Institutions.

2695. "Doomed Negroes Enjoy Feast, Unworried Over Who Dies First," *Nashville Tennessean*, August 14, 1936, p. 1.

2696. *James Smith v. State*, Memorandum opinion, Supreme Court, Middle Section, May 28, 1936. The death penalty statute in effect at the time was Chapter 5, Acts of 1919, section 1. Judge DeHaven's opinion said the court in *Gohlston v. State*, 223 S.W. 839 (Tenn. 1920), and *Mays v. State*, 226 S.W. 233 (Tenn. 1920), had ruled that because the statute did not specify penalties (sometimes referred to as mandatory sentences), the duty was upon the jury to "fix the penalty within certain limits": p. 9.

2697. *Anderson Berry v. State*, Memorandum opinion, Supreme Court, Middle Section, May 2, 1936, p. 6.

2698. *State of Tennessee v. Anderson Berry*, Memorandum opinion, Supreme Court, Middle Section, January 30, 1937, p. 4.

2699. "Doomed Negroes Enjoy Feast, Unworried Over Who Dies First," *Tennessean*, August 14, 1936, pp. 1, 9; Richard Battle, "Three Negroes Electrocuted in Quick Succession at Prison Here; Two Protest Innocence," *Nashville Banner*, August 14, 1936, p. 2.

2700. "Negro Pays with Life for Slaying," *Tennessean*, March 18, 1937, p. 18.

2701. "First Execution Is No Worry for New Warden; Negro to Die," *Tennessean*, March 17, 1937, p. 2. The *Banner* appears not to have reported Berry's execution.

2702. Bill of Exceptions, *State v. James Clarke*, Tennessee Supreme Court, Western Division [n.d.], pp. 34, 47. State Library and Archives Box 3217.

2703. Richard Battle, "Three Negroes Electrocuted in Quick Succession at Prison Here; Two Protest Innocence," *Nashville Banner*, August 14, 1936, p. 4.

2704. "Doomed Negroes Enjoy Feast, Unworried Over Who Dies First," *Nashville Tennessean*, August 14, 1936, p. 1.

2705. *Justus v. State*, 130 Tenn. 540 (1914).

2706. *Elmer Barrett v. State*, Memorandum opinion, Supreme Court, Eastern Section, July 6, 1936, p. 2.

2707. "Negro Asks to See Chair in Which He Dies at Dawn," *Tennessean*, Nov. 18, 1936, p. 18.

2708. "Condemned Negro Dies for Slaying," Nashville Banner, November 18, 1936, p. 3.

2709. "Turner Given Death for Killing Officer," *Commercial Appeal*, March 11, 1936, p. 24.

2710. Motion for New Trial, *State v. James Turner*, Shelby County Criminal Court No. 41882, March 20, 1936.

2711. Judgment, *James Turner v. State*, Tennessee Supreme Court, Western Section, January 22, 1937. He was ordered executed March 5, 1937.

2712. "Memphis Negro Goes to Chair Denying Guilt," *Nashville Banner*, March 5, 1937, p. 8.

2713. Ibid.

2714. Reply Brief for the State, *James Taylor v. State*, Tennessee Supreme Court, Middle Section, January 2, 1937, pp. 2–3. State Library and Archives Box 3388.

2715. *James Taylor v. State*, Memorandum opinion, Supreme Court, Middle Section, January 30, 1937, p. 2.

2716. Ibid.

2717. "Negro Hunted; Condition of Victim Grave," *Nashville Tennessean*, February 19, 1936, p. 1.

2718. Ibid., p. 3.

2719. Ibid.

2720. Taylor was charged and convicted of two crimes: rape and assault and battery with intent to rape.

2721. Ibid., p. 5.

2722. "Negro Admits Attack After Capture Here," *Nashville Tennessean*, March 20, 1936, p. 1. Taylor was immediately taken to the main prison in Nashville for safekeeping, rather than being kept in the Nashville jail.

2723. Ibid., pp. 6–7.

2724. "Negro Hatchet Man to Die June 10," *Nashville Banner*, April 21, 1936, p. 1.

2725. "Negro Solves Killing Before Going to Chair," *Tennessean*, March 15, 1937, p. 1.

2726. "Two Men Shot by Negro Bandits," *Nashville Tennessean*, May 26, 1936, p. 1.

2727. Bill of Exceptions, *State v. Frank Haynie Jr. and Tom Franklin*, Supreme Court, Middle Section, August 11, 1936, p. 6. State Library and Archives File Box No. 1939.

2728. While the bloodhounds were given credit for tracking the pair, this is unlikely because the killers' confessions said they went to Baby's Place in South Nashville, where the dogs could not have tracked them. Then they went to the Moonlight Café on 8th Avenue, where someone may have given Pugh the tip. Then they went to the Red Eye Hotel and spent the night with a prostitute. Bill of Exceptions, p. 12.

2729. Ibid., pp. 1–9.

2730. "Negro Solves Killing Before Going to Chair," *Nashville Tennessean*, March 15, 1937, p. 1.

2731. "Negro Pays with Life for Slaying," *Nashville Tennessean*, March 18, 1937, p. 3.

2732. "Negro Slayer Pays with Life in Chair Here," *Nashville Banner*, March 18, 1937, p. 2. The newspaper was still using the term "death row" in quotes.

2733. *Crawford (Pete) Dean, Gus McCoig, and Frank Hopson v. State*, Memorandum opinion, Supreme Court, Eastern Section, February 15, 1937, p. 5.

2734. Kenneth L. Eagon, "Cumberland's Bloody Bunch," *American Detective* (November 1938): 86; Jack Martin, "Tennessee's Murdering Troubadours," *Master Detective* (December 1938): 10.

2735. Ibid., p. 8.

2736. Ibid., p. 10.

2737. Ibid., p. 11.

2738. Ibid.

2739. Ibid., p. 11. The statute was Code Section 11840. The governor commuted the sentences.
2740. "East Tennessee Bandit-Killer Goes to Chair," *Nashville Banner*, April 8, 1937, p. 17.
2741. "Slain Sheriff's Wife, Children Hoped to See McCoig in Chair," *Nashville Tennessean*, April 9, 1937, p. 8.
2742. "Negro Solves Killing Before Going to Chair," *Nashville Tennessean*, March 15, 1937, p. 1. Franklin explained the knife was hidden in bread given to Haynie by McCoig.
2743. *Roy Wilburn Eatmon, Cecil Curtis Causie and Melvin D. Gilbert v. State*, Memorandum opinion, Supreme Court, Middle Section, February 4, 1937, p. 7.
2744. "Thomasson Slaying Outlined by State," *Commercial Appeal*, June 16, 1936, p. 4.
2745. "Jury Debating Fate of Eatmon, Friends," *Commercial Appeal*, June 18, 1936, p. 14.
2746. Ibid., p. 3.
2747. "Eatmon Convicted in Holdup-Slaying: Gets Death Verdict," *Commercial Appeal*, June 19, 1936, p. 1.
2748. Ibid., p. 6.
2749. "Memphis Killer Pays with Life in Death Chair," *Nashville Banner*, April 16, 1937, p. 14.
2750. Dunn had served a sixteen-month sentence. Sent again, he escaped a few months later and went home. Police made no attempt to arrest him. Transcript, *State v. Farmer and Dunn*, Supreme Court, Middle Section [n.d.], pp. 229–231. State Library and Archives Box 3387.
2751. John Cavanaugh, "Killers in the Dead Man's Shoes," *True Detective* (July 1946): 24, 92.
2752. John Lipscomb, "Slayers Calm as Witnesses Tell of Crime," *Nashville Tennessean*, April 10, 1936, p. 1.
2753. Transcript, *State v. Farmer and Dunn*, Supreme Court, Middle Section [n.d.], pp. 187–197.
2754. John Lipscomb, "Farmer Claims to be Insane, Attorneys Say," *Nashville Tennessean*, April 11, 1936, p. 1. The precise plea was hereditary insanity.
2755. Transcript, p. 239.
2756. John Lipscomb, "Slayers Calm as Witnesses Tell of Crime," *Nashville Tennessean*, April 10, 1936, p. 1.
2757. John Lipscomb, "Youths Laugh When Verdict Is Given Court," *Nashville Tennessean*, April 12, 1936, p. 1.
2758. *William Farmer and Howard Dunn v. State*, Memorandum Opinion, Supreme Court, Middle Section, January 30, 1937, pp. 2–7.
2759. Ibid., pp. 8–9.
2760. "Farmer, Dunn Calm as They Await Death," *Nashville Tennessean*, April 29, 1937, p. 1.
2761. Ibid., p. 5.
2762. Richard Battle, "Dunn and Farmer, Steadfast to the End, Go to Their Death for Slaying of J.K. Milliken," *Nashville Banner*, April 30, 1937, p. 1.
2763. Ibid.
2764. Bill of Exceptions, *State of Tennessee v. Jimmy Lee Parrish*, Supreme Court, Middle Section [n.d.], Case No. 8452, pp. 19–20. State Library and Archives Box 3375. See, "Negro Confesses Assault Attempt," *Nashville Tennessean*, Dec. 17, 1936, p. 1.
2765. Ibid., "Defendant's Proof," p. 21.
2766. Inmate Record Number 30435 (Jimmie Lee Parrish), Tennessee Department of Corrections, no date.
2767. *Jimmie Lee Parrish v. State*, Memorandum opinion, Supreme Court, Middle Section, June 17, 1937.
2768. Assault with intent to commit rape of a child under twelve was punishable as rape. But the rape statute, Code Section 10781, which provided for the death penalty, also said, "The jury before whom the offender is tried and convicted, may, if they think proper, commute the punishment for the offense to imprisonment in the penitentiary for life, or for a period of not less than ten years."
2769. Death Statement of Jimmie Lee Parrish, August 9, 1937.
2770. Ibid.
2771. "Attacker Is Calm During Last Walk," *Nashville Tennessean*, August 9, 1937, p. 12.
2772. "Negro Attacker of White Girl Dies in Chair," *Nashville Banner*, August 9, 1937, p. 12. The Banner reported that Parrish had twice been convicted of assault with intent to ravish.
2773. Bill of Exceptions, *State v. Richie*, Supreme Court, Middle Section, December 28, 1936, p. 17. State Library and Archives Box 3375.
2774. Ibid., p. 20.
2775. Ibid.
2776. *State v. Fred Richie*, Bill of Exceptions, December 28, 1936, p. 77.
2777. "Tennessee to Adopt 'Humanized' Executions," *Nashville Banner*, April 30, 1937, p. 8.
2778. "State Claims Ritchie's Life at Daybreak," *Nashville Tennessean*, August 10, 1937, p. 14.
2779. "Wife Slayer Put to Death in Chair Here," *Nashville Banner*, August 10, 1937, p. 13.
2780. Ibid.
2781. "Joe Richie, 37, Kills His Wife," *Nashville Tennessean*, August 1, 1938, p. 1.
2782. Ibid., p. 2.
2783. Inmate Record No. 37177 (Joe Ritchie), Tennessee Department of Corrections.
2784. "Young Negro Slayer Gets Death Sentence," *Commercial Appeal*, April 23, 1937, p. 9.
2785. "Condemned Negro Watched Closely," *Nashville Tennessean*, April 15, 1938, p. 10.
2786. Memphis Negro Dies in Electric Chair for Slaying," *Nashville Banner*, April 15, 1938, p. 16.
2787. "Death Penalty Fixed in Negro's Conviction," *Commercial Appeal*, January 20, 1938, p. 1. In the days before credit cards became popular, club plan purchasing was a method of purchasing on credit. This plan was for Goldsmith's Department Store.
2788. "Death Verdict in Attack Case," *Memphis Press-Scimitar*, January 20, 1938, p. 4.
2789. "Attacker Nervous as Death Nears," *Nashville Tennessean*, July 25, 1938, p. 3.
2790. "Negro Executed," *Nashville Times*, July 25, 1938, p. 4.
2791. *Ernest Stanley v. State*, Memorandum opinion, Supreme Court, Eastern Section, November 25, 1938.
2792. "Man Electrocuted for Killing Guard," *Nashville Banner*, January 10, 1939, p. 16.
2793. While these were their full names, they were generally known as Miller Tollett, Church Lester, Lee Walker, and Ulysses Walling. The Tennessee Supreme Court's opinion spelled Walling's name as "Wallin," and that will be used throughout this discussion of the case.
2794. The most complete discussion of the case is Jack Martin, "Mountain Murder: The Inside Story of Tennessee's Dynamite Massacre," *True Detective Mysteries* (September 1938): 12. See also "Dynamite Death," *True Detective Mysteries* (April 1938): 65; W.L. Hicklin, "Harvest of Revenge," *American Detective* (June 1938): 14.
2795. The picture of the destroyed house and the three girls with their mother appeared in newspapers nationally. See also "The 'PIC' Album of Notorious American Murders: The Gouge Case," *PIC Magazine* (June 28, 1938): 43; "When the Tolletts and the Gouges Clashed," *Actual Detective Stories of Women in Crime* (April 6, 1938): 12.
2796. The outcome of the case against Gouge is unknown. He was scheduled to stand trial on April 11, 1939, four months after Miller Tollett and Church Lester were sentenced to die for killing his girls.
2797. This alibi may have persuaded the jury but for the fact that the male friend named Vaughn did not testify at the trial. *White Miller Tollett v. State*, Memorandum opinion, Supreme Court, Eastern Section, November 25, 1938, p. 6. Tollett operated a restaurant in Pikeville and usually slept in that building.
2798. The statement was actually a transcript of his words, taken by a court stenographer.
2799. *White Miller Tollett v. State*, Memorandum opinion, Supreme Court, Eastern Section, November 25, 1938, pp. 10–11.
2800. On October 26, 1944, the (now) former sheriff went to his ex-wife's home and shot and killed her. The occupants of the house engaged in a gun battle in which Walling was also killed and they were badly wounded.
2801. *State v. Tollett*, 121 S.W.2d 525 (Tenn. 1938). Accessories before the fact may be prosecuted in any county where the principal felony was committed, but accessories after the fact must be prosecuted in the county where they committed their offense.
2802. He was a brother of White Miller Tollett and had been charged as an accessory before the fact.

2803. Church Lester as told to Grover Kidwell, "I Confess, but the Law Won't Get Me," *Crime Confessions* (August 1940): 10. The account is not really an authentic confession, but a purported description of the case from Lester's view, spoken in Appalachian vernacular, with accompanying pictures, notably of Church Lester hanging in his cell. See also "Self-Executed," *Dynamic Detective* (June 1938): 32–33. Another view of Lester hanging in his cell. Church Lester, white, was forty-four.

2804. *White Miller Tollett v. State*, Memorandum opinion, Supreme Court, Eastern Section, November 25, 1938, pp. 4–9.

2805. Ibid., p. 12.

2806. Ibid., p. 12.

2807. In support, it cited the Cumberland County case of Sullivan v. State, "decided this day, to which reference is made." Ibid., p. 15.

2808. Woodson Knight, "Tollett Maintains Innocence, Still Has Hopes of Clemency," *Nashville Tennessean*, January 10, 1939, p. 1. This was Gov. Gordon Browning.

2809. Ibid. He was referring to either Wallin or Walker, but it cannot be determined which he meant.

2810. James S. Metcalfe, "Tollett Dies for Dynamite Killing of Girls," *Nashville Banner*, January 11, 1939, p. 1.

2811. Ibid., p. 2.

2812. Ibid., p. 2.

2813. Morgan James, "Ride, Rob and Kill," *Real Detective* (November 1951): 18–19, 45, 48–49.

2814. *Hyman Johnson and Frank Murray v. State*, Memorandum opinion, Supreme Court, Middle Section, February 4, 1939.

2815. "Two Negroes Are Executed in Gordon Case," *Nashville Banner*, March 28, 1939, p. 5.

2816. "Two Negroes Facing Electric Chair Are Satisfied with Death," *Nashville Tennessean*, March 28, 1939, p. 1.

2817. Ibid.

2818. Ibid.

2819. *Hubert Harris and James Thompson v. State*, Memorandum opinion, Supreme Court, Middle Section, February 18, 1939, p. 1.

2820. Ibid., p. 2.

2821. Bill of Exceptions, *State v. Hubert Harris and James Thompson*, Supreme Court, Middle Section [n.d.] p. 34–40; State Library and Archives Box 3572.

2822. Ibid., note 1, p. 7.

2823. Bill of Exceptions, *State v. Hubert Harris and James Thompson*, Tennessee Supreme Court [n.d.], p. 24. During this era, Ed Pugh was famous for his bloodhounds, which caught many criminals. His son was a deputy sheriff.

2824. Ibid., note 1, p. 9.

2825. "Cooper Saves Life of Negro," *Nashville Tennessean*, April 2, 1939, A-9.

2826. "Hubert Harris Executed for Murder Here," *Nashville Banner*, April 4, 1939, p. 12; "Negro Will Die in Chair Today; Killed Farmer," *Nashville Tennessean*, April 4, 1939, p. 6.

2827. Jack DeWitt, "Please Stop Insuring My Life," *Official Detective* (February 1939): 8, 10.

2828. Ibid., p. 9. See also W.F. Glisson, "Calling All Cars: Trapped by a Random Shot," *Master Detective* (February 1939): 17–21, 56–58.

2829. *J.O. Martin, Joe McKay and James Willis Smith v. State*, Memorandum opinion, Supreme Court, Western Section, February 18, 1939, pp. 2, 10–12.

2830. Ibid., p. 34.

2831. Ibid., p. 21.

2832. Ibid., p. 34.

2833. Ibid., pp. 10–13.

2834. Ibid., p. 30.

2835. Ibid., p. 3.

2836. Ibid., p. 43.

2837. William D. Sisson, "Martin Dies in Chair, Blames Murder on 'Joke' to the End," *Commercial Appeal*, April 11, 1939, p. 1.

2838. William D. Sisson, "Martin Numb, Negroes Cool in Presence of Electric Chair," *Commercial Appeal*, April 10, 1939, p. 1.

2839. William D. Sisson, "Martin Dies in Chair, Blames Murder on 'Joke' to the End," *Commercial Appeal*, April 11, 1939, p. 1.

2840. *George v. Protective Life Insurance Company*, 136 S.W.2d 52 (Tenn. 1940).

2841. "Negro Bandits Get $1,100 at James' Place," *Nashville Tennessean*, June 9, 1937, p. 17.

2842. This was owned by the victim's son, also known as William James, Jr. He inherited his father's numbers running operation until a crackdown in August 1936. The robbery was probably an inside job because the money was never removed on the same day of the week and several witnesses linked the insider with Williams. The probable insider testified at trial but did not incriminate himself. The son was also wounded in the robbery-murder.

2843. *State v. Willie Williams and Henry Crockett*, Memorandum opinion, Supreme Court, Middle Section, January 2, 1939, p. 3. Both Brown and McKnight lived at the club.

2844. Ibid., p. 8.

2845. Ibid.

2846. Ibid.

2847. Ibid., p. 9.

2848. Ibid.

2849. Ibid., p. 11.

2850. "Willie Williams' Death Set Today," *Nashville Tennessean*, April 15, 1939, p. 3. This was the first time the term "last mile" was used in a local newspaper.

2851. "Convicted Negro Slayer Seeks to Cheat Chair — By Starvation," *Nashville Tennessean*, April 12, 1939, p. 8.

2852. Statement of Willie Williams [n.d.], Papers of Gov. Prentice Cooper, Box 21, folder 5. The statement was typewritten and someone clearly helped Williams compose it. The newspapers ignored the statement, if Swafford actually gave it to reporters.

2853. "Negro Slayer of James' Father Is Executed," *Nashville Banner*, April 15, 1939, p. 2.

2854. Bill of Exceptions, *State v. Henry Crockett and Willie Williams*, Supreme Court, Middle Section [n.d.]. State Library and Archives Box 3568.

2855. *Harley Evans v. State*, Memorandum opinions, Supreme Court, Eastern Section, July 1, 1939, pp. 5–6.

2856. Ibid., p. 3

2857. "Slayer of Two Is Electrocuted at State Prison," *Banner*, August 28, 1939, p. 9.

2858. Ibid.

2859. Ibid.

2860. Ibid.

2861. "Posse Takes Man in Hold-Up Attacks on Two Couples," *Knoxville News-Sentinel*, December 7, 1938, p. 1.

2862. "Man Confesses 'Date' Attack," *Knoxville News-Sentinel*, December 8, 1938, p. 1.

2863. *Clyde Wills v. State*, Memorandum opinion, Supreme Court, Eastern Division, November 2, 1939.

2864. "Clyde Wills Is Executed at Penitentiary," *Nashville Banner*, January 10, 1940, p. 2; "Knoxville Man Dies in Chair; Is Baptized," *Nashville Tennessean*, January 11, 1940, p. 3.

2865. Inmate Record No. 34105 (A. C. Mobley), Tennessee Department of Corrections.

2866. *A.C. Mobley v. State*, Memorandum opinion, Supreme Court, Western Division, January 2, 1940.

2867. "Negro Executed in State Prison," *Nashville Banner*, March 15, 1940, p. 37.

2868. Ibid.

2869. "Prison Death Row Emptied by Execution," *Nashville Tennessean*, March 15, 1940, p. 32.

2870. *William Henry alias Clay Nelson v. State*, Memorandum opinion, Supreme Court, Western Section, June 8, 1940, p. 2. Most published accounts of this execution describe the defendant as "William Henry Clay Nelson." Henry had used the Nelson alias for several years and his wife was always referred to as Mrs. Nelson. Curry was the local undertaker.

2871. This is not the neighbor's real name but was used in contemporary accounts of the case. K.K. O'Neal, "Love Riddle of the Lowlands," *Daring Detective* 16 (April 1942): 44, 65. See also David Kent, "Riddle of the Twilight Gunman," *Current Detective* (February 1946): 29. These accounts refer to Clay Nelson.

2872. This was not this neighbor's name but was used in contemporary accounts of the crime. Ibid.

2873. *William Henry, alias Clay Nelson v. State*, Memorandum opinion, Supreme Court, Western Section, June 8, 1940, p. 11.

2874. Ibid., p. 5.

2875. Ibid., p. 9.

2876. Ibid., p. 13.

2877. Ibid., p. 12.

2878. Ibid., p. 15.

2879. Ibid., p. 13

2880. "Two Die in Chair in State Prison," *Nashville Tennessean*, Sept. 5, 1940, p. 20.

2881. Payne was actually both. He was the blacksmith at the Memphis stockyards, and a friend of the liquor store owner, Bob Cartmell, sometimes doing work for him. Jack DeWitt, "The Strange Case of 'Trigger Slim,'" *Front Page Detective* (August 1940): 8, 9.

2882. Ibid.

2883. Ibid., p. 9.

2884. One of them was detective Lt. W.J. Raney, famous for his capture of Machine Gun Kelly.

2885. "'Trigger Slim' Goes to Death for Killing of Memphis Man," *Nashville Tennessean*, September 5, 1940, p. 6.

2886. *James Goodin, Alias v. State*, Memorandum opinion, Supreme Court, Western Division, June 8, 1940.

2887. "Two Die in Chair in State Prison," *Nashville Tennessean*, September 5, 1940, p. 6.

2888. *Van Gilmore v. State*, Memorandum opinion, Supreme Court, Western Section, March 20, 1941, p. 2.

2889. Ibid., p. 5.

2890. Ibid.

2891. Ibid.

2892. "Negro Will Die at Dawn for Criminal Attack," *Nashville Tennessean*, April 18, 1941, p. 7.

2893. Ibid., p. 6.

2894. Ibid.

2895. Ibid.

2896. Inmate Record No. 35427 (Van Gilmore), Tennessee Department of Corrections, photocopy.

2897. "State Offers Sixteen Witnesses in Reed Trial," *Chattanooga Times*, May 15, 1941, p. 3.

2898. "Negro Dies in Electric Chair," *Nashville Banner*, July 18, 1941, p. 4.

2899. "Cathy Photos Are Admitted," *Chattanooga Times*, May 16, 1941, p. 1; "Death Verdict Is Given Reed," *Chattanooga Times*, May 17, 1941, p. 1.

2900. Ibid., note 2; "Negro Executed for Woman's Death," *Nashville Tennessean*, July 20, 1941, p. 20.

2901. Porter v. State, 177 Tenn. 515, 519 (1941).

2902. Ibid., p. 519.

2903. Ibid., p. 520.

2904. Ibid., p. 523.

2905. *Porter v. State*, 177 Tenn. 515, 524 (1941).

2906. "Two Negro Youths Electrocuted for Killing Watchman," *Nashville Banner*, July 24, 1941, p. 22.

2907. *Lawrence West v. State*, Memorandum Opinion, Supreme Court, Middle Section, June 14, 1941, p. 1.

2908. Ibid., p. 2.

2909. Ibid.

2910. Ibid., p. 3.

2911. Ibid., p. 4.

2912. Ibid., p. 6.

2913. Ibid., p. 8.

2914. Ibid., p. 13.

2915. Letter from Thomas P. Gore, Warden to Honorable Prentice Cooper, Governor, July 8, 1941.

2916. Ibid., p. 1.

2917. Ibid.

2918. "Montgomery Negro Scheduled to Die in Electric Chair," *Nashville Banner*, July 24, 1941, p. 4; "Clarksville Negro, Who Killed Farm Couple, Executed," *Nashville Banner*, July 30, p. 1941, p. 16; "Negro Facing Chair Admits Slayings," *Nashville Tennessean*, July 31, 1941, p. 16.

2919. The court described the business as a lunchroom. It would be described as a family café today, in part, because it was not licensed to sell alcohol.

2920. *Walden v. State*, 156 S.W.2d 385, 386 (Tenn. 1941).

2921. Ibid., p. 386.

2922. Ibid.

2923. Ibid., p. 387.

2924. Ibid., p. 388.

2925. Ibid.

2926. Tenn. Department of Corrections Record No. 35135 (Roy Walden), no date.

2927. "One of Three to Die in Chair Pleads for Last Minute Break," *Nashville Tennessean*, February 12, 1942, p. 4.

2928. The court declined to describe the details of the rapes, saying an excellent statement of the facts was contained in the Attorney General's brief and "an even fuller statement of the facts is contained in the brief of counsel appointed by the Court, who, it should be said have ably and faithfully discharged their duty": *Ernest Dixon and John Dockery v. State*, Memorandum opinion, Supreme Court, Eastern Section, November 29, 1941, p. 4.

2929. *Ernest Dixon and John Dockery v. State*, Memorandum opinion, Supreme Court, Eastern Section, November 29, 1941, pp. 2–3.

2930. Ibid., p. 4.

2931. Ibid., p. 1.

2932. Ibid., p. 6. The court was applying the rule newly announced in Bellis v. State, 157 Tenn. 177.

2933. Ibid., p. 8.

2934. Ibid., p. 9.

2935. Ibid., p. 10.

2936. "Knox Youth Admits Assault of Mute as Two Electrocuted," *Nashville Tennessean*, February 15, 1942, p. 8.

2937. The opinion gives the son's name as "Roberta" but seems likely an error.

2938. *Clarence May v. State*, Memorandum Opinion, Supreme Court, Eastern Section, January 17, 1942. 5 pp. The decision in John Henry Goode's case was issued this day as well, with his execution set for March 3, 1942.

2939. "Farmer, Negro Die in Chair for Murder," *Nashville Tennessean*, March 21, 1942, p. 35; "Two Die in Chair at State Prison," *Nashville Banner*, March 20, 1942, p. 8.

2940. *John Henry Goode v. State*, Memorandum opinion, Supreme Court, Western Section, January 17, 1942, 5 pp.

2941. "Two Die in Chair at State Prison," *Nashville Banner*, March 20, 1942, p. 8; "Farmer, Negro Die in Chair for Murder," *Nashville Tennessean*, March 21, 1942, p. 35.

2942. "Two Die in Chair at State Prison," *Nashville Banner*, March 20, 1942, p. 8.

2943. The Tennessee Supreme Court opinion describes the murder victim as Mrs. Arlene Dillard, but newspaper accounts call her Mrs. Arlene Dillard Glowan. *William Hedden v. State*, Memorandum opinion, Supreme Court, Eastern Section, January 30, 1943, p. 2; Henry Gillespie, "He Was Keeping the Fellows Away," *Intimate Detective* (March 1942): 9; Herbert Rudlin, "Too Many Suitors for the Estranged Wife," *All-Fact Detective* (May 1942): 10; Eugene Pawley, "Blood Stains the Welcome Mat," *Sensation* (October 1942): 26; L.D. Miller, "Murder at Twilight," *Master Detective* (March 1944): 36; Eloise C. Mackey, "Triple Death and the Sex-Crazed Suitor," *Dynamic Detective* (April 1942): 14.

2944. A constable is an elected county official who serves as an undersheriff for a portion of the county, hence the saying, "One sheriff and many constables." Duties include serving process, enforcing the law against carrying deadly weapons, arresting tramps and vagrants, suppressing riot and breach of the peace and acting with all the power of a Sheriff. *Tennessee Sheriff and Constable Guide* (Nashville: McQuiddy, 1912). The constable was not a full-time job, and Hedden's prison record says that he was a farmer with a third-grade education.

2945. Robert Rudlin, "Too Many Suitors for the Estranged Wife," *All-Fact Detective* (May 1942): 10, 12.

2946. Ibid.

2947. L.D. Miller, "Murder at Twilight," *Master Detective* (March 1944): 36, 40.

2948. Accounts are conflicting, but the other man was identified as Floyd Breeden, his cousin. LD. Miller, "Murder at Twilight," *Master Detective* (March 1944): 36, 39.

2949. The drink of water explanation was not very convincing. He admitted there were creeks and springs along the way from which he could have obtained a drink of water, but he had nothing to drink with, and he was "well acquainted with Jack and his wife, but not particularly acquainted with Mrs. Dillard, having known her only about four days": *William Hedden v. State*, p. 15.

2950. *William Hedden v. State*, p. 14.

2951. *William Hedden v. State*, p. 9.

2952. Ibid., p. 9. According to one account, Hedden said, "She'll never give herself to another man and then act so holy with me. There's not a one left to tell the tale!" Herbert Rudlin, "Too Many Suitors for the Estranged Wife," *All-Fact Detective* (May 1942): 10, 40.

2953. Ibid., p. 10. The defendant was the first to say that the money was missing.

2954. Ibid., p. 15.

2955. Herbert Rudlin, "Too Many Suitors for the Estranged Wife," *All-Fact Detective* (May 1942): 40. According to this account, a pistol of this caliber had been loaned by Jack Hedden to his brother William Hedden about two weeks before the killings.

2956. Ibid.

2957. Bates lived two hundred yards away. *William Hedden v. State*, p. 11.

2958. It is not clear which of these men was Lawrence Breeden.

2959. *William Hedden v. State*, 11, 12. Bates was certain the shootings happened at this time because he had just heard a popular radio show, *Amos and Andy*, which ended at 6:15. L.D. Miller, "Murder at Twilight," *Master Detective* (March 1944): 36, 39.

2960. The coroner's jury proceeding consisted of the neighbors present standing outside around a fire that had been built to keep them warm and discussing the facts they saw. Another account said that Goforth was asked to serve on the coroner's jury but failed to do so, having left in the car with the defendant, ostensibly to tell family members about the killings. L.D. Miller, "Murder at Twilight," *Master Detective* (March 1944): 36, 38.

2961. *William Hedden v. State*, p. 16.

2962. Ibid., p. 28. Hedden's four defense counsel vigorously cross-examined all the witnesses against him.

2963. Henry Gillespie, "He Was Keeping the Fellows Away," *Intimate Detective* (March 1942): 9, 44. He also confirmed he had thrown the chewed match sticks on the ground while waiting in the car.

2964. Elmer Hinton, "Two to Die in State Chair Today; One Maintains Innocence," *Nashville Tennessean* (March 30, 1943), p. 1. The newspaper also published a letter Hedden sent to his mother in which he said he would see her in heaven and said the liars would have to "face a just judge some day and give an answer for the lies they swore on me."

2965. "2 Convicted Slayers Die in Electric Chair," *Nashville Banner*, March 30, 1943, p. 16. Hedden was the first person to receive a death sentence from Polk County since 1908.

2966. *Robert Cannon v. State*, Memorandum opinion, Supreme Court, Western Section, January 30, 1943, p. 3.

2967. "Hold-Up Killer Arrested," *Memphis Press-Scimitar*, May 11, 1942, p. 1.

2968. Ibid., p. 3.

2969. Tennessee Constitution, Article 1, Section 19.

2970. *Robert Cannon v. State*, Memorandum opinion, Supreme Court, Western Section, January 30, 1943, p. 4.

2971. 101 Tenn. 454 (1898)

2972. Ibid., p. 6, citing *Ford and Harris v. State*, 75 Tenn. 538 (1881), and *Dale v. State*, 18 Tenn. 550 (1837).

2973. Citing *Hannah v. State*, 79 Tenn. (1883)

2974. *Robert Cannon v. State*, Memorandum opinion, Supreme Court, Western Section, January 30, 1943, p. 7.

2975. Elmer Hinton, "Two to Die in State Chair Today; One Maintains Innocence," *Nashville Tennessean*, March 30, 1943, p.1.

2976. The couple rented two rooms in the house. *James Felix Tucker v. State*, Memorandum opinion, May 29, 1943, p. 1. Their landlord was the father of the salesman mentioned in the case.

2977. Stuart MacDonald, "The Green Eyed Monster and the Brunette Beauty," *Headquarters Detective* (September 1946): 39.

2978. Ibid., p. 72.

2979. Robert M. Seals and Beasley Thompson, "Tucker, Spigener Die Calmly; Memphian Confesses Crime," *Nashville Tennessean*, July 16, 1943, p. 5.

2980. *James Felix Tucker v. State*, Memorandum opinion, Supreme Court, Middle Section, May 29, 1943, p. 3

2981. Ibid., p. 6.

2982. Jack Setters, "Fugitive's Masquerade," *Human Detective* (September 1944): 18, 37; E.B. Moody, "The Strangled Beauty in Room 1011," *Sensational Detective Cases* (April 1, 1943): 20; Elton Whisenhunt, "Girl in the Strangler's Grip," *True Police Cases* (July 1956): 30.

2983. Nelson Stein, "Naked and Dead in Room 1011," *Detective Cases* (July 1964): 12, 13.

2984. *Marshall Spigener v. State*, Memorandum opinion, Supreme Court, Western Section, May 29, 1943, p. 3.

2985. A later investigation showed that the couple had gone to a second restaurant that evening as well, and Spigener was identified by a waitress there. See Opinion, p. 3. The hotel bellman also identified Spigener as the person who he saw at the hotel with Roberts.

2986. The girlfriend was Mrs. Evelyn Weible, a married woman, whom Spigener had met through his sister-in-law, Mrs. A.J. Spigener. Mrs. Weible gave conflicting testimony about whether she was Spigener's girlfriend, explaining that he had simply given her the rings for safekeeping. She told police Spigener had forced her to accept the rings because the owner had threatened him with arrest after they were lost in a card game. According to one account, Weible buried the rings in her back yard but told police their location. Jack Setters, "Fugitive's Masquerade," *Human Detective* (September 1944): 18, 37.

2987. Fred G. Millette, "Given Name, Marshall — Residence, Memphis — Bring Him In," *Intimate Detective* (December 1942): 6, 40.

2988. Jack Clements, "Tennessee's Weak-Eyed Strangler," *Detective Cases* (August 1980): 24, 45. According to this version, Spigener gave this information in a confession, explaining that the elderly man did not know of the attempt to manipulate him into selling the house.

2989. Opinion, p. 7.

2990. Ibid., p. 6.

2991. Ibid., p. 5. According to one account, the failure of the county commission to give the public defender money to pay for a psychiatric evaluation of Spigener caused the public defender to publicly denounce the commission and withdraw from the case, another public defender taking his place. Ken Carpenter, "Lie Back and Die, Darling," *Detective Files* (January 1992): 16, 38.

2992. The bellman had brought whiskey and mixers to the room. Spigener was also linked to the crime because two telephone calls had been made from the room, according to telephone operator records. One call was made to Spigener's sister and another to his sister-in-law. Opinion, p. 4.

2993. Jack Clements, "Tennessee's Weak-Eyed Strangler," *Detective Cases* (August 1980): 24.

2994. Judge L.D. Miller, "Murder in Room 1011," *True Detective* (January 1949): 21, 69.

2995. Robert M. Seals and Beasley Thompson, "Tucker, Spigener Die Calmly; Memphian Confesses to Crime," *The Nashville Tennessean*, July 16, 1943, p.8.

2996. Nelson Stein, "Naked and Dead in Room 1011," *Detective Cases* (July 1964): 12; Jack Clements, "Tennessee's Weak-Eyed Strangler," *Detective Cases* (August 1980): 24; Ken Carpenter, "Lie Back and Die, Darling," *Detective Files* (January 1992): 16; Ken Carpenter, "Lie Back and Die, My Darling," *True Police Cases* (June 2000): 54.

2997. 18 U.S.C.A. Section 253, 452, 453.

2998. *Arwood v. United States*, 134 F2d 1007 (6th Cir. 1943), cert. denied, 63 S. Ct. 1436, 319 U.S. 776, 87 L. Ed. 1722 (1945).

2999. Elmer Hinton and Gloria Root, "Arwood Calm, Refuses to Talk as He Goes to Chair Unmoved," *Nashville Tennessean*, August 15, 1943, p. 10; James E. McKee, "Clyde Arwood Executed at State Prison," *Nashville Banner*, August 14, 1943, p. 2.

3000. *Robert Hall v. State*, Memorandum opinion, Supreme Court, Eastern Section, September 16, 1943. Hall's lawyers made an unsuccessful petition to the United States Supreme Court, which denied certiorari in October 1943.

3001. "Police Slayer to Die in Chair," *Nashville Tennessean*, December 15, 1943, p. 20.

3002. Ibid.

3003. "Governor Refuses Clemency to Hall," *Chattanooga Times*, December 15, 1943, pp. 1, 17.

3004. "Negro Executed at State Prison," *Nashville Banner*, December 15, 1943, p. 1.

3005. "Police Slayer to Die in Chair," *Nashville Tennessean*, December 15, 1943, p. 20.

3006. Ibid.

3007. "Negro Executed at State Prison," *Nashville Banner*, December 15, 1943, p. 1.

3008. As a felon sentenced to more than a year's incarceration, he should have been held at the prison, but the common practice was to allow persons with short sentences to serve them in the county jail or workhouse. The newspapers said Hambrick was serving a short sentence, but there is also conflicting evidence about that. On October 13, 1939, a man named George Hambrick shot and killed Vernon Poole in Nashville after a back-alley dice game and pled guilty to second-degree murder on February 14, 1940, receiving a twenty-year sentence. It cannot be determined whether this is the same George Hambrick. John Cavanaugh, "He Gambled with Death,"

Master Detective (September 1946): 50–55, 89–91.
3009. "Negro Goes on Trial in McGrew Death," *Nashville Banner*, November 30, 1943, p. 15.
3010. "Negro Convicted of Killing Guard," *Nashville Tennessean*, December 4, 1943, p. 5.
3011. *Hambrick v. State*, 181 S.W.2d 957, 958 (Tenn. 1944).
3012. *Hambrick v. State*, 181 Tenn. 544, 549–60 (1944). This is the corrected opinion.
3013. A one-paragraph "Memorandum on Petition to Rehear" cannot be understood because it relates to language in the opinion that is not self-explanatory, with the court concluding, "upon reflection, has been stricken from the opinion." George Hambrick v. State, Memorandum on Petition to Rehear, August 4, 1944, p. 1. The corrected opinion is *Hambrick v. State*, 181 S.W. 2nd 957 (Tenn. 1944).
3014. The issue before the United States Supreme Court was whether Tennessee's infamy statute (Code Section 11762) violated the due process clause because it barred fellow inmates (felons) from testifying for Hambrick. The original opinion was made part of his petition for certiorari but was not available to this author.
3015. "Negro Slayer Executed at State Prison," *Nashville Banner*, April 24, 1945, p. 13.
3016. The "official" Tennessee Department of Corrections list of persons executed says this occurred on December 15, 1943, the same day as Robert Hall's execution, but this is an error. "Negro Electrocuted for Killing Here," *Nashville Tennessean*, April 25, 1945, p. 13: "This was the first electrocution in Tennessee during the administration of Gov. Jim McCord."
3017. "Negro Sentenced to Die in Chair on February 16; to Appeal to High Court," *Clarksville Leaf-Chronicle*, January 20, 1945, p. 1. The newspaper account called the defendant Billy Dixon Hickman.
3018. *Billy Dixon v. State*, Memorandum Opinion, Supreme Court, Middle Section, June 9, 1945.
3019. "Billie Dixon Dies in Chair for Assault," *Clarksville Leaf-Chronicle*, July 16, 1945, p. 1.
3020. Neither was charged with rape in this prosecution.
3021. Everett Amis, "Negroes in Parked-Car Slaying Receive Speedy Death Penalty," *Commercial Appeal*, May 10, 1945, pp. 1, 2.
3022. Motion for a Severance, *State v. Johnnie Outlow, alias Outlaw and Thomas Walker*, Shelby County Criminal Court No. 54581.
3023. *Johnnie Outlaw and Thomas Walker v. State*, Memorandum opinion, Supreme Court, Western Section, January 5, 1946, 3 pp. Outlaw was his street name.
3024. Margaret Vandiver and Michel Coconis, "Sentenced to the Punishment of Death: Pre-Furman Capital Crimes and Executions in Shelby County, Tennessee," *University of Memphis Law Review* 31 (Summer 2001): 861–918, 915.
3025. "Two Negroes Electrocuted for Shelby Murder," *Nashville Banner*, March 1, 1946, p. 6.
3026. Reply Brief on Behalf of the State, *George Douglass v. State*, Supreme Court, Western Section, November 2, 1945, pp. 2, 5, 6, 11, 14. State Library and Archives Box 117.
3027. Petition for Clemency, *State v. George Douglass*, June 19, 1946. State Library and Archives Box 117. The Supreme Court rejected this issue on a petition to rehear.
3028. "The Facts," Exhibit No. 10, in *George Douglass v. State*, Supreme Court, Western Section [n.d.], State Library and Archives Box 117.
3029. *George Douglass v. State*, Opinion, Supreme Court, Middle Section, January 19, 1946, p. 8.
3030. Ibid., p. 12.
3031. Ibid., p. 15.
3032. "McCord Grants Execution Stay in Douglass Case," *Tennessean*, June 20, 1946, p. 4.
3033. "Douglass to Die Unless Reprieved," *Tennessean*, July 5, 1946, p. 16; "Memphis Negro Electrocuted," *Nashville Banner*, July 5, 1946, p. 4.
3034. *Alvin Hicks and John Luffman v. State*, Memorandum opinion, Supreme Court, Middle Section, June 1, 1946, p. 3.
3035. Hicks had served a one year prison term in 1941 but the nature of the crime is unknown. One source says it was for attempted assault on a young girl. See Seymour J. Ettman, "Death Was a Party Guest," *Startling Detective* (March 1952): 10, 60; Norman Welton, "The Postman's Wife and the Unregistered Males," *Headquarters Detective* (April 1964): 32–33, 44–47; John Smithson, "Suicide Said the Coroner, Murder Said the Corpse," *Headquarters Detective* (August 1948): 18–23; John S. Thorp, "Bullets for Two," *Front Page Detective* (November 1945): 26–29, 49–53; H.L. Foote, "One Man Called It Murder," *True Crime Detective*, (November 1946): 17–19, 83–84; Michael Hand, "Killers Should Walk Alone," *Crime Year Book* (1950): 30–33, 45–50; D.L. Champion, "Mystery of the Two Bullets," *Master Detective* (February 1955): 44–46, 64–66.
3036. "Two Dover Men to Walk 'Last Mile,'" *Nashville Tennessean*, Aug. 30, 1946, pp. 1, 7.
3037. The Supreme Court opinion mentions only the stolen pistol, but the written confessions of Luffman and Hicks indicate that Luffman had carried a second pistol which was used to kill Grady. Hicks used the smaller weapon on Ruphine. Luffman threw his pistol into the river. John S. Thorp, "Bullets for Two," *Front Page Detective* (November 1945): 26, 53.
3038. Wilma Ericson, "Here Is Your Niece — Dead," *Vital Detective Cases* (January 1946): 50.
3039. *Alvin Hicks and John Luffman v. State*, Memorandum opinion, Supreme Court, Middle Section, June 1, 1946, p. 1.
3040. L.D. Miller, "Killers' Combine," *Expose Detective* (April 1946): 6. L.D. Miller was a circuit/criminal court judge who frequently wrote true crime stories for detective magazines.
3041. Ibid., p. 43.
3042. Wilma Ericson, "Here's Your Niece — Dead," *Vital Detective Cases* (January 1946): 24, 50; Jack Sellers, "When Fish-Hooked 'T's Spelled Murder," *Official Detective Stories* (January 1946): 30–32, 40–41.
3043. Fred Menagh, "One for the Inspector," *True Detective* (December 1946): 16, 95. Confessions transcribed verbatim.
3044. Ibid., p. 45. See Phil Bryant, "Somebody Was Sex Crazy," *Detective Dragnet* (October 1969): 20, 47.
3045. "Defendant Hicks was sent to a reformatory for some offense and was later convicted and sent to the penitentiary for assault with intent to commit rape": *Alvin Hicks and John Luffman v. State*, Memorandum opinion, Supreme Court, Middle Section, June 1, 1946, p. 10.
3046. *Alvin Hicks and John Luffman v. State*, Memorandum opinion, Supreme Court, Middle Section, June 1, 1946, p. 3.
3047. *Alvin Hicks and John Luffman v. State*, Memorandum opinion, Supreme Court, June 1, 1946, p. 4.
3048. "Luffman and Hicks Under Death Sentence for Slaying Tharpe Couple," *Stewart County Times*, Aug. 9, 1945, p. 1.
3049. Ibid., p. 5.
3050. Ibid., p. 8.
3051. Ibid., p. 9.
3052. Ibid.
3053. Ibid., p. 10.
3054. Ibid.
3055. Affidavit of Alvin Hicks [n.d.], Hicks and Luffman file, Circuit Court, Stewart County, p. 4.
3056. "2 Executed for Killing Cherry, Wife," *Nashville Banner*, Aug. 30, 1946, p. 8.
3057. Ibid.
3058. "Luffman Says Hicks Killed Mrs. Cherry, Both Executed," *Stewart County Times*, Sept. 5, 1946, p. 1.
3059. Because Rutherford County was a dry county, persons wishing to purchase liquor got it from persons like Duboise, who made large purchases of taxed liquor in Nashville. A method of distribution was to call a cab and the driver would deliver the bottle. According to one account, the real motive behind threatening Willis was to intimidate him into becoming a liquor courier, which he steadfastly refused. Duboise wanted to be something of a "crime lord" in Rutherford County. Jack Setters, "What's One More Killing?" *Front Page Detective* (March 1950): 26, 54; L.D. Miller, "Case of the Sinister Trio," *Amazing Detective* (January 1947): 42; Ken McLean, "Deadly Slash of the Nebulous Knifeman," *Real Detective* (December 1946): 58.

3060. *James "Wren" Miller, Albert Duboise, and Claude Higdon v. State*, Memorandum opinion, Supreme Court, Middle Section, February 1, 1947, p. 4.

3061. "While Duboise stated he had been on dope for ten years, using from two to six grains a day, he did not claim at the trial or at any other time he was under the influence of either a narcotic or whiskey on the day of the tragedy": *James "Wren" Miller, Albert Duboise, and Claude Higdon v. State*, Memorandum opinion, Supreme Court, Middle Section, February 1, 1947, p. 14.

3062. Ibid., p. 5.

3063. Ibid., p. 6.

3064. Jack Setters, "What's One More Killing?" *Front Page Detective* (March 1950): 26, 55. According to another source, he had been sentenced to a term of two to eight years for second-degree murder. Wayne Whitt, "Duboise to Die at Dawn for Taxi Driver Slaying," *Nashville Tennessean*, April 11, 1947, p. 1.

3065. Ibid., p. 9.

3066. Ibid., p. 16.

3067. Ibid., p. 18.

3068. Wayne Whitt, "Duboise to Die at Dawn for Taxi Driver Slaying," *Nashville Tennessean*, April 11, 1947, p. 1.

3069. "Chair, Gas Chamber Snuff Out 2 Lives," *Tennessean*, April 12, 1947, p. 1.

3070. "John Hodge, Jr., Sentenced to Die in Electric Chair," *Lauderdale County Enterprise*, October 11, 1946, p. 1.

3071. "Local Negro Dies in Chair," *Nashville Banner*, June 19, 1947, p. 3.

3072. "Negro Attacker Dies in Electric Chair," *Nashville Tennessean*, June 20, 1947, p. 4.

3073. Clell Morgan, "Mystery of the Killer of Shady Grove Road," *Uncensored Detective* (December 1947): 36, 57.

3074. *Fred Jackson v. State*, Memorandum opinion, Supreme Court, Eastern Section, Jan. 11, 1947, p. 5. The opinion uses the term "ravished."

3075. Herbert Mason, "One Crime Can't Hide Three Others," *Official Detective Stories* (May 1946): 9.

3076. *Fred Jackson v. State of Tennessee*, Memorandum opinion, Supreme Court, Eastern Section, Jan. 11, 1947, p. 7.

3077. Herbert Mason, "One Crime Can't Hide Three Others," *Official Detective Stories* (May 1946): 9–11, 42.

3078. Ibid., note 2, p. 43.

3079. Ibid., p. 8.

3080. An attempt was made to appeal the case to the United States Supreme Court.

3081. "Fred Jackson Admits Assault, Dies in Chair Without Emotion," *Commercial Appeal*, August 12, 1947, p. 8.

3082. *James Sandusky and John Kelly v. State*, Memorandum opinion, Supreme Court, Middle Section, Feb. 28, 1948, p. 2. All media accounts give the latter's name as Kelley. Jack Setters, "Murder for Laughs," *True Crime Cases* (December 1947): 22; T.S. Johns, "Highway to Homicide," *Real Detective* (August 1947): 20–23; 88–90.

3083. "Murder for Laughs," p. 44.

3084. Opinion, p. 3.

3085. Opinion, p. 3.

3086. "Murder for Laughs," p. 44.

3087. Monte Gurwit, "And Now Who Laughs at Death?" *Official Detective Stories* (April 1950): 37, 38.

3088. "Murder for Laughs," p. 44. According to another source, Bomar said, "Cut it! Don't try that stuff on me. We found Sprouse's body not more than an hour ago!" Gurwit, p. 45.

3089. Ibid.

3090. Opinion, p. 4.

3091. "Murder for Laughs," p. 45. According to this source, this was the first time the death penalty had been meted out in Hickman County.

3092. Opinion, page 6.

3093. Ibid., p. 7.

3094. Ibid., p. 9.

3095. Ibid.

3096. Wayne Whitt, "Sandusky, Kelley Manage Shaky Boldness on Death Eve," *Nashville Tennessean*, April 21, 1948, p. 1.

3097. Ibid., p. 2.

3098. Ibid.

3099. John Means, "Sandusky, Kelley Die in Electric Chair," *Nashville Banner*, April 22, 1948, p. 4; John Means, "Revenge Is Bitter at the Death House," *Fairfax (Virginia) Journal*, August 9, 1991, p. 4. Descriptions of the executions.

3100. "Sandusky, Kelley Manage Shaky Boldness on Death Eve," p. 1.

3101. From their vantage point it was possible to see the lights at a baseball field called Sulphur Dell. This was their given reason for going to the Capitol. Couples also used the Capitol grounds as a place to engage in petting because it was deemed safe.

3102. "Statement of the Case," *William J.C. Turner, James M. Scribner, and Thomas Howard Taylor v. State*, Supreme Court, Middle Section [n.d.], pp. 2–3; *Turner v. State*, 213 S.W. 2d 281 (Tenn. 1948): "From tears and lacerations of the vagina and hymeneal ring that the vagina had been penetrated and that the young lady had been a virgin prior to the intercourse": p. 282.

3103. While the opinion does not explain it, court officer Justice had noticed a pattern of strong-arm robberies around the Capitol and when the trio was brought in on some lesser charges about the same time as this crime, he became suspicious and decided to conduct his own search.

3104. *Turner v. State*, 213 S.W. 2d 281, 282 (Tenn. 1948).

3105. "Statement of Facts," note , p. 7.

3106. *Turner v. State*, 213 S.W.2d 281, 282–283 (Tenn. 1948).

3107. Ibid., p. 283.

3108. Ibid.

3109. *William J.C. Turner, James M. Scribner, and Thomas Howard Taylor v. State*, Opinion on Petition to Rehear, Supreme Court, Middle Section, August 14, 1948, p. 2.

3110. Ibid., p. 3.

3111. "3 Local Negroes Die in Chair for Criminal Assault," *Nashville Banner*, August 31, 1948, p. 6.

3112. *Barney Thompson v. State*, Memorandum opinion, Supreme Court, Eastern Section, Dec. 11, 1948, pp. 1–2.

3113. Ibid., p. 3

3114. Ibid.

3115. Ibid., p. 5, citing, *Mullendore v. State*, 183 Tenn. 53, 191 S.W.2d 149 (1945).

3116. Ibid., p. 5.

3117. Ibid., p. 7.

3118. Ibid., p. 9.

3119. "Barney Thompson Executed," *Nashville Banner*, February 17, 1949, p. 8; "Cleveland Killer Dies in Chair Today," *Nashville Tennessean*, February 17, 1949, p. 4.

3120. *Ashcraft v. Tennessee*, 322 U.S. 143 (1944).

3121. *Bruce Edward Watson v. State*, Memorandum opinion, Supreme Court, Western Section, January 17, 1949, p. 5.

3122. Ibid., p. 8.

3123. The family had been brought to the jail for questioning regarding Watson's whereabouts the night of the rape and to confirm the hat found was Watson's. Ibid., p. 8.

3124. Ibid. p. 6.

3125. 318 U.S. 332 (1943). As a matter of federal law applicable to persons charged with a federal crime, a suspect must not be subject to "unnecessary delay." A 1968 federal statute said no longer than six hours.

3126. *Bruce Edward Watson v. State*, Memorandum opinion, Supreme Court, Western Section, January 17, 1949, p. 9.

3127. Ibid., p. 13.

3128. Ibid., p. 12.

3129. "Shelby County Negro Dies in Electric Chair," *Nashville Banner*, June 10, 1949, p. 17.

3130. Margaret Vandiver and Michel Coconis, "Sentenced to the Punishment of Death: Pre–Furman Capital Crimes and Executions in Shelby County, Tennessee," *University of Memphis Law Review* 31 (Summer 2001); 861, 916–918.

3131. E.V. Aimes, "Buried in Alibis," *Official Detective* (January 1951): 12, 13. See also, "Maury Woman Assaulted, Killed; Suspects Nabbed," *Maury Democrat*, September 28, 1949, p. 1.

3132. Ibid., p. 55.

3133. Ibid., p. 56

3134. Robert W. Ikard, *No More Social Lynchings* (Franklin, TN: Hillsboro Press, 1997), 180 pp.

3135. "Lacy to Chair November 25, Bass Delayed," *Maury Democrat*, October 28, 1949, p. 1.

3136. Albert Cason, "Lacy Denies His Guilt as Last Hours Tick Off," *Nashville Tennessean*, November 25, 1949, p. F2; "Paul Lacy Executed for Murder," *Nashville Tennessean*, November 26, 1949, p. 6.

3137. Ibid.

3138. "Paul Lacy Dies in Electric Chair Denying Guilt," *Nashville Banner*, November 25, 1949, p. 16. Lacy told the warden, "Well, I just don't want to talk about it any more."

3139. Jack Dealy, "Odd Facts Mark First Two Death Sentences Given in Maury Court," *Maury Democrat*, October 25, 1949, p. 4.

3140. *Steele v. State*, 225 S.W.2d 260, 261 (Tenn. 1949).
3141. Ibid.
3142. Ibid.
3143. Ibid.
3144. Ibid., p. 262.
3145. *Clyde Steele and Herbert Bearden v. State*, Memorandum opinion, Supreme Court, Eastern Section, December 11, 1948, p. 2.
3146. *Steele v. State*, p. 262.
3147. Ibid.
3148. Ibid.
3149. Ibid., p. 263.
3150. Ibid.
3151. "Negro Is Electrocuted for Criminal Assault," *Nashville Banner*, January 24, 1950, p. 4; "Execution Set at Prison Today," *Nashville Tennessean*, January 24, 1950, p. 1.
3152. *Voss v. State*, 278 S.W.2d 667 (Tenn. 1955). Discussion of Hutchison murder; the record is not clear whether Voss was actually executed for this killing or that of Cox, described below.
3153. E.V. Aimes, "She Stepped in Murder," *Official Detective* (April 1954): 40.
3154. *Voss v. State*, 278 S.W.2d 667, 669 (Tenn. 1955).
3155. Aimes, p. 64. "I told him to lie down on the floor and I told him to keep his head down. But he looked around at me, like he recognized me, and I let him have it."
3156. Aimes, p. 42.
3157. Snell's family expressed concern for his safety because the older Voss had served a prison sentence for larceny. Aimes, p. 63.
3158. Reply Brief for the State, *Samuel L. Voss v. State*, June 7, 1954, p. 4.
3159. Ibid., p. 5.
3160. Ibid.
3161. *Samuel L. Voss v. State*, Memorandum opinion, Supreme Court, Middle Section, July 23, 1954, p. 2. The opinion was originally published at 270 S.W.2d 644, but was withdrawn when the court granted a second petition to rehear. It cannot be located under the earlier citation and was never republished.
3162. Ibid., p. 4.
3163. Ibid., pp. 4, 5.
3164. Ibid., p. 6.
3165. *Samuel L. Voss v. State*, Minutes, Supreme Court, December Term, 1953, July 23, 1954, p. 519.
3166. "Samuel Voss Walks to Death Chair Today," *Nashville Tennessean*, April 15, 1955, p. 4: "Voss, Negro, is the only man in Tennessee history to be twice sentenced to the electric chair."
3167. *Voss v. State*, 278 S.W.2d 667, 669 (Tenn. 1955).
3168. Ibid.
3169. Brice Runyon, "Voss Goes Calmly to Execution," *Nashville Banner*, April 15, 1955, p. 10.
3170. A constable was akin to an under-sheriff; elected from a district, each county could have as many as twenty-five, but only one sheriff. Duties included serving process, apprehending criminals and putting down "routs, riots and tumults." See *Tennessee Sheriff and Constable Manual* (Nashville: McQuiddy, 1912), p. 30.
3171. *Kirkendoll v. State*, 281 S.W.2d 243, 247. (Tenn. 1955).
3172. E.V. Aimes, "Right Out of Eddie's Little Book," *Official Detective* (October 1953): 46.
3173. *Kirkendoll v. State*, 281 S.W.2d 245 (Tenn. 1955).
3174. Ibid., p. 247.
3175. Ibid., p. 248.
3176. Ibid., p. 248. Citing *Kennedy v. State*, 186 Tenn. 310, 210 S.W.2d 132; *Hall v. United States*, 168 F.2d 161, 4 A.L.R. 2d 1193.
3177. Ibid., p. 244.
3178. Ibid., p. 245.
3179. Ibid., p. 246.
3180. Ibid., p. 244.
3181. Ibid., p. 245.
3182. "Families Visit Condemned Men," *Nashville Tennessean*, August 1, 1955, p. 3.
3183. John Seigenthaler, "13 Steps to Death," Nashville Tennessean Sunday Magazine, November 14, 1954, p. 8–9, 26. (Hale was in the Shelby County jail at this time.)
3184. Mickey McLinden, "Chair Claims 2 in Murder of Ed Collier," *Nashville Banner*, August 1, 1955, p. 1. Another of Sullins's last requests was that Kirkendoll's sentence be commuted to life in prison.
3185. Ibid.
3186. Ibid., p. 2.
3187. *Robert Crenshaw v. State*, Memorandum opinion, Supreme Court, Middle Section, August 2, 1955, p. 1.
3188. Ibid., p. 2.
3189. Ibid.
3190. Ibid., p. 3.
3191. Ibid., p. 4.
3192. "Crenshaw Executed for Housewife Rape," *Nashville Banner*, September 15, 1955, p. 14.
3193. *Crenshaw v. State*, Memorandum opinion, Supreme Court, Middle Section, August 2, 1955, p. 5.
3194. Ibid., p. 6.
3195. Ibid., pp. 7, 8.
3196. "Crenshaw Executed for Housewife Rape," *Nashville Banner*, September 15, 1955, p. 14.
3197. "You Prove It, Suspect Tells Murder Probers," *Nashville Tennessean*, June 28, 1955, p. 1.
3198. *Jimmy Allen v. State*, Memorandum opinion, Supreme Court, Middle Section, February 8, 1957, pp. 4–5.
3199. Ibid., p. 6.
3200. Ibid.
3201. Larry Brinton, "Murderer Confesses in Electric Chair," *Nashville Banner*, March 16, 1957, p. 1.
3202. "Text of Gibbs Confession," *Southern Standard*, March 31, 1955, p. 1. In another version, Gibbs said he had hid in a bush and shot Bratcher on impulse, explaining, "I never done nothin' like this before. I don't know what got into me. I always been a peaceful man": W.W. Ward, "House of Horror," *Front Page Detective* (July 1955): 52, 87.
3203. *Gibbs v. State*, 300 S.W.2d 890, 891 (Tenn. 1957).
3204. Sid Thiel, "Bloody Day," *Headquarters Detective* (September 1955): 43, 64.
3205. Sid Thiel, "Bloody Day," *Headquarters Detective* (September 1955): 43, 63. Another version says that Gibbs was arrested at his home on Sunday after the bodies were discovered, at which time he admitted that he had taken the animals and sold them because he needed money, but the family was gone, and he knew nothing about a note. W.W. Ward, "House of Horror," *Front Page Detective* (July 1955): 52, 86.
3206. Jack Settles, "For Him the Dead Talk," *Front Page Detective* (January 1956): 50, 53. Suggests Gibbs confessed only when confronted with a re-creation of the killing offered in a face-to-face meeting with the Davidson County coroner.
3207. "Scant Hope Held for Billy Gibbs," *Nashville Tennessean*, May 6, 1957, p. 1.
3208. *Gibbs v. State*, 300 S.W.890, 892 (Tenn. 1957).
3209. Ibid., p. 892.
3210. Ibid.
3211. Prisoner record, inmate number 48302, Billy Thomas Gibbs, Tennessee Department of Corrections.
3212. "Chaplain Says Gibbs Happy Before Chair," *Nashville Tennessean*, May 7, 1957, p. 12.
3213. Larry Brinton, "Billy Gibbs Dies Reciting Prayer," *Nashville Banner*, May 6, 1957, p. 1.
3214. Ibid.
3215. *Thomas Rutledge v. State*, Memorandum opinion, Supreme Court, Middle Section, April 8, 1959, p. 5.
3216. Ibid., p. 5.
3217. E.V. Aimes, "Over the Rails to Her Grave," *Official Detective Stories* (April 1961): 40, 62. The sheriff did not have legal authority to seek a court order for an autopsy because at this time there was no evidence of homicide.
3218. Ibid., p. 3.
3219. T.C.A. 39-2402.
3220. Ibid., p. 6.
3221. Judge John Sweptson wrote the opinion.
3222. Ibid., p. 7.
3223. Ibid.
3224. "Rutledge Dies Today Barring Late Stay," *Nashville Tennessean*, June 15, 1959, p. 4.
3225. Larry Brinton, "Thomas Rutledge Put to Death in Electric Chair," *Nashville Banner*, June 15, 1959, p. 1.
3226. Richard Urban, "Ultimate Penalty: The Story of William Tines, Tennessee's Last 'Dead Man Walking,' Prologue and Part I, The Horror on Highway 61," *Nashville Scene*, November 7, 1996, pp. 26–32. Richard Urban, "Ultimate Penalty: The Story of William Tines, Tennessee's Last 'Dead Man Walking,' Part 2 and Epilogue, Brought to Trial," *Nashville Scene*, November 14, 1996, pp. 25–31. This is a thorough and accurate account of the Tines case. See also Jim Andrews, "The Last Walk to the End of the Hall," *Nashville Tennessean Magazine*, September 6, 1970, pp. 8–10.

3227. Tines v. State, 315 S.W.2d 111, 112 (Tenn. 1958), cert. denied, 79 S. Ct. 134, 358 U.S. 889, 3 L.Ed2d 117.
3228. Ibid., p. 113.
3229. Ibid., pp. 113–114.
3230. No opinion can be located.
3231. Larry Brinton, "Tines Executed After Three Years on "Death Row," *Nashville Banner*, November 7, 1960, p. 1.
3232. "Ultimate Penalty: Part 2," p. 29.
3233. Max York, "Seven Men from Memphis," *Nashville Tennessean Magazine*, August 23, 1963, pp. 8–9. Description of seven men waiting execution at the time.
3234. Julie Hollabaugh, "Witness to 84 Raps Executions," *Tennessean*, March 18, 1965, p. 1.
3235. Josephine Murphey, "Prison Chaplain," *Tennessean Sunday Magazine*, March 10, 1946, pp. 5–6; James Ewing, "They Still Disagree on Capital Punishment," *Nashville Magazine* (November 1969): 20–24.
3236. Sam McPherson, "Death Penalty Repealer Argued; Action Uncertain," *Nashville Banner*, March 8, 1963, p. 1. Gov. Clement had endorsed repeal but did not lobby for it and the measure failed in committee. James M. Talley, "Four Men Wait to Die," *Tennessean*, March 10, 1963, p. 4; Max York, "Seven Men from Memphis," *Nashville Tennessean Sunday Magazine*, August 25, 1963, p. 4–6.
3237. Frank G. Clement, "Address from the Governor," 1965 Tenn. House J. 1st ex. Sess. 937, 938–941 (March 16, 1965); "End Death Law, Pleads Clement," *Nashville Banner*, March 17, 1965, p. 1. The House rejected the bill 47-43. When action was taken to reconsider the bill, a motion to table passed 48-47. Many people erroneously insist that repeal was rejected by one vote. The House had passed a bill repealing the death penalty in 1895.
3238. Ken Morrell, "Death Repeal Fails House," *Nashville Banner*, March 18, 1965, p. 1; Ken Morrell, "Five Death Sentences Commuted," *Nashville Banner*, March 19, 1965, p. 1. Three of the men had been scheduled to die in four days. The sentences were commuted to ninety-nine years. Bill Kovach and Larry Daughtrey, "House Rejects Death Bill," *Tennessean*, March 11, 1965, p. 1. Repeal also failed in 1967 and 1971. Charles Overby, "Death Law Repeal Refused," *Nashville Banner*, April 22, 1971, p. 1.
3239. Michael Meltsner, *Cruel & Unusual: The Supreme Court and Capital Punishment* (New York: Random House, 1973). See Roy Brasfield Herron, "Defending Life in Tennessee Death Penalty Cases," *Tennessee Law Review* 51 (1984): 681–768.
3240. "Federal Prisons Bureau Reports 1968 Marks 1st Year Without an Execution," *New York Times*, December 31, 1968, p. 17. The bureau began collecting these data in 1938.
3241. "To Abolish the Death Penalty," *Hearings before the Subcommittee on Criminal Laws and Procedures of the Committee on the Judiciary, United States Senate, March 20, 21 and July 2, 1968* (GPA: Washington, D.C., 1970), 240 pp. This contains a purported list of everyone executed at a state penal institution from 1864 to 1966. The list is woefully incomplete and does not include Tennessee executions. See also Thorsten Sellin, "Murder and the Penalty of Death," *Annals of the American Academy of Political and Social Science* 284 (November 1952), 238 pp.
3242. Dwight Aarons, "Adjudicating Claims of Innocence for the Capitally Condemned in Tennessee: Embracing a Truth Forum," *Tennessee Law Review* 76 (2009) 511, 516; Gary L. Anderson, "Post-Conviction Relief in Tennessee — Fourteen Years of Judicial Administration Under the Post-Conviction Procedure Act," *Tennessee Law Review* 48 (1981): 605–613. By statute, the filing of a post-conviction petition operates as a stay.
3243. *Furman v. Georgia*, 408 U.S. 238 (1972).
3244. Frances Meeker, "21 on Death Row Spared," *Nashville Banner*, July 18, 1972, p. 1.
3245. *Collins v. State*, 550 S.W.2d 643 (Tenn. 1977). Mandatory death penalty void.
3246. "Thirty-Five Condemned Men Taken Off Death Row," *Nashville Banner*, January 25, 1977, p. 1.
3247. Following a journey which included carnival side shows, it now reposes at the National Museum of Crime & Punishment in Washington, D.C., where it is misnamed "Old Smokey."
3248. *Gregg v. Georgia*, 428 U.S. 153 (1976). The standard is "guided discretion." Tennessee passed its current death penalty law the next year over Gov. Blanton's veto. Patricia Welch, "Assembly to Consider Revised Death Statute," *Tennessean*, January 9, 1977, p. 4.
3249. American Bar Association, *Evaluating Fairness and Accuracy in State Death Penalty Systems: The Tennessee Death Penalty Assessment Report, An Analysis of Tennessee's Death Penalty Laws, Procedures, and Practices* (March 2007). Comprehensive look at modern law.
3250. *Coker v. Georgia*, 433 U.S. 584 (1977).
3251. *Emmund v. Florida*, 458 U.S. 454 (1981).
3252. *Godfrey v. Georgia*, 446 U.S. 420 (1980).
3253. Act of Mar. 18, 1982, ch. 638, 1982 Tenn. Pub. Acts 141; *Roper v. Simmons* 543 U.S. 551 (2005).
3254. Act of Apr. 12, 1990, ch. 1038, 1990 Tenn. Pub. Acts 730.
3255. *Baze v. Rees*, 553 U.S. _____ (2008).
3256. William P. Redick, Jr., Bradley A. MacLean, and M. Shane Truett, "Pretend Justice — Representation in Tennessee Death Penalty Cases," *University of Memphis Law Review* 38 (2008): 303–463.
3257. Lawrence C. Marshall, "The Innocence Revolution and the Death Penalty," *Ohio State Journal of Criminal Law* 1 (2004): 573. For a discussion, see Aarons, "Adjudicating," supra, note 7, pp. 527–534.
3258. Tenn. Code Ann. Section 40-30-102(b). Passed in 2001.
3259. Innocence and the Death Penalty, DPIC (Death Penalty Info. Ctr.), Washington, D.C., at http://www.deathpenaltyinfo.org/innoc.html. Asserts there have been 139 exonerations since 1973.
3260. Donald F. Paine, "Eyewitness Identification Testimony: The Trials of Douglas MacArther Forbes," *Tenn. B. Jr.* 39 (April 2003): 11.
3261. Sarah Kelley, "Dead Wrong," *Nashville Scene*, June 26, 2008, pp. 16–24.
3262. *House v. Bell*, 547 U.S. 518 (2006).
3263. Lee Davis and Bryan Hoss, "Tennessee's Death Penalty: An Overview of the Procedural Safeguards," *University of Memphis Law Review* 31 (2001): 779.
3264. Steven J. Mulroy, "The Safety Net: Applying Coram Nobis Law to Prevent the Execution of the Innocent," *Virginia Journal of Social Policy and Law* 11 (2003): 1. This procedure can be used to bring new evidence before a court in order to show innocence.
3265. Called Section 1983 cases, this law has been used to challenge the lethal injection three-drug "cocktail." *Harbison v. Little*, 511 F. Supp. 2d 872 (M.D. Tenn. 2007). Litigants have asserted that the Tennessee death squad has not properly mixed thiopental in the past. They assert that Philip Workman continued talking for two minutes after he received the drug, which should have rendered him unconscious in a few seconds. They assert that post-mortem blood samples from Robert Coe showed thiopental levels far below those needed to induce anesthesia.
3266. Roy B. Morgan, Jr., "Death Penalty in Tennessee: Recent Developments," *Memphis State University Law Review* 8 (1977): 107–120. This statute also mandated the Supreme Court conduct a proportionality review, that is, comparing the person's sentence with others. Penny J. White, "A Survey of Tennessee Supreme Court Death Penalty Cases in the 1990s," *Tennessee Law Review* 61 (1994): 733.
3267. Glenda Washam, "Tracing an Execution," *The Tennessean*, April 19, 2000, 5A. Contains a time line of Coe's case, including his elopement from Vanderbilt University hospital after undergoing dental surgery in 1983.
3268. Benson Murray, "Little Girl Who Prayed During Her Sex Kill," *Detective Dragnet* (February 1984): 18–19, 41–42, 44.
3269. *State v. Coe*, 655 S.W.2d 903, 906 (Tenn. 1983). Autopsy report showed both vaginal and anal injury.
3270. Vicki Brown, "Clock Again Ticking on Coe's Date with Death," *Knoxville News-Sentinel*, April 4, 2000, p. 1.
3271. John Brannon, "Coe's Crimes Cost Taxpayers," *Weakley County Press*, July 22, 1999, p. 1. The deputy sheriff who drove the car said, "I hauled him back and forth to Fort Pillow. He delighted in telling me what he did. I advised him of his rights and told him not

to talk about it. He said, 'I don't care. I did it,' like he was proud of it."

3272. *Coe v. State*, 1986 WL 14453 (Tenn. Crim. App. Dec. 23, 1986); *Coe v. State*, 1991 WL 2873 (Tenn. Crim. App. Jan. 16, 1991). In 1996, a Nashville federal court found several jury instruction errors in Coe's case and ordered a new trial, but this was reversed by the Sixth Circuit Court of Appeals. *Coe v. Bell*, 161 F. 3d 320 (6th Cir. 1998).

3273. "Coe Gets Chair in Slaying," *Tennessean*, February 28, 1981, p. 1.

3274. "12 Jurors Pray for Convicted Coe, Then Sentence Him to Die in Chair," *Tennessean*, March 1, 1981, p. 1.

3275. "Coe's Wish Said Death: Not Appeal," *Nashville Banner*, April 10, 1981, p. 1.

3276. Coe v. State, 17 S.W. 3d 193. The December 15, 1999 order set a 55-day limit for the competency hearing and set Coe's execution date for March 23, 1999.

3277. Dylan T. Lovan, "Defense: Outbursts Prove Coe Insane," *Jackson Sun*, January 29, 2000, p. 1.

3278. Woody Baird, "Memphis Judge Rules Robert Glen Coe Is Competent to be Executed," *Buffalo River Review*, February 5, 2000, p. 1. The Tennessee Supreme Court refused to grant a stay. A stay was also refused by a Nashville federal judge. *Coe v. Bell*, 89 F. Supp. 2d 922 (M.D. Tenn. 2000). "Although he maintains his innocence, it has been made quite clear to this court that petitioner understands that he was found guilty of murder and was sentenced to die," ruled Judge Aleta Traugher. This was affirmed. *Coe v. State*, 208 F. 3d 815 (6th Cir. 2000); "Coe Begins 'Death Watch' as U.S. Judge Refuses Stay," *Chattanooga Times*, March 20, 2000, p. 1; Woody Baird, "Time Running Out on Coe's Efforts to Skirt Death Penalty," *Knoxville News-Sentinel*, March 19, 2000, p. 1.

3279. Kathy Carlson and Beth Warren, "No Clemency Hearing for Coe," *Tennessean*, March 21, 2000, p. A1. The board members had been sent copies of his commutation materials but declined to hold a hearing, sending their refusals by facsimile machine.

3280. The Tennessee Supreme Court refused to issue a certificate recommending commutation by the governor. *Coe v. State*, 17 S.W. 3rd 249 (Tenn. 2000).

3281. *Coe v. State*, 17 S.W. 3d 251 (Tenn. 2000).

3282. "Robert Glen Coe: The Early Years," in *Application for Executive Pardon or Executive Commutation*, n.d. [2000]. This is a narrative unaccompanied by affidavits.

3283. Robert L. Hutton, "The Right to Have Counsel Present at Execution," *University of Memphis Law Review* 31 (2001): 757. A month later the legislature passed a law allowing counsel to be present at executions.

3284. John Shiffman and Leon M. Tucker, "Midnight Ruling Caps Day of Legal Wrangling," *Tennessean*, April 19, 2000, 4A.

3285. Tom Shapp, "Coe Prepares for Final Day," *Clarksville Leaf-Chronicle*, March 22, 2000, p. 1.

3286. Kirk Loggins, "Media Get Tour of Death Row," *Tennessean*, October 14, 1999, p. 1A. The official witnesses were the Weakley County sheriff, seven media witnesses and Coe's immediate family. Rebecca Ferrar, "Execution Procedure Is Strict," *Knoxville News-Sentinel*, October 14, 1999, p. 1.

3287. Kent Flanaghan, "Reporter Describes Coe's Execution in Detail," *Chattanooga Times*, April 23, 2000, p. B5.

3288. Jack G. Heise, "The Freaky Mutilation of the Pretty Marine," *Front Page Detective* (September 1987): 34–35, 50–52.

3289. *State v. Alley*, 776 S.W.2d 506, 510 (Tenn. 1989).

3290. Ibid., p. 513.

3291. *Alley v. State*, 882 S.W.2d 811, 821–823 (Tenn. Crim. App. 1994).

3292. *Alley v. State*, 958 S.W.2d 138 (Tenn. Crim. App. 1997).

3293. *Alley v. Bell*, 101 F. Supp. 2d 588 (W. D. Tenn. 2000).

3294. *Alley v. Bell*, 307 F. 3d 380 (6th Cir. 2002).

3295. *Alley v. State*, 2004 WL 1196095 (Tenn. Crim. App. 2004).

3296. *Alley v. Bell*, 405 F. 3d 371 (6th Cir. 2005).

3297. Alley called this a civil rights lawsuit, not a habeas petition.

3298. *Alley v. Key*, 431 F. Supp. 2d 790 (W.D. 2006).

3299. *Alley v. Bell*, 178 Fed. Appx. 538 (6th Cir. 2006).

3300. *Alley v. Key*, 2006 WL 1313364 (6th Cir. 2006).

3301. Chris Lewis, "Bredesen Grants Alley 15-Day Reprieve," *The City Paper*, May 17, 2006, p. 3.

3302. "Innocent Man?" *Nashville Scene*, May 11, 2006, pp. 21–28. According to one account, much of this evidence had been discarded in 1999 when the refrigerator holding it had malfunctioned. Jeff Woods, "Capital Crimes," *Nashville Scene*, October 2, 2008, p. 9.

3303. *Alley v. State*, 2006 WL 1703820 (Tenn. Crim. App. 2006).

3304. Brief of Appellant Sedley Alley, Sixth Circuit No. 06-5552, n.d., p. 6. Filed with the petition.

3305. "Affidavit of April Higuera, April 27, 2004" in *Appendix to Appellant's Brief*, p. 51. The affidavit does not state whether the civilian boyfriend knew she had another boyfriend then in California at the time of her death.

3306. Letter from Barry C. Scheck to Robert E. Cooper, Jr., May 12, 2006, p. 3, 4.

3307. Sheila Burke, "State Appeals Late-Night Stay," *Tennessean*, June 28, 2006, 1A. The judge was an outspoken opponent of the death penalty. Gilbert S. Merritt, Jr., "Prosecutorial Error in Death Penalty Cases," *Tennessee Law Review* 76 (Spring 2009): 677–684.

3308. Brad Schrade, "State Readies Death Chamber for Reid, Alley," *Tennessean*, June 27, 2006, p. 1A. The other man's execution was stayed by the United States Supreme Court.

3309. Brad Schrade, "Alley's Defense Fight Outlives Him," *Tennessean*, June 29, 2006, p. 1A.

3310. *State v. Workman*, 667 S.W.2d 44 (Tenn. 1984).

3311. Sarah Kelley, "Running Out of Time," *City Paper*, April 26, 2007, pp. 9, 11.

3312. Letter from John W. Campbell to Tennessee Board of Probation and Parole, January 16, 2001. Police reports were attached.

3313. *Workman v. State*, 1987 WL 6724 (Tenn. Crim. App. 1987).

3314. *Workman v. State*, 868 S.W.2d 705 (Tenn. Crim. App. 1993)

3315. *Workman v. State*, 41 S.W.3d 100, 103 (Tenn. 2001).

3316. *Workman v. Bell*, 178 F. 3d 759 (6th Cir. 1998).

3317. Kirk Loggins, "Workman Argues Evidence Raises Doubts About Shooting," *Tennessean*, April 4, 2000, p. 1A. He also had another hearing on January 25, 2001.

3318. *Workman v. State*, 22 S.W. 3d 807 (Tenn. 2000).

3319. *Workman v. Bell*, 209 F. 3d 940 (6th Cir. 2000).

3320. *Workman v. Bell*, 227 F. 3d 331 (6th Cir. 2000)

3321. *Workman v. Bell*, 245 F. 3d 849, (6th Cir. 2001).

3322. John Shiffman, "Workman Loses Clemency Bid, Files Suit," *Tennessean*, March 28, 2001, p. 1A.

3323. *Workman v. Summers*, 136 F. Supp. 896 (M.D. Tenn. 2001); *Workman v. Summers*, 8 Fed. Apex. 371 (6th Cir. 2001). He had also challenged the fairness of the clemency hearing, but the Nashville federal court dismissed this suit as well. *Workman v. Summers*, 2001 WL 1782877 (M.D. 2001); *Workman v. Summers*, 111 Fed. Apex. 369 (6th Cir. 2004)

3324. In re Philip Workman, 532 U.S. 955 (2001).

3325. Rebecca Farrar, "Workman Set to Be Executed," *Knoxville News-Sentinel*, March 30, 2001, p. 1.

3326. *Workman v. State*, 41 SW. 3d 100 (2001); Marta W. Aldrich, "Last-Minute Reprieve for Workman," *Cookeville Harold-Citizen*, p. 1; "Order for Workman's Stay Was Issued at 12:11 A.M.," *Tennessean*, April 5, 2001; Tom Sharp, "Workman Receives Stay of Execution," *Chattanooga Free Press*, April 1, 2001, p. 1.

3327. "Ill Witness Delays Workman Hearing," *Daily News Journal*, August 16, 2001, p. 1.

3328. Lawrence Buser, "Workman Witnesses Finish with Little Clarified," *Memphis Commercial Appeal*, August 17, 2001, p. 1.

3329. "Forensic Expert Testifies Workman Did Not Kill Memphis Police Officer," *Paris Post-Intelligencer*, August 16, 2001, p. 1.

3330. Karin Miller, "Witness in Hearing Former Juror in Trial," *Johnson City Press*, November 11, 2001, p. 1. The judge said he would not consider the testimony of a former juror who said the new evidence would have influenced his decision not to impose the death penalty.

3331. *Workman v. State*, 111 S.W. 3d 10 (Tenn. Crim. App. 2002).
3332. Request for Clemency Filed on Behalf of Philip Ray Workman, August 12, 2003.
3333. A Petition for Clemency Signed by Professionals and Professors of Criminal Justice and Closely Related Fields (submitted by Dr. Margaret Vandiver, University of Memphis).
3334. Submission of the District Attorney General in Opposition to the Application for Commutation of Philip Ray Workman, February 28, 2000, p. 3.
3335. Ibid., p. 9.
3336. It was later shown the medical examiner had staged a purported assault.
3337. *Workman v. Bell*, 484 F. 3d 837 (6th Cir. 2002).
3338. Jared Allen, "Sixth Circuit Paves Way for Execution Wednesday," *City Paper*, May 5, 2007, p. 3.
3339. Sarah Kelley, "Witness to an Execution," *City Paper*, May 17, 2007, pp. 8, 13.
3340. Leon Alligood, "Workman's Bequest Sends Pizza to Homeless," *Tennessean*, May 9, 2007, p. 1A.
3341. Sheila Burke, Brad Schrade, and Sheila Wissner, "Workman Executed," *Tennessean*, May 9, 2007, p. A1
3342. Sarah Kelley, "Witness to an Execution," *City Paper*, May 17, 2007, pp. 8, 11.
3343. Ibid., p. 13.
3344. Ibid., p. 8.
3345. *State v. Holton*, 126 SW. 3d 845 (Tenn. 2004).
3346. The court cited seven other child murder cases including Coe.
3347. *Holton v. State*, 201 S.W. 3d 626 (Tenn. 2006).
3348. Clint Brewer, "Electric Chair Questions Remain Ahead of Execution," *City Paper*, September 11, 2007, p. 5.
3349. Jared Allen, "Examiner: Execution Was Swift," *City Paper*, September 13, 2007, pp. 3, 4.
3350. David Raybin, "This Should Be State's Last Electric Chair Execution," *Tennessean*, September 23, 2007.
3351. Sheila Burke, "Minor Burns During Execution Called Normal," *Tennessean*, September 11, 2007, p. 1A.
3352. *State v. Henley*, 774 S.W.2d 908, 912 (Tenn. 1989).
3353. Brantley Hargrove, "Charred Bodies in the Remote Tennessee Farm Country Leave Lingering Questions About the Execution of Steve Henley," *Nashville Scene*, March 4, 2009, pp. 1–4.
3354. *Henley v. State*, 960 S.W. 572 (Tenn. 1997). Henley's original lawyer was deceased.
3355. *Henley v. Bell*, 487 F. 3d 379 (6th Cir. 2007).
3356. Response to Motion to Set Execution Date, In re Steve Henley, M1987-0016-SC-DPE-DD (October 6, 2008), p. 6.
3357. Order, *State v. Henley*, No. M1987-0016-SC-DPE-DD (October 20, 2008).
3358. *Steve Henley v. George Little*, Application for Stay of Execution, United States Supreme Court, filed February 3, 2009. Federal defenders could file such petitions ruled the Supreme Court, a month after Henley's execution. *Harbison v. Bell*, 556 U.S. ____ (2009).
3359. Letter from Paul S. Davidson to Gov. Philip Bredesen, February 3, 2009, pp. 2, 3.
3360. Kate Howard, "Tennessee Executes Man Who Killed Couple," *Tennessean*, February 5, 2009, p. B1.
3361. Clint Brewer and Amy Griffith Graydon, "Henley Maintains His Innocence Until the End," *The City Paper*, February 5, 2009, p. 22.
3362. Kate Howard, "Watching Man's Execution Tears at Her Heart," *Tennessean*, February 8, 2009, pp.17A, 20A.
3363. *Johnson v. Bell*, 525 F.3d 466 (6th Cir. 2008).
3364. Mary Ann Hea, "Lawyers Pledge an Appeal in Johnson Death Case," *Nashville Banner*, January 21, 1981, p. 1. This was the first death penalty verdict in Nashville since 1976.
3365. Kirk Loggins, "Consecutive Terms Ruled for Slayer," *Tennessean*, March 10, 1981, p. 1.
3366. John Taylor, "Killer Tries Not to Think of Chair," *Nashville Banner*, March 30, 1981, p. 1. A Tennessee Bar Association official formed a sixteen-year friendship with him. Suzanne Craig Robertson, "An Odd Combination," *Tennessee Bar Journal* 45 (September 2009): 17, 20.
3367. *State v. Johnson*, 632 S.W.2d 542, 546 (Tenn. 1982).
3368. Donald F. Paine, "The Trial of Cecil Johnson," *Tennessee Bar Journal* 46 (February 2010): 32.
3369. *State v. Bobo*, 814 S.W.2d 353 (Tenn. 1991).
3370. *Johnson v. State*, 1988 WL 3632.
3371. *Johnson v. State*, 797 S.W.2d 578 (Tenn. 1990).
3372. *State v. Johnson*, 1997 WL 738586 (1997).
3373. *Johnson v. Bell*, 525 F. 3d 466 (6th Cir. 2008).
3374. Statement of Justice Stevens, On Application for Stay and on Petition for a Writ of Certiorari, Cecil C. Johnson v. Phil Bredesen, et al., United States Supreme Court, 558 U.S. _____ (December 2, 2009). Justices Stevens and Breyer would have granted a stay and heard the case. Justice Thomas disagreed.
3375. Cover Letter, Supplement to Petition for Executive Clemency, Sept. 30, 2009.
3376. Letter from Suzanne Craig Robertson to Governor, July 20, 2009: "It was then I became convinced of Cecil's innocence."
3377. Petition for Commutation of Sentence of Death, August 27, 2009, p. 6.
3378. In *State v. Thomas*, 158 S.W.3d 361 (2005) the Tennessee Supreme Court held that in the sentencing phase of a trial a "residual doubt" instruction must be given the jury. This is "lingering uncertainty about facts, a state of mind that exists somewhere between beyond a reasonable doubt and absolute certainty."
3379. Report of John C. Brigham, Ph.D., in Petition for Commutation, Exhibit G, p. 12.
3380. Petition for Commutation, p. 48.

Index

Names of perpetrators are in *italics*.

Aaron 90–91
Abe see *Henry, Abe*
Abongpohigo see *Obongpohego*
Ackerman, William 61
admission cards (tickets) needed to attend executions 124, 227; *see also* corpses of perpetrators, charging money to see; execution(s), paying to watch
age of people executed: oldest man 263–64; youngest female 25; *see also* minors
"Alas, and Did My Savior Bleed?" (hymn) 53, 110
alcohol intoxication 13, 19, 20, 28, 46, 71, 82, 85, 86, 89, 98, 100, 101, 133, 149, 150, 158–60, 170, 185, 191, 197, 198, 204, 208, 210, 211, 227, 239, 244, 245, 250, 251, 255–57, 268, 273, 307, 313, 314, 316, 340, 343, 344, 354, 355, 362, 365, 367, 368, 376, 377, 384, 387, 390, 393, 401, 402, 407, 415–16; of people attending executions 129, 132 (*see also* saloons closed on the days of executions); of perpetrator on day of execution 150, 163, 173, 174, 176, 204, 218; of sheriff performing execution 238
alcoholic beverages: purchasing 462n3059; saloons closed on the days of executions 112, 129; *see also* moonshine
Alec see *Ellick*
Alexander, Emmet 263
Alexander, George R. 195
Alexander, Gov. Lamar 405
Alfred see *Stephens, Alfred*
Alfred (slave) 45
Allbright, John T. (victim) 88–89
Allen, George 273–74
Allen, Harry H. (victim) 273
Allen, Captain Henry W. (victim) 82
Allen, Jeanette Patricia (victim) 398–99
Allen, Jim 319
Allen, Jimmy 398–99
Allen, Louise "Carrie" (victim) 321, 322
Allen, Will 273–74
Allen Russell see *Russell, Allen*
Alley, Sedley 406–9
Allison, John 133
Allison, Russell (victim) 132–33
Aloysius, Father 156
Alsup, Eddie James 269–70
"Am I Born to Die, to Lay This Body Down?" (hymn) 110, 172
"Amazing Grace" (hymn) 115, 211–13
"Amen" (spoken to signal death) 156
American Legion 292, 320
Amos (slave) 46–48
amphetamines 407, 409
Anders (aka Andries or Adres), Evan (victim) 15
Anderson (slave) 46–48
Anderson, Gideon 33
Anderson, Judge Joseph 8
Anthony (slave) 45
appeals, declining to pursue 3
Applewhite, Lewis 178, 179
Armstrong, Captain 75, 76
Armstrong, John 185–86
Arnold, Frank (victim) 165
arson 12, 39, 142, 385–86, 415
Arthur, Marion (victim) 320
Arwood, Clyde 376
Ashcraft v. Tennessee 390–91
Ashmore, Maggie (victim) 389
assault: with intent to kill 86–88; with intent to kill white person 42; with intent to murder white person 27–29; with intent to rape 38 (*see also* rape); with intent to rape child under age twelve 26, 271–72 (*see also* child rape); with intent to rape free white woman 41–42, 44–45; with intent to rape white woman 50
assisted suicide 239
Atchley, Arthur 355
atheists, legal restrictions placed on 22–23
Athens, McMinn County 46, 238
audiences (at executions): faintings in 42; hangings in front of large 1, 3, 10, 12, 13, 18, 19, 21–24, 26, 29, 30, 32–34, 37, 39, 44, 46, 50, 51, 53, 65, 76, 84, 97–99, 101–6, 108, 110, 112, 114–16, 118, 119, 122–24, 126, 129, 131, 132, 134, 136, 137, 139, 140, 143–45, 147, 148, 150, 153, 154, 159, 160, 170, 179, 180, 190, 199, 202, 219, 234, 246, 296; inability to view hangings 170, 172, 173, 178, 180, 183, 185, 186–88, 190, 191, 195, 199, 207, 209, 211–15, 217, 222, 223, 246; largest crowds 110, 116, 119, 134, 246; predominantly black 105, 106, 112, 113, 122–24, 139, 178, 187, 192–94, 205, 215, 217, 224; reasons for attending 129; violence, chaos, and injuries in 103, 113, 125, 139, 196; *see also* corpses of perpetrators
Ausmus, Thomas (victim) 117, 118
Austin see *Williams, Orton William*
Auton see *Williams, Orton William*
ax *see* murder, methods of

Bailey, John 261–63
Baird, Charles W. 234–35, 253, 446n1826
Baird, Col. John Pierson 66, 67
Baird, Mary Roper (victim) 234–35
Balentine, Benjamin see *Benjamin, Pvt. Valentine*
Ballard, Carl H. "Curly" 333–35
Ballard, Hardy 174–76
Ballard, Rosa 333–34
baptism prior to execution 18, 79, 88, 104, 108, 109, 111, 116, 122, 124, 125, 131, 132, 138, 143, 145, 148, 159, 164, 175, 178–80, 186, 188–89, 199, 200, 211, 213, 216, 217, 220, 225, 234, 236, 246, 253, 254, 257, 273, 296, 307, 320, 321, 330, 333, 357, 384, 388, 393, 398, 401
Bargus, Lt. George 76
Barham, William P. (victim) 44
Baron, Abraham (victim) 273
Barr, Charles 302–3
Barrett, Elmer "Moon Pie" 336
Barrows, Oscar 180
Bartlett, Shelby County 120, 122
Baskin (aka Bascom), Robert 114
Bass, Arthur Leonard 393
Bass, Ranier 393
Bates, Dol 133, 136
Battery's camp near Cripple Creek, Rutherford County 68
Battise, Babe H. 215–17
Bauden, Gideon (victim) 51
Baxter, Jim 164
Beadle (aka Beadles), Alexander M. 57–59
Beake, Erma (victim) 385
Bean Station, Grainger County 69
Bearden, Herbert 393, 394
Bearden, Joe 24
Beatty, Mary Jane (victim) 105–6
Beatty, Robert 105–6
Beck, Aaron (victim) 195–96
Bedau, Hugo Adam 280, 282, 283, 289
Bedford, K.G. "Cagey" 102–3
Bedford County 39, 65
Beggarly, Burr 124–25
beheading *see* decapitation; heads put on public display
Bell, Mourning Ann 101
Bell, Bob, Jr. (victim) 416–19
Bell, Sen. John 47

Bell, Robby (victim) 416–18
Bellamy, Mrs. P.F. 162
benefit of clergy 2, 428n433
Benjamin, Judah P. 54, 56
Benjamin, Pvt. Valentine 73
Bennecker, Edward L. (victim) 298, 299
Bennett, Charles L. 15–16
Bennett, Fannie (victim) 188
Bennett, Henry 188
Bennett, Henry (slave) 43–44
Bennett, James R. 19
Benton, Thomas Hart 25
Berry, Alzira "Allie" (victim) 116
Berry, Anderson 334–35
Berry, George 138
Berry, William Nicholas 116–19
Betsey (victim) 48
Bettis, Mariah (victim) 41–42
Bevins, Oscar 315–17
Bible 109, 113, 234, 263, 279, 311, 330, 331, 357; in pocket during execution 194
Bill see *Moore, Bill*
Billig, Otto 395
Billings, Rachael Fowler (victim) 108–10
bills of exceptions 17, 247–48, 270–71
Billy Goat Hill, Putnam County 134–35
Birch, Judge A.A. 417, 418
Bird, Wiley (slave) 25–26
Bird, William G. (victim) 25–26
Black, Samuel 11
black men who killed their black wives 4
"Black Panther" see *Barr, Charles*
Blackburn, Sheriff 110
Blackwell, Major 86, 87, 91–92
Blackwell, Mrs. 92
Blair, Anthony 139–40, 142; "Confessions" 140–42
Blair, Maggie (victim) *see* Walker, Maggie
Blair, Nancy (victim) 30
Blair, Samuel (victim) 30
Blanton, Gov. Ray 404
Blazer, David 68
Bledsoe County 42; Hangman's Basin/Gallows Bottom 42; Pikeville area 13, 42
bleeding on gallows 240
Blount County 14; Maryville 22, 30
Blountville, Sullivan County 72, 202
Blue Bills 207, 209
Bluff City Guards 52
Board of Mental Examiners 292–93
Bob (slave) 30–31
bodies *see* corpses
Bolivar, Hardeman County 22, 25
bombs/explosive devices, murders using 33, 347–48
Bond, Florence Robertson (victim) 258
Bond, Rev. Robert 124–25, 143
Bond, Love 257–59
Bonds, Duncan 21
Bone (aka Boone), Gen. 227–29
Book of Common Prayer 114
borderline personality disorder 406–9
Boring, Effie Viola 200, 201
Boring, William D. 200, 201
Bostic, Hyman see *Johnson, Hyman*
bounty hunters 34, 60, 64, 77
Bowman, Samuel 25
Boyd, Frank (victim) 359–60
Boyd, John 26, 280
Boyd, Walter (victim) 203–4
Bradford, Frederick 31
Bradford, Jake (slave) 31–32
Bradford, Matt 127
Bradford, Robert (victim) 31
Bradshaw, George W. 85–86
Bragg, Gen. Braxton 60, 61, 65, 67, 72, 74, 75
Brakefield, Pvt. W. S. 62
Branch, Thomas (victim) 36
Branner, Bob 242
Brassell, Amanda 134, 135
Brassell, George Andrew "Teek" 132–36
Brassell, Harriet Z. 133–34
Brassell, James 133–35
Brassell, Joseph Lewis 132–35
Bratcher, Cassie (victim) 399–401
Bratcher, Henry (victim) 399–401
Bray, Wilse 329, 330
Breckenridge, Gen. 60, 61
Bredesen, Gov. Philip 411
Brenish, Frank 174–77
bribery, murders involving 136
Brice, James 14
Bridges, Benjamin 15
Bridges, Lewis 215
bridges, destruction of 54–56
Brien, Rev. 109, 110
Brigance, Mary (victim) 15
Brinkley, Sgt. John G. (victim) 272
Bristow, Sarah (victim) 45
Broadway, Ida May (victim) 247–48
Broadway, Mrs. Leonard 247, 248
Brooks, Rev. G.K. 159
Brooks, Margaret (victim) 85–86
Brooks, Sam 250
brothers hanged together 50, 134–36, 154–55
Brown, Gov. Aaron V. 39
Brown, Ben 165–66
Brown, Bill 165, 166
Brown, Charlie (victim) 149
Brown, Eliza 106–7
Brown, Eloise (victim) 357–58
Brown, George W. (victim) 23
Brown, Mrs. George W. 23
Brown, Henry 308–9
Brown, Jane 106–7
Brown, Jerry (victim) 194
Brown, Jim 162
Brown, John "Bud" (victim) 211–13
Brown, Gov. John C. 107, 109
Brown, Mae (victim) 315, 316
Brown, Mary Fults (victim) 211–13
Brown, Mrs. (victim) 391–92
Brown, Thomas see *Williams, George W.*
Brown, Thomas Y. (victim) 92
Brown, Will see *Gohlston, Hamp*
Brown, William "Bill" 211–13
Brown, Rev. W.J. 151–52
Brown, Wyley 70
Browne, Gen. Thomas M. 94
Browning, Gov. Gordon 345, 376, 390
Brownlow, Gov. William G. "Parson" 55
Brown's Creek area, Davidson County 139
Brownsville, Haywood County 36, 43
Broyles, Sam (victim) 99
Brunner, Molly *see* Rogers, Molly
Bryant, Professor 110–12
Bryant, Progue see *Bryant, Professor*
Buchanan, Boyd 252, 253
Bucher, Simon (victim) 220
Buckner (slave) 36
Budzynski, Daniel 388
Bunch, Barzilla Daugherty (victim) 296–97
Bunch, Elmer 329
Bunch, Granville 296–97
Bunting, Robert F. 79
Burchfield, Ben 299–300
Burchfield, Charley (victim) 299, 300
Burchfield, Delia (victim) 299, 300
burglary 9, 13–14, 18, 142; *see also* robbery; theft
Burkley, Thornton (victim) 183
burning: death by 10; *see also* arson
burning bridges 54–56
Burrow, Mr. 12
Burrow, Mrs. Philip (victim) 12
bushwackers 58, 59, 81, 82, 89, 90, 92; *see also* guerrillas
Byrom, Ruth (victim) 259
Byrom, Thomas F. "Napper" 259–60

Cain, Francis D. 62
Caio, John 69
Callahan, John 85, 86
Callahan, Thomas (victim) 19
Calloway, Matthew 193–94
Camp, Pvt. Lawson 73–74
Camp Andrew Jackson, Davidson County 56
Campbell, David 11
Campbell, George Washington 10
Campbell County 46, 50
Cannon, Gov. Newton 28, 29
Cannon, Robert 372–73
"cards" (advertisements) 140
cards, admission *see* admission cards (tickets) needed to attend executions
Carlisle, Tampay (victim) 24, 51
Carlton, Cpl. Henry 63–64, 85
Carmack, Edward Ward 239
Carmack, John 242–43
Carman, Samuel 10
Carmichael, Daniel (victim) 178–79
Carmichael, Hicks 167–68
carnal knowledge 333; of female child under age twelve 246–50, 271–72; *see also* child rape; rape
Carney, Harry 79, 80
Carney, James 79, 80
Carney, Richard H. 79–81

Carney, Wright B. 80
Carr, Arlie Emerson "Toby" (victim) 376–78
Carr, Edward 173–76
Carr, Floyd 365
Carr, Sallie (victim) 173–74
Carroll, Willis Green 34–36
Carroll County 39, 160
Carter, Robert 105
Carter, Rev. William B. 54–56
Carthage area 63
Cartwright, Fred 381
Cartwright, Rev. 189, 190
Caruthers, Nathan 217–19
Cassell, Paul G. 453n2355
Casson, John 257
Cate, Sheriff William T. (victim) 156–57
Cates, Reuben L. 294
Cathey, Jane Fowler (victim) 361–62
Cathie, Cyrus Lee (aka Lee Cathey, Cyrus Lee Cathey) 86–88
Catholic cemeteries 156, 193
Catholic Church 123, 145
Catholic priests 35, 41, 94, 102, 119, 123, 124, 138, 139, 144, 153, 156, 163, 176, 215, 276, 336
Catholicism, conversion to and embracement of 122–24, 138, 153, 192, 215, 220, 223, 357, 372, 376, 383, 396
Catlett, Bob 207–10
Centerville, Hardin County 51
Centerville, Hickman County 24
Certain, Inez 108
certiorari, writ of 265, 266, 396
Champion, John 227–29
Chandler, Lizzie 207–10
Charles see *Maney, Charles*; Turner, Charles
Charlotte area, Dickson County 26
Chattanooga area 72, 77, 115–16, 148–49; federal camp 91; first civilian executed under civil authority in 115
Chattanooga jail 192, 252
Cheek, William 101
Cheney, Brainard 307
Cherokees 9
Cherry, Grady W. "Cotton" (victim) 382
Cherry, Ruphine Wallace (victim) 382
Chester, Nathaniel 14, 15
Chickasaw, Captain (L.H. Naron) 74, 75
child rape 161–62, 205, 269–70, 397, 402, 418; attempted 26, 199–200, 271–72 (*see also under* assault); rape of child 24, 25, 73, 240–42, 303–4, 311, 313–14, 323–25, 332–33, 381, 401–2; rape of child under age ten 136–38, 199–200, 218, 265–66, 343–44, 364–65; rape of child under age twelve 271–72, 305–6; rape of child under age twelve (statute) 458n2768; *see also* carnal knowledge; incest; rape; rape-murder
child rape statute 266, 458n2768
children: attending executions 139; *see also under* murder(s); rape-murder
Childrey, Warren 106
Choate, Isaac 7
choking/strangulation 9, 12, 30, 39, 193, 325–26, 398–99, 405
Christenson, Martin (victim) 257
Christian, Thomas 110
Christian, Will 178, 179
Christmas, Tom 3, 277–80, 295
Christmas Killers 3, 277–80, 295
Church, Andrew 164
Church, Robert R. 291–92
cigar smoking on gallows 180, 206
cigarette smoking on gallows 186, 187, 249
Civil War executions 5; first Union soldier executed during Civil War 56; *see also specific perpetrators*
Clapp, W.L. 292
Claricy/Clarissa (slave) 39; daughter of (victim) 39
Clark, Abagail Gardner (victim) 15
Clark, Ambrose 61
Clark, Evaline (victim) 136, 137
Clark, Hawson (aka Hanson Clark and Howson Clark) 125–26
Clark, Hubbard 104
Clark, Joseph 161
Clarke, James 334–36
Clarke, Lt. 58
Clarkston, George Middleton 8
Clarksville 46
Clayton (slave) 27
clemency 33, 66, 92, 97, 260, 265, 278, 291–92, 305, 364, 386, 388, 397, 412
clemency hearings 410, 411
clemency petitions/requests/pleas/appeals 56, 136, 229–30, 232, 248–49, 254, 279, 293, 295, 303, 306, 349, 405–6, 409–11, 416, 418; *see also* petitions
clemency recommendations 11, 23, 28, 280, 378
Clement, Gov. Frank 397, 398, 403
Clements, James 11
Clinton area, Monroe County 131, 203
closed-circuit television 405, 406
Coble, Rev. Brown 131–32
Cocke County 137–38, 144
Coe, Robert Glen 404–6
coffin, kneeling beside 72
"Coffin Handbill" 15
Coggins, Herman 305–6
Cole, Carl Leonard 362–63
Cole, Robert 202
Coleman, Captain (Henry B. Shaw) 75–77
Coleman, Pryor 101
Coleman's Scouts 59, 74, 76
Collier, Edward Martin (victim) 396, 397
Collins, Cal 184, 185
Collins, Charlie 198
Collins, Mack "River George" 257
Collins, Suzanne Marie (victim) 406–9
Coltart (Colhart), William (victim) 33–35
Colthorpe, Rev. G.H. 129
Colton, Judge John 411
Columbia area, Maury County 19, 29; Duck River 106
Comer, Edith (victim) 390, 391
Committee of Safety 47
competency hearing *see* mental competency hearing
Compiled Service Record (CSR) 3, 4
Condor, Thomas "Tom" Yates 172–73
Condra, Adley W. "Ed" (victim) 301, 302
Confederacy 3
confessions: allegations of coerced 25, 83, 243, 273, 303, 321, 326, 330, 352, 381, 389–91; published 2, 16, 23, 100, 110, 118, 140–42, 263; sold on execution day 140; sold to newspapers 158; written 18, 35, 104, 109, 114–15, 136, 150, 191, 209–10, 262, 263, 322, 323, 325, 342, 352, 358, 362, 382, 385, 386, 390, 392, 396, 400
Connel, Michael 56
Connell, Mr. 101–2
Conner, Sheriff Sam A. 251, 252
Connor, Miss 177
Connor, William 177
Conway, Deputy John J. (victim) 156–58
Cook, Dora Kinger (victim) 257–58
Cook, Moses B. 257–58
Cooke, Robert 260–61
Cooper, Duncan B. 239
Cooper, Gov. Prentice 354, 361, 364, 369, 377–78
Cooper, V.W. 61
coram nobis, petition for 411
Cornelius, Ada (victim) 311
Cornell, Joseph 79
Cornwell, Burrell 19–21
corpses of perpetrators 113–14, 192; attempts to revive 16, 139; audiences unable to view 205; charging money to see 192–93; exhibited to crowds 168, 174, 175, 177, 180, 187, 194, 203, 207, 215, 223–27, 233, 234, 240, 243, 265, 296, 349 (of predominantly black people 192–94, 215, 217, 223–27, 296); families refusing to claim 222, 334, 396; given to doctors 40, 136, 139; given to medical schools 259, 361; left hanging for days 54; slave corpses displayed to terrorize other slaves 32, 47; sold to doctors 24, 38
Couch, James P. 39
counsel, right to adequate 404
courthouse yard, executions in 112
court-martial files 3–5
court-martials 14, 15, 54–58, 60–64, 66–75, 77–79, 82, 93, 95, 101; *see also* military commissions; military executions
Cousan, Allen 186–87
Cousan, Mattie (victim) 186
cousins hanged together 188–89

Covington, Tipton County 36, 147
Cox, Charles (slave) 29–30
Cox, Clarence 190–91
Cox, James Buchanan 394, 395
Cox, Gov. John I. 280, 281
Cox, Tom 223
Cox, William (victim) 48
Crabb, George see *Craft, George*
Craft, George 96–97
Craig, John 202
Craighead, David 20
Crain, Sonnie 211–13
Crawford 194
Crawford, Sarah (victim) 9
Creeks 8–9
Creger, Martha (victim) 85
Crenshaw, Robert L. "Hambone" 397–98
Crite, George 353
Crittendon, Mandy 181
Crockett, Elizabeth (victim) 18
Crossland, Obed C. 89, 90
Cruise, David (victim) 159
Crume, Ed 272
Crumley, Andrew T. 277–78
Crunk, Felix (victim) 21
Crupper, Pvt. Thomas 69
crying 23, 24, 52, 53, 97, 110, 112, 115–16, 153, 154, 159, 174, 178, 185, 192, 199, 200, 211, 254, 264, 268, 276, 296, 345, 412
CSA executions 3–4
Cullum, Alvin 99
Cullum, Bill 99
Cumberland County jail 206–7
Cumberland River, gallows on bank of 17
Cummins, Woodson 26
Cunningham, John 13
Cunningham, Paul (victim) 331
Cunningham, Sumner A. 76
Curran, Frank (victim) 160, 161

Dabney, Pvt. William Franklin 72, 73
Daily, Erastus C. see *Daley, Pvt. Erastus C.*
Daley, Pvt. Erastus C. 73
Dandridge, Jefferson County 10, 42, 45
Daniel, Catherine (victim) 17
Darnell, Forrest 357, 358
David/Dave (slave) 42
Davidson, Adeline "Addie" (victim) 363
Davidson, Elizabeth "Etha" 363
Davidson, Robert (victim) 363
Davidson County 26; last triple hanging in 215–16; Nashville area 8, 11, 15, 21, 30, 32–36, 43–44, 63, 112–13 (Brown's Creek area 139; Camp Andrew Jackson 56; first triple execution in Nashville 32–36; gallows on bank of Cumberland River opposite Nashville 17; *see also* Main Prison); Nashville jail 109–10, 164, 166, 216–17; Nashville prison 71, 81, 82, 84–85, 88–93, 96–98, 414; public gallows at 10
Davidson County jail 195, 205, 215–16, 222–24
Davis, Captain Dick 93–94
Davis, Deputy Sheriff 208–10
Davis, Harold 410, 411
Davis, Jefferson 60
Davis, John W. (victim) 250
Davis, Samuel C. 74–77
Dawson, George (victim) 184–85
"dead men walking" 4
Deakins, David (slave) 40
Deakins, William (victim) 40
Deal, John 325–27
Dean, Crawford (Pete) 339
Dean, William see *Knight, James*
"death chamber" 268, 291, 412; *see also* "execution chamber"
"death house" 256, 260, 268, 277–79, 295, 305, 311, 345, 355; new 402, 403
"Death Is Only a Dream" 304, 305, 311
"death row" 272, 336, 337, 397, 403, 404
death warrant, hanging delayed due to forgetting 131
death watch 406, 412, 416, 419
DeBerry, Harvey 199–200, 250
decapitation: of perpetrators (*see* heads put on public display); of victims 130, 181–82
Deck, Evander Turner 98
Deering, Frank A. (victim) 235–36
DeKalb County 37, 110
Delap, Robert 17–18
Delk, David (victim) 95
Delp, Joe 219–20
desertion 14–15, 59–65, 67–73, 77; advising 71–72; executions for desertion not sent to president for review 63
devil, perpetrators talking about the 23, 24, 114, 126, 141, 153, 228; *see also* Satan
Dick see *Dyer, Dick*
Dickson County 26
Dillard, Arlene (victim) 370–72
Dillard, Ed 192
Dillard, Steven (victim) 370
disrobing 89, 90
Distow, Christian (victim) 8
Dixon, Billy Leon 378–79
Dixon, Ernest 365–66
Dixon, T.N. 158
Dixon, Zack (victim) 181–82
DNA testing 404, 408–9
Dockery, John 365–66
documentation, missing 2–4
Dodd, Ephraim Shelby 77–79
Dodge, Gen. Grenville M. 74, 75
Dodillet, Paula 412
domestic violence 24, 128, 154, 204, 220–21, 258, 367–69, 373, 374; *see also* murder(s), of wife
Donaldson, Nancy (victim) 148
double jeopardy 101, 132, 366
Dougherty, William 296, 297
Douglass, George 381
Dover area, Stewart County 47–48, 126
Dowell, Richard 119
Doyle, Constable Peter 245–46
Dran, William see *Knight, James*
Drew, Captain 20
drowning 7–8, 19, 325–27
drug intoxication 406–12, 415–16; *see also* alcohol intoxication
drunkenness *see* alcohol intoxication
Du Bois, W.E.B. 263, 289
Duboise, Albert "Bantam" 383–85
Duck River, Maury County 106
Duetch, Adolph (victim) 103–4
Duetch, Henry "Andy" 104
Dula, Bennett 26
Duncan, Dave 118–19
Duncan, Joseph 11
Dunlap, Sidney 264–65
Dunn, Helen (victim) 343
Dunn, Howard 341–43
Dunn, Gov. Winfield 404
Dupree, Mr. (victim) 38
Dutton, Lucille (victim) 303
Dwight, William 296–98
Dwyer, Professor M. 151
Dyer, Dick (slave) 31
Dyer, Emmett 283, 285
Dyer, Gertrude 283, 285, 286
Dyersburg, Dyer County 232

Earles, Gardner R. 46
Earles, Rhoda (victim) 46
Eatmon, Roy W. 340–41
Edgerton, John 280, 289
Edmondson, Young C. "Tobe" 59
Edmonson, Lizzie (victim) 204
Edwards, Dave D. 243, 250–52
Edwards, Grace Evelyn 369
Eelbeck, John G. (victim) 44
Eigiman, Elenora (victim) 199
electric chair 414; broken wire in 385; perpetrator begging jury for 375; removed from Main Prison 404; system short-circuited 323
electrocution 3, 5, 404; first white man from Shelby County electrocuted 341; last man executed in old corner chamber 399–402; of multiple people together 269–70, 274–75, 322–24, 327–30, 333–36, 350, 351–53, 358–63, 365–66, 370–73, 380–83, 386–89; number of people who died from 403; *see also* execution(s); *specific perpetrators*
Elias (slave) 45
Elkines, L. L. 77
Elkins, Deputy Sheriff 215
Eller, "Sam" 225
Ellick (slave) 44–45
Ellington, Gov. Buford 402
Ellis, Hannah 173
Ellis, Joe (victim) 173
Elrod, Peter (victim) 32–34
Emberlin, Mrs. 115
Emberlin, William (victim) 114–15
Emory, Joe 319–20
Erskin, Joe 313
Erwin, Diana (victim) 50
Erwin, Henry (slave) 50
Erwin, John Pinkney (victim) 50

espionage *see* spying
Espy, Major Watt, Jr. 5
Ethridge, John (victim) 36
Evans, Elzey (victim) 214
Evans, Harley 354–55
Evans, ("Slow") John 219–20
Evans, William 8, 11
Ewell, Mary H. (victim) 264
Ewing, Frank 270–71
"execution chamber" 273, 402, 412, 416, 419; *see also* "death chamber"; "hanging chamber"
execution fees 27, 40, 45, 194, 195
execution methods: burning 10; firing squads 15, 60–61, 67–68, 86; shootings 57, 59, 70, 72 (*see also* court-martials); *see also* electrocution; hanging(s)
execution(s): in bad weather 18, 41, 61, 76, 84, 113, 114, 131, 145–46, 170, 183, 185, 198, 243, 246; books on 3; compared with getting struck by lightning 1; cost of 10, 22, 40, 252; finding suitable locations for 112; greatest number on a single day 3; last quadruple 277–80, 295; missing cases of 2; most widely-known 94–96; paying to watch 103, 104, 143, 192–93 (*see also* corpses of perpetrators, charging money to see); perpetrators who died before the time of their 59; premature attempt to execute perpetrator 175–76; research on 1; semi-private 143, 156; summary executions ordered by Gen. Forest 59; *see also specific topics*
exoneration movement 404
explosive devices, murders using 33, 347–48

Fackenthal, Lt. J.W. 82
fact-based death penalty research 1, 4, 5
Fain, Isaac "Ike" 160–61
Fain, Louis 321–22
faintings prior to hanging 14, 24
Fallen, Littlebury 28
Fallen, William 28
family feuds 348
Farley, Ada (victim) 218–19
Farley, Dan 218–19
Farmer, John 128
Farmer, William 341–43
father and son executed together 56
Fayette County 126, 197
Fayette County jail 170
Fayetteville, Lincoln County 21–23, 51
federal government authority, executions under 8, 9, 376
felony murder 254, 314, 336, 372, 410
felony murder doctrine 254, 314, 387
Fenton, John (victim) 101, 102
Fenton, Mrs. 102, 103
Fentress County 107–8
Ferguson, Anna (victim) 270–71
Ferguson, Champ 94–96
Ferry, Thomas see *Perry, Thomas*
feuding 348
Fields, Asbury 276–77, 279, 295
Fields, Joe (victim) 121
Finnegan, Mike (victim) 351
fires *see* arson
Fishback, Buford 353
Fisher, Samuel 152
Fite, John A. 37
Flatt, Terry 414–16
Flippin, Dr. 38
Fogg, William (victim) 95
folklore 4
Forbes, Douglas 404
Ford, Joseph 69
Ford, Rhoda 25
Ford, Robert 194–95
Ford, William 25
forgiveness 21, 51, 52, 97, 104, 110–12, 116, 119, 125, 128, 135, 167, 168, 175, 186, 205, 211, 240, 249, 343, 406, 419; from God 52, 102, 103, 106, 119, 122, 125, 129, 141, 145, 150, 159, 180, 190, 193, 205, 209, 218, 219, 231, 240, 254, 258, 263, 264, 270, 275; *see also* God; Jesus Christ
Forrest, Armstead (victim) 39
Forrest, Jane (victim) 159
Forrest, Gen. Nathan Bedford 59, 86, 91–93
Forrest, Shim 159
Forrester, Samuel 11
Fort Donelson, Stewart County 71
Fort Pickering, Shelby County 83–84, 86, 93, 94
Foster, Gen. 78
Foster, James see *Clarke, James*
Foster, Mary Lee (victim) 313
Foust, Wiley F., Jr. 306
Foust, Wiley W. 307
Foust, Wylie W. (victim) 306, 307
Fowler, Ben "Two Gun" 306–7
Fowler, Constable Oder (victim) 354
Fowler, James A. 293, 294
Fox, Sheriff 186, 187
Fox, Simon 165, 166
Fraley, Captain Hugh (aka James F. Fraley) 84–85
Francis, Mack 169–70
Frank (slave) 12
Franklin, Mrs. (victim) 36
Franklin, Tom 338–39
Franklin, William C. (victim) 36
Franklin, Williamson County 12, 16, 18, 31, 65–67
Franklin County 2, 15; county jail 220; Tullahoma 61, 62, 64, 70, 79; Winchester 25, 39, 132, 220
Franklinites 8
Frazier, Hannah (victim) 46
Freeman, Judge 127, 142, 149–50, 158
Freeman, Sheriff M.H. 159
Friddle, Deputy Sheriff 318
Frierson, Jesse 179–81
Fritz, Lina 146
Fry, Henry 54, 55
Furman v. Georgia 1
Gaines, Samuel (victim) 225
Gaines, William (victim) 125
Gainesboro, Jackson County 27, 187
Galloway, Catherine (victim) 106–8
Galloway, James Hill 106, 107
Galloway, Lucinda (victim) 106, 107
Galloway, Walter (victim) 200–201
Galloway, William B. (victim) 106, 107
Gallows Bottom, Bledsoe County 42
Gallows Hollow, Clarksville 46
Galvin, James 101–3
gambling 70, 180, 194–95, 211–14, 216, 233, 274, 321, 402; *see also* Mays, Maurice
gangs 14, 26, 35, 86, 87, 92–95, 98, 142, 157, 216, 242, 382
Gardner, Elijah (victim) 13
Gardner, Felix (victim) 132
Garfield, Brig. Gen. James A. 66, 67
Garibaldi Guards 52
Garner, Granville (victim) 317–18
Garrison, Sheriff J.L. 206–7
Gaston, William 325, 326
General Assembly 8, 12–14
General Order (G.O.) 3
genital mutilation 137
George, Oliver James (victim) 351–53
George, Shawney 9
German, Columbus C. "Lum" 98–99
German, William 99
Gholson, Ham see *Gohlston, Hamp*
Gholston, Hamp see *Gohlston, Hamp*
Gibbs, Billy Thomas 399–401
Gibbs, Sheriff 131
Gibson, Mrs. Al 166
Gibson, Lillian (victim) 332
Gibson, Travis (victim) 49
Gibson County 36, 58
Giffen, J. Kelly 294
Gilbert (slave) 39
Gilbreath, Frank 252–54
Gilbreath, John 253, 254
Giles County: Pulaski 15, 74–76, 82, 111, 182; Pulaski jail 152
Gill, Alex (victim) 226
Gillespie, George 25
Gilmore, Van 361
Gist, Aaron 10
God: perpetrators crying out to 41, 96, 135, 145, 152, 161, 193, 228, 359; perpetrators speaking about 52, 53, 65, 67, 102, 103, 110, 113, 114, 116, 118, 119, 122, 125, 129, 131, 139–42, 145, 148, 150, 153, 155, 159, 160, 166–67, 170, 171, 175, 180, 183, 185–88, 190, 195, 198, 200, 205, 211, 213, 219–21, 230, 233, 236, 240, 242, 249, 252, 258, 261, 263, 264, 274, 275, 299, 323, 325, 350, 353, 354, 376, 378, 385, 392, 397, 401, 402, 405, 406; *see also* Jesus Christ
Godfrey, Hyde see *Godsey, Hiram*
Godsey, Hiram "Hyde" 42–43
Goeing, Rev. George A. 256
Goforth, Julius 370–72
Gohlston, Hamp 274–75
Goode, John Henry 368–70

Goodin, James "Trigger Slim" 360–61
Goodrich, Duncan (victim) 213
Goodrum, James R. (victim) 150–52
Goodspeed 27
Gordon, Isaac (victim) 350
Gordy, Joseph M. (victim) 329
Gore, Warden Thomas P. 361, 364, 373
Goss, Freddie J. (victim) 385, 386
Goss, Hazel 385, 386
Goss, I.T. (victim) 385, 386
Goss, Sammie M. (victim) 385
Gossett, Robert T. 88–90
Gouge, Harmon 347, 348
Gouge, Luena 347
Gouge, Roma Jean (victim) 347
Gouge, Sonia June 347
governors: commuting death sentence to life imprisonment 2; *see also specific governors*
Graham, Chesley 273–74
Graham, Jasper 323–25
Grainger County: Bean Station 69; Rutledge 9, 48, 101
grandchildren, murder of 7–8
grandparents, murder of 159, 328–29
Grandstaff, Sheriff 125
Grant, Gen. 97
graves, marked 108
Gray, Ed 264–65
Gray, Samuel 60–61
Green, Bart 196–97
Green, Judge Grafton 279, 293, 364
Green, John 295
Green, John 275–76, 279, 295
Green, Judge Nathan 34, 35, 41
Green, Thomas 24
Green, Willie (victim) 333
Greeneville, Greene County 32, 54, 136
Grey (slave) 46–48
Griffee (aka Griffey), Stephen 136–38, 144
Griffin, Deputy Sheriff Tom 265
Griffith, Rev. 248–49
Griffiths, Wiley P. (victim) 93
Grundy, Felix 16
guerrillas 57, 58, 64, 84–92, 94; *see also* bushwackers
Guinn, Sam 190–91
Gunn, Carey 311
Gunter, William 90

habeas corpus relief, seeking 101, 255, 303, 305, 403, 404, 408, 410, 411, 413–14, 416, 418
Hal see *Old Hal*
Hale, Harmon 321, 322
Hale, John Arthur 397
Hale, William Jasper 291
Hall, Hiram 206–7
Hall, Ida Belle Hassler (victim) 206
Hall, John 142–43
Hall, Minnie 220–21
Hall, Robert 376–78
Halliburton, Alf 213–14
Ham see *Hannibal*
Hamblen County, Morristown area in 79, 140
Hambrick, George Mansfield 378, 461n3008
Hamilton, Pvt. Abraham 72–73
Hamilton, Robert (victim) 124
Hamilton County: Chattanooga area 72, 77, 91, 115–16, 148–49; Chattanooga jail 192, 252; Harrison 99, 104
Hamilton County jail 180–81, 245
Hancock County, first legal hanging in 199
"hanging chamber" 263
hanging suicide 349
hanging(s): bodies left hanging as warning to others 19; collapse from fright prior to 14, 24; done twice 78–79; dual hanging of white and black man for same crime 21; keeping secret the date/time of 193, 214; of multiple people together 24, 32–36, 44, 45, 61, 65, 68, 73, 154, 173–76, 191, 192, 209–13, 215–17, 220, 223–29, 256–59; premature attempt to hang perpetrator 175–76; prolonged/botched 5, 9, 16, 42, 56, 67, 75, 78, 85, 96–98, 104, 108, 121, 122, 125, 127, 129, 136, 144, 148, 152, 158, 169–70, 178, 192, 195, 196, 206, 207, 210, 212, 215, 218, 222, 223, 234, 268, 374–75, 406–9 (*see also* hangman's rope); statute requiring (semi-) private 143, 156, 158, 166; time of day of 123, 193, 245; triple gallows 174; *see also* execution(s); *specific perpetrators*; *specific topics*
Hangman's Basin, Bledsoe County 42
"hangman's hill" in Maynardville 191
hangman's rope: demand for 13; giving away pieces of 187; same rope used to execute multiple perpetrators 129, 156, 253; superstitions about 13; *see also* hanging(s), prolonged/botched
Hanner, John 173
Hannibal (slave) 32
Harbert, Ben 46
Hardeman County 73, 220–21; Bolivar 22, 25, 114, 161
Hardin County: Centerville 51; Savannah area 24, 42, 62, 99
Hardwick, William M. (victim) 336
Harmon, Henry 55, 56
Harmon, Jacob, Jr. 55, 56
Harness, Jacob 129–31
Harriet (slave who drowned 5-year-old) 25
Harris, Austin 298
Harris, Benjamin 14
Harris, Dan 204–5
Harris, Dock 106
Harris, Ernest K. 332–33
Harris, Hubert 351
Harris, Joseph 149–50
Harris, Letha "Lettie" (victim) 174
Harris, Parker 174–75
Harris, Theodore James 311–13
Harrison, Charles 303–4
Harrison, Jo (slave) 50–51
Hart, Captain Dock 106
Hartsfield, Theresa Newman (victim) 322
Hatcher, John 283, 284, 289
hatchet *see* murder, methods of
Hatchey (Hatchett), Sam 194
Hatfield, Maired 198–99
Hauk, Judge 98
Haun, Charles Alexander 54–55
Hawkins County: Rogersville 18, 52, 116, 118, 119, 150; Rogersville jail 179
Hay, William T. (victim) 16
Hayes, Alexander 17
Hayes, O.B. 17
Hayley, James W. and Eliza, son of (victim) 36
Haynes, Edward M. 282–83
Haynes, Louisa (victim) 52
Haynes, Mary Hale (victim) 52
Haynes, Milton 35
Haynie, Frank, Jr. 338, 340
Hays, Solomon "Lee" (victim) 98
Haywood County 36, 43
Hazelwood, Crawford (victim) 95
heads put on public display 12, 15, 47; *see also* decapitation
Hearn model 3, 4
hearsay testimony 267, 289, 294, 295
Heck, Andy (victim) 149
Heck, John D. (victim) 202–3
Hedden, Lecie Mae Chastain (victim) 370–71
Hedden, William 370–72
Hedgecoth, Everett (victim) 304
Hedgecoth, Mrs. Everett 304, 305
Hedrick, Napoleon (victim) 90
Hefferman, William (victim) 97–98
Henderson, Bob 236, 237
Henderson County 18–19, 51; Lexington 51
Henley, Steve 414–16
Henning, Herman (victim) 266–67
Henry see *Bennett, Henry*; Erwin, Henry; Kelly, Henry
Henry, Abe (slave) 85
Henry, Rufus 85
Henry, William 359–61
Henry County 38–39, 159, 173
Hensley, Armstrong 218
Hensley, Matthew 328
Herndon, Newton K. "Jink" 381–83
Herrin, John A. 8
Hester, Evaline (victim) 170
Hibbert, Andrew 223–24
Hickey, Ellen 177
Hickman County 24
Hicks, Alvin 381–83
Hicks, Bettie 152–53
Hicks, Elisha (Lish) (victim) 236, 237
Higdon, Claude 384, 385
Hill, Jesse 356, 357
Hill, John (executed in 1849) see *Inman, John*
Hill, John (executed in 1905) 229–30
Hill, Sarah Catherine (victim) 229

Hill, Will 220–21
Hillis, James (victim) 210–11
Hindman, Squire H. William (victim) 254
Hinshaw, Jacob Madison 54, 55
Hodge, John, Jr. 385
Hodge, Milton 153–55
Hodge, Sam H. 356
Hodge, Samuel 153–55
Hodge, Welcome 8
Hodges, Elizabeth (victim) 31
Holliday, William D. (victim) 197
Hollis, Archibald 323, 324
Holmes, George M. 68–69
Holste, Charlene (victim) 381
Holt (jailor) 180, 181
Holt, Judge Advocate General 80–82, 84, 85, 88–92
Holt, William "Tom" 48
Holton, Brent (victim) 412–13
Holton, Daryl Keith 412–14
Holton, Eric (victim) 412–13
Holton, Kayla (victim) 412–13
Holton, Stephen (victim) 412–13
Homes, George M. see *Holmes, George M.*
Honeycutt, Ananias 117–19
Hood, Mantye E. (victim) 345
Hooper, Gov. Ben 260–63, 265–66
Hopson, Frank 339
horse stealing 7, 10–12, 14
horseback: corpses on 40; perpetrators on 9, 23, 50, 97, 109, 111–13, 116, 118–20, 125, 129, 131, 143, 196, 407; *see also* "swung off"
Horton, Gov. Henry 296, 306, 311
Hough, Joseph see *Huff, Joseph (aka Jacob)*
House, Charles H. (victim) 417, 418
House, Henderson 213–14
House, Paul Gregory 404
house burning (arson) 12, 39, 385–86
Houston, Robert L. (victim) 275
Houston, Gov. Sam 23, 25
Houston, William (victim) 260
Howell, George 136
Huckaby, Benjamin (victim) 43
Hudson, J.M. 252
Hudson, Mat 205
Huff, Alex (victim) 95
Huff, Joseph (aka Jacob) 99
Hughes, Owen (victim) 19–20
Hughes, Polly 24
Humes, David (victim) 29
Humphreys County: Reynoldsville 24; Waverly 145–46
Hunt, Andrew J. 128–29
Hunt, George see *Johnson, Will*
Hunt, Jack see *Hunt, Andrew J.*
Hunt, Jackson see *Hunt, Andrew J.*
Hunt, Margaret Ann Davis (victim) 128
Hunt, Thomas (victim) 27
Hunter, Polly 32, 33
Huntington, Carroll County 39, 160
Huntsville, Scott County 196
Hurst, Colonel Fielding 58
Hurt, Sheriff 216, 217
Hutchison, Louis (victim) 394–96
Hutchinson, Sheriff Louis B. (victim) 339
Hyde, Sheriff F. Scott 192
Hyde, Grey (victim) 86, 87, 92
Hyler, Bennie 345
hymn-singing 3, 22, 32, 52–53, 65, 103–6, 108, 110, 111, 121, 122, 125, 127, 131, 135, 142, 143, 145, 146, 154, 168, 175, 178, 180, 181, 183, 187, 188, 195, 200, 201, 205, 210–13, 232, 234, 258, 305, 306, 309, 311, 313, 357

"I Am Going Home to Die No More" (hymn) 168, 181
"I'm Going Home" 233, 240
"In the Sweet Bye and Bye" (hymn) 225, 226
inadequate counsel/inadequate defense 404
incest 152, 153, 382, 401–2
infamy statute 462n3014
infanticide 126; *see also under* murder(s)
Inman, John 41–42
Inman, Samuel 11
innocence, proclamations of 2, 3, 18, 29, 30, 33–35, 41, 44, 45, 53, 65, 66, 75, 78, 79, 84, 88, 92, 103, 106, 107, 109, 111, 113, 116, 118, 119, 124, 125, 131, 132, 134, 135, 137–38, 144, 145, 151–52, 164, 166, 170, 172, 178, 180, 182, 186, 191, 192, 197, 215, 216, 218, 219, 222–23, 230, 232–33, 235, 243, 246, 249, 255, 256, 258, 260–61, 264, 267, 270, 272, 274, 277, 279, 280, 301, 307, 308, 319, 321, 325, 327–30, 334, 337, 344, 349, 352, 354, 357, 366, 370, 374, 383, 391–92, 399, 409, 416–18; reasons for false 2–3; symbolic gestures 118; *see also* exoneration movement; Mays, Maurice; mistaken identity; self-defense
Innocence Project 409
innocence revolution 404
innocent, executed persons now suspected to have been 13–14, 249; *see also* Mays, Maurice; "wrong man" convictions vs. wrongful convictions
insanity 21, 67, 120, 128, 159, 166, 176, 183, 228, 229, 240, 244, 245, 258, 259, 268, 278, 293, 297, 301, 305, 308, 311, 312, 334, 336, 339, 342–43, 356, 357, 365, 375, 395, 396, 406–9, 413–14; by intoxication 19, 20, 211, 250–51 (*see also* alcohol intoxication; drug intoxication); partial 395; temporary 20, 211, 244, 250–51, 299, 374; *see also* mental capacity/incapacity
insurrection *see* slave insurrection/panic of 1856
intoxication: "cyclical" 250; *see also* alcohol intoxication; drug intoxication
Ipson, Henry (victim) *see* Thomas, J.H. "Henry"
Ipson, John (victim) *see* Thomas, J.H. "Henry"
Irving, Henry 93
Isaac (Isom) see *Isom*
Isaac (slave executed in 1861) 51–52
Isaac (victim) 36, 37
Isbell, Angeline Allison 132–34
Isbell, J.W. 132, 135
Ish, John (victim) 9
Isham see *Isom*
Ishmael (slave) 46–48
Isom (slave) 45
Israel (slave) 16–17
Itter, Henry (victim) *see* Thomas, J.H. "Henry"
Itter, John (victim) *see* Thomas, J.H. "Henry"
Ivie, Eliza (victim) 43
Ivy, Pvt. William 69

Jack (slave) 46
Jacksboro, Campbell County 46, 50
Jackson, Andrew 11, 14, 15
Jackson, Cyrenas 272–73
Jackson, Fred 385–86
Jackson, Judge Howell E. 120
Jackson, Captain John C. 57, 58
Jackson, R.C. 19
Jackson, Riley 304
Jackson, Madison County 21, 36, 127, 145, 222; county jail 197, 206
Jackson County 21; Gainesboro 27, 187
Jacob (slave) 30–31
Jacob/Jake see *Bradford, Jake*
jail/prison breaks 42, 46, 64, 71, 92, 94, 100, 101, 116, 128, 134, 136, 144, 145, 177, 189, 192, 212–14, 217, 257, 265, 267, 268, 302, 330, 338, 346, 355, 356, 375, 378, 385, 394, 402
Jake see *Bradford, Jake*
James, Frank 118
James, Harry 345
James, William "Cap," Jr. (victim) 353
Jameson, Thomas 21
Jamestown, Fentress County 107–8
Jasper area, Marion County 48, 183, 185, 190
Jefferson, Thomas 170–72, 174, 175
Jefferson County 10, 42, 45
Jenkins, Mary 48
Jessee/Jess (slave) 13–14
Jesus Christ, perpetrators speaking about 103, 113, 135, 145, 146, 150, 153, 155, 156, 168, 192, 197, 200, 225, 240, 263, 276, 327, 412
"Jesus, Lover of My Soul" (hymn) 232, 268
Jim see *Payne, Jim*; *Ragsdale, Jim*
Jobe, Dewitt Smith 59
Joe (slave executed 1833) 25
Joe (slave executed 1860) 50
John (slave) 48, 52
Johnson, Andrew 89, 97, 104
Johnson, Rev. B.H. 154, 155
Johnson, Cecil C., Jr. 416–19
Johnson, Coleman 348
Johnson, Dobson 133, 136

Johnson, Ethel 313
Johnson, Frank 197–98
Johnson, Glenn (victim) 346–47
Johnson, Henry (executed in 1908) 246–50
Johnson, Henry (executed in 1936) see *Clarke, James*
Johnson, Hyman 350
Johnson, James Weldon 289, 290
Johnson, John Lewis 402
Johnson, John W. 81–82
Johnson, Laura Wheaton 302
Johnson, Mary Louise (victim) 323, 324
Johnson, Rev. Pickens 306, 311, 324, 327, 328, 333, 334, 336, 339, 355, 374, 378, 384–86, 388, 403
Johnson, Richard "Dick" (victim) 232
Johnson, Thomas 85, 86
Johnson, Will 203–4
Johnson County 231
Johnston, James (victim) 9
Johnston, Thomas see *Johnson, Thomas*
Jones, Alice 394, 395
Jones, Barclay J. (victim) 311–12
Jones, Indiana (victim) 91
Jones, Gov. James "Lean Jimmy" 33
Jones, J.E. 244
Jones, John (executed in 1814) 14
Jones, John (executed in 1930) 309–11
Jones, Joseph A. 97
Jones, Lena Buffalow (victim) 311–12
Jones, Maggie (victim) 378–79
Jones, Orleans (Irene) (victim) 227
Jones, Robert 43
Jones, Sarah K. (victim) 50
Jones, Warren 130
Jones, Willie 317–19
Jonesborough, Washington County 7, 8, 40, 201, 202
Joslin, Foster 165
Joslin, Nelson 165
Judge, Henry (aka James Henry Judge) 219–20
judge sentencing 275, 285
judges, election and selection of 120
Julius (slave) 27–29
jurors 51–52, 397; atheist 22–23; citizenship 115; exclusion based on race 304, 331; perpetrator begging them for electric chair 375; standards to follow 404
jury sentencing 275, 285

Keener, Michael LaVoi see *LaVoi Keener, Michael*
Kefauver, Rev. J.P. 129
Keith, Ann (victim) 73
Kelley, Houston D. 178–79, 442n1464
Kelley, John T. 386–88
Kelly, Bill 112–14, 143
Kelly, George 124
Kelly, Henry (slave) 36
Kelly, William 58
Kemp, Ella 192
Kemp, Lawson see *Camp, Pvt. Lawson*
Kennedy, Annie (victim) 393
Kennedy, Pvt. Cornelius 62
Kennedy, Gen. 188–90
Kennedy, John S. 188–90
Kennedy, Josephus 189, 190
Kennedy, Sampson 52
Kennedy, Walter 329–30
Kenny, Samuel W. 61–62
Kerr, Dr. 244
Kerr, John C. 70
Kerr, Mr. 142–43
Key, Deputy Sheriff 318
kidnapping 330–31, 405
Killpatrick, John Jones (victim) 99
Kinchen see *Sullivan, Kinchen*
King, Elias, Jr. (victim) 105
King, Jacob 14
King, Mike L. 195–96
Kingston, Roane County 50, 160–61
Kinnon, Tom 261
Kirby, Archibald 32–35
Kirby, Officer Tom 283–86
Kirk, Lewis M. 58
Kirkendoll, Harry (aka Henry) 396–97
Kite, George Rufus (victim) 52
Knapp, George see *Mapp, George*
knifing/stabbing/cutting 13, 20–22, 31, 34, 36, 43, 44, 49, 50, 53, 71, 95, 105, 132, 138, 143–44, 165, 170–71, 174, 175, 178–79, 183, 188, 198, 204, 243, 266–67, 277–78, 321, 344, 380, 383–86, 389–90, 405–9
Knight, James 96, 97
Knox County: first white man legally executed after 1875 246; Knoxville 9–12, 23–25, 29, 55, 56, 69–70, 78–79, 85, 117–19, 154–55, 246 (county jail 168, 178, 186–87, 234, 240, 243); public gallows at 10
Kogier, Elijah (victim) 95
Kraft, George see *Craft, George*
Ku Klux Klan (KKK) 99, 119
Kyle, Marshall 402

Lacy, Paul 391–93
Lafayette, Macon County 38
Lahue, Dan 214
Lakin, Matthew 280–81
Lamar, Judge Lucius Q.C., Jr. 294
Lamar, Judge Lucius Q.C., Sr. 294
Lambert, Charley 269
Lambert, Emma (victim) 269
Lancaster, J. Larkin 181–82
land dispute, murder over 26, 359
Lane, George (victim) 311–12
Lane, John T. (victim) 166–67
Lane, Martha (victim) 164
Last Supper 210
Lauderdale, John W. (victim) 43
Lauderdale County 214–15
LaVoi Keener, Michael 62
Lawrence, David T. (victim) 46
Lawson, Henry 148–49
Lawson, Homer 270
lawyers: defense 16; executed 139–42
Lea, Edmund 105
Leach, Mynatt 202–3
Leadbetter, Colonel Danville 54, 56
League, Viola L. 361
Lebanon, Wilson County 124–25
Lee, Virgil 256
Lee, William 328–29
Leeper, Susan (victim) 365–66
legal counsel, defendants denied the right to 8
legislation 2; abolishing death penalty 403; law revised in 1807 14; placing on jury the burden of finding guilt and setting penalty 275, 285; *see also specific legislation*
Lemmons, William 86–87
Lemond, William P. see *Lemmons, William*
Lenoir City, Loudon County 158
Lester, Arnold 348
Lester, Church Calvin 347–49
Lester, Napoleon B. 166–67
Lester, Mrs. Napoleon *see* Gibson, Mrs. Al
lethal injection 404–19; protocol for 412, 416, 465n3265
letters, farewell 129
Levy, Isaac (victim) 274, 275
Lewis see *Louis*
Lewis, Pvt. Asa 60–61
Lewis, George A. (victim) 277–78
Lewis, Jesse 49–50
Lewis, John 49–50
Lewis, Mrs. Rufus (Luda) (victim) 177–78
Lexington, Henderson County 51
lie detector tests 399, 402, 415
life sentence vs. death penalty 2
Light Guards 170
Lincoln, Abraham 5, 52, 54–56, 59, 80–82, 84, 85, 88–93
Lincoln County 21–23, 51
Lincoln County jail 184, 235, 253
Lindsey, Rev. Isaac (victim) 35
Lindsey (or Lindsay), Bertie (victim) 281–83, 285–95
Litterall, William 60–61
Livingston, Overton County 98–99
Lize (slave) 38
locations of executions 3; Billy Goat Hill, Putnam County 134–35; Bledsoe County (Hangman's Basin/Gallows Bottom 42; Pikeville area 13, 42); Blount County 14 (Maryville 22, 30); Blountville, Sullivan County 72, 202; Brownsville, Haywood County 36, 43; Carthage area 63; Centerville, Hickman County 24; Charlotte area, Dickson County 26; Covington, Tipton County 36, 147; Cumberland County jail 206–7; Dandridge, Jefferson County 10, 42, 45; Dyersburg, Dyer County 232; Fayette County jail 170; Franklin County 2, 15 (county jail 220; Tullahoma 61, 62, 64, 70, 79; Winchester 25, 39, 132, 220); Gallows Hollow in Clarksville 46; Giles County (Pulaski 15, 74–76, 82, 111, 182; Pulaski jail 152); Grainger County

(Bean Station 69; Rutledge 9, 48, 101); Greeneville, Greene County 32, 54, 136; Hamilton County (Chattanooga area 72, 77, 91, 115–16, 148–49; Chattanooga jail 192, 252; Harrison 99, 104); Hamilton County jail 180–81, 245; "hangman's hill" in Maynardville, Union County 191; Hardeman County 73, 220–21 (Bolivar 22, 25, 114, 161); Hardin County (Centerville 51; Savannah area 24, 42, 62, 99); Hawkins County (Rogersville 18, 52, 116, 118, 119, 150; Rogersville jail 179); Henderson County 18–19 (Lexington 51); Humphreys County (Reynoldsville 24; Waverly 145–46); Huntington, Carroll County 39, 160; Huntsville, Scott County 196; Jacksboro, Campbell County 46, 50; Jackson County 21 (Gainesboro 27, 187); Jamestown, Fentress County 107–8; Jasper area, Marion County 48, 183, 185, 190; Jonesborough, Washington County 7, 8, 40, 201, 202; Kingston, Roane County 50, 160–61; Knox County (county jail 168, 178, 186–87, 234, 240, 243; Knoxville 9–12, 23–25, 29, 55, 56, 69–70, 78–79, 85, 117–19, 154–55, 168, 178, 186–87, 234, 240, 243, 246; public gallows at 10); Lafayette, Macon County 38; Lenoir City, Loudon County 158; Lincoln County (Fayetteville 21–23, 51; jail 184, 235, 253); Livingston, Overton County 98–99; Madison County 41(county jail 197, 206; Jackson 21, 36, 127, 145, 197, 206, 222); Marshall County 46; Maury County 19, 69 (Columbia 29; Columbia area 19, 106; Duck River 106); Maury County jail 193–94, 198; McMinn County 31 (Athens 46, 238); McMinn County jail 186; Monroe County (Clinton area 131, 203; Madisonville 129, 232–33); Montgomery County 45, 47; Montgomery County jail 162–63; Morristown area, Hamblen County 79, 140; Mountain City jail, Johnson County 231; Newport area, Cocke County 137–38, 144; Obion County 172–73; Paris, Henry County 38, 39, 159, 173; Purdy, McNairy County 50; Ripley, Lauderdale County 214–15; Rutherford County 27, 142–43 (Battery's camp near Cripple Creek 68; Murfreesboro 40, 43, 60–62, 65, 67–68); Sevier County jail 209–10; Shelby County 227–28 (Bartlett 120, 122; first legal executions in 51–52; Fort Pickering 83–84, 86, 93, 94; Memphis area 53, 83–84, 86, 93, 94, 103, 105, 122–24; Memphis jail 188, 228–29, 236); Shelby County jail 102, 153, 156, 163–64, 171–72, 174–77, 200, 204, 218, 219, 225–27, 249; Shelbyville, Bedford County 39, 65; Smithville, DeKalb County 37, 110; Sneedville area, Hancock County 199; Somerville area, Fayette County 126, 197; Sparta, White County 26; Springfield, Robertson County 38; Stewart County 47 (Dover area 47–48, 126; Fort Donelson 71); Tazewell 117–19; Tipton County jail 230; Trenton, Gibson County 36, 58; Unicoi County jail 218; Warren County jail 211–13; Waynesboro, Wayne County 242; Weakley County 45; Williamson County 18, 25 (Franklin 12, 16, 18, 31, 65–67); Wilson County 27, 124, 169–70 (Lebanon 124–25); Wilson County jail 167; *see also* Davidson County
Logan, Mrs. 82, 84
Logston, James Calvin 106–8
London, Prof see *Bryant, Professor*
London, Progue see *Bryant, Professor*
Long, Edward 144–45
Long, Elizabeth Manning (victim) 29
Long, George 29
Long, John 163
Long, Thomas C. 298
Lord's Prayer 153, 156, 162, 225, 275, 302, 406
Loudon County 158
Louis (slave) 36
Love, W.B. 160
Lowe, Colonel William W. 58
Lowery, Edward (victim) 330
Lowrie, John (victim) 189
Lucy (slave) 36
Luffman, John 381–83
Lum, Sam K. (victim) 327
Lunsford, Henry 22
Lurton, Horace 255
Lusk, John 17
Lyles, George 64–65
lynchings 50, 58, 59, 124, 126, 186, 214, 245, 266, 268, 428n419, 428n445; mobs and fears of 117, 138, 142, 150, 191, 197, 198, 204, 236, 247, 255, 269, 274, 284, 321, 332, 400; Pettigrew "lynching" 261–63; prevention of 168, 191, 197, 204, 218, 233, 255, 261, 266, 271, 400; threats of 177, 202, 204; *see also* vigilantes
Lysaught, James (aka James Lycought) 96–98
Lytle, John H. (victim) 329

Maburn, Mattie (victim) 228
Mac, Dave *see* McMahan, Dave
Macay, Judge Spruce 7
Macon County 38
Madison County 41 (county jail 197, 206; Jackson 21, 36, 127, 145, 197, 206, 222)
Madisonville, Monroe County 129, 232–33
Main Prison 3; electric chair removed from 404; executions in 3, 254–58, 260, 264, 268, 270–72, 274, 275, 280, 298, 301–8, 311, 312, 314, 317, 320, 327, 328, 331, 332, 336, 340, 341, 343, 344, 349, 350, 354, 363, 365, 368, 372, 378, 385, 390, 391, 394, 399, 403, 404, 417; law requiring executions to be held in 254; *see also* Riverbend Maximum Security Institution; *specific perpetrators*
Malloy, Pat 266–67
Malone, Burley 225
Maney, Charles (slave) 27
Manley, Grace (victim) 361
Manning, Jane 29
Manning, Joseph 64
manslaughter 7–8
Maples, Walter 207, 208
Mapp, George 191–93
Marcum, Mitchell 17
Marion County 48, 183, 185, 190
Markman, Stephen J. 453n2355
Marks, Gov. Albert 142
Marlow, John (victim) 114
Marshall County 46
Martin (slave) 45–46
Martin, Sen. Alexander 17
Martin, Eve (victim) 17–18
Martin, James Otha 351–53
Martin, Joseph (victim) 136
Martin, Mrs. Joseph 136
Martin, Rev. Joseph H. 79
Martin, Knox 138–39
Martin, Leonard (victim) 169
Mason, Rev. (pastor of Methodist Episcopal church) 251, 252
Mason, Rev. Luke 164, 166, 169, 195, 205, 215–16, 223
Massengill, George D. (victim) 201–2
Massey, Clem 184
Massey, John R. 59
Massey, Thomas 59
Maston, William Henry (victim) 90–91
Matlock, Hugh (victim) 334, 335
Matthews, John 27–29
Matthews, Rebecca (victim) 28
Matthews, Sandy 152–53, 156, 163, 174
Maury County 19, 69; Columbia 29; Columbia area 19 (Duck River 106); county jail 193–94, 198
May, Annie Savage (victim) 366–67
May, Clarence 366–68, 370
Mayers, Wesley 117–18
Maynardville, Union County 191
Mays, Fannie 313–14
Mays, Frank 323–25
Mays, Maurice 280; and the animus of Officer Andy White 286–87; appeals 284–86, 289–92, 295; apprehension of 283–84; back ground 280–81; and evidence of crimes by others/"wrong man" defense 287–89; eyewitness testimony 281–87, 290–91, 293, 295; hearsay testimony disallowed 289,

294, 295; identification of 284–86; insanity and 292–93; last hours and execution 296; lawyers 284–86, 289, 290, 293; letters on behalf of 280, 291–95; low heavy-set man in overalls 287, 289, 290, 294, 295; murder of Bertie Lindsey 281–83; NAACP and 289–90; "new" information tending to exonerate 293–95; physical evidence against 284–86; police testimony 282–84; respites granted to 293, 453n2384; second trial 285–89; state's brief 282–83, 286–89; struggle for a commutation 291–93, 453n2384; Tennessee Supreme Court and 280, 283, 284, 286–87, 289–94; time runs out for 295–96; and the "true" killer comes forward 289; why governor did not commute his sentence 3, 280, 295, 296; writings on 280
Mays, William 280, 281
Mays, William D. 201–2
McAlister, Gov. 319, 329
McAlister, W.D 336
McBee, Henry 154
McBee, William P. (victim) 99–100
McBride, Edward (victim) 22
McBride, James 14
McCallahan, Moses 19–20
McCarn, Daniel G. 42
McCarn, Elizabeth (victim) 42
McCarthy, Dan 272
McClish, Wiley (victim) 126
McClure, John 3, 277–80, 295
McClure, Samuel 22–23, 29
McClusky, William see *Knight, James*
McCoig, Gus 339–40
McCord, Gov. Jim 381
McCorkle, Warden A.A. 301
McCormick, Michael L. 404
McDaniel, Luther 304
McDonald, Bryce 256–57
McDonald, Tishie (victim) 256–57
McElroy, James 296, 298–99, 454n2441
McFarland, James (victim) 154
McFerrin, Rev. John B. 35–36
McFerrin, Rev. J.P. 134
McFerrin, Rev. Sumner 134–35
McGaughan, Delilah (victim) 44
McGee, Bulah 236–39
McGrain, Mr. 101, 102
McGrew, Robert (victim) 378
McKay, Joe 351–53
McKee, Hattie 177
McKeever, John 163–64, 171, 174, 175
McKenzie, Alexander, son of (victim) 25
McKinney, Bill 83
McKinney, Gus 345
McKinney, Robert J. 32
McKnight, L.D. 353
McLean, Pvt. Henry 71
McLean, Irvin E. (victim) 86–88, 92
McLean, Milton 120–21
McLendon, Sheriff 175, 177, 188
McMahan, Dave 143, 144
McMahan, Willis (victim) 143–44
McMahon, Esther (victim) 31
McMahon, John 31
McMahon, Mary (victim) 31
McMichael, Rev. William 170
McMillan, Clark 404
McMillan, Gov. 214
McMillan, May. John E. 280, 281, 287, 291
McMinn, Gov. 216, 254
McMinn County 31 (Athens 46, 238; county jail 186)
McNairy County 50
McNamara, Allen 279
McNight, Henry 12
McPherson, John 245–46
McQuillan, Dr. 244
Meador, Thomas J., Jr. (victim) 38
Meadows, Pvt. William M. 61
Medlin, Cary Ann (victim) 405
Memphis area 53, 103, 105, 122–24 (Fort Pickering 83–84, 86, 93, 94)
Memphis jail 188, 228–29, 236
Mendil, Mack (or Mark) 289–90
Mendil, Sadie 289–90
mental capacity/incapacity 211, 244, 258, 271, 278, 279, 290, 297, 305, 308, 312, 334, 339, 342, 347, 355–57, 360, 375–77, 395, 400–402, 405, 406, 413, 415; *see also* insanity; paranoia
mental competency hearing 405, 413–14
Mental Examiners, Board of 292–93
mental impairment 184; *see also* alcohol intoxication; insanity
mentally retarded persons 1, 404; *see also* insanity
Mentzler, Christian C. 260–61
Merchant, Elizabeth (victim) 355
mercy petitions *see* petitions
Merriman, Mr. 52
Merry, Rev. Nelson 111–13, 124–25, 138, 164
Messick, "Rooster" 384
Meyers, Sgt. John 82
Micci, Frank 272
Middleton, George (victim) 8
Milaka, Julien see *Milika, Julius*
Mileka, Julius see *Milika, Julius*
Miles, Abraham M. 224–26
Miles, Mattie Peoples (victim) 224
Milika, Julius 63–64
military commissions 59, 62, 64, 66, 75, 80, 81, 83–92, 94–98, 101, 300; *see also* court-martials
military crimes: conduct prejudicial to military discipline 62; corresponding with enemy 71–72; cowardice in face of enemy 62; desertion 14–15, 59–65, 67–73, 77; disobedience of officer in execution of his duties 68–69; guerrilla warfare 84–85, 90 (*see also* guerrillas); making false muster 71–72; offering violence to superior officer 68; quitting guard 71–72; sabotage in wartime 54–56; smuggling and trading with enemy 82–84; treason in wartime 57; willful failure to follow orders 61; *see also* bushwackers; spying
military executions 3; *see also* court-martials; military crimes
Miller, Bascomb H. 263
Miller, Cain (victim) 216
Miller, Clyde Othel (victim) 368–69
Miller, James L. (victim) 263
Miller, James "Wren" 384, 385
Miller, Jesse H. 146
Miller, Michael (victim) 146–47
Miller, Sidney 146
Millie (victim) 11
Milliken, Jasper K. (victim) 341–43
Mills, Major 225–27
Milroy, Gen. Robert H. 57
Milroyism 57
ministers 3
Minix, Pvt. William 67–68
Minnie (victim) 218
minors: execution of 1, 12, 24–25, 39, 40, 43–44, 46, 69, 90–91, 96–97, 108–9, 136, 265–66, 269–70, 345, 363–64 (prohibited 404); pardoned 11
Minott, Samuel (victim) 12
mistaken identity, claims of 13, 20, 94, 293, 316, 418–19; *see also* innocence, proclamations of; Mays, Maurice
Mitchell, Alida 178
Mitchell, Sgt. James (victim) 93
Mitchell, Jesse 26–27
Mitchell, John 231–32
Mitchell, Miles P. (victim) 196
Mitchell, William 254, 256
Mitchison, Andrew Jackson (victim) 380
Mitchum, John 22
Mitchum, Milley (victim) 22
mitigating circumstances 32, 49, 106, 125–26, 145, 162, 164, 172, 179, 182, 193, 203, 215, 216, 221, 224, 225, 227, 229, 235, 243, 246, 257, 281, 292, 332, 339, 415; legislation regarding 2, 249, 275; *see also* alcohol intoxication
Mobley, Asa Caldwell 357–58
mobs *see* lynchings: mobs and fears of
Mockbee, Bill 126
Mockbee, Robert 126
Molly (slave) 12
Monroe County: Clinton area 131, 203; Madisonville 129, 232–33
Monteverde, Sheriff 226–28, 236, 249
Montgomery County 45, 47
Montgomery County jail 162–63
Moody, Samuel 102–3
moonshine 196, 220, 276, 295, 306–7, 376
Moore, Ad 252, 253
Moore, Bill (slave) 38
Moore, Fred 205
Moore, James E. (victim) 417, 418
Moore, Sarah E. (victim) 112
Morgan, Gen. 63
Morgan, Julius 268–69
Morgan, Mitchell see *Mapp, George*

morphine: addiction to 229, 383–84; taken or requested prior to execution 152, 176, 186, 190, 191, 219
Morris, Absalom 8, 11
Morris, Gideon 8, 11
Morris, John D. (victim) 42
Morris, Polly 42
Morristown area, Hamblen County 79, 140
Morrow, Robert (victim) 161–62
Morrow, William 161–63
Morton, Mr. 52
Mosby, Arthur 345
Mosely, Captain 86
Mosely, Fanny 118
Mosely, Jourdan C. 91–93
Moser (Mozier), Washington (victim) 70–71
Moses (slave executed in 1850) 43
Moses (slave executed in 1851) 43–44
Moses (slave executed in 1861) 51, 52
Moses, William S. 232
Moss, Annie Lee (victim) 308
Mountain City jail, Johnson County 231
Muckelroy, Pvt. Joseph 15
multiple personality disorder 406–9
murder, methods of 16;
beating/striking 9, 16, 21–23, 25, 26, 32–34, 36, 38–40, 43, 46, 48, 50, 51, 104, 106, 108, 109, 111, 115, 117, 121, 138, 144, 161, 164, 165, 175, 183–84, 198, 204, 206, 212, 215, 217, 218, 222, 236–37, 242, 260, 263–64, 273–74, 276, 299–301, 311–12, 333–35, 351, 362, 385–86, 391–93, 406–9 (with ax/hatchet 8, 23, 24, 27, 31, 36, 38, 39, 44, 46, 50, 51, 106, 108, 109, 117, 126, 152–53, 159, 197, 215, 218, 298, 312, 378); bombs/explosive devices 33, 347–48; breaking victim's neck 320; choking/strangulation 9, 12, 30, 39, 193, 325–26, 398–99, 405; dragging 13; drowning 7–8, 19, 325–27; gunshot/shooting 8, 9, 11, 15, 17–19, 23, 29–30, 32–33, 36–37, 42, 49, 51, 52, 64, 80–82, 84, 86–95, 97–99, 101–3, 105, 114, 115, 119, 120, 123, 124, 127, 128, 130, 136, 140, 142, 145, 146, 151, 155, 157, 158, 160, 161, 163, 166, 167, 169, 170, 172–74, 178–79, 186, 187, 189–96, 201–14, 218–36, 239, 245–46, 250, 252–54, 256–59, 261–63, 272–76, 296–99, 301–2, 304, 306–7, 309–10, 317–20, 327–31, 334–42, 345–47, 350–55, 359–61, 363, 368–78, 381–83, 386–88, 394–97, 399–401, 409–19 (*see also* Mays, Maurice); knifing/stabbing/cutting 13, 20–22, 31, 34, 36, 43, 44, 49, 50, 53, 71, 95, 105, 132, 138, 143–44, 165, 170–71, 174, 175, 178–79, 183, 188, 198, 204, 243, 266–67, 277–78, 321, 344, 380, 383–86, 389–90, 405–9; poisoning 8, 18; *see also* arson; execution methods
murder(s): accessory before 216–17, 219–20; accessory to 21, 231–32; attempted (*see* assault); of best friend 354–55; of brother-in-law 220–21; of children 12, 36, 38, 39, 222, 399, 412–13 (*see also* murder[s]: of stepchildren); of cousins 401–2; double 27, 31, 49, 93–94, 138, 149, 156–57, 159, 190, 207–8, 212, 220, 329, 354, 363, 381–83, 385–86, 391–93, 399–401, 414–15; of employer by houseboy 311–12; of father-in-law 172, 226; of federal officers 376; of former employer 317–19; of girlfriend/lover 204, 227, 389–90 (*see also* sexual affairs and jealousy, murders related to); of girlfriend/lover's new lover 252–54, 280, 298; of grandchildren 7–8; of grandparents 159, 328–29; of husband 24; money-related 17, 26, 34–35, 46, 49, 53, 99, 117, 119, 121, 123, 126, 138, 142, 161, 169, 175, 183–84, 188–90, 194, 201–3, 210–17, 220, 232, 235–37, 298–301, 330–31, 333, 351–52, 381–83, 398–401, 414–16; (*see also* gambling; robbery-murders); of mother 159; of mother-in-law 223; multiple 90, 94–97, 106–7, 161–63, 190, 261–63, 275, 299–301, 311–12, 328, 347–48, 370–72, 374–78, 412–13, 416–19; over boundary dispute 26, 359; precipitated by animal abuse 105; of prison guard 346; as revenge for rape 161–62; sexual affairs, jealousy, and 23, 29, 39, 121, 132, 136, 146, 161, 166–67, 170, 172, 173, 178, 181–82, 185–86, 188, 193, 204, 205, 218–19, 225, 234–35, 239, 243–44, 252–54, 256, 280, 298, 344, 363–64, 368–70, 373–74, 381–83, 389–90, 412–14 (*see also* incest); of sheriffs 167, 339–40; of sheriff's constable 197; of sister-in-law 212, 256; of slave owners by slaves 24–26, 29–32, 36, 38, 40, 43, 46, 51; of stepchildren 139–41, 398–99; of stepson 299–301; of supervisor/boss 160, 235–36; of town constable 354–55; of uncle 125; of wife 4, 13, 22, 23, 29, 46, 128, 145, 173, 176, 188, 206, 218, 224, 227, 229, 234, 243, 257–60, 296–97, 299–301, 319–20, 344–45, 366–68, 373–74; of wife's lover 23 (*see also* sexual affairs and jealousy, murders related to); *see also specific murderers*
Murphy, John 22
Murphy, Lawrence P. (victim) 79–80
Murray, Frank 350
Murrell, Bob 47
Murrell gang 26, 35, 157
Musgrove, David Crockett (victim) 19
mute before court-martial, standing 79
Myers, William 14

Nance, John 99–101
Nancy (victim) 44
Napier, Charles (slave) 46–48
Naron, L.H. (Captain Chickasaw) 74, 75
Nashville *see* Davidson County
National Guard 204, 274, 311, 332
Neal, Taylor 272–73
"Nearer My God to Thee" (hymn) 200, 240, 276
Nearing, Jesse see *Neven, Jessee B.*
Nebe, Charles (victim) 217
Ned see *Walton, Ned*
Ned (slave) 52
Neely, Warden A.W. 318–19, 330, 332, 335, 336, 338–40
Nelson, George 91
Nelson, Thomas A. R. 104
Nerron, Jesse B. see *Neven, Jessee B.*
Ness see *Vest, Alexander*
Neven, Jessee B. 86–88
Newport area, Cocke County 137–38, 144
Nichols, Rev. John H. 134, 135
Nicholson, Alfred O.P. 28
Nicholson, Justice 100
Norfleet, James 227, 228
Norfleet, Lucy (victim) 227
Norman, Pvt. Edward P. 60–61
North Carolina, executions under authority of 7, 8
Norvell, Mary (victim) 223
Nunnelly, Andrew Jackson Baldwin (victim) 51
Nunnelly, Carter 24, 51
Nunnelly, Henry 24

Obion County 172–73; only legal execution in 173
Obongpohego (Native American) 8–9
O'Brien, Father 102
O'Bryant, Mrs. 17
O'Bryant (Obrien, O'Bryan), William (victim) 16–17
Old Hal (slave) 46–48
Olden, Rev. G.D. 180, 181
Oliver, Frank (slave) 39
Oliver, Ronald (victim) 409–12
organ donation 388
Orton, Lawrence Williams see *Williams, Orton William*
Osborn, Betsy (victim) 12
Osborn, Jane (victim) 98
Ould, John K. see *Caio, John*
Ould, Robert 88
Outlow, Johnnie (aka Johnnie Outlaw) 380
Overall, Rans "Ransom" (slave) 43
Overton County 98–99
Owens, Will 232

Paine, Don 280
Painter, Roy (victim) 319
Palmer, Cecil 254–56
Panky, Pvt. Frank (victim) 93
paranoia 299, 342
Parder, John T. (victim) 183
pardons 11, 15, 18, 19, 33, 34, 42, 59, 239, 280, 281, 294, 296; based on innocence 404; of Dave Sherman

238–39; requests/petitions for 28–29, 116, 294
Paris, Henry County 38, 39, 159, 173
Parker, Robert 9
Parrish, Jimmy Lee 343–44
Parsons, Ora Smyth 281–82, 286, 287, 293, 295; eyewitness testimony 282, 283, 290–91
Passagno, Giacomo (victim) 51
Pate, Jack (slave) 9–10
Pate, Stephen 9, 10
Patterson, Gov. Malcolm Rice ("Hamilton"/"Ham") 238–39, 251, 256
Patton, William (victim) 26
Payne, Jim (slave) 36–38
Payne, Raymond J. (victim) 360
Payne, Zebadiah 34–35
Pearlman, Jennie 273
Pearson, Arthur 240–42
Pearson, George 205–6
Pearson, Mitch 101
Peay, Austin ("Pardoning Gov.") 296, 301–4, 306
Peck, Judge 20–23, 27
pedophilia *see* carnal knowledge; child rape
Pegues, Annanias (victim) 221–22
Pennington, Elizabeth 23
Penrice, Moses (slave) 12
Pepper-Head see *Clarke, James*
Perkins, Earnest (victim) 233
Perkins, Sheriff George 127
Perkins, Captain Newton C. (victim) 126–27
Perkins, Thomas 88
perpetrators executed: allowing them as much time as possible on day of execution 245; *see also specific topics*
Perry, Captain James (victim) 102–3
Perry, Mrs. 102, 103
Perry, Thomas 96, 97
Perry, Virginia (victim) 337–38
Peter (slave) 31
Peter, Walter G. 65–67
Peters, Benjamin Franklin 293
petitions (signed by numerous people) 8, 10, 13–14, 25, 29, 48, 53, 78, 89, 92, 93, 102, 122, 137, 202, 216, 229–30, 242, 246, 249, 254, 278, 291, 293, 295; *see also* clemency petitions/requests/pleas/appeals; habeas corpus relief
Petree, Charles, Jr. 3, 277–80, 295
Pettigrew, Ben 261–63
Pettigrew, Fred 261–63
Pettigrew, Pearl (victim) 261–63
Petway, Abe 215–17
Philip Workman: A Case for Clemency (film) 412
Phillips, Charles 159–60
Phillips, James 230
Phillips, Pvt. Zachariah 60–61
Phillips, Ross (victim) 354–55
Phipps, Ransom (victim) 123
photographs of executions 1, 110, 212, 213, 230
Pickens, Dr. 245
Pickering, Jacob 13
Pierce, James R. (victim) 276
Pigg, Ed (victim) 252–53
Pikeville area, Bledsoe County 13, 42
Pillow, James 327
Pinkston, G. Emmett (victim) 175, 176
Pinkston, W.M. 176
Pirtle, Moses 196
Pledger, J. P. 71, 72
poems 142, 162, 231, 279
poisoning 8, 18
police brutality 352; *see also* confessions, allegations of coerced; torture
police informants, murder of 216
police officers: murder of 101–3, 126–27, 167, 179–81, 197, 272, 275, 336–37, 376–78; shooting at 387; *see also* sheriffs
Polk, Essiah (victim) 152–53
Pollock, Miss (victim) 39
Pollock, Preston 88–90
Pool, Moses 30
Pope, Thaddeus (victim) 120
Porter, Captain 89, 90
Porter, Emma (victim) 307–8
Porter, Gov. 120, 122
Pope, Warden Joe 335, 341, 343, 345, 349
Porter, Lee Willie 362–63
Porter, Susie 307, 308
Porter, Vivian 411
post-conviction relief 404, 408, 413, 415, 418
Poston, Wanda (victim) 388–89
Potter, Daniel C. 143–44
Powel, Charles 10–11
Powell, Phoebe (victim) 18
pregnant women: murder of 4, 128, 186, 206, 296–97; rape of 378–79
Prescott, Robert H. 247
Presswood, John, Jr. 108–10
Preston, Eb 230
Preston, Finley 230–31
Prewitt, Thomas see *Williams, John*
priests *see* Catholic priests
Prince, Frank (victim) 159, 160
Prince, Millard 315, 316
prison escapes *see* jail/prison breaks
prison guard, murder of 346
private execution: request for 137; *see also* public executions, vs. private executions
Prohibition 239
Pryor, Sampson 121
Psalms read 50, 105, 106, 111, 195, 218, 249, 306
psychiatric evaluations 308, 414; *see also* insanity; mental capacity/incapacity
psychiatric testimony 416; *see also* insanity; mental capacity/incapacity
psychiatrists 356, 413
public executions 45; vs. private executions 3, 137 (semi-public executions 151; statute requiring semi-private executions 143, 156, 158, 166); *see also* audiences
Puckett, Drury 14, 15
Puckett, Thomas 15
Pugh, Maj. Henry S. (victim) 142
Pugh, William Milton (victim) 376
Pulaski, Giles County 15, 74–76, 82, 111, 182
Pulaski jail 152
Pullum, Mae (victim) 388–89
Purdy, McNairy County 50
Putnam County 134–35
Pyle, Serene 190

Queen, Clara (victim) 265
Queen, Thomas F. 265
Queener, Sheriff Sampson D. (victim) 49
Quianthy, Detective Officer 326, 327

race riots 280
racial bias and discrimination 4, 256, 263, 390; *see also* Mays, Maurice
Radelet, Michael L. 280, 282, 283, 289
Ragland, William (victim) 170–71
Ragsdale, Jim (slave) 18
Rainwater, Sarah Abbie (victim) 320
Randal (slave) 21
Rankin, Frances (victim) 271
Rankin, Lt. 101
Ransom see *Overall, Rans*
rape 9–13, 17, 18, 27, 43, 46, 50, 91, 112–14, 148–49, 162, 177–78, 255–56, 261, 269–71, 307–9, 312, 315–17, 322–23, 337–38, 345, 355–58, 361, 385, 390–91, 393–94, 397–98, 402–3; of adult stepdaughter 140, 141, 152, 153; attempted 31, 162, 406; of cousin 401–2; of deaf-mute woman 365–66; death penalty legislation and 404; first white man executed for 136–38; of free white woman (age 17) 45; legal definition 333; multiple/serial 112, 268, 343–44, 361, 388–89, 391–93, 397–98; murder as revenge for 161–62; of pregnant woman 378–79; robbery and 91, 313–14, 355–58, 361, 365–66, 391–93; theft and 85–86, 91, 355–58; *see also* assault
rape-murder 36, 98, 138, 228, 320, 321–22, 380, 391–93; of child 24, 25, 218, 313–14, 401–2, 404–6
Raper, Treva Joyce (victim) 401–2
Rea, William W. 150–52
Record, Rev. John 25
Record, Paul 304
record-keeping 2–4
Red, George see *Craft, George*
Redd, George 120
Reed, Walter 361–62
Reeves, John "Alabama" 179, 181
Reeves, Sheriff 147
Reid, George see *Craft, George*
Reilly, Richard 388
religion 298–99; *see also* Catholicism; *specific topics*
religious conversion 179–80, 183,

186, 264, 412; *see also* baptism prior to execution; Catholicism
Remine, H.M. 237
respites 11, 21, 39, 71, 184, 200, 209, 215, 227, 243, 251, 256, 263, 293
Reuland, Thomas A. 235, 236
Revels, Rev. W. R. 103
Reynolds, Barbara 118, 119
Reynolds, Hiram 70–71
Reynolds, Richard F. (victim) 118–19
Rhea, John (victim) 32
Rhodes, Capt. Jabez R. 71–72
Rhodes, Mansfield see *Lyles, George*
Rice, Warden B.M. 254, 256–58, 260
Rice, Lewis 213–14
Richardson, Bud 198
Richie, Elsie Mae O'Brien (victim) 344
Richie, Fred 344–45
Richie, Joe 344, 345
Richie, Lafayette 187
Ridge, James (victim) 90
Ridge, William (victim) 90
Ridley, Bromfield 60
Riggs, Bertha (victim) 402–3
Riggs, Mary W. (victim) 45
Riley, Mrs. Jack 172, 173
Riley, Jackson (victim) 172
Riley, Jean 235
Riley, John Milton 40–41
Ripley, Lauderdale County 214–15
Ritchie, W. W. 51
Riverbend Maximum Security Institution 406, 414, 419
Roane, Archibald 10
Roane County 50, 160–61
robbery 71; highway 84–85; *see also* burglary; rape, robbery and; theft
robbery-murders 34, 36, 43, 46, 50, 64, 84, 88–90, 93, 100, 118–19, 132–33, 138, 142, 149, 155, 164, 184–85, 187, 190, 190–92, 195–98, 203, 217, 242, 254, 257, 260–64, 266–67, 272–80, 297–305, 313–14, 319, 321–22, 325–31, 334–43, 345, 350–54, 360–62, 372–76, 381–83, 386–88, 391–97, 409–12, 414–19; *see also* Mays, Maurice
Robert Blecker Wants Me Dead (film) 414
Roberts, Jewel Talley (victim) 374–76
Roberts, Pvt. Henry 72
Robertson, James see *Murray, Frank*
Robertson County 38
Robins, Deputy Sheriff 354
Robinson, Ellis (victim) 298
Rogers, Alice 170–72
Rogers, Bill Jeff Calhoun 212
Rogers, Molly 144–45
Rogers, Titus (Tito) (victim) 144
Rogersville, Hawkins County 18, 52, 116, 118, 119, 150; largest crowd ever assembled in 116; last public execution in 150
Rogersville jail 179
Roll, Pvt. James 77
rope *see* hangman's rope
Rose, George W. 263–64
Rose, Hicks 263–64
Rose, Mary 263, 264
Rosencrans, Gen. William 57, 61, 66, 71
Ross, Marion (victim) 191–92
Rossner, Agent 376
Rowland, William (victim) 46
Rule, William 292
Rumley, Elizabeth (victim) 39
Ruppell, Frank P. "Russell" (victim) 155
Russell (victim) *see* Ruppell, Frank P.
Russell, Allen (slave) 18
Russell, Rev. C.C. 154
Russell, John (victim) 345
Russell, Thomas 130
Rutherford County 27, 142–43; Battery's camp near Cripple Creek 68; Murfreesboro 40, 43, 60–62, 65, 67–68
Rutherford Rifles 76
Rutledge, Tom 401–2
Rutledge, Grainger County 9, 48, 101
Rye, Austin (victim) 197–98
Rye, Gov. 261, 268

sabotage in wartime 54–56
Safety, Committee of 47
Sain, John Fuller (victim) 8
saloons closed on the days of executions 112, 129
Samples, Frances M. 59–60
Sampson (slave) 26
Sanders, Dave 284, 289
Sanders, Francis (victim) 21
Sanders, Col. George M. 13
Sandusky, James D. 386–88
Sarah (slave) 39–40
Sartin, James L. (Rockwood Chief of Police) 309, 310
Sartin, Tom E. (victim) 309–10
Satan, perpetrators talking about 155; *see also* devil
Saunders, Andrew 146–48
Savannah area, Hardin County 24, 42, 62, 99
Schockman, John see *Shockman, John*
scientific evidence 3
Scott, Frank 120, 122–24
Scott, James Brandon (victim) 338
Scott, Lige 262
Scott, Minnie (victim) 239, 240
Scott, Roy A. (victim) 336
Scott, W.B. 239, 240
Scott County 196
Scribner, James M. 388–89
Scudder, James 222–23
Scudder, James Alfred (victim) 222
search warrants and illegal searches 376, 395–96
Searcy, Reuben 61
Sears, Rev. A.D. 162
Seiber, Dora (victim) 240–41
self-defense: claims of killing in 16, 22, 44, 71, 80, 91, 102, 111, 117, 118, 123, 124, 127, 147, 150, 160, 171, 174, 175, 206, 212, 217, 225, 236, 246, 250, 254, 256, 280, 298, 346–48, 359, 363, 372, 384; slaves killing owners in 31–32, 36, 40 (*see also* murder[s], of slave owners by slaves)
self-mutilation prior to execution 173, 315
Selkirk, William A. 64
Senter, Thomas 263, 264
Sevier, Gov. John 10
Sevier County jail 209–10
sexual abuse *see* carnal knowledge; child rape; rape
sexual affairs and jealousy, murders related to 23, 29, 39, 121, 132, 136, 146, 161, 166–67, 170, 172, 173, 178, 181–82, 185–86, 188, 193, 204, 205, 218–19, 225, 234–35, 239, 243–44, 252–54, 256, 280, 298, 344, 363–64, 368–70, 373–74, 381–83, 389–90, 412–14; *see also* incest
Shafter, Colonel 96
Shangles, Jim 83
Sharp, Ellen 185, 186
Sharp, French (victim) 185
Sharp, John 49
Sharp, Sheriff John 195, 205
Shaw, Henry B. (Captain Coleman) 75–77
Shaw, Howard 328
Shaw, Jasper (victim) 328
Shaw, John Thomas 313–15
Shaw, Lillian (victim) 230–31
Shaw, Nellie (victim) 328
Shaw, Wakeman O. 328
Sheehan, Richard Thomas (victim) 335–36
Shelby County 227–28; Bartlett 120, 122; county jail 102, 153, 156, 163–64, 171–72, 174–77, 200, 204, 218, 219, 225–27, 249; first legal executions in 51–52; first white man hanged in 53; Memphis area 53, 103, 105, 122–24 (Fort Pickering 83–84, 86, 93, 94); Memphis jail 188, 228–29, 236
Shelbyville, Bedford County 39, 65
Shell, Moody 332
Shelton, George 261–63
sheriffs: deputy sheriff executed for murder 306; murdered 167, 339–40; paid for performing executions (*see* execution fees); performing execution while drunk 238
Sherman, Dave 236–38
Shipe, Deputy Sheriff Doctor A. (John) (victim) 167, 168
Shipp, Sheriff 245, 249
Shirley, Sheriff 215
Shockman, John 68
shoes given to perpetrators, new 178, 195, 215, 221, 236, 252, 378
"Show Pity, Lord; Oh, Lord, Forgive" (hymn) 106, 205
Silvey, William R. 72, 73
Simms, Joseph L. 338
Sims, Robert 200–201
Skelt (slave) 38
slave corpses displayed to terrorize other slaves 32, 47

slave courts 9, 12, 16–18
slave insurrection: crime of 46–48; fear of 36, 52
slave insurrection/panic of 1856 47, 48
slave owners: compensation for execution of their slaves 13–14; killed by slaves 12, 24–26, 29–32, 36, 38, 40, 43, 46, 51 (in self-defense 31–32, 36, 40); reward for death of slave posted by 11; special juries consisting of 8, 12
slave stealing 14
slaveholder courts 21
slaves: execution of 7–19, 21, 27, 38–40, 50 (finances of 14, 28–29); request to sell rather than execute 28; witnessing executions 43 (*see also* corpses of perpetrators, slave corpses displayed to terrorize other slaves)
Slokum, Gen. 88
Smith, Bill 142, 143
Smith, Burrell 142–43
Smith, Catherine (victim) 39
Smith, Dewitt 59
Smith, Lt. Ezra C. (victim) 95
Smith, George 79
Smith, Grant 245
Smith, Henry 178, 179
Smith, James 283–87
Smith, James 334–35
Smith, James W. (victim) 299, 300
Smith, James Willis 351–53
Smith, John 182–83
Smith, John W. see *Davis, Captain Dick*
Smith, John Y. 27
Smith, Joseph 62–63
Smith, L.C. 335
Smith, Attorney Gen. L.D. 291
Smith, Louis (victim) 416–18
Smith, Mary (victim) 38
Smith, Mary E. (victim) 299–301
Smith, Ora *see* Parsons, Ora Smyth
Smith, Percy 322–24
Smith, Rubie (victim) 299
Smith, Samuel 13–14
Smith, Thomas Martin 82–84
Smith, Woody 273
Smithville, DeKalb County 37, 110
Smyth, Ora *see* Parsons, Ora Smyth
Sneedville area, Hancock County 199
Snell, Edward Lewis 395
Snellings, Will 212
Snodderly, Henry (victim) 190, 191
Snodderly, John 190
Snodderly, Lucinda 190
Snover, John (aka Jacob Snover) 85, 86
Snow, George G. 384
soldiers: largest execution of 14–15; *see also* court-martials
Somers, Captain Henry C. (victim) 93
Somerville area, Fayette County 126, 197
Sorrell, Nancy Ruth (victim) 364–65
Spain, William H. 40
Sparta, White County 26
spectators *see* audiences
speeches of perpetrators: on gallows 51, 52, 84, 106, 110, 113, 118, 122, 124, 125, 131, 135, 144–47, 155, 159–61, 170–72, 175, 180, 186–88, 206, 219, 221, 226, 228, 233, 236, 252, 264; prior to electrocution 312–13, 406
Spencer, William Obe (victim) 302
Sphynx, Burrell see *Beggarly, Burr*
Spigener, Marshall F. 374–76
Spinks, Burrell see *Beggarly, Burr*
Spraggins, R.F. 247–48
Springfield, Ben 221–22
Springfield, Robertson County 38
Springfield, Willie Pegues (victim) 221, 222
Sprouse, James Edward (victim) 386–88
spying 59–63, 65–67, 69, 74–79
Stafford, Edna (victim) 414–16
Stafford, Fred (victim) 414–16
Stanley, Ernest 346–47
Stanley, John 190–91
Staples, Jackson "Jack" 177–78, 186
statutory fees for hanging *see* execution fees
Stearns (Starnes), Aaron B. (victim) 53
Steel (Steele), Edward (victim) 11
Steele, Alexander (victim) 110–11
Steele, Clyde 393–94
Stephens, Alfred (slave) 51
Stephens, Otto 3, 277–80, 295
Stephens, William (murder victim of Albert Stephens) 51
Stephens, William (murder victim of Lafayette Richie) 187
Stephenson, Oliver 309, 310
Stewart County 47; Dover area 47–48, 126; Fort Donelson 71
Stielow, Charles E. 284
Stone, George 183–84
Stoner, George (victim) 297, 298
Stover, John 102
Stover, Levy 53
Stover, Mrs. Levy 53
strangulation/choking: murder by 9, 12, 30, 39, 193, 325–26, 398–99, 405; *see also* hanging(s), prolonged/botched
suicide: assisted 239; attempted 98, 176, 177, 186, 240, 315, 345, 395; hanging 349
Sullins, Charlie 396–97
Sullivan, Kinchen (slave) 18
Sullivan County 72, 202
Summerfield, Elizabeth Sangster (victim) 325–26
Summers, Squire J.M. 270
Supreme Court *see* Tennessee Supreme Court; United States Supreme Court
surplices (white shrouds) 52; *see also* "winding sheets"
Sutherland, Lura (victim) 268
Swafford, Deputy Warden Glenn 347, 349–50, 378, 392
Swafford, Warden Glenn 392
Swafford, J. Calhoun 348
Swafford, James (victim) 84
Swafford, Mrs. James 84
Swann, James 320–21
"swung off" method of hanging (body swinging) 18, 26, 46, 50, 99, 116, 118, 119, 129, 131, 136, 137, 140, 144, 150, 154

Talley, Annie 94
Talley, Rev. Robert 175
Tate, Robert 301–2
Taylor, Gov. Alfred A. 279, 280, 290–96
Taylor, Andrew 156–58
Taylor, George (victim) 220, 221
Taylor, Giles 220, 221
Taylor, James 337–38
Taylor, John 157, 158
Taylor, Pvt. Joel T. 69
Taylor, Pvt. Joseph C. 59
Taylor, Rev. Preston 256
Taylor, Robert 157
Taylor, Gov. Robert L. 274, 277–79, 286, 296
Taylor, Thomas H. 388–89
Taylor, Toots 225–27
Tazewell 117–19
Temple, Leo 265–66
Tennessee General Assembly *see* General Assembly
Tennessee Supreme Court 2, 14, 16, 17, 19, 21, 22; asking governor to commute sentence 2; power and scope of authority 4; written opinions of 4
Terrill, Will 307–8
territorial dispute, murder over a 26, 359
Terry, John 236, 237
"That Old-Time Religion" (hymn) 223, 224
theft 62–63, 71, 85–86; rape and 85–86, 91, 355–58; *see also* burglary; robbery
"There Is a Fountain Filled With Blood" (hymn) 103, 105, 121, 127, 168, 183
Thomas (slave) 39
Thomas, Gen. George 55–56, 97
Thomas, J.H. "Henry" ("Ipsom") (victim) 242, 243, 447n1895
Thomas, John 233–34
Thomason, Israel 19
Thomasson, Griffith C. (victim) 340
Thompson, Andrew "Duser" 215–17
Thompson, Barney (aka Bonnie) 389–90
Thompson, Berry (victim) 22
Thompson, Herbert (victim) *see* Thomas, J.H. "Henry"
Thompson, Jimmy 351
Thornhill, John 101
Thornton, Stewart W. 13
Thornton, W.W. "Tobe" 99
three-drug protocol (lethal injection) 412, 416, 465n3265
Thurman, Barnabas 29
Tidwell, Sarah E. (victim) 44

Tines, William James 402–3
Tipton, James Catlett 207–10
Tipton County 36, 147
Tipton County jail 230
Tiptonites 8
Todd, Mary Ann 32
Tollett, White Miller 347–50
Tom (slave) 8
torture, confessions allegedly obtain through 303, 321, 326, 381; *see also* confessions, allegations of coerced
Tracy, Mr. and Mrs. 97
Trail, Jonas (victim) 198
Trainor, William I. (victim) 163
trap-door gallows 33, 52, 75–76, 78–79, 84, 102–4, 108, 110, 112–14, 121, 124, 125, 134–37, 139, 143, 146–48, 153, 156, 158, 159, 161, 164, 167–70, 172–76, 178, 185–88, 190, 192–94, 196, 198–200, 203–5, 211–13, 215–16, 219, 222–27, 229, 230, 233, 234, 236, 244, 245, 251–53, 256, 260–61, 264
Travis, Chaplain R.E. 301–3, 305, 308, 309
treason *see* military crimes; spying
trees, hangings from 9, 23, 24, 38, 52, 54, 57, 66, 99, 140
Trenton, Gibson County 36, 58
"Tribute of Respect" 76
Trice, John Harrison (victim) 50–51
Tucker, James Felix "Jimmy" 373–74
Tucker, Minnie Margaret (victim) 373–74
Tucker, Ruby McElwain 302
Tull, Pvt. Abner (victim) 81
Tullahoma, Franklin County 61, 62, 64, 70, 79
Turner, Charles (slave) 24–25
Turner, Ed 243–45, 250
Turner, James 336–37
Turner, John 184–85
Turner, John (victim) 24–25
Turner, Lilly Burcham (victim) 243–45
Turner, Peter W. 239–40
Turner, Will 336
Turner, William J.C. 388–89
Turney, Jim "Blue Jim" 169–70
Turney, Sam 32

Unicoi County jail 218
Union County 191
Union executions 4
Union soldiers and partisans murdered 81, 94–95
Union soldiers executed 54, 56–59, 64–69, 72–73, 101; *see also* Davis, Dick
United States Supreme Court 404
Upton, Andrew "Drew" 232–33
Upton, Will 232–33

Valentine, Benjamin see *Benjamin, Pvt. Valentine*
Van Dorn, Gen. 67, 69
Vann, Ebb (Ed) 129–31
Vann, John 7
Vann, Pvt. Daniel 129–31
Vass see *Vest, Alexander*
Vernon, Grant (victim) 362
Vest see *Vest, Alexander*
Vest, Alexander 93
Videts, Stephen 118
vigilantes 59, 207; *see also* lynchings
Volatine, Benjamin see *Benjamin, Pvt. Valentine*
Volentine, Benjamin see *Benjamin, Pvt. Valentine*
"volunteers" 3
vomiting before execution 152, 280
Voss see *Vest, Alexander*
Voss, Samuel L. 394–96

Waddell, Joseph M. 245, 246
"The Wages of Sin is Death" (confession) 322
Wakefield, Samuel "Jack" (victim) 86, 87, 92
Walden, Roy 364–65
Walds, Moses 235–36
Walker, Maggie (victim) 139–41
Walker, Sam (victim) 205–6
Walker, Thomas 380
Walker, Thomas Lee 347–49
Walker, Deputy Sheriff William F. (victim) 245, 246
Walker, Winnifred 271–72
Wallace, Joe 182–83
Wallace, John Henry 304–5
Wallace, William 30
Wallin, Alva Ulysses 347–49
Walling, W.L. 349
Walters, James (victim) 193
Walters, Mary 193
Walton, Ned (slave) 38
War of 1812 14–15
Ward, Jesse (slave) 12
Warren, A. Dillard 214–15
Warren County jail 211–13
wartime *see* military crimes
Washington, Rev. George 200, 217, 219, 224–27, 229, 236, 249
Washington County 7, 8, 40, 201, 202
Waters, R.T. 301–2
Watkins, Desk Sgt. A.J. 283, 289
Watkins, Desk Sgt. O.J. *see* Watkins, Desk Sgt. A.J.
Watkins, Samuel 65, 67
Watson, Bruce Edward 390–91
Watson, Ida (victim) 261
Watson, John C. 210–13
Waynesboro, Wayne County 242
Weakley County 45
Weaver, Adam (victim) 64
Weaver, Sarah A. 64
Webb, Dick 129, 130
Webb, Eli 215
Webb, John 209
Webb, John C. 117–19, 129, 246
Webb, John Franklin 303–4
Weddell, Moses (victim) 231–32
Weddell, Will 231, 232
Weis, Margaret Catherine (victim) 305
Welch, James 62
Wells, Detective A.L. 285–86
West, Benjamin F. 86–88
West, George see *Johnson, Will*
West, Deputy John Wesley 306, 307
West, Lawrence 363–64
West, Michael 10, 11
West, Thomas R. 86–88
Westmoreland, Shade Woods 114–16
Whaley, Laura (victim) 207–8
Whaley, Mollie Lilliard 207, 208, 210
Whaley, William (victim) 207–9
Wheeler, Gen. "Fighting Joe" 96
Whelchel, Helen Hager (victim) 313, 315
White, Officer Andy 281, 283, 284–87, 289, 291–93; animus of 286–87
White, Hugh L. 11
White, Isaac (victim) 129–31
White, James 23, 24
White, Mrs. James 23
White, Lt. William H. 71, 72
White, William 7
White, William (victim) 86, 87, 92
White Caps 207–9, 444n1662
White County 26
white supremacists *see* Ku Klux Klan; White Caps
Whitehead, Pvt. William Jasper 69–71
Whitlock, William H. 197
Whittaker, Mr. 105, 106
Whitworth, Sheriff 113
wife-killers *see* murder(s): of wife
Wiggins, Patsy (victim) 25
Wilcoxen, Andrew 315–17
Wiley see *Bird, Wiley*
Williams, Rev. Blackman 106
Williams, George W. 64
Williams, Henry (aka Andy Williams) 103–4, 115
Williams, John 145–46
Williams, John D. 269–70
Williams, Orton William (aka Lawrence Orton Williams) 65–67
Williams, Rev. 161
Williams, Sallie (victim) 145
Williams, "Uncle" Jupiter 147
Williams, William 46
Williams, William "Billy" 120–24
Williams, William Henry "Willie" 353–54
Williamson, Porter 124
Williamson County 18, 25; Franklin 12, 16, 18, 31, 65–67
Willis, Albert (victim) 383–84
Willis, Lewis 330–31
Willis, William "Buck" (victim) 40, 41
Wills, Clyde 355–57
Wilson, Captain 283, 290
Wilson, Frank 126
Wilson, Dr. John A. 19
Wilson, Millard Filmore "Ninrod" 126–27
Wilson, Robert 155–56, 163
Wilson, Samuel (victim) 26–27
Wilson County 27, 124, 169–70; Lebanon 124–25
Wilson County jail 167

Winchester, Franklin County 25, 39, 132; county jail in 220
"winding sheets" (white shrouds) 33–35, 52
Wirt, Charles 170, 171
Wise, Bud 225
Withers, Jess 205
Witherspoon, Rufus 309
witnesses, trial; black, not allowed to testify against white persons 17; murder of 17
witnesses to executions *see* audiences
Wittemeier, John (victim) 138
Wittemeier, Lucinda Foster (victim) 138
Womack, Ernest, Jr. 331–32
women and girls executed 7–8, 12, 15, 18–19, 39; only white woman legally executed 24; youngest female executed 25
Wood, Reuben (victim) 95
Wood, R.R. 356
Wooden, Buddy 191–93
Woodly (aka Woodle), Floyd 184–85
Woods, Daniel 87–88
Woods, John 15
Woods, Roy Eldridge (victim) 372
Woods, Shade see *Westmoreland, Shade Woods*
Woods, W.J. 132
Wooten, Peter (victim) 161
Workman, Philip Ray 409–12
Wrenne, Michael C. (victim) 215
Wright, Rev. Absalom B. 108
Wright, Pvt. Solomon 65
written statements of perpetrators 131, 137–38, 191, 198, 251; *see also* confessions, published; letters
"wrong man" convictions vs. wrongful convictions 2–3, 280; *see also* innocence; Mays, Maurice
Wynn, Pleasant D. 207–10
Wynn, William 207

Yardley, William B. 136, 154
Yates, Sophronia J. (victim) 255
Young, John 14–15
Young, Joshua 23–24
Young, Margaret (victim) 23
youths *see* minors

Zachery, Peter (victim) 95